MOON OUTDOORS

WEST COAST
RV CAMPING

TOM STIENSTRA

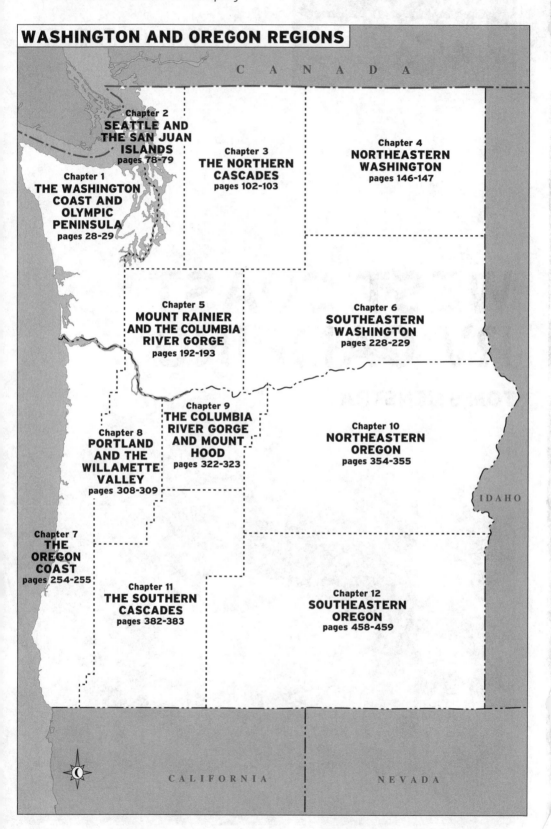

WASHINGTON AND OREGON REGIONS

CANADA

Chapter 2
SEATTLE AND
THE SAN JUAN
ISLANDS
pages 78-79

Chapter 1
THE WASHINGTON
COAST AND
OLYMPIC
PENINSULA
pages 28-29

Chapter 3
THE NORTHERN
CASCADES
pages 102-103

Chapter 4
NORTHEASTERN
WASHINGTON
pages 146-147

Chapter 5
MOUNT RAINIER
AND THE COLUMBIA
RIVER GORGE
pages 192-193

Chapter 6
SOUTHEASTERN
WASHINGTON
pages 228-229

Chapter 9
THE COLUMBIA
RIVER GORGE
AND MOUNT
HOOD
pages 322-323

Chapter 8
PORTLAND
AND THE
WILLAMETTE
VALLEY
pages 308-309

Chapter 10
NORTHEASTERN
OREGON
pages 354-355

IDAHO

Chapter 7
THE
OREGON
COAST
pages 254-255

Chapter 11
THE SOUTHERN
CASCADES
pages 382-383

Chapter 12
SOUTHEASTERN
OREGON
pages 458-459

CALIFORNIA

NEVADA

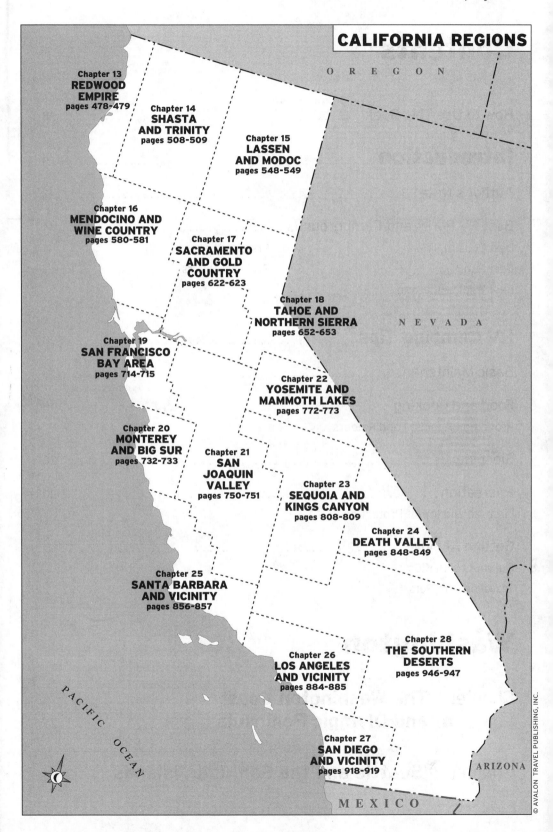

CALIFORNIA REGIONS

OREGON

Chapter 13
REDWOOD EMPIRE
pages 478-479

Chapter 14
SHASTA AND TRINITY
pages 508-509

Chapter 15
LASSEN AND MODOC
pages 548-549

Chapter 16
MENDOCINO AND WINE COUNTRY
pages 580-581

Chapter 17
SACRAMENTO AND GOLD COUNTRY
pages 622-623

Chapter 18
TAHOE AND NORTHERN SIERRA
pages 652-653

NEVADA

Chapter 19
SAN FRANCISCO BAY AREA
pages 714-715

Chapter 22
YOSEMITE AND MAMMOTH LAKES
pages 772-773

Chapter 20
MONTEREY AND BIG SUR
pages 732-733

Chapter 21
SAN JOAQUIN VALLEY
pages 750-751

Chapter 23
SEQUOIA AND KINGS CANYON
pages 808-809

Chapter 24
DEATH VALLEY
pages 848-849

Chapter 25
SANTA BARBARA AND VICINITY
pages 856-857

Chapter 28
THE SOUTHERN DESERTS
pages 946-947

PACIFIC OCEAN

Chapter 26
LOS ANGELES AND VICINITY
pages 884-885

Chapter 27
SAN DIEGO AND VICINITY
pages 918-919

ARIZONA

MEXICO

© AVALON TRAVEL PUBLISHING, INC.

Contents

How to Use This Book

ABOUT THE CAMPGROUND PROFILES

The campgrounds are listed in a consistent, easy-to-read format to help you choose the ideal camping spot. If you already know the name of the specific campground you want to visit, or the name of the surrounding geological area or nearby feature (town, national or state park, forest, mountain, lake, river, etc.), look it up in the index and turn to the corresponding page. Here is a sample profile:

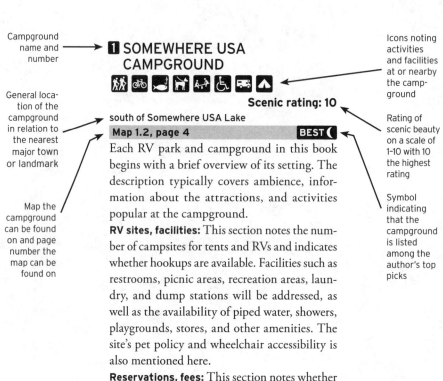

Campground name and number →

General location of the campground in relation to the nearest major town or landmark →

Map the campground can be found on and page number the map can be found on →

1 SOMEWHERE USA CAMPGROUND

Scenic rating: 10

south of Somewhere USA Lake
Map 1.2, page 4   BEST (

Each RV park and campground in this book begins with a brief overview of its setting. The description typically covers ambience, information about the attractions, and activities popular at the campground.

RV sites, facilities: This section notes the number of campsites for tents and RVs and indicates whether hookups are available. Facilities such as restrooms, picnic areas, recreation areas, laundry, and dump stations will be addressed, as well as the availability of piped water, showers, playgrounds, stores, and other amenities. The site's pet policy and wheelchair accessibility is also mentioned here.

Reservations, fees: This section notes whether reservations are accepted and provides rates. If there are additional fees for parking or pets, or discounted weekly or seasonal rates, they will also be noted here.

Directions: This section provides mile-by-mile driving directions to the campground from the nearest major town or highway.

Contact: This section provides an address, phone number, and website, if available, for each RV park or campground.

Icons noting activities and facilities at or nearby the campground →

Rating of scenic beauty on a scale of 1-10 with 10 the highest rating

Symbol indicating that the campground is listed among the author's top picks

ABOUT THE ICONS

The icons in this book are designed to provide at-a-glance information on activities, facilities, and services available on-site or within walking distance of each campground.

- Hiking trails
- Biking trails
- Swimming
- Fishing
- Boating
- Canoeing and/or kayaking
- Winter sports

- Hot Springs
- Pets permitted
- Playground
- Wheelchair accessible
- RV sites
- Tent sites

MAP SYMBOLS

======= Expressway	(80) Interstate Freeway	✗ Airfield
------- Primary Road	(101) U.S. Highway	✈ Airport
----- Secondary Road	(29) State Highway	○ City/Town
--------- Unpaved Road	[66] County Highway	▲ Mountain
············· Ferry	Lake	♦ Park
—·—·— National Border	Dry Lake	\ Pass
—··— State Border	Seasonal Lake	◉ State Capital

About the Scenic Rating

Each campground profile employs a scenic rating on a scale of 1 to 10, with 1 being the least scenic and 10 being the most scenic. A scenic rating measures only the overall beauty of the campground and environs. The scenic rating, whether a 1 or a 10, does not take into account noise level, facilities, maintenance, recreation options, or campground management. The setting of a campground with a lower scenic rating may simply not be as picturesque as that of a higher rated campground. However other factors, such as noise or recreation access, can still affect your camping trip.

If the noise levels or cleanliness of a campground—even a higher rated one—are unacceptable, it's best to contact the campground manager with your concerns. But because these elements can change from day to day, or simply with a new employee hired, these issues are not factored into the ratings. Consider both the scenic rating and the profile description before deciding which campground is perfect for you.

INTRODUCTION

Author's Note

"Moving is the closest thing to being free," wrote Billy Joe Shaver, an old Texas cowboy songwriter.

He got it.

It's not just the getaway destinations, adventures, and array of sights that makes roaming the West the greatest RV adventure in America. It's the way it makes you feel inside when you're on the road, the anticipation of the trip ahead, all the hopes and dreams that inspire road trips across the West—it's the closest thing to being free.

I understand these feelings. I've traveled more than a million miles across Washington, Oregon, and California in the past 25 years. Although I love hiking, boating, and fishing, the real underlying force is staying on the move, roaming around, free, always curious to see what is around the next bend in the road.

All along the Pacific Coast, from Mission Bay near San Diego to Orcas Island near the Canadian border north of the Olympic Peninsula, you can discover a series of beautiful park campgrounds that seem perfectly spaced for the trip. One of the greatest road trips anywhere is Highway 1 on the coast, the best of it venturing north along the slow, curving two-laner from Morro Bay to Fort Bragg, California. In the fall, the road is largely free of traffic, the skies often clear of fog, and the bluff-top perches furnish a procession of stunning views of the rocky coast, with unpeopled foothills on one side and an ocean that stretches to forever on the other. Traveling slowly, you'll discover, can be ecstasy.

Another option is to cruise up and down I-5, and then make side junctures into the Sierra Nevada in California, the Cascade Range in Oregon and Washington, or even a trip on a ferry boat out from Anacortes or Port Angeles in Washington to tour the San Juan Islands. Yosemite National Park is the No. 1 destination for most. Some of nature's most perfect artwork has been created in Yosemite and the adjoining eastern Sierra near Mammoth Lakes, as well as some of the most profound natural phenomena imaginable.

Cruising U.S. 395 along the Eastern Sierra is a preferred alternative for many, with the opportunity for easy side trips to many lakes. They include Bridgeport Reservoir, the June lakes, the Mammoth lakes, Convict Lake, and Crowley Lake. In addition, almost every lake's outlet stream provides prospects. This region has it all: beauty, variety, and a chance at the fish of a lifetime. There is also access to the Ansel Adams Wilderness, which features Banner and Ritter peaks, and lakes filled with fish.

Oregon and Washington feature similar stellar destinations, from pristine Crater Lake, a legend for its cobalt-blue waters, on north to Baker Lake in Mount Baker–Snoqualmie National Forest in Washington. These are just a handful amid more than a thousand lakes that provide RV access in Washington, Oregon, and California.

There's one catch. To make a road trip work, you have to be able to find a spot to stop every night. That's why this book is a must-have for every RV owner. You'll never get stuck again. One of the worst feelings imaginable is cruising down the road in the early evening without a clue where you will park for the night, without any knowledge of the array of spots available. I call that being a prisoner of hope. My advice is to never hope your way through a vacation.

This book details more than 1,800 campgrounds and parks with RV sites. The listings, directions, facilities, and highlights are far more detailed than any RV guide. To win your trust, we have done everything possible to make this book the most accurate guide in this field; every entry has been cross-checked with rangers and the owners of RV parks by our research editors.

Regardless, things are always changing at RV parks and camps, and getting it right in a book requires year-round vigilance. Most commonly, prices go up. The prices in this book are the most up-to-date possible, but if price is the bottom-line concern, always verify prior to your visit.

Some of the highlights of this book include:

- More than 1,800 campgrounds and parks for RV camping. These include sites in privately owned RV parks; local, county, state, and national parks; national forests; and, in some rare cases, land managed by the Bureau of Land Management and Washington Department of Natural Resources.

- More than 30 detailed maps.

- Directions that are written as if a passenger is reading them aloud to the person driving, making them extremely driver-friendly.

- Detailed information about each campground's facilities, fees, reservation policies, setting, and nearby recreation options.

- Icons that quickly identify activities available at each site.

- Up-to-date, fact-checked information.

- Not included are sites that are extremely remote, very difficult to reach, or where the access road is extremely narrow or twisty.

Over the years, I have received many comments from campers, rangers, and park owners about what they are looking for in an RV guidebook. That is exactly what we are delivering in this book. After all, this is my full-time job. I understand how seriously people take their trips and what you need to know to make your trips work, every time.

You can roam for just a day or two. Or you can just keep on going. The road, as songwriter Robert Earl Keen says, goes on forever. More Americans than ever are fulfilling the dream of taking to the highway. According to the Recreational Vehicle Industry Association's 2005 study (www.RVIA.org), sales of all styles of RVs are up 15 percent across the country. While most RVs are owned by those in the 35–54 age range (1 in every 10 Americans between the ages of 55–64 now owns at least one RV), the biggest increase in RV sales are to those under age 35.

Adventures are good for the soul. They can bond people for life. Adventures also make you feel good inside. Billy Joe Shaver was right. Moving really is the closest thing to being free.

—Tom Stienstra

Best RV Parks and Campgrounds

Can't decide where to stop this weekend? Following are some of my favorites spots, ranked 1–10 in five categories.

◖ Best Coastal Sites

1. Monterey Bay, California
Seacliff State Beach, Monterey and Big Sur, page 734.

2. Pacific Beach, Washington
Pacific Beach State Park, The Washington Coast and Olympic Peninsula, page 59.

3. Westport, Washington
American Sunset RV and Tent Resort, The Washington Coast and Olympic Peninsula, page 64.

4. Carlsbad, California
South Carlsbad State Beach, San Diego and Vicinity, page 928.

5. Coos Bay, Oregon
Sunset Bay State Park, The Oregon Coast, page 288.

6. Fort Stevens State Park on the Columbia River, Oregon
Fort Stevens State Park, The Oregon Coast, page 256.

7. Santa Barbara, California
Refugio State Beach, Santa Barbara and Vicinity, page 874.
El Capitan State Beach, Santa Barbara and Vicinity, page 874.

8. Fort Canby State Park, Washington
Ilwaco KOA, The Washington Coast and Olympic Peninsula, page 71.
Fisherman's Cove RV Park, The Washington Coast and Olympic Peninsula, page 72.

9. Prairie Creek Redwoods State Park, California
Prairie Creek Redwoods State Park: Gold Bluff Beach, Redwood Empire, page 488.

10. Pacifica, California
San Francisco RV Resort, San Francisco Bay Area, page 719.

◖ Best Fishing

1. Bass in the deep sea and lakes in and around San Diego, California
Campland on the Bay, San Diego and Vicinity, page 931.

2. Largemouth bass in the San Joaquin River Delta, California
Lundborg Landing, Sacramento and Gold Country, page 644.

3. Smallmouth bass in the Umpqua River, Oregon
Tyee, The Oregon Coast, page 286.

4. Sturgeon in the Columbia River, Washington
Beacon Rock State Park, Mount Rainier and the Columbia River Gorge, page 222.

5. Cutthroat trout in Omak Lake, Washington
Eastside Park and Carl Precht Memorial RV Park, Northeastern Washington, page 170.

6. Steelhead in Bogachiel River, Washington
Bogachiel State Park, The Washington Coast and Olympic Peninsula, page 43.

7. Rainbow trout in Rufus Woods Lake, Washington
Bridgeport State Park, Northeastern Washington, page 177.

8. Bass in Lake San Antonio, California
North Shore/South Shore San Antonio, Santa Barbara and Vicinity, page 858.

9. Salmon in Bodega Bay, California
Doran Regional Park, Mendocino and Wine Country, page 616.
Westside Regional Park, Mendocino and Wine Country, page 616.

10. Rainbow trout in the Sacramento River (Redding to Anderson), California
Marina RV Park, Shasta and Trinity, page 540.
Sacramento River RV Resort, Shasta and Trinity, page 541.

◖ Best Wildlife-Viewing

1. Tule elk, California
Olema Ranch Campground, San Francisco Bay Area, page 716.

2. Orcas, Washington
West Beach Resort Ferry-In, Seattle and the San Juan Islands, page 83.

3. Roosevelt elk, California
Prairie Creek Redwoods State Park: Elk Prairie, Redwood Empire, page 489.

4. Gray whales, California
MacKerricher State Park, Mendocino and Wine Country, page 586.
Caspar Beach RV Park, Mendocino and Wine Country, page 591.
Ocean Cove Campground, Mendocino and Wine Country, page 607.

5. Bald eagles, California
Indian Well, Lassen and Modoc, page 550.

6. Black bears, California
Dorst Creek, Sequoia and Kings Canyon, page 828.

7. Roosevelt elk, Washington
Bay Center/Willapa Bay KOA, The Washington Coast and Olympic Peninsula, page 66.

8. Black bears, California
White Wolf, Yosemite and Mammoth Lakes, page 775.
Tuolumne Meadows, Yosemite and Mammoth Lakes, page 775.

9. Antelope, Oregon
Adel Store and RV Park, Southeastern Oregon, page 472.

10. Deer and chukar, Oregon

Deschutes River State Recreation Area,
The Columbia River Gorge and Mount Hood, page328.
Chukar Park, Southeastern Oregon, page 461.

◖ Prettiest Lakes

1. Lake Tahoe, California

D. L. Bliss State Park, Tahoe and Northern Sierra, page 683.
Emerald Bay State Park and Boat-In, Tahoe and Northern Sierra, page 683.

2. Crater Lake, Oregon

Crater Lake Resort, The Southern Cascades, page 438

3. Baker Lake, Washington

Horseshoe Cove, The Northern Cascades, page 106.

4. Sardine Lake, California

Sardine Lake, Tahoe and Northern Sierra, page 662.

5. Crescent Lake, Oregon

Crescent Lake, The Southern Cascades, page 422.

6. Tenaya Lake, California

Porcupine Flat, Yosemite and Mammoth Lakes, page 776.

7. Lake Quinault, Washington

Falls Creek, The Washington Coast and Olympic Peninsula, page 51.

8. Lake Sabrina, California

Sabrina, Sequoia and Kings Canyon, page 820.

9. Donner Lake, California

Donner Memorial State Park, Tahoe and Northern Sierra, page 671.

10. Mountain Lake, Washington

Moran State Park Ferry-In, Seattle and the San Juan Islands, page 83.

◖ Prettiest Rivers

1. Umpqua River, Oregon

Umpqua Lighthouse State Park, The Oregon Coast, page 282.
Tyee, The Oregon Coast, page 286.
Horseshoe Bend, The Southern Cascades, page 425.

2. McCloud River, Califorinia

Fowler's Camp, Shasta and Trinity, page 519.

3. Smith River, California

Panther Flat, Redwood Empire, page 482.
Grassy Flat, Redwood Empire, page 482.

4. Bogachiel River, Washington

Bogachiel State Park, The Washington Coast and Olympic Peninsula, page 43.

5. McKenzie River, Oregon

Olallie, The Southern Cascades, page 391.

6. Owyhee River, Oregon

Rome Launch, Southeastern Oregon, page 468.

7. Trinity River, California

Bigfoot Campground and RV Park, Shasta and Trinity, page 527.

8. Rogue River, Oregon

Indian Mary Park, The Southern Cascades, page 435.
Schroeder, The Southern Cascades, page 439.
Whitehorse, The Southern Cascades, page 440.

9. Yuba River, California

Moonshine Campground, Sacramento and Gold Country, page 630.
Indian Springs, Tahoe and Northern Sierra, page 670.

10. Deschutes River, Oregon

Deschutes River State Recreation Area,
  The Columbia River Gorge and Mount Hood, page 328.
Tumalo State Park, The Southern Cascades, page 395.
Big River, The Southern Cascades, page 409.
LaPine State Park, The Southern Cascades, page 415.

RV Camping Tips

Many paths, one truth: There are nearly 40 styles of RVs in use, from the high-end 60-footers that resemble touring buses for rock stars, to the popular cab-over campers on pick-up trucks, to the pop-up trailers that can be towed by a small sedan. Regardless of what kind of rig you use, all share one similarity when you prepare for a trip: You must have good tires, brakes, and a cooling system for your engine.

During your trip, check fluid levels with every gas fill-up. These checks should include engine oil, brake fluid, engine coolant, transmission fluid, and power-steering fluid.

While these lists do not cover every imaginable item, they do serve as a checklist for primary items and a starting point to create your own list. My suggestion is to add items to these pages that are vital for your own vehicle.

BASIC MAINTENANCE

Here's a checklist for primary items; make sure that you have these and that they are in good working order before you go. Also be sure all mandatory routine maintenance is performed prior to your trip.

- All owner's manuals
- Batteries
- Brakes and brake fluid
- Cooling system and coolant
- Electrical system, lights
- Emergency flashers
- Fire extinguisher
- Gas filter
- Heater and air conditioner
- Lube
- Oil and filter
- Power-steering fluid
- Proof of insurance and registration
- Road service card
- Shocks
- Tire-changing equipment
- Tires (check air pressure, including spare tire)
- Transmission fluid
- Wheel bearings

Self-contained RVs
- Awning
- Dump valve and sewer hose
- Electrical system
- Extra battery if camping without hookups
- Fuses, including for slide-out motor
- Gray water tank and panel monitor
- Landing gear
- Lights
- Lube rollers or slider plates at the end of rams for slide-out rooms
- Pilot light
- Power converter
- Propane gas
- Refrigerator
- Stabilizer jacks
- Stove
- Toilet chemical and RV toilet paper
- Water system
- Windows and shades

Trailers and Fifth Wheels
- Lights
- Lube
- Perfect fit at tow junction
- Safety chains
- Self-adjusting brakes
- Wheel bearings

FOOD AND COOKING

When it comes to food, you are only limited by your imagination. So there is no reason to ever settle for less than what is ideal for you. Add to this list as necessary.

- Bottled water and drinks
- Can opener
- Charcoal
- Coffee maker and filters
- Cooking utensils
- Ice chest
- Kitchen towels

- Knives, forks, spoons
- Matches or lighters
- Napkins and paper towels
- Pots, pans, plates, glasses
- Primary foods for breakfasts, lunches, and dinners
- Seasoned pepper and salt, spices
- Trash bags
- Wash rack and detergent

Protection Against Food Raiders

Bears, raccoons, and even blue jays specialize in the food-raiding business at camps. Bears, in particular, can be a real problem for people new to RV camping at parks with high bear populations. In rare cases, bears have even been known to break into unattended RVs in the pursuit of human goodies, especially Swiss

Miss, Tang, butter, eggs, and ice cream. Raccoons can chew tiny holes in tents and destroy picnic baskets in their search. I've seen jays land on plastic bags hanging from tree limbs, rigged from rope as bear-proof food hangs, and then poke a hole in the plastic to get meat sticks. There are answers, of course. In the past few years, programs have been established at many state and national parks to reduce incidents with bears. The real problem, of course, is not bears, but the careless people who create incidents by not properly storing their food and disposing of garbage.

In areas with high bear density, owners of small truck campers or pop-up camper trailers can use a bear-proof food hang or bear-proof food canisters. When creating a bear-proof food hang, use the counter-balance method

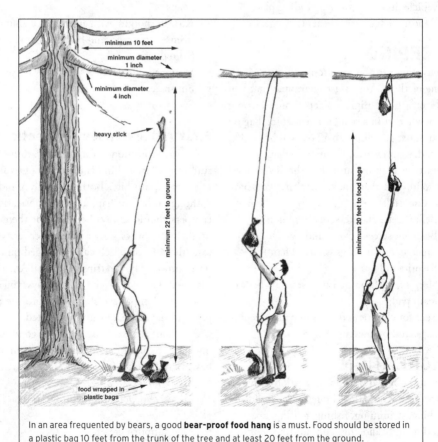

In an area frequented by bears, a good **bear-proof food hang** is a must. Food should be stored in a plastic bag 10 feet from the trunk of the tree and at least 20 feet from the ground.

with either double plastic bags or canvas bags. If no tree limb is suitable for the counter-balance method for a bear-proof food hang, put all your food in a double bag, hoist it up to a limb, and then tie the end off on a different tree.

Observe the following rules for proper food storage and disposal:
- Always use wildlife-proof metal food lockers available at major park campgrounds
- Do not leave food unattended on picnic tables or in camp
- Do not leave garbage unattended in camp
- Dispose of all garbage properly each day
- Do not leave food bags, cups, or anything that may appear as food within view of a bear who might peer into the window of an RV
- Do not put food inside a vehicle, under a vehicle, in a tent, or in a "hiding place"
- Report all aggressive bears to rangers

SLEEPING

Some things can't be compromised—ever. This is one of them. You must guarantee that you will get a good night's sleep. Your sleeping setup, whether in a bed or in a sleeping bag on a pad, must guarantee that you will be comfy, clean, dry, and warm, no matter what.

Start by making sure that the RV is level and solid, and then make sure that you have these essentials:
- Bed: sheets, blankets, or sleeping bag
- Blackout screens over windows
- Emergency ear plugs (snorers! hah!)
- Favorite pillows
- Sleeping surface: bed mattress, air bed, or foam pad
- Tent for children with foam pads, sleeping bags, and pillows

RECREATION

The most popular outdoor recreation activities on the West Coast are hiking, biking, wildlife-watching, swimming, fishing, golfing, boating, kayaking and canoeing, and hunting. For this checklist, you may wish to cross off items for activities that you do not take part in and add items essential for your favorites.
- Beach chair and towels
- Bike and tire repair kit
- Binoculars
- Boat with required safety equipment
- Camera, fresh battery, digital card or film
- Daypack
- Fishing rod, reel with fresh line, tackle, fishing license with appropriate tags, and state rulebook
- Flashlight and batteries
- Golf clubs and balls
- Hat
- Hiking boots and SmartWool (or equivalent) socks
- Identification guides
- Life vests
- Maps
- Rifle or shotgun with ammunition, hunting license with tags, and hunting regulations
- Sandals
- Sunglasses
- Sunscreen
- Swimsuit

First Aid and Insect Protection

The most common injury on vacations is a sunburn. Close behind is the result of scratching a mosquito bite. Both are easily avoided. Although other mishaps are rare on vacations, campers should always be ready for them. In bright sun, always wear a hat that covers your ears, the tops of which can get singed quickly on a summer day. On trips to Central America, I learned that even on the hottest days, you can wear light long-sleeve shirts that provide sun protection, yet are cool and ventilated.

A first-aid kit is a must. Here is a good starting list of basic sun and insect protection, plus basic first-aid supplies:
- Ace bandage
- Adhesive towels and medical tape
- AfterBite
- Aloe sunburn cream
- Antibiotic towels

- Aspirin
- Band-Aids
- Blood pressure monitoring equipment
- Burn ointment
- Chapstick
- Eye wash
- Moleskin or similar blister treatment
- Mosquito repellent
- Pain reliever such as Excedrin, Tylenol, Ibuprofen, Advil, Aleve, or similar
- Prescription medications (such as an inhaler for asthmatics)
- Scissors
- Sterile gloves
- Sun block
- Tums or other antacid
- Tweezers

GETTING ALONG

The most important element of any trip is the people you are with. That is why your choice of companions is so important. Your own behavior is equally consequential. Yet most people spend more time putting together their gear than considering why they enjoy or dislike the company of their chosen companions.

Here are a few rules of behavior for a great trip:

1. No whining: Nothing is more irritating than being around a whiner.

2. Activities must be agreed upon: Always have a meeting of the minds with your companions over the general game plan.

3. Nobody's in charge: It is impossible to be genuine friends if one person is always telling another what to do.

4. Equal chances at the fun stuff: There must be an equal distribution of the fun stuff and the not-fun stuff.

5. No heroes: Nobody cares about all your wonderful accomplishments. No gloating. The beauty of travel is simply how each person feels inside, the heart of the adventure.

6. Agree on a wake-up time: You can then proceed on course together without the risk of whining (see #1).

7. Think of the other guy: Count the number of times you say, "What do you think?"

8. Solo responsibilities: When it is time for you to cook, make a campfire, or clean a fish, it means you can do so without worrying about somebody else getting their mitts in the way.

9. Don't let money get in the way: Among friends, don't let somebody pay extra, because that person will likely try to control the trip, and yet at the same time, don't let somebody weasel out of paying a fair share.

10. Accordance on the food plan: Always have complete agreement on what you plan to eat each day, and always check for food allergies such as nuts, onions, or cheese.

Outdoors with Kids

I've put this list together with the help of my own kids, Jeremy and Kris, and their mother, Stephani. Some of the lessons are obvious, some are not, but all are important:

- Take children to places where there is a guarantee of action, such as a park with wildlife-viewing.
- Be enthusiastic. Enthusiasm is contagious—if you aren't excited about an adventure, you can't expect a child to be.
- Always be seated when talking to someone small, so the adult and child are on the same level.
- Always *show* how to do something—never tell.
- Let kids be kids by letting the adventure happen, rather than trying to force it within some preconceived plan.
- Use short attention spans to your advantage by bringing along a surprise bag of candy and snacks.
- Make absolutely certain the child's sleeping bag is clean, dry, and warm, and that they feel safe, protected, and listened to.
- Introduce kids to outdoor ethics; they quickly relate to the concepts and long remember when they do something right that somebody else has done wrong.
- Take close-up photographs of them holding

PREDICTING WEATHER

Weather lore can be valuable on trips. Small signs provided by nature and wildlife can be translated to provide a variety of weather information. By paying attention, I can often provide weather forecasts for specific areas that are more reliable than the broad-brush approach provided by weather services. Here is the list I have compiled over the years:

When the grass is dry at morning light,
Look for rain before the night.

No dew on the grass at 7?
Expect sign of rain by 11.

Short notice, soon to pass.
Long notice, long it will last.

When the wind is from the east,
'Tis fit for neither man nor beast.

When the wind is from the south,
The rain is in its mouth.

When the wind is from the west,
Then it is the very best.

Red sky at night, sailors' delight.
Red sky in the morning, sailors take warning.

When all the cows are pointed north,
Within a day rain will come forth.

Onion skins very thin, mild winter coming in.
Onion skins very tough, winter's going to
*   be very rough.*

When your boots make the squeak of
*   snow,*
Then very cold temperatures will surely
*   show.*

If a goose flies high, fair weather ahead.
If a goose flies low, foul weather will come
*   instead.*

fish they have caught, blowing on the campfire, or completing other camp tasks.

- Keep track of how often you say, "What do you think?"

Traveling with Pets

Many dogs and cats are considered members of the family. I recommend taking them along whenever possible. They always add to the trip. And after all, leaving them is a terrible moment, especially when they stare at you with those big, mournful eyes, and then you spend the next week thinking about them. My dog Rebel ended up traveling with me for 17 years. I believe one of the reasons he lived so long was because he was fit, happy, loved, had a job to do (camp security, or so he thought), and always had another adventure to look forward to. Of course, you just can't put your pet in the vehicle and figure everything will be fine. In addition, some pets

are built for travel or camping, and some are not. Know the difference. A few precautions can prevent a lot of problems.

Start with your pet's comfort. Make certain your pet is cool, comfortable, and can sleep while you are driving. Once you arrive at your destination, create similar sleeping quarters at camp as at home. Be sure to make frequent stops for exercise, sniffing, and bathroom breaks.

To avoid frustration, always confirm that pets are permitted at planned destinations before you head out. Plus keep these items in the RV:

- Clean and filled water and food dishes
- ID collar labeled with your cell phone number
- Leash
- Pooper-scooper
- Records of shots, licenses, and the vet's phone number

Washington

WASHINGTON

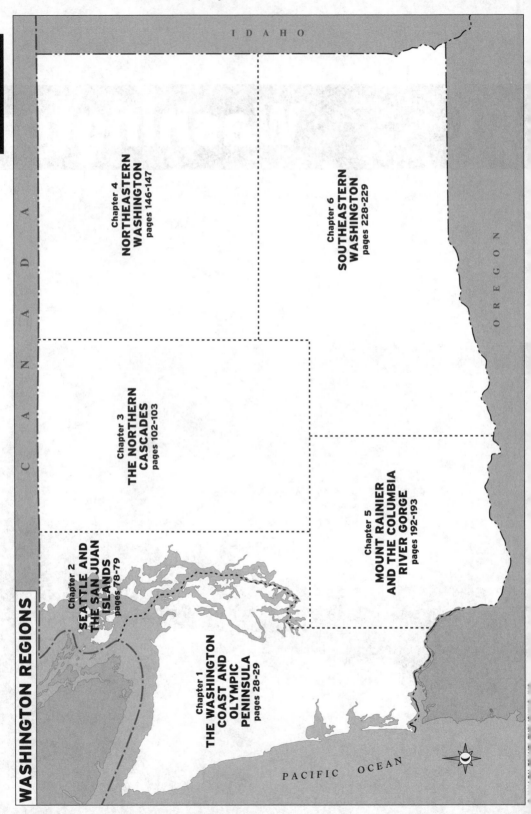

WASHINGTON REGIONS

Chapter 1
THE WASHINGTON COAST AND OLYMPIC PENINSULA
pages 28-29

Chapter 2
SEATTLE AND THE SAN JUAN ISLANDS
pages 78-79

Chapter 3
THE NORTHERN CASCADES
pages 102-103

Chapter 4
NORTHEASTERN WASHINGTON
pages 146-147

Chapter 5
MOUNT RAINIER AND THE COLUMBIA RIVER GORGE
pages 192-193

Chapter 6
SOUTHEASTERN WASHINGTON
pages 228-229

CANADA

IDAHO

OREGON

PACIFIC OCEAN

THE WASHINGTON COAST AND OLYMPIC PENINSULA

☽ **BEST RV PARKS AND CAMPGROUNDS**

Vast, diverse, and beautiful, the Olympic Peninsula is like no other landscape in the world. Water borders the region on three sides: the Pacific Ocean to the west, the Strait of Juan de Fuca to the north, and the inlets of the Hood Canal to the east. At its center are Olympic National Park and Mount Olympus, with rainforests on its slopes feeding rivers and lakes that make up the most dynamic river complex in America.

Only heavy rainfall for months on end from fall through spring and coastal fog in the summer have saved this area from a massive residential boom. At the same time, those conditions make it outstanding for getaways and virtually all forms of recreation. Stellar campgrounds ring the perimeter foothills of Mount Olympus, both in Olympic National Park and at the state parks and areas managed by the Department of Natural Resources. Your campsite can be your launch pad for adventure – just be sure to bring your rain gear.

In winter, campers can explore the largest array of steelhead rivers anywhere – there is no better place in America to fish for steelhead. Almost every one of these rivers provides campsites, often within walking distance of prime fishing spots.

Includes:

- Bainbridge Island
- Belfair State Park
- Big Quilcene River
- Bogachiel River and Bogachiel State Park
- Chehalis River
- Columbia River
- Dosewallips State Park
- Duckabush River
- Dungeness River and Recreation Area
- Elwha River
- Fay Bainbridge State Park
- Fort Canby State Park
- Fort Columbia State Park
- Fort Flagler State Park
- Fort Worden State Park
- Grayland Beach State Park
- Hamma Hamma River
- Harstine Island
- Hoh River
- Illahee State Park
- Jarrell Cove State Park
- Joemma Beach State Park
- Kitsap Memorial State Park
- Kopachuck State Park
- Lake Crescent
- Lake Cushman
- Lake Ozette
- Lake Quinault
- Lake Sylvia State Park
- Manchester State Park
- Ocean City State Park
- Old Fort Townsend State Park
- Olympic National Forest
- Olympic National Park
- Pacific Beach State Park
- Penrose Point State Park
- Potlatch State Park
- Puget Sound
- Quillayute River
- Quinault River
- Rainbow Falls State Park
- Satsop River
- Scenic Beach State Park
- Schafer State Park
- Sequim Bay State Park
- Skamokawa Vista Park
- Skokomish River
- Sol Duc River
- Strait of Juan de Fuca
- Twanoh State Park
- Twin Harbors State Park
- Wynoochee Lake

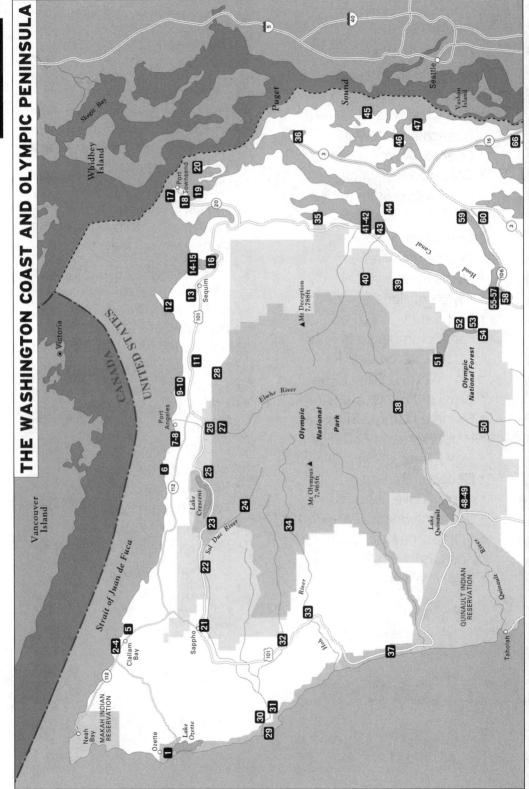

WASHINGTON

THE WASHINGTON COAST AND OLYMPIC PENINSULA

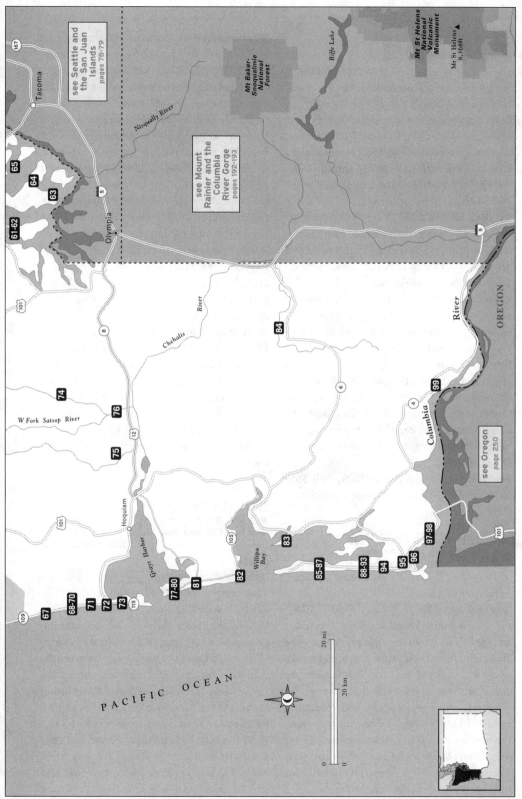

WASHINGTON

see Seattle and the San Juan Islands
pages 78-79

see Mount Rainier and the Columbia River Gorge
pages 192-193

see Oregon
page 250

Mt St Helens National Volcanic Monument

Mt St Helens
8,366ft

Mt Baker-Snoqualmie National Forest

Riffe Lake

Tacoma

Olympia

Nisqually River

Chehalis River

W Fork Satsop River

Hoquiam

Grays Harbor

Willapa Bay

Columbia River

OREGON

PACIFIC OCEAN

20 mi

20 km

© AVALON TRAVEL PUBLISHING, INC.

WASHINGTON

1 OZETTE

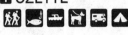

Scenic rating: 6

on Lake Ozette in Olympic National Park

See map page 28

Many people visit this site on the shore of Lake Ozette just a few miles from the Pacific Ocean. Set close to a trailhead road and ranger station, with multiple trailheads nearby, this camp is a favorite for both hikers and boaters and is one of the first to fill in the park.

RV sites, facilities: There are 15 sites for tents or RVs up to 21 feet (no hookups). Picnic tables and fire grills are provided. Vault toilets and drinking water (summer season only) are available. Leashed pets are permitted.

Reservations, fees: Reservations are not accepted. Sites are $12 per night, plus a $15 national park entrance fee per vehicle. Open year-round, weather permitting.

Directions: From Port Angeles, drive west on U.S. 101 to the junction with Highway 112. Bear right on Highway 112 and drive to Hoko-Ozette Road. Turn left and drive 21 miles to the ranger station. The camp parking lot is across from the ranger station on the northwest corner of Lake Ozette.

Contact: Olympic National Park, 360/565-3130, fax 360/565-3147, www.nps.gov/olym.

2 VAN RIPER'S RESORT

Scenic rating: 7

on Clallam Bay in Sekiu

See map page 28

Part of this campground hugs the waterfront and the other part sits on a hill overlooking the Strait of Juan de Fuca. Most sites are graveled, many with views of the strait. Other sites are grassy, without views. Note that some of the campsites are rented for the entire summer season. Hiking, fishing, and boating are among the options here, with salmon fishing being the principal draw. The beaches in the area, a mixture of sand and gravel, provide diligent rock hounds with agates and fossils.

RV sites, facilities: There are 100 sites for tents or RVs of any length with full or partial hookups (30 amps). Some sites are pull-through. Other lodging includes two cabins, a mobile home, a house, and 12 motel rooms. Picnic tables and cable TV are provided, and fire rings are available at some sites. Restrooms have flush toilets and showers. Drinking water, a dump station, modem access, firewood, and ice are available. A store, café, and coin laundry are within one mile. Boat docks, launching facilities, tackle shop, and rentals are available. Leashed pets are permitted; no pets are allowed in cabins or other buildings.

Reservations, fees: Reservations are not accepted for campsites. Sites are $12–24 per night. Open April–September. Some credit cards accepted.

Directions: From Aberdeen, drive north on U.S. 101 for 119 miles to Sappho and Highway 113. Turn north on Highway 113 and drive nine miles to a fork with Highway 112. Continue straight on Highway 112 for two miles to Sekiu and Front Street. Turn right and drive 0.25 mile to the resort on the right.

Contact: Van Riper's Resort, 360/963-2334, www.vanripersresort.com.

3 OLSON'S RESORT

Scenic rating: 5

in Sekiu

See map page 28

This camp is large and has full services. The nearby marina is salmon-fishing headquarters. In fact, the resort caters to anglers, offering all-day salmon fishing trips and boat moorage. Chartered trips can be arranged by reservation. A tackle shop, cabins, houses, and a motel are also available. (See the *Van Riper's Resort* listing in this chapter for details on the Sekiu area.)

RV sites, facilities: There are 45 sites for RVs up to 36 feet with full hookups (20 and 30 amps) and 55 sites for tents or RVs of any length (no hookups). Seven cabins, 14 motel rooms, and four houses are also available. Picnic tables are provided, and fire rings are available at some sites. Restrooms have flush toilets and showers. Drinking water, a dump station, a coin laundry, a convenience store, bait and tackle, and ice are available. Boat docks, launching facilities, bait, tackle, a fish-cleaning station, fish storage, gas, and diesel fuel are also available on-site. Two small cafés are within one block and a restaurant is one mile away. Leashed pets are allowed, with certain restrictions.

Reservations, fees: Reservations are not accepted. RV sites are $18–23 per night, $2 per person per night for more than two people. Some credit cards accepted. Open year-round.

Directions: From Aberdeen, drive north on U.S. 101 for 119 miles to Sappho and Highway 113. Turn north on Highway 113 and drive nine miles to a fork with Highway 112. Continue straight on Highway 112 for two miles to Sekiu and Front Street. Turn right and drive one block to the resort on the right.

Contact: Olson's Resort, 360/963-2311, www.olsonsresort.com.

4 COHO RESORT AND MARINA

Scenic rating: 5

near Sekiu
See map page 28

Set across the highway from water, this resort features campsites that are entirely concrete-free. They are mainly gravel, and some have grass. Coho is one of several camps in the immediate area. A full-service marina nearby provides boating access. (See the *Van Riper's Resort* and *Olson's Resort* listings in this chapter for information on the area.)

RV sites, facilities: There are 100 sites for tents or RVs of any length with full or partial hookups (30 amps). Cable TV is available at a few sites. A dump station, restrooms with flush toilets and coin showers, a restaurant, a coin laundry, and ice are available. A store is within one mile. A full-service marina with docks, launching facilities, and gas is available. Leashed pets are permitted.

Reservations, fees: Reservations are not accepted. Sites are $14–22 per night, $1 per person per night for more than two people, $3 per extra vehicle per night. Some credit cards are accepted. Open year-round, with limited winter facilities.

Directions: From Aberdeen, drive north on U.S. 101 for 119 miles to Sappho and Highway 113. Turn north on Highway 113 and drive nine miles to a junction with Highway 112. Continue straight on Highway 112 and continue toward Sekiu. The resort is between Mileposts 15 and 16, about three-quarters of a mile before the town of Sekiu.

Contact: Coho Resort and Marina, 360/963-2333.

5 SAM'S TRAILER AND RV PARK

Scenic rating: 5

on Clallam Bay
See map page 28

Sam's is an alternative to other resorts on Clallam Bay. It's a family-oriented park with grassy sites and many recreation options nearby. A mobile home park is adjacent to the RV park. Beaches are within walking distance. Those wanting to visit Cape Flattery, Hoh Rain Forest, or Port Angeles will find this a good central location.

RV sites, facilities: Sam's has one tent site and 21 sites with full hookups (30 amps) for RVs of any length. Some sites are pull-through. Picnic tables are provided. Restrooms have flush toilets and showers. Cable TV and a coin laundry are available. Gasoline, a store, a café, and ice are within one mile. Boat docks, launching facilities, and boat rentals are within two miles. Leashed pets are permitted.

Reservations, fees: Reservations are accepted. RV sites are $22 per night, the tent site is $12 per night, plus $2 per person per night for more than two people. No credit cards accepted. Open year-round.

Directions: From Aberdeen, drive north on U.S. 101 for 119 miles to Sappho and Highway

113. Turn north on Highway 113 and drive nine miles to Clallam Bay and Highway 112. Continue straight on Highway 112 and drive into Clallam Bay. Just as you come into town, the park is on the right at 17053 Highway 112.

Contact: Sam's Trailer and RV Park, 360/963-2402.

6 WHISKEY CREEK BEACH

Scenic rating: 7

on the Strait of Juan de Fuca

See map page 28

Located on a beach along the Strait of Juan de Fuca, this campground covers 30 acres and sits next to vast timberland. It is popular with rock hounds. Surf fishing for perch and other species draws anglers, and this is an excellent launch point for sea kayaking. The setting is rustic, with 1.25 miles of beach access. Olympic National Park is five miles away and offers numerous recreation opportunities, including miles of stellar hiking trails. This camp is a good option if the national park camps are full, but note that almost one-third of the campground is rented out to monthly and seasonal renters.

RV sites, facilities: There are eight sites for RVs of any length with full hookups (15 and 30 amps), seven sites with partial hookups, and 28 sites for tents or RVs of any length (no hookups), plus eight cabins on the beach. Picnic tables and fire rings are provided. Drinking water and pit toilets are available. Launching facilities for small boats are on-site. A store, a gas station, and a coin laundry are available within three miles. Leashed pets are permitted.

Reservations, fees: Reservations are accepted. Tent sites are $15 per night, RV sites are $25 per night, and it's $2 per pet per night. No credit cards accepted. Open May–late October; cabins available year-round.

Directions: From U.S. 101 in Port Angeles, drive north five miles to a fork with High-

way 112. Turn right (west) on Highway 112 and drive 13 miles (three miles past Joyce) to Whiskey Creek Beach Road. Turn right and continue 1.5 miles to the campground on the right (well marked).

Contact: Whiskey Creek Beach, 360/928-3489, fax 360/928-3218.

7 CRESCENT BEACH RV PARK

Scenic rating: 7

on the Strait of Juan de Fuca

See map page 28

Set on a half-mile stretch of sandy beach, this campground makes a perfect weekend spot. Popular activities include swimming, fishing, surfing, sea kayaking, and beachcombing. It borders Salt Creek Recreation Area, with direct access available. Numerous attractions and recreation options are available in Port Angeles.

RV sites, facilities: There are 41 sites for tents or RVs of any length with full or partial hookups (30 and 50 amps), and a grassy area for tent camping. Picnic tables and fire rings are provided. Restrooms have flush toilets and coin showers. A coin laundry, a pay phone, a recreation field, and horseshoe pits are available. A dump station is nearby. Leashed pets are permitted.

Reservations, fees: Reservations are accepted. Sites are $35–40 per night, $5 per person per night for more than two people, $5 per extra vehicle (one-time fee per stay) unless towed, and $5 per night per pet. Weekly and monthly rates available. Credit cards accepted. Open year-round.

Directions: From U.S. 101 in Port Angeles, drive north five miles to a fork with Highway 112. Turn right (west) on Highway 112 and drive 10 miles to Camp Hayden Road (between Mileposts 53 and 54). Turn right on Camp Hayden Road and drive four miles to the park on the left, on the beach.

Contact: Crescent Beach RV Park, 360/928-3344, www.olypen.com/crescent.

8 SALT CREEK RECREATION AREA

Scenic rating: 8

near the Strait of Juan de Fuca
See map page 28

The former site of Camp Hayden, a World War II–era facility, Salt Creek Recreation Area is a great spot for gorgeous ocean views, fishing, and hiking near Striped Peak, which overlooks the campground. Only a small beach area is available because of the rugged coastline, but there is an exceptionally good spot for tidepool viewing on the park's west side. The park covers 196 acres and overlooks the Strait of Juan de Fuca. It is known for its Tongue Point Marine Life Sanctuary. Recreation options include nearby hiking trails, swimming, fishing, horseshoes, and field sports. It's a good layover spot if you're planning to take the ferry out of Port Angeles to Victoria, British Columbia. The camp fills up quickly most summer weekends. Note that the gate closes at dusk.

RV sites, facilities: There are 39 sites for tents or RVs of any length with partial hookups (30 and 50 amps) and 51 sites for tents or RVs of any length (no hookups). Picnic tables and fire rings are provided. A restroom with flush toilets and coin showers, a dump station, firewood, a camp host, a playground, a baseball field, basketball and volleyball courts, horseshoe pits, and a reservable covered picnic shelter are available. Some facilities are wheelchair accessible. Leashed pets are permitted.

Reservations, fees: Reservations are not accepted. Sites are $14–16 per night, $4 per extra vehicle per night. Discount for Clallam County residents. No credit cards accepted. Open year-round.

Directions: From U.S. 101 in Port Angeles, drive north five miles to a fork with Highway 112. Turn right (west) on Highway 112 and drive nine miles to Camp Hayden Road. Turn right (north) near Mile Marker 54 and drive 3.5 miles to the park entrance on the left.

Contact: Salt Creek Recreation Area, Clallam County, 360/928-3441, www.clallam.net/CountyParks/.

9 PEABODY CREEK RV PARK

Scenic rating: 5

in Port Angeles
See map page 28

This three-acre RV park is right in the middle of town but offers a wooded, streamside setting. Nearby recreation options include salmon fishing, an 18-hole golf course, marked biking trails, a full-service marina, and tennis courts. The park is within walking distance of shopping and ferry services.

RV sites, facilities: There is a grassy area for tents and 30 sites with full hookups (30 and 50 amps) for RVs up to 40 feet, but note that 19 are permanent rentals. Restrooms have flush toilets and coin showers. Cable TV, ice, and a coin laundry are available. No open fires are allowed. A store and a café are within one block. Boat docks and launching facilities are within one mile. Leashed pets are permitted.

Reservations, fees: Reservations are accepted. RV sites are $25 per night, tent sites are $12 per night, plus $2 per person per night for more than two people. No credit cards accepted. Open year-round.

Directions: From U.S. 101 in Port Angeles, bear left on Lincoln Street and drive 0.5 mile to 2nd Street and the park entrance on the right at 127 South Lincoln Street.

Contact: Peabody Creek RV Park, tel./fax 360/457-7092 or 800/392-2361, www.peabodyrv.com.

10 AL'S RV PARK

Scenic rating: 8

near Port Angeles
See map page 28

This campground is a good choice for RV owners. The campground is set in the country at about 1,000 feet elevation yet is centrally

WASHINGTON

located and not far from the Strait of Juan de Fuca. Nearby recreation options include an 18-hole golf course and a full-service marina. Olympic National Park and the Victoria ferry are a short drive away.

RV sites, facilities: There are 31 sites with full hookups (20, 30, and 50 amps) for RVs up to 40 feet and a grassy area for tents. No open fires allowed. Picnic tables are provided. Restrooms have flush toilets and showers. Drinking water, cable TV, modem access, and a coin laundry are available. A store, a café, propane gas, and ice are within 0.5 mile. Boat docks and launching facilities are within two miles. Some facilities are wheelchair accessible. Leashed pets are permitted.

Reservations, fees: Reservations are accepted. RV sites are $26.70 per night, tent sites are $18 per night, and it's $3 per person per night for more than two people. Weekly and monthly rates available. No credit cards accepted. Open year-round.

Directions: From Port Angeles, take U.S. 101 east for two miles to North Brook Avenue. Turn left (north) on North Brook Avenue, then left (almost immediately) on Lees Creek Road, and drive 0.5 mile to the park on the right at 521 North Lees Creek Road.

Contact: Al's RV Park, 360/457-9844.

11 SEQUIM

Scenic rating: 5

near Port Angeles

See map page 28

This is a private, developed camp covering 13 acres in a country setting. A pleasant park, it features the typical KOA offerings, including a pool, recreation hall, and playground. Horseshoe pits and a sports field are also available. Hayrides are available in summer. Nearby recreation options include miniature golf, an 18-hole golf course, marked hiking trails, and tennis courts, and nearby side trips include Victoria, Butchart Gardens, and whale-watching tours.

RV sites, facilities: There are 82 sites for tents or RVs of any length with full and partial hookups

(20, 30, and 50 amps), 19 tent sites, 12 cabins, and one lodge. Some sites are pull-through. Picnic tables and fire pits are provided. Restrooms have flush toilets and showers. Drinking water, cable TV, Wi-Fi and modem access, propane gas, firewood, a dump station, a convenience store, a coin laundry, ice, a playground, miniature golf, organized activities, bicycle rentals, a recreation room, and a seasonal heated swimming pool and spa are available. A café is within two miles. Some facilities are wheelchair accessible. Leashed pets are permitted, with certain restrictions.

Reservations, fees: Reservations are accepted at 800/562-7558. Sites are $20–37 per night, $5 per person per night for more than two people (ages six and older), and $5 per extra vehicle per night. Some credit cards accepted. Open March–October.

Directions: From I-5 at Olympia, turn north on U.S. 101 and drive 116 miles to O'Brien Road, six miles southeast of Port Angeles. Turn left on O'Brien Road and drive half a block to the campground on the right.

Contact: KOA Port Angeles–Sequim, 360/457-5916, fax 360/452-4248, www.port angeleskoa.com.

12 DUNGENESS RECREATION AREA

Scenic rating: 5

near the Strait of Juan de Fuca

See map page 28

This 216-acre park overlooks the Strait of Juan de Fuca and is near the Dungeness National Wildlife Refuge. Quite popular, it fills up on summer weekends. The refuge sits on a seven-mile spit, and a highlight is the historic lighthouse at the end of the spit. Bird-watchers often spot bald eagles in the wildlife refuge. There is a one-mile bluff trail, and equestrian trails are available. A 100-acre upland hunting area is open during season. Nearby recreation options include marked hiking trails, fishing, and golfing. The toll ferry at Port Angeles can take you to Victoria, British Columbia.

RV sites, facilities: There are 67 sites, including five pull-throughs, for tents or RVs of any length (no hookups). Picnic tables and fire grills are provided. Restrooms have flush toilets and coin showers. Drinking water, firewood, a dump station, a playground, and a picnic area are available. Leashed pets are permitted.

Reservations, fees: Reservations are not accepted. Sites are $16 per night, $4 per extra vehicle per night. Clallam County residents receive a discount. Open February–September, with facilities limited to day use in the winter. Entrance gates close at dusk year-round.

Directions: From Sequim, drive north on U.S. 101 for four miles to Kitchen-Dick Road. Turn right on Kitchen-Dick Road and drive three miles to the park on the left.

Contact: Dungeness Recreation Area, Clallam County, 360/683-5847, www.clallam.net/CountyParks/.

13 SEQUIM WEST INN & RV PARK

Scenic rating: 5

near the Dungeness River
See map page 28

This two-acre camp is near the Dungeness River and within 10 miles of Dungeness National Wildlife Refuge. It's in town and is a pleasant spot with full facilities and an urban setting. An 18-hole golf course and a full-service marina at Sequim Bay are close by.

RV sites, facilities: There are 27 pull-through sites for RVs of any length with full hookups (30 and 50 amps), 14 cottages, and 21 motel rooms. Picnic tables are provided. No open fires are allowed. Restrooms have flush toilets and showers. Drinking water, cable TV, a coin laundry, a pay phone, and ice are available. Propane gas, gasoline, a store, and a café are within one mile. Leashed pets are permitted.

Reservations, fees: Reservations are accepted. Sites are $24 per night, $1 per person per night for more than two people (under 18 free). Some credit cards accepted. Open year-round.

Directions: From Sequim and U.S. 101, take the Washington Street exit and drive west on Washington Street for 2.7 miles to the park on the left.

Contact: Sequim West Inn & RV Park, 360/683-4144 or 800/528-4527, fax 360/683-6452.

14 RAINBOW'S END RV PARK

Scenic rating: 6

on Sequim Bay
See map page 28

This park on Sequim Bay is pretty and clean and features a pond (no fishing) and a creek running through the campground. There is a weekly potluck dinner in the summer, with free hamburgers and hot dogs, and a special landscaped area available for reunions, weddings, and other gatherings. Nearby recreation opportunities include an 18-hole golf course, marked bike trails, a full-service marina, fishing, and tennis courts.

RV sites, facilities: There are 43 sites with full or partial hookups (30 and 50 amps) for RVs up to 42 feet and 15 tent sites. Some sites are pull-through. Picnic tables are provided at all sites, and fire pits are provided at tent sites. Restrooms have flush toilets and showers. Drinking water, a dump station, cable TV, Wi-Fi, propane gas, firewood, a coin laundry, and a clubhouse are available. A store, a café, and ice are within one mile. Leashed pets are permitted.

Reservations, fees: Reservations are accepted at 877/683-3863. Tent sites are $20 per night, RV sites are $25–27 per night, plus $2 per person per night for more than two people and $2 per extra vehicle per night. Weekly and monthly rates are available. Some credit cards accepted. Open year-round.

Directions: From Sequim, drive west on U.S. 101 for one mile past the River Road exit to the park on the right (along the highway).

Contact: Rainbow's End RV Park, 360/683-3863 or 877/683-3863, fax 360/683-2150, www.rainbowsendrvpark.com.

15 SEQUIM BAY RESORT

Scenic rating: 5

on Sequim Bay

See map page 28

This is Sequim Bay headquarters for salmon anglers. The camp is in a wooded, hilly area, close to many activity centers, and with an 18-hole golf course nearby.

RV sites, facilities: There are 42 sites with full hookups (15 and 30 amps) for RVs of any length, plus eight cabins. Some sites are pull-through. No tent camping. Picnic tables and barbecue grills are provided. Restrooms have flush toilets and showers. Drinking water, cable TV, a community fire ring, Wi-Fi, and a coin laundry are available. Boat docks and launching facilities are across the street from the resort. Leashed pets are permitted, but not in cabins.

Reservations, fees: Reservations are accepted. Sites are $27 per night, $3 per person per night for more than two people. Weekly and monthly rates available. No credit cards accepted. Open year-round.

Directions: From Olympia on I-5, turn north on U.S. 101 and drive about 100 miles (near Sequim) to Whitefeather Way (between Mileposts 267 and 268, 2.5 miles east of Sequim). Turn right (north) on Whitefeather Way and drive 0.5 mile to West Sequim Bay Road. Turn left (west) and drive one block to the resort on the left at 2634 West Sequim Bay Road.

Contact: Sequim Bay Resort, 360/681-3853, www.sequimbayresort.com.

16 SEQUIM BAY STATE PARK

Scenic rating: 8

on Sequim Bay

See map page 28

Sequim translates to "quiet waters," which is an appropriate description of this area. Set in the heart of Washington's rain shadow, a region with far less rainfall than the surrounding areas, Sequim averages only 17 inches of rainfall a year. The 90-acre park features 4,909 feet of saltwater shoreline, and two natural overlapping sandbars protect the bay waters from the rough waves and currents of the Strait of Juan de Fuca. The park has one mile of hiking trails.

RV sites, facilities: There are 60 sites for tents or RVs (no hookups), 16 sites with full hookups (30 amps) for RVs up to 45 feet, a group tent site for up to 60 people, and three primitive tent sites. Picnic tables and fire grills are provided. Restrooms have flush toilets and coin showers. A dump station, firewood, ice, a picnic area with kitchen shelters, an amphitheater, athletic fields, a basketball court, tennis court, and a playground are available. Boat docks, launching facilities, and boat mooring are also available. Some facilities are wheelchair accessible. Leashed pets are permitted.

Reservations, fees: Reservations are accepted at 888/CAMP-OUT (888/226-7688) or www.parks.wa.gov/reservations ($7 reservation fee). Sites are $17–24 per night, $12 per night for hike-in/bike-in sites, $10 per extra vehicle per night; boat moorage is a minimum of $10 per night, plus $0.50 per foot for docking. Call for group rates. Some credit cards accepted. Open year-round.

Directions: From Olympia on I-5, turn north on U.S. 101 and drive 100 miles (near Sequim) to the park entrance on the right (along the highway). The park is 3.5 miles southeast of the town of Sequim.

Contact: Sequim Bay State Park, 360/683-4235; state park information 360/902-8844, www.parks.wa.gov.

17 FORT WORDEN STATE PARK

Scenic rating: 9

in Port Townsend

See map page 28

This park is on the northeastern tip of the Olympic Peninsula, at the northern end of Port Townsend, on a high bluff overlooking Puget Sound. Highlights include great lookouts and two miles of beach trails over the Strait of Juan de Fuca as it feeds into Puget Sound. The park covers 433 acres at historic Fort Worden (on which construction was begun in 1897 and decommissioned in 1953) and includes buildings from the turn of the 20th century. It has 11,020 feet of saltwater shoreline. Recreation options include 12 miles of marked hiking and biking trails, including five miles of wheelchair-accessible trails. The Coast Artillery Museum, Rothschild House, Commanding Officers Quarters, and the Marine Science Center and Natural History Museum are open during the summer season. A ferry at Port Townsend will take you across the strait to Whidbey Island. Special note on reservations: This is an extremely popular park and campground, and reservations are required via the Internet up to five months in advance or over the counter up to four months in advance.

RV sites, facilities: There are 80 sites for tents or RVs up to 60 feet with full or partial hook-ups (30 and 50 amps), five hike-in/bike-in sites, two nonmotorized boat-in sites, and one group camp for up to 200 people. Some sites are pull-through. Other lodging includes 40 Victorian-era houses and three dormitories. Picnic tables and fire grills are provided. Restrooms have flush toilets and coin showers. Drinking water, a store, firewood, and postal service are available. A restaurant, conference facilities, a sheltered amphitheater, athletic fields, and interpretive activities are available nearby. Boat docks, buoys, floats, and launching facilities are also nearby. Some facilities are wheelchair accessible. Several golf courses are nearby. Leashed pets are permitted.

Reservations, fees: Reservations are available by mail, fax, or Internet: www.fortworden.org (click on online camping reservations). Reservations are not available by phone. Sites are $24–31 per night, $12 per night for hike-in/bike-in and boat-in sites, $10 per extra vehicle per night; moorage is a minimum of $10 per night, plus $0.50 per foot for docking. Call for group rates. Open year-round, with fewer sites available during winter.

Directions: From Port Townsend follow Highway 20 north through town to Cherry Street. Turn left at Cherry Street and drive

1.75 miles to the park entrance at the end of the road.

Contact: Fort Worden State Park, 360/344-4400, fax 360/385-7248; state park information 360/902-8844, www.parks.wa.gov.

18 POINT HUDSON MARINA & RV PARK

Scenic rating: 6

in Port Townsend

See map page 28

Point Hudson RV Park is on the site of an old Coast Guard station near the beach in Port Townsend. This public facility is owned by the port of Port Townsend. The park features ocean views and 2,000 feet of beach frontage. Known for its Victorian architecture, Port Townsend is called Washington's Victorian seaport. Fishing and boating are popular here, and nearby recreation opportunities include an 18-hole municipal golf course, a full-service marina, Old Fort Townsend State Park, Fort Flagler State Park, and Fort Worden State Park.

RV sites, facilities: There are 45 sites with full hookups (30 amps) for RVs of any length. Some sites are pull-through. No tents are allowed. Picnic tables are provided at some sites. No fires are allowed. Restrooms have flush toilets and coin showers. Drinking water, cable TV, Wi-Fi and modem access, three restaurants, and a coin laundry are available. The on-site marina has 100-plus slips. Leashed pets are permitted.

Reservations, fees: Reservations are accepted. Sites are $30–37 per night, $5 per extra vehicle per night. Some credit cards accepted. Open year-round.

Directions: From Port Townsend on State Route 20, take the Water Street exit. Turn left (north) and continue (the road becomes Sims Way and then Water Street) to the end of Water Street at the marina. Turn left for registration.

Contact: Point Hudson Marina & RV Park, 360/385-2828 or 800/228-2803, fax 360/385-7331, www.portofpt.com.

WASHINGTON

19 OLD FORT TOWNSEND STATE PARK

Scenic rating: 10

near Quilcene

See map page 28

This 367-acre park features a thickly wooded landscape, nearly 4,000 feet of saltwater shoreline on Port Townsend Bay, and 6.5 miles of hiking trails. Built in 1856, the historic fort is one of the oldest remaining in the state. The scenic campground has access to a good clamming beach (check regulations), and visitors can take two different short self-guided walking tours. Note that the nearest boat ramps are at Port Townsend, Fort Flagler, and Hadlock. Mooring buoys are just offshore the park on the west side of Port Townsend Bay.

RV sites, facilities: There are 40 sites for tents or RVs up to 40 feet (no hookups), four hike-in/bike-in sites, and one group site for up to 80 people. Picnic tables and fire grills are provided. Restrooms have flush toilets and coin showers. Drinking water, a playground, boat buoys, seasonal firewood, a dump station, and a picnic area with a kitchen shelter are available. Some facilities are wheelchair accessible. Leashed pets are permitted.

Reservations, fees: Reservations are not accepted for individual sites. Group site reservations are required at 360/385-3595 (Fort Worden). Sites are $12–17 per night, plus $10 per extra vehicle per night. Call for group rates. Open mid-April–mid-October, weather permitting.

Directions: From Port Townsend and State Route 20, drive south on State Route 20 for two miles to Old Fort Townsend Road. Turn left and drive 0.5 mile to the park entrance road.

Contact: Old Fort Townsend State Park, 360/385-3595; state park information 360/902-8844, www.parks.wa.gov.

20 FORT FLAGLER STATE PARK

Scenic rating: 10

near Port Townsend

See map page 28

This beautiful park sits on a high bluff overlooking Puget Sound with views of the Olympic and Cascade Mountains. The park covers 784 acres and is surrounded on three sides by 19,100 feet of saltwater shoreline. Highlights include five miles of trails for hiking and biking, an interpretive trail, and a military museum featuring gun batteries that is open in the summer (limited winter schedule). Historic Fort Flagler is a pretty and unique state park, set on Marrowstone Island. The RV sites are right on the beach. Anglers like this spot for year-round rockfish and salmon fishing, and crabbing and clamming are good in season (check regulations). Fort Flagler, under construction on some level from 1897 until its closure in 1953, offers summer tours.

RV sites, facilities: There are 14 sites with partial hookups (30 amps) for RVs up to 50 feet, 101 tent sites, two hike-in/bike-in sites, a group tent site for up to 40 people, and a group site for tents or RVs up to 30 feet that can accommodate up to 100 people. Picnic tables and fire grills are provided. Restrooms have flush toilets and coin showers. Drinking water, interpretive activities, a dump station, a camp store, boat buoys, floats, and a launch are available. Some facilities are wheelchair accessible. Leashed pets are permitted.

Reservations, fees: Reservations are accepted at 888/CAMP-OUT (888/226-7688) or www.parks.wa.gov/reservations ($7 reservation fee). Sites are $17–24 per night, $12 per night for hike-in/bike-in sites, $10 per extra vehicle per night. Call for group rates. Some credit cards accepted. Open March–October, weather permitting.

Directions: From Port Townsend at Highway 20, drive east on Highway 20 for three miles to Ness' Corner Road (at the traffic light). Continue straight onto Highway 19 and drive eight miles to Oak Bay Road/State Route 116. Turn left and drive two miles through Port Hadlock (turning left to stay on State Route 116). Continue about eight miles to the entrance.

Contact: Fort Flagler State Park, 360/385-1259, fax 360/379-1746; state park information 360/902-8844, www.parks.wa.gov.

21 BEAR CREEK MOTEL AND RV PARK

Scenic rating: 7

on Bear Creek

See map page 28

This quiet little spot is set where Bear Creek empties into the Sol Duc River. It's private and developed, with a choice of sunny or shaded sites in a wooded setting. There are many recreation options in the area, including fishing, hunting, and nature and hiking trails leading to the ocean. Sol Duc Hot Springs is 25 miles north and well worth the trip. A restaurant next to the camp serves family-style meals.

RV sites, facilities: There are 12 pull-through sites for RVs of any length with full hookups (30 amps). Picnic tables and fire rings are provided. Restrooms have flush toilets and showers. Drinking water, a café, and firewood are available. A motel is on the premises. Boat-launching facilities are within 0.5 mile. Leashed pets are permitted.

Reservations, fees: Reservations are not accepted. Sites are $15 per night. Some credit cards accepted. Open year-round.

Directions: From Aberdeen, drive north on U.S. 101 to Forks. Continue past Forks for 15 miles to Milepost 205 (just past Sappho) to the park on the right at 205860 Highway 101 West.

Contact: Bear Creek Motel and RV Park, 360/327-3660, www.hungrybearcafemotel.com.

22 KLAHOWYA

Scenic rating: 9

on the Sol Duc River in Olympic National Forest

See map page 28

Klahowya features great views of Lake Crescent and Mount Olympus. It's a good choice if you don't want to venture far from U.S. 101 yet want to retain the feel of being in Olympic National Forest. Set along the Sol Duc River, this 32-acre camp is pretty and wooded, with hiking trails in the area. A favorite, Kloshe Nanitch Trail, is across the river and leads up to a lookout on Snider Ridge overlooking Sol Duc Valley. Pioneer's Path Trail, an easy, wheelchair-accessible, 0.3-mile loop with interpretive signs, starts in the camp. Fishing for salmon and steelhead, in season, can be good about one-quarter mile downstream from camp; always check regulations. This camp gets medium use.

RV sites, facilities: There are 54 sites for tents or RVs up to 30 feet (no hookups) and two walk-in sites requiring a 300-foot walk. Picnic tables are provided. Drinking water and vault and flush toilets are available. An amphitheater offers summer interpretive programs. A river boat ramp is nearby. Some facilities are wheelchair accessible. Leashed pets are permitted.

Reservations, fees: Reservations are not accepted. Sites are $12 per night, $6 per night for an additional vehicle. Open May–late September, weather permitting.

Directions: From U.S. 101 in Port Angeles, continue on for about 36 miles (10 miles west of Lake Crescent) to the campground on the right side of the road, close to Milepost 212. (Coming from the other direction on U.S. 101, drive eight miles east of Sappho to the campground.)

Contact: Olympic National Forest, Pacific Ranger District, 360/374-6522, fax 360/374-1250.

23 FAIRHOLME

Scenic rating: 9

on Lake Crescent in Olympic National Park

See map page 28

This camp is on the shore of Lake Crescent, a pretty lake within the boundary of Olympic National Park, at an elevation of 580 feet. The campsites lie along the western end of the lake,

WASHINGTON

in a cove with a boat ramp. Located less than one mile off U.S. 101, Fairholme gets heavy use during tourist months; some highway noise is audible at some sites. A naturalist program is often available in the summer. Waterskiing is permitted at Lake Crescent, but personal watercraft are prohibited.

RV sites, facilities: There are 88 sites for tents or RVs up to 21 feet (no hookups). Picnic tables and fire grills are provided. A dump station, restrooms with flush toilets (summer season), and drinking water are available. A store and a café are within one mile. Boat-launching facilities and rentals are nearby on Lake Crescent. Some facilities are wheelchair accessible. Leashed pets are permitted.

Reservations, fees: Reservations are not accepted. Sites are $12 per night, plus a $15 per vehicle national park entrance fee. Open May–October, weather permitting.

Directions: From Port Angeles, drive west on U.S. 101 for about 26 miles and continue along Lake Crescent to North Shore Road. Turn right and drive 0.5 mile to the camp on North Shore Road on the right.

Contact: Olympic National Park, 360/565-3130, fax 360/565-3147, www.nps.gov/olym.

24 SOL DUC

Scenic rating: 10

on the Sol Duc River in Olympic National Park
See map page 28

This site is a nice hideaway, with nearby Sol Duc Hot Springs a highlight. The problem is that this camp is very popular. It fills up quickly on weekends, and a fee is charged to use the hot springs, which have been fully developed since the early 1900s. The camp is at 1,680 feet along the Sol Duc River.

RV sites, facilities: There are 82 sites for tents or RVs up to 21 feet (no hookups), as well as one group site that can accommodate up to 30 people (nonprofit groups only). Picnic tables and fire grills are provided. Restrooms with flush toilets and drinking water are available

in the summer; there is no water in the winter, but pit toilets are available. A dump station is available nearby, and a store and a café are within one mile. Some facilities are wheelchair accessible. Leashed pets are permitted.

Reservations, fees: Reservations accepted for the group site only. Individual sites are $14 per night, plus a $15 national park entrance fee per vehicle. Group rates are $20 per night, plus $1 per person per night. Open year-round, with limited winter facilities.

Directions: From Port Angeles, continue on U.S. 101 for 27 miles, just past Lake Crescent. Turn left at the Sol Duc turnoff and drive 12 miles to the camp.

Contact: Olympic National Park, 360/327-3534 or 360/565-3130, fax 360/565-3147, www.nps.gov/olym.

25 LOG CABIN RESORT

Scenic rating: 10

on Lake Crescent in Olympic National Park
See map page 28

This pretty camp along the shore of Lake Crescent is a good spot for boaters as it features many sites near the water with excellent views. Fishing and swimming are two options at this family-oriented resort. It is home to a strain of Beardslee trout. Note that the fishing is catch-and-release. Waterskiing is permitted, but no personal watercraft are allowed. A marked hiking trail traces the lake's 22-mile shoreline. This camp is extremely popular in the summer months; you may need to make reservations 6–12 months in advance.

RV sites, facilities: There are 38 sites with full hookups (20 and 30 amps) for RVs of any length, four tent sites, and 28 cabins. Two sites are pull-through. Picnic tables and fire barrels are provided. A dump station, restrooms with flush toilets and coin showers, a store, a café, gift shop, a coin laundry, Wi-Fi, firewood, ice, and a recreation field are available. Boat docks, launching facilities, and boat rentals and hydrobikes are available. Some facilities are wheelchair accessible. Leashed pets are permitted.

Reservations, fees: Reservations are accepted. RV sites are $35 per night, tent sites are $22 per night, and it's $5 per person per night for more than two people, $2 per extra vehicle per night. Some credit cards accepted. Open Memorial Day weekend–September.

Directions: From I-5 at Olympia, turn north on U.S. 101 and drive about 122 miles to Port Angeles. Continue on U.S. 101 past Port Angeles for about 18 miles to East Beach Road. Turn right and drive three miles (along Lake Crescent) to the camp on the left.

Contact: Log Cabin Resort, 360/928-3325, fax 360/928-2088, www.logcabinresort.net.

26 ELWHA

Scenic rating: 7

on the Elwha River in Olympic National Park
See map page 28

The Elwha River is the backdrop for this popular camp with excellent hiking trails close by in Olympic National Park. The elevation is 390 feet. Fishing is good in season at nearby Lake Mills; check regulations. Check at one of the visitors centers for maps and backcountry information.

RV sites, facilities: There are 40 sites for tents or RVs up to 21 feet (no hookups). Picnic tables and fire grills are provided. Restrooms with flush toilets and drinking water are available during the summer; in winter there is no drinking water and pit toilets are available. Some facilities are wheelchair accessible. Leashed pets are permitted.

Reservations, fees: Reservations are not accepted. Sites are $12 per night, plus a $15 national park entrance fee per vehicle. Open year-round, with limited winter facilities.

Directions: From Port Angeles, drive west on U.S. 101 for about nine miles (just past Lake Aldwell) to the signed entrance road on the left. Turn left at the entrance road and drive three miles south along the Elwha River to the campground on the left.

Contact: Olympic National Park, 360/565-3130, fax 360/565-3147, www.nps.gov/olym.

27 ALTAIRE

Scenic rating: 8

on the Elwha River in Olympic National Park
See map page 28

A pretty and well-treed camp with easy highway access, Altaire is on the Elwha River about one mile from Lake Mills. Some sites are riverside. Fishing is good in season; check regulations. The elevation is 450 feet. Altaire also makes for a nice layover spot before taking the ferry at Port Angeles to Victoria, British Columbia.

RV sites, facilities: There are 30 sites for tents or RVs up to 21 feet (no hookups). Picnic tables and fire grills are provided. Drinking water and restrooms with flush toilets are available. Some facilities are wheelchair accessible. Leashed pets are permitted.

Reservations, fees: Reservations are not accepted. Sites are $12 per night, plus a $15 national park entrance fee per vehicle. Open May–October.

Directions: From Port Angeles, drive west on U.S. 101 for about nine miles (just past Lake Aldwell) to the signed entrance road on the left. Turn left at the signed entrance road and drive four miles south along the Elwha River.

Contact: Olympic National Park, 360/565-3130, fax 360/565-3147, www.nps.gov/olym.

28 HEART O' THE HILLS

Scenic rating: 9

in Olympic National Park
See map page 28

Heart O' the Hills is nestled on the northern edge of Olympic National Park at an elevation of 1,807 feet. You can drive into the park on Hurricane Ridge Road and take one of numerous hiking trails. Little Lake Dawn is less than 0.5 mile to the west, but note that most of the property around this lake is privately owned. Naturalist programs are available in summer months.

RV sites, facilities: There are 105 sites for tents or RVs up to 21 feet (no hookups). Picnic tables and fire grills are provided. Drinking water and

WASHINGTON

restrooms with flush toilets are available. Some facilities are wheelchair accessible. Leashed pets are permitted.

Reservations, fees: Reservations are not accepted. Sites are $12 per night, plus a $15 national park entrance fee per vehicle. Open year-round, weather permitting.

Directions: From U.S. 101 in Port Angeles at Hurricane Ridge Road, turn left and drive five miles to the camp on the left. (Access roads can be impassable in severe weather.)

Contact: Olympic National Park, 360/565-3130, fax 360/565-3147, www.nps.gov/olym.

29 LONESOME CREEK RV RESORT

Scenic rating: 8

north of Aberdeen on the Pacific Ocean
See map page 28

This private, developed park is along the Pacific Ocean and the coastal Dungeness National Wildlife Refuge. It has some of the few ocean sites available in the area and offers such recreation options as fishing, surfing, beachcombing, boating, whale-watching, and sunbathing.

RV sites, facilities: There are 42 sites for RVs of any length with full hookups (30 and 50 amps) and one tent site. Picnic tables and fire rings are provided. Restrooms have flush toilets and coin showers. A coin laundry, firewood, gasoline and propane gas, and a convenience store with a deli and ice are available. Boat docks, a marina, and launching facilities are within one mile. Leashed pets are permitted.

Reservations, fees: Reservations are accepted and are recommended for the 18 oceanfront sites. Tent sites are $15–18 per night and RV sites are $25–35 per night. Some credit cards accepted. Open year-round.

Directions: From Aberdeen, drive north on U.S. 101 for 108 miles to Forks. Continue past Forks for two miles to La Push Road/Highway 110. Turn left (west) and drive 14 miles to the resort on the left.

Contact: Lonesome Creek RV Resort, 360/374-4338.

30 MORA

Scenic rating: 8

near the Pacific Ocean in Olympic National Park
See map page 28

At an elevation of 50 feet, this is a good out-of-the-way choice near the Pacific Ocean and the Olympic Coast Marine Sanctuary. The Quillayute River feeds into the ocean near the camp, and upstream lies the Bogachiel, a prime steelhead river in winter months. A naturalist program is available during the summer. This camp includes eight sites that require short walks of up to 100 feet, and several of them are stellar.

RV sites, facilities: There are 94 sites for tents or RVs up to 21 feet (no hookups) and one walk-in site. Picnic tables and fire grills are provided. Restrooms have flush toilets. Drinking water and a dump station are available. Some facilities are wheelchair accessible. Leashed pets are permitted.

Reservations, fees: Reservations are not accepted. Sites are $12 per night, plus a $15 national park entrance fee per vehicle. Open year-round.

Directions: From Aberdeen, drive north on U.S. 101 for 108 miles to Forks. Continue past Forks for two miles to La Push Road/Highway 110. Turn left (west) and drive 12 miles to the campground on the left (well marked along the route).

Contact: Olympic National Park, 360/565-3130, fax 360/565-3147, www.nps.gov/olym.

31 THREE RIVERS RESORT

Scenic rating: 8

on the Quillayute River
See map page 28

This small, private camp is at the junction of three rivers: the Quillayute, Sol Duc, and

Bogachiel. Situated above this confluence, about six miles upstream from the ocean, this pretty spot features wooded, spacious sites. Hiking and fishing are popular here, and there is a fishing guide service. Salmon and steelhead migrate upstream, best on the Sol Duc and Bogachiel Rivers; anglers should check regulations. The coastal Dungeness National Wildlife Refuge and Pacific Ocean, which often offer good whale-watching in the spring, are a short drive to the west. Hoh Rain Forest, a worthwhile side trip, is about 45 minutes away.

RV sites, facilities: There are 10 sites for tents or RVs of any length (no hookups) and nine sites for tents or RVs of any length with full or partial hookups (30 and 50 amps), plus five rental cabins. Picnic tables and fire rings are provided. Restrooms have flush toilets and coin showers. A convenience store, gas station, a café, a coin laundry, firewood, and ice are available. Leashed pets are permitted.

Reservations, fees: Reservations are accepted. Tent sites are $10 per night, RV sites are $14–16 per night, plus $5 per night for an additional vehicle and $5 per pet per night. Some credit cards accepted. Open year-round.

Directions: From Aberdeen, drive north on U.S. 101 for 108 miles to Forks. Continue past Forks for two miles to La Push Road/Highway 110. Turn left (west) and drive eight miles to the resort on the right.

Contact: Three Rivers Resort, 360/374-5300, www.northolympic.com/threerivers.

32 BOGACHIEL STATE PARK

Scenic rating: 6

on the Bogachiel River

See map page 28   BEST (

A good base camp for salmon- or steelhead-fishing trips, this 123-acre park is on the Bogachiel River, with marked hiking trails in the area. It can be noisy at times because a logging mill is directly across the river from the campground. Also note that there is highway

noise, and you can see the highway from some campsites. A one-mile hiking trail is nearby, and opportunities for wildlife-viewing are outstanding in the park. Hunting is popular in the adjacent national forest. This region is heavily forested, with lush vegetation fed by an average of 140–160 inches of rain each year. This park was established in 1931.

RV sites, facilities: There are 30 sites for tents or RVs (no hookups), six sites with partial hookups (30 amps) for RVs up to 40 feet, two hike-in/bike-in sites, and one group tent camp with a covered shelter for up to 20 people. Picnic tables and fire grills are provided. Restrooms have flush toilets and coin showers. Drinking water, a dump station, and a picnic area are available. A store, ice, and firewood are within five miles. Some facilities are wheelchair accessible. Leashed pets are permitted.

Reservations, fees: Reservations are not accepted for individual sites but are required for the group camp at 360/374-6356. Sites are $17–24 per night, the hike-in/bike-in sites are $12 per night, plus $10 per extra vehicle per night. Call for group rates. Open year-round.

Directions: From Olympia on I-5, take Exit 104 and drive north on U.S. 101 to the Aberdeen/Highway 8 exit. Turn west on Highway 8 and drive 36 miles to Aberdeen. Continue through Aberdeen four miles to U.S. 101. Turn north on U.S. 101 and drive 102 miles to the park (six miles south of Forks) on the left side of the road.

Contact: Bogachiel State Park, Northwest Region, 360/374-6356; state park information 360/902-8844, www.parks.wa.gov.

33 HOH RIVER RESORT

Scenic rating: 6

on the Hoh River

See map page 28

This camp along U.S. 101 features a choice of grassy or graveled, shady sites and is most popular as a fishing camp. Although the Hoh River is nearby, you cannot see the river from the campsites. Marked hiking trails are in the area. This pleasant little park offers steelhead and salmon fishing in season as well as elk hunting in the fall. Horseshoe pits and a recreation field are available for campers.

RV sites, facilities: There are 23 sites for tents or RVs of any length with full or partial hookups (30 amps) and two cabins. Some sites are pull-through. Picnic tables and fire pits are provided. Restrooms have flush toilets and coin showers. A general store, propane gas, a gas station, firewood, and ice are available. A boat launch is available nearby. Leashed pets are permitted.

Reservations, fees: Reservations are accepted. RV sites are $17–24 per night, tent sites are $14–15 per night, and it's $5 per extra vehicle per night. Some credit cards accepted. Open year-round.

Directions: From Aberdeen, drive north on U.S. 101 for 90 miles to the resort (15 miles south of Forks) on the left.

Contact: Hoh River Resort, 360/374-5566, www.hohriverresort.com.

34 HOH

Scenic rating: 10

in Olympic National Park

See map page 28

This camp at a trailhead leading into the interior of Olympic National Park is in the beautiful heart of a temperate, old-growth rainforest. In the summer, there are naturalist programs, and a visitors center is nearby. This is one of the most popular camps in the park. The elevation is 578 feet.

RV sites, facilities: There are 88 sites for tents or RVs up to 21 feet (no hookups). Picnic tables and fire grills are provided. Restrooms have flush toilets, and drinking water is available. A dump station is nearby. Some facilities are wheelchair accessible. Leashed pets are permitted.

Reservations, fees: Reservations are not accepted. Sites are $12 per night, plus a $15 national park entrance fee per vehicle. Open year-round.

Directions: From Aberdeen, drive north on U.S. 101 for about 90 miles to Milepost 176. Turn east on Hoh River Road and drive 19 miles to the campground on the right (near the end of the road).

Contact: Olympic National Park, 360/565-3130, fax 360/565-3147, www.nps.gov/olym.

35 FALLS VIEW

Scenic rating: 8

on the Big Quilcene River in Olympic National Forest

See map page 28

A viewing area to a pretty waterfall on the Big Quilcene River, where you see a narrow, 100-foot cascade, is only a 150-foot walk from the campground. That explains why, despite the rustic setting, this spot on the edge of the Olympic National Forest has a host of facilities and is popular. Enjoy the setting of mixed conifers and rhododendrons along a one-mile scenic loop trail, which overlooks the river and provides views of the waterfall.

RV sites, facilities: There are 30 sites for tents or RVs up to 21 feet (no hookups). Picnic tables are provided. Drinking water and restrooms with flush toilets are available. Some facilities are wheelchair accessible. Leashed pets are permitted.

Reservations, fees: Reservations are not accepted. Sites are $10 per night, $5 per extra vehicle per night. Open mid-May–early September, weather permitting.

Directions: From Olympia on I-5, turn north on U.S. 101 and drive approximately 70 miles to the campground entrance on the left (about four miles south of Quilcene).

Contact: Olympic National Forest, Hood Canal Ranger District, Quilcene Office, 360/765-2200, fax 360/765-2202.

36 KITSAP MEMORIAL STATE PARK

Scenic rating: 10

on the Hood Canal

See map page 28

Kitsap Memorial State Park is a beautiful spot for campers along Hood Canal. The park covers only 58 acres but features sweeping views of Puget Sound and 1,797 feet of shoreline. The park has 1.5 miles of hiking trails and two open grassy fields for family play. Note that the nearest boat launch is four miles away, north on State Route 3 at Salisbury County Park. An 18-hole golf course and swimming, fishing, and hiking at nearby Anderson Lake Recreation Area are among the activities available. A short drive north will take you to historic Old Fort Townsend, which is an excellent day trip.

RV sites, facilities: There are 28 sites for tents or RVs up to 30 feet (no hookups), 18 sites with partial hookups (30 amps) for RVs up to 40 feet, three hike-in/bike-in sites, a group camp that can accommodate up to 56 people, and five cabins. Picnic tables and fire grills are provided. Restrooms have flush toilets and showers. Drinking water, a reservable picnic area and pavilion, firewood, and a playground are available. Two boat buoys are available. Gas stations and minimarts are nearby. Some facilities are wheelchair accessible. Leashed pets are permitted.

Reservations, fees: Reservations are accepted for individual campsites and cabins, and they're required for the group camp at 888/CAMP-OUT (888/226-7688) or www.parks.wa.gov/reservations ($7 reservation fee). Sites are $17–24 per night, $12 per night for hike-in/bike-in sites, $10 per extra vehicle per night. Call for group rates. Open year-round.

Directions: From Tacoma on I-5, turn north on Highway 16 and drive 44 miles (Highway 16 turns into Highway 3). Continue north on Highway 3 and drive six miles to Park Street. Turn left and drive 200 yards to the park entrance on the right (well marked).

The park is four miles south of the Hood Canal Bridge.

Contact: Kitsap Memorial State Park, 360/779-3205, fax 360/779-3161; state park information 360/902-8844, www.parks.wa.gov.

37 KALALOCH

Scenic rating: 10

near the Pacific Ocean in Olympic National Park

See map page 28

This camp, on a bluff above the beach, offers some wonderful ocean-view sites—which explains its popularity. It can fill quickly. As at other camps set on the coast of the Olympic Peninsula, heavy rain in winter and spring is common, and it's often foggy in the summer. A naturalist program is offered in the summer months. There are several good hiking trails in the area; check out the visitors center for maps and information.

RV sites, facilities: There are 170 sites for tents or RVs up to 21 feet (no hookups) and one group site for tents or RVs up to 21 feet that can accommodate up to 20 people. Picnic tables and fire grills are provided. Restrooms have flush toilets. Drinking water and a dump station are available. A store and a restaurant are within one mile. Some facilities are wheelchair accessible. Leashed pets are permitted in the campground.

Reservations, fees: Reservations are accepted for individual sites online at www.reservations.nps.gov, or for the group site at 360/962-2271. Sites are $14–18 per night, plus a $15 national park entrance fee per vehicle. The group site is $2 per person per night, plus a $20 reservation fee. Open year-round.

Directions: From Aberdeen, drive north on U.S. 101 for 83 miles to the campground on the left. It is near the mouth of the Kalaloch River five miles north of the U.S. 101 bridge over the Queets River.

Contact: Olympic National Park, 360/565-3130, fax 360/565-3147, www.nps.gov/olym.

38 GRAVES CREEK

Scenic rating: 6

near the Quinault River in Olympic National Park

See map page 28

This camp, at an elevation of 540 feet, sits a short distance from a trailhead leading into the backcountry of Olympic National Park. See an Olympic National Park and U.S. Forest Service map for details. The East Fork Quinault River is nearby, and there are lakes in the area.

RV sites, facilities: There are 30 sites for tents or RVs up to 21 feet (no hookups). Picnic tables and fire grills are provided. Drinking water and restrooms with flush toilets are available during the summer; in winter, there is no drinking water and pit toilets are available. Some facilities are wheelchair accessible. Leashed pets are permitted.

Reservations, fees: Reservations are not accepted. Sites are $12 per night, plus a $15 national park entrance fee per vehicle. Open year-round, with limited winter facilities.

Directions: From Aberdeen, drive north on U.S. 101 for 38 miles to the Lake Quinault turnoff and South Shore Road. Turn east on South Shore Road and drive 15 miles (the road becomes unpaved) to the campground at the end of the road. The Graves Creek Ranger Station is nearby.

Contact: Olympic National Park, 360/565-3130, fax 360/565-3147, www.nps.gov/olym.

39 HAMMA HAMMA

Scenic rating: 7

on the Hamma Hamma River in Olympic National Forest

See map page 28

This camp is on the Hamma Hamma River at an elevation of 600 feet. It's small and primitive, but it can be preferable to some of the developed camps on the U.S. 101 circuit. The Civilian Conservation Corps is memorialized in a wheelchair-accessible interpretive trail that begins in the campground and leads 0.25 mile along the river. The camps are set among conifers and hardwoods.

RV sites, facilities: There are 15 sites for tents or RVs up to 21 feet (no hookups). Picnic tables and fire rings are provided. Vault toilets are available, but there is no drinking water. Garbage must be packed out. Leashed pets are permitted.

Reservations, fees: Reservations are not accepted. Sites are $10 per night, $5 per night per additional vehicle. Open mid-May–early September, weather permitting.

Directions: From Olympia on I-5, turn north on U.S. 101 and drive 37 miles to Hoodsport. Continue on U.S. 101 for 14 miles north to Forest Road 25. Turn left on Forest Road 25 and drive seven miles to the camp on the left side of the road.

Contact: Olympic National Forest, Hood Canal Ranger District, Quilcene Office, 360/765-2200, fax 360/765-2202.

40 COLLINS

Scenic rating: 7

on the Duckabush River in Olympic National Forest

See map page 28

Most vacationers cruising U.S. 101 don't have a clue about this quiet spot set on a great launch point for adventure, yet it's only five or six miles from the highway. This four-acre camp is on the Duckabush River at 200 feet elevation. It has small, shaded sites, river access nearby, and plenty of fishing and hiking; check fishing regulations. Just one mile from camp is Duckabush Trail, which connects to trails in Olympic National Park. Murhut Falls Trail starts about three miles from the campground, providing access to a 0.8-mile trail to the falls. It's a 1.5-mile drive to Dosewallips State Park and a 30- to 35-minute drive to Olympic National Park.

RV sites, facilities: There are six tent sites and 10 sites with no hookups for RVs up to 21 feet. Picnic tables and fire rings are provided. Vault toilets are available, but there is no drinking water. Garbage must be packed out. Leashed pets are permitted.

Reservations, fees: Reservations are not accepted. Sites are $10 per night, $5 per night for each additional vehicle. Open May–September, weather permitting.

Directions: From Olympia on I-5, drive north on U.S. 101 for 59 miles to Forest Road 2510 (near Duckabush). Turn left on Forest Road 2510 and drive five miles west to the camp on the left.

Contact: Olympic National Forest, Hood Canal Ranger District, Quilcene Office, 360/765-2200, fax 360/765-2202.

41 COVE RV PARK

Scenic rating: 5

near Dabob Bay

See map page 28

This five-acre private camp enjoys a rural setting close to the shore of Dabob Bay, yet is fully developed. Sites are grassy and graveled with a few trees. Scuba diving is popular in this area, and the park sells air for scuba tanks. Dosewallips State Park is a short drive away and a possible side trip.

RV sites, facilities: There are 32 sites with full hookups (30 and 50 amps) for RVs up to 40 feet, as well as six tent sites. Some sites are pull-through. Picnic tables and fire rings (in season) are provided. Restrooms have flush toilets and coin showers. Drinking water, cable TV, propane gas, a convenience store, bait and tackle, a coin laundry, a sheltered picnic area, and ice are available. Boat docks and launching facilities are on Hood Canal 2.2 miles from the park. Leashed pets are permitted.

Reservations, fees: Reservations are accepted. Tent sites are $18 per night, RV sites are $25 per night. Some credit cards accepted. Open year-round.

Directions: From Olympia on I-5, drive north on U.S. 101 for 60 miles to Brinnon (about one mile north of Dosewallips State Park).

Continue three miles north on U.S. 101 to the park on the right (before Milepost 303).

Contact: Cove RV Park, 360/796-4723, fax 360/796-3452, www.covervpark.com.

42 SEAL ROCK

Scenic rating: 9

on Dabob Bay in Olympic National Forest

See map page 28

Seal Rock is a 30-acre camp set along the shore near the mouth of Dabob Bay. This is one of the few national forest campgrounds anywhere located on saltwater. It brings with it the opportunity to harvest oysters and clams in season, and makes an outstanding jumping-off point for scuba diving. Most campsites are along the waterfront, spaced among trees. Carry-in boats, such as kayaks and canoes, can be launched from the north landing. Native American Nature Trail and Marine Biology Nature Trail begin at the day-use area. These are short walks, each less than 0.5 mile. This camp is extremely popular in the summer, often filling up quickly.

RV sites, facilities: There are 40 sites for tents or RVs up to 30 feet (no hookups). Picnic tables and fire rings are provided. Restrooms have flush toilets. Drinking water and a picnic area are available. A camp host is on-site in summer. Boat docks and launching facilities are nearby on Hood Canal and in Dabob Bay. Some facilities, including viewing areas and trails, are wheelchair accessible. Leashed pets are permitted.

Reservations, fees: Reservations are not accepted. Sites are $12 per night, $5 per night for an additional vehicle. Open May–September.

Directions: From Olympia on I-5, drive north on U.S. 101 for 62 miles to Brinnon (about one mile north of Dosewallips State Park). Continue two miles north on U.S. 101 to Seal Rock and the camp on the right.

Contact: Olympic National Forest, Hood Canal Ranger District, Quilcene Office, 360/765-2200, fax 360/765-2202.

WASHINGTON

43 DOSEWALLIPS STATE PARK

Scenic rating: 8

on Dosewallips Creek
See map page 28

This 425-acre park is on the shore of Hood Canal at the mouth of Dosewallips River. It features 5,500 feet of saltwater shoreline on Hood Canal and 5,400 feet of shoreline on both sides of the Dosewallips River. Most campsites are grassy and located in scenic, rustic settings. Mushrooming is a seasonal activity. Check regulations for fishing and clamming, which fluctuate according to time, season, and supply. The park hosts an annual "Shellfish Shindig" every April. This camp is popular because it's right off a major highway; reservations or early arrival are advised. Access is not affected by the nearby slide area.

RV sites, facilities: There are 140 sites, including 40 with full hookups (30 amps), for tents or RVs up to 50 feet; two hike-in/bike-in sites; three platform tent rentals; and two group camps for up to 50 and 100 people, respectively. Picnic tables and fire rings are provided. Restrooms have flush toilets and coin showers. Drinking water, firewood, a sheltered picnic area, an amphitheater, interpretive activities, and a summer junior ranger program are available. A wildlife-viewing platform, horseshoe pits, saltwater boat-launching facilities, a recreation hall, a store, a café, and a coin laundry are available nearby. Some facilities are wheelchair accessible. Leashed pets are permitted.

Reservations, fees: Reservations are accepted at 888/CAMP-OUT (888/226-7688) or www.parks.wa.gov/reservations ($7 reservation fee). Sites are $17–24 per night, $12 per night for hike-in/bike-in sites, $45 per night for platform tents, $10 per extra vehicle per night. Call for group rates. Some credit cards accepted. Open year-round.

Directions: From Olympia on I-5, drive north on U.S. 101 for 61 miles (one mile south of Brinnon) to the state park entrance on the left.

Contact: Dosewallips State Park, 360/796-4415; state park information 360/902-8844, www.parks.wa.gov.

44 SCENIC BEACH STATE PARK

Scenic rating: 10

on the Hood Canal
See map page 28

Scenic Beach is an exceptionally beautiful state park with beach access and superb views of the Olympic Mountains. It features 1,500 feet of saltwater beachfront on Hood Canal. The park is also known for its wild rhododendrons in spring. Wheelchair-accessible paths lead to a country garden, gazebo, rustic bridge, and large trees. Many species of birds and wildlife can often be seen here. This camp is also close to Green Mountain Forest, where there is extensive hiking. A boat ramp is 0.5 mile east of the park. A nice touch here is that park staff will check out volleyballs and horseshoes during the summer.

RV sites, facilities: There are 52 sites for tents or RVs up to 60 feet (no hookups) and a group site that can accommodate up to 50 people. Some sites are pull-through. Picnic tables and fire grills are provided. Restrooms have flush toilets and coin showers. Drinking water and a dump station are available. A picnic area with reservable kitchen shelter, horseshoe pits, and volleyball fields are available nearby. Some facilities are wheelchair accessible. Leashed pets are permitted.

Reservations, fees: Reservations are accepted at 888/CAMP-OUT (888/226-7688) or www.parks.wa.gov/reservations ($7 reservation fee). Sites are $17–24 per night, $10 per extra vehicle per night. Call for group rates. Open April–mid-October, weather permitting.

Directions: From the junction at Highway 16 and Highway 3 in Bremerton, turn north on Highway 3 and drive about nine miles and take the first Silverdale exit (Newberry Hill Road). Turn left and drive approximately three miles to the end of the road. Turn right on Seabeck Highway and drive six miles to Scenic Beach Road. Turn right and drive one mile to the park.

Contact: Scenic Beach State Park, 360/830-5079, fax 360/830-2970; state park information 360/902-8844, www.parks.wa.gov.

45 FAY BAINBRIDGE STATE PARK

Scenic rating: 10

on Bainbridge Island

See map page 28

A beach park that offers beauty and great recreation, this camp is on the edge of Puget Sound. The park covers just 17 acres but features 1,420 feet of saltwater shoreline on the northeast corner of the island. You can hike several miles along the beach at low tide; the water temperature is typically about 55°F in summer. The primitive walk-in sites are heavily wooded, and the developed sites have great views of the sound. On clear days, campers can enjoy views of Mount Rainier and Mount Baker to the east, and at night the park provides beautiful vistas of the lights of Seattle. Clamming, diving, picnicking, beachcombing, and kite flying are popular here. In the winter months, there is excellent salmon fishing just offshore of the park.

RV sites, facilities: There are 26 water-hookup sites for tents or RVs up to 30 feet, 10 tent sites, and three hike-in/bike-in sites. Picnic tables and fire grills are provided. Restrooms have flush toilets and coin showers. Drinking water, a dump station, picnic areas with reservable kitchen shelter, firewood, horseshoes, and a playground are available. A store and a café are within one mile. Boat docks, launching facilities, and mooring buoys are nearby. Some facilities are wheelchair accessible. Leashed pets are permitted.

Reservations, fees: Reservations are not accepted. Sites are $17–24 per night, $10 per extra vehicle per night, and $10 per night for mooring buoys. Hike-in/bike-in sites are $12 per night. Open mid-April–early October, weather permitting.

Directions: From Tacoma at I-5, turn north on Highway 16 and drive 30 miles to Bremerton to the junction with Highway 3. Turn north on Highway 3 and drive 18 miles to Highway 305. Turn south on Highway 305 and drive over the bridge to Bainbridge Island and continue three miles to Day Road. Turn left and drive 1.5 miles to Sunrise Drive. Turn left and drive approximately 4.5 miles to the park on the right.

Note: From Seattle, this camp can be more easily accessed by taking the Bainbridge Island ferry and then Highway 305 north to the northeast end of the island.

Contact: Fay Bainbridge State Park, 206/842-3931; state park information 360/902-8844, www.parks.wa.gov.

46 ILLAHEE STATE PARK

Scenic rating: 9

near Bremerton

See map page 28

This 75-acre park, named for a Native American word for "earth" or "country," features the last stand of old-growth forest in Kitsap County, including one of the largest yew trees in America. The park also features 1,785 feet of saltwater frontage. The campsites are in a pretty, forested area, and some are grassy. The shoreline is fairly rocky, set on the shore of Port Orchard Bay, although there is a small sandy area for sunbathers. Clamming is popular here. A fishing pier is available for anglers. Note that large vessels can be difficult to launch at the ramp here.

RV sites, facilities: There are 23 sites for tents or RVs up to 35 feet (no hookups), two sites with full hookups (50 amps) for tents or RVs up to 35 feet, two hike-in/bike-in sites, and one group site for up to 40 people. Picnic tables and fire grills are provided. Restrooms have flush toilets and coin showers. Drinking water, firewood, and a pier are available. Boat docks, launching facilities, five mooring buoys, and 356 feet of moorage float space are available. A sheltered picnic area, horseshoes, volleyball, a field, and a playground are available nearby. A coin laundry and ice are within one mile. Some facilities are wheelchair accessible. Leashed pets are permitted.

Reservations, fees: Reservations are not accepted for family sites but are required for the group site at 360/478-6460. Sites are $17–24 per night, $12 per night for hike-in/bike-in sites, $10 per extra vehicle per night. Moorage is a minimum of $10 per night, plus a charge of $0.50 per foot for docking. Call for group rates. Open year-round.

Directions: On Highway 3, drive to Bremerton and the East Bremerton exit. Drive east for 7.5 miles to Sylvan Way. Turn left and drive 1.5 miles to the park entrance road.

Contact: Illahee State Park, 360/478-6460; state park information 360/902-8844, www.parks .wa.gov.

47 MANCHESTER STATE PARK

Scenic rating: 9

on Puget Sound

See map page 28

Manchester State Park is on the edge of Port Orchard, providing excellent lookouts across Puget Sound. The park covers 111 acres, with 3,400 feet of saltwater shoreline on Rich Passage in Puget Sound. The landscape is filled with fir maple, hemlock, cedar, alder, and ash, which are very pretty in the fall. There are approximately 2.5 miles of hiking trails, including an interpretive trail. Group and day-use reservations are available. Note that the beach is closed to shellfish harvesting. In the early 1900s, this park site was used as a U.S. Coast Guard defense installation. A gun battery remains from the park's early days, along with two other buildings that are on the register of National Historical Monuments.

RV sites, facilities: There are 15 sites for tents or RVs up to 50 feet with partial hookups (30 amps), 35 tent sites, three hike-in/bike-in sites, and one group site with hookups (30 amps) that can accommodate up to 130 people in tents or RVs. Picnic tables and fire grills are provided. Restrooms have flush toilets and coin showers. Drinking water, a dump station, firewood, horseshoe pits, volleyball, badminton, and a sheltered picnic area are available. Some facilities are wheelchair accessible. Leashed pets are permitted.

Reservations, fees: Reservations are accepted at 888/CAMP-OUT (888/226-7688) or www.parks.wa.gov/reservations ($7 reservation fee). Sites are $17–31 per night, $12 per night for hike-in/bike-in sites, $10 per extra vehicle per night. Call for group rates. Some credit cards accepted. Open year-round, with limited winter facilities.

Directions: From Tacoma on I-5, turn north on Highway 16 and drive to the Port Orford/ Sedgwick Road exit and Highway 160. Turn right (east) and drive one mile to Highway 166. Turn left and drive six miles on Highway 166 to Colby. Turn left and drive along the shore through Manchester, continuing for two miles to the park. The last part of the trip is well marked.

Contact: Manchester State Park, 360/871-4065; state park information 360/902-8844, www.parks.wa.gov.

48 WILLABY

Scenic rating: 8

on Lake Quinault in Olympic National Forest

See map page 28

This pretty, 14-acre wooded camp is on the shore of Lake Quinault, which covers about six square miles. The camp is at 200 feet in elevation, adjacent to where Willaby Creek empties into the lake. It's part of the Quinault Indian Reservation, and a boating permit and fishing license are required before fishing on the lake. The campsites vary, with some open and featuring lake views, while others are more private, with no views. The tree cover consists of Douglas fir, western red cedar, western hemlock, and bigleaf maple. The forest floor is covered with wall-to-wall greenery, with exceptional moss growth. Quinault Rain Forest Nature Trail and the Quinault National Recreation Trail System are nearby. This camp is concessionaire operated.

RV sites, facilities: There are 19 sites for tents or RVs up to 20 feet (no hookups), 10 overflow sites for RVs up to 32 feet, and two walk-in sites. Picnic tables and fire pits are provided. Drinking water and restrooms with flush toilets are available. Some facilities are wheelchair accessible. Launching facilities and rentals are available at nearby Lake Quinault. Leashed pets are permitted.

Reservations, fees: Reservations are not accepted. Sites are $14 per night, $5 per extra vehicle per night. Open Memorial Day weekend–September.

Directions: From Olympia on I-5, take Exit 104 and drive north on U.S. 101 to the Aberdeen/Highway 8 exit. Turn west on Highway 8 and drive 36 miles to Aberdeen. Continue through Aberdeen four miles to U.S. 101. Turn north on U.S. 101 and drive about 45 miles to the Lake Quinault turnoff and South Shore Road. Turn right (northeast) on South Shore Road and drive 1.5 miles to the camp set on the southern shore of the lake.

Contact: Olympic National Forest, Pacific Ranger District, Quinault Office, 360/288-2525, fax 360/288-0286.

49 FALLS CREEK

Scenic rating: 8

on Lake Quinault in Olympic National Forest

See map page 28   BEST (

This scenic, wooded three-acre camp is set where Falls Creek empties into Quinault Lake. A canopy of lush bigleaf maple hangs over the campground. The campground features both drive-in and walk-in sites, with the latter requiring about a 125-yard walk. Quinault Rain Forest Nature Trail and the Quinault National Recreation Trail System are nearby. The camp is adjacent to the Quinault Ranger Station and historic Lake Quinault Lodge at an elevation of 200 feet.

RV sites, facilities: There are 21 sites for tents or RVs up to 20 feet (no hookups) and 10 walk-in sites. Picnic tables and fire pits are provided. Drinking water and restrooms with flush toilets are available. A camp host has firewood for sale nearby. A picnic area, boat launching

facilities, and boat rentals are available at Lake Quinault. Some facilities are wheelchair accessible. Leashed pets are permitted.

Reservations, fees: Reservations are not accepted. Sites are $14 per night, $5 per extra vehicle per night. Open Memorial Day weekend–Labor Day weekend.

Directions: From Aberdeen, drive north on U.S. 101 for 38 miles to Quinault and South Shore Road. Turn right (northeast) and drive 2.5 miles to the camp on the southeast shore of Lake Quinault.

Contact: Olympic National Forest, Pacific Ranger District, Quinault Office, 360/288-2525, fax 360/288-0286.

50 COHO

Scenic rating: 10

on Wynoochee Lake in Olympic National Forest

See map page 28

This eight-acre camp sits on the shore of Wynoochee Lake, which is 4.4 miles long and covers 1,140 acres. The camp is at an elevation of 900 feet. The fishing season opens June 1 and closes October 31. Powerboats, waterskiing, and personal watercraft are permitted. Points of interest include Working Forest Nature Trail, Wynoochee Dam Viewpoint and exhibits, and 16-mile Wynoochee Lake Shore Trail, which circles the lake. This is one of the most idyllic drive-to settings you could hope to find.

RV sites, facilities: There are 46 sites for tents or RVs up to 36 feet (no hookups) and 10 walk-in sites. Picnic tables are provided. Drinking water and restrooms with flush toilets are available. There is a dump station nearby. Boat launching facilities are available at Wynoochee Lake. Some facilities are wheelchair accessible. Leashed pets are permitted.

Reservations, fees: Reservations are not accepted. Sites are $12 per night, $10 per night for walk-in sites, $5 per extra vehicle per night. Open May–September, weather permitting.

Directions: From Olympia on I-5, take Exit 104 and drive north on U.S. 101 to the Aberdeen/

Highway 8 exit. Turn west on Highway 8 and drive 36 miles (it becomes Highway 12 at Elma) to Montesano. Continue two miles on Highway 12 to Wynoochee Valley Road. Turn right (north) on Wynoochee Valley Road and drive 12 miles to Forest Road 22. Continue north on Forest Road 22 (a gravel road) to Wynoochee Lake. Just south of the lake, bear left and drive on Forest Road 2294 (which runs along the lake's northwest shore) for one mile to the camp on the west shore of Wynoochee Lake. Obtaining a U.S. Forest Service map is helpful.

Contact: Olympic National Forest, Hood Canal Ranger District, Quilcene Office, 360/765-2200, fax 360/765-2202.

51 STAIRCASE

Scenic rating: 9

on the North Fork of the Skokomish River in Olympic National Park

See map page 28

This camp is near the Staircase Rapids of the North Fork of the Skokomish River, about one mile from where it empties into Lake Cushman. The elevation is 765 feet. A major trailhead at the camp leads to the backcountry of Olympic National Park, and other trails are nearby. See an Olympic National Park and U.S. Forest Service map for details. Hiking trails along the river can be accessed nearby. Stock facilities are also available nearby.

RV sites, facilities: There are 56 sites for tents or RVs up to 21 feet (no hookups). Picnic tables and fire grills are provided. Restrooms with flush toilets and drinking water are available during the summer season only; pit toilets only are available during the winter. Some facilities are wheelchair accessible. Leashed pets are permitted in camp.

Reservations, fees: Reservations are not accepted. Sites are $12 per night, plus a $15 national park entrance fee per vehicle. Open year-round, with limited winter facilities.

Directions: From Olympia on I-5, take U.S. 101 and drive north about 37 miles to the town of

Hoodsport and Lake Cushman Road (County Road 119). Turn left (west) and drive 17 miles to the camp at the end of the road (set about one mile above the inlet of Lake Cushman). The last several miles of the road are unpaved.

Contact: Olympic National Park, 360/565-3130, fax 360/565-3147, www.nps.gov/olym.

52 BIG CREEK

Scenic rating: 7

near Lake Cushman in Olympic National Forest

See map page 28

Big Creek is an alternative to Staircase camp on the North Fork of Skokomish River and Camp Cushman and Recreation Park, both of which get heavier use. The sites here are large and well spaced for privacy over 30 acres, primarily of second-growth forest. Big Creek runs adjacent to the campground. A four-mile loop trail extends from camp and connects to Mount Eleanor Trail. A bonus: two walk-in sites along the creek.

RV sites, facilities: There are 23 sites for tents or RVs up to 30 feet (no hookups) and two walk-in sites (requiring a 0.25-mile walk). Picnic tables and fire grills are provided. Drinking water, vault toilets, and a sheltered picnic area are available. A boat dock and ramp are at nearby Lake Cushman. Garbage must be packed out. Leashed pets are permitted.

Reservations, fees: Reservations are not accepted. Sites are $10 per night, $5 per extra vehicle per night. Open May–September, weather permitting.

Directions: From Olympia on I-5, take Exit 104 for U.S. 101/Highway 8. Drive north on U.S. 101 for 37 miles to Hoodsport and Lake Cushman Road (Highway 119). Turn left on Lake Cushman Road and drive nine miles (two miles north of Camp Cushman) to the T intersection. Turn left and the campground is on the right.

Contact: Olympic National Forest, Hood Canal Ranger District, Quilcene Office, 360/765-2200, fax 360/352-2569.

53 CAMP CUSHMAN AND RECREATION PARK

Scenic rating: 10

on Lake Cushman

See map page 28

Set in the foothills of the Olympic Mountains on the shore of Lake Cushman, this 500-acre park features a 10-mile-long blue-water mountain lake, eight miles of park shoreline, forested hillsides, and awesome views of snowcapped peaks. Beach access and good trout fishing are other highlights. The park has eight miles of hiking trails. Windsurfing, waterskiing, and swimming are all popular. A nine-hole golf course is nearby. This park was previously Lake Cushman State Park.

RV sites, facilities: There are 53 sites for tents or RVs up to 30 feet (no hookups), 29 sites with full hookups (30 amps) for RVs up to 30 feet, two walk-in sites, and one group camp for up to 72 people. Picnic tables and fire grills are provided. Restrooms have flush toilets and coin showers. Drinking water, a camp store, a picnic area, horseshoe pits, badminton, ice, and firewood are available. A restaurant is within three miles. Boat docks and launching facilities are nearby on Lake Cushman. Some facilities are wheelchair accessible. Leashed pets are permitted.

Reservations, fees: Reservations are accepted. Sites are $18–24 per night, $6 per extra vehicle per night, $10 per pet per stay. The group camp is a minimum of $125 per night. Some credit cards accepted. Open mid-April–October, weather permitting.

Directions: From Olympia on I-5, take the U.S. 101 exit and drive north 37 miles to Hoodsport and Highway 119 (Lake Cushman Road). Turn left (west) on Lake Cushman Road and drive 7.5 miles to the park on the left.

Contact: Camp Cushman and Recreation Park, 360/877-6770 or 866/259-2900, fax 360/877-6550, www.lakecushman.com.

54 LAKE CUSHMAN RESORT

Scenic rating: 10

on Lake Cushman

See map page 28

This campground on Lake Cushman has full facilities for water sports, including boat launching and rentals. Waterskiing and fishing are popular. Lake Cushman Dam makes a good side trip. (See the listing in this chapter for *Camp Cushman and Recreation Park* for details about the area.)

RV sites, facilities: There are 50 sites for tents or RVs up to 22 feet (no hookups), 21 sites with partial hookups (20 amps) for RVs up to 40 feet, and 11 cabins. Picnic tables and fire grills are provided. Drinking water, flush and portable toilets, firewood, a convenience store, boat docks and launching facilities, mooring, and boat rentals are available. Groups can be accommodated. Some facilities are wheelchair accessible. Leashed pets are permitted.

Reservations, fees: Reservations are accepted. Tent sites are $18.50 per night, RV sites are $23–29.50 per night, plus $10 per pet per stay, and mooring is $10 per day. Some credit cards accepted. Open year-round.

Directions: From Olympia on I-5, take the U.S. 101 exit and drive north 37 miles to Hoodsport and Highway 119/Lake Cushman Road. Turn left (west) on Lake Cushman Road and drive 4.5 miles to the resort on the left.

Contact: Lake Cushman Resort, 360/877-9630 or 800/588-9630, fax 360/877-9356, www.lakecushman.com.

55 REST-A-WHILE RV PARK

Scenic rating: 6

on Hood Canal

See map page 28

This seven-acre park, at sea level on Hood Canal, offers waterfront sites and a private beach for clamming and oyster gathering, not to mention plenty of opportunities to fish, boat, and scuba dive. It's an alternative to Potlatch State Park and Glen-Ayr RV Park.

RV sites, facilities: There are 80 sites for RVs of any length with full hookups (30 amps), two tent sites, two rental trailers, and a bunkhouse. Some sites are pull-through. Picnic tables and fire rings are provided. Restrooms have flush toilets and showers. Drinking water, cable TV, modem access, Wi-Fi, propane gas, firewood, a clubhouse, a convenience store, a drive-in restaurant, a coin laundry, and ice are available. A café is within walking distance. Boat docks, launching facilities, seasonal boat and kayak rentals, and a private beach for clamming and oyster gathering (in season) are also available. Leashed pets are permitted.

Reservations, fees: Reservations are accepted. Sites are $25–33 per night, $2 per extra vehicle per night, and $5 per person per night for more than two people. Some credit cards accepted. Open year-round.

Directions: From Olympia on I-5, take Exit 104 for U.S. 101/Highway 8. Drive north on U.S. 101 for 37 miles to Hoodsport. Continue 2.5 miles north on U.S. 101 to the park at Milepost 329.

Contact: Rest-A-While RV Park, 360/877-9474 or 866/637-9474, www.restawhile.com.

56 GLEN-AYR RV PARK & MOTEL

Scenic rating: 6

on Hood Canal

See map page 28

This fully developed, nine-acre park is at sea level on Hood Canal, where there are opportunities to fish and scuba dive. Salmon fishing is especially excellent. Swimming and boating round out the options. The park has a spa, moorage, horseshoe pits, a recreation field, and a motel.

RV sites, facilities: There are 40 sites with full hookups (30 amps) for RVs of any length, 18 motel rooms, a townhouse, and two suites with kitchens. Some sites are pull-through. No tents. Picnic tables are provided. No open fires are allowed. Restrooms have flush toilets and showers. Drinking water, cable TV, Wi-Fi, propane gas, ice, a spa, a recreation hall, horseshoe pits,

seasonal organized activities, and a coin laundry are available. A store, a café, and ice are within one mile. A boat dock is across the street from the park. Leashed pets are permitted.

Reservations, fees: Reservations are accepted. Sites are $28–30 per night, $5 per person per night for more than two people, $5 per extra vehicle per night. Some credit cards accepted. Open year-round.

Directions: From Olympia on I-5, take Exit 104 for U.S. 101/Highway 8. Drive north on U.S. 101 for 37 miles to Hoodsport. Continue one mile north on U.S. 101 to the park on the left.

Contact: Glen-Ayr RV Park & Motel, 360/877-9522 or 866/877-9522, www.glenayr.com.

57 MINERVA BEACH RESORT

Scenic rating: 5

on Hood Canal

See map page 28

This resort is on Hood Canal, a layover spot if you're cruising up or down U.S. 101. Road noise is discernible from some sites. There are some long-term rentals here. Recreational opportunities at this resort include salmon fishing, crabbing, and digging for oysters and clams in season; check regulations. A winery is three miles to the north. Nearby Potlatch State Park provides a good side trip.

RV sites, facilities: There are 23 sites with full hookups (30 and 50 amps) for RVs up to 40 feet, along with 20 tent sites. Picnic tables and fire grills are provided. Restrooms have flush toilets and coin showers. Drinking water, cable TV, a coin laundry, horseshoe pits, and ice are available. Leashed pets are permitted, with certain restrictions.

Reservations, fees: Reservations are accepted. Sites are $18–25 per night, $2 per person per night for more than two people, $5 per extra vehicle per night. Winter rates are available. Some credit cards accepted. Open year-round.

Directions: From Tumwater/Olympia, take the U.S. 101 exit and drive north to Shelton. From Shelton, head north on U.S. 101 for 10 miles to the resort entrance on the left (just past Potlatch State Park).

Contact: Minerva Beach Resort, 360/877-5145 or 866/500-5145, www.minervabeach resort.com.

58 POTLATCH STATE PARK

🏃 🚴 🏖 🎣 🏕 🛶 🐴 ♿ 🚐 ⛰

Scenic rating: 8

on Hood Canal

See map page 28

This state park features good shellfish harvesting in season. The park has 9,570 feet of shoreline on Hood Canal. There are 1.5 miles of trails for hiking and biking, but the shoreline and water bring people here for the good kayaking, windsurfing, scuba diving, clamming, and fishing. The park is named for the potlatch, which is a Skyhomish gift-giving ceremony. There are four major rivers, the Skokomish, Hamma Hamma, Duckabush, and Dosewallips, within a 30-mile radius of the park. The park receives an annual rainfall of 64 inches.

RV sites, facilities: There are 18 sites with full hookups (30 and 50 amps) for RVs up to 45 feet, 17 tent sites, and two hike-in/bike-in sites. Picnic tables and fire grills are provided. Restrooms have flush toilets and coin showers. Drinking water, a dump station, firewood, an amphitheater, a picnic area, and seasonal interpretive programs are available. Five mooring buoys are located at the park, and boat docks are available nearby. Some facilities are wheelchair accessible. Leashed pets are permitted.

Reservations, fees: Reservations are not accepted. Sites are $17–24 per night, $12 per night for hike-in/bike-in sites, $10 per extra vehicle per night. Open year-round.

Directions: From Olympia on I-5, take Exit 104 for U.S. 101/Highway 8. Drive north on U.S. 101 for 22 miles to Shelton. Continue north on U.S. 101 for 12 miles to the park on the right (along the shoreline of Annas Bay on Hood Canal).

Contact: Potlatch State Park, 360/877-5361, fax 360/877-6346; state park information 360/902-8844, www.parks.wa.gov.

59 BELFAIR STATE PARK

🏃 🚴 🏊 🛶 🎣 🐴 🐕 ♿ 🚐 ⛰

Scenic rating: 8

on Hood Canal

See map page 28

Belfair State Park is situated along the southern edge of Hood Canal, spanning 65 acres with 3,720 feet of saltwater shoreline. This park is known for its saltwater tidal flats, wetlands, and wind-blown beach grasses. Beach walking and swimming are good. The camp sits primarily amid conifer forest and marshlands on Hood Canal with nearby streams, tideland, and wetlands. A gravel-rimmed pool that is separate from Hood Canal creates a unique swimming area; water level is determined by the tides. Note that the DNR Tahuya Multiple-Use Area is nearby with trails for motorcycles, mountain biking, hiking, horseback riding, and off-road vehicles. Big Mission Creek and Little Mission Creek, both in the park, are habitat for chum salmon during spawning season in fall.

RV sites, facilities: There are 137 sites for tents and 46 sites with full hookups (30 amps) for RVs up to 50 feet. Picnic tables and fire grills are provided. Restrooms have flush toilets and coin showers. Drinking water, a bathhouse, a dump station, firewood, a swimming lagoon, a playground, sports field, badminton, volleyball, and horseshoe pits are available. A store and a restaurant are nearby. Some facilities are wheelchair accessible. Leashed pets are permitted.

Reservations, fees: Reservations are accepted at 888/CAMP-OUT (888/226-7688) or www.parks.wa.gov/reservations ($7 reservation fee). Sites are $17–31 per night, $10 per extra vehicle per night. Some credit cards accepted. Open year-round.

Directions: From Tacoma on I-5, drive to the Highway 16 west exit. Take Highway 16 northwest and drive about 27 miles toward Bremerton and Belfair (after the Port Orchard exits, note that the highway merges into three lanes). Get in the left lane for the Belfair/State Route 3 south exit. Take that exit and turn left at the traffic signal. Take State Route 3 eight miles south to Belfair to State Route 300 (at the signal just after the Safeway). Turn right and drive three miles to the park entrance.

Contact: Belfair State Park, 360/275-0668; state park information 360/902-8844, www.parks .wa.gov.

60 TWANOH STATE PARK

Scenic rating: 8

near Union
See map page 28

This state park is on the shore of Hood Canal at one of the warmest saltwater bodies in Puget Sound and likely the warmest saltwater beach in the state. Twanoh, from a Native American word meaning "gathering place," covers 182 acres, with 3,167 feet of saltwater shoreline. Swimming and oyster and crab harvesting are popular here. No clamming is allowed. Winter smelting is also popular; check regulations. In late fall, the chum salmon can be seen heading up the small creek; fishing for them is prohibited. Most of the park buildings are made of brick, stone, and round logs. They were built by the Civilian Conservation Corps in the 1930s. You'll also see extensive evidence of logging from the 1890s. Amenities include a tennis court, horseshoe pits, and a concession stand.

RV sites, facilities: There are 22 sites with full or partial hookups (30 and 50 amps) for RVs up to 35 feet, 25 sites for tents or RVs (no hookups), and a group tent camp for up to 50 people. Picnic tables and fire grills are provided. Restrooms have flush toilets and coin showers. Drinking water, a seasonal snack bar, sheltered picnic area, and firewood are available. Some facilities are wheelchair accessible. Leashed pets are permitted.

Reservations, fees: Reservations are not accepted. Sites are $17–31 per night, $10 per extra vehicle per night. Call for group rates. Open April–October, weather permitting.

Directions: From Bremerton, take Highway 3 southwest to Belfair and Highway 106. Turn right (west) and drive eight miles to the park. If driving from U.S. 101, turn east on Highway 106 and drive 12 miles to the park.

Contact: Twanoh State Park, 360/275-2222; state park information 360/902-8844, www.parks.wa.gov.

61 JARRELL COVE STATE PARK

Scenic rating: 8

on Harstine Island
See map page 29

Most visitors to this park arrive by boat. Campsites are near the docks, set on a rolling, grassy area. The park covers just 43 acres but boasts 3,500 feet of saltwater shoreline on the northeast end of Harstine Island in South Puget Sound. The park's dense forest presses nearly to the water's edge at high tides—a beautiful setting. At low tides, tideland mud flats are unveiled. The beach is rocky and muddy—not exactly Hawaii. Hiking and biking are limited to just one mile of trail.

RV sites, facilities: There are 22 sites for tents or RVs up to 30 feet (no hookups), one boat-in site (nonmotorized), and a group camp for up to 64 people. Picnic tables and fire grills are provided. Restrooms have flush toilets and coin showers, and drinking water is available. Boat docks, a marine pump-out, and 14 mooring buoys are available. A picnic area, volleyball, badminton, and a horseshoe pit are nearby. Some facilities are wheelchair accessible. Leashed pets are permitted.

Reservations, fees: Reservations are accepted and are required for the group camp at 888/ CAMP-OUT (888/226-7688) or www.parks. wa.gov/reservations ($7 reservation fee). Sites are $17–24 per night, $10 per extra vehicle per night. Call for group rates. Open year-round.

Directions: From Olympia on I-5, turn north on U.S. 101 and drive 22 miles to Shelton and Highway 3. Turn north on Highway 3 and drive about eight miles to Pickering Road. Turn right and drive to the Harstine Bridge. Cross the bridge and continue to North Island Drive. Turn left and drive four miles to Wingert Road. Turn left and drive 0.25 mile to the park on the left.

Contact: Jarrell Cove State Park, 360/426-9226; state park information 360/902-8844, www.parks.wa.gov.

62 JARRELL'S COVE MARINA

Scenic rating: 6

near Shelton

See map page 29

The marina and nearby Puget Sound are the big draws here. This small camp features 1,000 feet of shoreline and half a mile of public beach. Clamming is available in season.

RV sites, facilities: There are three sites with partial hookups (30 amps) for RVs up to 40 feet. No tents. Picnic tables and barbecues are provided. Restrooms have flush toilets and coin showers. Drinking water, propane gas, a dump station, a seasonal convenience store, fishing licenses, bait and tackle, a coin laundry, gasoline, marine fuel, boat docks, and moorage are available. Leashed pets are permitted.

Reservations, fees: Reservations are accepted. Sites are $26 per night. Some credit cards accepted. Open year-round, with limited winter facilities.

Directions: From Olympia on I-5, turn north on U.S. 101 and drive 22 miles to Shelton and Highway 3. Turn north on Highway 3 and drive about eight miles to Pickering Road. Turn right and drive to the Harstine Bridge. Cross the bridge and continue to North Island Drive. Turn left on North Island Drive and drive 2.8 miles to Haskell Hill Road. Turn left (north) on Haskell Hill Road and drive one mile to the marina.

Contact: Jarrell's Cove Marina, 360/426-8823 or 800/362-8823.

63 JOEMMA BEACH STATE PARK

Scenic rating: 8

on Puget Sound

See map page 29

This beautiful camp set along the shore of the peninsula provides an alternative to nearby Penrose Point State Park. It covers 122 acres and features 3,000 feet of saltwater frontage on the southeast Kitsap Peninsula. This area is often excellent for boating, fishing, and crabbing. It is a forested park with the bonus of boat-in campsites. Hiking is limited to a trail that is less than a mile long.

RV sites, facilities: There are 19 sites for tents or RVs up to 35 feet (no hookups), two hike-in/bike-in sites, and two boat-in sites (nonmotorized). Picnic tables, fire grills, and tent pads are provided. Vault toilets, drinking water, boat-launching facilities, and a dock are available. A grocery store is approximately five miles away. Some facilities are wheelchair accessible. Leashed pets are permitted.

Reservations, fees: Reservations are not accepted. Sites are $17–24 per night, $12 per night for hike-in/bike-in and boat-in sites, $10 per extra vehicle per night. Moorage is a minimum of $10 per night, plus $0.50 per foot for docking. Open year-round.

Directions: From Tacoma, drive north on Highway 16 for about 10 miles to Highway 302/Key Peninsula Highway. Turn west and drive about five miles to Key Peninsula Highway. Turn left (south) and drive about 15 miles to Whiteman Road. Turn right and drive four miles to Bay Road. Turn right and drive one mile to the park entrance (stay on the asphalt road when entering the park).

Contact: Joemma Beach State Park, 253/884-1944; state park information 360/902-8844, www.parks.wa.gov.

64 PENROSE POINT STATE PARK

Scenic rating: 8

on Puget Sound

See map page 29

This park on Carr Inlet on Puget Sound, overlooking Lake Bay, has a remote feel, but it's actually not far from Tacoma. The park covers 152 acres, with two miles of saltwater frontage on Mayo Cove and Carr Inlet. The camp has impressive stands of fir and cedars nearby, along with ferns and rhododendrons. The park has 2.5 miles of trails for biking and hiking. Bay Lake is a popular fishing lake for trout and is one mile away; a boat launch is available there. Penrose is known for its excellent fishing, crabbing, clamming, and oysters. The nearest boat launch to Puget Sound is three miles away in the town of Home.

RV sites, facilities: There are 82 sites for tents or RVs up to 35 feet (no hookups), and a group camp for tents or RVs can accommodate up to 50 people. Picnic tables and fire grills are provided. Restrooms have flush toilets and coin showers. Drinking water, a dump station, horseshoe pits, sheltered picnic areas, lawn area, and a beach (no lifeguard or designated swimming area) are available. Boat docks, a marine pump-out, and mooring buoys are nearby. Some facilities are wheelchair accessible. Leashed pets are permitted.

Reservations, fees: Reservations are accepted and required for the group camp at 888/CAMP-OUT (888/226-7688) or www.parks.wa.gov /reservations ($7 reservation fee). Sites are $17–24 per night, $10 per extra vehicle per night. Call for group rates. Boat mooring is a minimum of $10 per night, plus $0.50 per foot for docking. Some credit cards accepted. Open April–August.

Directions: From Tacoma, drive north on Highway 16 for about 10 miles to Highway 302/Key Peninsula Highway. Turn west and drive about five miles to Key Peninsula Highway. Turn south and drive 9.2 miles through the towns of Key Center and Home to Cornwall Road KPS (second road after crossing the Home Bridge). Turn left and drive 1.25 miles to 158 Avenue KPS and the park entrance.

Contact: Penrose Point State Park, 253/884-2514; state park information 360/902-8844, www.parks.wa.gov.

and dramatic sunsets across Puget Sound and the Olympic Mountains. The park covers 109 acres, with 5,600 feet of saltwater shoreline. A unique element of this park is Cutts Island (also called Deadman's Island), which is a half mile from shore and is accessible only by boat. (There is no camping on the island.) The park has sandy beaches, about 250 yards down the hill from the camp. Approximately 2.5 miles of hiking trails are available. A boat launch is five miles southeast of the camp.

RV sites, facilities: There are 41 sites for tents or RVs up to 35 feet (no hookups), one primitive boat-in site (no motorized boats permitted), and one group site for up to 50 people. Picnic tables and fire grills are provided. Restrooms have flush toilets and coin showers. Drinking water, a dump station, covered picnic areas, a seasonal junior ranger program, interpretive activities, and boat buoys are available. A small store is approximately one mile away. Some facilities are wheelchair accessible. Leashed pets are permitted.

Reservations, fees: Reservations are not accepted for individual sites but are required for the group site at 253/265-3606. Sites are $19 per night, $12 per night for the boat-in site, and $10 per extra vehicle per night. Call for group rates. Open year-round.

Directions: From Tacoma on I-5, turn north on Highway 16. Drive seven miles north to the second Gig Harbor exit. Take that exit and look for the sign for Kopachuck State Park. At the sign, turn west and drive five miles (the road changes names several times) to the camp (well marked).

Contact: Kopachuck State Park, 253/265-3606; state park information 360/902-8844, www.parks.wa.gov.

65 KOPACHUCK STATE PARK

Scenic rating: 8

on Puget Sound
See map page 29

This park is on Henderson Bay on Puget Sound near Tacoma. Noteworthy are the scenic views

66 GIG HARBOR RV RESORT

Scenic rating: 7

near Tacoma
See map page 28

This is a popular layover spot for folks heading up to Bremerton. Just a short jaunt off the highway, it's pleasant, clean, and friendly. An 18-hole golf course, a full-service marina, and tennis courts are nearby. Look for the great view of Mount Rainier from the end of the harbor.

RV sites, facilities: There are 93 sites for tents or RVs of any length with full hookups (30 and 50 amps) including some long-term rentals, four sites for tents or RVs with partial hookups (30 amps), 10 tent sites, and one cabin. Some sites are pull-through. Restrooms have flush toilets and showers. Drinking water, cable TV, modem access, propane gas, a dump station, a club room, a coin laundry, ice, a playground, a sports field, and a seasonal heated swimming pool are available. Leashed pets are permitted.

Reservations, fees: Reservations are accepted October–April and required May–September. Tent sites are $20–25 per night, and RV sites are $34–37 per night. Some credit cards accepted. Open year-round.

Directions: From Tacoma, drive northwest on Highway 16 for 12 miles to the Burnham Drive NW exit. Take that exit and enter the roundabout to the first right and Burnham Drive NW. Turn right on Burnham Drive NW and drive 1.25 miles to the resort on the left.

Contact: Gig Harbor RV Resort, 253/858-8138 or 800/526-8311, fax 253/858-8399.

67 PACIFIC BEACH STATE PARK

Scenic rating: 10

near Pacific Beach

See map page 29   BEST (

This is the only state park campground in Washington where you can see the ocean from your campsite; about one-half of the sites are oceanfront. Set on just 10 acres, within the town of Pacific Beach, it boasts 2,300 feet of beachfront. This spot is great for long beach walks, although it can be windy, especially in the spring and early summer. Because of those winds, this is a great place for kite flying. Clamming (for razor clams) is permitted only in season. Note that rangers advise against swimming or body surfing because of strong

riptides. Vehicle traffic is allowed seasonally on the uppermost portions of the beach, but ATVs are not allowed in the park, on the beach, or on sand dunes. This camp is popular and often fills up quickly.

RV sites, facilities: There are 42 sites with partial hookups (30 amps) for RVs up to 50 feet, 22 tent sites and two hike-in/bike-in sites. Picnic tables are provided. Restrooms have flush toilets and coin showers. Drinking water, a dump station, and a picnic area are available. No fires are permitted, except on the beach. Some facilities are wheelchair accessible. Leashed pets are permitted.

Reservations, fees: Reservations are accepted at 888/CAMP-OUT (888/226-7688) or www.parks.wa.gov/reservations ($7 reservation fee). Sites are $17–31 per night, $12 per night for hike-in/bike-in sites, $10 per extra vehicle per night. Some credit cards accepted. Open year-round.

Directions: From Hoquiam, drive north on State Route 109 for 37 miles to Pacific Beach and the park on the right.

Contact: Pacific Beach State Park, 360/276-4297; state park information 360/902-8844, www.parks.wa.gov.

68 DRIFTWOOD ACRES OCEAN CAMPGROUND

Scenic rating: 7

in Copalis Beach

See map page 29

Driftwood Acres spreads over some 150 acres and features secluded tent sites and large RV sites. It is along a tidal river basin, out of the wind. Most find the rustic camp, with its beach access, old-growth forest, and marked hiking trails, to be family friendly. A bundle of firewood is provided for each night's stay. Clamming in season is often good in the area. Additional facilities within seven miles include an 18-hole golf course and a riding stable.

RV sites, facilities: There are 12 sites for tents or RVs of any length with partial hookups (20 and

WASHINGTON

30 amps) and 29 tent sites. Picnic tables and fire pits are provided. Restrooms have flush toilets and coin showers. Drinking water, a free bundle of firewood per day, horseshoe pits, badminton, volleyball, croquet, a dump station, and a clam-cleaning station are available. Propane gas, a tavern, and ice are within one mile. Leashed pets are permitted with certain restrictions.

Reservations, fees: Reservations are accepted. Sites are $25–30 per night, $5 per extra vehicle per night. Some credit cards accepted. Open year-round.

Directions: From Hoquiam, drive west on State Route 109 for 21 miles to Copalis Beach. Continue 0.5 mile north to the camp on the left, between Mileposts 21 and 22.

Contact: Driftwood Acres Ocean Campground, 360/289-3484 or 877/298-1916, www.driftwoodacres.com.

69 SURF AND SAND RV PARK

Scenic rating: 5

in Copalis Beach

See map page 29

Although not particularly scenic, this five-acre park is a decent layover for an RV vacation and will do the job if you're tired and ready to get off U.S. 101. It does have beach access, possible with a 15-minute walk. The surrounding terrain is flat and grassy.

RV sites, facilities: There are 50 sites with full or partial hookups (30 amps) for RVs of any length and 16 tent sites. Some sites are pull-through. Picnic tables and fire pits are provided. Restrooms have flush toilets and showers. Drinking water, seasonal cable TV, a coin laundry, firewood, a recreation room with kitchen facilities for groups, and ice are available. Propane gas is available within one mile. Leashed pets are permitted.

Reservations, fees: Reservations are accepted. RV sites are $25–38 per night, tent sites are $10–15 per night, $4 per extra vehicle per night. Some credit cards accepted. Open year-round.

Directions: From Hoquiam, drive west on State

Route 109 for 21 miles to Copalis Beach and Heath Road. Turn left (west) on Heath Road and drive 0.2 mile to the park.

Contact: Surf and Sand RV Park, 360/289-2707 or 866/787-2751, www.surfandsandrvpark.com.

70 RIVERSIDE RV RESORT

Scenic rating: 8

near Copalis Beach

See map page 29

River access is a bonus at this nice and clean six-acre resort. Most sites have a river view. Salmon fishing can be good in the Copalis River, and a boat ramp is available nearby for anglers. Other options include swimming and beachcombing.

RV sites, facilities: There are 53 sites with full hookups (30 amps) for RVs of any length and 15 tent sites. Some sites are pull-through. Picnic tables and fire grills are provided. Restrooms have flush toilets and coin showers. Drinking water, a dump station, a spa, modem access, firewood, ice, and a recreation hall are available. A café is within one mile. A boat dock, launching facilities, and boat rentals are nearby. Leashed pets are permitted.

Reservations, fees: Reservations are accepted. Tent sites are $16 per night, RV sites are $21 per night, plus $2 per person per night for more than two people. Some credit cards accepted. Open year-round.

Directions: From Hoquiam, drive west on State Route 109 for 22 miles to Copalis Beach. The park is off the highway on the left.

Contact: Riverside RV Resort, 360/289-2111 or 800/500-2111, www.riversidervresort.net.

71 TIDELANDS RESORT

Scenic rating: 7

near Copalis Beach

See map page 29

This flat, wooded resort covers 47 acres and provides beach access and a great ocean view.

It's primarily an RV park, and the sites are pleasant. Ten sites are set on sand dunes, while the remainder are in a wooded area. In the spring, azaleas and wildflowers abound. Horseshoe pits and a sports field offer recreation possibilities. Though more remote than at the other area campgrounds, clamming is an option in season. Various festivals are held in the area from spring through fall.

RV sites, facilities: There are 25 sites for tents or RVs (no hookups), 35 sites with partial or full hookups (20 and 30 amps) for tents or RVs of any length, one rental trailer, and three cottages. Some sites are pull-through. Picnic tables and fire pits are provided. Restrooms have flush toilets and coin showers. Drinking water, a dump station, firewood, cable TV, and a playground are available. A tavern is within one mile. A casino and horseback riding are within seven miles. A golf course is within six miles. Leashed pets are permitted.

Reservations, fees: Reservations are accepted. Sites are $17–23 per night. Some credit cards accepted. Open year-round.

Directions: From Hoquiam, drive west on State Route 109 for about 20 miles to the resort on the left. It is between Mileposts 20 and 21, about one mile south of Copalis Beach.

Contact: Tidelands Resort, 360/289-8963, www.tidelandsresort.com.

72 OCEAN MIST RESORT

Scenic rating: 9

on Conners Creek

See map page 29

Always call to determine whether space is available before planning a stay here. This is a membership resort RV campground, and members always come first. If space is available, they will rent sites to the public. Surf fishing is popular in the nearby Pacific Ocean, while the Copalis River offers salmon fishing and canoeing opportunities. It's about a one-block walk to the beach. There's a golf course within five miles.

RV sites, facilities: There are 116 sites, most with full hookups (30 amps), for RVs up to 40 feet, a grassy area for tents and RVs, and two cabins. Picnic tables are provided at some sites. Restrooms have flush toilets and showers. Drinking water, cable TV, modem access, a dump station, two community fire pits, a spa, clubhouse, and a coin laundry are available. A grocery store is within one mile in Ocean City. Leashed pets are permitted.

Reservations, fees: Reservations are required in the summer. Tent sites are $15 per night, RV sites are $30 per night. Some credit cards accepted. Open year-round.

Directions: From Hoquiam, drive west on State Route 109 for 19 miles to the resort on the left (one mile north of Ocean City).

Contact: Ocean Mist Resort, 360/289-3656, fax 360/289-2807, www.kmresorts.com.

73 OCEAN CITY STATE PARK

Scenic rating: 9

near Hoquiam

See map page 29

This 170-acre oceanfront camp, an excellent example of coastal wetlands and dune succession, features ocean beach, dunes, and dense thickets of pine surrounding freshwater marshes. The Ocean Shores Interpretive Center is on the south end of Ocean Shores near the marina (open summer only). This area is part of the Pacific Flyway, and the migratory route for gray whales and other marine mammals lies just offshore. Spring wildflowers are excellent and include lupine, buttercups, and wild strawberry. This is also a good area for surfing and kite flying, with spring typically windy. Beachcombing, clamming, and fishing are possibilities at this park. An 18-hole golf course, a horse stable, and moped rentals are nearby.

RV sites, facilities: There are 149 sites for tents or RVs (no hookups), 29 sites with full or partial hookups (30 amps) for RVs up to 55 feet, and two group tent camps that can accommodate 20–30 people each. Some sites are pull-through. Picnic tables and fire rings

WASHINGTON

are provided. Restrooms have flush toilets and coin showers. Drinking water, a dump station, a sheltered picnic area, lawn area, and firewood are available. Some facilities are wheelchair accessible. Leashed pets are permitted.

Reservations, fees: Reservations are accepted at 888/CAMP-OUT (888/226-7688) or www.parks.wa.gov/reservations ($7 reservation fee). Sites are $17–24 per night, $10 per extra vehicle per night. Call for group rates. Some credit cards accepted. Open year-round.

Directions: From Hoquiam, drive northwest on State Route 109 for 16 miles to State Route 115. Turn left and drive 1.2 miles south to the park on the right (1.5 miles north of Ocean Shores).

Contact: Ocean City State Park, 360/289-3553, fax 360/289-9405; state park information 360/902-8844, www.parks.wa.gov.

74 SCHAFER STATE PARK

Scenic rating: 8

on the Satsop River
See map page 29

This unique destination boasts many interesting features, including buildings constructed from native stone. A heavily wooded, rural camp, Schafer State Park covers 119 acres along the East Fork of the Satsop River. The river is well known for fishing and rafting. Fish for sea-run cutthroat in summer, salmon in fall, and steelhead in late winter. There are good canoeing and kayaking spots, some with Class II and III rapids, along the Middle and West Forks of the Satsop. Three miles of hiking trails are also available. At one time, this park was the Schafer Logging Company Park and was used by employees and their families.

RV sites, facilities: There are 42 tent sites, six sites with partial hookups (30 amps) for RVs up to 40 feet, two hike-in/bike-in sites, and two group camps for up to 100 people. Picnic tables and fire grills are provided. Restrooms have flush toilets and coin showers. Drinking water, reservable picnic shelters, interpretive

activities, a dump station, and horseshoe pits are available. Some facilities are wheelchair accessible. Leashed pets are permitted.

Reservations, fees: Reservations are not accepted for individual sites, but are required for the group camp at 360/482-3852. Sites are $17–24 per night, $12 per night for hike-in/bike-in sites, $10 per extra vehicle per night. Call for group rates. Open late April–early October, weather permitting.

Directions: From Olympia on I-5, take Exit 104 to U.S. 101. Drive west on U.S. 101 for six miles to Highway 8. Turn west on Highway 8 and drive to Elma (Highway 8 becomes Highway 12). Continue west on Highway 12 for five miles to the Brady exit/West Satsop Road (four miles east of Montesano). Turn right (north) on West Satsop Road and drive eight miles to Schafer Park Road. Turn right and drive two miles to the park.

Contact: Schafer State Park, tel./fax 360/482-3852; state park information 360/902-8844, www.parks.wa.gov.

75 LAKE SYLVIA STATE PARK

Scenic rating: 8

on Lake Sylvia
See map page 29

This 234-acre state park on the shore of Lake Sylvia features nearly three miles of freshwater shoreline. The park is in a former logging camp in a wooded area midway between Olympia and the Pacific Ocean. Expect plenty of rustic charm, with displays of old logging gear, a giant ball carved out of wood from a single log, and some monstrous stumps. The lake is good for fishing and ideal for canoes, prams, or small boats with oars or electric motors; no gas motors are permitted. Five miles of hiking trails and a 0.5-mile wheelchair-accessible trail meander through the park. Additional recreation options include trout fishing and swimming.

RV sites, facilities: There are 35 sites for tents or RVs up to 30 feet (no hookups), two hike-in/bike-in sites, and one group site for up to

60 people and 10 vehicles. Picnic tables and fire grills are provided. Restrooms have flush toilets and coin showers. Drinking water, a dump station, a boat launch, a picnic area, firewood, and a playground are available. A coin laundry, a grocery store, and ice are within two miles. Some facilities are wheelchair accessible. Leashed pets are permitted.

Reservations, fees: Reservations are accepted and required for the group camp at 888/CAMP-OUT (888/226-7688) or www.parks.wa.gov/reservations ($7 reservation fee). Sites are $17–24 per night, $12 per night for hike-in/bike-in sites, $10 per extra vehicle per night. Call for group rates. Open early April–early October, weather permitting.

Directions: From Olympia on I-5, take Exit 104 to U.S. 101. Drive west on U.S. 101 six miles to Highway 8. Turn west on Highway 8 (becomes Highway 12) and drive 26 miles to Montesano and West Pioneer Street (the only stoplight in town). Turn left on West Pioneer Street and drive three blocks to Third Street. Turn right and drive two miles to the park entrance (route is well signed).

Contact: Lake Sylvia State Park, 360/249-3621, fax 360/249-5571; state park information 360/902-8844, www.parks.wa.gov.

76 TRAVEL INN RESORT

Scenic rating: 7

on Lake Sylvia
See map page 29

This is a membership campground, which means sites for RV travelers are available only if there is extra space. It can be difficult to get a spot May–September, but the park opens up significantly in the off-season. There are five major rivers or lakes within 15 minutes of this camp (Satsop, Chehalis, Wynoochee, Black River, and Lake Sylvia). Nearby Lake Sylvia State Park provides multiple marked hiking trails. Additional recreation options include trout fishing, swimming, and golf (three miles away).

RV sites, facilities: There are 144 sites with full hookups (30 and 50 amps) for RVs of any length, plus 10 tent sites. Picnic tables are provided. Restrooms have flush toilets and showers. Drinking water, a coin laundry, two community fire pits, a gazebo, a seasonal heated swimming pool, two game rooms, cable TV, Wi-Fi, seasonal organized activities, and a clubhouse are available. A grocery store, gas station, propane, and restaurant are available within one mile. Some facilities are wheelchair accessible. Leashed pets are permitted.

Reservations, fees: Reservations are required May–September. Sites are $30 per night. No credit cards accepted. Open year-round.

Directions: From Olympia on I-5, take Exit 104 to U.S. 101. Drive west on U.S. 101 for six miles to Highway 8. Turn west on Highway 8 and drive to Elma (Highway 8 becomes Highway 12). Take the first Elma exit and drive to the stop sign and Highway 12/East Main Street. Turn right and drive about 200 yards to the end of the highway and a stop sign. Turn right and drive another 200 yards to the resort on the right.

Contact: Travel Inn Resort, 360/482-3877, www.kmresorts.com.

77 JOLLY ROGERS RV PARK

Scenic rating: 7

near Westport Harbor
See map page 29

A beachside RV park with concrete sites and nearby beach access, this camp covers one acre near Westport Harbor. It's a prime spot for watching ocean sunsets, and on clear days, snowcapped Mount Rainier is visible. Westport Light and Westhaven State Parks are nearby and offer day-use facilities along the ocean.

RV sites, facilities: There are 12 sites for RVs of any length with full hookups (20 and 30 amps). Some sites are pull-through. Restrooms have flush toilets and showers. Drinking water, cable TV, a picnic area, and boat docks and moorage are available. Propane gas, a store, a café, and a

WASHINGTON

coin laundry are within one mile. Leashed pets are permitted.

Reservations, fees: Reservations are accepted. Sites are $20–25 per night. No credit cards accepted. Open year-round.

Directions: From Aberdeen, drive south on State Route 105 for 22 miles to Westport and Neddie Rose Drive. Turn right (north) and drive a short distance to the park on the right (Westport Docks).

Contact: Jolly Rogers RV Park, tel./fax 360/268-0265.

78 AMERICAN SUNSET RV AND TENT RESORT

Scenic rating: 8

near Westport Harbor

See map page 29   BEST (

If location is everything, then this RV camp, set on a peninsula, is a big winner. It covers 32 acres and is 10 blocks from the ocean; hiking and biking trails are nearby. The park is divided into two areas: one for campers, another for long-term rentals. Nearby are Westhaven and Westport Light State Parks, popular with hikers, rock hounds, scuba divers, and surf anglers. Swimming (but not off the docks), fishing, and crabbing off the docks are also options. Monthly rentals are available in summer.

RV sites, facilities: There are 120 sites with full hookups (20, 30, and 50 amps) for RVs up to 45 feet, 50 sites for tents or RVs up to 30 feet (no hookups), and one rental trailer. Some sites are pull-through. Picnic tables and fire rings are provided. Restrooms have flush toilets and showers. Drinking water, satellite TV, Wi-Fi, a coin laundry, a convenience store, propane, a seasonal heated swimming pool, horseshoe pits, a playground, a fish-cleaning station, and a recreation hall are available. A marina is two blocks away. Leashed pets are permitted.

Reservations, fees: Reservations are accepted. Sites are $19–29 per night. Weekly rates

available. Some credit cards accepted. Open year-round.

Directions: From Aberdeen, drive south on State Route 105 for 22 miles to Westport and Montesano Street (the first exit in Westport). Turn right (northeast) on Montesano Street and drive three miles to the resort on the left.

Contact: American Sunset RV and Tent Resort, 360/268-0207 or 800/569-2267, www.americansunsetrv.com.

79 HOLAND CENTER

Scenic rating: 6

in Westport

See map page 29

This pleasant, 18-acre RV park is one of several in the immediate area. The sites are graveled or grassy with pine trees between and have ample space. There is no beach access from the park, but full recreational facilities are available nearby. About half of the sites are long-term rentals.

RV sites, facilities: There are 80 sites with full hookups (30 amps) for RVs of any length. No tents or open fires are allowed. Picnic tables are provided. Restrooms have flush toilets and coin showers. Cable TV, a coin laundry, and storage sheds are available. Propane gas, a store, a café, and ice are within one mile. Boat docks and launching facilities are nearby. Pets are not allowed.

Reservations, fees: Reservations are accepted. Sites are $25 per night. No credit cards accepted. Open year-round.

Directions: From Aberdeen, drive south on State Route 105 for 22 miles to Westport. Continue on State Route 105 to a Y intersection. Bear right on Montesano Street and drive approximately two miles to Wilson Street. The park is on the left, at the corner of State Route 105 and Wilson Street.

Contact: Holand Center, tel./fax 360/268-9582.

80 PACIFIC MOTEL AND RV PARK

Scenic rating: 5

near Twin Harbors

See map page 29

This five-acre park has shaded sites in a wooded setting. It's near Twin Harbors and Westport Light State Park, a day-use park nearby. Both parks have beach access. A full-service marina is within two miles. About 25 percent of the sites are occupied with long-term rentals.

RV sites, facilities: There are 80 sites with full hookups (20 and 30 amps) for RVs of any length and 12 tent sites. Some sites are pull-through. Picnic tables and fire rings are provided. Restrooms have flush toilets and coin showers. Drinking water, a dump station, propane gas, a fish-cleaning station, a recreation hall with a kitchen, cable TV, a pay phone, a coin laundry, and a seasonal heated swimming pool are available. A store, a café, and ice are within one mile. Boat-launching and boat docks are nearby in a full-service marina. Leashed pets are permitted.

Reservations, fees: Reservations are accepted. Sites are $19–25 per night, $2 per person per night for more than two people. Some credit cards accepted. Open year-round.

Directions: From Aberdeen, drive south on State Route 105 for approximately 18 miles to the State Route 105 spur road to Westport. Turn right (north) and drive 1.7 miles to the park on the right.

Contact: Pacific Motel and RV Park, 360/268-9325, fax 360/268-6227, www .pacificmotelandrv.com.

81 TWIN HARBORS STATE PARK

Scenic rating: 8

near Westport on the Pacific Ocean

See map page 29

The park covers 172 acres and is four miles south of Westhaven. It was a military training ground in the 1930s. The campsites are close together and often crammed to capacity in the summer. Highlights include beach access and marked hiking trails, including Shifting Sands Nature Trail. The most popular recreation activities are surf fishing, surfing, beachcombing, and kite flying. Fishing boats can be chartered nearby in Westport.

RV sites, facilities: There are 253 sites, including 49 with full hookups (30 amps) for tents or RVs up to 35 feet, four hike-in/bike-in sites, and one group site for up to 60 people. Picnic tables and fire grills are provided. Restrooms have flush toilets and coin showers. Drinking water, a dump station, interpretive activities, a picnic area with a kitchen shelter, a playground, and horseshoe pits are available. A store, a café, and ice are available within one mile. Some facilities are wheelchair accessible. Leashed pets are permitted.

Reservations, fees: Reservations are accepted and required for the group site at 888/CAMP-OUT (888/226-7688) or www.parks.wa.gov/reservations ($7 reservation fee). Sites are $17–31 per night, $12 per night for hike-in/bike-in sites, $10 per extra vehicle per night. Call for group rates. Some credit cards accepted. Open year-round.

Directions: From Aberdeen, drive south on State Route 105 for 17 miles to the park entrance on the left (three miles south of Westport).

Contact: Twin Harbors State Park, 360/268-9717; state park information 360/902-8844, www.parks.wa.gov.

82 GRAYLAND BEACH STATE PARK

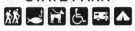

Scenic rating: 8

near Grayland on the Pacific Ocean

See map page 29

This state park features 7,500 feet of beach frontage. All the campsites are within easy walking distance of the ocean. The campsites are relatively spacious for a state park, but they are not especially private. This park is popular with out-of-towners, especially during summer. Recreation options include fishing, beachcombing, and kite flying. The best spot for surfing is five miles north at Westhaven State Park.

RV sites, facilities: There are 120 sites for tents or RVs up to 40 feet, including 102 with full or partial hookups (30 and 50 amps), four tent sites, four walk-in tent sites, and 10 yurts. Picnic tables and fire grills are provided. Drinking water, vault toilets, and restrooms with flush toilets and coin showers are available. Some facilities are wheelchair accessible. Leashed pets are permitted.

Reservations, fees: Reservations are accepted at 888/CAMP-OUT (888/226-7688) or www.parks.wa.gov/reservations ($7 reservation fee). Sites are $12–31 per night, $10 per extra vehicle per night. Yurts are $40 per night. Some credit cards accepted. Open year-round.

Directions: From Aberdeen, drive south on State Route 105 for 22 miles to the park entrance. The park is just south of the town of Grayland on the right (west).

Contact: Grayland Beach State Park, 360/267-4301; state park information 360/902-8844, www.parks.wa.gov.

83 BAY CENTER/ WILLAPA BAY KOA

Scenic rating: 7

on Willapa Bay

See map page 29   BEST (

This KOA is 200 yards from Willapa Bay, within walking distance of a beach that seems to stretch to infinity. A trail leads to the beach and from here you can walk for miles in either direction. The beach sand is mixed with agates, driftwood, and seaweed. Dungeness crabs, clams, and oysters all live within the nearshore vicinity. Another bonus is that herds of Roosevelt elk roam the nearby woods. Believe it or not, there are also black bears, although they are seldom seen here. The park covers five acres, and the campsites are graveled and shaded.

RV sites, facilities: There are 42 sites with full or partial hookups (20, 30, and 50 amps) for RVs of any length, 23 tent sites, and two cab-

ins. Some sites are pull-through. Picnic tables and fire rings are provided. Restrooms have flush toilets and showers. Drinking water, propane gas, a dump station, cable TV, Wi-Fi and modem access, a video arcade, a camp store, firewood, a coin laundry, and ice are available. A café, boat docks, and launching facilities are nearby. Some facilities are wheelchair accessible. Leashed pets are permitted, with certain restrictions.

Reservations, fees: Reservations are accepted at 800/562-7810. Sites are $21–35 per night, $4 per person per night for more than two people, $4 per extra vehicle per night. Some credit cards accepted. Open April–late October.

Directions: From Nemah on U.S. 101, drive north for five miles to Bay Center/Dike exit (between Mileposts 42 and 43, 16 miles south of Raymond). Turn left (west) and drive three miles to the campground.

Contact: Bay Center/Willapa Bay KOA, 360/875-6344, www.koa.com.

84 RAINBOW FALLS STATE PARK

Scenic rating: 8

on the Chehalis River Bay

See map page 29

This 139-acre park is on the Chehalis River and boasts 3,400 feet of shoreline. The camp features stands of old-growth cedar and fir and is named after a few small cascades with drops of about 10 feet. The park has 10 miles of hiking trails, including an interpretive trail, seven miles of bike trails, and seven miles of horse trails. A pool at the base of Rainbow Falls is excellent for swimming. Another attraction, a small fuchsia garden, has more than 40 varieties. Several log structures were built by the Civilian Conservation Corps in 1935.

RV sites, facilities: There are 45 sites for tents or RVs up to 32 feet (no hookups), eight sites with partial hookups (30 and 50 amps) for tents or RVs up to 32 feet, three hike-in/bike-in sites, three equestrian sites with hitching points and stock water, and one group site for up to 60 people. Picnic tables and fire rings are provided. Restrooms have flush toilets and coin showers. Drinking water, a dump station, firewood, a picnic area, interpretive activities, a playground with horseshoe pits, and a softball field are available. Some facilities are wheelchair accessible. Leashed pets are permitted.

Reservations, fees: Reservations are not accepted for individual sites but are required for the group site at 888/CAMP-OUT (888/226-7688) or www.parks.wa.gov/reservations ($7 reservation fee). Sites are $19–24 per night, $12 per night for hike-in/bike-in sites, $10 per extra vehicle per night. Call for group rates. Open year-round.

Directions: From Chehalis on I-5, take Exit 77 to Highway 6. Turn west and drive 16 miles to the park entrance on the right.

Contact: Rainbow Falls State Park, 360/291-3767; state park information 360/902-8844, www.parks.wa.gov.

85 OCEAN PARK RESORT

Scenic rating: 5

on Willapa Bay

See map page 29

This wooded, 10-acre campground is a half mile from Willapa Bay. With grassy, shaded sites, it caters primarily to RVs. Fishing, crabbing, and clamming are popular in season. Ocean Park has several festivals during the summer season. During these festivals, this resort fills up. To the north, Leadbetter Point State Park provides a side-trip option.

RV sites, facilities: There are 70 sites with full hookups (30 amps) for RVs of any length, seven tent sites, and two park-model cottages. Some sites are pull-through. Picnic tables are provided. Fire pits are provided at tent sites. Restrooms have flush toilets and coin showers. Drinking water, propane gas, a recreation hall, a coin laundry, a playground, firewood, a spa, and a seasonal heated swimming pool are available. A store and a café are available within one mile. Boat docks and launching facilities

are nearby on Willapa Bay. Leashed pets are permitted, with certain restrictions.

Reservations, fees: Reservations are accepted. Sites are $21–25 per night, $3 per person per night for more than two people. Some credit cards accepted. Open year-round.

Directions: From Kelso/Longview on I-5, turn west on Highway 4 and drive 63 miles to U.S. 101. Turn south on U.S. 101 and drive 13 miles to the junction with Highway 103. Turn right (north) on Highway 103 and drive 11 miles to the town of Ocean Park and 259th Street. Turn right (east) on 259th Street and drive two blocks to the resort at the end of the road.

Contact: Ocean Park Resort, 360/665-4585 or 800/835-4634, www.opresort.com.

86 WESTGATE CABIN & RV PARK

Scenic rating: 9

near Long Beach

See map page 29

Highlights at this pretty and clean four-acre camp include beach access, oceanfront sites, and all the amenities. There are 28 miles of beach that can be driven on. Additional facilities within five miles of the park include an 18-hole golf course.

RV sites, facilities: There are 38 sites with full hookups (30 amps) for RVs up to 50 feet, as well as six cabins. Some sites are pull-through. No tents. Picnic tables are provided. Restrooms have flush toilets and showers. Drinking water, cable TV, Wi-Fi and modem access, a coin laundry, a recreation hall, gas station, and ice are available. A store and a café are available about two miles away. Boat docks and launching facilities are nearby on Willapa Bay. Leashed pets are permitted, but not in cabins.

Reservations, fees: Reservations are accepted. Sites are $28–31 per night, $2 per person per night for more than two people. Some credit cards accepted. Open year-round.

Directions: From Kelso/Longview on I-5, turn west on Highway 4 and drive 63 miles to U.S. 101. Turn left (south) on U.S. 101 and

WASHINGTON

drive 13 miles to the junction with Highway 103. Turn right (north) on Highway 103 and drive nine miles to the park on the left (at the south edge of the town of Ocean Park).

Contact: Westgate Cabin & RV Park, 360/665-4211, fax 360/665-2451.

87 OCEAN AIRE RV PARK

Scenic rating: 4

near Willapa Bay

See map page 29

This camp is in town, a half mile from the shore of Willapa Bay. At the time of publication, this park was in escrow; check for current status. Tennis courts are a quarter mile away, and a golf course is three miles away. Leadbetter Point State Park, about eight miles north, is open for day use and provides footpaths for walking through the state-designated natural area and wildlife refuge. Two-thirds of the sites are long-term rentals, making reservations essential for the remaining sites during the summer.

RV sites, facilities: There are 46 sites with full hookups (20 amps), including eight drive-through, for RVs of any length. No tents are allowed. Restrooms, drinking water, flush toilets, showers, picnic tables, cell phone reception, an RV dump station, and a coin laundry are available. A store, ice, pay phone, and a café are available next door. Boat rentals are nearby on Willapa Bay. An ATM is within two blocks. Leashed pets are permitted.

Reservations, fees: Reservations are accepted. Call for current prices. Open year-round.

Directions: From Kelso/Longview on I-5, turn west on Highway 4 and drive 63 miles to U.S. 101. Turn south on U.S. 101 and drive 13 miles to the junction with Highway 103. Turn north on Highway 103 and drive 11 miles to the town of Ocean Park and 259th Street. Turn right on 259th Street and drive two blocks to the camp.

Contact: Ocean Aire RV Park, 25918 R Street, Ocean Park, WA 98640, 360/665-4027, www.opchamber.com.

88 LANDS END RV PARK

Scenic rating: 7

near Long Beach

See map page 29

This park covers six acres and features both beach access and spacious, grassy sites near the shore. A bonus is that the tent sites sit close to the ocean. Additional facilities found within five miles of the campground include an 18-hole golf course, marked bike trails, and a riding stable. This park was previously known as Ma and Pa's Pacific RV Park.

RV sites, facilities: There are 53 sites with full or partial hookups (30 amps) for RVs of any length and 68 tent sites. Picnic tables are provided and fire pits are available at some tent sites. Restrooms have flush toilets and coin showers. Drinking water, cable TV, modem access, a coin laundry, a recreation room, propane gas, and ice are available. A store and café are available within one mile. Leashed pets are permitted.

Reservations, fees: Reservations are accepted. Tent sites are $12–15 per night, RV sites are $15–25 per night, plus $2 per person per night for more than two people and $1 per pet per night. Some credit cards accepted. Open year-round.

Directions: From Kelso/Longview on I-5, turn west on Highway 4 and drive 63 miles to U.S. 101. Turn left (south) on U.S. 101 and drive 13 miles to the junction with Highway 103. Turn right (north) on Highway 103 and drive four miles to the park on the left (ocean side).

Contact: Lands End RV Park, 360/642-3253 or 877/300-3253, fax 360/642-5039, www.landsendrvpark.com.

89 ANDERSEN'S RV PARK ON THE OCEAN

Scenic rating: 7

near Long Beach

See map page 29

Timing is everything here. When the dates are announced for the local festivals, reservations start pouring in and the sites at this park can be booked a year in advance. Located 3.5 miles north of downtown Long Beach, this five-acre camp features a path through the dunes that will get you to the beach in a flash. It is in a flat, sandy area with gravel sites. Recreation options include beach bonfires, beachcombing, surf fishing, and clamming (seasonal). Additional facilities found within five miles of the park include marked dune trails, a nine-hole golf course, a riding stable, and tennis courts. The park is big-rig friendly and reservations are recommended.

RV sites, facilities: There are 60 sites with full hookups (20, 30, and 50 amps) for RVs of any length. No tent camping. Picnic tables and fire pits are provided. Restrooms have flush toilets and showers. Drinking water, cable TV, Wi-Fi, modem access, a dump station, a coin laundry, ice, propane gas, a fax machine, group facilities, a horseshoe pit, and a playground are available. A store and a café are available within two miles. Leashed pets are permitted.

Reservations, fees: Reservations are accepted. Sites are $27–42 per night, $2 per person per night for more than two people. Some credit cards accepted. Open year-round.

Directions: From Kelso/Longview on I-5, turn west on Highway 4 and drive 63 miles to U.S. 101. Turn left (south) on U.S. 101 and drive 13 miles to the junction with Highway 103. Turn right (north) on Highway 103 and drive five miles to the park on the left.

Contact: Andersen's RV Park on the Ocean, 360/642-2231 or 800/645-6795, www .andersensrv.com.

90 OCEANIC RV PARK

Scenic rating: 3

in Long Beach
See map page 29

This two-acre park is in the heart of downtown, within walking distance of restaurants and stores. It is also within five miles of an 18-hole golf course, marked bike trails, and a full-service marina.

RV sites, facilities: There are 18 pull-through sites with full hookups (30 and 50 amps) for RVs of any length. No tents or open fires are allowed. Restrooms have flush toilets and showers. Cable TV, a restaurant, and propane gas are available. A store, a coin laundry, and ice are within one mile. Boat docks, launching facilities, and boat rentals are nearby. Leashed pets are permitted.

Reservations, fees: Reservations are accepted. Sites are $25–30 per night, $3 per person per night for more than two people. Some credit cards accepted. Open year-round.

Directions: From Kelso/Longview on I-5, turn west on Highway 4 and drive 63 miles to U.S. 101. Turn left (south) on U.S. 101 and drive 13 miles to the junction with Highway 103. Turn right (north) on Highway 103 and drive two miles to Long Beach. Continue to the park at the south junction of Pacific Highway (Highway 103) and Fifth Avenue on the right.

Contact: Oceanic RV Park, 360/642-3836.

91 MERMAID INN AND RV PARK

Scenic rating: 3

near Long Beach
See map page 29

Situated along the highway, this three-acre park is within four blocks of the beach. It is also within five miles of an 18-hole golf course, a full-service marina, and a riding stable.

RV sites, facilities: There are 11 sites for RVs of any length with full hookups (20 and 30 amps), as well as 10 motel rooms. No tents are allowed. Picnic tables are provided. Restrooms have flush toilets and showers. Drinking water, cable TV, a picnic area, fish cleaning station, and a coin laundry are available. Propane gas, a gas station, a store, a restaurant, and ice are within one mile. Leashed pets are permitted, with certain restrictions.

Reservations, fees: Reservations are accepted. Sites are $21–25 per night, $2 per person per night for more than two people. Monthly rates

WASHINGTON

available. Some credit cards accepted. Open year-round.

Directions: From Kelso/Longview on I-5, turn west on Highway 4 and drive 63 miles to U.S. 101. Turn left (south) on U.S. 101 and drive 13 miles to the junction with Highway 103. Turn right (north) on Highway 103 and drive three miles to the park on the right at 1910 Pacific Avenue North.

Contact: Mermaid Inn and RV Park, 360/642-2600, www.mermaidinnatlongbeach wa.com.

92 DRIFTWOOD RV PARK

Scenic rating: 5

near Long Beach
See map page 29

This two-acre park features grassy, shaded sites and beach access close by. A fenced pet area is a bonus. Additional facilities within five miles of the park include a nine-hole golf course, hiking and bicycle trails, horseback riding, and a full-service marina.

RV sites, facilities: There are 56 sites with full hookups (30 amps) for RVs of any length. Some sites are pull-through. No tents are allowed. Picnic tables are provided and portable fire pits can be rented. Restrooms have flush toilets and showers. Drinking water, a coin laundry, cable TV, Wi-Fi, modem access, fish- and clam-cleaning station, group facilities, and a fenced pet area are available. Propane gas, a gas station, a store, and several restaurants are available within one mile. Leashed pets are permitted, with certain restrictions.

Reservations, fees: Reservations are required. Sites are $23.50–33 per night, $3 per person per night for more than two people. Weekly and monthly rates available. Credit cards are not accepted. Open year-round.

Directions: From Kelso/Longview on I-5, turn west on Highway 4 and drive 63 miles to U.S. 101. Turn left (south) on U.S. 101 and drive 13 miles to the junction with Highway 103. Turn right (north) on Highway 103 and

drive 2.25 miles to the park on the right, at 14th Street North and Pacific Avenue.

Contact: Driftwood RV Park, 360/642-2711 or 888/567-1902, www.driftwood-rvpark.com.

93 SAND CASTLE RV PARK

Scenic rating: 3

in Long Beach
See map page 29

This park is across the highway from the ocean. Although not particularly scenic, it is clean and does provide nearby beach access. The park covers two acres, has grassy areas, and is one of several in the immediate area. Additional facilities found within five miles of the park include a nine-hole golf course, marked bike trails, a full-service marina, and two riding stables.

RV sites, facilities: There are 38 sites with full hookups (20 and 30 amps) for RVs of any length, four sites with no hookups for RVs up to 25 feet, and two tent sites. Picnic tables are provided. Restrooms have flush toilets and coin showers. Drinking water, cable TV, Wi-Fi, a dump station, a coin laundry, and a pay phone are available. Propane gas, a gas station, a store, ice, and a café are available within one mile. Boat docks, launching facilities, and rentals are within five miles. Leashed pets are permitted, with certain restrictions.

Reservations, fees: Reservations are accepted. Tent sites are $12.50–15 per night, RV sites are $20–30 per night, plus $2 per person per night for more than two people and $2 per extra vehicle per night. Some credit cards accepted. Open year-round.

Directions: From Kelso/Longview on I-5, turn west on Highway 4 and drive 63 miles to U.S. 101. Turn left (south) on U.S. 101 and drive 13 miles to the junction with Highway 103. Turn right (north) on Highway 103 and drive two miles to the park on the right.

Contact: Sand Castle RV Park, 360/642-2174, www.sandcastlerv.com.

94 SOU'WESTER LODGE, CABINS, TCH TCH, AND TRAILER PARK

Scenic rating: 7

in Seaview on the Long Beach Peninsula

See map page 29

This one-of-a-kind place features a lodge that dates back to 1892, vintage trailers available for rent, and cottages. Various cultural events are held at the park throughout the year, including fireside evenings with theater and chamber music. The park covers three acres, provides beach access, and is one of the few sites in the immediate area that provides spots for tent camping. This park often attracts creative people such as musicians and artists, and some arrive for vacations in organized groups. It is definitely not for Howie and Ethel from Iowa. Fishing is a recreation option. The area features the Lewis and Clark Interpretive Center, a lighthouse, museums, fine dining, bicycle and boat rentals, bicycle and hiking trails, and bird sanctuaries. Additional facilities found within five miles of the park include an 18-hole golf course, a full-service marina, and a riding stable. The lodge was originally built for U.S. Senator Henry Winslow Corbett. Two side notes: Tch Tch stands for "trailers, classic, hodge-podge." The park owners also boast of a "t'ink tank," which they say is not quite a think tank. Like I said, the place is unique and management has a great sense of humor.

RV sites, facilities: There are 60 sites with full hookups (20 and 30 amps) for RVs of any length, 10 tent sites, a historic lodge, four cottages, and 12 1950s-style trailers in vintage condition. Some RV sites are pull-through. Picnic tables are provided at some sites. Restrooms have flush toilets and showers. Drinking water, cable TV, modem access, a classic video library, a picnic area with pavilion, and community fire pits and grills are available. Propane gas, a dump station, a store, a gas station, a café, and ice are within one mile. Boat-launching facilities are nearby. Leashed pets are permitted.

Reservations, fees: Reservations are accepted. Sites are $29.75–39.75 per night, $2–3 per person per night for more than two people. Some credit cards accepted. Open year-round.

Directions: From Kelso/Longview on I-5, turn west on Highway 4 and drive 63 miles to U.S. 101. Turn left (south) on U.S. 101 and drive 13 miles to the junction with Highway 103 (flashing light). Turn left to stay on U.S. 101 and drive one block to Seaview Beach Access Road (38th Place). Turn right and drive toward the ocean. Look for the campground on the left.

Contact: Sou'Wester Lodge, Cabins, Tch Tch, and Trailer Park, 360/642-2542, www.souwesterlodge.com.

95 ILWACO KOA

Scenic rating: 5

near Fort Canby State Park

See map page 29 | BEST (

This 17-acre camp is about three miles from the beach and includes a secluded area for tents. You'll find a boardwalk nearby, as well as the Lewis and Clark Museum, lighthouses, an amusement park, and fishing from a jetty or charter boats. The Washington State International Kite Festival is held in Long Beach the third week of August. The World Kit Museum and Hall of Fame, also in Long Beach, is open year-round. Additional facilities within five miles of the campground include a maritime museum, hiking trails, and a nine-hole golf course.

RV sites, facilities: There are 57 sites with full or partial hookups (20 and 30 amps) for RVs of any length, a tent area for up to 50 tents, and five cabins. Some sites are pull-through. Picnic tables and fire rings are provided. Restrooms have flush toilets and showers. Drinking water, cable TV, propane gas, a dump station, a recreation hall, seasonal organized activities and tours, a camp store, a coin laundry, ice, and a playground are available. Leashed pets are permitted.

Reservations, fees: Reservations are accepted

at 800/562-3258. Sites are $26–42 per night, $5 per person per night for more than two people, and $6.50 per extra vehicle per night. Some credit cards accepted. Open mid-May–mid-October.

Directions: From Kelso/Longview on I-5, turn west on Highway 4 and drive 63 miles to U.S. 101. Turn left (south) on U.S. 101 and drive 13 miles to the junction with Highway 103. The campground is at the junction.

Contact: Ilwaco KOA, tel./fax 360/642-3292, www.koa.com.

96 FISHERMAN'S COVE RV PARK

Scenic rating: 7

near Fort Canby State Park

See map page 29   BEST (

This five-acre park is by the docks, near where the Pacific Ocean and the Columbia River meet. It has fishing access nearby and caters to anglers. Fish- and clam-cleaning facilities are available in the park. Beach access is approximately one mile away. A maritime museum, hiking trails, a full-service marina, and a riding stable are within five miles of the park. About 15 percent of the sites are taken by monthly renters.

RV sites, facilities: There are 51 sites with full hookups (30 and 50 amps) for RVs of any length. Some sites are pull-through. Picnic tables are provided. Restrooms have flush toilets and coin showers. Drinking water, cable TV, Wi-Fi, a dump station, and a coin laundry are available. Propane gas, a gas station, a store, and a café are within one mile. Boat docks, launching facilities, and rentals are nearby. Leashed pets are permitted.

Reservations, fees: Reservations are accepted. Sites are $25 per night. Weekly and monthly rates available. No credit cards accepted. Open year-round.

Directions: From Kelso/Longview on I-5, turn west on Highway 4 and drive 63 miles to U.S. 101. Turn left (south) on U.S. 101 and drive 13 miles to the junction with Highway

103. Turn right (north) on Highway 103 and drive two miles to Highway 100/Spruce Street exit. Turn right (south) and drive into the town of Ilwaco. At the junction of Spruce Street SW and 1st Street, turn right (west) on Spruce Street and drive one block to 2nd Avenue SW. Turn left (south) on 2nd Avenue SW and drive four blocks south to the park on the right.

Contact: Fisherman's Cove RV Park, 360/642-3689.

97 RIVER'S END CAMPGROUND AND RV PARK

Scenic rating: 6

near Fort Columbia State Park

See map page 29

This wooded park spreads over five acres and has riverside access. Salmon fishing is available here. Additional facilities found within five miles of the campground include marked bike trails and a full-service marina. Also nearby is Fort Columbia State Park.

RV sites, facilities: There are 75 sites for tents or RVs of any length with full or partial hookups (30 amps). Some sites are pull-through. Picnic tables are provided and fire pits are available at some sites. Restrooms have flush toilets and coin showers. Drinking water, cable TV, a dump station, a recreation hall, a coin laundry, firewood, a fish-cleaning station, and ice are available. A gas station, a store, and a café are within one mile. Boat docks and launching facilities are nearby on the Columbia River. Leashed pets are permitted.

Reservations, fees: Reservations are accepted. Sites are $24 per night, $5 per person per night for more than two people. No credit cards accepted. Open April–late October.

Directions: From Kelso/Longview on I-5, turn west on Highway 4 and drive 60 miles to Highway 401. Turn left (south) on Highway 401 and drive 14 miles to the park entrance (just north of Chinook) on the left.

Contact: River's End Campground and RV Park, 360/777-8317.

98 MAUCH'S SUNDOWN RV PARK

Scenic rating: 5

near Fort Columbia State Park

See map page 29

This park has about 50 percent of the sites rented monthly, usually throughout the summer. The park covers four acres, has riverside access, and is in a wooded, hilly setting with grassy sites. Nearby fishing from shore is available. It's near Fort Columbia State Park.

RV sites, facilities: There are 44 sites for tents or RVs of any length with full or partial hookups (30 amps). Some sites are pull-through. Small pets are permitted. Picnic tables are provided. No open fires are allowed. Restrooms have flush toilets and coin showers. Drinking water, a dump station, cable TV, a coin laundry, a convenience store, propane gas, and ice are available. A café is within three miles. Boat docks and launching facilities are nearby on the Columbia River.

Reservations, fees: Reservations are accepted. Sites are $8–20 per night, $1.50 per person per night for more than two people, and $1.50 per extra vehicle per night. No credit cards accepted. Open year-round.

Directions: From Kelso/Longview on I-5, turn west on Highway 4 and drive 60 miles to Highway 401. Turn left (south) on Highway 401 and drive to U.S. 101. Take U.S. 101 to the right and continue for 0.5 mile (do not go over the bridge) to the park on the right.

Contact: Mauch's Sundown RV Park, 360/777-8713.

99 SKAMOKAWA VISTA PARK

Scenic rating: 7

near the Columbia River

See map page 29

This public camp covers 70 acres and features half a mile of sandy beach and a Lewis and Clark interpretive site. Reservations are recommended. A short hiking trail is nearby. The camp also has nearby access to the Columbia River, where recreational options include fishing, swimming, and boating. Additional facilities found within five miles of the park include a full-service marina and tennis courts. In Skamokawa, River Life Interpretive Center stays open year-round.

RV sites, facilities: There are 34 sites with full or partial hookups (30 amps) for RVs of any length, nine sites for tents or RVs of any length (no hookups), four tent sites, and five yurts. Picnic tables and fire grills are provided. Restrooms have flush toilets and coin showers. Drinking water, a dump station, ice, firewood, tennis courts, basketball courts, and a playground are available. A store and café are within one mile. Boat docks, launching facilities, and canoe and kayak rentals are nearby. Leashed pets are permitted.

Reservations, fees: Reservations are accepted. Tent sites are $16 per night, and RV sites are $19–23 per night. Some credit cards accepted. Open year-round.

Directions: From Kelso/Longview on I-5, turn west on Highway 4 and drive 35 miles to Skamokawa. Continue west on Highway 4 for 0.5 mile to the park on the left.

Contact: Skamokawa Vista Park, Port of Wahkiakum No. 2, 360/795-8605, fax 360/795-8611.

SEATTLE AND THE SAN JUAN ISLANDS

☾ BEST RV PARKS AND CAMPGROUNDS

☾ Wildlife-Viewing
West Beach Resort Ferry-In, page 83.

☾ Prettiest Lakes
Moran State Park Ferry-In, page 83.

No metropolitan area in the world offers a wider

array of recreation options than Seattle-Tacoma and its sphere of influence. At the center are water, woods, and islands. One of my favorite views anywhere is from the top of Mount Constitution on Orcas Island, where on a clear day you can look out over an infinity of sun-swept charm. Take one look and you'll know this is why you came.

The scope of parks, campgrounds, and recreation on the islands in this region is preeminent. Even in an RV you'll have an array of excellent destinations, including many available by ferry transport. Many state parks offer gorgeous water-view campsites. Well-furnished RV parks along the I-5 corridor offer respite for vacationers in need of a layover, and hidden lakes, such as Cascade Lake on Orcas Island, will surprise you with their beauty.

But spend even a short time here and you will realize that you need some kind of boat to do it right. A powerboat, sailboat, or kayak offers instant access to adventure. With a powerboat, you get freedom from the traffic on the I-5 corridor, as well as near-unlimited access to destinations in Puget Sound and the linked inlets, bays, and canals. Fishing can be good, too. On calm days with light breezes, roaming the peaceful waters in a sailboat amid dozens of islands provides a segue to instant tranquility. With near-perfect destinations like these, this area is quickly becoming the sea-kayaking capital of the world.

People who live here year-round, fighting the rat maze of traffic on I-5, can easily fall into the trap of tunnel vision, never seeing beyond the line of cars ahead of them. Escape that tunnel. Scan the maps and pages in this region, and in the process, reward yourself with the best water-based adventure anywhere.

Includes:

- Bay View State Park
- Birch Bay State Park
- Camano Island State Park
- Dash Point State Park
- Deception Pass State Park
- Fort Casey State Park
- Fort Ebey State Park
- Green River
- Lake Goodwin
- Lake Pleasant
- Lake Sammamish State Park
- Larrabee State Park
- Lopez Island
- Nooksack River
- Orcas Island
- Puget Sound
- Puyallup River
- Saltwater State Park
- Samish Bay
- San Juan Island
- Skagit River
- South Whidbey State Park
- Washington Park
- Wenberg State Park
- Whidbey Island

WASHINGTON

SEATTLE AND THE SAN JUAN ISLANDS

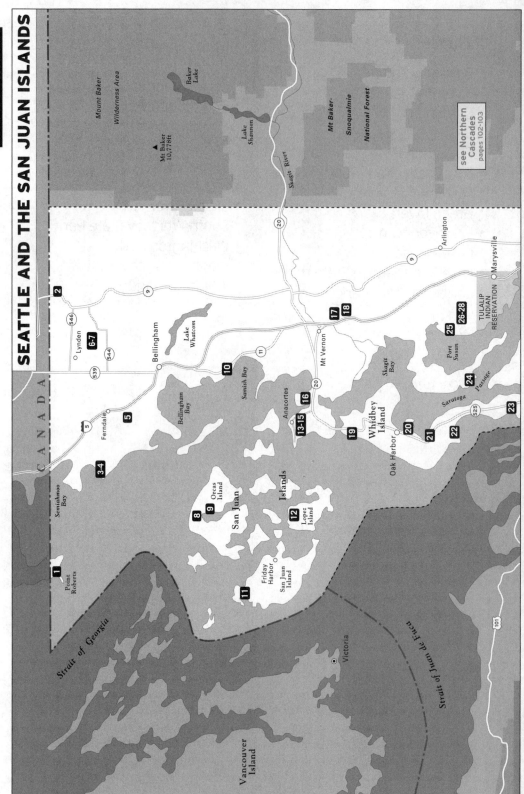

CANADA

Point Roberts **1**

Semiahmoo Bay

Strait of Georgia

Lynden **2**

546

6-7

544

539

Ferndale

Bellingham

5

3-4

Bellingham Bay

Lake Whatcom

9

Mount Baker Wilderness Area

Baker Lake

Mt Baker 10,778ft ▲

Lake Shannon

Mt Baker- Snoqualmie National Forest

Skagit River

20

see Northern Cascades pages 102-103

9

Arlington

Marysville

Samish Bay

10

11

Mt Vernon

20

17
18

9

TULALIP INDIAN RESERVATION

26-28

25

Port Susan

Orcas Island

8 **9**

San Juan Islands

Anacortes

16

13-15

19

Whidbey Island

Oak Harbor

20

21

22

24

Skagit Bay

Saratoga Passage

525

23

Lopez Island

12

Friday Harbor

San Juan Island

11

Victoria

Vancouver Island

Strait of Juan de Fuca

101

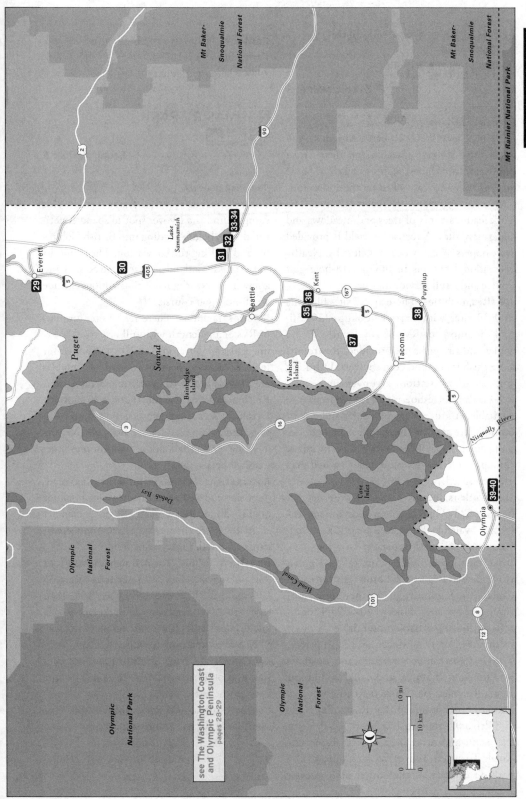

WASHINGTON

Mt Baker-
Snoqualmie
National Forest

Mt Baker-
Snoqualmie
National Forest

Mt Rainier National Park

2

90

Lake
Sammamish

31 32 33-34

Everett 30

405

29 5

Seattle

Kent

35 36

167

5

Puyallup

38

Tacoma

Puget

Sound

Bainbridge
Island

Vashon
Island

5

3

16

Nisqually River

Case
Inlet

39-40

Olympia

Dabob Bay

Olympic
National
Forest

Hood Canal

101

8

12

Olympic
National
Park

Olympic
National
Forest

see The Washington Coast
and Olympic Peninsula
pages 28-29

10 mi

10 km

0

1 WHALEN'S CAMPGROUND & RV PARK

Scenic rating: 6

on Point Roberts

See map page 78

This park is on Point Roberts, so remote you must drive through Canada and then return south into the United States to reach it. Some of the campsites are booked for the entire summer, so reservations are recommended. The park features a mix of trees and meadows and has grassy sites. A recreation field is provided for campers. A sandy beach is close by. Nearby recreational options include an 18-hole golf course and a full-service marina.

RV sites, facilities: There are 27 sites for tents and 49 sites with partial hookups (20, 30, and 50 amps) for RVs of any length. Picnic tables and fire grills are provided. Restrooms have flush toilets and coin showers. Drinking water, a dump station, a convenience store, Wi-Fi, ice, horseshoe pits, and firewood are available. A grocery store, a café, and a coin laundry are within three miles. Boat docks and launching facilities are within four miles. Groups can be accommodated. Leashed pets are permitted.

Reservations, fees: Reservations are accepted. Sites are $23–33 per night. Weekly and monthly rates available. Some credit cards accepted. Open March–late October.

Directions: From Bellingham, take I-5 north through Blaine and the border customs into Canada to Highway 99 northbound. Continue northwest on Highway BC 99N for 18 miles to BC 17. Turn left and drive six miles to the town of Tsawwassen and 56th Street. Turn left on 56th Street (and border customs into the United States) and drive to Johnson Road. Turn left on Johnson Road and drive one mile to Boundary Bay Road. Turn left and drive 0.5 mile to Bay View Road. Turn left again and drive 0.25 mile to Roosevelt Road. Turn left and drive 0.25 mile to the park on the left, at the corner of Roosevelt Road and Derby Avenue.

Contact: Whalen's Campground & RV Park, 360/945-2874, fax 360/945-0824, www.whalenspark.com.

2 SUMAS RV PARK

Scenic rating: 5

in Sumas

See map page 78

Located near the U.S.-Canada border, this campground is a layover spot to spend American dollars before heading into British Columbia and making the conversion. The camp sits in the grassy flatlands; it has graveled sites and a few trees. Nearby recreation options include an 18-hole golf course.

RV sites, facilities: There are 50 sites for tents or RVs of any length with full or partial hookups (30 and 50 amps) and a grassy area for tents. Some sites are pull-through. Picnic tables are provided, and fire rings are at most sites. Restrooms have flush toilets and coin showers. Drinking water, modem access, a dump station, and a coin laundry are available. A store, ice, café, and a ballpark are within one mile. Leashed pets are permitted.

Reservations, fees: Reservations are accepted. Tent sites are $10 per tent, sites with hookups are $17–20 per night, and it's $4 per person per night for more than two people. Some credit cards accepted. Open year-round.

Directions: From I-5 at Bellingham, take Exit 256 to Highway 539. Turn north on Highway 539 and drive 12 miles to Highway 546. Turn right (east) on Highway 546 (Badger Road) and drive 14 miles (the road becomes Highway 9) to Sumas and look for Cherry Street. Turn right (south) at Cherry Street (the road becomes Easterbrook Road) and drive two blocks to the park on the left.

Contact: Sumas RV Park, 360/988-8875 or 866/213-5180, www.sumasrvpark.com.

3 BIRCH BAY STATE PARK

Scenic rating: 8

on Birch Bay

See map page 78

Birch Bay State Park covers 198 acres and features nearly two miles of beach as well as great views of the Canadian coast range and some of the Canadian Gulf Islands. For water lovers it has the best of both worlds, with 8,255 feet of saltwater shoreline and 14,923 feet of freshwater shoreline on Terrell Creek. More than 100 different species of birds, many of which migrate on the Pacific Flyway, can be seen here. Terrell Creek Marsh Interpretive Trail extends 0.5 mile through a forest of red alder trees, Douglas fir, and western hemlock and one of the few remaining saltwater/freshwater estuaries in northern Puget Sound. Bald eagles and great blue herons feed along the banks of Terrell Creek. Several 18-hole golf courses are nearby. The campground is divided into two loops; hookups for RVs are in the North Loop.

RV sites, facilities: There are 147 sites for tents or RVs (no hookups), 20 sites with full or partial hookups (30 and 50 amps) for RVs up to 60 feet, and one group tent site that can accommodate up to 40 people. Picnic tables and fire grills are provided. Restrooms with flush toilets and coin showers are available, as is a dump station. A gravel boat launch (for boats less than 16 feet only), a picnic area with a sheltered kitchen with electricity, seasonal wildlife theater, basketball court, interpretive activities, and a camp host are available. Some facilities are wheelchair accessible. A store, a restaurant, a coin laundry, and ice are within one mile. Leashed pets are permitted.

Reservations, fees: Reservations are accepted (summer season only) and are required for groups at 888/CAMP-OUT (888/226-7688) or www.parks.wa.gov/reservations ($7 reservation fee). Sites are $17–31 per night, $10 per extra vehicle per night. Call for group rates. Some credit cards accepted. Open year-round.

Directions: From Bellingham, drive north on I-5 to Exit 266. At Exit 266 take Grandview west and continue seven miles to Jackson Road. Turn right on Jackson Road and drive one-half mile to Helweg Road. Turn left and drive 0.25 mile to the reservation office.

Contact: Birch Bay State Park, 360/371-2800, fax 360/371-0455; state park information 360/902-8844, www.parks.wa.gov.

4 BEACHSIDE RV PARK

Scenic rating: 8

on Birch Bay

See map page 78

This pretty park is surrounded by evergreens and bay views. Hiking, fishing, mountain biking, and nearby golf are also options. Note that most sites are filled with monthly renters.

RV sites, facilities: There are 68 pull-through sites with full hookups (30 and 50 amps) for RVs. Picnic tables are provided. Restrooms have flush toilets and showers. Drinking water, a group fire pit, modem access, barbecue area, and a coin laundry are available. A boat launch, a grocery store, and restaurant are within one mile. Leashed pets are permitted with certain restrictions.

Reservations, fees: Reservations are recommended at 800/596-9586. Sites are $25 per night. Some credit cards accepted. Open year-round.

Directions: From Bellingham, drive north on I-5 to Exit 270. Turn west on Birch Bay–Lynden Road and drive five miles to Birch Bay Drive. Turn left and drive one mile to the park on the left.

Contact: Beachside RV Park, tel./fax 360/371-5962.

5 THE CEDARS RV RESORT

Scenic rating: 5

in Ferndale

See map page 78

This resort provides more direct access from I-5 than Windmill Inn or KOA Lynden, and you can usually get a site here. It's a nice, clean park covering 22 acres with spacious sites and trees. Horseshoe pits, a game room, and a recreation field provide possible activities for campers. Several golf courses are nearby.

RV sites, facilities: There are 175 sites for tents or RVs of any length with full or partial hookup sites (20, 30, and 50 amps), including pull-through sites, and a dispersed tent camping area on grass. Picnic tables and fire pits are provided. Restrooms have flush toilets and showers. Drinking water, cable TV, Wi-Fi, modem access, a dump station, a coin laundry, a playground, horseshoe pits, badminton, a recreation room, an arcade, a seasonal heated pool, a convenience store, and ice are available. Leashed pets are permitted.

Reservations, fees: Reservations are accepted. Tent sites are $20 per night, RV sites are $27.50–29.50 per night, plus $2 per pet per night. Some credit cards accepted. Open year-round.

Directions: From Bellingham on I-5, drive north to Ferndale and Exit 263. Take Exit 263 and turn right (north) on Portal Way. Drive less than one mile to the resort on the left.

Contact: The Cedars RV Resort, 360/384-2622, fax 360/380-6365.

6 KOA LYNDEN/BELLINGHAM

Scenic rating: 9

in Lynden

See map page 78

Lynden is a quaint Dutch town with a windmill and the Pioneer Museum. The park features green lawns, flowers, and trees surrounding a miniature golf course and three fishing ponds, where you can fish for trout. This KOA stars as a unique layover spot for vacationers heading north to Canada via Highway 539 and Highway 546. Nearby recreational options include several golf courses. Bellingham, a historic waterfront town with good restaurants and Victorian mansions, is also close by.

RV sites, facilities: There are 31 sites for tents

or RVs (no hookups), 107 sites with full or partial hookups (30 and 50 amps) for RVs of any length, and 12 cabins. Some sites are pull-through. Picnic tables are provided, and most sites have fire pits. Restrooms have flush toilets and showers. Drinking water, Wi-Fi and modem access, propane gas, a dump station, firewood, a recreation hall, a convenience store, a café (summer only), an espresso bar, an ice cream parlor, a coin laundry, ice, a playground, miniature golf, horseshoe pits, volleyball, bicycle rentals, and a seasonal heated swimming pool are available. Fishing tackle and boat rentals are available. Leashed pets are permitted.

Reservations, fees: Reservations accepted at 800/562-4779. Sites are $31–39 per night, $4–5 per person per night for more than two people. Some credit cards accepted. Open year-round.

Directions: From I-5 at Bellingham, take Exit 256 to Highway 539. Turn north on Highway 539 and drive 12 miles to Highway 546. Turn east on Highway 546 (Badger Road) and drive three miles to Line Road. Turn right (south) on Line Road and drive 0.5 mile to the campground on the right.

Contact: KOA Lynden/Bellingham, 360/354-4772, fax 360/354-7050, www.koa.com.

7 WINDMILL INN

Scenic rating: 7

near the Nooksack River

See map page 78

This nice little spot, only 15 minutes from Puget Sound, is near the Nooksack River and Wiser Lake. As the last stop before the U.S.-Canada border, the camp serves primarily as a layover for people heading north. The quiet and pretty setting abounds with trees and flowers. Area attractions include Mount Baker, the quaint little shops of Lynden, and the nearby Birch Bay area, which offers many recreation options.

RV sites, facilities: There are eight sites with full hookups (30 amps) for RVs of any length, and 15 motel rooms. Picnic tables are provided.

Restrooms have flush toilets and coin showers. Drinking water, cable TV, Wi-Fi access, and a park are available. A store, propane gas, a café, a coin laundry, and ice are available within one mile. Boat-launching facilities are within 1.5 miles. Pets are not permitted.

Reservations, fees: Reservations are not accepted. Sites are $20 per night, $1 per person per night for more than two people. Some credit cards accepted. Open year-round.

Directions: In Bellingham on I-5, take Exit 256 for Highway 539 (called Meridian Street in Bellingham). Turn north on Highway 539 and drive 10 miles to Lynden. The RV park is on the right side of the road as you enter Lynden.

Contact: Windmill Inn, 360/354-3424, fax 360/354-8138.

8 WEST BEACH RESORT FERRY-IN

Scenic rating: 9

on Orcas Island

See map page 78   **BEST (**

Right on the beach, this resort offers salmon fishing, boating, swimming, and an apple orchard. Some sites are ocean views and rent by the week in July and August. An excellent alternative to Moran State Park, which is often full, it offers the same recreation opportunities. There is excellent fishing, crabbing, and scuba diving at the resort, and fishing charters and guided kayak tours are available. The beaches at Orcas Island are prime spots for whale-watching and beautiful views, especially at sunrise and sunset.

RV sites, facilities: There are 21 sites for tents or RVs of any length with partial hookups (20 and 30 amps), 21 tent sites, and eight overflow tent sites. There are also 20 cabins. Picnic tables and fire pits are provided. Restrooms have flush toilets and coin showers (April–October only). A pay phone, a convenience store, seasonal café, a playground, a coin laundry, ice, propane gas, Wi-Fi and modem access, a fish-cleaning station, and firewood are available. A spa is available for a fee. Also on-site are a boat ramp, a dock, a full-service marina, rentals, moorage, and dry storage. A dump station is nearby. Leashed pets are permitted.

Reservations, fees: Reservations are accepted by phone or online. Sites are $25–35 per night for up to three people, $5 per extra vehicle per night, and $5 per pet per night. Some credit cards accepted. Open year-round.

Directions: From Burlington and I-5, take Exit 230 (San Juan Islands) for Highway 20. Turn west on Highway 20 and drive 12 miles to the Highway 20 northbound spur, following signs to the San Juan Islands Ferry Terminal in Anacortes. Take the ferry to Orcas Island. From the ferry landing, turn left and drive nine miles on Horseshoe Highway/Orcas Road to the entrance of Eastsound. Continue 0.5 mile to Enchanted Forest Road. Turn left and drive 2.4 miles to the end of Enchanted Forest Road and the resort.

Contact: West Beach Resort, 360/376-2240 or 877/WEST-BCH (877/937-8224), fax 360/376-4746, www.westbeachresort.com; Washington State Ferries, 888/808-7977.

9 MORAN STATE PARK FERRY-IN

Scenic rating: 10

on Orcas Island

See map page 78   **BEST (**

This state park is drop-dead beautiful. It covers 5,252 acres, with surprise lakes, hiking trails, and the best mountaintop views anywhere in the chain of islands. There are actually four separate campgrounds plus a primitive area. You can drive to the summit of Mount Constitution, which tops out at 2,409 feet, then climb up the steps to a stone observation tower (built in 1936 by the Civilian Conservation Corps). The tower provides sensational 360-degree views of Vancouver, Mount Baker, the San Juan Islands, the Cascade Mountains, and several cities on the distant shores of mainland America and Canada. No RVs are allowed on the winding road to the top. There are five

WASHINGTON

freshwater lakes with fishing for rainbow trout, cutthroat trout, and kokanee salmon, 33 miles of hiking trails, 11 miles of biking trails, and six miles of horse trails. The landscape features old-growth forest, primarily lodgepole pine and Douglas fir, and several small waterfalls. Nearby recreation options include a nine-hole golf course.

RV sites, facilities: There are 136 sites for tents or RVs up to 45 feet (no hookups) (including some pull-through sites), 15 primitive hike-in/bike-in tent sites, one group camp for up to 60 people, and one cabin for up to 10 people. Picnic tables and fire grills are provided. Restrooms have flush toilets and coin showers. Drinking water, a dump station, a picnic area with log kitchen shelter, and firewood are available. Boat docks, limited fishing supplies, launching facilities, and boat rentals are at the concession stand in the park. Some facilities are wheelchair accessible. Leashed pets are permitted.

Reservations, fees: Reservations are accepted at 888/CAMP-OUT (888/226-7688) or www.parks.wa.gov/reservations ($7 reservation fee). Sites are $16–19 per night, $10 per night for bike-in/hike-in sites, plus $10 per extra vehicle per night. Reserve the cabin at 800/360-4240. Some credit cards accepted. Open year-round. Note that some campers consider the ferry-crossing fee for RVs to be very high; call ahead for prices.

Directions: From Seattle on I-5, drive north to Burlington and Highway 20. Turn west on Highway 20 and drive 12 miles to the Highway 20 northbound spur, following signs to the San Juan Islands Ferry Terminal in Anacortes. Take the ferry to Orcas Island. From the ferry landing, turn left on Horseshoe Highway/Orcas Road and drive 13 miles to Moran State Park (well marked). Stop at the campground registration booth for directions to your site.

Contact: Moran State Park Ferry-In, 360/376-2326; state park information 360/902-8844, www.parks.wa.gov; Washington State Ferries, 888/808-7977.

10 LARRABEE STATE PARK

🏃 🚴 🎣 🚐 🐕 ♿ 🚙 ⛺

Scenic rating: 9

on Samish Bay

See map page 78

This 2,683-acre state park sits on Samish Bay in Puget Sound and boasts 8,100 feet of saltwater shoreline. The park has two freshwater lakes, coves, and tidelands. Sunsets are often beautiful. The park has 13.7 miles of hiking trails and 11.7 miles of mountain-biking trails. The landscape is primarily forested with conifers, often with dense woodlands and vegetation, but also features marshlands, wetlands, streams, lakes, and includes Chuckanut Mountain. The area is known for Chuckanut sandstone. Fishing is available on Fragrance Lake and Lost Lake, which are hike-in lakes. Dating from 1915, this was the first state park established in Washington. The park lies on a beautiful stretch of coastline and offers prime spots for wildlife-viewing. A relatively short drive south will take you to Anacortes, where you can catch a ferry to islands in the San Juan chain.

RV sites, facilities: There are 26 sites for RVs up to 60 feet with full hookups (30 amps), 51 tent sites, eight primitive tent sites, and a group camp for up to 40 people. Picnic tables and fire grills are provided. Restrooms have flush toilets and coin showers. Drinking water, a dump station, a picnic area with electricity and a covered shelter, and firewood are available. Boat-launching facilities are available nearby. Some facilities are wheelchair accessible. Leashed pets are permitted.

Reservations, fees: Reservations are accepted at 888/CAMP-OUT (888/226-7688) or www.parks.wa.gov/reservations ($7 reservation fee). Primitive tent sites are $12 per night, tent sites are $17 per night, and hookup sites are $24–31 per night, plus $10 per extra vehicle per night. Some credit cards accepted. Open year-round with limited winter facilities.

Directions: From Bellingham on I-5, take Exit 250 and turn on Fairhaven Parkway. Drive less than a mile to State Route 11/Chuckanut Drive (second stoplight). Turn left (stay left at the next stoplight) and drive six miles to the park entrance on the right.

Contact: Larrabee State Park, 360/676-2093, fax 360/676-2061; state park information 360/902-8844, www.parks.wa.gov.

11 LAKEDALE RESORT FERRY-IN

Scenic rating: 7

on San Juan Island
See map page 78

This is a nice spot on 82 acres for visitors who want the solitude of an island camp, yet all the amenities of a privately run campground. Fishing, swimming, and boating are available at two of the three Lakedale lakes. Two volleyball courts and a grassy sports field are also on-site. Roche Harbor and Wescott Bay are nearby to the north, and Friday Harbor and its restaurants are nearby to the south.

RV sites, facilities: There are 12 sites for tents or RVs up to 40 feet with partial hookups (20 and 30 amps) and 88 sites for tents. There are also six group tent sites for up to 20–40 people each, 10 bike-in sites, six log cabins, one log house, and 10 luxury lodge rooms. Picnic tables and fire rings are provided. Restrooms have flush toilets and coin showers. Drinking water and firewood are available. A convenience store and ice are available. Boat docks, a swimming beach, and boat and fishing gear rentals are available on-site. Leashed pets are permitted.

Reservations, fees: Reservations accepted. Tent sites are $21–34 per night, RV sites are $32–39 per night, hike-in/bike-in sites are $16–20 per person per night, and it's $6 per extra vehicle per night. Some credit cards accepted. Open mid-March–mid-October for camping. Cabins and lodge rooms available year-round.

Directions: From Burlington and Highway 20, turn west on Highway 20 and drive 12 miles to the Highway 20 northbound spur, following signs to the San Juan Islands Ferry Terminal in Anacortes. Take the ferry to Friday Harbor on San Juan Island. From the ferry landing at Friday Harbor, drive two blocks on Spring Street

to 2nd Street. Turn right (northwest) on 2nd Street and drive a 0.5 mile to Tucker Avenue (it becomes Roche Harbor Road). Continue 4.5 miles to the resort on the left.

Contact: Lakedale Resort, 360/378-2350 or 800/617-CAMP (800/617-2267), fax 360/378-0944, www.lakedale.com; Washington State Ferries information, 888/808-7977.

12 SPENCER SPIT STATE PARK FERRY-IN

Scenic rating: 9

on Lopez Island
See map page 78

Spencer Spit State Park offers one of the few island campgrounds accessible to cars via ferry. It also features walk-in sites for privacy, which require anywhere from a 50-foot to a 200-yard walk to the tent sites. A sand spit extends far into the water and provides a lagoon and good access to prime clamming areas. The park covers 138 acres. Picnicking, beachcombing, and sunbathing are some pleasant activities for campers looking for relaxation.

RV sites, facilities: There are 37 sites for tents or RVs up to 32 feet (no hookups), seven walk-in sites, two Adirondacks for up to eight people each, and two group sites for up to 20 and 50 people respectively. No hookups are provided. Picnic tables and fire grills are provided. Restrooms have flush toilets. Drinking water, a picnic area, and a dump station are available, and 16 mooring buoys are available on the Cascadia Marine Trail. Boat docks and a launch are within two miles, and showers are approximately three miles away. Some facilities are wheelchair accessible. Leashed pets are permitted.

Reservations, fees: Reservations are accepted at 888/CAMP-OUT (888/226-7688) or www.parks.wa.gov/reservations ($7 reservation fee). Sites are $17 per night, $12 per night for walk-in sites, $24–31 per night for Adirondacks, $10 per extra vehicle per night, and $10 per night for mooring buoys. Call for group rates. Open year-round with limited winter facilities.

Directions: From Seattle on I-5, drive north to Burlington and Highway 20. Turn west on Highway 20 and drive 12 miles to the Highway 20 northbound spur, following signs to the San Juan Islands Ferry Terminal in Anacortes. Take the ferry to Lopez Island. The park is within four miles of the ferry terminal.

Contact: Spencer Spit State Park, 360/468-2251, fax 360/468-3176; state park information 360/902-8844, www.parks.wa.gov; Washington State Ferries, 888/808-7977.

13 PIONEER TRAILS RV RESORT & CAMPGROUND

Scenic rating: 9

near Anacortes on Fidalgo Island
See map page 78

This site offers resort camping in the beautiful San Juan Islands. Tall trees, breathtaking views, cascading waterfalls, and country hospitality can all be found here. Side trips include nearby Deception Pass State Park (eight minutes away) and ferries to Victoria, British Columbia, Friday Harbor, Orcas Island, and other nearby islands (it is imperative to arrive early at the ferry terminal). Nearby recreation activities include horseshoes, an 18-hole golf course, relaxing spas, and lake fishing.

RV sites, facilities: There are 98 sites with full hookups (30 and 50 amps) for RVs of any length, including some pull-through sites, plus 24 covered wagons and five cabins. No tents are allowed. Picnic tables and fire rings are provided. Restrooms have flush toilets and showers. Drinking water, a dump station, cable TV, modem and Wi-Fi access, a pay phone, and a coin laundry are available. A recreation hall, a playground, horseshoe pits, and a basketball court are available nearby. Leashed pets are permitted with certain restrictions.

Reservations, fees: Reservations recommended. A three-night minimum on holidays is required. Sites are $27.50 per night, $5 per extra vehicle per night, $2 per pet per night. Some credit cards accepted. Open year-round.

Directions: From Burlington and I-5, take Exit 230 for Highway 20 westbound. Drive west on Highway 20 for 12 miles. At the traffic signal, turn left (still Highway 20, toward Oak Harbor/Deception Pass) and drive 0.5 mile to Miller Road. Turn right (west) on Miller Road, drive 0.25 mile, and look for the park on the right side of the road.

Contact: Pioneer Trails RV Resort & Campground, 360/293-5355 or 888/777-5355, fax 360/299-2240, www.pioneertrails.com.

14 FIDALGO BAY RESORT

Scenic rating: 5

near Anacortes on Fidalgo Bay
See map page 78

This 40-acre park is five minutes from Anacortes and right on Fidalgo Bay, providing easy access to boating, fishing, and swimming. More than one mile of beach is available. A golf course is available two miles away. A number of sites are filled with monthly renters. This resort is owned by the Samish Indian Nation.

RV sites, facilities: There are 177 sites with full hookups (20, 30, and 50 amps), including many pull-through sites, for RVs of any length. Picnic tables are provided at most sites. Restrooms have flush toilets and showers. Drinking water, cable TV, modem and Wi-Fi access, a clubhouse, a large fire pit, a small boat launch, a convenience store, video rentals, propane, and a coin laundry are available. Leashed pets are permitted, with a maximum of two pets.

Reservations, fees: Reservations recommended at 800/727-5478. Sites are $30–47.50 per night. Some credit cards accepted. Open year-round.

Directions: From Burlington and Highway 20, turn west on Highway 20 and drive about 14 miles to Fidalgo Bay Road. Turn right on Fidalgo Bay Road and drive one mile to the resort on the right.

Contact: Fidalgo Bay Resort, 360/293-5353 or 800/727-5478, fax 360/299-3010, www.fidalgobay.com.

15 WASHINGTON PARK

Scenic rating: 6

in Washington Park

See map page 78

This 220-acre city park is in the woods on a peninsula at the west end of Fidalgo Island. It features many hiking trails. A 2.2-mile paved loop route for vehicles, hikers, and bicyclists stretches around the perimeter of the park. The Washington State Ferry terminals are 0.5 mile away, providing access to the San Juan Islands. This is a popular camp, and it's a good idea to arrive early to claim your spot.

RV sites, facilities: There are 73 sites for tents or RVs of any length, including 46 with partial hookups (20 and 30 amps), and one group tent site for up to 30 people. Some sites are pull-through. Restrooms have flush toilets and coin showers. Drinking water, a pay phone, a playground, a recreation field, a dump station, a reservable picnic area, a boat launch, and a coin laundry are available. Some facilities are wheelchair accessible. Leashed pets are permitted.

Reservations, fees: Reservations are not accepted. Sites are $16–20 per night; the group site is $77 per night. Open year-round.

Directions: From Burlington and I-5, turn west on Highway 20 and drive to Anacortes and Commercial Avenue. Turn right on Commercial Avenue and drive approximately 0.5 mile to 12th Street. Turn left and drive about three miles (west of the ferry landing the road changes names several times) to Sunset Avenue. Drive straight across road to Sunset Avenue to the park entrance and campground.

Contact: Washington Park, City of Anacortes, 360/293-1927; Parks and Recreation, 360/293-1918, www.cityofanacortes.org.

16 BAY VIEW STATE PARK

Scenic rating: 10

on Padilla Bay

See map page 78

This campground set on Padilla Bay has a large, grassy area for kids, making it a good choice for families. Bordering 11,000 acres of Padilla Bay and the National Estuarine Sanctuary, this 25-acre park boasts 1,285 feet of saltwater shoreline. From the park, you can enjoy views of the San Juan Islands fronting Padilla Bay. On a clear day, you can see the Olympic Mountains to the west and Mount Rainier to the south. Kayakers should note that Padilla Bay becomes a large mud flat during low tides. Windsurfing is becoming popular, but tracking tides and wind is required. The Breazeale Padilla Bay Interpretive Center is 0.5 mile north of the park. For a nice day trip, take the ferry at Anacortes to Lopez Island (there are several campgrounds there as well).

RV sites, facilities: There are 30 sites with full or partial (30 amps) hookups for RVs up to 60 feet, 46 sites for tents or RVs up to 40 feet (no hookups), one group tent site for up to 64 people, and four cabins. Picnic tables and fire rings are provided. Restrooms have flush toilets and coin showers. Drinking water, firewood, a dump station, and a picnic area with a beach shelter are available. Horseshoes, volleyball, interpretive activities, windsurfing, waterskiing, swimming, and boating are available. A store and a coin laundry are eight miles away in Burlington. Some facilities are wheelchair accessible. Leashed pets are permitted.

Reservations, fees: Reservations are accepted and required for groups at 888/CAMP-OUT (888/226-7688) or www.parks.wa.gov/reservations ($7 reservation fee). Sites are $17–31 per night, $10 per extra vehicle per night. Call for group rates. Cabins are $44 per night. Some credit cards accepted. Open year-round, but some campsites are closed in winter.

Directions: From Seattle on I-5, drive north to Burlington and Exit 230 for Highway 20. Turn west on Highway 20 and drive seven

WASHINGTON

miles west (toward Anacortes) to Bay View-Edison Road. Turn right (north) on Bay View-Edison Road and drive four miles to the park on the right.

Contact: Bay View State Park, 360/757-0227, fax 360/757-1967; state park information 360/902-8844, www.parks.wa.gov.

17 BURLINGTON/ ANACORTES KOA

Scenic rating: 5

in Burlington

See map page 78

This is a fine KOA campground, complete with all the amenities. The sites are spacious and comfortable. Possible side trips include tours of the Boeing plant in Everett (about 30 miles away), Victoria, Vancouver Island, and the San Juan Islands.

RV sites, facilities: There are 120 sites for tents or RVs of any length, most with full or partial hookups (30 and 50 amps), and 11 cabins. Some sites are pull-through. Restrooms have flush toilets and showers. Drinking water, a dump station, cable TV, Wi-Fi and modem access, a pay phone, a coin laundry, limited groceries, ice, propane gas, firewood, and a barbecue area are available. There are also an indoor heated pool, a spa, a recreation hall, a game room, a playground, nine-hole miniature golf, bicycle rentals, horseshoe pits, and a sports field. Leashed pets are permitted, with certain restrictions.

Reservations, fees: Reservations are recommended in the summer, 800/562-9154. Sites are $27–39 per night, $2.50–4 per person per night for more than two people. Some credit cards accepted. Open year-round.

Directions: From Burlington and I-5, take Exit 232/Cook Road. Turn right on Cook Road and drive 100 feet to Old Highway 99. Turn left and drive 3.5 miles to the campground on the right.

Contact: Burlington/Anacortes KOA, 360/724-5511, www.koa.com.

18 RIVERBEND RV PARK

Scenic rating: 5

on the Skagit River

See map page 78

Riverbend RV Park is a pleasant layover spot for I-5 travelers. While not particularly scenic, it is clean and spacious. Access to the Skagit River here is a high point, with fishing for salmon, trout, and Dolly Varden in season; check regulations. Nearby recreational options include a casino and an 18-hole golf course. Note that about half of the sites are filled with monthly renters.

RV sites, facilities: There are 90 sites with full hookups (30 and 50 amps) for RVs up to 45 feet and 25 tent sites. Most sites are pull-through. Picnic tables are provided at RV sites and barbecues are provided at some tent sites. Restrooms have flush toilets and coin showers. Drinking water, a dump station, a coin laundry, a playground, and horseshoe pits are available. A store, a café, and ice are within 0.25 mile. Leashed pets are permitted with certain restrictions.

Reservations, fees: Reservations accepted. Tent sites are $13 per night, and RV sites are $24.50 per night. Some credit cards accepted. Open year-round.

Directions: From Seattle on I-5, drive north to Mount Vernon and the College Way exit. Take the College Way exit and drive one block west to Freeway Drive. Turn right (north) and drive 0.25 mile to the park and Stewart Road. Turn left and drive a short distance to the park entrance on the right.

Contact: Riverbend RV Park, 360/428-4044.

19 DECEPTION PASS STATE PARK

Scenic rating: 10

on Whidbey Island

See map page 78

Located at beautiful Deception Pass on the west side of Whidbey Island, this state park encompasses 4,134 acres with almost 15 miles of saltwater shoreline and six miles of fresh-water shoreline on three lakes. The landscape ranges from old-growth forest to sand dunes. This diverse habitat has attracted 174 species of birds. An observation deck overlooks the Cranberry Lake wetlands. The park also features spectacular views of shoreline, mountains, and islands, often with dramatic sunsets. At one spot, rugged cliffs drop to the turbulent waters of Deception Pass. Recreation options include fishing at Pass Lake, a freshwater lake within the park. Fly-fishing for trout is a unique bonus for anglers. Note that each lake has different regulations for boating. Scuba diving is also popular. The park provides 38 miles of hiking trails, 1.2 miles of wheelchair-accessible trails, and six miles of equestrian and biking trails. There are several historic Civilian Conservation Corps buildings throughout the park.

RV sites, facilities: There are 167 sites for tents or RVs up to 50 feet (no hookups), 143 sites with partial hookups (15, 30, and 50 amps) for RVs up to 50 feet, three group camps for up to 64 people, and five hike-in/bike-in sites. Some sites are pull-through. Picnic tables and fire rings are provided. Restrooms have flush toilets and coin showers. Drinking water, a playground, firewood, and a dump station are available. A concession stand, an amphitheater, interpretive activities, sheltered picnic areas with electricity, a boat launch, boat rentals, and mooring buoys are nearby. Some facilities are wheelchair accessible. Leashed pets are permitted.

Reservations, fees: Reservations are accepted at 888/CAMP-OUT (888/226-7688) or www.parks.wa.gov/reservations ($7 reservation fee). Hike-in/bike-in sites are $12 per night, sites with no hookups are $17 per night, and sites with hookups are $24–31 per night, plus $10 per extra vehicle per night. Some credit cards accepted. Open year-round, with limited winter services.

Directions: From Seattle on I-5, drive north to Burlington and Exit 230/Highway 20. Take that exit and drive west on Highway 20 for 12 miles to Highway 20 southbound. Turn south on Highway 20, drive six miles (across the

bridge at Deception Pass), and continue to the park entrance (three miles south of the bridge) on the right.

Contact: Deception Pass State Park, 360/675-2417, fax 360/675-8991; state park information 360/902-8844, www.parks.wa.gov.

20 WINDJAMMER PARK

Scenic rating: 4

in Oak Harbor

See map page 78

This popular city park fills quickly on summer weekends. With graveled sites, it is geared toward RVers but is also suitable for tent campers. Fishing, swimming, boating, and sunbathing are all options at Windjammer Park. Several miles of paved trails run along the waterfront. A full-service marina is nearby. Within a few miles are tennis courts and an 18-hole golf course. Fort Ebey and Fort Casey State Parks are both a short drive away and make excellent side trips.

RV sites, facilities: There are 56 sites with full hookups (30 amps) for RVs of any length and five tent sites. Overflow camping is also available. Picnic tables are provided. No campfires are allowed. Restrooms have flush toilets and coin showers. Drinking water, a dump station, and a playground are available. Propane gas, a store, a café, a coin laundry, and ice are available within one mile. Boat-launching facilities, swimming, a lagoon, wading pools, a day-use area, and walking trails are available at Oak Harbor. Leashed pets are permitted.

Reservations, fees: Reservations are not accepted. Sites are $12–20 per night. Open year-round.

Directions: From Burlington and I-5, turn west on Highway 20 and drive 28 miles to the intersection of Highway 20 and Pioneer Way in the town of Oak Harbor on Whidbey Island. Drive straight through the intersection onto Beeksma Drive and continue about one block to the park on the left.

Contact: Windjammer Park, City of Oak Harbor, 360/279-4500, www.oakharbor.org.

WASHINGTON

21 FORT EBEY STATE PARK

Scenic rating: 9

on Whidbey Island

See map page 78

This park is situated on the west side of Whidbey Island at Point Partridge. It covers 645 acres and has access to a rocky beach that is good for exploring. There are also 28 miles of trails for hiking and biking. Fort Ebey is the site of a historic World War II bunker, where concrete platforms mark the locations of the historic gun batteries. Other options include fishing and wildlife-viewing. There is limited fishing available for smallmouth bass at Lake Pondilla, which is only about 100 yards away from the campground and a good place to see bald eagles. The saltwater shore access provides a good spot for surfing and paragliding.

RV sites, facilities: There are 40 sites for tents or RVs (no hookups), 10 sites for tents or RVs with partial hookups (50 amps), a group camp for up to 75 people, and three primitive tent sites. RVs up to 70 feet can be accommodated. Picnic tables and fire grills are provided. Restrooms have flush toilets and coin showers. Drinking water, firewood, ice, and a picnic area are available. Some facilities are wheelchair accessible. Leashed pets are permitted.

Reservations, fees: Reservations are accepted at 888/CAMP-OUT (888/226-7688) or www.parks.wa.gov/reservations ($7 reservation fee). Sites are $12 per night for primitive sites, $17–31 per night for sites with hookups, $10 per extra vehicle per night. Some credit cards accepted. Open year-round.

Directions: From Burlington and I-5, turn west on Highway 20 and drive 23 miles (Whidbey Island) to Libbey Road (eight miles past Oak Harbor). Turn right and drive 1.5 miles to Hill Valley Drive. Turn left and enter the park.

Contact: Fort Ebey State Park, 360/678-4636; state park information 360/902-8844, www.parks.wa.gov.

22 FORT CASEY STATE PARK

Scenic rating: 10

on Whidbey Island

See map page 78

Fort Casey State Park features a lighthouse and views of Admiralty Inlet and the Strait of Juan de Fuca. The park has a little more than 10,000 feet of shoreline on Puget Sound at Admiralty Inlet and includes Keystone Spit, a stretch of land that separates Admiralty Inlet from Crocket Lake. The park covers 467 acres, with just 1.8 miles of hiking trails, but as part of Ebey's Landing National Historic Reserve it contains a coast artillery post featuring four historic guns on display. Remote-control glider flying is allowed in a designated area, and there is a parade field perfect for kite flying. The lighthouse and interpretive center are open seasonally. Fishing is often good in this area, in season. The underwater park, another highlight, attracts divers. You can take a ferry from here to Port Townsend on the Olympic Peninsula.

RV sites, facilities: There are 35 sites for tents or RVs up to 40 feet and three hike-in/bike-in sites. Picnic tables and fire grills are provided. Restrooms have flush toilets and coin showers. Drinking water, an interpretive center, a picnic area, firewood, and an amphitheater are available. Some facilities are wheelchair accessible. Boat-launching facilities are in the park. Leashed pets are permitted.

Reservations, fees: Reservations are not accepted. Sites are $17–31 per night, $12 per night for hike-in/bike-in sites, $10 per extra vehicle per night. Open year-round.

Directions: From Burlington and I-5, turn west on Highway 20 and drive 35 miles to Coupeville. Continue south on Highway 20 (adjacent to Whidbey Island Naval Air Station) and then turn right (still Highway 20, passing Crockett Lake and the Camp Casey barracks) to the park entrance.

Contact: Fort Casey State Park, 360/678-4519; state park information 360/902-8844, www.parks.wa.gov.

23 SOUTH WHIDBEY STATE PARK

Scenic rating: 10

on Whidbey Island
See map page 78

This park is on the southwest end of Whidbey Island. It covers 347 acres and provides opportunities for hiking, picnicking, and beachcombing along a sandy beach. There are spectacular views of Puget Sound and the Olympic Mountains. The park features old-growth forest, tidelands for clamming and crabbing (check current regulations), and campsites set in the seclusion of a lush forest undergrowth. The park has 4,500 feet of saltwater shoreline on Admiralty Inlet and 3.5 miles of hiking trails.

RV sites, facilities: There are 46 sites for tents or RVs up to 45 feet (no hookups), eight sites for tents or RVs up to 45 feet with partial hookups (30 amps), six hike-in/bike-in sites, and one group site for tents or RVs up to 28 feet that can accommodate up to 100 people. Picnic tables and fire grills are provided. Restrooms have flush toilets and coin showers. Drinking water, a dump station, a convenience store, a picnic area with a log kitchen shelter, an amphitheater, interpretive activities, a junior ranger program, and firewood are available. Some facilities are wheelchair accessible. Leashed pets are permitted.

Reservations, fees: Reservations are accepted at 888/CAMP-OUT (888/226-7688) or www.parks.wa.gov/reservations ($7 reservation fee). Sites are $17–31 per night, $12 per night for hike-in/bike-in sites, $10 per extra vehicle per night. The group site is $2.10 per person per night with a minimum of 20 people. Some credit cards accepted. Open year-round, with fewer sites available in winter.

Directions: From Seattle on I-5, drive north to Burlington and the Highway 20 exit. Take Highway 20 west and drive 28 miles (past Coupeville on Whidbey Island) until it becomes Highway 525. Continue south on Highway 525 to Smugglers Cove Road (the park access road, well marked). Turn right and drive six miles to the park entrance. The park can also be reached easily with a ferry ride from Mukilteo (southwest of Everett) to Clinton (this also makes a great bike trip to the state park).

Contact: South Whidbey State Park, 360/331-4559, fax 360/331-7669; state park information 360/902-8844, www.parks.wa.gov.

24 CAMANO ISLAND STATE PARK

Scenic rating: 10

on Camano Island
See map page 78

This park features panoramic views of Puget Sound, the Olympic Mountains, and Mount Rainier. Set on the southwest point of Camano Island, near Lowell Point and Elger Bay along the Saratoga Passage, this wooded camp offers quiet and private campsites. The park covers 134 acres and features 6,700 feet of rocky shoreline and beach, three miles of hiking trails, and just one mile of bike trails. Good inshore angling for rockfish is available year-round, and salmon fishing is also good in season. A diving area with kelp is available. There is also a self-guided nature trail.

RV sites, facilities: There are 87 sites for tents or RVs up to 40 feet (no hookups), one group camp for up to 100 people, and five camping cabins. Picnic tables and fire grills are provided. Restrooms have flush toilets and coin showers. Drinking water, a dump station, firewood, a sheltered picnic area with a kitchen, summer interpretive programs, an amphitheater, and a large grassy play area in the day-use area are available. Boat-launching facilities are in the park. An 18-hole golf course is nearby. Some facilities are wheelchair accessible. Leashed pets are permitted.

Reservations, fees: Reservations are not accepted for family camping. Reservations are required for the group camp May–September at 360/387-3031. Sites are $17–24 per night, $10 per extra vehicle per night. Call for group rates. Open year-round.

Directions: From Seattle on I-5, drive north (17 miles north of Everett) to Exit 212. Take Exit

212 to Highway 532. Drive west on Highway 532 to Stanwood and continue three miles (to Camano Island) to a fork. Bear left at the fork and continue south for six miles on East Camano Drive, bearing to the right where the road becomes Elger Bay Road, to Mountain View Road. Turn right and drive two miles (climbs a steep hill) and continue to Lowell Point Road. Turn left and continue to the park entrance road. (The park is 14 miles southwest of Stanwood.)

Contact: Camano Island State Park, 360/387-3031; state park information 360/902-8844, www.parks.wa.gov.

25 KAYAK POINT COUNTY PARK

Scenic rating: 5

on Puget Sound
See map page 78

This camp usually fills on summer weekends. On the shore of Puget Sound, this large, wooded county park covers 428 acres on Port Susan. It provides good windsurfing and whale-watching as well as hiking and an 18-hole golf course nearby. Good for crabbing and fishing, a pier is also available. No alcohol is permitted in the park.

RV sites, facilities: There are 34 sites for tents or RVs up to 32 feet with partial hookups (30 amps), including some pull-through sites, and 10 yurts with heat and electricity that hold up to five people. Picnic tables and fire rings are provided. Restrooms have flush toilets and showers. Drinking water, firewood, a picnic area with covered shelter, and a 300-yard fishing pier are available. Boat docks and launching facilities are in the park. Some facilities are wheelchair accessible. Leashed pets are permitted.

Reservations, fees: Reservations are accepted at 425/388-6600 or online at www.snoco.org. Sites are $15–21 per night, additional tents are $6 per tent per night. Yurts are $40–60 per night. Some credit cards accepted. Open year-round.

Directions: From Everett and I-5, drive north to Exit 199 (Tulalip) at Marysville. Take Exit 199,

bear left on Tulalip Road, and drive west for 13 miles (road name changes to Marine Drive) through the Tulalip Indian Reservation to the park entrance road on the left (marked for Kayak Point). Turn left and drive mile to the park.

Contact: Kayak Point Regional Park, Snohomish County, 425/388-6600 or 360/652-7992, fax 425/388-6645, www.snoco.org.

26 WENBERG STATE PARK

Scenic rating: 8

on Lake Goodwin
See map page 78

This state park lies along the east shore of Lake Goodwin, where the trout fishing can be great. The park covers 46 acres with 1,140 feet of shoreline frontage on the lake. Powerboats are allowed, and a seasonal concession stand provides food. This is a popular weekend spot for Seattle-area residents.

RV sites, facilities: There are 30 sites with partial hookups (30 and 50 amps) for RVs up to 50 feet and 45 tent sites. Some sites are pull-through. Picnic tables and fire grills are provided. Restrooms have flush toilets and coin showers. Firewood, drinking water, a dump station, a sheltered picnic area, and a playground are available. Boat-launching facilities are on Lake Goodwin. Some facilities are wheelchair accessible. Leashed pets are permitted.

Reservations, fees: Reservations are accepted at 888/CAMP-OUT (888/226-7688) or www.parks.wa.gov/reservations ($7 reservation fee). Sites are $17–31 per night, $10 per extra vehicle per night. Some credit cards accepted. Open year-round.

Directions: From Everett on I-5, drive north to Exit 206. Take Exit 206/Smokey Point and turn west onto Highway 531. Drive five miles on Highway 531 to East Lake Goodwin Road. Turn left and drive 1.6 miles to the park entrance on the right.

Contact: Wenberg State Park, 360/652-7417; state park information 360/902-8844, www.parks.wa.gov.

27 CEDAR GROVE SHORES RV PARK

Scenic rating: 5

on Lake Goodwin

See map page 78

This wooded resort is on the shore of Lake Goodwin near Wenberg State Park. The camp is a busy place in summer, with highlights including trout fishing, waterskiing, and swimming. A security gate is closed at night. An 18-hole golf course is nearby.

RV sites, facilities: There are 48 sites with full hookups (30 and 50 amps), including some pull-through, for RVs of any length. No tents are permitted. Restrooms have flush toilets and coin showers. Drinking water, a coin laundry, a dump station, modem access, propane gas, ice, a clubhouse, a recreation room, horseshoe pits, and firewood are available. A store and a café are within one mile. Boat docks and launching facilities are available nearby on Lake Goodwin. Some facilities are wheelchair accessible. Leashed pets are permitted.

Reservations, fees: Reservations are accepted. Sites are $17–28 per night, $5 per adult per night for more than two people. Some credit cards accepted. Open year-round.

Directions: From Everett on I-5, drive north for 10 miles to Exit 206. Take Exit 206/Smokey Point and drive west for 2.2 miles to Lakewood Road. Turn right and drive 3.2 miles to Westlake Goodwin Road. Turn left (the park is marked) and drive 0.75 mile to the resort on the left.

Contact: Cedar Grove Shores RV Park, 360/652-7083 or 866/342-4981, www.cgsrvpark.com.

28 LAKE GOODWIN RESORT

Scenic rating: 5

on Lake Goodwin

See map page 78

This private campground is on Lake Goodwin, which is known for good trout fishing. Motorboats are permitted on the lake, and an 18-hole golf course is nearby. Other activities include swimming in the lake, horseshoe pits, shuffleboard, and a recreation field.

RV sites, facilities: There are 85 sites with full or partial hookups (30 and 50 amps) for RVs of any length, 11 tent sites, and four cabins. Some sites are pull-through. Picnic tables and fire grills are provided. Restrooms have flush toilets and coin showers. Drinking water, propane gas, a convenience store with recreation equipment, a coin laundry, ice, Wi-Fi, a playground, and firewood are available. Boat moorage and a fishing pier are nearby on Lake Goodwin. Leashed pets are permitted in RV sites only.

Reservations, fees: Reservations are accepted at 800/242-8169. Tent sites are $22 per night and RV sites are $30–45 per night. Some credit cards accepted. Open year-round.

Directions: From Everett on I-5, drive north for 10 miles to Exit 206. Take Exit 206/Smokey Point, turn west, and drive two miles to Highway 531/Lakewood Road. Bear right on Highway 531 and drive 3.5 miles to the resort on the left.

Contact: Lake Goodwin Resort, 360/652-8169, fax 360/652-4025, www.lakegoodwinresort.com.

29 LAKESIDE RV PARK

Scenic rating: 6

in the town of Everett

See map page 79

With 75–100 of the 150 RV spaces dedicated to permanent rentals, this camp can be a crapshoot for vacationers in summer; the remaining spaces get filled nightly with vacationers. The park is landscaped with annuals, roses, other perennials, and shrubs, which provide privacy and gardens for each site. There's a pond stocked with trout year-round, providing fishing for a fee.

RV sites, facilities: There are 150 sites, including some pull-through, with full hookups (20, 30, and 50 amps) for RVs of any length and nine tent sites. Restrooms have flush toilets

WASHINGTON

and showers. Drinking water, cable TV, a coin laundry, propane gas, a playground, off-leash dog area, horseshoe pits, modem access, and pay phones are available. Some facilities are wheelchair accessible. Leashed pets are permitted.

Reservations, fees: Reservations are recommended at 800/468-7275. Tent sites are $13.83–15.37 per night, and RV sites are $34.73–38.59 per night. Some credit cards accepted. Open year-round.

Directions: From Everett on I-5, drive north to Exit 186. Take Exit 186 and turn west on 128th Street. Drive about two miles to Old Highway 99. Turn left (south) on Old Highway 99 and drive 0.25 mile to the park on the left.

Contact: Lakeside RV Park, 425/347-2970 or 800/468-7275, fax 425/347-9052.

30 LAKE PLEASANT RV PARK

Scenic rating: 6

on Lake Pleasant
See map page 79

A large, developed camp geared primarily toward RVers, this park is on Lake Pleasant. The setting is pretty, with lakeside sites and plenty of trees. Just off the highway, it's a popular camp, so expect lots of company, especially in summer. This is a good spot for a little bass fishing. The lake is not suitable for swimming or boating. Note that half of the 196 sites are monthly rentals. All sites are paved.

RV sites, facilities: There are 196 sites with full hookups (30 and 50 amps), including half available for overnight use, for RVs up to 45 feet. Some sites are pull-through. No tents or campfires are allowed. Picnic tables are provided. Restrooms have flush toilets and showers. Drinking water, cable TV, modem and Wi-Fi access, a dump station, a pay phone, a coin laundry, a playground, and propane gas are available. Some facilities are wheelchair accessible. Leashed pets are permitted with certain restrictions.

Reservations, fees: Reservations recommended. Sites are $32 per night. Some credit cards accepted. Open year-round.

Directions: From the junction of I-5 and I-405 (just south of Seattle), take I-405 and drive to Exit 26. Take that exit to the Bothell/Everett Highway over the freeway and drive south for about one mile; look for the park on the left side. It's marked by a large sign.

Contact: Lake Pleasant RV Park, 425/487-1785 or 800/742-0386.

31 TRAILER INNS RV PARK/ BELLEVUE

Scenic rating: 5

near Lake Sammamish State Park
See map page 79

This park features all the amenities for RV travelers. Lake Sammamish State Park is about two miles away. Nearby recreation options include an 18-hole golf course, hiking trails, marked bike trails, and tennis courts.

RV sites, facilities: There are 103 sites, including half that are permanently rented, with full hookups (30 and one 50 amp) for RVs up to 45 feet. Some sites are pull-through. No tents are allowed. Picnic tables are provided. Restrooms have flush toilets and showers. Drinking water, propane gas, modem and Wi-Fi access, a recreation hall, an indoor swimming pool, spa, sauna, a coin laundry, ice, a picnic area, and a playground are available. A store and a café are within one mile. Leashed pets are permitted.

Reservations, fees: Reservations are accepted at 800/659-4684. Sites are $22–45 per night, $4 per person per night for more than two people. Some credit cards accepted. Open year-round.

Directions: At the junction of I-405 and I-90 south of Seattle, turn east on I-90 and drive 1.5 miles to Exit 11A. Take Exit 11A (a two-avenue exit) and stay in the right lane for 150th Avenue SE. After the lanes split, stay in the left lane and drive to the intersection of 150th Avenue SE and 37th. Continue straight through the light and look for the park entrance at the fifth driveway on the right (about one mile from I-90).

Contact: Trailer Inns RV Park and Recreation

Center, 425/747-9181 or 509/248-1142, fax 425/401-6565, www.trailerinnsrv.com.

32 VASA PARK RESORT

Scenic rating: 5

on Lake Sammamish
See map page 79

I was giving a seminar in Bellevue one evening when a distraught-looking couple walked in and pleaded, "Where can we camp tonight?" I answered, "Just look in the book," and they ended up staying at this camp. It was the easiest sale ever made. This is the most rustic of the parks in the immediate Seattle area. The resort is on the western shore of Lake Sammamish, and the state park is at the south end of the lake. Lake activities include fishing for smallmouth bass, waterskiing, and personal watercraft use. There is a two-week maximum stay during the summer. An 18-hole golf course, hiking trails, and marked bike trails are close by. The park is within easy driving distance of Seattle.

RV sites, facilities: There are 16 sites for tents or RVs of any length with partial hookups (20 amps) and six sites with full hookups (30 amps) for RVs of any length. Picnic tables are provided. Restrooms have flush toilets and coin showers. Drinking water, a dump station, a coin laundry, a playground, and a boat-launching facility are available. Propane gas, firewood, a store, and a café are within one mile. Leashed pets are permitted.

Reservations, fees: Reservations accepted. Sites are $22–27 per night, $3.50 per person per night for more than two people. Some credit cards are accepted. Open mid-May–mid-October.

Directions: From Bellevue, drive east on I-90 to Exit 13. Take Exit 13 to West Lake Sammamish Parkway SE and drive north for one mile; the resort is on the right. Note: Larger rigs should pull into the parking lot on the left.

Contact: Vasa Park Resort, 425/746-3260, fax 425/746-0301, www.vasaparkresort.com.

33 ISSAQUAH VILLAGE RV PARK

Scenic rating: 7

in Issaquah
See map page 79

Although Issaquah Village RV Park doesn't allow tents, it's set in a beautiful environment ringed by the Cascade Mountains, making it a scenic choice in the area. Lake Sammamish State Park is just a few miles north. Most of the sites are asphalt, and 20 percent are long-term rentals.

RV sites, facilities: There are 56 sites, including two pull-through sites, with full hookups (30 and 50 amps) for RVs of any length. No tents are allowed. Picnic tables are provided. Restrooms have flush toilets and showers. Drinking water, cable TV, a dump station, a pay phone, a coin laundry, picnic areas, a playground, Wi-Fi and modem access, and propane gas are available. Some facilities are wheelchair accessible. Leashed pets are permitted.

Reservations, fees: Reservations recommended. Sites are $40–45.56 per night. Weekly and monthly rates available. Some credit cards accepted. Open year-round.

Directions: From Seattle on I-405 (preferred) or I-5, drive to the junction of I-90. Take I-90 east and drive 17 miles to Issaquah and Exit 17. Take Exit 17 for Front Street and turn left; drive under the freeway and look for the first right at 229th Avenue SE. Turn right and drive for a very short distance and keep bearing right on the frontage road that parallels the freeway. Drive 0.25 mile to the park on the left.

Contact: Issaquah Village RV Park, 425/392-9233 or 800/258-9233, http://home.earthlink .net/~issaquahrv.

34 BLUE SKY RV PARK

Scenic rating: 5

near Lake Sammamish State Park
See map page 79

Blue Sky RV Park is in an urban setting just outside of Seattle. It provides a good off-the-beaten-path alternative to the more crowded

WASHINGTON

metro area, yet is still only a short drive from the main attractions in the city. Nearby Lake Sammamish State Park provides more rustic recreation opportunities, including hiking and fishing. All sites are paved and level, and about half are filled with monthly renters.

RV sites, facilities: There are 51 sites with full hookups (30 and 50 amps) for RVs of any length. Some sites are pull-through. No tents are allowed. Picnic tables are provided at some sites. Restrooms have flush toilets and showers. Drinking water, cable TV, a coin laundry, modem access, recreation room, and a covered picnic pavilion with barbecue are available. Leashed pets are permitted.

Reservations, fees: Reservations are accepted. Sites are $30 per night, $5 per person per night for more than two people. Monthly rates available. Open year-round.

Directions: From Seattle on I-5, drive to the junction with Highway 90. Turn east on Highway 90 and drive 22 miles to Exit 22 (Preston/Falls City exit). Take that exit to SE 82nd Street. Turn right on SE 82nd Street and drive a very short distance to 302nd Avenue SE. Turn left and drive 0.5 mile to the campground entrance at the end of the road.

Contact: Blue Sky RV Park, 425/222-7910, www.blueskypreston.com.

35 SALTWATER STATE PARK

Scenic rating: 7

near Seattle

See map page 79

This state park is halfway between Tacoma and Seattle. The cities literally buried a hatchet in the park to symbolize the end of a feud between the two of them. Campers still don't have it so peaceful, though. The camp is on the flight path of Seattle-Tacoma International Airport, so it is often noisy from the jets. The park features tidepools and marine life, including salmon spawning in McSorley Creek in the fall. Scuba diving is good here with a nearby underwater artificial reef. There are three trails for

hiking and biking, and four buildings from the 1930s were built by the Civilian Conservation Corps. Environmental walks are offered. You'll find beautiful views of Maury and Vashon Islands and of the Olympic Mountains. Beaches offer picnic facilities.

RV sites, facilities: There are 52 sites for tents or RVs up to 50 feet (no hookups). Picnic tables and fire grills are provided. Restrooms have flush toilets and coin showers. Drinking water, a dump station, a playground, a picnic area, horseshoe pits, volleyball, interpretive activities, and firewood are available. A store, a restaurant, and ice are within the park. Some facilities are wheelchair accessible. Boat buoys are nearby on Puget Sound. Leashed pets are permitted.

Reservations, fees: Reservations are not accepted. Sites are $17–24 per night, $10 per extra vehicle per night. Open year-round.

Directions: From the junction of I-5 and Highway 516 (between Seattle and Tacoma three miles south of Seattle-Tacoma International Airport), take Highway 516 and drive west for two miles to Highway 509. Turn left and drive one mile to the park access road on the right. Turn right (well marked) and drive 0.5 mile to the park on the shore of Puget Sound.

Contact: Saltwater State Park, 253/661-4956, fax 206/870-4294; state park information 360/902-8844, www.parks.wa.gov.

36 SEATTLE/TACOMA KOA

Scenic rating: 5

in Kent on the Green River

See map page 79

This is a popular urban campground, not far from the highway yet in a pleasant setting. The sites are spacious, and many are pull-throughs that accommodate large RVs. A public golf course is nearby. During the summer, take a tour of Seattle from the campground. The tour highlights include the Space Needle, Pike Place Market, Pioneer Square, Woodland Park Zoo, Seattle Aquarium, Boeing Museum of Flight, Safeco Field, and Puget Sound.

RV sites, facilities: There are 134 sites with full or partial hookups (30 and 50 amps) for RVs up to 65 feet, and eight tent sites. Cable TV is provided at some sites. Restrooms have flush toilets and showers. Drinking water, a dump station, a pay phone, a coin laundry, modem and Wi-Fi access, limited groceries, espresso bar, propane gas, ice, RV supplies, seasonal free movies, and a seasonal pancake breakfast are available. A large playground, a seasonal heated swimming pool, and seasonal three-wheel fun-cycle rentals are also available. No campfires are allowed. Some facilities are wheelchair accessible. Leashed pets are permitted with certain restrictions.

Reservations, fees: Reservations are recommended at 800/562-1892. Tent sites are $35.95–39.95 per night, and RV sites are $45.95–60.95 per night, plus $4–5 per person per night for more than two people. Some credit cards accepted. Open year-round.

Directions: From Seattle, drive south approximately 10 miles on I-5 and take Exit 152 for 188th Street/Orillia Road. Drive east on Orillia Road for three miles (the road becomes 212th Street) to the campground on the right.

Contact: Seattle/Tacoma KOA, 253/872-8652, fax 253/395-1782, www.seattlekoa.com.

37 DASH POINT STATE PARK

Scenic rating: 8

near Tacoma

See map page 79

This urban state park set on Puget Sound features unobstructed water views. The park covers 388 acres, with 3,300 feet of saltwater shoreline and 12 miles of trails for hiking and biking. Windsurfing, swimming, boating, and mountain biking are all popular. Tacoma offers a variety of activities and attractions, including the Tacoma Art Museum (with a children's gallery); the Washington State Historical Society Museum; the Seymour Botanical Conservatory at Wrights Park; Point Defiance Park, Zoo, and Aquarium; the Western Washington Forest Industries Museum; and the Fort Lewis Military Museum.

RV sites, facilities: There are 22 sites with partial hookups (30 amps) for RVs up to 40 feet, 114 tent sites, and a group camp for up to 100 people. Picnic tables and fire grills are provided. Restrooms have flush toilets and coin showers. Drinking water, an amphitheater, interpretive activities, two sheltered picnic areas, a store, and firewood are available. Some facilities are wheelchair accessible. Leashed pets are permitted.

Reservations, fees: Reservations are accepted at 888/CAMP-OUT (888/226-7688) or www.parks.wa.gov/reservations ($7 reservation fee). Sites are $17–31 per night, $10 per extra vehicle per night. Open year-round.

Directions: On I-5 in Tacoma, drive to Exit 143/320th Street. Take that exit and turn west on 320th Street and drive six miles to 47th Street (a T intersection). Turn right on 47th Street and drive two blocks to Highway 509 (another T intersection). Turn left on Highway 509/Dash Point Road and drive 0.5 mile to the park. Note: The camping area is on the south side of the road; the day-use area is on the north side of the road.

Contact: Dash Point State Park, 253/661-4955, fax 253/661-4995; state park information 360/902-8844, www.parks.wa.gov.

38 MAJESTIC MOBILE MANOR RV PARK

Scenic rating: 7

on the Puyallup River near Tacoma

See map page 79

This clean, pretty park along the Puyallup River and with limited views of Mount Rainier caters to RVers. Note that at least half of the sites are filled with monthly renters. Recreation options within 10 miles include an 18-hole golf course, a full-service marina, and tennis courts. For information on the attractions in Tacoma, see the *Dash Point State Park* listing in this chapter.

RV sites, facilities: There are 118 sites with full hookups (30 and 50 amps) for RVs of any

WASHINGTON

length, plus 12 tent sites available May–September only. Restrooms have flush toilets and showers. Drinking water, cable TV, Wi-Fi and modem access, propane gas, a recreation hall, a convenience store, a coin laundry, lending library, ice, and a seasonal heated swimming pool are available. Leashed pets are permitted.

Reservations, fees: Reservations accepted. Tent sites are $20 per night, hookup sites are $20–28 per night, and it's $2 per person per night for more than two people. Open year-round.

Directions: From the north end of Tacoma on I-5, take Exit 135 to Highway 167. Drive east on Highway 167 (River Road) for four miles to the park on the right.

Contact: Majestic Mobile Manor RV Park, 253/845-3144 or 800/348-3144, fax 253/841-2248, www.majesticrvpark.com.

39 OLYMPIA CAMPGROUND

Scenic rating: 7

near Olympia

See map page 79

This campground in a natural, wooded setting has all the comforts. Nearby recreation options include an 18-hole golf course, hiking trails, marked bike trails, and tennis courts.

RV sites, facilities: There are 95 sites for tents or RVs of any length with full or partial hookups (20 and 30 amps) and two cabins. Some sites are pull-through. Picnic tables are provided and fire rings are at some sites. Restrooms have flush toilets and showers. Drinking water, modem and Wi-Fi access, propane gas, a dump station, a recreation hall, a convenience store, a coin laundry, ice, a playground, a seasonal heated swimming pool, a gas station, and firewood are available. A café is within two miles. Leashed pets are permitted.

Reservations, fees: Reservations accepted. Sites are $19–26 per night, $4 per person per night for more than two people. Some credit cards accepted. Open year-round.

Directions: From Olympia on I-5, take Exit 101 to Tumwater Boulevard. Bear east and drive for 0.25 mile to Center Street. Turn right on Center Street and drive one mile to 83rd Avenue. Turn right on 83rd Avenue and drive an eighth of a mile to the park on the left at 1441 83rd Avenue SW.

Contact: Olympia Campground, 360/352-2551, www.olympiacampground.com.

40 NISQUALLY PLAZA RV PARK

Scenic rating: 5

near McAlister Creek

See map page 79

This campground is near McAlister Creek, where salmon fishing and boating are popular. Nearby recreation opportunities include an 18-hole golf course and the Nisqually National Wildlife Refuge (admission is charged), which offers seven miles of foot trails for viewing a great variety of flora and fauna.

RV sites, facilities: There are 51 sites with full hookups (20, 30, and 50 amps) for RVs of any length. Some sites are pull-through. No tents are allowed. Picnic tables are provided. Restrooms have flush toilets and coin showers. Drinking water, cable TV, a convenience store, a café, a coin laundry, ice, and a seasonal swimming pool are available. Some facilities are wheelchair accessible. Small, hand-launched boat facilities are nearby. Leashed pets are permitted.

Reservations, fees: Reservations are accepted. Sites are $25 per night, $2 per person per night for more than two people. Weekly and monthly rates available. Open year-round.

Directions: In Olympia on I-5, take Exit 114 and drive a short distance to Martin Way. Turn right and drive a short distance to the first road (between two gas stations), a private access road for the park. Turn right and drive a short distance to the park.

Contact: Nisqually Plaza RV Park, 360/491-3831.

THE NORTHERN CASCADES

(BEST RV PARKS AND CAMPGROUNDS

(Prettiest Lakes
Horseshoe Cove, page 106.

Mount Baker is the centerpiece in a forested landscape with hundreds of lakes, rivers, and hidden campgrounds. The only limit here is weather. The Northern Cascades are deluged with the nation's highest snowfall in winter; Mount Baker often receives a foot a day for weeks. Although that shortens the recreation season to just a few months in summer, it has another effect as well. With so many recreation destinations available for such a short time — literally hundreds over the course of three or four months — many remain largely undiscovered.

The vast number of forests, lakes, and streams can make choosing your destination the most difficult decision of all. With so many stellar spots to pick from, newcomers will be well served starting at the state parks, which offer beautiful settings that are easy to reach. Many camps set along roads provide choice layover spots for vacationing travelers.

After a while, though, searching for the lesser-known camps in the national forests becomes more appealing. Many beautiful spots are set alongside lakes and streams, often with trailheads for hikes into nearby wilderness. These areas are among the wildest in America, featuring abundant wildlife, good fishing, and great hiking.

It's true that anybody can get an overview of the area by cruising the highways and camping at the roadside spots I list. But you can take this one the extra mile. Your dream spot may be waiting out there.

Includes:

- Alpine Lakes Wilderness
- Baker Lake
- Beckler River
- Blackpine Lake
- Chewuch River
- Chiwawa River
- Cle Elum Lake
- Columbia River
- Daroga State Park
- Diablo Lake
- Entiat River
- Green River
- Icicle River
- Kachess Lake
- Kanaskat-Palmer State Park
- Lake Chelan State Park
- Lake Easton State Park
- Lake Entiat
- Lake Wapato
- Lake Wenatchee State Park
- Lincoln Rock State Park
- Little Naches River
- Methow River
- Mount Baker – Snoqualmie National Forest
- Napeequa River
- Nooksack River
- Okanogan and Wenatchee National Forests
- Pearrygin Lake State Park
- Rasar State Park
- Rockport State Park
- Ross Lake National Recreation Area
- Sauk River
- Skagit River
- Skykomish River
- Snoqualmie River
- Stillaguamish River
- Suiattle River
- Twin Lakes
- Twisp River
- Wenatchee Confluence State Park
- Wenatchee National Forest
- Wenatchee River
- White River
- Yakima River

WASHINGTON

THE NORTHERN CASCADES

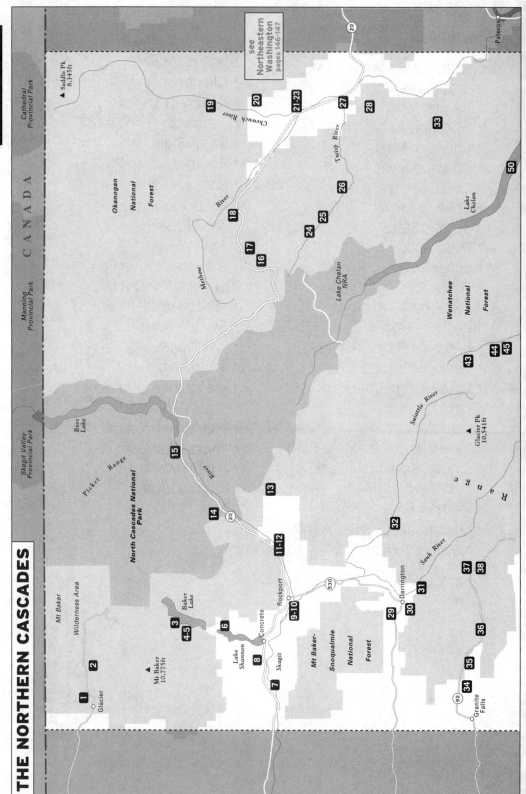

see
**Northeastern
Washington**
pages 146-147

CANADA

Cathedral
Provincial Park

Manning
Provincial Park

Skagit Valley
Provincial Park

▲ Saddle Pk
8,345ft

Okanogan
National
Forest

Chewuch River

Twisp River

Methow River

Lake Chelan
NRA

Lake
Chelan

Wenatchee
National
Forest

Ross
Lake

Picket Range

North Cascades National
Park

River

Suiattle River

▲ Glacier Pk
10,541ft

Range

Mt Baker
Wilderness Area

Glacier

▲ Mt Baker
10,775ft

Baker
Lake

Lake
Shannon

Concrete

Rockport

Skagit

Sauk River

Darrington

Mt Baker-
Snoqualmie
National
Forest

Granite
Falls

Pateros

20

20

92

530

20

WASHINGTON

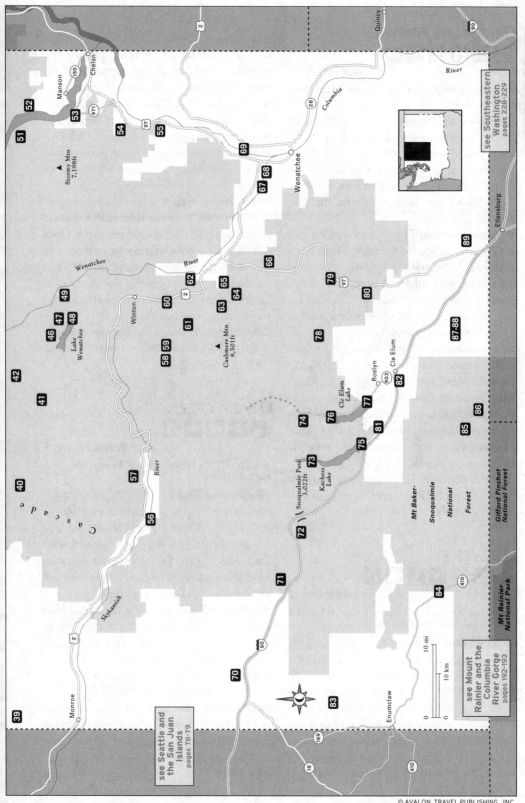

see Southeastern
Washington
pages 228-229

Quincy

2

90

River

Columbia

28

Chelan

150

Manson

971

97

Wenatchee

52

53

54

55

51

69

68

67

Stormy Mtn
7,196ft

Ellensburg

89

Wenatchee

River

66

62

65

64

79

97

80

49

60

63

61

Winton

87-88

78

Cle Elum

46

47

48

Lake
Wenatchee

58

59

Cashmere Mtn
8,501ft

Roslyn

903

82

42

Cle Elum
Lake

77

86

41

76

74

81

85

75

57

River

73

72

Snoqualmie Pass
3,022ft

Kachess
Lake

Mt Baker-
Snoqualmie
National
Forest

Gifford Pinchot
National Forest

40

56

C a s c a d e

71

84

410

Mt Rainier
National Park

39

Monroe

Skykomish

2

90

70

83

Enumclaw

169

410

18

410

see Seattle and
the San Juan
Islands
pages 78-79

see Mount
Rainier and the
Columbia
River Gorge
pages 192-193

10 mi

10 km

0

0

© AVALON TRAVEL PUBLISHING, INC.

WASHINGTON

1 DOUGLAS FIR

Scenic rating: 10

on the Nooksack River in Mount Baker-Snoqualmie National Forest

See map page 102

Set along the Nooksack River, this camp features river views from some campsites. It is a beautiful camp, surrounded by old-growth Douglas fir, silver fir, and western hemlock. Trout fishing is available on the river, and there are hiking trails in the area.

RV sites, facilities: There are 29 sites for tents or RVs up to 35 feet (no hookups). Picnic tables and fire grills are provided. Drinking water and vault toilets are available. A store, a café, a coin laundry, and ice are within five miles at Glacier. Some facilities are wheelchair accessible. Leashed pets are permitted.

Reservations, fees: Reservations are accepted at 877/444-6777 or www.ReserveUSA.com ($9 reservation fee). Sites are $16 per night. Open May–September, weather permitting.

Directions: From Bellingham on I-5, take the Highway 542 exit and drive 33 miles to Glacier. Continue two miles northeast on Highway 542 to the campground on the left.

Contact: Mount Baker–Snoqualmie National Forest, Mount Baker Ranger District, 360/856-5700, fax 360/856-1934.

2 SILVER FIR

Scenic rating: 9

on the North Fork of the Nooksack River in Mount Baker-Snoqualmie National Forest

See map page 102

This campground is on the North Fork of the Nooksack River. It is within 30 minutes of the Heather Meadows area, which provides some of the best hiking trails in the entire region. In addition, a one-mile round-trip to Artist Ridge promises views of Mount Baker and Mount Shuksan. The first part of the trail to the first viewpoint is wheelchair accessible. Fishing is available nearby, and in the winter the area offers cross-country skiing. You're strongly advised to obtain a U.S. Forest Service map in order to take maximum advantage of the recreational opportunities in the area.

RV sites, facilities: There are 20 sites for tents or RVs up to 30 feet (no hookups). Picnic tables and barbecue grills are provided. Drinking water, vault toilets, and a group picnic shelter are available. Some facilities are wheelchair accessible. Leashed pets are permitted.

Reservations, fees: Reservations are accepted at 877/444-6777 or www.ReserveUSA.com ($9 reservation fee). Sites are $16 per night. Open May–early October, weather permitting.

Directions: From I-5 at Bellingham, turn east on Highway 542 and drive 33 miles to Glacier. Continue east on Highway 542 for 12.5 miles to the campground on the right.

Contact: Mount Baker–Snoqualmie National Forest, Mount Baker Ranger District, 360/856-5700, fax 360/856-1934.

3 PARK CREEK

Scenic rating: 6

near Baker Lake in Mount Baker-Snoqualmie National Forest

See map page 102

This pretty camp is at an elevation of 800 feet on Park Creek amid a heavily wooded area comprising old-growth Douglas fir and western hemlock. Park Creek is a feeder stream to nearby Baker Lake. The camp is primitive and small but gets its fair share of use.

RV sites, facilities: There are 11 sites for tents or RVs up to 22 feet (no hookups). Picnic tables are provided. Vault toilets are available, but there is no drinking water. Boat docks, launching facilities, and rentals are nearby on Baker Lake. Leashed pets are permitted.

Reservations, fees: Reservations are accepted at 877/444-6777 or www.ReserveUSA.com ($9 reservation fee). Sites are $12 per night. Open mid-May–early September, weather permitting.

Directions: From I-5 at Burlington, turn east on Highway 20 and drive approximately 24 miles to Milepost 82 and Baker Lake Highway (Forest Road 11). Turn north on Baker Lake Highway and drive about 19.5 miles to Forest Road 1144. Turn left (northwest) and drive about 200 yards to the campground on the left. Obtaining a U.S. Forest Service map is helpful.

Contact: Mount Baker–Snoqualmie National Forest, Mount Baker Ranger District, 360/856-5700, fax 360/856-1934.

◢ BOULDER CREEK

Scenic rating: 8

near Baker Lake in Mount Baker-Snoqualmie National Forest

See map page 102

This camp provides an alternative to Horseshoe Cove (see the *Horseshoe Cove* listing in this chapter). It is on Boulder Creek about one mile from the shore of Baker Lake. Fishing is fair here for rainbow trout, but typically it's far better at Baker Lake. A boat launch is located at Panorama Point, about 15 minutes away. Wild berries can be found in the area in season. The campground offers prime views of Mount Baker.

RV sites, facilities: There are eight sites for tents or RVs up to 22 feet (no hookups) and one group site that can accommodate up to 25 people. Picnic tables and fire grills are provided. Vault toilets are available, but there is no drinking water. Boat docks and launching facilities are nearby on Baker Lake. Leashed pets are permitted.

Reservations, fees: Reservations are required for the group site and are available for some individual sites at 877/444-6777 or www.Reserve USA.com ($9 reservation fee). Sites are $12 per night; the group site is $40 per night. Open mid-May–early September, weather permitting.

Directions: From I-5 at Burlington, turn east on Highway 20 and drive approximately 24 miles to Milepost 82 and Baker Lake Highway (Forest Road 11). Turn north on Baker Lake

Highway and drive 17.4 miles to the campground on the right.

Contact: Mount Baker–Snoqualmie National Forest, Mount Baker Ranger District, 360/856-5700, fax 360/856-1934.

◢ PANORAMA POINT

Scenic rating: 10

on Baker Lake in Mount Baker-Snoqualmie National Forest

See map page 102

With incredible scenic views of Mount Baker, Mount Shuk, Baker Lake, and Anderson Mountain, this camp is true to its name. Panorama Point is a well-maintained campground on the northwest shore of Baker Lake. The reservoir is one of the better fishing lakes in the area, often with good prospects for rainbow trout. Powerboating and waterskiing are permitted. Hiking trails are nearby.

RV sites, facilities: There are 15 sites for tents or RVs up to 25 feet (no hookups). Picnic tables are provided. Drinking water and vault toilets are available. A convenience store and ice are within one mile. A boat ramp is adjacent to the camp. Boat docks and rentals are nearby. Some facilities are wheelchair accessible. Leashed pets are permitted.

Reservations, fees: Reservations are accepted for some sites at 877/444-6777 or www .ReserveUSA.com ($9 reservation fee). Sites are $16 per night. Open mid-May–mid-September, weather permitting.

Directions: From I-5 at Burlington, turn east on Highway 20 and drive approximately 24 miles to Milepost 82 and Baker Lake Highway (Forest Road 11). Turn north on Baker Lake Highway and drive 18.7 miles to the campground entrance on the right on the shore of Baker.

Contact: Mount Baker–Snoqualmie National Forest, Mount Baker Ranger District, 360/856-5700, fax 360/856-1934.

WASHINGTON

6 HORSESHOE COVE

Scenic rating: 9

on Baker Lake in Mount Baker-Snoqualmie National Forest

See map page 102   BEST

This camp is along 5,000-acre Baker Lake. Anglers will often find good fishing for rainbow trout and kokanee salmon. Other highlights include swimming access from the campground and a boat ramp. Some hiking trails can be found nearby. The Baker Lake Basin has many trails, and the Mount Baker National Recreation area is within 30 minutes.

RV sites, facilities: There are 36 sites for tents or RVs up to 25 feet (no hookups), and three group sites can accommodate up to 25 people each. Picnic tables and fire grills are provided. Drinking water and flush toilets are available. A boat ramp and swimming beach are adjacent to camp. Canoes, kayaks, and pedal boats are available for rent; check with the camp host. Some facilities are wheelchair accessible. Leashed pets are permitted.

Reservations, fees: Reservations required for group sites and accepted for family sites at 877/444-6777 or www.ReserveUSA.com ($9 reservation fee). Sites are $16 per night, and group sites are $75 per night. Open May–September, weather permitting. The campground is gated in the winter, but one loop remains open through the off-season on a no-service, no-fee basis for walk-in campers.

Directions: From I-5 at Burlington, turn east on Highway 20 and drive approximately 24 miles to Milepost 82 and the Baker Lake Highway (Forest Road 11). Turn north on Baker Lake Highway and drive about 14.8 miles to Forest Road 1118. Turn right (east) on Forest Road 1118 and drive two miles to the campground. A U.S. Forest Service map is recommended.

Contact: Mount Baker–Snoqualmie National Forest, Mount Baker Ranger District, 360/856-5700, fax 360/856-1934.

7 RASAR STATE PARK

Scenic rating: 8

on the Skagit River

See map page 102

This park borders North Cascade National Park and is also near 10,778-foot Mount Baker and the Baker River watershed. Fishing and hiking are the attractions here. The elevation is 4,000 feet.

RV sites, facilities: There 22 sites for RVs up to 40 feet with full hookups (30 amps), three primitive hike-in/bike-in sites, 10 walk-in sites at which two four-person Adirondack shelters are available, and three group sites for up to 80–120 people per site. Picnic tables and fire grills are provided. Restrooms have flush toilets and coin showers. Drinking water, a dump station, and a kitchen shelter are available. Firewood gathering is prohibited. Some facilities are wheelchair accessible. Leashed pets are permitted.

Reservations, fees: Reservations are required for the group site and accepted for the other sites at 888/CAMP-OUT (888/226-7688) or www.parks.wa.gov/reservations ($7 reservation fee). Sites are $17–31 per night, $12 per night for hike-in/bike-in sites, $10 per extra vehicle per night. Call for group rates. Open year-round.

Directions: From I-5 at Burlington, turn east on Highway 20/North Cascade Highway, and drive 20 miles to Lusk Road. Turn right on Lusk Road and drive 0.75 mile to Cape Horn Road. Turn left on Cape Horn Road and drive one mile to the park entrance.

Contact: Rasar State Park, 360/826-3942; state park information 360/902-8844, www.parks.wa.gov.

8 CREEKSIDE CAMPGROUND

Scenic rating: 6

near the Skagit River

See map page 102

This pretty, wooded campground is centrally located to nearby recreational opportunities at Baker Lake and the Skagit River. Trout fishing is good here, and tackle is available nearby. Horseshoe pits and a recreation hall are also available. About half of the sites are filled with monthly renters.

RV sites, facilities: There are 29 sites for tents, trailers, or RVs up to 40 feet with full or partial hookups (20 and 30 amps). Picnic tables and fire rings are provided. Restrooms have flush toilets and showers. Drinking water, a dump station, a coin laundry, horseshoe pits, and a recreation hall are available. A café is within one mile. Leashed pets are permitted.

Reservations, fees: Reservations are recommended. Sites are $12–16 per night for tent sites, $18–25 per night for RV sites. Open year-round.

Directions: From Seattle, drive north on I-5 to Exit 232 (Cook Road). Take the exit up and over the highway to the flashing light and Highway 20. Turn left on Highway 20/North Cascades Highway and drive 17 miles to Baker Lake Road, between Mileposts 182 and 183. Turn left on Baker Lake Road and drive 0.25 mile to the camp on the right.

Contact: Creekside Campground, 360/826-3566.

9 ROCKPORT STATE PARK

Scenic rating: 8

near the Skagit River

See map page 102

This state park covers 670 acres and is at the foot of 5,400-foot Sauk Mountain. This natural forest was never logged and as a result has grown a thick canopy that allows only minimal sunlight to reach the forest floor. The park features more than 600 acres of old-growth Douglas firs. There are five miles of hiking trails amid this forest, and a steep but climbable trail extends three miles (one-way) to the top of Sauk Mountain. Access for these trails is outside the park. The summit offers good views of the Skagit Valley and the Northern Cascades. A bonus at this camp: four Adirondack shelters, which have three sides and a roof. The Skagit River,

a good steelhead stream, runs nearby. Rafting and kayaking are allowed on the Skagit, with the put-in not at the park, but on nearby Highway 20 at Howard Miller Steelhead Park.

RV sites, facilities: There are 50 sites with full hookups (30 amps) for RVs up to 38 feet, three tent sites, eight walk-in tent sites, four Adirondack shelters, and a group tent site for up to 40 people. Picnic tables and fire grills are provided. Restrooms have flush toilets and coin showers. A dump station and firewood are available. Some facilities are wheelchair accessible. A store, gas, and ice are within one mile. Leashed pets are permitted.

Reservations, fees: Reservations are required for the group site and two wheelchair-accessible sites only at 360/853-8461. Sites are $17–24 per night, $12 per night for hike-in/bike-in sites, $10 per extra vehicle per night. Adirondack shelters are $21 per night. Call for group rates. Open April–late October.

Directions: From I-5 at Burlington, turn east on Highway 20 and drive 37 miles to Milepost 96. Look for the park entrance (one mile west of Rockport) on the left.

Contact: Rockport State Park, 360/853-8461; state park information 360/902-8844, www.parks.wa.gov.

10 HOWARD MILLER STEELHEAD PARK

Scenic rating: 5

on the Skagit River

See map page 102

This Skagit County Park provides grassy sites and access to the Skagit River and some good walking trails. The river is designated a Wild and Scenic River. The salmon and steelhead fishing is often good in season. Campsites at this spot are sunny and spacious. Groups can be accommodated. A bald eagle sanctuary is nearby, just east of the park. November–January is the best time to see bald eagles here. This camp is most popular in July, August, and September, when the weather is best, but

WASHINGTON

also attracts visitors in early winter who arrive primarily for bald eagle watching.

RV sites, facilities: There are 49 sites for tents or RVs of any length with full or partial hookups (30 amps), 10 walk-in tent sites, and two Adirondack sleeping shelters. Picnic tables and fire pits are provided. Restrooms have flush toilets and coin showers. Drinking water, a dump station, a clubhouse, a picnic shelter, two playgrounds, a dog run, and horseshoe pits are available. A store and ice are within one mile. Boat-launching facilities are on the Skagit River, within the park. Some facilities are wheelchair accessible. Leashed pets are permitted.

Reservations, fees: Reservations are recommended ($6 reservation fee). Sites are $18–20 per night, Adirondacks are $20 per night, plus $5 per extra vehicle per night. Some credit cards accepted. Open year-round.

Directions: On I-5, drive to Exit 230/Highway 20 at Burlington. Turn east on Highway 20, and drive 44 miles to Rockport and Rockport-Darrington Road (Highway 530). Turn right (south) and drive three blocks to the camp on the right.

Contact: Howard Miller Steelhead Park, 360/853-8808, fax 360/853-7315; Skagit County Parks, 360/336-9414, fax 360/336-9493.

11 WILDERNESS VILLAGE AND RV PARK

Scenic rating: 6

near the Skagit River

See map page 102

This RV park is near the Skagit River. Cool and wooded, it offers nice, grassy sites and nearby access to the river and fishing. Horseshoe pits and a sports field provide recreation alternatives. Rockport State Park and hiking trails are nearby. Bald eagles can often be viewed on the Skagit River in December and January. A one-mile trail (round-trip) can be accessed along the river.

RV sites, facilities: There are 32 pull-through sites with full hookups (30 amps) for RVs of any length and 20 tent sites. Picnic tables and

fire rings are provided. Restrooms have flush toilets and coin showers. Cable TV, a recreation hall, and a coin laundry are available. A café and ice are within two miles. Leashed pets are permitted.

Reservations, fees: Reservations are accepted. Sites are $11–19 per night. Open year-round.

Directions: From Burlington, drive east on Highway 20 for 44 miles to Rockport. Continue east on Highway 20 for five miles to the park. The park is between Mileposts 102 and 103 on the right at 57588 State Route 20.

Contact: Wilderness Village and RV Park, 360/873-2571.

12 SKAGIT RIVER RESORT

Scenic rating: 9

on the Skagit River

See map page 102

This beautiful camp nestles in the trees along the Skagit River. The resort covers 125 acres, including 1.5 miles of river frontage. A restaurant called "The Eatery" has received awards for its pecan pie and is also known for its home-style meals. Fishing, river walks, and nearby hiking trails among the glaciers and waterfalls can be accessed close to the campground. Three hydroelectric plants nearby offer tours. Recreational facilities include horseshoes and a sports field for volleyball, croquet, and badminton. This resort is popular July–September, when reservations are often required to get a spot.

RV sites, facilities: There are 48 sites for tents or RVs of any length with full hookups, including some pull-through sites, plus 34 cabins and mobile homes. Restrooms have flush toilets and coin showers. Drinking water, a dump station, modem access, a pay phone, a coin laundry, horseshoe pits, and a restaurant are available. A sports field is set up for volleyball, croquet, and badminton. Leashed pets are permitted.

Reservations, fees: Reservations are recommended. Sites are $20–25 per night, $10 per pet per night. Some credit cards accepted. Open year-round.

Directions: From Burlington, drive east on Highway 20 for 44 miles to Rockport. Continue east on Highway 20 for six miles to the resort on the left (between Mileposts 103 and 104).

Contact: Skagit River Resort, 360/873-2250 or 800/273-2606, fax 360/873-4077, www.northcascades.com.

13 MARBLE CREEK

Scenic rating: 7

on Marble Creek in Mount Baker-Snoqualmie National Forest

See map page 102

This primitive campground is on Marble Creek amid old-growth Douglas fir and western hemlock. Fishing for rainbow trout is possible. A trailhead to Hidden Lake just inside the boundary of North Cascades National Park can be found about five miles from camp at the end of Forest Road 1540. See a U.S. Forest Service map for details.

RV sites, facilities: There are 22 sites for tents or RVs up to 22 feet (no hookups). Picnic tables and fire grills are provided. Vault toilets are available, but there is no drinking water. Some facilities are wheelchair accessible. Leashed pets are permitted.

Reservations, fees: Reservations are accepted at 877/444-6777 or www.ReserveUSA.com ($9 reservation fee). Sites are $12 per night, $6 per night for an additional vehicle. Open mid-May–mid-September, weather permitting.

Directions: From I-5 in Burlington, take Exit 230/Highway 20. Turn east on Highway 20 and drive 46 miles to Marblemount and Forest Road 15 (Cascade River Road). Cross the bridge, turn east on Cascade River Road, and drive eight miles to Forest Road 1530. Turn right (south) on Forest Road 1530 and drive one mile to the campground. Obtaining a U.S. Forest Service map is advised.

Contact: Mount Baker–Snoqualmie National Forest, Mount Baker Ranger District, 360/856-5700, fax 360/856-1934.

14 NEWHALEM CREEK & NEWHALEM CREEK GROUP

Scenic rating: 7

near the Skagit River in Ross Lake National Recreation Area

See map page 102

This spot is along the Skagit River west of Newhalem at an elevation of 500 feet. Good hiking possibilities abound in the immediate area, and naturalist programs are available. Be sure to visit the North Cascades Visitor Center at the top of the hill from the campground. No firewood gathering is permitted. If this camp is full, try Goodell Creek Campground, just one mile west on Highway 20.

RV sites, facilities: There are 108 sites for tents or RVs up to 32 feet (no hookups), and two group sites for tents or RVs up to 26 feet can accommodate up to 24 people each. Picnic tables and fire grills are provided. Restrooms have flush toilets. Drinking water and a dump station are available. The group camp has a covered pavilion. Some facilities are wheelchair accessible. Leashed pets are permitted.

Reservations, fees: Reservations are accepted for some of the individual sites and are required for group camps at 877/444-6777 or www.ReserveUSA.com ($9 reservation fee). Sites are $12 per night, group sites are $32 per night. Open mid-May–mid-October.

Directions: On I-5, drive to Exit 230/Highway 20 at Burlington. Turn east on Highway 20, and drive 46 miles to Marblemount. Continue 14 miles east on Highway 20 to the camp.

Contact: North Cascades National Park, 360/856-5700, fax 360/856-1934, www.nps.gov/noca/.

15 COLONIAL CREEK

Scenic rating: 7

on Diablo Lake in Ross Lake National Recreation Area

See map page 102

Colonial Creek Campground sits at an elevation of 1,200 feet along the shore of Diablo

Lake in the Ross Lake National Recreation Area. The five-mile-long lake offers many hiking and fishing opportunities. A naturalist program and guided walks are available during the summer months. No firewood gathering is permitted at this campsite.

RV sites, facilities: There are 129 sites for tents or RVs up to 45 feet (no hookups), including a few walk-in tent sites. Picnic tables and fire grills are provided. Restrooms have flush toilets. Drinking water, a dump station, three boat docks, fishing cleaning station, wheelchair accessible fishing pier, and a boat ramp are available. Some facilities are wheelchair accessible. Leashed pets are permitted.

Reservations, fees: Reservations are not accepted. Sites are $12 per night. Open mid-April–mid-October; 18 lakefront sites are open through the winter (no services provided).

Directions: From I-5 at Burlington, take Exit 230 and drive east to Highway 20. Turn east on Highway 20 and drive 46 miles to Marblemount. Continue east on Highway 20 for 24 miles to the campground entrance.

Contact: North Cascades National Park, 360/856-5700, fax 360/856-1934, www.nps.gov/noca.

16 LONE FIR

Scenic rating: 9

on Early Winters Creek in Okanogan and Wenatchee National Forests

See map page 102

Lone Fir sits at 3,640 feet elevation along the banks of Early Winters Creek. The area has had some timber operations in the past, but there are no nearby clear-cuts. To the west, Washington Pass Overlook offers a spectacular view. Anglers can fish in the creek, and many hiking and biking trails crisscross the area, including the trailhead for Cutthroat Lake. A U.S. Forest Service map will provide details. A loop trail through the campground woods is wheelchair accessible for 0.4 mile. (See the *Early Winters* listing in this chapter for more area information.)

RV sites, facilities: There are 27 sites for tents or RVs up to 36 feet (no hookups). Picnic tables and fire grills are provided. Vault toilets and drinking water are available. Some facilities are wheelchair accessible. Leashed pets are permitted.

Reservations, fees: Reservations are not accepted. Sites are $8 per night per vehicle. Open late May–September with full services, weather permitting; camping is allowed during the off-season with no fees and reduced services.

Directions: From Burlington, drive east on Highway 20 for 107 miles to the campground (11 miles west of Mazama) on the right.

Contact: Okanogan and Wenatchee National Forests, Methow Valley Ranger District, 509/996-4003, fax 509/996-2208; Methow Valley Visitor Center, 509/996-4000, fax 509/996-4051.

17 KLIPCHUCK

Scenic rating: 7

on Early Winters Creek in Okanogan and Wenatchee National Forests

See map page 102

This camp is at an elevation of 3,000 feet along Early Winters Creek. The camp area nestles amid majestic trees, primarily Douglas fir and subalpine firs. Klipchuck provides hiking aplenty, but note that rattlesnakes are occasionally seen in this area. A short loop trail from the camp leads about five miles up and over Delancy Ridge to Driveway Butte and down to the creek, although the trail is somewhat overgrown. Another trail starts nearby on Forest Road 200 (Sandy Butte-Cedar Creek Road) and goes two miles up Cedar Creek to lovely Cedar Creek Falls. Still another option from the campground is a four-mile trail along Early Winters Creek. This region is best visited in the spring and fall, with summer hot and dry. (See the listing for *Early Winters* in this chapter for more information.)

RV sites, facilities: There are 46 sites for tents or RVs up to 34 feet (no hookups). Sites can be combined to accommodate groups. Picnic tables and fire grills are provided. Drinking water and vault toilets are available. Some facilities are wheelchair accessible. Leashed pets are permitted.

Reservations, fees: Reservations are not accepted. Sites are $8 per night per vehicle. Open late May–late September, with full services, weather permitting; camping is allowed during the off-season with no fees and reduced services.

Directions: From Burlington, drive east on Highway 20 for 115 miles to Forest Road 300. (If you reach the Methow River Valley, you have gone four miles past the turnoff.) Turn left (marked) and drive northwest one mile to the camp at the end of the road.

Contact: Okanogan and Wenatchee National Forests, Methow Valley Ranger District, 509/996-4003, fax 509/996-2208; Methow Valley Visitor Center, 509/996-4000, fax 509/996-4051.

18 EARLY WINTERS

Scenic rating: 6

on Early Winters Creek in Okanogan and Wenatchee National Forests

See map page 102

Located on each side of the highway, this campground has an unusual configuration. The confluence of Early Winters Creek and the Methow River marks the site of this campground. The elevation is 2,160 feet. You'll find great views of Goat Wall here. Campsites are flat, and the open landscape, set in a sparse lodgepole pine and fir forest, provides an arid feel to the area. Several hiking trails can be found within five miles, including one that leads south to Cedar Creek Falls. Other possible side trips include Goat Wall to the north and the town of Winthrop to the south, which boasts a historical museum, a state fish hatchery, and Pearrygin Lake State Park.

RV sites, facilities: There are 12 sites for tents or RVs up to 24 feet (no hookups). Picnic tables and fire grills are provided. Drinking water and vault toilets are available. There is a small store and snack bar in Mazama, about two miles away. Some facilities are wheelchair accessible. Leashed pets are permitted.

Reservations, fees: Reservations are not accepted. Sites are $5 per night per vehicle. Open mid-May–October, weather permitting.

Directions: From Burlington, drive east on Highway 20 for 116 miles to the campground (if you reach County Road 1163 near Mazama, you have gone two miles too far).

Contact: Okanogan and Wenatchee National Forests, Methow Valley Ranger District, 509/996-4003, fax 509/996-2208; Methow Valley Visitor Center, 509/996-4000, fax 509/996-4051.

19 CHEWUCH

Scenic rating: 6

on the Chewuch River in Okanogan and Wenatchee National Forests

See map page 102

Chewuch camp sits along the Chewuch River at an elevation of 2,278 feet and is surrounded by ponderosa pines. It is a small camp where catch-and-release fishing is a highlight. Hiking and biking trails explore the area. By traveling north, you can access trailheads that lead into the Pasayten Wilderness. See a U.S. Forest Service map for specific locations.

RV sites, facilities: There are 16 sites for tents or RVs up to 35 feet (no hookups). Picnic tables and fire grills are provided. Vault toilets and drinking water are available. Some facilities are wheelchair accessible. Leashed pets are permitted.

Reservations, fees: Reservations are not accepted. Sites are $5 per vehicle per night. Open late May–October, weather permitting.

Directions: From Burlington, drive east on Highway 20 for 134 miles to Winthrop and County Road 1213/West Chewuch Road. Turn north on County Road 1213/West Chewuch Road and drive 6.5 miles (where it merges with Forest Road 51). Continue north on Forest Road 51 for seven miles to the campground on the right.

Contact: Okanogan and Wenatchee National Forests, Methow Valley Ranger District,

WASHINGTON

509/996-4003, fax 509/996-2208; Methow Valley Visitor Center, 509/996-4000, fax 509/996-4051.

20 PEARRYGIN LAKE STATE PARK

Scenic rating: 8

on Pearrygin Lake
See map page 102

Pearrygin Lake is fed from underground springs and Pearrygin Creek, the lifeblood for this setting and the adjacent 696-acre state park. Located in the beautiful Methow Valley, it's ringed by the Northern Cascade Mountains. The park is known for its expansive green lawns, which lead to 11,000 feet of waterfront and sandy beaches. Old willows and ash provide shade. The camp is frequented by red-winged and yellow-headed blackbirds, as well as by marmots. Wildflower- and wildlife-viewing are excellent in the spring. The campground has access to a sandy beach and facilities for swimming, boating, waterskiing, fishing, and hiking. The sites are close together and don't offer much privacy, but they are spacious, and the variety of recreation options makes it worth the crunch.

RV sites, facilities: There are 70 sites for RVs up to 60 feet with full hookups (15 and 30 amps), 93 tent sites, two hike-in/bike-in sites, two group sites for up to 48 and 80 people, and two cabins. Picnic tables and fire grills are provided. Restrooms have flush toilets and coin showers. Drinking water, a dump station, firewood for a fee, and junior ranger and seasonal campfire programs are available. A store, pay telephone, a deli, and ice are within one mile. Some facilities are wheelchair accessible. Boat-launching and dock facilities are available. Leashed pets are permitted.

Reservations, fees: Reservations are accepted for individual sites and required for group camps at 888/CAMP-OUT (888/226-7688) or www.parks.wa.gov/reservations ($7 reservation fee). Tent sites are $17–19 per night, RV hookup sites are $24–31 per night, plus $10 per extra vehicle per night. Hike-in/bike-in sites are

$12 per night. Call for group rates. Some credit cards accepted. Open April–early November.

Directions: From Winthrop and Highway 20, drive north through town (road changes to East Chewuch Road). Continue 1.5 miles north from town to Bear Creek Road. Turn right and drive 1.5 miles to the end of the pavement and look for the cattle guard and the park entrance on the right. Turn right, drive over the cattle guard, and continue to the campground.

Contact: Pearrygin Lake State Park, 509/996-2370, fax 509/996-2630; state park information 360/902-8844, www.parks.wa.gov.

21 PINE-NEAR RV PARK

Scenic rating: 7

on the Methow River
See map page 102

This camp is an adequate layover spot for Highway 20 cruisers and a good alternative camp to the more crowded sites at Pearrygin Lake. The Methow River is nearby; see the *KOA Winthrop* listing in this chapter for information on the various activities available in the Winthrop area.

RV sites, facilities: There are 28 sites with full hookups (30 and 50 amps) for RVs of any length and 40 tent sites. Some sites are pull-through. Three mobile homes are for rent on a per-night basis. Picnic tables are provided and fire rings are available on request. Restrooms have flush toilets and coin showers. A dump station and a coin laundry are available. A store, propane gas, and a café are within one mile. Leashed pets are permitted.

Reservations, fees: Reservations accepted. Sites are $13–24 per night, $2 per person per night for more than two people, $2 per extra vehicle per night. Some credit cards accepted. Open year-round.

Directions: From Winthrop, drive east for a short distance on Highway 20 to Castle Avenue. Turn right (east) and drive half a block to the park on the left.

Contact: Pine-Near RV Park, 509/996-2391, www.pinenear.com.

22 KOA WINTHROP

Scenic rating: 7

on the Methow River
See map page 102

Here's another campground set along the Methow River, which offers opportunities for fishing, boating, swimming, and rafting. The park has a free shuttle into Winthrop, an interesting town with many restored, early-1900s buildings lining the main street. One such building, the Shafer Museum, displays an array of period items. If you would like to observe wildlife, take a short, two-mile drive southeast out of Winthrop on County Road 9129 on the east side of the Methow River. Turn east on County Road 1631 into Davis Lake and follow the signs to the Methow River Habitat Management Area Headquarters. Depending on the time of year, you may see mule deer, porcupines, bobcats, mountain lions, snowshoe hares, black bears, red squirrels, and many species of birds. If you're looking for something tamer, other nearby recreation options include a nine-hole golf course and tennis courts.

RV sites, facilities: There are 60 sites with full or partial hookups (30 and 50 amps) for RVs of any length, 15 sites with no hookups for RVs of any length, and 35 tent sites. There are also 17 one- and two-room cabins. Some sites are pull-through. Picnic tables and fire grills are provided. Restrooms have flush toilets and showers. Drinking water, firewood, a dump station, a recreation hall, high-speed modem and Wi-Fi access, bike rentals, a convenience store, a coin laundry, ice, a playground, and a seasonal heated swimming pool are available. Propane gas and a café are within one mile. There is a courtesy shuttle to and from Winthrop. Leashed pets are permitted.

Reservations, fees: Reservations are accepted at 800/562-2158. Sites are $24–35 per night, $2–5 per person per night for more than two people. Some credit cards accepted. Open mid-April–November.

Directions: From Winthrop, drive east on High-way 20 for one mile to the camp on the left. The camp is between Mileposts 194 and 195.

Contact: KOA Winthrop, 509/996-2258, www.koa.com.

23 BIG TWIN LAKE CAMPGROUND

Scenic rating: 5

on Twin Lakes
See map page 102

As you might figure from the name, this campground is along the shore of Big Twin Lake. With its sweeping lawn and shade trees, the camp features views of the lake from all campsites. No gas motors are permitted on the lake. Fly-fishing is good for rainbow trout, with special regulations in effect: one-fish limit, single barbless hook, artificials only. This is an ideal lake for a float tube, rowboat with a casting platform, or a pram. (See the *KOA Winthrop* listing in this chapter for information on the various activities available in the Winthrop area.)

RV sites, facilities: There are 50 sites with full or partial hookups (30 amps) for RVs of any length, as well as 35 tent sites. Some sites are pull-through. Picnic tables and fire grills are provided. Restrooms have flush toilets and coin showers. Drinking water, two dump stations, Wi-Fi, firewood, ice, and a playground are available. Boat docks, launching facilities, and boat rentals can be obtained on Big Twin Lake. Leashed pets are permitted.

Reservations, fees: Reservations are accepted. Sites are $16–22 per night, $4 per person per night for more than two people, $5 per extra vehicle per night. Weekly and monthly rates available. Open mid-April–October.

Directions: From Winthrop, drive east on Highway 20 for one mile to Twin Lakes Road. Turn right (west) on Twin Lakes Road and drive 1.25 miles to the campground on the left, at 210 Twin Lakes Road.

Contact: Big Twin Lake Campground, 509/996-2650, www.methownet.com/bigtwin.

24 SOUTH CREEK

Scenic rating: 6

on the Twisp River in Okanogan and Wenatchee
National Forests

See map page 102

Although small, quiet, and little known, South
Creek Campground packs a wallop with good
recreation options. It's set at the confluence of the
Twisp River and South Creek at a major trailhead
that accesses the Lake Chelan–Sawtooth Wilderness. The South Creek Trailhead provides a hike
to Louis Lake. The elevation at the camp is 3,100
feet. See a U.S. Forest Service map for details.

RV sites, facilities: There are four sites for tents
or RVs up to 24 feet (no hookups). Picnic tables
and fire grills are provided. A vault toilet is available. There is no drinking water, and garbage
must be packed out. Some facilities are wheelchair accessible. Leashed pets are permitted.

Reservations, fees: Reservations are not accepted. Sites are $5 per vehicle per night. Open
late May–early October, weather permitting.

Directions: From Burlington, drive east on
Highway 20 for 145 miles to Twisp and County
Road 9114 (Twisp River Road). Turn right
on County Road 9114 and drive 17.5 miles
(becomes Forest Road 44). Continue west (becomes Forest Road 4440 and a dirt road) for 4.5
miles to the campground on the left.

Contact: Okanogan and Wenatchee National Forests, Methow Valley Ranger District,
509/996-4003, fax 509/996-2208; Methow
Valley Visitor Center, 509/996-4000, fax
509/996-4051.

25 POPLAR FLAT

Scenic rating: 7

on the Twisp River in Okanogan and Wenatchee
National Forests

See map page 102

This campground is at 2,900 feet elevation
along the Twisp River. This area provides many
wildlife-viewing opportunities for deer, black
bears, and many species of birds. Several trails

in the area, including Twisp River Trail, follow
streams, and some provide access to the Lake
Chelan–Sawtooth Wilderness. Twisp River
Horse Camp, across the river from the campground, has facilities for horses.

RV sites, facilities: There are 16 sites for tents
or RVs up to 30 feet (no hookups) and one
double site for up to 12 people. Picnic tables
and fire grills are provided. Drinking water
and vault toilets are available. A day-use picnic
area with a shelter is nearby. Some facilities
are wheelchair accessible. Leashed pets are
permitted.

Reservations, fees: Reservations are not accepted. Sites are $8 per vehicle per night. Open
mid-May–October, weather permitting.

Directions: From Burlington, drive east on
Highway 20 for 145 miles to Twisp and County
Road 9114 (Twisp River Road). Turn west on
County Road 9114 and drive 11 miles (becomes
Forest Road 44). Continue west for 9.5 miles to
the campground on the left.

Contact: Okanogan and Wenatchee National Forests, Methow Valley Ranger District,
509/996-4003, fax 509/996-2208; Methow
Valley Visitor Center, 509/996-4000, fax
509/996-4051.

26 WAR CREEK

Scenic rating: 6

on the Twisp River in Okanogan and Wenatchee
National Forests

See map page 102

This trailhead camp is at 2,400 feet eleva-
tion and provides several routes into the Lake
Chelan–Sawtooth Wilderness. War Creek
Trail, Eagle Creek Trail, and Oval Creek Trail
all offer wilderness access and trout fishing.
Backpackers can extend this trip into Lake
Chelan National Recreation Area, for a 15-
mile trek that finishes off at the shore of Lake
Chelan and the National Park Service outpost.
Rattlesnakes are occasionally spotted in this
region in the summer.

RV sites, facilities: There are 10 sites for tents

or RVs up to 22 feet (no hookups). Picnic tables and fire grills are provided. Vault toilets and drinking water are available. Garbage must be packed out. Some facilities are wheelchair accessible. Leashed pets are permitted.

Reservations, fees: Reservations are not accepted. Sites are $5 per vehicle per night. Open May–September, weather permitting.

Directions: From Burlington, drive east on Highway 20 for 145 miles to Twisp and County Road 9114 (Twisp River Road). Turn west on County Road 9114 and drive 11 miles (becomes Forest Road 44). Continue west on Forest Road 44 for 3.5 miles to the campground on the left.

Contact: Okanogan and Wenatchee National Forests, Methow Valley Ranger District, 509/996-4003, fax 509/996-2208; Methow Valley Visitor Center, 509/996-4000, fax 509/996-4051.

27 RIVERBEND RV PARK

Scenic rating: 6

near the Methow River

See map page 102

The shore of the Methow River skirts this campground, and there is a nice separate area for tent campers set right along the river. Some of the RV sites are also riverfront. Trout fishing, river rafting, and swimming are popular here. (The *KOA Winthrop* listing in this chapter details the recreation possibilities available within 10 miles.)

RV sites, facilities: There are 69 sites with full hookups (20, 30, and 50 amps) for RVs of any length, and 12 tent sites. Some sites are pull-through. Picnic tables and fire pits are provided. Restrooms have flush toilets and coin showers. An RV dump station, firewood, a convenience store, a coin laundry, ice, a playground, horseshoe pits, propane gas, Wi-Fi access, and RV storage are available. Groups can be accommodated. Leashed pets are permitted.

Reservations, fees: Reservations are accepted at 800/686-4498. Sites are $20–29 per night, $3 per person per night for more than two people, $3 per night per extra vehicle, $2 per night per pet. Some credit cards accepted. Open year-round.

Directions: From Twisp, drive west on Highway 20 for two miles to the park on the right, between Mileposts 199 and 200.

Contact: Riverbend RV Park, 509/997-3500 or 800/686-4498, www.riverbendrv.com.

28 BLACKPINE LAKE

Scenic rating: 7

on Blackpine Lake in Okanogan and Wenatchee National Forests

See map page 102

This campground features great views of some local peaks. About one-third of the campsites have views; the rest are set in a forest of Douglas fir and ponderosa pine. This popular spot often fills up on summer weekends and occasionally even during the week. Fishing is available for stocked rainbow trout. Note that boating is permitted, but no gas motors are allowed, only electric motors. Less than 0.25 mile long, an interpretive trail leads around the north end of the lake.

RV sites, facilities: There are 23 sites for tents or RVs up to 30 feet (no hookups). Picnic tables and fire grills are provided. Drinking water and vault toilets are available. A boat launch and two floating docks are available nearby. Some facilities are wheelchair accessible. Leashed pets are permitted.

Reservations, fees: Reservations are not accepted. Sites are $8 per night per vehicle. Open May–mid-October, weather permitting.

Directions: From Burlington, drive east on Highway 20 for 145 miles to Twisp and County Road 9114 (Twisp River Road). Turn west on County Road 9114 and drive 10 miles to County Road 1090. Turn left and drive over a bridge (becomes Forest Road 43) and continue eight miles to the campground on the right.

Contact: Okanogan and Wenatchee National Forests, Methow Valley Ranger District, 509/996-4003, fax 509/996-2208; Methow Valley Visitor Center, 509/996-4000, fax 509/996-4051.

WASHINGTON

29 SQUIRE CREEK COUNTY PARK

Scenic rating: 7

on Squire Creek

See map page 102

This pretty park sits amid old-growth forest, primarily Douglas fir and cedar, along Squire Creek. A family-oriented park, it often fills on summer weekends. The park covers 53 acres and features several nearby trailheads. A trail from the park provides a 4.5-mile loop that heads toward White Horse Mountain. Other trailheads are within five miles in nearby Mount Baker–Snoqualmie National Forest, about three miles from the boundaries of the Boulder River Wilderness. No alcohol is permitted in this park.

RV sites, facilities: There are 34 sites for tents or RVs up to 35 feet (no hookups). Picnic tables and fire rings are provided. Restrooms have flush toilets. Drinking water and firewood are available. Some facilities are wheelchair accessible. A store is three miles east in Darrington. Leashed pets are permitted.

Reservations, fees: Reservations are not accepted. Sites are $15 per night. Open year-round, with limited winter facilities.

Directions: From Seattle, drive north on I-5 to Exit 208 and the junction with Highway 530. Turn east on Highway 530 and drive 26 miles to the park on the left. The park is at Milepost 45.2, approximately three miles west of the town of Darrington.

Contact: Squire Creek County Park, 360/436-1283; Snohomish County Parks, 425/388-6600, www.co.snohomish.wa.us/.

30 CASCADE KAMLOOPS TROUT FARM AND RV PARK

Scenic rating: 5

in Darrington

See map page 102

Campers will find a little bit of both worlds at this campground—a rustic quietness and a family atmosphere with all facilities available.

A bonus is the trout pond, which is stocked year-round. No boats are allowed. Nearby recreation options include marked hiking trails, snowmobiling, cross-country skiing, river rafting, and tennis.

RV sites, facilities: There are 32 sites with full hookups (20 and 30 amps) for RVs of any length, plus 12 tent sites. A loft apartment is also available. Picnic tables and fire rings are provided for tent sites only. Restrooms have flush toilets and showers. Drinking water, a dump station, firewood, a coin laundry, Wi-Fi access, a community fire pit, a trout pond, and a recreation hall are available. Propane gas, a store, a café, and ice are within one mile. Leashed pets are permitted.

Reservations, fees: Reservations are accepted. Sites are $18–22 per night, $2 per person per night for more than two people, $2 per extra vehicle per night, $1 per pet per night. Some credit cards accepted. Open year-round.

Directions: From Seattle, drive north on I-5 to Exit 208 and the junction with Highway 530. Turn east on Highway 530 and drive 32 miles to Darrington and Madison Street. Turn right on Madison Street and drive about four blocks to Darrington Street. Turn right and drive two blocks to the park on the right.

Contact: Cascade Kamloops Trout Farm and RV Park, 360/436-1003, www.glacierview.net/kamloops.

31 CLEAR CREEK

Scenic rating: 8

on Clear Creek and the Sauk River in Mount Baker-Snoqualmie National Forest

See map page 102

This nice, secluded spot is in old-growth fir on the water, but it doesn't get heavy use. It's at the confluence of Clear Creek and the Sauk River, a designated Wild and Scenic River. Fishing is available for rainbow trout, Dolly Varden, whitefish, and steelhead in season. A trail from camp leads about one mile up to Frog Pond.

RV sites, facilities: There are 12 sites for tents or RVs up to 25 feet (no hookups). Picnic tables

and fire grills are provided. Vault toilets and firewood are available. There is no drinking water. A store, a café, a coin laundry, and ice are within four miles. Some facilities are wheelchair accessible. Leashed pets are permitted.

Reservations, fees: Reservations are accepted at 877/444-6777 or www.ReserveUSA.com ($9 reservation fee). Sites are $12 per night, $6 per extra vehicle per night. Open late May–mid-September, weather permitting.

Directions: From Seattle, drive north on I-5 to Exit 208 and the junction with Highway 530. Turn east on Highway 530 and drive 32 miles to Darrington and Forest Road 20 (Mountain Loop Highway). Turn right (south) on Forest Road 20 and drive 3.3 miles to the campground entrance on the left.

Contact: Mount Baker–Snoqualmie National Forest, Darrington Ranger District, 360/436-1155, fax 360/436-1309.

32 BUCK CREEK

Scenic rating: 9

near the Suiattle River in Mount Baker-Snoqualmie National Forest

See map page 102

Quiet and remote, this primitive campground is along Buck Creek near its confluence with the Suiattle River in the Glacier Peak Wilderness. An interpretive trail runs along Buck Creek and provides access to fishing on the stream for rainbow trout, Dolly Varden, whitefish, and steelhead in season. There's a large (18 feet by 18 feet) Adirondack shelter by the creek and stands of old-growth timber. A zigzagging trail routed into the Glacier Peak Wilderness is accessible about one mile west of camp. See a U.S. Forest Service map for specifics.

RV sites, facilities: There are 29 sites for tents or RVs up to 30 feet (no hookups); some sites are pull-through. Picnic tables and fire grills are provided. Vault toilets and firewood are available. No drinking water is available. Some facilities are wheelchair accessible. Leashed pets are permitted.

Reservations, fees: Reservations are accepted at 877/444-6777 or www.ReserveUSA.com ($9 reservation fee). Sites are $12 per night, $6 per extra vehicle per night. Open June–mid-September, weather permitting.

Directions: From Seattle, drive north on I-5 to Exit 208 and the junction with Highway 530. Turn east on Highway 530 and drive 32 miles to Darrington. Continue 7.5 miles on Highway 530 to Forest Road 26 (Suiattle River Road). Turn right (southeast) on Forest Road 26 and drive 14 miles to the campground on the left. Obtaining a U.S. Forest Service map is essential.

Contact: Mount Baker–Snoqualmie National Forest, Darrington Ranger District, 360/436-1155, fax 360/436-1309.

33 FOGGY DEW

Scenic rating: 6

on Foggy Dew Creek in Okanogan and Wenatchee National Forests

See map page 102

This private, remote campground is at the confluence of Foggy Dew Creek and the North Fork of Old Creek. The elevation is 2,400 feet. Several trails for hiking and horseback riding nearby provide access to various backcountry lakes and streams. To get to the trailheads, follow the forest roads near camp. Bicycles are allowed on Trails 417, 429, and 431. There is also access to a motorcycle-use area. See a U.S. Forest Service map for options.

RV sites, facilities: There are 12 sites for tents or RVs up to 22 feet (no hookups). Picnic tables and fire grills are provided. Vault toilets are available. No drinking water is available. Garbage must be packed out. Some facilities are wheelchair accessible. Leashed pets are permitted.

Reservations, fees: Reservations are not accepted. Sites are $5 per night per vehicle. Open late May–October, weather permitting.

Directions: From Burlington, drive east on Highway 20 for 145 miles to Twisp. Continue east on Highway 20 for three miles to Highway 153. Turn south on Highway 153 and drive 12

WASHINGTON

miles to County Road 1029 (Gold Creek Road). Turn right (south) and drive one mile to Forest Road 4340. Turn right (west) and drive four miles to the campground on the left.

Contact: Okanogan and Wenatchee National Forests, Methow Valley Ranger District, 509/996-4003, fax 509/996-2208; Methow Valley Visitor Center, 509/996-4000, fax 509/996-4051.

34 TURLO

Scenic rating: 8

on the South Fork of the Stillaguamish River in Mount Baker-Snoqualmie National Forest

See map page 102

The westernmost camp on this stretch of Highway 92, Turlo is at 900 feet elevation along the South Fork of the Stillaguamish River. A U.S. Forest Service Public Information Center is nearby. Riverside campsites are available, and the fishing can be good here. A few hiking trails can be found in the area; see a U.S. Forest Service map or consult the nearby information center for trail locations.

RV sites, facilities: There are 18 sites for tents or RVs up to 35 feet (no hookups). Picnic tables are provided. Vault toilets, drinking water, and firewood are available. Some facilities are wheelchair accessible. A store, a café, and ice are one mile away. Leashed pets are permitted.

Reservations, fees: Reservations are accepted at 877/444-6777 or www.ReserveUSA.com ($9 reservation fee). Sites are $16 per night, $8 per extra vehicle per night. Open mid-May–early September, weather permitting.

Directions: From I-5 and Everett, turn east on U.S. 2 and drive five miles to Highway 9. Turn north and drive four miles to Highway 92. Turn east on Highway 92 and drive approximately 15 miles to the town of Granite Falls. Continue another 11 miles east on Highway 92 to the campground entrance on the right.

Contact: Mount Baker–Snoqualmie National Forest, Darrington Ranger District, 360/436-1155, fax 360/436-1309.

35 VERLOT

Scenic rating: 9

on the South Fork of the Stillaguamish River in Mount Baker-Snoqualmie National Forest

See map page 102

This pretty campground is along the South Fork of the Stillaguamish River. Some campsites provide river views. The camp is a short distance from the Lake Twenty-Two Research Natural Area and Maid of the Woods Trail. A U.S. Forest Service map details back roads and hiking trails. Fishing is another recreation option.

RV sites, facilities: There are 25 sites for tents or RVs up to 31 feet (no hookups). Picnic tables and fire rings are provided. Restrooms have flush toilets. Drinking water and firewood are available. A store, a café, and ice are within one mile. Some facilities are wheelchair accessible. Leashed pets are permitted.

Reservations, fees: Reservations are accepted at 877/444-6777 or www.ReserveUSA.com ($9 reservation fee). Sites are $16 per night, $7 per extra vehicle per night. Open mid-May–mid-September, weather permitting.

Directions: From I-5 and Everett, turn east on U.S. 2 and drive five miles to Highway 9. Turn north and drive four miles to Highway 92. Turn east on Highway 92 and drive approximately 15 miles to the town of Granite Falls, and continue another 11.6 miles east on Highway 92 to the campground entrance on the right.

Contact: Mount Baker–Snoqualmie National Forest, Darrington Ranger District, 360/436-1155, fax 360/436-1309.

36 GOLD BASIN

Scenic rating: 9

on the South Fork of the Stillaguamish River in Mount Baker-Snoqualmie National Forest

See map page 102

This is the largest campground in Mount Baker–Snoqualmie National Forest; since it's loaded with facilities, it's a favorite with RVers. At an elevation of 1,100 feet along the South

Fork of the Stillaguamish River, the campground features riverside sites, easy access, and a wheelchair-accessible interpretive trail. This area once provided good fishing, but a slide upstream put clay silt into the water, and it has hurt the fishing. Rafting and hiking are options.

RV sites, facilities: There are 94 sites for tents or RVs up to 60 feet (no hookups) and one group site for up to 50 people. Picnic tables and fire rings are provided. Drinking water, restrooms with flush toilets and coin showers, and firewood are available. A store, a café, and ice are within 2.5 miles. Some facilities are wheelchair accessible. Leashed pets are permitted.

Reservations, fees: Reservations are accepted at 877/444-6777 or www.ReserveUSA.com ($9 reservation fee). Sites are $18 per night, $8 per extra vehicle per night. The group site is $75 per night. Open mid-May–early October, weather permitting.

Directions: From I-5 and Everett, turn east on Highway 92 and drive about 15 miles to the town of Granite Falls and Mountain Loop Highway. Continue east on Mountain Loop Highway for 13.5 miles to the campground entrance on the left.

Contact: Mount Baker–Snoqualmie National Forest, Darrington Ranger District, 360/436-1155, fax 360/436-1309.

37 BEDAL

Scenic rating: 9

on the Sauk River in Mount Baker-Snoqualmie National Forest

See map page 102

This campground sits at the confluence of the North and South Forks of the Sauk River. It offers shaded sites, river views, and good fishing. It's a bit primitive. North Fork Falls is about one mile up the North Fork from camp and worth the trip.

RV sites, facilities: There are 22 sites for tents or RVs up to 21 feet (no hookups). Picnic tables and fire grills are provided. Vault toilets, a picnic shelter, and firewood are available. No

drinking water is available. Some facilities are wheelchair accessible. Leashed pets are permitted. A U.S. Forest Service district office is 17 miles from the campground, in Darrington.

Reservations, fees: Reservations are accepted at 877/444-6777 or www.ReserveUSA.com ($9 reservation fee). Sites are $12 per night, $6 per extra vehicle per night. Open May–early September, weather permitting.

Directions: From Seattle, drive north on I-5 to Exit 208 and the junction with Highway 530. Turn east on Highway 530 and drive 32 miles to Darrington and Forest Road 20 (Mountain Loop Highway). Turn right (south) on Forest Road 20 and drive 17 miles to the campground on the right. Obtaining a U.S. Forest Service map is advised.

Contact: Mount Baker–Snoqualmie National Forest, Darrington Ranger District, 360/436-1155, fax 360/436-1309.

38 RED BRIDGE

Scenic rating: 9

on the South Fork of Stillaguamish River in Mount Baker-Snoqualmie National Forest

See map page 102

Red Bridge is a classic spot, one of several in the vicinity, and a good base camp for a backpacking expedition. The campground is at 1,300 feet elevation on the South Fork of the Stillaguamish River near Mallardy Creek. It has pretty, riverside sites with old-growth fir. A trailhead two miles east of camp leads to Granite Pass in the Boulder River Wilderness.

RV sites, facilities: There are 16 sites for tents or RVs up to 35 feet (no hookups). Picnic tables are provided. Vault toilets, drinking water, and firewood are available. Some facilities are wheelchair accessible. Leashed pets are permitted.

Reservations, fees: Reservations are accepted at 877/444-6777 or www.ReserveUSA.com ($9 reservation fee). Sites are $12 per night, $6 per extra vehicle per night. Open mid-May–mid-September, weather permitting.

Directions: From I-5 and Everett, turn east

on Highway 92 and drive about 15 miles to the town of Granite Falls and Mountain Loop Highway. Continue northeast on Mountain Loop Highway for 18 miles to the campground entrance on the right.

Contact: Mount Baker–Snoqualmie National Forest, Darrington Ranger District, 360/436-1155, fax 360/436-1309.

39 FLOWING LAKE COUNTY PARK

Scenic rating: 6

near Snohomish

See map page 103

This campground has a little something for everyone, including swimming, powerboating, waterskiing, and good fishing on Flowing Lake. The campsites are in a wooded setting (that is, no lake view), and it is a 0.25-mile walk to the beach. A one-mile nature trail is nearby. Note the private homes on the lake; all visitors are asked to respect the privacy of the owners.

RV sites, facilities: There are 40 sites, most with partial hookups (20 and 30 amps), for tents or RVs up to 40 feet, and a walk-in group site for up to 50 people. Some sites are pull-through. Four cabins are also available. Picnic tables and fire grills are provided. Restrooms have flush toilets and coin showers. Drinking water, a dump station, and firewood are available. Picnic shelters, a fishing dock, a playground, boat docks, and launching facilities are available nearby. Some facilities are wheelchair accessible. Leashed pets are permitted.

Reservations, fees: Reservations are accepted for family sites by phone or online. Sites are $15–21 per night, $6 per night for a second tent. Reservations required for the group site, $20 per night plus $2 per person per night. Open year-round with limited winter facilities.

Directions: From I-5 and Everett, take the Snohomish-Wenatchee exit and turn east on U.S. 2; drive to Milepost 10 and look for 100th

Street SE (Westwick Road). Turn left and drive two miles (the street becomes 171st Avenue SE) to 48th Street SE. Turn right and drive about one-half mile into the park at the end of the road.

Contact: Flowing Lake County Park, 360/568-2274 or Snohomish County Parks, 425/388-6600, fax 425/388-6645, www.snoco.org.

40 TROUBLESOME CREEK

Scenic rating: 9

on the North Fork of the Skykomish River in Mount Baker-Snoqualmie National Forest

See map page 103

This campground is along the North Fork of the Skykomish River among old-growth pine and fir. Highlights include a 0.5-mile nature trail adjacent to the camp as well as rafting and good fishing in the river. A must-do trip here is the hike out to Blanca Lake. The trailhead is a short drive; then hike 3.5 miles to the lake, which is drop-dead beautiful with blue-green water fed by glacier-melt.

RV sites, facilities: There are 24 sites for tents or RVs up to 45 feet (no hookups) and six walk-in tent sites requiring about a 100-foot walk. Some sites are pull-through. Picnic tables and fire rings are provided. Drinking water and vault toilets are available. Some facilities are wheelchair accessible. Leashed pets are permitted.

Reservations, fees: Reservations are accepted at 877/444-6777 or www.ReserveUSA.com ($9 reservation fee). Sites are $16 per night, $7 per extra vehicle per night. Open mid-May–mid-September, weather permitting.

Directions: From I-5 and Everett, turn east on U.S. 2 and drive 35.5 miles to the town of Index and Forest Road 63 (Index-Galena Road). Turn left (northeast) on Forest Road 63 and drive 12 miles to the campground on the right.

Contact: Mount Baker–Snoqualmie National Forest, Skykomish Ranger District, 360/677-2414, fax 425/744-3265.

41 LAKE CREEK (LAKE WENATCHEE)

Scenic rating: 6

on the Little Wenatchee River in Wenatchee National Forest

See map page 103

Fishing for rainbow trout sometimes can be good, though difficult, at this camp, which lies in a remote and primitive spot along the Little Wenatchee River. Berry picking is a bonus in late summer. The elevation is 2,300 feet. Note that there is another Lake Creek Camp in the Entiat Ranger District.

RV sites, facilities: There are eight sites for tents or RVs of any length (no hookups). Picnic tables and fire grills are provided, but there is no drinking water. Vault toilets are available. Garbage must be packed out. Leashed pets are permitted.

Reservations, fees: Reservations are not accepted. There is no fee for camping. Open May–late October, weather permitting.

Directions: From I-5 and Everett, turn east on U.S. 2 and drive 87 miles to Highway 207. Turn north on Highway 207 and drive 11 miles to Forest Road 6500. Turn left (west) on Forest Road 6500 and drive 9.5 miles to the campground on the left.

Contact: Okanogan and Wenatchee National Forests, Wenatchee River Ranger District, Lake Wenatchee Ranger Station, 509/763-3103, fax 509/763-3211.

42 NAPEEQUA CROSSING

Scenic rating: 8

on the White and Napeequa Rivers in Wenatchee National Forest

See map page 103

A trail across the road from this camp on the White River heads east for about 4.3 miles to Twin Lakes in the Glacier Peak Wilderness. It's definitely worth the hike, with scenic views and wildlife observation as your reward. But note that Twin Lakes is closed to fishing. Sightings

of ospreys, bald eagles, and golden eagles can brighten the trip. This is an excellent spot for fall colors.

RV sites, facilities: There are five sites for tents or RVs up to 30 feet (no hookups). Picnic tables and fire grills are provided. Vault toilets are available, but there is no drinking water. Garbage must be packed out. Leashed pets are permitted.

Reservations, fees: Reservations are not accepted. There is no fee for camping. Open year-round, weather and snow level permitting.

Directions: From Leavenworth, drive west on U.S. 2 for 14 miles to Coles Corner and Highway 207. Turn north and drive 10 miles to Forest Road 6400 (White River Road). Turn right and drive 5.9 miles to the campground on the left.

Contact: Okanogan and Wenatchee National Forests, Wenatchee River Ranger District, Lake Wenatchee Ranger Station, 509/763-3103, fax 509/763-3211.

43 PHELPS CREEK & PHELPS CREEK EQUESTRIAN

Scenic rating: 7

on the Chiwawa River in Wenatchee National Forest

See map page 102

These camps are set at an elevation of 2,800 feet at the confluence of Phelps Creek and the Chiwawa River. There's a key trailhead for backpackers and horseback riders nearby that provides access to the Glacier Peak Wilderness and Spider Meadows. Phelps Creek Trail is routed out to Spider Meadows, a five-mile hike one-way, and Buck Creek Trail extends into the Glacier Peak Wilderness. The Chiwawa River is closed to fishing to protect endangered species. A U.S. Forest Service map is advisable.

RV sites, facilities: There are seven sites for tents or RVs up to 30 feet at Phelps Creek and six sites for tents or RVs up to 30 feet at Phelps Creek Equestrian. There are no hookups at either camp. Picnic tables and fire grills are provided. Vault toilets are available, but there is

WASHINGTON

no drinking water. Garbage must be packed out to the dumpster at the park exit road. Horse facilities, including loading ramps and high lines, are nearby. Leashed pets are permitted.

Reservations, fees: Reservations are not accepted. Sites are $7 per vehicle per night. Open mid-June–mid-October, weather permitting.

Directions: From I-5 and Everett, turn east on U.S. 2 and drive 87 miles to Highway 207. Turn north on Highway 207 and drive four miles to Chiwawa Loop Road. Turn right (east) on Chiwawa Loop Road and drive 1.4 miles to Chiwawa River Road (Forest Road 6200). Bear left (north) and continue for 23.6 miles to the campground.

Contact: Okanogan and Wenatchee National Forests, Wenatchee River Ranger District, Lake Wenatchee Ranger Station, 509/763-3103, fax 509/763-3211.

44 LAKE CREEK (ENTIAT)

Scenic rating: 7

on the Entiat River in Wenatchee National Forest

See map page 102

This camp is at the confluence of Lake Creek and the Entiat River, at a trail crossroads. It ties into the Mad Lake trail system, where all-purpose trails are available for hiking, horseback riding, and mountain biking. Another trail ties into a loop system that features the Devils Backbone to Ramona Park. There is also linkage available to a network of trails in the Lake Creek Basin in the Chelan Mountains, and several others head south and west into the Entiat Mountains. Consult a U.S. Forest Service map for more details on backcountry routes. Fishing is available on the Entiat River, but not in the vicinity of Entiat Falls. Check fishing regulations. Note that there is another Lake Creek Camp in the Lake Wenatchee and Leavenworth Ranger District.

RV sites, facilities: There are 18 sites for tents or RVs up to 30 feet (no hookups). Picnic tables and fire grills are provided. Drinking water and composting toilets are available. Some facilities are wheelchair accessible. Leashed pets are permitted.

Reservations, fees: Reservations are not accepted. Sites are $8 per night per vehicle. Open May–mid-October, weather permitting.

Directions: From I-5 and Everett, turn east on U.S. 2 and drive 120 miles to U.S. 97-A. Turn north on U.S. 97-A and drive 18.5 miles to Entiat River Road. Turn northwest and drive 28 miles to the campground on the left.

Contact: Okanogan and Wenatchee National Forests, Entiat Ranger District, 509/784-1511, fax 509/784-1150.

45 FOX CREEK

Scenic rating: 7

on the Entiat River in Wenatchee National Forest

See map page 102

This camp is along the Entiat River near Fox Creek. Fishing is prohibited in the vicinity of Entiat Falls; check regulations. This camp features several campsites that are closer to the river than those at nearby Lake Creek, making it the more popular campground of the two. The elevation is 2,100 feet. Contact the U.S. Forest Service for details.

RV sites, facilities: There are 16 sites for tents or RVs up to 32 feet (no hookups). Picnic tables and fire grills are provided. Drinking water and composting toilets are available. Some facilities are wheelchair accessible. Leashed pets are permitted.

Reservations, fees: Reservations are not accepted. Sites are $8 per night per vehicle. Open May–mid-October, weather permitting.

Directions: From I-5 and Everett, turn east on U.S. 2 and drive 120 miles to U.S. 97-A. Turn north on U.S. 97-A and drive 18.5 miles to Entiat River Road. Turn left (northwest) and drive 27 miles to the campground on the left.

Contact: Okanogan and Wenatchee National Forests, Entiat Ranger District, 509/784-1511, fax 509/784-1150.

46 LAKE WENATCHEE STATE PARK

Scenic rating: 8

on Lake Wenatchee
See map page 103

Lake Wenatchee is the centerpiece for a 489-acre park with two miles of waterfront. Glaciers and the Wenatchee River feed Lake Wenatchee, and the river, which bisects the park, helps make it a natural wildlife area. Visitors should be aware of bears; all food must be stored in bearproof facilities. Lake Wenatchee is in a transition zone between the wet, western Washington woodlands and the sparse pine and fir of the eastern Cascades. Thanks to a nice location and pull-through sites that are spaced just right, you can expect plenty of company at this campground. The secluded campsites are set at the southeast end of Lake Wenatchee, which offers plenty of recreation opportunities, with a boat ramp nearby. A swimming beach is available at the south shore. There are eight miles of hiking trails, seven miles of bike trails, five miles of horse trails in and around the park, plus a 1.1-mile interpretive snowshoe trail in winter. Note that no horse facilities are available right in the park, but horse rentals are nearby. In winter, there are 11 miles of multi-use trails and 23 miles of groomed cross-country skiing trails.

RV sites, facilities: In the South Camp there are 100 sites for tents or RVs up to 30 feet (no hookups). In the North Camp there are 55 sites for tents or RVs up to 45 feet (no hookups), 42 pull-through sites with partial hookups (30 and 50 amps) for RVs of any length, and one group site for up to 80 people. Picnic tables and fire grills are provided. Restrooms have flush toilets and showers. Drinking water, a dump station, a store, ice, firewood, a restaurant, and a playground are available. Some facilities are wheelchair accessible. Boat docks, launching facilities, boat and raft rentals, shuttle service, and golf are nearby. Leashed pets are permitted.

Reservations, fees: Reservations are accepted for individual sites and required for the group camp at 888/CAMP-OUT (888/226-7688) or www.parks.wa.gov/reservations ($7 reservation fee). Sites are $17–31 per night, $10 per extra vehicle per night. Call for group rates. Open year-round, with limited winter facilities.

Directions: From Leavenworth, drive west on U.S. 2 for 15 miles to Highway 207 at Coles Corner. Turn right (north) and drive 3.5 miles to the south park entrance and 4.5 miles to the north park entrance.

Contact: Lake Wenatchee State Park, 509/763-3101; state park information 360/902-8844, www.parks.wa.gov.

47 MIDWAY VILLAGE AND GROCERY

Scenic rating: 5

near the Wenatchee River
See map page 103

This private campground is about one-quarter mile from the Wenatchee River, and one mile from Lake Wenatchee State Park and Fish Lake, which is noted for good fishing year-round. There is good hiking and mountain biking out of the camp. Nearby recreation options include boating, fishing, waterskiing, swimming, windsurfing, hiking, and bike riding. The average annual snowfall is 12 feet. There is a snowmobile trail across the road from Midway Village. Winter options include cross-country skiing, dogsledding, snowshoeing, and ice fishing. The Stevens Pass Ski Area is 25 miles to the west.

RV sites, facilities: There are 17 sites, 10 with full hookups (30 amps) for RVs up to 36 feet. No tents are allowed. Restrooms have flush toilets and showers. A convenience store, gasoline, firewood, an espresso shop, a coin laundry, Wi-Fi, ice, propane gas, and picnic area are available. Boat docks, launching facilities, and rentals are nearby. Leashed pets are permitted with certain restrictions.

Reservations, fees: Reservations are accepted.

WASHINGTON

Sites are $22.50–24.50 per night. Some credit cards accepted. Open year-round.

Directions: From I-5 and Everett, turn east on U.S. 2 and drive 88 miles over Stevens Pass to Coles Corner at Highway 207. Turn left (north) on Highway 207 and drive four miles, crossing the bridge over the Wenatchee River to a Y intersection. Turn right at the Y and drive 0.25 mile to the campground on the right, at 14193 Chiwawa Loop Road.

Contact: Midway Village and Grocery, 509/763-3344, fax 509/763-3519.

48 NASON CREEK

Scenic rating: 7

near Lake Wenatchee in Wenatchee National Forest
See map page 103

This campground is on Nason Creek near Lake Wenatchee, bordering Lake Wenatchee State Park. Recreation activities include swimming and waterskiing. Boat rentals, horseback riding, and golfing are available nearby.

RV sites, facilities: There are 73 sites for tents or RVs of any length (no hookups). Some sites are pull-through. Picnic tables and fire grills are provided. Drinking water and restrooms with flush toilets are available. Some facilities are wheelchair accessible. Boat-launching facilities are nearby.

Reservations, fees: Reservations are not accepted. Sites are $14 per night, $11 per night per extra vehicle. Open mid-May–mid-October, weather permitting.

Directions: From I-5 and Everett, turn east on U.S. 2 and drive 87 miles to Highway 207, one mile west of Winton. Turn north on Highway 207 and drive 3.5 miles to Cedar Brae Road. Turn left (west) and drive 100 yards to the campground.

Contact: Okanogan and Wenatchee National Forests, Wenatchee River Ranger District, Lake Wenatchee Ranger Station, 509/763-3103, fax 509/763-3211.

49 GOOSE CREEK

Scenic rating: 7

on Goose Creek in Wenatchee National Forest
See map page 103

With trails for dirt bikes available directly from the camp, Goose Creek is used primarily by motorcycle riders. A main trail links to the Entiat off-road vehicle trail system, so this camp gets high use during the summer. The camp is near a small creek.

RV sites, facilities: There are 29 sites for tents or RVs of any length (no hookups). Picnic tables and fire rings are provided. Drinking water and vault toilets are available. Leashed pets are permitted.

Reservations, fees: Reservations are not accepted. Sites are $7 per vehicle per night. Open mid-May–mid-October, weather permitting.

Directions: From I-5 and Everett, turn east on U.S. 2 and drive 87 miles to Highway 207, one mile west of Winton. Turn north on Highway 207 and drive five miles to Chiwawa Loop Road. Turn right and drive 1.5 miles to Chiwawa River Road/Forest Road 6200. Turn left and drive three miles to Forest Road 6100. Turn right and drive 0.25 mile to the camp on the right.

Contact: Okanogan and Wenatchee National Forests, Wenatchee River Ranger District, Lake Wenatchee Ranger Station, 509/763-3103, fax 509/763-3211.

50 SNOWBERRY BOWL

Scenic rating: 7

near Lake Chelan in Wenatchee National Forest
See map page 102

Snowberry Bowl is less than four miles from Twenty-Five Mile Creek State Park and Lake Chelan. Nestled amid a forest of Douglas fir and ponderosa pine, which provide privacy screening, it sits at an elevation of 2,000 feet.

RV sites, facilities: There are seven sites for tents or RVs up to 40 feet (no hookups) and two double sites for up to 15 people each. Picnic tables, fire grills, and tent pads on sand are provided. Drinking water and vault toilets are available. Some facilities are wheelchair accessible. Leashed pets are permitted.

Reservations, fees: Reservations are not accepted. Sites are $10 per night, $20 per night for double sites. Open year-round, with limited winter facilities.

Directions: From Chelan, drive south on Highway 97-A for three miles to South Lakeshore Road. Turn right and drive 13.5 miles (passing the state park) to Shady Pass Road. Turn left and drive 2.5 miles to a Y intersection with Slide Ridge Road. Bear left and drive 0.5 mile to the campground on the right.

Contact: Okanogan and Wenatchee National Forests, Chelan Ranger District, 509/682-2576, fax 509/682-9004.

51 TWENTY-FIVE MILE CREEK STATE PARK

Scenic rating: 8

near Lake Chelan

See map page 103

This campground is on Twenty-Five Mile Creek near where it empties into Lake Chelan. A 235-acre marine camping park, it sits on the forested south shore of Lake Chelan. The park sits between the mountains and the lake and is surrounded by spectacular scenery, featuring a rocky terrain with forested areas. It's known for its boat access. You can use this park as your launching point for exploring the up-lake wilderness portions of Lake Chelan. Fishing access for trout and salmon is close by. Fishing supplies, a dock, a modern marina, and boat moorage are available. There is also a small wading area for kids. Forest Road 5900, which heads west from the park, accesses several trailheads leading into the U.S. Forest Service lands of the Chelan Mountains. Obtain a U.S. Forest Service map of Wenatchee National Forest for details. Note that a ferry can take visitors to a roadless community at the head of the lake.

RV sites, facilities: There are 46 sites for tents and 21 sites with full or partial hookups (30 amps) for RVs up to 38 feet. Picnic tables and fire grills are provided. Drinking water and flush toilets are available. A dump station, firewood, a boat dock, a fishing pier, a marina, a boat ramp, boat moorage, a picnic area, gasoline, and a grocery store are available nearby. Some facilities are wheelchair accessible. Leashed pets are permitted.

Reservations, fees: Reservations are accepted at 888/CAMP-OUT (888/226-7688) or www.parks.wa.gov/reservations ($7 reservation fee). Sites are $17–31 per night, $10 per night per extra vehicle. Some credit cards accepted. Open April–October, weather permitting.

Directions: From Chelan, drive south on Highway 97A for three miles to South Lakeshore Road. Turn right and drive 15 miles to the park on the right.

Contact: Twenty-Five Mile Creek State Park, 509/687-3610; state park information 360/902-8844, www.parks.wa.gov; Lake Chelan Boat Company, 509/682-2224, www.ladyofthelake.com.

52 KAMEI RESORT

Scenic rating: 6

on Lake Wapato

See map page 103

This resort is on Lake Wapato, about four miles from Lake Chelan. Note that this is a seasonal lake that closes in early September. No open fires are allowed. If you have an extra day, take the ferryboat ride on Lake Chelan.

RV sites, facilities: There are 50 sites for tents or RVs of any length with partial hookups (30 amps). A rental trailer is also available. Picnic tables are provided. Restrooms have flush toilets and showers. Drinking water and ice are available. Boat docks, launching facilities, and rentals are nearby. Leashed pets are permitted.

Reservations, fees: Reservations accepted beginning in January. Sites are $19–20 per night. Open late April–early September.

Directions: From Chelan, drive west on Highway

WASHINGTON

150 for seven miles to Wapato Lake Road. Turn right (north) on Wapato Lake Road and drive four miles to the resort on the right, at 5000 Wapato Lake Road.

Contact: Kamei Resort, 509/687-3690.

53 LAKE CHELAN STATE PARK

Scenic rating: 10

on Lake Chelan

See map page 103

This is the recreation headquarters for Lake Chelan—the third deepest lake in North America, reaching a depth of 1,500 feet. The park provides boat docks and concession stands on the shore of the 55-mile-long lake. The park covers 127 acres, featuring 6,000 feet of shoreline on the forested south shore. Summers tend to be hot and dry, but expansive lawns looking out on the lake provide a fresh feel, especially in the early evenings. A daily ferry service nearby provides access to the roadless community at the head of the lake. "Chelan" is a Chelan Indian word that translates to both "lake" and "blue water." Water sports include fishing, swimming, scuba diving, and waterskiing.

RV sites, facilities: There are 35 sites with full or partial hookups (30 amps) for RVs up to 32 feet, 109 tent sites, and two primitive tent sites. Picnic tables and fire grills are provided. Restrooms have flush toilets and coin showers. Drinking water, firewood, a picnic area with a kitchen shelter, a dump station, a store, pay telephone, concession stand, ice, a playground, a beach area, a boat dock, and launching facilities and moorage are available. Some facilities are wheelchair accessible. Leashed pets are permitted.

Reservations, fees: Reservations are accepted at 888/CAMP-OUT (888/226-7688) or www.parks.wa.gov/reservations ($7 reservation fee). Sites are $12 per night for primitive tent sites, $17 per night for tent sites, $24–31 per night for hookup sites, $10 per extra vehicle per night. Some credit cards accepted. Open year-round, weather permitting.

Directions: From Wenatchee, drive north on U.S. 97-A for 27 miles to State Route 971 (Navarre Coulee Road). Turn left (north) and drive seven miles to the end of the highway at South Lakeshore Road. Turn right, then immediately look for the park entrance to the left.

Contact: Lake Chelan State Park, 509/687-3710; state park information 360/902-8844, www.parks.wa.gov; Lake Chelan Boat Company, 509/682-2224, www.ladyofthelake.com.

54 DAROGA STATE PARK

Scenic rating: 6

on the Columbia River

See map page 103

This 90-acre state park is along 1.5 miles of shoreline on the Columbia River. It sits on the elevated edge of the desert scablands. This camp fills up quickly on summer weekends. Desert Canyon Golf Course is two miles away. Fishing, walking, and biking are available out of the camp.

RV sites, facilities: There are 28 sites for tents or RVs up to 45 feet with partial hookups (30 amps), 17 walk-in or boat-in sites (requiring a 0.25-mile trip), and two group sites for up to 150 people each. Some sites are pull-through. Picnic tables and fire pits are provided. Restrooms have flush (near RV sites) and vault (near walk-in sites) toilets and coin showers. Drinking water, a dump station, a swimming beach, boat-launching facilities and docks, a playground, baseball field, basketball courts, tennis courts, softball and soccer fields, and a picnic area with a kitchen shelter are available. Some facilities are wheelchair accessible. Leashed pets are permitted.

Reservations, fees: Reservations are not accepted for individual sites but are required for group sites at 888/CAMP-OUT (888/226-7688) or www.parks.wa.gov/reservations ($7 reservation fee). Sites are $17–31 per night, $12 per night for walk-in/boat-in sites, $10 per extra vehicle per night; call for group rates. Open mid-March–mid-October, weather permitting.

Directions: From East Wenatchee, drive north on Highway 97 (east side of the Columbia River) for 18 miles to the camp. For boat-in camps, launch boats from the ramp at the park and go 0.25 mile.

Contact: Daroga State Park, 509/664-6380; state park information 360/902-8844, www.parks.wa.gov.

55 ENTIAT CITY PARK

Scenic rating: 8

on the Columbia River
See map page 103

If you're hurting for a spot for the night, you can usually find a campsite here. The campground is on Lake Entiat, which is a dammed portion of the Columbia River. Access to nearby launching facilities makes this a good camping spot for boaters. Waterskiing and personal watercraft are allowed. A dirt trail leads from the lake to the town of Entiat. Note: This campground may be closed for renovations in 2007; check the status before planning a trip.

RV sites, facilities: There are 31 sites with partial hookups (30 amps) for RVs of any length and 25 tent sites. Picnic tables are provided. Restrooms have flush toilets and coin showers. Drinking water, a dump station, and a playground are available. Boat docks and launching facilities are nearby. A store, café, propane gas, and coin laundry are available within 1.5 miles. Some facilities are wheelchair accessible. Open fires, dogs, and alcohol are prohibited.

Reservations, fees: Reservations are available at 800/736-8428 ($5 reservation fee). Sites are $22–27.50 per night, $2 per extra vehicle per night. Open mid-April–mid-October.

Directions: From Wenatchee, drive north on U.S. 97-A for 16 miles to Entiat; the park entrance is on the right (Shearson Street is adjacent on the left). Turn right and drive a short distance to the park along the shore of Lake Entiat.

Contact: Entiat City Park, 800/736-8428, City Hall, 509/784-1500.

56 MONEY CREEK CAMPGROUND

Scenic rating: 5

on the Skykomish River in Mount Baker-Snoqualmie National Forest
See map page 103

You have a little surprise waiting for you here. Trains go by regularly day and night, and the first time it happens while you're in deep sleep, you might just launch a hole right through the top of your roof. The Burlington Northern rail runs along the western boundary of the campground. By now you've got the picture: This can be a noisy camp. Money Creek Campground is on the Skykomish River, with hiking trails a few miles away. The best of these is Dorothy Lake Trail.

RV sites, facilities: There are 25 sites for tents or RVs up to 45 feet (no hookups); some sites are pull-through. Picnic tables are provided. Vault toilets and drinking water are available. A store, a café, and ice are 3.5 miles to the east. Some facilities are wheelchair accessible. Leashed pets are permitted.

Reservations, fees: Reservations are accepted at 877/444-6777 or www.ReserveUSA.com ($9 reservation fee). Sites are $16 per night, $7 per extra vehicle per night. Open mid-May–early October, weather permitting.

Directions: From I-5 and Everett, turn east on U.S. 2 and drive 46 miles to Old Cascade Highway, 11 miles east of Index. Turn right (south) on Old Cascade Highway and drive across the bridge to the campground.

Contact: Mount Baker-Snoqualmie National Forest, Skykomish Ranger District, 360/677-2414, fax 425/744-3265.

57 BECKLER RIVER

Scenic rating: 7

on the Beckler River in Mount Baker-Snoqualmie National Forest
See map page 103

Located on the Beckler River at an elevation of 900 feet, this camp has scenic riverside sites

WASHINGTON

in second-growth timber, primarily Douglas fir, cedar, and bigleaf maple. Fishing at the campground is poor; it's better well up the river. The Skykomish Ranger Station is just a couple of miles away; maps are available for sale.

RV sites, facilities: There are 27 sites for tents or RVs up to 45 feet (no hookups); some sites are pull-through. Picnic tables and fire grills are provided. Vault toilets and drinking water are available. A store, a café, and ice are within two miles. Some facilities are wheelchair accessible. Leashed pets are permitted.

Reservations, fees: Reservations are accepted at 877/444-6777 or www.ReserveUSA.com ($9 reservation fee). Sites are $16 per night, $7 per extra vehicle per night. Open late May–early September, weather permitting.

Directions: From I-5 and Everett, turn east on U.S. 2 and drive 49 miles to Skykomish. Continue east on U.S. 2 for 0.5 mile to Forest Road 65. Turn left (north) on Forest Road 65 and drive 1.6 miles to the camp on the left.

Contact: Mount Baker–Snoqualmie National Forest, Skykomish Ranger District, 360/677-2414, fax 425/744-3265.

58 ROCK ISLAND

Scenic rating: 8

near the Alpine Lakes Wilderness in Wenatchee National Forest

See map page 103

Rock Island is one of several campgrounds in the immediate area along Icicle Creek and is about one mile from the trailhead that takes hikers into the Alpine Lakes Wilderness. This is a pretty spot with good fishing access. The elevation is 2,900 feet.

RV sites, facilities: There are 22 sites for tents or RVs up to 22 feet (no hookups). Picnic tables and fire grills are provided. Drinking water and vault toilets are available. Some facilities are wheelchair accessible. Leashed pets are permitted.

Reservations, fees: Reservations are not ac-

cepted. Sites are $12 per vehicle per night, $9 per night per extra vehicle. Open May–late October, weather permitting.

Directions: From I-5 and Everett, turn east on U.S. 2 and drive 103 miles to Leavenworth and County Road 7600/Icicle River Road. Turn right (south) and drive 17.7 miles to the campground.

Contact: Okanogan and Wenatchee National Forests, Wenatchee River Ranger District, Leavenworth Ranger Station, 509/548-6977, fax 509/548-5817.

59 CHATTER CREEK

Scenic rating: 8

near the Alpine Lakes Wilderness in Wenatchee National Forest

See map page 103

Icicle and Chatter Creeks are the backdrop for this creek-side campground. The elevation is 2,800 feet. Trails lead out in several directions from the camp into the Alpine Lakes Wilderness.

RV sites, facilities: There are 12 sites for tents or RVs up to 22 feet (no hookups) and one group site for up to 45 people. Picnic tables and fire grills are provided. Drinking water and vault toilets are available. Leashed pets are permitted.

Reservations, fees: Reservations are required for the group site at 888/CAMP-OUT (888/226-7688) or www.parks.wa.gov/reservations ($7 reservation fee). Rates are $12 per night, $9 per night per extra vehicle, and $75 per night for the group site. Open May–late October, weather permitting.

Directions: From I-5 and Everett, turn east on U.S. 2 and drive 103 miles to Leavenworth and County Road 7600/Icicle River Road. Turn right (south) and drive 16.1 miles to the campground on the right.

Contact: Okanogan and Wenatchee National Forests, Wenatchee River Ranger District, Leavenworth Ranger Station, 509/548-6977, fax 509/548-5817.

60 TUMWATER

Scenic rating: 7

near the Alpine Lakes Wilderness in
Wenatchee National Forest

See map page 103

This large, popular camp provides a little bit of
both worlds. It's a good layover spot for campers
cruising U.S. 2, but it also features two nearby
forest roads, each less than a mile long, which
end at trailheads that provide access to the
Alpine Lakes Wilderness. The camp is on the
Wenatchee River in Tumwater Canyon. This
section of river is closed to fishing. The elevation is 2,050 feet.

RV sites, facilities: There are 84 sites for tents
or RVs up to 50 feet (no hookups) and one
group site for up to 75 people. Picnic tables
and fire grills are provided. Drinking water and
restrooms with flush toilets are available. Some
facilities are wheelchair accessible. Leashed pets
are permitted.

Reservations, fees: Reservations are required for the group site at 888/CAMP-OUT
(888/226-7688) or www.parks.wa.gov/reser-
vations ($7 reservation fee). Sites are $14 per
night, $11 per night per extra vehicle, and $85
per night for the group site. Open May–mid-
October, weather permitting.

Directions: From I-5 and Everett, turn east on
U.S. 2 and drive 93 miles to the campground
(10 miles west of Leavenworth).

Contact: Okanogan and Wenatchee National
Forests, Wenatchee River Ranger District,
Leavenworth Ranger Station, 509/548-6977,
fax 509/548-5817.

61 IDA CREEK

Scenic rating: 8

on Icicle Creek in Wenatchee National Forest

See map page 103

This campground is one of several small, quiet
camps along Icicle and Ida Creeks, with recreation
options similar to those detailed in the *Chatter
Creek* and *Rock Island* listings in this chapter.

RV sites, facilities: There are 10 sites for tents
or RVs up to 30 feet (no hookups). Picnic
tables and fire grills are provided. Drinking
water and vault toilets are available. Some facilities are wheelchair accessible. Leashed pets
are permitted.

Reservations, fees: Reservations are not accepted. Sites are $12 per night, $9 per night per
extra vehicle. Open May–late October, weather
permitting.

Directions: From I-5 and Everett, turn east on
U.S. 2 and drive 103 miles to Leavenworth
and County Road 7600/Icicle River Road.
Turn right (south) and drive 14.2 miles to the
campground on the left.

Contact: Okanogan and Wenatchee National
Forests, Wenatchee River Ranger District,
Leavenworth Ranger Station, 509/548-6977,
fax 509/548-5817.

62 LEAVENWORTH KOA

Scenic rating: 8

near the Wenatchee River

See map page 103

This lovely resort on 30 acres is near the
Bavarian-themed village of Leavenworth, to
which the park provides a free shuttle in the
summer. The spectacularly scenic area is surrounded by the Cascade Mountains and sits
among ponderosa pines. The camp has access to the Wenatchee River, not to mention
many luxurious extras, including a spa and a
heated pool. The park allows campfires and
has firewood available. Nearby recreation options include an 18-hole golf course, horseback
riding, white-water rafting, and hiking trails.
Make a point to spend a day in Leavenworth if
possible; it offers authentic German food and
architecture, along with music and art shows
in the summer.

RV sites, facilities: There are 60 sites with
full hookups and 60 sites with partial hookups (30 and 50 amps) for RVs up to 65 feet,
40 tent sites, 20 cabins, and nine cottages.
Some sites are pull-through. Picnic tables are

WASHINGTON

provided and fire grills are available at some sites. Restrooms have flush toilets and showers. Drinking water, a dump station, Wi-Fi access, bicycle rentals, firewood, a recreation hall, cable TV, a convenience store, a coin laundry, ice, a playground, horseshoe pits, volleyball, a spa, a seasonal heated swimming pool, a snack bar, and a beach area are available. Some facilities are wheelchair accessible. Propane gas and a café are within one mile. Leashed pets are permitted.

Reservations, fees: Reservations are accepted at 800/562-5709. RV sites are $26–42 per night, tent sites are $22–35 per night, plus $5 per extra vehicle per night and $4–5 per person per night for more than two people. Some credit cards accepted. Open mid-March–November.

Directions: From I-5 and Everett, turn east on U.S. 2 and drive 103 miles to Leavenworth. Continue east on U.S. 2 for 0.25 mile to River Bend Drive. Turn left (north) and drive 0.5 mile to the campground on the right, at 11401 River Bend Drive.

Contact: Leavenworth KOA, tel./fax 509/548-7709, www.koa.com.

63 JOHNNY CREEK
🚶 🏊 🐕 ♿ 🚐 ⛺

Scenic rating: 8

on Icicle Creek in Wenatchee National Forest

See map page 103

This campground is split into two parts, and sits on both sides of the road, along Icicle and Johnny Creeks. It is fairly popular. Upper Johnny has a forest setting, whereas Lower Johnny is alongside the creek, with adjacent forest. The elevation is 2,300 feet.

RV sites, facilities: There are 65 sites for tents or RVs up to 50 feet (no hookups). Picnic tables and fire grills are provided. Drinking water and vault toilets are available. Some facilities are wheelchair accessible. Leashed pets are permitted.

Reservations, fees: Reservations are not accepted. Sites are $11–12 per night, $8–9 per

night per extra vehicle. Open May–late October, weather permitting.

Directions: From I-5 and Everett, turn east on U.S. 2 and drive 103 miles to Leavenworth and County Road 7600/Icicle River Road. Turn right (south) and drive 12.4 miles to the campground (with camps on each side of the road).

Contact: Okanogan and Wenatchee National Forests, Wenatchee River Ranger District, Leavenworth Ranger Station, 509/548-6977, fax 509/548-5817.

64 EIGHTMILE

Scenic rating: 8

near the Alpine Lakes Wilderness in Wenatchee National Forest

See map page 103

Trailheads are within two miles of this campground along Icicle and Eightmile Creeks, providing access to fishing, as well as a backpacking route into the Alpine Lakes Wilderness. The elevation is 1,800 feet. Horseback-riding opportunities are within four miles, and golf is within five miles.

RV sites, facilities: There are 45 sites for tents or RVs up to 50 feet (no hookups) and one group site for up to 70 people. Picnic tables and fire grills are provided. Drinking water and vault toilets are available. Some facilities are wheelchair accessible. Leashed pets are permitted.

Reservations, fees: Reservations are required for the group site at 888/CAMP-OUT (888/226-7688) or www.parks.wa.gov/reservations ($7 reservation fee). Sites are $13 per night, $10 per night per extra vehicle, and $75 per night for the group site. Open mid-April–late October.

Directions: From I-5 and Everett, turn east on U.S. 2 and drive 103 miles to Leavenworth and County Road 7600/Icicle River Road. Turn right (south) and drive eight miles to the campground on the left.

Contact: Okanogan and Wenatchee National Forests, Wenatchee River Ranger District, Leavenworth Ranger Station, 509/548-6977, fax 509/548-5817.

65 ICICLE RIVER RV RESORT

Scenic rating: 9

on Icicle River

See map page 103

This pretty, wooded spot is along the Icicle River, where fishing and swimming are available. The 50-acre resort is clean and scenic. An 18-hole golf course and hiking trails are nearby.

RV sites, facilities: There are 100 sites with full or partial hookups (30 and 50 amps) for RVs of any length and six rustic cabins for rent. No tents are allowed. Picnic tables and fire pits (at some sites) are provided. Restrooms have flush toilets and coin showers. Drinking water, cable TV, modem and Wi-Fi access, a spa, firewood, and propane gas are available. Horseshoe pits and two pavilions are available nearby. Leashed pets are permitted in the campground.

Reservations, fees: Reservations accepted. Sites are $30–34 per night, $4 per extra vehicle per night, $3–4 per person per night for more than two people. Some credit cards accepted. Open April–mid-October, weather permitting.

Directions: From I-5 and Everett, turn east on U.S. 2 and drive 103 miles to Leavenworth and County Road 7600/Icicle River Road. Turn right (south) and drive three miles to the resort on the left, at 7305 Icicle Road.

Contact: Icicle River RV Resort, 509/548-5420, fax 509/548-6207, www.icicleriverrv.com.

66 BLU-SHASTIN RV PARK

Scenic rating: 6

near Peshastin Creek

See map page 103

This 13-acre park is in a mountainous area near Peshastin Creek. Gold-panning in the river is a popular activity here; during the gold rush, the Peshastin was the best-producing river in the state—and it still is. The camp has sites on the riverbank and plenty of shade trees. A heated pool, a recreation field, and horseshoe pits provide possible activities in the park. Hiking trails and marked bike trails are nearby. Rafting

and tubing nearby are popular in the summer. Snowmobiling is an option during the winter.

RV sites, facilities: There are 85 sites, including four pull-through sites, for tents or RVs of any length with full hookups (30 amps). Picnic tables and fire rings are provided. Restrooms have flush toilets and showers. Drinking water, modem access, a recreation hall, firewood, a coin laundry, ice, a playground, horseshoes, badminton, volleyball, and a seasonal heated swimming pool are available. Propane gas, a store, and a café are within seven miles. Leashed pets are permitted.

Reservations, fees: Reservations are accepted at 888/548-4184. Sites are $21.99–26.85 per night. Some credit cards accepted. Open year-round.

Directions: From Leavenworth, drive east on U.S. 2 for five miles to U.S. 97. Turn right (south) on U.S. 97 and drive seven miles to the park on the right, at 3300 Highway 97.

Contact: Blu-Shastin RV Park, 509/548-4184 or 888/548-4184, www.blushastin.com.

67 WENATCHEE RIVER COUNTY PARK

Scenic rating: 5

on the Wenatchee River

See map page 103

This camp lies along the Wenatchee River, situated between the highway and the river. Though not the greatest setting, with some highway noise, it is convenient for RV campers. You can usually get a tree-covered site in the campground, despite it being a small park. The adjacent river is fast-moving and provides white-water rafting in season, with a put-in spot at the park. A boat launch is available for nonmotorized boats such as kayaks and rafts. Fishing is not allowed.

RV sites, facilities: There are 47 sites with full or partial hookups (50 amps) for tents or RVs up to 40 feet, two sites with no hookups, and one cabin. Several sites are pull-through. Cabins are also available. Picnic tables and fire pits are

WASHINGTON

provided. Drinking water, restrooms with flush toilets and coin showers, a recreation room, and Wi-Fi and modem access are available. A convenience store and a restaurant are within 0.5 mile. Leashed pets are permitted.

Reservations, fees: Reservations are available at 509/667-7503. Sites are $17–24 per night, $5 per extra vehicle per night. Some credit cards accepted. Open April–October.

Directions: From Wenatchee and U.S. 2, drive west on U.S. 2 for 4.7 miles to the park on the left.

Contact: Chelan County Commissioner, 509/667-6215, fax 509/667-6599; Wenatchee River County Park, 509/667-7503, www.co .chelan.wa.us/.

68 WENATCHEE CONFLUENCE STATE PARK

Scenic rating: 10

on the Columbia River

See map page 103

This 197-acre state park is at the confluence of the Wenatchee and Columbia Rivers. The park features expansive lawns shaded by deciduous trees and fronted by the two rivers. Wenatchee Confluence has something of a dual personality: The north portion of the park is urban and recreational, while the southern section is a designated natural wetland area. There are 10.5 miles of paved trail for hiking, biking, and in-line skating. A pedestrian bridge crosses the Wenatchee River. An interpretive hiking trail is available in the Horan Natural Area. Other recreation possibilities include fishing, swimming, boating, and waterskiing. Sports enthusiasts will find playing fields as well as tennis and basketball courts. Daroga State Park and Lake Chelan to the north offer side-trip possibilities.

RV sites, facilities: There are 51 sites with full hookups (30 amps) for RVs of any length, eight tent sites, and a group tent site for up to 300 people. Picnic tables and fire grills are provided. Restrooms have flush toilets and

coin showers. Drinking water, a boat launch, a dump station, a swimming beach, a playground, and athletic fields are available. Some facilities are wheelchair accessible. Leashed pets are permitted.

Reservations, fees: Reservations are accepted at 888/CAMP-OUT (888/226-7688) or www.parks.wa.gov/reservations ($7 reservation fee). Tent sites are $17 per night, RV sites are $24–31 per night, plus $10 per extra vehicle per night. Call for group rates. Some credit cards accepted. Open year-round, with limited services in winter.

Directions: From Wenatchee and U.S. 2, take the Easy Street exit and drive south to Penny Road. Turn left and drive a short distance to Chester Kimm Street. Turn right and drive to a T intersection and Old Station Road. Turn left on Old Station Road and drive past the railroad tracks to the park on the right. The park is 1.3 miles from U.S. 2.

Contact: Wenatchee Confluence State Park, 509/664-6373, fax 509/662-0459; state park information 360/902-8844, www.parks.wa.gov.

69 LINCOLN ROCK STATE PARK

Scenic rating: 5

on Lake Entiat

See map page 103

Lincoln Rock State Park is an 80-acre park set along the shore of Lake Entiat. The lake was created by the Rocky Reach Dam on the Columbia River. The name of the park comes from a basalt outcropping within the park that is thought to resemble the profile of Abraham Lincoln. The park features lawns and shade trees amid an arid landscape. There are two miles of paved, flat trails suitable for both hiking and biking. Water sports include swimming, boating, and waterskiing. Beavers are occasionally visible in the Columbia River.

RV sites, facilities: There are 67 sites with partial or full hookups (30 amps) for RVs up to 65 feet and 27 sites for tents or RVs up to 60 feet (no hookups). Picnic tables and fire grills are provided. Restrooms have flush toilets and coin showers. Drinking water, a dump station, a playground, athletic fields, horseshoe pits, a swimming beach, an amphitheater, three picnic shelters, and firewood are available. Boat docks, moorage, and launching facilities are on Lake Entiat. Some facilities are wheelchair accessible. Leashed pets are permitted.

Reservations, fees: Reservations are accepted at 888/CAMP-OUT (888/226-7688) or www.parks.wa.gov/reservations ($7 reservation fee). Sites are $17–31 per night, $10 per extra vehicle per night. Some credit cards accepted. Open March–mid-October, weather permitting.

Directions: From East Wenatchee, drive northeast on U.S. 2 for seven miles to the park on the left.

Contact: Lincoln Rock State Park, 509/884-8702; state park information 360/902-8844, www.parks.wa.gov.

70 SNOQUALMIE RIVER RV PARK & CAMPGROUND

Scenic rating: 7

on the Snoqualmie River

See map page 103

If you're in the Seattle area and stuck for a place for the night, this pretty 10-acre park set along the Snoqualmie River might be a welcome option. Approximately one-third of the sites are filled with monthly renters. Activities include fishing, swimming, road biking, and rafting. Nearby recreation options include several nine-hole golf courses. A worthwhile side trip is beautiful Snoqualmie Falls, 3.5 miles away in the famed Twin Peaks country.

RV sites, facilities: There are 92 sites with full or partial hookups (30 and 50 amps) for RVs of any length, as well as 32 tent sites. Picnic tables and fire rings are provided. Restrooms have flush toilets and showers. Drinking water, a dump station, firewood, and a playground are available. Propane gas, a store, a café, a coin laundry, and ice are

within 3.5 miles. Boat-launching facilities are within 0.5 mile. Leashed pets are permitted with certain restrictions.

Reservations, fees: Reservations accepted. Sites are $24–36 per night, $4 per person per night for more than two people, and $3 per pet per night. Some credit cards accepted. Open year-round with limited winter facilities.

Directions: From the junction of I-5 and I-90 south of Seattle, turn east on I-90. Drive east for 26 miles to Exit 22 (Preston-Fall City). Take that exit and turn north on Preston-Fall City Road and drive 4.5 miles to SE 44th Place. Turn right (east) and drive one mile to the park at the end of the road, at 34807 SE 44th Place.

Contact: Snoqualmie River RV Park & Campground, 425/222-5545, www.srcghsg.com.

71 TINKHAM

Scenic rating: 9

on the Snoqualmie River in Mount Baker-Snoqualmie National Forest

See map page 103

About half the campsites here face the Snoqualmie River, making this a pretty spot. Fishing can be good; check regulations. The camp is at an elevation of 1,600 feet. The creek provides hiking options. This camp is often used as an overflow for Denny Creek camp (see the *Denny Creek Camp* listing in this chapter). Wilderness trails for the Alpines Lakes Wilderness are 5–10 miles away from the camp.

RV sites, facilities: There are 46 sites for tents or RVs up to 35 feet (no hookups). Picnic tables and fire pits are provided. Drinking water and vault toilets are available. Some facilities are wheelchair accessible. Leashed pets are permitted.

Reservations, fees: Reservations are accepted at 877/444-6777 or www.ReserveUSA.com ($9 reservation fee). Sites are $16 per night, $7 per extra vehicle per night. Open mid-May–mid-September, weather permitting.

Directions: In Seattle on I-5, turn east on I-90.

WASHINGTON

Drive east on I-90 to Exit 42. Take that exit and turn right on Tinkham Road (Forest Road 55), and drive southeast 1.5 miles to the campground on the left. Obtaining a U.S. Forest Service map is advisable.

Contact: Mount Baker–Snoqualmie National Forest, Snoqualmie Ranger District, North Bend office, 425/888-1421, fax 425/888-1910.

72 DENNY CREEK

Scenic rating: 9

on Denny Creek

See map page 103

This camp is at 1,900 feet elevation along Denny Creek, which is pretty and offers nearby recreation access. The campground is secluded in an area of Douglas fir, hemlock, and cedar, with hiking trails available in addition to swimming opportunities. Denny Creek Trail starts from the campground and provides a 4.5-mile round-trip hike that features Keck-wulee Falls and Denny Creek Waterslide. You can climb to Hemlock Pass and Melakwa Lake. There is access for backpackers into the Alpine Lakes Wilderness.

RV sites, facilities: There are 33 sites, some with partial hookups (30 amps), for tents or RVs up to 40 feet and one group site for up to 40 people. Picnic tables and fire grills are provided. Drinking water, flush toilets, and firewood are available. Some facilities are wheelchair accessible. Leashed pets are permitted.

Reservations, fees: Reservations are accepted at 877/444-6777 or www.ReserveUSA.com ($9 reservation fee). Sites are $16–20 per night, $8 per extra vehicle per night. The group site is $75 per night. Open mid-May–early October, weather permitting.

Directions: In Seattle on I-5, turn east on I-90. Drive east on I-90 to Exit 47. Take that exit, cross the freeway, and at the T intersection turn right and drive 0.25 mile to Denny Creek Road (Forest Road 58). Turn left on Denny Creek Road and drive two miles to the campground on the left.

Contact: Mount Baker–Snoqualmie National Forest, Snoqualmie Ranger District, North Bend office, 425/888-1421, fax 425/888-1910.

73 KACHESS & KACHESS GROUP

Scenic rating: 8

on Kachess Lake in Wenatchee National Forest

See map page 103

This is the only campground on the shore of Kachess Lake, but note that the water level can drop significantly in summer during low-rain years. It is the most popular campground in the local area, often filling in July and August, especially on weekends. Recreation opportunities include waterskiing, fishing, hiking, and bicycling. There is a lakeshore trail and self-guided interpretive nature trails. A trail from camp heads north into the Alpine Lakes Wilderness; see a U.S. Forest Service map for details. The elevation is 2,300 feet.

RV sites, facilities: There are 120 sites, including 30 double sites, for tents or RVs up to 32 feet (no hookups). A group site for up to 50 people is also available. Picnic tables and fire grills are provided. Drinking water, flush toilets, a boat ramp, swimming beach, and camp host are available. Restrooms and dump stations are at Kachess Lake. Some facilities are wheelchair accessible. Leashed pets are permitted but aren't allowed in swimming areas.

Reservations, fees: Reservations are accepted for family sites and required for the group site at 877/444-6777 or www.ReserveUSA.com ($9 reservation fee). Sites are $16 per night, $8 per extra vehicle per night. The group fee is $100 per night. Open late May–mid-September, weather permitting.

Directions: In Seattle on I-5, turn east on I-90. Drive east on I-90 for 59 miles to Exit 62. Take that exit to Forest Road 49 and turn northeast; drive 5.5 miles to the campground on the right at the end of the paved road.

Contact: Okanogan and Wenatchee National Forests, Cle Elum Ranger District, 509/852-1100, fax 509/852-1080.

74 SALMON LA SAC

Scenic rating: 6

on the Cle Elum River in Wenatchee National Forest

See map page 103

This is a base camp for backpackers and day hikers and is also popular with kayakers. It's along the Cle Elum River at 2,400 feet elevation, about one-quarter mile from a major trailhead, the Salmon La Sac Trailhead. Hikers can follow creeks heading off in several directions, including into the Alpine Lakes Wilderness. A campground host is available for information.

RV sites, facilities: There are 99 sites, including 12 double sites, for tents or RVs up to 21 feet (no hookups). Picnic tables and fire grills are provided. Drinking water and vault toilets are available. Some facilities are wheelchair accessible. Leashed pets are permitted.

Reservations, fees: Reservations are accepted at 877/444-6777 or www.ReserveUSA.com ($9 reservation fee). Sites are $16–32 per night, $8 per extra vehicle per night. Open late May–early September, weather permitting.

Directions: In Seattle on I-5, turn east on I-90. Drive east on I-90 for 78 miles to Exit 80 (two miles before Cle Elum). Take that exit, turn north on Bullfrog Road, and drive four miles to Highway 903. Continue north on Highway 903 for 21 miles to the campground on the left.

Contact: Okanogan and Wenatchee National Forests, Cle Elum Ranger District, 509/852-1100, fax 509/852-1080.

75 CRYSTAL SPRINGS

Scenic rating: 5

on the Yakima River in Wenatchee National Forest

See map page 103

This campground is just off I-90, and if you think that means lots of highway noise, well, you are correct. This camp is worth knowing as an overflow campground from the more desirable Kachess campground (see listing in this chapter for *Kachess & Kachess Group*). It is at 2,400 feet elevation and features the Yakima River

and some old-growth trees. It's a short drive to Kachess and Keechelus Lakes. Both lakes have boat ramps. The Snoqualmie Summit Ski Area is at the north end of Keechelus Lake.

RV sites, facilities: There are 22 sites, including some pull-through sites, and two double sites for tents or RVs up to 40 feet (no hookups). Picnic tables and fire grills are provided. Drinking water, vault toilets, camp host, and firewood are available. Leashed pets are permitted.

Reservations, fees: Reservations are not accepted. Sites are $13–26 per night, $8 per extra vehicle per night. Open mid-May–mid-September, weather permitting.

Directions: In Seattle on I-5, turn east on I-90. Drive east on I-90 for 60 miles to Exit 62. Take that exit and turn right (south) on Forest Road 54, and drive 0.5 mile to the campground on the right.

Contact: Okanogan and Wenatchee National Forests, Cle Elum Ranger District, 509/852-1100, fax 509/852-1080.

76 CLE ELUM RIVER & CLE ELUM GROUP

Scenic rating: 6

on the Cle Elum River in Wenatchee National Forest

See map page 103

The gravel roads in the campground make this setting a bit more rustic than nearby Salmon La Sac. It serves as a valuable overflow campground for Salmon La Sac (see the *Salmon La Sac* listing in this chapter) and is similar in setting and opportunities. The group site fills on most summer weekends. A nearby trailhead provides access into the Alpine Lakes Wilderness.

RV sites, facilities: There are 23 sites, including some pull-through, for tents or RVs up to 30 feet (no hookups), along with a group site for up to 100 people. Picnic tables and fire grills are provided. Drinking water and vault toilets are available. Leashed pets are permitted.

Reservations, fees: Reservations are not accepted for individual sites but are required for the group site at 877/444-6777 or www.ReserveUSA.com ($9 reservation fee). Sites are $13–26 per night, $6 per extra vehicle per night. The group site is $100 per night. Open late May–mid-September, weather permitting.

Directions: In Seattle on I-5, turn east on I-90. Drive east on I-90 for 78 miles to Exit 80 (two miles before Cle Elum). Take that exit, turn north on Bullfrog Road, and drive four miles to Highway 903. Continue north on Highway 903 for 17 miles to the campground on the left.

Contact: Okanogan and Wenatchee National Forests, Cle Elum Ranger District, 509/852-1100, fax 509/852-1080.

77 WISH POOSH

Scenic rating: 7

on Cle Elum Lake in Wenatchee National Forest

See map page 103

This popular camp is on the shore of Cle Elum Lake. It fills up on summer weekends and holidays. It is great during midweek, when many sites are usually available. While the lake is near the camp, note that the lake level can lower significantly in low-rainfall years. Waterskiing, sailing, fishing, and swimming are among recreation possibilities. The camp sits at an elevation of 2,400 feet.

RV sites, facilities: There are 34 sites, including five double sites, for tents or RVs up to 30 feet (no hookups). Picnic tables and fire grills are provided. Restrooms have flush toilets and showers. Drinking water, a camp host, and firewood are available. Boat-launching facilities are on Cle Elum Lake. A restaurant and ice are available nearby. Leashed pets are permitted.

Reservations, fees: Reservations are not accepted. Sites are $16–32 per night, $8 per extra vehicle per night. Open mid-May–mid-September, weather permitting.

Directions: In Seattle on I-5, turn east on I-90. Drive east on I-90 for 78 miles to Exit 80 (two miles before Cle Elum). Take that exit, turn north on Bullfrog Road, and drive four miles to

Highway 903. Continue north on Highway 903 for nine miles to the campground on the left.

Contact: Okanogan and Wenatchee National Forests, Cle Elum Ranger District, 509/852-1100, fax 509/852-1080.

78 BEVERLY

Scenic rating: 8

on the North Fork of the Teanaway River in Wenatchee National Forest

See map page 103

This primitive campground is on the North Fork of the Teanaway River, a scenic area of the river. It is primarily a hiker's camp, with several trails leading up nearby creeks and into the Alpine Lakes Wilderness. The elevation is 3,100 feet.

RV sites, facilities: There are 14 sites for tents or RVs up to 21 feet (no hookups). Picnic tables and fire grills are provided. Vault toilets are available, but there is no drinking water. Garbage must be packed out. Leashed pets are permitted.

Reservations, fees: Reservations are not accepted. Sites are $8 per night per vehicle. Open June–mid-November, weather permitting.

Directions: In Seattle on I-5, turn east on I-90. Drive east on I-90 for 80 miles to Cle Elum and Exit 86. Take Exit 86 to Highway 970. Turn east on Highway 970 and drive eight miles to Teanaway Road (Highway 970). Turn left (north) on Teanaway Road and drive 13 miles to the end of the paved road. Bear right (north) on Forest Road 9737 and drive four miles to the campground on the left.

Contact: Okanogan and Wenatchee National Forests, Cle Elum Ranger District, 509/852-1100, fax 509/852-1080.

79 SWAUK

Scenic rating: 6

on Swauk Creek in Wenatchee National Forest

See map page 103

Fishing is marginal, and there is some highway noise from U.S. 97. A one-mile round-trip interpretive trail can be found along Swauk Creek. The elevation is 3,200 feet. Three miles east of the camp on Forest Road 9716 is Swauk Forest Discovery Trail. This three-mile interpretive trail explains some of the effects of logging and U.S. Forest Service management of the forest habitat.

RV sites, facilities: There are 22 sites, including two double sites, for tents or RVs up to 30 feet (no hookups). Fire grills and picnic tables are provided. Vault toilets, drinking water, and firewood are available. Leashed pets are permitted.

Reservations, fees: Reservations are not accepted. Sites are $13 per night, double sites are $26 per night, and it's $6 per extra vehicle per night. Open late May–early September, weather permitting.

Directions: In Seattle on I-5, turn east on I-90. Drive east on I-90 for 80 miles to Cle Elum and Exit 86. Take Exit 86 to Highway 970. Turn east on Highway 970 and drive 12 miles to U.S. 97. Turn north on U.S. 97 and drive 10 miles to the campground on the right (near Swauk Pass).

Contact: Okanogan and Wenatchee National Forests, Cle Elum Ranger District, 509/852-1100, fax 509/852-1080.

80 MINERAL SPRINGS

Scenic rating: 6

on Swauk Creek in Wenatchee National Forest
See map page 103

This campground is at the confluence of Medicine and Swauk Creeks. Note that this camp is along a highway, so there is some highway noise. Fishing, berry picking, and hunting are good in season in this area. It is at an elevation of 2,800 feet. Most use the camp as a one-night layover spot.

RV sites, facilities: There are 12 sites for tents or RVs up to 21 feet (no hookups) and one group site for up to 50 people. Picnic tables and fire rings are provided. Drinking water, vault toilets, and a camp host are available. Leashed pets are permitted. A restaurant is nearby.

Reservations, fees: Reservations are not accepted for individual sites but are required for the group site at 888/CAMP-OUT (888/226-7688) or www.parks.wa.gov/reservations ($7 reservation fee). Sites are $13 per night, $6 per extra vehicle per night. The group site is $80 per night. Open mid-May–late September, weather permitting.

Directions: From Seattle, drive east on I-90 for 80 miles to Cle Elum and Exit 85 and Highway 970. Turn northeast on Highway 970 and drive 12 miles to U.S. 97. Continue northeast (the road becomes U.S. 97) and drive about seven miles to the campground on the left.

Contact: Okanogan and Wenatchee National Forests, Cle Elum Ranger District, 509/852-1100, fax 509/852-1080.

81 LAKE EASTON STATE PARK

Scenic rating: 8

on Lake Easton
See map page 103

This campground offers many recreational opportunities. For starters, it's set along the shore of Lake Easton on the Yakima River in the Cascade foothills. The landscape features old-growth forest, dense vegetation, and freshwater marshes, and the park covers 516 acres of the best of it. Six miles of trails for hiking and biking are available. The park provides opportunities for both summer and winter recreation, including swimming, fishing, boating, cross-country skiing, and snowmobiling. Note that high-speed boating is not allowed because Lake Easton is a shallow reservoir with stumps often hidden just below the water surface; boat motors are limited to 10 horsepower. Nearby recreation options include several 18-hole golf courses and hiking trails. Kachess Lake and Keechelus Lake are just a short drive away.

RV sites, facilities: There are 137 sites, including 45 sites with hookups (30 amps) for RVs up to 60 feet, two primitive walk-in tent sites, and one group tent site for up to 50 people. Picnic tables and fire grills are provided. Restrooms have flush toilets and showers. Drinking water, pay telephone, a dump station, an amphitheater with seasonal interpretive programs, a playground, basketball, horseshoe pits, and firewood are available. Boat-launching facilities and floats are on Lake Easton. A café and ice are within one mile. Some facilities are wheelchair accessible. Leashed pets are permitted.

Reservations, fees: Reservations are accepted and required for the group site at 888/CAMP-OUT (888/226-7688) or www.parks.wa.gov/reservations ($7 reservation fee). Sites are $17–31 per night, $12 per night for the walk-in sites, $10 per extra vehicle per night. Call for group rates. Some credit cards accepted. Open year-round, with limited winter facilities.

Directions: From Seattle, drive east on I-90 for 68 miles to Exit 70; the park entrance is on the right (it is one mile west of the town of Easton).

Contact: Lake Easton State Park, 509/656-2586, fax 509/656-2294; state park information 360/902-8844, www.parks.wa.gov.

82 TRAILER CORRAL RV PARK

Scenic rating: 7

near the Yakima River
See map page 103

This wooded campground about one mile from the Yakima River offers a choice of grassy or graveled sites. Nearby recreation options include an 18-hole golf course, marked hiking trails, and tennis courts.

RV sites, facilities: There are 23 sites with full or partial hookups (30 amps) for RVs of any length, three tent sites, and six cabins. Picnic tables and cable TV are provided, and fire rings are available on request. Restrooms have flush toilets and showers, and a coin laundry is available. A store is within one mile. Boat-launching facilities are nearby. Leashed pets are permitted.

Reservations, fees: Reservations are not accepted. Sites are $15–20 per night, $1.50 per person per night for more than two people. Open year-round.

Directions: From Seattle, drive east on I-90 for 80 miles to Cle Elum and Exit 85 and Highway 970. Turn east on Highway 970 and drive 1.5 mile to the park on the left.

Contact: Trailer Corral RV Park, 509/674-2433.

83 KANASKAT-PALMER STATE PARK

Scenic rating: 8

on the Green River
See map page 103

This wooded campground offers private campsites near the Green River. The park covers 320 acres with two miles of river frontage; the river can be accessed from the day-use area but not from the campground. It is on a small, low, forested plateau. In summer, the river is ideal for expert-level rafting and kayaking, and the park is used as a put-in spot for the rafting run down the Green River Gorge. This area has much mining history, and coal mining continues, as does cinnabar mining (the base ore for mercury). Nearby Flaming Geyser gets its name from a coal seam. In winter, the river attracts a run of steelhead and salmon. The park has three miles of hiking trails.

RV sites, facilities: There are 19 pull-through sites with partial hookups (30 amps) for RVs up to 50 feet, 31 tent sites, and one group camp for up to 80 people, which includes two Adirondack shelters, a picnic shelter, and a community fire ring. Picnic tables are provided. Restrooms have flush toilets and showers. Drinking water, a sheltered picnic area, horseshoe pits, and a dump station are available. Some facilities are wheelchair accessible. Leashed pets are permitted.

Reservations, fees: Reservations are accepted and are required for the group camp at 888/CAMP-OUT (888/226-7688) or www.parks.wa.gov/reservations ($7 reservation fee). Sites are $17–31 per night, $10 per extra vehicle per night. Call for group rates. Some credit cards accepted. Open year-round, weather permitting, with a 10-day stay limit.

Directions: From Puyallup at the junction of Highway 167 and Highway 410, turn southeast on Highway 410 and drive 25 miles to Enumclaw and Farman Road. Turn northeast on Farman Road and drive 10 miles to the park on the left.

Contact: Kanaskat-Palmer State Park, 360/886-0148; state park information 360/902-8844, www.parks.wa.gov.

84 DALLES

Scenic rating: 10

in Mount Baker-Snoqualmie National Forest

See map page 103

This campground is at the confluence of Minnehaha Creek and the White River. Aptly, its name means "rapids." A nature trail is nearby, and the White River entrance to Mount Rainier National Park is about 14 miles south on Highway 410. The camp sits amid a grove of old-growth trees; a particular point of interest is a huge old Douglas fir that is 9.5 feet in diameter and more than 235 feet tall. This is one of the prettiest camps in the area. It gets moderate use in summer.

RV sites, facilities: There are 44 sites for tents or RVs up to 25 feet (no hookups), and one group tent site can accommodate up to 60 people. Picnic tables and fire grills are provided. Vault toilets, drinking water, and firewood are available. There is a large shaded picnic area for day use. Leashed pets are permitted.

Reservations, fees: Reservations are accepted for individual sites and are required for the group site at 877/444-6777 or www.ReserveUSA.com ($9 reservation fee). Sites are $16 per night, $7 per extra vehicle per night. The group site is $50 per night. Open mid-May–early September, weather permitting.

Directions: From Enumclaw, drive east on Highway 410 for 25.5 miles to the campground (three miles inside the forest boundary) on the right.

Contact: Mount Baker–Snoqualmie National Forest, White River Ranger District, 360/825-6585, fax 360/825-0660.

85 CROW CREEK

Scenic rating: 5

on the Little Naches River in Wenatchee National Forest

See map page 103

This campground on the Little Naches River is popular with off-road bikers and four-wheel-drive enthusiasts; it's similar to Kaner Flat (see the *Kaner Flat* listing in this chapter), except that there is no drinking water. It is at 2,900 feet elevation. A trail nearby leads into the backcountry and then forks in several directions. One route leads to the American River, another follows West Quartz Creek, and another goes along Fife's Ridge into the Norse Peak Wilderness (where no motorized vehicles are permitted). See a U.S. Forest Service map for details. There is good seasonal hunting and fishing in this area.

RV sites, facilities: There are 15 sites for tents or RVs up to 30 feet (no hookups). Picnic tables and fire grills are provided. Vault toilets are available, but there is no drinking water. Downed firewood may be gathered when fire closures are not in effect. Leashed pets are permitted.

Reservations, fees: Reservations are not accepted. Sites are $7 per night, $5 per extra vehicle per night. Open mid-April–late September, weather permitting.

Directions: From Yakima, drive northwest on U.S. 12 for 18 miles to Highway 410. Bear northwest on Highway 410 and drive 24.5 miles to Forest Road 1900. Turn northwest and drive 2.5 miles to Forest Road 1902. Turn left (west) and drive 0.5 mile to the campground on the right.

Contact: Okanogan and Wenatchee National Forests, Naches Ranger District, 509/653-1400, fax 509/653-2638.

WASHINGTON

86 KANER FLAT

Scenic rating: 7

near the Little Naches River in Wenatchee
National Forest

See map page 103

This campground is near the Little Naches
River, at an elevation of 2,678 feet. It is at the
site of a wagon-train camp on the Old Naches
Trail, a route used in the 1800s by wagon trains,
Native Americans, and the U.S. Cavalry on their
way to west side markets. The narrow-clearance
Naches Trail is now used by motorcyclists and
four-wheel-drive enthusiasts. Kaner Flat is popular among them, and is larger and more group-
friendly than nearby Crow Creek campground.

RV sites, facilities: There are 41 sites for tents
or RVs up to 30 feet (no hookups). Picnic tables
and fire grills are provided. Drinking water
and flush and vault toilets are available. Some
facilities are wheelchair accessible. Leashed pets
are permitted.

Reservations, fees: Reservations are not accepted. Sites are $10 per night, $5 per night for
each additional vehicle. Open mid-May–late
November, weather permitting.

Directions: From Yakima, drive northwest on
U.S. 12 for 18 miles to Highway 410. Bear
northwest on Highway 410 and drive 25 miles
to Forest Road 1900. Turn right (northwest)
and drive 2.5 miles to the campground on
the right.

Contact: Okanogan and Wenatchee National
Forests, Naches Ranger District, 509/653-1400,
fax 509/653-2638.

87 TANEUM

Scenic rating: 7

on Taneum Creek in Wenatchee National Forest

See map page 103

This rustic spot is along Taneum Creek, at an
elevation of 2,400 feet. It is several miles away
from the camps popular with the off-road vehicle crowd. This is more of a quiet getaway, not
a base camp. Ponderosa pines add to the setting.

Trout fishing is popular here in the summer.
The camp receives moderate use.

RV sites, facilities: There are 13 sites for tents
or RVs up to 21 feet (no hookups) and one
double site. Picnic tables and fire rings are
provided. Drinking water, vault toilets, camp
host, and firewood are available. Leashed pets
are permitted.

Reservations, fees: Reservations are not accepted. Sites are $13 per night, $26 per night
for double sites, $6 per night for each additional
vehicle. Open May–late September, weather
permitting.

Directions: From Ellensburg, drive northwest
on U.S. 90 for approximately five miles to the
Thorp Prairie Road exit. Take that exit and turn
west on Thorp Prairie Road and drive four miles
(crossing back over the freeway) to Taneum
Road. Turn right and drive west for three miles
(it becomes Forest Road 33). Continue west for
five miles to the campground on the left.

Contact: Okanogan and Wenatchee National
Forests, Cle Elum Ranger District, 509/852-
1100, fax 509/852-1080.

88 ICEWATER CREEK

Scenic rating: 7

on Taneum Creek in Wenatchee National Forest

See map page 103

Icewater Creek camp is similar to Taneum
camp (see the *Taneum* listing in this chapter),
except that the trees are smaller and the sites are
a bit more open. It is most popular with off-road
motorcyclists because there are two ORV trails
leading from the camp, both of which network
with an extensive system of off-road riding
trails. The best route extends along the South
Fork Taneum River area. Fishing is fair, primarily for six- to eight-inch cutthroat trout.

RV sites, facilities: There are 14 sites for tents
or RVs up to 26 feet (no hookups), including
three double sites. Picnic tables and fire rings
are provided. Drinking water and firewood are
available. Leashed pets are permitted.

Reservations, fees: Reservations are not

WASHINGTON

accepted. Rates are $13 per night for single sites, $26 per night for double sites, and $6 per night for each additional vehicle. Open May–late September, weather permitting.

Directions: From Ellensburg, drive northwest on U.S. 90 for about five miles to the Thorp Prairie Road exit. Take that exit and turn west (right) on Thorp Prairie Road and drive four miles (crossing back over the freeway) to Taneum Road. Turn right and drive west for three miles (it becomes Forest Road 33). Continue west for 4.5 miles to the campground on the left.

Contact: Okanogan and Wenatchee National Forests, Cle Elum Ranger District, 509/852-1100, fax 509/852-1080.

89 ELLENSBURG KOA

Scenic rating: 8

on the Yakima River

See map page 103

This KOA is one of the few campgrounds in a 25-mile radius. Exceptionally clean and scenic, it offers well-maintained, shaded campsites along the Yakima River. Rafting and fly-fishing on the nearby Yakima River are popular. Other nearby recreation options include an 18-hole golf course and tennis courts. The Kittitas County Historical Museum is in town at 3rd and Pine Streets.

RV sites, facilities: There are 100 sites with full or partial hookups (30 and 50 amps) for RVs of any length, plus 40 tent sites. Some sites are pull-through. A trailer and an apartment are also available. Picnic tables are provided. Restrooms have flush toilets and showers. Cable TV, a dump station, propane, Wi-Fi and modem access, firewood, bicycle rentals, a video arcade, a convenience store, seasonal snack bar, a coin laundry, ice, a playground, video rentals, a horseshoe pit, volleyball, a seasonal wading pool, and a seasonal heated swimming pool are available. Breakfast is available during the summer season. A café is within one mile. Extra parking is available for horse trailers, vans, and boats. Leashed pets are permitted.

Reservations, fees: Reservations are accepted at 800/562-7616. Sites are $19–40 per night, $3–4 per person per night for more than two people, and $3 per extra vehicle per night. Some credit cards accepted. Open year-round.

Directions: From Seattle, drive east on I-90 for 106 miles to Exit 106 (near Ellensburg). Take that exit and continue 0.25 mile to Thorp Highway. Turn right at Thorp Highway and drive a short distance to the KOA entrance (well marked).

Contact: Ellensburg KOA, 509/925-9319, fax 509/925-3607, www.koa.com.

NORTHEASTERN WASHINGTON

(BEST RV PARKS AND CAMPGROUNDS

(Fishing

A lot of people call this area "God's country." You know why? Because nobody else could have thought of it. The vast number of lakes, streams, and national forests provides an unlimited land of adventure. You could spend a lifetime here – your days hiking, fishing, and exploring, your nights camping out and staring up at the stars.

And that's exactly what some people do, like Rich Landers, the outdoors writer for the *Spokane Spokesman-Review*. People know they have it good here, living on the threshold of a fantastic land of adventure, but with a population base in Spokane that creates a financial center with career opportunities.

The landscape features a variety of settings. The national forests (Colville, Kaniksu, Wenatchee), in the northern tier of the state, are ideal for a mountain hideaway. You'll find remote ridges and valleys with conifers, along with many small streams and lakes. In the valleys, the region is carved by the Pacific Northwest's largest river system, featuring the Columbia River, Franklin D. Roosevelt Lake, and the Spokane River. These waterways are best for campers interested in water views, boating, and full facilities.

While many well-known destinations are stellar, my favorites are the lesser-known sites. There are dozens of such camps in this area, often along the shore of a small lake, that provide good fishing and hiking. You could search across the land and not find a better region for outdoor adventure. This is a wilderness to enjoy.

Includes:

- Alta Lake State Park
- Banks Lake
- Beaver Lake
- Beth Lake
- Big Meadow Lake
- Blue Lake
- Bonaparte Lake
- Bridgeport State Park
- Browns Lake
- Chopaka Lake
- Clear Lake
- Columbia River
- Colville National Forest
- Conconully State Park
- Crawfish Lake
- Curlew Lake State Park
- Franklin Roosevelt Lake
- Grand Coulee Dam
- Jump Off Joe Lake
- Lake Chelan
- Lake Ellen
- Lake Gillette
- Lake Roosevelt National Recreation Area
- Lake Thomas
- Leader Lake
- Little Spokane River
- Long Lake
- Loon Lake
- Lost Lake
- Okanogan National Forest
- Okanogan River
- Osoyoos Lake State Park
- Park Lake
- Pend Oreille River
- Pierre Lake
- Riverside State Park
- Rufus Woods Lake
- Sanpoil River
- Sherman Pass
- Silver Lake
- South Skookum Lake
- Spectacle Lake
- Spokane River
- Steamboat Rock State Park
- Sullivan Lake
- Sun Lakes State Park
- Swan Lake
- Upper Conconully Reservoir
- Waitts Lake
- Wannacut Lake
- West Medical Lake

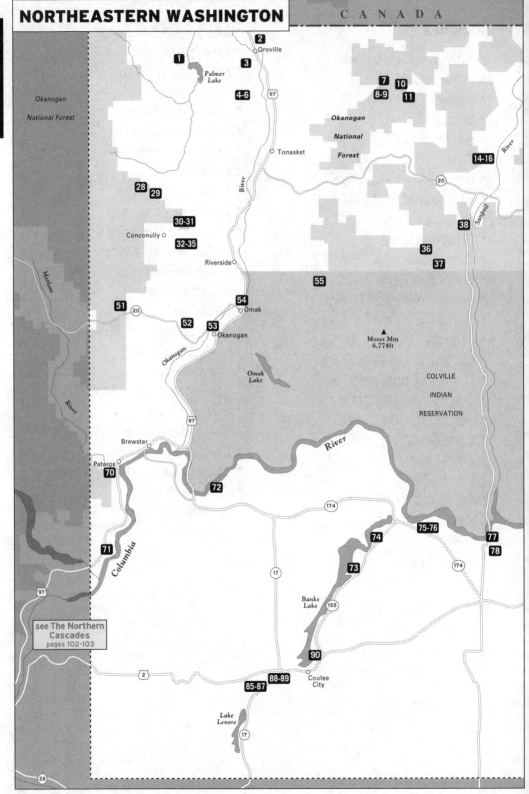

WASHINGTON

NORTHEASTERN WASHINGTON

CANADA

Oroville

2

1

3

Palmer
Lake

4-6

97

7

10

8-9

11

Okanogan
National Forest

Okanogan

National

Forest

14-16

River

River

Tonasket

20

28

29

38

Sanpoil

30-31

Conconully

32-35

36

Riverside

37

55

51

54

20

Omak

52

53

Okanogan

Methow

Okanogan

Moses Mtn
6,774ft

River

Omak
Lake

COLVILLE

INDIAN

RESERVATION

River

97

Brewster

River

Pateros

70

72

River

174

75-76

74

77

71

78

Columbia

73

174

17

Banks
Lake

155

see The Northern
Cascades
pages 102-103

90

97

88-89

Coulee
City

2

85-87

Lake
Lenore

17

28

WASHINGTON

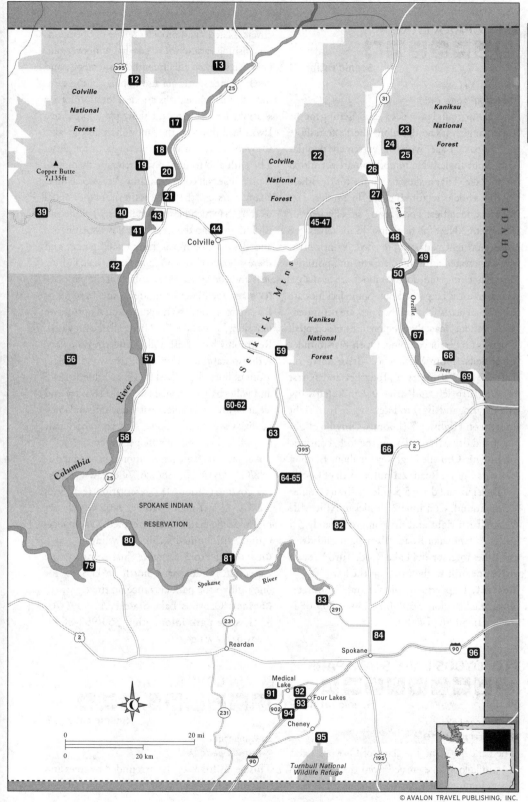

Colville
National
Forest

Kaniksu
National
Forest

Copper Butte
7,135ft

IDAHO

Colville
National
Forest

Pend

Colville

Oreille

S e l k i r k   M t n s

Kaniksu
National
Forest

River

River

Columbia

SPOKANE INDIAN
RESERVATION

Spokane
River

Reardan

Spokane

Medical
Lake

Four Lakes

Cheney

Turnbull National
Wildlife Refuge

0   20 mi

0   20 km

© AVALON TRAVEL PUBLISHING, INC.

WASHINGTON

1 CHOPAKA LAKE

Scenic rating: 8

on Chopaka Lake

See map page 146

This campground provides a classic setting for the expert angler. It's nestled along the western shore of Chopaka Lake, which is extremely popular with trout anglers. No motorboats are permitted on the lake. That makes it a winner for fly fishers (barbless hooks required) using float tubes.

RV sites, facilities: There are 17 sites for tents or RVs up to 20 feet (no hookups). Picnic tables, fire grills, and tent pads are provided. Vault toilets, drinking water, a fishing platform, and primitive boat-launching and dock facilities are available. Garbage must be packed out. Some facilities are wheelchair accessible. Leashed pets are permitted.

Reservations, fees: Reservations are not accepted. There is no fee for camping. Open year-round.

Directions: From Wenatchee, drive north on U.S. 97 for 120 miles to Tonasket and Forest Street. Turn left and drive 0.2 mile (crossing the Okanogan River) to Highway 7. Turn right (north) on Highway 7 (Loomis-Oroville Highway) and drive five miles. At the fork, continue on Loomis-Oroville Highway for about 12 miles to Toats Coulee Road, 2.1 miles north of Loomis. Turn left and drive 5.5 miles to Touts Coulee campground. Continue 2.1 miles to Nine Mile Road. Turn right and drive approximately 3.5 miles to Chopaka Road. Turn right and drive 3.5 miles to Chopaka Lake Road. Turn left and drive one mile to the camp on the left.

Contact: Department of Natural Resources, Northeast Region, 360/902-1234 or 509/684-7474, fax 509/684-7484.

2 OSOYOOS LAKE STATE PARK

Scenic rating: 9

on Osoyoos Lake

See map page 146

The park lies along the shore of Osoyoos Lake, a 14-mile-long lake created from the Okanogan River, south of the Canadian Rockies. The park covers 47 acres and provides a base of operations for a fishing vacation. The lake has rainbow trout, kokanee salmon, smallmouth bass, crappie, and perch. Water sports are also popular in the summer, and in winter, it is an ideal location for ice skating, ice fishing, and snow play. Expansive lawns lead down to the sandy shore of the lake. Osoyoos Lake is a winter nesting area for geese. The park also features a war veteran's memorial. A nine-hole golf course is nearby. A historical note: Many years ago, the area was the site of the annual okanogan (which means "rendezvous") of the Salish Indians from the area that is now Washington and British Columbia. They would gather and share supplies of fish and game for the year. Fishing gear and concessions are available at the park.

RV sites, facilities: There are 86 sites for tents or RVs up to 45 feet (no hookups) and six primitive tent sites. Picnic tables and fire grills are provided. Restrooms have flush toilets and coin showers. A dump station, a store, a café, firewood, a playground, horseshoes, basketball, an athletic field, and volleyball are available. A coin laundry and ice are within one mile. Boat-launching and dock facilities are nearby. Some sites are wheelchair accessible. Leashed pets are permitted.

Reservations, fees: Reservations are accepted at 888/CAMP-OUT (888/226-7688) or www.parks .wa.gov/reservations ($7 reservation fee). Sites are $12–19 per night, $10 per extra vehicle per night. Some credit cards accepted. Open year-round, with limited facilities in winter.

Directions: From Oroville, just south of the Canadian border, drive north on U.S. 97 for one mile to the park entrance on the right.

Contact: Osoyoos Lake State Park, 509/476-3321; state park information 360/902-8844, www.parks.wa.gov.

3 SUN COVE RESORT

Scenic rating: 9

on Wannacut Lake

See map page 146

This beautiful resort is surrounded by trees and hills and set along the shore of Wannacut Lake, a spring-fed lake that doesn't get much traffic. The lake is approximately three miles long and 2.5 miles wide. An eight-mph speed limit is enforced for boats. Fishing, swimming, boating, and hiking are all summertime options. The park provides full facilities, including a heated pool, a playground, and a recreation hall. For the horse-riding set, a guided trail and overnight rides are available one mile from the resort.

RV sites, facilities: There are 22 sites for tents or RVs (no hookups), 28 pull-through sites with full hookups (30 amps) for RVs of any length, two cottages, and 10 motel units with kitchens. Picnic tables are provided. No wood fires are allowed. Restrooms have flush toilets and coin showers. A dump station, a recreation hall, a general store, a café, a coin laundry, ice, fishing supplies, a playground, and a seasonal heated swimming pool are available. Some facilities are wheelchair accessible. Boat docks, launching facilities, and rentals are also available. Leashed pets are permitted in the campground.

Reservations, fees: Reservations are accepted. Sites are $25 per night. Some credit cards accepted. Open late April–mid-October.

Directions: From Oroville, just south of the Canadian border, drive west on Ellemehan Mountain Road for about six miles to Wannacut Lake Road. Turn left (south) and drive five miles to the resort at the end of the road.

Contact: Sun Cove Resort, tel./fax 509/476-2223.

4 SPECTACLE LAKE RESORT

Scenic rating: 7

on Spectacle Lake

See map page 146

This pleasant resort on the shore of long, narrow Spectacle Lake has grassy, shaded sites. Space is usually available here, although reservations are accepted. Recreation options include boating, fishing, swimming, waterskiing, riding personal watercraft, and hunting (in season).

RV sites, facilities: There are 40 sites for RVs of any length with full hookups (20 and 30 amps) and 16 motel rooms with kitchenettes. Picnic tables and fire pits are provided. Restrooms have flush toilets and showers. A dump station, a convenience store, a coin laundry, ice, a playground, a recreation hall, horseshoe pits, volleyball, an exercise room, and a seasonal heated swimming pool are available. Boat docks, launching facilities, and rentals are also available nearby. Leashed pets are permitted.

Reservations, fees: Reservations are accepted. Sites are $20 per night. Some credit cards accepted. Open April–October.

Directions: In Tonasket on U.S. 97, turn west (left if arriving from south), cross the bridge, and continue to Highway 7. Turn right on Highway 7 and drive about 12 miles to Holmes Road. Turn left (south) on Holmes Road and drive 0.5 mile to McCammon Road. Turn right (west) and drive one block to the resort at the end of the road.

Contact: Spectacle Lake Resort, 509/223-3433, www.spectaclelakeresort.com.

5 RAINBOW RESORT

Scenic rating: 7

on Spectacle Lake

See map page 146

This resort on Spectacle Lake is an alternative to Spectacle Lake Resort. The camp features pretty lake views and full facilities. Nearby activities include swimming, fishing, hunting, and horseback riding, including overnight trail rides.

RV sites, facilities: There are 35 sites with full hookups (30 amps) for RVs of any length and 14 sites for tents or RVs of any length (partial hookups). Some sites are pull-through. Picnic tables are provided. Restrooms have flush toilets and showers. Ice, a recreation room, volleyball, boat docks, and launching facilities are available. Leashed pets are permitted.

Reservations, fees: Reservations are accepted. Sites are $25 per night. Some credit cards accepted. Open April–October.

WASHINGTON

Directions: From Ellisford, turn west on Ellisford Bridge Road. Drive 0.5 mile to Highway 7. Turn left (south) and drive one mile to Loomis Highway. Turn right and drive 6.5 miles to the resort on the left.

Contact: Rainbow Resort, 509/223-3700.

6 SPECTACLE FALLS RESORT

Scenic rating: 8

on Spectacle Lake

See map page 146

Spectacle Falls Resort sits on the shore of Spectacle Lake. It is open only as long as fishing is available, which means it closes in late July. Be sure to phone ahead of time to verify that the resort is open. Nearby recreation options include hiking, swimming, fishing, tennis, and horseback riding, including guided trails and overnight rides. Rainbow Resort is an alternative.

RV sites, facilities: There are 20 pull-through sites with full hookups (30 and 50 amps) for RVs of any length, 10 tent sites, and four mobile homes available for rent. Picnic tables are provided. Restrooms have flush toilets and showers. Ice, boat docks, launching facilities, and boat rentals are available. Leashed pets are permitted.

Reservations, fees: Reservations are accepted. Sites are $17 per night, $2 per person per night for more than two people, $2 per extra vehicle per night. Open April–July.

Directions: From Tonasket on U.S. 97, turn northwest on Loomis Highway and drive 15 miles to the resort on the left.

Contact: Spectacle Falls Resort, 509/223-4141.

7 LOST LAKE

Scenic rating: 7

on Lost Lake in Okanogan National Forest

See map page 146

This camp is on the shore of Lost Lake at an elevation of 3,800 feet. As a launch point for fishing, swimming, hiking, hunting, and horseback riding, it keeps visitors happy. Only electric motors are permitted on the lake (that is, no gas motors). The lake is similar to Beth Lake and Beaver Lake but is rounder. The Big Tree Botanical Area is about one mile away. Note that the group site is often booked one year in advance.

RV sites, facilities: There are 18 single and double sites for tents or RVs up to 31 feet. There is also one group site for up to 100 people. No hookups. Picnic tables and fire rings are provided. Drinking water and vault toilets are available. Boat-launching facilities and swimming platforms are nearby. Leashed pets are permitted.

Reservations, fees: Reservations are not available for single and double sites but are required for the group site at 877/444-6777 or www.ReserveUSA.com ($9 reservation fee). Single and double sites are $8 per vehicle per night; group rates are $40–80 per night. Open mid-May–mid-October, weather permitting.

Directions: From East Wenatchee, drive north on U.S. 97 for 120 miles to Tonasket and Highway 20. Turn east on Highway 20 and drive 24 miles to Bonaparte Lake Road (County Road 4953). Turn left (north) and drive six miles to Forest Road 32. Turn right (north) and drive four miles to Forest Road 33. Bear left (northwest) and drive five miles to a four-way intersection. Turn left on Forest Road 33-050 and drive 0.3 mile to the campground on the right.

Contact: Okanogan and Wenatchee National Forests, Tonasket Ranger District, 509/486-2186, fax 509/486-5161.

8 BONAPARTE LAKE

Scenic rating: 7

on Bonaparte Lake in Okanogan National Forest

See map page 146

This campground is on the southern shore of Bonaparte Lake at an elevation of 3,600 feet. The lake is stocked with rainbow trout, brook trout, and Mackinaw trout. (See the listing for *Bonaparte Lake Resort* for lake recreation information.) Several trails nearby provide access to Mount Bonaparte Lookout. Consult a U.S. Forest Service map for details.

RV sites, facilities: There are 25 single and multiple sites for tents or RVs up to 31 feet, three bike-in/hike-in sites (requiring a walk of less than 100 feet), and one group site that can accommodate up to 30 people. No hookups. Picnic tables and fire grills are provided. Drinking water and vault toilets are available. A dump station, a store, a café, and ice are available within one mile. Boat docks and launching facilities are also available. Some facilities are wheelchair accessible. Leashed pets are permitted.

Reservations, fees: Reservations are not accepted. Sites are $8 per night per vehicle, $8 for bike-in/hike-in sites. The group site is $8 per vehicle per night.

Directions: From East Wenatchee, drive north on U.S. 97 for 120 miles to Tonasket and Highway 20. Turn east on Highway 20 and drive 24 miles to Bonaparte Lake Road (County Road 4953). Turn left (north) and drive six miles to Bonaparte Lake and Forest Road 32 and the campground on the left.

Contact: Okanogan and Wenatchee National Forests, Tonasket Ranger District, 509/486-2186, fax 509/486-5161.

9 BONAPARTE LAKE RESORT

Scenic rating: 6

on Bonaparte Lake

See map page 146

Fishing is popular at this resort, which is on the southeast shore of Bonaparte Lake. A 10-mph speed limit keeps the lake quiet, ideal for fishing. Other recreational activities include hiking and hunting in the nearby U.S. Forest Service lands and snowmobiling, cross-country skiing, and ice fishing in the winter. Poker tournaments are held occasionally.

RV sites, facilities: There are 35 sites with full or partial hookups (20 and 30 amps) for RVs of any length, 10 tent sites, and 10 cabins. Some sites are pull-through. Picnic tables and fire

rings are provided. Restrooms, flush toilets, showers, propane gas, a dump station, firewood, a convenience store, a restaurant, a coin laundry, ice, a playground, boat docks, launching facilities, and boat rentals are available. Leashed pets are permitted.

Reservations, fees: Reservations are accepted. Sites are $10–20 per night. Some credit cards accepted. Open year-round, with limited winter facilities.

Directions: From East Wenatchee, drive north on U.S. 97 for 120 miles to Tonasket and Highway 20. Turn east on Highway 20 and drive 20 miles to Bonaparte Lake Road (County Road 4953). Turn left (north) and drive six miles to Bonaparte Lake and the resort on the left.

Contact: Bonaparte Lake Resort, 509/486-2828, www.bonaparte-lake-resort.com.

10 BETH LAKE
Scenic rating: 7

on Beth Lake in Okanogan National Forest

See map page 146

This campground is between Beth Lake and Beaver Lake, both small, narrow lakes stocked with rainbow trout and brook trout. The elevation is 2,800 feet. A 1.9-mile-long hiking trail (one-way) connects the two lakes. Other side trips in the area include Lost Lake, Bonaparte Lake, and several hiking trails, one of which leads up to the Mount Bonaparte Lookout.

RV sites, facilities: There are 14 sites for tents or RVs up to 31 feet (no hookups), plus one multiple site. Picnic tables and fire rings are provided. Drinking water and vault toilets are available. Garbage must be packed out. Boat-launching facilities are available nearby. Some facilities are wheelchair accessible. Leashed pets are permitted.

Reservations, fees: Reservations are not accepted. Sites are $6 per vehicle per night. Open mid-May–mid-October, weather permitting.

Directions: From East Wenatchee, drive north on U.S. 97 for 120 miles to Tonasket and Highway 20. Turn east on Highway 20 and drive 24

WASHINGTON

miles to Bonaparte Lake Road (County Road 4953). Turn left (north) and drive six miles to Bonaparte Lake and Forest Road 32. Continue (north) on Forest Road 32 and drive six miles to County Road 9480. Turn left (northwest) and drive one mile to the campground on the left.

Contact: Okanogan and Wenatchee National Forests, Tonasket Ranger District, 509/486-2186, fax 509/486-5161.

11 BEAVER LAKE

Scenic rating: 7

on Beaver Lake in Okanogan National Forest

See map page 146

This camp calls the southeastern shore of long, narrow Beaver Lake home. Situated at 2,700 feet elevation, it is one of several lakes in this area. Beth Lake is nearby and accessible with an hour-long hike. Both Beaver and Beth Lakes are stocked with trout. Fishing, swimming, hunting, and hiking are all possibilities here. (See the *Lost Lake* and *Bonaparte Lake* listings in this chapter for information on the other lakes in the area.)

RV sites, facilities: There are nine single and two multiple sites for tents or RVs up to 21 feet (no hookups). Picnic tables are provided. Vault toilets and drinking water are available. Boat-launching facilities are within 100 yards of the campground. No boats with gas engines are permitted; electric motors are allowed. Leashed pets are permitted.

Reservations, fees: Reservations are not accepted. Sites are $6 per vehicle per night. Open mid-May–mid-October, weather permitting.

Directions: From East Wenatchee, drive north on U.S. 97 for 120 miles to Tonasket and Highway 20. Turn east on Highway 20 and drive 24 miles to Bonaparte Lake Road (County Road 4953). Turn left (north) and drive six miles to Bonaparte Lake and Forest Road 32. Continue (north) on Forest Road 32 and drive six miles to the campground on the left.

Contact: Okanogan and Wenatchee National Forests, Tonasket Ranger District, 509/486-2186, fax 509/486-5161.

12 PIERRE LAKE

Scenic rating: 8

on Pierre Lake in Colville National Forest

See map page 147

Pierre Lake, just 105 acres, is a quiet jewel of a camp near the Canadian border. It's only a short drive from U.S. 395, yet the campground gets relatively little use. The camp is on the west shore of the lake. It is popular and usually fills on summer weekends. The lake has fishing for rainbow trout, cutthroat trout, brook trout, crappie, bass, and catfish. While there is no speed limit, the lake is too small for big, fast boats.

RV sites, facilities: There are 15 sites for tents or RVs up to 24 feet (no hookups). Picnic tables and fire grills are provided. Vault toilets are available. No drinking water is available. Garbage must be packed out. Boat docks and launching facilities are available on-site. Some facilities are wheelchair accessible. A convenience store and ice are within seven miles. Leashed pets are permitted.

Reservations, fees: Reservations are not accepted. Sites are $6 per night. Open mid-April–mid-October, weather permitting.

Directions: From Spokane, drive north on U.S. 395 for 74 miles to Colville. Continue north on U.S. 395 for about 25 miles to Barstow and Pierre Lake Road (County Road 4013). Turn right (north) on Pierre Lake Road and drive nine miles to the campground on the west side of Pierre Lake.

Contact: Colville National Forest, Three Rivers Ranger District, 509/738-7700, fax 509/738-7780.

13 SHEEP CREEK

Scenic rating: 8

near the Columbia River and the Canadian border

See map page 147

This campground is in a forested area along Sheep Creek, about four miles from the Columbia River and close to the Canadian border. Although a primitive camp, it has drinking water and is crowded with locals on the Fourth of July weekend. A wheelchair-accessible fishing platform and trail are available. Sheep Creek provides opportunities for trout fishing. Huckleberry picking is good in August.

RV sites, facilities: There are 11 sites for tents or RVs up to 30 feet (no hookups). Picnic tables, fire grills, and tent pads are provided. Vault toilets, drinking water, a fishing platform, and a group picnic shelter with barbecues are available. Garbage must be packed out. Restaurants and stores are within five miles. Some facilities are wheelchair accessible. Leashed pets are permitted.

Reservations, fees: Reservations are not accepted. There is no fee for camping. Open mid-April–November, weather permitting.

Directions: From Spokane, drive north on U.S. 395 for 87 miles to Kettle Falls and Highway 25. Turn north on Highway 25 and drive 33 miles to Northport. Continue north on Highway 25 for 0.75 mile to Sheep Creek Road (across the Columbia River Bridge). Turn left on Sheep Creek Road and drive 4.3 miles (on a gravel road) to the campground entrance on the right.

Contact: Department of Natural Resources, Northeast Region, 509/684-7474, fax 509/684-7484.

14 CURLEW LAKE STATE PARK

Scenic rating: 8

on Curlew Lake

See map page 146

Boredom is banned at this park, which lies on the eastern shore of Curlew Lake. The park covers 123 acres, and the lake is 5.5 miles long. Fishing is often good for trout and largemouth bass at the lake, and there are additional fishable lakes and streams in the immediate region. There is also beach access, swimming, waterskiing, and hiking, with two miles of hiking and biking trails in the park. The park is also used as a base for bicycle tour groups, with mountain biking available on a fairly steep trail that provides a view of the valley. An active osprey nest can be viewed from the park. Nearby recreation options include a nine-hole golf course. The

park borders an airfield and is in the heart of a historic gold-mining district.

RV sites, facilities: There are 25 sites with full or partial hookups (30 amps) for RVs up to 35 feet, 52 developed tent sites, and five primitive tent sites. Picnic tables are provided. Restrooms have flush toilets and coin showers. A dump station, drinking water, firewood, ice, and boat-launching and dock facilities are available. Boat fuel is available at the marina on the north side of the lake. Some facilities are wheelchair accessible. An amphitheater with interpretive activities is available nearby. Leashed pets are permitted.

Reservations, fees: Reservations are not accepted. Sites are $17–31 per night, $10 per extra vehicle per night. Open April–October, weather permitting.

Directions: From Spokane on I-90, turn north on U.S. 395 and drive 87 miles to Kettle Falls and Highway 20. Turn west on Highway 20 and continue 34 miles to Highway 21 (two miles east of Republic). Turn right (north) and drive six miles to the park entrance on the left.

Contact: Curlew Lake State Park, 509/775-3592; state park information 360/902-8844, fax 509/775-0822, www.parks.wa.gov.

15 TIFFANYS RESORT

Scenic rating: 7

on Curlew Lake

See map page 146

Tiffanys Resort is in a pretty, wooded setting along the western shore of Curlew Lake. This 6.5-mile-long lake is good for waterskiing. Fishing can be good for rainbow trout and largemouth bass. Most of the sites are fairly spacious. This is a smaller, more private alternative to Black Beach Resort.

RV sites, facilities: There are 15 sites for RVs of any length with full hookups (30 and 50 amps), four tent sites, and 19 cabins. Picnic tables are provided, and fire pits are available on request. Restrooms have flush toilets and showers. Firewood, a convenience store, a coin laundry, ice, a playground, and a swimming beach are available.

Boat docks, launching facilities, and rentals are available. Leashed pets are permitted.

Reservations, fees: Reservations are accepted. Sites are $22–24 per night. Some credit cards accepted. Open April–late October.

Directions: From Colville, drive west on Highway 20 for 36 miles into the town of Republic and Klondike Road. Turn right on Klondike Road and drive 10.2 miles (Klondike Road will turn into West Curlew Lake Road) to Tiffany Road. Turn right and drive 0.5 mile to the resort at the end of the road.

Contact: Tiffanys Resort, 509/775-3152, www.tiffanysresort.com.

16 BLACK BEACH RESORT

Scenic rating: 7

on Curlew Lake

See map page 146

Here's another resort along Curlew Lake. This one is much larger than Tiffanys Resort, with beautiful waterfront sites and full facilities. Waterskiing, personal watercraft, swimming, and fishing are all options. Fossil digging near the town of Republic is also popular.

RV sites, facilities: There are 112 sites for RVs of any length with full hookups (20 and 30 amps), nine sites for tents or RVs of any length (no hookups), and 13 lodging units. Some sites are pull-through. Picnic tables are provided and fire pits are available at some sites. Restrooms have flush toilets and coin showers. A dump station, a convenience store, a coin laundry, ice, volleyball, basketball, tetherball, horseshoes, and a playground are available. Boat docks, launching facilities, and boat rentals are at the resort. Leashed pets are permitted.

Reservations, fees: Reservations are accepted. RV sites are $20–22 per night, tent sites are $18 per night, plus $5 per pet per stay. Some credit cards accepted. Campground open April–October; two campsites and three cabins are available in winter.

Directions: From Colville, drive west on Highway 20 for approximately 36 miles to the town of Re-

public and Klondike Road. Turn right on Klondike Road (which becomes West Curlew Lake Road) and drive 7.5 miles to Black Beach Road. Turn right and drive 0.75 mile to the resort.

Contact: Black Beach Resort, tel./fax 509/775-3989, www.blackbeachresort.com.

17 NORTH GORGE

Scenic rating: 7

on Franklin Roosevelt Lake in Lake Roosevelt National Recreation Area

See map page 147

This is the first and northernmost of many campgrounds I discovered along the west shore of 130-mile-long Franklin Roosevelt Lake, which was formed by damming the Columbia River at Coulee. Recreation options include waterskiing and swimming, plus fishing for walleye, trout, bass, and sunfish. During the winter, the lake level lowers; for a unique trip, walk along the lake's barren edge. Note that this campground provides full facilities May–September, then limited facilities in the off-season. (See the *Spring Canyon* listing in this chapter for more recreation information.)

RV sites, facilities: There are 12 sites for tents or RVs up to 26 feet (no hookups). Picnic tables and fire grills are provided. Drinking water, vault toilets, boat docks, and launching facilities are available. Some facilities are wheelchair accessible. Note that if the lake level drops below an elevation of 1,272 feet, there is no drinking water. Leashed pets are permitted.

Reservations, fees: Reservations are not accepted. Sites are $10 per night ($5 per night in off-season), with a $6 boat-launch fee (good for seven days). Open year-round.

Directions: From Spokane on I-90, drive north on U.S. 395 for 84 miles to the town of Kettle Falls and Highway 25. Turn right (north) on Highway 25 and drive 20 miles to the campground entrance.

Contact: Lake Roosevelt National Recreation Area, 509/633-9441, fax 509/633-9332, www.nps.gov/laro.

WASHINGTON

18 SNAG COVE

Scenic rating: 8

on Franklin Roosevelt Lake in Lake Roosevelt
National Recreation Area

See map page 147

Snag Cove has a setting similar to North Gorge campground, amid ponderosa pines along the west shore of Franklin Roosevelt Lake. This small camp has just nine sites, but the nearby boat launch makes it a find.

RV sites, facilities: There are nine sites for tents or RVs up to 26 feet (no hookups). Picnic tables and fire grills are provided. Vault toilets are available. When the lake level drops, there is no drinking water. Some facilities are wheelchair accessible. Boat-launching facilities and docks are nearby. Leashed pets are permitted.

Reservations, fees: Reservations are not accepted. Sites are $5–10 per night, and the boat-launch fee is $6 (good for seven days). Open year-round, weather permitting.

Directions: From Spokane, turn north on U.S. 395 and drive 84 miles to the town of Kettle Falls. Continue north on U.S. 395 (crossing the Columbia River) for seven miles to the Hedlund Bridge turnoff. Turn right, cross Hedlund Bridge, and drive 7.5 miles to the campground on the right.

Contact: Lake Roosevelt National Recreation Area, 509/633-9441, fax 509/633-9332, www.nps.gov/laro.

19 NORTH LAKE ROOSEVELT RESORT

Scenic rating: 7

on Franklin Roosevelt Lake

See map page 147

This campground is along the long, narrow Kettle River Arm of Franklin Roosevelt Lake. A country resort, it is usually quiet and peaceful. A highlight is easy access to the lake. There is no steep walk like at so many other campgrounds at this lake. A one-mile loop nature trail is available along the lakeshore, where wild turkeys and deer are often spotted. It's close to a full-service marina and tennis courts. Riding stables are available 20 miles away, and a golf course is within 15 miles. Colville National Forest East Portal Interpretive Area, 10 miles away, is a good side trip. (Drive south to the junction of Highway 20 and continue southwest for about six miles.) Highlights include a nature trail and the Bangs Mountain auto tour, a five-mile drive that takes you through old-growth forest to Bangs Mountain Vista overlooking the Roosevelt Lake–Kettle Falls area.

RV sites, facilities: There are 42 sites for RVs of any length with full hookups (30 and 50 amps), 15 sites for tents or RVs of any length (no hookups), two cabins, three rental trailers, and two motel rooms with kitchens. All sites are pull-through. An overflow camping area is also available. Picnic tables and fire grills are provided. Restrooms have flush toilets and coin showers. Drinking water, a coin laundry, horseshoe pits, volleyball, modem hookups, a convenience store, and firewood are available. Lake swimming and fishing are on-site. Leashed pets are permitted. A restaurant is available within five miles.

Reservations, fees: Reservations are accepted. Sites are $13–22 per night, $2 per person per night for more than two people. Weekly and monthly rates are available. Open year-round.

Directions: From Spokane, turn north on U.S. 395 and drive 84 miles to the town of Kettle Falls. Continue north on U.S. 395 for 6.5 miles (toward Canada) to Roosevelt Road. Turn right (east) and drive 300 yards to the resort on the right.

Contact: North Lake Roosevelt Resort, tel./fax 509/738-2593 or 800/597-4423.

20 EVANS

Scenic rating: 9

on Franklin Roosevelt Lake in Lake Roosevelt
National Recreation Area

See map page 147

This campground is another along the shore of Franklin Roosevelt Lake. This one sits along

WASHINGTON

the eastern shoreline, just south of the town of Evans. Fishing, swimming, and waterskiing are among the activities here. (See the *Spring Canyon* listing in this chapter for more information.)

RV sites, facilities: There are 43 sites for tents or RVs up to 26 feet and one group site for tents or RVs up to 26 feet that can accommodate up to 25 people. No hookups. Picnic tables and fire grills are provided. Seasonal drinking water and flush toilets are available, with vault toilets available during the off-season. A boat dock, launch facilities, a dump station, and a picnic area are available nearby. Some facilities are wheelchair accessible. Leashed pets are permitted.

Reservations, fees: Reservations are not accepted for individual sites but are required for the group site at 877/444-6777 or www.ReserveUSA.com ($9 reservation fee). Sites are $5–10 per night, with a $6 boat-launch fee (good for seven days). Open year-round, with limited facilities in the winter.

Directions: From Spokane on I-90, drive north on U.S. 395 for 84 miles to the town of Kettle Falls and Highway 25. Turn right (north) on Highway 25 and drive eight miles to the campground entrance on the left.

Contact: Lake Roosevelt National Recreation Area, 509/633-9441, fax 509/633-9332, www.nps.gov/laro.

21 MARCUS ISLAND

Scenic rating: 8

on Franklin Roosevelt Lake in Lake Roosevelt National Recreation Area

See map page 147

This campground, south of Evans camp on the eastern shore of Franklin Roosevelt Lake, is quite similar to that camp. Waterskiing, fishing, and swimming are the primary recreation options. (See the *Spring Canyon* listing for information about the park and side-trip options in the area.)

RV sites, facilities: There are 27 sites for tents

or RVs up to 20 feet (no hookups). Picnic tables and fire grills are provided. Drinking water, vault toilets, and a picnic area are available. A boat launch and dock are available nearby. Some facilities are wheelchair accessible. Note that if the lake level drops below an elevation of 1,272 feet, there is no drinking water. Leashed pets are permitted.

Reservations, fees: Reservations are not accepted. Sites are $5–10 per night, and there's a $6 boat-launch fee (good for seven days). Open year-round, weather permitting.

Directions: From Spokane on I-90, drive north on U.S. 395 for 84 miles to the town of Kettle Falls and Highway 25. Turn right (north) on Highway 25 and drive four miles to the campground entrance on the left.

Contact: Lake Roosevelt National Recreation Area, 509/633-9441, fax 509/633-9332, www.nps.gov/laro.

22 BIG MEADOW LAKE

Scenic rating: 8

on Big Meadow Lake in Colville National Forest

See map page 147

Big Meadow Lake is at 3,400 feet elevation and has 71 surface acres. The camp, in a scenic area, is quiet, remote, and relatively unknown, and the lake provides trout fishing. The U.S. Forest Service has built a wildlife-viewing platform, where ospreys, ducks, geese, and occasionally even moose, elk, and cougars may be spotted. A camp host is on-site during the summer season.

RV sites, facilities: There are 16 sites for tents or RVs up to 32 feet (no hookups). Fire grills, picnic tables, and vault toilets are provided, but there is no drinking water. A boat launch, restrooms, and a wheelchair-accessible nature trail and fishing pier are available. Leashed pets are permitted.

Reservations, fees: Reservations are not accepted. There is no fee for camping. Open May–November, weather permitting.

Directions: From Spokane, drive north on U.S. 395 for 87 miles to Colville and Highway

20. Turn east on Highway 20 and drive one mile to Colville-Aladdin Northpoint Road (County Road 9435). Turn north and drive 20 miles to Meadow Creek Road. Turn right (east) and drive six miles to the campground on the right. Note: The surface of the access road changes dramatically depending on the season.

Contact: Colville National Forest, Three Rivers Ranger District, Colville Office, 509/684-7000 or 509/684-7010, fax 509/684-7280.

23 EAST SULLIVAN

Scenic rating: 7

on Sullivan Lake in Colville National Forest

See map page 147

This campground is the largest one on Sullivan Lake and by far the most popular. It fills up in summer. The camp is on the lake's north shore. Some come here to try to catch giant brown trout or smaller, more plentiful rainbow trout. The boating and hiking are also good. The beautiful Salmo-Priest Wilderness is just three miles to the east. It gets light use, which means quiet, private trails. This is a prime place to view wildlife, so carry binoculars while hiking for a chance to spot the rare woodland caribou and Rocky Mountain bighorn sheep.

RV sites, facilities: There are 38 sites for tents or RVs up to 40 feet, including some pull-through sites, and one group site for up to 30 people. No hookups. Picnic tables and fire grills are provided. Drinking water and vault toilets are available. A boat dock, launching facilities, a picnic area, a swimming area and floating platform, and a camp host are nearby. Some facilities are wheelchair accessible. Leashed pets are permitted.

Reservations, fees: Reservations are accepted for individual sites and required for the group site at 877/444-6777 ($9 reservation fee) or www.ReserveUSA.com. Sites are $12 per night, double sites are $24 per night, it's $6 per night for extra vehicle, and the group site is $50 per night. Open late May–September, weather permitting.

Directions: From Spokane, drive north on U.S. 395 for six miles to U.S. 2. Turn northeast on U.S. 2 and drive 30 miles to the Metaline turnoff and Highway 211 northbound. Turn northwest on Highway 211 and drive 15 miles to Usk and Highway 20. Turn left (northwest) and drive 34 miles to Tiger and Highway 31. Continue (north) on Highway 31 and drive 15 miles to the town of Metaline Falls (Highway 31 is also known as Lehigh Avenue in town). Continue 2.5 miles to Sullivan Lake Road/County Road 9345. Turn right and drive a short distance, cross the bridge over the Pend Oreille River, and continue 12 miles to the campground on the left.

Contact: Colville National Forest, Sullivan Lake Ranger District, 509/446-7500, fax 509/446-7580.

24 WEST SULLIVAN

Scenic rating: 7

on Sullivan Lake in Colville National Forest

See map page 147

This small campground is along the northwestern shore of Sullivan Lake and is a popular destination for boating, fishing, swimming, sailing, waterskiing, and hiking. (See the listing for *East Sullivan* in this chapter for recreation and local details.)

RV sites, facilities: There are 10 sites for tents or RVs up to 30 feet (no hookups). Picnic tables and fire grills are provided. Drinking water and vault toilets, a picnic shelter, a developed swimming beach, a floating swim platform, and a camp host are available. Some facilities are wheelchair accessible. Leashed pets are permitted.

Reservations, fees: Reservations are accepted at 877/444-6777 ($9 reservation fee) or www.ReserveUSA.com. Call for current rates. Open late May–late September, weather permitting.

Directions: From Spokane, drive north on U.S. 395 for six miles to U.S. 2. Turn northeast on U.S. 2 and drive 30 miles to the Metaline

WASHINGTON

turnoff and Highway 211 northbound. Turn northwest on Highway 211 and drive 15 miles to Usk and Highway 20. Turn left (northwest) and drive 34 miles to Tiger and Highway 31. Continue (north) on Highway 31 and drive 15 miles to the town of Metaline Falls (Highway 31 is also known as Lehigh Avenue in town). Continue 2.5 miles to Sullivan Lake Road/ County Road 9345. Turn right and drive a short distance, cross the bridge over the Pend Oreille River, and continue 12 miles to the campground on the left (at the foot of Sullivan Lake, just across the road from the Sullivan Lake Ranger Station).

Contact: Colville National Forest, Sullivan Lake Ranger District, 509/446-7500, fax 509/446-7580.

25 NOISY CREEK AND NOISY CREEK GROUP

Scenic rating: 7

on Sullivan Lake in Colville National Forest
See map page 147

This campground is on the southeast end of Sullivan Lake, adjacent to where Noisy Creek pours into Sullivan Lake. Note that the lake level can be drawn down for irrigation, leaving this camp well above the lake. Noisy Creek Trail near camp heads east along Noisy Creek and then north up to Hall Mountain (elevation 6,323 feet), a distance of 5.3 miles; this is bighorn sheep country. The Lakeshore Trailhead is at the nearby day-use area. Waterskiing is allowed on the 3.5-mile-long lake, and the boat ramp near the camp provides a good launch point.

RV sites, facilities: There are 19 sites for tents or RVs up to 45 feet and one group camp for up to 40 people. No hookups. If the group camp is not reserved, it is available as an overflow area. Picnic tables and fire grills are provided. Drinking water and vault toilets are available. A camp host is on-site. Boat-launching facilities and a picnic area are nearby. Some facilities are wheelchair accessible. Leashed pets are permitted.

Reservations, fees: Reservations are accepted for individual sites and required for the group camp at 877/444-6777 ($9 reservation fee) or www.ReserveUSA.com. Sites are $12 per night, $6 per night extra vehicle fee. Group site is $50 per night. Open May–September, weather permitting.

Directions: From Spokane, drive north on U.S. 395 for six miles to U.S. 2. Turn northeast on U.S. 2 and drive 30 miles to the Metaline turnoff and Highway 211 northbound. Turn northwest on Highway 211 and drive 15 miles to Usk and Highway 20. Turn left (northwest) and drive 34 miles to Tiger and Highway 31. Continue (north) on Highway 31 and drive 15 miles to the town of Metaline Falls (Highway 31 is also known as Lehigh Avenue in town). Continue 2.5 miles to Sullivan Lake Road/County Road 9345. Turn right and drive a short distance, cross the bridge over the Pend Oreille River, and continue nine miles to the campground on the right (on the south end of Sullivan Lake).

Contact: Colville National Forest, Sullivan Lake Ranger District, 509/446-7500, fax 509/446-7580.

26 EDGEWATER

Scenic rating: 6

on the Pend Oreille River in Colville National Forest
See map page 147

Edgewater Camp is on the shore of the Pend Oreille River about two miles upstream from the Box Canyon Dam. Although not far out of Ione, the camp has a primitive feel to it. Fishing for largemouth bass, rainbow trout, and brown trout is popular here, though suckers and squawfish present somewhat of a problem.

RV sites, facilities: There are 20 sites for tents or RVs up to 40 feet (no hookups). Picnic tables and fire grills are provided. Drinking water and vault toilets are available. A boat launch and a picnic area are available nearby. Leashed pets are permitted.

Reservations, fees: Reservations are accepted at 877/444-6777 ($9 reservation fee) or www

.ReserveUSA.com. Sites are $12 per night, $6 per extra vehicle per night. Open late May–early September, weather permitting.

Directions: From Spokane, drive north on U.S. 395 for six miles to U.S. 2. Turn northeast on U.S. 2 and drive 30 miles to the Metaline turnoff and Highway 211 northbound. Turn northwest on Highway 211 and drive 15 miles to Usk and Highway 20. Turn left (northwest) and drive 34 miles to Tiger and Highway 31. Continue on Highway 31 and drive 15 miles to the town of Metaline Falls (Highway 31 is known as Lehigh Avenue in town); continue 2.5 miles to Sullivan Lake Road (County Road 9345). Turn right (east) on Sullivan Lake Road and drive 0.25 mile to County Road 3669. Turn left (north) on County Road 3669 and drive two miles to the campground entrance road on the left. Turn left and drive 0.25 mile to the campground.

Contact: Colville National Forest, Sullivan Lake Ranger District, 509/446-7500, fax 509/446-7580.

27 IONE RV PARK AND MOTEL

Scenic rating: 8

on the Pend Oreille River

See map page 147

This camp is a good layover spot for campers with RVs or trailers who want to stay in town. The park sits on the shore of the Pend Oreille River, which offers fishing, swimming, several bike trails, and boating. The city park is adjacent to this property. In the winter, bighorn sheep may be spotted north of town.

RV sites, facilities: There are 19 sites for tents or RVs of any length with full hookups (15, 20, and 30 amps), seven tent sites, and 11 motel rooms. Picnic tables are provided. Restrooms have flush toilets and showers. Drinking water, a dump station, a pay phone, and a coin laundry are available. A store, a café, and ice are within one mile. Boat docks, launching facilities, and a park with a playground are nearby. Leashed pets are permitted.

Reservations, fees: Reservations are accepted. RV sites are $18 per night, and tent sites are $5 per night. Some credit cards accepted. Open year-round.

Directions: From Spokane, drive north on U.S. 2 for 48 miles to the junction with Highway 211 at the Washington/Idaho border. Turn west on Highway 211 and drive 48 miles northwest to Tiger and Highway 31. Turn right (north) on Highway 31 and drive four miles to Ione. Cross a spillway (it looks like a bridge) on Highway 31 and continue a short distance to the park on the right.

Contact: Ione RV Park and Motel, 509/442-3213.

28 KERR

Scenic rating: 6

on Salmon Creek in Okanogan National Forest

See map page 146

This camp sits at an elevation of 3,100 feet along Salmon Creek, about four miles north of Conconully Reservoir, and is one of many campgrounds near the lake. Fishing prospects are marginal for trout here. There are numerous recreation options available at Conconully Reservoir, including far better fishing. Note: At the time of publication, the campground was closed because of the Tripod Complex fire, and it is scheduled to reopen in 2007; check status before planning a trip.

RV sites, facilities: There are 13 sites for tents or RVs up to 21 feet (no hookups). Picnic tables and fire grills are provided. Vault toilets are available, but there is no drinking water. Garbage must be packed out. Some facilities are wheelchair accessible. Leashed pets are permitted.

Reservations, fees: Reservations are not accepted. Sites are $5 per night per vehicle. Open mid-May–mid-October, weather permitting.

Directions: From East Wenatchee, drive north on U.S. 97 for 88 miles to Okanogan and County Road 9229. Turn left (north) on County Road 9229 and drive 17.5 miles to

WASHINGTON

Conconully and County Road 2361. Continue northwest on County Road 2361 and drive four miles (the road becomes Forest Road 38) to the campground on the left.

Contact: Okanogan and Wenatchee National Forests, Tonasket Ranger District, 509/486-2186, fax 509/486-5161.

29 ORIOLE

Scenic rating: 6

on Salmon Creek in Okanogan National Forest
See map page 146

This camp is at 2,900 feet elevation along Salmon Creek and offers a creek view from some of the campsites. This forest setting features well-spaced campsites among western larch and lodgepole pine. This is a primitive camp, similar to Kerr, which is also on Salmon Creek. Note: At the time of publication, the campground was closed because of the Tripod Complex fire, and it is scheduled to reopen in 2007; check status before planning a trip.

RV sites, facilities: There are 10 sites for tents or RVs up to 25 feet (no hookups). Picnic tables and fire grills are provided. Vault toilets are available, but there is no drinking water. Garbage must be packed out. Some facilities are wheelchair accessible. Leashed pets are permitted.

Reservations, fees: Reservations are not accepted. Sites are $5 per night per vehicle. Open mid-May–October, weather permitting.

Directions: From East Wenatchee, drive north on U.S. 97 for 88 miles to Okanogan and County Road 9229. Turn left (north) on County Road 9229 and drive 17.5 miles to Conconully and County Road 2361. Continue northwest on County Road 2361 and drive 2.5 miles to Forest Road 025. Turn left and drive 0.5 mile (crossing the creek) to the campground on the left.

Contact: Okanogan and Wenatchee National Forests, Tonasket Ranger District, 509/486-2186, fax 509/486-5161.

30 JACK'S RV PARK & MOTEL

Scenic rating: 5

near Conconully Reservoir
See map page 146

This park is in the town of Conconully, set between Conconully Reservoir and Conconully Lake. Horseshoe pits can be found in the park, and nearby recreation options include hiking trails, fishing, hunting (in season), and water sports (summer and winter) at the lake. Snowmobiling is popular in winter.

RV sites, facilities: There are 30 sites with full hookups (30 amps) for RVs of any length and six motel rooms with kitchenettes. Some sites are pull-through. Picnic tables are provided. Restrooms have flush toilets and coin showers. A covered barbecue building, community fire pits, and a five-hole putting green are available. A store, a café, and ice are within two blocks. Boat docks, launching facilities, and rentals are nearby. Leashed pets are permitted.

Reservations, fees: Reservations are accepted. Sites are $25 per night. Some credit cards accepted. Open mid-April–October, weather permitting.

Directions: From U.S. 97 in Okanogan, turn north (left if arriving from the south) on Pine Street and drive 17.5 miles northwest to Conconully and Broadway Street. Turn right (east) and drive one block to A Avenue. Turn left (north) on A Avenue and drive less than one block to the park on the right.

Contact: Jack's RV Park & Motel, 509/826-0132 or 800/893-5668, www.jacksrv.com.

31 KOZY KABINS AND RV PARK

Scenic rating: 7

near Conconully Reservoir
See map page 146

This quiet and private park in Conconully has a small creek running through it and plenty of greenery. A full-service marina is close by. There is hunting in season and snowmobiling is an option in the winter. If you continue northeast of town on County Road 4015, the road will get a bit narrow for a while but widens again when you enter the Sinlahekin Habitat Management Area, which is managed by the Department of Fish and Wildlife. There are some primitive campsites in this valley, especially along the shores of the lakes in the area.

RV sites, facilities: There are 15 sites with full hookups (30 amps) for RVs up to 40 feet, two tent sites, and eight cabins. Picnic tables are provided. Restrooms have flush toilets and coin showers. A community fire pit and firewood are available. Propane gas, a dump station, a general store, a café, a coin laundry, and ice are within one block. Boat docks, launching facilities, and boat rentals are nearby. Leashed pets are permitted.

Reservations, fees: Reservations are accepted at 888/502-2246. RV sites are $20 per night, and tents are $10 per night. Some credit cards accepted. Open year-round.

Directions: From U.S. 97 in Okanogan, turn north (left if arriving from the south) on Pine Street/Conconully Highway and drive 17.5 miles northwest to Conconully and Broadway Street. Turn right (east) and drive one block to A Avenue. The park is at the junction of A Avenue and Broadway Street.

Contact: Kozy Kabins and RV Park, 509/826-6780.

32 CONCONULLY STATE PARK

Scenic rating: 9

on Conconully Reservoir
See map page 146

This park is considered a fisherman's paradise, with trout, bass, and kokanee salmon. The park is along Conconully Reservoir and covers 81 acres, with 5,400 feet of shoreline. A boat launch, beach access, swimming, and fishing provide all sorts of water sports possibilities. A 0.5-mile nature trail is available. This park dates to 1910. A side-trip option is to Sinlahekin Habitat Management Area, which is accessible via County Road 4015. This route heads northeast along the shore of Conconully Reservoir on

the other side of U.S. 97. The road is narrow at first but then becomes wider as it enters the habitat management area.

RV sites, facilities: There are 82 sites for tents or RVs up to 60 feet (no hookups). Picnic tables and fire grills are provided. Restrooms have flush toilets and coin showers. A dump station and a playground are available. A store, a café, a coin laundry, and ice are within one mile. Boat-launching and dock facilities are nearby. A sheltered picnic area, horseshoe pits, a baseball field, and interpretive activities are available nearby. Some facilities are wheelchair accessible. Leashed pets are permitted.

Reservations, fees: Reservations are not accepted. Sites are $17 per night, $10 per extra vehicle per night. Open year-round.

Directions: On U.S. 97 at Omak, take the North Omak exit. At the base of the hill, turn right and drive two miles until you reach Conconully Road. Turn right and drive 19 miles north to the park entrance.

Contact: Conconully State Park, 509/826-7408; state park information 360/902-8844, www.parks.wa.gov.

33 CONCONULLY LAKE RESORT

Scenic rating: 6

on Upper Conconully Reservoir
See map page 146

This is the only resort along the shore of Conconully Lake, which is 3.5 miles long. Tents are permitted, but this is a prime vacation destination for RVers. Trout fishing, swimming, boating, waterskiing, and riding personal watercraft are all options here. There are ATV trails in the area.

RV sites, facilities: There are 11 sites for RVs of any length with full hookups (30 amps), four cabins, and one apartment. Picnic tables and fire rings are provided. Restrooms have flush toilets and coin showers, and ice is available. Propane gas. Gasoline, a dump station, limited groceries, a gift shop, bait and tackle, a café, and a coin laundry are within one mile. Boat docks, launching

WASHINGTON

facilities, moorage, and a variety of boat rentals are available. Leashed pets are permitted.

Reservations, fees: Reservations are accepted. Sites are $23 per night, $2 per person per night for more than two people. Some credit cards accepted. Open late April–October.

Directions: From U.S. 97 in Okanogan, turn north (left if arriving from the south) on Pine Street/Conconully Highway and drive 17.5 miles northwest to Conconully and Lake Street. Turn right on Lake Street and drive one mile to the resort on the right.

Contact: Conconully Lake Resort, 509/826-0813 or 800/850-0813, fax 509/826-1292.

❸❹ LIAR'S COVE RESORT

Scenic rating: 6

on Conconully Reservoir

See map page 146

Roomy sites for RVs can be found at this camp on the shore of Conconully Reservoir. Tents are allowed, too. Fishing, swimming, boating, and hiking opportunities are nearby.

RV sites, facilities: There are 28 sites for RVs of any length with full hookups (30 amps), two cabins, one mobile home, and three motel rooms. Picnic tables and fire pits are provided. Restrooms have flush toilets and coin showers. Cable TV, modem access, ice, boat docks, launching facilities, moorage, and boat rentals are available. Propane gas, a dump station, a store, and a café are within one mile. Some facilities are wheelchair accessible. Leashed pets are permitted.

Reservations, fees: Reservations are accepted. Sites are $23–25 per night, tents are $17 per night, plus $2 per person per night for more than two people. Weekly rates available. Some credit cards accepted. Open April–October.

Directions: From U.S. 97 in Okanogan, turn north (left if arriving from the south) on Pine Street/Conconully Highway and drive 16.5 miles northwest to Conconully and look for the park on the left. It's 0.25 mile south of Conconully.

Contact: Liar's Cove Resort, 509/826-1288 or 800/830-1288, www.liarscr.com.

❸❺ SHADY PINES RESORT

Scenic rating: 6

on Conconully Reservoir

See map page 146

This camp is on the western shore of Conconully Reservoir; some sites are lakeside. It is near Conconully State Park and provides a possible option if the state park campground is full—a common occurrence in summer. But note that on summer weekends, this camp often fills as well. See the *Kozy Kabins and RV Park* and *Conconully State Park* listings in this chapter for area information.

RV sites, facilities: There are 21 sites with full hookups (30 and 50 amps) for RVs up to 40 feet, two tent sites, and six cabins. Some sites are pull-through. Picnic tables and fire rings are provided. Restrooms have flush toilets and coin showers. Ice, firewood, a gift shop, Wi-Fi, massage therapy, boat-launching facilities, and boat rentals are available. Propane gas, a dump station, a store, a café, and a coin laundry are within one mile. Leashed pets are permitted.

Reservations, fees: Reservations are accepted at 800/552-2287. RV sites are $21–23 per night, tent sites are $19 per night. Some credit cards accepted. Open mid-April–late October.

Directions: From U.S. 97 in Okanogan, turn north (left if arriving from the south) on Pine Street/Conconully Highway and drive 16.5 miles northwest to Conconully and Broadway Street. Turn left (west) and drive one mile. The park is on the west shore of the lake.

Contact: Shady Pines Resort, 509/826-2287, www.shadypinesresort.com.

❸❻ SWAN LAKE

Scenic rating: 8

on Swan Lake in Colville National Forest

See map page 146

Scenic views greet visitors on the drive to Swan Lake and at the campground as well. The camp is on the shore of Swan Lake, at an elevation of 3,700 feet. Swan Lake Trail, a beautiful hiking trail, circles the lake. Fishing for rainbow trout is an option. Swimming, boating (gas motors prohibited), mountain biking, and hiking are some of the possibilities here. This is a good out-of-the-way spot for RV cruisers seeking a rustic setting. It commonly fills on summer weekends.

RV sites, facilities: There are 25 sites for tents or RVs up to 31 feet (no hookups). Picnic tables and fire grills are provided. Drinking water and vault toilets are available. A reservable picnic shelter with barbecue, firewood, a fishing dock, and launching facilities are available nearby. Gas motors are prohibited on the lake. Some facilities are wheelchair accessible. Leashed pets are permitted.

Reservations, fees: Reservations are not accepted. Sites are $10 per night, $2 per extra vehicle per night; fees are charged Memorial Day weekend–Labor Day weekend. Open May–September, weather permitting.

Directions: From Spokane on I-90, turn north on U.S. 395 and drive 87 miles to Highway 20. Turn west on Highway 20 and drive 36 miles to the town of Republic and Highway 21. Turn south on Highway 21 and drive seven miles to Forest Road 53 (Scatter Creek Road). Turn right (southwest) on Forest Road 53 and drive eight miles to the campground at the end of the road.

Contact: Colville National Forest, Republic Ranger District, 509/775-3305, fax 509/775-7401.

37 LONG LAKE
🥾 🚴 🏊 🎣 🛶 🐕 🚐 ⛺

Scenic rating: 9

on Long Lake in Colville National Forest
See map page 146

Long Lake is one of the three lakes in this area (the others are Swan Lake and Ferry Lake). Expert anglers can have a quality experience here fly-fishing for cutthroat trout. No motors are allowed on the lake, and fishing is restricted (fly-fishing only), but it's ideal for a float tube or a pram. The lake is adjacent to little Fish Lake, and a 0.5-mile trail runs between the two. The drive on Highway 21 south of Republic is particularly beautiful, with views of the Sanpoil River.

RV sites, facilities: There are 12 sites for tents or RVs up to 21 feet (no hookups). Picnic tables and fire grills are provided. Drinking water and vault toilets are available. Primitive launching facilities are nearby. Leashed pets are permitted.

Reservations, fees: Reservations are not accepted. Sites are $8 per night, $2 per extra vehicle per night; fees are charged Memorial Day weekend–Labor Day weekend. Open May–September, weather permitting.

Directions: From Spokane on I-90, turn north on U.S. 395 and drive 87 miles to Highway 20. Turn west on Highway 20 and drive 36 miles to the town of Republic and Highway 21. Turn south on Highway 21 and drive seven miles to Forest Road 53 (Scatter Creek Road). Turn right (southwest) on Forest Road 53 and drive seven miles to Forest Road 400. Turn left (south) and drive 1.5 miles to the camp on the right.

Contact: Colville National Forest, Republic Ranger District, 509/775-3305, fax 509/775-7401.

38 TEN MILE
🥾 🎣 🐕 🚐 ⛺

Scenic rating: 7

on the Sanpoil River in Colville National Forest
See map page 146

This spot is secluded and primitive. Located about nine miles from Swan Lake, Ferry Lake, and Long Lake, this campground along the Sanpoil River is a good choice for a multiday trip visiting each of the lakes. The Sanpoil River provides fishing for rainbow trout, and a hiking trail leads west from camp for about 2.5 miles.

RV sites, facilities: There are nine sites for tents or RVs up to 21 feet (no hookups). Picnic tables and fire rings are provided. Vault toilets are available. No drinking water is available. Leashed pets are permitted.

Reservations, fees: Reservations are not accepted. Sites are $6 per night, $2 per extra vehicle per night; fees are charged Memorial Day weekend–Labor Day weekend. Open mid-May–mid-October, weather permitting.

WASHINGTON

Directions: From Spokane on I-90, turn north on U.S. 395 and drive 87 miles to Highway 20. Turn west on Highway 20 and drive 36 miles to Republic and Highway 21. Turn south on Highway 21 and drive 10 miles to the campground entrance on the left.

Contact: Colville National Forest, Republic Ranger District, 509/775-3305, fax 509/775-7401.

39 SHERMAN PASS OVERLOOK

Scenic rating: 6

at Sherman Pass in Colville National Forest

See map page 147

Sherman Pass Scenic Byway (Highway 20) runs through here, so the camp has some road noise. This roadside campground is near Sherman Pass (5,575 feet elevation), one of the few high-elevation mountain passes open year-round in Washington. Several nearby trails provide access to various peaks and vistas in the area. One of the best is the Kettle Crest National Recreation Trail, with the trailhead one mile from camp. This trail extends for 45 miles, generally running north to south, and provides spectacular views of the Cascades on clear days. No other campgrounds are in the immediate vicinity.

RV sites, facilities: There are nine sites for tents or RVs up to 24 feet (no hookups). Picnic tables and fire grills are provided. Vault toilets are available. No drinking water is available. Garbage must be packed out. Some facilities are wheelchair accessible. Leashed pets are permitted.

Reservations, fees: Reservations are not accepted. Sites are $6 per night. Open mid-May–October, weather permitting; campground may be open until snowfall with no fee and limited services.

Directions: From Spokane on I-90, turn north on U.S. 395 and drive 87 miles to Highway 20. Turn west on Highway 20 and drive 19.5 miles to the campground on the right.

Contact: Colville National Forest, Three Rivers Ranger District, 509/738-7700, fax 509/738-7780.

40 CANYON CREEK

Scenic rating: 7

near the East Portal Historical Site in Colville National Forest

See map page 147

This campground is almost half a mile from the highway, just far enough to keep it from road noise. It's a popular spot among campers looking for a layover spot, with the bonus of trout fishing in the nearby creek. Canyon Creek lies within hiking distance of the East Portal Historical Site. The camp is set in a pretty area not far from the Columbia River, which offers myriad recreation options.

RV sites, facilities: There are 12 sites for tents or RVs up to 30 feet (no hookups). Picnic tables and fire grills are provided. Vault toilets are available. No drinking water is available. Garbage must be packed out. Some facilities are wheelchair accessible. Leashed pets are permitted.

Reservations, fees: Reservations are not accepted. Sites are $6 per night. Open late April–early October, weather permitting; campground may be open until snowfall with no fee and limited services.

Directions: From Spokane, drive north on U.S. 395 for 87 miles to Highway 20. Turn west on Highway 20 and drive 18 miles (crossing the Columbia River) to Forest Road 136. Turn left (south) and drive for 0.3 mile to the campground on the left.

Contact: Colville National Forest, Three Rivers Ranger District, 509/738-7700, fax 509/738-7780.

41 HAAG COVE

Scenic rating: 8

on Franklin Roosevelt Lake in Lake Roosevelt National Recreation Area

See map page 147

This campground is tucked away in a cove along the western shore of Franklin Roosevelt Lake (Columbia River), about two miles south of Highway 20. A good side trip is to the Sherman Creek Habitat Management Area, just north of camp. It's rugged and steep, but a good place to see and photograph wildlife, including bald eagles, golden eagles, and 200 other species of birds, along with the occasional black bear, cougar, and moose. Note that no boat launch is available at this camp, but boat ramps are available at Kettle Falls and French Rock. Also note that no drinking water is available if the lake level drops below an elevation of 1,275 feet.

RV sites, facilities: There are 16 sites for tents or RVs up to 26 feet (no hookups). Picnic tables and fire grills are provided. Seasonal drinking water and vault toilets are available. Boat docks are available nearby. Leashed pets are permitted.

Reservations, fees: Reservations are not accepted. Sites are $5–10 per night. Open year-round, weather permitting.

Directions: From Spokane, drive north on U.S. 395 for 84 miles to the town of Kettle Falls and Highway 20. Continue on Highway 20 and drive 7.5 miles to Kettle Falls Road. Turn left (south) and drive two miles to the campground on the right.

Contact: Lake Roosevelt National Recreation Area, 509/633-9441, fax 509/633-9332, www.nps.gov/laro.

42 LAKE ELLEN & LAKE ELLEN WEST

Scenic rating: 7

on Lake Ellen in Colville National Forest

See map page 147

This 82-acre lake is a favorite for fishing for rainbow trout, which are a good size and plentiful early in the season. There are two small camps available here. The boat launch is at the west end of the lake. It is about three miles west of the Columbia River and the Lake Roosevelt National Recreation Area. See a U.S. Forest Service map for details.

RV sites, facilities: There are 11 sites at Lake Ellen and five sites at Lake Ellen West for tents or RVs up to 22 feet (no hookups). Picnic

tables are provided, but there is no drinking water. Vault toilets and boat docks are available. Garbage must be packed out. Some facilities are wheelchair accessible. Leashed pets are permitted.

Reservations, fees: Reservations are not accepted. Sites are $6 per night. Open mid-April–October, weather permitting; campsites may be open until snowfall with no fee and limited services.

Directions: From Spokane, drive north on U.S. 395 for 87 miles to Colville and Highway 20. Turn west on Highway 20 and drive 14 miles (crossing the Columbia River) to County Road 3. Turn left and drive south for 4.5 miles to County Road 412. Turn right on County Road 412 and drive five miles to the Lake Ellen Campground or continue another 0.7 mile to Lake Ellen West Campground.

Contact: Colville National Forest, Three Rivers Ranger District, 509/738-7700, fax 509/738-7780.

43 KETTLE FALLS

Scenic rating: 8

on Franklin Roosevelt Lake in Lake Roosevelt National Recreation Area

See map page 147

This campground only occasionally fills. It's along the eastern shore of Roosevelt Lake, about two miles south of the highway bridge near West Kettle Falls. In the summer, the rangers offer campfire programs in the evenings. Waterskiing, swimming, and fishing are all options. Local side trips include St. Paul's Mission in Kettle Falls, which was built in 1846 and is one of the oldest churches in Washington.

RV sites, facilities: There are 76 sites for tents or RVs up to 26 feet and two group sites for tents or RVs up to 26 feet that can accommodate up to 50 and 75 people respectively. No hookups. Picnic tables and fire grills are provided. Seasonal flush toilets, seasonal drinking water, a dump station, firewood, a small marina with a store, and a playground are available.

WASHINGTON

A store is within one mile. Some facilities are wheelchair accessible. Boat docks, fuel, and launching facilities are available. Leashed pets are permitted.

Reservations, fees: Reservations are accepted for individual sites and required for group sites at 877/444-6777 or www.ReserveUSA.com ($9 reservation fee). Sites are $5–10 per night, with a $6 boat-launch fee (good for seven days). Open year-round, with limited winter facilities.

Directions: From Spokane, drive north on U.S. 395 for 84 miles to the town of Kettle Falls. Continue on U.S. 395 for three miles to Kettle Park Road. Turn left and drive two miles to the campground on the right.

Contact: Lake Roosevelt National Recreation Area, 509/633-9441, fax 509/633-9332, www.nps.gov/laro.

44 DOUGLAS FALLS

Scenic rating: 8

on Mill Creek

See map page 147

This campground is just outside of Colville in a wooded area along Mill Creek. A 0.2-mile walk from the campground takes you to a beautiful overlook of Douglas Falls. Another unique highlight is a cabled free-span bridge. And best of all, this camp is free!

RV sites, facilities: There are 12 sites for tents or RVs up to 30 feet (no hookups). Picnic tables, fire grills, and tent pads are provided. Vault toilets, drinking water, and a group picnic shelter are available. Garbage must be packed out. A camp host is on-site. A baseball field is nearby. Some facilities are wheelchair accessible. Leashed pets are permitted.

Reservations, fees: Reservations are not accepted. There is no fee for camping. Open Memorial Day weekend–November, weather permitting.

Directions: From Spokane, drive north on U.S. 395 for 87 miles to Colville and Highway 20. Turn east on Highway 20 and drive 1.1 miles to Aladdin Road. Turn left (north) and

drive two miles to Douglas Falls Road. Turn left and drive three miles to the campground on the left.

Contact: Department of Natural Resources, Northeast Region, 509/684-7474, fax 509/684-7484.

45 LAKE GILLETTE

Scenic rating: 8

on Lake Gillette in Colville National Forest

See map page 147

This pretty and popular camp is right on the shore of Lake Gillette. Like neighboring East Gillette Campground, it fills up quickly in the summer. The camp is popular with off-road vehicle (ORV) users, primarily motorcyclists. An ORV system can't be accessed directly from the campground but is close. Note that ORV riding in and out of camp is prohibited. Fishing at Lake Gillette is best for cutthroat trout.

RV sites, facilities: There are 14 sites for tents or RVs up to 31 feet (no hookups). Drinking water, fire grills, and picnic tables are provided. Vault toilets and a camp host are available. A store and ice are within one mile. Some facilities are wheelchair accessible. Boat docks, launching facilities, and rentals are nearby. Leashed pets are permitted.

Reservations, fees: Reservations are not accepted. Sites are $12 per night, double sites are $24 per night, plus $6 per extra vehicle per night. Open mid-May–early September, weather permitting; campground may be open until snowfall with no fee and limited services.

Directions: From Spokane, drive north on U.S. 395 for 74 miles to Colville and Highway 20. Turn east on Highway 20 and drive 20 miles to County Road 4987 (Lake Gillette Road). Turn right (east) on Lake Gillette Road and drive 0.5 mile to the campground on the left.

Contact: Colville National Forest, Three Rivers Ranger District, Colville Office, 509/684-7000 or 509/684-7010, fax 509/684-7280.

WASHINGTON

46 GILLETTE

Scenic rating: 7

near Lake Gillette in Colville National Forest
See map page 147

This beautiful and extremely popular campground, just south of Beaver Lodge Resort and Lake Thomas, is near Lake Gillette, one in a chain of four lakes. There are a few hiking trails in the area. (See the listing for *Beaver Lodge Resort* for other recreation information.)

RV sites, facilities: There are 28 sites for tents or RVs up to 31 feet (no hookups). Picnic tables and fire grills are provided. Drinking water, vault toilets, and a camp host are available. A store and ice are within one mile. Some facilities are wheelchair accessible. Boat docks, launching facilities, and rentals are nearby. Leashed pets are permitted.

Reservations, fees: Reservations are not accepted. Sites are $12 per night, $6 per extra vehicle per night. Open mid-May–early September, weather permitting; campground may be open until snowfall, with no fee and limited services.

Directions: From Spokane, drive north on U.S. 395 for 74 miles to Colville and Highway 20. Turn east on Highway 20 and drive 20 miles to County Road 4987 (Lake Gillette Road). Turn right (east) on Lake Gillette Road and drive 0.5 mile to the campground on the right.

Contact: Colville National Forest, Three Rivers Ranger District, Colville Office, 509/684-7000 or 509/684-7010, fax 509/684-7280.

47 BEAVER LODGE RESORT

Scenic rating: 9

on Lake Thomas
See map page 147

This developed camp sits along the shore of Lake Gillette, one in a chain of four lakes. A highlight in this area: the numerous opportunities for off-road vehicles (ORVs) provided by a network of ORV trails. In addition, hiking trails and marked bike trails are close to the camp. In winter, downhill and cross-country skiing is available.

RV sites, facilities: There are 18 sites for tents or RVs up to 34 feet with full or partial hookups (30 amps), 23 sites for tents or RVs up to 40 feet (no hookups), and 10 cabins. Picnic tables and fire pits are provided. Restrooms have flush toilets and coin showers. Drinking water, gasoline, propane gas, firewood, a gift and convenience store, a café, ice, boat rentals, and a playground are available. A dump station is within one mile. Boat docks and launching facilities are nearby. Leashed pets are permitted.

Reservations, fees: Reservations are accepted. Sites are $12–20 per night, $5 per extra vehicle per night, $5 per pet per night. Some credit cards accepted. Open year-round.

Directions: From Spokane, drive north on U.S. 395/Division Street for 74 miles to Colville and Highway 20. Turn east on Highway 20 and drive 25 miles to the resort on the right.

Contact: Beaver Lodge Resort, 509/684-5657, fax 509/685-9426.

48 BLUESLIDE RESORT

Scenic rating: 7

on the Pend Oreille River
See map page 147

This resort is along the western shore of the Pend Oreille River. It offers a headquarters for anglers and vacationers. Four or five bass tournaments are held each spring during May and June, and the river is stocked with both rainbow trout and bass. The resort offers full facilities for anglers, including tackle, and a marina with the only boat gas for 53 miles. The park is lovely, with grassy, shaded sites, and is along the waterfowl migratory path. Lots of groups camp here in the summer. Recreation options include bicycling nearby. See the listing in this chapter for *The Outpost Resort* for the only other campground in the vicinity.

RV sites, facilities: There are 49 for tents or RVs of any length with full or partial hookups

(20, 30, and 50 amps), including four pull-through sites. There are also three tent sites, four motel units, and five cabins. Picnic tables and fire pits are provided. Restrooms have flush toilets and showers. Drinking water, a dump station, a meeting hall, modem access, several sports fields, a convenience store, propane, a coin laundry, ice, firewood, a playground, basketball, tetherball, volleyball, horseshoe pits, a seasonal heated swimming pool, boat docks, launching facilities, and boat fuel are available. Leashed pets are permitted.

Reservations, fees: Reservations are accepted. Sites are $17–22 per night. Some credit cards accepted. Open year-round, but only cabins are available in the winter.

Directions: From Spokane, drive north on Division Street for six miles to U.S. 2. Turn north on U.S. 2 and drive 26 miles northeast to Highway 211. Turn left and drive 18 miles to Highway 20. Turn left and drive 22 miles to the park (on the right at Milepost 400).

Contact: Blueslide Resort, 509/445-1327, fax 509/445-0202, www.blueslideresort.com.

49 PANHANDLE

🚶 🏊 🎣 🚐 🐕 ♿ 🚙 ⛺

Scenic rating: 9

on the Pend Oreille River in Colville National Forest
See map page 147

Among tall trees and with views of the river, this is a scenic spot to set up camp along the eastern shore of the Pend Oreille River. This camp makes a good base for a fishing or water-skiing trip. Fishing for largemouth and small-mouth bass is popular, with an annual bass tournament held every summer in the area. The campground is in an area of mature trees directly across the river from The Outpost Resort. A network of hiking trails can be accessed by taking forest roads to the east. See a U.S. Forest Service map for details.

RV sites, facilities: There are 13 sites for tents or RVs up to 38 feet (no hookups). Picnic tables and fire grills are provided. Drinking water and vault toilets are available. A camp host is on-site. A small boat launch is nearby. Some facilities are wheelchair accessible. Leashed pets are permitted.

Reservations, fees: Reservations are accepted at 877/444-6777 ($9 reservation fee) or www.ReserveUSA.com. Sites are $12 per night, $6 per extra vehicle per night. Open late May–late September, weather permitting.

Directions: From Spokane, drive north on U.S. 395/Division Street for six miles to U.S. 2. Turn north on U.S. 2 and drive 30 miles to the Metaline turnoff and Highway 211 northbound. Take Highway 211 north and drive 15 miles to the junction of Highway 20. Cross Highway 20, driving through the town of Usk. Continue across the Pend Oreille River to Le Clerk Road. Turn left and drive 15 miles north on Le Clerk Road to the campground on the left.

Contact: Colville National Forest, Newport Ranger District, 509/447-7300, fax 509/447-7301.

50 THE OUTPOST RESORT

🚶 🏊 🎣 🚐 ❄️ 🐕 🚴 🚙 ⛺

Scenic rating: 8

on the Pend Oreille River
See map page 147

This comfortable campground in a pretty setting along the west shore of the Pend Oreille River has fairly spacious sites and views of snowcapped mountains. The tent sites are closer to the river than the RV sites. Winter sports, including snowmobiling, are available nearby. Blueslide Resort, the nearest alternative if this camp is full, is about five miles north (see the *Blueslide Resort* listing in this chapter).

RV sites, facilities: There are 12 sites for tents or RVs of any length with full or partial hookups (30 amps), 10 tent sites, four cabins, and a bunkhouse. Some sites are pull-through. Picnic tables are provided, and fire rings are available at some sites. Restrooms have flush toilets and coin showers. A dump station, a convenience store, a café, ice, drinking water, a playground, horseshoe pits, a swimming area, nonmotorized boat rentals, boat docks, and launching facilities are available. Leashed pets are permitted.

Reservations, fees: Reservations are accepted. Sites are $15–20 per night, $5 per night per extra vehicle or tent. Some credit cards accepted. Open year-round, with limited winter facilities.

Directions: From Spokane, drive north on Division Street for six miles to U.S. 2. Turn north on U.S. 2 and drive 34 miles to Highway 211. Turn left and drive 18 miles to Highway 20. Turn left and drive 17 miles to the resort (between Mileposts 405 and 406) on the right.

Contact: The Outpost Resort, 509/445-1317 or 888/888-9064, www.theoutpostresort.com.

51 LOUP LOUP

Scenic rating: 6

near Loup Loup Ski Area in Okanogan National Forest

See map page 146

This camp provides a good setup for large groups of up to 100 people. It is next to the Loup Loup Ski Area at 4,200 feet elevation. The camp features a setting of western larch trees, along with good access to biking and hiking trails as well as the ski area.

RV sites, facilities: There are 25 sites for tents or RVs up to 36 feet (no hookups). Picnic tables and fire rings are provided. Drinking water and vault toilets are available. Some facilities are wheelchair accessible. Leashed pets are permitted.

Reservations, fees: Reservations are not accepted. Sites are $8 per night per vehicle. Open May–mid-October, weather permitting.

Directions: From East Wenatchee, drive north on U.S. 97 for 88 miles to Okanogan and Highway 20. Turn west and drive 21 miles to Forest Road 42. Turn right (north) on Forest Road 42 and drive one mile to the campground on the left.

Contact: Okanogan and Wenatchee National Forests, Methow Valley Ranger District, 509/996-4003, fax 509/996-2208; Methow Valley Visitor Center, 509/996-4000, fax 509/996-4051.

52 LEADER LAKE

Scenic rating: 7

on Leader Lake

See map page 146

This primitive but pretty camp is along the shore of Leader Lake. It is just far enough off the beaten path to get missed by many travelers. The camp has forest cover. The boat ramp is a bonus, and trout fishing can be good in season. Note that the water level often drops in summer because of irrigation use.

RV sites, facilities: There are 14 sites for tents or RVs up to 30 feet (no hookups). Picnic tables and fire pits are provided. Vault toilets, a boat ramp, and a fishing pier are available, but there is no drinking water. Boat-launching facilities are nearby. Garbage must be packed out. Some facilities are wheelchair accessible. Leashed pets are permitted.

Reservations, fees: Reservations are not accepted. There is no fee for camping. Open year-round.

Directions: From East Wenatchee, drive north on U.S. 97 for 88 miles to Okanogan and Highway 20. Turn west and drive eight miles to Leader Lake Road. Turn left and drive 0.4 mile to the campground.

Contact: Department of Natural Resources, Northeast Region, 509/684-7474, fax 509/684-7484.

53 AMERICAN LEGION PARK

Scenic rating: 6

on the Okanogan River

See map page 146

This city park is along the shore of the Okanogan River in an urban setting. The sites are graveled and sunny. Anglers may want to try their hand at the excellent bass fishing here. There is a historical museum at the park. A local farmers market is held on summer weekends.

RV sites, facilities: There are 35 sites for tents or RVs of any length (no hookups). Picnic tables are provided. Restrooms have flush toilets and coin showers. Drinking water and a boat ramp are available. A store, a café, a coin laundry, gasoline, and ice are within one mile. Some facilities are wheelchair accessible. Leashed pets are permitted.

Reservations, fees: Reservations are not accepted. Sites are $3 per tent and $5 per vehicle per night. Open May–October, weather permitting.

Directions: From East Wenatchee, drive north on U.S. 97 for 88 miles to Okanogan and Highway 215. Turn left (north) on Highway 215/2nd Avenue and drive about three miles to the campground on the right.

Contact: Okanogan City Hall, 509/422-3600, fax 509/422-0747.

54 EASTSIDE PARK AND CARL PRECHT MEMORIAL RV PARK

Scenic rating: 6

on the Okanogan River

See map page 146   BEST (

This city park is in the town of Omak, along the shore of the Okanogan River. It covers about 76 acres and features campsites positioned on concrete pads surrounded by grass. Trout fishing is often good here, and there is a boat ramp near the campground. Nearby recreation options include an 18-hole golf course, a swimming pool, and a sports field.

RV sites, facilities: There are 76 pull-through sites with full hookups (30 amps) for RVs of any length and 25 tent sites. Picnic tables are provided. Restrooms have flush toilets and coin showers. A dump station, a picnic area, a seasonal heated swimming pool, a playground, horseshoe pits, a skateboarding park, and a fitness trail are available. A store, a café, a coin laundry, gasoline, and ice are within one mile. Boat-launching facilities are nearby. Some facilities are wheelchair accessible. Leashed pets are permitted.

Reservations, fees: Reservations are not accepted. RV sites are $16 per night, and tent sites are $11 per night. Open April–October, weather permitting.

Directions: From U.S. 97 in Omak, turn west (left, if coming from the south) on Highway 155 and drive 0.3 mile to the campground on the left.

Contact: City of Omak, 509/826-1170, fax 509/826-6531.

55 CRAWFISH LAKE

Scenic rating: 8

on Crawfish Lake in Okanogan National Forest

See map page 146

This pretty, remote, and primitive camp is at 4,500 feet elevation along the shore of Crawfish Lake. Crawdads were once abundant here, but overfishing has depleted their numbers. Swimming and fishing for trout are more popular.

RV sites, facilities: There are 19 sites for tents or RVs up to 31 feet (no hookups). Picnic tables and fire grills are provided. Vault toilets are available, but there is no drinking water. Garbage must be packed out. Boat-launching facilities are on the lake. Leashed pets are permitted.

Reservations, fees: Reservations are not accepted. There is no fee for camping. Open mid-May–mid-October, weather permitting.

Directions: From East Wenatchee, drive north on U.S. 97 for 102 miles to Riverside and County Road 9320. Turn right (east) on County Road 9320 and drive 20 miles (the road becomes Forest Road 30) to Forest Road 30-100. Turn right and drive 0.5 mile to the campground on the right.

Contact: Okanogan and Wenatchee National Forests, Tonasket Ranger District, 509/486-2186, fax 509/486-5161.

56 RAINBOW BEACH RESORT

Scenic rating: 8

on Twin Lakes Reservoir

See map page 147

This quality resort is along the shore of Twin Lakes Reservoir in the Colville Indian Reservation. Busy in summer, the camp fills up virtually every day in July and August. Nearby recreation options include hiking trails, marked bike trails, a full-service marina, and tennis courts.

RV sites, facilities: There are 11 sites with full hookups (30 amps), including five pull-through sites for RVs of any length, seven tent sites, and 26 cabins. Picnic tables and fire pits are provided. Restrooms have flush toilets and coin showers. Drinking water, propane gas, gasoline, firewood, a convenience store, a coin laundry, ice, a roped swimming area, boat rentals, docks and launching facilities, a playground, volleyball, and horseshoe pits are available. Leashed pets are permitted.

Reservations, fees: Reservations are accepted. Sites are $15–20 per night, $10 per pet per stay. Some credit cards accepted. Campsites are available April–October; cabins are available year-round.

Directions: From Spokane, drive north on U.S. 395 for 84 miles to the town of Kettle Falls and Highway 20. Turn east on Highway 20 and drive five miles to the turnoff for Inchelium Highway. Turn left (south) and drive about 20 miles to Inchelium and Bridge Creek-Twin Lakes County Road. Turn right (west) and drive two miles to Stranger Creek Road. Turn left and drive a quarter mile to the resort on the right.

Contact: Rainbow Beach Resort, 509/722-5901, fax 509/722-7080.

57 GIFFORD

Scenic rating: 7

on Franklin Roosevelt Lake in Lake Roosevelt National Recreation Area

See map page 147

Fishing and waterskiing are two of the draws at this camp on the eastern shore of Franklin Roosevelt Lake (Columbia River). The nearby boat ramp is a big plus.

RV sites, facilities: There are 42 sites for tents or RVs up to 20 feet and one group site for tents or RVs up to 20 feet that can accommodate up to 50 people. No hookups. Picnic tables and fire grills are provided. Seasonal drinking water and vault toilets are available. Boat docks and launching facilities, a dump station, and a picnic area are nearby. Some facilities are wheelchair accessible. Leashed pets are permitted.

Reservations, fees: Reservations are not accepted for individual sites but are required for the group site at 877/444-6777 or www.ReserveUSA.com ($9 reservation fee). Sites are $5–10 per night, with a $6 boat-launch fee (good for seven days). Open year-round, with limited winter facilities.

Directions: From Spokane on I-90, drive west for four miles to U.S. 2. Turn west on U.S. 2 and drive 34 miles to Davenport and Highway 25. Turn right (north) on Highway 25 and drive 60 miles to the campground (about three miles south of Gifford) on the left.

Contact: Lake Roosevelt National Recreation Area, 509/633-9441, fax 509/633-9332, www.nps.gov/laro.

58 HUNTERS

Scenic rating: 8

on Franklin Roosevelt Lake in Lake Roosevelt National Recreation Area

See map page 147

This campground, on a shoreline point along Franklin Roosevelt Lake (Columbia River), offers good swimming, fishing, and waterskiing. It is on the east shore of the lake, adjacent to the mouth of Hunters Creek and near the town of Hunters. Note: No drinking water is available if the lake level drops below an elevation of 1,245 feet.

RV sites, facilities: There are 39 sites for tents or RVs up to 26 feet and three group sites for tents or RVs up to 26 feet that can accommodate up to 25 people each. No hookups. Picnic tables are provided. Drinking water and vault toilets are available. Flush toilets, a dump station, and a picnic area are available. Some facilities are wheelchair accessible. A store and ice are available within one mile. Boat docks and launching facilities are nearby. Leashed pets are permitted.

Reservations, fees: Reservations are not accepted for individual sites but are required for group sites at 877/444-6777 or www.ReserveUSA.com ($9 reservation fee). Sites are $5–10 per night, plus a $6 boat-launch fee (good for seven days). Open year-round, with limited winter facilities. Call for group rates.

Directions: From Spokane on I-90, drive west for four miles to U.S. 2. Turn west on U.S. 2 and drive 34 miles to Davenport and Highway 25. Turn north on Highway 25 and drive 47 miles to Hunters and the campground access road on the left (west) side of the road (well marked). Turn left at the access road and drive two miles to the campground at the end of the road.

Contact: Lake Roosevelt National Recreation Area, 509/633-9441, fax 509/633-9332, www.nps.gov/laro.

59 THE 49ER MOTEL & RV PARK

Scenic rating: 6

near Chewelah

See map page 147

This region is the heart of mining country. The park has grassy sites and is next to a motel in a mountainous setting. Nearby recreation options include a 27-hole golf course, hiking trails, and marked bike trails. This park is a good deal for RV cruisers—a rustic setting right in town. In winter, note that the 49 Degrees North Ski & Snowboard Park is 12 miles to the east.

RV sites, facilities: There are 27 sites for RVs up to 40 feet with full hookups (20 and 30 amps), including mostly pull-through sites, and 13 motel rooms. Picnic tables are provided. Restrooms have flush toilets and showers. Drinking water, a dump station, cable TV, a spa, a recreation hall, and an indoor heated swimming pool are available. Propane gas, gasoline, a store, a café, ice, and a coin laundry are within one mile. Leashed pets are permitted.

Reservations, fees: Reservations are accepted. RV sites are $17.50 per night, tent sites are $4 per person per night, and it's $4 per pet per night. Weekly and monthly rates available. Some credit cards accepted. Open year-round.

Directions: From Spokane, drive north on U.S. 395 for 44 miles to Chewelah; the park is on the right (on U.S. 395 at the south edge of town, well marked).

Contact: The 49er Motel & RV Park, 509/935-8613 or 888/412-1994, fax 509/935-8705, www.49er-motel.com.

60 WINONA BEACH RESORT

Scenic rating: 9

on Waitts Lake

See map page 147

This beautiful and comfortable resort on the shore of Waitts Lake has spacious sites and friendly folks. The park fills up in July and August, and note that cabins here are available during this time by the week, not the night. In the spring, fishing for brown trout and rainbow trout can be quite good. The trout head to deeper water in the summer, and bluegill and perch are easier to catch then. Waterskiing is also popular.

RV sites, facilities: There are 54 sites for RVs up to 40 feet with full hookups (30 amps), including 20 lakeside sites, as well as seven tent sites and seven cabins. Picnic tables and fire rings are provided. Restrooms have flush toilets and coin showers. Drinking water, a dump station, firewood, a snack bar, a general store, a playground, volleyball, horseshoe pits, basketball, a swimming beach, an antiques store, and ice are available. Boat docks, launching facilities, and boat rentals are on-site. Leashed pets are permitted.

Reservations, fees: Reservations are accepted. RV sites are $25 per night, tent sites are $16 per night, plus $3 per extra vehicle per night and $3 per pet per night. Some credit cards accepted. Open April–September.

Directions: From Spokane, drive north on

U.S. 395 for 42 miles to the Valley–Waitts Lake exit. Turn left (west) at that exit and drive one mile to Highway 231. Turn right (north) on Highway 231 and drive 1.5 miles to the town of Valley and Valley–Waitts Lake Road. Turn left and drive three miles to Winona Beach Road. Turn left and drive 0.25 mile to the resort at the end of the road.

Contact: Winona Beach Resort, 509/937-2231 or 888/271-4693, fax 509/937-2215.

61 SILVER BEACH RESORT

Scenic rating: 6

on Waitts Lake
See map page 147

Silver Beach Resort offers grassy sites on the shore of Waitts Lake, where fishing and water-skiing are popular. (See the listing for *Winona Beach Resort* in this chapter for information about the lake.)

RV sites, facilities: There are 41 sites with full hookups (30 amps) for RVs up to 36 feet, including four pull-through sites, and seven cabins. Picnic tables are provided, and fire pits can be rented. Restrooms have flush toilets and coin showers. Drinking water, modem access, propane gas, a dump station, a convenience store, a restaurant, a coin laundry, ice, a play-ground, swimming area, boat docks, launching facilities, and boat rentals are available. Leashed pets are permitted.

Reservations, fees: Reservations are accepted. Sites are $24 per night, $2 per person per night for more than two people, and $2 per pet per night. Weekly and monthly rates available. Some credit cards accepted. Open mid-April–mid-September.

Directions: From Spokane, drive north on U.S. 395 for 42 miles to the Valley-Waitts Lake exit. Turn left (west) at that exit and drive six miles to Waitts Lake and the resort on the left-hand side near the shore of the lake.

Contact: Silver Beach Resort, 509/937-2811 or 800/937-2816, fax 509/937-2816, www.silverbeachresort.net.

62 TEALS WAITTS LAKE RESORT

Scenic rating: 7

on Waitts Lake
See map page 147

The shore of Waitts Lake is home to this clean, comfortable resort, where lake views are available and ice fishing is popular in the winter. Hunting is possible in the fall. (See the *Winona Beach Resort* listing in this chapter for information about the lake.)

RV sites, facilities: There are 21 sites for RVs up to 40 feet with full hookups (30 amps). Picnic tables and fire rings are provided. Restrooms have flush toilets and showers. Drinking water, a camp store, a restaurant, firewood, boat docks, boat rentals, launching facilities, and ice are available. Leashed pets are allowed.

Reservations, fees: Reservations are accepted. Sites are $24.50 per night, $5 per pet per night. Some credit cards accepted. Open year-round.

Directions: From Spokane, drive north on U.S. 395 for 42 miles to the Valley–Waitts Lake exit. Turn left (west) at that exit and drive one mile to Highway 231. Turn right (north) on Highway 231 and drive 1.5 miles to the town of Valley and Valley–Waitts Lake Road. Turn left and drive three miles to the resort on the left.

Contact: Teals Waitts Lake Resort, 509/937-2400.

63 JUMP OFF JOE LAKE RESORT

Scenic rating: 7

on Jump Off Joe Lake
See map page 147

On the edge of Jump Off Joe Lake, this wooded campground offers lake views and easy boating access. Recreational activities include boating, fishing, and swimming. Spokane and Grand Coulee Dam are both within a short drive and provide excellent side-trip options. Within 10 miles to the north are an 18-hole golf course and casino.

RV sites, facilities: There are 20 sites for RVs of any length with full hookups (30 amps), 20 sites for tents, and five cabins. Picnic tables and fire rings are provided. Restrooms have flush toilets and coin showers. Drinking water, horseshoe pits, a recreation field, a convenience store, a swimming beach, and a picnic area are available. The resort also rents boats and has a boat ramp and dock. Leashed pets are permitted.

Reservations, fees: Reservations are accepted. Sites are $19–21 per night, $2.50 per pet per night. Some credit cards accepted. Open April–October.

Directions: From Spokane, drive north on U.S. 395 for about 40 miles (three miles south of the town of Valley) to the Jump Off Joe Road exit (Milepost 198). Take that exit, turn west, and drive 1.2 miles to the resort on the right.

Contact: Jump Off Joe Lake Resort, 509/937-2133.

64 SHORE ACRES RESORT

Scenic rating: 8

on Loon Lake
See map page 147

Located on Loon Lake at 2,400 feet elevation, this family campground has a long beach and offers an alternative to Granite Point Park across the lake. Some sites have lake views. The lake is approximately four miles long, and waterskiing, wakeboarding, and personal watercraft are allowed. See the *Granite Point Park* listing in this chapter for details about the fishing opportunities.

RV sites, facilities: There are 30 sites for tents or RVs up to 40 feet with full hookups (20, 30, and 50 amps) and 10 cabins. Picnic tables are provided. Restrooms have flush toilets and showers. Drinking water, a dump station, cable TV, a general store, tackle, firewood, propane, marine fuel, ice, community fire pits, a playground, volleyball, a swimming area, boat docks, personal watercraft and boat rentals, moorage, and launching facilities are available. Leashed pets are permitted with certain restrictions.

Reservations, fees: Reservations are accepted. Sites are $26 per night, $2.50 per pet per night. Some credit cards accepted. Open mid-April–September.

Directions: From Spokane, drive north on U.S. 395 for 30 miles to Highway 292. Turn left (west) on Highway 292 and drive two miles to Shore Acres Road. Turn left and drive another two miles to the resort.

Contact: Shore Acres Resort, 509/233-2474 or 800/900-2474, www.shoreacresresort.com.

65 GRANITE POINT PARK

Scenic rating: 8

on Loon Lake
See map page 147

This camp is on the shore of Loon Lake, a clear, clean, spring-fed lake that covers 1,200 acres and features a sandy beach and swimming area. The RV park features grass sites, no concrete. In the spring, Mackinaw trout range 4–30 pounds and can be taken by deepwater trolling (downriggers suggested). Easier to catch are kokanee salmon and rainbow trout in the 12- to 14-inch class. A few perch, sunfish, and bass come out of their hiding places when the weather heats up. Waterskiing and windsurfing are popular in summer months, and personal watercraft are allowed.

RV sites, facilities: There are 80 sites with full hookups (30 and 50 amps) for RVs up to 40 feet and 25 cottages with kitchens. No tents are allowed. Picnic tables are provided. Restrooms have flush toilets and showers. Drinking water, a recreation hall, a convenience store, a café, a coin laundry, ice, a playground, basketball, volleyball, and horseshoe pits, three swimming areas with a 0.75-mile beach, two swimming docks, boat docks, boat rentals, mooring, and launching facilities are available. Propane gas is within one mile. Pets are not permitted.

Reservations, fees: Reservations are accepted. Sites are $25 per night, $2–4 per person per night for more than two people. Open May–September.

Directions: From Spokane, drive north on U.S. 395/Division Street for 26 miles (eight miles past the town of Deer Park) to the park on the left.

Contact: Granite Point Park, 509/233-2100, www.granitepointpark.com.

66 PEND OREILLE COUNTY PARK

Scenic rating: 6

near Newport

See map page 147

This 440-acre park is wooded and features eight miles of trails throughout for hikers, bicyclists, and equestrians. There is some road noise from U.S. 2, but it's not intolerable. Pend Oreille is the only campground around, and it's not a bad choice if you're looking for a layover spot. It's a good alternative to the often-crowded Mount Spokane State Park. Nearby activities include fishing and hunting.

RV sites, facilities: There are 35 sites for tents or RVs up to 30 feet (no hookups). Picnic tables and fire pits are provided. Restrooms have flush toilets and showers. Drinking water and a picnic area are available. Leashed pets are permitted.

Reservations, fees: Reservations are accepted at 509/292-0121. Sites are $10 per night, $5 per extra vehicle per night. Open May–September, weather permitting.

Directions: From Spokane, drive north on U.S. 395/Division Street for six miles to U.S. 2. Turn north on U.S. 2 and drive 31 miles to the county park entrance on the left (west side).

From Newport, drive east on U.S. 2 for 15 miles (past County Road 211) to the park entrance on the right.

Contact: Pend Oreille County Park, 509/292-0121; Pend Oreille County, Department of Public Works, 509/447-4821.

67 SOUTH SKOOKUM LAKE

Scenic rating: 7

on South Skookum Lake in Colville National Forest

See map page 147

This camp is on the western shore of South Skookum Lake, at the foot of Kings Mountain (elevation 4,383 feet). This is a good fishing lake, stocked with cutthroat trout; it's popular with families. A 1.3-mile hiking trail circles the water. South Baldy Lookout is nearby.

RV sites, facilities: There are 25 sites for tents or RVs up to 30 feet (no hookups). Picnic tables and fire rings are provided. Drinking water and vault toilets are available. A camp host is on-site. A boat ramp for small boats, two docks, and a wheelchair-accessible fishing dock are available nearby. Some facilities are wheelchair accessible. Leashed pets are permitted.

Reservations, fees: Reservations are not accepted. Sites are $12 per night, $6 per extra vehicle per night. Open late May–late September, weather permitting.

Directions: From Spokane, drive north on U.S. 395/Division Street for six miles to U.S. 2. Turn north on U.S. 2 and drive 30 miles to the Metaline turnoff and Highway 211. Turn northwest on Highway 211 and drive 15 miles to Usk and Highway 20. Drive north on Highway 20 a short distance to Kings Lake–Boswell Road (County Road 3389). Turn right (east) on Kings Lake–Boswell Road and drive eight miles (over the Pend Oreille River) to the campground entrance road on the right. Turn right and drive 0.25 mile to the campground.

Contact: Colville National Forest, Newport Ranger District, 509/447-7300, fax 509/447-7301.

68 BROWNS LAKE

Scenic rating: 8

on Browns Lake in Colville National Forest

See map page 147

This campground is along the shore of Browns Lake, with lakeside sites bordering old-growth hemlock and cedar. No motorized boats are permitted on the lake, and only fly-fishing is allowed, so it can be ideal for float tubes, canoes, and prams. A 1.25-mile hiking trail leaves the campground and ties into a wheelchair-accessible interpretive trail with beautiful views along the way. At the end of the trail sits a fishing-viewing platform in Browns Creek, which feeds into the lake. South Skookum Lake is about five miles away.

RV sites, facilities: There are 18 sites for tents or RVs up to 28 feet (no hookups). Picnic tables and fire grills are provided. Vault toilets are available. No drinking water is available. A primitive boat launch is available for small boats, such as canoes, rowboats, and inflatables. Some facilities are wheelchair accessible. Leashed pets are permitted.

Reservations, fees: Reservations are not accepted. Sites are $10 per night, $5 per extra vehicle per night. Open late April–late October, weather permitting.

Directions: From Spokane, drive north on U.S. 395/Division Street for six miles to U.S. 2. Turn north on U.S. 2 and drive 30 miles to the Metaline turnoff and Highway 211 northbound. Turn northwest on Highway 211 and drive 15 miles to Usk and Highway 20. Drive north on Highway 20 a short distance to County Road 3389. Turn right (east) on Kings Lake-Boswell Road (County Road 3389) and drive (over the Pend Oreille River) five miles to a fork with Forest Road 5030. Turn left and drive three miles to the campground at the end of the road.

Contact: Colville National Forest, Newport Ranger District, 509/447-7300, fax 509/447-7301.

69 PIONEER PARK

🥾 🏊 🎣 🚐 🐕 ♿ 🚙 ⛺

Scenic rating: 8

on the Pend Oreille River in Colville National Forest

See map page 147

Pioneer Park Campground is along the shore of Box Canyon Reservoir on the Pend Oreille River near Newport. The launch and adjoining parking area are suitable for larger boats. Waterskiing and water sports are popular here. There is a wheelchair-accessible interpretive trail with a boardwalk and beautiful views of the river. Signs along the way explain the history of the Kalispel tribe.

RV sites, facilities: There are 17 sites for tents

or RVs up to 38 feet (no hookups). Picnic tables and fire rings are provided. Drinking water, vault toilets, and a sheltered picnic area are available. A camp host is on-site. Some facilities are wheelchair accessible. Boat docks and launching facilities are nearby. Leashed pets are permitted.

Reservations, fees: Reservations are accepted at 877/444-6777 ($9 reservation fee) or www.ReserveUSA.com. Sites are $12 per night, $6 per extra vehicle per night. Open early May–late September, weather permitting.

Directions: From Spokane, drive north on U.S. 395 for six miles to U.S. 2. Turn north on U.S. 2 and drive 41 miles to Newport. Continue across the Pend Oreille River to Le Clerc Road (County Road 9305). Turn left on Le Clerc Road and drive two miles to the campground on the left.

Contact: Colville National Forest, Newport Ranger District, 509/447-7300, fax 509/447-7301.

70 ALTA LAKE STATE PARK

🥾 🏊 🎣 🚐 🐕 ♿ 🚙 ⛺

Scenic rating: 8

on Alta Lake

See map page 146

This state park nestles among the pines along the shore of Alta Lake. The park covers 186 acres, and the lake is two miles long and a quarter mile wide. Alta Lake brightens a region where the mountains and pines meet the desert and features good trout fishing in summer, along with a boat launch and a 100-yard long swimming beach. Windsurfing, waterskiing, and personal watercraft use are often excellent on windy afternoons. Because of many hidden rocks just under the lake surface, waterskiing can be dangerous. An 18-hole golf course and a riding stable are close by, and a nice one-mile hiking trail leads up to a scenic overlook. Lake Chelan is about 30 minutes away. Note that open fires are prohibited at times during fire season, so campers are encouraged to bring gas stoves or barbecues.

RV sites, facilities: There are 168 developed

tent sites, 32 sites with partial hookups (30 amps) for RVs up to 40 feet, and a group site for 20–88 people. Picnic tables and fire grills are provided. Restrooms have flush toilets and coin showers. Firewood, a dump station, a store, and ice are available. A sheltered picnic area is available nearby. Some facilities are wheelchair accessible. Boat-launching facilities are nearby. Leashed pets are permitted.

Reservations, fees: Reservations are not accepted for family sites but are required for the group site at 509/923-2473. Sites are $17–24 per night, $10 per extra vehicle per night. Call for group rates. Open April–October, weather permitting.

Directions: From East Wenatchee, drive north on U.S. 97 for 64 miles to Highway 153 (just south of Pateros). Turn left (northwest) on Highway 153 and drive two miles to Alta Lake Road. Turn left (southwest) and drive two miles to the park.

Contact: Alta Lake State Park, 509/923-2473; state park information 360/902-8844, www.parks.wa.gov.

71 LAKESHORE RV PARK AND MARINA

Scenic rating: 7

on Lake Chelan
See map page 146

This municipal park and marina on Lake Chelan is a popular family camp, with fishing, swimming, boating, waterskiing, personal watercraft, and hiking among the available activities. City amenities are within walking distance. The camp fills up in the summer, including on weekdays in July and August. This RV park covers 22 acres, featuring a large marina and a 15-acre day-use area. An 18-hole championship golf course and putting green, lighted tennis courts, a water slide park, and a visitors center are nearby. A casino is six miles west of Chelan. A trip worth taking, the ferry ride goes to several landings on the lake; the ferry terminal is 0.5 mile from the park.

RV sites, facilities: There are 163 sites for RVs of any length with full hookups (30 and 50 amps). Some sites are pull-through. Picnic tables are provided. Restrooms have flush toilets and coin showers. Cable TV, Wi-Fi, a dump station, ice, post office, a covered picnic area, swimming beaches, a playground, tennis courts, volleyball, and basketball are available. A store, a café, a coin laundry, ice, a playground, and propane gas are available within one mile. Boat docks and launching facilities are on-site. Some facilities are wheelchair accessible. Leashed pets are permitted, except during some holiday periods.

Reservations, fees: Reservations are accepted. RV sites are $19–38 per night, tent sites are $13–29 per night. Monthly rates available. Some credit cards accepted. Open year-round.

Directions: From Wenatchee, drive north on U.S. 97-A for 38 miles to Chelan (after crossing the Dan Gordon Bridge, the road name changes to Saunders Street). Continue for 0.1 mile to Johnson Street. Turn left and drive 0.2 mile (becomes Highway 150/Manson Highway) to the campground on the left, at 619 West Manson Highway.

Contact: City of Chelan, Lakeshore RV Park and Marina, 509/682-8023, fax 509/682-8248, www.chelancityparks.com.

72 BRIDGEPORT STATE PARK

Scenic rating: 8

on Rufus Woods Lake
See map page 146   BEST (

Bridgeport State Park is along the shore of Rufus Woods Lake, a reservoir on the Columbia River above Chief Joseph Dam. It's a big place, covering 748 acres, including 7,500 feet of shoreline and 18 acres of lawn, with some shade amid the desert landscape. Highlights include beach access and a boat launch. The "haystacks," unusual volcanic formations that resemble their name, stand out as the park's most striking characteristic. Fishing is best by boat because shore fishing requires a Colville

WASHINGTON

Tribe fishing license (for sale at the Bridgeport Hardware Store), in addition to a state fishing license. The lake has plenty of rainbow trout and walleye. Windsurfing in the afternoon wind and waterskiing are popular at the lake. Nearby recreation options include a nine-hole golf course.

RV sites, facilities: There are 14 sites for tents or RVs (no hookups), 20 sites with partial hook-ups (30 amps) for RVs up to 45 feet, and a group site for up to 72 people. Picnic tables and fire grills are provided. Restrooms have flush toilets and coin showers. Firewood, a picnic area, and a dump station are available. Some facilities are wheelchair accessible. A store, a café, and ice are within two miles. Boat docks and launching facilities are nearby on both the upper and lower portions of the reservoir. Interpretive programs are available in summer. Leashed pets are permitted.

Reservations, fees: Reservations are not accepted for individual sites but are required for group sites at 509/686-7231. Sites are $17–24 per night. Call for group rates. Open April–October.

Directions: From East Wenatchee, drive north on U.S. 97 for 71 miles to Highway 17. Turn south on Highway 17 and drive eight miles southeast to the park entrance on the left.

Contact: Bridgeport State Park, 509/686-7231; state park information 360/902-8844, www.parks.wa.gov.

73 STEAMBOAT ROCK STATE PARK

Scenic rating: 10

on Banks Lake
See map page 146

Steamboat Rock State Park is surrounded by desert. The park covers 3,522 acres and features nine miles of shoreline along Banks Lake, a reservoir created by the Grand Coulee Dam. A column of basaltic rock, with a surface area of 600 acres, rises 800 feet above the lake. Two

campground areas and a large day-use area are set on green lawns sheltered by tall poplars. The park has 13 miles of hiking and biking trails, as well as 10 miles of horse trails. There is also a swimming beach. Fishing and waterskiing are popular; so is rock climbing. A hiking trail leads to Northrup Lake. Horse trails are also available in nearby Northrup Canyon. Note that the one downer is mosquitoes, which are very prevalent in early summer. During the winter, the park is used by snowmobilers, cross-country skiers, and ice anglers.

RV sites, facilities: There are 100 sites with full hookups (50 amps) for RVs up to 50 feet, 26 sites for tents or RVs up to 30 feet (no hookups), 80 primitive sites, 12 hike-in/boat-in sites, and a group camp for up to 50 people. Picnic tables and fire grills are provided. Restrooms have flush toilets and coin showers. A dump station, a café, store, firewood, ice, fishing supplies, a playground, and volleyball are available. Some facilities are wheelchair accessible. Boat-launching facilities, docks, and a marine dump station are nearby. Leashed pets are permitted.

Reservations, fees: Reservations are accepted at 888/CAMP-OUT (888/226-7688) or www.parks.wa.gov/reservations ($7 reservation fee). Sites are $12–31 per night, $10 per extra vehicle per night. Call for group rates. Some credit cards accepted. Open year-round, with limited winter facilities.

Directions: From East Wenatchee, drive north on U.S. 2 for 70 miles to Highway 155 (five miles east of Coulee City). Turn north and drive 18 miles to the park on the left.

Contact: Steamboat Rock State Park, 509/633-1304, fax 509/633-1294; state park information 360/902-8844, www.parks.wa.gov.

74 COULEE PLAYLAND RESORT

Scenic rating: 7

near the Grand Coulee Dam
See map page 146

This park on North Banks Lake, south of the Grand Coulee Dam, is pretty and well treed, with spacious sites for both tents and RVs. The Grand Coulee Laser Light Show (seasonal) is just three miles away and is well worth a visit. Boating, fishing for many species, waterskiing, and personal watercraft are all popular. In addition, hiking trails, marked bike trails, a full-service marina, and tennis courts are close by.

RV sites, facilities: There are 58 sites for tents or RVs of any length with full or partial hookups (15 and 30 amps), seven tent sites, and one yurt. Some sites are pull-through. Picnic tables and fire grills are provided. Restrooms have flush toilets and coin showers. A dump station, modem access, a general store, a coin laundry, firewood, ice, a playground, boat docks, launching facilities, boat rentals, gas, and a bait and tackle shop are available. Propane gas and a café are within one mile. Leashed pets are permitted.

Reservations, fees: Reservations are accepted. Sites are $24–30 per night, $15 per extra vehicle per night. The yurt is $79 per night. Some credit cards accepted. Open year-round, with limited winter facilities.

Directions: From the junction of Highway 17 and U.S. 2 (north of Ephrata), drive east on U.S. 2 for five miles to Highway 155. Turn left (north) and drive 26 miles to Grand Coulee and Electric City. The resort is just off the highway on the left.

Contact: Coulee Playland Resort, 509/633-2671 or 888/633-2671, www.couleeplayland.com.

75 SPRING CANYON

🥾 🎣 🚐 🐕 🔥 ♿ 🚙 ⛺

Scenic rating: 6

on Franklin Roosevelt Lake in Lake Roosevelt National Recreation Area

See map page 146

This large, developed campground is a popular vacation destination. Fishing for bass, walleye, trout, and sunfish is popular at Franklin Roosevelt Lake, as is waterskiing. The campground is not far from Grand Coulee Dam. Lake Roosevelt National Recreation Area offers numerous recreation options, such as free programs conducted by rangers that include guided canoe trips, his-

torical tours, campfire talks, and guided hikes. This lake is known as a prime location to view bald eagles, especially in winter. Side-trip options include visiting the Colville Tribal Museum in the town of Coulee Dam and touring the Grand Coulee Dam Visitor Center. Almost one mile long and twice as high as Niagara Falls, the dam is one of the largest concrete structures ever built. It is open for self-guided tours.

RV sites, facilities: There are 87 sites for tents or RVs up to 26 feet and one group site for tents or RVs up to 26 feet that can accommodate up to 25 people. No hookups. Picnic tables and fire grills are provided. Seasonal flush toilets, drinking water, a dump station, a picnic area, and a playground are available. Some facilities are wheelchair accessible. Boat docks, launching facilities, marine fuel, and a marine dump station are available nearby. Leashed pets are permitted.

Reservations, fees: Reservations are accepted for individual sites at 877/444-6777 and required for the group site at 509/633-3830 or www.ReserveUSA.com ($9 reservation fee). Sites are $5–10 per night, with a $6 boat-launch fee (good for seven days). Open year-round, weather permitting.

Directions: From the junction of I-90 and Highway 17 (just south of Moses Lake), drive north on Highway 17 for 45 miles to U.S. 2. Turn east on U.S. 2 and drive five miles to Highway 155. Turn left (north) and drive 26 miles to Grand Coulee and Highway 174. Turn right (east) on Highway 174 and drive three miles to the campground entrance on the left.

Contact: Lake Roosevelt National Recreation Area, 509/633-9441, fax 509/633-5125, www.nps.gov/laro.

76 LAKEVIEW TERRACE MOBILE AND RV PARK

🥾 🏊 🎣 🚐 🐕 🔥 🚙 ⛺

Scenic rating: 6

near Franklin Roosevelt Lake

See map page 146

This pleasant resort is near Franklin Roosevelt Lake, which was created by Grand Coulee

Dam. It provides a slightly less crowded alternative to the national park camps in the vicinity. A mobile home park is also on the property. A full-service marina is nearby. See the *Spring Canyon* listing in this chapter for recreation options on the water.

RV sites, facilities: There are 20 pull-through sites with full hookups (30 and 50 amps) for RVs of any length and 10 tent sites. Picnic tables are provided. Restrooms have flush toilets and showers. A coin laundry and a playground are available. Boat docks, launching facilities, and rentals are nearby. Leashed pets are permitted, with certain restrictions.

Reservations, fees: Reservations are accepted. Sites are $20–25 per night. Credit cards are not accepted. Open year-round.

Directions: From Grand Coulee, drive east on Highway 174 for 3.5 miles to the park entrance on the left.

Contact: Lakeview Terrace Mobile and RV Park, 509/633-2169.

77 KELLER FERRY

Scenic rating: 7

on Franklin Roosevelt Lake in Lake Roosevelt National Recreation Area

See map page 146

This camp is along the shore of Franklin Roosevelt Lake, a large reservoir created by Grand Coulee Dam, which sits about 15 miles west of camp. Franklin Roosevelt Lake is known for its walleye fishing; although more than 30 species live in this lake, 90 percent of those caught are walleye. They average 1–4 pounds and always travel in schools. Trout and salmon often swim below the bluffs near Keller Ferry. Waterskiing, fishing, and swimming are all recreation options here.

RV sites, facilities: There are 50 sites for tents or RVs up to 16 feet and two group sites for tents or RVs up to 16 feet that can accommodate up to 50 people each. No hookups. Picnic tables and fire grills are provided. Drinking water and vault toilets are available. A dump station, ice, a picnic area, a pay telephone, and a playground

are available nearby. Boat docks, launching facilities, fuel, and a marine dump station are also available. Some facilities are wheelchair accessible. Leashed pets are permitted.

Reservations, fees: Reservations are accepted for individual sites and required for group sites at 877/444-6777 or www.ReserveUSA.com ($9 reservation fee). Call for current rates. Open year-round, weather permitting.

Directions: From Spokane on U.S. 90, turn west on U.S. 2 and drive 71 miles to Wilbur and Highway 21. Turn north and drive 14 miles to the campground on the left.

Contact: Lake Roosevelt National Recreation Area, 509/633-9441, fax 509/633-9332, www.nps.gov/laro.

78 RIVER RUE RV PARK

Scenic rating: 7

near the Columbia River

See map page 146

This camp is in high desert terrain yet is surrounded by lots of trees. You can fish, swim, water-ski, or rent a houseboat at Lake Roosevelt, which is one mile away. Personal watercraft are allowed. Another nearby side trip is to the Grand Coulee Dam. A nine-hole golf course is available in Wilbur.

RV sites, facilities: There are 48 sites for tents or RVs of any length with full or partial hookups (20 and 30 amps) and 29 sites for tents or RVs of any length (no hookups). Some sites are pull-through. Picnic tables and fire rings are provided. Restrooms have flush toilets and showers. A dump station, a pay phone, limited groceries, ice, a snack bar, RV supplies, fishing tackle, and propane gas are available. Recreational facilities include a playground and volleyball. Some facilities are wheelchair accessible. Leashed pets are permitted.

Reservations, fees: Reservations are accepted. Sites are $15–25 per night, $2 per person per night for more than two people. Monthly rates available. Some credit cards accepted. Open April–October.

WASHINGTON

Directions: On U.S. 2 at Wilbur, drive west on U.S. 2 for one mile to Highway 174. Turn right (north) on Highway 174 and drive 0.25 mile to Highway 21. Turn right (north) on Highway 21 and drive 13 miles to the park on the right.
Contact: River Rue RV Park, 509/647-2647, www.riverrue.com.

79 FORT SPOKANE

Scenic rating: 8

on Franklin Roosevelt Lake in Lake Roosevelt National Recreation Area

See map page 147

Rangers offer evening campfire programs and guided daytime activities at this modern campground on the shore of Roosevelt Lake. This park also hosts living-history demonstrations. Fort Spokane is one of more than two dozen campgrounds on the 130-mile-long lake. A 190-mile scenic vehicle route encircles most of the lake.

RV sites, facilities: There are 67 sites for tents or RVs up to 26 feet and two group sites for tents or RVs up to 26 feet that can accommodate up to 30 people each. No hookups. Picnic tables and fire grills are provided. Seasonal flush toilets, drinking water, a dump station, and a playground are available. A picnic area is nearby. A store and ice are within one mile. Some facilities are wheelchair accessible. Boat docks, launching facilities, and a marine dump station are nearby. Leashed pets are permitted.

Reservations, fees: Reservations are accepted for individual sites, and are required for group sites at 877/444-6777 or www.ReserveUSA.com ($9 reservation fee). Sites are $5–10 per night; there is a $6 boat-launch fee (good for seven days). Open year-round, with limited winter facilities.

Directions: From Spokane on I-90, drive west for four miles to U.S. 2. Turn west on U.S. 2 and drive 34 miles to Davenport and Highway 25. Turn right (north) on Highway 25 and drive 22 miles to the campground entrance on the right.
Contact: Lake Roosevelt National Recreation

Area, 509/633-9441, fax 509/633-9332, www.nps.gov/laro.

80 PORCUPINE BAY

Scenic rating: 8

on Franklin Roosevelt Lake in Lake Roosevelt National Recreation Area

See map page 147

This camp is extremely popular, and the sites are filled most of the summer. Its proximity to a nearby dock and launch makes it an especially good spot for campers with boats. A swimming beach is adjacent to the campground.

RV sites, facilities: There are 31 sites for tents or RVs up to 20 feet (no hookups). Picnic tables and fire grills are provided. Drinking water and vault toilets are available. Restrooms have flush toilets. Drinking water, a dump station, a picnic area, a pay telephone, and a playground are available. Boat docks and launching facilities are nearby. Some facilities are wheelchair accessible. Leashed pets are permitted.

Reservations, fees: Reservations are not accepted. Call for current rates. Open year-round, weather permitting.

Directions: From Spokane on I-90, drive west for four miles to U.S. 2. Turn west on U.S. 2 and drive 34 miles to Davenport and Highway 25. Turn right (north) on Highway 25 and drive 19 miles to Porcupine Bay Road. Turn right (east) and drive 4.3 miles to the campground at the end of the road.
Contact: Lake Roosevelt National Recreation Area, 509/633-9441, fax 509/633-9332, www.nps.gov/laro.

81 LAKE SPOKANE CAMPGROUND

Scenic rating: 8

on the Spokane River

See map page 147

This campground is about 45 minutes from Spokane. The camp sits on a terrace above Lake

Spokane (Spokane River), where fishing can be good for rainbow trout and the occasional brown trout. This area is also popular for power boating, waterskiing, and personal watercraft. Crowded in summer, it gets a lot of use from residents of the Spokane area.

RV sites, facilities: There are 11 sites for tents or RVs up to 30 feet (no hookups). Picnic tables, fire grills, and tent pads are provided. Drinking water and vault toilets are available. Garbage must be packed out. A camp host is on-site. A boat launch, dock, swimming beach, and a day-use area are nearby. Some facilities are wheelchair accessible. Leashed pets are permitted.

Reservations, fees: Reservations are not accepted. There is no fee for camping. Open May–September, weather permitting.

Directions: From Spokane on I-90, drive west for four miles to U.S. 2. Turn west on U.S. 2 and drive 21 miles to Reardan and Highway 231. Turn right (north) on Highway 231 and drive 14.2 miles to Highway 291. Turn right and drive 4.7 miles to the campground entrance on the right.

Contact: Department of Natural Resources, Northeast Region, 509/684-7474, fax 509/684-7484.

82 DRAGOON CREEK

Scenic rating: 5

near the Little Spokane River

See map page 147

This spot is frequented by locals but is often missed by out-of-town vacationers. The camp is along Dragoon Creek, a tributary to the Little Spokane River. Its campsites are situated in a forest of ponderosa pine and Douglas fir. Although fairly close to U.S. 395, it remains quiet and rustic. The Department of Natural Resources offers a map that details the region.

RV sites, facilities: There are 22 sites for tents or RVs up to 30 feet (no hookups). Picnic tables, fire grills, and tent pads are provided. Vault toilets and drinking water are available. Garbage must be packed out. Some fa-

cilities are wheelchair accessible. Leashed pets are permitted.

Reservations, fees: Reservations are not accepted. There is no fee for camping. Open May–September, weather permitting.

Directions: From Spokane, drive north on U.S. 395 for 10.2 miles to North Dragoon Creek Road. Turn left on North Dragoon Creek Road and drive 0.4 mile to the campground entrance at the end of the road.

Contact: Department of Natural Resources, Northeast Region, 509/684-7474, fax 509/684-7484.

83 RIVERSIDE STATE PARK

Scenic rating: 8

near Spokane

See map page 147

This 10,000-acre park is along the Spokane and Little Spokane Rivers and features freshwater marshes and beautiful countryside. There are many recreation options, including fishing for bass, crappie, and perch. There are 55 miles of hiking and biking trails and 25 miles of trails for horseback riding. The 37-mile Centennial Trail can be accessed from the park. The park also has a 600-acre riding area for dirt bikes in summer and snowmobiles in winter. An 18-hole golf course is nearby. A local point of interest is the unique Bowl and Pitcher lava formation in the Spokane River.

RV sites, facilities: There are 15 sites for tents or RVs up to 45 feet with partial hookups (30 and 50 amps), 15 tent sites, and two group tent sites that can accommodate up to 30 and 60 people. Picnic tables and fire grills are provided. Restrooms have flush toilets and showers. Drinking water, a picnic area with a kitchen shelter, a dump station, interpretive programs, a seasonal store, and firewood are available. A store, a restaurant, and ice are within three miles. Boat-launching facilities and a dock are eight miles north of the campground. Some facilities are wheelchair accessible. Leashed pets are permitted.

Reservations, fees: Reservations are accepted for individual sites and are required for group sites at 888/CAMP-OUT (888/226-7688) or www.parks.wa.gov/reservations ($7 reservation fee). Sites are $17–24 per night, $10 per extra vehicle per night. Call for group rates. Open year-round.

Directions: In Spokane on I-90, take Exit 280/Maple Street North (cross the Maple Street Bridge) and drive north 1.1 miles to Maxwell Street. Turn left (west) and drive 1.9 miles, bearing left along the Spokane River to the park entrance. From the park entrance, continue for 1.5 miles on Aubrey L. White Parkway to the campground.

Alternative route for long RVs: In Spokane on I-90, take Exit 280/Maple Street North (cross the Maple Street Bridge) and drive north 4.5 miles to Francis Avenue. Turn left and drive three miles to Rifle Club Road. Turn left and drive to Aubrey L. White Parkway and the park entrance. From the entrance, continue 1.5 miles to the campground.

Contact: Riverside State Park, 509/465-5064, www.riversidestatepark.org; state park information 360/902-8844, www.parks.wa.gov.

84 TRAILER INNS RV PARK/ SPOKANE

Scenic rating: 5

in Spokane

See map page 147

This large RV park makes a perfect layover spot on the way to Idaho. It's as close to a hotel as an RV park can get. The pull-through sites are shaded. Nearby recreation options include several 18-hole golf courses, a racquet club, and tennis courts. Note that only about one-third of the sites are available for overnight campers.

RV sites, facilities: There are 97 sites for tents or RVs up to 40 feet with full hookups (15, 30, and 50 amps); approximately 30 sites are available for overnight campers. Some sites are pull-through. Picnic tables are provided. Restrooms have flush toilets and showers. Drink-

ing water, propane gas, cable TV, Wi-Fi and modem access, a TV room, a coin laundry, ice, a picnic area, and a playground are available. A dump station, a convenience store, gasoline, and a café are within one mile. Leashed pets are permitted.

Reservations, fees: Reservations are accepted at 800/659-4864. Sites are $18–30 per night, $4 per person per night for more than two people. Weekly rates available. Some credit cards accepted. Open year-round.

Directions: Note that your route will depend on the direction you're heading: In Spokane eastbound on I-90, take Exit 285 (Thierman Road) to Eastern Road. Drive 0.2 mile on Thierman Road to 4th Avenue. Turn right (west) on 4th Avenue and drive two blocks to the park. In Spokane westbound on I-90, take Exit 285 and turn right onto Sprague Avenue. Drive 0.3 mile to Thierman Road. Turn left (east) on Thierman Road and drive one mile to the park.

Contact: Trailer Inns RV Park/Spokane, 509/535-1811 or 509/248-1142, www.trailer innsrv.com.

85 BLUE LAKE RESORT

Scenic rating: 6

on Blue Lake

See map page 146

Blue Lake Resort is in a desertlike area along the shore of Blue Lake between Sun Lakes State Park and Lake Lenore Caves State Park. Both parks make excellent side trips. Activities at Blue Lake include trout fishing, swimming, boating, waterskiing, and riding personal watercraft. Tackle and boat rentals are available at the resort.

RV sites, facilities: There are 60 sites with full or partial hookups (30 amps) for RVs of any length, including six pull-through sites; 30 tent sites; and 10 cabins. Picnic tables and fire pits are provided. Restrooms have flush toilets and showers. A dump station, firewood, a store, ice, tackle, RV and boat storage, a roped swimming

WASHINGTON

area, volleyball, a playground, horseshoe pits, a marina, boat docks, launching facilities, and boat rentals are available. Leashed pets are permitted.

Reservations, fees: Reservations are accepted at 877/287-7937. Sites are $18 per night, $3 per person per night for more than two people, $4 per night for an additional vehicle, $3 per pet per night. Some credit cards accepted. Open April–September.

Directions: From the junction of I-90 and Highway 17 (just south of Moses Lake), drive north on Highway 17 for 36 miles to the resort on the right. The resort is 15 miles south of Coulee City.

Contact: Blue Lake Resort, 509/632-5364 or 509/632-5388, www.bluelakeresort washington.com.

86 LAURENT'S SUN VILLAGE RESORT

Scenic rating: 6

on Blue Lake
See map page 146

Like Blue Lake Resort, this campground is along the shore of Blue Lake. The hot desert setting is perfect for swimming and fishing. Late July and early August are the busiest times of the year here. (See the *Sun Lakes State Park* listing in this chapter for information on the nearby state parks and other recreation options.)

RV sites, facilities: There are 95 sites, most with full hookups (30 amps), for RVs of any length and four tent sites. Some sites are pull-through. Picnic tables are provided. Restrooms have flush toilets and coin showers. Group fire pits, propane gas, a dump station, a coin laundry, a store, bait and tackle, ice, firewood, a playground, boat docks, launching facilities, and boat rentals are available. Leashed pets are permitted.

Reservations, fees: Reservations are accepted. Sites are $20 per night, $4 per night for an additional vehicle. Some credit cards accepted. Open late April–late September.

Directions: From the junction of I-90 and Highway 17 (just south of Moses Lake), drive north on Highway 17 for 36 miles to Blue Lake and Park Lake Road. Turn right (east) on Park Lake Road (the south entrance) and drive 0.5 mile to the resort on the right.

Contact: Laurent's Sun Village Resort, 509/632-5664, 509/632-5360, or 888/632-5664, www.laurentsresort.com.

87 COULEE LODGE RESORT

Scenic rating: 8

on Blue Lake
See map page 146

This camp is at Blue Lake, which often provides outstanding fishing for a mix of stocked rainbow trout and brown trout in early spring. Blue Lake offers plenty of summertime recreation options, including a swimming beach. (See the *Sun Lakes State Park* listing in this chapter for details.)

RV sites, facilities: There are 22 sites for RVs up to 35 feet with full hookups (30 amps), as well as 14 tent sites. Some sites are pull-through. Picnic tables and fire pits are provided. Restrooms have flush toilets and coin showers. Propane gas, a dump station, a convenience store, firewood, a coin laundry, boat docks, boat and personal watercraft rentals, launching facilities, and ice are available. A café is within five miles. Leashed pets are permitted.

Reservations, fees: Reservations are accepted. Sites are $20–25 per night, $3 per extra vehicle per night, and $2 per pet per night. Some credit cards accepted. Open mid-April–September.

Directions: From the junction of I-90 and Highway 17 (just south of Moses Lake), drive north on Highway 17 for 39 miles to the north end of Blue Lake.

Contact: Coulee Lodge Resort, 509/632-5565, fax 509/632-8607, www.couleelodgeresort.com.

WASHINGTON

88 SUN LAKES STATE PARK

Scenic rating: 10

on Park Lake
See map page 146

Sun Lakes State Park is on the shore of Park Lake, which is used primarily by anglers, boaters, and water-skiers. This 4,027-acre park near the foot of Dry Falls features 12 miles of shoreline. Dry Falls, a former waterfall, is now a stark 400-foot climb, 3.5 miles wide. During the ice age floods, this waterfall was 10 times as large as Niagara Falls. An interpretive center at Dry Falls is open May–September. Now, back to the present: There are nine lakes in the park and 15 miles of hiking trails. A trail at the north end of Lake Lenore (a 15-minute drive by vehicle) leads to the Lake Lenore Caves. Nearby recreation possibilities include a nine-hole golf course and miniature golf.

Insider's tip: Be prepared for heavy winds.

RV sites, facilities: There are 152 sites for tents or RVs (no hookups), 39 sites with full hookups (30 and 50 amps) for RVs up to 50 feet, and one group camp for up to 75 people. Picnic tables and fire pits are provided. Restrooms have flush toilets and coin showers. A dump station, a snack bar, a coin laundry, ice, drinking water, and firewood are available. A store is within one mile. Some facilities are wheelchair accessible. Boat docks, launching facilities, moorage, and boat rentals are nearby. Leashed pets are permitted.

Reservations, fees: Reservations are accepted at 888/CAMP-OUT (888/226-7688) or www.parks.wa.gov/reservations ($7 reservation fee). Sites are $17–24 per night. Call for the group rate. Some credit cards accepted. Open year-round.

Directions: From Ephrata, drive northeast on Highway 28 to Soap Lake and Highway 17. Turn left (north) on Highway 17 and drive 17 miles to the park on the right.

Contact: Sun Lakes State Park, 509/632-5583, fax 509/632-5971; state park information 360/902-8844, www.parks.wa.gov.

89 SUN LAKES PARK RESORT

Scenic rating: 8

Sun Lakes State Park
See map page 146

Run by the concessionaire that operates within Sun Lakes State Park, this camp offers full facilities and is a slightly more developed alternative to the state park's campground.

RV sites, facilities: There are 110 sites for RVs of any length with full hookups (30 and 50 amps) and 59 cabins. Some sites are pull-through. Picnic tables and fire grills are provided. Restrooms have flush toilets and coin showers. Propane gas, a dump station, a convenience store, firewood, a snack bar, a coin laundry, ice, a playground, boat rentals, a seasonal heated swimming pool, miniature golf, and a nine-hole golf course are available. Boat docks and launching facilities are nearby. Some facilities are wheelchair accessible. Leashed pets are permitted.

Reservations, fees: Reservations are accepted. Sites are $20–30 per night, $5 per extra vehicle per night. Open mid-April–mid-October, weather permitting.

Directions: From Ephrata, drive northeast on Highway 28 to Soap Lake and Highway 17. Turn left (north) on Highway 17 and drive 17 miles to the Sun Lakes Park on the right. Enter the park and drive to the resort (well marked).

Contact: Sun Lakes Park Resort, 509/632-5291, www.sunlakesparkresort.com.

90 COULEE CITY PARK

Scenic rating: 6

on Banks Lake
See map page 146

Coulee City Park is a well-maintained park in shade trees on the southern shore of 30-mile-long Banks Lake. You can see the highway from the park, and there is some highway noise. Campsites are usually available. The busiest time of the year is Memorial Day weekend because of the local rodeo. Boating, fishing, waterskiing, and riding personal watercraft are popular. A one-mile walking trail leads from the campground and meanders along the eastern shore of the lake. A nine-hole golf course is close by.

RV sites, facilities: There are 55 sites for RVs up to 35 feet with full hookups (30 and 50 amps) and a large grassy area for tents. Some sites are pull-through. Picnic tables and fire rings are provided. Restrooms have flush toilets and showers. Group fire pits, a dump station, and a playground are available. Propane gas, gasoline, firewood, a store, a restaurant, a café, a coin laundry, and ice are within one mile. Some facilities are wheelchair accessible. Boat docks and launching facilities are on-site. Leashed pets are allowed.

Reservations, fees: Reservations are not accepted. Sites are $15–20 per night, $2 per extra vehicle per night. Open April–late October, weather permitting.

Directions: From Coulee City, drive east on U.S. 2 for 0.5 mile to the park on the left. The park is within the city limits.

Contact: Coulee City Park, 509/632-5331.

91 WEST MEDICAL LAKE RESORT

Scenic rating: 7

on West Medical Lake

See map page 147

This resort functions primarily as a fish camp for anglers. There are actually two lakes: West Medical is the larger of the two and has better fishing, with boat rentals available; Medical Lake is just a quarter mile wide and half a mile long, and boating is restricted to rowboats, canoes, kayaks, and sailboats. The lakes got their names from the wondrous medicinal powers once attributed to their waters. This family-operated shorefront resort, one of several campgrounds on these lakes, is a popular spot for Spokane locals.

RV sites, facilities: There are 20 sites for RVs up to 40 feet with full hookups (30 amps) and 20 tent sites. Picnic tables are provided at all sites, and fire pits are provided at tent sites. Restrooms have flush toilets and showers. Drinking water, a café, bait, tackle, and ice are available. Boat

and fishing docks, launching facilities, a fish-cleaning station, and boat and barge rentals are nearby. Leashed pets are permitted.

Reservations, fees: Reservations are accepted. Sites are $17 per night. Some credit cards accepted. Open late April–September.

Directions: In Spokane on I-90, drive west to Exit 264 and Salnave Road. Take that exit and turn north on Salnave Road; drive six miles to Fancher Road. Turn right (west) and drive 200 yards. Bear left on Fancher Road and drive 200 yards to the resort.

Contact: West Medical Lake Resort, 509/299-3921.

92 PICNIC PINES ON SILVER LAKE

Scenic rating: 8

on Silver Lake

See map page 147

This shorefront resort on Silver Lake caters primarily to RVers, although tent campers are welcome. Fishing can be excellent here. Nearby recreation options include marked bike trails, a full-service marina, and tennis courts. See the *West Medical Lake Resort* listing in this chapter for further details about the area.

RV sites, facilities: There are 18 sites with full or partial hookups (30 amps) for RVs up to 35 feet and 13 tent sites. Hookups are available only mid-March–mid-October. Picnic tables are provided and fire pits are available at some sites. Flush toilets, drinking water, a store, a restaurant, a lounge, a bait shop, boat docks, boat rentals, launching facilities, ice, and a swimming beach are available. Propane gas and a coin laundry are within two miles. Leashed pets are permitted.

Reservations, fees: Reservations are accepted. Sites are $17–20 per night. Some credit cards accepted. Open year-round.

Directions: In Spokane on I-90, drive west to Exit 270 and Medical Lake Road. Take that exit and turn west on Medical Lake Road; drive three miles to Silver Lake Road. Turn left and drive 0.5 mile to the park on the left.

Contact: Picnic Pines on Silver Lake, tel./fax 509/299-6902 or tel. 509/299-3223.

93 MALLARD BAY RESORT

Scenic rating: 8

on Clear Lake
See map page 147

This popular fishing resort is on the shore of Clear Lake, which is two miles long, a half mile wide, and used for waterskiing, personal watercraft, windsurfing, and sailing. Most of the campsites are lakeshore sites on a 20-acre peninsula. Marked bike trails are nearby.

RV sites, facilities: There are 50 sites for tents or RVs of any length with partial hookups (20 and 30 amps), plus two cabins. Picnic tables and fire pits are provided. Restrooms have flush toilets and showers. Drinking water, propane gas, a dump station, a camp store, bait and tackle, ice, swimming facilities with a diving board, a playground, a basketball court, boat docks, launching facilities, a fishing pier, fish-cleaning stations, and boat rentals are available. Leashed pets are permitted.

Reservations, fees: Reservations are accepted. Sites are $17.95 per night. Open mid-April–Labor Day weekend.

Directions: In Spokane on I-90, drive west to Exit 264 and Salnave Road. Take that exit and turn north on Salnave Road; drive 1.5 miles to a junction and Mallard Bay Lane. Turn right on Mallard Bay Lane and drive 0.5 mile (bearing right at the intersection) on a dirt road to the resort at the end of the road.

Contact: Mallard Bay Resort, 509/299-3830.

94 DAN'S LANDING

Scenic rating: 7

on Clear Lake
See map page 147

This resort at Clear Lake features a 300-foot dock with benches that can be used for fishing. If you figured that most people here are anglers,

well, that is correct. Fishing can be good for rainbow trout, brown trout, largemouth bass, crappie, bullhead, and catfish. Most of the campsites are at least partially shaded. Summer weekends are often busy.

RV sites, facilities: There are 17 sites with full or partial hookups (30 and 50 amps) for RVs up to 40 feet, four tent sites, and two rustic cabins. Picnic tables and fire pits are provided. Restrooms have flush toilets and coin showers. Drinking water, a café, ice, bait and tackle, boat docks and launch, boat rentals, and moorage are available. Leashed pets are permitted.

Reservations, fees: Reservations are accepted. Call for current rates. Some credit cards accepted. Open mid-April–mid-September.

Directions: In Spokane on I-90, drive west to Exit 264 and Salnave Road. Take that exit and turn right (north) on Salnave Road; drive a short distance to Clear Lake Road. Turn right (north) on Clear Lake Road and drive three miles to the resort on the left (well signed).

Contact: Dan's Landing, 509/299-3717.

95 PONDEROSA FALLS RESORT

Scenic rating: 6

west of Spokane
See map page 147

This resort is 10 minutes from downtown Spokane, yet provides a wooded, rural setting. It features towering ponderosa pines. Highlights include an 18-hole golf course nearby and several other courses within 20 minutes of the resort.

RV sites, facilities: There are 168 sites for RVs up to 40 feet with full hookups (30 and 50 amps), five cabins, and six bungalows. Picnic tables are provided. No open fires are allowed. Restrooms have flush toilets and showers. Drinking water, cable TV, Wi-Fi and modem access, propane, a coin laundry, an RV wash station, and three playgrounds are available. Other facilities include a camp store, an activity center with an indoor pool, a spa, an exercise room, a game room, and various sports facilities

WASHINGTON

(volleyball, basketball, badminton, miniature golf, and daily, seasonal organized recreational activities). Some facilities are wheelchair accessible. Leashed pets are permitted.

Reservations, fees: Reservations are accepted. Tent sites are $25 per night and RV sites are $25–35 per night. Some credit cards accepted. Open year-round.

Directions: In Spokane on I-90, drive to Exit 272. Take that exit, turn east on Hayford Road (becomes Aero Road), and drive approximately two miles to Thomas Mallen Road. Turn right (south) on Thomas Mallen Road and drive 0.25 mile to the resort on the right.

Contact: Ponderosa Falls Resort, 509/747-9415 or 800/494-7275 (800/494-PARK), fax 509/459-0148, www.kmresorts.com.

96 SPOKANE KOA

Scenic rating: 5

on the Spokane River

See map page 147

This KOA campground is close to the shore of the Spokane River. Nearby you'll find the 37-mile Centennial Trail along the river, as well as an 18-hole golf course and tennis courts. Other options include touring the gardens of Manito Park or visiting Riverfront Park, which has an IMAX theater and aerial gondola rides over the Spokane River.

RV sites, facilities: There are 150 sites with full hookups (30 and 50 amps) for RVs of any length, 50 tent sites, and three cabins. Some sites are pull-through. Picnic tables are provided. No wood fires are allowed. Restrooms have flush toilets and showers. Drinking water, cable TV, a dump station, a recreation hall, a playground, a convenience store, a coin laundry, ice, Wi-Fi and modem access, a pet walk, volleyball, horseshoe pits, basketball, bicycle rentals, and a seasonal heated swimming pool are available. Some facilities are wheelchair accessible. A café and gasoline are within two miles. Leashed pets are permitted.

Reservations, fees: Reservations are accepted at 800/562-3309. Sites are $26–35 per night, $2–3 per night per person for more than two people. Some credit cards accepted. Open year-round.

Directions: From Spokane, drive east on I-90 for 13 miles to Barker/Exit 293. Take that exit to Barker Road. Turn north on Barker Road and drive 1.5 miles to the campground on the left.

Contact: KOA Spokane, 509/924-4722, www.spokanekoa.com.

MOUNT RAINIER AND THE COLUMBIA RIVER GORGE

☾ Fishing
Beacon Rock State Park, **page 222.**

As you stand at the rim of Mount St. Helens, the greatest natural spectacle anywhere on the planet is at your boot tips. The top 1,300 feet of the old volcano, along with the entire north flank, was blown clean off. The half-moon crater walls drop almost 2,100 feet straight down to a lava plug dome, a mile across and still building, where a wisp of smoke emerges from its center. At its edges, the rising plumes of dust from continuous rock falls can be deceptive – you may think a small eruption is in progress. It's like looking inside the bowels of the earth.

The plug dome gives way to the blast zone, where the mountain has completely blown out its side and spreads out across 230 square miles of devastation. From here, it's largely a moonscape but for Spirit Lake on the northeast flank, where thousands of trees are still floating, log-jammed from the eruption in May 1980. Beyond this scene rises 14,411-foot Mount Rainier to the north, 12,276-foot Mount Adams to the northeast, and 11,235-foot Mount Hood to the south, all pristine jewels in contrast to the nearby remains.

I've hiked most of the Pacific Crest Trail and climbed most of the West's highest mountains, but no view compares to this. You could explore this sweeping panorama of a land for years. The most famous spots in this region are St. Helens, Rainier, and Adams; the latter are two of the three most beautiful mountains in the Cascade Range (Mount Shasta in Northern California is the third). All of them offer outstanding touring and hiking, with excellent camps of all kinds available around their perimeters. St. Helens provides the most eye-popping views and most developed visitors centers, Rainier the most pristine wilderness, and Adams some of the best lakeside camps.

That's just the beginning. The Western Cascades span down river canyons and up mountain subridges, both filled with streams and lakes. There are camps throughout. At the same time, the I-5 corridor and its network of linked highways provide many privately developed RV parks fully furnished with everything a vacationer could desire.

Includes:

- Alder Lake Recreation Area
- American River
- Battle Ground Lake State Park
- Beacon Rock State Park
- Black Lake
- Blue Lake
- Bumping Lake and Bumping River
- Cispus River
- Clear Lake
- Columbia Hills State Park
- Columbia River
- Cowlitz River
- Deep Lake
- Dog Lake
- Gifford Pinchot National Forest
- Ike Kinswa State Park
- Indian Heaven Wilderness
- Kalama River
- Leech Lake
- Lewis and Clark State Park
- Lewis River
- Little White Salmon River
- Mayfield Lake
- Millersylvania State Park
- Mount Baker – Snoqualmie National Forest
- Mount Rainier National Park
- Naches River
- Newaukum River
- Offut Lake
- Ohanapecosh River
- Paradise Point State Park
- Riffe Lake
- Rimrock Lake
- Seaquest State Park
- Silver Lake
- Takhlakh Lake
- Tanwax Lake
- Toutle River
- Walupt Lake
- Wenatchee National Forest
- White River
- Wind River
- Yale Lake

WASHINGTON

MOUNT RAINIER AND THE COLUMBIA RIVER GORGE

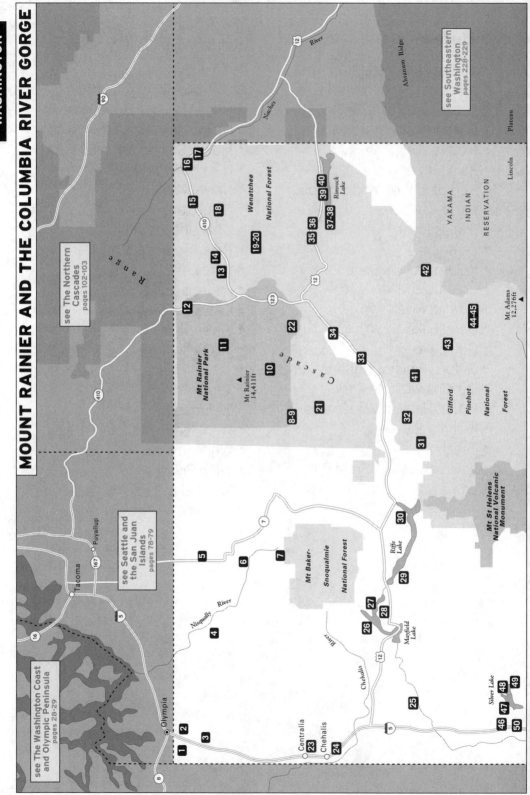

see The Northern
Cascades
pages 102-103

see Seattle and
the San Juan
Islands
pages 78-79

see The Washington Coast
and Olympic Peninsula
pages 28-29

see Southeastern
Washington
pages 228-229

Cascade Range

Wenatchee National Forest

Mt Rainier National Park
Mt Rainier 14,411ft

Mt Baker-Snoqualmie National Forest

Gifford Pinchot National Forest

Mt St Helens National Volcanic Monument

YAKAMA INDIAN RESERVATION

Mt Adams 12,276ft

Ahtanum Ridge

Lincoln Plateau

Nisqually River
Naches River
Chehalis River
Riffe Lake
Mayfield Lake
Rimrock Lake
Silver Lake

Tacoma
Puyallup
Olympia
Centralia
Chehalis

WASHINGTON

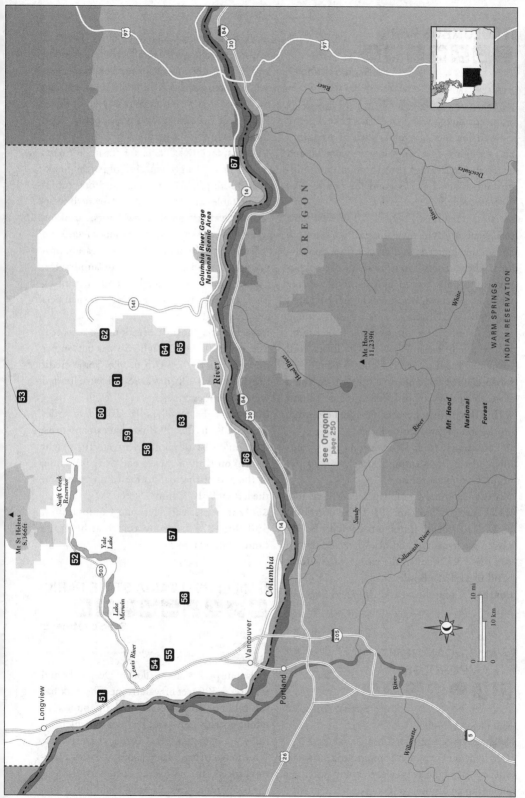

Columbia River Gorge National Scenic Area

OREGON

Deschutes River

WARM SPRINGS INDIAN RESERVATION

White River

Hood River

▲ Mt Hood 11,239ft

Mt Hood National Forest

River

see Oregon
page 250

Sandy River

Collawash River

River

Willamette River

Columbia

River

Vancouver

Portland

Mt St Helens
8,366ft ▲

Swift Creek Reservoir

Yale Lake

Lake Merwin

Lewis River

Longview

10 mi

10 km

0

© AVALON TRAVEL PUBLISHING, INC.

WASHINGTON

1 COLUMBUS PARK

Scenic rating: 7

on Black Lake

See map page 192

This spot along the shore of Black Lake is pretty enough for special events, such as weddings and reunions. The campsites are wooded, and a stream (no fishing) runs through the campground. Black Lake is good for fishing. An 18-hole golf course is nearby.

RV sites, facilities: There are 29 sites for tents or RVs up to 40 feet with partial hookups (30 amps), one tent site, and an overflow camping area. There are also 46 sites with full hookups that are usually rented by the month. Picnic tables are provided. Restrooms have flush toilets and showers. Drinking water, a dump station, a coin laundry, ice, firewood, a playground, volleyball, horseshoe pits, boat docks, and launching facilities are available. A picnic area for special events is nearby. Propane gas and a store are within one mile; there is a restaurant within three miles. Leashed pets are permitted, but not on the swimming beach.

Reservations, fees: Reservations are recommended during summer. Sites are $20 per night. Open year-round.

Directions: From I-5 in Olympia, take Exit 104, which merges onto U.S. 101. Drive northwest on U.S. 101 for 1.7 miles to Black Lake Boulevard. Turn left (south) on Black Lake Boulevard and drive 3.5 miles to the park on the left, at 5700 Black Lake Boulevard.

Contact: Columbus Park, 360/786-9460 or 866/848-9460, www.columbuspark.net.

2 AMERICAN HERITAGE CAMPGROUND

Scenic rating: 7

near Olympia

See map page 192

This spacious, wooded campground just half mile off the highway is close to many activities, including an 18-hole golf course, hiking trails, marked bike trails, and tennis courts. The park features novelty cycle rentals, free wagon rides, and free nightly movies during the summer season. It's pretty and exceptionally clean, making for a pleasant layover on your way up or down I-5. The park has a 5,000-square-foot pavilion for special events or groups.

RV sites, facilities: There are 72 sites for tents or RVs of any length with full or partial hookups (30 amps), 23 tent sites, and one cabin. Picnic tables and fire rings are provided. Restrooms have flush toilets and showers. Drinking water, propane gas, a dump station, a recreation hall, a group pavilion, seasonal recreation programs, a convenience store, a coin laundry, ice, a playground, a seasonal heated swimming pool, and firewood are available. Leashed pets are permitted.

Reservations, fees: Reservations are accepted. Sites are $20–28 per night, $4 per person per night for more than two people. Some credit cards accepted. Open year-round, with limited winter facilities.

Directions: From Olympia, drive five miles south on I-5 to Exit 99. Take that exit and drive 0.25 mile east to Kimmie Street. Turn right (south) on Kimmie Street and drive 0.25 mile to the end of the road to the campground on the left, at 9610 Kimmie Street SW.

Contact: American Heritage Campground, 360/943-8778, www.americanheritage campground.com.

3 MILLERSYLVANIA STATE PARK

Scenic rating: 8

on Deep Lake

See map page 192

This state park is on the shore of Deep Lake and features 3,300 feet of waterfront. The park has 8.6 miles of hiking trails amid an abundance of old-growth cedar and fir trees, of which 7.6 miles are open to bikes. Boating at Deep Lake is restricted to hand-launched boats, with a five-mph speed limit. A fishing dock is available at the boat-launch area. Another highlight: a one-mile fitness trail. Remnants of a narrow-gauge railroad and several skid trails used in the 1800s by the logging industry are still present.

RV sites, facilities: There are 120 sites for tents or RVs up to 35 feet (no hookups), 48 sites with partial hookups (30 amps) for RVs up to 45 feet, and four hike-in/bike-in sites. Picnic tables and fire grills are provided. Restrooms have flush toilets and coin showers. Drinking water, a dump station, boat docks and launching facilities, and firewood are available. A picnic area, boat rentals, summer interpretive activities, and horseshoe pits are nearby. A store, a restaurant, and ice are within one mile. Some facilities are wheelchair accessible. Leashed pets are permitted.

Reservations, fees: Reservations are accepted at 888/CAMP-OUT (888/226-7688) or www.parks.wa.gov/reservations ($7 reservation fee). Sites are $17–31 per night, $12 per night for hike-in/bike-in sites, $10 per extra vehicle per night. Some credit cards accepted. Open year-round.

Directions: From Olympia, drive south on I-5 for 10 miles to Exit 95 and Highway 121. Turn east on Maytown Road (Highway 121) and drive 2.7 miles to Tilley Road. Turn left (north) and drive 1.3 miles to the park.

Contact: Millersylvania State Park, 360/753-1519, fax 360/664-2180; state park information 360/902-8844, www.parks.wa.gov.

4 OFFUT LAKE RESORT

Scenic rating: 8

on Offut Lake

See map page 192

This wooded campground is on Offut Lake, just enough off the beaten track to provide a bit of seclusion. Fishing, swimming, and boating are favorite activities here. Anglers will find everything they need at the resort, including tackle, licenses, and boat rentals. Boating is restricted to a five-mph speed limit, and no gas motors are permitted at the resort. Several fishing derbies are held here every year.

RV sites, facilities: There are 31 sites with full or partial hookups (30 and 50 amps) for RVs up to 40 feet, 25 tent sites, and six cabins. Picnic tables, fire rings, and cable TV are provided. Restrooms have flush toilets and coin showers. Drinking water, modem access, a picnic shelter, a dump station, firewood, a convenience store, bait and tackle, propane gas, a coin laundry, ice, a playground, basketball, and horseshoe pits are available. Boat rentals and docks are available; no gas motors permitted. Some facilities are wheelchair accessible. Leashed pets are permitted.

Reservations, fees: Reservations are accepted. Sites are $17–24 per night, $5 per person per night for more than two adults and two children, $2 per extra vehicle per night, and $2 per pet per night. Some credit cards accepted. Open year-round.

Directions: From Olympia, drive south on I-5 for seven miles to Exit 99. Take that exit and turn east on 93rd Avenue; drive four miles to Old Highway 99. Turn right (south) and drive four miles to Offut Lake Road. Turn left (east) and drive 1.5 miles to the resort.

Contact: Offut Lake Resort, 360/264-2438, www.offutlakeresort.com.

5 RAINBOW RV RESORT

Scenic rating: 8

on Tanwax Lake

See map page 192

This wooded park along the shore of Tanwax Lake has spacious sites with views of mountains, forest, and lake. Highlights include good fishing for trout, perch, crappie, bass, bluegill, catfish, and bullhead. Powerboating and waterskiing are popular on hot summer weekends.

RV sites, facilities: There are about 50 sites with full hookups for RVs up to 40 feet. No tents are allowed. Picnic tables are provided at most sites and portable fire pits are available. Restrooms have flush toilets and coin showers. Drinking water, propane gas, a recreation hall, a convenience store, a coin laundry, a café, ice, cable TV, Wi-Fi access, boat docks and launch, boat rentals, and boat moorage are available. Leashed pets are permitted.

Reservations, fees: Reservations are accepted. Sites are $23–25 per night. Some credit cards accepted. Open year-round.

Directions: From Tacoma, drive south on I-5 to Exit 127 and Highway 512. Turn east on Highway 512 and drive to Highway 161. Turn right (south) on Highway 161 and drive to Tanwax Drive. Turn left (east) on Tanwax Drive and continue 200 yards to the resort.

Contact: Rainbow RV Resort, 360/879-5115, fax 360/879-5116.

6 HENLEY'S SILVER LAKE RESORT

Scenic rating: 7

on Silver Lake

See map page 192

Silver Lake is a 150-acre spring-fed lake that can provide good trout fishing. This full-facility resort is set up as a family vacation destination. A rarity, this private campground caters both to tent campers and RVers. Silver Lake is beautiful and stocked with trout. Highlights include a 250-foot fishing dock and rental rowboats.

RV sites, facilities: There are 36 sites with full or partial hookups for RVs, including two pull-through; a very large area for dispersed tent camping; and six cabins. Picnic tables are provided, and fire pits are available at most sites. Restrooms have flush toilets. Drinking water, snacks, bait and tackle, boat rentals, a boat ramp, and a dock are available. No showers are available. A grocery store, gasoline, and supplies are available within 3.5 miles. Leashed pets are permitted except in the cabins.

Reservations, fees: Reservations are accepted. Sites are $20 per night. Open the first day of fishing season in late April–October, weather permitting.

Directions: From Tacoma, drive south on I-5 for five miles to Exit 127 and Highway 512. Turn east on Highway 512 and drive two miles

to Highway 7. Turn right (south) on Highway 7 and drive 19 miles (two miles straight beyond the blinking light) to Silver Lake Road on the right (well marked). Turn right and drive 0.25 mile to the resort entrance on the left.

Contact: Henley's Silver Lake Resort, 360/832-3580.

7 ALDER LAKE PARK

Scenic rating: 6

on Alder Lake

See map page 192

The 161-acre recreation area at Alder Lake features four camping areas and a group camp; one of the camps is four miles east of the main park entrance. Alder Lake is a 3,065-acre lake (7.5 miles long) often with good fishing for kokanee salmon, rainbow trout, and cutthroat trout. Rocky Point features a sunny beach and is near the mouth of feeder streams, often the best fishing spots on the lake. At the west end of the lake, anglers can catch catfish, perch, and crappie. The campsites have lots of trees and shrubbery. On clear, warm summer weekends, these camps can get crowded. They're always booked full for summer holiday weekends as soon as reservations are available in January. Another potential downer, the water level fluctuates here. Powerboating, waterskiing, and personal watercraft are allowed at this lake. Mount Rainier Scenic Railroad leaves from Elbe regularly and makes its way through the forests to Mineral Lake. It features open deck cars, live music, and restored passenger cars.

RV sites, facilities: There are four camping areas with approximately 110 sites for tents or RVs up to 40 feet with full or partial hookups (30 and 50 amps), 62 tent sites, and one group area (20 sites with full hookups) for tents or RVs. Picnic tables and fire rings are provided. Restrooms have flush toilets and coin showers. Drinking water and vault toilets are available. Boat docks and launching facilities are available nearby. A swimming beach, picnic area, playground, fishing dock, small convenience store, and dump station are also available nearby. Some facilities are wheelchair accessible. Leashed pets are permitted.

Reservations, fees: Reservations are accepted at 888/CAMP-OUT (888/226-7688) or www.tacomapower.com ($7 reservation fee). For group reservations, phone 360/569-2778 ($15 group reservation fee). Sites are $16–23 per night, $10 per extra vehicle per night. The group camp is $23 per site per night, with a five-site minimum. Some credit cards accepted. Open year-round, excluding December 20–January 1.

Directions: From Chehalis, drive south on I-5 for six miles to U.S. 12. Turn east and drive 31 miles to Morton and Highway 7. Turn north on Highway 7 and drive 17 miles to Elbe. Bear left on Highway 7 and drive to the park entrance road on the left (on the east shore of Alder Lake). Turn left and drive 0.2 mile to the park entrance gate.

Contact: Alder Lake Park, Tacoma Power, 360/569-2778 or 888/502-8690, fax 253/502-8631, www.tacomapower.com.

⑧ MOUNTHAVEN RESORT

🥾 ❄️ 🐕 ⛵ 🚐 ⛺

Scenic rating: 7

near Mount Rainier National Park

See map page 192

This campground is within a half mile of the Nisqually (southwestern) entrance to Mount Rainier National Park. In turn, it can provide a launching point for your vacation. One option: Enter the park at the Nisqually entrance, then drive on Nisqually Paradise Road for about five miles to Longmire Museum; general park information and exhibits about the plants and geology of the area are available. If you then continue into the park for 10 more miles, you'll arrive at the Jackson Visitor Center in Paradise, which has more exhibits and an observation deck. This road is the only one into the park that's open year-round. Winter activities in the park include cross-country skiing, snowshoeing,

and inner-tube sledding down slopes. A creek runs through this wooded camp.

RV sites, facilities: There are 16 sites with full hookups (20 and 30 amps) for RVs of any length, one tent site, and nine furnished cabins. Picnic tables and fire grills are provided. Restrooms have flush toilets and showers. Drinking water, a coin laundry, a pay telephone, firewood, and a playground are available. A restaurant and a store are within one mile. Leashed pets are permitted.

Reservations, fees: Reservations are accepted at 800/456-9380. Sites are $25 per night, $2 per pet per night. Some credit cards accepted. Open year-round.

Directions: From Chehalis, drive south on I-5 for 10 miles to U.S. 12. Turn east and drive 31 miles to Morton and Highway 7. Turn left (north) on Highway 7 and drive 17 miles to Elbe and Highway 706. Turn right (east) on Highway 706 and drive to Ashford; continue for six miles to the resort on the right.

Contact: Mounthaven Resort, 360/569-2594, fax 360/569-2949, www.mounthaven.com.

⑨ SUNSHINE POINT

🥾 🎣 ❄️ 🐕 ♿ 🚐 ⛺

Scenic rating: 7

in Mount Rainier National Park

See map page 192

This campground is one of several in Mount Rainier National Park near the Nisqually entrance. The others include Ipsut Creek, Cougar Rock, White River, and Ohanapecosh. The elevation is 2,000 feet. See the *Mounthaven Resort* listing in this chapter for information about nearby sights and facilities.

RV sites, facilities: There are 18 sites for tents or RVs up to 25 feet (no hookups). Picnic tables and fire grills are provided. Drinking water and vault toilets are available. Some facilities are wheelchair accessible. Leashed pets are permitted in the camp but not on trails or in the wilderness.

Reservations, fees: Reservations are not accepted. Sites are $10 per night, plus a $10 per vehicle park entrance fee. Some credit cards accepted. Open year-round.

Directions: From Chehalis, drive south on I-5 for 10 miles to U.S. 12. Turn east and drive 31 miles to Morton and Highway 7. Turn left (north) on Highway 7 and drive 17 miles to Elbe and Highway 706. Turn left (east) on Highway 706 and drive 12 miles to the park entrance. The campground is just inside the park entrance on the right.

Contact: Mount Rainier National Park, 360/569-2211, fax 360/569-2170, www.nps .gov/mora.

10 COUGAR ROCK

Scenic rating: 9

in Mount Rainier National Park
See map page 192

Cougar Rock is a national park campground set at 3,180 feet elevation at the foot of awesome Mount Rainier. To the east lies the Nisqually Vista Trail, a beautiful 1.2-mile loop trail. It begins at the visitors center at Paradise and provides stellar views of Mount Rainier and the Nisqually Glacier. Fishing tends to be marginal. As in all national parks, no trout are stocked, and lakes without natural fisheries provide zilch. See the *Mounthaven Resort* listing in this chapter for information about nearby sights and facilities.

RV sites, facilities: There are 173 sites for tents or RVs up to 35 feet (no hookups) and five group sites for up to 24–40 people each. Picnic tables and fire grills are provided. Restrooms have flush toilets. Drinking water, a dump station, and an amphitheater are available. A general store is two miles away at Longmire. Some facilities are wheelchair accessible. Leashed pets are permitted.

Reservations, fees: Reservations are accepted at 800/365-CAMP (800/365-2267) or http:// reservations.nps.gov/. Sites are $12–15 per night, plus a $10 per vehicle park entrance fee. Group sites are $40–64 per night. Open late-May–mid-October.

Directions: From Tacoma, drive south on I-5 for five miles to Highway 512. Turn east on

Highway 512 and drive two miles to Highway 7. Turn right (south) on Highway 7 and drive to Elbe and Highway 706. Continue east on Highway 706 and drive 12 miles to the park entrance. Continue 11 miles to the campground entrance on the left (about two miles past the Longmire developed area).

Contact: Mount Rainier National Park, 360/569-2211, fax 360/569-2170, www.nps. gov/mora.

11 WHITE RIVER

Scenic rating: 7

on the White River in Mount Rainier National Park
See map page 192

This campground is on the White River at 4,400 feet elevation. The Glacier Basin Trail, a seven-mile round-trip, starts at the campground and leads along the Emmons Moraine for a short distance before ascending above it. A view of the Emmons Glacier, the largest glacier in the continental United States, can be attained by hiking the spur trail, the Emmons Moraine Trail. It is sometimes possible to spot mountain goats, as well as mountain climbers, on the surrounding mountain slopes. Note that another trail near camp leads a short distance (but vertically, for a rise of 2,200 feet) to the Sunrise Visitor Center. Local rangers recommend that trailers be left at the White River Campground and the 11-mile road trip to the visitors center be made by car. From there, you can take several trails that lead to backcountry lakes and glaciers. Also note that this campground is in what is considered to be a geo-hazard zone, where there is risk of a mudflow, although it hasn't happened in recent years.

RV sites, facilities: There are 112 sites for tents or RVs up to 20 feet (no hookups). Picnic tables and fire grills are provided. Flush toilets and drinking water are available. A small amphitheater is nearby. Some facilities are wheelchair accessible. Leashed pets are permitted in camp but not on trails or in the wilderness.

Reservations, fees: Reservations are not accepted. Sites are $12 per night, plus the $10

per vehicle park entrance fee. Some credit cards accepted. Open late-June–mid-September.
Directions: From Enumclaw, drive southeast on Highway 410 to the entrance of Mount Rainier National Park and White River Road. Turn right and drive seven miles to the campground on the left.
Contact: Mount Rainier National Park, 360/569-2211, fax 360/569-2170, www.nps.gov/mora.

12 SILVER SPRINGS

Scenic rating: 9

in Mount Baker–Snoqualmie National Forest
See map page 192

This campground along the White River on the northeastern border of Mount Rainier National Park offers a good alternative to the more crowded camps in the park. It's in a beautiful section of old-growth forest, primarily with Douglas fir, cedar, and hemlock, and is very scenic. Recreational options are limited to hiking. A U.S. Forest Service information center is one mile away from the campground entrance on Highway 410.
RV sites, facilities: There are 55 sites for tents or RVs up to 21 feet (no hookups) and one group tent site for up to 25 people. Picnic tables and fire grills are provided. Flush toilets, drinking water, and downed firewood for gathering are available. The group site has a picnic shelter. Some facilities are wheelchair accessible. Leashed pets are permitted.
Reservations, fees: Reservations are accepted and required for the group site at 877/444-6777 or www.ReserveUSA.com ($9 reservation fee). Sites are $16 per night, $7 per night extra vehicle fee. The group site is $75 per night. Open mid-May–early October, weather permitting.
Directions: From Enumclaw, drive east on Highway 410 for 31 miles (one mile south of the turnoff for Corral Pass) to the campground entrance on the right.
Contact: Mount Baker–Snoqualmie National Forest, White River Ranger District, 360/825-6585, fax 360/825-0660.

13 LODGEPOLE

Scenic rating: 6

on the American River in Wenatchee National Forest
See map page 192

This campground lies at an elevation of 3,500 feet along the American River, just eight miles east of the boundary of Mount Rainier National Park. See the description of Gateway Inn and RV Park for information on Mount Rainier. Fishing access is available nearby.
RV sites, facilities: There are 33 sites for tents or RVs up to 20 feet (no hookups). Picnic tables and fire grills are provided. Drinking water, vault toilets, garbage service, and firewood are available. Some facilities are wheelchair accessible. Leashed pets are permitted.
Reservations, fees: Reservations are accepted at 877/444-6777 or www.ReserveUSA.com ($9 reservation fee). Sites are $15–17 per night, $5 per night for each additional vehicle. Open mid-May–mid-September, weather permitting.
Directions: From Yakima, drive northwest on U.S. 12 for 18 miles to Highway 410. Bear northwest on Highway 410 and drive 40.5 miles (eight miles east of the national park boundary) to the campground on the right.
Contact: Okanogan and Wenatchee National Forests, Naches Ranger District, 509/653-1400, fax 509/653-2638.

14 PLEASANT VALLEY

Scenic rating: 7

on the American River in Wenatchee National Forest
See map page 192

This campground, at an elevation of 3,300 feet, provides a good base camp for a hiking or fishing trip. A trail from the camp follows Kettle Creek up to the American Ridge and Kettle Lake in the William O. Douglas Wilderness. It joins another trail that follows the ridge and then drops down to Bumping Lake. A U.S. Forest Service map is essential. You can fish

WASHINGTON

here for whitefish, steelhead, trout, and salmon in season; check regulations. In the winter, the area is popular with cross-country skiers.

RV sites, facilities: There are 16 sites for tents or RVs up to 32 feet (no hookups). Picnic tables and fire grills are provided. Drinking water, garbage service, vault toilets, and a picnic shelter are available. Downed firewood may be gathered. Some facilities are wheelchair accessible. Leashed pets are permitted.

Reservations, fees: Reservations are accepted at 877/444-6777 or www.ReserveUSA.com ($9 reservation fee). Sites are $15–17 per night, $5 per night for each additional vehicle. Open mid-May–late October, weather permitting.

Directions: From Yakima, drive northwest on U.S. 12 for 18 miles to Highway 410. Bear northwest on Highway 410 and drive 37 miles to the campground on the left.

Contact: Okanogan and Wenatchee National Forests, Naches Ranger District, 509/653-1400, fax 509/653-2638.

15 CEDAR SPRINGS

Scenic rating: 6

on the Bumping River in Wenatchee National Forest

See map page 192

The Bumping River runs alongside this camp, set at an elevation of 2,800 feet. Fishing here follows the seasons for trout, steelhead, and whitefish; check regulations. If you continue driving southwest for 11 miles on Forest Road 1800/Bumping River Road, you'll reach Bumping Lake, where recreation options abound.

RV sites, facilities: There are 15 sites for tents or RVs up to 22 feet (no hookups), including two double sites. Picnic tables and fire grills are provided. Drinking water and vault toilets are available. Leashed pets are permitted.

Reservations, fees: Reservations are accepted at 877/444-6777 or www.ReserveUSA.com ($9 reservation fee). Sites are $15–17 per night for single sites, $26 per night for double sites, and $5 per night for each additional vehicle. Open mid-May–mid-September, weather permitting.

Directions: From Yakima, drive northwest on U.S. 12 for 18 miles to Highway 410. Bear northwest on Highway 410 and drive 28.5 miles to the campground access road (Forest Road 1800/Bumping River Road). Turn left (southwest) and drive 0.5 mile to the campground on the left.

Contact: Okanogan and Wenatchee National Forests, Naches Ranger District, 509/653-1400, fax 509/653-2638.

16 LITTLE NACHES

Scenic rating: 5

on the Little Naches River in Wenatchee National Forest

See map page 192

This campground on the Little Naches River near the American River is just 0.1 mile off the road and 24 miles from Mount Rainier. The easy access is a major attraction for highway cruisers, but the location also means you can sometimes hear highway noise, and at four sites, you can see highway vehicles. Trees act as a buffer between the highway and the campground at other sites. Fishing access is available from camp. The elevation is 2,562 feet.

RV sites, facilities: There are 21 sites for tents or RVs up to 20 feet (no hookups) and two double sites. Picnic tables and fire grills are provided. Drinking water, vault toilets, and garbage service are available. Some facilities are wheelchair accessible. Leashed pets are permitted.

Reservations, fees: Reservations are accepted at 877/444-6777 or www.ReserveUSA.com ($9 reservation fee). Call for current rates. Open mid-May–mid-September, weather permitting.

Directions: From Yakima, drive northwest on U.S. 12 for 18 miles to Highway 410. Bear northwest on Highway 410 and drive 25 miles to the campground access road (Forest Road 1900). Turn left and drive 100 yards to the campground on the left.

Contact: Okanogan and Wenatchee National Forests, Naches Ranger District, 509/653-1400, fax 509/653-2638.

17 SAWMILL FLAT

Scenic rating: 6

on the Naches River in Wenatchee National Forest
See map page 192

This campground on the Naches River near Halfway Flat is used by motorcyclists more than by other types of campers. It offers fishing access and a hiking trail that leads west from Halfway Flat campground for several miles into the backcountry. Fishing is primarily for trout in summer, whitefish in winter; check regulations. Another trailhead is at Boulder Cave to the south. See a U.S. Forest Service map for details.

RV sites, facilities: There are 24 sites for tents or RVs up to 24 feet (no hookups). Picnic tables and fire grills are provided. Drinking water, vault toilets, and an Adirondack group shelter are available. Downed firewood may be gathered. Some facilities are wheelchair accessible. A camp host is available in summer. Leashed pets are permitted.

Reservations, fees: Reservations are accepted at 877/444-6777 or www.ReserveUSA.com ($9 reservation fee). Sites are $15–17 per night, $5 per night for each additional vehicle. Open mid-May–late October, weather permitting.

Directions: From Yakima, drive northwest on U.S. 12 for 18 miles to Highway 410. Bear northwest on Highway 410 and drive 23.5 miles to the campground on the left.

Contact: Okanogan and Wenatchee National Forests, Naches Ranger District, 509/653-1400, fax 509/653-2638.

18 SODA SPRINGS

Scenic rating: 6

on the Bumping River in Wenatchee National Forest
See map page 192

Highlights at this camp along Bumping River include natural mineral springs and a nature trail. The mineral spring is next to a trail across the river from the campground, where the water bubbles up out of the ground. This cold-water spring is popular with some campers for soaking

and drinking. Many campers use this camp for access to nearby Bumping Lake. Fishing access is available. A sheltered picnic area is provided.

RV sites, facilities: There are 26 sites for tents or RVs up to 30 feet (no hookups). Picnic tables and fire grills are provided. Drinking water, vault toilets, a picnic shelter with a fireplace, and garbage service are available. Some facilities are wheelchair accessible. Leashed pets are permitted.

Reservations, fees: Reservations are accepted at 877/444-6777 or www.ReserveUSA.com ($9 reservation fee). Sites are $15–17 per night, $5 per night for each additional vehicle. Open mid-May–late October, weather permitting.

Directions: From Yakima, drive northwest on U.S. 12 for 18 miles to Highway 410. Turn left (northwest) on Highway 410 and drive 28.5 miles to Forest Road 1800. Turn left (southwest) and drive five miles (along the Bumping River) to the campground on the left.

Contact: Okanogan and Wenatchee National Forests, Naches Ranger District, 509/653-1400, fax 509/653-2638.

19 LOWER BUMPING LAKE

Scenic rating: 7

on Bumping Lake in Wenatchee National Forest
See map page 192

This popular campground is at an elevation of 3,200 feet near Bumping Lake amid a forest of primarily lodgepole pine. Bumping Lake features water activities such as waterskiing, fishing for salmon and trout, and swimming. A boat ramp is available near the camp. Several hiking trails go into the William O. Douglas Wilderness surrounding the lake.

RV sites, facilities: There are 23 sites for tents or RVs up to 50 feet (no hookups). Picnic tables and fire grills are provided. Drinking water, vault toilets, and a dump station are available. Some facilities are wheelchair accessible. Boat-launching facilities are nearby (see the listing in this chapter for *Upper Bumping Lake*). Leashed pets are permitted.

Reservations, fees: Reservations are accepted

at 877/444-6777 or www.ReserveUSA.com ($9 reservation fee). Sites are $15–17 per night, $32 for a double site, and $5 per night for each additional vehicle. Open mid-May–mid-September, weather permitting.

Directions: From Yakima, drive northwest on U.S. 12 for 18 miles to Highway 410. Turn left (northwest) on Highway 410 and drive 28.5 miles to Forest Road 1800. Turn left (southwest) and drive 11 miles (along the Bumping River); look for the campground entrance road on the right.

Contact: Okanogan and Wenatchee National Forest, Naches Ranger District, 509/653-1400, fax 509/653-2638.

20 UPPER BUMPING LAKE

Scenic rating: 7

on Bumping Lake in Wenatchee National Forest
See map page 192

Woods and water—this spot has them both. The cold lake is stocked with trout, and the nearby boat launch makes it a winner for campers with boats. This popular camp fills up quickly on summer weekends. Various water activities are allowed at Bumping Lake, including waterskiing, fishing (for salmon and trout), and swimming. A picnic area is adjacent to the boat facilities. In addition, several hiking trails lead into the William O. Douglas Wilderness surrounding the lake. This is one of the more developed camps in the area.

RV sites, facilities: There are 45 sites for tents or RVs up to 30 feet (no hookups). Picnic tables and fire grills are provided. Drinking water, vault toilets, and firewood are available. Boat docks, launching facilities, and a dump station are nearby. Some facilities are wheelchair accessible. Leashed pets are permitted.

Reservations, fees: Reservations are accepted at 877/444-6777 or www.ReserveUSA.com ($9 reservation fee). Sites are $15–17 per night, $5 per night for each additional vehicle. Open mid-May–late September, weather permitting.

Directions: From Yakima, drive northwest on U.S. 12 for 18 miles to Highway 410. Turn left (northwest) on Highway 410 and drive 28.5 miles

to Forest Road 1800. Turn left (southwest) and drive 11 miles (along the Bumping River); look for the campground entrance road on the right.

Contact: Okanogan and Wenatchee National Forests, Naches Ranger District, 509/653-1400, fax 509/653-2638.

21 BIG CREEK

Scenic rating: 8

on Big Creek in Gifford Pinchot National Forest
See map page 192

This camp is useful as an overflow spot for Mount Rainier Sound–area campers. It is along a stream next to a rural residential area in a forest setting made up of Douglas fir, western hemlock, western red cedar, and bigleaf and vine maple.

RV sites, facilities: There are 29 sites for tents or RVs up to 22 feet (no hookups). Picnic tables and fire rings are provided. Drinking water, vault toilets, and firewood are available. Leashed pets are permitted.

Reservations, fees: Reservations are accepted at 877/444-6777 or www.ReserveUSA.com ($9 reservation fee). Sites are $15 per night, $30 for a double site per night, and $5 per night for each additional vehicle. Open mid-May–mid-September.

Directions: On I-5, drive to Exit 68 (south of Chehalis) and U.S. 12. Turn east on U.S. 12 and drive 62 miles to Packwood and Forest Road 52/Skate Creek Road. Turn left (northwest) and drive 23 miles to the campground on the left.

Contact: Gifford Pinchot National Forest, Cowlitz Valley Ranger District, 360/497-1100, fax 360/497-1102.

22 OHANAPECOSH

Scenic rating: 8

on the Ohanapecosh River in Mount Rainier National Park
See map page 192

This camp is at an elevation of 1,914 feet at the foot of North America's most beautiful volcano,

14,411-foot Mount Rainier. It is also set along the Ohanapecosh River, adjacent to the Ohanapecosh Visitor Center, which features exhibits on the history of the forest, plus visitor information. A 0.5-mile loop trail leads from the campground, behind the visitors center, to Ohanapecosh Hot Springs. The Silver Falls Trail, a three-mile loop trail, follows the Ohanapecosh River to 75-foot Silver Falls. Warning: Do not climb on the wet rocks near the waterfall; they are wet and slippery. Note that Stevens Canyon Road heading west and Highway 123 heading north are closed by snowfall in winter.

RV sites, facilities: There are 188 sites for tents or RVs up to 32 feet (no hookups) and one group site for up to 25 people. Picnic tables and fire rings are provided. Flush toilets, drinking water, and a dump station are available. An amphitheater is nearby. Some facilities are wheelchair accessible. Leashed pets are permitted in camp but not on trails.

Reservations, fees: Reservations are accepted at 800/365-CAMP (800/365-2267) or http://reservations.nps.gov. Sites are $12–15 per night, plus a $10 per vehicle park entrance fee. The group site is $40 per night. Some credit cards accepted. Open mid-May–September.

Directions: On I-5, drive to Exit 68 (south of Chehalis) and U.S. 12. Turn east on U.S. 12 and drive 72 miles (seven miles past Packwood) to Highway 123. Turn left (north) and drive 6.5 miles to the Ohanapecosh entrance to the park. As you enter the park, the camp is on the left, next to the visitors center.

Contact: Mount Rainier National Park, 360/569-2211, fax 360/569-2170, www.nps.gov/mora.

23 PEPPERTREE WEST MOTOR INN & RV PARK

Scenic rating: 5

in Centralia

See map page 192

If you're driving I-5 and looking for a stopover, this spot is a good choice for tent campers and RVers. Surrounded by Chehalis Valley farmland, it's near an 18-hole golf course, hiking trails, and tennis courts.

RV sites, facilities: There are 42 sites with full or partial hookups (30 amps) for RVs of any length, a grassy area for tents, and 26 motel rooms. Most sites are pull-through. Restrooms have flush toilets and coin showers. Drinking water, cable TV, a dump station, a coin laundry, and ice are available. Boat-launching facilities are nearby. A store, propane, and a café are also nearby. Leashed pets are permitted.

Reservations, fees: Reservations are accepted. Call for current rates. Some credit cards accepted. Open year-round.

Directions: From Centralia on I-5, take Exit 81 to Melon Street. Turn west and then take the first right (Alder Street) to the park (in the southeast corner of Centralia).

Contact: Peppertree West Motor Inn & RV Park, 360/736-1124, fax 360/807-9779.

24 STAN HEDWALL PARK

Scenic rating: 5

on the Newaukum River

See map page 192

This park is along the Newaukum River, and its proximity to I-5 makes it a good layover spot for vacation travelers. Recreational opportunities include fishing, hiking, and golf; an 18-hole course and hiking trails are nearby.

RV sites, facilities: There are 29 sites for tents or RVs of any length with partial hookups (30 and 50 amps). Picnic tables are provided, and some sites have fire pits. Restrooms have flush toilets and coin showers. Drinking water, a dump station, cable TV, and a playground are available. Propane gas, a store, a café, and a coin laundry are within one mile. Leashed pets are permitted.

Reservations, fees: Reservations are accepted. Sites are $15 per night. Open April–November, weather permitting.

Directions: From Chehalis on I-5, take Exit 76 to Rice Road. Turn south and drive just over 0.1 mile to the park.

WASHINGTON

Contact: Stan Hedwall Park, City of Chehalis, 360/748-0271, fax 360/748-6993.

25 LEWIS AND CLARK STATE PARK

Scenic rating: 8

near Chehalis
See map page 192

The highlight of this state park is an immense old-growth forest that contains some good hiking trails and a 0.5-mile nature trail. This famous grove lost half of its old-growth trees along the highway when they were blown down in the legendary 1962 Columbus Day storm. This was a cataclysmic event for what is one of the last major stands of old-growth forest in the state. The park covers 621 acres and features primarily Douglas fir and red cedar, wetlands, and dense vegetation. There are eight miles of trails, including five miles of horse trails. June is Youth Fishing Month, when youngsters age 14 and younger can fish the creek. Jackson House tours, in which visitors can see a pioneer home built in 1845 north of the Columbia River, are available year-round by appointment.

RV sites, facilities: There are 25 sites for tents or RVs (no hookups), eight sites with full hookups (30 amps) for RVs up to 60 feet, five equestrian sites, and two group camps for up to 50 people each. A bunkhouse is also available. Picnic tables and fire grills are provided. Restrooms have flush toilets and coin showers. Drinking water, a small store, firewood, a picnic area, an amphitheater, reservable day-use area, horseshoe pits, volleyball, and badminton are available. Leashed pets are permitted.

Reservations, fees: Reservations are not accepted for individual sites. Reservations for the bunkhouse are accepted at 360/902-8600. Sites are $15–21 per night, equestrian sites are $10 per night, plus $10 per extra vehicle per night. Group sites are $2.15 per person per night with a 20-person minimum. Open year-round, weather permitting.

Directions: From Chehalis, drive south on I-5

six miles to Exit 68 and U.S. 12. Turn east on U.S. 12 for 2.5 miles to Jackson Highway. Turn right and drive two miles to the park entrance on the right.

Contact: Lewis and Clark State Park, 360/864-2643, fax 360/864-2515; state park information 360/902-8844, www.parks.wa.gov.

26 IKE KINSWA STATE PARK

Scenic rating: 8

on Mayfield Lake
See map page 192

This state park sits alongside the north shore of Mayfield Lake. The park features 8.5 miles of shore, forested campsites, 2.5 miles of hiking trails, and two miles of bike trails. Mayfield Lake is a treasure trove of recreational possibilities. Fishing is a year-round affair here, with trout and tiger muskie often good. Boating, waterskiing, swimming, and driftwood collecting are all popular. The park is named after Ike Kinswa, a prominent member of the Cowlitz tribe. Two fish hatcheries are nearby. A spectacular view of Mount St. Helens can be found at a vista point 11 miles east. This popular campground often fills on summer weekends. Be sure to reserve well in advance.

RV sites, facilities: There are 28 developed tent sites, 73 sites with full or partial hookups (30 amps) for RVs up to 32 feet, and two primitive tent sites. Picnic tables and fire grills are provided. Restrooms have flush toilets and coin showers. Drinking water, a dump station, a seasonal store, a playground, a picnic area, horseshoe pits, and firewood are available. Some facilities are wheelchair accessible. Boat docks and launching facilities are nearby. Leashed pets are permitted.

Reservations, fees: Reservations are accepted at 888/CAMP-OUT (888/226-7688) or www.parks.wa.gov/reservations ($7 reservation fee). Sites are $16 per night for tent sites, $22–27 per night for RV sites, $10 per night for hike-in/bike-in sites, $6 per extra vehicle per night. Some credit cards accepted. Open year-round.

Directions: From Chehalis, drive south on I-5

six miles to Exit 68 and U.S. 12. Turn east on U.S. 12 and drive 14 miles to Silver Creek Road (State Route 122). Turn left (north) and drive 1.9 miles to a Y intersection. Bear right on State Route 111/Harmony Road and drive 1.6 miles to the park entrance.

Contact: Ike Kinswa State Park, 360/983-3402, fax 360/983-3332; state park information 360/902-8844, www.parks.wa.gov.

27 HARMONY LAKESIDE RV PARK

Scenic rating: 7

near Mayfield Lake
See map page 192

This park fills up on weekends in July, August, and September. It is on Mayfield Lake, a 10-mile-long lake with numerous recreational activities, including fishing, boating, riding personal watercraft, and waterskiing. Some sites feature lake views. Nearby Ike Kinswa State Park is a side-trip option.

RV sites, facilities: There are 80 sites for tents or RVs of any length with full or partial hookups (30 and 50 amps). Some sites are pull-through. Picnic tables and fire grills are provided. Restrooms have coin showers. Drinking water, a dump station, cable TV, modem and Wi-Fi access, ice, firewood, a pay phone, boat docks, and launching facilities are available. Group facilities, including a banquet and meeting room, are also available. Leashed pets are permitted.

Reservations, fees: Reservations are recommended. Sites are $32–48 per night, plus $2.50 per pet per night. Winter and monthly rates available. Some credit cards accepted. Open year-round.

Directions: From Chehalis, drive south on I-5 for six miles to Exit 68 and U.S. 12. Turn east on U.S. 12 and drive 21 miles to Mossyrock (Highway 122). Turn left (north) and drive 3.5 miles to the park on the left.

Contact: Harmony Lakeside RV Park, 360/983-3804, fax 360/983-8345, www.mayfield lake.com.

28 MAYFIELD LAKE PARK

Scenic rating: 7

on Mayfield Lake
See map page 192

Mayfield Lake is the centerpiece of this 50-acre park. Insider's tip: Campsites 42–54 are set along the lake's shoreline. The camp has a relaxing atmosphere and comfortable, wooded sites. Fishing is primarily for trout, bass, and silver salmon. Other recreational activities include waterskiing, swimming, and boating. For a great side trip, tour nearby Mount St. Helens.

RV sites, facilities: There are 54 sites for tents or RVs up to 45 feet (no hookups) and a group camp (15 sites) for tents or RVs up to 45 feet. Picnic tables and fire rings are provided. Restrooms have flush toilets and coin showers. Drinking water, a pay phone, and a day-use area with a reservable picnic shelter, a playground, horseshoe pits, and a volleyball court are available. A dump station is within 0.5 mile. Some facilities are wheelchair accessible. Leashed pets are permitted.

Reservations, fees: Reservations are accepted at 888/CAMP-OUT (888/226-7688) or www.tacomapower.com; $7 reservation fee and $15 group reservation fee. Sites are $16–20 per night, $10 per extra vehicle per night. The group camp is $150 per night. Open mid-April–mid-October; the group camp is open Memorial Day weekend–mid-October.

Directions: From Longview, drive north on I-5 to Exit 68 and U.S. 12. Turn east on U.S. 12 and drive approximately 17 miles to Beach Road. Turn left and drive 0.25 mile to the park entrance.

Contact: Mayfield Lake Park, 360/985-2364 or 888/502-8690, fax 360/985-7825, www.tacomapower.com.

29 MOSSYROCK PARK

Scenic rating: 8

on Riffe Lake
See map page 192

This park is along the southwest shore of Riffe Lake. It is an extremely popular campground.

For anglers, it provides the best of both worlds: a boat launch on Riffe Lake, which offers coho salmon, rainbow trout, and bass, and nearby Swofford Pond, a 240-acre pond stocked with rainbow trout, brown trout, bass, catfish, and bluegill. Swofford Pond is south of Mossyrock on Swofford Road; no gas motors are permitted. This campground provides access to a 0.5-mile loop nature trail. Bald eagles and osprey nest on the north side of the lake in the 14,000-acre Cowlitz Wildlife Area.

RV sites, facilities: There are 76 sites for tents or RVs of any length with partial hookups (30 amps), 76 sites for tents or RVs (no hookups), 12 walk-in sites, one group camp (60 sites) for tents or RVs of any length that has partial hookups, and a primitive group camp (10 sites) for tents or RVs of any length. Picnic tables and fire rings are provided. Restrooms have flush toilets and coin showers. Drinking water, a dump station, seasonal convenience store, seasonal snack bar, a coin laundry, fish-cleaning stations, a boat launch, a playground, reservable picnic area, a swimming area, a horseshoe pit, a volleyball net, BMX track, camp host, and interpretive displays are available. Some facilities are wheelchair accessible. Leashed pets are permitted.

Reservations, fees: Reservations are accepted at 888/CAMP-OUT (888/226-7688) or www.tacomapower.com ($7 reservation fee and $15 group reservation fee). Sites are $16–22 per night, walk-in sites are $11 per night, and it's $10 per extra vehicle per night. The primitive group camp is $100 per night, and the other group camp is $16–20 per site per night with a minimum of five sites. Some credit cards accepted in summer. Open year-round, excluding December 20–January 1.

Directions: From Chehalis, drive south on I-5 six miles to Exit 68 and Highway 12 eastbound. Take Highway 12 east and drive 21 miles to Williams Street (flashing yellow light). Turn right and drive several blocks in the town of Mossyrock to a T intersection with State Street. Turn left and drive 3.5 miles

(becomes Mossyrock Road East, then Ajlune Road) to the park. Ajlune Road leads right into the park.

Contact: Mossyrock Park, Tacoma Power, 360/983-3900 or 888/502-8690, fax 360/983-3906, www.tacomapower.com.

30 TAIDNAPAM PARK

Scenic rating: 8

on Riffe Lake

See map page 192

This 50-acre park is at the east end of Riffe Lake. Nestled in a cover of Douglas fir and maple, it is surrounded by thousands of acres of undeveloped greenbelt. Fishing is permitted year-round at the lake, with coho salmon, rainbow trout, and bass available. This camp was named after the Upper Cowlitz Indians, also known as "Taidnapam."

RV sites, facilities: There are 52 sites for tents or RVs of any length with full or partial hookups (30 amps), 16 walk-in sites, and one group camp (22 sites) for tents or RVs of any length that has full or partial hookups. Picnic tables and fire rings are provided. Restrooms have flush toilets and coin showers. Drinking water, a dump station, a fishing bridge, fish-cleaning stations, a boat launch, a reservable picnic shelter, a playground, a swimming beach, a horseshoe pit, a volleyball net, and interpretive displays are available. Some facilities are wheelchair accessible. Leashed pets are permitted.

Reservations, fees: Reservations are accepted at 888/CAMP-OUT (888/226-7688) or www.tacomapower.com ($7 reservation fee). Group reservations are accepted at 360/497-7707 ($15 group reservation fee). Sites are $22–23 per night, $10 per extra vehicle per night, and walk-in sites are $11 per night. The group camp is $22–23 per site per night with a minimum of 10 sites. Some credit cards accepted in summer season. Open year-round, excluding December 20–January 1.

Directions: From Chehalis, drive south on I-5

to Exit 68 and Highway 12 eastbound. Take Highway 12 east and drive 37 miles (five miles past Morton) to Kosmos Road. Turn right and drive 200 yards to No. 100 Champion Haul Road. Turn left and drive four miles to the park entrance on the right.

Contact: Taidnapam Park, Tacoma Power, 360/497-7707 or 888/502-8690, fax 360/497-7708, www.tacomapower.com.

31 IRON CREEK

Scenic rating: 7

on the Cispus River in Gifford Pinchot National Forest

See map page 192

This popular U.S. Forest Service campground is along the Cispus River near its confluence with Iron Creek. Trout fishing is available. The landscape features primarily Douglas fir, western red cedar, and old-growth forest on fairly flat terrain. The camp is also along the access route that leads to the best viewing areas on the eastern flank for Mount St. Helens. Take a 25-mile drive to Windy Ridge Vista Point for a breathtaking view of Spirit Lake and the blast zone of the volcano.

RV sites, facilities: There are 98 sites for tents or RVs up to 40 feet (no hookups). Picnic tables and fire rings are provided. Drinking water, vault toilets, and firewood are available. Some facilities are wheelchair accessible. Leashed pets are permitted.

Reservations, fees: Reservations are accepted at 877/444-6777 or www.ReserveUSA.com ($9 reservation fee). Sites are $16–18 per night, $32 per night for a double site, $5 per extra vehicle per night. Open mid-May–mid-September, weather permitting.

Directions: From Chehalis, drive south on I-5 for six miles to Exit 68 and U.S. 12. Turn east on U.S. 12 and drive 48 miles to Randle and Highway 131. Turn south on Highway 131 and drive one mile (the highway becomes Forest Road 25). Continue south on Forest Road 25 and drive nine miles to a fork. Bear left at

the fork, continue across the bridge, turn left, and drive two miles to the campground entrance on the left (along the south shore of the Cispus River).

Contact: Gifford Pinchot National Forest, Cowlitz Valley Ranger District, 360/497-1100, fax 360/497-1102.

32 TOWER ROCK

Scenic rating: 5

on the Cispus River in Gifford Pinchot National Forest

See map page 192

This campground along the Cispus River is an alternative to nearby Iron Creek and North Fork. It has shaded and sunny sites, with lots of trees and plenty of room. The camp is fairly close to the river, and some sites feature river frontage. It is also fairly flat and forested with Douglas fir, western hemlock, red cedar, and bigleaf maple. Fishing for trout is popular here.

RV sites, facilities: There are 22 sites for tents or RVs up to 22 feet (no hookups). Picnic tables and fire grills are provided. Drinking water, vault toilets, and firewood are available. Leashed pets are permitted.

Reservations, fees: Reservations are accepted at 877/444-6777 or www.ReserveUSA.com ($9 reservation fee). Call for current rates. Open mid-May–mid-September, weather permitting.

Directions: From Chehalis, drive south on I-5 for six miles to Exit 68 and U.S. 12. Turn east on U.S. 12 and drive 48 miles to Randle and Highway 131. Turn right (south) on Highway 131 and drive one mile to Forest Road 23. Turn left on Forest Road 23 and drive eight miles to Forest Road 28. Turn right and drive two miles to Forest Road 76. Turn right and drive two miles to the campground entrance road on the right.

Contact: Gifford Pinchot National Forest, Cowlitz Valley Ranger District, 360/497-1100, fax 360/497-1102.

33 PACKWOOD RV PARK

Scenic rating: 6

in Packwood

See map page 192

This is a pleasant campground, especially in the fall when the maples turn color. Groups are welcome. Mount Rainier National Park is just 25 miles north, and this camp provides a good alternative if the park is full. Nearby recreation options include a riding stable. Note that some sites are filled with monthly renters.

RV sites, facilities: There are 88 sites for RVs of any length, most with full hookups (30 amps), and 15 tent sites. Some sites are pull-through. Picnic tables are provided at some sites, and portable fire pits are available on request. Restrooms have flush toilets and showers. Cable TV and a coin laundry are available. A café, store, diesel and propane gas, restaurants, and library with modem access are available within walking distance. Leashed pets are permitted.

Reservations, fees: Reservations are accepted. Sites are $16–26 per night, $3 per person per night for more than two people. Open year-round.

Directions: On I-5, drive to Exit 68 (south of Chehalis) and U.S. 12. Turn east on U.S. 12 and drive 65 miles to Packwood. The park is on the left (north) side of the highway in town at 12985 U.S. 12.

Contact: Packwood RV Park, 360/494-5145.

34 LA WIS WIS

Scenic rating: 9

on the Cowlitz River in Gifford Pinchot National Forest

See map page 192

This camp is ideally located for day trips to Mount Rainier and Mount St. Helens. It's set at an elevation of 1,400 feet along the Clear Fork of the Cowlitz River, near the confluence with the Ohanapecosh River. Trout fishing is an option. The landscape features an old-growth forest of Douglas fir, western hemlock, western red

cedar, and Pacific yew, with an undergrowth of bigleaf maple. A 200-yard trail provides access to the Blue Hole on the Ohanapecosh River, a deep pool designated by an observation point and interpretive signs. Another trail leads less than 0.25 mile to Purcell Falls. The entrance to Mount Rainier National Park is about seven miles south of the camp.

RV sites, facilities: There are 115 sites for tents or RVs up to 24 feet (no hookups). Picnic tables and fire rings are provided. Flush and vault toilets, drinking water, and firewood are available. Some facilities are wheelchair accessible. Leashed pets are permitted.

Reservations, fees: Reservations are accepted at 877/444-6777 or www.ReserveUSA.com ($9 reservation fee). Sites are $16–32 per night, $5 per extra vehicle per night. Open mid-May–mid-September, weather permitting.

Directions: On I-5, drive to Exit 68 (south of Chehalis) and U.S. 12. Turn east on U.S. 12 and drive 69 miles (about six miles past Packwood) to Forest Road 1272. Turn left and drive 0.5 mile to the campground on the left.

Contact: Gifford Pinchot National Forest, Cowlitz Valley Ranger District, 360/497-1100, fax 360/497-1102.

35 WHITE PASS

Scenic rating: 7

on Leech Lake in Wenatchee National Forest

See map page 192

This campground on the shore of Leech Lake sits at an elevation of 4,500 feet and boasts nearby trails leading into the Goat Rocks Wilderness to the south and the William O. Douglas Wilderness to the north. A trailhead for the Pacific Crest Trail is also nearby. Beautiful Leech Lake is popular for fly-fishing for rainbow and Eastern brook trout. Note that this is the only type of fishing allowed here; check regulations. No gas motors are permitted on Leech Lake. White Pass Ski Area is across the highway, less than 0.25 mile away.

RV sites, facilities: There are 10 sites for tents

or RVs up to 20 feet (no hookups). Picnic tables and fire grills are provided. Vault toilets and firewood are available, but there is no drinking water. A store, a coin laundry, and ice are within one mile. Boat-launching facilities are nearby. No gas motors on boats are allowed; electric motors are permitted. Leashed pets are permitted.

Reservations, fees: Reservations are not accepted. Sites are $5 per night per vehicle. Open mid-May–mid-September, weather permitting.

Directions: On I-5, drive to Exit 68 (south of Chehalis) and U.S. 12. Turn east on U.S. 12 and drive 81 miles (one mile past the White Pass Ski Area) to the campground entrance road on the left side. Turn left (north) and drive 200 yards to Leech Lake and the campground.

Contact: Okanogan and Wenatchee National Forests, Naches Ranger District, 509/653-1400, fax 509/653-2638.

36 DOG LAKE

Scenic rating: 5

on Dog Lake in Wenatchee National Forest
See map page 192

This campground is on the shore of Dog Lake at 3,400 feet elevation. Fishing can be good for native rainbow trout, and the lake is good for hand-launched boats, such as canoes and prams. Nearby trails lead into the William O. Douglas Wilderness. See a U.S. Forest Service map for details.

RV sites, facilities: There are 11 sites for tents or RVs up to 20 feet (no hookups). Picnic tables and fire grills are provided. Vault toilets are available, but there is no drinking water. Leashed pets are permitted. No horses are allowed in the campground.

Reservations, fees: Reservations are not accepted. Call for current rates. Open mid-May–late September, weather permitting.

Directions: On I-5, drive to Exit 68 (south of Chehalis) and U.S. 12. Turn east on U.S. 12 and drive 84 miles (three miles past the White Pass Ski Area) to the campground entrance road on the left side.

Contact: Okanogan and Wenatchee National Forests, Naches Ranger District, 509/653-1400, fax 509/653-2638.

37 CLEAR LAKE SOUTH

Scenic rating: 7

in Wenatchee National Forest
See map page 192

This campground (elevation 3,100 feet) is near the east shore of Clear Lake, which is the forebay for Rimrock Lake. Fishing and swimming are recreation options. For winter travelers, several Sno-Parks in the area offer snowmobiling and cross-country skiing. Many hiking trails lie to the north; see a U.S. Forest Service map.

RV sites, facilities: There are 32 sites for tents or RVs up to 22 feet (no hookups). Picnic tables and fire grills are provided. Drinking water and vault toilets are available. Downed firewood may be gathered. Boat-launching facilities are nearby. Some facilities are wheelchair accessible. Leashed pets are permitted.

Reservations, fees: Reservations are not accepted. Sites are $10 per night, $5 per extra vehicle per night. Open mid-May–late October, weather permitting.

Directions: From Yakima, drive northwest on I-82 for 17 miles to the junction with Highway 410. Turn west on U.S. 12 and drive 31 miles to Forest Road 1200. Turn left (south) and drive one mile to Forest Road 1200-740. Continue south and drive 0.25 mile to the campground.

Contact: Okanogan and Wenatchee National Forests, Naches Ranger District, 509/653-1400, fax 509/653-2638.

38 CLEAR LAKE NORTH

Scenic rating: 7

on Clear Lake in Wenatchee National Forest
See map page 192

This primitive campground is along the shore of Clear Lake at an elevation of 3,100 feet; it gets relatively little use. A five-mph speed limit keeps the lake quiet and ideal for fishing, which is often good for rainbow trout. It is stocked regularly in the summer. Clear Lake is the forebay for Rimrock Lake. Swimming is allowed.

RV sites, facilities: There are 33 sites for tents or RVs up to 22 feet (no hookups). Picnic tables and fire grills are provided. Vault toilets and garbage service are available. There is no drinking water at Clear Lake North, but there is drinking water at Clear Lake South campground. Some facilities are wheelchair accessible. Boat docks and launching facilities are nearby. Leashed pets are permitted.

Reservations, fees: Reservations are not accepted. Call for current rates. Open mid-May–mid-September, weather permitting.

Directions: From Yakima, drive northwest on I-12 for 17 miles to the junction with Highway 410. Turn west on U.S. 12 and drive 31 miles to Forest Road 1200. Turn left (south) and drive 0.25 mile to Forest Road 1200-740. Continue south for 0.5 mile to the campground.

Contact: Okanogan and Wenatchee National Forests, Naches Ranger District, 509/653-1400, fax 509/653-2638.

39 SILVER BEACH RESORT

Scenic rating: 8

on Rimrock Lake
See map page 192

This resort along the shore of Rimrock Lake is one of several camps in the immediate area. It's very scenic, with beautiful lakefront sites. Hiking trails, marked bike trails, a full-service marina, a sandy swimming beach, and a riding stable are close by.

RV sites, facilities: There are 46 sites for tents or RVs up to 40 feet with full or partial hookups (20 and 30 amps), 46 sites for tents or RVs up to 40 feet (no hookups), three cabins with kitchens, and 16 motel rooms. Some sites are pull-through. Picnic tables and fire pits are provided. Restrooms have flush toilets and coin showers. A café, a convenience store, a

dump station, bait and tackle, propane gas, ice, a playground, boat docks, launching facilities, and boat and personal watercraft rentals are available. Leashed pets are permitted.

Reservations, fees: Reservations are accepted. Sites are $15–20 per night, $5 per extra vehicle per night. Some credit cards accepted. Open year-round, with limited winter facilities.

Directions: From Yakima, drive northwest on U.S. 12 for 40 miles to the resort on the left.

Contact: Silver Beach Resort, 509/672-2500, www.silverbeach.biz.

40 INDIAN CREEK

Scenic rating: 7

on Rimrock Lake in Wenatchee National Forest
See map page 192

Fishing, swimming, and waterskiing are among the activities at this shorefront campground on Rimrock Lake (elevation 3,000 feet). The camp is adjacent to Rimrock Lake Marina and Silver Beach Resort. This is a developed lake and an extremely popular campground, often filling on summer weekends. Fishing is often good for rainbow trout. The treasured Indian Creek Trail and many other excellent hiking trails about 5–10 miles north of the campground lead into the William O. Douglas Wilderness.

RV sites, facilities: There are 39 sites for tents or RVs up to 45 feet (no hookups). Picnic tables and fire grills are provided. Drinking water and vault toilets are available. Downed firewood may be gathered. A café, a store, ice, boat docks, launching facilities, and rentals are nearby. Leashed pets are permitted.

Reservations, fees: Reservations are accepted at 877/444-6777 or www.ReserveUSA.com ($9 reservation fee). Sites are $15–17 per night, $5 per extra vehicle per night. Open mid-May–mid-September, weather permitting.

Directions: From Yakima, drive northwest on I-82 for 17 miles to the junction with Highway 410. Turn west on U.S. 12 and drive 20 miles to Rimrock Lake and the campground entrance at the lake.

Contact: Okanogan and Wenatchee National Forests, Naches Ranger District, 509/653-1400, fax 509/653-2638.

41 NORTH FORK & NORTH FORK GROUP

🚶 🚴 🎣 🐕 ♿ 🚙 ⛺

Scenic rating: 6

on the Cispus River in Gifford Pinchot National Forest

See map page 192

This campground offers single sites, double sites, and group camps, with the North Cispus River flowing between the sites for individual and group use. The elevation is 1,500 feet. The campsites are set back from the river in a well-forested area. A national forest map details the backcountry access to the Valley Trail, which is routed up the Cispus River Valley for 16.7 miles. This trailhead provides access for hikers, bikers, all-terrain vehicles, and horses. Note that if you explore Road 2300-083 15 miles west you will find Layser Cave, a Native American archaeological site that is open to the public.

RV sites, facilities: There are 33 sites for tents or RVs up to 32 feet (no hookups) and three group camps that can accommodate up to 20–40 people each. Picnic tables and fire grills are provided. Drinking water, vault toilets, and firewood are available. Some facilities are wheelchair accessible. Leashed pets are permitted.

Reservations, fees: Reservations are accepted at 877/444-6777 or www.ReserveUSA.com ($9 reservation fee). Sites are $16–18 per night, $32 per night for double sites, $5 per extra vehicle per night, and $75–88 per night for group sites. Open mid-May–mid-September, weather permitting.

Directions: From Chehalis, drive south on I-5 for six miles to Exit 68 and U.S. 12. Turn east on U.S. 12 and drive 48 miles to Randle and Highway 131. Turn right (south) on Highway 131 and drive one mile to Forest Road 23. Bear left and drive 11 miles to the campground on the left.

Contact: Gifford Pinchot National Forest,

Cowlitz Ranger District, 360/497-1100, fax 360/497-1102.

42 WALUPT LAKE

🚶 🚣 🎣 🚤 🐕 🚙 ⛺

Scenic rating: 8

on Walupt Lake in Gifford Pinchot National Forest

See map page 192

This popular spot, set at 3,900 feet elevation along the shore of Walupt Lake, is a good base camp for a multiday vacation. The trout fishing is often good here; check regulations. But note that only small boats are advisable here because the launch area at the lake is shallow, and it can take a four-wheel-drive vehicle to get a boat in and out. A small swimming beach is nearby. In addition, several nearby trails lead into the backcountry and to other smaller alpine lakes. One trail out of the campground leads to the upper end of the lake, then launches off to the Goat Rocks Wilderness; it's an outstanding hike, and the trail is also excellent for horseback rides. See a U.S. Forest Service map for details.

RV sites, facilities: There are 34 sites for tents or RVs up to 22 feet (no hookups) and 10 walk-in sites. Picnic tables are provided. Drinking water and vault toilets are available. Fire rings are next to the campground. There is primitive boat access with a 10-mph speed limit; no waterskiing is allowed. Leashed pets are permitted.

Reservations, fees: Reservations are accepted at 877/444-6777 or www.ReserveUSA.com ($9 reservation fee). Call for current rates. Open mid-June–mid-September.

Directions: On I-5, drive to Exit 68 (south of Chehalis) and U.S. 12. Turn east on U.S. 12 and drive 62 miles to Forest Road 21 (2.5 miles southwest of Packwood). Turn right (southeast) and drive 20 miles to Forest Road 2160. Turn left (east) and drive 4.5 miles to the campground.

Contact: Gifford Pinchot National Forest, Cowlitz Valley Ranger District, 360/497-1100, fax 360/497-1102.

WASHINGTON

43 BLUE LAKE CREEK

Scenic rating: 7

near Blue Lake in Gifford Pinchot National Forest

See map page 192

This camp is at an elevation of 1,900 feet along Blue Lake Creek. With access to a network of all-terrain vehicle (ATV) trails, it is a significant camp for ATV owners. There is nearby access to 16.7-mile Valley Trail. This camp is also near the launch point for the 3.5-mile hike to Blue Lake; the trailhead lies about one-half mile from camp.

RV sites, facilities: There are 11 sites for tents or RVs up to 22 feet (no hookups). Picnic tables and fire rings are provided. Drinking water and vault toilets are available. Firewood can be gathered outside of the campground area. Some facilities are wheelchair accessible. Leashed pets are permitted.

Reservations, fees: Reservations are accepted at 877/444-6777 or www.ReserveUSA.com ($9 reservation fee). Sites are $15 per night, $5 per extra vehicle per night. Open mid-May–mid-September, weather permitting.

Directions: From Chehalis, drive south on I-5 for six miles to Exit 68 and U.S. 12. Turn east on U.S. 12 and drive 48 miles to Randle and Highway 131. Turn right (south) on Highway 131 and drive one mile to Forest Road 23. Turn south and drive about 10 miles to the campground on the left.

Contact: Gifford Pinchot National Forest, Cowlitz Ranger District, 360/497-1100, fax 360/497-1102.

44 ADAMS FORK

Scenic rating: 7

on the Cispus River in Gifford Pinchot National Forest

See map page 192

This campground is at 2,600 feet elevation along the Upper Cispus River near Adams Creek and is popular with off-road vehicle (ORV) enthusiasts. There are many miles of

trails designed for use by ORVs. A trail that is just 0.5 mile away leads north to Blue Lake, which is about a five-mile hike (one-way) from the camp. Most of the campsites are small, but a few are large enough for comfortable RV use. The area has many towering trees. The Cispus River provides trout fishing.

RV sites, facilities: There are 24 sites for tents or RVs up to 22 feet (no hookups) and two group camps for up to 20 people each. Picnic tables and fire grills are provided. Drinking water and vault toilets are available. Firewood may be gathered outside the campground area. Some facilities are wheelchair accessible. Leashed pets are permitted.

Reservations, fees: Reservations are accepted at 877/444-6777 or www.ReserveUSA.com ($9 reservation fee). Sites are $16 per night, and group sites are $22–35 per night, plus $5 per extra vehicle per night. Open May–mid-September, weather permitting.

Directions: On I-5, drive to Exit 68 (south of Chehalis) and U.S. 12. Turn east on U.S. 12 and drive 48 miles to Randle and U.S. 131. Turn right (south) and drive one mile to Forest Road 23. Turn left (southeast) and drive 18 miles to Forest Road 21. Turn left (southeast) on Forest Road 21 and drive five miles to Forest Road 56. Turn right on Forest Road 56 and drive 200 yards to the campground on the left.

Contact: Gifford Pinchot National Forest, Cowlitz Valley Ranger District, 360/497-1100, fax 360/497-1102.

45 TAKHLAKH LAKE

Scenic rating: 9

on Takhlakh Lake in Gifford Pinchot National Forest

See map page 192

This campground is along the shore of Takhlakh Lake, one of five lakes in the area, all accessible by car. It's a beautiful place, set at 4,500 feet elevation, but alas, mosquitoes abound until late July. A viewing area (Mount Adams is visible across the lake) is available for visitors, while the more ambitious can go berry picking, fishing, and hiking. This lake is much better than nearby Horseshoe Lake, and in turn, the fishing is much better, especially for trout early in the season. The Takhlakh Meadow Loop Trail, a barrier-free trail, provides a 1.5-mile hike.

RV sites, facilities: There are 54 sites for tents or RVs up to 22 feet (no hookups). Drinking water and picnic tables are provided. Vault toilets are available. Firewood may be gathered outside the campground area. Boat-launching facilities are available in the day-use area, but gasoline motors are prohibited on the lake. Some facilities are wheelchair accessible. Leashed pets are permitted.

Reservations, fees: Reservations are accepted at 877/444-6777 or www.ReserveUSA.com ($9 reservation fee). Call for current rates. Open mid-June–late September, weather permitting.

Directions: From Chehalis, drive south on I-5 for 10 miles to Exit 68 and U.S. 12. Turn east on U.S. 12 and drive 48 miles to Randle and U.S. 131. Turn right (south) and drive one mile to Forest Road 23. Turn left (southeast) and drive 29 miles to Forest Road 2329. Turn left (northeast) and drive 1.5 miles to the campground entrance road on the right.

Contact: Gifford Pinchot National Forest, Cowlitz Valley Ranger District, 360/497-1100, fax 360/497-1102.

46 RIVER OAKS RV PARK & CAMPGROUND

Scenic rating: 8

on the Cowlitz River
See map page 192

This camp is right on the Cowlitz River, with opportunities for boating and fishing for sturgeon, steelhead, and salmon in season. Swimming is not recommended because of the cold water. The park provides nearby access to Mount St. Helens. Note that some sites are filled with monthly renters.

RV sites, facilities: There are 50 sites for tents

or RVs of any length (no hookups) and 30 sites with full hookups (30 and 50 amps) for RVs of any length. Some sites are pull-through. Picnic tables and fire rings are provided. Restrooms have flush toilets and showers. Drinking water, firewood, and horseshoe pits are available. Propane gas, a store, bait and tackle, and a café are within one-third mile. Boat-launching facilities, mooring buoys, and a fishing shelter are nearby. Leashed pets are permitted.

Reservations, fees: Reservations are accepted. Sites are $15–22 per night, $2.50 per person per night for more than two people. Weekly and monthly rates available. Open year-round.

Directions: From Castle Rock on I-5, take Exit 59 for Highway 506. Turn west on Highway 506 and drive 0.3 mile to the park on the left.

Contact: River Oaks RV Park & Campground, 360/864-2895, www.riveroaksrvpark.com.

47 MOUNT ST. HELENS RV PARK

Scenic rating: 6

near Silver Lake
See map page 192

This RV park is just outside Castle Rock, only three miles from the Mount St. Helens Visitor Center. It is close to the highway. Fishing and boating are available nearby on Silver Lake. Note that some sites are filled with monthly renters.

RV sites, facilities: There are 90 sites for tents or RVs up to 40 feet with full or partial hookups (20 and 30 amps). Picnic tables are provided. Restrooms have flush toilets and coin showers. Drinking water, cable TV, modem access, a coin laundry, a meeting room, and a dump station are available. A convenience store and gasoline are available nearby. Some facilities are wheelchair accessible. Leashed pets are permitted.

Reservations, fees: Reservations are recommended in the summer. Sites are $21–23 per night, $1 per person per night for more than two people. Some credit cards accepted. Open year-round.

Directions: From Longview, drive 10 miles

WASHINGTON

north on I-5 to Castle Rock and Exit 49 and Highway 504. Take Exit 49 and drive east on Highway 504 for two miles to Tower Road. Turn left (well signed) and drive a short distance to a Y intersection and Schaffran Road. Bear right and drive approximately 300 yards to the park on the right.

Contact: Mount St. Helens RV Park, 360/274-8522, fax 360/274-4529, www.mtsthelens rvpark.com.

48 SEAQUEST STATE PARK

Scenic rating: 6

near Silver Lake
See map page 192

This camp fills nightly because it is along the paved road to the awesome Johnston Ridge Observatory, the premier lookout of Mount St. Helens. This state park is adjacent to Silver Lake, one of western Washington's finest fishing lakes for bass and trout. But that's not all. The Mount St. Helens Visitor Center, which opened in 2000, is across the road from the park entrance. This heavily forested, 425-acre park features more than one mile of lake shoreline and 5.5 miles of trails for hiking and biking. The irony of the place is that some out-of-towners on vacation think that this park is on the ocean because of its name, Seaquest. The park has nothing to do with the ocean, of course. It is named after Alfred L. Seaquest, who donated the property to the state for parkland. One interesting fact: He stipulated in his will that if liquor were ever sold on the property the land would be transferred to Willamette University. The park is popular for day use as well as camping. No hunting or fishing is allowed. There is public access to the lake but no boat launch.

RV sites, facilities: There are 92 sites for tents or RVs, including 16 with partial hookups (30 amps), and four hike-in/bike-in sites. Yurts also may be available. Picnic tables and fire grills are provided. Restrooms have flush toilets and coin showers. Drinking water, a picnic area, a

playground, horseshoe pits, a dump station, and firewood are available. A store is within five miles. Some facilities are wheelchair accessible. Leashed pets are permitted.

Reservations, fees: Reservations are accepted at 888/CAMP-OUT (888/226-7688) or www.parks.wa.gov/reservations ($7 reservation fee). Sites are $16–22 per night, $10 per night for hike-in/bike-in sites, $6 per extra vehicle per night. Some credit cards accepted. Open year-round.

Directions: From Longview, drive 10 miles north on I-5 to Castle Rock and Exit 49 and Highway 504. Take Exit 49 and drive east on Highway 504 for 5.5 miles to the park.

Contact: Seaquest State Park, 360/274-8633, fax 360/274-0962; state park information 360/902-8844, www.parks.wa.gov.

49 SILVER LAKE MOTEL AND RESORT

Scenic rating: 8

on Silver Lake
See map page 192

This park is near the shore of Silver Lake and features a view of Mount St. Helens. One of Washington's better lakes for largemouth bass and trout, Silver Lake also has perch, crappie, and bluegill. Powerboating, personal-watercraft riding, and waterskiing are popular. This spot is considered a great angler's camp. The grassy sites are set along a horseshoe-shaped driveway. Access is quick to Mount St. Helens, which is nearby to the east.

RV sites, facilities: There are 20 sites with partial hookups (30 amps) for RVs of any length, 11 tent sites, five cabins, and six motel rooms. Picnic tables are provided. Restrooms have flush toilets and showers. Drinking water, a convenience store, bait and tackle, a fish-cleaning station, ice, boat docks, boat rentals, launching facilities, and a playground are available. A dump station is within one mile, and a café is within four miles. Leashed pets are permitted in the campground.

Reservations, fees: Reservations are accepted. Sites are $17–27 per night, $5 per extra vehicle per night. Some credit cards accepted. Open year-round.

Directions: From Longview, drive 10 miles north on I-5 to Castle Rock and Exit 49 and Highway 504. Take Exit 49 and drive east on Highway 504 for six miles to the resort on the right.

Contact: Silver Lake Motel and Resort, 360/274-6141, fax 360/274-2183, www.silver lake-resort.com.

50 PARADISE COVE RESORT & RV PARK

Scenic rating: 7

near the Toutle River

See map page 192

This wooded park is about 400 yards from the Toutle River and a half mile from the Cowlitz River. Take your pick: Seaquest State Park and Silver Lake to the east provide two excellent, activity-filled side-trip options. This is a major stopover for visits to Mount St. Helens.

RV sites, facilities: There are 48 sites for tents or RVs of any length with full hookups (20, 30, and 50 amps) and a large dispersed tent camping area. Some sites are pull-through. Picnic tables are provided. Restrooms, drinking water, flush toilets, showers, a coin laundry, and ice are available. Boat-launching facilities are nearby. Leashed pets are permitted.

Reservations, fees: Reservations are accepted. Sites are $12–32 per night. Monthly rates available. Some credit cards accepted. Open year-round.

Directions: From Longview, drive 10 miles north on I-5 to Castle Rock and Exit 52. Take Exit 52 and turn right on the frontage road and drive a short distance to Burma Road. Turn left and drive a short distance to the resort, just off the freeway (within view of the freeway).

Contact: Paradise Cove Resort & RV Park, 360/274-6785, fax 360/274-4031.

51 CAMP KALAMA RV PARK AND CAMPGROUND

Scenic rating: 6

on the Kalama River

See map page 193

This campground has a rustic setting, with open and wooded areas and some accommodations for tent campers. It's set along the Kalama River, where salmon and steelhead fishing is popular. A full-service marina is nearby. Note that some sites are filled with monthly renters.

RV sites, facilities: There are 114 sites with full or partial hookups (30 and 50 amps) for RVs of any length and 50 tent sites. Some sites are pull-through. Picnic tables and fire pits are provided. Restrooms have flush toilets and coin showers. Drinking water, cable TV, propane gas, a dump station, a general store, a café, a banquet room, firewood, a coin laundry, ice, boat-launching facilities, a beach area, and a playground are available. Some facilities are wheelchair accessible. Leashed pets are permitted, with certain restrictions.

Reservations, fees: Reservations are accepted. Sites are $18.10–28.05 per night, $1.50 per person per night for more than two adults, $1.50 per night per extra vehicle, and $1 per pet per night. Weekly and monthly rates available. Some credit cards accepted. Open year-round.

Directions: From the north end of Kalama (between Kelso and Woodland) on I-5, take Exit 32 and drive south on the frontage road for one block to the campground.

Contact: Camp Kalama RV Park and Campground, 360/673-2456 or 800/750-2456, fax 360/673-2324, www.kalama.com/~camp kalama/.

52 LONE FIR RESORT

Scenic rating: 4

near Yale Lake

See map page 193

This private campground is near Yale Lake (the smallest of four lakes in the area) and, with grassy sites and plenty of shade trees, is designed primarily for RV use. Mount St. Helens provides a side-trip option. The trailhead for the summit climb is nearby at Climber's Bivouac on the south flank of the volcano; a primitive campground with dispersed sites for hikers only is available. Note: This trailhead is the only one available for the summit climb. Though it happens infrequently, the trail to the summit can be closed because of volcanic activity at the plug dome.

RV sites, facilities: There are 32 sites with full hookups (30 and 50 amps) for RVs of any length, a grassy area for tents, six cabins, and 12 motel rooms. Some sites are pull-through. Picnic tables are provided, and fire pits are at some sites. Restrooms have flush toilets and coin showers. Satellite TV, drinking water, a coin laundry, clubhouse, Wi-Fi, community fire pit, horseshoe pits, ice, snowshoe rentals, a restaurant, and a seasonal heated swimming pool and spa are available. Propane gas, a store, boat docks, and launching facilities are nearby. Leashed pets are permitted.

Reservations, fees: Reservations are accepted. Sites are $27 per night, $15 per night for tents. Some credit cards accepted. Open year-round.

Directions: In Woodland on I-5, take Exit 21 for Highway 503. Drive east on Highway 503 for 29 miles to Cougar and the resort turnoff (marked, in town, with the park visible from the road) on the left.

Contact: Lone Fir Resort, 360/238-5210, fax 360/238-5120, www.lonefirresort.com.

53 LOWER FALLS

Scenic rating: 10

on the Lewis River in Gifford Pinchot National Forest

See map page 193

This camp is at 1,400 feet elevation in the primary viewing area for six major waterfalls on the Lewis River. The spectacular Lewis River Trail is available for hiking or horseback riding, and it features a wheelchair-accessible loop.

Several other hiking trails in the area branch off along backcountry streams. The sites are paved and set among large fir trees on gently sloping ground; access roads were designed for easy RV parking. Note that above the falls, the calm water in the river looks safe, but it is not! Stay out. In addition, the Lewis River Trail goes along cliffs, providing beautiful views but potentially dangerous hiking.

RV sites, facilities: There are 42 sites for tents or RVs up to 60 feet (no hookups) and two group sites for up to 20 people each. Picnic tables and fire grills are provided. Drinking water and composting toilets are available. Some facilities are wheelchair accessible. Leashed pets are permitted.

Reservations, fees: Reservations are not accepted. Sites are $15 per night for single sites, $35 per night for double sites, and $5 per extra vehicle per night. Group sites are $34 per night. Open May–November, weather permitting.

Directions: From Woodland on I-5, take Exit 21 for Highway 503. Drive east on Highway 503 for 23 miles to the Highway 503 spur. Drive northeast on the Highway 503 spur for seven miles (the highway becomes Forest Road 90). Continue east on Forest Road 90 for 30 miles to the campground (along the Lewis River) on the right.

Contact: Gifford Pinchot National Forest, Mount St. Helens National Volcanic Monument, 360/449-7800, fax 360/449-7801.

54 PARADISE POINT STATE PARK

Scenic rating: 8

on the East Fork of the Lewis River

See map page 193

This park is named for the serenity that once blessed this area. Alas, it has lost much of that peacefulness since the freeway went in next to the park. To reduce traffic noise, stay at one of the wooded sites in the small apple orchard. The sites in the grassy areas have little noise buffer. This park covers 88 acres and features 1,680 feet of river frontage. The two-mile hiking trail is good for families and children. Note that the dirt boat ramp is primitive and non-functional when the water level drops, and is recommended for car-top boats only. Fishing on the East Fork of the Lewis River is a bonus.

RV sites, facilities: There are 58 sites for tents or RVs up to 50 feet (no hookups), 20 sites for tents or RVs up to 50 feet with partial hookups (30 and 50 amps), and nine hike-in/bike-in sites. Picnic tables and fire grills are provided. Restrooms have flush toilets and coin showers. Drinking water, a dump station, firewood, an amphitheater, and summer interpretive programs are available. A primitive, dirt boat-launching area is nearby on the East Fork of the Lewis River. Some facilities are wheelchair accessible. Leashed pets are permitted.

Reservations, fees: Reservations are accepted at 888/CAMP-OUT (888/226-7688) or www.parks.wa.gov/reservations ($7 reservation fee). Sites are $16–22 per night, $12 per night for hike-in/bike-in sites, $10 per extra vehicle per night. Some credit cards accepted. Open year-round.

Directions: From Vancouver, Washington, drive north on I-5 for 15 miles to Exit 16 (La Center/Paradise Point State Park exit). Take that exit and turn right, then almost immediately at Paradise Park Road, turn left and drive one mile to the park.

Contact: Paradise Point State Park, tel./fax 360/263-2350; state park information 360/902-8844, www.parks.wa.gov.

55 BIG FIR CAMPGROUND AND RV PARK

🚶 🚣 🚐 🐕 🚍 ⛺

Scenic rating: 6

near Paradise Point State Park

See map page 193

This campground lies in a heavily wooded, rural area not far from Paradise Point State Park. It's nestled among hills and features shaded gravel sites and wild berries. (See the listing in this chapter for *Paradise Point State Park* for details on the area.)

RV sites, facilities: There are 37 sites with full hookups (30 and 50 amps) for RVs of any length, along with 33 tent sites. Some sites are pull-through. Picnic tables and barbecues are provided; no wood fires are allowed. Restrooms have flush toilets and coin showers. Drinking water, volleyball, croquet, a horseshoe pit, board games, limited groceries, and ice are available. Boat-launching facilities are within 1.5 miles. Leashed pets are permitted.

Reservations, fees: Reservations are accepted. Sites are $16–22 per night, $2 per night per extra vehicle. Some credit cards accepted. Open year-round, except for the tent area, which is open Memorial Day weekend–Labor Day weekend.

Directions: From Vancouver, Washington, drive north on I-5 to Exit 9/10th Street. Take that exit and drive north on 10th Street for two miles to 259th Street. Turn right and drive two miles to the park.

Contact: Big Fir Campground and RV Park, 360/887-8970.

56 BATTLE GROUND LAKE STATE PARK

🚶 🚴 🏊 🎣 🚣 🐎 🛝 ♿ 🚍 ⛺

Scenic rating: 8

on Battle Ground Lake

See map page 193

The centerpiece of this state park is Battle Ground Lake, a spring-fed lake that is stocked with trout but is popular for bass and catfish fishing as well. The lake is fed by water from underground lava tubes and is similar to Crater Lake in Oregon, though smaller. The park covers 280 acres, primarily forested with conifers, in the foothills of the Cascade Mountains. There are 10 miles of trails for hiking and biking, including a trail around the lake, and an additional five miles of trails that are also for horses; a primitive equestrian camp is available. The lake is good for swimming and fishing, and it has a nice beach area; no gas motors on boats are allowed. If you're traveling on I-5 and looking for a layover, this camp, just 15 minutes

WASHINGTON

from the highway, is ideal. In July and August, the area hosts several fairs and celebrations. Like many of the easy-access state parks on I-5, this one fills up quickly on weekends. The average annual rainfall is 35 inches.

RV sites, facilities: There are 25 sites for tents or RVs up to 50 feet (no hookups), six sites with partial hookups (50 amps) for RVs, 15 hike-in/bike-in sites, a horse camp with four sites, a group site that can accommodate up to 32 people, and four cabins. Picnic tables and fire grills are provided. Restrooms have flush toilets and coin showers. Drinking water, a dump station, a store, firewood, a seasonal snack bar, a seasonal store with fishing supplies, ice, firewood, a sheltered picnic area, an amphitheater, summer interpretive programs, a playground, horseshoe pits, and an athletic field are available. Some facilities are wheelchair accessible. Boat-launching facilities and rentals are nearby. Leashed pets are permitted.

Reservations, fees: Reservations are accepted at 888/CAMP-OUT (888/226-7688) or www.parks.wa.gov/reservations ($7 reservation fee). Sites are $16–22 per night, $10 per night for hike-in/bike-in sites, $10 per night per extra vehicle. Some credit cards accepted. Open year-round.

Directions: Take Exit 14 from I-5 southbound (or Exit 9 from I-5 northbound) and drive to the city of Battle Ground (well marked); continue to the east end of town to Grace Avenue. Turn left and drive three miles (a marked route) to the park.

Contact: Battle Ground Lake State Park, tel./fax 360/687-4621; state park information 360/902-8844, www.parks.wa.gov.

57 SUNSET

Scenic rating: 9

on the East Fork of the Lewis River in Gifford Pinchot National Forest

See map page 193

This campground is at an elevation of 1,000 feet along the East Fork of the Lewis River.

Fishing, hiking, and huckleberry and mushroom picking are some of the favored pursuits of visitors. Scenic Sunset Falls is just upstream of the campground. A barrier-free viewing trail leads to an overlook.

RV sites, facilities: There are 16 sites for tents or RVs up to 22 feet (no hookups). Picnic tables and fire grills are provided. Vault toilets are available. There is no drinking water. Some facilities are wheelchair accessible. Leashed pets are permitted.

Reservations, fees: Reservations are not accepted. Sites are $14 per night, $5 per extra vehicle per night. Open year-round.

Directions: From Vancouver, Washington, drive north on I-5 about seven miles to County Road 502. Turn east on Highway 502 and drive six miles to Highway 503. Turn left and drive north for five miles to Lucia Falls Road. Turn right and drive eight miles to Moulton Falls and Old County Road 12. Turn right on Old County Road 12 and drive seven miles to the Forest Boundary and the campground entrance on the right.

Contact: Gifford Pinchot National Forest, Mount St. Helens National Volcanic Monument, 360/449-7800, fax 360/449-7801.

58 BEAVER

Scenic rating: 7

on the Wind River in Gifford Pinchot National Forest

See map page 193

This is the closest campground north of Stevenson in the Columbia Gorge. Set along the Wind River at an elevation of 1,100 feet, it features pretty, shaded sites. No fishing is permitted. The campsites are paved, and a large grassy day-use area is nearby. Hiking highlights include two nearby trailheads. Two miles north lies the trailhead for the Trapper Creek Wilderness, with 30 miles of trails, including a loop possibility. Three miles north is the Falls Creek Trail.

RV sites, facilities: There are 24 sites for tents or RVs up to 25 feet (no hookups) and one group site for up to 40 people. Picnic tables and fire grills are provided. Drinking water, flush and vault toilets, horseshoe pits, and swings are available. Some facilities are wheelchair accessible. Leashed pets are permitted.

Reservations, fees: Reservations are accepted and required for the group site at 877/444-6777 or www.ReserveUSA.com ($9 reservation fee). Sites are $15–17 per night, $30 per night for double sites, $5 per extra vehicle per night. The group site is $91 per night. Open mid-May–early September.

Directions: From Vancouver, Washington, take Highway 14 east and drive 50 miles to Carson and the Wind River Highway (County Road 30). Turn left (north) and drive 12 miles to the campground entrance (five miles past Stabler) on the left.

Contact: Gifford Pinchot National Forest, Mount Adams Ranger Station, 509/427-3200, fax 509/427-4633.

59 PARADISE CREEK

Scenic rating: 9

on Paradise Creek and the Wind River in Gifford Pinchot National Forest

See map page 193

This camp is deep in Gifford Pinchot National Forest at the confluence of Paradise Creek and the Wind River. It gets light use despite easy access and easy RV parking. The well-shaded campsites are set among old-growth woods, primarily Douglas fir, cedar, and western hemlock. Lava Butte, a short distance from the camp, is accessible by trail; the 1.2-mile round-trip hike from the campground provides a good view of the valley. Fishing is closed here. The elevation is 1,500 feet.

RV sites, facilities: There are 42 sites for tents or RVs up to 25 feet (no hookups). Picnic tables and fire grills are provided. Drinking water and vault toilets are available. Some facilities are wheelchair accessible. Leashed pets are permitted.

Reservations, fees: Reservations are accepted at 877/444-6777 or www.ReserveUSA.com ($9 reservation fee). Sites are $15–17 per night,

double sites are $30 per night, and it's $5 per extra vehicle per night. Open mid-May–mid-September, weather permitting.

Directions: From Vancouver, Washington, take Highway 14 east and drive 50 miles to Carson and the Wind River Highway (County Road 30). Turn left (north) on the Wind River Highway and drive 20 miles to the camp on the right.

Contact: Gifford Pinchot National Forest, Mount Adams Ranger District, 509/395-3400, fax 509/395-3424.

60 CULTUS CREEK

Scenic rating: 7

near the Indian Heaven Wilderness in Gifford Pinchot National Forest

See map page 193

This camp is at an elevation of 4,000 feet along Cultus Creek on the edge of the Indian Heaven Wilderness. It offers nearby access to trails that will take you into the backcountry, which has numerous small meadows and lakes among old-growth stands of fir and pine. Horse trails are available as well. Access to the Pacific Crest Trail requires a two-mile climb. This camp is popular during the fall huckleberry season, when picking is good, but gets light use the rest of the year. Situated amid gentle terrain, the sites are graveled and level.

RV sites, facilities: There are 51 sites for tents or RVs up to 32 feet (no hookups). Picnic tables and fire grills are provided. Vault toilets and firewood are available. There is no drinking water. Some facilities are wheelchair accessible. Leashed pets are permitted.

Reservations, fees: Reservations are not accepted. Sites are $5 per night. Open late June–late September, weather permitting.

Directions: From Vancouver, Washington, on I-205, take Highway 14 east and drive 66 miles to State Route 141-A. Turn left (north) on State Route 141-A and drive 28 miles (becomes Forest Road 24); continue two miles to a junction. Turn right (staying on Forest Road 24) and drive 13.5 miles to the campground.

Contact: Gifford Pinchot National Forest, Mount Adams Ranger District, 509/395-3400, fax 509/395-3424.

61 PETERSON PRAIRIE & PETERSON PRAIRIE GROUP

Scenic rating: 8

near the town of Trout Lake in Gifford Pinchot National Forest

See map page 193

Here's a good base camp if you want to have a short ride to town as well as access to the nearby wilderness areas. Peterson Prairie is a prime spot for huckleberry picking in the fall. A trail from the camp leads about one mile to nearby ice caves; a stairway into the caves provides access to a variety of ice formations. The camp is closed in winter, but an area Sno-Park with snowmobiling and cross-country skiing trails is open for winter recreation. The elevation is 2,800 feet.

RV sites, facilities: There are 23 sites with no hookups for RVs up to 32 feet or tents, one group site for up to 50 people, and one historic cabin. Picnic tables and fire grills are provided. Drinking water, vault toilets, cell phone reception, and firewood are available. A camp host is available in summer. Leashed pets are permitted.

Reservations, fees: Reservations are required for the group site only; phone 877/444-6777 or reserve online at www.ReserveUSA.com ($9 reservation fee). The fees are $13–26 per night for individual and double sites, plus $5 per additional vehicle per night. It's $32–67 per night for the group site. Open May–late September.

Directions: From Hood River, Oregon, drive north on Highway 35 (over the Columbia River) to Highway 14. Turn left and drive two miles to Highway 141. Turn right (north) on Highway 141 and drive 23 miles to Forest Road 24 (five miles beyond and southwest of the town of Trout Lake). Bear right (west) and drive 2.5 miles to the campground on the left.

Contact: Gifford Pinchot National Forest, Mount Adams Ranger District, 509/395-3400, fax 509/395-9384.

62 TROUT LAKE CREEK

Scenic rating: 7

on Trout Lake Creek in Gifford Pinchot National Forest

See map page 193

This spot makes a popular base camp for folks fishing at Trout Lake (five miles away). Many anglers will spend the day at the lake, where fishing is good for stocked rainbow trout, then return to this camp for the night. Some bonus brook trout are occasionally caught at Trout Lake. The camp is along a creek in a forest of Douglas fir. In season, berry picking can be good here.

RV sites, facilities: There are 16 sites for tents or RVs up to 28 feet (no hookups). Picnic tables and fire rings are provided. Vault toilets are available. There is no drinking water. Leashed pets are permitted.

Reservations, fees: Reservations are not accepted. Sites are $5 per night. Open mid-May–mid-September, weather permitting.

Directions: From Hood River, Oregon, drive north on Highway 35 (over the Columbia River) to Highway 14. Turn left and drive two miles to Highway 141-A. Turn right (north) on Highway 141-A and drive 25 miles north to Forest Road 88. Turn right and drive four miles to Forest Road 8810. Turn right and drive 1.5 miles to Forest Road 8810-010. Turn right and drive 0.25 mile to the campground on the right. Note that the access road is rough.

Contact: Gifford Pinchot National Forest, Mount Adams Ranger District, 509/395-3400, fax 509/395-3424.

63 PANTHER CREEK AND PANTHER CREEK HORSE CAMP

Scenic rating: 8

on Panther Creek in Gifford Pinchot National Forest

See map page 193

This campground sits along Panther Creek in a second-growth forest of Douglas fir and western hemlock, adjacent to an old-growth forest. The sites are well defined, but despite a paved road to the campground and easy parking and access, it gets light use. The camp lies 3.5 miles from the Wind River, an option for those who enjoy fishing, hiking, and horseback riding. The Pacific Crest Trail is accessible from the adjacent Panther Creek Horse Camp. The elevation is 1,000 feet.

RV sites, facilities: There are 33 sites for tents or RVs up to 25 feet (no hookups) and one equestrian site with a stock-loading ramp at the adjacent horse camp. Picnic tables and fire rings are provided. Drinking water and pits toilets are available. Garbage must be packed out. Some facilities are wheelchair accessible. Leashed pets are permitted.

Reservations, fees: Reserve at 877/444-6777 or www.ReserveUSA.com ($9 reservation fee). Sites are $15–30 per night, $5 per extra vehicle per night. Open mid-May–early September.

Directions: From Vancouver, Washington, take Highway 14 east and drive 50 miles to Carson and the Wind River Highway (County Road 30). Turn north and drive nine miles to Forest Road 6517 (just past Stabler). Turn right (east) on Forest Road 6517 and drive 1.5 miles to the campground entrance road on the right.

Contact: Gifford Pinchot National Forest, Mount Adams Ranger District, 509/427-3200, fax 509/427-4633.

64 OKLAHOMA

Scenic rating: 7

on the Little White Salmon River in Gifford Pinchot National Forest

See map page 193

This pretty campground is along the Little White Salmon River at an elevation of 1,700 feet. Fishing can be excellent in this area, and the river is stocked in the spring with rainbow trout. The camp gets light use. It features some open meadow but is generally flat. Close to the Columbia River Gorge, it features paved road all the way into the campground and easy RV parking. As to why they named the camp "Oklahoma," who knows? If you do, drop me a line.

RV sites, facilities: There are 23 sites for tents or RVs up to 22 feet (no hookups). Drinking water, fire rings, and picnic tables are provided. Vault toilets are available. Some facilities are wheelchair accessible. Leashed pets are permitted.

Reservations, fees: Reservations are accepted at 877/444-6777 or www.ReserveUSA.com ($9 reservation fee). Sites are $15 per night, $5 per night for each additional vehicle. Open mid-May–mid-September, weather permitting.

Directions: From Hood River, Oregon, drive north on Highway 35 for one mile over the Columbia River to Highway 14. Turn left on Highway 14 and drive about five miles to Cook and County Road 1800. Turn right (north) and drive 14 miles (becomes Cook-Underwood Road, then Willard Road, then Oklahoma Road) to the campground entrance at the end of the paved road.

Contact: Gifford Pinchot National Forest, Mount Adams Ranger District, 509/395-3400, fax 509/395-3424.

65 MOSS CREEK

Scenic rating: 7

on the Little White Salmon River in Gifford Pinchot National Forest

See map page 193

This campground is at 1,300 feet elevation about one mile from the Little White Salmon River. Although it's a short distance from Willard and Big Cedars County Park, the camp gets light use. The river provides good fishing prospects for trout in the spring, usually with few other people around. The sites are generally small but are shaded and still functional for most RVs. The road is paved all the way to the campground.

RV sites, facilities: There are 18 sites for tents or RVs up to 32 feet (no hookups). Picnic tables and fire grills are provided. Drinking water and vault toilets are available. Some facilities are wheelchair accessible. A camp host is available in the summer. Leashed pets are permitted.

Reservations, fees: Reservations are accepted at 877/444-6777 or www.ReserveUSA.com ($9 reservation fee). Sites are $15 per night, $5 per night for each additional vehicle. Open mid-May–mid-September, weather permitting.

Directions: From Hood River, Oregon, drive north on Highway 35 for one mile over the Columbia River to Highway 14. Turn left on Highway 14 and drive about five miles to Cook and County Road 1800. Turn right (north) and drive 10 miles (becomes Cook-Underwood Road, then Willard road, then Oklahoma Road) to the campground entrance on the right.

Contact: Gifford Pinchot National Forest, Mount Adams Ranger District, 509/395-3400, fax 509/395-3424.

66 BEACON ROCK STATE PARK

Scenic rating: 8

on the Columbia River

See map page 193   BEST (

This state park features Beacon Rock, the second-largest monolith in the world, which overlooks the Columbia River Gorge. Lewis and Clark gave Beacon Rock its name on their expedition to the Pacific Ocean in 1805. The park is in the heart of the Columbia River Gorge National Scenic Area. The Beacon Rock Summit Trail, a 1.8-mile round-trip hike, provides panoramic views of the gorge. The rock is excellent for rock climbing, with the climbing season running mid-July–January. The park covers nearly 5,000 acres and includes 9,500 feet of shoreline along the Columbia River and more than 22 miles of nearby trails open for hiking, mountain biking, and horseback riding. An eight-mile loop trail to Hamilton Mountain (2,300 feet elevation) is one of the best hikes, featuring even better views than from Beacon Rock. Fishing for sturgeon, salmon, steelhead, smallmouth bass (often excellent), and walleye is available in season on the Lower Columbia River below Bonneville Dam; check regulations.

RV sites, facilities: There are 29 sites for tents or small RVs (no hookups), six sites with full hookups (30 amps) for RVs, one hike-in/bike-in site, and one group site for up to 200 people. Picnic tables and fire grills are provided. Restrooms have flush toilets and coin showers. Drinking water, picnic areas (one is reservable), and a playground are available. Some facilities are wheelchair accessible. Boat docks and launching facilities are on-site. Leashed pets are permitted.

Reservations, fees: Reservations are not accepted for individual sites but are required for the group camp at 888/CAMP-OUT (888/226-7688) or www.parks.wa.gov/reservations ($7 reservation fee). Sites are $16–22 per night, $10 per night for hike-in/bike-in sites, $10 per night per extra vehicle. The group site is $2 per person per night with a 20-person minimum. There's a $5 launch fee, $10 minimum for boat mooring plus $0.50 per foot per boat. Open April–October, with two campsites available year-round.

Directions: From Vancouver, Washington, take Highway 14 and drive east for 35 miles. The park straddles the highway; follow the signs to the campground.

Contact: Beacon Rock State Park, 509/427-8265, fax 509/427-4471; state park information 360/902-8844, www.parks.wa.gov.

67 COLUMBIA HILLS STATE PARK

Scenic rating: 10

near the Dalles Dam

See map page 193

You may remember this park by its former name: Horsethief Lake State Park. The 338-acre park boasts 7,500 feet of Columbia River shoreline. It also adjoins the 3,000-acre Dalles Mountain Ranch State Park. Horsethief Lake, created by the Dalles Dam, covers approximately 100 acres and is part of the Columbia River. Horsethief Butte, adjacent to the lake, dominates the skyline. The blooms of lupine and balsam root in mid-April create stunning views. Rock climbing in the park is popular, but the river canyon is often windy, especially in late spring and early summer. Most people find the place as a spot to camp while driving along the Columbia River Highway. There are hiking trails and access to both the lake and the Columbia River. The boat speed limit is five mph, and anglers can try for trout and bass. Guided tours on weekends feature pictographs and petroglyphs; reservations are required at 509/767-1159.

RV sites, facilities: There are eight sites for tents or RVs up to 45 feet, with partial hookups (15 amps, convertors available), three sites for tents or RVs up to 30 feet (no hookups), three tent sites, and one hike-in/bike-in site. Picnic tables and fire grills are provided. Drinking water, flush toilets, firewood, a dump station, a horseshoe pit, and a picnic area are available. No showers are available. A store is within three miles. Boat-launching facilities are on both the lake and the river. Leashed pets are permitted.

Reservations, fees: Reservations are not accepted. Sites are $16–22 per night, $10 per night for the hike-in/bike-in site, $10 per extra vehicle per night. Open April–late October.

Directions: From The Dalles in Oregon, turn north on Highway 197, cross over the Columbia River, and drive four miles to Highway 14. Turn right (east) and drive two miles to Milepost 85 and the park entrance on the right.

Contact: Columbia Hills State Park, 509/767-1159, fax 509/767-4304; state park information 360/902-8844, www.parks.wa.gov.

SOUTHEASTERN WASHINGTON

The expansive domain of southeastern Washington is a surprise for many newcomers. Instead of the high mountains of the Cascades, there are rolling hills. Instead of forests, there are miles of wheat fields (Washington's second-largest export crop behind lumber). Instead of a multitude of streams, there are giant rivers – the Columbia and Snake. Just one pocket of mountains and a somewhat sparse forest sit in the southeast corner of the state, in a remote sector of Umatilla National Forest.

The Lewis and Clark expedition was routed through this area some 200 years ago, and today, several major highways, including I-82 and U.S. 395, bring out-of-town visitors through the region en route to other destinations. A network of camps is set along these highways, including RV parks created to serve the needs of travelers. Of the area parks, the state parks offer the best campgrounds. The prettiest picture you will find is of Palouse Falls, where a gorgeous fountain of water pours through a desert gorge.

Includes:

- Brooks Memorial State Park
- Columbia River
- Fields Spring State Park
- Ginkgo Petrified Forest State Park
- Lake Bryan
- Lake Sacajawea
- Lake Wallula
- Lewis and Clark Trail State Park
- Lower Granite Lake
- Maryhill State Park
- Moses Lake State Park
- Naches River
- Palouse Falls State Park
- Potholes State Park
- Snake River
- Soap Lake
- Sprague Lake
- Tieton River
- Touchet River
- Umatilla National Forest
- Wanapum State Recreation Area
- Wenatchee National Forest
- Williams Lake
- Yakima River
- Yakima Sportsman State Park

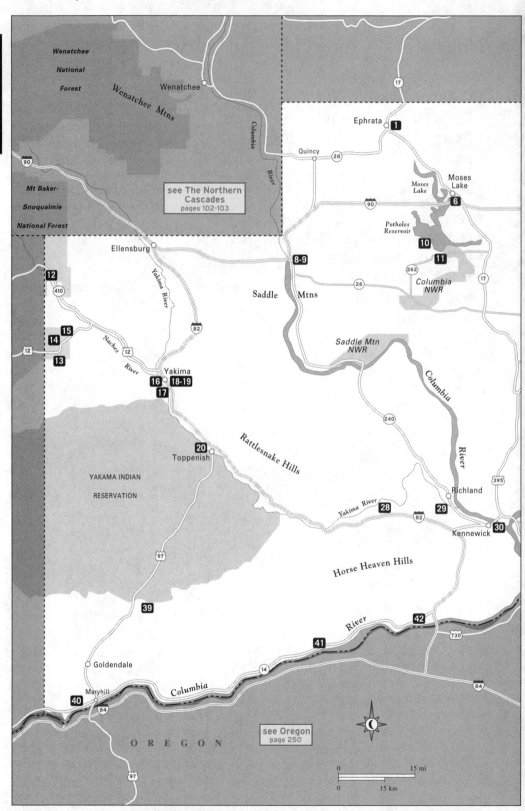

WASHINGTON

Wenatchee National Forest

Wenatchee Mtns

Wenatchee

Columbia River

17

Ephrata **1**

90

Quincy

28

Mt Baker-Snoqualmie National Forest

Moses Lake

Moses Lake

6

see The Northern Cascades
pages 102-103

90

Potholes Reservoir

10

11

Ellensburg

8-9

26

262

Columbia NWR

17

12

410

Yakima River

82

Saddle Mtns

Saddle Mtn NWR

Columbia River

15

Naches River

14

12

12

13

Yakima

16 **18-19**

17

240

Rattlesnake Hills

20

Toppenish

YAKAMA INDIAN RESERVATION

Yakima River

28

29

82

Richland

395

30

Kennewick

97

Horse Heaven Hills

39

River

42

730

41

14

84

Goldendale

Maryhill

Columbia

40

84

see Oregon
page 250

O R E G O N

97

0   15 mi
0   15 km

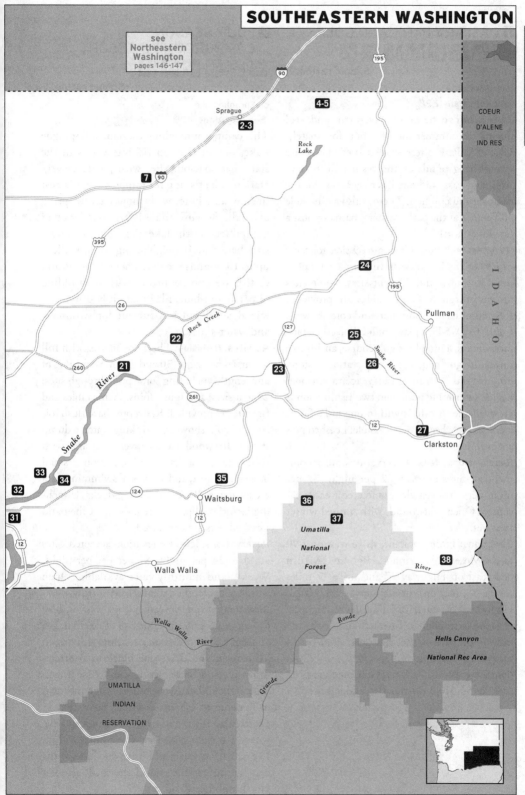

SOUTHEASTERN WASHINGTON

see
Northeastern
Washington
pages 146-147

WASHINGTON

Sprague

Rock
Lake

2-3

4-5

7

Rock Creek

24

Pullman

22

127

25

23

26

Snake River

21

River

261

27

Clarkston

Snake

33

34

124

35

Waitsburg

36

32

12

37

Umatilla

31

Walla Walla

National

38

Forest

River

COEUR
D'ALENE
IND RES

IDAHO

Hells Canyon

National Rec Area

Walla Walla River

Ronde

Grande

UMATILLA

INDIAN

RESERVATION

WASHINGTON

1 OASIS RV PARK AND GOLF

Scenic rating: 5

near Soap Lake

See map page 228

This area can be extremely warm and arid during the summer months, but, fortunately, Oasis RV Park offers shaded sites. There are two fishing ponds at the resort: Both have trout and bass, and one has easy access for the disabled and children. There is also a nine-hole golf course at the park. Mineral baths are just a few miles north.

RV sites, facilities: There are 69 sites for tents or RVs of any length with full or partial hookups (30 amps) and 12 tent sites. Some sites are pull-through. Picnic tables are provided. Restrooms have flush toilets and coin showers. Cable TV, Wi-Fi, a playground, horseshoe pits, picnic areas, a nine-hole golf course, an 18-hole miniature golf course, a dump station, a store, propane gas, a coin laundry, ice, a seasonal heated swimming pool, and two fishing ponds are available. A café is within one mile. Some facilities are wheelchair accessible. Leashed pets are permitted.

Reservations, fees: Reservations are recommended. Sites are $17–22 per night, $2 per night per extra vehicle. Some credit cards accepted. Open year-round, with limited winter facilities.

Directions: From Spokane, drive west on I-90 to the Moses Lake exit and Highway 17. Turn northeast on Highway 17 and drive 17 miles to the Y junction with Highway 282. Take Highway 282 and drive four miles to Highway 281/283 (a stoplight). Turn left and drive 1.25 miles to the park on the right (just before reaching the town of Ephrata).

Contact: Oasis RV Park and Golf, 509/754-5102 or 877/754-5102, www.oasisrvandgolf.net.

2 FOUR SEASONS CAMPGROUND & RESORT

Scenic rating: 7

on Sprague Lake

See map page 229

This campground along the shore of Sprague Lake, one of the top fishing waters in the state, has spacious sites with plenty of vegetation. The fishing for rainbow trout is best in May and June, with some bass in spring and fall. Because there is an abundance of natural feed in the lake, the fish reach larger sizes here than in neighboring lakes. Walleye up to 10 pounds are taken here. Crappie and catfish are also abundant, with a sprinkling of perch and bluegill. In late July–August, a fair algae bloom is a turnoff for swimmers and water-skiers.

RV sites, facilities: There are 38 sites with full or partial hookups (30 and 50 amps) for RVs of any length, including some pull-through sites; 25 tent sites; and four cabins. Picnic tables and fire pits are provided. Restrooms have flush toilets and coin showers. Drinking water, a dump station, firewood, ice, a convenience store with fishing tackle, a fish-cleaning station, a small basketball court, and a seasonal swimming pool are available. Boat and fishing docks, launching facilities, slips, and rentals are at the park. Leashed pets are permitted.

Reservations, fees: Reservations accepted. Sites are $18–24 per night, $1 per pet per night. Weekly and monthly rates available. Open April–mid-October, weather permitting.

Directions: From Spokane, drive west on I-90 for about 40 miles to Exit 245. Take Exit 245 and drive a short distance south to 4th Street. Turn right and drive one block to B Street. Turn left and drive two blocks to 1st Street. Turn right and drive one mile through the town of Sprague to a Y intersection. Bear right to Doerschlag Road and drive two miles to Lake Road. Turn left and drive three miles to Bob Lee Road. Turn left and drive one mile to the campground at the end of the road, at 2384 North Bob Lee Road.

Contact: Four Seasons Campground & Resort, 509/257-2332, www.fourseasons campground.com.

③ SPRAGUE LAKE RESORT

Scenic rating: 5

on Sprague Lake
See map page 229

This developed campground is on the shore of Sprague Lake, about 35 miles from Spokane. It offers a pleasant, grassy setting with about 30 cottonwood and native trees on the property. (See listing in this chapter for *Four Seasons Campground & Resort* for more information about Sprague Lake.)

RV sites, facilities: There are 30 pull-through sites with full or partial hookups (30 amps) for RVs of any length and 50 tent sites. Picnic tables and fire grills are provided. Restrooms have flush toilets and coin showers. Drinking water, a small store, a coin laundry, ice, firewood, a playground, boat docks, launching facilities, and rentals are available. Leashed pets are permitted.

Reservations, fees: Reservations are accepted. Sites are $18–25 per night, $1 per person per night for more than two people. Open April–mid-October.

Directions: From Spokane, drive west on I-90 to the Sprague Business Center exit. Take that exit to Sprague Lake Road and continue two miles to the resort on the left (well signed), at 1999 Sprague Lake Resort Road.

Contact: Sprague Lake Resort, 509/257-2864, www.spraguelakeresort.com.

④ KLINK'S WILLIAMS LAKE RESORT

Scenic rating: 6

on Williams Lake
See map page 229

This family-oriented resort is on the shore of Williams Lake, which is less than three miles long and is popular for fishing, swimming,

and waterskiing. The resort has a swimming area with a floating dock and slide. This lake is also one of the top fishing lakes in the region for rainbow and cutthroat trout. Rocky cliffs border the lake in some areas. Note that about 100 permanent residents live at the resort.

An option for a side trip is Turnbull National Wildlife Refuge, an expanse of marsh and pine that is a significant stopover point for migratory birds on the Pacific Flyway. This is a prime spot and only a 30-minute drive out of Spokane, yet it is relatively unknown.

RV sites, facilities: There are 60 sites with full or partial hookups (30 and 50 amps) for RVs of any length, 15 tent sites, and three log cabins. Picnic tables and fire grills are provided. Restrooms have flush toilets and coin showers. Drinking water, Wi-Fi access, propane gas, a dump station, firewood, a general store, a restaurant, ice, a playground, boat docks, launching facilities, and boat rentals are available. Leashed pets are permitted.

Reservations, fees: Reservations are recommended at 800/274-1540. Sites are $16.95–23.95 per night, $2 per pet per night. Some credit cards accepted. Open mid-April–October.

Directions: From Spokane, drive west on I-90 for 10 miles to Exit 270 and Highway 904. Turn south on Highway 904 and drive four miles to Cheney and Cheney Plaza Road. Turn left (south) on Cheney Plaza Road and drive 11.2 miles to Williams Lake Road. Turn right (west) and drive 3.2 miles to the resort on the left, at 18617 West Williams Lake Road.

Contact: Klink's Williams Lake Resort, 509/235-2391 or 800/274-1540, www.klinks resort.com.

⑤ BUNKER'S RESORT

Scenic rating: 8

on Williams Lake
See map page 229

This campground is on the shore of Williams Lake. The lake is stocked with rainbow, cutthroat, and triploid trout, and fishing season is from the last Saturday in April through September. Waterskiing, wakeboarding, and personal watercraft are allowed. (See the listing in this chapter for *Klink's Williams Lake Resort* for information on the area.)

RV sites, facilities: There are 10 sites with full or partial hookups (30 amps) for RVs up to 32 feet, seven tent sites, and four cottages. Picnic tables and fire pits are provided. Restrooms have flush toilets and coin showers. Drinking water, propane gas, a dump station, a restaurant, a convenience store, bait and tackle, ice, boat and fishing docks, launching facilities, and boat rentals are available. Leashed pets are permitted.

Reservations, fees: Reservations are accepted. Sites are $15–30 per night. Some credit cards accepted. Open mid-April–September.

Directions: From Spokane, drive west on I-90 for 10 miles to Exit 270 and Highway 904. Turn south on Highway 904 and drive six miles to Cheney and Mullinex Road. Turn left (south) on Mullinex Road and drive 12 miles to the resort, at 36402 Bunkers Landing Road.

Contact: Bunker's Resort, 509/235-5212 or 800/404-6674, www.bunkersresort.com.

6 WILLOWS TRAILER VILLAGE

Scenic rating: 5

near Moses Lake State Park

See map page 228

This campground has grassy, shaded sites, horseshoe pits, barbecues, and a recreation field. Note that there are some permanent site rentals at this RV park, but a landscape barrier separates them from the other sites. The primary appeal is Moses Lake, Washington's largest freshwater lake, where you will find shady picnic spots with tables and fire grills, beach access, and moorage floats. Waterskiing and personal watercraft are allowed on the lake. Bird hunting is popular in season. Sand dunes are a few miles away and can be used for all-terrain vehicle (ATV) activities.

RV sites, facilities: There are 65 pull-through sites, most with full hookups (30 and 50 amps) for RVs of any length, and 20 tent sites. Picnic tables are provided. A restroom with flush toilets and coin showers, propane gas, a convenience store, ice, a coin laundry, a playground, and horseshoe pits are available. There is also a hair salon on-site. Leashed pets are permitted.

Reservations, fees: Reservations are accepted. Sites are $14.50–20.50 per night, $3 per person per night for more than two people. Open year-round.

Directions: From Spokane, drive west on I-90 to Moses Lake and Exit 179 and Highway 17. Turn south on Highway 17 and drive 2.5 miles to Road M SE. Turn right and drive 0.5 mile to the park on the left, at 1347 Road M SE.

Contact: Willows Trailer Village, tel./fax 509/765-7531.

7 LA QUINTA INN/ RITZVILLE RV PARK

Scenic rating: 7

in Ritzville

See map page 229

If you have an RV, well, this might be the only site to stake it on within a radius of 25 miles. The RV park is adjacent to the motel. The nearest fishing is at Sprague Lake, 22 miles east on U.S. 395. Burroughs Historical Museum is a possible side trip in town. A nine-hole golf course is just across the street, and tennis courts are available a few blocks away.

RV sites, facilities: There are 39 pull-through sites for RVs of any length with full hookups (30 and 50 amps). Picnic tables are provided. Restrooms have flush toilets and showers. Cable TV, a dump station, a coin laundry, modem access, ice, a playground, a spa, and a seasonal heated swimming pool are available. Some facilities are wheelchair accessible. Propane gas, a store, a gift shop, a café, and a restaurant are within one mile. Leashed pets are permitted.

Reservations, fees: Reservations are accepted for groups only. Sites are $15–25 per night. Some credit cards accepted. Open year-round, with limited winter facilities.

Directions: From Pasco, take U.S. 395 and drive 85 miles north to Ritzville and I-90. Take I-90 east and drive 0.5 mile to Exit 221. Take that exit and drive 0.25 mile to Smitty's Boulevard. Turn right and drive a short distance to the motel/RV check-in on the left, at 1515 Smitty's Boulevard.

Contact: La Quinta Inn/Ritzville RV Park, 509/659-1007, fax 509/659-1025.

8 WANAPUM STATE RECREATION AREA/GINKGO PETRIFIED FOREST STATE PARK

Scenic rating: 7

on the Columbia River and Wanapum Lake

See map page 228

Ginkgo Petrified Forest State Park is one of the most unusual fossil forests in the world, and it is registered as a National Natural Landmark. Although a completely separate park, it is linked to Wanapum State Recreation Area. Camping is permitted only at the Wanapum Recreation Area, which is three miles south of I-90. Ginkgo Petrified Forest State Park features an interpretive center and trail; it is open weekends and holidays November–March. The petrified forest is along Wanapum Lake in the course of the Columbia River. Ginko is a huge park, covering 7,740 acres and surrounding the 27,000 feet of shoreline of Wanapum Lake. Camping is not allowed at Ginko. Recreation options include hiking (three miles of trails), swimming, boating, waterskiing, and fishing. Several Civilian Conservation Corps structures date from the 1930s. The campground at Wanapum is set up primarily for RVs, with full hookups, restrooms, and showers. Note that the park always fills up during the Gorge concert season.

RV sites, facilities: There are 50 sites with full hookups (30 amps) for RVs up to 60 feet. Picnic tables and fire grills are provided. Restrooms have flush toilets and coin showers. Firewood is available. Boat docks, launching facilities, and a picnic area are nearby. Some facilities are wheelchair accessible. Leashed pets are permitted.

Reservations, fees: Reservations are accepted at 888/CAMP-OUT (888/226-7688) or www.parks.wa.gov/reservations ($7 reservation fee). Sites are $26–31 per night, $10 per extra vehicle per night. Open April–October, weather permitting, and on weekends and holidays November–March.

Directions: From Ellensburg, drive east on I-90 to Vantage Highway/Huntzinger Road (Exit 136). Take that exit, turn south on Huntzinger Road, and drive three miles to the campground on the left.

Contact: Wanapum State Recreation Area, 509/856-2700; state park information 360/902-8844, www.parks.wa.gov.

9 VANTAGE RIVERSTONE RESORT

Scenic rating: 6

on the Columbia River

See map page 228

This resort offers pleasant, grassy sites overlooking the Columbia River and lies a short distance from Ginkgo Petrified Forest State Park (see listing in this chapter for *Wanapum State Recreation Area*). This campground is the only one in the immediate area that provides space for tent camping.

RV sites, facilities: There are 50 sites with full hookups (30 amps) for RVs of any length and 200 tent sites. Four vacation homes, one cabin, and 14 motel rooms are also available. Picnic tables and fire rings are provided at most sites. A restroom with flush toilets and showers, modem access, a dump station, a recreation hall, horseshoe pits, a coin laundry, ice, a playground, and an indoor swimming pool are available. A store and a café are next to the resort. Boat docks and launching facilities are nearby. Leashed pets are permitted.

Reservations, fees: Reservations are accepted. RV sites are $27–37 per night, tent sites are $20–30 per night, plus $10–15 per person per

WASHINGTON

night for more than two people. Some credit cards accepted. Open year-round.

Directions: From Ellensburg, drive east on I-90 for approximately 24 miles to Vantage and the Vantage Highway (Exit 136). Take that exit, turn north, and drive three blocks to the resort on the left.

Contact: Vantage Riverstone Resort, 509/856-2230, fax 509/856-2800.

10 POTHOLES STATE PARK

Scenic rating: 8

on Potholes Reservoir
See map page 228

This park is on Potholes Reservoir, also known as O'Sullivan Reservoir (because of the O'Sullivan Dam), where fishing is the highlight. Trout, walleye, bass, crappie, and perch are among the species taken here. Waterskiing and hiking (on three miles of hiking trails) are other recreation options. The surrounding terrain is desertlike with freshwater marshes. A side trip to the Columbia Wildlife Refuge, two miles southeast of the park, is recommended. Note that Potholes Reservoir is often confused with the Potholes Lakes, which are a 30- to 45-minute drive from the park.

RV sites, facilities: There are 60 sites for tents or RVs up to 50 feet (no hookups), 60 sites for RVs up to 50 feet with full hookups (30 amps), and a group camp that accommodates up to 50 people. Picnic tables and fire grills are provided. Restrooms have flush toilets and showers. A dump station, a playground, firewood, and a sheltered picnic area are available. Boat-launching facilities and rentals are nearby. Some facilities are wheelchair accessible. Leashed pets are permitted.

Reservations, fees: Reservations are accepted at 888/CAMP-OUT (888/226-7688) or www.parks.wa.gov/reservations ($7 reservation fee). Sites are $10–22 per night, $10 per extra vehicle per night. Open year-round.

Directions: From I-90 at Moses Lake, take Exit 179 and Highway 17. Turn south and drive nine

miles to Highway 262. Turn right (west) and drive 11 miles to the resort on the southern shore of Potholes Reservoir (well signed).

Contact: Potholes State Park, 509/346-2759, fax 509/346-1732; state park information 360/902-8844, www.parks.wa.gov.

11 MAR DON RESORT

Scenic rating: 7

on Potholes Reservoir
See map page 228

This resort is on Potholes Reservoir and provides opportunities for fishing, swimming, and boating. A marina, tackle, and boat rentals are all available. Hiking trails are close by. Many visitors find the café and cocktail lounge a nice bonus. The Columbia National Wildlife Refuge is nearby to the south and provides exceptional bird-watching; pelicans and kingfishers are common, and bald eagles and migratory sandhill cranes are often seen.

RV sites, facilities: There are 187 sites for tents or RVs of any length with full or partial hookups (30 amps) and 88 sites for tents or RVs of any length (no hookups). Some sites are pull-through. Three rental homes, three cottages, and 24 motel rooms are also available. Picnic tables and fire rings are provided. A restroom with flush toilets and coin showers, drinking water, propane gas, a dump station, a small convenience store, a boutique, a coin laundry, ice, a playground, fish cleaning station, boat moorage, boat rentals, and launching facilities are available. Some facilities are wheelchair accessible. Leashed pets are permitted, with certain restrictions.

Reservations, fees: Reservations are accepted. Sites are $22–28 per night, $5 per extra vehicle per night, and $3 per pet per night. Some credit cards accepted. Open year-round.

Directions: From Highway 17 in Moses Lake, drive south nine miles to Highway 262. Turn right (west) and drive 10 miles to the resort on the southern shore of Potholes Reservoir, at 8198 Highway 262 SE.

Contact: Mar Don Resort, 509/346-2651 or 800/416-2736, www.mardonresort.com.

12 SQUAW ROCK RESORT

Scenic rating: 8

on the Naches River

See map page 228

This park, in a stand of old-growth fir and pine on the Naches River, is close to a host of activities, including trout fishing, hiking trails, marked bike trails, and a riding stable. The park has a pool and spa. The nearby town of Naches, southeast of the campground on State Route 410, offers all services.

RV sites, facilities: There are 65 sites with full or partial hookups (20, 30, and 50 amps) for RVs of any length, 25 tent sites, six cabins, and four motel rooms. Picnic tables and fire pits are provided. Restrooms have flush toilets and showers. Propane gas, gasoline, diesel, a dump station, cable TV, a recreation hall, a convenience store, a café, ice, a playground, a spa, and a seasonal heated swimming pool are available. Leashed pets are permitted.

Reservations, fees: Reservations are accepted at 800/546-2848. Sites are $16–24 per night, $3 per person per night for more than two people. Some credit cards accepted. Open year-round.

Directions: From Yakima, drive northwest on U.S. 12 for 18 miles to State Route 410. Continue straight on State Route 410 and drive 15 miles to the resort on the left, Mile Marker 102, at 15070 State Route 410.

Contact: Squaw Rock Resort, 509/658-2926 or 800/546-2848, fax 509/658-2927, www.squawrockresort.net.

13 HAUSE CREEK

Scenic rating: 7

on the Tieton River in Wenatchee National Forest

See map page 228

Several creeks converge at this campground along the Tieton River (elevation 2,500 feet).

The Tieton Dam, which creates Rimrock Lake, is just upstream. Hause Creek is one of the larger, more developed camps in the area.

RV sites, facilities: There are 42 sites for tents or RVs up to 30 feet (no hookups). Picnic tables and fire grills are provided. Drinking water, flush toilets, firewood, and a camp host are available. Boat docks, launching facilities, and rentals are on Rimrock Lake. Some facilities are wheelchair accessible. Leashed pets are permitted.

Reservations, fees: Reservations are accepted at 877/444-6777 or www.ReserveUSA.com ($9 reservation fee). Sites are $15–17 per night, $30 per night for double sites, and $5 per extra vehicle per night. Open mid-May–September, weather permitting.

Directions: From Yakima, drive northwest on U.S. 12 for 18 miles to the junction with Highway 410. Turn west on U.S. 12 and drive 22 miles to the campground on the left.

Contact: Okanogan and Wenatchee National Forests, Naches Ranger District, 509/653-1400, fax 509/653-2638.

14 WILLOWS

Scenic rating: 5

on the Tieton River in Wenatchee National Forest

See map page 228

This primitive, beautiful, and easily accessible camp can be found on the Tieton River at 2,400 feet elevation. Rimrock Lake to the west provides many recreation options, and hiking trails leading into the William O. Douglas Wilderness are within driving distance.

RV sites, facilities: There are 16 sites for tents or RVs up to 20 feet (no hookups). Picnic tables and fire grills are provided. Drinking water, vault toilets, and garbage service are available. Leashed pets are permitted.

Reservations, fees: Reservations are not accepted. Call for current rates. Open late May–September, weather permitting.

Directions: From Yakima, drive northwest on I-82 for 17 miles to the junction with Highway

410. Turn west on U.S. 12 and drive 16 miles to the campground on the left.

Contact: Okanogan and Wenatchee National Forests, Naches Ranger District, 509/653-1400, fax 509/653-2638.

15 WINDY POINT

Scenic rating: 5

on the Tieton River in Wenatchee National Forest
See map page 228

This campground, along the Tieton River at an elevation of 2,000 feet, is more isolated than the camps set westward toward Rimrock Lake. Drinking water is a bonus. Fishing access is available.

RV sites, facilities: There are 15 sites for tents or RVs up to 35 feet (no hookups). Picnic tables and fire grills are provided. Drinking water and vault toilets are available. Firewood is available nearby. Leashed pets are permitted.

Reservations, fees: Reservations are accepted at 877/444-6777 or www.ReserveUSA.com ($9 reservation fee). Sites are $15–17 per night, $5 per extra vehicle per night. Open late May–September, weather permitting.

Directions: From Yakima, drive northwest on I-82 for 17 miles to the junction with Highway 410. Turn west on U.S. 12 and drive nine miles to the campground on the left.

Contact: Okanogan and Wenatchee National Forests, Naches Ranger District, 509/653-1400, fax 509/653-2638.

16 CIRCLE H RV RANCH

Scenic rating: 8

in Yakima
See map page 228

This pleasant, centrally located, and clean park with a Western flavor has comfortable, spacious sites among ornamental trees and roses. Nearby recreation options include an 18-hole golf course, hiking trails, and marked bike trails. See the *Yakima KOA* listing in this

chapter for information on points of interest in Yakima.

RV sites, facilities: There are 64 sites with full hookups (30 and 50 amps) for RVs of any length, and 12 tent sites. Some sites are pull-through. Picnic tables and barbecues are provided. Restrooms have flush toilets and showers. Cable TV, a recreation hall, a coin laundry, a spa, modem and Wi-Fi access, clubhouse, seasonal café, playgrounds, horseshoes, a tennis court, volleyball and basketball, a video arcade, an 18-hole mini-golf course, and a seasonal heated swimming pool are available. Propane gas, a store, casino, and shopping center are within one mile. Mini-storage units are available for a fee. Leashed pets are permitted.

Reservations, fees: Reservations accepted. Sites are $24–25 per night, $3 per person per night for more than two people. Some credit cards accepted. Open year-round.

Directions: In Yakima on I-82, take Exit 34 west and drive one block to South 18th Street. Turn right (north) and drive 0.25 mile to the campground on the right.

Contact: Circle H RV Ranch, 509/457-3683, www.circlehrvranch.com.

17 TRAILER INNS RV PARK/ YAKIMA

Scenic rating: 7

in Yakima
See map page 228

This spot has many of the luxuries you'd find in a hotel, including a pool, a spa, on-site security, and a large-screen TV. An 18-hole golf course, hiking trails, marked bike trails, and tennis courts are close by. Local pond fishing, as well as fishing in the Yakima River, is available. It's especially pretty in the fall when the sycamores turn color. The region has become known for its wineries and breweries. Fresh produce is available in the local area in season. See the *Yakima KOA* listing in this chapter for information on points of interest in Yakima.

RV sites, facilities: There are 135 sites for tents

or RVs of any length with full hookups (20, 30, and 50 amps). Some sites are pull-through. Picnic tables are provided, and some sites have gas barbecues. Restrooms have flush toilets and showers. Cable TV, Wi-Fi and modem access, propane gas, a dump station, a recreation hall, a coin laundry, ice, an indoor heated swimming pool, a whirlpool, a TV room, a dog walk, an enclosed barbecue area (no open fires permitted), and a playground are available. A store and a café are within one block. Leashed pets are permitted.

Reservations, fees: Reservations accepted. Sites are $18–35 per night, $5 per person per night for more than two people, and $5 per extra vehicle per night. Some credit cards accepted. Open year-round.

Directions: In Yakima on I-82, take Exit 31 and drive south for one block on North 1st Street to the park on the right (west side of the road), at 1610 North 1st Street.

Contact: Trailer Inns RV Park, 509/452-9561; corporate office, 509/248-1142, www.trailerinnsrv.com.

18 YAKIMA SPORTSMAN STATE PARK

Scenic rating: 8

on the Yakima River
See map page 228

This park is on the floodplain of the Yakima River and is an irrigated area in an otherwise desert landscape. Several deciduous trees shade the camping and picnic areas. More than 140 bird species have been identified in the park. It is a popular layover spot for visitors attending events in the Yakima area. There is a fishing pond for children (no anglers over age 14 are allowed). Hiking is permitted along five miles of unpaved roadway on the river dike. No swimming is allowed. Nearby recreation options include an 18-hole golf course and hiking trails. (See the *Yakima KOA* listing in this chapter for information on other points of interest in Yakima.)

RV sites, facilities: There are 37 sites with full

hookups (20, 30, and 50 amps) for RVs up to 60 feet and 30 sites for tents or RVs (no hookups). Some sites are pull-through. Picnic tables and fire grills are provided. Restrooms have flush toilets and coin showers. A dump station, firewood, a playground, volleyball, horseshoe pits, ranger-led nature walks, and seasonal campfire programs are available. Some facilities are wheelchair accessible. A store and ice are within one mile. Leashed pets are permitted.

Reservations, fees: Reservations are accepted at 888/CAMP-OUT (888/226-7688) or www.parks.wa.gov/reservations ($7 reservation fee). Sites are $16–22 per night, $10 per extra vehicle per night. Some credit cards accepted. Open year-round.

Directions: In Yakima, drive on I-82 to Milepost 34 and the Highway 24 exit. Turn east on Highway 24 and drive two miles to South 33rd Street. Turn left and drive approximately one mile to the park entrance on the left.

Contact: Yakima Sportsman State Park, 509/575-2774, fax 509/454-4114; state park information 360/902-8844, www.parks.wa.gov.

19 YAKIMA KOA

Scenic rating: 6

on the Yakima River
See map page 228

This campground along the Yakima River offers well-maintained, shaded sites and fishing access. Some points of interest in Yakima are the Yakima Valley Museum and the Yakima Trolley Lines, which offer rides on restored trolley cars originally built in 1906. Indian Rock Paintings State Park is five miles west of Yakima on U.S. 12. Nearby recreation options include an 18-hole golf course, hiking trails, marked bike trails, and tennis courts. A casino is two miles west.

RV sites, facilities: There are 120 sites with full or partial hookups (30 and 50 amps) for RVs of any length, 40 tent sites, and 10 cabins. Picnic tables and fire rings are provided. Restrooms have flush toilets and showers. Propane gas, a dump station, a convenience store, a coin

WASHINGTON

laundry, modem access, ice, a seasonal heated swimming pool, a playground, horseshoe pits, a basketball hoop, fishing ponds, firewood, bike rentals, and boat rentals including pedal boats are available. Leashed pets permitted.

Reservations, fees: Reservations are accepted at 800/562-5773. Sites are $22–33 per night, $3 per person per night for more than two people. Some credit cards accepted. Open year-round.

Directions: In Yakima, drive on I-82 to Milepost 34 and the Highway 24 exit. Turn east on Highway 24 and drive one mile to Keys Road. Turn left (north) on Keys Road and drive 300 yards to the campground on the left.

Contact: Yakima KOA, 509/248-5882, fax 509/469-3986, www.koa.com.

20 YAKAMA NATION RV RESORT

Scenic rating: 3

near the Yakima River
See map page 228

The park is within the Yakama Indian Reservation (the tribe spells its name differently from the river and town), close to a casino and movie theater. The Toppenish National Wildlife Refuge, the best side trip, is almost always a good spot to see a large variety of birds. For information, phone 509/545-8588. Nearby Toppenish, a historic Old West town with a museum, is also worth a side trip.

RV sites, facilities: There are 125 sites with full hookups (20, 30, and 50 amps) for RVs of any length, a tent area, and 14 tepees for up to 10 people each. Picnic tables and fire pits are provided. Restrooms have flush toilets and showers. Cable TV, modem and Wi-Fi access, a dump station, a playground, a recreation room, an exercise room, a jogging track, basketball, volleyball, a seasonal heated swimming pool, spa, sauna, and a coin laundry are available. A picnic shelter is available in the tent area. A restaurant and a grocery store are within 1.5 miles. Some facilities are wheelchair accessible. Leashed pets are permitted.

Reservations, fees: Reservations are accepted

at 800/874-3087. Tent sites are $20 per night, and hookup sites are $26–28 per night, plus $2 per person per night for more than two people. Tepees are $50 per night for five campers, plus $5 per night for each additional person. Some credit cards accepted. Open year-round.

Directions: From Yakima, drive south on U.S. 97 for 16 miles to the resort on the right, at 280 Buster Road.

Contact: Yakama Nation RV Resort, 509/865-2000 or 800/874-3087, www.yakama nation.com.

21 WINDUST

Scenic rating: 6

on Lake Sacajawea
See map page 229

With no other campgrounds within a 30-mile radius, Windust is the only game in town. The camp is along the shore of Lake Sacajawea near the Lower Monumental Dam on the Snake River. The park covers 54 acres. Swimming, waterskiing, and fishing are popular.

RV sites, facilities: There are 24 sites for tents or RVs up to 40 feet (no hookups). Picnic tables and fire grills are provided. Flush toilets are available May–September, and vault toilets are provided the remainder of the year. Drinking water (summer season only), a dump station, garbage bins, a playground, a swimming beach, and covered sun shelters are available nearby. No alcohol is permitted. Some facilities are wheelchair accessible. Boat docks and launching facilities are nearby. Leashed pets are permitted.

Reservations, fees: Reservations are accepted at 877/444-6777 or www.ReserveUSA.com ($9 reservation fee). Sites are $12 per night, and boat camping is $8 per night. Open year-round, with limited facilities and no fee October–April.

Directions: From Pasco, drive east on U.S. 12 for 2.5 miles to Pasco/Kahlotus Highway. Turn east and drive 28 miles to Burr Canyon Road. Turn right on Burr Canyon Road and drive 5.2 miles to the park (from the north, Burr Canyon Road becomes Highway 263).

WASHINGTON

Contact: U.S. Army Corps of Engineers, Walla Walla District, 509/547-7781, www.nww.usace.army.mil; Natural Resources Management Office, 509/547-2048.

22 PALOUSE FALLS STATE PARK

Scenic rating: 10

on the Snake and Palouse Rivers

See map page 229

This remote state park is well worth the trip. Spectacular 198-foot Palouse Falls is a sight not to miss. A half-mile wheelchair-accessible trail leads to a waterfall overlook. The park is at the confluence of the Snake and Palouse Rivers, and it does not receive heavy use, even in summer. The park covers 1,282 acres and features a waterfall observation shelter, shaded picnic facilities, historical displays, and an abundance of wildlife.

RV sites, facilities: There are 10 sites for tents or RVs up to 40 feet (no hookups). Picnic tables and fire grills are provided. Vault toilets, a picnic area, and a dump station are available. Some facilities are wheelchair accessible. Leashed pets are permitted.

Reservations, fees: Reservations are not accepted. Sites are $15 per night, $10 per extra vehicle per night. Open April–late September, weather permitting.

Directions: From Starbuck, drive northwest on Highway 261 for 15 miles (crossing the river) to the park entrance and Palouse Falls Road. Turn right and drive to the park.

Contact: Palouse Falls State Park, 509/646-9218; state park information 360/902-8844, www.parks.wa.gov.

23 CENTRAL FERRY PARK

Scenic rating: 8

on the Snake River

See map page 229

This campground is the only one within a 20-mile radius, yet it's a great spot to hunker down and enjoy the world. This 185-acre park is near 10,000-acre Lake Bryan, a reservoir on the Snake River created by Little Goose Dam. With summer daytime temperatures in the 90s and even 100s occasionally, boating is popular at the desert lake. The surrounding terrain is dry, courtesy of just eight inches of average rainfall per year, as well as basaltic lava flows, according to geologic evidence. The park is named after a ferry that once operated in this area. A beach, swimming, boating, waterskiing, and fishing for bass and catfish are all options here. This was formerly a state park but is now owned by the U.S. Army Corps of Engineers.

RV sites, facilities: There are eight primitive tent sites and 60 sites with full hookups (30 amps) for RVs up to 45 feet. One group camp accommodates up to 200 people. Picnic tables and fire grills are provided. Restrooms have flush toilets and coin showers. A dump station, a group fire ring, firewood, camp host, a day-use picnic area, covered shelters, a swimming beach and bathhouse, beachside shade structures, volleyball courts, and horseshoe pits are available. A store and a restaurant are within five miles. Some facilities are wheelchair accessible. Boat docks, launching facilities, and a fishing pier are within the park. Leashed pets are permitted.

Reservations, fees: Reservations are accepted at 877/444-6777 or www.ReserveUSA.com ($9 reservation fee). Sites are $20–26.50 per night, $5.38 per extra vehicle per night. The group camp is $118 per night, plus $3.25 per person per night for more than 50 people. Some credit cards accepted. Open May–October, weather permitting.

Directions: From Spokane, drive south on U.S. 195 for 59 miles to Highway 26. Turn west on Highway 26 and drive 17 miles southwest to the town of Dusty and Highway 127. Turn south on Highway 127 and drive 17 miles to the park entrance on the right (on the north shore of the Snake River).

Contact: Central Ferry Park, 509/549-3551; U.S. Army Corps of Engineers, Walla Walla District, 509/547-7781, www.nww.usace.army.mil.

WASHINGTON

24 PALOUSE EMPIRE FAIRGROUNDS & HORSE CAMP

Scenic rating: 6

west of Colfax, Whitman County

See map page 229

The camp consists primarily of a large lawn area with shade trees. It is just off the road, but the highway noise, surprisingly, is relatively limited. All sites are on grass. The park covers 47 acres, with paved trails available around the adjacent fairgrounds. This area is agricultural, with rolling hills, and it is considered the "Lentil Capital of the World." With wash racks, corrals, arenas, and water troughs, the camp encourages horse campers to stay here. It fills up for the Whitman County Fair in early September. They turn back the clock every Labor Day weekend with the annual "Threshing Bee," where there are demonstrations of historical farming practices dating back to the early 1900s, including the use of draft horses.

RV sites, facilities: There are 60 sites for RVs of any length with full hookups (30 amps). Large groups can be accommodated. Picnic tables are provided. Restrooms have flush toilets and showers. Drinking water and a dump station are available. Some facilities are wheelchair accessible. Restaurants, gas, and supplies are available 4.5 miles away in Colfax. Leashed pets are permitted.

Reservations, fees: Reservations are accepted for groups only. Sites are $15 per night, $5 per night per extra vehicle. Horse stalls cost $10 per night. Open year-round with limited winter facilities.

Directions: From Colfax and Highway 26, drive west on Highway 26 for 4.5 miles to the fairgrounds on the right.

Contact: Palouse Empire Fairgrounds & Horse Camp, Whitman County, 509/397-6238 or 509/397-3753, www.palouseempirefair.org.

25 BOYER PARK AND MARINA

Scenic rating: 7

on Lake Bryan on the Snake River

See map page 229

This 56-acre park on the north shore of Lake Bryan is two miles from the Lower Granite Dam. It features 3.5 miles of trails for hiking and biking, and the lake is popular for waterskiing and fishing for sturgeon, steelhead, and salmon. Most campsites are shaded, and all are paved and bordered by a grassy day-use area. The landscape is flat and open, and it gets hot here in summer. The camp is well above the water level, typically about 100 feet above the lakeshore. It commonly fills on summer weekends.

RV sites, facilities: There are 32 sites for tents or RVs up to 40 feet with full or partial hookups (30 and 50 amps) and eight tent sites. Four motel rooms and an apartment are also available. Picnic tables and fire grills are provided. Restrooms have flush toilets and coin showers. Drinking water and a dump station are available. Some facilities are wheelchair accessible. A coin laundry, covered shelters, a swimming area, a snack bar, a convenience store, ice, gas, and pay phones are available. A marina, boat docks, a boat launch, moorage, and a marine dump station are nearby. Leashed pets are permitted.

Reservations, fees: Reservations are accepted at 509/397-3208 ($10 reservation fee). Tent sites are $12–13 per night, $6 per night per additional tent. RV sites are $18.95–27.95 per night, $6 per night per extra vehicle. Moorage is $12–16 per night. Winter rates available. Some credit cards accepted. Open year-round, with limited winter facilities.

Directions: From U.S. 195 at Colfax, turn southwest on Almota Road and drive 17 miles to the park and campground.

Contact: Boyer Park and Marina, 509/397-3208, fax 509/397-3181; Port of Whitman County, 509/397-3791, fax 509/397-4758, www.portwhitman.com.

26 WAWAWAI COUNTY PARK

Scenic rating: 7

on Lower Granite Lake, Whitman County

See map page 229

This park covers 49 acres and is near the inlet to Lower Granite Lake, about one-quarter mile from the lake. The camp itself is on a hillside, and all sites are paved. Some sites have views of a bay, but not the entire lake. Tree cover is a plus. So is a 0.5-mile loop trail that leads to a bird-viewing platform. The mix of wildlife and geology is diverse. One strange note: An underground house built in 1980 has been converted to a ranger's residence. This camp often fills on summer weekends. No campfires are permitted during the summer season.

RV sites, facilities: There are nine sites for tents or RVs up to 24 feet (no hookups). Some sites are pull-through. Picnic tables and fire grills are provided. Drinking water (mid-April–mid-October) and vault toilets are available. A volleyball net, reservable group picnic shelter, and a boat launch are available nearby. Some facilities are wheelchair accessible. Leashed pets are permitted.

Reservations, fees: Reservations are not accepted; sites are $15 per night, $5 per extra vehicle per night. Open year-round, with limited winter facilities and no fee mid-October–mid-April.

Directions: From Colfax, drive south on U.S. 195 for 15 miles to Wawawai-Pullman Road (just west of Pullman). Turn right (west) and drive approximately 9.5 miles to Wawawai Road. Turn right on Wawawai Road (signed) and drive 5.5 miles to the park.

Contact: Wawawai County Park, Whitman County Parks and Recreation, 509/397-6238, www.whitmancounty.org.

27 CHIEF TIMOTHY PARK

Scenic rating: 8

on the Snake River

See map page 229

This unusual park is on an island composed of glacial tills in the Snake River; it is accessible by car over a bridge. The park covers 282 acres with two miles of shoreline and features a desert landscape. There are 2.5 miles of hiking trails, plus docks for boating campers and a beach area. Water sports include fishing, swimming, boating, waterskiing, and sailing. Outfitters in Clarkston will take you sightseeing up the Grand Canyon of the Snake River. Call the Clarkston Chamber of Commerce at 509/758-7712 for details. This was formerly a state park but is now a U.S. Army Corps of Engineers facility.

RV sites, facilities: There are 66 sites for tents or RVs up to 40 feet, including 33 with full or partial hookups (30 amps), and one group tent camp for up to 60 people. Picnic tables and fire grills are provided. Restrooms have flush toilets and coin showers. A dump station, a picnic area, a small store, firewood, a playground, and horseshoe pits are available. Some facilities are wheelchair accessible. Boat docks and launching facilities are nearby. Leashed pets are permitted.

Reservations, fees: Reservations are accepted at 877/444-6777 or www.ReserveUSA.com ($9 reservation fee). Sites are $20–26.50 per night, $5.36 per extra vehicle per night. The group camp is $5.36 per vehicle. Some credit cards accepted. Open May–November, weather permitting.

Directions: From Clarkston on the Washington/Idaho border, drive west on U.S. 12 for seven miles to the signed park entrance road on the right. Turn right (north) and drive one mile to the park, which sits on a bridged island in the Snake River.

Contact: Chief Timothy Park, 509/758-9580; U.S. Army Corps of Engineers, Walla Walla District, 509/547-7781, www.nww.usace.army.mil.

28 BEACH RV PARK

Scenic rating: 8

on the Yakima River

See map page 228

This park along the shore of the Yakima River is a pleasant spot with spacious RV sites, a large grassy area, and poplar trees and shrubs that provide privacy between many of the sites.

WASHINGTON

Fishing for bass and trout is available in season. Nearby recreation options include an 18-hole golf course and a full-service marina, both within 12 miles.

RV sites, facilities: There are 59 sites with full hookups (30 and 50 amps) for RVs of any length and six tent sites. Some sites are pull-through. Picnic tables are provided. Restrooms have flush toilets and free showers. Cable TV, Wi-Fi, a dump station, and a coin laundry are available. Propane gas, a store, and a café are within one mile. Boat-launching facilities are nearby. Leashed pets are permitted.

Reservations, fees: Reservations are accepted. RV sites are $26–29 per night, tent sites are $15–18 per night, and it's $2 per person per night for more than two people, $2 per night per extra vehicle, and $2 per night per pet. No credit cards accepted. Open year-round.

Directions: From Pasco, drive west on U.S. 12 past Richland and continue eight miles to Exit 96 and the Benton City/West Richland exit. Take that exit and drive one block north to Abby Avenue. Turn left (west) and drive one and a half blocks to the park, at 113 Abby Avenue.

Contact: Beach RV Park, tel./fax 509/588-5959, www.beachrv.net.

29 DESERT GOLD RV PARK AND MOTEL

Scenic rating: 6

near the Columbia River
See map page 228

Desert Gold is a nice RV park about one mile from the Columbia River. Nearby recreation options include an 18-hole golf course, hiking trails, and a full-service marina. You can also visit the Department of Energy public information center at the Hanford Science Center. The RV park has a pool and spa if you just want to relax without going anywhere. Note that some sites are filled with monthly renters.

RV sites, facilities: There are 90 sites with full hookups (30 amps) for RVs of any length; some sites are pull-through. There are also 29 motel rooms, including 19 with kitchenettes. Picnic tables are provided. Restrooms have flush toilets and showers. Cable TV, wireless and modem access, propane gas, a dump station, a store, a coin laundry, ice, a game/meeting room, video rentals, a picnic area, and a seasonal spa and swimming pool are available. A café is within one mile. Boat docks and launching facilities are nearby on the Columbia River. Leashed pets are permitted.

Reservations, fees: Reservations are accepted. Sites are $24 per night, $1.50 per person per night for more than two people. Some credit cards accepted. Open year-round.

Directions: In Richland on I-182, take Exit 3 (Queensgate). Turn right and drive to Columbia Park Trail (the first left). Turn left and drive about two miles to the park, at 611 Columbia Park Trail.

Contact: Desert Gold RV Park and Motel, 509/627-1000 or 800/788-GOLD (800/788-4653).

30 ARROWHEAD RV PARK

Scenic rating: 5

near the Columbia River
See map page 228

Arrowhead provides a decent layover spot in Pasco. Nearby recreation options include an 18-hole golf course, a full-service marina, and tennis courts.

RV sites, facilities: There are 80 sites with full hookups (30 amps) for RVs of any length, including 33 drive-through sites, and 35 tent sites. Drinking water, sewer hookups, cell phone reception, and picnic tables are provided. Flush toilets, showers, a pay phone, and a coin-operated laundry are available. A store, an ATM, and a café are within walking distance. Small pets are permitted (no pit bulls, Rottweilers, or Doberman pinschers).

Reservations, fees: Reservations are accepted. The fee is $20–30 per night for two people, plus $5 per person and $3 per child per night for more than two people and $1 per pet per night. Open year-round.

Directions: In Pasco on U.S. 395 northbound, take the Hillsboro Street exit, turn east, and drive a short distance to Commercial Avenue. Turn right (south) and drive 0.25 mile to the park entrance on the right.

Contact: Arrowhead RV Park, 3120 Commercial Avenue, Pasco, WA 99301, 509/545-8206.

31 GREENTREE RV & MOBILE HOME PARK

Scenic rating: 6

in Pasco

See map page 229

This shady park in urban Pasco is close to an 18-hole golf course, hiking trails, and a full-service marina. The Franklin County Historical Museum, which is in town, and the Sacajawea State Park Museum and Interpretive Center, three miles southeast of town, both offer extensive collections of Native American artifacts. Note that most sites are filled with monthly rentals.

RV sites, facilities: There are 40 sites with full hookups for RVs of any length. No tents are allowed. A coin laundry and coin showers are available, but no toilets are available. A mini-storage facility is on-site. Propane gas, a store, a café, and ice are within one mile. Boat docks, launching facilities, and rentals are nearby. Leashed pets are permitted, with certain restrictions.

Reservations, fees: Reservations are accepted. Call for current rates. Weekly and monthly rates available. Open year-round.

Directions: In Pasco on I-182, take Exit 13 onto 4th Avenue and continue a short distance to the park entrance driveway on the right.

Contact: Greentree RV & Mobile Home Park, tel./fax 509/547-6220.

32 HOOD PARK

Scenic rating: 6

on Lake Wallula

See map page 229

This 99-acre developed park on Lake Wallula provides access for swimming and boating. Some sites are near the shoreline, and shaded sites are available. No alcohol is permitted. There are hiking trails throughout the park, along with fishing ponds. Other recreation options include basketball and horseshoes. McNary Wildlife Refuge is right next door, and Sacajawea State Park is within four miles.

RV sites, facilities: There are 69 sites for tents or RVs of any length with partial hookups (20, 30, and 50 amps); an overflow camping area has some pull-through sites. Picnic tables and fire grills are provided. Drinking water, restrooms with flush toilets and showers, a dump station, a playground, horseshoe pits, a basketball court, a swimming beach, a reservable covered picnic area, pay phone, and an amphitheater are available. A restaurant and convenience store are within two miles. Some facilities are wheelchair accessible. Boat docks and launching facilities are at the park. Leashed pets are permitted.

Reservations, fees: Reservations are accepted at 877/444-6777 or www.ReserveUSA.com ($9 reservation fee). Sites are $18–20 per night or $8 per night in the overflow area and for boat camping. Open May–September.

Directions: In Pasco, drive southeast on U.S. 12 for five miles to the junction with Highway 124. Turn left (east) on Highway 124 and drive to the park entrance on the left (just before the town of Burbank). Drive 0.5 mile to the gate entrance.

Contact: U.S. Army Corps of Engineers, Walla Walla District, 509/547-7781, www.nww.usace.army.mil; Natural Resources Management Office, 509/547-2048.

WASHINGTON

33 CHARBONNEAU PARK

Scenic rating: 6

on the Snake River
See map page 229

This shorefront camp is the centerpiece of a 244-acre park set along the Snake River just above Ice Harbor Dam. It is a good spot for fishing, boating, swimming, and waterskiing. An overflow camping area provides an insurance policy if the numbered sites are full. No alcohol is permitted. At Lake Sacajawea, the dam's visitors center (open daily April–October) features exhibits and a view through Lucite of a salmon fish ladder.

RV sites, facilities: There are 54 sites for tents or RVs up to 60 feet with full or partial hookups (20 and 30 amps) and an overflow camping area. Some sites are pull-through. Picnic tables and fire grills are provided. Restrooms have flush toilets and showers. A dump station, a pay telephone, a playground, and a volleyball net are available. A marina with boat docks, launching facilities, a marine dump station, a swimming beach, fishing tackle, seasonal snack bar, ice, and a reservable day-use area and picnic shelters are nearby. Some facilities are wheelchair accessible. Leashed pets are permitted.

Reservations, fees: Reservations are accepted at 877/444-6777 or www.ReserveUSA.com ($9 reservation fee). Sites are $18–22 per night. Overflow camping is $8 per night. Open April–October with full facilities; there are limited facilities and no fee the rest of the year.

Directions: From Pasco, drive southeast on U.S. 12 for five miles to Highway 124. Turn left (east) and drive eight miles to Sun Harbor Road. Turn left (north) and drive two miles to the park.

Contact: U.S. Army Corps of Engineers, Walla Walla District, 509/547-7781, www.nww.usace.army.mil; Natural Resources Management Office, 509/547-2048.

34 FISHHOOK PARK

Scenic rating: 6

on the Snake River
See map page 229

If you're driving along Highway 124 and you need a spot for the night, check out this wooded camp along the Snake River. It is a nice spot within a 46-acre park set on Lake Sacajawea, which is a dammed portion of the Snake River. The park provides some lawn area, along with places to swim, fish, and water-ski. A one-mile walk along railroad tracks will take you to a fishing pond. This park is popular on summer weekends.

RV sites, facilities: There are 41 sites for tents or RVs up to 45 feet with partial hookups (20 and 30 amps), 20 tent sites, and one group tent site that can accommodate up to 16 people. Some sites are pull-through. Picnic tables and fire grills are provided. Drinking water, restrooms with flush toilets and showers, a dump station, and playgrounds are available. Boat docks, launching facilities, a swimming beach, and reservable group picnic shelters are at the park. Some facilities are wheelchair accessible. Leashed pets are permitted.

Reservations, fees: Reservations are accepted at 877/444-6777 or www.ReserveUSA.com ($9 reservation fee). Tent sites are $12 per night, hookup sites are $14–20 per night, the group tent site is $22 per night, and boat camping is $8 per night. Open May–September. Park gates are locked 10 P.M.–6 A.M.

Directions: From Pasco, drive southeast on U.S. 12 for five miles to Highway 124. Turn left (east) and drive 18 miles to Fishhook Park Road. Turn left on Fishhook Park Road and drive four miles to the park.

Contact: U.S. Army Corps of Engineers, Walla Walla District, 509/547-7781, www.nww.usace.army.mil; Natural Resources Management Office, 509/547-2048.

35 LEWIS AND CLARK TRAIL STATE PARK

Scenic rating: 8

on the Touchet River

See map page 229

Fishing for rainbow trout and brown trout can be excellent here. The park is on 37 acres with frontage along the Touchet River. The landscape is an unusual mixture of old-growth forest and riparian habitat, featuring long-leafed ponderosa pine and cottonwood amid the surrounding arid prairie grasslands. An interpretive display explains much of it, as well as the history of the area. A seasonal Saturday evening living-history program depicts the story of Lewis and Clark and the site's history here on the original Lewis and Clark Trail. In winter, cross-country skiing and snow-shoeing are good. Note: If it's getting late and you need to stop, consider this camp because it's the only one within 20 miles.

RV sites, facilities: There are 24 sites for tents or RVs up to 28 feet (no hookups), 17 hike-in sites for tents, and two group camps for up to 100 people each. Picnic tables and fire grills are provided. Restrooms have flush toilets and coin showers. Firewood and a dump station are available. Two fire circles, an amphitheater, a picnic area, badminton, a baseball field, and a volleyball court are available nearby. A store, a café, and ice are within one mile. Leashed pets are permitted.

Reservations, fees: Reservations are not accepted for individual sites but are required for group sites at 509/337-6457 or www.parks.wa.gov/reservations. Sites are $17–19 per night, $10–14 per night for hike-in sites, $10 per extra vehicle per night. Open late May–mid-September, with primitive sites open mid-September–March.

Directions: From Walla Walla, drive east on U.S. 12 for 22 miles to Waitsburg. Bear right on U.S. 12 and drive east for 4.5 miles to the park entrance on the left.

Contact: Lewis and Clark Trail State Park, 509/337-6457; state park information 360/902-8844, www.parks.wa.gov.

36 TUCANNON

Scenic rating: 8

in Umatilla National Forest

See map page 229

For people willing to rough it, this backcountry camp in Umatilla National Forest is the place. It has plenty of hiking, fishing, and hunting, all in a rugged setting. The camp is along the Tucannon River, which offers myriad recreation options for vacationers. It is popular from early spring (the best time for fishing) through fall (when it makes a good hunting camp). In summer, several nearby ponds are stocked with trout, making it a good family destination. There is some tree cover. The elevation is 2,600 feet.

RV sites, facilities: There are 16 sites for tents and five sites with no hookups for RVs up to 21 feet. Picnic tables and fire rings are provided. Vault toilets are available, but there is no drinking water. Garbage must be packed out. Two covered shelters are available nearby. Some facilities are wheelchair accessible. Leashed pets are permitted.

Reservations, fees: Reservations are not accepted. Sites are $5 per night per vehicle. Open year-round, weather permitting.

Directions: From Clarkston, drive west on U.S. 12 for 37 miles to Pomeroy. Continue west for five miles to Tatman Mountain Road (signed for Camp Wooten). Turn left (south) and drive 19 miles (the road becomes Forest Road 47). Once inside the national forest boundary, continue southwest on Forest Road 47 for four miles to the campground on the left.

Contact: Umatilla National Forest, Pomeroy Ranger District, 509/843-1891, fax 509/843-4621.

37 TEAL SPRING

Scenic rating: 8

in Umatilla National Forest

See map page 229

The views of the Tucannun drainage and the Wenaha-Tucannon Wilderness are astonishing

WASHINGTON

from the nearby drive-to lookout. Teal Spring Camp is at 5,600 feet elevation and is one of several small, primitive camps in the area. Trails in the immediate area provide a variety of good day-hiking options. A U.S. Forest Service map details the backcountry roads, trails, and streams. Hunting is popular in the fall.

RV sites, facilities: There are five sites for tents or RVs up to 35 feet (no hookups). Vault toilets are available, but there is no drinking water. Picnic tables and fire rings are provided. Garbage must be packed out. Some facilities are wheelchair accessible. Leashed pets are permitted.

Reservations, fees: Reservations are not accepted. There is no fee for camping. Open late May–mid-November, weather permitting.

Directions: From Clarkston, drive west on U.S. 12 for 37 miles to Pomeroy and Highway 128. Turn left (south) and drive 25 miles to Forest Road 42 (to the Clearwater Lookout Tower). Turn left on Forest Road 40 and drive one mile to the campground entrance road. Turn right and drive 200 yards to the campground.

Contact: Umatilla National Forest, Pomeroy Ranger District, 509/843-1891, fax 509/843-4621.

38 FIELDS SPRING STATE PARK

Scenic rating: 8

near Puffer Butte

See map page 229

This 792-acre state park is in the Blue Mountains and is in a forested landscape atop and surrounding Puffer Butte, offering a spectacular view of three states and the Grande Ronde River. Two hiking trails lead up to Puffer Butte at 4,500 feet elevation, providing a panoramic view of the Snake River Canyon, the Wallowa Mountains in Washington, and Idaho, Oregon, and Washington. This park is noted for its variety of birdlife and wildflowers. There are seven miles of mountain-biking trails, along with three miles of hiking trails. In winter, nonmotorized recreation opportunities include cross-country skiing (groomed trails), snowshoeing, and general snow play; warming huts are available. Basalt dominates the landscape. Not many people know about this spot, yet it's a good one, tucked away in the southeast corner of the state. It also has a retreat center with two reservable lodges. Two day-use areas with boat launches, managed by the Department of Fish and Wildlife, are within about 25 miles of the park.

RV sites, facilities: There are 20 sites for tents or RVs up to 30 feet (no hookups), two primitive tent sites, and two tepees. Picnic tables and fire grills are provided. Drinking water, restrooms with flush toilets and coin showers, firewood, a dump station, two picnic shelters, a fire circle, a playground, horseshoe pits, a softball field, and volleyball courts are available. A café and ice are within four miles. Some facilities are wheelchair accessible. Leashed pets are permitted.

Reservations, fees: Reservations are not accepted for campsites or tepees. Sites are $10–15 per night, tepees are $20 per night, plus $10 per extra vehicle per night. Open March–October.

Directions: From Clarkston, turn south on Highway 129 and drive 30 miles (just south of Rattlesnake Summit) to the park entrance on the left (east) side of the road.

Contact: Fields Spring State Park, 509/256-3332; state park information 360/902-8844, www.parks.wa.gov.

39 BROOKS MEMORIAL STATE PARK

Scenic rating: 7

near the Goldendale Observatory

See map page 228

This 700-acre park is near the South Yakima Valley and within the pine forests of the Simcoe Mountains. It is at an elevation of nearly 3,000 feet. The campground is on the Little Klickitat River. Highlights include nine miles of hiking trails. You can extend your trip into the mountains, where you'll find open meadows with a panoramic view of Mount Hood. Activities near the park include stargazing at the Goldendale Observatory, visiting the Maryhill Museum, viewing the replica of Stonehenge on State Route 14, and driving the historic Columbia Highway in nearby Oregon. The Yakama Indian Nation is two miles north of the park.

RV sites, facilities: There are 23 sites with full hookups (20, 30, and 50 amps) for RVs up to 60 feet, 22 sites for tents or RVs (no hookups), and a group site that can accommodate up to 50 people. Picnic tables and fire grills are provided. Restrooms have flush toilets and coin showers. A dump station and a playground are available. A sheltered picnic area, volleyball court, a ball field, a café, and a store are nearby. Leashed pets are permitted.

Reservations, fees: Reservations are not accepted for individual sites but are required for the group site at 509/773-4611. Sites are $17–24 per night, $10 per extra vehicle per night. Open year-round, with limited winter facilities.

Directions: From Toppenish, drive south on U.S. 97 for 40 miles to the park on the right (well signed).

Contact: Brooks Memorial State Park, 509/773-4611, fax 509/773-6428; state park information 360/902-8844, www.parks.wa.gov.

40 MARYHILL STATE PARK

Scenic rating: 8

on the Columbia River

See map page 228

This 99-acre park has 4,700 feet of frontage along the Columbia River. Fishing, waterskiing, and windsurfing are among the recreation possibilities. Two interesting places can be found near Maryhill: a full-scale replica of Stonehenge, on a bluff overlooking the Columbia River about one mile from the park, and the historic Mary Hill home, which is open to the public. Mary Hill's husband, Sam Hill, constructed the Stonehenge replica.

RV sites, facilities: There are 50 sites with full hookups (30 and 50 amps) for RVs up to 50 feet, 20 tent sites, three hike-in/bike-in sites, and one group camp for up to 200 people. Picnic tables and fire pits are provided. Restrooms have flush toilets and showers. A dump station and a picnic area with covered shelters are available. A café and store are within one mile. Some facilities are wheelchair accessible. Boat docks and launching facilities are nearby. Leashed pets are permitted.

Reservations, fees: Reservations are accepted and are required for the group camp at 888/CAMP-OUT (888/226-7688) or www.parks.wa.gov/reservations ($7 reservation fee). Sites are $19–31 per night, $14 per night for hike-in/bike-in sites, $10 per extra vehicle per night. The group camp is $55–440 per night. Some credit cards accepted. Open year-round.

Directions: From Goldendale and U.S. 97, drive 12 miles south to the park on the left.

Contact: Maryhill State Park, 509/773-5007, fax 509/773-6337; state park information 360/902-8844, www.parks.wa.gov.

41 CROW BUTTE PARK

Scenic rating: 8

on the Columbia River

See map page 228

How would you like to be stranded on a romantic island? Well, this park offers that possibility. The park is on an island in the Columbia River and is the only campground in a 25-mile radius. Sometimes referred to as the "Maui of the Columbia," the park covers 1,312 acres and has several miles of shoreline. It is on the Lewis and Clark Trail, with the camp situated alongside a partially protected bay. The highlight of 3.5 miles of hiking trails is a mile-long path that leads to the top of a butte, where you can see Mount Hood, Mount Adams, and the Columbia River Valley. Waterskiing, sailboarding, fishing, swimming, and hiking are among the possibilities here. One downer: Keep an eye out for rattlesnakes, which are occasionally spotted. The Umatilla National Wildlife Refuge is adjacent to the park and allows fishing and hunting in specified areas. Note that Crow Butte Park was formerly a state park but is now run by the Crow Butte Park Association.

RV sites, facilities: There are 50 sites for RVs up to 60 feet with full hookups (30 amps), one primitive tent site, and one group camp that can accommodate up to 100 people. Some sites are pull-through. Fire grills and picnic tables are provided. Restrooms have flush toilets and coin showers. A sheltered picnic area, a swimming beach, and a dump station are available. Some facilities are wheelchair accessible. Boat-launching and moorage facilities are nearby. A seasonal convenience store is open on weekends. Leashed pets are permitted.

Reservations, fees: Reservations are accepted at 509/875-2644. Sites are $25 per night, $5 per extra vehicle per night. The group site is $60 per night. Open year-round, with limited winter facilities.

Directions: From the junction of I-82/U.S. 395 and Highway 14 at Plymouth, just north of the Columbia River, turn west on Highway 14. Drive to Paterson and continue west for 13 miles to Sonora Road. Turn right (north) and drive 100 feet to Butte Road. Turn right and drive one mile (across the bridge) to the park on the island.

Contact: Crow Butte Park, 509/875-2644, www.crowbutte.com.

42 PLYMOUTH PARK

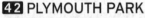

Scenic rating: 7

near Lake Umatilla, Benton County

See map page 228

Plymouth Park is a family and RV-style campground set near Lake Umatilla on the Columbia River. The 112-acre park is not on the shore of the lake, rather about a quarter-mile drive from the water. The camp has tree cover, which is a nice plus, and it fills up on most summer weekends. Each campsite has a tent pad.

RV sites, facilities: There are 32 sites for tents or RVs up to 40 feet with full or partial hookups (30 amps). Most sites are pull-through. Picnic tables and fire grills are provided. Restrooms have flush toilets and showers. Drinking water, a dump station, a playground, and a coin laundry are available. A boat dock, boat launch, swimming areas, and covered picnic shelters are available nearby. A store and a restaurant are within two miles. Some facilities are wheelchair accessible. Leashed pets are permitted.

Reservations, fees: Reservations are accepted at 877/444-6777 or www.ReserveUSA.com ($9 reservation fee). Sites are $18–20 per night, $2 per night for an additional vehicle. Some credit cards accepted. Open April–October.

Directions: From Richland and I-82, drive south on I-82 for about 30 miles to Highway 14. Turn west on Highway 14 and drive two miles to the Plymouth exit. Take that exit and drive to Christy Road; turn right and continue 200 yards to the campground entrance on the left.

Contact: U.S. Army Corps of Engineers, Portland District, 509/783-1270 or 541/506-7816.

Oregon

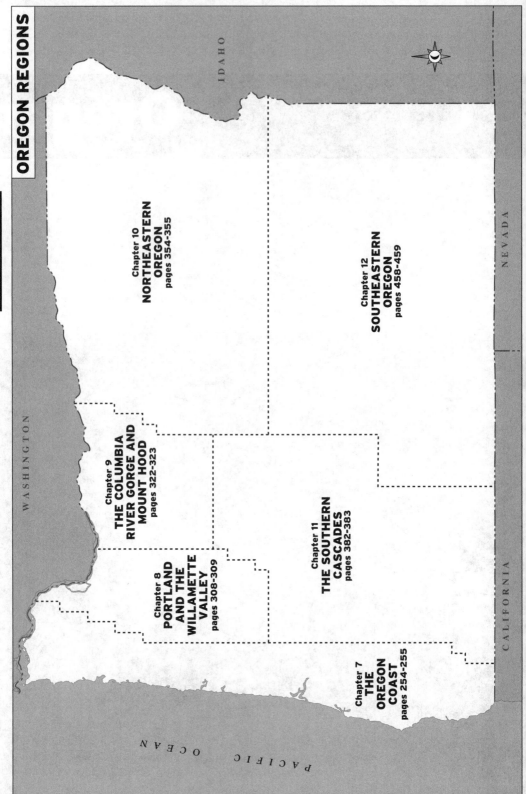

OREGON

OREGON REGIONS

IDAHO

NEVADA

WASHINGTON

CALIFORNIA

Chapter 10
NORTHEASTERN
OREGON
pages 354-355

Chapter 12
SOUTHEASTERN
OREGON
pages 458-459

Chapter 9
THE COLUMBIA
RIVER GORGE AND
MOUNT HOOD
pages 322-323

Chapter 11
THE SOUTHERN
CASCADES
pages 382-383

Chapter 8
PORTLAND
AND THE
WILLAMETTE
VALLEY
pages 308-309

Chapter 7
THE
OREGON
COAST
pages 254-255

PACIFIC OCEAN

THE OREGON COAST

If you want to treat yourself to vacation memories you'll treasure forever, take a drive (and then stop overnight) along U.S. 101 on the Oregon coast. Here you'll see some of the most dramatic coastal frontage in North America: tidewater rock gardens, cliff-top views that seem to stretch to forever, vast sand dunes, protected bays, beautiful streams with giant salmon and steelhead (in fall and winter), and three major national forests. I prefer cruising north to south, in the right lane close to the coastline and with the wind behind me; it often seems I'm on the edge of never-never land.

On the way, you'll cross the Columbia River on the border of Oregon and Washington. The river is so wide here that it looks like an inland sea. I find that the best way to appreciate this massive waterway is to get off the main highway and explore the many coastal streams by two-lane road. There are numerous routes, from tiny Highway 15 on the Little Nestucca River to well-known Highway 38 along the beautiful Umpqua.

The most spectacular region on the coast may be the Oregon Dunes National Recreation Area, which spans roughly from Coos Bay north past Florence to near the mouth of the Siuslaw River. Whenever I visit, I feel like I'm instantly transported to another universe. I have a photo of the dunes in my office. While I'm writing, I often look at the image of a lone raptor soaring past a pyramid of sand — it's my window to this wonderful otherworld.

OREGON

Includes:

- Alder Lake
- Alfred A. Loeb State Park
- Alsea River
- Bastendorff Beach Park
- Beachside State Park
- Beverly Beach State Park
- Bluebill Lake
- Bullards Beach State Park
- Cape Arago State Park
- Cape Blanco State Park
- Cape Kiwanda State Park
- Cape Lookout State Park
- Carl G. Washburne State Park
- Carter Lake
- Chetco River
- Cleowax Lake
- Columbia River
- Coquille River
- Devil's Lake State Park
- Ecola State Park
- Eel Lake
- Elk River
- Fort Stevens State Park
- Harris Beach State Park
- Humbug Mountain State Park
- Jessie M. Honeyman
  Memorial State Park
- Kilchis River
- Lake Umatilla
- Loon Lake Recreation Area
- Mercer Lake
- Neawanna River
- Nehalem Bay State Park
- Nestucca River
- Oregon Dunes National
  Recreation Area
- Rogue River
- Seal Rock State Park
- Siltcoos Lake
- Siskiyou National Forest
- Siuslaw National Forest
- Siuslaw River
- Sixes River
- South Beach State Park
- Squaw Lake
- Sunset Bay State Park
- Sutton Lake
- Tahkenitch Lake
- Tenmile Lake
- Tillamook River
- Tillamook State Forest
- Umpqua Lighthouse State Park
- Umpqua River
- William M. Tugman State Park
- Wilson River
- Winchuck River
- Woahink Lake

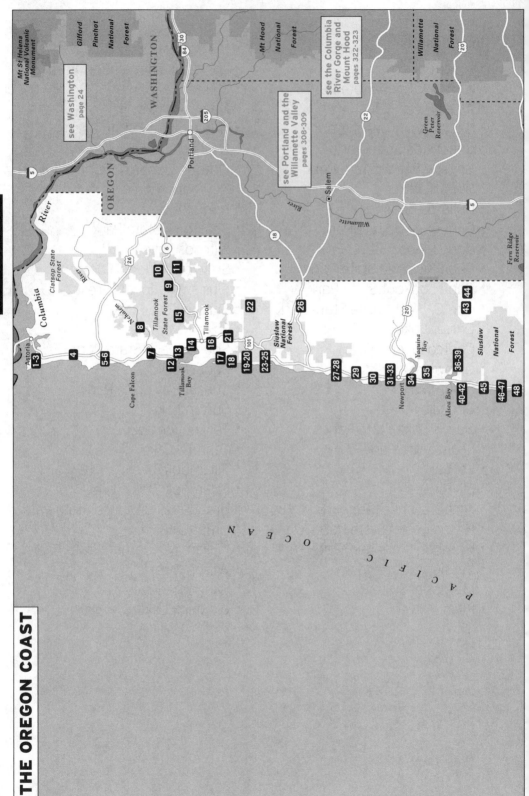

THE OREGON COAST

OREGON

see Washington
page 24

see Portland and the
Willamette Valley
pages 308-309

see the Columbia
River Gorge and
Mount Hood
pages 322-323

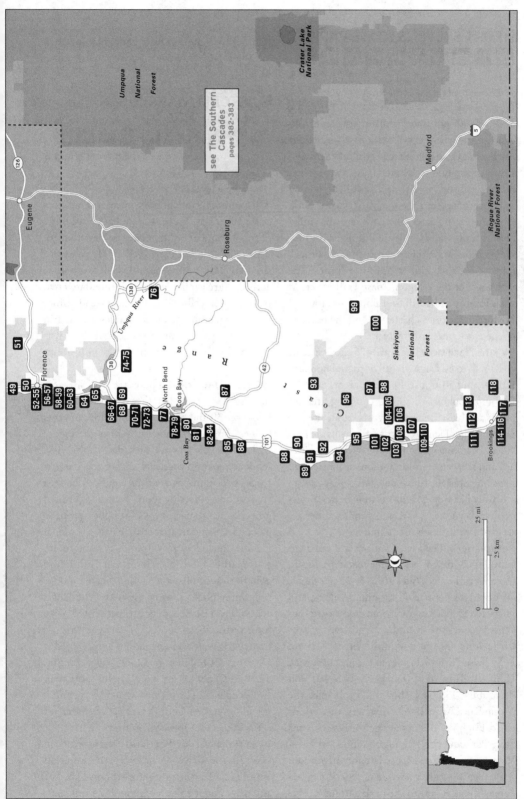

OREGON

OREGON

1 FORT STEVENS STATE PARK

Scenic rating: 8

at the mouth of the Columbia River

See map page 254   BEST (

This classic spot is at the northern tip of Oregon, right where the Columbia River enters the Pacific Ocean. A historic military area and shipwreck site, freshwater lake, swimming, beachcombing, trails, and wildlife-viewing make Fort Stevens a uniquely diversified park. Covering 3,700 acres, the park has nine miles of bike trails and six miles of hiking trails, providing exploration through spruce and hemlock forests, wetlands, dunes, and shore pines. The trailhead for the Oregon Coast Trail is here as well. History buffs will find a museum, tours of the fort and artillery batteries, and the remains of the *Peter Iredale* shipwreck.

RV sites, facilities: There are 476 sites for tents or RVs up to 50 feet with full or partial hookups (20, 30, and 50 amps), 19 sites for tents or small RVs (no hookups), a special camping area for hikers and bicyclists, and 15 yurts. Some sites are pull-through. Picnic tables and fire grills are provided. Drinking water, restrooms with flush toilets and showers, a dump station, a transfer and recycling station, firewood, and a playground are available. Some facilities are wheelchair accessible. Boat docks and launching facilities are nearby. Leashed pets are permitted.

Reservations, fees: Reservations are accepted at 800/452-5687 or www.oregonstateparks.org ($6 reservation fee). Sites are $13–22 per night, $4 per night per person for hikers/bikers, and yurts are $30 per night. Some credit cards accepted. Open year-round.

Directions: From Portland, turn west on U.S. 26 and drive 73 miles to the junction with U.S. 101. Turn right (north) on U.S. 101 and drive about 15 miles (about 0.25 mile past the Camp Rilea Army Base). Turn west on Perkins Road/Highway 104 at the sign for Fort Stevens State Park and drive about one mile to Ocean View Cemetery Road. Turn left and drive about 2.5 miles (Ocean View Cemetery Road becomes Ridge Road) to the park entrance.

Contact: Fort Stevens State Park, 503/861-1671 or 800/551-6949, www.oregonstateparks.org.

2 ASTORIA/WARRENTON SEASIDE KOA

Scenic rating: 3

near Fort Stevens State Park

See map page 254

This campground nestles in a wooded area adjacent to Fort Stevens State Park, and tours of that historical military site can be arranged. This camp provides an excellent alternative if the state park campground is full. Numerous activities are available in the immediate area, including bicycling, hiking, deep-sea fishing, and beachcombing. Horse stables are within 10 miles. See the *Fort Stevens State Park* listing in this chapter for further details about the area.

RV sites, facilities: There are 311 sites for tents or RVs of any length with full or partial hookups (30 and 50 amps), 54 cabins, and two lodges. Some sites are pull-through. Picnic tables and fire pits are provided. Cable TV, modem hookups, wireless Internet service, restrooms with showers, security, a public phone, a coin laundry, meeting room, firewood, limited groceries, ice, a snack bar, RV supplies, propane gas, and a picnic area are available. Recreational facilities include a playground, a game room, a recreation field, bicycle rentals, miniature golf, horseshoe pits, a spa, and a heated indoor swimming pool. Some facilities are wheelchair accessible. Leashed pets are permitted with some restrictions.

Reservations, fees: Reservations are accepted at 800/562-8506. Sites are $23.95–53 per night, $3.50–4.50 per person per night for more than two people, $2 per pet per night, $5 per night per additional vehicle unless towed. Some credit cards accepted. Open year-round.

Directions: From Portland, turn west on U.S. 26 and drive 73 miles to the junction with U.S. 101. Turn right (north) on U.S. 101 and drive about 15 miles (about 0.25 mile past the Camp Rilea Army Base). Turn west on Perkins Road/Highway 104 at the sign for Fort Stevens State Park and drive about one mile to Ocean View Cemetery Road. Turn left and drive about 2.5 miles (Ocean View Cemetery Road becomes Ridge Road) to the campground directly across from the state park.

Contact: Astoria/Warrenton Seaside KOA, 503/861-2606, fax 503/861-3209, www.astoria koa.com.

3 KAMPERS WEST RV PARK

Scenic rating: 7

near Fort Stevens State Park
See map page 254

Just four miles from Fort Stevens State Park, this privately run camp offers full RV services. Nearby recreation possibilities include an 18-hole golf course, hiking trails, and marked bike trails.

RV sites, facilities: There are 180 sites with full or partial hookups (30 amps) for RVs of any length, including a small area for tents only, and three park-model cabins. Drinking water and picnic tables are provided, and some sites have fire pits. Restrooms have flush toilets and showers. Propane gas, a dump station, a coin laundry, and ice are available. A store and a café are within one mile. Leashed pets are permitted.

Reservations, fees: Reservations accepted. RV sites are $33 per night and tent sites are $28 per night. Some credit cards accepted. Open year-round.

Directions: From Portland, turn west on U.S. 30 and drive 105 miles north and west to Astoria and the junction of U.S. 101. Turn south and drive 6.5 miles to the Warrenton/Hammond Junction. Turn right (west) on Warrenton and drive 1.5 miles to the campground on the right.

Contact: Kampers West RV Park, 503/861-1814, fax 503/861-3620, www.kamperswest.com.

4 VENICE RV PARK

Scenic rating: 3

on the Neawanna River
See map page 254

This park along the Neawanna River—one of two rivers running through Seaside—is less than a mile from the beach. A great bonus: Crab pot rentals are available. Seaside offers beautiful ocean beaches for fishing and surfing, moped and bike rentals, shops, and a theater. The city provides swings and volleyball nets on the beach. An 18-hole golf course is nearby.

RV sites, facilities: There are 31 sites with full hookups (30 amps), some pull-through, for RVs of any length and six tent sites. Drinking water, cable TV, and picnic tables are provided. Restrooms have flush toilets and showers. A picnic area and a coin laundry are available. A store and a café are within one mile. Leashed pets are permitted.

Reservations, fees: Reservations are accepted. RV sites are $25.09 per night, tent sites are $16 per night, plus $2 per person per night for more than two people, $2 per night per additional vehicle, $2 per pet per stay. Some credit cards accepted. Open year-round.

Directions: From Portland on I-5, turn west on U.S. 26 and drive 73 miles to the junction with U.S. 101. Turn north on U.S. 101 and drive 5.25 miles to Seaside. Continue to the north end of town and bear left (west) on 24th Avenue. The campground is on the corner (do not cross the bridge) at 1032 24th Avenue.

Contact: Venice RV Park, 503/738-8851.

5 SEA RANCH RV PARK

Scenic rating: 9

near the Pacific Ocean
See map page 254

This park lies in a wooded area with nearby access to the beach. Activities at the camp include stream fishing, horseback riding, and swimming on the seashore. A golf course is six miles away, and the historic Lewis and Clark Trail

OREGON

is nearby. Elk hunters camp here in season. The beach and the town of Cannon Beach are within walking distance of the park.

RV sites, facilities: There are 80 sites for tents or RVs up to 40 feet with full or partial hookups, along with seven cabins. Picnic tables and fire rings are provided. Restrooms have showers. Horse rentals and a dump station are available. Supplies are available within two miles. Leashed pets are permitted.

Reservations, fees: Reservations are accepted. RV sites are $26–27 per night, tent sites are $23 per night, plus $2 per person per night for more than two people, $3 per night per additional vehicle, and $2 per pet per night. Some credit cards accepted. Open year-round.

Directions: From Portland on I-5, turn west on U.S. 26 and drive 73 miles to the junction with U.S. 101. Turn south on U.S. 101 and drive three miles to the Cannon Beach exit. Take that exit and drive on Fir Street for 0.3 mile to the park on the left.

Contact: Sea Ranch RV Park, 503/436-2815, www.searanchrv.com.

6 RV RESORT AT CANNON BEACH

Scenic rating: 9

near Ecola State Park
See map page 254

This private resort is about seven blocks from one of the nicest beaches in the region and about two miles from Ecola State Park. From the town of Cannon Beach you can walk for miles up or down the coast. Nearby recreational facilities include marked bike trails, a riding stable, and tennis courts. The city shuttle service stops here.

RV sites, facilities: There are 100 sites with full hookups (30 and 50 amps) for RVs of any length; some are pull-through sites. No tents are permitted. Picnic tables and fire pits are provided. Restrooms have flush toilets and showers. Cable TV, propane gas, firewood, a recreation hall, a playground, horseshoe pits, basketball court, a convenience store, a spa, a coin laundry, ice, gasoline, and a heated swimming pool (year-round) are available. Leashed pets are permitted.

Reservations, fees: Reservations are accepted at 800/847-2231. Sites are $26.75–38.52 per night, $3 per person per night for more than two people, $3 per night for an additional vehicle. Some credit cards accepted. Open year-round.

Directions: From Portland on I-5, turn west on U.S. 26 and drive 73 miles to the junction with U.S. 101. Turn south on U.S. 101 and drive four miles to the second Cannon Beach exit at Milepost 29.5. Exit on the left (east) and drive 200 feet to the resort.

Contact: RV Resort at Cannon Beach, 503/436-2231, fax 503/436-1527, www.cbrvresort.com.

7 NEHALEM BAY STATE PARK

Scenic rating: 7

west of Portland on the Pacific Ocean
See map page 254

This state park on a sandy point separating the Pacific Ocean from Nehalem Bay features six miles of beach frontage. There is no ocean view from the campsites, but the sites are about 150 yards from the ocean. Crabbing and fishing on the bay are popular. The neighboring towns of Manzanita and Nehalem offer fine dining and shopping. The Oregon Coast Trail passes through the park. A horse camp with corrals and a 7.5-mile equestrian trail are available. There is also a two-mile bike trail. An airport is adjacent to the park, and there are airstrip fly-in campsites.

RV sites, facilities: There are 265 sites for tents or RVs up to 60 feet with partial hookups (30 amps), a special camping area for hikers and bicyclists, and six primitive fly-in sites next to the airport. There are also 18 yurts and 17 sites with stock corrals. Drinking water, picnic tables, and fire grills are provided. Restrooms have flush toilets and showers. A dump station, playgrounds, and firewood are available. Some facilities are wheelchair accessible. Boat-launching facilities are nearby on Nehalem Bay, and an airstrip is adjacent to the park. Leashed pets are permitted.

Reservations, fees: Reservations are accepted at 800/452-5687 or www.oregonstateparks.org ($6 reservation fee). Sites are $16–20 per night, $5 per night per additional vehicle, and $4 per person per night for hikers/bikers. Yurts are $27 per night; horse sites are $12–16 per night. Fly-in sites are $8 per night, not including tie-down. Some credit cards accepted. Open year-round.

Directions: From Portland, drive west on U.S. 26 for 73 miles to the junction with U.S. 101. Turn south on U.S. 101 and drive 19 miles to Manzanita. Continue south on U.S. 101 for 0.75 mile to Necarney City Road. Turn right and drive 0.2 mile to a stop sign. Turn right and drive 0.75 mile to the park entrance.

Contact: Nehalem Bay State Park, 503/368-5154 or 800/551-6949, www.oregonstateparks.org.

8 NEHALEM FALLS

🚶 🚴 🏊 🎣 🐕 ♿ 🚐 ⛺

Scenic rating: 10

in Tillamook State Forest

See map page 254

This beautiful campground, amid old-growth hemlock and spruce, is within a two-minute walk of lovely Nehalem Falls. Note that swimming in the pool below the falls is hazardous and not advised. A half-mile loop trail follows the Nehalem River, where fishing and swimming are options.

RV sites, facilities: There are 14 sites for tents or RVs up to 40 feet (no hookups), four walk-in tent sites, and one group site. Drinking water, picnic tables, garbage bins, a recycling center, fire grills, and vault toilets are available. A camp host is on-site. Some facilities are wheelchair accessible. Leashed pets are permitted.

Reservations, fees: Reservations are not accepted. Sites are $10 per night, $2 per night per additional vehicle. Walk-in sites are $5 per

night. Reservations are required for the group site at 503/842-2545; $25 per night. Open May–October.

Directions: From Tillamook on U.S. 101 northbound, drive 22 miles to Highway 53. Turn right (east) and drive 1.3 miles to Miami Foley Road. Turn right (south) and drive one mile to Foss Road (narrow and rough). Turn left and drive seven miles to the campground on the left.

Contact: Tillamook State Forest, Tillamook District, 503/842-2545, fax 503/842-3143.

9 JONES CREEK

🚶 🎣 🐕 ♿ 🚐 ⛺

Scenic rating: 7

on the Wilson River in Tillamook State Forest

See map page 254

Set in a forest of fir, hemlock, spruce, and alder, campsites here are spacious and private. The adjacent Wilson River provides opportunities for steelhead and salmon fishing (artificial lures only). A scenic 3.8-mile trail runs along the riverfront. The camp fills up on weekends from July through Labor Day.

RV sites, facilities: There are 29 sites for tents or RVs (no hookups); 27 sites are for RVs up to 50 feet and one pull-through site is for RVs up to 72 feet). There are also nine walk-in tent sites and one group site for up to 20 people. Drinking water, picnic tables, and fire grills are provided. Vault toilets, garbage bins, firewood, and a horseshoe pit are available. A camp host is on-site. Some facilities are wheelchair accessible. Leashed pets are permitted.

Reservations, fees: Reservations are not accepted. Sites are $10 per night, $2 per night per additional vehicle. Walk-in sites are $5 per night. Reservations are required for the group site at 503/842-2545; $25 per night. Open May–October.

Directions: From Portland, turn west on U.S. 26 and drive 24 miles to Highway 6. Turn west on Highway 6 and drive 28 miles to Milepost 22.7 and North Fork Road. Turn right and drive 0.25 mile to the campground on the left.

Contact: Tillamook State Forest, Tillamook District, 503/842-2545, fax 503/842-3143.

10 GALES CREEK

Scenic rating: 7

on Gales Creek in Tillamook State Forest
See map page 254

Gales Creek runs through this heavily forested camp. The Gales Creek Trailhead is accessible from camp, providing access to hiking and mountain biking opportunities. A day-use picnic area is also available.

RV sites, facilities: There are 19 sites for tents or RVs up to 35 feet (no hookups) and four walk-in tent sites. Drinking water, picnic tables, fire grills, garbage bins, and vault toilets are available. Some facilities are wheelchair accessible. Leashed pets are permitted.

Reservations, fees: Reservations are not accepted. Sites are $10 per night, walk-in sites are $5 per night, and an additional vehicle is $2 per night. Open early May–October.

Directions: From Portland, turn west on U.S. 26 and drive 24 miles to Highway 6. Turn west on Highway 6 and drive 17 miles to the campground entrance road (Rogers Road) on the right at Milepost 35. Turn right on Rogers Road and drive one mile to the campground.

Contact: Tillamook State Forest, Forest Grove District, 503/357-2191.

11 BROWNS CAMP

Scenic rating: 6

in Tillamook State Forest
See map page 254

This camp is next to the Devil's Lake Fork of the Wilson River and has sites with and without tree cover. Surrounded by miles of off-highway vehicle (OHV) trails, it caters to OHV campers. Don't expect peace and quiet. No fishing is allowed here.

RV sites, facilities: There are 29 sites for tents or RVs up to 45 feet (no hookups). Drinking water,

picnic tables, fire grills, garbage bins, and vault toilets are available. Some facilities are wheelchair accessible. Leashed pets are permitted.

Reservations, fees: Reservations are not accepted. Sites are $10 per night, $2 per night per additional vehicle. Open March–November.

Directions: From Portland, turn west on U.S. 26 and drive 24 miles to Highway 6. Turn west on Highway 6 and drive 19 miles to Beaver Dam Road. Turn left (south) and drive 2.5 miles to Scoggins Road. Turn left (southeast) and drive one-half mile to the campground.

Contact: Tillamook State Forest, Forest Grove District, 503/357-2191.

12 BARVIEW JETTY PARK

Scenic rating: 7

near Garibaldi
See map page 254

This Tillamook County park covers 160 acres and is near the beach, in a wooded area adjacent to Tillamook Bay. The sites are on grassy hills. Nearby recreation options include an 18-hole golf course, surf and scuba fishing, and a full-service marina.

RV sites, facilities: There are 69 sites for tents or RVs of any length with full hookups (15, 30, and 50 amps), 219 tent sites, and four hiker/bicyclist sites. Some sites are pull-through. Drinking water, picnic tables, and fire pits are provided. Restrooms have flush toilets and showers. A dump station and a day-use area are available. Groups can be accommodated. Some facilities are wheelchair accessible. Propane gas, a store, a café, and ice are within one mile. Leashed pets are permitted.

Reservations, fees: Reservations are accepted ($5 reservation fee). Sites are $10–25 per night, $5 per night for each additional vehicle or tent, $5 per person per night for hikers/bikers. Some credit cards accepted. Open year-round.

Directions: From Tillamook, drive north on U.S. 101 for 12 miles to the park on the left (two miles north of the town of Garibaldi).

Contact: Barview Jetty Park, Tillamook

County, 503/322-3522, www.co.tillamook.or.us/gov/parks.

13 BIAK-BY-THE-SEA RV PARK

Scenic rating: 7

on Tillamook Bay

See map page 254

This park along the shore of Tillamook Bay is a prime retreat for deep-sea fishing, crabbing, clamming, surf fishing, scuba diving, and beachcombing. The nearby town of Tillamook is home to a cheese factory and a historical museum. A good side trip is to Cape Meares State Park, where you can hike through the national wildlife preserve and see how the seabirds nest along the cliffs. There is also a golf course nearby. Note that most of the sites are monthly rentals.

RV sites, facilities: There are 65 sites with full hookups (15 and 30 amps) for RVs of any length, including 45 pull-through sites, and a grassy area for tents. Drinking water and cable TV are provided. Restrooms have flush toilets and coin showers, and a coin laundry is available. Propane gas, a store, a café, and ice are within one mile. Boat docks, launching facilities, and rentals are nearby. Leashed pets are permitted.

Reservations, fees: Reservations are accepted. Sites are $25 per night. Some credit cards accepted. Open year-round.

Directions: From Tillamook and U.S. 101, drive north for 10 miles to 7th Street. Turn left on 7th Street and drive to the park on the left (just over the tracks).

Contact: Biak-by-the-Sea RV Park, 503/322-2111.

14 PACIFIC CAMPGROUND & RV PARK

Scenic rating: 6

on Tillamook Bay

See map page 254

This campground is near Tillamook Bay, about 17 miles inland from the ocean, not far from the Wilson River. The Tillamook Cheese Factory—the place for cheese tours—is just south of the park. An 18-hole golf course is also nearby. See the *Biak-by-the-Sea RV Park* listing in this chapter for more information about the area.

RV sites, facilities: There are 30 pull-through sites with full hookups (20, 30, and 50 amps) for RVs of any length and 21 tent sites. Drinking water and picnic tables are provided, and there are fire rings at the tent sites. Restrooms have flush toilets and showers. Cable TV, wireless Internet service, business services, a covered gazebo, firewood, and ice are available. A store and a café are within one mile. Leashed pets are permitted.

Reservations, fees: Reservations accepted. RV sites are $25–28 per night, tent sites are $18 per night, plus $2 per person per night for more than two people and $5 per night per additional vehicle. Some credit cards accepted. Open year-round.

Directions: From Tillamook, drive north on U.S. 101 for two miles to the campground entrance across from the Tillamook Cheese Factory.

Contact: Pacific Campground & RV Park, 503/842-5201, fax 503/842-0588.

15 KILCHIS RIVER PARK

Scenic rating: 8

on the Kilchis River

See map page 254

Riverfront campsites are the highlight at this Tillamook County campground. The campground is forested and gets moderate use. Hiking trails are available. Other recreational options include boating, fishing, and swimming.

RV sites, facilities: There are 36 sites for tents or RVs of any length (no hookups) and two hiker/bicyclist sites. Picnic tables, drinking water, flush toilets, and fire pits are provided. A playground, garbage bins, a boat launch, a day-use area, a pay phone, horseshoe pits, and a volleyball court are available. A camp host is on-site. Leashed pets are permitted.

Reservations, fees: Reservations are accepted during the summer season at 503/842-6694 and at 503/322-3522 when the park is closed ($5 reservation fee). Sites are $10 per night, $5 per night per additional vehicle, and $5 per person per night for hikers and bicyclists. Open May–September.

Directions: From Tillamook and U.S. 101, take the Alderbrook Loop/Kilches Park exit. Turn onto Alderbrook Loop and drive northeast for approximately one mile to Kilches River Road. Turn right and drive approximately four miles to the park at the end of the road.

Contact: Kilchis River Park, Tillamook County, 503/842-6694, www.co.tillamook.or.us/gov/parks.

16 PLEASANT VALLEY RV PARK

Scenic rating: 8

on the Tillamook River

See map page 254

This campground along the Tillamook River is very clean and features many recreation options in the immediate area.

RV sites, facilities: There are 74 pull-through sites with full or partial hookups (50 amps) for RVs of any length, 10 tent sites, and two cabins. Drinking water and picnic tables are provided, and some sites have fire rings. Restrooms have flush toilets and showers. Propane gas, a dump station, firewood, a meeting room, cable TV, modem access, a convenience store, a coin laundry, ice, and a playground are available. Boat-launching facilities are nearby. Leashed pets are permitted.

Reservations, fees: Reservations are accepted. RV sites are $28 per night, tent sites are $18 per night, plus $2 per person per night for more than two people; cabins are $29 per night. Some credit cards accepted. Open year-round.

Directions: From Tillamook and U.S. 101, drive south on U.S. 101 for 6.5 miles to the campground entrance on the right (west).

Contact: Pleasant Valley RV Park, 503/842-4779, fax 503/842-2293, www.pleasantvalley rvpark.com.

17 NETARTS BAY RV PARK & MARINA

Scenic rating: 8

on Netarts Bay

See map page 254

This camp is one of three on the east shore of Netarts Bay. A golf course is eight miles away. Sunsets and wildlife-viewing are notable here. Some sites are filled with rentals for the summer season. No tent campers permitted.

RV sites, facilities: There are 83 sites with full hookups (20, 30, and 50 amps) for RVs of any length; some are pull-through sites. Drinking water and picnic tables are provided, and fire rings are available at some sites. Restrooms have flush toilets and showers. Propane gas, a meeting room, a coin laundry, a playground, horseshoe pits, crab-cooking facilities, crab bait, and ice are available. Boat docks, launching facilities, and rentals are available on-site. A store and a café are within one mile. Leashed pets (up to 40 pounds) are permitted with a two-pet maximum.

Reservations, fees: Reservations recommended. Sites are $28–30 per night, $5 per night per additional vehicle. Some credit cards accepted. Monthly rentals available. Open year-round.

Directions: From Tillamook and Netarts Highway/Highway 131, drive west on Netarts Highway for six miles to the campground entrance.

Contact: Netarts Bay RV Park & Marina, 503/842-7774, www.netartsbay.com.

18 CAPE LOOKOUT STATE PARK

Scenic rating: 8

near Netarts Bay

See map page 254

The park is on a sand spit between Netarts Bay and the ocean. Cape Lookout has more than eight miles of hiking and walking trails that wind through old-growth forest. The Cape Lookout Trail follows the headland for more than two miles. Another walk will take you out through a variety of estuarine habitats along the five-mile sand spit that extends between the ocean and Netarts Bay. With many species to view, this area is a paradise for bird-watchers. You might also catch the local hang gliders and para gliders that frequent the park. Fishing is another option.

RV sites, facilities: There are 173 sites for tents or RVs (no hookups), 34 sites with full hookups (20, 30, and 50 amps) for RVs up to 50 feet, a special tent-camping area for hikers and bicyclists, four group tent sites for up to 25 people each, three cabins, and 13 yurts. Picnic tables and fire grills are provided. Restrooms have flush toilets and showers. A dump station, garbage bins, a playground, reservable meeting hall, reservable picnic shelter, summer interpretive programs, and firewood are available. A restaurant is within one mile. Some facilities are wheelchair accessible. Leashed pets are permitted.

Reservations, fees: Reservations are accepted at 800/452-5687 or www.oregonstateparks.org ($6 reservation fee). Sites are $12–20 per night, $5 per night per additional vehicle, $4 per person per night for hikers/bikers, $40–61 for group sites, $45–66 for cabins, and $27 per night for yurts. Some credit cards accepted. Open year-round.

Directions: From Tillamook and U.S. 101, turn east on 3rd Street (becomes Netarts Highway). Drive approximately five miles to Whiskey Creek Road. Turn left and drive approximately seven miles to the park on the right.

Contact: Cape Lookout State Park, 503/842-4981, www.oregonstateparks.org.

19 WHALEN ISLAND PARK

Scenic rating: 6

in the Sandlake Estuary
See map page 254

This park is in the Sandlake Estuary and is close to the beach and Nestucca Bay. The campground is fairly open and has a few trees.

RV sites, facilities: There are 36 sites for tents or RVs of any length (no hookups) and a hiker/ bicyclist site. Picnic tables and fire pits are provided. Drinking water, flush and chemical toilets, a dump station, a day-use area, and a boat launch are available. A camp host is on-site during the summer. Some facilities are wheelchair accessible. Leashed pets are permitted.

Reservations, fees: Reservations are accepted ($5 reservation fee). Sites are $10 per night, $5 per night per additional vehicle, and $5 per person per night for hikers and bicyclists. Open May–September; check for current status at other times of year.

Directions: From Tillamook and U.S. 101, drive south for 11 miles to Sand Lake Road. Turn right (west) and drive approximately 55 miles to a stop sign. Turn left to stay on Sand Lake Road. Continue 4.75 miles south to the park entrance road on the right.

Contact: Whalen Island Park, Tillamook County, 503/965-6085, www.co.tillamook .or.us/gov/parks.

20 SANDBEACH

Scenic rating: 5

in Siuslaw National Forest
See map page 254

This area is known for its beaches with large sand dunes, which are popular with off-road-vehicle enthusiasts. It's noisy and can be windy. The campground sits along the shore of Sand Lake, which is actually more like an estuary than a lake since the ocean is just around the bend. This is the only coastal U.S. Forest Service campground for many miles, and it's quite popular. If you're planning a trip for midsummer, be sure to reserve far in advance. Holiday permits are required ($10 at the district office) for three-day holiday weekends.

RV sites, facilities: There are 101 sites for tents or RVs of any length (no hookups). If these sites are full, the east (East Dunes) and west (West Wind) parking lots provide additional sites for RVs. Dispersed camping is also available at the adjacent Derrick Road campground. Picnic tables and fire pits are provided. Drinking

OREGON

water, garbage bins, and flush toilets are available. Leashed pets are permitted.

Reservations, fees: Reservations are accepted during the summer season at 877/444-6777 or www.ReserveUSA.com ($9 reservation fee). Sandbeach sites are $16 per night, $8 per night per additional vehicle. The east and west parking lots are $10 per night, and dispersed camping is $5 per night. Open year-round.

Directions: From Tillamook on U.S. 101, drive south for 11 miles to County Road 8. Turn right (west) on County Road 8 and drive approximately 12 miles to the campground.

Contact: Siuslaw National Forest, Hebo Ranger District, 503/392-3161, fax 503/392-4203.

21 CAMPER COVE RV PARK AND CAMPGROUND

Scenic rating: 6

on Beaver Creek

See map page 254

This small, wooded campground along Beaver Creek is just far enough off the highway to provide quiet. The park can be used as a base camp for anglers, with seasonal steelhead and salmon fishing in the nearby Nestucca River. It gets crowded here, especially in the summer, so be sure to make a reservation whenever possible. Ocean beaches are four miles away.

RV sites, facilities: There are 17 sites with full hookups for RVs up to 40 feet, five tent sites, and three cabins. Drinking water, fire pits, and picnic tables are provided. Restrooms have flush toilets and coin showers. A dump station, firewood, a recreation hall, a coin laundry, and ice are available. Leashed pets are permitted.

Reservations, fees: Reservations accepted. RV sites are $23 per night, tent sites are $16 per night, plus $3 per person per night for more than two people and $3 per night per additional vehicle. Open year-round.

Directions: From Tillamook and U.S. 101, drive south on U.S. 101 for 12.5 miles to the park entrance on the right (west), 2.5 miles north of Beaver.

Contact: Camper Cove RV Park and Campground, 503/398-5334, www.campercove campground.com.

22 DOVRE, FAN CREEK, ALDER GLEN

Scenic rating: 5

on the Nestucca River

See map page 254

This is a series of three BLM campgrounds set along the Nestucca River. The camps, separated by alder trees and shrubs, are near the river, and some have river views. Tourists don't know about these spots. The Nestucca is a gentle river, with the water not deep enough for swimming.

RV sites, facilities: Dovre has 10 sites, Fan Creek has 11 sites, and Alder Glen has 10 sites for tents or small RVs. No hookups. Picnic tables and fire grills are provided. Drinking water and vault toilets are available. Garbage must be packed out. Some facilities, including a fishing pier at Alder Glen, are wheelchair accessible. Leashed pets are permitted.

Reservations, fees: Reservations are not accepted. Sites are $10 per night, $4 per night per additional vehicle with a limit of two vehicles per site. Open year-round.

Directions: On U.S. 101 southwest of Portland, drive to the tiny town of Beaver and Blaine Road. Turn east on Blaine Road (keep right; Blaine Road turns into Nestucca River Access Road) and drive 17.5 miles to Alder Glen. Continue east for seven more miles to reach Fan Creek and nine more miles to reach Dovre.

Contact: Bureau of Land Management, Salem District, 503/375-5646, fax 503/375-5622.

23 WOODS PARK

Scenic rating: 6

on the Kilchis River

See map page 254

This small, Tillamook County park is not well known outside the local area and gets fairly light use. The campground is grassy with few trees. Salmon fishing is a possibility; check current regulations.

RV sites, facilities: There are four tent sites and five sites with no hookups for RVs up to 40 feet. Picnic tables and fire pits are provided. Drinking water, flush toilets, garbage containers, a covered picnic shelter, and a reservable day-use area are available. A camp host is on-site. Leashed pets are permitted.

Reservations, fees: Reservations are accepted ($5 reservation fee). Sites are $10–15 per night, plus $5 per night per additional vehicle. Open May–September, weather permitting.

Directions: From Tillamook and U.S. 101, drive approximately 25 miles south to Resort Drive. Turn right (west) and drive three miles (road changes to Brooten Drive) to the park on the right.

Contact: Webb Park (no contact phone number at Woods Park), Tillamook County, 503/965-5001, www.co.tillamook.or.us/gov/parks.

24 CAPE KIWANDA RV RESORT

Scenic rating: 8

near Cape Kiwanda State Park on the Pacific Ocean
See map page 254

This park is a short distance from Cape Kiwanda State Park, which is open for day use only. Highlights at the park include a boat launch and hiking trails that lead out to the cape. Four miles south at Nestucca Spit, there is another day-use park, providing additional recreational options. The point extends about three miles and is a good spot for bird-watching. The campsites do not have ocean views, but the ocean is across the road and within walking distance. Surfing is an option.

RV sites, facilities: There are 120 sites with full hookups (30 and 50 amps), 10 sites with partial hookups for RVs up to 65 feet, 10 tent sites, and 14 camping cabins. Some sites are pull-through. Drinking water, fire rings, and picnic tables are provided. Restrooms have flush toilets and showers. A dump station, modem access,

heated swimming pool (year-round), Jacuzzi, exercise room, firewood, a recreation hall, a coin laundry, propane, a seafood market, deli, gift shop, an ATM, sandboard rentals, volleyball, basketball, tetherball, horseshoe pits, and a playground are available. Gasoline, a store, and a café are within one mile. Boat docks, launching facilities, and rentals are nearby. Leashed pets are permitted.

Reservations, fees: Reservations are accepted. RV sites are $34.95–36.95 per night, tent sites are $21 per night, plus $2–4 per person per night for more than two people and $4 per night per additional vehicle. Weekly and monthly rates available. Some credit cards accepted. Open year-round.

Directions: From Tillamook and U.S. 101, drive south on U.S. 101 for 25 miles to the Pacific City exit and Brooten Road. Turn right on Brooten Road and drive three miles toward Pacific City and Three Capes Drive. Turn left, cross the bridge, and bear right on Three Capes Drive. Continue one mile north to the park on the right.

Contact: Cape Kiwanda RV Resort, 503/965-6230, fax 503/965-6235, www.capekiwandarvresort.com.

25 WEBB PARK

Scenic rating: 7

near the Pacific Ocean
See map page 254

This public campground provides an excellent alternative to the more crowded commercial RV parks off U.S. 101. Although not as developed, it offers a quiet, private setting and access to the ocean. Fishing and swimming are among your options here. The camp is adjacent to Cape Kiwanda and the beach.

RV sites, facilities: There are 30 sites for tents or RVs (no hookups), seven sites with partial hookups (30 amps) for RVs up to 40 feet, and a hiker/bicyclist site. Picnic tables and fire pits are provided. Drinking water, a dump station, a fish-cleaning station, and restrooms with flush toilets and showers are available. Beach launching is nearby. Leashed pets are permitted.

Reservations, fees: Reservations are accepted at 503/965-5001 ($5 reservation fee). Sites are $15–20 per night, $5 per night per additional vehicle, and $5 per person per night for hikers/bikers. Some credit cards accepted. Open year-round.

Directions: From Tillamook and U.S. 101, drive south on U.S. 101 for 25 miles to the Pacific City exit and Highway 30. From Pacific City, turn right (north) and drive to the four-way stop at McPhillips Drive. Turn left on McPhillips Drive and drive one-half mile to Cape Kiwanda and the park on the right.

Contact: Webb Park, Tillamook County Parks, 503/965-5001, www.co.tillamook.or .us/gov/parks.

26 WANDERING SPIRIT RV PARK

Scenic rating: 6

on Rock Creek

See map page 254

The major draw here is the nearby casino, but there is the added benefit of shaded sites next to Rock Creek, which provides fishing and swimming options. The Yamhill River is a half mile away. Fishing is good for steelhead and salmon in season. Golf courses and wineries are available within 10 miles. There is a combination of monthly rentals and overnighters at this park.

RV sites, facilities: There are 106 sites with full hookups (30 and 50 amps) for RVs up to 45 feet, 10 tent sites, and four park-model cabins. Some sites are pull-through. Drinking water, cable TV, wireless Internet service, modem access, restrooms with showers, a dump station, a coin laundry, RV storage, RV supplies, and a convenience store are available. Propane, a clubhouse, a basketball hoop, an exercise room, and a game room are also on-site. A 24-hour free bus shuttles campers to and from the Spirit Mountain Casino, restaurants, and shops less than two miles away. Some facilities are wheelchair accessible. Leashed pets are permitted.

Reservations, fees: Reservations are accepted at 800/390-6980. Tent sites are $16 per night, RV sites are $25 per night, and it's $2 per person per night for more than two people. Monthly rates available. Some credit cards accepted. Open year-round.

Directions: From Salem, drive west on Highway 22 about 25 miles to Highway 18. Turn west on Highway 18 and drive seven miles to the park on the left.

Contact: Wandering Spirit RV Park, 503/879-5700, fax 503/879-5171, www.wanderingspirit rvpark.com.

27 DEVIL'S LAKE STATE PARK

Scenic rating: 7

on Devil's Lake

See map page 254

Oregon's only coastal camp in the midst of a city, Devil's Lake is the center of summertime activity. A take-your-pick deal: You can boat, canoe, kayak, fish, or water-ski. A walking path extends from the campground to the boat launch a quarter mile away. For something different, head west and explore the seven miles of beaches. Lincoln City has arts and crafts galleries as well as a weekend farmers market during the summer. East Devil's Lake is two miles east and offers a boat ramp and picnic facilities.

RV sites, facilities: There are 54 sites for tents or small RVs (no hookups), 31 sites for RVs up to 60 feet with full hookups (50 amps), 10 yurts, and a separate area for hikers and bikers. Picnic tables and fire grills are provided. Drinking water, cable TV, garbage bins, restrooms with flush toilets and showers, an amphitheater, and firewood are available. Some facilities are wheelchair accessible. Boat docks and launching facilities are nearby. Leashed pets are permitted.

Reservations, fees: Reservations are accepted at 800/452-5687 or www.oregonstateparks.org ($6 reservation fee). Sites are $13–22 per night, plus $5 per night per additional vehicle and $4 per person per night for hikers/bikers. Yurts are

$29 per night. Boat mooring is $7 per night. Some credit cards accepted. Open year-round.
Directions: From Lincoln City and U.S. 101, take the 6th Street exit. Drive east on 6th Street for one block to the park on the right.
Contact: Devil's Lake State Park, 503/994-2002 or 800/551-6949, www.oregonstateparks.org.

28 KOA LINCOLN CITY

Scenic rating: 7

near the Pacific Ocean
See map page 254

This area offers opportunities for beachcombing, tidepool viewing, and fishing along a seven-mile stretch of beach. Nearby recreation options include a golf course, tennis courts, skateboard park, factory outlets, and a casino.
RV sites, facilities: There are 52 sites with full or partial hookups (20, 30, and 50 amps) for RVs up to 60 feet; some are pull-through sites. There are also 15 tent sites and 14 cabins. Picnic tables and fire pits are provided. Drinking water, cable TV, modem access, restrooms with flush toilets and showers, a dump station, public phones, a convenience store, a snack bar, a gift shop, propane gas, ice, RV supplies, video and DVD rentals, a game room, a coin laundry, meeting room, firewood, and a playground are available. Leashed pets are permitted.
Reservations, fees: Reservations are accepted at 800/562-2791. Tent sites are $20–28 per night, RV sites are $20–35 per night, plus $4 per person per night for more than two people and $8 per night per additional vehicle. Some credit cards accepted. Open year-round.
Directions: From Portland, drive south on Highway 99 West to Highway 18. Turn west on Highway 18 and drive 47 miles to U.S. 101. Turn south on U.S. 101 and drive 1.5 miles to East Devil's Lake Road. Turn east on East Devil's Lake Road and drive one mile to the park on the left.
Contact: KOA Lincoln City, 541/994-2961, fax 541/994-9454, www.koa.com.

29 SEA AND SAND RV PARK

Scenic rating: 9

near Siletz Bay
See map page 254

Beachcombing for fossils and agates is popular at this oceanfront park near Gleneden Beach on Siletz Bay. Some sites have ocean views and pleasant terraces. The Siletz River and numerous small creeks are in the area. The park is 3.5 miles north of Depoe Bay.
RV sites, facilities: There are 109 sites with full hookups (30 amps) for RVs up to 36 feet. Drinking water, cable TV, fire pits, and picnic tables are provided. Restrooms have flush toilets and showers. A dump station, firewood, and a coin laundry are available. A store, a café, and ice are within one mile. Leashed pets are permitted.
Reservations, fees: Reservations are accepted. Sites are $31–34 per night, plus $2 per person per night for more than two people and $5 per night per additional vehicle unless towed. Monthly rates available. Open year-round.
Directions: From Lincoln City and U.S. 101, drive south for nine miles on U.S. 101 to the park entrance (on the beach side of the highway).
Contact: Sea and Sand RV Park, 541/764-2313, www.seaandsandrvpark.com.

30 BEVERLY BEACH STATE PARK

Scenic rating: 7

north of Newport on the Pacific Ocean
See map page 254

This beautiful campground nestles in a wooded, grassy area on the east side of U.S. 101. Giant, wind-sculpted trees surround the campsites along Spencer Creek. Magically, you walk through a tunnel under the roadway and emerge on a beach that extends from Yaquina Head to the headlands of Otter Rock and from which a lighthouse is visible. A one-mile hiking trail is available. Just a mile to the north lies a small day-use state park called Devil's Punchbowl, named for an unusual bowl-shaped rock formation with caverns under it where the waves

OREGON

rumble about. For some great ocean views, head north one more mile to the Otter Crest Wayside. The Oregon Coast Aquarium is within a few minutes' drive.

RV sites, facilities: There are 128 sites for tents or small RVs, 128 sites for tents or RVs up to 65 feet with full or partial hookups (20 and 30 amps), a special camping area for hikers and bicyclists, and five group sites for tents or RVs (no hookups) that can accommodate up to 25 people each. There is also a village of 21 yurts. Picnic tables and fire grills are provided. Drinking water, restrooms with flush toilets and showers, cable TV, a playground, day-use area, garbage bins, and a dump station are available. Some facilities are wheelchair accessible. Leashed pets are permitted.

Reservations, fees: Reservations are accepted at 800/452-5687 or www.oregonstateparks.org ($6 reservation fee). Sites are $13–21 per night, $5 per night per additional vehicle, $4 per person per night for hikers/bikers, $29 per night for yurts, and $43–64 per night for group sites. Some credit cards accepted. Open year-round.

Directions: From Newport and U.S. 101, drive north on U.S. 101 for seven miles to the park entrance on the east side.

Contact: Beverly Beach State Park, 541/265-9278 or 800/551-6949, www.oregonstateparks.org.

31 AGATE BEACH RV PARK

Scenic rating: 6

near the Pacific Ocean
See map page 254

This park is about a half mile from Agate Beach Wayside, a small state park with beach access. Agate hunting can be good. Sometimes a layer of sand covers the agates, and you have to dig a bit. But other times wave action will clear the sand, unveiling the agates at low tides. Beverly Beach State Park is 4.5 miles north. About half of the sites are filled with monthly rentals. There are no ocean views from the campsites.

RV sites, facilities: There are 32 sites with full or partial hookups (30 amps) for RVs

up to 40 feet. No tent camping is permitted. Drinking water, cable TV, and picnic tables are provided. Restrooms have flush toilets and showers. A dump station, and a coin laundry room are available. A store and ice are within one mile. Leashed pets are permitted, with some restrictions.

Reservations, fees: Reservations accepted. Sites are $22.50 per night, $1 per person per night for more than two people, and $1 per night per additional vehicle. Some credit cards accepted. Open year-round.

Directions: From Newport and U.S. 101, drive to the north end of town and the park on the east side of the road.

Contact: Agate Beach RV Park, 541/265-7670.

32 HARBOR VILLAGE RV PARK

Scenic rating: 6

on Yaquina Bay
See map page 254

This wooded and landscaped park is near the shore of Yaquina Bay. See the *Port of Newport Marina and RV Park* listing in this chapter for information on attractions in Newport. Nearby recreation options include clamming, crabbing, deep-sea fishing, an 18-hole golf course, hiking trails, and a full-service marina. No tent campers are permitted.

RV sites, facilities: There are 40 sites with full hookups (30 amps) for RVs up to 40 feet. There are also 100 sites for full-time renters and a mobile-home park for ages 55 and up. Drinking water, cable TV, wireless Internet service, modem access, and picnic tables are provided. Restrooms have flush toilets and showers, and a coin laundry is available. Propane gas, a store, and a café are within one mile. Boat docks, launching facilities, and rentals are nearby. Leashed pets are permitted.

Reservations, fees: Reservations accepted at 888/818-0002. Sites are $25 per night, $5 per person per night for more than two people. Some credit cards accepted. Open year-round.

Directions: From Newport and John Moore Road (lighted intersection), drive south on John Moore Road for one-half mile to the bay and Bay Boulevard. Bear left and drive a short distance to the park entrance on the left.

Contact: Harbor Village RV Park, 541/265-5088, fax 541/265-5895, www.harborvillagerv park.com.

33 PORT OF NEWPORT MARINA AND RV PARK

Scenic rating: 7

on Yaquina Bay
See map page 254

This public park lies along the shore of Yaquina Bay near Newport, a resort town that offers a variety of attractions, such as ocean fishing, a museum and aquarium at the nearby Hatfield Marine Science Center, the Undersea Garden, the Waxworks, Ripley's Believe It or Not, and the Lincoln County Historical Society Museum. Nearby recreation options include an 18-hole golf course, hiking trails, and a full-service marina.

RV sites, facilities: There are 152 sites with full hookups (30 and 50 amps) for RVs up to 45 feet. No tents are allowed. Restrooms have flush toilets and showers. Cable TV, modem and wireless access, a convenience store, a coin laundry, and ice are available. A marina with boat docks and launching facilities is available on-site. Leashed pets are permitted.

Reservations, fees: Reservations are accepted at 541/867-3321. Sites are $26.50–36.80 per night, $1 per person per night for more than two people. Some credit cards accepted. Open year-round.

Directions: From Newport and U.S. 101, drive south for one-half mile (over the bridge) to Marine Science Drive. Turn right (east) and drive one-half mile to the park entrance on the left.

Contact: Port of Newport Marina and RV Park, 541/867-3321, fax 541/867-3352, www.portof newport.com.

34 SOUTH BEACH STATE PARK

Scenic rating: 7

south of Newport on the Pacific Ocean
See map page 254

This park along the beach offers opportunities for beachcombing, fishing, crabbing, windsurfing, boating, and hiking. In fact, the Oregon Coast Trail passes right through the park. A nature trail circles the campground, and there are hiking and bicycling trails to the beach. A primitive hike-in campground is also available. The park is within walking distance of Oregon Aquarium. A naturalist provides campground talks during the summer season. Kayak trips are an option during the summer. For information on attractions in Newport, see the *Port of Newport Marina and RV Park* listing in this chapter.

RV sites, facilities: There are 244 sites for tents or RVs up to 45 feet with partial hookups (30 amps), 10 sites for hikers and bicyclists, and an overflow area for RVs. There are also three group sites for up to 25 people each and 27 yurts. Picnic tables and fire grills are provided. Drinking water, restrooms with flush toilets and showers, garbage bins, recycling, a dump station, a playground, day-use area, reservable meeting hall, and firewood are available. Some facilities are wheelchair accessible. Leashed pets are permitted.

Reservations, fees: Reservations are accepted at 800/452-5687 or www.oregonstateparks.org ($6 reservation fee). Sites are $17–22 per night, $5 per night per additional vehicle, $4 per person per night for hikers/bicyclists (three-night limit), $44–65 per night for group sites, and $29 per night for yurts. Some credit cards accepted. Open year-round.

Directions: From Newport and U.S. 101, drive south for three miles to the park entrance on the right.

Contact: South Beach State Park, 541/867-4715; Oregon State Parks, 800/551-6949, www.oregon stateparks.org.

OREGON

OREGON

35 SEAL ROCKS RV COVE

Scenic rating: 8

near Seal Rock State Park

See map page 254

This RV park is on the rugged coastline near Seal Rock State Park (open for day use only), where you may find seals, sea lions, and birds. The ocean views are stunning, and some sites have views.

RV sites, facilities: There are 28 sites with full hookups (30 and 50 amps) for RVs of any length and 15 tent sites with electricity. Drinking water, picnic tables, and fire rings are provided. Restrooms have flush toilets and showers, and firewood is available. A store, a café, and ice are within one mile. Leashed pets are permitted.

Reservations, fees: Reservations accepted. Tent sites are $20–24 per night, RV sites are $28–33, $1–3 per person per night for more than two people, $3 one-time fee for an additional vehicle unless towed. Winter rates available. Open year-round.

Directions: From Newport and U.S. 101, drive south for 10 miles to the town of Seal Rock. Continue south on U.S. 101 for 0.25 mile to the park entrance on the left.

Contact: Seal Rocks RV Cove, 541/563-3955, www.sealrocksrv.com.

36 DRIFT CREEK LANDING

Scenic rating: 6

on the Alsea River

See map page 254

This campground is along the shore of the Alsea River in a heavily treed and mountainous area. The Oregon Coast Aquarium is 15 miles away, and an 18-hole golf course is nearby. There are 10 mobile homes on this property with long-term renters, and more than one-third of the RV sites are taken by monthly renters. For more information on the area, see the *Waldport/Newport KOA* listing in this chapter.

RV sites, facilities: There are 49 sites with full hookups (30 amps) for RVs of any length, an area for tent camping, and three cabins. Drinking water and picnic tables are provided. Restrooms have flush toilets and showers. Cable TV, propane gas, a recreation hall, a convenience store, a snack bar, a coin laundry, boat docks, boat rentals, and launching facilities are available. Leashed pets are permitted.

Reservations, fees: Reservations accepted. RV sites are $22 per night, tent sites are $15 per night, plus $2 per person per night for more than two people and $5 per night per additional vehicle. Some credit cards accepted. Open year-round.

Directions: From Newport and U.S. 101, drive south for 14 miles to Waldport and Highway 34. Turn east on Highway 34 and drive 3.8 miles to the campground.

Contact: Drift Creek Landing, 541/563-3610, fax 541/563-5234.

37 ALSEA RIVER RV PARK & MARINA

Scenic rating: 6

on the Alsea River

See map page 254

This park is one of several along the shore of the Alsea River and was previously known as Fishin' Hole RV Park & Marina. Kayaking and canoeing are popular. Some of the sites here are filled with monthly rentals. For information on the area, see the *Waldport/Newport KOA* listing in this chapter.

RV sites, facilities: There are 27 sites with full or partial hookups (30 amps) for RVs of any length, an area for tent campers, one rental home, and one cabin. Drinking water and picnic tables are provided, and fire pits are available on request. Restrooms have flush toilets and showers. A coin laundry, Wi-Fi access, recreation room, bait and tackle, boat docks, boat rentals, and launching facilities are available. Leashed pets are permitted.

Reservations, fees: Reservations are accepted at 877/770-6137. Tent sites are $17 per night, RV

OREGON

sites are $21–23 per night, plus $5 per person per night for more than two people and $5 per night per additional vehicle. Some credit cards accepted. Open year-round.

Directions: From Newport and U.S. 101, drive south for 14 miles to Waldport and Highway 34. Turn east on Highway 34 and drive four miles to the entrance on the left.

Contact: Alsea River RV Park & Marina, 541/563-3401, www.alseariverrvpark.com.

38 CHINOOK RV PARK

Scenic rating: 7

on the Alsea River

See map page 254

This park is along the shore of the Alsea River, about 3.5 miles from the ocean. The park is filled primarily with monthly rentals although several RV sites are reserved for short-term campers. Campsites are rented on a space-available basis. For more information on the area, see the *Waldport/Newport KOA* listing in this chapter.

RV sites, facilities: There are six sites for tents and 34 sites with full or partial hookups (30 amps) for RVs up to 40 feet. Picnic tables are provided. Drinking water, cable TV, Wi-Fi access, restrooms with flush toilets and showers, a picnic area, ice, and a coin laundry are available. A store is within 1.5 miles. Boat docks are nearby. Propane gas and boat-launching facilities are available 3.5 miles away. Leashed pets are permitted.

Reservations, fees: Reservations are accepted. RV sites are $18–23 per night, tent sites are $14–16 per night, and it's $2 per person per night for more than two people. Open year-round.

Directions: From Newport and U.S. 101, drive south for 14 miles to Waldport and Highway 34. Turn east on Highway 34 and drive 3.3 miles to the park entrance on the left.

Contact: Chinook RV Park, 541/563-3485, www.chinookrvpark.com.

39 TAYLOR'S LANDING RV PARK

Scenic rating: 9

on the Alsea River

See map page 254

This campground is along the Alsea River. Fall, when the salmon fishing is best, is the prime time here, and the park often fills up. For more information on the area, see the *Waldport/Newport KOA* listing in this chapter.

RV sites, facilities: There are 28 sites for RVs of any length with full hookups (30 amps). Drinking water, cable TV, and picnic tables are provided. Restrooms have flush toilets and showers. Propane gas, a café, a coin laundry, community fire ring, and boat docks and rentals are available. Boat launching facilities are nearby. Leashed pets are permitted.

Reservations, fees: Reservations accepted. Sites are $21.08 per night, $1 per person per night for more than two people. Monthly rates available. Open year-round.

Directions: From Newport and U.S. 101, drive south for 14 miles to Waldport and Highway 34. Turn east on Highway 34 and drive seven miles to the entrance on the right.

Contact: Taylor's Landing RV Park, tel./fax 541/528-3388, www.taylorslandingrvpark.com.

40 WALDPORT/NEWPORT KOA

Scenic rating: 8

on Alsea Bay

See map page 254

This pretty park, set amid some of the oldest pine trees in Oregon, is within walking distance of the beach, the bay, and downtown Waldport—and to top it off, some of the campsites have beautiful ocean views. Alsea Bay's sandy and rocky shoreline makes this area a favorite with anglers. The crabbing and clamming can also be quite good. Kite flying is popular. South Beach State Park, about five miles north on U.S. 101, offers more fishing and a boat ramp along Beaver Creek. It's open for day use only. Other nearby recreation options include hiking

OREGON

trails, marked bike trails, the Oregon Coast Aquarium, the Sea Lion Caves, and a marina.

RV sites, facilities: There are 76 sites with full hookups (30 and 50 amps) for RVs up to 45 feet, 13 tent sites, and 15 cabins. Picnic tables and fire pits are provided; drinking water and cable TV are also available. Restrooms have flush toilets and showers. Wireless Internet service, modem access, a recreation room, propane gas, a dump station, a store, a café, a coin laundry, a playground, and ice are available. Boat docks, launching facilities, and boat rentals are nearby. A café is within one mile. Some facilities are wheelchair accessible. Leashed pets are permitted, with certain restrictions.

Reservations, fees: Reservations are accepted at 800/562-3443. Tent sites are $18–19 per night, RV sites are $29–52 per night, and it's $2–5 per person per night for more than two people. Some credit cards are accepted. Open year-round.

Directions: From Newport and U.S. 101, drive south for approximately 14 miles to Milepost 155 at the north end of the Alsea Bay Bridge. The park is on the west side of the bridge.

Contact: Waldport/Newport KOA, 541/563-2250, fax 541/563-4098, www.koa.com.

41 BEACHSIDE STATE PARK

Scenic rating: 7

near Alsea Bay

See map page 254

This state park offers about nine miles of beach and is not far from Alsea Bay and the Alsea River. Every site is seconds from the beach. Within 30 miles in either direction, you'll find clamming, crabbing, and fishing, as well as hiking and driving tours, tidepools, and an aquarium, three lighthouses, science centers, and visitors centers. (See the *Waldport/Newport KOA* listing in this chapter for more information on fishing opportunities in the area.)

RV sites, facilities: There are 28 sites for tents or RVs, 33 sites for tents or RVs up to 40 feet with partial hookups (30 amps), two yurts, and a special camping area for hikers and bicyclists. Picnic

tables and fire grills are provided. Drinking water, garbage bins, restrooms with flush toilets and showers, recycling, and firewood are available. A horseshoe pit is nearby. Some facilities are wheelchair accessible. Leashed pets are permitted.

Reservations, fees: Reservations are accepted at 800/452-5687 or www.oregonstateparks.org ($6 reservation fee). Sites are $13–21 per night, $5 per night per additional vehicle, and $4 per person per night for hikers/bicyclists; yurts are $29 per night. Some credit cards are accepted. Open mid-March–October, weather permitting.

Directions: From Newport and U.S. 101, drive south for 16 miles to Waldport. Continue south on U.S. 101 for four miles to the park entrance on the west side of the road.

Contact: Beachside State Park, 541/563-3220, fax 541/563-3657; Oregon State Parks, 800/551-6949, www.oregonstateparks.org.

42 TILLICUM BEACH

Scenic rating: 8

in Siuslaw National Forest

See map page 254

Ocean-view campsites are a big draw at this campground just south of Beachside State Park. Nearby forest roads provide access to streams in the mountains east of the beach area. A U.S. Forest Service map details the possibilities. Since it's just off the highway and along the water, this camp fills up very quickly in the summer, so expect crowds.

RV sites, facilities: There are 60 sites for tents or RVs up to 40 feet; some sites have partial hookups (25 amps). Picnic tables and fire rings are provided. Flush toilets, garbage bins, and drinking water are available. Leashed pets are permitted.

Reservations, fees: Reservations are accepted at 877/444-6777 or www.ReserveUSA.com ($9 reservation fee). Sites are $17 per night, $5 per night per additional vehicle. Open year-round, with reduced capacity in winter; there's a 14-day stay limit.

Directions: From Newport and U.S. 101, drive south for 14 miles to Waldport. Continue south on U.S. 101 for 4.5 miles to the campground entrance on the right.

Contact: Siuslaw National Forest, Waldport Ranger District, 541/563-3211 or 541/547-3679 (concessionaire), fax 541/563-8449.

43 BLACKBERRY

Scenic rating: 7

on the Alsea River in Siuslaw National Forest
See map page 254

Blackberry makes a good base camp for a fishing trip on the Alsea River. The U.S. Forest Service provides boat launches and picnic areas at several spots along this stretch of river. Often, there is a camp host, who can give you inside information on nearby recreational opportunities. Large fir trees and lawn separate the sites.

RV sites, facilities: There are 32 sites for tents or RVs up to 25 feet (no hookups). Picnic tables and fire grills are provided. Drinking water, garbage bins, and flush toilets are available. There is no firewood. A boat ramp is on-site. Leashed pets are permitted.

Reservations, fees: Reservations are not accepted. Sites are $15 per night, $5 per night per additional vehicle. Open mid-May–early October, with a 14-day stay limit.

Directions: From Albany, drive west on U.S. 20 for 15 miles to Philomath and Highway 34. Turn south on Highway 34 and drive 41 miles to the campground entrance on the left.

Contact: Siuslaw National Forest, Waldport Ranger District, 541/563-3211, fax 541/563-3124.

44 ALSEA FALLS

Scenic rating: 8

adjacent to the South Fork of the Alsea River
See map page 254

Enjoy the beautiful surroundings of Alsea Falls by exploring the trails that wander through this park and lead to a picnic area by the falls. Trails to McBee Park and Green Peak Falls are accessible from the campground along the South Fork of the river. The campsites are in a 1950s-era forest of Douglas fir and vine maple. On a warm day, Alsea Falls offers cool relief along the river. The area was named after its original inhabitants, the Alsea people.

RV sites, facilities: There are 16 sites for tents or RVs up to 32 feet (no hookups). Fire pits are provided. Drinking water, vault toilets, garbage bins, and fireplaces for wood and charcoal are available. Leashed pets are permitted.

Reservations, fees: Reservations are not accepted. Sites are $10 per night, $5 per night per additional vehicle. Open mid-May–late September.

Directions: From Albany, drive west on U.S. 20 for nine miles to Corvallis. Turn left (south) onto Highway 99 and drive 15 miles to County Road 45120. Turn right (west) and drive five miles to Alpine Junction. Continue along the South Fork Alsea Access Road for nine miles to the campground on the right.

Contact: Bureau of Land Management, Salem District Office, 503/375-5646, fax 503/375-5622.

45 CAPE PERPETUA

Scenic rating: 8

on Cape Creek in Siuslaw National Forest
See map page 254

This U.S. Forest Service campground is along Cape Creek in the Cape Perpetua Scenic Area. The visitor information center provides hiking and driving maps to guide you through this spectacular region. Maps highlight the tidepool and picnic spots. The coastal cliffs are perfect for whale-watching December–March. Neptune State Park is just south and offers additional rugged coastline vistas.

RV sites, facilities: There are 38 sites for tents or RVs up to 22 feet (no hookups), plus one group site that can accommodate up to 100 people and 12 vehicles. Picnic tables and fire grills are provided. Flush toilets, drinking water, and garbage bins are available. Leashed pets are permitted.

Reservations, fees: Reservations are not accepted for family sites but are required at the group site at 877/444-6777 or www.Reserve USA.com ($9 reservation fee). Group sites are $125 per night, regular sites are $17 per night, and it's $5 per night per additional vehicle. Open mid-May–early October, with a 14-day stay limit.

Directions: From Newport and U.S. 101, drive south for 23 miles to Yachats. Continue three miles south on U.S. 101 to the entrance on the left.

Contact: Siuslaw National Forest, Waldport Ranger District, 541/563-3211 or 541/822-3799 (concessionaire), fax 541/563-3124.

46 SEA PERCH RV PARK

Scenic rating: 8

near Cape Perpetua

See map page 254

Sea Perch sits right in the middle of one of the most scenic areas on the Oregon coast. This private park just south of Cape Perpetua has sites 75 feet from the beach and in lawn areas, plus its own shell museum and gift shop. Big rigs are welcome here. No tent camping is permitted. Surf fishing and windsurfing are options here. For more information on the area, see the *Cape Perpetua* listing in this chapter.

RV sites, facilities: There are 36 sites with full or partial hookups for RVs of any length. Some sites are pull-through. Drinking water and picnic tables are provided. Restrooms have flush toilets and coin showers. A dump station, firewood, a recreation hall, a coin laundry, ice, a convenience store, wireless Internet access, modem hookups, a picnic area, and a beach are available. Leashed pets are permitted.

Reservations, fees: Reservations are accepted. Sites are $26–36 per night, $2 per person per night for more than two people, and $5 per night for an additional vehicle. Some credit cards are accepted. Open year-round.

Directions: From Newport and U.S. 101, drive south for 23 miles to Yachats. Continue south

on U.S. 101 for 6.5 miles to the campground at Milepost 171 on the right.

Contact: Sea Perch RV Park, 541/547-3505, fax 541/547-3368, www.seaperchrvpark.com.

47 ROCK CREEK

Scenic rating: 7

on Rock Creek in Siuslaw National Forest

See map page 254

This little campground is along Rock Creek just a quarter mile from the ocean. It's a premium spot for coastal-highway travelers, although it can get packed very quickly. An excellent side trip is to Cape Perpetua, a designated scenic area a few miles up the coast. The cape offers beautiful ocean views and a visitors center that will supply you with information on nature trails, picnic spots, tidepools, and where to find the best viewpoints in the area.

RV sites, facilities: There are 15 sites for tents or RVs up to 22 feet (no hookups). Fire grills and picnic tables are provided. Flush toilets, garbage bins, and drinking water are available. Leashed pets are permitted.

Reservations, fees: Reservations are not accepted. Sites are $17 per night, $5 per night per additional vehicle. Open mid-May–early October, with a 15-day stay limit.

Directions: From Newport and U.S. 101, drive south for 23 miles to Yachats. Continue south on U.S. 101 for 10 miles to the campground entrance on the left.

Contact: Siuslaw National Forest, Waldport Ranger District, 541/563-3211 or 541/547-3679 (concessionaire), fax 541/563-3124.

48 CARL G. WASHBURNE STATE PARK

Scenic rating: 7

near Yachats

See map page 254

These spacious campsites feature a buffer of native plants between campers and the highway.

At night, you can hear the pounding surf. A creek runs through the campground, and elk have been known to wander through. Short hikes lead from the campground to a two-mile-long beach, extensive tidepools along the base of the cliffs, and a three-mile trail to Heceta Head Lighthouse. Just three miles south of the park are the Sea Lion Caves, where an elevator takes visitors down into a cavern for an insider's view of the life of a sea lion.

RV sites, facilities: There are 58 sites for RVs up to 45 feet with full hookups (20 amps), seven primitive walk-in sites, and two yurts. A special area is available for hikers and bicyclists. Picnic tables, fire pits, drinking water, garbage bins, and a dump station are provided. Restrooms have flush toilets and showers, and firewood is available. Leashed pets are permitted.

Reservations, fees: Reservations are not accepted, except for yurts. Sites are $13–22 per night, $5 per night per additional vehicle, and $4 per person per night for hikers/bicyclists; yurts are $29 per night. Some credit cards are accepted. Open year-round.

Directions: From Florence and U.S. 101, drive north for 12.5 miles to the park entrance road (well signed, 10 miles south of the town of Yachats). Turn east and drive a short distance to the park.

Contact: Carl G. Washburne State Park, 541/547-3416 or 800/551-6949, www.oregons tateparks.org.

49 ALDER DUNE

Scenic rating: 7

near Alder Lake in Siuslaw National Forest
See map page 255

This wooded campground is near four lakes—Alder Lake, Dune Lake, Mercer Lake (the largest), and Sutton Lake. A boat launch is available at Sutton Lake. An excellent recreation option is to explore the expansive sand dunes in the area by foot. There is no off-road-vehicle access here. (See the *Harbor Vista*

Campground listing in this chapter for more information on the area.)

RV sites, facilities: There are 38 sites for tents or RVs up to 30 feet (no hookups). Picnic tables and fire grills are provided. Flush toilets, garbage bins, and drinking water are available. Leashed pets are permitted.

Reservations, fees: Reservations are accepted at 877/444-6777 or by website at www.Reserve USA.com ($9 reservation fee). Sites are $20 per night. Open early May–early October, weather permitting, with a 14-day stay limit.

Directions: From Florence and U.S. 101, drive north for eight miles to the campground on the left.

Contact: Siuslaw National Forest, Mapleton Ranger District, 541/902-8526, fax 541/902-6946.

50 SUTTON

Scenic rating: 7

near Sutton Lake in Siuslaw National Forest
See map page 255

This campground is adjacent to Sutton Creek, not far from Sutton Lake. Vegetation provides some privacy between sites. Holman Vista on Sutton Beach Road offers a beautiful view of the dunes and ocean. Wading and fishing are both popular. A hiking trail system leads from the camp out to the dunes. There is no off-road-vehicle access here. An alternative camp is Alder Dune to the north.

RV sites, facilities: There are 80 sites for tents or RVs up to 30 feet, 20 with partial hookups (20 amps), and two group sites for up to 50 and 100 people, respectively. Picnic tables and fire grills are provided. Flush toilets, garbage bins, and drinking water are available. A boat ramp is nearby. Some facilities are wheelchair accessible. Leashed pets are permitted.

Reservations, fees: Reservations are accepted at 877/444-6777 or www.ReserveUSA.com ($9 reservation fee). Sites are $20–22 per night and $75–125 per night for group sites. Open year-round, with a 14-day stay limit.

Directions: From Eugene, drive west on Highway 126 for 61 miles to Florence and U.S. 101. Turn north on U.S. 101 and drive six miles to Sutton Beach Road (Forest Road 794). Turn left (northwest) and drive 1.5 miles to the campground entrance.

Contact: Siuslaw National Forest, Mapleton Ranger District, 541/902-8526, fax 541/902-6946.

51 MAPLE LANE RV PARK AND MARINA

Scenic rating: 5

on the Siuslaw River
See map page 255

This park along the shore of the Siuslaw River in Mapleton is close to hiking trails. The general area is surrounded by Siuslaw National Forest land. A U.S. Forest Service map details nearby backcountry side-trip options. Fall is the most popular time of the year here, as it's prime time for salmon fishing on Siuslaw. Most sites are taken by monthly renters.

RV sites, facilities: There are two tent sites and 46 sites with full hookups for RVs up to 35 feet. Some sites are pull-through. Drinking water, restrooms with flush toilets and showers, and propane gas are available. A bait and tackle shop is open during the fishing season. Boat docks and launching facilities are on-site. A store, a café, and ice are nearby. Small pets (under 15 pounds) are permitted.

Reservations, fees: Reservations are accepted. Tent sites are $7 per night, RV sites are $14 per night, and it's $1.50 per person per night for more than two people and $2 per night per additional vehicle. Monthly rates are available. Open year-round.

Directions: From Eugene, drive west on Highway 126 for 47 miles to Mapleton. Continue on Highway 126 for 0.25 mile past the business district to the park entrance on the left.

Contact: Maple Lane RV Park and Marina, 541/268-4822.

52 HARBOR VISTA CAMPGROUND

Scenic rating: 6

near Florence
See map page 255

This county park out among the dunes near the entrance to the harbor offers a great lookout point from its observation deck. The park is perched above the North Jetty of the Siuslaw River and encompasses 15 acres. Beach access is one mile away. Side trips include the Sea Lion Caves, Darlington State Park, Jessie M. Honeyman Memorial State Park, and the Indian Forest, just four miles north. Florence also has displays of Native American dwellings and crafts.

RV sites, facilities: There are 38 sites for tents or RVs up to 60 feet with partial hookups (30 and 50 amps). Picnic tables, fire rings, and garbage bins are provided. Restrooms have flush toilets and coin showers. A dump station, drinking water, a pay phone, and a playground are available. A camp host is on-site. Some facilities are wheelchair accessible. Leashed pets are permitted.

Reservations, fees: Reservations are accepted at 541/682-2000 ($10 reservation fee). Sites are $20 per night, $6.50 per night per additional vehicle. Some credit cards are accepted. Open year-round.

Directions: From Florence and U.S. 101, drive north for four miles to 35th Street. Turn left and drive to where it dead-ends into Rhododendron Drive. Turn right and drive 1.4 miles to North Jetty Road. Turn left and drive half a block to Harbor Vista Road. Turn left and continue to the campground at 87658 Harbor Vista Road.

Note: Follow these exact directions. Part of Harbor Vista Road is now gated, blocking a route previous visitors to this park may have taken.

Contact: Harbor Vista Campground, 541/997-5987, www.lanecounty.org/parks/harbor.htm.

OREGON

53 B AND E WAYSIDE MOBILE HOME AND RV PARK

Scenic rating: 5

near Florence

See map page 255

Adjacent to this landscaped RV park is a 28-unit mobile home park for ages 55 and up. Some sites at the RV park are taken by monthly rentals. Nearby recreation options include two golf courses and a riding stable, two miles away. (See the *Harbor Vista Campground* and *Port of Siuslaw RV Park and Marina* listings in this chapter for side-trip ideas.)

RV sites, facilities: There are 24 sites with full hookups (30 amps) for RVs of any length. There are no tent sites. Picnic tables are provided. Restrooms have flush toilets and showers. A dump station, a recreation room, modem and wireless access, and a coin laundry are available. Propane gas, a store, ice, a café, and a restaurant are within two miles. Boat-launching facilities are nearby. Some facilities are wheelchair accessible. Small, leashed pets are permitted.

Reservations, fees: Reservations are accepted. Sites are $25 per night, $2 per person per night for more than two people. Weekly and monthly rates are available. Open year-round.

Directions: From Florence and U.S. 101, drive north for 1.8 miles to the park on the right.

Contact: B and E Wayside Mobile Home and RV Park, 541/997-6451.

54 PORT OF SIUSLAW RV PARK AND MARINA

Scenic rating: 8

on the Siuslaw River

See map page 255

This public resort can be found along the Siuslaw River in a grassy, urban setting. Anglers with boats will find that the U.S. 101 bridge support pilings make good spots for crabbing as well as fishing for perch and flounder. New docks with drinking water, electricity, gasoline, security, and a fish-cleaning station are available. The Sea Lion Caves and estuary are a bonus for wildlife lovers, and nearby lakes make swimming and waterskiing a possibility. Golf is within driving distance, and horses can be rented about nine miles away.

RV sites, facilities: There are 85 sites for tents or RVs of any length with full or partial hookups (20 and 30 amps) and 10 tent sites. Drinking water, cable TV, and picnic tables are provided. Restrooms have flush toilets and showers. A dump station, a coin laundry, Wi-Fi, and boat docks are available. A café, a grocery store, and ice are within one mile. Some facilities are wheelchair accessible. Leashed pets are permitted.

Reservations, fees: Reservations are accepted at 541/997-3040. RV sites are $22 per night, and tent sites are $10 per night. Some credit cards are accepted. Open year-round.

Directions: From Florence and U.S. 101, drive south to Nopal Street. Turn left (east) and drive two blocks to 1st Street. Turn left and drive 0.25 mile to the park at the end of the road.

Contact: Port of Siuslaw RV Park and Marina, 541/997-3040, www.portofsiuslaw.com.

55 JESSIE M. HONEYMAN MEMORIAL STATE PARK

Scenic rating: 7

near Cleowax Lake

See map page 255

This popular state park is within walking distance of the shore of Cleowax Lake and adjacent to the dunes of the Oregon Dunes National Recreation Area. Dunes stretch for two miles between the park and the ocean. The dunes are quite impressive, with some reaching to 500 feet. In the winter, the area is open to OHV use. For thrill seekers, sandboard rentals (for sandboarding on the dunes) are available in nearby Florence. The two lakes in the park offer facilities for boating, fishing, and swimming. A one-mile hiking trail with access to the dunes is available in the park, and off-road-vehicle trails are nearby in the sand dunes.

RV sites, facilities: There are 188 sites for tents or RVs (no hookups), 168 sites with full or partial hookups (20, 30, and 50 amps) for RVs up to 60 feet, a special camping area for hikers and bicyclists, six group tent areas for up to 25 people and 10 vehicles each, and 10 yurts. Picnic tables, garbage bins, and fire grills are provided. Drinking water, restrooms with flush toilets and showers, a dump station, seasonal interpretive programs, a playground, day-use areas, an amphitheater, and firewood are available. Some facilities are wheelchair accessible. Boat docks and launching facilities are nearby. Leashed pets are permitted.

Reservations, fees: Reservations are accepted at 800/452-5687 or www.oregonstateparks.org ($6 reservation fee). Sites are $13–22 per night, plus $5 per night per additional vehicle; $4 per person per night for hikers/bicyclists; $29 per night for yurts; and $43–65 per night for group sites. Some credit cards are accepted. Open year-round.

Directions: From Florence and U.S. 101, drive south for three miles to the park entrance on the west side of the road.

Contact: Jessie M. Honeyman Memorial State Park, 541/997-3641 or 800/551-6949, www.oregonstateparks.org.

56 LAKESHORE RV PARK

Scenic rating: 5

on Woahink Lake

See map page 255

Here's a prime area for vacationers. This park is along the shore of Woahink Lake, a popular spot to fish for bass, bluegill, catfish, crappie, perch, and trout. It's adjacent to Jessie M. Honeyman Memorial State Park and the Oregon Dunes National Recreation Area. Off-road-vehicle access to the dunes is four miles northeast and three miles south of the park. Hiking trails through the dunes can be found at Honeyman Memorial State Park. Some sites are filled with monthly rentals. No tent camping is available.

RV sites, facilities: There are 20 sites with full hookups (30 amps) for RVs of any length; some are pull-through sites. Picnic tables and cable TV are provided. Drinking water, restrooms with flush toilets and showers, modem access, Wi-Fi, and a coin laundry are available. A café is within three miles. Boat docks are nearby. Leashed pets are permitted.

Reservations, fees: Reservations are accepted at 866/240-4269. Sites are $25 per night, $2 per person per night for more than two people. Monthly rentals are available. Open year-round.

Directions: From Florence and U.S. 101, drive south for four miles to Milepost 195. The park is on the left (east) side of the road.

Contact: Lakeshore RV Park, 541/997-2741, www.lakeshorerv.com.

57 WOAHINK LAKE RV RESORT

Scenic rating: 7

on Woahink Lake

See map page 255

One of several RV parks in the Florence area, this quiet, clean camp is across from Woahink Lake, where trout fishing is an option. Sand dunes can be accessed from the resort. Nearby Oregon Dunes National Recreation Area makes a good side trip.

RV sites, facilities: There are 76 sites with full hookups for RVs of any length and one cabin. Most sites are pull-through. No tent camping is allowed. Picnic tables and cable TV are provided. Drinking water, restrooms with showers, modem access, a community fire ring, and a coin laundry are available. Recreational facilities include horseshoe pits, a recreation hall, a game room, and a boat dock. Leashed pets are permitted, with some restrictions.

Reservations, fees: Reservations are accepted at 541/997-6454. Sites are $27 per night, $2 per person per night for more than two people, and $6 per night per additional vehicle. Some credit cards are accepted. Open year-round.

Directions: From Florence and U.S. 101, drive south for 5.1 miles to the resort on the right (west side of road).

Contact: Woahink Lake RV Resort, 541/997-6454, fax 541/902-0481.

58 MERCER LAKE RESORT

Scenic rating: 7

on Mercer Lake

See map page 255

This resort is in a forested setting above the shore of Mercer Lake, one of a number of lakes that have formed among the ancient dunes in this area. The 375-acre lake has 11 miles of shoreline and numerous coves. Fishing for rainbow trout and largemouth bass is the most popular activity, and the lake is stocked. A sandy swimming beach is also available, and the ocean is four miles away.

RV sites, facilities: There are 10 sites with full or partial hookups for RVs up to 40 feet and 10 cabins. Some sites are pull-through. There is no tent camping. No open fires are allowed. Drinking water, cable TV, and picnic tables are provided. Restrooms have flush toilets and showers. A dump station, a convenience store, a coin laundry, and ice are available. Boat docks, launching facilities, and fishing boat rentals are on-site. Leashed pets are permitted.

Reservations, fees: Reservations are accepted at 800/355-3633. Sites are $22–35 per night for up to six people, plus $5 per night per additional vehicle and $5 per night per pet. Some credit cards are accepted. Open year-round.

Directions: From Florence and U.S. 101, drive north for five miles to Mercer Lake Road. Turn east and drive just under one mile to Bay Berry Lane. Turn left and drive to the resort.

Contact: Mercer Lake Resort, 541/997-3633, www.mlroregon.com.

59 CARTER LAKE

Scenic rating: 9

on Carter Lake in Oregon Dunes National Recreation Area

See map page 255

This campground sits on the north shore of Carter Lake, and you can fish almost right from your campsite. Boating and fishing are permitted on this long, narrow lake, which sits among

dunes overgrown with vegetation. The nearby Taylor Dunes Trail is a half-mile wheelchair-accessible trail to the dunes past Taylor Lake. Hiking is allowed in the dunes, but there is no off-road-vehicle access here. If you want off-road access, head north one mile to Siltcoos Road, turn west, and drive 1.3 miles to Driftwood II.

RV sites, facilities: There are 23 sites for tents or RVs up to 35 feet (no hookups). Picnic tables, garbage service, and fire grills are provided. Drinking water and flush toilets are available. Some facilities are wheelchair accessible. Leashed pets are permitted.

Reservations, fees: Reservations are accepted at 877/444-6777 or www.ReserveUSA.com ($9 reservation fee). Sites are $17 per night, $7 per night per additional vehicle. Open May–September, with a 14-day stay limit.

Directions: From Florence and U.S. 101, drive south for 8.5 miles to Forest Road 1084. Turn right on Forest Road 1084 and drive west 200 yards to the camp.

Contact: Oregon Dunes National Recreation Area, Visitors Center, 541/271-3611, fax 541/750-7244, www.fs.fed.us/r6/siuslaw/recreation.

60 DRIFTWOOD II

Scenic rating: 6

near Siltcoos Lake in Oregon Dunes National Recreation Area

See map page 255

Primarily a campground for off-road vehicles, Driftwood II is near the ocean, but without an ocean view, in the Oregon Dunes National Recreation Area. It has off-road-vehicle access. Several small lakes, the Siltcoos River, and Siltcoos Lake are nearby. Note that ATV use is prohibited 10 P.M.–6 A.M.

RV sites, facilities: There are 69 sites for tents or RVs up to 50 feet (no hookups). Picnic tables, garbage service, and fire grills are provided. Drinking water and restrooms with flush toilets and showers are available. A dump station is within five miles. Some facilities are wheelchair

OREGON

accessible. Boat docks, launching facilities, and rentals can be found about four miles away on Siltcoos Lake. Leashed pets are permitted.

Reservations, fees: Reservations are accepted at 877/444-6777 or www.ReserveUSA.com ($9 reservation fee). Sites are $20 per night. Open year-round.

Directions: From Florence and U.S. 101, drive south for seven miles to Siltcoos Beach Road. Turn right and drive 1.5 miles west to the campground.

Contact: Oregon Dunes National Recreation Area, Visitors Center, 541/271-3611, fax 541/750-7244, www.fs.fed.us/r6/siuslaw/recreation.

61 LAGOON

Scenic rating: 9

near Siltcoos Lake in Oregon Dunes National Recreation Area

See map page 255

One of several campgrounds in the area, this camp is along the lagoon, about one mile from Siltcoos Lake and half a mile inland. The Lagoon Trail offers prime wildlife-viewing for marine birds and other aquatic species.

RV sites, facilities: There are 39 sites for tents or RVs up to 35 feet (no hookups); some sites are pull-through. Picnic tables, garbage service, and fire grills are provided. Drinking water and flush and vault toilets are available. A telephone and a dump station are within five miles. Boat docks, launching facilities, and rentals are nearby on Siltcoos Lake. Some facilities are wheelchair accessible. Leashed pets are permitted.

Reservations, fees: Reservations are not accepted. Sites are $20 per night. Open year-round, with a 14-day stay limit.

Directions: From Florence and U.S. 101, drive south for seven miles to Siltcoos Beach Road. Turn right on Siltcoos Beach Road and drive west for 1.2 miles to the campground.

Contact: Oregon Dunes National Recreation Area, 541/271-3611, fax 541/750-7244, www.fs.fed.us/r6/siuslaw/recreation.

62 DARLINGS RESORT AND MARINA

Scenic rating: 7

on Siltcoos Lake

See map page 255

This park, in a rural area along the north shore of Siltcoos Lake, is adjacent to the extensive Oregon Dunes National Recreation Area. Sites are right on the lake; fish from your picnic table. An access point to the dunes for hikers and off-road vehicles is just across the highway. The lake has a full-service marina. About half the sites are taken by monthly rentals. There is no tent camping.

RV sites, facilities: There are 14 sites with partial hookups (20 and 30 amps) for RVs up to 38 feet. Cable TV, drinking water, fire pits, and picnic tables are provided. Restrooms have flush toilets and coin showers. Firewood, a convenience store, a tavern, a deli, boat docks, boat rentals, launching facilities, and a coin laundry are available. Leashed pets are permitted.

Reservations, fees: Reservations are accepted. Sites are $28.08–30.24 per night, $5 per night per additional vehicle. Some credit cards are accepted. Open year-round.

Directions: From Florence and U.S. 101, drive south for five miles to North Beach Road. Turn left (east) and drive 0.25 mile to Darlings Loop Road. Turn right and drive 0.25 mile to the resort.

Contact: Darlings Resort and Marina, 541/997-2841, www.darlingsresortrv.com.

63 WAXMYRTLE

Scenic rating: 7

near Siltcoos Lake in Oregon Dunes National Recreation Area

See map page 255

One of three camps in the immediate vicinity, Waxmyrtle is adjacent to Lagoon and less than a mile from Driftwood II. The camp is near the Siltcoos River and a couple of miles from Siltcoos Lake, a good-sized lake with boating facilities where you can fish. A pleasant hiking trail meanders through the dunes and along the estuary.

RV sites, facilities: There are 55 sites for tents or RVs up to 35 feet (no hookups). Picnic tables, garbage service, and fire grills are provided. Drinking water and flush toilets are available. Boat docks, launching facilities, and rentals are nearby on Siltcoos Lake. Leashed pets are permitted.

Reservations, fees: Reservations are not accepted. Sites are $20 per night. Open late May–September, with a 14-day stay limit.

Directions: From Florence and U.S. 101, drive south for seven miles to Siltcoos Beach Road. Turn right and drive 1.3 miles west to the campground.

Contact: Oregon Dunes National Recreation Area, 541/271-3611, fax 541/750-7244, www.fs.fed.us/r6/siuslaw/recreation.

64 TAHKENITCH LANDING

Scenic rating: 6

near Tahkenitch Lake in Oregon Dunes National Recreation Area

See map page 255

This camp overlooking Tahkenitch Lake (which means "lake of many fingers") has easy access to excellent fishing.

RV sites, facilities: There are 27 sites for tents or RVs up to 30 feet (no hookups). Picnic tables and garbage service are provided. Vault toilets, boat-launching facilities, and a floating dock are available, but there is no drinking water. Some facilities are wheelchair accessible. Leashed pets are permitted.

Reservations, fees: Reservations are accepted at 877/444-6777 or www.ReserveUSA.com ($9 reservation fee). Sites are $17 per night and $7 per night for an additional vehicle. Open year-round, with a 14-day stay limit.

Directions: From Florence and U.S. 101, drive south for 14 miles to the campground on the east side of the road.

Contact: Oregon Dunes National Recreation Area, 541/271-3611, fax 541/750-7244, www.fs.fed.us/r6/siuslaw/recreation.

65 TAHKENITCH

Scenic rating: 7

near Tahkenitch Lake in Oregon Dunes National Recreation Area

See map page 255

This very pretty campground with dense vegetation is in a wooded area across the highway from Tahkenitch Lake, which has numerous coves and backwater areas for fishing. A hiking trail close to the camp goes through the dunes out to the beach, as well as to Threemile Lake. If this camp is full, Tahkenitch Landing provides space nearby.

RV sites, facilities: There are 34 sites for tents or RVs up to 30 feet (no hookups). Picnic tables, garbage service, and fire grills are provided. Drinking water and flush toilets are available. Boat docks and launching facilities are on the lake across the highway. Leashed pets are permitted.

Reservations, fees: Reservations are accepted at 877/444-6777 or www.ReserveUSA.com ($9 reservation fee). Sites are $17 per night and $7 per night for an additional vehicle. Open mid-May–September, with a 14-day stay limit.

Directions: From Florence and U.S. 101, drive south for 14 miles. The campground entrance is on the right.

Contact: Oregon Dunes National Recreation Area, Visitors Center, 541/271-3611, fax 541/750-7244, www.fs.fed.us/r6/siuslaw/recreation.

66 DISCOVERY POINT RESORT & RV PARK

Scenic rating: 7

on Winchester Bay

See map page 255

This resort sits on the shore of Winchester Bay, adjacent to sandy dunes, in a fishing village near the mouth of the Umpqua River. The park was designed around motor sports, and ATVs are available for rent. It is somewhat noisy, but that's what most people come for here.

RV sites, facilities: There are three tent sites, 60 sites with full hookups (15 and 30 amps) for RVs of any length, and eight cabins. Some sites are pull-through. Picnic tables and fire pits are provided at most sites. Restrooms have flush toilets and showers. Drinking water, cable TV, a convenience store, a coin laundry, a weekend snack bar, and ice are available. A dump station and propane gas are within one mile. Boat docks and launching facilities are nearby. Leashed pets are permitted.

Reservations, fees: Reservations are accepted. Sites are $16–18 per night for tent sites, $28–33 per night for RV sites, and $7 per night for an additional vehicle. Some credit cards are accepted. Open year-round.

Directions: From Reedsport and U.S. 101, drive south for three miles to the Windy Cove exit near Winchester Bay. Take that exit and drive west 1.5 miles to the resort.

Contact: Discovery Point Resort & RV Park, 541/271-3443, www.discoverypointresort.com; ATV rentals, 541/271-9357.

67 WINDY COVE COUNTY PARK

Scenic rating: 7
near Winchester Bay on the Pacific Ocean
See map page 255

This Douglas County park comprises two campgrounds, Windy Cove A and B. Set near ocean beaches and sand dunes, both offer a variety of additional recreational opportunities, including an 18-hole golf course, hiking trails, and a lighthouse.

RV sites, facilities: There are 69 sites with full or partial hookups (30 amps) for RVs up to 60 feet and 29 tent sites. Drinking water and picnic tables are provided. Fire pits are provided at some Windy A sites and all Windy B sites. Restrooms have flush toilets and showers, and cable TV is available. Propane gas, a dump sta-

tion, a store, a café, a coin laundry, and ice are within one mile. Boat docks, launching facilities, boat charters, and rentals are nearby. Some facilities are wheelchair accessible. Leashed pets are permitted.

Reservations, fees: Reservations are accepted for Windy B sites only at 541/957-7001 ($10 reservation fee). Sites are $12–18 per night, $3 per night per additional vehicle. Some credit cards are accepted. Open year-round.

Directions: From Reedsport and U.S. 101, drive south for three miles to the Windy Cove exit near Winchester Bay. Take that exit and drive west to the park on the left.

Contact: Windy Cove County Park, Windy B, 541/271-5634; Windy A, 541/271-4138, www.co.douglas.or.us/parks.asp.

68 UMPQUA LIGHTHOUSE STATE PARK

Scenic rating: 7
on the Umpqua River
See map page 255   BEST (

This park is near Lake Marie and less than a mile from Salmon Harbor on Winchester Bay. A one-mile trail circles Lake Marie, and swimming and nonmotorized boating are allowed. Near the mouth of the Umpqua River, this unusual area features dunes as high as 500 feet. Hiking trails lead out of the park and into the Oregon Dunes National Recreation Area. The park offers more than two miles of beach access on the ocean and a half mile along the Umpqua River. The adjacent lighthouse is still in operation; tours are available during the summer season.

RV sites, facilities: There are 24 sites for tents or RVs up to 45 feet (no hookups), 20 sites with full hookups (20 and 30 amps) for RVs up to 45 feet, a hiker/bicyclist camp, two cabins, two yurts, and six deluxe yurts. Picnic tables and fire pits are provided. Drinking water, garbage bins, restrooms with flush toilets and showers, and firewood are available. Boat docks and launching facilities are on the Umpqua River. Leashed pets are permitted.

Reservations, fees: Reservations are accepted at 800/452-5687 or www.oregonstateparks.org ($6 reservation fee). Sites are $12–20 per night, $5 per night for an additional vehicle, $4 per person per night for hikers/bikers, $35 per night for cabins, and $27–66 per night for yurts. Some credit cards are accepted. Open year-round.

Directions: From Reedsport and U.S. 101, drive south for six miles to Umpqua Lighthouse Road. Turn right (west) and drive one mile to the park.

Contact: Umpqua Lighthouse State Park, 541/271-4118; Oregon State Parks, 800/551-6949, www.oregonstateparks.org.

69 WILLIAM M. TUGMAN STATE PARK

Scenic rating: 7

on Eel Lake

See map page 255

This campground is along the shore of Eel Lake, which offers almost five miles of shoreline for boating, fishing, sailing, and swimming. It's perfect for bass fishing. A boat ramp is available, but there is a 10-mph speed limit for boats. Oregon Dunes National Recreation Area is across the highway. Hiking is available just a few miles north at Umpqua Lighthouse State Park. A developed, 2.5-mile trail along the south end of the lake allows hikers to get away from the developed areas of the park and explore the lake's many outlets.

RV sites, facilities: There are 99 sites for tents or RVs up to 50 feet (partial hookups), a special camping area for hikers and bicyclists, and 13 yurts. Drinking water, fire rings, and picnic tables are provided. Restrooms have flush toilets and showers. A dump station, firewood, and a reservable picnic shelter are available. Some facilities are wheelchair accessible. Boat docks and launching facilities are nearby. Leashed pets are permitted.

Reservations, fees: Reservations are accepted at 800/452-5687 or www.oregonstateparks.org

($6 reservation fee). Sites are $12–16 per night, $5 per night per additional vehicle, $4 per person per night for hikers/bicyclists, and $27 per night for yurts. Some credit cards are accepted. Open year-round.

Directions: From Reedsport and U.S. 101, drive south for eight miles to the park entrance on the left (east side of the road).

Contact: William M. Tugman State Park, 541/759-3604; Oregon State Parks, 800/551-6949, www.oregonstateparks.org.

70 NORTH LAKE RESORT AND MARINA

Scenic rating: 8

on Tenmile Lake

See map page 255

This 40-acre resort along the shore of Tenmile Lake is wooded and secluded, with a private beach, and makes the perfect layover spot for U.S. 101 travelers. The lake has a full-service marina, and bass fishing can be good here. About 25 percent of the sites are taken by summer season rentals.

RV sites, facilities: There are 75 sites with full or partial hookups (50 amps) for RVs of any length and 20 tent sites. Picnic tables are provided, and there are fire pits at most sites. Restrooms have flush toilets and coin showers. A dump station, firewood, a convenience store, ice, phone/modem hookups, cable TV, drinking water, a coin laundry, horseshoe pits, and a volleyball court are available. Boat docks, launching facilities, and a marina are available. A café and boat rentals are nearby. Leashed pets are permitted.

Reservations, fees: Reservations are accepted. Tent sites are $20 per night, and RV sites are $27 per night. Some credit cards are accepted. Open April–October.

Directions: From Reedsport and U.S. 101, drive south on U.S. 101 for 11 miles to the Lakeside exit. Take that exit east into town for 0.75 mile (across the railroad tracks) to North Lake Road. Turn left (north) and drive 0.5 mile to the resort on the left.

OREGON

OREGON

Contact: North Lake Resort and Marina, 541/759-3515, fax 541/759-3326, www.north lakeresort.com.

7.1 OSPREY POINT RV RESORT

Scenic rating: 7

on Tenmile Lake

See map page 255

Tenmile is one of Oregon's premier bass-fishing lakes and yet is only three miles from the ocean. The resort is in a large, open area adjacent to Tenmile Lake and half a mile from North Lake. A navigable canal connects the lakes. The Oregon Dunes National Recreation Area provides nearby hiking trails, and Elliot State Forest offers wooded trails. With weekend barbecues and occasional live entertainment, Osprey Point is more a destination resort than an overnight stop.

RV sites, facilities: There are 132 sites for tents or RVs of any length with full hookups (30 and 50 amps) and a grassy area for tents. There are also five park-model cabins. Drinking water, picnic tables, and fire pits are provided. Cable TV, modem access, restrooms with flush toilets and showers, a dump station, a coin laundry, a restaurant, a cocktail lounge, a convenience store, a full-service marina with boat docks, a launch, a fishing pier, a fish-cleaning station, horseshoe pits, volleyball, tetherball, a recreation hall, a video arcade, and a pizza parlor are available. Some facilities are wheelchair accessible. Leashed pets are permitted.

Reservations, fees: Reservations are accepted. RV sites are $25–36 per night, tent sites are $20 per night, and it's $3.50 per person per night for more than two people. Monthly rates are available. Some credit cards are accepted. Open year-round.

Directions: From Coos Bay, drive north on U.S. 101 for 13 miles to the Lakeside exit. Take that exit east into town for 0.75 mile (across the railroad tracks) to North Lake Road. Turn left (north) on North Lake Road and drive 0.5 mile to the resort on the right.

Contact: Osprey Point RV Resort, 541/759-2801, fax 541/759-3198, www.ospreypoint.net.

7.2 EEL CREEK

Scenic rating: 8

near Eel Lake in Oregon Dunes National Recreation Area

See map page 255

This campground along Eel Creek is near both Eel and Tenmile Lakes. Although Tenmile Lake allows waterskiing, Eel Lake does not. Nearby trails offer access to the Umpqua Dunes Scenic Area, where you'll find spectacular scenery in an area closed to off-road vehicles. Off-road access is available at Spinreel.

RV sites, facilities: There are 52 sites for tents or RVs up to 35 feet (no hookups). Picnic tables, garbage service, and fire grills are provided. Drinking water and flush toilets are available. Boat docks, launching facilities, and rentals are nearby. Leashed pets are permitted.

Reservations, fees: Reservations are accepted at 877/444-6777 or www.ReserveUSA.com ($9 reservation fee). Sites are $17 per night and $7 per night for an additional vehicle. Open mid-May–September, with a 14-day stay limit.

Directions: From Reedsport and U.S. 101, drive south for 10.5 miles to the park entrance.

Contact: Oregon Dunes National Recreation Area, Visitors Center, 541/271-3611, fax 541/750-7244, www.fs.fed.us/r6/siuslaw /recreation.

7.3 SPINREEL

Scenic rating: 6

on Tenmile Creek in Oregon Dunes National Recreation Area

See map page 255

This campground, primarily for off-road-vehicle enthusiasts, is several miles inland at the outlet of Tenmile Lake in the Oregon Dunes National Recreation Area. A boat launch (for drift boats and canoes) is near the camp. Other recreational opportunities include hiking trails and off-road-vehicle access to the dunes. Off-road-vehicle rentals are available adjacent to the camp.

RV sites, facilities: There are 36 sites for tents or RVs up to 40 feet (no hookups). Drinking water, garbage service, and flush toilets are available. Picnic tables and fire grills are provided. Firewood, a store, and a coin laundry are nearby. Boat docks, launching facilities, and rentals are on Tenmile Lake. Some facilities are wheelchair accessible. Leashed pets are permitted.

Reservations, fees: Reservations are accepted at 877/444-6777 or www.ReserveUSA.com ($9 reservation fee). Sites are $20 per night. Open year-round.

Directions: From Coos Bay, drive north on U.S. 101 for 10 miles to the campground entrance road (well signed). Turn northwest and drive one mile to the campground.

Contact: Oregon Dunes National Recreation Area, Visitors Center, 541/271-3611, fax 541/750-7244, www.fs.fed.us/r6/siuslaw/recreation.

74 LOON LAKE RECREATION AREA

Scenic rating: 8

on Loon Lake

See map page 255

Loon Lake was created 1,400 years ago when a nearby mountain crumbled and slid downhill, damming a creek with house-sized boulders. Today, the lake is half a mile wide and nearly two miles long, covers 260 acres, and is more than 100 feet deep in places. Its ideal location provides a warm, wind-sheltered summer climate for various water activities. A nature trail leads to a waterfall about half a mile away. Evening interpretive programs are held during summer weekends.

RV sites, facilities: There are 61 sites for tents or RVs of any length (no hookups). There are also five group sites for up to 15 people per site. Picnic tables and fire pits are provided.

Drinking water, restrooms with flush toilets and showers, garbage bins, a dump station, a sand beach, and a boat ramp and moorings are available. Some facilities are wheelchair accessible, including the fishing pier. Leashed pets are permitted in the campground but not on the beach or in the day-use area.

Reservations, fees: Reservations are required for most sites at 877/444-6777 or www.ReserveUSA.com ($9 reservation fee). Sites are $18 per night, $7 per night per additional vehicle, and $45 per night for group sites. Open late May–October, weather permitting.

Directions: From Eugene, drive south on I-5 to Exit 162 and Highway 38. Turn west on Highway 38 and drive 43 miles to Milepost 13.5 and the County Road 3 exit. Turn left (south) and drive 7.5 miles to the campground on the right.

Contact: Bureau of Land Management, Coos Bay District Office, 541/756-0100, fax 541/751-4303.

75 LOON LAKE LODGE AND RV RESORT

Scenic rating: 8

on Loon Lake

See map page 255

This resort boasts one mile of lake frontage and nestles among the tall trees on pretty Loon Lake. It's not a long drive from either U.S. 101 or I-5, making it an ideal layover spot for travelers eager to get off the highway. The lake offers good bass fishing, boating, swimming, and waterskiing.

RV sites, facilities: There are 70 sites for tents or RVs up to 40 feet with full or partial hookups (50 amps), 30 tent sites, four group sites for up to 20–30 people each, nine cabins, and a six-unit motel. Some RV sites are pull-through. Picnic tables and fire rings are provided. Pit toilets and drinking water are available. A restaurant, a general store, wireless Internet service, ice, gas, a beach, a boat ramp, a dock, a marina, and boat rentals are also available. Leashed pets are permitted, with certain restrictions.

OREGON

Reservations, fees: Reservations are accepted. Tent sites are $20 per night, RV sites are $27–33 per night, and it's $5 per night per additional vehicle. Some credit cards are accepted. Open year-round.

Directions: From Eugene, drive south on I-5 to Exit 162 and Highway 38. Turn west on Highway 38 and drive 43 miles to Milepost 13.5 and the County Road 3/Loon Lake Road exit. Turn left (south) and drive 8.2 miles to the resort on the left.

Contact: Loon Lake Lodge and RV Resort, 541/599-2244, fax 541/599-2274, www.loonlakerv.com.

76 TYEE

Scenic rating: 7

on the Umpqua River

See map page 255   BEST (

Here's a classic spot set along the Umpqua River, which has great salmon, smallmouth bass, and steelhead fishing in season. Boat launches are available a few miles upstream and downstream of the campground. Eagleview Group camp, a BLM campground, is one mile away.

RV sites, facilities: There are 15 sites for tents or RVs of any length (no hookups). Drinking water, garbage service, fire grills, and picnic tables are provided. Vault toilets, a day-use area with horseshoe pits, and a pavilion are available. A camp host is on-site. A store is within one mile. Some facilities are wheelchair accessible. Leashed pets are permitted.

Reservations, fees: Reservations are not accepted. Sites are $8 per night, $3 per night for each additional vehicle. Open year-round.

Directions: From Roseburg, drive north on I-5 to Exit 136 and Highway 138. Take that exit and drive west on Highway 138 for 12 miles. Cross Bullock Bridge and continue to County Road 57. Turn right and drive 0.5 mile to the campground entrance.

Contact: Bureau of Land Management, Roseburg District, 541/440-4930, fax 541/440-4948.

77 OREGON DUNES KOA

Scenic rating: 5

six miles north of North Bend, next to the Oregon Dunes National Recreation Area

See map page 255

This ATV-friendly park has direct access to Oregon Dunes National Recreation Area, which offers miles of ATV trails. The fairly open campground features a landscape of grass, young trees, and a small lake. The ocean is a 15-minute drive away. Mill Casino is about six miles south on U.S. 101. Freshwater and ocean fishing are nearby. A golf course is about five miles away.

RV sites, facilities: There are 63 sites for tents or RVs of any length with full hookups, seven tent sites, and six cabins. Most sites are pull-through, and 30- and 50-amp service is available. RV sites have drinking water, picnic tables, fire pits, and cable TV provided. Drinking water, restrooms with flush toilets and showers, wireless Internet service, modem access, a coin laundry, a convenience store, a game room, a playground, seasonal organized activities, a snack bar, firewood, propane gas, horseshoe pits, volleyball, and a picnic shelter are available. Some facilities are wheelchair accessible. ATV rentals are nearby. Leashed pets are permitted, except in cabins.

Reservations, fees: Reservations are accepted at 800/562-4236. Tent sites are $17–33 per night, RV sites are $24–51 per night, and it costs $4.25–5 per person per night for more than two people and $4.50–5 per night per additional vehicle. Some credit cards are accepted. Open year-round.

Directions: From Coos Bay, drive north on U.S. 101 past North Bend for nine miles to Milepost 229. The campground entrance road is on the left.

Contact: Oregon Dunes KOA, 541/756-4851, fax 541/756-8838, www.oregonduneskoa.com.

OREGON

78 WILD MARE HORSE CAMP

Scenic rating: 7

in Oregon Dunes National Recreation Area

See map page 255

This horse camp has paved parking, with single and double corrals. No off-road vehicles are allowed within the campground. Horses can be ridden straight out into the dunes and to the ocean—they cannot be ridden on developed trails, such as Bluebill Lake Trail. The heavily treed shoreline gives rise to treed sites with some bushes.

RV sites, facilities: There are 12 horse campsites for tents or RVs up to 35 feet (no hookups). There is a maximum of two vehicles per site. Picnic tables and fire pits are provided. Drinking water, vault toilets, and garbage bins are available. Leashed pets are permitted.

Reservations, fees: Reservations are accepted at 877/444-6777 or www.ReserveUSA.com ($9 reservation fee). Sites are $20 per night. Some credit cards are accepted. Open year-round, with a 14-day stay limit.

Directions: From Coos Bay, drive north on U.S. 101 for 1.5 miles to Horsfall Dunes and Beach Access Road. Turn left and drive west for one mile to the campground access road. Turn right and drive 0.75 mile to the campground on the left.

Contact: Oregon Dunes National Recreation Area, Visitors Center, 541/271-3611, fax 541/750-7244, www.fs.fed.us/r6/siuslaw/recreation.

79 BLUEBILL

Scenic rating: 6

on Bluebill Lake in Oregon Dunes National Recreation Area

See map page 255

This campground gets very little camping pressure although there are some good hiking trails available. It's next to little Bluebill Lake, which sometimes dries up during the summer. A one-mile trail goes around the lake bed. The camp is a short distance from Horsfall Lake, which is surrounded by private property. If you continue west on the forest road, you'll come to a picnicking and parking area near the beach. This spot provides off-road-vehicle access to the dunes at the Horsfall day-use area and Horsfall Beach.

RV sites, facilities: There are 18 sites for tents or RVs up to 30 feet (no hookups). Picnic tables, garbage service, and fire grills are provided. Flush toilets and drinking water are available. Leashed pets are permitted.

Reservations, fees: Reservations are not accepted. Sites are $20 per night. Open May–September.

Directions: From Coos Bay, drive north on U.S. 101 for 1.5 miles north to Horsfall Dunes and Beach Access Road. Turn west and drive one mile to Horsfall Road. Turn northwest and drive two miles to the campground entrance.

Contact: Oregon Dunes National Recreation Area, Visitors Center, 541/271-3611, fax 541/750-7244, www.fs.fed.us/r6/siuslaw/recreation.

80 HORSFALL

Scenic rating: 4

in Oregon Dunes National Recreation Area

See map page 255

This campground is a nice, large paved area for parking RVs. It's the staging area for off-road-vehicle access into the southern section of Oregon Dunes National Recreation Area. If Horsfall is full, try nearby Horsfall Beach, an overflow area with 34 tent and RV sites.

RV sites, facilities: There are 70 sites with no hookups for RVs up to 50 feet. No tents. Drinking water, garbage service, restrooms with flush toilets and coin showers, and a pay phone are available. Some facilities are wheelchair accessible. Leashed pets are permitted.

Reservations, fees: Reservations are accepted at 877/444-6777 or www.ReserveUSA.com ($9 reservation fee). Sites are $20 per night. Open year-round, with a 14-day stay limit.

Directions: From Coos Bay, drive north on

U.S. 101 for 1.5 miles to Horsfall Road. Turn west on Horsfall Road and drive about one mile to the campground access road. Turn on the campground access road (well signed) and drive 0.5 mile to the campground.

Contact: Oregon Dunes National Recreation Area, Visitors Center, 541/271-3611, fax 541/750-7244, www.fs.fed.us/r6/siuslaw/recreation.

81 SUNSET BAY STATE PARK

🥾 🚲 🏊 🎣 🐕 ♿ 🚐 ⛺

Scenic rating: 8

near Sunset Bay
See map page 255   BEST (

Situated in one of the most scenic areas on the Oregon Coast, this park features beautiful, sandy beaches protected by towering sea cliffs. A network of hiking trails connects Sunset Bay with nearby Shore Acres and Cape Arago Parks. Clamming, fishing, golfing, and swimming are some of the recreation options.

RV sites, facilities: There are 66 sites for tents or RVs (no hookups), 65 sites for tents or RVs up to 47 feet with full or partial hookups (20 and 30 amps), a separate area for hikers and bicyclists, eight yurts, and two group camps for up to 25 and 250 people, respectively. Drinking water, picnic tables, garbage bins, and fire grills are provided. Restrooms have flush toilets and showers. A reservable gazebo, a boat ramp, and firewood are available. A restaurant is within three miles. Some facilities are wheelchair accessible. Leashed pets are permitted, except in yurts.

Reservations, fees: Reservations are accepted at 800/452-5687 or www.oregonstateparks.org ($6 reservation fee). Sites are $12–20 per night plus $5 per night per additional vehicle, $4 per person per night for hikers/bicyclists, $27 per night for yurts, and $40–61 per night for group camps plus $2.40 per person per night for more than 25 people. Some credit cards are accepted. Open year-round.

Directions: In Coos Bay, take the Charleston/State Parks exit to Empire Coos Bay Highway. Drive west to Newmark Avenue. Bear left and

continue to Cape Arago Highway. Turn left and drive about five miles south to Charleston and cross the South Slough Bridge. Continue on Cape Arago Highway about three miles to the park entrance on the left.

Contact: Sunset Bay State Park, 541/888-4902; Oregon State Parks, 800/551-6949, www.oregonstateparks.org.

82 BASTENDORFF BEACH PARK

🥾 🚲 🏊 🎣 🚐 🐕 🏄 ♿ 🚐 ⛺

Scenic rating: 8

near Cape Arago State Park
See map page 255

This campground is surrounded by large trees and provides access to the ocean and a small lake. Nearby activities include boating, clamming, crabbing, dune buggy riding, fishing, golfing, swimming, and whale-watching. Swimmers should be aware of undertows and sneaker waves. Horses may be rented near Bandon. A nice side trip is to Shore Acres State Park and Botanical Gardens, about 2.5 miles away.

RV sites, facilities: There are 76 sites for tents or RVs of any length with partial hookups (30 and 50 amps), 25 tent sites, and two cabins. Group camping is available. Picnic tables and fire pits are provided. Drinking water, restrooms with flush toilets and coin showers, a dump station, and a public phone are provided. A fish-cleaning station, horseshoe pits, a playground, basketball courts, and a picnic area are also available. Some facilities are wheelchair accessible. Leashed pets are permitted.

Reservations, fees: Reservations are accepted for groups, cabins, and the picnic area only at 541/396-3121, ext. 354. Sites are $15–20 per night, $5 per night per additional vehicle. Group sites start at $160 per night, and cabins are $30 per night. Some credit cards are accepted. Open year-round.

Directions: In Coos Bay, take the Charleston/State Parks exit to Empire Coos Bay Highway. Drive west to Newmark Avenue. Bear left and continue to Cape Arago Highway. Turn left and drive about five miles south to Charleston and cross the South Slough Bridge. Continue on Cape Arago Highway about two miles to the park entrance.

Contact: Bastendorff Beach Park, 541/888-5353, www.co.coos.or.us/.

83 CHARLESTON MARINA RV PARK

Scenic rating: 7

on Coos Bay
See map page 255

This large, developed public park and marina is near Charleston on the Pacific Ocean. Recreational activities in and near the campground include boating, clamming, crabbing, fishing (halibut, salmon, and tuna), hiking, huckleberry and blackberry picking, and swimming.

RV sites, facilities: There are 108 sites for tents or RVs up to 50 feet with full hookups (20, 30, and 50 amps), four tent sites, and two yurts. Picnic tables are provided. No open fires are allowed. Drinking water, satellite TV, modem access, restrooms with showers, a dump station, a public phone, a coin laundry, a playground, a fish cleaning station, crab-cooking facilities, and propane gas are available. A marina with a boarding dock and launch ramp are on-site. Some facilities are wheelchair accessible. Leashed pets are permitted.

Reservations, fees: Reservations are accepted. RV sites are $21–23 per night, tent sites are $12 per night, and yurts are $32 per night. Weekly and monthly rates are available. Some credit cards are accepted. Open year-round.

Directions: In Coos Bay, take the Charleston/State Parks exit to Empire Coos Bay Highway. Drive west to Newmark Avenue. Bear left and continue to Cape Arago Highway. Turn left and drive about five miles south to Charleston and cross the South Slough Bridge. Continue to Boat Basin Drive. Turn right and drive 0.2 mile to Kingfisher Drive. Turn right and drive 200 feet to the campground on the left.

Contact: Charleston Marina RV Park, 541/888-9512, fax 541/888-6111, www.charlestonmarina.com.

84 OCEANSIDE RV PARK

Scenic rating: 7

near the Pacific Ocean
See map page 255

One of several private, developed parks in the Charleston area, this park is within walking distance of the Pacific Ocean, with opportunities for boating, clamming, crabbing, fishing, and swimming. A marina is 1.5 miles away.

RV sites, facilities: There are 71 sites with full hookups (30 or 50 amps) for RVs up to 45 feet and 10 tent sites. Picnic tables and fire rings are provided. Restrooms have coin showers. Limited groceries, a public phone, modem and wireless access, video and DVD rentals, a fish-cleaning station, and propane gas are available. Equipment for crabbing and clamming is also available. Some facilities are wheelchair accessible. Leashed pets are permitted.

Reservations, fees: Reservations are accepted at 800/570-2598. Tent sites are $16.16 per night, RV sites are $19.19–27.27 per night, and it costs $5 per night for an extra vehicle or tent. Some credit cards are accepted. Open year-round.

Directions: In Coos Bay, take the Charleston/State Parks exit to Empire Coos Bay Highway. Drive west to Newmark Avenue. Bear left and continue to Cape Arago Highway. Turn left and drive about five miles south to Charleston and cross the South Slough Bridge. Continue on Cape Arago Highway for 1.8 miles to the park entrance on the right.

Contact: Oceanside RV Park, 541/888-2598 or 800/570-2598, fax 541/888-8323.

85 BULLARDS BEACH STATE PARK

Scenic rating: 7

on the Coquille River
See map page 255

The Coquille River, which has good fishing in season for both boaters and crabbers, is the centerpiece of this park with four miles of shore access. If fishing is not your thing, the park

OREGON

also has several hiking trails. The Coquille River Lighthouse is at the end of the road that wanders through the park. During the summer, there are tours to the tower. Equestrians can explore the seven-mile horse trail.

RV sites, facilities: There are 185 sites for tents or RVs up to 64 feet with full or partial hookups (20 and 30 amps), a hiker/bicyclist camping area, a primitive horse camp with corrals, and 13 yurts. Drinking water, garbage bins, picnic tables, and fire grills are provided. Restrooms have flush toilets and showers. A dump station, a playground, firewood, a reservable yurt meeting hall, and picnic shelters are available. Some facilities are wheelchair accessible. Boat docks and launching facilities are in the park on the Coquille River. Leashed pets are permitted.

Reservations, fees: Reservations are accepted at 800/452-5687 or www.oregonstateparks.org ($6 reservation fee). Sites are $16–20 per night plus $5 per additional vehicle per night, it's $4 per person per night for hikers/bicyclists, and yurts are $27 per night. Horse camping is $12–16 per night. Some credit cards are accepted. Open year-round.

Directions: In Coos Bay, drive south on U.S. 101 for about 22 miles to the park on the right (west side of road), two miles north of Bandon.

Contact: Bullards Beach State Park, 541/347-2209; Oregon State Parks, 800/551-6949, www.oregonstateparks.org.

86 BANDON RV PARK

Scenic rating: 6

near Bullards Beach State Park
See map page 255

This in-town RV park is a good base for many adventures. Some sites are filled with renters, primarily anglers, for the summer season. Rock hounds will enjoy combing for agates and other semiprecious stones hidden along the beaches, while kids can explore the West Coast Game Park Walk-Through Safari petting zoo seven miles south of town. Bandon State Park, four

miles south of town, has a nice wading spot in the creek at the north end of the park. Nearby recreation opportunities include two 18-hole golf courses, a riding stable, and tennis courts. Bullards Beach is about 2.5 miles north. Nice folks run this place.

RV sites, facilities: There are 44 sites with full hookups (30 amps) for RVs of any length; some are pull-through sites. Picnic tables are provided at most sites. No tents or open fires are allowed. Restrooms have flush toilets and showers. A dump station, cable TV, modem access, and a coin laundry are available. Propane gas and a store are within two blocks. Boat docks and launching facilities are nearby. Leashed pets are permitted.

Reservations, fees: Reservations are accepted at 800/393-4122. Sites are $22–24 per night, $2 per person per night for more than two people. Some credit cards are accepted. Open year-round.

Directions: From Coos Bay, drive south on U.S. 101 for 26 miles to Bandon and the Highway 42S junction. Continue south on U.S. 101 for one block to the park (on the right at 935 2nd Street Southeast).

Contact: Bandon RV Park, 541/347-4122.

87 LAVERNE AND WEST LAVERNE GROUP CAMP

Scenic rating: 9

in Fairview on the North Fork of the Coquille River
See map page 255

This beautiful, 350-acre park sits on a river with a small waterfall and many trees, including a myrtle grove and old-growth Douglas fir. Mountain bikers can take an old wagon road, and golfers can enjoy any of several courses. There are a few hiking trails and a very popular swimming hole. Fishing includes salmon, steelhead, and trout, and the wildlife includes bear, cougar, deer, elk, and raccoon. You can take a side trip to the museums at Myrtle Point and Coos Bay, which display local indigenous items, or an old stagecoach house in Dora.

RV sites, facilities: There are 46 sites for RVs of any length with partial hookups (20 and 30 amps) and 30 sites for tents or RVs (no hookups). There is also a large group site at West Laverne B with 22 RV hookups (20 and 30 amps). One cabin is also available. Drinking water, picnic tables, and fire pits are provided. Restrooms have flush toilets and coin showers. Garbage bins, a dump station, a playground, a reservable picnic area, a swimming hole (unsupervised), horseshoe pits, and volleyball and softball areas are available. Some facilities are wheelchair accessible. Ice and a restaurant are within 1.5 miles. Propane gas, a store, and gasoline are within five miles. Leashed pets are permitted.

Reservations, fees: Reservations are not accepted for family sites but are accepted for the group site and cabin ($10 reservation fee) at 541/396-3121, ext. 354. Sites are $10–16 per night, $5 per night per additional vehicle. The group site is $140 per night for the first six camping units, then $16 per unit per night. The cabin is $30 per night. Some credit cards are accepted. Open year-round.

Directions: From Coos Bay, drive south on U.S. 101 for six miles to the junction with Highway 42. Turn east and drive 11 miles to Coquille and West Central. Turn left and drive 0.5 mile to Fairview McKinley Road. Turn right and drive eight miles to the Fairview Store. Continue east another five miles (past the store) to the park on the right.

Contact: Laverne County Park, Coos County, 541/396-2344, www.co.coos.or.us/.

88 BANDON/PORT ORFORD KOA

🚶 🚵 🐕 🎣 🚐 ⛺

Scenic rating: 7

near the Elk River
See map page 255

This spot is considered to be just a layover camp, but it offers large, secluded sites nestled among big trees and coastal ferns. A pool and spa are available. During the summer season, a daily pancake breakfast and ice cream social are held. The Elk and Sixes Rivers, where the fishing can be good, are minutes away, and Cape Blanco State Park is just a few miles down the road.

RV sites, facilities: There are 26 pull-through sites with full hookups (20, 30, and 50 amps) for RVs of any length and 46 tent sites. Six cabins are also available. Picnic tables and fire rings are provided. Restrooms have flush toilets and showers. Cable TV, modem access, a snack bar, propane gas, a dump station, firewood, a recreation hall, a convenience store, a coin laundry, a seasonal heated swimming pool, a hot tub, horseshoe pits, a basketball court, ice, and a playground are available. Leashed pets are permitted.

Reservations, fees: Reservations are accepted at 800/562-3298. Sites are $26–32 per night, $3–5 per person per night for more than two people, and $5 per night per additional vehicle. Some credit cards are accepted. Open March–November.

Directions: From Bandon, drive south on U.S. 101 for 16 miles to the campground at Milepost 286 near Langlois, on the west side of the highway.

Contact: Bandon/Port Orford KOA, 541/348-2358, www.bandonkoa.com.

89 CAPE BLANCO STATE PARK

🚶 🚵 🎣 🛶 🐕 ♿ 🚐 ⛺

Scenic rating: 8

between the Sixes and Elk Rivers
See map page 255

This large park is named for the white *(blanco)* chalk appearance of the sea cliffs here, which rise 200 feet above the ocean. Sea lions inhabit the offshore rocks, and trails and a road lead to the black-sand beach below the cliffs. Another highlight is the good access to the Sixes River, which runs for more than two miles through the meadows and forests of the park. There are also seven miles of trails for horseback riding; more than eight miles of hiking trails lead through woodland and wetland settings and feature spectacular ocean vistas. Lighthouse and historic Hughes House tours are nearby.

OREGON

RV sites, facilities: There are 54 sites for tents or RVs up to 65 feet (partial hookups). Other options include an equestrian camp, a hiker/bicyclist camping area, four cabins, and one primitive group site for tents or RVs that can accommodate up to 50 people. Garbage bins, picnic tables, drinking water, and fire grills are provided. Firewood and restrooms with flush toilets and showers are available. Some facilities are wheelchair accessible. Leashed pets are permitted.

Reservations, fees: No reservations are taken for single sites. Reservations are accepted for cabins, the group site, and the horse camp at 800/452-5687 or www.oregonstateparks.org ($6 reservation fee). Sites are $12–16 per night, $5 per night per additional vehicle; the horse camp is $10–14 per night, and it's $4 per person per night for hikers/bikers. The group site is $40–61 per night for the first 25 people, then $2.40 per person per night. Cabins are $35 per night. Some credit cards are accepted. Open year-round.

Directions: From Coos Bay, turn south on U.S. 101 and drive approximately 46 miles (south of Sixes, five miles north of Port Orford) to Cape Blanco Road. Turn right (northwest) and drive five miles to the campground on the left.

Contact: Humbug Mountain State Park, 541/332-6774, www.oregonstateparks.org. (This park is under the same management as Humbug Mountain State Park.)

90 EDSON

Scenic rating: 6

on the Sixes River

See map page 255

This is a popular campground along the banks of the Sixes River. Edson is similar to Sixes River Campground, except it has less tree cover and Sixes River has the benefit of a boat ramp.

RV sites, facilities: There are 25 sites for tents or RVs up to 30 feet (no hookups) and three group sites for up to 100 people. Picnic tables and fire grills are provided. Drinking water, vault toilets, garbage service, a boat launch, and a camp host

are available. Some facilities are wheelchair accessible. Leashed pets are permitted.

Reservations, fees: Reservations are not accepted for single sites but are required for group sites at 541/332-8027. Sites are $8 per night and $4 per night for each additional vehicle. Group sites are $15–30 per night. Open year-round, weather permitting, with a 14-day stay limit.

Directions: From Coos Bay, drive south on U.S. 101 for 40 miles to Sixes and Sixes River Road/County Road 184. Turn left (east) on Sixes River Road and drive four miles to the campground entrance on the left. It's before the Edson Creek bridge.

Contact: Bureau of Land Management, Coos Bay District, 541/756-0100, fax 541/751-4303.

91 SIXES RIVER

Scenic rating: 6

on the Sixes River

See map page 255

Set along the banks of the Sixes River at an elevation of 4,303 feet, this camp is a favorite of anglers, miners, and nature lovers. There are opportunities to pan or sluice for gold year-round or through a special limited permit. Dredging is permitted July 15–September. The camp roads are paved.

RV sites, facilities: There are 19 sites for tents or RVs up to 30 feet (no hookups). Picnic tables, garbage service, and fire grills are provided. Drinking water and vault toilets are available. A camp host is on-site. Some facilities are wheelchair accessible. Leashed pets are permitted.

Reservations, fees: Reservations are not accepted. Sites are $8 per night, $4 per night for an additional vehicle, with a 14-day stay limit. Open year-round, weather permitting.

Directions: From Coos Bay, drive south on U.S. 101 for 40 miles to Sixes and Sixes River Road/County Road 184. Turn left (east) on Sixes River Road and drive 11 miles to the campground on the right. The last 0.5 mile is an unpaved road.

Contact: Bureau of Land Management, Coos Bay District, 541/756-0100, fax 541/751-4303.

92 ELK RIVER CAMPGROUND

Scenic rating: 7

near the Elk River

See map page 255

This quiet and restful camp makes an excellent base for fall and winter fishing on the Elk River, which is known for its premier salmon fishing. A one-mile private access road goes to the river, so guests get their personal fishing holes. About half of the sites are taken by monthly rentals.

RV sites, facilities: There are 50 sites with full hookups (30 amps) for RVs up to 55 feet; some sites are pull-through. No tents. Picnic tables are provided. No open fires are allowed. Drinking water, restrooms with showers, a dump station, a public phone, modem hookups, cable TV, and a coin laundry are available. Recreational facilities include a sports field, horseshoe pits, a recreation hall, and a boat ramp. Some facilities are wheelchair accessible. Leashed pets are permitted.

Reservations, fees: Reservations are recommended. Sites are $18.18–20.20 per night. Weekly and monthly rates are available. Open year-round.

Directions: From Port Orford, drive north on U.S. 101 for 1.5 miles to Elk River Road (Milepost 297). Turn right (east) on Elk River Road and drive 1.8 miles to the campground on the left.

Contact: Elk River Campground, 541/332-2255.

93 POWERS COUNTY PARK

Scenic rating: 9

near the South Fork of the Coquille River

See map page 255

This private and secluded public park in a wooded, mountainous area is a great stop for travelers going between I-5 and the coast. A 30-acre lake at the park provides a spot for visitors to boat and fish for trout. The lake is stocked with bass, catfish, crappie, and trout. Only electric boat motors are allowed. Swimming is not recommended because of the algae in the lake. A bike trail is available. On display at the park are an old steam donkey and a hand-carved totem pole. The biggest cedar tree in Oregon is reputed to be about 12 miles away.

RV sites, facilities: There are 30 sites for tents or RVs up to 54 feet and 40 sites with partial hookups (20 and 30 amps). A cabin is also available. Picnic tables, fire pits, drinking water, restrooms with showers, a dump station, a fish-cleaning station, picnic shelters, and a public phone are provided. Recreational facilities include a boat ramp, horseshoe pits, a playground, basketball and volleyball courts, tennis courts, and a softball field. Supplies are available within one mile. Some facilities are wheelchair accessible. Leashed pets are permitted.

Reservations, fees: Reservations are accepted for the cabin only at 541/396-3121, ext. 354 ($10 reservation fee). Sites are $10–16 per night, and cabins are $30 per night. Some credit cards are accepted. Open year-round.

Directions: From Coos Bay, drive south on U.S. 101 for six miles to the junction with Highway 42. Turn east and drive 20 miles to Myrtle Point. Continue on Highway 42 to the Powers Highway (Highway 242) exit. Turn right (southwest) and drive 19 miles to the park on the right.

Contact: Powers County Park, Coos County, 541/439-2791, www.co.coos.or.us/.

94 PORT ORFORD RV VILLAGE

Scenic rating: 5

near the Elk and Sixes Rivers

See map page 255

Each evening, an informal group campfire and happy hour enliven this campground. Other nice touches include a small gazebo where you can get free coffee each morning and a patio where you can sit. Fishing is good during the

OREGON

fall and winter on the nearby Elk and Sixes Rivers, and the campground has a smokehouse, a freezer, and a fish-cleaning station. Some sites are taken by summer season rentals, and some are taken by permanent residents.

RV sites, facilities: There are 49 sites with full or partial hookups (30 amps) for RVs of any length and seven tent sites. Some sites are pull-through. Picnic tables are provided, and fire pits are available on request. Restrooms have flush toilets and showers. Propane gas, a dump station, horseshoe pits, a recreation hall, and a coin laundry are available. Boat docks and launching facilities are nearby. Lake, river, and ocean are all within 1.5 miles. Leashed pets are permitted.

Reservations, fees: Reservations are accepted. Sites are $18–26 per night, $3 per person per night for more than two people. Open year-round.

Directions: In Port Orford on U.S. 101, drive to Madrona Avenue. Turn east and drive one block to Port Orford Loop. Turn left (north) and drive 0.5 mile to the camp on the left side.

Contact: Port Orford RV Village, 541/332-1041, www.portorfordrv.com.

95 HUMBUG MOUNTAIN STATE PARK

Scenic rating: 7

near the Pacific Ocean

See map page 255

This park and its campground are dominated by Humbug Mountain (1,756 feet elevation) and surrounded by forested hills. The campground enjoys some of the warmest weather on the Oregon coast. Windsurfing and scuba diving are popular, as is hiking the three-mile trail to Humbug Peak. Both ocean and freshwater fishing are accessible nearby.

RV sites, facilities: There are 62 sites for tents or RVs (no hookups), 32 sites with partial hookups for RVs up to 55 feet, and a hiker/bicyclist camp. Some sites are pull-through. Fire grills, picnic tables, garbage bins, and drinking water are provided. Restrooms have flush toilets and

showers, and firewood is available. Some facilities are wheelchair accessible. Leashed pets are permitted.

Reservations, fees: Reservations are accepted at 800/452-5687 or www.oregonstateparks.org ($6 reservation fee). Sites are $10–16 per night, $5 per night per additional vehicle, and $4 per person per night for hikers/bicyclists. The group camp is $60 per night for up to 25 people, plus $2.40 per person per night for additional persons. Some credit cards are accepted. Open year-round.

Directions: From Port Orford, drive south on U.S. 101 for six miles to the park entrance on the left.

Contact: Humbug Mountain State Park, 541/332-6774 or 800/551-6949, www.oregonstate parks.org.

96 DAPHNE GROVE

Scenic rating: 7

on the South Fork of the Coquille River in Siskiyou National Forest

See map page 255

This prime spot is far enough out of the way to attract little attention. At 1,000 feet elevation, it sits along the South Fork of the Coquille River and is surrounded by old-growth cedar, Douglas fir, and maple. No fishing is allowed. The road is paved all the way to, and in, the campground, a plus for RVs and "city cars."

RV sites, facilities: There are 14 sites for tents or RVs up to 30 feet (no hookups). Picnic tables, garbage bins, and fire grills are provided. Vault toilets and drinking water are available. Some facilities are wheelchair accessible. Leashed pets are permitted.

Reservations, fees: Reservations are not accepted. Sites are $8 per night from late May to late September, $6 per night if drinking water is not available, and it costs $3 per night per additional vehicle. Sites are free October–April. Open year-round.

Directions: From Coos Bay, drive south on U.S. 101 for six miles to the junction with Highway 42. Turn east and drive 20 miles to Myrtle Point. Continue on Highway 42 to Powers Highway (Highway 242). Turn right (southwest) and drive 18 miles (the highway becomes County Road 90) to Powers. Continue for 4.3 miles (the road becomes Forest Road 33). Continue for 10.5 miles to the campground entrance.

Contact: Siskiyou National Forest, Powers Ranger District, 541/439-6200, fax 541/439-6217.

97 SQUAW LAKE

Scenic rating: 8

on Squaw Lake in Siskiyou National Forest

See map page 255

This campground (at 2,200 feet elevation) along the shore of one-acre Squaw Lake sits in rich, old-growth forest. Squaw is more of a pond than a lake, but it is stocked with trout in the spring. Get there early; the fish are generally gone by midsummer. The trailheads for the Panther Ridge Trail and Coquille River Falls Trail are a 10-minute drive from the campground. It's strongly advised that you obtain a U.S. Forest Service map detailing the backcountry roads and trails.

RV sites, facilities: There are seven sites for tents or RVs up to 21 feet (no hookups). Picnic tables and fire rings are provided. Pit toilets are available. There is no drinking water, and all garbage must be packed out. Leashed pets are permitted.

Reservations, fees: Reservations are not accepted. There is no fee for camping. Open year-round.

Directions: From Coos Bay, drive south on U.S. 101 for six miles to the junction with Highway 42. Turn east and drive 20 miles to Myrtle Point. Continue on Highway 42 to Powers Highway (Highway 242). Turn right (southwest) and drive 18 miles to Powers and County Road 90. Turn south and drive 4.3 miles to Forest Road 33. Turn south and drive 12.5 miles to Forest Road 3348. Turn southeast and drive 4.5 miles to the campground entrance road. Turn east and

drive one mile to the campground. The road is paved for all but the last 0.5 mile.

Contact: Siskiyou National Forest, Powers Ranger District, 541/439-6200, fax 541/439-6217.

98 ILLAHE

Scenic rating: 7

on the Rogue River in Siskiyou National Forest

See map page 255

This quiet and isolated camping area has great hiking opportunities, beginning at the nearby Upper Rogue River Trail. Boating and fishing are just a mile away at Foster Bar Campground. This pretty spot offers privacy between sites and is hidden from the majority of tourists. Deer are in abundance here.

RV sites, facilities: There are 14 sites for tents or RVs up to 21 feet (no hookups). Drinking water, fire rings, garbage bins, and picnic tables are provided. Flush toilets are available. A camp host is on-site. A store is within five miles. Boat docks are nearby. Leashed pets are permitted.

Reservations, fees: Reservations are not accepted. Sites are $10 per night, plus $3 per night for each additional vehicle. Open year-round, weather permitting.

Directions: From Gold Beach on U.S. 101, turn east on County Road 595. Drive east for 35 miles (the county road becomes Forest Road 33) to a junction for Illahe, Illahe Campground, and Foster Bar. Turn right on County Road 375 and drive five miles to the campground.

Contact: Siskiyou National Forest, Gold Beach Ranger District, 541/247-3600, fax 541/247-3617.

99 ALMEDA PARK

Scenic rating: 6

on the Rogue River

See map page 255

This rustic park, along the Rogue River and featuring a grassy area, is popular for rafting

OREGON

and swimming. One of the main put-in points for floating the lower section of the river can be found right here. Fishing is also available. The Rogue River Trail is four miles west.

RV sites, facilities: There are 34 sites for tents or RVs of any length (no hookups), two group sites for tents or RVs that can accommodate up to 12 people, and one yurt. Some sites are pull-through. Picnic tables and fire pits are provided. Drinking water, vault toilets, garbage bins, horseshoe pits, and a boat ramp are available. A seasonal camp host is on-site. Leashed pets are permitted.

Reservations, fees: Reservations are accepted at 800/452-5687 or www.reserveamerica.com ($6 reservation fee). Sites are $15 per night, and the yurt is $28 per night. The group site is $30 per night for up to 12 people, plus $3 per person per night for each additional person. Open year-round.

Directions: From Grants Pass, drive north on I-5 for 3.5 miles to Exit 61 (Merlin-Galice Road). Take that exit and drive on Merlin-Galice Road for 19 miles to the park on the right. The park is approximately 16 miles west of Merlin.

Contact: Josephine County Parks, 541/474-5285, fax 541/474-5288, www.co.josephine .or.us/.

100 SAM BROWN AND SAM BROWN HORSE CAMP

Scenic rating: 4

near Grants Pass in Siskiyou National Forest

See map page 255

This campground is in an isolated area near Grants Pass along Briggs Creek in a valley of pine and Douglas fir. It is at an elevation of 2,500 feet. Many sites lie in the shade of trees, and a creek runs along one side of the campground. Briggs Creek Trail, Dutchy Creek Trail, and Taylor Creek Trail are nearby and are popular for hiking and horseback riding. An amphitheater is available for small group presentations. Although the campground was spared, the Biscuit Fire of 2002 did burn nearby areas.

RV sites, facilities: There are 29 sites for tents or

RVs of any length (no hookups) at Sam Brown and seven equestrian tent sites with small corrals across the road at Sam Brown Horse Camp. Picnic tables and fire rings or grills are provided. Drinking water and vault toilets are available. A picnic shelter, solar shower, and an amphitheater are available. Leashed pets are permitted.

Reservations, fees: Reservations are not accepted. Sites are $5 per night, $2 per night per additional vehicle. Open late May–mid-October, weather permitting.

Directions: From Grants Pass, drive north on I-5 for 3.5 miles to Exit 61 (Merlin-Galice Road). Take that exit and drive northwest for 12.5 miles to Forest Road 25. Turn left on Forest Road 25 and head southwest for 14 miles to the campground.

Contact: Siskiyou National Forest, Galice Ranger District, 541/471-6500, fax 541/471-6514.

101 ARIZONA BEACH CAMPGROUND

Scenic rating: 7

near Gold Beach

See map page 255

This campground offers grassy, tree-lined sites along half a mile of ocean beach frontage. Many of the RV sites are along the beach frontage. A creek runs through the campground, and you can swim at the mouth of it in the summer. Elk and deer roam nearby. A small lake is available for fishing. That is the good part; now for the bad. This camp does not take reservations. I also found that the staff don't answer the phone or return phone messages. I hope that the customer service improves once you reach the campground.

RV sites, facilities: There are 130 sites (30 and 50 amps) for RVs of any length, 35 tent sites, and furnished trailer rentals. Drinking water and picnic tables are provided, and RV sites have fire rings. Restrooms have flush toilets and showers. Propane gas, a dump station, a clubhouse, firewood, a store, a coin laundry, a recreation room, and a playground are available. Leashed pets are permitted.

Reservations, fees: Reservations are not accepted. Tent sites are $16–20 per night, and RV sites are $25–30 per night; it costs $3 per person per night for more than two people, $5 per night for an additional vehicle, and $4 per night for an additional tent. Some credit cards are accepted. Monthly rates are available. Open year-round.

Directions: From Gold Beach, drive north on U.S. 101 for 14 miles to the campground on the right (west side of road).

Contact: Arizona Beach Campground, 541/332-6491, www.arizonabeachrv.com.

102 HONEY BEAR CAMPGROUND & RV RESORT

Scenic rating: 10

near Gold Beach

See map page 255

This campground offers wooded sites with ocean views. The owners have built a huge, authentic chalet, which contains a German deli, a recreation area, and a big dance floor. On summer nights, they hold dances with live music. A restaurant is on-site serves German food. A fishing pond is stocked with trout.

RV sites, facilities: There are 20 sites for tents or RVs (no hookups) and 65 sites with full hookups for RVs of any length. Thirty are pull-through sites with full hookups, and 15 have patios. Picnic tables and fire rings are provided. Restrooms have flush toilets and showers. Drinking water, cable TV, modem access, a dump station, firewood, a recreation hall, a restaurant, a convenience store, a coin laundry, ice, and a playground are available. Leashed pets are permitted.

Reservations, fees: Reservations are accepted at 800/822-4444. RV sites are $18–27 per night, tent sites are $13–16 per night, plus $3 per person per night for more than two people and $1 per night per additional vehicle. Open year-round, weather permitting.

Directions: From Gold Beach, drive north on U.S. 101 for eight miles to Ophir Road near

Milepost 321. Turn right and drive two miles to the campground on the right side of the road.
Contact: Honey Bear Campground & RV Resort, 541/247-2765, www.honeybearrv.com.

103 NESIKA BEACH RV PARK

Scenic rating: 7

near Gold Beach

See map page 255

This campground next to Nesika Beach is a good layover spot for U.S. 101 cruisers. An 18-hole golf course is close by. There are many long-term rentals here.

RV sites, facilities: There are six tent sites and 32 sites with full or partial hookups (30 amps) for RVs up to 40 feet; some sites are pull-through. Drinking water, cable TV, and picnic tables are provided; some tent sites have fire rings. Restrooms have flush toilets and showers. A dump station, a convenience store, a coin laundry, and ice are available. Leashed pets are permitted.

Reservations, fees: Reservations are accepted. Tent sites are $15 per night, RV sites are $21–23 per night, and it's $1 per person per night for more than two people. Monthly rates are available. Open year-round.

Directions: From Gold Beach, drive north on U.S. 101 for six miles to Nesika Road. Turn left and drive 0.75 mile west to the park on the right.

Contact: Nesika Beach RV Park, 541/247-6077.

104 QUOSATANA

Scenic rating: 6

on the Rogue River in Siskiyou National Forest

See map page 255

This campground is along the banks of the Rogue River, upstream from the much smaller Lobster Creek Campground. The campground features a large, grassy area and a barrier-free trail with interpretive signs. Ocean access is just

OREGON

a short drive away, and the quaint town of Gold Beach offers a decent side trip. Nearby Otter Point State Park (day use only) has further recreation options. The Shrader Old-Growth Trail and Myrtle Tree Trail provide nearby hiking opportunities. Quosatana makes a good base camp for a hiking or fishing trip.

RV sites, facilities: There are 43 sites for tents or RVs up to 34 feet (no hookups). Drinking water, fire grills, garbage bins, and picnic tables are provided. Flush toilets, a dump station, a fish-cleaning station, and a boat ramp are available. A camp host is on-site. Some facilities are wheelchair accessible. Leashed pets are permitted.

Reservations, fees: Reservations are not accepted. Sites are $10 per night, plus $3 per night per additional vehicle. Open year-round.

Directions: From Gold Beach on U.S. 101, turn east on County Road 595 and drive 13 miles (it becomes Forest Road 33) to the campground on the left.

Contact: Siskiyou National Forest, Gold Beach Ranger District, 541/247-3600, fax 541/247-3617.

105 LOBSTER CREEK

Scenic rating: 6

on the Rogue River in Siskiyou National Forest
See map page 255

This small campground on a river bar along the Rogue River is about a 15-minute drive from Gold Beach, and it makes a good base for a fishing trip. The area is heavily forested with myrtle and Douglas fir, and the Shrader Old-Growth Trail and Myrtle Tree Trail are nearby.

RV sites, facilities: There are six sites for tents or RVs up to 21 feet (no hookups). Fire rings and picnic tables are provided. Flush toilets are available. There is no drinking water. A boat launch is available. A camp host is on-site. Leashed pets are permitted.

Reservations, fees: Reservations are not accepted. Sites are $6 per night, $3 per night per additional vehicle. Camping is also permitted

on a gravel bar area for $5 per night. Open year-round, weather permitting.

Directions: From Gold Beach on U.S. 101, turn east on County Road 595 and drive 10 miles (the road becomes Forest Road 33) to the campground on the left.

Contact: Siskiyou National Forest, Gold Beach Ranger District, 541/247-3600, fax 541/247-3617.

106 KIMBALL CREEK BEND RV RESORT

Scenic rating: 6

on the Rogue River
See map page 255

This campground on the scenic Rogue River is just far enough from the coast to provide quiet and its own distinct character. The resort offers guided fishing trips and sells tickets for jet-boat tours. Nearby recreation options include an 18-hole golf course, hiking trails, and boating facilities. Note that about one-third of the sites are monthly rentals.

RV sites, facilities: There are 56 sites with full hookups (30 amps) for RVs of any length, 13 tent sites, and three motel rooms. Drinking water and picnic tables are provided, and fire rings are at some sites. Restrooms have flush toilets and showers. Modem access, propane gas, a dump station, a recreation hall, a store, a coin laundry, ice, and a playground are available. Boat docks are on-site and launching facilities are nearby. Leashed pets are permitted.

Reservations, fees: Reservations are accepted at 888/814-0633. RV sites are $24.50–36.50 per night, tent sites are $20 per night, and it's $1–3 per person per night for more than two people. Some credit cards are accepted. Open year-round.

Directions: From Gold Beach, drive north on U.S. 101 for one mile (on the north side of the Rogue River) to Rogue River Road. Turn right (east) and drive about eight miles to the resort on the right.

Contact: Kimball Creek Bend RV Resort, 541/247-7580, www.kimballcreek.com.

107 LUCKY LODGE RV PARK

Scenic rating: 6

on the Rogue River
See map page 255

Lucky Lodge is a good layover spot for U.S. 101 travelers who want to get off the highway circuit. Set on the shore of the Rogue River, it offers opportunities for boating, fishing, and swimming. Most sites have a view of the river. Nearby recreation options include hiking trails. About one-third of the sites are occupied by monthly renters.

RV sites, facilities: There are 32 sites with full hookups (30 and 50 amps) for RVs of any length, four tent sites, and two cabins. Most sites are pull-through. Drinking water and picnic tables are provided. Restrooms have flush toilets and showers. Propane gas, a recreation hall, and a coin laundry are available. Boat docks and rentals are within eight miles. Leashed pets are permitted.

Reservations, fees: Reservations are accepted. Sites are $24–27 per night for RVs, $17 per night for tents, and $4 per person per night for more than two people. Open year-round.

Directions: From Gold Beach, drive north on U.S. 101 for four miles (on the north side of the Rogue River) to Rogue River Road. Turn right (east) and drive 3.5 miles to North Bank River Road. Turn right and drive 4.5 miles to the park on the right.

Contact: Lucky Lodge RV Park, 541/247-7618.

108 INDIAN CREEK RESORT

Scenic rating: 7

on the Rogue River
See map page 255

This campground is along the Rogue River on the outskirts of the town of Gold Beach. A few sites have river views. Nearby recreation options include boat trips on the Rogue.

RV sites, facilities: There are 100 sites with full hookups (30 amps) for RVs up to 40 feet; some sites are pull-through. There are also 25 tent sites. Drinking water, cable TV hookups, and picnic tables are provided. Fire pits are provided at some sites. Restrooms have flush toilets and showers. Modem access, firewood, a recreation hall, a convenience store, a sauna, a café, a coin laundry, ice, and a playground are available. Propane gas is within two miles. Boat docks, launching facilities, and rentals are nearby. Leashed pets are permitted.

Reservations, fees: Reservations are accepted at 877/537-7704. Tent sites are $17 per night, RV sites are $24–27 per night, and it's $2 per person per night for more than two people. Some credit cards are accepted. Open year-round, with limited winter facilities.

Directions: On U.S. 101, drive to the northern end of Gold Beach to Jerry's Flat Road (just south of the Patterson Bridge). Turn left (east) on Jerry's Flat Road and drive 0.5 mile to the resort.

Contact: Indian Creek Resort, 541/247-7704, www.indiancreekrv.com.

109 IRELAND'S OCEAN VIEW RV PARK

Scenic rating: 8

in Gold Beach
See map page 255

This spot is on the beach in the quaint little town of Gold Beach, only one mile from the famous Rogue River. The park is very clean and features blacktop roads and grass beside each site. Recreation options include beachcombing, boating, and fishing. Great ocean views are possible from the observatory/lighthouse.

RV sites, facilities: There are 33 sites with full hookups (20, 30, and 50 amps) for RVs up to 40 feet; some sites are pull-through. Picnic tables are provided. No open fires are allowed. Cable TV, restrooms with showers, a coin laundry, a

OREGON

OREGON

recreation room, horseshoe pits, and modem access are available. Leashed pets are permitted.

Reservations, fees: Reservations are recommended. Sites are $17–30 per night. Monthly and weekly rates are available. Open year-round.

Directions: On U.S. 101, drive to the southern end of Gold Beach (U.S. 101 becomes Ellensburg Avenue). The park is at 20272 Ellensburg Avenue, across from the U.S. Forest Service office.

Contact: Ireland's Ocean View RV Park, 541/247-0148, www.irelandsrvpark.com.

110 OCEANSIDE RV PARK

Scenic rating: 5

in Gold Beach

See map page 255

Set 100 yards from the ocean, this park is close to beachcombing terrain, marked bike trails, and boating facilities. The park is also adjacent to the mouth of the Rogue River, in the Port of Gold Beach. No tent camping is permitted.

RV sites, facilities: There are 80 sites with full or partial hookups (30 amps) for RVs up to 40 feet and two yurts; some sites are pull-through. There are no tent sites. Drinking water and picnic tables are provided. Restrooms have flush toilets and showers. A coin laundry, cable TV, a convenience store, a picnic area, and ice are available. Propane gas, a store, and a café are within two miles. Boat docks, launching facilities, and rentals are nearby. Leashed pets are permitted.

Reservations, fees: Reservations are recommended. Sites are $18.18–24.24 per night, $1 per person per night for more than two people; yurts are $35.35 per night. Some credit cards are accepted. Open year-round.

Directions: On U.S. 101, drive to central Gold Beach and the intersection with Moore Street. Turn west and drive two blocks to Airport Way. Turn right and drive three blocks to South Jetty Road. Turn left and look for the park on the left.

Contact: Oceanside RV Park, 541/247-2301.

111 WHALESHEAD BEACH RESORT

Scenic rating: 7

near the Pacific Ocean

See map page 255

This resort, about a quarter mile from the beach, is in a forested area with a small stream nearby. Activities at and around the camp include ocean and river fishing, jet-boat trips, whale-watching excursions, and a golf course (13 miles away). Each campsite has a deck, and many cabins have an ocean view. One unique feature is a tunnel that connects the campground to a trail to the beach.

RV sites, facilities: There are 45 sites with full hookups (30 and 50 amps) for RVs up to 60 feet and 36 cabins. No tent sites. Picnic tables are provided, and fire rings are available on request. Cable TV, restrooms with showers, a coin laundry, modem access, limited groceries, ice, snacks, RV supplies, propane gas, and a restaurant are available. A dump station is six miles away. Some facilities are wheelchair accessible. Leashed pets are permitted.

Reservations, fees: Reservations are recommended. Sites are $22–25 per night, plus $2 per person per night for more than two people; cable TV is $1.50 per night. Some credit cards are accepted. Open year-round.

Directions: From Brookings, drive seven miles north on U.S. 101 to Milepost 349.5 and look for the resort on the right.

Contact: Whaleshead Beach Resort, 541/469-7446, fax 541/469-7447, www.whaleshead resort.com.

112 ALFRED A. LOEB STATE PARK

Scenic rating: 8

near the Chetco River

See map page 255

This park is in a canyon formed by the Chetco River. The campsites nestle in a beautiful old myrtle grove. The 0.75-mile, self-guided River

View Trail adjacent to the Chetco River leads to the northernmost redwood grove in the United States. Nature programs and interpretive tours are available by request.

RV sites, facilities: There are 48 sites for tents or RVs up to 50 feet with partial hookups (30 amps) as well as three log cabins. Picnic tables, drinking water, garbage bins, and fire grills are provided. Restrooms have flush toilets and showers, and firewood is available. Leashed pets are permitted.

Reservations, fees: Reservations are accepted only for cabins at 800/452-5687 or www .oregonstateparks.org ($6 reservation fee). Sites are $12–16 per night, plus $5 per night per additional vehicle; cabins are $35 per night. Some credit cards are accepted. Open year-round.

Directions: On U.S. 101, drive to south Brookings and County Road 784 (North Bank Chetco River Road). Turn northeast and drive eight miles northeast on North Bank Road to the park entrance on the right.

Contact: Harris Beach State Park (no contact phone number at Loeb), 541/469-2021 or 800/551-6949, www.oregonstateparks.org.

113 LITTLE REDWOOD

Scenic rating: 7

on the Chetco River in Siskiyou National Forest
See map page 255

This campground sits among old-growth fir trees near the banks of the Chetco River. An official put-in spot for rafting and river boats, the camp is also on the main western access route to the Kalmiopsis Wilderness (pass required), which is about 20 miles away. Campsites are fairly private, though close together.

RV sites, facilities: There are 11 sites for tents or RVs up to 20 feet (no hookups). Picnic tables, garbage containers, and fire grills are provided. Drinking water and vault toilets are available. Leashed pets are permitted.

Reservations, fees: Reservations are not accepted. Sites are $10 per night, $2 per night

per additional vehicle. Open mid-May–late September, weather permitting.

Directions: On U.S. 101, drive to south Brookings and County Road 784 (North Bank Chetco River Road). Turn northeast on North Bank Chetco River Road and drive 13.5 miles (the road becomes Forest Road 1376) to the campground.

Contact: Siskiyou National Forest, Chetco Ranger District, 541/412-6000, fax 541/412-6025.

114 HARRIS BEACH STATE PARK

Scenic rating: 8

north of Brookings on the Pacific Ocean
See map page 255

This park boasts the largest island off the Oregon coast. Bird Island (also called Goat Island) is a breeding site for such rare birds as the tufted puffin. The park's sandy beaches are interspersed with eroded sea stacks. Tide-pooling is popular. The park's beauty changes with the seasons. Wildlife-viewing opportunities are abundant (gray whales, harbor seals, and sea lions). In the fall and winter, the nearby Chetco River attracts good runs of salmon and steelhead, respectively.

RV sites, facilities: There are 63 sites for tents or RVs up to 20 feet (no hookups), 84 sites with full or partial hookups for RVs up to 60 feet, three group areas for tents, a hiker/bicyclist camp, and six yurts. Picnic tables, garbage bins, and fire grills are provided. Drinking water, cable TV, restrooms with flush toilets and showers, a dump station, a coin laundry, and firewood are available. Some facilities are wheelchair accessible. Leashed pets are permitted.

Reservations, fees: Reservations are accepted at 800/452-5687 or www.oregonstateparks.org ($6 reservation fee). Sites are $13–21 per night, $5 per night per additional vehicle; it's $4 per night per person for hikers/bikers; group tent sites are $17 per night; and yurts are $29 per night. Some credit cards are accepted. Open year-round.

Directions: From Brookings, drive north on U.S. 101 for two miles to the park entrance on the left (west side of road).

Contact: Harris Beach State Park, 541/469-2021; Oregon State Parks, 800/551-6949, www.oregonstateparks.org.

115 BEACHFRONT RV PARK

Scenic rating: 8

south of Brookings on the Pacific Ocean
See map page 255

This park, just past the Oregon/California border on the Pacific Ocean, makes a great layover spot. Oceanfront sites are available, and recreational activities include boating, fishing, and swimming. Beach access is available from the park. Plan your trip early as sites usually book up for the entire summer season. Nearby Harris Beach State Park, with its beach access and hiking trails, makes a good side trip.

RV sites, facilities: There are 138 sites with full or partial hookups (30 and 50 amps) for RVs of any length; some sites are pull-through. Picnic tables and fire rings are provided. Restrooms have showers. A dump station, a public phone, modem access, a coin laundry, a restaurant, ice, and a marina with a boat ramp, a boat dock, and snacks are available. Supplies are available nearby. Some facilities are wheelchair accessible. Leashed pets are permitted.

Reservations, fees: Reservations are accepted at 800/441-0856. RV sites are $33–35 per night. Some credit cards are accepted. Open year-round.

Directions: From Brookings, drive south on U.S. 101 for 2.5 miles to Benham Lane. Turn west on Benham Lane and drive 1.5 miles (it becomes Lower Harbor Road) to Boat Basin Road. Turn left and drive two blocks to the park on the right.

Contact: Beachfront RV Park, 541/469-5867 or 800/441-0856 in Oregon; Port of Brookings Harbor, 541/469-2218, www.port-brookings-harbor.org.

116 AT RIVERS EDGE RV RESORT

Scenic rating: 7

on the Chetco River
See map page 255

This resort lies along the banks of the Chetco River, just upstream from Brookings Harbor. A favorite spot for anglers, it features salmon and steelhead trips on the Chetco in the fall and winter. Deep-sea trips for salmon or rockfish are available nearby in the summer. This resort looks like the Rhine Valley in Germany, a pretty canyon between the trees and the river. A golf course is nearby.

RV sites, facilities: There are 122 sites with full hookups (20, 30, and 50 amps) for RVs of any length; some are pull-through. Eight cabins are available. Picnic tables are provided, and fire rings are at most sites. Restrooms have flush toilets and showers. Wireless Internet service, modem access, propane gas, a dump station, a recreation hall with exercise equipment, a coin laundry, a recycling station, a small boat launch, and cable TV are available. Leashed pets are permitted.

Reservations, fees: Reservations are recommended at 888/295-1441. Sites are $33 per night and $2 per person per night for more than two people. Some credit cards are accepted. Open year-round.

Directions: On U.S. 101, drive to the southern end of Brookings (harbor side) and to South Bank Chetco River Road (a cloverleaf exit). Turn east on South Bank Chetco River Road and drive 1.5 miles to the resort entrance on the left (a slanted left turn, through the pillars, well signed).

Contact: At Rivers Edge RV Resort, 541/469-3356, www.atriversedge.com.

117 SEA BIRD RV PARK

Scenic rating: 5

in Brookings on the Pacific Ocean
See map page 255

This is one of several parks in the area. Nearby recreation options include marked bike trails, a full-service marina, and tennis courts. A nice, neat park, it features paved roads and gravel/granite sites. There is also a beach for surfing near the park. In summer, most of the sites are reserved for the season. No tent camping is permitted. An 18-hole golf course is within 2.5 miles.

RV sites, facilities: There are 60 sites with full or partial hookups (30 amps) for RVs of any length; some are pull-through sites. Picnic tables are provided. No open fires are allowed. Restrooms have flush toilets and showers. A dump station, high-speed modem access, a recreation hall, and a coin laundry are available. Boat docks, launching facilities, and rentals are nearby. Leashed pets are permitted.

Reservations, fees: Reservations are accepted. Sites are $20 per night, $2 per person per night for more than two people. Open year-round.

Directions: In Brookings, drive south on U.S. 101 to the Chetco River Bridge. Continue 0.25 mile south on U.S. 101 to the park entrance on the left.

Contact: Sea Bird RV Park, 541/469-3512, www.seabirdrv.com.

Directions: From Brookings, drive south on U.S. 101 for 5.5 miles to County Road 896. Turn left (east) and drive six miles to Forest Road 1107. Turn left (east) and drive one mile to the campground.

Contact: Siskiyou National Forest, Chetco Ranger District, 541/412-6000, fax 541/412-6025.

118 WINCHUCK

Scenic rating: 6

on the Winchuck River in Siskiyou National Forest

See map page 255

This forested campground hugs the banks of the Winchuck River, an out-of-the-way stream that out-of-towners don't know exists. It's quiet, remote, and not that far from the coast, although it feels like an inland spot. If this camp is full, Ludlum Campground is about two miles away on Forest Road 1108.

RV sites, facilities: There are 15 sites for tents or RVs up to 30 feet (no hookups). Picnic tables, garbage bins, and fire grills are provided. Vault toilets and drinking water are available. Leashed pets are permitted.

Reservations, fees: Reservations are not accepted. Sites are $10 per night, plus $2 per night per additional vehicle. Open mid-May–late September, weather permitting.

PORTLAND AND THE WILLAMETTE VALLEY

OREGON

For most tourists, Oregon is little more than a stretch of I-5 from Portland to Cottage Grove. Although there are some interesting things about this particular part of the state – it's Oregon's business center and most of my relatives and pals live there – the glimpse provided from I-5 doesn't capture its beauty. Residents, however, know the secret: Not only can you earn a good living here, but it's also a great jump-off point to adventure.

To discover what the locals know, venture east to west on the slow two-lane highways that border the streams. Among the most notable are Highway 26 along the Nacanticum River, little Highway 6 along the Wilson, little Highway 22 along Three Rivers, tiny Highway 15 on the Little Nestucca, Highway 18 on the Salmon River, Highway 34 on the Alsea, Highway 126 on the Siuslaw, and Highway 38 on the Umpqua (my favorite). These roads provide routes to reach the coast and can be used to create beautiful loop trips, with many hidden campgrounds to choose from while en route.

There are also parks and a number of lakes set in the foothills along dammed rivers. The highlight is Silver Falls State Park, Oregon's largest state park, with a seven-mile hike that is routed past 10 awesome waterfalls, some falling more than 100 feet from their brinks. Lakes are plentiful, too.

Portland is a great hub for finding recreation in the region. To the east is the Columbia River corridor and Mount Hood, with its surrounding wilderness and national forest. To the south is Eugene, which leads to the McKenzie and Willamette Rivers and offers a good launch station to the Three Sisters in the east.

Includes:

- Cascadia State Park
- Champoeg State Heritage Area
- Clackamas River
- Columbia River
- Fern Ridge Reservoir
- Foster Reservoir
- Green Peter Reservoir
- Molalla River
- Santiam River
- Silver Falls State Park
- Willamette River
- Yamhill River

OREGON

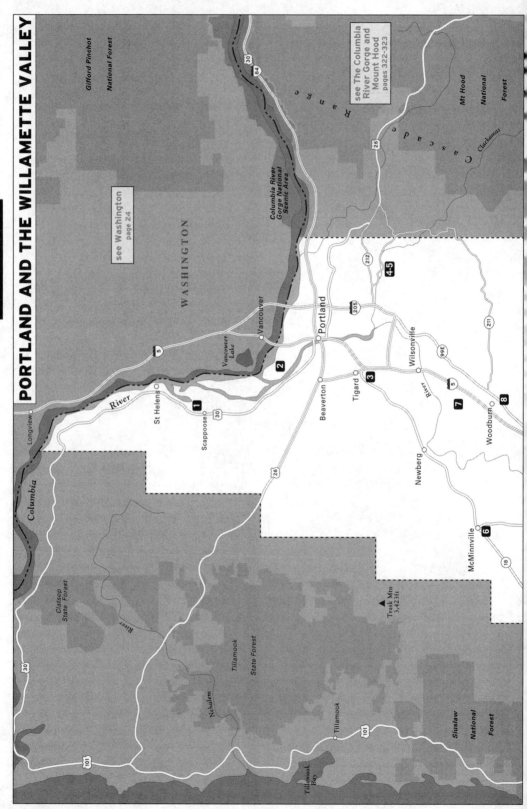

see The Columbia
River Gorge and
Mount Hood
pages 322–323

see Washington
page 24

PORTLAND AND THE WILLAMETTE VALLEY

OREGON

Gifford Pinchot

National Forest

WASHINGTON

Columbia River
Gorge National
Scenic Area

Cascade Range

Mt Hood

National

Forest

Cluckamas

Vancouver

Vancouver
Lake

Portland

Beaverton

Tigard

Wilsonville

Newberg

Woodburn

McMinnville

St Helens

Scappoose

Longview

Columbia River

Clatsop
State Forest

River

Nehalem

Tillamook
State Forest

Trask Mtn
3,423 ft

Siuslaw

National

Forest

Tillamook

Tillamook Bay

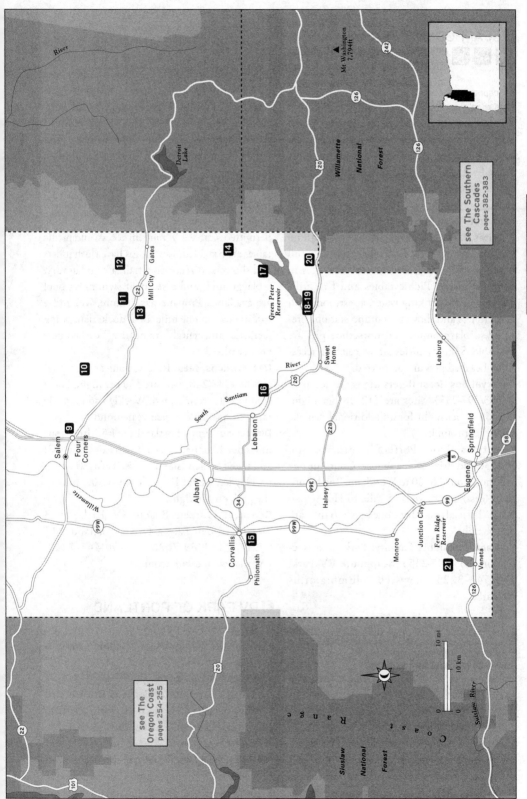

OREGON

Mt. Washington
7,794ft

Willamette National Forest

see The Southern Cascades
pages 382-383

Detroit Lake

Gates

Mill City

Green Peter Reservoir

Sweet Home

River

Santiam

South

Lebanon

Salem

Four Corners

Leaburg

Springfield

Eugene

Albany

Halsey

Willamette

Corvallis

Philomath

Monroe

Junction City

Fern Ridge Reservoir

Veneta

see The Oregon Coast
pages 254-255

Coast Range

Siuslaw National Forest

Siuslaw River

10 mi

10 km

© AVALON TRAVEL PUBLISHING, INC.

OREGON

1 SCAPPOOSE RV PARK

Scenic rating: 6

in Scappoose

See map page 308

This county-operated RV park neighbors the rural Scappoose airport, making it a convenient spot for private pilots. The sites are partially shaded with maple, oak, and spruce trees. Set on the edge of a dike, it is less than a mile from the Columbia River and about a 30-minute drive from Portland.

RV sites, facilities: There are six sites with no hookups for RVs up to 35 feet, six with full hookups (30 amps), and several tent sites in dispersed areas. Picnic tables and fire grills are provided. Drinking water, a restroom with flush toilets and showers, a dump station, firewood, a playground, and horseshoe pits are available. Some facilities are wheelchair accessible. Leashed pets are permitted.

Reservations, fees: Reservations are accepted at 503/397-2353. Sites are $12–18 per night, plus $4–7 per night for an additional vehicle. Open year-round.

Directions: From Portland, turn west on U.S. 30 and drive to Scappoose. Continue one mile north on U.S. 30 to West Lane Road. Turn right (east) and drive 0.75 mile to Honeyman Road. Turn left and drive one block to the park on the right.

Contact: Columbia County, Parks and Recreation, 503/397-2353; Scappoose RV Park, 503/543-3225, www.co.columbia.or.us/colparks.

2 JANTZEN BEACH RV PARK

Scenic rating: 6

near the Columbia River

See map page 308

This RV campground, near the banks of the Columbia River on the outskirts of Portland, offers seasonal swimming. An 18-hole golf course and tennis courts are close by. Many recreation opportunities are available in the Portland area. Numerous marinas on the Willamette and Columbia Rivers offer boat trips and rentals, and the city parks and nearby state parks have bicycling, hiking, and horseback riding possibilities. If golf is your game, Portland has 18 public golf courses. The Columbia River Highway (U.S. 30) is a scenic drive. The winter ski areas at Mount Hood are within an hour's drive.

RV sites, facilities: There are 169 sites with full hookups (20, 30, and 50 amps) for RVs of any length; some sites are pull-through. No tents are permitted. Cable TV, modem access, and picnic tables are provided. Restrooms have flush toilets and showers. A recreation hall, a coin laundry, a playground, and a seasonal swimming pool are available. Propane gas, a store, ice, and a café are within one mile. Boat docks, launching facilities, and rentals are nearby. Leashed pets are permitted.

Reservations, fees: Reservations are accepted at 800/443-7248. Sites are $30 per night. Some credit cards are accepted. Weekly and monthly rates are available. Open year-round.

Directions: From Portland on I-5, drive four miles north to the Jantzen Beach exit (Exit 308) and take Hayden Island Drive. Turn left (west) on Hayden Island Drive and drive 0.5 mile to the park on the right.

Contact: Jantzen Beach RV Park, 1503 North Hayden Island Drive, Portland, OR 97217, 503/289-7626 or 800/443-7248, www.jantzenbeachrv.com.

3 RV PARK OF PORTLAND

Scenic rating: 6

in Tualatin

See map page 308

This park, just south of Portland in a wooded setting, has spacious sites, all with access to lawn areas. More than half of the sites are taken by monthly rentals.

RV sites, facilities: There are 112 sites, most of them with full hookups (20, 30, and 50 amps), for RVs of any length; many sites are pull-through. No tents are permitted. Cable TV and picnic tables are provided. Restrooms have flush toilets and showers. A dump station, a coin laundry, modem access, and wireless Internet service are available. Propane gas, a store, a café, and ice are within one mile. Leashed pets are permitted.

Reservations, fees: Reservations are accepted at 800/856-2066. Sites are $33.39 per night, plus $2.50 per person per night for more than two people. Monthly rates are available. Some credit cards are accepted. Open year-round.

Directions: From Portland, drive south on I-5 to Tualatin and Exit 289. Take Exit 289 and turn left (east) on Nyberg Road. Drive 0.25 mile to Nyberg Lane. Turn left and drive a short distance to the park on the left.

Contact: RV Park of Portland, 503/692-0225, www.rvparkofportland.com.

4 BARTON PARK

Scenic rating: 6

near the Clackamas River

See map page 308

Getting here may seem a bit of a maze, but the trip is well worth it. This camp is on the Clackamas River and is surrounded by woods and tall trees. The river can provide good salmon and steelhead fishing.

RV sites, facilities: There are 98 sites for tents or RVs of any length with partial hookups (20, 30, and 50 amps); some sites are pull-through. Picnic tables and fire rings are provided. Restrooms have showers. A dump station, a picnic area, and reservable picnic shelters are available. Recreational facilities include horseshoe pits, a playground, a volleyball court, a softball field, and a boat ramp. Supplies are available within one mile. A camp host is on-site. Some facilities are wheelchair accessible. Leashed pets are permitted.

Reservations, fees: Reservations are recommended. Sites are $12–16 per night, plus $2 per night per additional vehicle. Some credit cards are accepted for reservations. Open May–September.

Directions: From Portland, drive south on I-5 to I-205. Turn east and drive about 20 miles to Exit 12, the Clackamas/Estacada exit (Highway 212). Turn east on Highway 212/224 and drive 3.2 miles to the Carver exit/Rock Creek junction. Turn right on Highway 224 and drive about 6.5 miles to the town of Barton and Baker's Ferry Road. Turn right and drive 0.2 mile to Barton Park Road. Turn left and drive to the park on the left.

Contact: Clackamas County Parks Department, 503/353-4414, fax 503/353-4420, www.co.clackamas.or.us.

5 METZLER PARK

Scenic rating: 8

on Clear Creek

See map page 308

This county campground on a small stream not far from the Clackamas River is a hot spot for fishing, picnicking, and swimming. Be sure to make your reservation early at this very popular park.

RV sites, facilities: There are 70 sites for tents or RVs up to 40 feet (partial hookups). Picnic tables and fire pits are provided. Restrooms have flush toilets and showers. A dump station, a playground, reservable picnic areas, and a recreation field with baseball, basketball, and volleyball are available. Propane, ice, and a coin laundry are within five miles. Some facilities are wheelchair accessible. Leashed pets are permitted.

Reservations, fees: Reservations are recommended. Sites are $12–16 per night. Some credit cards are accepted with reservations. Open May–September.

Directions: From Portland, drive south on I-5 to I-205. Turn east and drive about 20 miles to Exit 12, the Clackamas/Estacada exit (Highway 212). Turn east on Highway 212/224 and drive 3.2 miles to the Carver exit/Rock Creek junction. Turn right on Highway 224 and drive approximately 15 miles to Estacada and Highway 211. Turn right, crossing a bridge, and drive four miles to Tucker Road. Turn right and drive

OREGON

OREGON

0.5 mile to Metzler Park Road. Turn left and drive 1.6 miles to the park entrance.

Contact: Clackamas County Parks Department, 503/353-4414, fax 503/353-4420, www.co.clackamas.or.us.

6 MULKEY RV PARK

Scenic rating: 7

near the South Yamhill River

See map page 308

This wooded park sits near the South Yamhill River. Nearby recreation options include an 18-hole golf course, tennis courts, and the Western Deer Park and Arboretum, which has a playground. Most sites are taken by monthly renters.

RV sites, facilities: There are 70 sites with full hookups (30 and 50 amps) for RVs of any length; some sites are pull-through. No tents. Drinking water and picnic tables are provided. Restrooms have flush toilets and showers. Wi-Fi, a grocery store, propane gas, ice, and a coin laundry are available. Leashed pets are permitted.

Reservations, fees: Reservations are accepted at 877/472-2475. Sites are $24 per night, $3 per person per night for more than two people. Monthly rates are available. Some credit cards are accepted. Open year-round.

Directions: From Portland, turn south on Highway 99 and drive about 31 miles to McMinnville and Highway 18. Turn southwest on Highway 18 and drive 3.5 miles to the park entrance.

Contact: Mulkey RV Park, 503/472-2475, fax 503/472-0718.

7 CHAMPOEG STATE HERITAGE AREA

Scenic rating: 7

on the Willamette River

See map page 308

Situated on the south bank of the Willamette River, this state park features an interpretive center, a botanical garden with native plants, and hiking and bike trails. A junior ranger program is available during the summer. The log cabin museum, the historic Newell House, and the visitors center are also worth a tour.

RV sites, facilities: There 79 sites for tents or RVs up to 50 feet with full or partial hookups (30 amps). There are also three group tent areas that accommodate a maximum of 25 people each, six walk-in sites, six cabins, six yurts, a hiker/biker camp, and a 10-site tent and RV group area with electric hookups only. Picnic tables and fire grills are provided. Restrooms have flush toilets and showers. Drinking water, garbage bins, a dump station, a reservable meeting hall, a picnic area, an off-leash dog park, disc golf, ice, and firewood are available. Some facilities are wheelchair accessible. Boat docking facilities are nearby. Leashed pets are permitted.

Reservations, fees: Reservations are accepted at 800/452-5687 ($6 reservation fee) or www.oregonstateparks.org. Sites are $16–20 per night, $5 per night per additional vehicle; it's $4 per person per night for hiker/biker sites; the group tent camps are $61 per night; the group RV and tent camp is $81 per night and $8 per RV after the first 10 units; yurts are $27 per night; and cabins are $35 per night. Some credit cards are accepted. Open year-round.

Directions: From Portland, drive south on I-5 to Exit 278, the Donald/Aurora exit. Take that exit and turn right (west) on Ehlen Road and drive three miles to Case Road. Turn right (north) and drive 4.5 miles (the road becomes Champoeg Road) to the park on the right.

Contact: Champoeg State Heritage Area, 503/678-1251; Oregon State Parks, 800/551-6949, www.oregonstateparks.org.

8 FEYRER MEMORIAL PARK

Scenic rating: 5

on the Molalla River

See map page 308

On the scenic Molalla River, this county park offers swimming and excellent salmon fishing.

A superb option for weary I-5 cruisers, the park is only 30 minutes off the highway and provides a peaceful, serene environment.

RV sites, facilities: There are 20 sites for tents or RVs up to 40 feet with partial hookups (30 and 50 amps). Picnic tables and fire rings are provided. Drinking water, restrooms with showers, a dump station, and reservable picnic areas are available. Other amenities include a playground, horseshoe pits, volleyball, and softball. A boat ramp is nearby. Some facilities are wheelchair accessible. Supplies are available within three miles. Leashed pets are permitted.

Reservations, fees: Reservations are recommended. Sites are $12–16 per night. Some credit cards are accepted with reservations. Open May–September.

Directions: From Portland, drive south on I-5 to Woodburn and Exit 271. Take that exit and drive east on Highway 214; continue (the road changes to Highway 211 at the crossing with Highway 99E) to Molalla and Mathias Road. Turn right and drive 0.25 mile to Feyrer Park Road. Turn right and drive three miles to the park on the left.

Contact: Clackamas County Parks Department, 503/353-4414, fax 503/353-4420, www.co.clackamas.or.us.

9 SALEM CAMPGROUND AND RVS
🥾 🚴 ⛵ 🎣 🐕 🛶 🚐 ⛺

Scenic rating: 5

in Salem

See map page 309

This park with shaded sites is next to I-5 in Salem; expect to hear traffic noise. A picnic area and a lake for swimming are within walking distance, and a nine-hole golf course, hiking trails, a riding stable, and tennis courts are nearby. This is a good overnight campground but not a destination place.

RV sites, facilities: There are 190 sites for RVs of any length, most with full hookups (20, 30, and 50 amps) and 31 tent sites; most sites are pull-through. Picnic tables are provided, and barbecues are available on request. Restrooms have flush toilets and showers. Propane gas, a dump station, a recreation hall with a game room, a convenience store, a coin laundry, ice, a playground, and drinking water are available. A café is within one mile. Leashed pets are permitted; no pit bulls or Rottweilers are allowed.

Reservations, fees: Reservations are accepted at 800/826-9605. Sites are $17–28 per night, plus $2 per person per night for more than two people. Weekly, monthly, and group rates are available. Some credit cards are accepted. Open year-round.

Directions: From Salem on I-5, take Exit 253 to Highway 22. Turn east and drive 0.25 mile to Lancaster Drive. Turn right on Lancaster Drive and continue 0.1 mile to Hagers Grove Road. Turn right on Hagers Grove Road and drive a short distance to the campground at the end of the road.

Contact: Salem Campground and RVs, 503/581-6736 or 800/826-9605, fax 888/581-9945, www.salemrv.com.

10 SILVER FALLS STATE PARK
🥾 🚴 ⛵ 🐎 🛶 ♿ 🚐 ⛺

Scenic rating: 8

near Salem

See map page 309

Oregon's largest state park, Silver Falls covers more than 8,700 acres. Numerous trails crisscross the area. One, a seven-mile jaunt, meanders past 10 majestic waterfalls (some more than 100 feet high) in the rainforest of Silver Creek Canyon. Four of these falls have an amphitheater-like surrounding where you can walk behind the falls and feel the misty spray. A horse camp and a 14-mile equestrian trail are available in the park. Fitness-conscious campers can check out the three-mile jogging trail or the four-mile bike trail. A rustic nature lodge and group lodging facilities round out the options. Pets are not allowed on the Canyon Trail.

RV sites, facilities: There are 46 sites for tents or RVs (no hookups), 47 sites for tents or RVs up to 60 feet with partial hookups (30 amps), three group tent sites for up to 50–75 people

OREGON

OREGON

each, two group RV areas, five horse sites, a group horse camp, and 14 cabins. Picnic tables and fire grills are provided. Drinking water, garbage bins, restrooms with flush toilets and showers, a dump station, an amphitheater, firewood, ice, and a playground are available. Some facilities are wheelchair accessible. Leashed pets are permitted in the campground.

Reservations, fees: Reservations are accepted at 800/452-5687 or www.oregonstateparks.org ($6 reservation fee). Sites are $16–20 per night, the group tent site is $61 per night, the group RV sites are $80 per night for the first 10 units and then $8 per additional unit, horse campsites are $16 per night, the group horse camp is $48 per night, and it's $5 per night for an additional vehicle. Cabins are $35 per night. Some credit cards are accepted. Open year-round.

Directions: From Salem on I-5, take Exit 253 to Highway 22. Turn east and drive five miles to Highway 214. Turn left (east) and drive 15 miles to the park.

Contact: Silver Falls State Park, 503/873-8681, 503/873-4395, or 503/873-3890 (trail rides); Oregon State Parks, 800/551-6949, www.oregonstateparks.org.

11 FISHERMEN'S BEND
🚶 🚴 🎣 🚤 🐕 ⛺ ♿ 🚐 ⛺

Scenic rating: 7

on the North Santiam River

See map page 309

Fishermen's Bend is a popular spot for anglers of all ages, and the sites are spacious. The campground was renovated in 2005. A barrier-free fishing and river-viewing area and a network of trails provide access to more than a mile of river. There's a one-mile, self-guided nature trail, and the nature center has a variety of displays. The amphitheater has films and activities on weekends. The front gate closes at 10 P.M.

RV sites, facilities: There are 52 sites, some with full hookups (30 and 50 amps), for tents or RVs up to 40 feet; some sites are pull-through. Three group sites hold up to 60 people each, and there are two cabins. Drinking water, picnic

tables, and fire pits are provided. Restrooms have flush toilets and showers. A dump station and garbage containers are available. A boat ramp, a day-use area with playgrounds, baseball, volleyball, and basketball courts and fields, horseshoe pits, firewood, and a reservable picnic shelter are also available. Some facilities are wheelchair accessible. Leashed pets are permitted.

Reservations, fees: Reservations are accepted at 877/444-6777 or www.ReserveUSA.com ($9 reservation fee). Sites are $12–18 per night, $5 per night for an additional vehicle. Group sites are $65–85 per night. Cabins are $35 per night. Open April–October, with a 14-day stay limit.

Directions: From Salem on I-5, take Exit 253 to Highway 22. Turn east and drive 30 miles to the campground on the right.

Contact: Bureau of Land Management, Salem District Office, 503/375-5646, fax 503/375-5622.

12 ELKHORN VALLEY
🚶 🏊 🎣 🐕 ♿ 🚐 ⛺

Scenic rating: 7

on the Little North Santiam River

See map page 309

This pretty campground along the Little North Santiam River, not far from the North Fork of the Santiam River, has easy access and on-site hosts and is only a short drive away from a major metropolitan area. Swimming is good here during the summer, and the campground is popular with families. The front gate is locked 10 P.M.–7 A.M. daily.

RV sites, facilities: There are 24 sites for tents or RVs up to 18 feet (no hookups). Picnic tables, garbage bins, fire grills, vault toilets, and drinking water are available. Firewood is available for purchase. Some facilities are wheelchair accessible. Leashed pets are permitted.

Reservations, fees: Reservations are not accepted. Sites are $10 per night, plus $5 per night for an additional vehicle. There is a 14-day stay limit. Open mid-May–late September.

Directions: From Salem on I-5, take Exit 253 to Highway 22. Turn east and drive 25 miles to Elkhorn Road (Little North Fork Road). Turn left (northeast) and drive nine miles to the campground on the left.

Contact: Bureau of Land Management, Salem District Office, 503/375-5646, fax 503/375-5622.

13 JOHN NEAL MEMORIAL PARK

Scenic rating: 6

on the North Santiam River

See map page 309

This camp is on the banks of the North Santiam River, offering good boating and trout-fishing possibilities. The park covers about 27 acres and there are hiking trails. Other recreation options include exploring lakes and trails in the adjacent national forest land or visiting Silver Falls State Park.

RV sites, facilities: There are 40 sites for tents or RVs up to 30 feet (no hookups), and 14 sites can be reserved as a group area. Some sites are pull-through. Picnic tables and fire pits are provided. Restrooms have flush toilets and showers. Garbage bins and drinking water are available. Recreational facilities include a boat ramp, a playground, horseshoe pits, a picnic area, and a recreation field. A camp host is on-site. Ice and a grocery store are within one mile. Leashed pets are permitted.

Reservations, fees: Reservations are accepted by Internet at www.co.linn.or.us (reservation fees are $11 for single sites and $50 for groups). Sites are $15 per night, plus $5 per night per additional vehicle. The group site is $100 per night. Some credit cards are accepted for reservations. Open mid-April–mid-September, weather permitting.

Directions: From Salem, drive east on Highway 22 for about 20 miles to Highway 226. Turn right and drive south for two miles to Lyons and John Neal Park Road. Turn left (east) and drive a short distance to the campground on the left.

Contact: Linn County Parks Department, 541/967-3917, fax 541/924-6915, www.co.linn.or.us.

14 YELLOWBOTTOM

Scenic rating: 7

on Quartzville Creek

See map page 309

Out-of-town visitors always miss this campground across the road from Quartzville Creek. It nestles under a canopy of old-growth forest. The Rhododendron Trail, which is just under a mile, provides a challenging hike through forest and patches of rhododendrons. Some folks pan for gold here, and swimming is popular in the creek. Though primitive, the camp is ideal for a quiet getaway weekend.

RV sites, facilities: There are 20 sites for tents or RVs up to 25 feet (no hookups); some sites are pull-through. Picnic tables, garbage bins, and fire grills are provided. Drinking water and vault toilets are available. Some facilities are wheelchair accessible. Leashed pets are permitted.

Reservations, fees: Reservations are not accepted. Sites are $8 per night, with a 14-day stay limit, and $5 per night for an additional vehicle. Open mid-May–late September.

Directions: From Albany, drive east on U.S. 20 for about 35 miles (through Sweet Home) to Quartzville Road. Turn left (northeast) on Quartzville Road and drive 24 miles to the campground on the left.

Contact: Bureau of Land Management, Salem District, 503/375-5646, fax 503/375-5622.

15 WILLAMETTE CAMPGROUND

Scenic rating: 8

on the Willamette River

See map page 309

This 40-acre city park is adjacent to the Willamette River, just outside Corvallis. The camping area is actually a large clearing near the entrance to the park, which has been left in its

OREGON

OREGON

natural state. Trails lead down to the river, and the bird-watching is good here. Hiking and bicycling are options and a path goes from the park to nearby Crystal Lake.

RV sites, facilities: There are 15 sites for tents or RVs of any length (no hookups). Picnic tables are provided, and fire pits are available at some sites. Vault toilets and drinking water are available. Propane gas, a store, a café, a coin laundry, and ice are within one mile. Boat docks and launching facilities are also within three miles. Leashed pets are permitted.

Reservations, fees: Reservations are not accepted. Sites are $9 per night, plus $5 per night per additional vehicle. Open April–October.

Directions: On I-5, take Exit 228 (five miles south of Albany) to Highway 34. Turn west and drive nine miles to Corvallis and Highway 99S. Turn left (south) and drive 1.3 mile to Goodnight Avenue. Turn left (east) and drive one mile to the campground on the left.

Contact: Corvallis Department of Parks and Recreation, 541/766-6918, fax 541/754-1701, www.ci.corvallis.or.us.

16 WATERLOO COUNTY PARK

Scenic rating: 8

on the South Santiam River

See map page 309

This campground features more than a mile of South Santiam River frontage. Field sports, fishing, picnicking, and swimming are options. Small boats with trolling motors are the only boats usable here.

RV sites, facilities: There are 120 sites for tents or RVs of any length; most have partial hookups (30 amps). Drinking water, fire pits, and picnic tables are provided. Restrooms have showers. A dump station, boat ramps, a playground, a day-use area, and picnic shelters are available. A small grocery store is within one mile. Some facilities are wheelchair accessible. Leashed pets are permitted.

Reservations, fees: Reservations are accepted ($11 reservation fee). Sites are $13–18 per night, plus $5 per night for an additional vehicle.

Some credit cards are accepted for reservations. Open year-round.

Directions: From Albany, drive east on U.S. 20 for about 20 miles through Lebanon to the Waterloo exit. Turn left (north) at the Waterloo exit and drive approximately two miles to the camp on the right. The camp is on the south side of the South Santiam River, five miles east of Lebanon.

Contact: Linn County Parks Department, 541/967-3917, fax 541/924-6915, www.co.linn .or.us.

17 WHITCOMB CREEK COUNTY PARK

Scenic rating: 8

on Green Peter Reservoir

See map page 309

This camp, on the north shore of Green Peter Reservoir, is in a wooded area with lots of ferns, which gives it a rainforest feel. Recreation options include hiking, picnicking, sailing, swimming, and waterskiing. Two boat ramps are on the reservoir about a mile from camp.

RV sites, facilities: There are 39 sites for tents or RVs up to 30 feet (no hookups) and one group tent and RV area for up to 100 people. Picnic tables and fire pits are provided. Drinking water is available to haul; vault toilets, garbage bins, and a boat ramp are also available. Supplies are within 15 miles. Leashed pets are permitted.

Reservations, fees: Reservations are accepted (reservation fees are $11 for single sites and $50 for groups) at 541/967-3917. Sites are $13 per night, and the group site is $100 per night. Some credit cards are accepted for reservations. Open mid-April–mid-October.

Directions: From Albany, drive east on U.S. 20 for about 35 miles (through Lebanon and Sweet Home) to the Quartzville Road exit (near Foster Reservoir). Turn left (north) on Quartzville Road and drive 15 miles to the park.

Contact: Linn County Parks Department, 541/967-3917, fax 541/924-6915, www.co.linn .or.us.

18 RIVER BEND COUNTY PARK

Scenic rating: 8

on the South Santiam River
See map page 309

This park opened in 2005, and it is already popular. The river current is calm here in the summer and there are swimming beaches. Additional water activities include fishing and inner tubing, a favorite activity. The campground is in a woodsy setting of firs and ferns, and the park features hiking trails. Additional facilities are planned.

RV sites, facilities: There are 10 sites for tents or RVs (no hookups) and 35 sites for tents or RVs of any length with partial hookups. Picnic tables and fire pits are provided. Drinking water, restrooms with flush toilets and showers, a dump station, a picnic area, an athletic field, an interpretive display, a fishing area, and a swimming and tubing area are available. Some facilities are wheelchair accessible. Leashed pets are permitted.

Reservations, fees: Reservations are accepted at 541/967-3917 or by Internet at www.co.linn.or.us ($11 reservation fee). Sites are $13–18 per night, plus $5 per night per additional vehicle. Some credit cards are accepted for reservations. Open year-round.

Directions: From Albany, drive east on U.S. 20 to Sweet Home. Continue east on U.S. 20 for five miles to the park on the left.

Contact: Linn County Parks Department, 541/967-3917, fax 541/924-6915, www.co.linn.or.us.

19 SUNNYSIDE COUNTY PARK

Scenic rating: 8

on Foster Reservoir
See map page 309

This is Linn County's most popular park. Recreation options at this 98-acre park include boating, fishing, swimming, and waterskiing. A golf course is within 15 miles.

RV sites, facilities: There are 165 sites for tents or RVs of any length; most sites have partial hookups (30 and 50 amps). There are 27 sites available for groups, who must take a minimum of eight sites, with a maximum of eight people per site. Picnic tables are provided, and community fire rings are available. Drinking water, restrooms with flush toilets and showers, a dump station, a playground, a reservable picnic shelter, volleyball courts, firewood, a boat ramp, and moorage are available. Supplies are within two miles. Some facilities are wheelchair accessible. Leashed pets are permitted.

Reservations, fees: Reservations are accepted ($11 for a site reservation and $50 for a group reservation). Sites are $13–18 per night, plus $5 per night for an additional vehicle. Open April–October.

Directions: From Albany, drive east on U.S. 20 for about 35 miles (through Lebanon and Sweet Home) to the Quartzville Road exit (near Foster Reservoir). Turn left (north) on Quartzville Road and drive one mile to the campground on the right. The camp is on the south side of Foster Reservoir.

Contact: Linn County Parks Department, 541/967-3917, fax 541/924-0202, www.co.linn.or.us.

20 CASCADIA STATE PARK

Scenic rating: 7

on the Santiam River
See map page 309

The highlight of this 258-acre park is Soda Creek Falls, with a fun 0.75-mile hike to reach it. The park is along the banks of the Santiam River. A newer trail ushers you through Douglas fir trees along the river, a good place to fish and swim. It's a great spot for a more intimate getaway for hikers and also for reunions and meetings for families, Boy Scouts, and other groups.

RV sites, facilities: There are 25 sites for tents or RVs up to 30 feet (no hookups), a hike-in/bike-in area, and two group tent areas for up to 100 people each. Picnic tables, garbage bins,

OREGON

and fire grills are provided. Drinking water, vault toilets, firewood, and ice are available. A camp host is on-site. Some facilities are wheelchair accessible. Leashed pets are permitted.

Reservations, fees: Reservations are accepted only for group tent areas at 800/452-5687. Sites are $14 per night, $5 per night for an additional vehicle, and $4 per person for hike-in/bike-in sites. Group sites are $61 per night for up to 25 people and $2.40 per night for each additional person. Some credit cards are accepted. Open May–September, weather permitting.

Directions: From Albany, drive east on U.S. 20 for 40 miles to the park on the left (14 miles east of the town of Sweet Home).

Contact: Cascadia State Park, 541/367-6021 or 800/551-6949, www.oregonstateparks.org.

21 RICHARDSON PARK

Scenic rating: 7

on Fern Ridge Reservoir

See map page 309

This pretty Lane County park is a favorite for sailing and sailboarding, as the wind is consistent. Boating and waterskiing are also popular. A walking trail doubles as a bike trail. A kiosk display in the park features the historic Applegate Trail. Additional activities include fishing, swimming (unsupervised), and wildlife-viewing. The Corps of Engineers has wildlife areas nearby. Note: At the time of publication, the reservoir had been drained for repairs; check for current status.

RV sites, facilities: There are 88 sites for tents or RVs of any length with partial hookups (30 and 50 amps); some sites are pull-through. Group sites are double campsites. Drinking water, picnic tables, and fire pits are provided. Restrooms have flush toilets and coin showers. A dump station, picnic areas, a seasonal snack bar, sand volleyball, and garbage bins are available. Some facilities are wheelchair accessible. A part-time attended marina with minimal supplies—including ice, a boat launch, and transient boat docks—and a playground are also available in the park. There is a small town within five miles. Leashed pets are permitted.

Reservations, fees: Reservations are accepted at 541/682-2000 or by Internet at www.ecomm .lanecounty.org/parks ($10 reservation fee). Sites are $20 per night, plus $6.50 per night per additional vehicle. Maximum stay is 14 days in a 30-day period. Some credit cards are accepted. Open mid-April–mid-October.

Directions: In Eugene on I-5, drive to Exit 195B and Belt Line Road. Turn west on Belt Line Road and drive 6.5 miles to the Junction City Airport exit and Highway 99. Take that exit, turn left on Highway 99, and drive north for 0.5 mile to Clear Lake Road (the first stoplight). Turn left and drive 8.25 miles to the campground on the left.

Contact: Richardson Park, 541/935-2005 or 541/682-2000, www.co.lane.or.us/parks.

THE COLUMBIA RIVER GORGE AND MOUNT HOOD

The Columbia River area is at once a living history

lesson, a geological wonder, and a recreation paradise. The waterway is probably best known as the route the Lewis and Clark expedition followed two centuries ago. It's also famous for carving out a deep gorge through the Cascade Range that divides Oregon. Nearby Mount Hood and its surrounding national forest and many lakes provide almost unlimited opportunities for camping, hiking, and fishing.

The Columbia spans hundreds of square miles and is linked to a watershed that in turn is connected to the Snake River, which covers thousands of square miles. I-84 provides a major route along the southern shore of the Columbia, but the river view is not what you will remember. After you depart the traffic of the Portland area, driving west to east, you will pass along the wooded foothills of the Cascade Range to the south. When you pass Hood River, the world suddenly changes. The trees disappear. In their place are rolling grasslands that seem to extend for as far as you can see. It is often hot and dry here, with strong winds blowing straight down the river.

However, the entire time you are within the realm of Mount Hood. At 11,239 feet, Hood is a beautiful mountain, shaped like a diamond, its flanks supporting many stellar destinations with campsites and small lakes set in forest. Snowmelt feeds many major rivers as well as numerous smaller streams, which roll down Mount Hood in every direction.

The transformation of the Gorge-area landscape from forest to grasslands to high desert is quick and striking. Particularly remarkable is how the Deschutes River has cut a path through the desert bluffs. And while the Deschutes is one of Oregon's better steelhead streams, unless you're fishing, you are more likely to encounter a desert chukar on a rock perch than anything water-bound.

Includes:

- Ainsworth State Park
- Breitenbush River
- Clackamas River
- Collawash River
- Columbia River
- Columbia Wilderness
- Cove Palisades State Park
- Deschutes National Forest
- Deschutes River State Recreation Area
- Detroit Lake State Park
- Hood River
- John Day River
- Lake Billy Chinook
- Lake Harriet
- Lake Simtustus
- Little Crater Lake
- Lost Lake
- Memaloose State Park
- Milo McIver State Park
- Mount Hood National Forest
- Mount Jefferson Wilderness
- Olallie Lake
- Roaring River
- Salmon River
- Sandy River
- Santiam River
- Timothy Lake
- Trillium Lake
- Viento State Park
- Willamette National Forest
- Zigzag River

OREGON

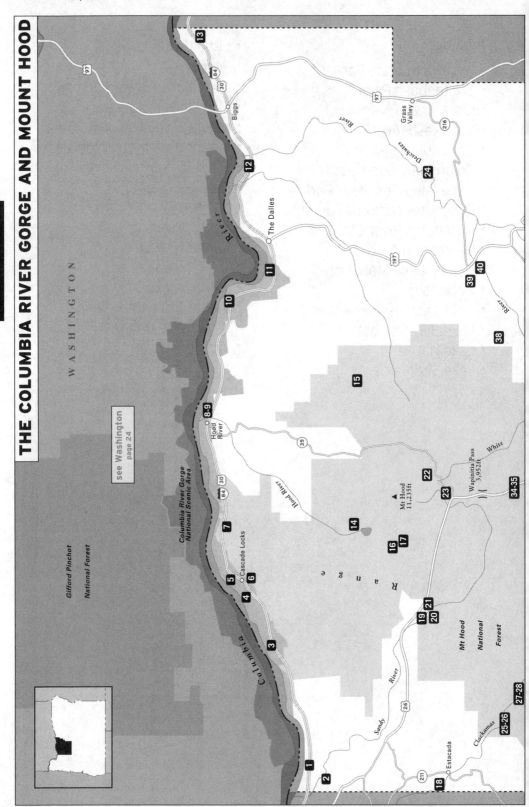

OREGON

THE COLUMBIA RIVER GORGE AND MOUNT HOOD

WASHINGTON

see Washington
page 24

Gifford Pinchot
National Forest

Columbia River Gorge
National Scenic Area

Cascade Locks

Columbia

Hood River

Hood River

River

Biggs

The Dalles

Deschutes River

Grass Valley

97

84

30

97

216

197

24

39

40

38

15

35

River

White

Wapinitia Pass
3,952ft

Mt Hood
11,235ft

Range

22

23

34-35

14

16 17

19
20 21

Mt Hood
National

Forest

Sandy River

Clackamas

26

211

Estacada

18

25-26

27-28

1

2

3

4

5

6

7

8-9

10

11

12

13

30

84

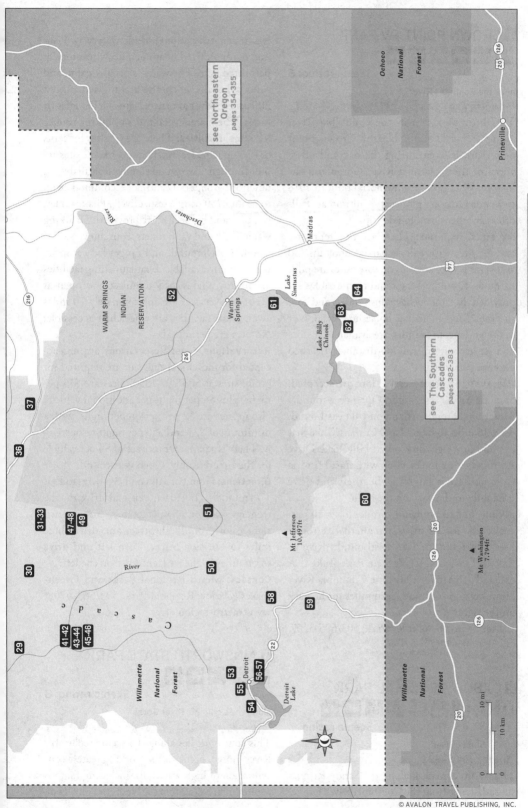

OREGON

see Northeastern
Oregon
pages 354-355

see The Southern
Cascades
pages 382-383

Ochoco National Forest

Prineville

Madras

WARM SPRINGS INDIAN RESERVATION

Warm Springs

Lake Simtustus

Lake Billy Chinook

Deschutes River

Willamette National Forest

Willamette National Forest

Detroit

Detroit Lake

Mt Jefferson
10,497ft

Mt Washington
7,794ft

Cascade River

52

61

63

64

62

37

36

31-33

47-48

49

30

51

50

58

59

22

53

56-57

55

54

29

41-42

43-44

45-46

60

20 126

97

20

124

126

20

10 mi

10 km

0

0

1 CROWN POINT RV PARK

Scenic rating: 6

near the Columbia River

See map page 322

This little park is near the Columbia River along scenic U.S. 30. Nearby Crown Point State Park is open during the day and offers views of the Columbia River Gorge and the historic Vista House, a memorial built in 1918 to honor Oregon's pioneers. Multnomah Falls offers another possible side trip.

RV sites, facilities: There are five tent sites and 22 sites with full or partial hookups (30 amps) for RVs of any length; some sites are pull-through. Drinking water and picnic tables are provided. Restrooms have flush toilets and coin showers. Modem access, horseshoe pits, a hair salon, and a coin laundry are available. A store and ice are within walking distance. Leashed pets are permitted.

Reservations, fees: Reservations are accepted. Sites are $15–25 per night. Open year-round.

Directions: From Portland on I-84 eastbound, drive 16 miles to Exit 22 and Corbett. Take that exit and turn right on Corbett Hill Road. Drive 1.5 miles to a Y intersection with East Historic Columbia River Highway. Bear left and drive 0.25 mile to the park on the right.

Note: The recommended route has a 10 percent grade for 1.5 miles. An alternative route: From Portland on I-84 eastbound, drive to Exit 18/Lewis and Clark State Park. Take that exit and drive to East Historic Columbia River Highway and continue seven miles to the park on the right.

Contact: Crown Point RV Park, 503/695-5207, fax 503/695-3217.

2 OXBOW REGIONAL PARK

Scenic rating: 7

on the Sandy River

See map page 322

This 1,200-acre park along the Sandy River, a short distance from the Columbia River Gorge,
is a designated national scenic waterway. Fishing, nonmotorized boating, and swimming are permitted here. The water is usually calm, and canoes, kayaks, and rafts are allowed. About 200 acres of the park are old-growth Douglas fir forest. There are several miles of hiking trails.

RV sites, facilities: There are 67 sites for tents or RVs up to 35 feet (no hookups); some sites are pull-through. Two group camps are available for nonprofit groups only and can accommodate up to 35 and 250 people respectively. Picnic tables, fire pits, and barbecues are provided. Drinking water, flush and vault toilets, coin showers, firewood, a playground, and ranger-led campfire programs are available. Boat-launching facilities are nearby. Gates lock at sunset and open at 6:30 A.M. Services are approximately 10 miles away. Some facilities are wheelchair accessible. No pets are permitted.

Reservations, fees: Reservations are not accepted for individual sites but are required for group sites at 503/797-1850. Sites are $15 per night, plus $4 per night per additional vehicle. Group sites are $2 per person per night, with a minimum of $25 and $50 per night respectively. There is a park entrance fee of $4 per vehicle for the first day only. Open year-round.

Directions: From Portland on I-84, drive to Exit 17/Troutdale. Take that exit and drive on the frontage road for 0.5 mile to 257th Street. Turn right (south) on 257th Street and drive three miles to Division Street. Turn left and drive seven miles to the park entrance on the left.

Contact: Metro Regional Parks and Greenspaces, Oxbow Regional Park, 503/663-4708, www.metro-region.org.

3 AINSWORTH STATE PARK

Scenic rating: 8

along the Columbia River Gorge

See map page 322

This state park lies along the scenic Columbia River Gorge, home to the world's greatest concentration of high waterfalls, including famous Multnomah Falls. From the Nesmith Point Trail, enjoy a great view of St. Peter's Dome. A 1.3-mile trail leads from the campground to Horsetail Falls. Anglers should check out the Bonneville Fish Hatchery about five miles away.

RV sites, facilities: There are 32 sites with full hookups (30 amps) for RVs up to 60 feet and six walk-in sites. Picnic tables and fire grills are provided. Drinking water, restrooms with flush toilets and showers, garbage bins, a dump station, a playground, a camp host, an amphitheater with occasional interpretive and junior ranger programs, and firewood are available. Leashed pets are permitted.

Reservations, fees: Reservations are not accepted. Sites are $16 per night, $14 per night for walk-in tent sites, and $5 per night per additional vehicle. Some credit cards are accepted. Open mid-March–late October, weather permitting.

Directions: From Portland on I-84 eastbound, drive 35 miles to Exit 35. Turn southwest on the Columbia River Scenic Highway and continue a short distance to the park; the park is 17 miles east of Troutdale. An alternative route is to take the historic Columbia River Highway, a designated scenic highway, all the way from Portland (37 miles).

Contact: Ainsworth State Park, 503/695-2301 or 800/551-6949, www.oregonstateparks.org.

4 EAGLE CREEK

Scenic rating: 8

near the Columbia Wilderness in Mount Hood National Forest

See map page 322

Eagle Creek is the oldest Forest Service Camp in America. Set at 400 feet elevation among old-growth Douglas fir and hemlock, it makes a good base camp for a hiking trip. The Eagle Creek Trail leaves the campground and goes 13 miles to Wahtum Lake, where it intersects with the Pacific Crest Trail. A primitive campground sits at the 7.5-mile point. The upper seven miles of the trail pass through the Hatfield Wilderness.

RV sites, facilities: There are 20 sites for tents or RVs up to 20 feet (no hookups) and one

group site. Picnic tables and fire grills are provided. Drinking water, garbage bins, and flush toilets are available. A camp host is on-site. Boat docks and launching facilities are nearby on the Columbia River. Some facilities are wheelchair accessible. Leashed pets are permitted.

Reservations, fees: Reservations are not accepted for individual sites but are required for groups at 877/444-6777 or www.ReserveUSA.com ($9 reservation fee). Sites are $10 per night for sites, plus $5 per night per additional vehicle. Open mid-April–September.

Directions: From Portland, drive east on I-84 for 41 miles to Bonneville. Continue east for two miles to the campground.

Contact: Columbia River Gorge National Scenic Area, 541/308-1700, fax 541/386-1916, www.fs.fed.us/r6/columbia/forest/.

5 CASCADE LOCKS MARINE PARK

Scenic rating: 8

in Cascade Locks

See map page 322

This public riverfront park covers 23 acres and offers a museum and boat rides. The salmon fishing is excellent here. Stern-wheeler dinner cruises are available. Hiking trails and tennis courts are nearby; the Pacific Crest Trail is within one mile.

RV sites, facilities: There are 16 sites for tents or RVs of any length; some sites have partial hookups (30 amps). Picnic tables are provided. Drinking water, restrooms with flush toilets and showers, a dump station, boat docks, launching facilities, a picnic area, and a playground are available. A camp host is on-site. Propane gas, gasoline, a store, a café, a coin laundry, and ice are within one mile. Leashed pets are permitted.

Reservations, fees: Reservations are not accepted. Sites are $15–25 per night. Some credit cards are accepted. Open year-round, with limited winter facilities.

Directions: From Portland, drive east on I-84 for 44 miles to Cascade Locks. Take Exit 44/ Cascade Locks to Wanapa Street. Turn left and

OREGON

drive 0.5 mile to the sign for the park on the left (well signed).

Contact: Port of Cascade Locks, Cascade Locks Marine Park, 541/374-8619, fax 541/374-8428, www.portofcascadelocks.org.

6 KOA CASCADE LOCKS

Scenic rating: 5

near the Columbia River
See map page 322

This KOA is a good layover spot for RVers touring the Columbia River corridor. The campground offers level, shaded RV sites and grassy tent sites. A pancake breakfast is available on weekends during the summer season. Nearby recreation options include bike trails, hiking trails, and tennis courts. The 200-acre Cascade Locks Marine Park is close by and offers everything from museums to boat trips.

RV sites, facilities: There are 33 sites for tents, 78 sites with full or partial hookups (30 and 50 amps) for RVs of any length, nine cabins, and two cottages. Most RV sites are pull-through. Picnic tables and fire pits are provided. Restrooms have flush toilets and showers. Drinking water, propane gas, a dump station, firewood, a spa, cable TV, wireless Internet service, a recreation hall, a convenience store, a coin laundry, ice, a playground, bicycle rentals, and a heated seasonal swimming pool are available. A café is within one mile. Some facilities are wheelchair accessible. Leashed pets are permitted, with certain restrictions.

Reservations, fees: Reservations are accepted at 800/562-8698. Sites are $23–33 per night, plus $3 per person per night for more than two people. Some credit cards are accepted. Open February–November.

Directions: From Portland, drive east on I-84 for 44 miles to Cascade Locks and Exit 44. Take that exit to Forest Lane. Turn east on Forest Lane and drive one mile to the campground on the left.

Contact: KOA Cascade Locks, 541/374-8668, www.koa.com.

7 WYETH

Scenic rating: 5

on Gordon Creek in Mount Hood National Forest
See map page 322

Wyeth makes a good layover spot for Columbia River corridor cruisers. The camp (100 feet elevation) borders Gordon Creek, near the Columbia River. There are many recreation options nearby, including biking, boating, fishing, and hiking.

RV sites, facilities: There are 14 sites for tents or RVs up to 30 feet (no hookups) and three group sites. Fire grills and picnic tables are provided. Drinking water and flush toilets are available. A camp host is on-site. Leashed pets are permitted.

Reservations, fees: Reservations are not accepted. Sites are $10 per night, plus $5 per night per additional vehicle. Group sites are $15 per night. Open April–mid-October.

Directions: From Portland, drive east on I-84 for 44 miles to Cascade Locks. Continue east on I-84 for seven miles to Wyeth and Exit 51. Turn right and drive 0.25 mile to the campground entrance.

Contact: Columbia River Gorge National Scenic Area, 541/308-1700, fax 541/386-1916, www.fs.fed.us/r6/columbia/forest/.

8 VIENTO STATE PARK

Scenic rating: 8

along the Columbia River Gorge
See map page 322

This park along the Columbia River Gorge offers scenic hiking trails and some of the best windsurfing in the Gorge. Just 12 miles to the east, old U.S. 30 skirts the Columbia River, offering a picturesque drive. Viento has a day-use picnic area right next to a babbling creek. Look for weekend interpretive programs during the summer. There are several other day-use state parks along I-84 just west of Viento, including Seneca Fouts, Vinzenz Lausmann, and Wygant. All offer quality hiking trails and scenic views.

RV sites, facilities: There are 56 sites with partial hookups (20 and 30 amps) for RVs up to 30 feet, with some sites accessible for RVs up to 40 feet, and 18 tent sites. Picnic tables and fire grills are provided. Drinking water, garbage bins, restrooms with flush toilets and showers, firewood, and a playground are available. Some facilities are wheelchair accessible. Leashed pets are permitted.

Reservations, fees: Reservations are not accepted. Tent sites are $14 per night, RV sites are $16 per night, and it costs $5 per night per additional vehicle. Some credit cards are accepted. Open early May–October, weather permitting.

Directions: From Portland, drive east on I-84 for 56 miles to Exit 56 (eight miles west of Hood River). Take Exit 56 and drive to the park entrance. The park flanks I-84.

Contact: Viento State Park, 541/374-8811; Oregon State Parks, 800/551-6949, www.oregonstateparks.org.

9 TUCKER COUNTY PARK

Scenic rating: 6

on the Hood River

See map page 322

This county park along the banks of the Hood River is just far enough out of the way to be missed by most of the tourist traffic. Many people who choose this county park come for the windsurfing. Other recreation opportunities include rafting and kayaking. Fishing is not allowed at the park.

RV sites, facilities: There are 14 sites for tents or RVs up to 30 feet with partial hookups (30 amps) and 80 tent sites. Picnic tables and fire rings are provided. Drinking water, restrooms with flush toilets and showers, firewood, and a playground are available. A store, a café, a coin laundry, gasoline, and ice are within two miles. Some facilities are wheelchair accessible. Leashed pets are permitted.

Reservations, fees: Reservations are not accepted. Sites are $18–19 per night, and it costs $8

per night per additional tent and $5 per night per additional vehicle. Open April–October.

Directions: From Portland, turn east on I-84 and drive about 65 miles to the town of Hood River and Exit 62. Take the exit and drive east on Cascade Street, continuing to 13th Street (first light). Turn right (south) and drive through and out of town; 13th Street becomes Tucker Road and then Dee Highway (Highway 281). Follow the signs to Parkdale. The park is four miles out of town on the right.

Contact: Hood River County Parks, 541/387-6889 or 541/386-4477, fax 541/386-6325.

10 MEMALOOSE STATE PARK

Scenic rating: 7

in the Columbia River Gorge

See map page 322

This park borrows its name from nearby Memaloose Island, which ancient Native Americans used as a sacred burial ground. Situated along the hottest part of the scenic Columbia River Gorge, it makes a prime layover spot for campers cruising the Oregon-Washington border. Nature programs and interpretive events are also held here. This popular camp receives a good deal of traffic, so plan on arriving early to claim a spot even if you have a reservation.

RV sites, facilities: There are 44 sites with full hookups (30 amps) for RVs up to 60 feet and 66 tent sites. Picnic tables and fire grills are provided. Drinking water, garbage bins, restrooms with flush toilets and showers, a dump station, and firewood are available. Leashed pets are permitted.

Reservations, fees: Reservations are accepted at 800/452-5687 or www.oregonstateparks.org ($6 reservation fee). Sites are $16–20 per night, plus $5 per night per additional vehicle. Some credit cards are accepted. Open mid-March–October.

Directions: This park is accessible only to westbound traffic on I-84. From The Dalles, drive west on I-84 for 11 miles to the signed turnoff. (The park is about 75 miles east of Portland.)

OREGON

OREGON

Contact: Memaloose State Park, 541/478-3008; Oregon State Parks, 800/551-6949, www.oregonstateparks.org.

11 LONE PINE RV PARK

Scenic rating: 7

near the Columbia River
See map page 322

This private park isn't far from the Columbia River, where boating, fishing, and swimming are options. The area gets hot weather and occasional winds shooting through the river canyon during summer. Nearby recreation possibilities include an 18-hole golf course and tennis courts.

RV sites, facilities: There are 22 pull-through sites with full hookups for RVs of any length. Restrooms have flush toilets and showers. Cable TV, a café, a coin laundry, ice, and a playground are available. Propane gas and a dump station are within one mile. Boat docks and launching facilities are nearby. Leashed pets are permitted.

Reservations, fees: Reservations are accepted. Sites are $22–25 per night. Open mid-April–September.

Directions: From Portland, turn east on I-84 and drive about 90 miles to The Dalles and Exit 87. Take Exit 87 to U.S. 197 and drive less than a quarter mile to the park at 335 U.S. 197.

Contact: Lone Pine RV Park, 541/506-3755.

12 DESCHUTES RIVER STATE RECREATION AREA

Scenic rating: 7

on the Deschutes River
See map page 322   BEST (

This tree-shaded park along the Deschutes River in the Deschutes Canyon offers bicycling and hiking trails and good steelhead fishing in season. The river-level Atiyeh Deschutes River Trail is a favorite jaunt for hikers. A small day-use state park called Heritage Landing, which

has a boat ramp and restroom facilities, is across the river. Good rafting is a bonus from above the state recreation area to here. For 25 miles upstream, the river is mostly inaccessible by car. Many anglers launch boats here and then go upstream to steelhead fishing grounds. Note that boat fishing is not allowed in the Deschutes River; you must wade into the river or fish from shore. However, anglers can launch here and fish from their boats in the Columbia River.

RV sites, facilities: There are 35 sites for tents or RVs of any length (no hookups) and 34 sites for tents or RVs of any length with partial hookups (20, 30, and 50 amps). There are also four group areas for RVs and tents, which can hold up to 25 people and five RVs each. Picnic tables and fire grills are provided. Drinking water, garbage bins, and flush toilets are available. Leashed pets are permitted.

Reservations, fees: Reservations are accepted at 800/452-5687 or www.oregonstateparks.org ($6 reservation fee). Sites without hookups are $5–8 per night, sites with partial hookups are $12–16, and it's $5 per night per additional vehicle. Group sites are $41–61 per night. Some credit cards are accepted. Open year-round, with limited services November–March.

Directions: From Portland, turn east on I-84 and drive about 90 miles to The Dalles. Continue east on I-84 for 12 miles to Exit 97/ Deschutes State Recreation Area, turn right, and drive 50 feet to Biggs-Rufus Highway. Turn left and drive about three miles, cross the Deschutes River, and turn right to the campground entrance.

Contact: Deschutes River State Recreation Area, 541/739-2322; Oregon State Parks, 800/452-5687, www.oregonstateparks.org.

13 LE PAGE PARK

Scenic rating: 6

on the John Day River
See map page 322

Half of the campsites are adjacent to the John Day River, and the other half are on the opposite side of the road at this partially shaded campground. The John Day River feeds into the Columbia just one-eighth of a mile north of the campground. Rattlesnakes are occasionally seen in the area but are not abundant. Anglers come for the smallmouth bass and catfish during the summer. The day-use area has a swimming beach, a lawn, a boat launch, and boat docks. There are several other campgrounds nearby.

RV sites, facilities: There are 22 sites for tents or RVs up to 40 feet with partial hookups (30 amps); some sites are pull-through. There is also a grassy area for tents (weekends only). Picnic tables and fire pits are provided. Drinking water, restrooms with flush toilets and showers, and pit toilets are available. A boat ramp, docks, a dump station, and garbage containers are also available. Food, gasoline, and coin laundry are available five miles away in the town of Rufus. Leashed pets are permitted.

Reservations, fees: Reservations are accepted at 877/444-6777 or www.ReserveUSA.com ($9 reservation fee). RV sites are $17–18 per night, tent sites are $12 per night, and it costs $5 per night per additional vehicle. Some credit cards are accepted. Open April–October.

Directions: From Portland on I-84, drive east 120 miles (30 miles past The Dalles) to Exit 114, the John Day River Recreation Area. The campground is just off I-84.

Contact: Army Corps of Engineers, Portland District, 503/808-5150, fax 503/808-4515; Le Page Park, 541/739-2713.

14 LOST LAKE RESORT

🚶 🚲 🛶 🎣 ⛴ 🐕 ♿ 🚐 ⛺

Scenic rating: 9

on Lost Lake, Mount Hood National Forest, Hood River District

See map page 322

Only nonmotorized boats are allowed on this clear, 240-acre lake set against the Cascade Range. The campground is nestled in an old-growth forest of cedar, Douglas fir, and hemlock trees at 3,200 feet elevation. Many sites

have a lake view, and the campground affords a great view of Mount Hood.

RV sites, facilities: There are 125 sites for tents or RVs up to 32 feet (no hookups), and three group sites can accommodate up to 15 people and five vehicles each. Picnic tables and fire rings with grills are provided. Drinking water, vault toilets, garbage containers, a dump station, and a covered picnic shelter are available. Cabins, a grocery store, showers, beach picnic areas, a boat launch, and boat rentals are nearby. Some facilities are wheelchair accessible, including a barrier-free boat launch and fishing pier, as well as 3.5 miles of barrier-free trails. Leashed pets are permitted.

Reservations, fees: Reservations are not accepted for single sites but are required for the group sites at 541/386-6366. Sites are $18–25 per night, plus $6 per night per additional vehicle. The group sites are $65–100 per night. Some credit cards are accepted. Open mid-May–mid-October, weather permitting.

Directions: From Portland, drive 62 miles east on I-84 to the city of Hood River. Take Exit 62/Westcliff to Cascade Street. Drive east on Cascade Street to 13th Street. Turn right on 13th Street and drive through Hood River Heights. The road turns into Dee Highway. Continue seven miles to Lost Lake Road/Forest Road 1340. Turn right and drive seven miles to the campground.

Contact: Mount Hood National Forest, Hood River Ranger District, 541/352-6002, fax 541/352-7365; Lost Lake Resort, 541/386-6366.

15 EIGHTMILE CROSSING

🚶 🚲 🛶 🐕 ♿ 🚐 ⛺

Scenic rating: 7

on Eightmile Creek in Mount Hood National Forest

See map page 322

This campground sits at an elevation of 4,200 feet along Eightmile Creek. Although pretty and shaded, with sites scattered along the banks of the creek, it gets relatively little camping pressure. From the day-use area, you have access to a nice hiking trail that runs along Eightmile Creek. In addition, a 0.75-mile wheelchair-accessible trail links Eightmile Campground to Lower Crossing Campground. The fishing can be good here, so bring your gear.

RV sites, facilities: There are 21 sites for tents or RVs up to 30 feet (no hookups). Picnic tables and fire grills are provided. Vault toilets are available. No drinking water is available, and garbage must be packed out. Leashed pets are permitted.

Reservations, fees: Reservations are not accepted. Sites are $10 per night. Open June–mid-October, weather permitting.

Directions: From Portland, turn east on I-84 and drive about 90 miles to Exit 87. Take Exit 87 and turn south on U.S. 197; drive 13 miles to Dufur and Dufur Valley Road. Turn right on Dufur Valley Road and drive west for 12 miles to Forest Road 44. Continue west on Forest Road 44 for four miles to Forest Road 4430. Turn right and drive 0.5 mile to the campground.

Contact: Mount Hood National Forest, Barlow Ranger District, 541/467-2291, fax 541/467-2271.

16 McNEIL

Scenic rating: 5

on the Clear Fork of the Sandy River in Mount Hood National Forest

See map page 322

This campground (2,040 feet elevation) is in Old Maid Flat, a special geological area along the Clear Fork of the Sandy River. There's a good view of Mount Hood from the campground entrance. Several trails nearby provide access to the wilderness backcountry. See a U.S. Forest Service map for details.

RV sites, facilities: There are 34 sites for tents or RVs up to 22 feet (no hookups). Picnic tables and vault toilets are provided. There is no drinking water. Leashed pets are permitted.

Reservations, fees: Reservations are not accepted. Sites are $12 per night, plus $6 per

night per additional vehicle. Open May–late September, weather permitting.

Directions: From Portland, drive 40 miles east on U.S. 26 to Zigzag. Turn left on County Road 18/East Lolo Pass Road and drive 4.5 miles to Forest Road 1825. Turn right on Forest Road 1825, drive less than one mile, bear right onto a bridge to stay on Forest Road 1825, and drive 0.25 mile to the campground on the left.

Contact: Mount Hood National Forest, Zigzag Ranger District, 503/622-3191, fax 503/622-5622.

17 LOST CREEK

Scenic rating: 8

on Lost Creek in Mount Hood National Forest

See map page 322

This campground near McNeil has some of the same opportunities. Set in a cool, lush area on a creek at 2,600 feet elevation, it's barrier-free and offers an interpretive nature trail about one mile long as well as a wheelchair-accessible fishing pier.

RV sites, facilities: There are 16 sites for tents or RVs up to 22 feet (no hookups); some are walk-in sites. Picnic tables and fire grills are provided. Drinking water, garbage service, and vault toilets are available. Some facilities are wheelchair accessible. Leashed pets are permitted.

Reservations, fees: Reservations are accepted at 877/444-6777 or www.ReserveUSA.com ($9 reservation fee). Sites are $16 for a single site, $32 for a double site, and $8–9 per night per additional vehicle. Open May–late September.

Directions: From Portland, drive 40 miles east on U.S. 26 to Zigzag. Turn left (northeast) on County Road 18/East Lolo Pass Road and drive 4.5 miles to Forest Road 1825. Turn right and drive two miles to a fork. Bear right and drive 0.25 mile to the campground on the right.

Contact: Mount Hood National Forest, Zigzag Ranger District, 503/622-3191, fax 503/622-5622.

18 MILO McIVER STATE PARK

Scenic rating: 7

on the Clackamas River
See map page 322

Though only 45 minutes from Portland, this park is far enough off the beaten track to provide a feeling of separation from the metropolitan area. It sits along the banks of the Clackamas River and has a boat ramp. There is fishing for salmon and steelhead in season; check current regulations. Trails for hiking are available, and a 4.5-mile equestrian trail is also accessible; bicycles are not allowed on trails. A fish hatchery is a nearby point of interest. Every April, actors participate in a Civil War reenactment here.

RV sites, facilities: There are nine tent sites and 44 sites with partial hookups (30 amps) for RVs up to 50 feet, one hike-in/bike-in site, and three group tent areas for up to 50 people each. Picnic tables and fire grills are provided. Drinking water, garbage bins, restrooms with flush toilets and showers, a dump station, dog run, picnic shelters, and firewood are available. Boat-launching facilities (canoes, inflatables, and kayaks) and a 27-hole disc golf course are nearby. Group facilities are available. Some facilities are wheelchair accessible. Leashed pets are permitted.

Reservations, fees: Reservations are accepted at 800/452-5687 or www.oregonstateparks.org ($6 reservation fee). Tent sites are $8 per night, RV sites are $17 per night, and it's $5 per night per additional vehicle. Hike-in/bike-in sites are $4 per person per night, and group sites are $64 per night for each increment of up to 25 people. Some credit cards are accepted. Open mid-March–October.

Directions: From Portland, drive east on U.S. 26 to Gresham. Continue 11 miles to Sandy and Highway 211. Turn right (south) and drive six miles to a junction. Turn south (still Highway 211) and drive one mile to Hayden Road. Turn right and drive one mile to Springwater Road. Turn right and drive one mile to the park on the right.

Contact: Milo McIver State Park, 503/630-6147, 503/630-7150, or 800/551-6949.

19 TOLL GATE

Scenic rating: 8

on the Zigzag River in Mount Hood National Forest
See map page 322

This shady campground along the banks of the Zigzag River near Rhododendron is extremely popular, and finding a site on a summer weekend can be next to impossible. Luckily, you can make a reservation. There are numerous hiking trails in the area. The nearest one leads east for several miles along the river. The campground features a historic Civilian Conservation Corps shelter from the 1930s, which can be used by campers for day use.

RV sites, facilities: There are 15 sites for tents or RVs up to 16 feet (no hookups). Picnic tables and fire grills are provided. Drinking water, garbage service, and vault toilets are available. Some facilities are wheelchair accessible. Leashed pets are permitted.

Reservations, fees: Reservations are accepted at 877/444-6777 or www.ReserveUSA.com ($9 reservation fee). Sites are $16–18 per night, plus $8–9 per night per additional vehicle. Open late May–late September, weather permitting.

Directions: From Portland, drive east on U.S. 26 for 40 miles to Zigzag. Continue 2.5 miles southeast on U.S. 26 to the campground entrance.

Contact: Mount Hood National Forest, Zigzag Ranger District, 503/622-3191, fax 503/622-5622.

20 GREEN CANYON

Scenic rating: 8

on the Salmon River in Mount Hood National Forest
See map page 322

Few out-of-towners know about this winner. But the locals do, and they keep the place hopping in the summer. The camp sits at 1,600 feet elevation along the banks of the Salmon River. A long trail cuts through the area and parallels the river, passing through a magnificent old-growth forest. See a U.S. Forest Service map for details.

OREGON

OREGON

RV sites, facilities: There are 15 sites for tents or RVs up to 22 feet (no hookups). Picnic tables, garbage service, and fire grills are provided. Vault toilets are available. Drinking water is intermittently available. A store, a café, and ice are within five miles. Some facilities are wheelchair accessible. Leashed pets are permitted.

Reservations, fees: Reservations are not accepted. Sites are $14–16 per night, plus $7–8 per night per additional vehicle. Open May–September, weather permitting.

Directions: From Portland, drive east on U.S. 26 for 39 miles to Forest Road 2618 (Salmon River Road) near Zigzag. Turn right and drive 4.5 miles to the campground on the right.

Contact: Mount Hood National Forest, Zigzag Ranger District, 503/622-3191, fax 503/622-5622.

21 CAMP CREEK

Scenic rating: 8

near the Zigzag River in Mount Hood
National Forest

See map page 322

This campground (2,200 feet elevation) sits along Camp Creek, not far from the Zigzag River. It looks similar to Toll Gate, but it's larger and farther from the road. A hiking trail runs through camp and along the river; another one leads south to Still Creek. This campground, along with Toll Gate to the west, is very popular, and you'll probably need a reservation.

RV sites, facilities: There are 25 sites for tents or RVs up to 22 feet (no hookups). Picnic tables and fire grills are provided. Drinking water, vault toilets, and garbage bins are available. Some facilities are wheelchair accessible. Leashed pets are permitted.

Reservations, fees: Reservations are accepted at 877/444-6777 or www.ReserveUSA.com ($9 reservation fee). Sites are $16–18 per night, $32 for a double site, and $8–9 per night per additional vehicle. Open May–September, weather permitting.

Directions: From Portland, drive east on U.S. 26 for 40 miles to Zigzag. Continue southeast on U.S. 26 for about four miles to the camp on the right.

Contact: Mount Hood National Forest, Zigzag Ranger District, 503/622-3191, fax 503/622-5622.

22 NOTTINGHAM

Scenic rating: 7

near the East Fork of the Hood River

See map page 322

This campground, at 3,300 feet in elevation on the East Fork of the Hood River, has a variety of shady and sunny spots. The primary tree cover is Douglas fir and ponderosa pine. The Tamanawas Falls Trail (near Sherwood Camp) is three miles away, and the Gumjuwac Trail is 1.5 miles north. Fishing is merely fair because of the swift water and lack of pools.

RV sites, facilities: There are 23 sites for tents or RVs up to 32 feet (no hookups). Picnic tables and fire rings are provided. Vault toilets are available. There is no drinking water. Garbage must be packed out. Leashed pets are permitted.

Reservations, fees: Reservations are not accepted. Sites are $10 per night, plus $3 per night per additional vehicle. Open May–October, weather permitting.

Directions: From Mount Hood, drive south on Highway 35 for 13 miles to the camp on the right.

Contact: Mount Hood National Forest, Hood River Ranger District, 541/352-6002, fax 541/352-7365.

23 STILL CREEK

Scenic rating: 6

on Still Creek in Mount Hood National Forest

See map page 322

This primitive camp, shaded primarily by fir and hemlock, sits along Still Creek where the creek pours off Mount Hood's south slope.

Adjacent to Summit Meadows and the site of a pioneer gravesite from the Oregon Trail days, it's a great place for mountain views, sunsets, and wildlife. Anglers should bring along their rods: The fishing in Still Creek can be excellent. The camp sits at 3,600 feet elevation.

RV sites, facilities: There are 27 sites for tents or RVs up to 16 feet (no hookups). Picnic tables and fire grills are provided. Vault toilets, drinking water, and garbage service are available. Some facilities are wheelchair accessible. Leashed pets are permitted.

Reservations, fees: Reservations are accepted at 877/444-6777 or www.ReserveUSA.com ($9 reservation fee). Sites are $16–18 per night, plus $8–9 per night per additional vehicle. Open mid-June–mid-September, weather permitting.

Directions: From Portland, drive 55 miles east on U.S. 26 to Government Camp. Continue east on U.S. 26 for one mile to Forest Road 2650. Turn right and drive south for 500 yards to the campground.

Contact: Mount Hood National Forest, Zigzag Ranger District, 503/622-3191, fax 503/622-5622, www.oregonstateparks.org.

Deschutes River Road. The hardest part is getting used to the freight trains that rumble through the canyon at night.

RV sites, facilities: There are 15 sites for tents or RVs up to 30 feet (no hookups) and two group sites for up to 16 people. Picnic tables, garbage bins, and fire grills are provided. Drinking water and vault toilets are available. Boat-launching facilities are nearby. Some facilities are wheelchair accessible. Leashed pets are permitted.

Reservations, fees: Reservations are not accepted. Sites are $8–12 per night, plus $2 per night for an additional vehicle. Group sites are $25–35 per night. Open year-round, with a 14-day stay limit.

Directions: From Portland, drive east on U.S. 84 to The Dalles and Highway 197. Turn south and drive to Maupin. Continue through Maupin, cross the bridge, and within a mile look for Deschutes River Road on your left. Turn left on Deschutes River Road and drive 21 miles northeast to the campground.

Contact: Bureau of Land Management, Prineville District, 541/416-6700, fax 541/416-6798.

24 BEAVERTAIL

Scenic rating: 6

on the Deschutes River
See map page 322

This isolated campground is at an elevation of 2,900 feet along the banks of the Deschutes River, one of the classic steelhead streams in the Pacific Northwest. The camp provides fishing and rafting options. The open landscape affords canyon views. This is my favorite put-in spot for a drift boat for fishing float trips on the Deschutes. I've made the trip from Beavertail to the mouth of the Deschutes, ideal in four days, camping at BLM boat-in sites along the river and fly-fishing for steelhead. A boating pass is required to float the river. There are 12 other BLM campgrounds along upper and lower

25 PROMONTORY

Scenic rating: 7

on North Fork Reservoir
See map page 322

This Portland General Electric camp on North Fork Reservoir is part of a large recreation area and park. The reservoir, actually a dammed-up overflow of the Clackamas River, encompasses 350 acres. The water is calm and ideal for boating, and the trout fishing is excellent. A trail connects the campground to the marina. A one-acre lake is available for children's fishing.

RV sites, facilities: There are 40 sites for tents or RVs up to 32 feet (no hookups) and 10 yomes (which are a cross between a yurt and a dome). There is also a group area for up to 35 people for tents or small RVs. There are

OREGON

no RV hookups. Picnic tables and fire rings are provided. Restrooms have flush toilets and showers. Garbage bins, limited groceries, ice, a playground, horseshoes, covered picnic shelters, and snacks are available. A fish-cleaning station, a fishing pier, a children's fishing pond, a boat ramp, a dock, and boat rentals are also on-site. Some facilities, including the boat ramp and the fishing pier, are wheelchair accessible. Leashed pets are permitted.

Reservations, fees: Reservations are accepted at 503/630-7229 or by www.portlandgeneral.com. Sites are $16 per night, $25 per night for a yome. Some credit cards are accepted. Open mid-May–September.

Directions: From Portland, drive east on U.S. 26 to Gresham. Continue 11 miles to Sandy and Highway 211. Turn right (south) and drive six miles to a junction. Turn south (still Highway 211) and drive six miles to Estacada. Continue south on Highway 224 and drive seven miles to the campground on the right. The route is well signed.

Contact: Portland General Electric, 503/464-8515, fax 503/464-2944; store and marina, 503/630-5152, www.portlandgeneral.com.

26 LAZY BEND

Scenic rating: 8

on the Clackamas River in Mount Hood National Forest

See map page 322

This campground is at 800 feet elevation along the banks of the Clackamas River near the large North Fork Reservoir. It's far enough off the highway to provide a secluded, primitive feeling, though it fills quickly on weekends and holidays. There's only catch-and-release fishing in the Clackamas.

RV sites, facilities: There are 21 sites for tents or RVs up to 16 feet (no hookups). Picnic tables, garbage service, and fireplaces are provided. Drinking water and flush toilets are available. Leashed pets are permitted.

Reservations, fees: Reservations are accepted

at 877/444-6777 or www.ReserveUSA.com ($9 reservation fee). Sites are $16 per night, plus $8 per night per additional vehicle. Open late April–early September, weather permitting.

Directions: From Portland, drive south on U.S. 205 to the junction with Highway 24. Take the Highway 224/Estacada exit and turn left (south) onto Highway 224. Drive approximately 13 miles to Estacada. Continue south on Highway 224 for 10.5 miles to the campground on the right.

Contact: Mount Hood National Forest, Clackamas River Ranger District, 503/630-6861, fax 503/630-2299.

27 CARTER BRIDGE

Scenic rating: 5

on the Clackamas River in Mount Hood National Forest

See map page 322

This small, flat campground is popular with anglers. The Clackamas River flows along one end, and the other end borders the highway, with the attendant traffic noise.

RV sites, facilities: There are 15 sites for tents or RVs up to 28 feet (no hookups). Picnic tables and fire pits are provided. Drinking water, vault toilets, and garbage bins are available. Some facilities are wheelchair accessible. Leashed pets are permitted.

Reservations, fees: Reservations are not accepted. Sites are $14 per night, plus $7 per night per additional vehicle. Open late May–early September, weather permitting.

Directions: From Portland, drive south on U.S. 205 to the junction with Highway 24. Take the Highway 224/Estacada exit and turn left (south) onto Highway 224. Drive approximately 13 miles to Estacada. Continue south on Highway 224 for 15.2 miles to the campground on the left.

Contact: Mount Hood National Forest, Clackamas River Ranger District, 503/630-6861, fax 503/630-2299.

28 LOCKABY

Scenic rating: 6

on the Clackamas River in Mount Hood National Forest

See map page 322

This campground sits at an elevation of 900 feet along the banks of the Clackamas River, next to Armstrong Campground. Fishing in the Clackamas River is catch-and-release only.

RV sites, facilities: There are 30 sites for tents or RVs up to 16 feet (no hookups). Picnic tables, fireplaces, drinking water, garbage service, and vault toilets are available. Leashed pets are permitted.

Reservations, fees: Reservations are accepted at 877/444-6777 or www.ReserveUSA.com ($9 reservation fee). Sites are $16 per night, plus $8 per night per additional vehicle. Open late May–early September.

Directions: From Portland, drive south on U.S. 205 to the junction with Highway 24. Take the Highway 224/Estacada exit and turn left (south) onto Highway 224. Drive approximately 13 miles to Estacada. Continue south on Highway 224 for 15.3 miles to the campground on the left.

Contact: Mount Hood National Forest, Clackamas River Ranger District, 503/630-6861, fax 503/630-2299.

29 ROARING RIVER

Scenic rating: 8

on the Roaring River in Mount Hood National Forest

See map page 323

This campground, set among old-growth cedars at the confluence of the Roaring and Clackamas Rivers at an elevation of 1,000 feet, has access to the Dry Ridge Trail. The trail starts in camp, and it's a butt-kicker of an uphill climb. Several other trails into the adjacent roadless area are accessible from camp. See a U.S. Forest Service map for details.

RV sites, facilities: There are 19 sites for tents or RVs up to 16 feet (no hookups). Picnic tables and fireplaces are provided. Garbage service, drinking water, and vault toilets are available. Leashed pets are permitted.

Reservations, fees: Reservations are accepted at 877/444-6777 or www.ReserveUSA.com ($9 reservation fee). Sites are $14 per night, plus $7 per night per additional vehicle. Open mid-May–mid-September, weather permitting.

Directions: From Portland, drive south on U.S. 205 to the junction with Highway 24. Take the Highway 224/Estacada exit and turn left (south) onto Highway 224. Drive approximately 13 miles to Estacada. Continue south on Highway 224 for 18 miles to the campground on the left.

Contact: Mount Hood National Forest, Clackamas River Ranger District, 503/630-6861, fax 503/630-2299.

30 LAKE HARRIET

Scenic rating: 5

on Lake Harriet in Mount Hood National Forest

See map page 323

Formed by a dam on the Oak Grove Fork of the Clackamas River, this little lake is a popular spot during the summer. Rowboats and boats with small motors are permitted, but only nonmotorized boats are encouraged. The lake is stocked regularly and can provide good fishing for a variety of trout, including brook, brown, cutthroat, and rainbow. Anglers often stand shoulder to shoulder in summer.

RV sites, facilities: There are 13 sites for tents or RVs up to 30 feet (no hookups). Picnic tables and fire grills are provided. Drinking water and vault toilets are available. Garbage service is provided in the summer. A fishing pier and boat-launching facilities are on the lake. Some facilities are wheelchair accessible. Leashed pets are permitted.

Reservations, fees: Reservations are accepted at 877/444-6777 or www.ReserveUSA.com ($9 reservation fee). Sites are $16 per night, plus $7 per night per additional vehicle. Open year-round, with limited winter services.

Directions: From Portland, drive south on U.S. 205 to the junction with Highway 224/Estacada. Take the exit and turn left onto

Highway 224, heading south. Drive approximately 13 miles to Estacada. Continue south on Highway 224 and drive 27 miles to Forest Road 57. Turn east and drive 7.5 miles to Forest Road 4630. Turn left and drive two miles to the campground on the left.

Contact: Mount Hood National Forest, Clackamas River Ranger District, 503/630-6861, fax 503/630-2299.

31 GONE CREEK

Scenic rating: 8

on Timothy Lake in Mount Hood National Forest
See map page 323

This campground, along the south shore of Timothy Lake at 3,200 feet elevation, is one of five camps at the lake. Timothy Lake provides good fishing for brook trout, cutthroat trout, kokanee salmon, and rainbow trout. Boats with motors are allowed, but a 10-mph speed limit keeps it quiet. Several trails in the area—including the Pacific Crest Trail—provide access to small mountain lakes.

RV sites, facilities: There are 50 sites for tents or RVs up to 32 feet (no hookups). Picnic tables and fire grills are provided. Drinking water, garbage service, vault toilets, and firewood are available. A boat ramp is nearby. Some facilities are wheelchair accessible. Leashed pets are permitted.

Reservations, fees: Reservations are accepted at 877/444-6777 or www.ReserveUSA.com ($9 reservation fee). Sites are $16–18 per night, plus $8–9 per night per additional vehicle. Open mid-May–mid-September, weather permitting.

Directions: From Portland, drive on U.S. 26 for 55 miles (just past the town of Government Camp) to the junction with Highway 35. Bear southeast, staying on U.S. 26, and drive 15 miles to Forest Road 42 (Skyline Road). Turn right and drive eight miles to Forest Road 57. Turn right and drive one mile west to the campground on the right.

Contact: Mount Hood National Forest, Zigzag Ranger District, 503/622-3191, fax 503/622-5622.

32 OAK FORK

Scenic rating: 8

on Timothy Lake in Mount Hood National Forest
See map page 323

Heavy timber and bear grass surround this forested camp along the south shore of Timothy Lake. It's just east of Hoodview and Gone Creek campgrounds at an elevation of 3,200 feet. Refer to the *Hoodview* and *Gone Creek* listings in this chapter for more details.

RV sites, facilities: There are 47 sites for tents or RVs up to 32 feet (no hookups). Picnic tables and fire grills are provided. Drinking water, firewood, and vault toilets are available. A boat ramp and launching facilities are nearby; the speed limit on the lake is 10 mph. Some facilities are wheelchair accessible. Leashed pets are permitted.

Reservations, fees: Reservations are accepted at 877/444-6777 or www.ReserveUSA.com ($9 reservation fee). Sites are $16–18 per night, plus $8–9 per night per additional vehicle. Open June–mid-September, weather permitting.

Directions: From Portland, turn east on U.S. 26 and drive 57 miles (just past the town of Government Camp) to the junction with Highway 35. Bear southeast, staying on U.S. 26, and drive 15 miles to Forest Road 42 (Skyline Road). Turn right and drive eight miles to Forest Road 57. Turn right and drive three miles to the camp on the right.

Contact: Mount Hood National Forest, Zigzag Ranger District, 503/622-3191, fax 503/622-5622.

33 PINE POINT

Scenic rating: 8

on Timothy Lake in Mount Hood National Forest
See map page 323

One of five camps on Timothy Lake, this spot sits at an elevation of 3,200 feet on the southwest shore and has lake access and more open vegetation than the other Timothy Lake campgrounds. The trail that leads around the lake and to the Pacific Crest Trail passes along this campground. (See the *Gone Creek* listing in this chapter for boating and fishing details.)

RV sites, facilities: There are 25 sites for tents or RVs up to 32 feet (no hookups) (10 single sites, 10 double sites, and five group sites). Picnic tables, garbage service, and fire grills are provided. Drinking water, vault toilets, and firewood are available. A boat ramp, launching facilities, and fishing pier are nearby; the speed limit on the lake is 10 mph. Some facilities are wheelchair accessible, including a fishing pier. Leashed pets are permitted.

Reservations, fees: Reservations are accepted at 877/444-6777 or www.ReserveUSA.com ($9 reservation fee). The fees are $16–18 per night for a single site, $32 per night for a double site, plus $8–9 per night per additional vehicle; group sites are $48 per night. Open late May–mid-September, weather permitting.

Directions: From Portland, turn east on U.S. 26 and drive 57 miles (just past the town of Government Camp) to the junction with Highway 35. Bear southeast, staying on U.S. 26, and drive 15 miles to Forest Road 42 (Skyline Road). Turn right and drive eight miles to Forest Road 57. Turn right and drive four miles to the park on the right.

Contact: Mount Hood National Forest, Zigzag Ranger District, 503/622-3191, fax 503/622-5622.

34 TRILLIUM LAKE

Scenic rating: 9

on Trillium Lake in Mount Hood National Forest

See map page 322

This campground (3,600 feet elevation) hugs the shores of Trillium Lake, which is about half a mile long and a quarter mile wide. Fishing is good in the evening here, and the nearby boat ramp makes this an ideal camp for anglers. The lake is great for canoes, rafts, and small rowboats. Trillium Lake is an extremely popular vacation destination, so expect plenty of company. Reservations are highly recommended.

RV sites, facilities: There are 57 sites for tents or RVs up to 40 feet (no hookups). Picnic tables and fire grills are provided. Vault toilets and drinking water are available. Boat docks and launching facilities are available on the lake, but no motors are allowed. Some facilities are wheelchair accessible. Leashed pets are permitted.

Reservations, fees: Reservations are accepted at 877/444-6777 or www.ReserveUSA.com ($9 reservation fee). Sites are $16–18 per night, double sites are $32 per night, and it's $8–9 per night per additional vehicle. Open late May–late September, weather permitting.

Directions: From Portland, drive east on U.S. 26 for 55 miles to the small town of Government Camp. Continue east on U.S. 26 for 1.5 miles to Forest Road 2656. Turn right and drive 1.3 miles to the campground on the right.

Contact: Mount Hood National Forest, Zigzag Ranger District, 503/622-3191, fax 503/622-5622.

35 FROG LAKE

Scenic rating: 6

near the Pacific Crest Trail in Mount Hood National Forest

See map page 322

This classic spot in the Cascade Range is on the shore of little Frog Lake (more of a pond than a lake), at an elevation of 3,800 feet and a short distance from the Pacific Crest Trail. Several other trails lead to nearby lakes. Clear Lake, to the south, provides a possible day trip and offers more recreation options.

RV sites, facilities: There are 33 sites for tents or RVs up to 22 feet (no hookups). Drinking water and picnic tables are provided. Vault toilets, garbage bins, and firewood are available. Boat-launching facilities are nearby; no motorized boats are allowed. Some facilities are wheelchair accessible. Leashed pets are permitted.

Reservations, fees: Reservations are accepted at 877/444-6777 or www.ReserveUSA.com ($9 reservation fee). Sites are $16–18 per night, plus

OREGON

$8–9 per night per additional vehicle. Open mid-May–mid-September, weather permitting.
Directions: From Portland, drive east on U.S. 26 for 57 miles to the junction with Highway 35 (two miles past Government Camp). Take that exit, bear right onto Highway 35, and drive seven miles to Forest Road 2610. Turn left and drive 0.5 mile to the campground.
Contact: Mount Hood National Forest, Hood River Ranger District, 541/352-6002, fax 541/352-7365.

36 CLEAR LAKE

Scenic rating: 4

near the Pacific Crest Trail in Mount Hood National Forest

See map page 323

This campground is along the shore of Clear Lake, a spot favored by anglers, swimmers, and windsurfers, but as a reservoir, it is subject to water-level fluctuations. The boating speed limit is 10 mph. This wooded camp features shady sites and is at 3,600 feet elevation. The camp sometimes gets noisy from the revels of the party set. If you want quiet, this spot is probably not for you. A nearby trail heads north from the lake and provides access to the Pacific Crest Trail and Frog Lake, both good recreation options.
RV sites, facilities: There are 28 sites for tents or RVs up to 32 feet (no hookups). Picnic tables and fire grills are provided. Drinking water, garbage bins, firewood, and vault toilets are available. Some facilities are wheelchair accessible. Boat-launching facilities are nearby. Leashed pets are permitted.
Reservations, fees: Reservations are accepted at 877/444-6777 or www.ReserveUSA.com ($9 reservation fee). Sites are $16–18 per night, plus $8–9 per night per additional vehicle. Open mid-May–late September, weather permitting.
Directions: From Portland, drive east on U.S. 26 for 57 miles to the junction with Highway 35 (two miles past Government Camp). Bear right (southeast) on U.S. 26 and drive nine miles to

Forest Road 2630. Turn right (south) and drive one mile to the campground on the right.
Contact: Mount Hood National Forest, Hood River Ranger District, 541/352-6002, fax 541/352-7365.

37 BEAR SPRINGS

Scenic rating: 6

on Indian Creek in Mount Hood National Forest

See map page 323

This campground is along the banks of Indian Creek on the border of the Warm Springs Indian Reservation. The camp features both secluded and open sites in old-growth forest. The elevation is 3,000 feet.
RV sites, facilities: There are 21 sites for tents or RVs up to 32 feet (no hookups). Picnic tables and fire grills are provided. Drinking water, garbage bins, vault toilets, and firewood are available. Leashed pets are permitted.
Reservations, fees: Reservations are not accepted. Sites are $12 per night and $6 per night for each additional vehicle. Open June–September, weather permitting.
Directions: From Portland, drive east on U.S. 26 for 55 miles to Government Camp. Continue three miles to a junction and bear right, staying on U.S. 26, and drive south for 12 miles to Highway 216. Turn left (east) on Highway 216 and drive four miles to Reservation Road. Turn right (east) on Reservation Road and look for the campground on the right.
Contact: Mount Hood National Forest, Barlow Ranger District, 541/467-2291, fax 541/467-2271.

38 ROCK CREEK RESERVOIR

Scenic rating: 7

on Rock Creek Reservoir in Mount Hood National Forest

See map page 322

Fishing is excellent, and the environment is perfect for canoes or rafts at this campground along the shore of Rock Creek Reservoir. Enjoy views of Mount Hood from the day-use area (Northwest Forest Pass required). No hiking trails are in the immediate vicinity, but there are many old forest roads that are ideal for walking or mountain biking. The camp sits at 2,200 feet elevation.

RV sites, facilities: There are 33 sites for tents or RVs up to 18 feet (no hookups). Picnic tables, garbage service, and fire grills are provided. Vault toilets, drinking water, and firewood are available. Some of the facilities are wheelchair accessible. There are boat docks nearby, but no motorboats are allowed on the reservoir. Leashed pets are permitted.

Reservations, fees: Reservations are accepted at 877/444-6777 or www.ReserveUSA.com ($9 reservation fee). Sites are $14–16 per night, plus $7–8 per night per additional vehicle. Open mid-April–early October.

Directions: From Portland, turn east on I-84 and drive 91 miles to The Dalles/Exit 87/Highway 197. Turn south and drive 31 miles to Tygh Valley and Wamic Market Road. Turn right and drive west for six miles to Forest Road 48. Turn west and drive one mile to Forest Road 4820. Turn west and drive a short distance to the campground.

Contact: Mount Hood National Forest, Barlow Ranger District, 541/467-2291, fax 541/467-2271.

39 PINE HOLLOW LAKESIDE RESORT

Scenic rating: 8

on Pine Hollow Reservoir
See map page 322

This resort on the shore of Pine Hollow Reservoir is the best game in town for RV campers, with some shaded lakefront sites and scenic views. Year-round boating, fishing, swimming, and waterskiing are some recreation options here.

RV sites, facilities: There are 75 sites with partial hookups (30 and 50 amps) for RVs of any length, 35 tent sites, and 10 cabins. Picnic

tables and fire pits are provided. Drinking water, restrooms with flush toilets and coin showers, propane gas, a dump station, firewood, a convenience store, a café, a coin laundry, and ice are available. Boat docks, launching facilities, and boat and personal watercraft rentals are nearby. Leashed pets are permitted.

Reservations, fees: Reservations are accepted. Sites are $18–20 per night, $2 per person per night for more than two people, $2 per night per additional vehicle, and $2 per pet per night. Some credit cards are accepted. Open mid-March–October.

Directions: From Portland, turn east on I-84 and drive 91 miles to The Dalles/Exit 87/Highway 197. Turn south on Highway 197 and drive 31 miles to Tygh Valley and Wamic Market Road. Turn right (west) and drive 4.5 miles to Ross Road. Turn right (north) and drive 3.5 miles to the resort on the right.

Contact: Pine Hollow Lakeside Resort, 541/544-2271, www.pinehollowlakeside.com.

40 WASCO COUNTY FAIRGROUNDS

Scenic rating: 6

near Badger Creek
See map page 322

This county campground is near the confluence of Badger and Tygh Creeks. Hiking trails, marked bike trails, and tennis courts are nearby.

RV sites, facilities: There are 120 pull-through sites with partial hookups (20 and 30 amps) for RVs of any length and 150 tent sites. Picnic tables are provided. Drinking water, restrooms with flush toilets and coin showers, a dump station, garbage bins, and reservable picnic shelters are available. Horse facilities, including stalls and an arena, are also available. A store, a café, and ice are within one mile. Some facilities are wheelchair accessible. Leashed pets are permitted.

Reservations, fees: Reservations are accepted only for RV sites and for groups booking multiple sites. Sites are $12–15 per night,

$3 per night per additional vehicle. Open mid-April–November.

Directions: From Portland, turn east on I-84 and drive 91 miles to The Dalles/Exit 87/Highway 197. Turn south on Highway 197 and drive 31 miles to Tygh Valley and Main Street. Turn right on Main Street and drive two blocks to Fairgrounds Road. Turn right and drive one mile to the fairgrounds on the right.

Contact: Wasco County, 541/483-2288.

41 SUNSTRIP

Scenic rating: 3

on the Clackamas River in Mount Hood National Forest

See map page 323

This campground on the banks of the Clackamas River offers fishing and rafting access. One of several camps along the Highway 224 corridor, Sunstrip is a favorite with rafting and kayaking enthusiasts and can fill up quickly on weekends. The elevation is 1,000 feet. Note: This campground, squeezed between the river and the highway and traversed by power lines, may be a turnoff for those wanting another kind of experience.

RV sites, facilities: There are nine sites for tents or RVs up to 18 feet (no hookups). Picnic tables and fireplaces are provided. Garbage service, drinking water, and vault toilets are available. Leashed pets are permitted.

Reservations, fees: Reservations are accepted at 877/444-6777 or www.ReserveUSA.com ($9 reservation fee). Sites are $16 per night, plus $8 per night per additional vehicle. Open year-round, with limited winter services.

Directions: From Portland, drive south on U.S. 205 to the junction with Highway 24. Take the Highway 224/Estacada exit and turn left (south) onto Highway 224. Drive approximately 13 miles to Estacada. Continue south on Highway 224 for 19 miles to the campground.

Contact: Mount Hood National Forest, Clackamas River Ranger District, 503/630-6861, fax 503/630-2299.

42 RAINBOW

Scenic rating: 6

on the Oak Grove Fork of the Clackamas River in Mount Hood National Forest

See map page 323

This campground sits at an elevation of 1,400 feet along the banks of the Oak Grove Fork of the Clackamas River, not far from where it empties into the Clackamas River. The camp is less than a quarter mile from Ripplebrook Campground.

RV sites, facilities: There are 17 sites for tents or RVs up to 16 feet (no hookups). Picnic tables and fire grills are provided. Vault toilets are available. Garbage service is available during the summer. There is no drinking water. Leashed pets are permitted.

Reservations, fees: Reservations are accepted at 877/444-6777 or www.ReserveUSA.com ($9 reservation fee). Sites are $14 per night, plus $7 per night per additional vehicle. Open year-round, with limited winter services.

Directions: From Portland, drive south on U.S. 205 to the junction with Highway 24. Take the Highway 224/Estacada exit and turn left (south) onto Highway 224. Drive approximately 13 miles to Estacada. Continue south on Highway 224 and drive 27 miles in national forest (the road becomes Forest Road 46). Continue south and drive about 100 yards to the campground on the right.

Contact: Mount Hood National Forest, Clackamas River Ranger District, 503/630-6861, fax 503/630-2299.

43 INDIAN HENRY

Scenic rating: 8

on the Clackamas River in Mount Hood National Forest

See map page 323

One of the most popular campgrounds in the Clackamas River Ranger District, Indian Henry hugs the banks of the Clackamas River at an elevation of 1,250 feet and has a wheelchair-accessible trail. Group campsites and an amphitheater are available. The nearby Clackamas River Trail has fishing access.

RV sites, facilities: There are 86 sites for tents or RVs up to 36 feet (no hookups) and eight group tent sites. Picnic tables, garbage service, and fire grills are provided. Flush toilets, a dump station, and drinking water are available. Some facilities are wheelchair accessible. Leashed pets are permitted.

Reservations, fees: Reservations are accepted at 877/444-6777 or www.ReserveUSA.com ($9 reservation fee). Sites are $16 per night, plus $8 per night per additional vehicle; group sites are $42 per night. Open late May–early September, weather permitting.

Directions: From Portland, drive south on U.S. 205 to the junction with Highway 24. Take the Highway 224/Estacada exit and turn left (south) onto Highway 224. Drive approximately 13 miles to Estacada. Continue south on Highway 224 for 23 miles to Forest Road 4620. Turn right and drive 0.5 mile southeast to the campground on the left.

Contact: Mount Hood National Forest, Clackamas River Ranger District, 503/630-6861, fax 503/630-2299.

44 RIPPLEBROOK

Scenic rating: 7

on the Oak Grove Fork of the Clackamas River in Mount Hood National Forest

See map page 323

Shaded sites with river views are a highlight at this campground along the banks of the Oak Grove Fork of the Clackamas River, where anglers are limited to artificial lures and catch-and-release only. Note: The road to this camp experiences slides and washouts; check current status before making the trip.

RV sites, facilities: There are 13 sites with no hookups for RVs up to 16 feet. Picnic tables, garbage service, and fire grills are provided. Vault toilets are available, but there is no drinking water. Leashed pets are permitted; horses are not allowed in the campground.

Reservations, fees: Reservations are accepted at 877/444-6777 or www.ReserveUSA.com ($9 reservation fee). Sites are $14 per night, plus $7 per night per additional vehicle. Open late April–late September, weather permitting.

Directions: From Portland, drive south on U.S. 205 to the junction with Highway 224. Take the Highway 224/Estacada exit and turn left (south) onto Highway 224. Drive approximately 13 miles to Estacada. Continue south on Highway 224 for 26.5 miles to the campground entrance on the left.

Contact: Mount Hood National Forest, Clackamas River Ranger District, 503/630-6861, fax 503/630-2299.

45 RIVERSIDE

Scenic rating: 8

on the Clackamas River in Mount Hood National Forest

See map page 323

The banks of the Clackamas River are home to this campground (elevation 1,400 feet). A worthwhile trail leaves the camp and follows the river for four miles north. Fishing is another option here, and several old forest roads in the vicinity make excellent mountain-biking trails.

RV sites, facilities: There are 16 sites for tents or RVs up to 22 feet (no hookups). Picnic tables, garbage service, and fire grills are provided. Vault toilets and drinking water are available. Leashed pets are permitted; no horses are allowed in the campground.

Reservations, fees: Reservations are accepted at 877/444-6777 or www.ReserveUSA.com ($9 reservation fee). Sites are $16 per night, plus $8 per night per additional vehicle. Open mid-May–late September, weather permitting.

Directions: From Portland, drive south on U.S. 205 to the junction with Highway 24. Take the Highway 224/Estacada exit and turn left (south) onto Highway 224. Drive approximately 13 miles to Estacada. Continue south on Highway 224 for 27 miles and into national forest (Highway 224 becomes Forest Road 46).

OREGON

Continue 2.5 miles south on Forest Road 46 to the campground on the right.

Contact: Mount Hood National Forest, Clackamas River Ranger District, 503/630-6861, fax 503/630-2299.

46 KINGFISHER

Scenic rating: 7

on the Hot Springs Fork of the Collawash River in Mount Hood National Forest

See map page 323

This pretty campground, surrounded by old-growth forest, sits on the banks of the Hot Springs Fork of the Collawash River and provides fishing access. It's about three miles from Bagby Hot Springs, a U.S. Forest Service day-use area. The hot springs are an easy 1.5-mile hike from the day-use area. The camp sits at 1,250 feet elevation.

RV sites, facilities: There are 23 sites for tents or RVs up to 16 feet (no hookups). Picnic tables and fireplaces are provided. Garbage service is provided during the summer. Vault toilets and drinking water are available. Leashed pets are permitted.

Reservations, fees: Reservations are accepted at 877/444-6777 or www.ReserveUSA.com ($9 reservation fee). Sites are $16 per night, plus $8 per night per additional vehicle. Open year-round, with limited winter facilities.

Directions: From Portland, drive south on U.S. 205 to the junction with Highway 24. Take the Highway 224/Estacada exit and turn left (south) onto Highway 224. Drive approximately 13 miles to Estacada. Continue south on Highway 224 for 27 miles in national forest (the road becomes Forest Road 46). Continue south on Forest Road 46 for 3.5 miles to Forest Road 63. Turn right and drive three miles to Forest Road 70. Turn right again and drive one mile to the campground on the left.

Contact: Mount Hood National Forest, Clackamas River Ranger District, 503/630-6861, fax 503/630-2299.

47 HOODVIEW

Scenic rating: 9

on Timothy Lake in Mount Hood National Forest

See map page 323

Here's another camp along the south shore of Timothy Lake; this one is at 3,200 feet elevation. Motorized boats are allowed, and the speed limit is 10 mph. A trail out of camp branches south for a few miles and, if followed to the east, eventually leads to the Pacific Crest Trail. (See the *Gone Creek* listing in this chapter for boating and fishing information.)

RV sites, facilities: There are 43 sites for tents or RVs up to 32 feet (no hookups). Picnic tables and fire grills are provided. Vault toilets, drinking water, garbage service, and firewood are available. A boat ramp is nearby. Some facilities are wheelchair accessible. Leashed pets are permitted.

Reservations, fees: Reservations are accepted at 877/444-6777 or www.ReserveUSA.com ($9 reservation fee). Sites are $16–18 per night, plus $8–9 per night per additional vehicle. Open mid-May–mid-September, weather permitting.

Directions: From Portland, turn east on U.S. 26 and drive 57 miles (just past the town of Government Camp) to the junction with Highway 35. Bear southeast, staying on U.S. 26, and drive 15 miles to Forest Road 42 (Skyline Road). Turn right and drive eight miles to Forest Road 57. Turn right and drive three miles to the campground on the right.

Contact: Mount Hood National Forest, Zigzag Ranger District, 503/622-3191, fax 503/622-5622.

48 LITTLE CRATER

Scenic rating: 5

on Little Crater Lake in Mount Hood National Forest

See map page 323

Little Crater campground (3,200 feet elevation) nestles against Crater Creek and scenic Little Crater Lake. This camp is popular with hunters in the fall. Both the drinking water and the lake water are spring fed, and the water is numbingly cold. The Pacific Crest Trail is near camp, providing hiking trail access. Fishing is poor at Little Crater Lake. Little Timothy Lake lies about 10 miles away; note the 10-mph speed limit for boats. Bring your mosquito repellent; you'll need it.

RV sites, facilities: There are 16 sites for tents or RVs up to 22 feet (no hookups). Picnic tables, garbage bins, and fire grills are provided. Vault toilets, firewood, and drinking water are available. Some facilities are wheelchair accessible. Leashed pets are permitted.

Reservations, fees: Reservations are accepted at 877/444-6777 or www.ReserveUSA.com ($9 reservation fee). Sites are $16 per night, plus $8 per night per additional vehicle. Open June–mid-September, weather permitting.

Directions: From Portland, drive east on U.S. 26 for 57 miles to the junction with Highway 35 (two miles past Government Camp). Bear right (southeast), staying on U.S. 26, and drive 15 miles to Forest Road 42 (Skyline Road). Turn right and drive about six miles to Forest Road 58. Turn right and drive about 2.5 miles to the campground on the left.

Contact: Mount Hood National Forest, Zigzag Ranger District, 503/622-3191, fax 503/622-5622.

49 CLACKAMAS LAKE

Scenic rating: 7

near the Clackamas River in Mount Hood National Forest

See map page 323

This camp, set at 3,400 feet elevation, is a good place to go to escape the hordes of people at the lakeside sites in neighboring camps. The Pacific Crest Trail passes nearby, and Timothy Lake requires little more than a one-mile hike from camp. The Clackamas Lake Historic Ranger Station, a visitors center, is worth a visit and is still using the old, hand crank–style phones once used in lookout towers and guard stations. This is a popular spot for campers with horses, although the facilities could use

some updating and repairs. (See the *Gone Creek* listing in this chapter for information on Timothy Lake.)

RV sites, facilities: There are 46 sites for tents, horse trailers, or RVs up to 32 feet (no hookups). Some sites have hitch rails, and horses are permitted at the first 19 sites. Drinking water, garbage service, fire grills, and picnic tables are provided. Vault toilets and firewood are available. Boat docks and launching facilities are nearby at Timothy Lake, but only nonmotorized boats are allowed. Some facilities are wheelchair accessible. Leashed pets are permitted.

Reservations, fees: Reservations are accepted at 877/444-6777 or www.ReserveUSA.com ($9 reservation fee). Sites are $14 per night, plus $7 per night per additional vehicle. Open June–mid-September, weather permitting.

Directions: From Portland, turn east on U.S. 26 and drive 57 miles (just past the town of Government Camp) to the junction with Highway 35. Bear southeast, staying on U.S. 26, and drive 15 miles to Forest Road 42 (Skyline Road). Turn right and drive eight miles to Forest Road 57. Continue 500 feet (on Forest Road 42) past the Clackamas Lake Historic Ranger Station to Forest Road 4270. Turn left and drive 0.5 mile to the campground on the left.

Contact: Mount Hood National Forest, Zigzag Ranger District, 503/622-3191, fax 503/622-5622.

50 BREITENBUSH

Scenic rating: 8

on the Breitenbush River in Willamette National Forest

See map page 323

There is fishing access at this campground along the Breitenbush River. Nearby recreation options include the South Breitenbush Gorge National Recreation Trail, three miles away, and Breitenbush Hot Springs, just over a mile away. If this campground is crowded, try nearby Cleator Bend.

RV sites, facilities: There are 30 sites for tents or RVs up to 24 feet (no hookups) (longer trailers may be difficult to park and turn). Picnic tables, garbage service (summer only), and fire grills are provided. Drinking water, vault toilets, and firewood are available. Some facilities are wheelchair accessible. Leashed pets are permitted.

Reservations, fees: Reservations are not accepted. Sites are $10 per night for a single site, $20 per night for a double site, and $5 per night per additional vehicle. Open May–September, with a gate preventing access during the off-season.

Directions: From Salem on I-5, take Exit 253, turn east on Highway 22, and drive 50 miles to Detroit. Turn left (north) on Forest Road 46/Breitenbush Road and drive 10 miles to the campground on the right.

Contact: Willamette National Forest, Detroit Ranger District, 503/854-3366, fax 503/854-4239.

51 PENINSULA

Scenic rating: 10

on Olallie Lake in Mount Hood National Forest

See map page 323

Peninsula, the largest of several campgrounds along Olallie Lake, is at an elevation of 5,000 feet on the south shore. An amphitheater is near camp, and during the summer rangers present campfire programs. Boats without motors are permitted on the lake. Nearby trails lead to a number of smaller lakes in the area.

RV sites, facilities: There are 31 sites for tents or RVs up to 24 feet (no hookups), five walk-in tent sites, and one group site for up to 25 people and five vehicles. Picnic tables, garbage service, and fire grills are provided. Vault toilets are available. There is no drinking water. Boat docks, launching facilities, and rentals are nearby. Some facilities are wheelchair accessible. Leashed pets are permitted.

Reservations, fees: Reservations are not accepted. Sites are $10 per night, $6 per night per additional vehicle, $6 per night for walk-in sites,

and $36 per night for the group site. Open mid-June–late September, weather permitting.

Directions: From Portland, drive south on U.S. 205 to the junction with Highway 24. Take the Highway 224/Estacada exit and turn left (south) onto Highway 224. Drive approximately 13 miles to Estacada. Continue south on Highway 224 and drive 27 miles in national forest (the road becomes Forest Road 46). Continue south on Forest Road 46 for 20 miles to Forest Road 4690. Turn left and drive southeast for 8.2 miles to Forest Road 4220. Turn right (south) and drive 6.5 miles of rough road to the campground on the left.

Contact: Mount Hood National Forest, Clackamas River Ranger District, 503/630-6861, fax 503/630-2299.

52 KAH-NEE-TA RESORT

Scenic rating: 7

on the Warm Springs Indian Reservation

See map page 323

This resort features a stellar-rated, full-concept spa, with the bonus of a nearby casino. It is also the only public camp on the east side of the Warm Springs Indian Reservation; there are no other camps within 30 miles. The Warm Springs River runs nearby. Recreation options in the area include an 18-hole golf course, miniature golf, biking and hiking trails, a riding stable, and tennis courts.

RV sites, facilities: There are 50 sites with full hookups (50 amps) for RVs of any length; most sites are pull-through. No tents are allowed. A motel, tepees, and a cottage are also available. Cable TV, restrooms with flush toilets and coin showers, propane gas, a dump station, a concession stand, a coin laundry, ice, a playground, a spa with a therapist, mineral baths, and an Olympic-sized, spring-fed swimming pool with a 140-foot water slide are available. Some facilities are wheelchair accessible. Leashed pets are permitted, but some areas are restricted.

Reservations, fees: Reservations are accepted

at 800/554-4786. Sites are $38 per night for three people. Some credit cards are accepted. Open year-round.

Directions: From Portland, turn east on U.S. 26 and drive about 105 miles to Warm Springs and Agency Hot Springs Road on the left. Turn left and drive 11 miles northeast to Kah-Nee-Ta and the resort on the right.

Contact: Kah-Nee-Ta Resort, 541/553-1112.

53 HUMBUG

Scenic rating: 9

on the Breitenbush River in Willamette National Forest

See map page 323

Fishing and hiking are popular at this campground along the banks of the Breitenbush River, about four miles from where it empties into Detroit Lake. The lake offers many other recreation opportunities. The Humbug Flat Trailhead is behind sites 9 and 10, and a scenic stroll through an old-growth forest follows the Breitenbush River. The rhododendrons put on a spectacular show May–July.

RV sites, facilities: There are 22 sites for tents or RVs up to 30 feet (no hookups). Picnic tables and fire grills are provided. Garbage service (summer only), drinking water, and pit toilets are available. Leashed pets are permitted.

Reservations, fees: Reservations are not accepted. Sites are $10 per night, plus $5 per night per additional vehicle. Open year-round, weather permitting, with limited winter facilities.

Directions: From Salem on I-5, take Exit 253, turn east on Highway 22, and drive 52 miles to Detroit. Turn left on Forest Road 46/Breitenbush Road and drive five miles northeast to the campground on the right.

Contact: Willamette National Forest, Detroit Ranger District, 503/854-3366, fax 503/854-4239.

54 DETROIT LAKE STATE PARK

Scenic rating: 7

on Detroit Lake

See map page 323

This campground lies at 1,600 feet elevation along the shore of Detroit Lake, which is 400 feet deep, nine miles long, and has more than 32 miles of shoreline. The park offers two fishing docks and a moorage area, and a boat ramp and bathhouse are available nearby at the Mongold Day Use Area. The lake is crowded on the opening day of trout season in late April because it's heavily stocked.

RV sites, facilities: There are 178 sites with full or partial hookups (20, 30, and 50 amps) for RVs up to 60 feet, 133 tent sites, and 82 boat slips. Drinking water, garbage bins, fire grills, and picnic tables are provided. Restrooms have flush toilets and showers. Two playgrounds, swimming areas, a gift shop, a visitors center, and firewood are available. Two boat docks and launching facilities are nearby. Leashed pets are permitted.

Reservations, fees: Reservations are accepted at 800/452-5687 or www.oregonstateparks.org ($6 reservation fee). Sites are $12–20 per night, plus $5 per night per additional vehicle. Boating moorage is $7 per night. Some credit cards are accepted. Open March–November, weather permitting.

Directions: From Salem, drive east on Highway 22 for 50 miles to the park entrance on the right (two miles west of Detroit).

Contact: Detroit Lake State Park, 503/854-3406; Oregon State Parks, 503/854-3346, www.oregonstateparks.org.

55 SOUTHSHORE

Scenic rating: 9

on Detroit Lake in Willamette National Forest

See map page 323

This popular camp hugs the south shore of Detroit Lake, where fishing, swimming, and waterskiing are some of the recreation options.

OREGON

OREGON

The Stahlman Point Trailhead is about half a mile from camp. There's a day-use area for picnicking and swimming. The views of the lake and surrounding mountains are outstanding.

RV sites, facilities: There are eight walk-in tent sites and 24 sites for tents or RVs up to 30 feet (no hookups). Fire grills, garbage service, and picnic tables are provided. Vault toilets and drinking water are available. Boat-launching facilities are nearby at a day-use area. Some facilities are wheelchair accessible. Leashed pets are permitted.

Reservations, fees: Reservations are not accepted. Sites are $14 for a single site, $28 for a double site, and $5 per night per additional vehicle. Open mid-May–late September, with a gate preventing access during the off-season.

Directions: From Salem, drive east on Highway 22 for 52 miles to Detroit. Continue southeast on Highway 22 for 2.5 miles to Forest Road 10 (Blowout Road). Turn right and drive four miles to the campground on the right.

Contact: Willamette National Forest, Detroit Ranger District, 503/854-3366, fax 503/854-4239.

56 COVE CREEK

Scenic rating: 10

on Detroit Lake in Willamette National Forest
See map page 323

Cove Creek is a popular campground, and it gets high use in the summer. The campground is in a forest and is on the south side of the lake, about one mile from both Hoover and Southshore campgrounds. Water sports are popular, and both waterskiing and personal watercraft are allowed. (See the *Hoover* and *Southshore* listings in this chapter for more recreation options.)

RV sites, facilities: There are 63 sites for tents or RVs of any length (no hookups) and one group site for up to 70 people. Picnic tables, garbage service, and fire rings are provided. Drinking water, restrooms with flush toilets and coin showers, garbage bins, firewood, and a boat

ramp are available. Some facilities are wheelchair accessible. Leashed pets are permitted.

Reservations, fees: Reservations are required for the group site at 877/444-6777 or www.ReserveUSA.com ($9 reservation fee) but are not accepted for family sites. Sites are $16 per night for single sites, $32 per night for double sites, and $5 per night per additional vehicle. Group sites are $150 per night. Open mid-April–late September, with a gate preventing access in the off-season.

Directions: From Salem, drive east on Highway 22 for 52 miles to Detroit. Continue southeast on Highway 22 for 2.5 miles to Forest Road 10 (Blowout Road). Turn right and drive three miles to the campground on the right.

Contact: Willamette National Forest, Detroit Ranger District, 503/854-3366, fax 503/854-4239.

57 HOOVER

Scenic rating: 9

on Detroit Lake in Willamette National Forest
See map page 323

This campground is along the eastern arm of Detroit Lake, near the mouth of the Santiam River. The elevation is 1,600 feet. It features a wheelchair-accessible fishing area and interpretive trail. You're likely to see osprey fishing during the day, a truly special sight. (See the *Southshore* listing in this chapter for other recreation options.)

RV sites, facilities: There are 37 sites for tents or RVs up to 30 feet (no hookups). Picnic tables, garbage service, and fire grills are provided. Flush toilets and drinking water are available. Some facilities are wheelchair accessible. Boat docks and launching facilities are nearby. Leashed pets are permitted.

Reservations, fees: Reservations are not accepted. Sites are $14 per night, $28 per night for double sites, and $5 per night per additional vehicle. Open mid-April–late September; a gate prevents access in the off-season.

Directions: From Salem, drive east on Highway 22 for 52 miles to Detroit. Continue southeast on Highway 22 for 2.5 miles to Forest Road 10 (Blowout Road). Turn right and drive one mile to the campground on the right.

Contact: Willamette National Forest, Detroit Ranger District, 503/854-3366, fax 503/854-4239.

58 WHISPERING FALLS

Scenic rating: 10

on the North Santiam River near Detroit Lake in Willamette National Forest

See map page 323

This popular campground sits on the banks of the North Santiam River, where you can fish. If the campsites at Detroit Lake are crowded, this camp provides a more secluded option, and it's only about a 10-minute drive from the lake. Ospreys sometimes nest near the campground.

RV sites, facilities: There are 16 sites for tents or RVs up to 30 feet (no hookups). Picnic tables, garbage service, and fire grills are provided. Drinking water and flush toilets are available. Leashed pets are permitted.

Reservations, fees: Reservations are not accepted. Sites are $12 per night, plus $5 per night per additional vehicle. Open mid-April–late September; a gate prevents access in the off-season.

Directions: From Salem, drive east on Highway 22 for 50 miles to Detroit. Continue east on Highway 22 for eight miles to the campground on the right.

Contact: Willamette National Forest, Detroit Ranger District, 503/854-3366, fax 503/854-4239.

59 RIVERSIDE

Scenic rating: 7

on the North Santiam River in Willamette National Forest

See map page 323

This campground is at an elevation of 2,400 feet along the banks of the North Santiam River, where the fishing can be good. A point of interest, the Marion Forks Fish Hatchery and interpretive site, lies just 2.5 miles south; a campground there has 15 sites for tents or RVs up to 24 feet. Other day-trip options include the Mount Jefferson Wilderness, directly to the east in Willamette National Forest, and Minto Mountain Trail, three miles to the east.

RV sites, facilities: There are 37 sites for tents or RVs up to 24 feet (no hookups). Picnic tables and fire grills are provided. Drinking water and vault toilets are available. Leashed pets are permitted.

Reservations, fees: Reservations are not accepted. Sites are $10 per night, plus $5 per night per additional vehicle. Open mid-April–late September, with limited facilities until snowfall; a gate prevents access during the off-season.

Directions: From Salem, drive east on Highway 22 for 50 miles to Detroit. Continue southeast on Highway 22 for 14 miles to the campground on the right.

Contact: Willamette National Forest, Detroit Ranger District, 503/854-3366, fax 503/854-4239.

60 JACK CREEK

Scenic rating: 5

near Mount Jefferson Wilderness in Deschutes National Forest

See map page 323

A more primitive alternative to the other camps in the area, this campground sits along the banks of Jack Creek in an open setting among ponderosa pine. The elevation is 3,100 feet. To protect the bull trout habitat, no fishing is permitted here.

RV sites, facilities: There are 11 sites for tents or RVs up to 50 feet (no hookups). Picnic tables and fire grills are provided. Vault toilets are available. There is no drinking water, and garbage must be packed out. Leashed pets are permitted.

Reservations, fees: Reservations are not accepted. Sites are $10 per night, plus $5 per night per additional vehicle. Open mid-April–mid-October.

Directions: From Albany, drive east on U.S. 20

OREGON

for 87 miles to the sign for Jack Lake (one mile east of Suttle Lake) and Suttle-Sherman Road. Turn left on Forest Road 12 and drive five miles to Forest Road 1230. Turn left and drive 0.75 mile to Forest Road 1232. Turn left and drive 0.25 mile to the campground on the left.

Contact: Deschutes National Forest, Sisters Ranger District, 541/549-7700, fax 541/549-7746.

61 PELTON

Scenic rating: 8

on Lake Simtustus in Deschutes National Forest
See map page 323

This campground claims 0.5 mile of shoreline along the north side of Lake Simtustus. Campsites here are shaded with juniper in an area of rolling hills and sagebrush. One section of the lake is accessible for water skis and personal watercraft. Simtustus is a trophy fishing lake for kokanee and brown, bull, and rainbow trout. Just north of the park is the Pelton Wildlife Overlook, where you can view a variety of waterfowl, such as great blue herons, ducks, geese, and shore birds, as well as eagles and other raptors. Cove Palisades State Park, about 15 miles south, provides additional recreational opportunities.

RV sites, facilities: There are 71 sites for tents or RVs up to 40 feet, some with partial hookups (30 amps); three group sites for up to 12–35 people; and eight yomes (which are a cross between a yurt and a dome). Drinking water, picnic tables, garbage service, and fire grills are provided. Restrooms have flush toilets and showers. A restaurant, a snack bar, a general store, ice, fishing supplies, gasoline, and a picnic shelter are available. Also, a full-service marina with boat rentals, marine fuel, a boat launch, boat dock, fishing pier, moorage, swimming beach, volleyball courts, horseshoe pits, and a playground are available. Some facilities are wheelchair accessible. Leashed pets are permitted.

Reservations, fees: Reservations are accepted at 541/475-0517 or www.portlandgeneral.com. Sites are $16–21 per night, the group site is

$32–65 per night, and yomes are $25 per night. Some credit cards are accepted. Open mid-April–September.

Directions: From Portland, drive south on U.S. 26 for 108 miles to the town of Warm Springs. Continue south two miles to Pelton Dam Road. Turn right and drive three miles to the campground on the right.

Contact: Portland General Electric, 503/464-8515 or 541/475-0516 (store and marina), fax 503/464-2944, www.portlandgeneral.com/parks.

62 COVE PALISADES STATE PARK

Scenic rating: 7

on Lake Billy Chinook
See map page 323

Note that there are two campgrounds at this state park: Crooked River and Deschutes. This park is a mile away from the shore of Lake Billy Chinook, where some lakeshore cabins are available. Here in Oregon's high-desert region, the weather is sunny and warm in the summer and chilly but generally mild in the winter. Towering cliffs surround the lake, and about 10 miles of hiking trails crisscross the area. Two popular special events are held here annually: Lake Billy Chinook Day in September and the Eagle Watch in February.

RV sites, facilities: There are 173 sites with full or partial hookups (30 amps) for RVs up to 60 feet, 92 tent sites, three cabins, and three group tent areas for up to 25 people each. Picnic tables and fire grills are provided. Drinking water, garbage bins, restrooms with flush toilets and showers, a dump station, firewood, dog run, a convenience store, and ice are available. Some facilities are wheelchair accessible. Boat docks, launching facilities, a marina, slip and boat rentals, and a restaurant are nearby. Leashed pets are permitted.

Reservations, fees: Reservations are accepted at 800/452-5687 or www.oregonstateparks.org ($6 reservation fee). Tent sites are $13–17 per night, and RV sites are $17–21 per night, plus $5 per night per additional vehicle; cabins are $48–70 per night; and the group areas are $64 per night. Some credit cards are accepted. Open year-round, with fewer sites available during the winter season.

Directions: From Bend, drive north on U.S. 97 for 13 miles to Redmond and continue north for 15 miles to the Culver Highway. Take the Culver Highway north to Culver and continue two miles to Gem Lane. Turn left and drive two miles to Frazier Drive. Turn left and drive a short distance to Peck Road. Turn right and drive to the park entrance.

Contact: Cove Palisades State Park, 541/546-3412; Oregon State Parks, 800/551-6949, www.oregonstateparks.org.

63 PERRY SOUTH

Scenic rating: 6

on Lake Billy Chinook in Deschutes National Forest
See map page 323

This campground is near the shore of the Metolius arm of Lake Billy Chinook. The lake can get very crowded and noisy; it attracts powerboat/water-ski enthusiasts. The lake borders the Warm Springs Indian Reservation. (See the descriptions of *KOA Madras/Culver* in this chapter and *Crooked River Ranch RV Park* in the *Southern Cascades* chapter for recreation details.)

RV sites, facilities: There are four tent sites and 59 sites for tents or RVs up to 50 feet (no hookups). Picnic tables, garbage service, and fire grills are provided. Drinking water, vault toilets, a fish-cleaning station, boat docks, and launching facilities are available. Some facilities are wheelchair accessible. Leashed pets are permitted.

Reservations, fees: Reservations are accepted at 877/444-6777 or www.ReserveUSA.com ($9 reservation fee). Sites are $16 per night, plus $8 per night per additional vehicle. Open May–September, weather permitting.

Directions: From Bend, drive north on U.S. 97 to Redmond, then continue north for 15 miles to the Culver Highway. Take the Culver Highway north to Culver and continue two miles to Gem Lane. Turn left and drive two miles to Frazier Drive. Turn left and drive a short distance to Peck Road. Turn right and drive through Cove

Palisades State Park to Jordan Road at the shore of Lake Billy Chinook. Turn left on Jordan Road and drive about 10 miles (over the bridge) to County Road 64. Continue (bearing left) and drive about eight miles to the campground entrance on the left (on the upper end of the Metolius Fork of Lake Billy Chinook).

Contact: Deschutes National Forest, Sisters Ranger District, 541/549-7700, fax 541/549-7746.

64 KOA MADRAS/CULVER

Scenic rating: 6

near Lake Billy Chinook
See map page 323

This campground has a relaxing atmosphere, with some mountain views. It is about three miles from Lake Billy Chinook, a steep-sided reservoir formed where the Crooked River, Deschutes River, Metolius River, and Squaw Creek all merge. Like much of the country east of the Cascades, this is a high-desert area.

RV sites, facilities: There are 58 pull-through sites with full or partial hookups (30 and 50 amps) for RVs of any length and 22 tent sites; most sites are pull-through. There are also three cabins. Drinking water, fire pits, and picnic tables are provided. Restrooms have flush toilets and showers. Propane gas, a dump station, firewood, a convenience store, a coin laundry, ice, and a playground are available. Recreational activities include a recreation hall, seasonal heated pool, bicycle rentals, volleyball, horseshoe pits, and basketball. Boat docks and launching facilities are nearby. Leashed pets are permitted.

Reservations, fees: Reservations are accepted at 800/562-1992. Sites are $19–36 per night, plus $2–4 per person per night for more than two people. Some credit cards are accepted. Open year-round.

Directions: From Madras, drive south on U.S. 97 for nine miles to Jericho Lane. Turn left (east) and drive 0.5 mile to the campground on the right.

Contact: KOA Madras/Culver, 541/546-3046, fax 541/546-7972, www.madras-koa.com.

OREGON

NORTHEASTERN OREGON

It might be difficult to believe that there are many places left in America that are little known and little traveled. Yet that is how it is in northeastern Oregon. Even longtime residents often overlook this area of Oregon (the same is true with the southeastern portion of the state, detailed in the *Southeastern Oregon* chapter). With its high desert abutting craggy Blue Mountains, it just doesn't look like the archetypal Oregon.

In this corner of the state you'll find Wallowa-Whitman National Forest and little-known sections of Umatilla, Malheur, and Ochoco National Forests. Idaho, the Snake River, and the Hells Canyon National Recreation Area border this region to the east. My favorite destinations are the Wallowa Mountains and the Eagle Cap Wilderness, a wildlife paradise with deer, elk, bears, mountain lions, and bighorn sheep.

This region covers a huge swatch of land, most of it explored by few. But those few have learned to love it for its unique qualities. Among the highlights are the John Day River and its headwaters, the Strawberry Mountain Wilderness in Malheur National Forest, and various sections of the linked John Day Fossil Beds National Monument. One of the prettiest spots in northeastern Oregon is Wallowa Lake State Park, where 9,000-foot snowcapped mountains surround a pristine lake on three sides.

Includes:

- Antelope Flat Reservoir
- Anthony Lake
- Bull Prairie Lake
- Burnt River
- Columbia River
- Crooked River
- Emigrant Springs State Heritage Park
- Farewell Bend State Recreation Area
- Fish Lake
- Grande Ronde River
- Imnaha River
- Jasper Point State Park
- John Day River
- Jubilee Lake
- Langdon Lake
- Lostine River
- Magone Lake
- Malheur National Forest
- Minam State Park
- Ochoco Lake
- Ochoco National Forest
- Olive Lake
- Phillips Lake
- Prineville Reservoir State Park
- Snake River
- Umatilla National Forest
- Umatilla River
- Walla Walla River
- Wallowa Lake
- Wallowa Lake State Park
- Wallowa-Whitman National Forest
- Walton Lake
- Wolf Creek

OREGON

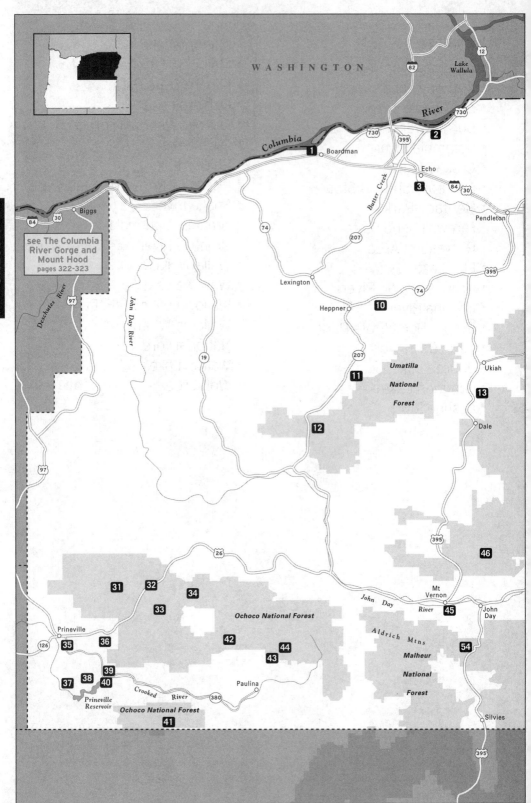

OREGON

WASHINGTON

Lake
Wallula

82

12

Columbia

River

730

2

395

1 Boardman

730

Echo

84 30

3

Pendleton

Biggs

84 30

74

Butter Creek

395

207

see The Columbia
River Gorge and
Mount Hood
pages 322-323

97

Lexington

74

Deschutes River

Heppner

10

John Day River

19

Umatilla

207

Ukiah

11

National

13

Forest

Dale

12

97

395

46

26

31 32

34

John Day River

Mt
Vernon

31

Ochoco National Forest

45

John
Day

33

42

Aldrich Mtns

54

Prineville

44

Malheur

126

35 36

43

National

37 38 39

Crooked River

Paulina

Forest

40

380

Prineville
Reservoir

Silvies

Ochoco National Forest

41

395

NORTHEASTERN OREGON

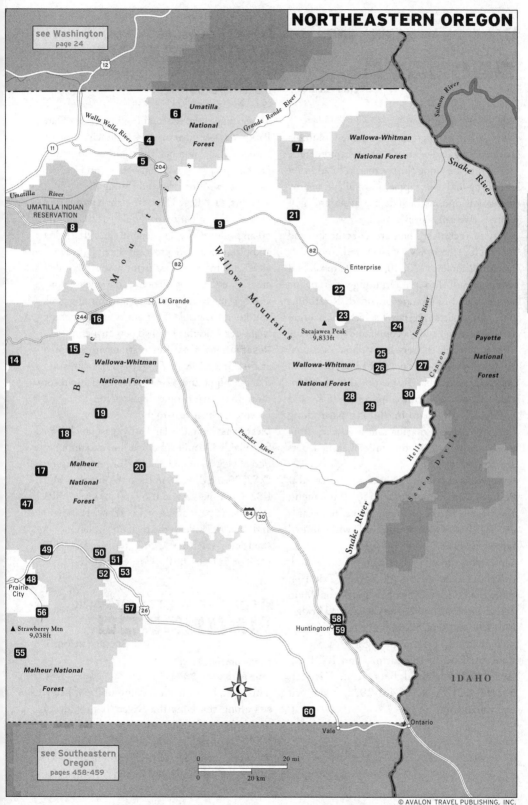

see Washington
page 24

OREGON

Umatilla
National
Forest

6

4

5

204

11

Walla Walla River

Umatilla   River

Umatilla River

UMATILLA INDIAN
RESERVATION

8

Grande Ronde River

7

Wallowa-Whitman
National Forest

Salmon River

Snake River

9

21

82

Enterprise

22

82

La Grande

244

16

15

14

Blue

Mountains

Wallowa   Mountains

Sacajawea Peak
9,833ft

23

24

Imnaha River

Payette
National
Forest

Wallowa-Whitman

National Forest

25
26

28

29

27

30

Hells

Canyon

Seven Devils

Wallowa-Whitman

National Forest

19

18

17

Malheur

National

Forest

20

47

Powder River

49

50

51

48
Prairie
City

52

53

84   30

56

57   26

▲ Strawberry Mtn
9,038ft

Snake River

55

Malheur National

Forest

58
59

Huntington

IDAHO

60

Ontario

Vale

see Southeastern
Oregon
pages 458-459

0   20 mi

0   20 km

1 BOARDMAN MARINA AND RV PARK

Scenic rating: 7

on the Columbia River

See map page 354

This public campground is on the Columbia River among linden, maple, and sycamore trees. Some sites are along the riverbank. In addition to fishing for bass, crappie, and walleye, nearby recreation options include a marina and golf course (five miles away).

RV sites, facilities: There are four tent sites and 63 sites for tents or RVs of any length; most sites have full hookups (20, 30, and 50 amps), and some are pull-through. Drinking water, picnic tables, and fire pits are provided. Restrooms have flush toilets and showers. Fire pits, a dump station, garbage bins, a coin laundry, a day-use area with picnic shelters, a pay phone, seasonal firewood and ice for sale, and a boat dock and launch are available. Recreational facilities include a basketball court, horseshoe pits, sand volleyball, and a hiking/biking path along the river. A boat marina and a grocery store are available within one mile. Leashed pets are permitted.

Reservations, fees: Reservations are accepted at 888/481-7217. Tent sites are $10.40 per night; RV sites are $22.88 per night. Some credit cards are accepted. Open year-round, with limited winter facilities.

Directions: From Portland on I-84 eastbound, drive 164 miles to Boardman and Exit 164. Take that exit and turn left (north) on Main Street. Drive 0.25 mile over the railroad bridge, bear left, and continue 0.2 mile to the Y intersection and the park on the right.

Contact: Boardman Marina and RV Park, Boardman Park and Recreation District, 541/481-7217, fax 541/481-2828, www.visit boardman.com.

2 HAT ROCK CAMPGROUND

Scenic rating: 7

near the Columbia River

See map page 354

This campground is not far from Hat Rock State Park, a day-use area with a boat launch along the banks of the Columbia River. The campground itself is very pretty, with lots of trees, and it offers close access to the river and fishing.

RV sites, facilities: There are eight tent sites and 60 sites with full or partial hookups (20, 30, and 50 amps) for RVs of any length. Drinking water and picnic tables are provided. Fire pits are provided at some sites. Restrooms have flush toilets and showers. A dump station, a convenience store, a café, a coin laundry, a seasonal swimming pool, and ice are available. Boat docks and launching facilities are nearby. Leashed pets are permitted.

Reservations, fees: Reservations are accepted at 541/567-4188 or 541/567-0917. Sites are $18 per night and $2 per person per night for more than two people. Some credit cards are accepted. Open year-round.

Directions: From Portland, drive east on U.S. 84 for roughly 170 miles past Boardman to the junction of U.S. 84 and U.S. 730. Turn northeast on U.S. 730 and drive 18 miles to the junction with I-82. Continue east on U.S. 730 for seven miles to the state park access road. Turn left (north) and drive 0.5 mile to the park on the left.

Contact: Hat Rock Campground, 541/567-4188 or 541/567-0917 (Hat Rock Store).

3 FORT HENRIETTA RV PARK

Scenic rating: 7

on the Umatilla River

See map page 354

This park, in the historic community of Echo, sits along the Umatilla River. It provides a quiet, pleasant layover spot for travelers cruising I-84. The river has some good trout fishing.

RV sites, facilities: There are seven sites with full or partial hookups (30 and 50 amps) for RVs of any length and an area for dispersed tent

OREGO

camping. Picnic tables are provided, and cable TV is available at some sites. Drinking water, restrooms with showers, and a dump station are available. Some facilities are wheelchair accessible. The camp is within walking distance of two restaurants. Leashed pets are permitted.

Reservations, fees: Reservations are not accepted. Sites are $15–19 per night, $2 per person per night for more than two people. Open year-round.

Directions: From Pendleton, drive west on I-84 to Exit 188 and the Echo Highway. Take the exit, turn left (southeast), and drive one mile; cross the railroad tracks and continue 0.5 mile to Dupont Street. Turn right (south) and drive 0.3 mile to Main Street. Turn left (west) and drive one block to the park on the left.

Contact: Echo City Hall, 541/376-8411, fax 541/376-8218; camp hosts, 541/571-3597, www.echo-oregon.com.

4 WOODWARD

Scenic rating: 7

near Langdon Lake in Umatilla National Forest
See map page 355

Nestled among the trees at an elevation of 4,950 feet, with some privacy screening between campsites, this popular campground has a view of Langdon Lake (though campers do not have access to the private lake). A flat trail circles the camp.

RV sites, facilities: There are 18 sites for tents or RVs up to 28 feet (no hookups). Drinking water, picnic tables, garbage bins, fire grills, and vault toilets are provided. A picnic shelter is available. Some facilities are wheelchair accessible. Leashed pets are permitted.

Reservations, fees: Reservations are not accepted. Sites are $10 per night, $5 per night for an additional vehicle. Open June–mid-September, weather permitting.

Directions: From Pendleton on I-84, turn north on Highway 11 and drive approximately 27 miles to Weston and Highway 204. Turn right (southeast) on Highway 204 and drive 17 miles to the campground on the right (near Langdon Lake).

Contact: Umatilla National Forest, Walla Walla Ranger District, 509/525-6290, fax 509/522-6000; Bluewood Recreation Management, 509/382-4725.

5 TARGET MEADOWS

Scenic rating: 6

near the South Fork of the Walla Walla River in Umatilla National Forest
See map page 355

This quiet campground with shady sites and a sunny meadow is at 4,800 feet elevation and is adjacent to the Burnt Cabin Trailhead, which leads to the South Fork of the Walla Walla River. An old military site can be viewed here.

RV sites, facilities: There are 16 sites for tents or RVs up to 28 feet (no hookups). Drinking water, picnic tables, and fire grills are provided. Garbage bins and vault toilets are available. Leashed pets are permitted.

Reservations, fees: Reservations are not accepted. Sites are $10 per night, $5 per night for an additional vehicle. Open June–mid-November, weather permitting.

Directions: From Pendleton, drive north on Highway 11 for 16 miles to Highway 204 near Weston. Turn right (southeast) on Highway 204 and drive 17.5 miles to Forest Road 64. Turn left and drive 0.5 mile to Forest Road 6401. Turn left (north) and drive two miles to Road 6401-050. Turn right (north) and drive 0.5 mile to the camp.

Contact: Umatilla National Forest, Walla Walla Ranger District, 509/522-6290, fax 509/522-6000; Bluewood Recreation Management, 509/382-4725.

6 JUBILEE LAKE

Scenic rating: 8

on Jubilee Lake in Umatilla National Forest
See map page 355

This campground along the shore of 90-acre Jubilee Lake (elevation 4,800 feet) is a good area for fishing, hiking, and swimming. The largest and most popular campground in Umatilla National Forest, it fills up on weekends and holidays. Electric boat motors are permitted, but gas-powered motors are prohibited. A 2.8-mile trail loops around the lake and provides different levels of wheelchair accessibility for people with disabilities. Fishing access is available along the trail.

RV sites, facilities: There are 51 sites for tents or RVs up to 28 feet (no hookups). Picnic tables and fire grills are provided. Drinking water, firewood, picnic areas, and restrooms with flush toilets are available. Some facilities are wheelchair accessible. Boat docks and launching facilities are nearby. Garbage bins are available during the summer. Leashed pets are permitted.

Reservations, fees: Reservations are not accepted. Sites are $15 per night, plus $5 per night for each additional vehicle. Open mid-June–mid-October, weather permitting.

Directions: From Pendleton, drive north on Highway 11 for 16 miles to Highway 204 near Weston. Turn right (southeast) on Highway 204 and drive 17.5 miles to Forest Road 64. Turn left and drive 12 miles northeast to Forest Road 6400-250. Turn right (south) and drive 0.5 mile to the camp.

Contact: Umatilla National Forest, Walla Walla Ranger District, 509/522-6290, fax 509/522-6000; Bluewood Recreation Management, 509/382-4725.

◼ DOUGHERTY SPRINGS

Scenic rating: 5

near Dougherty Springs in Wallowa-Whitman National Forest

See map page 355

This wooded, primitive campground (elevation 5,100 feet) adjacent to Dougherty Springs is one in a series of remote camps set near natural springs. The camp is in an open area with sparse Douglas and white fir. Birds, deer, elk, and small mammals can be seen in the area. Hells Canyon National Recreation Area to the east provides many recreation options.

RV sites, facilities: There are 12 sites for tents or RVs up to 22 feet (no hookups). Picnic tables and fire grills are provided. Vault toilets are available. There is no drinking water, and garbage must be packed out. Leashed pets are permitted.

Reservations, fees: Reservations are not accepted. There is no fee for camping. Open June–late November, weather permitting.

Directions: From LaGrande, drive northeast on Highway 82 for 62 miles to Enterprise and Highway 3. Turn north on Highway 3 and drive 15 miles to Forest Road 46. Turn right (northeast) and drive 30 miles to the campground on the left.

Contact: Hells Canyon National Recreation Area, Wallowa Mountains Visitors Center, 541/426-5546, www.fs.fed.us/hellscanyon/.

◼ EMIGRANT SPRINGS STATE HERITAGE PARK

Scenic rating: 7

near the Umatilla Indian Reservation

See map page 355

Perched near the summit of the Blue Mountains, Emigrant Springs provides an opportunity to explore a popular pioneer stopover along the Oregon Trail. The park is nestled in an old-growth forest, lush with flora and teeming with native wildlife. From here, you can explore nearby attractions, such as the Blue Mountain Crossing Oregon Trail interpretive park or the Pendleton Woolen Mills and underground tours. Horse campers frequent this park.

RV sites, facilities: There are 19 sites with full hookups (20 and 30 amps) for RVs of any length, 33 tent sites, a designated horse camp, and eight cabins. Picnic tables, fire grills, and horse corrals are provided. Drinking water, garbage bins, restrooms with flush toilets and showers, firewood, a coin laundry, some horse facilities, a community building with a kitchen, a basketball court, an amphitheater, and a baseball field are available. Some facilities are wheelchair accessible. Leashed pets are permitted.

Reservations, fees: Reservations are accepted at 800/452-5687 or www.oregonstateparks.org ($6 reservation fee). Sites are $10–16 per night, horse campsites are $10–14 per night, plus $5 per night per additional vehicle. Cabins are $20–35 per night. Some credit cards are accepted. Open year-round, with limited facilities during winter.

Directions: From Pendleton, drive southeast on I-84 for 26 miles to Exit 234. Take that exit to Old Oregon Trail Road (frontage road) and drive 0.5 mile to the park on the right.

Contact: Emigrant Springs State Heritage Park, 541/983-2277 or 800/551-6949, www.oregonstateparks.org.

9 MINAM STATE PARK

Scenic rating: 7

near the Grande Ronde River

See map page 355

In a remote, steep valley, this park has a landscape dominated by large pine trees. The Wallowa River flows through the park and is noted for its rafting and fishing, especially for steelhead in the spring and fall. Wildlife is abundant, including bear, cougar, deer, elk, and, occasionally, mountain sheep downriver. The park is small and pretty, well worth the detour off I-84 necessary to get here.

RV sites, facilities: There are 12 sites for tents or RVs of any length (no hookups). Picnic tables and fire grills are provided. Drinking water is available May–mid-October. Garbage bins and vault toilets are available. Raft rentals are available nearby. Leashed pets are permitted.

Reservations, fees: Reservations are not accepted. Sites are $8 per night, plus $5 per night for an additional vehicle. Open April–October.

Directions: From LaGrande, drive northeast on Highway 82 for 18 miles to Elgin, then continue 14 miles to the park entrance road. Turn left (north) and drive two miles to the park.

Contact: Minam State Park, 541/432-8855; Oregon State Parks, 800/551-6949, www.oregonstateparks.org.

10 CUTSFORTH PARK

Scenic rating: 8

on Willow Creek

See map page 355

This county park is secluded and private. It's set beside a small, wheelchair-accessible pond in a quiet, wooded area. Trout fishing is available in the stocked pond. Three of the campsites have corrals available. (See the *Anson Wright Memorial Park* listing in this chapter for details on the area.)

RV sites, facilities: There are 45 sites for tents or RVs up to 30 feet with full or partial hookups (30 amps). A large building with kitchen facilities is available for rent by groups. Picnic tables and fire rings are provided. Restrooms have coin showers. Horseshoe pits, firewood, ice, and a playground are available. Some facilities are wheelchair accessible. Supplies are available in Heppner (22 miles away). Leashed pets are permitted.

Reservations, fees: Reservations are accepted at 541/989-9500. Sites are $10–18 per night, plus $2 per night per additional vehicle and $3 per night per horse. Weekly rates are available. Open mid-May–mid-November, weather permitting.

Directions: From Pendleton on I-84, drive west for 27 miles to Exit 182 and Highway 207 (Heppner Highway). Turn south and drive 32 miles to Lexington and Highway 74. Turn left (southeast) on Highway 74 (becomes Highway 207) and drive 10 miles to Heppner. Continue south on Highway 207 for 0.5 mile to Willow Creek Road. Turn left on Willow Creek Road and drive 23 miles to the park.

Contact: Morrow County Public Works, 541/989-9500, fax 541/989-8352, www.morrowcountyparks.org.

11 ANSON WRIGHT MEMORIAL PARK

Scenic rating: 7

on Rock Creek

See map page 354

Set among wooded hills along a small stream, this county park offers visitors prime trout fishing in several stocked ponds as well as hiking opportunities. One of the fishing ponds is wheelchair accessible. Attractions in the area include Emigrant Springs State Park, Hardman Ghost Town (10 miles away), and the Pendleton Mills. There's also a nearby opal mine.

RV sites, facilities: There are 49 sites for tents or RVs up to 40 feet; some sites have full hookups (30 amps) and/or are pull-through. Picnic tables and fire rings are provided. Restrooms have coin showers. A picnic area, firewood, ice, and a playground are provided. Some facilities are wheelchair accessible. Leashed pets are permitted.

Reservations, fees: Reservations are accepted at 541/989-9500. Sites are $10–18 per night and $2 per night per additional vehicle. Weekly rates are available. Open mid-May–mid-November, weather permitting.

Directions: From Pendleton, drive west on I-84 for 27 miles to Exit 182 and Highway 207 (Heppner Highway). Turn south and drive 32 miles to Lexington and Highway 74. Turn left (south) on Highway 74 (becomes Highway 20) and drive 10 miles to Heppner. Continue south on Highway 207 for 11 miles to Ruggs and a fork. Bear left at the fork (still Highway 207) and drive 12 miles to the park on the right.

Contact: Morrow County Public Works, 541/989-9500, fax 541/989-8352, www.morrowcountyparks.org.

12 BULL PRAIRIE LAKE

Scenic rating: 8

on Bull Prairie Lake in Umatilla National Forest
See map page 354

This campground is on the shore of Bull Prairie Lake, a 24-acre lake at 4,000 feet elevation. Boating (no motors permitted), fishing, hunting, and swimming are some of the options. A hiking trail circles the lake. This spot attracts little attention from out-of-towners, yet it offers plenty of recreation opportunities, making it an ideal vacation destination for many.

RV sites, facilities: There are 28 sites for tents or RVs up to 31 feet (no hookups). Picnic tables

and fire grills are provided. Drinking water, garbage bins (summer only), firewood, and vault toilets are available. Boat docks, launching facilities, and a boat ramp are on-site. Some facilities are wheelchair accessible, including the boat ramp. Leashed pets are permitted.

Reservations, fees: Reservations are not accepted. Sites are $14 per night, double sites are $19 per night, and it's $5–8 per night for an additional vehicle. Open May–October, weather permitting.

Directions: From Heppner, drive south on Highway 207 for roughly 35 miles to the national forest boundary and continue four miles to Forest Road 2039 (paved). Turn left and drive three miles northeast to the campground on the right.

Contact: Umatilla National Forest, Heppner Ranger District, 541/676-9187, fax 541/676-2105; Bluewood Recreation Management, 509/382-4725.

13 UKIAH-DALE FOREST STATE SCENIC CORRIDOR

Scenic rating: 7

near the North Fork of the John Day River
See map page 354

Fishing is a prime activity at this Camas Creek campground, nestled near the banks of the North Fork of the John Day River at an elevation of 3,140 feet. It's a good layover for visitors cruising U.S. 395 looking for a spot for the night. Emigrant Springs State Park near Pendleton is a possible side trip.

RV sites, facilities: There are 27 sites for tents or RVs up to 50 feet (no hookups). Picnic tables and fire pits are provided. Drinking water, firewood, and restrooms with flush toilets are available. Leashed pets are permitted.

Reservations, fees: Reservations are not accepted. Sites are $5–8 per night, plus $5 per night per additional vehicle. Open mid-April– late October.

Directions: From Pendleton, drive south on U.S. 395 for 50 miles to Highway 244 (near Ukiah). Continue south on U.S. 395 for three miles to the park.

Contact: Emigrant Springs State Heritage Area, 541/983-2277; Oregon State Parks, 800/551-6949, www.oregonstateparks.org.

14 LANE CREEK

Scenic rating: 4

on Camas Creek in Umatilla National Forest

See map page 355

This campground (3,850 feet elevation) borders Camas Creek and Lane Creek, just inside the forest boundary, and provides easy access to all the amenities of town. It's a popular stop for overnighters passing through the area. Some of the sites close to the highway get traffic noise. Highlights in the area include hot springs (privately owned) and good hunting and fishing. A U.S. Forest Service map details the back roads.

RV sites, facilities: There are six sites for tents or RVs up to 28 feet (no hookups) and one group site. Picnic tables, garbage bins, and fire grills are provided. Vault toilets are available. There is no drinking water. Some facilities are wheelchair accessible. Leashed pets are permitted.

Reservations, fees: Reservations are not accepted. Sites are $5 per night, and it's $10 per night for the group site. Open April–November, weather permitting.

Directions: From Pendleton, drive south on U.S. 395 for 50 miles to Ukiah and Highway 244. Turn east on Highway 244 and drive nine miles to the campground on the left.

Contact: Umatilla National Forest, North Fork John Day Ranger District, 541/427-3231, fax 541/276-5026.

15 SPOOL CART

Scenic rating: 6

on the Grande Ronde River in Wallowa-Whitman National Forest

See map page 355

This campground on the banks of the Grande Ronde River gets its name from the large cable spools that were left on a cart here for some years. It sits at 3,500 feet elevation. Hilgard Junction State Park to the north provides numerous recreation options, and the Oregon Interpretive Trail Park at Blue Crossing is nearby. This camp is popular with hunters in the fall. It's advisable to obtain a map of Wallowa-Whitman National Forest, which details the back roads and other side trips.

RV sites, facilities: There are nine sites for tents or RVs up to 22 feet (no hookups). Picnic tables and fire grills are provided. Vault toilets are available. There is no drinking water, and garbage must be packed out. Some facilities are wheelchair accessible. Leashed pets are permitted.

Reservations, fees: Reservations are not accepted. Sites are $5 per night per vehicle. Open late May–late November.

Directions: From Pendleton, drive southeast on U.S. 84 for 42 miles to Highway 244. Turn southwest on Highway 244 and drive 13 miles to Forest Road 51. Turn left (south) and drive five miles to the campground on the right.

Contact: Wallowa-Whitman National Forest, LaGrande Ranger District, 541/963-7186, fax 541/962-8580.

16 BIRD TRACK SPRINGS

Scenic rating: 7

near the Grande Ronde River in Wallowa-Whitman National Forest

See map page 355

Located at an elevation of 3,100 feet about a five-minute walk from the Grande Ronde River, this campground has open, spacious sites right off the highway. The surrounding woods are primarily ponderosa pine and white fir. The Bird Track Springs Interpretive Trail provides a hiking option.

RV sites, facilities: There are 26 sites for tents or RVs up to 22 feet (no hookups). Picnic tables, garbage service (summer only), and fire rings are provided. Drinking water and vault toilets are available. A summer camp host is on-site. Some facilities are wheelchair accessible. Leashed pets are permitted.

OREGON

OREGON

Reservations, fees: Reservations are not accepted. Sites are $5 per night per vehicle. Open mid-May–November, weather permitting.

Directions: From Pendleton, drive southeast on U.S. 84 for 42 miles to Highway 244. Turn right (southwest) and drive seven miles to the campground on the left.

Contact: Wallowa-Whitman National Forest, LaGrande Ranger District, 541/963-7186, fax 541/962-8580.

17 OLIVE LAKE

Scenic rating: 9

on Olive Lake in Umatilla National Forest

See map page 355

This campground (6,100 feet elevation) nestles along the shore of Olive Lake, between two sections of the North Fork John Day Wilderness. Dammed to hold an increased volume of water, the glacial lake is a beautiful tint of blue. Motorized boats are allowed, but waterskiing is prohibited. Fishing is fair for kokanee salmon and brook, cutthroat, and rainbow trout. A 2.5-mile trail circles the lake. Nearby trails provide access to the wilderness; motorbikes and mountain bikes are not permitted in the wilderness. Sections of the old wooden pipeline for the historic Fremont Powerhouse can still be seen. The old mining town of Granite is 12 miles east of camp.

RV sites, facilities: There are 23 sites for tents or RVs up to 28 feet (no hookups) and two group sites. Picnic tables and fire grills are provided. Vault toilets are available. There is no drinking water, and garbage must be packed out. Boat docks, launching facilities, and two picnic areas are available. Leashed pets are permitted.

Reservations, fees: Reservations are not accepted. Sites are $5 per night, with a 14-day stay limit; the fee is $10 for a group camp. Open June–early October, weather permitting.

Directions: From Pendleton, drive south on U.S. 395 for 62 miles to Forest Road 55 (one

mile north of Dale). Turn right and drive 0.5 mile to Forest Road 10. Turn right on Forest Road 10 and drive 26 miles to Forest Road 480. Turn right and drive 0.5 mile to the campground.

Contact: Umatilla National Forest, North Fork John Day Ranger District, 541/427-3231, fax 541/276-5026.

18 NORTH FORK JOHN DAY

Scenic rating: 6

on the North Fork of the John Day River in Umatilla National Forest

See map page 355

This campground is in a conifer stand along the banks of the North Fork of the John Day River and makes an ideal base camp for a wilderness backpacking trip. Trails from camp lead into the North Fork John Day Wilderness. A horse-handling area is available for wilderness users. No motorbikes are permitted in the wilderness. In the fall, it has a great view of salmon spawning in the river. The camp is at an elevation of 5,200 feet at the intersection of Elkhorn and Blue Mountain National Forest Scenic Byways.

RV sites, facilities: There are 17 sites for tents or RVs up to 28 feet (no hookups). Picnic tables and fire rings are provided. Vault toilets are available. There is no drinking water. Garbage must be packed out. Leashed pets are permitted.

Reservations, fees: Reservations are not accepted. Sites are $5 per night, with a 14-day stay limit. Open June–November, weather permitting. For trailhead use only, a Northwest Forest Pass ($5 daily fee or $30 annual fee per parked vehicle) is required.

Directions: From Pendleton, drive south on U.S. 395 for 50 miles to Highway 244. Turn east on Highway 244 and drive one mile to Ukiah and Forest Road 52. Turn right (south) on Forest Road 52 and drive 36 miles to the campground on the right.

Contact: Umatilla National Forest, North Fork

John Day Ranger District, 541/427-3231, fax 541/276-5026.

19 ANTHONY LAKES

Scenic rating: 10

on Anthony Lake in Wallowa-Whitman National Forest

See map page 355

This campground (7,100 feet elevation) is adjacent to Anthony Lake, where boating without motors is permitted. Sites are wooded, providing good screening between them. Alas, mosquitoes are often in particular abundance. Several smaller lakes within two miles by car or trail are ideal for trout fishing from a canoe, float tube, or raft. Sometimes mountain goats can be seen from the Elkhorn Crest Trail, which begins near here. Weekends and holidays are full.

RV sites, facilities: There are 37 sites for tents or RVs up to 22 feet (no hookups) and one group site for up to 75 people. Drinking water, fire grills, garbage bins (summer only), and picnic tables are provided. Vault toilets are available. Garbage must be packed out. Some facilities are wheelchair accessible. Boat-launching facilities are nearby. Leashed pets are permitted.

Reservations, fees: Reservations are required for the group site at 541/894-2505 but are not accepted for family sites. Sites are $8 per night, $5 per night per additional vehicle, and $35–55 per night for the group site. Open June–late September, weather permitting.

Directions: From Baker City on I-84, turn north on U.S. 30. Drive north for 10 miles to Haines and County Road 1146 (signed for Anthony Lakes Ski Resort). Turn left on County Road 1146 and drive 20 miles (the road becomes Forest Road 73) to the campground on the left.

Contact: Wallowa-Whitman National Forest, Baker Ranger District, 541/523-4476, fax 541/523-1965.

20 UNION CREEK

Scenic rating: 8

on Phillips Lake in Wallowa-Whitman National Forest

See map page 355

This campground along the north shore of Phillips Lake is easy to reach, yet missed by most I-84 travelers. It's the largest of three camps on the lake and the only one with drinking water. An old narrow-gauge railroad has been restored and runs up the valley from McEwen Depot (six miles from the campground) to Sumpter (10 miles away). Visit Sumpter to see an old dredge.

RV sites, facilities: There are 58 sites for tents or RVs up to 32 feet and one group site; some sites have full hookups (20 amps). Drinking water, garbage bins (summer only), and picnic tables are provided. Flush toilets, a dump station, firewood, and ice are available. There is a seasonal concession stand for packaged goods and fishing tackle. Some facilities are wheelchair accessible. Boat docks and launching facilities are adjacent to the campground. Leashed pets are permitted.

Reservations, fees: Reservations are required for the group site at 541/894-2505 but are not accepted for family sites. Sites are $12–20 per night, $5 per night per additional vehicle, and $55 per night for group sites. Open May–September, weather permitting.

Directions: From Baker City, drive southwest on Highway 7 for 20 miles to the campground on the left.

Contact: Wallowa-Whitman National Forest, Baker Ranger District, 541/523-4476 or 541/894-2505 (concessionaire, Recreation Resource Management), fax 541/523-1965.

21 SHADY

Scenic rating: 6

on the Lostine River in Wallowa-Whitman National Forest

See map page 355

This campground, set along the banks of the Lostine River at an elevation of 5,400 feet, is

OREGON

close to trails that provide access to the Eagle Cap Wilderness, a beautiful and pristine area that's perfect for an extended backpacking trip. The camp has wooded as well as meadow areas. Mountain sheep can sometimes be spotted.

RV sites, facilities: There are 12 sites for tents or RVs up to 30 feet (no hookups). Picnic tables and fire grills are provided. Vault toilets are available. There is no drinking water, and garbage must be packed out. Leashed pets are permitted.

Reservations, fees: Reservations are not accepted. Sites are $6 per night. Open mid-June–November, weather permitting.

Directions: From LaGrande, turn north on Highway 82 and drive 52 miles to Lostine and Forest Road 8210. Turn right (south) and drive 15 miles to the campground.

Contact: Wallowa-Whitman National Forest, Eagle Cap Ranger District; Wallowa Mountains Visitors Center, 541/426-5546.

22 MOUNTAIN VIEW MOTEL AND RV PARK

Scenic rating: 3

near Wallowa Lake
See map page 355

This park is centrally located for exploring the greater Wallowa Lake area. Enjoy views of the Seven Devils Mountains and of the Eagle Cap Wilderness from here. Nearby recreational facilities include bike paths, a golf course, hiking trails, and a riding stable. Fishing and jet boating are also one mile away at Wallowa Lake.

RV sites, facilities: There are 30 sites with full hookups (15, 20, and 50 amps) for RVs of any length, including some pull-through; a grassy area for tents; and nine cabins. Picnic tables and fire pits are provided. Restrooms have flush toilets and showers. A dump station and coin laundry are available. Propane gas, a store, and a café are within two miles. Leashed pets are permitted.

Reservations, fees: Reservations are accepted. RV sites are $21.95 per night, tent sites are $15.95 per night, and it's $3 per person per

night for more than two people. Some credit cards are accepted. Open year-round.

Directions: From LaGrande, turn north on Highway 82 and drive 62 miles to Enterprise and the junction with Highway 3. Continue north on Highway 82 for four miles to the campground on the right (1.5 miles north of Joseph).

Contact: Mountain View Motel and RV Park, 866/262-9891 (toll free) or tel./fax 541/432-2982, www.rvmotel.com.

23 WALLOWA LAKE STATE PARK

Scenic rating: 8

on Wallowa Lake
See map page 355

Surrounded on three sides by 9,000-foot, snow-capped mountains and large, clear Wallowa Lake, this area is popular for fishing and boating recreation, including waterskiing and parasailing. You can also enjoy bumper boats, canoes, hikes, horseback rides, miniature golf, or a tram ride up 4,000 feet to a mountaintop. A nearby artist community makes world-class bronze castings, and tours are available. This is also the gateway to Hells Canyon, the deepest gorge in North America. Other highlights include a pretty one-mile nature trail and trailheads that provide access into the Eagle Cap Wilderness. A marina is nearby for boaters and anglers. Picnicking, swimming, and wildlife-viewing are a few of the other activities available to visitors.

RV sites, facilities: There are 121 sites for RVs of any length with full hookups, 89 tent sites, some hike-in/bike-in sites, three group tent areas for up to 25 people each, two yurts, and one deluxe cabin. Picnic tables and fire rings are provided. Garbage bins, drinking water, restrooms with flush toilets and showers, a dump station, and firewood are available. A store, a café, and ice are within one mile. Some facilities are wheelchair accessible. Boat docks, launching facilities, and rentals are nearby. Leashed pets are permitted.

Reservations, fees: Reservations are accepted at 800/452-5687 or www.oregonstateparks.org

($6 reservation fee). Sites are $13–21 per night, plus $5 per night for an additional vehicle; hike-in/bike-in sites are $4 per person per night; group areas are $64 per night; yurts are $29 per night; and the deluxe cabin is $58–80 per night. Some credit cards are accepted. Open year-round.

Directions: From LaGrande, turn north on Highway 82 and drive 62 miles to Enterprise and the junction with Highway 3. Continue south on Highway 82 to Joseph. Continue for six miles to the south shore of the lake and the campground.

Contact: Wallowa Lake State Park, 541/432-4185; Oregon State Parks, 800/551-6949, www.oregonstateparks.org.

24 BLACKHORSE

Scenic rating: 7

on the Imnaha River in Wallowa-Whitman National Forest

See map page 355

This campground along the banks of the Imnaha River in Hells Canyon National Recreation Area is in a secluded section of Wallowa-Whitman National Forest at an elevation of 4,000 feet.

RV sites, facilities: There are 16 sites for tents or RVs up to 30 feet (no hookups). Picnic tables and fire grills are provided. Vault toilets are available. There is no drinking water, and garbage must be packed out. Leashed pets are permitted.

Reservations, fees: Reservations are not accepted. Sites are $8 per night. Open June–late November, weather permitting.

Directions: From I-84 at LaGrande, turn north on Highway 82 and drive 62 miles to Enterprise. Continue six miles south to Joseph and Highway 350. Turn left (east) and drive eight miles on Highway 350 to Forest Road 39. Turn right (south) on Forest Road 39 and drive 29 miles to the campground.

Contact: Hells Canyon National Recreation Area, Wallowa Mountains Visitors Center, 541/426-5546, www.fs.fed.us/hellscanyon/.

25 LICK CREEK

Scenic rating: 7

on Lick Creek in Wallowa-Whitman National Forest

See map page 355

This campground sits at an elevation of 5,400 feet in parklike surroundings along the banks of Lick Creek in Hells Canyon National Recreation Area. It is secluded and pretty. Tall Douglas fir, lodgepole pine, tamarack, and white fir are interspersed throughout the campground, providing habitat for some of the birds and small mammals you might see.

RV sites, facilities: There are seven tent sites and five sites with no hookups for RVs up to 30 feet. Picnic tables and fire grills are provided. Vault toilets are available. There is no drinking water, and garbage must be packed out. Leashed pets are permitted.

Reservations, fees: Reservations are not accepted. Sites are $6 per night. Open mid-June–late November, weather permitting.

Directions: From LaGrande, turn north on Highway 82 and drive 62 miles to Enterprise and the junction with Highway 3. Continue south on Highway 82 to Joseph and Highway 350. Turn left (east) and drive 7.5 miles to Forest Road 39. Turn right (south) and drive 15 miles to the campground.

Contact: Hells Canyon National Recreation Area, Wallowa Mountains Visitors Center, 541/426-5546, www.fs.fed.us/hellscanyon/.

26 OLLOKOT

Scenic rating: 5

on the Imnaha River in Wallowa-Whitman National Forest

See map page 355

This campground sits on the banks of the Imnaha River in Hells Canyon National Recreation Area at an elevation of 4,000 feet. It's named for Chief Joseph's brother, a member of the Nez Perce tribe. For those seeking a little more solitude, this could be the spot.

RV sites, facilities: There are 12 sites for tents or

OREGON

RVs up to 30 feet (no hookups). Picnic tables and fire grills are provided. Vault toilets are available. There is no drinking water, and garbage must be packed out. Leashed pets are permitted.

Reservations, fees: Reservations are not accepted. Sites are $8 per night. Open June–late November, weather permitting.

Directions: From I-84 at LaGrande, turn north on Highway 82 and drive 62 miles to Enterprise. Continue six miles south to Joseph and Highway 350. Turn left (east) and drive eight miles to Forest Road 39. Turn right (south) on Forest Road 39 and drive 30 miles to the campground on the left.

Contact: Hells Canyon National Recreation Area, Wallowa Mountains Visitors Center, 541/426-5546, www.fs.fed.us/hellscanyon/.

27 INDIAN CROSSING

Scenic rating: 6

on the Imnaha River in Wallowa-Whitman National Forest

See map page 355

This campground is at an elevation of 4,500 feet. A trailhead for the Eagle Cap Wilderness is near this camp. Obtain a U.S. Forest Service map for side-trip possibilities.

RV sites, facilities: There are 14 sites for tents or RVs up to 30 feet (no hookups). Picnic tables and fire grills are provided. Vault toilets and horse facilities are available. There is no drinking water, and garbage must be packed out. Leashed pets are permitted.

Reservations, fees: Reservations are not accepted. Sites are $8 per night. Open June–late November, weather permitting.

Directions: From LaGrande, turn north on Highway 82 and drive 62 miles to Enterprise and the junction with Highway 3. Continue on Highway 82 for six miles to Joseph and Highway 350. Turn left (east) on Highway 350 and drive eight miles to Forest Road 39. Turn right (south) and drive about 30 miles to Forest Road 3960. Turn right and drive 10 miles to the campground at the end of the road.

Contact: Hells Canyon National Recreation Area, Wallowa Mountains Visitors Center, 541/426-5546, www.fs.fed.us/hellscanyon/.

28 TAMARACK

Scenic rating: 5

on Eagle Creek in Wallowa-Whitman National Forest

See map page 355

On the banks of Eagle Creek in a beautiful area with lush vegetation and abundant wildlife, this camp (4,600 feet elevation) is a good spot for a fishing and hiking trip in a remote setting.

RV sites, facilities: There are 15 sites for tents or RVs up to 25 feet (no hookups). Picnic tables and fire grills are provided. Drinking water and vault toilets are available. Garbage must be packed out. Leashed pets are permitted.

Reservations, fees: Reservations are not accepted. Sites are $5 per night. Open June–late October, weather permitting.

Directions: From Baker City, drive north on I-84 for six miles to Highway 203. Turn east on Highway 203 and drive 17 miles to Medical Springs and Big Springs Road (Forest Road 67). Turn left on Forest Road 67 and drive 15.5 miles (staying on Forest Road 67 at all Y junctions) to Forest Road 77. Turn right and drive 0.25 mile to the camp on the right.

Contact: Wallowa-Whitman National Forest, Pine Ranger District, 541/742-7511, fax 541/742-6705.

29 McBRIDE

Scenic rating: 6

on Brooks Ditch in Wallowa-Whitman National Forest

See map page 355

This campground is along the banks of Brooks Ditch at an elevation of 4,800 feet. It is little used, primitive, and obscure. Though not particularly scenic, it will work as a quick, free layover spot.

RV sites, facilities: There are 11 sites for tents

OREGON

or RVs up to 25 feet (no hookups). Picnic tables and fire grills are provided. Drinking water and vault toilets are available. Garbage must be packed out. Leashed pets are permitted.

Reservations, fees: Reservations are not accepted. There is no fee for camping. Open June–late October, weather permitting.

Directions: From Baker City, drive east on Highway 86 for 52 miles to Halfway. Turn northwest on Highway 413 and drive six miles to Forest Road 7710. Turn left (west) and drive 2.5 miles to the campground on the left.

Contact: Wallowa-Whitman National Forest, Pine Ranger District, 541/742-7511, fax 541/742-6705.

30 FISH LAKE

Scenic rating: 6

on Fish Lake in Wallowa-Whitman National Forest

See map page 355

This pretty, well-forested camp with comfortable sites along the shore of Fish Lake makes a good base for a fishing trip. Side-trip options include hiking on nearby trails that lead to mountain streams. The campground sits at an elevation of 6,600 feet.

RV sites, facilities: There are 15 sites for tents or RVs up to 20 feet (no hookups). Picnic tables and fire grills are provided. Drinking water and vault toilets are available. Garbage must be packed out. Boat-launching facilities are nearby. Leashed pets are permitted.

Reservations, fees: Reservations are not accepted. Sites are $5 per night. Open July–late October, weather permitting.

Directions: From Baker City, drive north on I-84 for four miles to Highway 86. Turn east on Highway 86 and drive 52 miles to Halfway and County Road 733. Turn right (north) on County Road 733 and drive five miles to Forest Road 66. Continue north on Forest Road 66 for 18.5 miles to the campground on the left.

Contact: Wallowa-Whitman National Forest, Pine Ranger District, 541/742-7511, fax 541/742-6705.

31 WILDCAT

Scenic rating: 4

on the East Fork of Mill Creek in Ochoco National Forest

See map page 354

This quiet, cool campground, surrounded by conifer forest, sits at an elevation of 3,700 feet in a canyon. Situated along the East Fork of Mill Creek, the camp is near the Twin Pillars Trailhead, which provides access into the Mill Creek Wilderness. No climbing is allowed in the wilderness. Ochoco Lake and Ochoco Lake State Park to the south provide side-trip possibilities.

RV sites, facilities: There are 17 sites for tents or RVs up to 30 feet (no hookups). Picnic tables and fire grills are provided. Drinking water and vault toilets are available. Garbage must be packed out. Leashed pets are permitted.

Reservations, fees: Reservations are not accepted. Sites are $8 per night, plus $3 per night for each additional vehicle. Open mid-April–late October, weather permitting.

Directions: From Prineville, drive east on U.S. 26 for nine miles to Mill Creek Road (Forest Road 33). Turn left on Mill Creek Road and drive about 10 miles to the campground.

Contact: Ochoco National Forest, Lookout Mountain Ranger District, 541/416-6500, fax 541/416-6695.

32 OCHOCO DIVIDE

Scenic rating: 5

in Ochoco National Forest

See map page 354

This camp is at an elevation of 4,700 feet amid an old-growth stand of ponderosa pine just off scenic U.S. 26. An unused forest road on the far side of the campground provides an easy stretch walk after a long day of driving. Most visitors arrive late in the day and leave early in the morning, so the area is normally quiet during the day. Marks Creek is nearby, and the Bandit Springs Rest Stop, one mile west, is the jumping-off point for a network of trails.

OREGON

RV sites, facilities: There are 28 sites for tents or RVs up to 30 feet (no hookups), with a separate hike-in/bike-in area. Picnic tables and fire pits are provided. Drinking water and vault toilets are available. Garbage must be packed out. Some facilities are wheelchair accessible. Leashed pets are permitted.

Reservations, fees: Reservations are not accepted. Sites are $10 per night, plus $5 per night for an additional vehicle. Hike-in/bike-in sites are $3 per person per night. Open late May–mid-November, weather permitting.

Directions: From Prineville, drive east on U.S. 26 for 30 miles to the campground at the summit of Ochoco Pass.

Contact: Ochoco National Forest, Lookout Mountain Ranger District, 541/416-6500, fax 541/416-6695.

33 OCHOCO FOREST CAMP

Scenic rating: 4

in Ochoco National Forest

See map page 354

Campsites here nestle along Ochoco Creek in a lush setting of ponderosa pine and aspen. The camp sits at an elevation of 4,000 feet. Fishing for rainbow trout is fair. A large group picnic area with a beautiful log shelter, perfect for weddings, family reunions, and other group events, is available for reservation. The nearby Lookout Mountain Trail provides access to the Lookout Mountain Recreation Area, 15,000 acres without roads. But hey, the truth is, don't expect privacy and solitude at this campground.

RV sites, facilities: There are six sites for tents or RVs up to 24 feet (no hookups). Picnic tables and fire rings are provided. Drinking water, garbage bins, vault toilets, and a reservable picnic shelter are available. Some facilities are wheelchair accessible. Leashed pets are permitted.

Reservations, fees: Reservations are not accepted. Sites are $10 per night, plus $5 per night for an additional vehicle. Open mid-May–November, weather permitting.

Directions: From Prineville, drive east on U.S. 26 for 16.5 miles to County Road 23. Turn right on County Road 23 and drive nine miles (County Road 23 becomes Forest Road 42) to the campground, across from the Ochoco Ranger Station.

Contact: Ochoco National Forest, Lookout Mountain Ranger District, 541/416-6500, fax 541/416-6695.

34 WALTON LAKE

Scenic rating: 7

on Walton Lake in Ochoco National Forest

See map page 354

This campground, surrounded by old-growth ponderosa pine and mountain meadows, borders the shore of small Walton Lake, where fishing and swimming are popular. Only non-motorized boats or those with electric motors are allowed. Hikers can explore a nearby trail that leads south to Round Mountain. The lake is stocked with rainbow trout, and the fishing can range from middle-of-the-road fair right up to downright excellent.

RV sites, facilities: There are 30 sites for tents or RVs up to 31 feet (no hookups) and one group site. Picnic tables, garbage bins, and fire grills are provided. Drinking water and vault toilets are available. Some facilities are wheelchair accessible. Boat-launching facilities are nearby (only electric motors are allowed). Leashed pets are permitted.

Reservations, fees: Reservations are required for the group sites at 877/444-6777 or www.ReserveUSA.com ($9 reservation fee) but are not accepted for family sites. Sites are $10–12 per night, plus $7 per night for an additional vehicle. Group sites are $25 per night. Open June–late September, weather permitting.

Directions: From Prineville, drive east on U.S. 26 for 16.5 miles to County Road 23. Turn right (northeast) and drive nine miles (County Road 23 becomes Forest Road 42) to the Ochoco Ranger Station and Forest Road

22. Turn left and drive north on Forest Road 22 for seven miles to the campground.

Contact: Ochoco National Forest, Lookout Mountain Ranger District, 541/416-6500, fax 541/416-6695.

35 CROOK COUNTY RV PARK

Scenic rating: 6

near the Crooked River
See map page 354

This public campground is in a landscaped and grassy area near the Crooked River, where fly-fishing is popular. The camp is right next to the Crook County Fairgrounds, where, in season, expositions, horse races, and rodeos take place.

RV sites, facilities: There are 81 sites for RVs up to 70 feet with full hookups (30 and 50 amps); most sites are pull-through. Two cabins are also available. Picnic tables are provided. Fire pits are provided at the tent sites. Restrooms have flush toilets and showers. A dump station, cable TV, modem access, and vending machines are available. A convenience store, a restaurant, a coin laundry, ice, gasoline, and propane are available within one mile. Some facilities are wheelchair accessible. Leashed pets are permitted.

Reservations, fees: Reservations are accepted at 800/609-2599. The fees are $9 per night for tent sites, $24 per night for RVs, and $3 per night per additional vehicle. Weekly and monthly rates are available. Some credit cards are accepted. Open year-round.

Directions: From Redmond, drive east on Highway 126 for 18 miles to Prineville (Highway 126 becomes 3rd Street) and Main Street. Turn right on Main Street and drive about 0.5 mile south to the campground on the left, before the fairgrounds.

Contact: Crook County RV Park, 541/447-2599, fax 541/416-9022, www.co.crook.or.us/.

36 OCHOCO LAKE

Scenic rating: 6

on Ochoco Lake
See map page 354

This is one of the nicer camps along U.S. 26 in eastern Oregon. The campground is on the shore of Ochoco Lake, where boating and fishing are popular pastimes. Some quality hiking trails can be found in the area.

RV sites, facilities: There are 22 sites for tents or RVs up to 30 feet (no hookups) and four sites for hikers and bicyclists. Picnic tables, garbage bins, and fire grills are provided. Drinking water, firewood, restrooms with showers and flush toilets, a fish-cleaning station, and boat-launching facilities are available. Leashed pets are permitted.

Reservations, fees: Reservations are not accepted. Sites are $16 per night, $5 per person per night for hike-in/bike-in sites, and $7 per night per additional vehicle. Some credit cards are accepted. Open April–October, weather permitting.

Directions: From Prineville, drive east on U.S. 26 for seven miles to the park entrance on the right.

Contact: Crook County Parks and Recreation, 541/447-1209, fax 541/447-9894, www.co.crook.or.us/.

37 CHIMNEY ROCK

Scenic rating: 6

on the Crooked River
See map page 354

This well-spaced campground is a favorite for picnicking and wildlife-viewing. The Chimney Rock Trailhead, just across the highway, is the jumping-off point for the 1.7-mile, moderately difficult hike to Chimney Rock. There are numerous scenic overlooks along the trail, and wildlife sightings are common. The elevation is 3,000 feet. Chimney Rock Campground is one of eight BLM camps along a six-mile stretch of Highway 27.

OREGON

RV sites, facilities: There are 20 sites for tents or RVs of any length (no hookups). Picnic tables are provided. Vault toilets, drinking water, and garbage bins are available. Some facilities are wheelchair accessible, including a fishing dock. Leashed pets are permitted.

Reservations, fees: Reservations are not accepted. Sites are $8 per night, plus $2 per night for an additional vehicle. Open year-round.

Directions: In Prineville, drive south on Highway 27 for 16.4 miles to the campground.

Contact: Bureau of Land Management, Prineville District, 541/416-6700, fax 541/416-6798.

38 PRINEVILLE RESERVOIR STATE PARK

Scenic rating: 7

on Prineville Reservoir
See map page 354

This state park is along the shore of Prineville Reservoir, which formed with the damming of the Crooked River. Boating, fishing, swimming, and waterskiing are among the activities here. The nearby boat docks and ramp are a bonus. The reservoir supports rainbow and cutthroat trout, small- and largemouth bass, catfish, and crappie. You can even ice fish in the winter. This is one of two campgrounds on the lake; the other is Prineville Reservoir Resort (see listing in this chapter).

RV sites, facilities: There are 42 sites with full or partial hookups (30 amps) for RVs up to 40 feet, 23 tent sites, two rustic cabins, and three deluxe cabins. Picnic tables and fire pits are provided. Drinking water, garbage bins, restrooms with flush toilets and showers, ice, and firewood are available. Boat docks and launching facilities are nearby. Some facilities are wheelchair accessible. Leashed pets are permitted.

Reservations, fees: Reservations are accepted at 800/452-5687 or www.oregonstateparks.org ($6 reservation fee). Sites are $12–20 per night, cabins are $35–66 per night, and it's $5 per

night per additional vehicle. Some credit cards are accepted. Open year-round.

Directions: From Prineville, drive east on U.S. 26 for one mile to Combs Flat Road. Turn right (south) and drive one mile to Juniper Canyon Road. Turn right (south) and drive 18 miles to the campground.

Contact: Prineville Reservoir State Park, 541/447-4363 or 800/551-6949, www.oregon stateparks.org.

39 PRINEVILLE RESERVOIR RESORT

Scenic rating: 6

on Prineville Reservoir
See map page 354

This resort sits on the shore of Prineville Reservoir in the high desert, a good spot for water sports and fishing. The mostly shaded sites are a combination of dirt and gravel. The camp features easy access to the reservoir and some colorful rock formations to check out.

RV sites, facilities: There are 71 sites for tents or RVs of any length with partial hookups (30 amps) including four pull-through sites. There are also seven motel rooms and one primitive cabin. Drinking water, fire pits, and picnic tables are provided. Restrooms have flush toilets and coin showers. Propane gas, a dump station, firewood, a convenience store, a café, and ice are available. A full-service marina, a boat ramp, and boat rentals, including personal watercraft, are on-site. Leashed pets are permitted.

Reservations, fees: Reservations are accepted at 541/447-7468. Sites are $14–21 per night. Some credit cards are accepted. Open May–mid-October, weather permitting.

Directions: From Prineville, drive east on U.S. 26 for one mile to Combs Flat Road. Turn right (south) and drive one mile to Juniper Canyon Road. Turn right (south) and drive 18 miles to the resort at the end of the road.

Contact: Prineville Reservoir Resort, tel./fax 541/447-7468.

40 JASPER POINT STATE PARK

Scenic rating: 7

on Prineville Reservoir
See map page 354

Here is a quiet alternative to Prineville Reservoir State Park. This park is not as popular as Prineville, although it does fill up on summer weekends. It's used mainly by locals. Although this park is named Jasper Point, the setting is in a cove and the views are not as good as at Prineville Reservoir State Park. A 1.75-mile trail connects the two campgrounds, and another 0.7-mile trail runs along the shoreline.

RV sites, facilities: There are 28 sites for tents or RVs of any length (no hookups). Picnic tables and fire pits are provided. Drinking water, vault toilets, garbage containers, a day-use area, and a boat launch are available. Leashed pets are permitted.

Reservations, fees: Reservations are not accepted. Sites are $18 per night and $5 per night per additional vehicle. Open May–September.

Directions: From Prineville, drive east on U.S. 26 for one mile to Combs Flat Road. Turn right (south) and drive one mile to Juniper Canyon Road. Turn right (south) and drive 21 miles to the campground.

Contact: Prineville Reservoir State Park (no contact phone number at Jasper), 541/447-4363; Oregon State Parks, 800/551-6949, www.oregonstateparks.org.

41 ANTELOPE FLAT RESERVOIR

Scenic rating: 6

on Antelope Flat Reservoir in Ochoco
National Forest

See map page 354

This pretty spot is along the west shore of Antelope Flat Reservoir amid ponderosa pine and juniper. The campground is on the edge of the high desert at an elevation of 4,600 feet. It features wide sites and easy access to the lake. Trout fishing can sometimes be good in the spring, and boating with motors is permitted. This is also a good lake for canoes.

RV sites, facilities: There are 25 sites for tents or RVs up to 30 feet (no hookups). Picnic tables and fire grills are provided. Drinking water and vault toilets are available. Garbage must be packed out. Boat-launching facilities are nearby. Leashed pets are permitted.

Reservations, fees: Reservations are not accepted. Sites are $8 per night, plus $3 per night for each additional vehicle. Open early May–late October, weather permitting.

Directions: From Prineville, drive southeast on Combs Flat Road (Paulina Highway) for 30 miles to Forest Road 17 (Antelope Reservoir Junction). Turn right on Forest Road 17 and drive about 10 miles to Forest Road 1700-600. Drive 0.25 mile on Forest Road 1700-600 to the campground.

Contact: Ochoco National Forest, Lookout Mountain Ranger District, 541/416-6500, fax 541/416-6695.

42 DEEP CREEK

Scenic rating: 5

on the North Fork of the Crooked River in Ochoco National Forest

See map page 354

This small camp on the edge of high desert gets little use, but it's in a nice spot—the confluence of Deep Creek and the North Fork of the Crooked River. The elevation is 4,200 feet. Highlights include pretty, shady sites and river access. Fishing is possible.

RV sites, facilities: There are six sites for tents or RVs up to 22 feet (no hookups). Picnic tables and fire grills are provided. Drinking water and vault toilets are available. Garbage must be packed out. Leashed pets are permitted.

Reservations, fees: Reservations are not accepted. Sites are $8 per night, plus $3 per night per additional vehicle. Open June–mid-October, weather permitting.

Directions: From Prineville, drive east on U.S. 26 for 16.5 miles to County Route 23.

Turn right (northeast) and drive 8.5 miles (it becomes Forest Road 42). Continue east on Forest Road 42 (paved road) for 23.5 miles to the campground on the right.
Contact: Ochoco National Forest, Lookout Mountain Ranger District, 541/416-6500, fax 541/416-6695.

43 WOLF CREEK

Scenic rating: 5

on Wolf Creek in Ochoco National Forest
See map page 354

This campground, at 4,000 feet elevation, sits along the banks of Wolf Creek, a nice trout stream that runs through Ochoco National Forest. A quality spot, it features some excellent hiking trails to the northeast in the Black Canyon Wilderness.
RV sites, facilities: There are 10 sites for tents or RVs up to 22 feet (no hookups). Picnic tables and fire grills are provided. Vault toilets are available. There is no drinking water, and garbage must be packed out. Leashed pets are permitted.
Reservations, fees: Reservations are not accepted. Sites are $6 per night, with a 14-day stay limit, and $3 per night for an additional vehicle. Open May–November, weather permitting.
Directions: From Prineville, drive southeast on Combs Flat Road (Paulina Highway) for 55 miles to Paulina. Continue east for 3.5 miles to County Road 112. Turn left (north) and drive 6.5 miles to Forest Road 42. Turn left (north) and drive 1.5 miles to the campground on the right.
Contact: Ochoco National Forest, Paulina Ranger District, 541/477-6900, fax 541/477-6949.

44 SUGAR CREEK

Scenic rating: 6

on Sugar Creek in Ochoco National Forest
See map page 354

This small, quiet, and remote campground sits along the banks of Sugar Creek at an elevation of 4,000 feet. A 0.75-mile trail loops along the creek. The camp also offers a covered group shelter in the day-use area and a wheelchair-accessible trail. Because of the presence of bald eagles, there may be seasonal closures on land access in the area. Be sure to check posted notices.
RV sites, facilities: There are 17 sites for tents or RVs up to 22 feet (no hookups). Picnic tables, garbage bins, and fire grills are provided. Drinking water, a picnic shelter, and vault toilets are available. Some facilities are wheelchair accessible. Leashed pets are permitted.
Reservations, fees: Reservations are not accepted. Sites are $8 per night, with a 14-day stay limit, and $3 per night for an additional vehicle. Open May–November.
Directions: From Prineville, drive southeast on Combs Flat Road (Paulina Highway) for 55 miles to Paulina. Continue east and drive 3.5 miles to a fork with County Road 112. Bear left at the fork onto County Road 112 and drive 7.5 miles to Forest Road 58. Bear right on Forest Road 58 and continue for 2.25 miles to the campground on the right.
Contact: Ochoco National Forest, Paulina Ranger District, 541/477-6900, fax 541/477-6949.

45 CLYDE HOLLIDAY STATE RECREATION SITE

Scenic rating: 7

near the John Day River
See map page 354

Think of this campground as an oasis. Its tall, willowy cottonwood trees provide shade and serenity, giving you that private, secluded feeling. It borders the John Day River, and you're as likely to have wildlife neighbors as human ones; Rocky Mountain elk and mule deer are frequent visitors. You might also see steelhead rushing upriver to spawn.
RV sites, facilities: There are 31 sites for tents or RVs up to 60 feet with partial hookups (20, 30, and 50 amps), a hike-in/bike-in tent

area, and two tepees. Picnic tables and fire grills are provided. Drinking water, firewood, a dump station, and restrooms with showers and flush toilets are available. Leashed pets are permitted.

Reservations, fees: Reservations are not accepted. Sites are $12–17 per night, $5 per night for an additional vehicle, $4 per person per night for hike-in/bike-in sites, and $27–28 per night for tepees. Open March–November, weather permitting.

Directions: From John Day, drive west on U.S. 26 for six miles to the park on the left.

Contact: Clyde Holliday State Recreation Site, 541/932-4453 or 800/551-6949, www.oregon stateparks.org.

46 MAGONE LAKE

Scenic rating: 8

on Magone Lake in Malheur National Forest

See map page 354

This campground is along the shore of little Magone Lake at an elevation of 5,500 feet. A 1.8-mile trail rings the lake, and the section extending from the beach area to the campground (about 0.25 mile) is wheelchair accessible. A 0.5-mile trail leads to Magone Slide, an unusual geological formation. Canoeing, fishing, sailing, and swimming are some of the popular activities at this lake. Easy-access bike trails can be found within 0.25 mile of the campground.

RV sites, facilities: There are 20 sites for tents or RVs up to 40 feet (no hookups); some are pull-through sites. There is a separate group camping site designed for 10 families and a picnic shelter. Picnic tables and fire grills are provided. Drinking water, composting toilets, a boat ramp, and a beach area are available. Some facilities are wheelchair accessible. Boat docks and launching facilities are nearby. Leashed pets are permitted.

Reservations, fees: Reservations are required for the group site and group picnic shelter at 541/820-3863 but are not accepted for family

sites. Sites are $10 per night, and it's $60 per night for the group site. Open May–November, weather permitting.

Directions: From John Day, drive east on U.S. 26 for eight miles to County Road 18. Turn north and drive 10 miles to Forest Road 3620. Turn left (west) on Forest Road 3620 and drive 1.5 miles to Forest Road 3618. Turn right (northwest) and drive 1.5 miles to the campground.

Contact: Malheur National Forest, Blue Mountain Ranger District, 541/575-3000.

47 MIDDLE FORK

Scenic rating: 6

on the Middle Fork of the John Day River in Malheur National Forest

See map page 355

Scattered along the banks of the Middle Fork of the John Day River at 4,100 feet elevation, these rustic campsites are easy to reach off a paved road. Besides wildlife-watching and berry picking, the main activity at this camp is fishing, so bring along your fly rod and pinch down your barbs for catch-and-release. The John Day is a state scenic waterway.

RV sites, facilities: There are 10 sites for tents or RVs up to 30 feet (no hookups). Picnic tables and fire grills are provided. Vault toilets are available. There is no drinking water, and garbage must be packed out. Some facilities are wheelchair accessible. Leashed pets are permitted.

Reservations, fees: Reservations are not accepted. Sites are $5 per night, plus $2.50 per night per additional vehicle. Open May–November, weather permitting.

Directions: From John Day, drive northeast on U.S. 26 for 28 miles to Highway 7. Turn left (north) and drive one mile to County Road 20. Turn left and drive five miles to the campground on the left.

Contact: Malheur National Forest, Blue Mountain Ranger District, 541/575-3000.

OREGON

48 DEPOT PARK

Scenic rating: 6

on the John Day River

See map page 355

This urban park on grassy flatlands provides access to the John Day River, a good trout fishing spot. The camp is a more developed alternative to the many U.S. Forest Service campgrounds in the area. Depot Park features a historic rail depot on the premises as well as a related museum. A nearby attraction, the Strawberry Mountain Wilderness, has prime hiking trails.

RV sites, facilities: There are 20 sites for RVs up to 35 feet with full hookups (30 and 50 amps); some sites are pull-through. There is also a grassy area for hikers/bikers. Picnic tables and fire rings are provided. Restrooms have showers. A dump station, a gazebo, and a picnic area are provided. Some facilities are wheelchair accessible. Leashed pets are permitted.

Reservations, fees: Reservations are not accepted. Sites are $12–16 per night, plus $5 per night for an additional vehicle, and it's $6 per night for the hike-in/bike-in area. Open May–November, weather permitting.

Directions: From John Day, drive east on U.S. 26 for 13 miles to Prairie City and the junction of U.S. 26 and Main Street. Turn right (south) on Main Street and drive 0.5 mile to the park (well signed).

Contact: Prairie City Hall, 541/820-3605 or 541/820-4687 (camp hosts), www.prairie cityoregon.com.

49 DIXIE

Scenic rating: 5

near Dixie Summit in Malheur National Forest

See map page 355

This campground is perched at Dixie Summit (elevation 5,000 feet) near Bridge Creek, where you can toss in a fishing line. The camp is just off U.S. 26, close enough to provide easy access.

It draws overnighters but otherwise gets light use. The Sumpter Valley Railroad interpretive site is one mile west on U.S. 26.

RV sites, facilities: There are 11 sites for tents or RVs up to 30 feet (no hookups). Picnic tables, vault toilets, and fire grills are provided. Drinking water is available, but garbage must be packed out. A store, a café, gas, and ice are available within nine miles. Some facilities are wheelchair accessible. Leashed pets are permitted.

Reservations, fees: Reservations are not accepted. Sites are $5 per night, plus $2.50 per night for an additional vehicle. Open May–November, weather permitting.

Directions: From John Day, drive northeast on U.S. 26 for 24 miles to Forest Road 365. Turn left and drive 0.25 mile to the campground on the left.

Contact: Malheur National Forest, Blue Mountain Ranger District, 541/575-3000.

50 WETMORE

Scenic rating: 7

on the Middle Fork of the Burnt River in Wallowa-Whitman National Forest

See map page 355

This campground, at an elevation of 4,320 feet near the Middle Fork of the Burnt River, makes a nice base camp for a fishing or hiking trip. The stream can provide good trout fishing. Trails are detailed on a map of Wallowa-Whitman National Forest. In addition, an excellent 0.5-mile, wheelchair-accessible trail passes through old-growth forest. Watch for bald eagles.

RV sites, facilities: There are 16 sites for tents or RVs up to 28 feet (no hookups). Picnic tables and fire grills are provided. Drinking water and vault toilets are available. Garbage must be packed out. Some facilities are wheelchair accessible. Leashed pets are permitted.

Reservations, fees: Reservations are not accepted. Sites are $5 per night. Open late May–September, weather permitting.

Directions: From John Day, drive east on U.S. 26 for 29 miles to Austin Junction. Continue east on U.S. 26 for 10 miles to the campground on the left.

Contact: Wallowa-Whitman National Forest, Unity Ranger District, 541/446-3351, fax 541/523-1479.

51 OREGON

Scenic rating: 6

near Austin Junction in Wallowa-Whitman National Forest

See map page 355

This campground at 4,880 feet elevation is just off U.S. 26 and is the staging area for all-terrain-vehicle (ATV) enthusiasts; several ATV trails crisscross the area. The camp is surrounded by hillside as well as Douglas fir, tamarack, and white fir. Bald eagles nest in the area.

RV sites, facilities: There are 11 sites for tents or RVs up to 28 feet (no hookups). Picnic tables and fire grills are provided. Vault toilets are available. There is no drinking water, and garbage must be packed out. Leashed pets are permitted.

Reservations, fees: Reservations are not accepted. Sites are $5 per night. Open May–September, weather permitting.

Directions: From John Day, drive east on U.S. 26 for 29 miles to Austin Junction. Continue east for 20 miles to the campground.

Contact: Wallowa-Whitman National Forest, Unity Ranger District, 541/446-3351, fax 541/523-1479.

52 YELLOW PINE

Scenic rating: 7

near the Middle Fork Burnt River

See map page 355

Highlights of this camp include easy access and good recreation potential. The camp offers a number of hiking trails; a 0.5-mile-long, wheelchair-accessible trail connects to the Wetmore Campground. Yellow Pine is similar to Oregon Campground, but larger. Keep an eye out for bald eagles in this area.

RV sites, facilities: There are 21 sites for tents or RVs up to 28 feet (no hookups). Picnic tables and fire grills are provided. Drinking water, a dump station, and vault toilets are available. Garbage must be packed out. Leashed pets are permitted.

Reservations, fees: Reservations are not accepted. Sites are $5 per night. Open late May–September, weather permitting.

Directions: From John Day, drive east on U.S. 26 for 29 miles to Austin Junction. Continue east for 21 miles to the campground.

Contact: Wallowa-Whitman National Forest, Unity Ranger District, 541/446-3351, fax 541/523-1479.

53 UNITY LAKE STATE RECREATION SITE

Scenic rating: 7

on Unity Reservoir

See map page 355

This camp, set along the east shore of Unity Reservoir, is a popular spot in good weather. Campers can choose from boating, fishing, hiking, picnicking, swimming, and enjoying the scenic views. Set in the high desert, this grassy park provides a contrast to the sagebrush and cheat grass of the bordering land.

RV sites, facilities: There are 35 sites for tents or RVs of any length with partial hookups (30 and 50 amps), a separate area for hikers and bicyclists, and two cabins. Some sites are pull-through. Picnic tables, garbage bins, and fire grills are provided. Drinking water, restrooms with flush toilets and showers, a dump station, and firewood are available. Some facilities are wheelchair accessible. Boat docks and launching facilities are nearby. Leashed pets are permitted.

Reservations, fees: Reservations are not accepted. Sites are $13–17 per night, $5 per night for an additional vehicle, $5 per person per night for hike-in/bike-in sites, $29 per night for cabins. Open April–late October.

Directions: From John Day, drive east on U.S. 26 for 50 miles to Highway 245. Turn left (north) on Highway 245 and drive three miles to the park on the left.

Contact: Clyde Holliday State Recreation Site, 541/932-4453; Oregon State Parks, 800/551-6949, www.oregonstateparks.org.

54 STARR

Scenic rating: 4

on Starr Ridge in Malheur National Forest
See map page 354

A good layover spot for travelers on U.S. 395, Starr happens to be adjacent to Starr Ridge, a snow play area that is popular in winter for skiing and sledding. The camp itself doesn't offer much in the way of recreation, but to the northeast is the Strawberry Mountain Wilderness, which has a number of lakes, streams, and trails. The camp sits at an elevation of 5,100 feet.

RV sites, facilities: There are eight sites for tents or RVs up to 22 feet (no hookups). Picnic tables and fire grills are provided. Vault toilets are available. There is no drinking water, and garbage must be packed out. Some facilities are wheelchair accessible. Leashed pets are permitted.

Reservations, fees: Reservations are not accepted. Sites are $4 per night. Open early May–November, weather permitting.

Directions: From John Day, drive south on U.S. 395 for 15 miles to the campground on the right.

Contact: Malheur National Forest, Blue Mountain Ranger District, 541/573-4300, fax 541/573-4398.

55 PARISH CABIN

Scenic rating: 6

on Little Bear Creek in Malheur National Forest
See map page 355

This campground along the banks of Little Bear Creek (elevation of 4,900 feet) is in a pretty spot that's not heavily used. The creek offers limited fishing. The road is paved all the way to the campground. This spot is popular with groups of families and hunters in season.

RV sites, facilities: There are 16 sites for tents or RVs up to 32 feet (no hookups) and one group site for up to 50 people. Picnic tables and fire grills are provided. Drinking water, vault toilets, and horse facilities are available. Garbage must be packed out. Some facilities are wheelchair accessible. Leashed pets are permitted.

Reservations, fees: Reservations are not accepted. Sites are $6 per night, plus $3 per night per additional vehicle. Open mid-May–late November, weather permitting.

Directions: From John Day, drive south on U.S. 395 for 10 miles to Forest Road 15. Turn left and drive 16 miles southeast to Forest Road 16. Turn right onto Forest Road 16 and drive a short distance to the campground on the right.

Contact: Malheur National Forest, Blue Mountain Ranger District, 541/573-4300, fax 541/573-4398.

56 TROUT FARM

Scenic rating: 6

near Prairie City in Malheur National Forest
See map page 355

This campground (4,900 feet elevation) is on the Upper John Day River, which provides good trout fishing with easy access for people who don't wish to travel off paved roads. A picnic shelter is available for family picnics, and a small pond at the campground has a wheelchair-accessible trail.

RV sites, facilities: There are six sites for tents or RVs up to 21 feet (no hookups). Picnic tables and fire grills are provided. Drinking water and vault toilets are available. Garbage must be packed out. Some facilities are wheelchair accessible. Leashed pets are permitted.

Reservations, fees: Reservations are not accepted. Sites are $6 per night. Open June–mid-October, weather permitting.

Directions: From John Day, drive east on U.S. 26 for 13 miles to Prairie City and County Road 62. Turn right and drive 15 miles to the campground entrance on the right.

Contact: Malheur National Forest, Prairie City Ranger District, 541/820-3800, fax 541/820-3838.

57 SOUTH FORK

Scenic rating: 5

on the South Fork of the Burnt River in Wallowa-Whitman National Forest

See map page 355

This campground (4,400 feet elevation) is on the banks of the South Fork of the Burnt River, a nice trout creek with good evening bites for anglers who know how to sneak-fish. Off-highway-vehicle (OHV) trail access is across the road from the campground. A gem of a spot, it offers drinking water, privacy, and scenery.

RV sites, facilities: There are 21 sites for tents or RVs up to 28 feet (no hookups); some sites are pull-through. Picnic tables and fire grills are provided. Drinking water and vault toilets are available. Garbage must be packed out. Leashed pets are permitted.

Reservations, fees: Reservations are not accepted. Sites are $5 per night. Open late May–September, weather permitting.

Directions: From John Day, drive east on U.S. 26 for 49 miles to Unity and County Road 600. Turn right on County Road 600 and drive west for six miles (the road becomes Forest Road 6005/South Fork Road). Continue past the forest boundary for one mile to the campground on the left.

Contact: Wallowa-Whitman National Forest, Unity Ranger District, 541/446-3351, fax 541/523-1479.

58 SPRING RECREATION SITE

Scenic rating: 5

on the Snake River

See map page 355

One of two camps in or near Huntington, this campground hugs the banks of the Brownlee Reservoir. A more developed alternative, Farewell Bend State Recreation Area, offers showers and all the other luxuries a camper could want. Fishing is popular at this reservoir.

RV sites, facilities: There are 35 sites for tents or RVs of any length (no hookups). Picnic tables, garbage service, and fire grills are provided. Drinking water (summer only), a dump station, and vault toilets are available. Boat-launching facilities and a fish-cleaning station are on-site. A seasonal camp host is on-site. Leashed pets are permitted.

Reservations, fees: Reservations are not accepted. Sites are $5 per night per vehicle, with a 14-day stay limit. Open year-round, weather permitting.

Directions: From Ontario (near the Oregon-Idaho border), drive northwest on I-84 for 28 miles to Huntington and Snake River Road. Turn right (northeast) on Snake River Road and drive five miles (paved road) to the campground.

Contact: Bureau of Land Management, Baker City Office, 541/523-1256, fax 541/523-1965.

59 FAREWELL BEND STATE RECREATION AREA

Scenic rating: 7

on the Snake River

See map page 355

This campground offers a green desert experience on the banks of the Snake River's Brownlee Reservoir. Situated along the Oregon Trail, it offers historic interpretive displays and an evening interpretive program at the amphitheater during the summer. Among the amenities are basketball hoops, horseshoe pits, and a sand volleyball court.

RV sites, facilities: There are 101 sites with partial hookups for RVs of any length, 30 tent sites, a hike-in/bike-in area, and overflow camping in the parking lot. There are also two tepees, two cabins, two covered camper wagons, and one group tent area for up to 50 people. Drinking water, garbage bins, fire rings, and picnic tables are provided. Restrooms have flush toilets and showers. A dump station, firewood, and boat-launching facilities are available. Some facilities are wheelchair accessible. Leashed pets are permitted.

Reservations, fees: Reservations are accepted at 800/452-5687 or www.oregonstateparks.org ($6 reservation fee). Sites are $11–17 per night, $5 per night for an additional vehicle, $4 per person per night for the hike-in/bike-in area, and $65 per night for group sites. Tepees or covered wagons are $29 per night, and cabins are $38 per night. Some credit cards are accepted. Open year-round, with limited winter facilities.

Directions: From Ontario (near the Oregon-Idaho border), drive northwest on I-84 for 21 miles to Exit 353. Take that exit and drive one mile to the park.

Contact: Farewell Bend State Recreation Area, 541/869-2365; Oregon State Parks, 800/551-6949, www.oregonstateparks.org.

60 BULLY CREEK PARK

Scenic rating: 7

on Bully Creek Reservoir

See map page 355

Bully Creek reservoir is in a kind of high-desert area with sagebrush and poplar trees for shade. People come here to boat, fish (mostly for warm-water fish, such as crappie and large- and smallmouth bass), swim, and water-ski. You can bike on the gravel roads. It's beautiful if you like the desert, and the sunsets are worth the trip. The primitive setting is home to deer, jackrabbits, squirrels, and many birds. The elevation is 2,300 feet. No monthly rentals are permitted here, a big plus for overnighters.

RV sites, facilities: There are 40 double sites for tents or RVs up to 45 feet in length with partial hookups (20, 30, and 50 amps); some sites are pull-through. There are also four group sites. Picnic tables and fire pits are provided. Drinking water, restrooms with flush toilets and showers, ice, garbage bins, a dump station, a picnic area, and a boat ramp and dock are available. A restaurant, a café, a convenience store, gasoline, propane gas, charcoal, and a coin laundry are within 10 miles. Bring your own firewood. Some facilities are wheelchair accessible. Leashed pets are permitted.

Reservations, fees: Reservations are accepted ($10 deposit). Sites are $10 per night. Open April–mid-November, weather permitting.

Directions: From Ontario (near the Oregon-Idaho border), drive west on U.S. 20/26 for 12 miles to Vale and Graham Boulevard. Turn right (northwest) on Graham Boulevard and drive five miles to Bully Creek Road. Turn right (west) and drive three miles to the park on the left.

Contact: Bully Creek Park, 541/473-2969, fax 541/473-9462.

THE SOUTHERN CASCADES

This region of Oregon is famous for one of its lakes, but it holds many fantastic recreation secrets. The crown jewel is Crater Lake, of course, and visitors come from all over the world to see its vast cobalt-blue waters within the clifflike walls. The lake's Rim Drive is one of those trips that everybody should have on their life's to-do list.

Cottage Grove Reservoir, Dorena Lake, and Fall Creek Reservoir are further examples of some of the region's ample lakes. Beyond the lakes, though, you'll find stellar camping, hiking, and fishing spots. The best among them are neighboring Mount Washington Wilderness and Three Sisters Wilderness in Willamette National Forest, accessible via a beautiful drive on the McKenzie River Highway (Highway 126) east from Eugene and Springfield.

But wait, there's more. Wickiup Reservoir, Crane Prairie, and Waldo Lake provide camping, boating, and good fishing. Wickiup, in turn, feeds into the headwaters of the Deschutes River, a prime steelhead locale. The Umpqua and Rogue River National Forests offer some great water-sport destinations, including the headwaters of the North Umpqua, one of the prettiest rivers in North America; Diamond Lake; and the headwaters of the Rogue River. Upper Klamath Lake and the Klamath Basin are the No. 1 wintering areas in America for bald eagles. Klamath Lake also provides a chance to catch huge but elusive trout, as does the nearby Williamson River out of Chiloquin. The best still-water canoeing and fly-fishing is at Fall River, Big Lake, and Ahjumawi State Park. All of this is but a small sampling of one of Oregon's best regions for adventure.

This region is all the more special for me because it evokes powerful personal memories. One of these is of a time at Hills Creek Reservoir southeast of Eugene. My canoe flipped on a cold winter day, and I almost drowned after 20 minutes in the icy water. After I'd gone down for the count twice, my brother Bob jumped in, swam out, grabbed the front of the flipped canoe, and towed me to shore. Then, once ashore, he kept me awake, preventing me from lapsing into a coma from hypothermia.

Thanks, Bob.

Includes:

- Agency Lake
- Applegate River
- Big Lake
- Blue River Reservoir
- Branchwater Lake
- Clear Lake
- Clearwater River
- Collier Memorial State Park
- Crater Lake National Park
- Crescent Lake
- Crooked River National Grassland
- Cultus Lake
- Davis Lake
- Deschutes National Forest
- Deschutes River
- Dexter Reservoir
- Diamond Lake
- Dorena Lake
- East Lake
- Elk Lake
- Emigrant Lake
- Fall Creek Reservoir State Recreation Area
- Fish Lake
- Fourmile Lake
- Gold Lake
- Hemlock Lake
- Hosmer Lake
- Howard Prairie Lake
- Hyatt Lake
- Illinois River
- Jackson F. Kimball State Park
- Joseph H. Stewart State Park
- Lake Selmac
- LaPine State Park
- Lava Lake
- Lemolo Lake
- Little Cultus Lake
- Little Lava Lake
- Little River
- McKenzie River
- Metolius River
- Miller Lake
- Odell Lake
- Oregon Caves National Monument
- Paulina Lake
- Rogue River
- Rogue River National Forest
- Santiam River
- Siuslaw River
- Smith Rock State Park
- Sparks Lake
- Sprague River
- Suttle Lake
- Three Creeks Lake
- Three Sisters Wilderness
- Toketee Lake
- Trailbridge Reservoir
- Tumalo State Park
- Twin Lakes
- Umpqua National Forest
- Umpqua River
- Upper Klamath Lake
- Valley of the Rogue State Park
- Waldo Lake
- Wickiup Reservoir
- Willamette National Forest
- Williamson River
- Willow Lake
- Winema National Forest
- Wood River

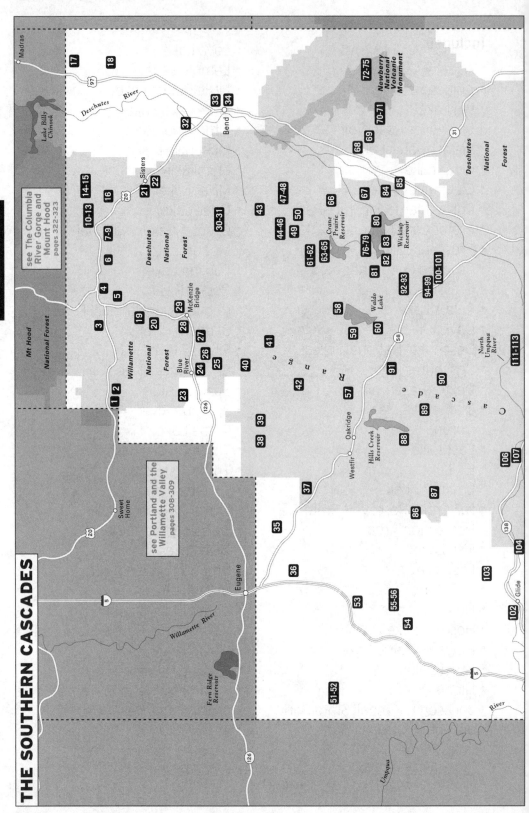

OREGON

THE SOUTHERN CASCADES

see The Columbia River Gorge and Mount Hood pages 322–323

see Portland and the Willamette Valley pages 308–309

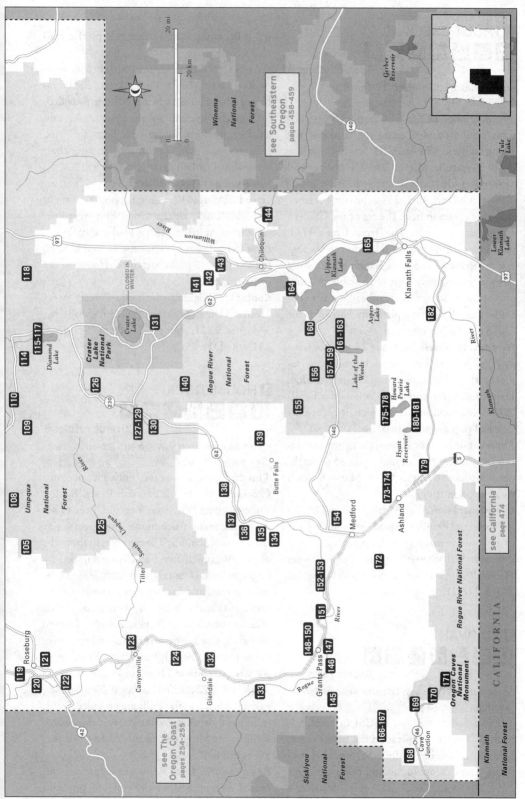

OREGON

20 mi

20 km

0

0

Winema

National

Forest

see Southeastern
Oregon
pages 458–459

Gerber
Reservoir

Tule
Lake

118

Williamson River

144

CLOSED IN WINTER

143

142

141

Chiloquin

165

Upper Klamath Lake

Lower Klamath Lake

97

164

Crater Lake

131

62

160

Aspen Lake

Klamath Falls

182

115-117

Crater Lake National Park

126

161-163

Lake of the Woods

Klamath River

114

Diamond Lake

140

157-159

156

Howard Prairie Lake

110

230

155

175-178

180-181

109

127-129

130

Rogue River National Forest

179

5

108

Umpqua National Forest

62

139

Hyatt Reservoir

South Umpqua River

138

Butte Falls

173-174

125

137

154

Medford

Ashland

105

136

135

134

see California
page 474

172

119

Roseburg

121

123

Rogue River

152-153

Rogue River National Forest

120

122

Canyonville

124

132

151

148-150

147

Grants Pass

146

Oregon Caves National Monument

171

Glendale

133

145

169

170

42

see The
Oregon Coast
pages 254–255

166-167

46

Cave
Junction

168

Siskiyou National Forest

CALIFORNIA

Klamath National Forest

© AVALON TRAVEL PUBLISHING, INC.

❶ TROUT CREEK

Scenic rating: 8

on the South Santiam River in Willamette National Forest

See map page 382

This campground is along the banks of the South Santiam River at 1,200 feet in elevation, about seven miles east of Cascadia. Fishing and swimming are some of the recreation possibilities. A historic shelter and the ruins of some stonework remain from the era of the Civilian Conservation Corps. The Trout Creek Trail, just across the highway, leads into the Menagerie Wilderness. The Long Ranch Elk Viewing Area is immediately west of the campground, and at the Trout Creek Trailhead a short trail leads to an elk-viewing platform. Nearby is the Old Santiam Wagon Road.

RV sites, facilities: There are 24 sites for tents or RVs up to 32 feet (no hookups). Picnic tables, garbage bins, and fire grills are provided. Drinking water and vault toilets are available. Some facilities are wheelchair accessible. Leashed pets are permitted.

Reservations, fees: Reservations are not accepted. Sites are $10 per night, plus $5 per night per additional vehicle. Open May–October, weather permitting.

Directions: From Albany, drive east on U.S. 20 for 45 miles (19 miles past Sweet Home) to the campground entrance on the right.

Contact: Willamette National Forest, Sweet Home Ranger District, 541/367-5168, fax 541/367-9221.

❷ YUKWAH

Scenic rating: 7

on the Santiam River in Willamette National Forest

See map page 382

Yukwah campground is nestled in a second-growth Douglas fir forest on the banks of the Santiam River. The camp is 0.25 mile east of Trout Creek campground and offers the same recreation possibilities. The camp features a 0.5-mile, compacted-surface interpretive trail that's barrier-free.

RV sites, facilities: There are 20 sites for tents or RVs up to 32 feet (no hookups). Picnic tables, garbage bins, and fire grills are provided. Drinking water, vault toilets, a picnic area, and a fishing platform are available. Some facilities, including the fishing platform, are wheelchair accessible. Leashed pets are permitted.

Reservations, fees: Reservations are not accepted. Sites are $10 per night, plus $5 per night per additional vehicle. Open May–October, weather permitting, with a 14-day stay limit.

Directions: From Albany, drive east on U.S. 20 for 45 miles (19 miles past Sweet Home) to the campground.

Contact: Willamette National Forest, Sweet Home Ranger District, 541/367-5168, fax 541/367-9221; South Santium Services, 541/466-5511.

❸ HOUSE ROCK

Scenic rating: 8

on the Santiam River in Willamette National Forest

See map page 382

This campground is at the confluence of Sheep Creek and the South Santiam River. Botany students come here from long distances to see firsthand many uncommon and spectacular specimens of plantlife. The camp sits in the midst of an old-growth forest and is surrounded by huge, majestic Douglas fir. Trout fishing can be good, particularly during summer evenings. History buffs should explore the short loop trail out of camp, which passes by House Rock, a historic rock shelter for Native Americans, and continues to the historic Old Santiam Wagon Road.

RV sites, facilities: There are 17 sites for tents or RVs up to 22 feet (no hookups). Picnic tables, garbage bins, and fire grills are provided. Vault toilets and drinking water are available. Some facilities are wheelchair accessible. Leashed pets are permitted.

Reservations, fees: Reservations are not accepted. Sites are $10 per night, plus $5 per night per additional vehicle. Open May–October, weather permitting.

Directions: From Albany drive east on U.S. 20 for 52.5 miles (26 miles past Sweet Home) to Latiwi Road (Forest Road 2044). Turn right and drive a short distance to the campground.

Contact: Willamette National Forest, Sweet Home Ranger District, 541/367-5168, fax 541/367-9221.

◢ COLDWATER COVE

Scenic rating: 10

on Clear Lake in Willamette National Forest
See map page 382

This campground sits at 3,000 feet elevation on the south shore of Clear Lake, a spring-fed lake formed by a natural lava dam and the source of the McKenzie River. No motors are permitted on the lake, making it ideal for anglers in rowboats or canoes. The northern section of the McKenzie River National Recreation Trail passes by the camp.

RV sites, facilities: There are 35 sites for tents or RVs up to 30 feet (no hookups). Picnic tables, garbage service, and fire grills are provided. Drinking water and vault toilets are available. Some facilities are wheelchair accessible. Boat docks, launching facilities, rowboats, a store, a café, and cabin rentals are available nearby at Clear Lake Resort. Leashed pets are permitted.

Reservations, fees: Reservations are accepted at 877/444-6777 or www.ReserveUSA.com ($9 reservation fee). Sites are $14 per night for single sites, $7 per night per additional vehicle, and $25 per night for double sites. Open mid-May–mid-October, weather permitting.

Directions: From Eugene, drive east on Highway 126 for 47 miles to the town of McKenzie Bridge. Continue on Highway 126 for 14 miles to Forest Road 770. Turn right (east) and drive to the campground.

Contact: Willamette National Forest, McKenzie Ranger District, 541/822-3381, fax 541/822-7254.

◢ ICE CAP

Scenic rating: 9

on Carmen Reservoir in Willamette National Forest
See map page 382

This campground (3,000 feet elevation) is perched on a hill above Carmen Reservoir, which was created by a dam on the McKenzie River. The McKenzie River National Recreation Trail passes by the camp, and Koosah Falls and Sahalie Falls are nearby. Clear Lake, a popular local vacation destination, is two miles away.

RV sites, facilities: There are 22 sites for tents or RVs up to 30 feet (no hookups). Picnic tables, garbage service, and fire grills are provided. Drinking water and flush toilets are available. Boat-launching facilities and boat rentals are about two miles away at Clear Lake Resort (541/967-5030). Only nonmotorized boats are allowed on Carmen Reservoir. Leashed pets are permitted.

Reservations, fees: Reservations are not accepted. Sites are $14 per night, plus $7 per night per additional vehicle. Open mid-May–September, weather permitting.

Directions: From Eugene, drive east on Highway 126 for 47 miles to the town of McKenzie Bridge. Continue on Highway 126 for 19 miles to the campground entrance road on the left. Turn left and drive 200 yards to the campground.

Contact: Willamette National Forest, McKenzie Ranger District, 541/822-3381, fax 541/822-7254.

◢ BIG LAKE

Scenic rating: 9

on Big Lake in Willamette National Forest
See map page 382

This jewel of a spot on the north shore of Big Lake at 4,650 feet elevation offers a host of activities, including fishing, hiking, swimming, and waterskiing. Big Lake has heavy motorized boat use. One of the better hikes is the five-mile wilderness loop trail (Patjens Lakes Trail) that heads out from the south shore of the lake and cuts past a few small lakes before returning. There's a great view of Mount Washington from the lake. The Pacific Crest Trail is only 0.5 mile away.

RV sites, facilities: There are 49 sites for tents or RVs up to 35 feet (no hookups). Picnic tables, garbage service, and fire grills are provided. Drinking water and vault and flush toilets are available. Boat ramps and launching facilities are nearby. Leashed pets are permitted.

Reservations, fees: Reservations are accepted at 877/444-6777 or www.ReserveUSA.com ($9 reservation fee). Sites are $14 per night for single sites, $7 per night per additional vehicle, and $25 per night for double sites. Open late May–mid-October, weather permitting.

Directions: From Eugene, drive east on Highway 126 for 47 miles to the town of McKenzie Bridge. Continue northeast on Highway 126 for 40 miles to Big Lake Road (Forest Road 2690). Turn right and drive three miles to the campground on the left.

Contact: Willamette National Forest, McKenzie Ranger District, 541/822-3381, fax 541/822-7254.

7 LINK CREEK

Scenic rating: 6

on Suttle Lake in Deschutes National Forest
See map page 382

This campground (elevation 3,450 feet) is at the west end of Suttle Lake. The high-speed boating area is on this end of the lake, making it a popular spot with water-skiers. (See the *South Shore* listing in this chapter for recreation details.)

RV sites, facilities: There are 33 sites for tents or RVs up to 50 feet (no hookups). Picnic tables, garbage service, and fire grills are provided. Drinking water and vault toilets are available. Boat docks, launching facilities, and rentals are nearby. Leashed pets are permitted.

Reservations, fees: Reservations are accepted at 877/444-6777 or www.ReserveUSA.com

($9 reservation fee). Sites are $14 per night, plus $7 per night per additional vehicle. Open April–mid-October, weather permitting.

Directions: From Albany, drive east on U.S. 20 for 74 miles to the junction of U.S. 20 and Highway 126. Continue east on Highway 126 for 12 miles to Forest Road 2070 (Suttle Lake). Turn right and drive a short distance to the campground.

Contact: Deschutes National Forest, Sisters Ranger District, 541/549-7700, fax 541/549-7746; Hoodoo Recreation Services, 541/822-3799.

8 SOUTH SHORE

Scenic rating: 6

on Suttle Lake in Deschutes National Forest
See map page 382

This campground is at 3,500 feet elevation on the south shore of Suttle Lake, where waterskiing is permitted. A hiking trail winds around the lake. Other popular activities include fishing and windsurfing. The camp often fills up on weekends and holidays; reserve early.

RV sites, facilities: There are 39 sites for tents or RVs up to 50 feet (no hookups). Picnic tables, garbage service, and fire grills are provided. Drinking water and vault toilets are available. A fish-cleaning station, boat docks, launching facilities, and rentals are nearby. Leashed pets are permitted.

Reservations, fees: Reservations are accepted at 877/444-6777 or www.ReserveUSA.com ($9 reservation fee). Sites are $14 per night, plus $7 per night per additional vehicle. Open May–September, weather permitting.

Directions: From Albany, drive east on U.S. 20 to the junction with Highway 126. Continue east on Highway 126 for 12 miles to Forest Road 2070 (Suttle Lake). Turn right and proceed a short distance to the campground.

Contact: Deschutes National Forest, Sisters Ranger District, 541/549-7700, fax 541/549-7746; Hoodoo Recreation Services, 541/822-3799.

9 BLUE BAY

Scenic rating: 7

on Suttle Lake in Deschutes National Forest

See map page 382

This campground is along the south shore of Suttle Lake, the low-speed end of the lake. It's a quieter campground, with more tree cover than South Shore or Link Creek. (See the *South Shore* listing in this chapter for recreation details.)

RV sites, facilities: There are 25 sites for tents or RVs up to 50 feet (no hookups). Picnic tables, garbage service, and fire grills are provided. Drinking water and vault toilets are available. A fish-cleaning station, boat docks, launching facilities, and rentals are nearby. Leashed pets are permitted.

Reservations, fees: Reservations are accepted at 877/444-6777 or www.ReserveUSA.com ($9 reservation fee). Sites are $14 per night, plus $7 per night per additional vehicle. Open May–mid-September, weather permitting.

Directions: From Albany, drive east on U.S. 20 for 74 miles to the junction of U.S. 20 and Highway 126. Continue east on Highway 126 for 12 miles to Forest Road 2070 (Suttle Lake). Turn right and drive a short distance to the campground.

Contact: Deschutes National Forest, Sisters Ranger District, 541/549-7700, fax 541/549-7746; Hoodoo Recreation Services, 541/822-3799.

10 BLACK BUTTE RESORT MOTEL AND RV PARK

Scenic rating: 6

near the Metolius River

See map page 382

This RV park offers a choice of graveled or grassy sites in a clean, scenic environment. (See the *Camp Sherman* listing in this chapter for more area information.)

RV sites, facilities: There are 41 sites for tents or RVs of any length with full or partial hookups (30 and 50 amps). Motel rooms are also

available. Picnic tables and barbecues are provided. Restrooms have flush toilets and showers. A dump station, recreation room, firewood, and a coin laundry are available. Propane gas, an additional dump station, a store, a café, and ice are within one block. Leashed pets are permitted.

Reservations, fees: Reservations are accepted. Sites are $21.50–24.50 per night, plus $3 per person per night for more than two people. Some credit cards are accepted. Open year-round.

Directions: From Albany, drive east on U.S. 20 for 87 miles (near Black Butte) to the sign for Camp Sherman. Turn left (north) on Forest Road 1419 and drive four miles to a stop sign and the resort access road. Turn right and drive 0.25 mile to the park on the right.

Contact: Black Butte Resort Motel and RV Park, 541/595-6514, fax 541/595-5971.

11 SMILING RIVER

Scenic rating: 5

on the Metolius River in Deschutes National Forest

See map page 382

Another camp along the banks of the Metolius River, this one sits at an elevation of 2,900 feet. (See the *Camp Sherman* listing in this chapter for more area details.)

RV sites, facilities: There are 35 sites for tents or RVs up to 50 feet (no hookups). Picnic tables, garbage service, and fire grills are provided. Vault toilets and drinking water are available. Leashed pets are permitted.

Reservations, fees: Reservations are not accepted. Sites are $14 per night, plus $7 per night per additional vehicle. Open May–September, weather permitting.

Directions: From Albany, drive east on U.S. 20 for 87 miles (near Black Butte) to the sign for Camp Sherman and Forest Road 14. Turn left on Forest Road 14 and drive five miles to Camp Sherman, the store, and Forest Road 900. Turn left on Forest Road 900 and drive one mile to the campground on the left.

OREGON

OREGON

Contact: Deschutes National Forest, Sisters Ranger District, 541/549-7700, fax 541/549-7746; Hoodoo Recreation Services, 541/822-3744.

12 PIONEER FORD

Scenic rating: 7

on the Metolius River in Deschutes National Forest

See map page 382

This quiet and serene wooded campground is along the banks of the Metolius River and features grassy sites. (See the *Camp Sherman* listing in this chapter for recreation options.)

RV sites, facilities: There are 20 sites for tents or RVs up to 40 feet (no hookups). Drinking water, garbage service, and fire grills are provided. Vault toilets and a picnic shelter are available. Some facilities are wheelchair accessible. Leashed pets are permitted.

Reservations, fees: Reservations are not accepted. Sites are $14 per night, plus $7 per night per additional vehicle. Open May–September, weather permitting.

Directions: From Albany, drive east on U.S. 20 for 87 miles (near Black Butte) to the sign for Camp Sherman and Forest Road 14. Turn left on Forest Road 14 and drive 11 miles to the campground on the left.

Contact: Deschutes National Forest, Sisters Ranger District, 541/549-7700, fax 541/549-7746; Hoodoo Recreation Services, 541/822-3799.

13 COLD SPRINGS RESORT AND RV PARK

Scenic rating: 7

on the Metolius River

See map page 382

This pretty, wooded RV park on the Metolius River is world-famous for its fly-fishing and features an acre of riverfront lawn. Bird-watching is also popular. Recreation options in the area include boating, swimming, waterskiing,

and windsurfing. In addition, nearby facilities include a golf course, hiking and biking trails, a riding stable, and tennis courts. Winter activities vary from alpine and Nordic skiing to sledding, snowmobiling, and winter camping. A private foot bridge leads from the resort to Camp Sherman; the towns of Sisters and Bend are nearby (15 miles and 35 miles away, respectively).

RV sites, facilities: There are 45 sites with full hookups (20 and 30 amps) for RVs of any length, a grassy area for tents, and five cabins on the river. Fire pits, picnic tables, and patios are provided. Restrooms have showers. A coin laundry, wireless Internet service, firewood, and a riverfront picnic facility are available. Propane gas, a convenience store, fishing and sport supplies, a café, a post office, and ice are within 0.25 mile. Leashed pets are permitted.

Reservations, fees: Reservations are accepted. Sites are $24–28 per night, $2 per person per night for more than two people, and $1 per pet per night. Some credit cards are accepted. Open year-round.

Directions: From Albany, drive east on U.S. 20 for 87 miles (near Black Butte) to the sign for Camp Sherman/Metolius River. Turn left (north) on Forest Road 14 and drive 4.5 miles to a stop sign. Turn right (still Forest Road 14) and drive about 300 feet to Cold Springs Resort Lane. Turn right and drive through the forest and the meadow, crossing Cold Springs Creek, to the resort.

Contact: Cold Springs Resort and RV Park, 541/595-6271, fax 541/595-1400, www.coldsprings-resort.com.

14 CAMP SHERMAN

Scenic rating: 6

on the Metolius River in Deschutes National Forest

See map page 382

Camp Sherman is at an elevation of 2,950 feet along the banks of the Metolius River, where you can fish for wild trout. This place is for expert fly anglers seeking a quality fishing experience. It's advisable to obtain a map of the Deschutes National Forest that details back roads, streams, and trails. Camp Sherman is one of five camps in the immediate area.

RV sites, facilities: There are 15 sites for tents or RVs up to 40 feet (no hookups). Picnic tables, garbage service, and fire grills are provided. Vault toilets, drinking water, and a picnic shelter are available. Leashed pets are permitted.

Reservations, fees: Reservations are not accepted. Sites are $10–14 per night, plus $5–7 per night per additional vehicle. Open April–mid-October, weather permitting.

Directions: From Albany, drive east on U.S. 20 for 87 miles (near Black Butte) to the sign for Camp Sherman and Forest Road 14. Turn left on Forest Road 14 and drive five miles to Camp Sherman, the store, and Forest Road 900. Turn left on Forest Road 900 and drive 0.5 mile to the campground on the left.

Contact: Deschutes National Forest, Sisters Ranger District, 541/549-7700, fax 541/549-7746; Hoodoo Recreation Services, 541/822-3799.

15 ALLEN SPRINGS

Scenic rating: 7

on the Metolius River in Deschutes National Forest
See map page 382

This shady campground is nestled in a conifer forest along the banks of the Metolius River, where fishing and hiking can be good. For an interesting side trip, head to the Wizard Falls Fish Hatchery about a mile away.

RV sites, facilities: There are 17 sites for tents or RVs up to 36 feet (no hookups). Picnic tables, garbage service, and fire grills are provided. Vault toilets and drinking water are available. A store, a café, and ice are within five miles. Leashed pets are permitted.

Reservations, fees: Reservations are not accepted. Sites are $10–14 per night, plus $5–7 per night per additional vehicle. Open April–October, weather permitting.

Directions: From Albany, drive east on U.S. 20

for 87 miles (near Black Butte) to the sign for Camp Sherman and Forest Road 14. Turn left on Forest Road 14 and drive about nine miles to the campground on the left.

Contact: Deschutes National Forest, Sisters Ranger District, 541/549-7700, fax 541/549-7746; Hoodoo Recreation Services, 541/822-3799.

16 KOA SISTERS/BEND

Scenic rating: 7

on Branchwater Lake
See map page 382

This park is amid wooded mountains outside of Sisters at an elevation of 3,200 feet. Branchwater Lake, a three-acre lake at the campground, offers good trout fishing. (See the *Belknap Hot Springs Resort* listing in this chapter for information about the surrounding area.)

RV sites, facilities: There are 64 sites for RVs of any length with full hookups (30 amps); many sites are pull-through. There are also three cabins. Picnic tables and fire pits are provided. Drinking water, air-conditioning, cable TV, modem access, restrooms with showers, a dump station, a coin laundry, a convenience store, ice, RV supplies, and propane gas are available. Recreational facilities include a playground, a game room, horseshoes, table tennis, a spa, and a seasonal heated swimming pool. Leashed pets are permitted.

Reservations, fees: Reservations are accepted at 800/562-0363. RV sites are $35–40 per night, tent sites are $18 per night, plus $2–4 per person per night for more than two people, and it's $7 per night per additional vehicle. Some credit cards are accepted. Open late March–November, weather permitting.

Directions: From Eugene, drive east on Highway 126 to its junction with U.S. 20. Turn east on U.S. 20 and drive 26 miles to Sisters. Continue southeast on U.S. 20 for three miles to the park on the right side of the highway.

Contact: KOA Sisters/Bend, 541/549-3021, fax 541/549-8144, www.koa.com.

OREGON

OREGON

17 HAYSTACK RESERVOIR

Scenic rating: 5

on Haystack Reservoir in Crooked River
National Grassland

See map page 382

This campground can be found in the high
desert along the shore of Haystack Reservoir,
a bright spot in an expansive desert landscape.
The camps feature a moderate amount of privacy, as well as views of nearby Mount Jefferson. Haystack Reservoir receives moderate
numbers of people who boat, camp, fish, swim,
and water-ski.

RV sites, facilities: There are 24 sites for tents
or RVs up to 22 feet (no hookups); some sites
are pull-through. Picnic tables and fire grills
are provided. Vault toilets and covered picnic
shelters are available. At the time of publication,
there was no drinking water; call for current
status. A store, a café, and ice are within five
miles. Boat docks and launching facilities are
nearby. Leashed pets are permitted.

Reservations, fees: Reservations are not accepted. Sites are $5 per night, plus $3 per
night per additional vehicle. If drinking
water is available, sites are $8 per night. Open
mid-May–mid-September.

Directions: From Madras, drive south on
U.S. 97 for nine miles to Jericho Lane. Turn
left and drive one mile to County Road 100.
Turn right and drive two miles to Forest Road
96. Turn left (north) and drive 0.5 mile to
the campground.

Contact: Crooked River National Grassland, 541/475-9272 or 541/416-6640, fax
541/416-6694.

18 CROOKED RIVER RANCH RV PARK

Scenic rating: 6

near Smith Rock State Park

See map page 382

Spectacular wildlife abounds in this area. This
campground is a short distance from Smith

Rock State Park, which contains unusual,
colorful volcanic formations overlooking the
Crooked River Canyon. Lake Billy Chinook
to the north is a good spot for waterskiing and
fishing for bass and panfish. The park has a basketball court and a softball field, and seasonal
horseback riding is available. Nearby recreation
options include fishing, golf, and tennis. One of
Oregon's nicest golf courses is nearby.

RV sites, facilities: There are 92 sites with full
or partial hookups (20, 30, and 50 amps) for
RVs of any length and 20 tent sites; some are
pull-through sites. Picnic tables are provided.
No open fires are allowed; propane is permitted. Restrooms have flush toilets and coin
showers. A dump station, cable TV, modem
access, a convenience store, a coin laundry, ice, a
covered picnic shelter, a playground, horseshoe
pits, a tennis court, and a seasonal swimming
pool are available. A café is nearby. Leashed pets
are permitted, with certain restrictions.

Reservations, fees: Reservations are accepted
at 800/841-0563. Sites are $20–28 per night.
Some credit cards are accepted. Open mid-
March–October, weather permitting.

Directions: From Redmond, drive north on
U.S. 97 for six miles to Terrebonne and Lower
Bridge Road. Turn left (west) on Lower Bridge
Road and drive approximately two miles to
43rd Street. Turn right and drive two miles
to a T intersection. Turn left on Chinook and
drive approximately five miles (becomes Clubhouse Road, then Hays Lane) to the ranch on
the right.

Contact: Crooked River Ranch RV Park,
541/923-1441 or 800/841-0563, www.crooked
riverranch.com.

19 TRAILBRIDGE

Scenic rating: 6

on Trailbridge Reservoir in Willamette
National Forest

See map page 382

This campground along the shore of Trailbridge
Reservoir (2,000 feet elevation) offers boating,

fishing, and hiking among its recreation options. From this camp, there is access to the McKenzie River National Recreation Trail. Highway 126 east of McKenzie Bridge is a designated scenic route, providing a pleasant trip to the camp and making Trailbridge an exceptional spot for car campers. For a good side trip, take the beautiful 40-minute drive east to the little town of Sisters.

RV sites, facilities: There are 27 sites for tents and 19 sites with no hookups for RVs up to 45 feet, along with a large camping area at Trailbridge Flats. Picnic tables, garbage service, and fire grills are provided. Drinking water and vault and flush toilets are available. Boat ramps are nearby. Some facilities are wheelchair accessible. Leashed pets are permitted.

Reservations, fees: Reservations are not accepted. Sites are $6 per night, plus $3 per night per additional vehicle. Open late April–September, weather permitting.

Directions: From Eugene, drive east on Highway 126 for 47 miles to the town of McKenzie Bridge. Continue on Highway 126 for 13 miles to Forest Road 1477. Turn left on Forest Road 1477 and drive a short distance, then bear left and continue 0.25 mile to the campground on the left.

Contact: Willamette National Forest, McKenzie Ranger District, 541/822-3381, fax 541/822-7254.

20 OLALLIE

Scenic rating: 7

on the McKenzie River in Willamette National Forest
See map page 382   **BEST (**

This campground (2,000 feet elevation) along the banks of the McKenzie River features boating, fishing, and hiking among its recreational opportunities. Other bonuses include easy access from Highway 126. Fishing for rainbow trout usually is good. The campground is two miles southwest of Trailbridge Reservoir off Highway 126.

RV sites, facilities: There are 16 sites for tents or RVs up to 50 feet (no hookups). Picnic tables, garbage service, and fire grills are provided.

Vault toilets and drinking water are available. A boat launch is nearby (nonmotorized boats only). Leashed pets are permitted.

Reservations, fees: Reservations are accepted at 877/444-6777 or www.ReserveUSA.com ($9 reservation fee). Sites are $12 per night, plus $6 per night per additional vehicle. Open late April–October, weather permitting.

Directions: From Eugene, drive east on Highway 126 for 47 miles to the town of McKenzie Bridge. Continue on Highway 126 for 11 miles to the campground on the left.

Contact: Willamette National Forest, McKenzie Ranger District, 541/822-3381, fax 541/822-7254; Hoodoo Recreation Services, 541/822-3799.

21 INDIAN FORD

Scenic rating: 4

on Indian Ford Creek in Deschutes National Forest
See map page 382

This campground is on the banks of Indian Ford Creek at an elevation of 3,250 feet. It is sprinkled with aspen trees and provides great bird-watching opportunities. The camp is used primarily by overnighters on their way to the town of Sisters. There's a lot of traffic noise from U.S. 20.

RV sites, facilities: There are 25 sites for tents or RVs up to 50 feet (no hookups). Picnic tables, garbage service, and fire grills are provided. Vault toilets are available. There is no drinking water. Leashed pets are permitted.

Reservations, fees: Reservations are not accepted. Sites are $10 per night, plus $5 per night per additional vehicle. Open May–mid-October, weather permitting.

Directions: From Albany, drive east on U.S. 20 to the junction with Highway 126. Continue east on Highway 126 and drive 21 miles to the campground on the left.

Contact: Deschutes National Forest, Sisters Ranger District, 541/549-7700, fax 541/549-7746; Hoodoo Recreation Services, 541/822-3799.

OREGON

OREGON

22 COLD SPRINGS

Scenic rating: 7

in Deschutes National Forest
See map page 382

This wooded campground is at 3,400 feet elevation at the source of a small seasonal creek. It's just far enough off the main drag to be missed by many campers. Spring and early summer are the times for great bird-watching in the area's abundant aspen trees.

RV sites, facilities: There are 23 sites for tents or RVs up to 50 feet (no hookups). Picnic tables, fire grills, and garbage service are provided. Vault toilets and drinking water are available. Leashed pets are permitted.

Reservations, fees: Reservations are not accepted. Sites are $12 per night, plus $6 per night per additional vehicle. Open May–mid-October, weather permitting.

Directions: From Albany, drive east on U.S. 20 to the junction with Highway 126. Continue east on Highway 126 and drive 26 miles to Sisters and Highway 242. Turn right and drive 4.2 miles to the campground on the right.

Contact: Deschutes National Forest, Sisters Ranger District, 541/549-7700, fax 541/549-7746; Hoodoo Recreation Services, 541/822-3799.

23 MONA

Scenic rating: 8

near Blue River Reservoir in Willamette
National Forest

See map page 382

This forested campground (1,360 feet elevation) is along the shore of Blue River Reservoir, close to where the Blue River joins it. A boat ramp is across the river from the campground (at Lookout Campground); another boat ramp is at the south end of the reservoir. After launching a boat, campers can ground it near their campsite. This camp is extremely popular when the reservoir is full. Lookout Campground is another option if this camp is full.

RV sites, facilities: There are 23 sites for tents or RVs up to 50 feet (no hookups). Picnic tables, garbage bins, and fire grills are provided. Drinking water and flush toilets are available. Some facilities are wheelchair accessible. Leashed pets are permitted.

Reservations, fees: Reservations are not accepted. Sites are $14 per night for single sites, $25 per night for double sites, and $7 per night per additional vehicle. Open May–mid-September, weather permitting.

Directions: From Eugene, drive east on Highway 126 for 41 miles to Blue River. Continue east on Highway 126 for three miles to Forest Road 15. Turn left (north) and drive three miles to the campground on the left.

Contact: Willamette National Forest, McKenzie River Ranger District, 541/822-3381, fax 541/822-7254; Hoodoo Recreation Services, 541/822-3799.

24 PATIO RV PARK

Scenic rating: 7

near the South Fork of the McKenzie River
See map page 382

This RV park is near the banks of the South Fork of the McKenzie River, not far from Cougar Lake, which offers opportunities for fishing, swimming, and waterskiing. Nearby recreation options include a golf course, hiking trails, and bike paths. The Hoodoo Ski Area is approximately 30 miles away.

RV sites, facilities: There are 60 sites with full hookups (30 and 50 amps) for RVs of any length and a grassy area for tents. Picnic tables are provided. Restrooms have flush toilets and coin showers. Ice, firewood, a recreation hall, video rentals, group kitchen facilities, cable TV, modem access, a community fire pit, horseshoe pits, and a coin laundry are available. A store, gasoline, propane, and a café are within two miles. Leashed pets are permitted.

Reservations, fees: Reservations are accepted at 541/822-3596. RV sites are $27–33 per night, tent sites are $16 per night, plus $7 per night

per additional vehicle. Some credit cards are accepted. Open year-round, weather permitting.
Directions: From Eugene, drive east on Highway 126 for 37 miles to the town of Blue River. Continue east on Highway 126 for six miles to McKenzie River Drive. Turn right and drive two miles to the park on the right.
Contact: Patio RV Park, 541/822-3596, fax 541/822-8392.

25 SLIDE CREEK

Scenic rating: 6

on Cougar Reservoir in Willamette National Forest
See map page 382

This campground sits on a hillside overlooking Cougar Reservoir, which covers about 1,300 acres, has a paved boat landing, and offers opportunities for fishing, swimming, and waterskiing. This pretty lakeside camp at 1,700 feet in elevation is quite popular, so plan to arrive early on weekends.
RV sites, facilities: There are 16 sites for tents or RVs up to 50 feet (no hookups). Picnic tables, garbage bins, and fire grills are provided. Drinking water and vault toilets are available. A boat ramp is also available. Leashed pets are permitted.
Reservations, fees: Reservations are not accepted. Sites are $14 per night, $7 per night per additional vehicle, and $25 per night for double sites. Open May–September, weather permitting.
Directions: From Eugene, drive east on Highway 126 for 41 miles to the town of Blue River. Continue east on Highway 126 for five miles to Aufderheide Scenic Byway. Turn right (south) and drive 11 miles (along the west shore of Cougar Reservoir, crossing the reservoir bridge) to Eastside Road (Forest Road 500). Turn left and drive 1.5 miles northeast to the campground set on the southeast shore of the lake.
Contact: Willamette National Forest, McKenzie River Ranger District, 541/822-3381, fax 541/822-7254; Hoodoo Recreation Services, 541/822-3799.

26 DELTA

Scenic rating: 8

on the McKenzie River in Willamette National Forest
See map page 382

This popular campground sits along the banks of the McKenzie River. This spot is heavily forested, primarily with old-growth Douglas fir. The Delta Old Growth Nature Trail, a 0.5-mile wheelchair-accessible interpretive trail, is adjacent to the campground. The camp also features an amphitheater. Blue River and Cougar Reservoirs are seven and five miles away, respectively; both offer swimming, trout fishing, and waterskiing.
RV sites, facilities: There are 38 sites for tents or RVs up to 60 feet (no hookups). Picnic tables, garbage bins, and fire grills are provided. Drinking water and vault toilets are available. Some facilities are wheelchair accessible. Leashed pets are permitted.
Reservations, fees: Reservations are not accepted. Sites are $12 per night for single sites, $20 per night for double sites, and $6 per night per additional vehicle. Open late April–October, weather permitting.
Directions: From Eugene, drive east on Highway 126 for 37 miles to the town of Blue River. Continue east on Highway 126 for five miles to Forest Road 19 (Aufderheide Scenic Byway). Turn right (south) and drive 0.25 mile to Forest Road 400. Turn right and drive one mile to the campground.
Contact: Willamette National Forest, McKenzie River Ranger District, 541/822-3381, fax 541/822-7254; Hoodoo Recreation Services, 541/822-3799.

27 McKENZIE BRIDGE

Scenic rating: 8

on the McKenzie River in Willamette National Forest
See map page 382

This campground (1,400 feet elevation) is along the banks of the McKenzie River, one mile from the town of McKenzie Bridge. During

OREGON

OREGON

the summer, this stretch of river provides good evening fly-fishing for trout. Only nonmotorized boats are permitted.

RV sites, facilities: There are 19 sites for tents or RVs up to 40 feet (no hookups). Picnic tables, garbage service, and fire rings are provided. Vault toilets and drinking water are available. A grocery store and restaurants are available within one mile. Leashed pets are permitted.

Reservations, fees: Reservations are accepted at 877/444-6777 or www.ReserveUSA.com ($9 reservation fee). Sites are $12 per night, plus $6 per night per additional vehicle. Open April–September, weather permitting.

Directions: From Eugene, drive east on Highway 126 for 46 miles to the campground entrance on the right (one mile west of the town of McKenzie Bridge).

Contact: Willamette National Forest, McKenzie River Ranger District, 541/822-3381, fax 541/822-7254; Hoodoo Recreation Services, 541/822-3799.

28 PARADISE

Scenic rating: 9

on the McKenzie River in Willamette National Forest
See map page 382

This campground (1,600 feet elevation) along the banks of the McKenzie River may be right off the highway, but it offers a rustic, streamside setting with access to the McKenzie River National Recreation Trail. Trout fishing can be good here.

RV sites, facilities: There are 64 sites for tents or RVs up to 40 feet (no hookups). Picnic tables, garbage service, and fire rings are provided. Flush and vault toilets, drinking water, a boat ramp, and firewood are available. Leashed pets are permitted.

Reservations, fees: Reservations are accepted at 877/444-6777 or www.ReserveUSA.com ($9 reservation fee). Sites are $14 per night, plus $7 per night per additional vehicle. Double sites are $25 per night. Open April–mid-October, weather permitting.

Directions: From Eugene, drive east on Highway 126 for 47 miles to the town of McKenzie Bridge. Continue east on Highway 126 for 3.5 miles to the campground on the left.

Contact: Willamette National Forest, McKenzie Ranger District, 541/822-3381, fax 541/822-7254; Hoodoo Recreation Services, 541/822-3799.

29 BELKNAP HOT SPRINGS RESORT

Scenic rating: 9

on the McKenzie River
See map page 382

This beautiful park, with 60 acres of developed and landscaped gardens, has been featured on at least one magazine cover. It's in a wooded, mountainous area on the McKenzie River. Trout fishing can be excellent. If you're looking for hiking opportunities, the McKenzie River Trail can be accessed from camp. Other hiking opportunities include the Three Sisters and Mount Washington Wilderness Areas, both accessible by driving west of Sisters on Highway 242. Exceptionally scenic and pristine expanses of forest, they are well worth exploring. The Pacific Crest Trail runs north and south through both wilderness areas.

RV sites, facilities: There are 15 sites for tents, 42 sites with full or partial hookups (30 amps) for RVs of any length, a lodge with 18 rooms, and six cabins. Picnic tables and fire pits are provided. Drinking water, restrooms with showers, and a dump station are available. Recreational facilities include two hot-spring fed swimming pools, massage therapy on weekends, and a recreation field. Some facilities are wheelchair accessible. Leashed pets are permitted at the campground and in some of the cabins; pets are not permitted in the other cabins and lodge rooms.

Reservations, fees: Reservations are accepted at 541/822-3512. Sites are $20–25 per night, plus $8 per person per night for more than two people. Some credit cards are accepted. Open year-round.

Directions: From Eugene, drive east on Highway 126 for 56 miles to Belknap Springs Road. Turn left and drive 0.5 mile until the road deadends at the lodge.

Contact: Belknap Hot Springs Resort, 541/822-3512, fax 541/822-3327, www.belknaphotsprings.com.

30 DRIFTWOOD

Scenic rating: 9

on Three Creeks Lake in Deschutes National Forest
See map page 382

This wooded campground (6,600 feet elevation) is often blocked by snowdrifts until July. At this high elevation, the views of Tam McArthur Rim are spectacular. Although located on the lakeshore and hidden from outsiders, the area can get very crowded. The campground is full most weekends July 4–Labor Day. Some of the recreation options include boating (nonmotorized only), fishing, hiking, and swimming.

RV sites, facilities: There are 17 sites for tents or RVs up to 40 feet (no hookups). Picnic tables, garbage service, and fire grills are provided. Vault toilets are available. There is no drinking water. Boats with motors are not allowed. Leashed pets are permitted.

Reservations, fees: Reservations are not accepted. Sites are $12 per night, plus $6 per night per additional vehicle. Open June–September, weather permitting.

Directions: From Eugene, drive east on Highway 126 to its junction with U.S. 20. Turn east and drive 26 miles to Sisters and Forest Road 16. Turn right and drive 16.4 miles to the campground.

Contact: Deschutes National Forest, Sisters Ranger District, 541/549-7700, fax 541/549-7746; Hoodoo Recreation Services, 541/822-3799.

31 THREE CREEKS LAKE

Scenic rating: 8

on Three Creeks Lake in Deschutes National Forest
See map page 382

This wooded campground sits along the south shore of Three Creek Lake in a pretty spot at 6,600 feet elevation. Boating (nonmotorized only), fishing, hiking, and swimming are the highlights. (See the *Driftwood* listing in this chapter for additional details.)

RV sites, facilities: There are 10 sites for tents or RVs up to 40 feet (no hookups). Picnic tables, garbage service, and fire grills are provided. Vault toilets are available. There is no drinking water. Boats with motors are not allowed. Leashed pets are permitted.

Reservations, fees: Reservations are not accepted. Sites are $12 per night, plus $6 per night per additional vehicle. Open June–October, weather permitting.

Directions: From Eugene, drive east on Highway 126 to its junction with Highway 20. Turn east and drive 26 miles to Sisters and Forest Road 16. Turn right and drive 17 miles to the campground.

Contact: Deschutes National Forest, Sisters Ranger District, 541/549-7700, fax 541/549-7746; Hoodoo Recreation Services, 541/822-3799.

32 TUMALO STATE PARK

Scenic rating: 7

on the Deschutes River
See map page 382   BEST (

Trout fishing can be good at this camp along the banks of the Deschutes River, just five miles from Bend. Bird-watching is popular. The swimming area is generally safe and a good spot for children. Rafting is also an option here. Mount Bachelor is just up the road and provides plenty of winter recreation opportunities.

RV sites, facilities: There are 54 sites for tents or RVs (no hookups), 23 sites with full hookups (20 and 30 amps) for RVs up to 44 feet,

OREGON

OREGON

a hiker/bicyclist area, seven yurts, and two group tent areas for up to 25 people. Drinking water, fire grills, and picnic tables are provided. Restrooms have flush toilets and showers. Firewood and a playground are available. Some facilities are wheelchair accessible. A store, a café, and ice are within one mile. Leashed pets are permitted.

Reservations, fees: Reservations are accepted at 800/452-5687 or www.oregonstateparks.org ($6 reservation fee). Sites are $13–22 per night for single sites, $4 per person per night for hikers/bikers, $29 per night for yurts, $43–65 per night for the group areas, and $5 per night per additional vehicle. Some credit cards are accepted. Open year-round.

Directions: From Bend, drive north on U.S. 97 for two miles to U.S. 20 westbound. Turn west and drive five miles to Tumalo Junction. Turn left at Tumalo Junction onto Cook Avenue (the road becomes O. B. Riley), and drive one mile to the campground.

Contact: High Desert Management Unit, Oregon State Parks, 541/388-6055; Oregon State Parks Information, 800/551-6949, www.oregon stateparks.org.

33 SCANDIA RV AND MOBILE PARK

Scenic rating: 5

near the Deschutes River

See map page 382

This in-town park near the Deschutes River is close to bike paths, a golf course, a stable, and tennis courts.

RV sites, facilities: There are 75 sites for tents or RVs of any length with full hookups (20, 30, and 50 amps); some are pull-through sites. Picnic tables and cable TV are provided. Restrooms have flush toilets and showers. Modem access, a picnic area, and a coin laundry are available. Propane gas, a dump station, a store, a café, and ice are within one mile. Leashed pets are permitted.

Reservations, fees: Reservations are accepted.

Sites are $33–39.60 per night, plus $2.75 per person per night for more than two people. Some credit cards are accepted. Open year-round.

Directions: In Bend, drive south on Business U.S. 97 (3rd Street) for 0.5 mile to the park entrance on the right.

Contact: Scandia RV and Mobile Park, 541/382-6206, fax 541/382-4087.

34 CROWN VILLA RV RESORT

Scenic rating: 6

near Bend

See map page 382

This RV park offers large and landscaped grassy sites. Nearby recreation options include horse-back riding and golf.

RV sites, facilities: There are 116 sites with full or partial hookups (50 amps) for RVs of any length; some sites are pull-through. No tent camping is permitted. Picnic tables are provided. Restrooms have flush toilets and showers. Cable TV, wireless Internet service, a coin laundry, a bistro, propane gas, and ice are available. A store and a café are within one mile. Some facilities are wheelchair accessible. Leashed pets are permitted.

Reservations, fees: Reservations are accepted. Sites are $35–55 per night, plus $2.50 per person per night for more than two people. Weekly and monthly rates available. Some credit cards are accepted. Open year-round.

Directions: From Bend, drive south on Business U.S. 97 (3rd Street) for two miles to Broster-hous Road. Turn left (east) and drive approximately one mile to a T intersection. Bear right to stay on Brosterhous Road. Continue about one mile to the park on the right.

Contact: Crown Villa RV Resort, 541/388-1131, www.crownvillarvresort.com.

35 DEXTER SHORES RV PARK

Scenic rating: 7

near Dexter Reservoir
See map page 382

If you're traveling on I-5, this RV park is well worth the 15-minute drive out of Springfield. It's across the street from Dexter Reservoir, where fishing and boating are permitted year-round. Speedboat races are held at Dexter in the summer. There is seasonal fishing for salmon and steelhead below Dexter dam. The local area is good for bird-watching. Nearby Lookout and Fall Creek Lakes offer sailing, swimming, waterskiing, and windsurfing. There are three authentic Sioux tepees on the property in the summer and two cabins. Many of the campsites have a lake view.

RV sites, facilities: There are five tent sites, 57 sites with full or partial hookups (30 and 50 amps) for RVs up to 40 feet, three group tent sites, and two one-bedroom cabins. Drinking water, cable TV and telephone hookups, picnic tables, and fire pits are provided. Restrooms have flush toilets and showers. A dump station, modem access, a clubhouse, a lending library, video rentals, firewood, and a coin laundry are available. Propane gas, a café, a restaurant, and ice are within one mile. Boat docks and launching facilities are nearby. Leashed pets are permitted in the campground, but not in the cabins or tepees.

Reservations, fees: Reservations are accepted at 866/558-9777. Tent sites are $20 per night and RV sites are $30 per night; it's $5 per night for an additional vehicle and $1 per pet per night. Weekly and monthly rates are available. Some credit cards are accepted. Open year-round.

Directions: From south Eugene on I-5, drive to Exit 188A and Highway 58. Take Highway 58 east and drive 11.5 miles to Lost Creek Road. Turn right (south) and drive several hundred feet to Dexter Road. Turn left (in front of the café) and drive east for half a block to the park on the right.

Contact: Dexter Shores RV Park, 866/558-9777 or 541/937-3711, fax 541/937-1724, www .dextershoresrvpark.com.

36 PASS CREEK COUNTY PARK

Scenic rating: 7

near Cottage Grove
See map page 382

This decent layover spot for travelers on I-5 is in a wooded, hilly area and features many shaded sites. Mountain views give the park scenic value. There is a reservable covered pavilion and gazebo with barbecue grills for get-togethers. A bonus is a fishing pond with bluegill, crappie, and largemouth bass. You can find more fishing and other water activities 11 miles away; history buffs can look for a covered bridge eight miles away. There are no other campgrounds in the immediate area, so if it's late and you need a place to stay, grab this one.

RV sites, facilities: There is a grassy area for tents and 30 sites with full hookups (50 amps) for RVs up to 45 feet. Drinking water, picnic tables, and fire rings or barbecues are provided. Restrooms have flush toilets and showers. A coin laundry and a playground are available. A store and ice are within one mile. Some facilities are wheelchair accessible. Leashed pets are permitted.

Reservations, fees: Reservations are not accepted. Sites are $11–16 per night, plus $3 per night for an additional vehicle unless towed. Some credit cards are accepted. Open year-round.

Directions: On I-5, drive to Exit 163 (between Roseburg and Eugene). Take Exit 163 and turn west on Curtin Park Road. Drive west (under the freeway) for a very short distance to the park entrance.

Contact: Pass Creek County Park, 541/942-3281, www.co.douglas.or.us.

37 BLACK CANYON

Scenic rating: 7

on the Middle Fork of the Willamette River in Willamette National Forest

See map page 382

This campground is along the banks of the Middle Fork of the Willamette River, not far

OREGON

above Lookout Point Reservoir, where fishing and boating are available. The elevation is 1,000 feet. The camp is pretty and wooded and has comfortable sites. Within the camp is a one-mile-long nature trail with interpretive signs. You will hear train noise from the other side of the river.

RV sites, facilities: There are 72 sites for tents or RVs up to 32 feet (no hookups). Picnic tables, garbage service, and fire grills are provided. Drinking water, vault toilets, and firewood are available. A dump station, a café, and a coin laundry are within six miles. Launching facilities are nearby at the south end of Lookout Point Reservoir. Some facilities are wheelchair accessible. Leashed pets are permitted.

Reservations, fees: Reservations are accepted. Sites are $14 per night for single sites, $7 per night per additional vehicle, and $20 per night for double sites. Open late April–early October, weather permitting.

Directions: From south Eugene on I-5, take Exit 188 to Highway 58. Drive southeast on Highway 58 for 27 miles to the camp on the left (six miles west of Oakridge).

Contact: Willamette National Forest, Middle Fork Ranger District, 541/782-2283, fax 541/782-5306.

38 BEDROCK

Scenic rating: 6

on Fall Creek in Willamette National Forest

See map page 382

This campground along the banks of Fall Creek is one of the access points for the scenic, 13.7-mile Fall Creek National Recreation Trail, which in turn offers access to Jones Trail, a six-mile uphill climb. The Fall Creek trail varies between 960 and 1,385 feet in elevation. This campground suffered damage in the Clark Fire but has reopened.

RV sites, facilities: There are 21 sites for tents or RVs up to 40 feet (no hookups). Picnic tables, garbage service, and fire grills are provided. Vault toilets and drinking water are available. Leashed pets are permitted.

Reservations, fees: Reservations are not accepted. Sites are $14 per night for single sites, $7 per night per additional vehicle, and $25 per night for double sites. Open May–mid-September, weather permitting.

Directions: From south Eugene on I-5, take Exit 188 to Highway 58. Drive 11 miles south to Lowell and Pioneer Street (at the covered bridge). Turn left and drive less than a quarter mile to West Boundary Road. Turn left and drive one block to Lowell Jasper Road. Turn right and drive 1.5 miles to Unity and Place Road. Turn right and drive about one mile to a fork with North Shore Road. Bear left onto North Shore Road (Big Fall Creek Road) and drive about 14 miles (the road becomes Forest Road 18) to the campground on the left.

Contact: Willamette National Forest, Middle Fork Ranger District, 541/782-2283, fax 541/782-5336.

39 PUMA

Scenic rating: 6

on Fall Creek in Willamette National Forest

See map page 382

This campground hugs the banks of Fall Creek, across from the Fall Creek National Recreation Trail. The elevation is 1,100 feet. It's one of four camps in the immediate area. (See the *Bedrock* listing in this chapter for more information.)

RV sites, facilities: There are 11 sites for tents or RVs up to 36 feet (no hookups). Picnic tables, garbage containers, and fire grills are provided. Vault toilets and drinking water are available. Leashed pets are permitted.

Reservations, fees: Reservations are not accepted. Sites are $12 per night, plus $6 per night per additional vehicle. Open late May–September, weather permitting.

Directions: From I-5 south of Eugene, take Exit 188 to Highway 58. Drive about 11 miles to Lowell. Turn left at Pioneer Street (at the covered bridge), drive 0.2 mile, and turn left on West Boundary Road. Drive one block and turn right at Lowell Jasper Road. Drive 1.5 miles to

Place Road and turn right. Drive about one mile to a fork and bear left onto North Shore Road (Big Fall Creek Road). Drive about 16 miles (the road becomes Forest Road 18) to the campground on the left.

Contact: Willamette National Forest, Middle Fork Ranger District, 541/782-2283, fax 541/782-5336.

40 FRENCH PETE

Scenic rating: 8

on the South Fork of the McKenzie River in Willamette National Forest

See map page 382

This quiet, wooded campground is on the banks of the South Fork of the McKenzie River and French Pete Creek at 1,800 feet in elevation. Fishing is catch-and-release only. A trail across the road from the campground provides access to the Three Sisters Wilderness (permit required; contact district office). French Pete is only two miles from Cougar Reservoir, and the camp attracts campers wanting to use Cougar Reservoir facilities. Frissell Crossing (see listing in this chapter) is a few miles southeast on the same road.

RV sites, facilities: There are 17 sites for tents or RVs up to 50 feet (no hookups). Picnic tables, garbage containers, and fire grills are provided. Drinking water and vault toilets are available. Some facilities are wheelchair accessible. Leashed pets are permitted.

Reservations, fees: Reservations are not accepted. The fees are $12 per night for single sites, $6 per night per additional vehicle, and $20 per night for double sites. Open May–September, weather permitting.

Directions: From Eugene, drive east on Highway 126 for 41 miles to the town of Blue River. Continue east on Highway 126 for five miles to Forest Road 19 (Aufderheide Scenic Byway). Turn right (south) and drive 12 miles to the campground on the right.

Contact: Willamette National Forest, McKenzie River Ranger District, 541/822-3381, fax

541/822-7254; Hoodoo Recreation Services, 541/822-3799.

41 FRISSELL CROSSING

Scenic rating: 8

near the Three Sisters Wilderness in Willamette National Forest

See map page 382

This campground (elevation 2,600 feet) sits on the banks of the South Fork of the McKenzie River, adjacent to a trailhead that provides access to the backcountry of the Three Sisters Wilderness. Frissell Crossing is the only camp in the immediate area that has drinking water. If you're looking for solitude, this place should be heaven to you.

RV sites, facilities: There are 12 sites for tents or RVs up to 22 feet (no hookups). Picnic tables, garbage bins, and fire grills are provided. Drinking water and vault toilets are available. Leashed pets are permitted.

Reservations, fees: Reservations are not accepted. Sites are $10 per night, plus $5 per night per additional vehicle. Open mid-May–mid-September, weather permitting.

Directions: From Eugene, drive east on Highway 126 for 37 miles to Blue River. Continue east on Highway 126 for five miles to Forest Road 19 (Aufderheide Scenic Byway). Turn right (south) and drive 21.5 miles to the camp on the left.

Contact: Willamette National Forest, McKenzie River Ranger District, 541/822-3381, fax 541/822-7254.

42 KIAHANIE

Scenic rating: 5

on the North Fork of the Willamette River in Willamette National Forest

See map page 382

This is one heck of a spot for fly-fishing (the only kind allowed). This remote campground sits at 2,200 feet elevation along the North Fork

OREGON

OREGON

of the Willamette River, a designated Wild and Scenic River. If you want beauty and quiet among enormous Douglas fir trees, you came to the right place.

RV sites, facilities: There are 19 sites for tents or RVs up to 24 feet (no hookups). Picnic tables and fire rings are provided. Drinking water, vault toilets, garbage bins, and a recycling center are available. Leashed pets are permitted.

Reservations, fees: Reservations are not accepted. Sites are $10 per night, plus $5 per night per additional vehicle. Open late May–September, weather permitting.

Directions: From south Eugene on I-5, take Exit 188 to Highway 58. Drive 31 miles southeast on Highway 58 to Westfir. Take the Westfir exit and drive two miles to Westfir and the junction with Aufderheide Scenic Byway (Forest Road 19). Bear left (northeast) and drive 19 miles to the campground.

Contact: Willamette National Forest, Middle Fork Ranger District, 541/782-2283, fax 541/782-5306.

43 SODA CREEK

Scenic rating: 5

near Sparks Lake in Deschutes National Forest
See map page 382

This campground, nestled between two meadows in a pastoral setting, is on the road to Sparks Lake. Boating—particularly canoeing—is ideal at Sparks Lake, about a two-mile drive away. Also at the lake, a loop trail hugs the shore; about 0.5 mile of it is paved and barrier-free. Only fly-fishing is permitted. The camp sits at 5,450 feet elevation.

RV sites, facilities: There are 10 sites for tents or RVs up to 30 feet (no hookups). Picnic tables and fire grills are provided. Vault toilets are available. There is no drinking water, and garbage must be packed out. Leashed pets are permitted.

Reservations, fees: Reservations are not accepted. There is no fee. Open June–October, weather permitting.

Directions: From Bend, drive southwest on Cas-

cades Lakes Highway (also called Century Drive Highway and County Road 46) for 26.2 miles to Forest Road 400 (at a sign for Sparks Lake). Turn left (east) and drive 25 yards to the campground.

Contact: Deschutes National Forest, Bend–Fort Rock Ranger District, 541/383-4000, fax 541/383-4700.

44 POINT

Scenic rating: 8

on Elk Lake in Deschutes National Forest
See map page 382

This campground is along the shore of Elk Lake at an elevation of 4,900 feet. Fishing for kokanee salmon and brook trout can be good; hiking is another option. Swimming and water sports are popular during warm weather.

RV sites, facilities: There are 10 sites for tents or RVs up to 26 feet (no hookups). Picnic tables, garbage service, and fire grills are provided. Vault toilets and drinking water are available. Boat docks and launching facilities are on-site. A store, a restaurant, and propane are at Elk Lake Resort, one mile away. Leashed pets are permitted.

Reservations, fees: Reservations are not accepted. Sites are $10–12 per night, $5 per night per additional vehicle, and $10–12 per night for an additional RV. Open late May–late September, weather permitting.

Directions: From Bend, drive southwest on Cascades Lakes Highway (Century Drive Highway, which becomes County Road 46) for 34 miles to the campground on the left.

Contact: Deschutes National Forest, Bend–Fort Rock Ranger District, 541/383-4000, fax 541/383-4700.

45 ELK LAKE

Scenic rating: 8

on Elk Lake in Deschutes National Forest
See map page 382

This campground hugs the shore of Elk Lake at 4,900 feet elevation. It is adjacent to Elk Lake

Resort, which has a store, a restaurant, and propane. Elk Lake is popular for windsurfing and sailing. (See the *Point* listing in this chapter for recreation options.)

RV sites, facilities: There are 25 sites for tents or RVs up to 26 feet (no hookups). Picnic tables, garbage service, and fire grills are provided. Vault toilets and drinking water are available. Boat-launching facilities are on-site. Boat rentals can be obtained nearby. Leashed pets are permitted.

Reservations, fees: Reservations are not accepted. Sites are $10–12 per night, $5 per night per additional vehicle, and $10–12 per night per additional RV. Open late May–September, weather permitting.

Directions: From Bend, drive southwest on Cascades Lakes Highway (Century Drive Highway, which becomes County Road 46) and drive 33.1 miles to the campground at the north end of Elk Lake.

Contact: Deschutes National Forest, Bend–Fort Rock Ranger District, 541/383-4000, fax 541/383-4700.

46 LITTLE FAWN

Scenic rating: 5

on Elk Lake in Deschutes National Forest

See map page 382

Choose between sites on the water's edge or nestled in the forest at this campground along the eastern shore of Elk Lake. Afternoon winds are common here, making this a popular spot for sailing and windsurfing. A play area for children can be found at one of the lake's inlets. The camp sits at 4,900 feet elevation. Little Fawn Group Camp is just beyond Little Fawn campground. (See the *Point* listing in this chapter for recreation options.)

RV sites, facilities: There are 20 sites for tents or RVs up to 30 feet (no hookups) and one group site that can accommodate up to 50 campers. Picnic tables and fire grills are provided. Vault toilets, drinking water, and garbage service are available. Boat-launching

facilities and rentals are on-site. Leashed pets are permitted.

Reservations, fees: Reservations are required for the group site at 877/444-6777 or www.ReserveUSA.com ($9 reservation fee) but are not accepted for individual sites. Sites are $8 per night, $5 per night per additional vehicle, $8 per night per additional RV, and $70 per night for the group site. Open late May–September, weather permitting.

Directions: From Bend, drive southwest on Cascades Lakes Highway (Century Drive Highway, which becomes County Road 46) and drive 35.5 miles to Forest Road 4625. Turn left (east) and drive 1.7 miles to the campground.

Contact: Deschutes National Forest, Bend–Fort Rock Ranger District, 541/383-4000, fax 541/383-4700.

47 SOUTH

Scenic rating: 8

on Hosmer Lake in Deschutes National Forest

See map page 382

This campground is along the shore of Hosmer Lake, adjacent to Mallard Marsh. (See the *Mallard Marsh* listing in this chapter for recreation details.)

RV sites, facilities: There are 23 sites for tents or RVs up to 26 feet (no hookups). Picnic tables, garbage service, and fire grills are provided. Vault toilets and boat-launching facilities are available. No drinking water is provided. Leashed pets are permitted.

Reservations, fees: Reservations are not accepted. Sites are $5 per night per vehicle. Open late May–early October, weather permitting.

Directions: From Bend, drive southwest on Cascades Lakes Highway (Century Drive Highway, which becomes County Road 46) and drive 35.5 miles to Forest Road 4625. Turn left (east) and drive 1.2 miles to the campground on the right.

Contact: Deschutes National Forest, Bend–Fort Rock Ranger District, 541/383-4000, fax 541/383-4700.

OREGON

OREGON

48 MALLARD MARSH

Scenic rating: 8

on Hosmer Lake in Deschutes National Forest

See map page 382

This quiet campground is on the shore of Hosmer Lake, elevation 5,000 feet. The lake is stocked with brook trout and Atlantic salmon and reserved for catch-and-release fly-fishing only. You'll get a pristine, quality fishing experience here. The lake is ideal for canoeing. Only nonmotorized boats are allowed.

RV sites, facilities: There are 15 sites for tents or RVs up to 26 feet (no hookups). Picnic tables, garbage service, and vault toilets are provided. No drinking water is available. Boat-launching facilities are nearby. Leashed pets are permitted.

Reservations, fees: Reservations are not accepted. Sites are $5 per night per vehicle. Open late May–October, weather permitting.

Directions: From Bend, drive southwest on Cascades Lakes Highway (Century Drive Highway, which becomes County Road 46) and drive 35.5 miles to Forest Road 4625. Turn left (southeast) and drive 1.3 miles to the camp.

Contact: Deschutes National Forest, Bend–Fort Rock Ranger District, 541/383-4000, fax 541/383-4700.

49 LITTLE LAVA LAKE

Scenic rating: 8

on Little Lava Lake in Deschutes National Forest

See map page 382

Boating, fishing, hiking, and swimming are some of the recreation options here. This lake feeds into the Deschutes River. Some sites are lakeside and some are riverside. The elevation is 4,750 feet.

RV sites, facilities: There are 12 sites for tents or RVs up to 30 feet (no hookups). Picnic tables, garbage service, and fire grills are provided. Vault toilets and drinking water are available. A boat launch, docks, and rentals are nearby. There are also launching facilities on-site. Leashed pets are permitted.

Reservations, fees: Reservations are not ac-

cepted. Sites are $8 per night, plus $5 per night per additional vehicle. Open April–October, weather permitting.

Directions: From Bend, drive southwest on Cascades Lakes Highway (Century Drive Highway, which becomes County Road 46) and drive 38.4 miles to Forest Road 4600-500. Turn left (east) and drive 0.7 mile to Forest Road 4600-520. Continue east for 0.4 mile to the campground.

Contact: Deschutes National Forest, Bend–Fort Rock Ranger District, 541/383-4000, fax 541/383-4700.

50 LAVA LAKE

Scenic rating: 10

on Lava Lake in Deschutes National Forest

See map page 382

This well-designed campground sits on the shore of pretty Lava Lake at 4,750 feet elevation. Mount Bachelor and the Three Sisters are in the background, making a classic picture. Boating and fishing are popular here. A bonus is nearby Lava Lake Resort, which has showers, laundry facilities, an RV dump station, a store, gasoline, and propane.

RV sites, facilities: There are 43 sites for tents or RVs up to 45 feet (no hookups). Picnic tables, garbage service, and fire grills are provided. Vault toilets, drinking water, and a fish-cleaning station are available. Some facilities are wheelchair accessible. Boat docks and launching facilities are on-site. Boat rentals are nearby. Leashed pets are permitted.

Reservations, fees: Reservations are not accepted. Sites are $10–12 per night, $5 per night per additional vehicle, and $10–12 per night per additional RV. Open late April–October, weather permitting.

Directions: From Bend, drive southwest on Cascades Lakes Highway (Century Drive Highway, which becomes County Road 46) and drive 38.4 miles to Forest Road 4600-500. Turn left (east) and drive one mile to the campground.

Contact: Deschutes National Forest, Bend–

OREGON

Fort Rock Ranger District, 541/383-4000, fax 541/383-4700.

51 WHITTAKER CREEK

Scenic rating: 7

near the Siuslaw River

See map page 382

This campground is home to one of the area's premier salmon spawning grounds, where annual runs of chinook, coho salmon, and steelhead can be viewed. The (Whitaker Creek) Old Growth Ridge Trail, a national recreation trail, is accessible from the campground. This moderately difficult trail ascends 1,000 feet above the Siuslaw River through a stand of old-growth Douglas fir. Fishing is for trout and crayfish.

RV sites, facilities: There are 31 sites for tents or RVs up to 35 feet (no hookups). Picnic tables and fire pits are provided. A camp host is onsite, and drinking water, vault toilets, garbage bins, a boat ramp, a swimming beach, a playground, and a picnic shelter are available. Leashed pets are permitted. Some facilities are wheelchair accessible.

Reservations, fees: Reservations are not accepted. Sites are $10 per night, plus $5 per night for each additional vehicle. Open mid-May–mid-October, weather permitting.

Directions: From Eugene, drive west on Highway 126 for 33 miles to Siuslaw River Road. Turn left (south) and drive two miles to the first junction. Turn right and drive a short distance across Siuslaw River to the campground on the right.

Contact: Bureau of Land Management, Eugene District Office, 541/683-6600 or 888/442-3061, fax 541/683-6981.

52 CLAY CREEK

Scenic rating: 7

near the Siuslaw River

See map page 382

Clay Creek Trail, a two-mile loop, takes you to a ridge overlooking the river valley and is well worth the walk. Fishing for trout and crayfish is popular. Sites are in a forest of cedars, Douglas fir, and maple trees. The campground gets a medium amount of use.

RV sites, facilities: There are 21 sites for tents or RVs up to 35 feet (no hookups). Picnic tables and fire pits are provided. Drinking water, vault toilets, garbage bins, a swimming beach with changing rooms, a softball field, horseshoe pits, a playground, and two reservable group picnic shelters with fireplaces are available. There is a camp host. Leashed pets are permitted. Some facilities are wheelchair accessible.

Reservations, fees: Reservations are not accepted. Sites are $10 per night, plus $5 per night for each additional vehicle. Open mid-May–mid-October, weather permitting.

Directions: From Eugene, drive west on Highway 126 for 33 miles to Siuslaw River Road. Turn left (south) and drive 16 miles to BLM Road 19-7-2001 (signed for Clay Creek). Turn right and drive a short distance to the campground on the right.

Contact: Bureau of Land Management, Eugene District Office, 541/683-6600 or 888/442-3061, fax 541/683-6981.

53 CASCARA AND FISHERMAN'S PARK GROUP CAMP

Scenic rating: 7

in Fall Creek Reservoir State Recreation Area

See map page 382

There are two campgrounds here: Cascara and the group camp area, Fisherman's Park. Most of these spacious sites have Douglas fir and white fir tree cover. Water recreation is the primary activity here. Personal watercraft and water skis are allowed. The lake level drops in August, and water temperatures are ideal for summer swimming.

RV sites, facilities: There are 42 sites for tents or RVs (no hookups); some sites can accommodate RVs of any length. There are also five walk-in sites for tents and a group area for RVs of any length and up to 16 vehicles. There are no pull-through sites. Picnic tables, garbage service, and fire rings are provided. Drinking water, vault toilets, and firewood are available, and there is a camp host. A boat launch, dock, and swimming area are also available. Leashed pets are permitted.

Reservations, fees: Reservations are accepted for the RV group area only at 800/452-5687. Sites are $15 per night, plus $5 per night for an additional vehicle. The group RV area is $87 per night for up to 10 RVs and $8 per unit per night for each additional RV. Walk-in sites are $9 per night. Some credit cards are accepted. Open May–September.

Directions: From south Eugene on I-5, take Exit 188 to Highway 58. Drive 11 miles south to Lowell and Pioneer Street (at the covered bridge). Turn left on Pioneer Street and drive less than 0.25 mile to West Boundary Road. Turn left and drive one block to Lowell Jasper Road. Turn right and drive 1.5 miles to Unity and Place Road. Turn right and drive about one mile to a fork with North Shore Road (Big Fall Creek Road). Bear left onto Big Fall Creek Road and drive about eight miles to the head of Fall Creek Reservoir and Peninsula Road (Forest Road 6250). Turn right and drive 0.5 mile to the campground. The park is approximately 27 miles southeast of Eugene.

Contact: Fall Creek State Recreation Area, 541/937-1173 or 800/551-6949, www.oregonstateparks.org.

54 COTTAGE GROVE LAKE/ PINE MEADOWS

Scenic rating: 6

on Cottage Grove Reservoir

See map page 382

This campground is surrounded by a varied landscape—forest, grassland, and marshland—near the banks of Cottage Grove Reservoir. Campsites are within 200 feet of the water. Boating, fishing, swimming, and waterskiing are among the recreation options. It's an easy hop from I-5.

RV sites, facilities: There are 85 sites for tents

or RVs of any length (no hookups), with some pull-through sites. Drinking water, picnic tables, garbage bins, and fire rings are provided. Restrooms have flush toilets and showers. A dump station, a children's play area, an amphitheater, interpretive displays, and a swimming area are available. A boat dock, launching facilities, and a small store are nearby. Leashed pets are permitted.

Reservations, fees: Reservations are accepted at 877/444-6777 or www.ReserveUSA.com ($9 reservation fee). Sites are $15 per night, plus $5 per night for an additional vehicle. Open mid-May–mid-September.

Directions: From Eugene, drive south on I-5 past Cottage Grove to Exit 172. Take that exit to London Road and drive south for 4.5 miles to Reservoir Road. Turn left and drive three miles to the camp entrance on the right.

Contact: U.S. Army Corps of Engineers, Recreation Information, Cottage Grove, 541/942-8657 or 541/942-5631, fax 541/942-1305, www.nwp.usace.army.mil.

55 BAKER BAY COUNTY PARK

Scenic rating: 6

on Dorena Lake

See map page 382

This campground is along the shore of Dorena Lake, where boating, canoeing, fishing, sailing, swimming, and waterskiing are among the recreation options. Row River Trail follows part of the lake for a hike or bike ride, and there are covered bridges in the area. For golf, head to Cottage Grove.

RV sites, facilities: There are 49 sites for tents or RVs of any length (no hookups), plus two group sites for up to 25 people each. Picnic tables and fire grills are provided. Drinking water, restrooms with flush toilets and coin showers, firewood, garbage bins, and a dump station are available. Some facilities are wheelchair accessible. A concession stand with ice is in the park. A store is within two miles. Boat docks, launching facilities, and rentals are nearby, with seasonal on-shore facilities for catamarans. Leashed pets are permitted.

Reservations, fees: Reservations are accepted only for group sites at 541/682-2000 ($14 reservation fee). Single sites are $16 per night and $6.50 for an additional vehicle. Group sites are $50 per night. Open April–October.

Directions: From Eugene, drive south on I-5 for 22 miles to Cottage Grove and Exit 174 (Dorena Lake exit). Take that exit to Row River Road and drive east for 4.4 miles (the road becomes Shore View Drive). Bear right on Shore View Drive and continue 2.8 miles to the campground entrance on the left.

Contact: Baker Bay Park, 541/942-7669, www.co.lane.or.us/parks.

56 SCHWARZ PARK

Scenic rating: 7

on Dorena Lake
See map page 382

This large campground sits below Dorena Lake on the Row River, where boating, fishing, swimming, and waterskiing are among the recreation options at the lake. Note that chances of rain are high May to mid-June and that there is a posted warning for consumption of fish from Dorena Lake. The Row River Trail parallels Dorena Lake's north shoreline for 6.2 miles. This paved trail is excellent for walking, bike riding, and shoreline access.

RV sites, facilities: There are 72 sites for tents or RVs of any length (no hookups) and six group sites for up to 15–50 people; some sites are pull-through. Drinking water, garbage bins, picnic tables, and fire rings are provided. Restrooms have flush toilets and showers. A playground, interpretive displays, and a dump station are available. Boat-launching facilities are on the lake about two miles upstream. Some facilities are wheelchair accessible. Leashed pets are permitted.

Reservations, fees: Reservations are accepted at 877/444-6777 or www.ReserveUSA.com. Sites are $13 per night, group sites are $100 per night, and an additional vehicle is $5 per night. Open late April–late September.

Directions: From Eugene, drive south on I-5 for 22 miles to Cottage Grove and Exit 174. Take that exit to Shoreview Drive and drive one mile to Row River Road. Turn left and drive four miles east to the campground entrance.

Contact: U.S. Army Corps of Engineers, Recreation Information, Cottage Grove, 541/942-1418 or 541/942-5631, fax 541/942-1305.

57 SALMON CREEK FALLS

Scenic rating: 8

on Salmon Creek in Willamette National Forest
See map page 382

This pretty campground sits in a lush, old-growth forest, right along Salmon Creek at 1,500 feet in elevation. The rocky gorge area creates two small but beautiful waterfalls and several deep pools in the clear, blue-green waters. Springtime brings a full range of wildflowers and wild thimbleberries; hazelnuts abound in the summer. This area is a popular recreation spot.

RV sites, facilities: There are 14 sites for tents or RVs up to 40 feet (no hookups). Picnic tables, garbage bins, and fire grills are provided. Drinking water and vault toilets are available. A store, a café, a coin laundry, and ice are available within five miles. Leashed pets are permitted.

Reservations, fees: Reservations are not accepted. Sites are $12 per night, plus $6 per night per additional vehicle. Open late April–mid-September, weather permitting.

Directions: From south Eugene on I-5, take Exit 188 to Highway 58. Drive southeast on Highway 58 for 35 miles to Oakridge and the signal light for downtown. Turn left on Crestview Street and drive 0.25 mile to 1st Street. Turn right and drive five miles (the road becomes Forest Road 24, then Salmon Creek Road) to the campground entrance on the right.

Contact: Willamette National Forest, Middle Fork Ranger District, 541/782-2283, fax 541/782-5306; Hoodoo Recreation Services, 541/822-3799.

OREGON

58 NORTH WALDO

Scenic rating: 10

on Waldo Lake in Willamette National Forest

See map page 382

This camp, at an elevation of 5,400 feet, is the most popular of the Waldo Lake campgrounds. The drier environment supports fewer mosquitoes, but they can still be plentiful in season. The boat launch is deeper than the others on the lake, making it more accommodating for large sailboats. North Waldo is also a popular starting point to many wilderness trails and lakes, most notably the Rigdon, Torrey, and Wahanna Lakes. Waldo Lake has the special distinction of being one of the three purest lakes in the world. Of those three lakes, two are in Oregon (the other is Crater Lake), and the third is in Siberia. Amphitheater programs are presented here on weekends late July–Labor Day.

RV sites, facilities: There are 58 sites for tents or RVs up to 40 feet (no hookups). Picnic tables and fire rings are provided. Drinking water, vault and composting toilets, garbage bins, a recycle center, a swimming area, and an amphitheater are available. Boat-launching facilities are available. Leashed pets are permitted.

Reservations, fees: Reservations are not accepted. Sites are $14 per night for single sites, $7 per night per additional vehicle, and $25 per night for double sites. Northwest Forest Pass ($5 daily fee or $30 annual fee per parked vehicle) is required at the nearby boat launch and trailheads. Open mid-June–mid-October, weather permitting.

Directions: From Eugene, drive south on I-5 for four miles to Exit 188 and Highway 58. Turn southeast and drive about 60 miles to Waldo Lake Road (Forest Road 5897). Turn left and drive north on Waldo Lake Road for 14 miles to Forest Road 5898. Turn left and drive about two miles to the campground at the northeast end of Waldo Lake.

Contact: Willamette National Forest, Middle Fork Ranger District, 541/782-2283, fax 541/782-5306; Hoodoo Recreation Services, 541/822-3799.

59 ISLET

Scenic rating: 10

on Waldo Lake in Willamette National Forest

See map page 382

You'll find sandy beaches and an interpretive sign at this campground at the north end of Waldo Lake. The winds blow consistently every afternoon. A picnic table placed strategically on the rock jetty provides a great spot to enjoy a sunset. A one-mile shoreline trail stretches between Islet and North Waldo Campground. Bring your mosquito repellent June–August; you'll need it. (For more information, see the *North Waldo* listing in this chapter.)

RV sites, facilities: There are 55 sites for tents or RVs up to 40 feet (no hookups). Picnic tables, garbage bins, a recycling center, and fire rings are provided. Drinking water and vault toilets are available. Boat-launching facilities are available. Leashed pets are permitted.

Reservations, fees: Reservations are not accepted. Sites are $14 per night, plus $7 per night per additional vehicle. Double sites are $25 per night. A Northwest Forest Pass ($5 daily fee or $30 annual fee per parked vehicle) is required at the nearby boat launch and trailheads. Open July–September, weather permitting.

Directions: From Eugene, drive south on I-5 for four miles to Exit 188 and Highway 58. Turn southeast and drive about 60 miles to Waldo Lake Road (Forest Road 5897). Turn left and drive north on Waldo Lake Road for 14 miles to Forest Road 5898. Turn left and continue 1.5 miles to the campground at the northeast end of Waldo Lake.

Contact: Willamette National Forest, Middle Fork Ranger District, 541/782-2283, fax 541/782-5306; Hoodoo Recreation Services, 541/822-3799.

60 SHADOW BAY

Scenic rating: 10

on Waldo Lake in Willamette National Forest
See map page 382

This campground, at 5,400 in elevation, is on a large bay at the south end of Waldo Lake. It has a considerably wetter environment than either North Waldo or Islet, supporting a more diverse and prolific ground cover as well as more mosquitoes. The camp receives considerably lighter use than North Waldo. You have access to the Shore Line Trail and then the Waldo Lake Trail from here. The boating speed limit is 10 mph for all of Waldo Lake.

RV sites, facilities: There are 92 sites for tents or RVs up to 40 feet (no hookups). Picnic tables, garbage bins, a recycle center, and fire grills are provided. Vault and composting toilets are available. Drinking water is available intermittently. Boat-launching facilities are nearby. Leashed pets are permitted.

Reservations, fees: Reservations are accepted at 877/444-6777 or www.ReserveUSA.com ($9 reservation fee). Sites are $14 per night for single sites, $7 per night per additional vehicle, and $25 per night for double sites. Camping fees are reduced if there is no drinking water. A Northwest Forest Pass ($5 daily fee or $30 annual fee per parked vehicle) is required at the nearby boat launch and trailheads. Open July–mid-September, weather permitting.

Directions: From Eugene, drive south on I-5 for four miles to Exit 188 and Highway 58. Turn southeast and drive about 60 miles to Waldo Lake Road (Forest Road 5897). Turn left on Waldo Lake Road and drive north for 6.5 miles to the Shadow Bay turnoff. Turn left and drive on Forest Road 5896 to the campground at the south end of Waldo Lake.

Contact: Willamette National Forest, Middle Fork Ranger District, 541/782-2283, fax 541/782-5306; Hoodoo Recreation Services, 541/822-3799; Hoodoo Recreation Services, 541/822-3799.

61 LITTLE CULTUS LAKE

Scenic rating: 7

on Little Cultus Lake in Deschutes National Forest
See map page 382

This campground is near the shore of Little Cultus Lake at an elevation of 4,800 feet. It's a popular spot for boating (10-mph speed limit), fishing, hiking, and swimming. Nearby trails offer access to numerous backcountry lakes, and the Pacific Crest Trail passes about six miles west of the camp.

RV sites, facilities: There are 20 sites for tents or RVs up to 45 feet (no hookups). Picnic tables, garbage service, and fire grills are provided. Drinking water, vault toilets, and a boat launch are available. Leashed pets are permitted.

Reservations, fees: Reservations are not accepted. Sites are $8 per night, $5 per night per additional vehicle, and $8 per night per additional RV. Open late May–October, weather permitting.

Directions: From Bend, drive southwest on Cascades Lakes Highway (Century Drive Highway, which becomes County Road 46) and drive 46 miles to Forest Road 4635. Turn right (west) and drive two miles to Forest Road 4630. Turn left (south) and drive 1.7 miles to Forest Road 4636. Turn left (west) and drive one mile to the campground.

Contact: Deschutes National Forest, Bend–Fort Rock Ranger District, 541/383-4000, fax 541/383-4700.

62 CULTUS LAKE

Scenic rating: 7

on Cultus Lake in Deschutes National Forest
See map page 382

This camp along the east shore of Cultus Lake is at 4,700 feet elevation. It is a popular spot for fishing, hiking, swimming, waterskiing, and windsurfing. The campsites fill up early on weekends and holidays.

RV sites, facilities: There are 55 sites for tents or RVs up to 50 feet (no hookups). Picnic tables,

OREGON

garbage service, and fire grills are provided. Drinking water and vault toilets are available. Boat docks and launching facilities are on-site. Boat rentals are nearby. A restaurant, gasoline, and cabins are available nearby at Cultus Lake Resort nearby. Leashed pets are permitted.

Reservations, fees: Reservations are not accepted. Sites are $12–14 per night, $6 per night per additional vehicle, and $12–14 per night per additional RV. Open May–September, weather permitting.

Directions: From Bend, drive southwest on Cascades Lakes Highway (Century Drive Highway, which becomes County Road 46) and drive 46 miles to Forest Road 4635. Turn right (west) and drive two miles to the campground.

Contact: Deschutes National Forest, Bend–Fort Rock Ranger District, 541/383-4000, fax 541/383-4700.

63 CRANE PRAIRIE

Scenic rating: 6

on Crane Prairie Reservoir in Deschutes National Forest

See map page 382

This campground along the north shore of Crane Prairie Reservoir is a good spot for anglers and boaters. World-renowned for rainbow trout fishing, this reservoir is also popular for bass fishing.

RV sites, facilities: There are 146 sites for tents or RVs up to 50 feet (no hookups). Four group sites can accommodate up to 75–150 people each, depending on the site. Picnic tables, garbage service, and fire grills are provided. Drinking water and vault toilets are available. Boat docks, launching facilities, and a fish-cleaning station are available on-site. Boat rentals, showers, gas, and a coin laundry are nearby. Some facilities are wheelchair accessible. Leashed pets are permitted.

Reservations, fees: Reservations are accepted only for group sites at 877/444-6777 or www.ReserveUSA.com ($9 reservation fee). Single sites are $10–12 per night, $5 per night

per additional vehicle, and $10–12 per night per additional RV. Group sites are $80–175 per night. Open April–October, weather permitting.

Directions: From Bend, drive south on U.S. 97 for 26.8 miles to Wickiup Junction and County Road 43. Turn right (west) on County Road 43 and drive 11 miles to Forest Road 42. Continue west on Forest Road 42 for 5.4 miles to Forest Road 4270. Turn right (north) and drive 4.2 miles to the campground on the left.

Contact: Deschutes National Forest, Bend–Fort Rock Ranger District, 541/383-4000, fax 541/383-4700.

64 QUINN RIVER

Scenic rating: 5

on Crane Prairie Reservoir in Deschutes National Forest

See map page 382

This campground is along the western shore of Crane Prairie Reservoir, a popular spot for anglers and a great spot for bird-watching. A separate, large parking lot is available for boats and trailers. Boat speed is limited to 10 mph here. The elevation is 4,450 feet.

RV sites, facilities: There are 41 sites for tents or RVs up to 45 feet (no hookups). Picnic tables, garbage service, and fire grills are provided. Drinking water and vault toilets are available. Boat-launching facilities are available. Some facilities are wheelchair accessible. Leashed pets are permitted.

Reservations, fees: Reservations are not accepted. Sites are $10–12 per night, $5 per night per additional vehicle, and $10–12 per night per additional RV. Open late April–September, weather permitting.

Directions: From Bend, drive southwest on Cascade Lakes Highway (Century Drive Highway, which becomes County Road 46) for 48 miles to the campground.

Contact: Deschutes National Forest, Bend–Fort Rock Ranger District, 541/383-4000, fax 541/383-4700.

65 ROCK CREEK

Scenic rating: 5

on Crane Prairie Reservoir in Deschutes
National Forest

See map page 382

This campground is along the west shore of
Crane Prairie Reservoir at an elevation of 4,450
feet. (See the *Quinn River* listing in this chapter
for area details.)

RV sites, facilities: There are 31 sites for tents
or RVs up to 30 feet (no hookups). Picnic
tables, garbage service, and fire grills are provided. Drinking water, a fish-cleaning station,
and vault toilets are available. Boat docks and
launching facilities are on-site. Some facilities are wheelchair accessible. Leashed pets
are permitted.

Reservations, fees: Reservations are not accepted. Sites are $10–12 per night, $5 per night
per additional vehicle, and $10–12 per night per
additional RV. Open April–October, weather
permitting.

Directions: From Bend, drive southwest on
Cascade Lakes Highway (Century Drive Highway, which becomes County Road 46) for 48.8
miles to the campground.

Contact: Deschutes National Forest, Bend–
Fort Rock Ranger District, 541/383-4000, fax
541/383-4700.

66 FALL RIVER

Scenic rating: 5

on the Fall River in Deschutes National Forest

See map page 382

This campground is on the Fall River, where
fishing is restricted to fly-fishing only. Check
the regulations for other restrictions. Fall River
is beautiful, crystal clear, and cold. The Fall
River Trail meanders along the river for 3.5
miles and is open for bicycling. The elevation
is 4,300 feet.

RV sites, facilities: There are 10 sites for tents
or RVs up to 30 feet (no hookups). Picnic tables,
garbage service, and fire grills are provided.

Vault toilets are available. There is no drinking
water. Leashed pets are permitted.

Reservations, fees: Reservations are not accepted. Sites are $5 per night per vehicle. Open
mid-April–October, weather permitting.

Directions: From Bend, drive south on U.S. 97
for 17.3 miles to the Vandevert Road exit. Take
that exit and turn right on Vandevert Road.
Drive 1.5 miles to Forest Road 42. Turn left and
drive 12.2 miles to the campground.

Contact: Deschutes National Forest, Bend–
Fort Rock Ranger District, 541/383-4000, fax
541/383-4700.

67 BIG RIVER

Scenic rating: 4

on the Deschutes River in Deschutes
National Forest

See map page 382   BEST (

This is a good spot. Located between the banks
of the Deschutes River and the road, it has
easy access and is popular as an overnight
camp. Fishing, motorized boating, and rafting
are permitted.

RV sites, facilities: There are 11 sites for tents
or RVs up to 26 feet (no hookups). Picnic tables,
garbage service, and fire grills are provided.
Vault toilets are available. There is no drinking water. Boat-launching facilities are on-
site. Some facilities are wheelchair accessible.
Leashed pets are permitted.

Reservations, fees: Reservations are not accepted. Sites are $5 per night per vehicle, plus
$5 per vehicle monument entrance fee. Open
April–late September, weather permitting.

Directions: From Bend, drive south on U.S. 97
for 17.3 miles to the Vandervert Road exit. Take
that exit and turn right on Vandervert Road.
Drive 1.5 miles to Forest Road 42. Turn left
and drive 7.9 miles to the campground.

Contact: Deschutes National Forest, Bend–
Fort Rock Ranger District, 541/383-4000, fax
541/383-4700.

OREGON

68 PRAIRIE

Scenic rating: 4

on Paulina Creek in Deschutes National Forest

See map page 382

Here's another good overnight campground that is quiet and private. This camp along the banks of Paulina Creek is about 0.5 mile from the trailhead for the Peter Skene Ogden National Recreation Trail. The elevation is 4,300 feet.

RV sites, facilities: There are 16 sites for tents or RVs up to 30 feet (no hookups). Picnic tables, garbage service, and fire grills are provided. Drinking water, firewood, and vault toilets are available. Leashed pets are permitted.

Reservations, fees: Reservations are not accepted. Sites are $10 per night, $5 per night per additional vehicle, and $10 per night per additional RV. There is a $5 per vehicle monument entrance fee. Open April–early October, weather permitting.

Directions: From Bend, drive south on U.S. 97 for 23.5 miles to County Road 21 (Paulina/East Lake Road). Turn left (east) and drive 3.1 miles to the campground.

Contact: Deschutes National Forest, Bend–Fort Rock Ranger District, 541/383-4000, fax 541/383-4700.

69 McKAY CROSSING

Scenic rating: 6

on Paulina Creek in Deschutes National Forest

See map page 382

This pleasant little campground borders Paulina Creek. An outstanding site for bird-watching, it sits at an elevation of 4,750 feet. The nearby Peter Skene Ogden National Recreation Trail travels east for six miles to Paulina Lake (also reachable by car). This spot is the gateway to Newberry National Volcanic Monument, about 10 miles east on County Road 21.

RV sites, facilities: There are 10 sites for tents or RVs up to 26 feet (no hookups). Picnic tables, garbage service, and fire grills are provided.

Vault toilets are available. There is no drinking water. Leashed pets are permitted.

Reservations, fees: Reservations are not accepted. Sites are $5 per night per vehicle. There also is a $5 per vehicle monument entrance fee. Open April–late September, weather permitting.

Directions: From Bend, drive south on U.S. 97 for 23.5 miles to County Road 21 (Paulina/East Lake Road). Turn left (east) and drive 3.2 miles to Forest Road 2120. Continue east for 2.7 miles to the campground.

Contact: Deschutes National Forest, Bend–Fort Rock Ranger District, 541/383-4000, fax 541/383-4700.

70 PAULINA LAKE

Scenic rating: 8

on Paulina Lake in Deschutes National Forest

See map page 382

This campground (6,350 feet elevation) is along the south shore of Paulina Lake and within the Newberry National Volcanic Monument. The camp is adjacent to Paulina Lake Resort. The lake itself sits in a volcanic crater. Nearby trails provide access to the remains of volcanic activity, including craters and obsidian flows. My longtime friend, Guy Carl, caught the state's record brown trout here, right after I'd written a story about his unique method of using giant Rapala and Rebel bass lures for giant browns. The recreation options here include boating, fishing, hiking, mountain biking, and sailing. The boat speed limit is 10 mph. Note that food-raiding bears are common at all the campgrounds in the Newberry Caldera area and that all food must be kept out of reach. Do not store food in vehicles.

RV sites, facilities: There are 69 sites with no hookups for RVs up to 30 feet. Picnic tables, garbage service, and fire grills are provided. Drinking water and flush and vault toilets are available. Some facilities are wheelchair accessible. Boat docks, launching facilities, boat rentals, coin showers, a coin laundry, a small store, a restaurant, cabins, gas, and propane are within five miles. The Newberry RV dump station is nearby. Leashed pets are permitted.

Reservations, fees: Reservations are not accepted. Sites are $12–14 per night, $6 per night for each additional vehicle. There is also a $5 per vehicle park entrance fee. Open May–late October, weather permitting.

Directions: From Bend, drive south on U.S. 97 for 23.5 miles to County Road 21 (Paulina/East Lake Road). Turn left (east) and drive 12.9 miles to the campground on the left.

Contact: Deschutes National Forest, Bend–Fort Rock Ranger District, 541/383-4000, fax 541/383-4700.

71 LITTLE CRATER

Scenic rating: 8

near Paulina Lake in Deschutes National Forest
See map page 382

This campground (6,350 feet elevation) is near the east shore of Paulina Lake in Newberry National Volcanic Monument, a caldera. This camp is very popular. (See the *Paulina Lake* listing in this chapter for more information.)

RV sites, facilities: There are 50 sites for tents or RVs up to 30 feet (no hookups). Picnic tables, garbage service, and fire grills are provided. Drinking water and vault toilets are available. Boat docks and launching facilities are on-site, and boat rentals are nearby. Some facilities are wheelchair accessible. Leashed pets are permitted.

Reservations, fees: Reservations are not accepted. Sites are $14 per night and $5 per night for each additional vehicle. Parking at the nearby trailhead requires an additional fee ($5 daily fee or $30 annual fee per parked vehicle). Open late May–late October, weather permitting.

Directions: From Bend, drive south on U.S. 97 for 23.5 miles to County Road 21 (Paulina/East Lake Road). Turn left (east) and drive 14.5 miles to Forest Road 2100. Turn left (north) and drive 0.5 mile to the campground on the left.

Contact: Deschutes National Forest, Bend–Fort Rock Ranger District, 541/383-4000, fax 541/383-4700.

72 CINDER HILL

Scenic rating: 7

on East Lake in Deschutes National Forest
See map page 382

This campground hugs the northeast shore of East Lake at an elevation of 6,400 feet. Located within the Newberry National Volcanic Monument, Cinder Hill makes a good base camp for area activities. Boating, fishing, and hiking are among the recreation options. Boat speed is limited to 10 mph.

RV sites, facilities: There are 110 sites for tents or RVs up to 26 feet (no hookups). Picnic tables, garbage service, and fire grills are provided. Drinking water and flush and vault toilets are available. Boat docks and launching facilities are on-site, and boat rentals, a store, a restaurant, coin showers, a coin laundry, and cabins are nearby at East Lake Resort. Some facilities are wheelchair accessible. Leashed pets are permitted.

Reservations, fees: Reservations are not accepted. Sites are $12–14 per night. Parking at the nearby trailhead requires an additional fee ($5 daily fee or $30 annual fee per parked vehicle). Open late May–late October, weather permitting.

Directions: From Bend, drive south on U.S. 97 for 23.5 miles to County Road 21 (Paulina/East Lake Road). Turn left (east) and drive 17.6 miles to Forest Road 2100-700. Turn left (north) and drive 0.5 mile to the campground.

Contact: Deschutes National Forest, Bend–Fort Rock Ranger District, 541/383-4000, fax 541/383-4700.

73 EAST LAKE

Scenic rating: 8

on East Lake in Deschutes National Forest
See map page 382

This campground lies along the south shore of East Lake at an elevation of 6,400 feet. Boating and fishing are popular here, and hiking trails provide access to signs of former volcanic activity in the area. East Lake Campground is

OREGON

OREGON

similar to Cinder Hill but smaller. Boat speed is limited to 10 mph.

RV sites, facilities: There are 29 sites for tents or RVs up to 26 feet (no hookups). Picnic tables, garbage service, and fire grills are provided. Drinking water and flush and vault toilets are available. Some facilities are wheelchair accessible. Boat docks, launching facilities, and rentals are nearby. Leashed pets are permitted.

Reservations, fees: Reservations are not accepted. Sites are $12–14 per night, $5 per night for an additional vehicle. There is also a $5 per vehicle park entrance fee. Open late May–late October, weather permitting.

Directions: From Bend, drive south on U.S. 97 for 23.5 miles to County Road 21 (Paulina/East Lake Road). Turn left (east) and drive 16.6 miles to the campground on the left.

Contact: Deschutes National Forest, Bend–Fort Rock Ranger District, 541/383-4000, fax 541/383-4700.

74 EAST LAKE RESORT AND RV PARK

Scenic rating: 7

on East Lake

See map page 382

This resort offers shaded sites in a wooded, mountainous setting on the east shore of East Lake. Opportunities for boating, fishing, and swimming abound.

RV sites, facilities: There are 38 sites for tents or RVs up to 40 feet with partial hookups (30 amps) and 16 cabins. Some sites are pull-through. Drinking water, barbecues, and picnic tables are provided. Restrooms have flush toilets and coin showers. Propane gas, firewood, a dump station, a convenience store, a café, a coin laundry, ice, boat-launching facilities, boat rentals, moorage, and a playground are available. Leashed pets are permitted.

Reservations, fees: Reservations are accepted. Sites are $20 per night, plus $5 per night for a second vehicle. Some credit cards are accepted. Open mid-May–September, weather permitting.

Directions: From Bend, drive south on U.S. 97 for 23.5 miles to County Road 21 (Paulina/East Lake Road). Turn left (east) and drive 18 miles to the park at the end of the road.

Contact: East Lake Resort and RV Park, 541/536-2230, www.eastlakeresort.com.

75 HOT SPRINGS

Scenic rating: 5

near East Lake in Deschutes National Forest

See map page 382

Don't be fooled by the name. There are no hot springs at this campsite. It lies across the road from East Lake at 6,400 feet elevation. (See the listing in this chapter for *East Lake Resort and RV Park* for additional recreation information.)

RV sites, facilities: There are 52 sites for tents or RVs up to 26 feet (no hookups). Picnic tables, garbage service, and fire grills are provided. Drinking water and vault toilets are available. Boat docks, launching facilities, and rentals are nearby. Leashed pets are permitted.

Reservations, fees: Reservations are not accepted. Sites are $10 per night, plus $5 per night per additional vehicle and $7 per night for additional RV. There is a $5 per vehicle monument entrance fee. Open July–late September, weather permitting.

Directions: From Bend, drive south on U.S. 97 for 23.5 miles to County Road 21 (Paulina/East Lake Road). Turn left (east) and drive 17.2 miles to the campground on the right.

Contact: Deschutes National Forest, Bend–Fort Rock Ranger District, 541/383-4000, fax 541/383-4700.

76 NORTH TWIN LAKE

Scenic rating: 6

on North Twin Lake in Deschutes National Forest

See map page 382

This campground on the shore of North Twin Lake is a popular weekend spot for families. Although small and fairly primitive, it has lake access and a pretty setting. Only nonmotorized boats are permitted. The elevation is 4,350 feet.

RV sites, facilities: There are 19 sites for tents or RVs up to 30 feet (no hookups). Picnic tables and fire grills are provided. Vault toilets are available. There is no drinking water. Boat-launching facilities are on-site. Leashed pets are permitted.

Reservations, fees: Reservations are not accepted. Sites are $5 per night per vehicle. Open April–late September, weather permitting.

Directions: From Bend, drive southwest on Cascade Lakes Highway (Century Drive Highway, which becomes County Road 46) for 52 miles and drive past Crane Prairie Reservoir to Forest Road 42. Turn east and drive four miles to Forest Road 4260. Turn right (south) and drive 0.25 mile to the campground.

Contact: Deschutes National Forest, Bend–Fort Rock Ranger District, 541/383-4000, fax 541/383-4700.

⁊⁊ TWIN LAKES RESORT

🚶 🚴 🏊 🎣 🛥 🛶 🐕 🚐

Scenic rating: 8

on Twin Lakes

See map page 382

This resort is a popular family vacation destination with a full-service marina and all the amenities, including beach areas. Recreational activities vary from hiking to boating, fishing, and swimming on Wickiup Reservoir. Nearby South Twin Lake is popular with pedal boaters and kayakers. It's stocked with rainbow trout. (See the listings in this chapter for *South Twin Lake* and *West South Twin* for additional details.)

RV sites, facilities: There are 22 sites with full hookups (30 amps) for RVs of any length. There are also 14 cabins. Picnic tables and fire rings are provided. Restrooms have flush toilets and coin showers. A dump station, a coin laundry, a convenience store, a restaurant, ice, snacks, some RV supplies, propane gas, and gasoline are available. A boat ramp, rentals, and a dock are provided; no motors are permitted on South Twin Lake. Leashed pets are permitted.

Reservations, fees: Reservations are recom-

mended. Sites are $30 per night, plus $15 per tent in addition to RV. There are no tent-only sites. Some credit cards are accepted. Open late April–mid-October, weather permitting.

Directions: From Bend, drive south on U.S. 97 for 26.8 miles to Wickiup Junction. Turn right (west) on County Road 43 and drive 11 miles to Forest Road 42. Turn left and continue 4.6 miles west on Forest Road 42 to Forest Road 4260. Turn left (south) and drive two miles to the resort.

Contact: Twin Lakes Resort, 541/593-6526, fax 541/410-4688, www.twinlakesresort oregon.com.

⁊⁸ SOUTH TWIN LAKE

🚶 🚴 🏊 🎣 🛶 🚐 🐕 ♿ 🚐 ⛺

Scenic rating: 6

on South Twin Lake in Deschutes National Forest

See map page 382

This campground is on the shore of South Twin Lake, a popular spot for boating (nonmotorized only), fishing, and swimming. The elevation is 4,350 feet. (See the listing in this chapter for *West South Twin* for more area details.)

RV sites, facilities: There are 24 sites for tents or RVs up to 26 feet (no hookups). Picnic tables, garbage service, and fire grills are provided. Drinking water and vault and flush toilets are available. Some facilities are wheelchair accessible. Boat-launching facilities (small boats only), boat rentals, showers, and laundry facilities are nearby. Leashed pets are permitted.

Reservations, fees: Reservations are not accepted. Sites are $14 per night, $6 per night per additional vehicle, and $14 per night per additional RV. Open April–October, weather permitting.

Directions: From Bend, drive south on U.S. 97 for 26.8 miles to Wickiup Junction. Turn right (west) on County Road 43 and drive 11 miles to Forest Road 42. Continue west on Forest Road 42 for 4.6 miles to Forest Road 4260. Turn left (south) and drive two miles to the campground on the left.

Contact: Deschutes National Forest, Bend–Fort Rock Ranger District, 541/383-4000, fax 541/383-4700.

79 WEST SOUTH TWIN

Scenic rating: 4

on South Twin Lake in Deschutes National Forest
See map page 382

A major access point to the Wickiup Reservoir, this camp is on South Twin Lake adjacent to the reservoir. It's a popular angling spot with very good kokanee salmon fishing. Twin Lakes Resort is adjacent to West South Twin. The elevation is 4,350 feet.

RV sites, facilities: There are 24 sites with no hookups for RVs up to 30 feet. Picnic tables, garbage service, and fire grills are provided. Drinking water and flush toilets are available. Boat-launching facilities are on-site, and boat rentals, a restaurant, showers, a coin laundry, gas, propane, cabins, and a store are nearby. Leashed pets are permitted.

Reservations, fees: Reservations are not accepted. Sites are $10–12 per night, $5 per night per additional vehicle, and $10–12 per night per additional RV. Open April–mid-October, weather permitting.

Directions: From Bend, drive southwest on Cascade Lakes Highway (Century Drive Highway, which becomes County Road 46) for 52 miles (past Crane Prairie Reservoir) to Forest Road 42. Turn left (east) and drive four miles to Forest Road 4260. Turn right (south) and drive 0.25 mile to the campground.

Contact: Deschutes National Forest, Bend–Fort Rock Ranger District, 541/383-4000, fax 541/383-4700.

80 GULL POINT

Scenic rating: 5

on Wickiup Reservoir in Deschutes National Forest
See map page 382

This campground sits in an open ponderosa stand on the north shore of Wickiup Reservoir. You'll find good fishing for kokanee salmon here. About two miles from West South Twin campground, Gull Point is the most popular campground on Wickiup Reservoir.

RV sites, facilities: There are 81 sites for tents or RVs up to 30 feet (no hookups) and two group sites for up to 25 people each. Picnic tables, garbage service, and fire grills are provided. Drinking water, a dump station, and flush and vault toilets are available. Boat-launching facilities and fish-cleaning stations are on-site. Some facilities are wheelchair accessible. Leashed pets are permitted.

Reservations, fees: Reservations are required for the group sites at 541/382-9443 but are not accepted for family sites. Sites are $12–14 per night for single sites, $6 per night per additional vehicle, $12–14 per night per additional RV, and $65 per night for group sites. Open mid-April–October, weather permitting.

Directions: From Bend, drive south on U.S. 97 for about 26.8 miles to County Road 43 (three miles north of LaPine). Turn right (west) on County Road 43 and drive 11 miles to Forest Road 42. Turn west on Forest Road 42 and drive 4.6 miles to Forest Road 4260. Turn left (south) and drive three miles to the campground on the right.

Contact: Deschutes National Forest, Bend–Fort Rock Ranger District, 541/383-4000, fax 541/383-4700.

81 GOLD LAKE

Scenic rating: 8

on Gold Lake in Willamette National Forest
See map page 382

This campground wins the popularity contest for high use. Although motors are not allowed on this small lake (100 acres, 25 feet deep), rafts and rowboats provide excellent fishing access. A primitive log shelter built in the early 1940s provides a dry picnic area. In the spring and summer, this area abounds with wildflowers and huckleberries. The Gold Lake Bog is another special attraction where one can often see deer, elk, and smaller wildlife.

RV sites, facilities: There are 25 sites for tents or RVs up to 30 feet (no hookups). Picnic tables, garbage bins, and fire grills are provided.

Drinking water and vault toilets are available. Boat docks and launching facilities are nearby. Leashed pets are permitted.

Reservations, fees: Reservations are not accepted. Sites are $14 per night, plus $7 per night per additional vehicle. Open June–September, weather permitting.

Directions: From Eugene, drive south on I-5 for five miles to Exit 188 and Highway 58. Turn east and drive 35 miles to the town of Oakridge. From Oakridge, continue east on Highway 58 for 28 miles to Gold Lake Road (Forest Road 500). Turn left (north) and drive two miles to the campground on the right.

Contact: Willamette National Forest, Middle Fork Ranger District, 541/782-2283, fax 541/782-5306; Hoodoo Recreation Services, 541/822-3799.

82 NORTH DAVIS CREEK

Scenic rating: 4

on North Davis Creek in Deschutes National Forest
See map page 382

This remote, secluded campground is along a western channel that feeds into Wickiup Reservoir. Fishing for brown and rainbow trout as well as kokanee salmon is good here. In late summer, the reservoir level tends to drop. The elevation is 4,350 feet. It receives little use and makes a good overflow camp if campsites are filled at Wickiup Reservoir.

RV sites, facilities: There are 15 sites for tents or RVs up to 26 feet (no hookups). Picnic tables, garbage service, and fire grills are provided. Drinking water and vault toilets are available. Boat-launching facilities are on-site. Leashed pets are permitted.

Reservations, fees: Reservations are not accepted. Sites are $8 per night, $5 per night per additional vehicle, and $8 per night per additional RV. Open April–early September.

Directions: From Bend, drive southwest on Cascade Lake Highway (Highway 46/Forest Road 46) for 56.2 miles to the campground on the left.

Contact: Deschutes National Forest, Bend–Fort Rock Ranger District, 541/383-4000, fax 541/383-4700.

83 RESERVOIR

Scenic rating: 4

on Wickiup Reservoir in Deschutes National Forest
See map page 382

You'll find this campground along the south shore of Wickiup Reservoir, where the kokanee salmon fishing is good. The camp is best in early summer, before the lake level drops. This camp gets little use, so you won't find crowds here. The elevation is 4,350 feet.

RV sites, facilities: There are 28 sites for tents or RVs up to 30 feet (no hookups). Picnic tables, garbage service, and fire grills are provided. Boat-launching facilities and vault toilets are available, but there is no drinking water. Leashed pets are permitted.

Reservations, fees: Reservations are not accepted. Sites are $5 per night per vehicle. Open April–September, weather permitting.

Directions: From Bend, drive southwest on Cascade Lakes Highway (Century Drive Highway, which becomes County Road 46) for 57.8 miles to Forest Road 44. Turn left (east) and drive 1.7 miles to the campground.

Contact: Deschutes National Forest, Bend–Fort Rock Ranger District, 541/383-4000, fax 541/383-4700.

84 LaPINE STATE PARK

Scenic rating: 7

on the Deschutes River
See map page 382   **BEST (**

This clean, quiet campground sits next to a twisting, cold river brimming with trout, a nearby legendary fly-fishing spot, and Oregon's "Big Tree," the largest ponderosa pine in the state. The camp is in a subalpine pine forest, and you just might see an eagle or red-tailed hawk grabbing breakfast right in front of you.

Many high mountain lakes are in proximity, and skiing is a popular wintertime option in the area.

RV sites, facilities: There are 137 sites for tents or RVs of any length with full or partial hookups (20 amps); some sites are pull-through. There are also 10 cabins. Picnic tables and fire grills are provided. Drinking water, restrooms with flush toilets and showers, garbage bins, a dump station, a seasonal store, a day-use area with a sandy beach, a reservable meeting hall, and firewood are available. A boat launch is nearby. Leashed pets are permitted.

Reservations, fees: Reservations are accepted at 800/452-5687 or www.oregonstateparks.org ($6 reservation fee). Sites are $13–17 per night, plus $5 per night per additional vehicle. Cabins are $38–70 per night. Some credit cards are accepted. Open year-round.

Directions: From Bend, turn south on U.S. 97 and drive 23 miles to State Recreation Road. Turn right and drive four miles to the park.

Contact: LaPine State Park, 541/536-2071; Oregon State Parks, 800/551-6949, www.oregonstateparks.org.

85 HIDDEN PINES RV PARK

Scenic rating: 7

near the Little Deschutes River
See map page 382

So you think you've come far enough, eh? If you want a spot in a privately run RV park two miles from the bank of the Little Deschutes River, you've found it. Within a 30-minute drive are two reservoirs, four lakes, and a golf course. The nearby town of LaPine is the gateway to the Newberry National Volcanic Monument.

RV sites, facilities: There is an area for tents and 25 sites with full or partial hookups (30 amps) for RVs of any length; most are pull-through sites. Drinking water, cable TV, and picnic tables are provided. Restrooms have flush toilets and showers. A dump station, a coin laundry, RV supplies, propane gas, a community fire ring with firewood, and ice

are available. The full-service community of LaPine is about five miles away. Leashed pets are allowed.

Reservations, fees: Reservations are accepted. Sites are $19.44–25.92 per night, plus $2.50 per person per night for more than two people. Some credit cards are accepted. Open year-round.

Directions: From Bend, drive south on U.S. 97 for 24 miles to Wickiup Junction, Milepost 165, and County Road 43/Burgess Road (lighted). Turn right (west) on County Road 43 (Burgess Road) and drive 2.4 miles to Pine Forest Road. Turn left and drive 0.7 mile to Wright Avenue. Turn left and drive one block to the park on the left.

Contact: Hidden Pines RV Park, tel./fax 541/536-2265.

86 SHARPS CREEK

Scenic rating: 5

on Sharps Creek
See map page 382

Like nearby Rujada, this camp on the banks of Sharps Creek is just far enough off the beaten path to be missed by most campers. It's quiet, primitive, and remote, and fishing, gold-panning, and swimming are popular activities in the day-use area.

RV sites, facilities: There are 10 sites for tents or RVs up to 30 feet (no hookups). Picnic tables and fire pits are provided. Drinking water and vault toilets are available. A camp host is here in summer. Some facilities are wheelchair accessible. Leashed pets are permitted.

Reservations, fees: Reservations are not accepted. Sites are $8 per night, with a 14-day stay limit, and it's $3 per night per additional vehicle. Open mid-May–September, weather permitting.

Directions: From Eugene, drive south on I-5 to Cottage Grove and Exit 174. Take that exit and drive east on Row River Road for 18 miles to Sharps Creek Road. Turn right (south) and drive four miles to the campground.

Contact: Bureau of Land Management, Eugene District, 541/683-6600, fax 541/683-6981.

87 RUJADA

Scenic rating: 7

on Layng Creek in Umpqua National Forest

See map page 382

This campground is nestled on a river terrace on the banks of Layng Creek, right at the national forest border. The Swordfern Trail follows Layng Creek through a beautiful forest within a lush fern grotto. There is a fair swimming hole near the campground. Those with patience and persistence can fish in the creek. By continuing east on Forest Road 17, you reach a trailhead that leads 0.5 mile to beautiful Spirit Falls, a spectacular 60-foot waterfall. A bit farther east is another easy trail, which leads to Moon Falls, even more awe-inspiring at 125 feet. Another campground option is Cedar Creek, about six miles southeast on Brice Creek Road (County Road 2470).

RV sites, facilities: There are 15 sites for tents or RVs up to 22 feet (no hookups). Picnic tables, garbage bins, and fire pits are provided. Flush and vault toilets, drinking water, and a softball field are available. Some facilities are wheelchair accessible. Leashed pets are permitted.

Reservations, fees: Reservations are not accepted. Sites are $8 per night, plus $3 per night per additional vehicle. Open late May–late September, weather permitting.

Directions: From Eugene, drive south on I-5 to Cottage Grove and Exit 174. Take that exit and drive east on Row River Road for 19 miles to Layng Creek Road (Forest Road 17). Turn left and drive two miles to the campground on the right.

Contact: Umpqua National Forest, Cottage Grove Ranger District, 541/767-5000, fax 541/767-5075.

88 PACKARD CREEK

Scenic rating: 6

on Hills Creek Reservoir in Willamette National Forest

See map page 382

Situated on a large flat beside Hills Creek Reservoir, this campground is extremely popular with families and fills up on weekends and holidays. The mix of vegetation in the campground includes an abundance of poison oak. The speed limit around the swimming area and boat ramp is 5 mph. The elevation is 1,600 feet.

RV sites, facilities: There are 37 sites for tents or RVs up to 40 feet (no hookups). Picnic tables and fire rings are provided. Drinking water, vault toilets, garbage bins, a recycling center, and firewood are available. Some facilities are wheelchair accessible. Fishing and boat docks, boat-launching facilities, a roped swimming area, a picnic shelter, and an amphitheater are available. Some sites have their own docks. Leashed pets are permitted.

Reservations, fees: Reservations are accepted at 877/444-6777 or www.ReserveUSA.com ($9 reservation fee). Sites are $14 per night for single sites, $7 per night per additional vehicle, and $25 per night for double sites. Groups can be accommodated. Open mid-April–mid-September, weather permitting.

Directions: From Eugene, drive south on I-5 for four miles to Exit 188 and Highway 58. Turn southeast and drive 35 miles to Oakridge. Continue east on Highway 58 for two miles to Kitson Springs Road. Turn right and drive 0.5 mile to Forest Road 21. Turn right and continue six miles to the campground on the left.

Contact: Willamette National Forest, Middle Fork Ranger District, 541/782-2283, fax 541/782-5306; Hoodoo Recreation Services, 541/822-3799.

89 SAND PRAIRIE

Scenic rating: 6

on the Willamette River in Willamette National Forest

See map page 382

Situated at 1,600 feet elevation in a mixed stand of cedar, dogwood, Douglas fir, hazelnut, and western hemlock, this campground provides easy access to the Middle Fork of the Willamette River. An access road leads to the south (upstream) end of the Hills Creek Reservoir.

OREGON

OREGON

The 27-mile Middle Fork Trail begins at the south end of the campground. Fishing is good here; you can expect to catch large-scale cutthroat trout, rainbow trout, and suckers in the Middle Fork.

RV sites, facilities: There are 21 sites for tents or RVs up to 40 feet (no hookups). Picnic tables, garbage bins, and fire rings are provided. Vault and flush toilets, a group picnic area, and drinking water are available. Some facilities are wheelchair accessible. A boat launch is nearby on Hills Creek Reservoir. Leashed pets are permitted.

Reservations, fees: Reservations are not accepted. Sites are $12 per night, plus $6 per night per additional vehicle. Open late May–early September, weather permitting.

Directions: From Eugene, drive south on I-5 for four miles to Exit 188 and Highway 58. Turn southeast and drive 35 miles to Oakridge. Continue east on Highway 58 for two miles to Kitson Springs Road. Turn right and drive 0.5 mile to Forest Road 21. Turn right and continue 11 miles to the campground on the right.

Contact: Willamette National Forest, Middle Fork Ranger District, 541/782-2283, fax 541/782-5306.

90 SACANDAGA

Scenic rating: 5

on the Willamette River in Willamette National Forest

See map page 382

This campground sits along the Middle Fork of the Willamette River, where a segment of the historic Oregon Central Military Wagon Road is visible. Two trails from the campground access the Willamette River, and the Middle Fork Trail is in close proximity. Also, a short trail leads to a viewpoint with a bench, great for a short break. This campground gets low use, and the sites are well separated by vegetation. Count on solitude here. The elevation is 2,400 feet.

RV sites, facilities: There are 17 sites for tents

or RVs up to 24 feet (no hookups). Picnic tables and fire rings are provided. Drinking water, vault toilets, and firewood are available. Leashed pets are permitted.

Reservations, fees: Reservations are not accepted. Sites are $8 per night, plus $4 per night per additional vehicle. Open mid-May–mid-September, weather permitting.

Directions: From Eugene, drive south on I-5 for four miles to Exit 188 and Highway 58. Turn southeast and drive 35 miles to Oakridge. Continue east on Highway 58 for two miles to Kitson Springs Road. Turn right and drive 0.5 mile to Forest Road 21. Turn right and drive 24 miles to the campground on the right.

Contact: Willamette National Forest, Middle Fork Ranger District, 541/782-2283, fax 541/782-5306.

91 BLUE POOL

Scenic rating: 4

on Salt Creek in Willamette National Forest

See map page 382

This campground is in an old-growth forest alongside Salt Creek at 1,900 feet elevation. The camp features a large picnic area along the creek with picnic tables, a large grassy area, and fire stoves built in the 1930s by the Civilian Conservation Corps. One-half mile east of the campground on Highway 58 is McCredie Hot Springs. This spot is undeveloped, without any facilities. Exercise caution when using the hot springs; they can be very hot.

RV sites, facilities: There are 24 sites for tents or RVs up to 40 feet (no hookups). Picnic tables, garbage bins, a recycling center, and fire rings are provided. Drinking water and vault and flush toilets are available. Leashed pets are permitted.

Reservations, fees: Reservations are not accepted. Sites are $12 per night, plus $6 per night per additional vehicle. Open mid-May–September, weather permitting.

Directions: From Eugene, drive south on I-5 for four miles to Exit 188 and Highway 58.

Turn southeast and drive 35 miles to Oakridge. Continue east on Highway 58 for eight miles to the campground on the right.

Contact: Willamette National Forest, Middle Fork Ranger District, 541/782-2283, fax 541/782-5306; Hoodoo Recreation Services, 541/822-3799.

92 NORTH LAVA FLOW

Scenic rating: 8

on Davis Lake in Deschutes National Forest
See map page 382

This campground is surrounded by old-growth forest along the northeast shore of Davis Lake, a very shallow lake formed by lava flow. The water level fluctuates here, and this campground can sometimes be closed in summer. There's good duck hunting during the fall. Fishing can be decent, but only fly-fishing is allowed. Boat speed is limited to 10 mph.

RV sites, facilities: There are 25 sites for tents or RVs up to 30 feet (no hookups). Picnic tables and fire grills are provided. Vault toilets, garbage bins, and firewood (to be gathered from the surrounding area) are available. There is no drinking water. A primitive boat ramp is nearby. Leashed pets are permitted.

Reservations, fees: Reservations are not accepted. There is no fee for camping. Open May–early October, weather permitting.

Directions: From Eugene, drive south on I-5 for five miles to Exit 188 and Highway 58. Turn east on Highway 58 and drive 86 miles to County Road 61. Turn left and drive three miles to Forest Road 46. Turn left and drive 7.7 miles to Forest Road 850. Turn left and drive 1.8 miles to the campground.

Contact: Deschutes National Forest, Crescent Ranger District, 541/433-3200, fax 541/433-3224.

93 EAST DAVIS LAKE

Scenic rating: 9

on Davis Lake in Deschutes National Forest
See map page 382

This campground is nestled in the lodgepole pines along the south shore of Davis Lake. Recreation options include boating (speed limit 10 mph), fly-fishing, and hiking. Leeches prevent swimming here. Bald eagles and sandhill cranes are frequently seen.

RV sites, facilities: There are 33 sites for tents or RVs up to 22 feet (no hookups). Picnic tables, garbage service, fire grills, drinking water, and vault toilets are provided. Firewood may be gathered from the surrounding area. Primitive boat-launching facilities are available on-site. Leashed pets are permitted.

Reservations, fees: Reservations are not accepted. Sites are $9–11 per night, plus $5 per night per additional vehicle. Open May–late October, weather permitting.

Directions: From Eugene, drive south on I-5 for five miles to Exit 188 and Highway 58. Turn east and drive 73 miles to County Road 61. Turn left (east) and drive three miles to Forest Road 46. Turn left and drive 7.7 miles to Forest Road 850. Turn left and drive 0.25 mile to the campground entrance road on the right.

Contact: Deschutes National Forest, Crescent Ranger District, 541/433-3200, fax 541/433-3224.

94 TRAPPER CREEK

Scenic rating: 8

on Odell Lake in Deschutes National Forest
See map page 382

The west end of Odell Lake is the setting for this camp. Boat docks and rentals are available nearby at the Shelter Cove Resort. One of Oregon's prime fisheries for kokanee salmon and Mackinaw (lake trout), this lake also has some huge brown trout.

RV sites, facilities: There are 32 sites for tents or RVs up to 22 feet (no hookups). Picnic tables,

OREGON

garbage service, and fire grills are provided. Drinking water, vault toilets, and a boat launch are available. Firewood may be gathered from the surrounding area. A store, a coin laundry, and ice are within one mile. Leashed pets are permitted.

Reservations, fees: Reservations are not accepted. Sites are $13–15 per night, double sites are $26–30 per night, plus $5 per night per additional vehicle. Open June–early October, weather permitting.

Directions: From Eugene, drive south on I-5 for five miles to Exit 188 and Highway 58. Turn east and drive 61 miles to the turnoff for Odell Lake and Forest Road 5810. Turn right on Forest Road 5810 and drive 1.9 miles to the campground on the left.

Contact: Deschutes National Forest, Crescent Ranger District, 541/433-3200, fax 541/433-3224.

95 SHELTER COVE RESORT

Scenic rating: 9

on Odell Lake
See map page 382

This private resort along the north shore of Odell Lake is at the base of the Diamond Peak Wilderness and offers opportunities for fishing, hiking, and swimming. The cabins sit right on the lakefront. A general store and tackle shop are available.

RV sites, facilities: There are three tent sites and 64 sites with partial hookups (30 amps) for RVs up to 40 feet; some sites are pull-through. There are also 13 cabins. Picnic tables and fire rings are provided. Drinking water, restrooms with flush toilets and showers, a dump station, wireless Internet service, an ATM, a convenience store, a coin laundry, and ice are available. Boat docks, launching facilities, and boat rentals are on-site. Leashed pets are permitted.

Reservations, fees: Reservations are accepted at 800/647-2729. Sites are $14–24 per night. Some credit cards are accepted. Open year-round.

Directions: From Eugene, drive south on I-5 for

five miles to Exit 188 and Highway 58. Turn east and drive 61 miles to the turnoff for Odell Lake and West Odell Lake Road. Turn right and drive south for 1.8 miles to the resort at the end of the road.

Contact: Shelter Cove Resort, 541/433-2548, www.sheltercoveresort.com.

96 ODELL CREEK

Scenic rating: 9

on Odell Lake in Deschutes National Forest
See map page 382

You can fish, hike, and swim at this campground (4,800 feet elevation) along the east shore of Odell Lake. A trail from the nearby Crater Buttes trailhead leads southwest into the Diamond Peak Wilderness and provides access to several small lakes in the backcountry. Another trail follows the north shore of the lake. Boat docks, launching facilities, and rentals are available at the Odell Lake Lodge and Resort, adjacent to the campground. Windy afternoons are common here.

RV sites, facilities: There are 26 sites for tents or RVs up to 50 feet (no hookups). Picnic tables, garbage service, and fire grills are provided. Drinking water and vault toilets are available. Firewood may be gathered from the surrounding area. Leashed pets are permitted.

Reservations, fees: Reservations are required at 541/433-2540. Sites are $15 per night, $5 per night per additional vehicle. Weekly rates are available. Open mid-May–late September, weather permitting.

Directions: From Eugene, drive south on I-5 for five miles to Exit 188 and Highway 58. Turn east and drive 68 miles to Odell Lake and Forest Road 680 (at the east end of the lake). Turn right on Forest Road 680 and drive 400 yards to the campground on the right.

Contact: Deschutes National Forest, Crescent Ranger District, 541/433-3200, fax 541/433-3224; Odell Lake Lodge, 541/433-2540.

97 SUNSET COVE

Scenic rating: 8

on Odell Lake in Deschutes National Forest
See map page 382

This campground borders the northeast shore of Odell Lake. Boat docks and rentals are available nearby at Odell Lake Lodge and Resort. Campsites are surrounded by large Douglas fir and some white pine. The camp backs up to the highway; expect to hear the noise.

RV sites, facilities: There are 20 sites for tents or RVs up to 22 feet (no hookups). Picnic tables and fire grills are provided. Drinking water, vault toilets, a boat launch and day-use area, and fish-cleaning facilities are available. Firewood may be gathered from the surrounding area. Some facilities are wheelchair accessible. Leashed pets are permitted.

Reservations, fees: Reservations are not accepted. Sites are $13 per night, plus $5 per night per additional vehicle. Open mid-May–mid-October, weather permitting.

Directions: From Eugene, drive south on I-5 for five miles to Exit 188 and Highway 58. Turn east and drive 67 miles to the campground on the right.

Contact: Deschutes National Forest, Crescent Ranger District, 541/433-3200, fax 541/433-3224.

98 PRINCESS CREEK

Scenic rating: 9

on Odell Lake in Deschutes National Forest
See map page 382

This wooded campground is on the northeast shore of Odell Lake, but it backs up to the highway; expect traffic noise. Boat docks and rentals are available nearby at the Shelter Cove Resort. (See the *Odell Creek* listing in this chapter for recreation details.)

RV sites, facilities: There are 46 sites for tents or RVs up to 22 feet (no hookups). Picnic tables and fire grills are provided. Drinking water, vault toilets, and boat-launching facilities are available.

Firewood may be gathered from the surrounding area. Showers, a store, a coin laundry, and ice are within five miles. Leashed pets are permitted.

Reservations, fees: Reservations are not accepted. Sites are $12–14 per night, plus $5 per night per additional vehicle. Open mid-May–September, weather permitting.

Directions: From Eugene, drive south on I-5 for five miles to Exit 188 and Highway 58. Turn east and drive 64 miles to the campground on the right.

Contact: Deschutes National Forest, Crescent Ranger District, 541/433-3200, fax 541/433-3224.

99 SPRING

Scenic rating: 8

on Crescent Lake in Deschutes National Forest
See map page 382

This campground nestles in a lodgepole pine forest on the southern shore of Crescent Lake. Sites are open, and some are on the lake with Diamond Peak views. The camp is at an elevation of 4,850 feet. Boating, swimming, and waterskiing are among the summer pastimes. A number of trails from the nearby Windy-Oldenburg Trailhead provide access to lakes in the Oregon Cascades Recreation Area. Motorized vehicles are restricted to open roads only.

RV sites, facilities: There are 73 sites for tents or RVs up to 22 feet (no hookups). Picnic tables, garbage service, and fire grills are provided. Drinking water, vault toilets, boat-launching facilities, and firewood (to be gathered from the surrounding area) are available. Leashed pets are permitted.

Reservations, fees: Reservations are not accepted. Sites are $13–15 per night, double sites are $26–30 per night, plus $5 per night per additional vehicle. Open May–September, weather permitting.

Directions: From Eugene, drive south on I-5 for five miles to Exit 188 and Highway 58. Turn east and drive 70 miles to Crescent Lake Highway (Forest Road 60). Turn right and drive

OREGON

eight miles west to the campground entrance road on the left. Turn left and drive one mile to the campground.

Contact: Deschutes National Forest, Crescent Ranger District, 541/433-3200, fax 541/433-3224.

100 CONTORTA FLAT

🚶 🚴 ⛵ 🎣 🛶 🏕 🐕 ♿ 🚐 ⛺

Scenic rating: 8

on Crescent Lake in the Deschutes National Forest
See map page 382

This campground on Crescent Lake was named for the particular species of lodgepole pine *(pinus contorta)* that grows here. The elevation is 4,850 feet.

RV sites, facilities: There are 18 sites for tents or RVs up to 35 feet (no hookups). Picnic tables and fire grills are provided. Vault toilets and garbage bins are available. There is no drinking water. Some facilities are wheelchair accessible. Leashed pets are permitted.

Reservations, fees: Reservations are not accepted. Sites are $9–11 per night, plus $5 per night per additional vehicle. Open May–October, weather permitting.

Directions: From Eugene, drive south on I-5 for five miles to Exit 188 and Highway 58. Turn east and drive 69 miles to County Road 60. Turn right (west) and drive 10 miles to the camp on the left.

Contact: Deschutes National Forest, Crescent Ranger District, 541/433-3200, fax 541/433-3224.

101 CRESCENT LAKE

🚶 ⛵ 🎣 🛶 🐕 🚐 ⛺

Scenic rating: 8

on Crescent Lake in Deschutes National Forest
See map page 382   BEST (

This campground is along the north shore of Crescent Lake, and it is often windy here in the afternoon. Boat docks, launching facilities, and rentals are available at Crescent Lake Resort, adjacent to the campground. A trail from camp

heads into the Diamond Peak Wilderness (free permit required; available on-site) and also branches north to Odell Lake.

RV sites, facilities: There are 47 sites for tents or RVs up to 35 feet (no hookups). Picnic tables, garbage service, and fire grills are provided. Drinking water, vault toilets, and boat-launching facilities are available. Firewood may be gathered from the surrounding area. Leashed pets are permitted.

Reservations, fees: Reservations are not accepted. Sites are $13–15 per night, plus $5 per night per additional vehicle. Open mid-May–late October, weather permitting.

Directions: From Eugene, drive south on I-5 for five miles to Exit 188 and Highway 58. Turn east and drive 70 miles to Crescent Lake Highway (Forest Road 60). Turn right (west) and drive 2.2 miles southwest. Bear right to remain on Forest Road 60, and drive another 0.25 mile to the campground on the left.

Contact: Deschutes National Forest, Crescent Ranger District, 541/433-3200, fax 541/433-3224.

102 WHISTLER'S BEND

🚶 🎣 🚐 🏕 🐕 🛶 ♿ 🚐 ⛺

Scenic rating: 7

on the North Umpqua River
See map page 382

This 175-acre county park along the banks of the North Umpqua River is an idyllic spot because it gets little pressure from outsiders, yet it is just a 20-minute drive from I-5. Two boat ramps accommodate boaters, and fishing is a plus. A wildlife reserve provides habitat for deer.

RV sites, facilities: There are 23 sites for tents or RVs up to 35 feet (no hookups) and two yurts. Group camping is available. Picnic tables and fire grills are provided. Drinking water, restrooms with flush toilets and showers, a playground, disc golf, and launching facilities are available. Some facilities are wheelchair accessible. Leashed pets are permitted.

Reservations, fees: Reservations are accepted

for yurts and group camps at 541/440-4500 but are not accepted for tent or RV sites. Sites are $10–12 per night, $3 per night per additional vehicle, $28 per night for yurts, $40 per night for the group camp for up to 25 people, $70 per night for the group camp for 26–50 people, and $100 per night for the group camp for 51 or more people. Some credit cards are accepted. Open year-round.

Directions: From Roseburg, drive east on Highway 138 for 12 miles to Whistler's Bend Park Road (well signed). Turn left and drive two miles to the end of the road and the park entrance.

Contact: Whistler's Bend, 541/673-4863, www.co.douglas.or.us.

103 MILLPOND

Scenic rating: 8

on Rock Creek

See map page 382

Rock Creek flows past Millpond and empties into the North Umpqua River five miles downstream. Just above this confluence is the Rock Creek Fish Hatchery, which is open year-round to visitors, with free access. This campground along the banks of Rock Creek is the first camp you'll see along Rock Creek Road, which accounts for its relative popularity in the area. Like Rock Creek Campground, which is two miles north, it's primitive and remote. No fishing is allowed in Rock Creek.

RV sites, facilities: There are 12 sites for tents or RVs up to 45 feet (no hookups). Picnic tables, garbage service, and fire grills are provided. A camp host is on-site, and flush and vault toilets, drinking water, firewood, a ball field, a playground, and a pavilion are available. Some facilities are wheelchair accessible. Leashed pets are permitted.

Reservations, fees: Reservations are not accepted. Sites are $8 per night, with a 14-day stay limit, and $3 per night per additional vehicle. Open mid-May–mid-October.

Directions: From Roseburg, drive east on High-

way 138 for 22 miles to Rock Creek Road. Turn right (north) and drive five miles to the campground on the right.

Contact: Bureau of Land Management, Roseburg District, 541/440-4930, fax 541/440-4948.

104 SUSAN CREEK

Scenic rating: 9

on the North Umpqua River

See map page 382

This popular and pretty campground borders the North Umpqua Wild and Scenic River. This lush setting features plenty of trees and river access. Highlights include two barrier-free trails, one traveling 0.5 mile to the day-use area. From there, a hike of about 0.75 mile leads to the 50-foot Susan Creek Falls. Another 0.4 mile up the trail are the Susan Creek Indian Mounds. These moss-covered rocks are believed to be a spiritual site and are visited by Native Americans in search of guardian spirit visions. This area also boasts an excellent osprey interpretive site with a viewing platform along the river.

RV sites, facilities: There are 30 sites with no hookups for RVs up to 65 feet. No tent camping. Picnic tables, garbage service, and fire grills are provided. Restrooms have flush toilets and showers. Drinking water and firewood are available, and there is a camp host. Some facilities and trails are wheelchair accessible. Leashed pets are permitted.

Reservations, fees: Reservations are not accepted. Sites are $11 per night, with a 14-day stay limit, and $3 per night per additional vehicle. Open early May–late October.

Directions: From Roseburg, drive east on Highway 138 for 29.5 miles to the campground (turnoff well signed).

Contact: Bureau of Land Management, Roseburg District, 541/440-4930, fax 541/440-4948, www.or.blm.gov/roseburg.

OREGON

OREGON

105 WOLF CREEK

Scenic rating: 6

on the Little River in Umpqua National Forest

See map page 383

This pretty Little River camp is at the entrance to the national forest, near the Wolf Creek Civilian Conservation Center. It is at an elevation of 1,100 feet, with easy access to civilization. The campground has abundant wildflowers in the spring. If you want to get deeper into the Cascades, Hemlock Lake and Lake of the Woods are about 21 and 15 miles east, respectively.

RV sites, facilities: There are eight sites for tents or RVs up to 30 feet (no hookups) and one group site for up to 130 people. Picnic tables and fire grills are provided. Flush toilets, drinking water, a covered pavilion for groups, garbage bins, horseshoe pits, a softball field, and a volleyball court are available. Some facilities are wheelchair accessible. Leashed pets are permitted.

Reservations, fees: Reservations are required for the group site at 877/444-6777 or www.ReserveUSA.com ($9 reservation fee) but are not accepted for individual sites. Sites are $10 per night, $4 per night per additional vehicle, and $70 per night for the group site. Open mid-May–September, weather permitting.

Directions: From Roseburg on I-5, take Exit 120. Drive east on Highway 138 for 18 miles to Glide and County Road 17. Turn right (southeast) and drive 12 miles (the road becomes Little River Road) to the campground on the right.

Contact: Umpqua National Forest, North Umpqua Ranger District, 541/496-3532, fax 541/496-3534.

106 STEAMBOAT FALLS

Scenic rating: 8

on Steamboat Creek in Umpqua National Forest

See map page 382

This Steamboat Creek campground boasts some excellent scenery. Beautiful Steamboat Falls features a fish ladder that provides passage for steelhead and salmon on their upstream migration. No fishing is permitted in Steamboat Creek.

RV sites, facilities: There are 10 sites for tents or RVs up to 20 feet (no hookups). Picnic tables, garbage bins, vault toilets, and fire grills are provided. There is no drinking water. Leashed pets are permitted.

Reservations, fees: Reservations are not accepted. Sites are $7 per night, plus $4 per night per additional vehicles. Open year-round, weather permitting.

Directions: From Roseburg on I-5, take Exit 120 to Highway 138. Drive east on Highway 138 to Steamboat and Forest Road 38. Turn left on Forest Road 38 (Steamboat Creek Road) and drive six miles to a fork with Forest Road 3810. Turn right and drive one mile on a paved road to the campground.

Contact: Umpqua National Forest, North Umpqua Ranger District, 541/496-3532, fax 541/496-3534.

107 EAGLE ROCK

Scenic rating: 9

on the North Umpqua River in Umpqua National Forest

See map page 382

This camp sits next to the North Umpqua River and adjacent to the Boulder Creek Wilderness. It is named after Eagle Rock, which, along with Rattlesnake Rock, towers above the campground. The camp offers outstanding views of these unusual rock formations. It gets moderate use, even heavy on weekends. The camp sits at 1,676 feet elevation near Boulder Flat, a major launch point for rafting. Fishing here is restricted to the use of artificial lures with a single barbless hook.

RV sites, facilities: There are 25 sites for tents or RVs up to 30 feet (no hookups). Picnic tables and fire grills are provided. Vault toilets and garbage bins are available. There is no drinking water. A store, propane, and ice are within five miles. Some facilities are wheelchair accessible. Leashed pets are permitted.

Reservations, fees: Reservations are not accepted. Sites are $10 per night, plus $4 per night per additional vehicle. Open mid-May–September, weather permitting.

Directions: From Roseburg, drive east on Highway 138 for 53 miles to the campground on the left.

Contact: Umpqua National Forest, North Umpqua Ranger District, 541/496-3532, fax 541/496-3534.

108 HEMLOCK LAKE

Scenic rating: 8

on Hemlock Lake in Umpqua National Forest

See map page 383

This is a little-known jewel of a spot. For starters, it's along the shore of Hemlock Lake at 4,400 feet elevation. This is a 28-acre, manufactured reservoir that is 33 feet at its deepest point. An eight-mile loop trail called the Yellow Jacket Loop is just south of the campground. Another trail leaves camp and heads north for about three miles to the Lake in the Woods campground. From there, it's just a short hike to either Hemlock Falls or Yakso Falls, both spectacularly scenic.

RV sites, facilities: There are 13 sites for tents or RVs up to 35 feet (no hookups). Picnic tables, fire grills, and garbage bins are provided. Vault toilets are available, but there is no drinking water. Boat docks and launching facilities are nearby. No motors are allowed on the lake. Leashed pets are permitted.

Reservations, fees: Reservations are not accepted. Sites are $8 per night, plus $4 per night per additional vehicle. Open year-round, weather permitting.

Directions: From Roseburg on I-5, take Exit 120. Drive east on Highway 138 for 18 miles to Glide and County Road 17. Turn right (southeast) and drive 32 miles to the campground on the right.

Contact: Umpqua National Forest, North

Umpqua Ranger District, 541/496-3532, fax 541/496-3534.

109 HORSESHOE BEND

Scenic rating: 8

on the Umpqua River in Umpqua National Forest

See map page 383   BEST (

This campground, at an elevation of 1,300 feet, is in the middle of a big bend in the North Umpqua River. This spot is a major launching point for white-water rafting. Fly-fishing is popular.

RV sites, facilities: There are 22 sites for tents or RVs up to 35 feet (no hookups) and one group site for up to 70 people. Picnic tables, fire grills, garbage bins, drinking water, and flush toilets are provided. A store, gas, and propane are available one mile east. Some facilities are wheelchair accessible. Raft-launching facilities are nearby. Leashed pets are permitted.

Reservations, fees: Reservations are required for the group site at 877/444-6777 or www.ReserveUSA.com ($9 reservation fee) but are not accepted for individual sites. Sites are $12 per night, $4 per night per additional vehicle, and $85 per night for group sites. Open mid-May–late September, weather permitting.

Directions: From Roseburg on I-5, take Exit 120. Drive east on Highway 138 for 47 miles to Forest Road 4750. Turn right and drive south a short distance to the campground entrance road on the right.

Contact: Umpqua National Forest, North Umpqua Ranger District, 541/496-3532, fax 541/496-3534.

110 TOKETEE LAKE

Scenic rating: 7

on Toketee Lake in Umpqua National Forest

See map page 383

This campground is just north of Toketee Lake and sits at an elevation of 2,200 feet. The North

OREGON

Umpqua River Trail passes near camp and continues east along the river for many miles. Diehard hikers can also take the trail west toward the Boulder Creek Wilderness. Toketee Lake, a 97-acre reservoir, offers a good population of brown and rainbow trout and many recreation options. A worthwhile point of interest is Toketee Falls, just west of the lake turnoff. Another is Umpqua Hot Springs, a few miles northeast of the camp. The area sustains a wide variety of wildlife; you might see bald eagles, beavers, ducks and geese, great blue herons, kingfishers, and otters in fall and winter.

RV sites, facilities: There are 33 sites for tents or RVs up to 30 feet (no hookups) and one group site for up to 30 people. Picnic tables, garbage bins, and fire grills are provided. Vault toilets are available, but there is no drinking water. Boat docks and launching facilities are nearby. Leashed pets are permitted.

Reservations, fees: Reservations are required for the group site at 541/498-2531 but are not accepted for individual sites. Sites are $7 per night, $3 per night per additional vehicle, and $18 per night for the group site. Open year-round.

Directions: From Roseburg, drive east on Highway 138 for 59 miles to Forest Road 34. Turn left (north) and drive 1.5 miles to the campground on the right.

Contact: Umpqua National Forest, Diamond Lake Ranger District, 541/498-2531, fax 541/498-2515.

111 EAST LEMOLO

Scenic rating: 8

on Lemolo Lake in Umpqua National Forest
See map page 382

This campground is on the southeastern shore of Lemolo Lake, where boating and fishing are some of the recreation possibilities. Boats with motors and personal watercraft are allowed. The North Umpqua River and its adjacent trail lie just beyond the north shore of the lake. If you hike for two miles northwest of the lake, you can reach spectacular Lemolo Falls. Large

German brown trout, a wild, native fish, can be taken on troll and fly. Lemolo Lake also provides fishing for brook trout, kokanee, and a sprinkling of rainbow trout.

RV sites, facilities: There are 15 sites for tents or small RVs up to 22 feet (no hookups). No drinking water is available. Picnic tables, garbage bins, and fire rings are provided. Vault toilets are available. Boat docks, launching facilities, boat rentals, restaurants, a store, a coin laundry, and showers are nearby. Leashed pets are permitted.

Reservations, fees: Reservations are not accepted. Sites are $7 per night, plus $3 per night per additional vehicle. Open mid-May–late October, weather permitting.

Directions: From Roseburg, drive east on Highway 138 for 73 miles to Forest Road 2610 (three miles east of Clearwater Falls). Turn left (north) and drive three miles to Forest Road 2614. Turn right and drive two miles to Forest Road 2614-430. Turn left and drive a short distance to the campground at the end of the road.

Contact: Umpqua National Forest, Diamond Lake Ranger District, 541/498-2531, fax 541/498-2515.

112 POOLE CREEK

Scenic rating: 8

on Lemolo Lake in Umpqua National Forest
See map page 382

This campground on the western shore of Lemolo Lake isn't far from Lemolo Lake Resort, which is open for recreation year-round. The camp is just south of the mouth of Poole Creek in a lodgepole pine, mountain hemlock, and Shasta red fir forest. This is by far the most popular U.S. Forest Service camp at the lake, especially with water-skiers, who are allowed to ski in designated areas of the lake. (See the listing in this chapter for *East Lemolo* for more information.)

RV sites, facilities: There are 59 sites for tents or RVs up to 35 feet (no hookups) and a group site for up to 60 people. Picnic tables and fire grills are provided. Drinking water and vault toilets are available. A grocery store, a restaurant, a lounge, boat docks, launching facilities, and rentals are nearby. Leashed pets are permitted.

Reservations, fees: Reservations are not accepted for single sites but are required for the group camp at 877/444-6777 or www.ReserveUSA.com ($9 reservation fee). Sites are $11–14 per night, $4 per night per additional vehicle, and $72 per night for the group camp. Open late April–late October, weather permitting.

Directions: From Roseburg, drive east on Highway 138 for 73 miles to Forest Road 2610 (Bird's Point Road). Turn left (north) and drive four miles to the signed turnoff for the campground entrance on the right.

Contact: Umpqua National Forest, Diamond Lake Ranger District, 541/498-2531, fax 541/498-2515.

113 INLET

Scenic rating: 5

on Lemolo Lake in Umpqua National Forest
See map page 382

This campground sits on the eastern inlet of Lemolo Lake, hidden in the deep, green, and quiet forest where the North Umpqua River rushes into Lemolo Reservoir. The lake exceeds 100 feet in depth in some spots. The camp is just across the road from the North Umpqua River Trail, which is routed east into the Oregon Cascades Recreation Area and the Mount Thielsen Wilderness. (See the *East Lemolo* listing in this chapter for more recreation details.)

RV sites, facilities: There are 14 sites for tents or RVs up to 25 feet (no hookups). Vault toilets are available, but there is no drinking water. Picnic tables, garbage bins, and fire grills are provided. Boat docks, launching facilities, rentals, a restaurant, a lounge, groceries, and a gas station are available nearby. Leashed pets are permitted.

Reservations, fees: Reservations are not accepted. Sites are $7 per night, plus $3 per night per additional vehicle. Open mid-May–late October, weather permitting.

Directions: From Roseburg, drive east on Highway 138 for 73 miles to Forest Road 2610. Turn left (north) and drive three miles to Forest Road 2614. Turn right (east) and drive three miles to the campground.

Contact: Umpqua National Forest, Diamond Lake Ranger District, 541/498-2531, fax 541/498-2515.

114 CLEARWATER FALLS

Scenic rating: 8

on the Clearwater River in Umpqua National Forest
See map page 383

The main attraction at this campground along the banks of the Clearwater River is the nearby cascading section of stream called Clearwater Falls. The camp sits at an elevation of 4,100 feet. Other recreation options include fishing and hiking.

RV sites, facilities: There are 12 sites for tents or RVs up to 30 feet (no hookups). Picnic tables, fire grills, and garbage bins are provided. Vault toilets are available, but there is no drinking water. Leashed pets are permitted.

Reservations, fees: Reservations are not accepted. Sites are $7 per night, plus $3 per night per additional vehicle. Open mid-May–October, weather permitting.

Directions: From Roseburg, drive east on Highway 138 for 70 miles to a signed turn for Clearwater Falls. Turn right and drive to the campground.

Contact: Umpqua National Forest, Diamond Lake Ranger District, 541/498-2531, fax 541/498-2515.

115 BROKEN ARROW

Scenic rating: 6

on Diamond Lake in Umpqua National Forest
See map page 383

This campground sits at 5,190 feet elevation near the south shore of Diamond Lake, the largest natural lake in Umpqua National Forest.

OREGON

OREGON

Set back from the lake, it is surrounded by lodgepole pine and features views of Mount Bailey and Mount Thielsen. Bicycling, boating, fishing, hiking, and swimming keep visitors busy here. Diamond Lake is adjacent to Crater Lake National Park, Mount Bailey, and the Mount Thielsen Wilderness, all of which offer a variety of recreation opportunities year-round. Diamond Lake is quite popular with anglers because of its good trout trolling, particularly in early summer.

RV sites, facilities: There are 147 sites for tents or RVs up to 35 feet (no hookups) and four group sites for 40–104 people. Picnic tables, fire grills, and garbage bins are provided. Restrooms have flush toilets and showers. A dump station and drinking water are available. Some facilities are wheelchair accessible. Boat docks, launching facilities, and rentals are nearby. Leashed pets are permitted.

Reservations, fees: Reservations are required for group sites at 877/444-6777 or www.Reserve USA.com ($9 reservation fee) but are not accepted for individual sites. Sites are $11–14 per night, $4 per night per additional vehicle, and $54–132 per night for group sites. Open late May–mid-September.

Directions: From Roseburg, drive east on Highway 138 for 78.5 miles to Diamond Lake Loop (Forest Road 4795). Turn right (south) and drive four miles (along the east shore) to the campground turnoff road. Turn right and continue one mile to the camp on the left at the southern end of the lake.

Contact: Umpqua National Forest, Diamond Lake Ranger District, 541/498-2531, fax 541/498-2515.

116 THIELSEN VIEW

Scenic rating: 7

on Diamond Lake in Umpqua National Forest

See map page 383

This campground sits along the west shore of Diamond Lake in the shadow of majestic Mount Bailey. There is a beautiful view of Mount Thielsen from here. (See the *Broken Arrow* listing in this chapter for information on recreation opportunities.)

RV sites, facilities: There are 60 sites for tents or RVs up to 30 feet (no hookups). Picnic tables, fire grills, and garbage bins are provided. Drinking water and vault toilets are available. Some facilities are wheelchair accessible. Boat docks, launching facilities, and rentals are about five miles away. Leashed pets are permitted.

Reservations, fees: Reservations are not accepted. Sites are $11–14 per night, plus $4 per night per additional vehicle. Open late May–late September, weather permitting.

Directions: From Roseburg, drive east on Highway 138 for 78.5 miles to Diamond Lake Loop (Forest Road 4795). Turn right and drive a short distance to the junction with the loop road. Continue on the loop road and drive four miles to the campground on the left.

Contact: Umpqua National Forest, Diamond Lake Ranger District, 541/498-2531, fax 541/498-2515.

117 DIAMOND LAKE

Scenic rating: 9

on Diamond Lake in Umpqua National Forest

See map page 383

This extremely popular camp along the east shore of Diamond Lake has all the luxuries: flush toilets, showers, and drinking water. There are campfire programs every Friday and Saturday night in the summer. Personal watercraft are not allowed. (See the *Broken Arrow* listing in this chapter for recreation information.)

RV sites, facilities: There are 238 sites for tents or RVs up to 45 feet (no hookups). Picnic tables, garbage bins, and fire grills are provided. Restrooms have flush toilets and showers. Drinking water, a dump station, firewood, and an amphitheater are available. Some facilities are wheelchair accessible. Boat docks, launching facilities, boat rentals, and a fish-cleaning station are nearby. Leashed pets are permitted.

OREGON

Reservations, fees: Reservations are accepted at 877/444-6777 or www.ReserveUSA.com ($9 reservation fee). Sites are $12–18 per night, $6 per night per additional vehicle. Open late April–late October, weather permitting.

Directions: From Roseburg, drive east on Highway 138 for 78.5 miles to Diamond Lake Loop (Forest Road 4795). Turn right and drive a short distance to the junction with a loop road. Turn right (south) and drive two miles (along the east shore) to the campground on the right.

Contact: Umpqua National Forest, Diamond Lake Ranger District, 541/498-2531, fax 541/498-2515.

118 DIGIT POINT

Scenic rating: 7

on Miller Lake in Winema National Forest

See map page 383

This campground is nestled in a lodgepole pine and mountain hemlock forest at 5,600 feet elevation on the shore of Miller Lake, a popular spot for boating, fishing, and swimming. Nearby trails provide access to the Mount Thielsen Wilderness and the Pacific Crest Trail.

RV sites, facilities: There are 64 sites for tents or RVs up to 30 feet (no hookups). Picnic tables, garbage bins, and fire grills are provided. Drinking water, a dump station, and flush toilets are available. Boat docks and launching facilities are nearby. Leashed pets are permitted.

Reservations, fees: Reservations are not accepted. Sites are $12 per night, plus $6 per night per additional vehicle. Open Memorial Day–mid-October, weather permitting.

Directions: From Eugene, drive southeast on Highway 58 for 86 miles to U.S. 97. Turn south and drive seven miles to Forest Road 9772 (one mile north of Chemult). Turn right and drive 12 miles west to the campground.

Contact: Winema National Forest, Chemult Ranger District, 541/365-7001, fax 541/365-7019.

119 JOHN P. AMACHER COUNTY PARK

Scenic rating: 5

on the Umpqua River

See map page 383

This prime layover spot for I-5 RV cruisers is in a wooded Douglas County park, set along the banks of the North Umpqua River. Tent sites are underneath the freeway next to the railroad tracks. Trains come by intermittently. This park has one of the few myrtlewood groves in the country. An 18-hole golf course and tennis courts are close by. Riding stables are within a 20-minute drive, and Winchester Dam is within 0.25 mile.

RV sites, facilities: There are 20 sites with full or partial hookups (20-amp service only) for RVs up to 30 feet and 10 sites for tents or RVs (no hookups). Drinking water and picnic tables are provided; some sites have fire rings. Restrooms have flush toilets and showers. A reservable gazebo and a picnic area are available. Propane gas, a store, a café, a coin laundry, and ice are within one mile. Boat-launching facilities are available. Some facilities are wheelchair accessible. Leashed pets are permitted.

Reservations, fees: Reservations are not accepted. Sites are $11–14 per night, plus $3 per night per additional vehicle. Open May–October.

Directions: From Roseburg, drive five miles north on I-5 to Exit 129. Take that exit and drive south on Old Highway 99 for 0.25 mile to the park on the right (just across Winchester Bridge).

Contact: John P. Amacher County Park, 541/672-4901; Douglas County, 541/957-7001, www.co.douglas.or.us.

120 TWIN RIVERS VACATION PARK

Scenic rating: 6

near the Umpqua River

See map page 383

This wooded campground is near the Umpqua River. It features large shaded pull-through sites and more than 100 kinds of trees on the property. Groups are welcome, and clubhouses are available for group use. Nearby recreation options include bike paths, a county park, and a golf course.

RV sites, facilities: There are 72 sites with full or partial hookups (30 and 50 amps) for RVs of any length; many are pull-through sites. Cable TV, fire pits, and picnic tables are provided. Restrooms have flush toilets and showers. Modem access, propane gas, firewood, a convenience store, a coin laundry, ice, and a playground are available. Boat-launching facilities are nearby. Leashed pets are permitted.

Reservations, fees: Reservations are accepted. Sites are $24–31 per night, plus $3 per person per night for more than two people. Some credit cards are accepted. Open year-round.

Directions: In Roseburg on I-5, take Exit 125 to Garden Valley Road. Drive west for five miles (over the river) to Old Garden Valley Road. Turn left and drive 1.5 miles to River Forks Road. Turn left and drive a short distance to the park entrance on the left.

Contact: Twin Rivers Vacation Park, 541/673-3811, www.twinriversrvpark.com.

121 DOUGLAS COUNTY FAIRGROUNDS RV PARK

Scenic rating: 8

on the South Umpqua River

See map page 383

This 74-acre county park is very easily accessible off the highway. Nearby Umpqua River, one of Oregon's prettiest rivers, often has good fishing in season. Bike paths, a golf course, and tennis courts are nearby. Horse stalls and a boat ramp are available at the nearby fairgrounds.

RV sites, facilities: There are 50 sites for tents or RVs of any length with partial hookups (50 amps). Tent camping is limited to two nights. Drinking water and picnic tables are provided. Restrooms have flush toilets and showers, and a dump station is available. A store, a café, a coin laundry, and ice are within one mile. Some facilities are wheelchair accessible. Leashed pets are permitted.

Reservations, fees: Reservations are not accepted. Sites are $20 per night, with a 14-day stay limit. Open year-round, except one week in August during the county fair. Phone ahead to confirm current status.

Directions: Heading south on I-5 in Roseburg, take Exit 123 and drive south under the freeway to Frear Street. Turn right and enter the park.

Contact: Douglas County Fairgrounds & Speedway, 541/957-7010, fax 541/440-6023, www.douglasfairgrounds.com.

122 WILDLIFE SAFARI RV PARK

Scenic rating: 6

near Roseburg

See map page 383

This park is part of Wildlife Safari in Winston (near Roseburg), which offers a walk-through zoo, a petting zoo, and a drive-through wildlife park. Nearby recreation options include an 18-hole golf course, hiking trails, fishing, and marked bike trails.

RV sites, facilities: There are 15 sites for tents or RVs (no hookups); a few sites have partial hookups (20 and 30 amps), and some are pull-through. A portable toilet is available. A café is on-site. There is no drinking water. A restaurant, gift shop, and dump station are nearby. Leashed pets are permitted.

Reservations, fees: Reservations are not accepted. Sites are $10–12 per night. Open March–September, weather permitting.

Directions: From Roseburg, drive south on I-5 for five miles to Exit 119 and Highway 42. Take Highway 42 southwest for three miles to Looking Glass Road (just before reaching Winston). Turn right and drive one block to Safari Road. Turn right and enter the park.

Contact: Wildlife Safari RV Park, 541/679-6761, fax 541/679-9210, www.wildlifesafari.org.

123 CHARLES V. STANTON PARK

Scenic rating: 7

on the South Umpqua River

See map page 383

This campground, along the banks of the South Umpqua River, is an all-season spot with a nice beach for swimming in the summer and good steelhead fishing in the winter.

RV sites, facilities: There are 20 sites with full hookups (30 amps) for RVs up to 60 feet, 20 sites for tents or RVs (no hookups), and one group area for up to 13 camping units. Picnic tables and fire pits or barbecues are provided. Drinking water, restrooms with flush toilets and showers, a dump station, a reservable pavilion, a picnic area, and a playground are available. Some facilities are wheelchair accessible. Propane gas, a store, a café, a coin laundry, and ice are within one mile. Leashed pets are permitted.

Reservations, fees: Reservations are required for the group site ($10 reservation fee) at 541/440-4500 but are not accepted for individual sites. Sites are $11–16 per night and $180 per night for the group site. Some credit cards are accepted. Open year-round.

Directions: Depending on your heading on I-5, there are two routes to reach this campground. In Canyonville northbound on I-5, take Exit 99 and drive one mile north on the frontage road to the campground on the right.

In Canyonville southbound on I-5, take Exit 101. Turn right at the first stop sign, and almost immediately turn right again onto the frontage road. Drive one mile south on the frontage road to the campground on the left.

Contact: Charles V. Stanton Park, Douglas County Parks, 541/839-4483, fax 541/440-4500, www.co.douglas.or.us/parks.

124 MEADOW WOOD RV PARK

Scenic rating: 6

in Glendale

See map page 383

Meadow Wood is a good option for RVers looking for a camping spot along I-5. It features 80 wooded acres and all the amenities. Nearby attractions include a ghost town, gold panning, and Wolf Creek Tavern.

RV sites, facilities: There are 64 pull-through sites for tents or RVs of any length with full or partial hookups (50 amps). Drinking water and picnic tables are provided. Restrooms have flush toilets and showers. Propane gas, a dump station, modem access, firewood, a coin laundry, ice, a playground, and a seasonal heated swimming pool are available. Leashed pets are permitted.

Reservations, fees: Reservations are accepted at 800/606-1274. Sites are $17–25 per night. Monthly rentals available. Open year-round.

Directions: Depending on your heading on I-5, there are two routes to reach this campground. From Roseburg, drive south on I-5 to Exit 86 (near Glendale). Take that exit and drive over the freeway and turn right onto the frontage road. Continue for three miles to Barton Road. Turn left (east) and drive one mile to Autumn Lane. Turn right (south) on Autumn Lane and drive 0.75 mile to the park. Otherwise: From Grants Pass, drive north on I-5 to Exit 83 (near Glendale) and drive east for 0.25 mile to Autumn Lane. Turn right (south) on Autumn Lane and drive one mile to the park.

Contact: Meadow Wood RV Park, 541/832-3114 or 800/606-1274, fax 541/832-2454.

125 BOULDER CREEK

Scenic rating: 4

on the South Umpqua River in Umpqua National Forest

See map page 383

This campground hugs the banks of the South Umpqua River near Boulder Creek. No fishing is allowed here. It is at 1,400 feet elevation. A

OREGON

good side trip is nearby South Umpqua Falls, a beautiful, wide waterfall featuring a fish ladder and a platform so you can watch the fish struggle upstream.

RV sites, facilities: There are eight sites for tents or RVs up to 25 feet (no hookups). Picnic tables, fire grills, and garbage bins are provided. Vault toilets and drinking water are available. Leashed pets are permitted.

Reservations, fees: Reservations are not accepted. Sites are $6 per night, plus $3 per night per additional vehicle. Open year-round, with limited services in winter.

Directions: At Canyonville on I-5, take Exit 99 to County Road 1. Drive east on County Road 1 for 25 miles to Tiller and County Road 46. Turn left and drive six miles northeast (County Road 46 turns into South Umpqua Road/Forest Road 28). Continue northeast and drive seven miles to the camp.

Contact: Umpqua National Forest, Tiller Ranger District, 541/825-3100, fax 541/825-3110.

126 HAMAKER

Scenic rating: 8

near the Upper Rogue River in Rogue River National Forest

See map page 383

Set at 4,000 feet elevation near the Upper Rogue River, Hamaker is a beautiful little spot high in a mountain meadow. Wildflowers and wildlife abound in the spring and early summer. One of the least-used camps in the area, it's a prime camp for Crater Lake visitors.

RV sites, facilities: There are 10 sites for tents or RVs up to 30 feet (no hookups). Picnic tables, fire grills, garbage service, and stoves are provided. Drinking water and vault toilets are available. Firewood is available for purchase. Leashed pets are permitted.

Reservations, fees: Reservations are not accepted. Sites are $10 per night, plus $5 per night per additional vehicle. Open late May–late October, weather permitting.

Directions: From Medford, drive northeast

on Highway 62 for 57 miles (just past Union Creek) to Highway 230. Turn left (north) and drive 11 miles to a junction with Forest Road 6530. Continue on Forest Road 6530 for 0.5 mile to Forest Road 6530-900. Turn right and drive 0.5 mile to the campground.

Contact: Rogue River National Forest, Prospect Ranger District, 541/560-3400, fax 541/560-3444.

127 FAREWELL BEND

Scenic rating: 7

on the Upper Rogue River in Rogue River National Forest

See map page 383

This extremely popular campground is at an elevation of 3,400 feet along the banks of the Upper Rogue River near the Rogue River Gorge. A 0.25-mile barrier-free trail leads from camp to the Rogue Gorge Viewpoint and is definitely worth the trip. The Upper Rogue River Trail passes near camp. This spot attracts a lot of the campers visiting Crater Lake. (See the *Union Creek* listing for more information.)

RV sites, facilities: There are 61 sites for tents or RVs up to 40 feet (no hookups). Picnic tables, fire grills, and fire rings are provided. Drinking water, firewood, and flush toilets are available. Some facilities are wheelchair accessible. Leashed pets are permitted.

Reservations, fees: Reservations are not accepted. Sites are $15 per night, plus $7 per night per additional vehicle. Open mid-May–late October, weather permitting.

Directions: From Medford, drive northeast on Highway 62 for 57 miles (near Union Creek) to the campground on the left.

Contact: Rogue River National Forest, Prospect Ranger District, 541/560-3400, fax 541/560-3444.

128 UNION CREEK

Scenic rating: 8

near the Upper Rogue River in Rogue River National Forest

See map page 383

One of the most popular camps in the district, this spot is more developed than the nearby camp of Natural Bridge. It sits at 3,200 feet elevation along the banks of Union Creek, where the creek joins the Upper Rogue River. The Upper Rogue River Trail passes near camp. Interpretive programs are offered in the summer, and a convenience store and a restaurant are within walking distance. A private riding stable is less than one mile away at Farewell Bend Campground.

RV sites, facilities: There are 78 sites for tents or RVs up to 30 feet (no hookups). Picnic tables, garbage service, and fire grills are provided. Drinking water and vault toilets are available. Firewood is available for purchase. A store and a restaurant are within walking distance. Some facilities are wheelchair accessible. Leashed pets are permitted.

Reservations, fees: Reservations are not accepted. Sites are $10 per night, plus $5 per night per additional vehicle. Open mid-May–mid-October, weather permitting.

Directions: From Medford, drive northeast on Highway 62 for 56 miles (near Union Creek) to the campground on the left.

Contact: Rogue River National Forest, Prospect Ranger District, 541/560-3400, fax 541/560-3444.

129 NATURAL BRIDGE

Scenic rating: 8

on the Upper Rogue River Trail in Rogue River National Forest

See map page 383

Expect lots of company in midsummer at this popular camp, which sits at an elevation of 3,200 feet, where the Upper Rogue River runs underground. The Upper Rogue River Trail passes by the camp and follows the river for many miles to the Pacific Crest Trail in Crater Lake National Park. There is an interpretive area and a spectacular geological viewpoint adjacent to the camp. A 0.25-mile, barrier-free trail is also available.

RV sites, facilities: There are 17 sites for tents or RVs up to 30 feet (no hookups). Picnic tables, garbage service, and fire grills are provided. Vault toilets are available, but there is no drinking water. Some facilities are wheelchair accessible. Leashed pets are permitted.

Reservations, fees: Reservations are not accepted. Sites are $6 per night, plus $3 per night per additional vehicle. Open May–early November, weather permitting.

Directions: From Medford, drive northeast on Highway 62 for 55 miles (near Union Creek) to Forest Road 300. Turn left and drive one mile west to the campground on the right.

Contact: Rogue River National Forest, Prospect Ranger District, 541/560-3400, fax 541/560-3444.

130 ABBOTT CREEK

Scenic rating: 8

on Abbott and Woodruff Creeks in Rogue River National Forest

See map page 383

At the confluence of Abbott and Woodruff Creeks about two miles from the Upper Rogue River, this camp is a better choice for visitors with children than some of the others along the Rogue River. Abbott Creek is small and tame compared to the roaring Rogue. The elevation here is 3,100 feet.

RV sites, facilities: There are 25 sites for tents or RVs up to 22 feet (no hookups). Picnic tables, garbage service, and fire grills are provided. Drinking water, vault toilets, and firewood are available. Leashed pets are permitted.

Reservations, fees: Reservations are not accepted. Sites are $10 per night, plus $5 per night per additional vehicle. Open mid-May–late October, weather permitting.

OREGON

Directions: From Medford, drive northeast on Highway 62 for 50 miles (near Union Creek) to Forest Road 68. Turn left and drive 3.5 miles west to the campground on the left.

Contact: Rogue River National Forest, Prospect Ranger District, 541/560-3400, fax 541/560-3444.

131 MAZAMA

Scenic rating: 6

near the Pacific Crest Trail in Crater Lake National Park

See map page 383

One of two campgrounds at Crater Lake—the other being Lost Creek—this camp sits at 6,000 feet elevation and is known for cold nights, even in late June and early September. I once got caught in a snowstorm here at the opening in mid-June. A nearby store is a great convenience. Seasonal boat tours and junior ranger programs are available. The Pacific Crest Trail passes through the park, but the only trail access down to Crater Lake is at Cleetwood Cove. Note that winter access to the park is from the west only on Highway 62 to Rim Village.

RV sites, facilities: There are 213 sites for tents or RVs up to 32 feet (no hookups); some sites have partial hookups (20 and 30 amps). Picnic tables, fire grills, bearproof food lockers, and garbage bins are provided. Drinking water, restrooms with flush toilets and coin showers, a dump station, a coin laundry, gasoline, a minimart, firewood, and ice are available. Some facilities are wheelchair accessible. Leashed pets are permitted in the campground and on paved roads only.

Reservations, fees: Reservations are not accepted. Sites are $18–23 per night, plus a $10 park-entrance fee per vehicle and $3.50 per person per night for more than two people. Some credit cards are accepted. Open late June–early October.

Directions: From I-5 at Medford, turn east on Highway 62 and drive 72 miles into Crater Lake National Park and to Annie Springs junction. Turn left and drive a short distance to the national park entrance kiosk. Just beyond the kiosk, turn right to the campground and Mazama store entrance.

Contact: Crater Lake National Park, 541/594-3000, www.nps.gov/crla.

132 WOLF CREEK PARK

Scenic rating: 6

near the town of Wolf Creek

See map page 383

This rustic campground is on Wolf Creek near the historic Wolf Creek Inn. A hiking trail leads to the top of London Peak through old-growth forest. Although close to I-5 and the town of Wolf Creek, this spot gets low–average use.

RV sites, facilities: There are 32 sites for tents or RVs (no hookups) and 16 sites for tents or RVs up to 40 feet with partial hookups (30 amps). Picnic tables and fire pits are provided. Drinking water, vault toilets, a dump station, a softball field, a playground, horseshoe pits, disc golf, and a reservable picnic shelter are available. Supplies are available nearby. Some facilities are wheelchair accessible. Leashed pets are permitted.

Reservations, fees: Reservations are accepted at 800/452-5687 or www.reserveamerica.com ($6 reservation fee). Sites are $15–18 per night, plus $5 per night for an additional vehicle. Open year-round.

Directions: From Grants Pass, drive north on I-5 for approximately 18 miles to Exit 76/Wolf Creek. Take that exit to Wolf Creek Road. Turn left and drive 0.5 mile to the town of Wolf Creek and Main Street. Turn left and drive 0.25 mile to the park.

Contact: Josephine County Parks, 541/474-5285, fax 541/474-5288, www.co.josephine.or.us/.

133 INDIAN MARY PARK

Scenic rating: 9

on the Rogue River

See map page 383   BEST (

This park is the crown jewel of the Josephine County parks. Set right on the Rogue River at an elevation of 900–1,000 feet, the park offers disc golf (Frisbee golf), fishing, hiking trails, a historic mining town nearby, a reservable picnic shelter, a swimming beach (unsupervised), and volleyball. Rogue River is famous for its rafting, which can be done commercially or on your own.

RV sites, facilities: There are 56 sites for tents or RVs up to 40 feet with full or partial hookups (30 and 50 amps), 34 sites for tents or RVs (no hookups), two yurts, and a house. Picnic tables and fire pits are provided. Drinking water, restrooms with flush toilets and coin showers, garbage bins, a dump station, a boat ramp, a day-use area, a reservable picnic shelter, a playground, ice, and firewood are available. A camp host is on-site. Some facilities are wheelchair accessible. A store and café are seven miles away, and a coin laundry is 16 miles away. Leashed pets are permitted.

Reservations, fees: Reservations are accepted at 800/452-5687 or www.reserveamerica.com ($6 reservation fee). Sites are $15–20 per night, $5 per night for an additional vehicle, $26–28 per night for yurts, and $120 per night for the house. Open year-round.

Directions: From Grants Pass, drive north on I-5 for 3.5 miles to Exit 61 (Merlin-Galice Road). Take that exit and drive west on Merlin-Galice Road for 10 miles to Indian Mary Park on the right.

Contact: Josephine County Parks, 541/474-5285, fax 541/474-5288, www.co.josephine.or.us.

134 SHADY TRAILS RV PARK

Scenic rating: 7

on the Rogue River

See map page 383

This grassy park with many shaded sites is along the banks of the Rogue River in a wooded, mountainous area. Recreation options include fishing on the Rogue River and exploring Casey State Park. Most of the sites are taken by monthly renters. No tents are allowed.

RV sites, facilities: There are 54 sites with full hookups (30 and 50 amps) for RVs of any length. Picnic tables are provided. Restrooms have flush toilets and showers. Cable TV, propane gas, a dump station, a coin laundry, vending machines, and a playground are available. A restaurant, a grocery store, and gasoline are within one mile. Boat-launching facilities are nearby. Leashed pets are permitted.

Reservations, fees: Reservations are accepted. RV sites are $25 per night, plus $2 per person per night for more than two people. Some credit cards are accepted. Open year-round.

Directions: From I-5 at Medford, drive northeast on Highway 62 for 23 miles to the park on the right.

Contact: Shady Trails RV Park, 541/878-2206.

135 FLY CASTERS RV PARK

Scenic rating: 6

on the Rogue River

See map page 383

This spot along the banks of the Rogue River is a good base camp for RVers who want to fish or hike. The county park, across the river in Shady Cove, offers picnic facilities and a boat ramp. Lost Creek Lake is about a 15-minute drive northeast. No tent camping is permitted at this park. Note that about half of the sites are taken by long-term rentals.

RV sites, facilities: There are 47 sites with full hookups (30 and 50 amps) for RVs of any length; two are pull-through sites. Picnic tables are provided. Restrooms have flush toilets and showers. Propane gas, cable TV, wireless Internet service, a clubhouse, a barbecue area, and coin laundry are available. A store, a café, and ice are within one mile. Boat-launching facilities are nearby. Leashed pets are permitted.

OREGON

OREGON

Reservations, fees: Reservations are accepted. Sites are $25–34 per night. Some credit cards are accepted. Monthly rates are available. Open year-round.

Directions: From Medford, drive northeast on Highway 62 for 21 miles to the park on the left.

Contact: Fly Casters RV Park, 541/878-2749, fax 541/878-2742.

136 BEAR MOUNTAIN RV PARK

Scenic rating: 7

on the Rogue River

See map page 383

This campground sits in an open, grassy area on the Rogue River about six miles from Lost Creek Lake, where boat ramps and picnic areas are available for day use. The campsites are spacious and shaded.

RV sites, facilities: There is a grassy area for tent sites and 37 sites with full or partial hookups (30 and 50 amps) for RVs of any length. Drinking water and picnic tables are provided. Restrooms have flush toilets and showers. Propane gas, a coin laundry, ice, and a playground are available. A store and a café are within one mile. Boat docks and launching facilities are nearby. Leashed pets are permitted.

Reservations, fees: Reservations are accepted at 541/878-2400 (from Oregon) or 800/586-2327 (from outside Oregon). Sites are $20–24 per night, plus $2 per person per night for more than two adults. Some credit cards are accepted. Open year-round.

Directions: From Medford, drive northeast on Highway 62 to the junction with Highway 227. Continue east on Highway 62 for 2.5 more miles to the park on the left.

Contact: Bear Mountain RV Park, 541/878-2400.

137 ROGUE ELK CAMPGROUND

Scenic rating: 8

on the Rogue River east of the city of Trail

See map page 383

Right on the Rogue River at an elevation of 1,476 feet, the park has creek swimming (unsupervised), a Douglas fir forest, fishing, hiking trails, rafting, and wildlife. With 33 acres of space and 0.75 mile of river frontage, this is Jackson County's most popular park. The forest is very beautiful here. Lost Creek Lake on Highway 62 makes a good side trip.

RV sites, facilities: There are 37 sites for tents or RVs up to 25 feet; some have partial hookups (50 amps). Picnic tables and fire pits are provided. Drinking water, restrooms with flush toilets and coin showers, garbage bins, a dump station, a boat ramp, and a playground are available. Some facilities are wheelchair accessible. A café, a minimart, ice, a coin laundry, and firewood are available within three miles. Leashed pets are permitted.

Reservations, fees: Reservations are not accepted. Family sites are $16–18 per night and $1 per pet per night. Open mid-April–mid-October.

Directions: From Medford, take Exit 30 for the Crater Lake Highway (Highway 62) and drive northeast on Highway 62 for 29 miles to the park entrance on the right.

Contact: Jackson County Parks, 541/774-8183, fax 541/774-6320, www.jacksoncounty parks.com.

138 JOSEPH H. STEWART STATE PARK

Scenic rating: 7

on Lost Creek Reservoir

See map page 383

This state park is on the shore of Lost Creek Reservoir, a lake with a beach, boat rentals, and a marina. Home to eight miles of hiking and biking trails, the park is about 40 miles from Crater Lake National Park and makes an excellent jumping-off point for an exploration of southern Oregon.

RV sites, facilities: There are 151 sites for tents or RVs with partial hookups (20 and 30 amps), including some sites for RVs of any length, and 50 sites with water for tents or RVs. There are also two group areas for tents or RVs that can accommodate up to 50 people each. Picnic tables and fire grills are provided. Restrooms have flush toilets and showers. Garbage bins, drinking water, a dump station, firewood, and a playground are available. Boat rentals, launching facilities, a swimming area, and a reservable picnic area are nearby. Some facilities are wheelchair accessible. Leashed pets are permitted.

Reservations, fees: Reservations are accepted at 800/452-5687 or www.oregonstateparks.org ($6 reservation fee). Sites are $10–16 per night, plus $5 per night per additional vehicle, and $40–60 per night for group sites, plus $2.40 per person per night for more than 25 people. Some credit cards are accepted. Open March–October.

Directions: From Medford, drive northeast on Highway 62 for 34 miles to the Lost Creek Reservoir and the campground on the left.

Contact: Joseph H. Stewart State Park, 541/560-3334; Oregon State Parks, 800/551-6949, www.oregonstateparks.org.

139 WHISKEY SPRINGS

Scenic rating: 9

near Butte Falls in Rogue River National Forest

See map page 383

This campground at Whiskey Springs is one of the larger, more developed backwoods U.S. Forest Service camps in the area. A one-mile, wheelchair-accessible nature trail passes nearby. You can see beaver dams and woodpeckers here. The camp is at 3,200 feet elevation.

RV sites, facilities: There are 34 sites for tents or RVs up to 30 feet (no hookups). Picnic tables, garbage service, and fire grills are provided. Drinking water, vault toilets, and firewood are available. Boat docks, launching facilities, and rentals are within 1.5 miles. Some facilities are wheelchair accessible. Leashed pets are permitted.

Reservations, fees: Reservations are not accepted. Sites are $10 per night, plus $5 per night per additional vehicle. Open mid-May–September, weather permitting.

Directions: From Medford, drive northeast on Highway 62 for 14 miles to the Butte Falls Highway. Turn right and drive east for 16 miles to the town of Butte Falls. Continue southeast on Butte Falls Highway for nine miles to Forest Road 3065. Turn left on Forest Road 3065 and drive 300 yards to the campground on the left.

Contact: Rogue River National Forest, Butte Falls Ranger District, 541/865-2700, fax 541/865-2795.

OREGON

140 HUCKLEBERRY MOUNTAIN

Scenic rating: 6

near Crater Lake National Park in Rogue River National Forest

See map page 383

Here's a hideaway for Crater Lake visitors. The camp is at the site of an old 1930s Civilian Conservation Corps camp, and an ATV trail runs through and next to the campground. Set at an elevation of 5,400 feet, this spot, about 15 miles from the entrance to Crater Lake National Park, really does get overlooked by highway travelers, so you have a good shot at privacy.

RV sites, facilities: There are 25 sites for tents or RVs up to 26 feet (no hookups). Picnic tables and fireplaces are provided. Drinking water and vault toilets are available. Garbage must be packed out. Leashed pets are permitted.

Reservations, fees: Reservations are not accepted. There is no fee for camping. Open June–late October, weather permitting.

Directions: From Medford, drive north on Highway 62 for 50 miles (near Union Creek) to Forest Road 60. Turn right and drive 12 miles to the campground.

Contact: Rogue River National Forest, Prospect Ranger District, 541/560-3400, fax 541/560-3444.

OREGON

141 JACKSON F. KIMBALL STATE PARK

Scenic rating: 7

on the Wood River
See map page 383

This primitive state campground at the headwaters of the Wood River is another nice spot just far enough off the main drag to remain a secret. Wood River offers fine fishing that's accessible from the park by canoe. A walking trail leads from the campground to a clear spring bubbling from a rocky hillside.

RV sites, facilities: There are 10 sites for tents or RVs up to 45 feet (no hookups). Picnic tables, fire grills, and garbage bins are provided. Vault toilets are available. There is no drinking water. Leashed pets are permitted.

Reservations, fees: Reservations are not accepted. Sites are $5–8 per night, plus $5 per night per additional vehicle. Open mid-April–October.

Directions: From Klamath Falls, drive north on U.S. 97 for 21 miles to Highway 62. Turn left (northwest) on Highway 62 and drive 10 miles to Highway 232/Sun Pass Road (near Fort Klamath). Turn right (north) and drive three miles to the campground.

Contact: Collier Memorial State Park, 541/783-2471; Oregon State Parks, 800/551-6949, www.oregonstateparks.org. This park is managed by Collier Memorial State Park.

142 CRATER LAKE RESORT

Scenic rating: 6

on the Wood River
See map page 383   BEST (

This campground, dotted with huge pine trees, is on the banks of the beautiful, crystal-clear Fort Creek. It's just outside Fort Klamath, the site of numerous military campaigns against the Modoc people in the late 1800s.

RV sites, facilities: There are 23 sites with full or partial hookups (30 amps) for RVs of any length, six tent sites, nine cabins, and one log cabin. Drinking water, picnic tables, and fire rings are provided. Restrooms have flush toilets and showers. Modem access, a recreation hall, and a coin laundry are available. Propane gas, a store, a café, and ice are within one mile. Leashed pets are permitted.

Reservations, fees: Reservations are accepted. RV sites are $25 per night, $3 per person per night for more than two people, and $3 per pet per night. Tent sites are $20 per night. Some credit cards are accepted. Open mid-April–mid-October.

Directions: From Klamath Falls, drive north on U.S. 97 for 21 miles to Highway 62. Bear left on Highway 62 and drive 12.5 miles north to the resort (just before reaching Fort Klamath).

Contact: Crater Lake Resort, 541/381-2349, www.craterlakeresort.com.

143 COLLIER MEMORIAL STATE PARK

Scenic rating: 7

on the Williamson River
See map page 383

This campground sits at the confluence of Spring Creek and the Williamson River, both of which are superior trout streams. An area for equestrian campers is situated at a trailhead for horses. A nature trail is also available. The park features a pioneer village and one of the state's finer logging museums. Movies about old-time logging and other activities are shown on weekend nights during the summer.

RV sites, facilities: There are 50 sites for RVs of any length with full hookups (30 amps), 18 sites for tents or RVs (no hookups), and an area for equestrian campers that can accommodate up to four camping units. Some sites are pull-through. Picnic tables, fire grills, garbage bins, and drinking water are provided. Restrooms have flush toilets and showers. A dump station, firewood, a coin laundry, a playground, and a day-use hitching area are available. Some facilities are wheelchair accessible. Leashed pets are permitted.

Reservations, fees: Reservations are not accepted. Sites are $11–17 per night, plus $5 per night per additional vehicle. The equestrian area is $10–15 per night and $1.50 per night per horse. Some credit cards are accepted. Open April–late October, weather permitting.

Directions: From Klamath Falls, drive north on U.S. 97 for 28 miles to the park (well signed).

Contact: Collier Memorial State Park, 541/783-2471; Oregon State Parks, 800/551-6949, www.oregonstateparks.org.

144 POTTER'S PARK

Scenic rating: 6

on the Sprague River
See map page 383

This park on a bluff overlooking the Sprague River is in a wooded setting and bordered by the Winema National Forest. Canoeing and rafting are options. For the most part, the area east of Klamath Lake doesn't get much attention.

RV sites, facilities: There are 22 sites with full hookups (20 amps) for RVs of any length and 17 tent sites. Drinking water, picnic tables, and fire pits are provided. Restrooms have flush toilets and showers. Firewood, a convenience store, a coin laundry, a pay telephone, and ice are available. Leashed pets are permitted.

Reservations, fees: Reservations are accepted. Sites are $15–20 per night, plus $3–5 per person per night for more than one adult. Monthly rates are available for RV sites. Open year-round, with limited winter facilities.

Directions: From Klamath Falls, drive north on U.S. 97 for 27 miles to Chiloquin and Sprague River Highway. Turn right (east) on Sprague River Highway and drive 12 miles to the park on the right.

Contact: Potter's Park, 541/783-2253.

145 GRANTS PASS/REDWOOD HIGHWAY KOA

Scenic rating: 8

near Grants Pass
See map page 383

This KOA campground along a stream in the hills outside of Grants Pass attracts bird-watchers. It also makes a perfect layover spot for travelers who want to get away from the highway for a while. For an interesting side trip, drive south down scenic U.S. 199 to Cave Junction or Illinois River State Park.

RV sites, facilities: There are 40 sites for tents or RVs of any length with full or partial hookups (30 and 50 amps), one cabin, and one RV rental. Some sites are pull-through. Picnic tables are provided, and tent sites have fire pits. Restrooms have showers. Drinking water, a dump station, a coin laundry, a convenience store, ice, RV supplies, propane gas, and modem access are available. Amenities include a recreation hall, a playground, and a recreation field. Leashed pets are permitted with certain restrictions.

Reservations, fees: Reservations are accepted at 800/562-7566. Sites are $22–35 per night, plus $2–3 per person per night for more than two people. Some credit cards are accepted. Open year-round.

Directions: In Grants Pass on I-5, take the U.S. 199 exit. Turn southwest on U.S. 199 and drive 14.5 miles to the campground on the right (at Milepost 14.5).

Contact: Grants Pass/Redwood Highway KOA, 541/476-6508, www.koa.com.

146 SCHROEDER

Scenic rating: 9

on the Rogue River
See map page 383   BEST (

Steelhead and salmon fishing, swimming, and boating are among the possibilities at this popular camp along the Rogue River. Just a short jog off the highway, it makes an excellent

OREGON

layover for I-5 travelers. A bonus for RVers is 50-amp service. The park is close to Hellgate Excursions, which provides jet-boat trips on the Rogue River. Tennis courts are close by.

RV sites, facilities: There are 25 sites for RVs of any length with full hookups (30 and 50 amps), and 22 sites with no hookups, as well as two yurts. Restrooms have flush toilets and coin showers, and a reservable picnic shelter is available. Recreational facilities include ball fields, tennis and basketball courts, horseshoe pits, a recreation field, a picnic area, a playground, and a boat ramp. A camp host is on-site. Some facilities, including a fishing pier, are wheelchair accessible. Leashed pets are permitted.

Reservations, fees: Reservations are accepted at 800/452-5687 or www.reserveamerica.com ($6 reservation fee). Sites are $15–20 per night, $5 per night for an additional vehicle, and yurts are $26–28 per night. Open year-round.

Directions: In Grants Pass on I-5, take Exit 58 to U.S. 199. Drive west on U.S. 199 for 0.7 mile to Redwood Avenue. Turn right and drive 1.5 miles to Willow Lane. Turn right and drive 0.9 mile to Schroeder Lane and the park.

Contact: Josephine County Parks, 541/474-5285, fax 541/474-5288, www.co.josephine.or.us.

147 ROGUE VALLEY OVERNITERS

Scenic rating: 5

near the Rogue River

See map page 383

This park is just off the freeway in Grants Pass, the jumping-off point for trips down the Rogue River. The summer heat in this part of Oregon can surprise visitors in late June and early July. This is a nice, comfortable park with shade trees. About one-half of the sites are taken by monthly renters.

RV sites, facilities: There are 110 sites for RVs of any length with full hookups (50 amps); some are pull-through sites. Cable TV and

picnic tables are provided. Restrooms have flush toilets and showers. Modem access, a dump station, and a coin laundry are available. Propane gas, a store, a café, and ice are available within one mile. Leashed pets are permitted.

Reservations, fees: Reservations are accepted. Sites are $25.30–30.25 per night, plus $2 per person per night for more than two people. Weekly and monthly rates are available. Open year-round.

Directions: In Grants Pass on I-5, take Exit 58 to 6th Street. Drive south on 6th Street for 0.25 mile to the park on the right.

Contact: Rogue Valley Overniters, 541/479-2208.

148 WHITEHORSE

Scenic rating: 9

near the Rogue River

See map page 383   BEST (

This pleasant county park about 0.25 mile from the banks of the Rogue River is one of several parks in the Grants Pass area that provide opportunities for salmon and steelhead fishing, hiking, and boating. This is a popular bird-watching area. Wildlife Images, a wildlife rehabilitation center, is nearby. Possible side trips include Crater Lake National Park (two hours away), Kerby Museum, and Oregon Caves.

RV sites, facilities: There are 34 sites for tents or RVs of any length (no hookups), eight sites with full hookups (30 amps) for RVs of any length, one group site for up to 18 people, and one yurt. Picnic tables and fire pits are provided. Restrooms have flush toilets and coin showers. A boat ramp, horseshoe pits, volleyball, a reservable picnic shelter, and a playground are available. A camp host is on-site. Some facilities are wheelchair accessible. Leashed pets are permitted.

Reservations, fees: Reservations are accepted at 800/452-5687 or www.reserveamerica.com ($6 reservation fee). Sites are $15–20 per night, $5 per night for an additional vehicle, and $26–28 per night for the yurt. The group site is $30 per night for up to 12 people and $2–3 per person per night for additional people. Open year-round, but only to self-contained RVs in the winter.

Directions: In Grants Pass on I-5, take Exit 58 to 6th Street. Drive south on 6th Street to G Street. Turn right (west) and drive approximately seven miles (the road becomes Upper River Road, then Lower River Road). The park is on the left at 7600 Lower River Road.

Contact: Josephine County Parks, 541/474-5285, fax 541/474-5288, www.co.josephine.or.us.

149 GRANTS PASS OVERNITERS

Scenic rating: 6

near Grants Pass
See map page 383

This wooded park, in a rural area just outside Grants Pass, is mostly shaded. Several other campgrounds are in the area. Don't let the name mislead you; whereas several spaces are reserved for overnighters, there are many monthly rentals at the park.

RV sites, facilities: There are 26 pull-through sites with full hookups (20, 30, and 50 amps) for RVs of any length. There are no tent sites. Picnic tables are provided. Restrooms have flush toilets and coin showers. A coin laundry and a seasonal heated swimming pool are available. A store is within one mile. Leashed pets are permitted.

Reservations, fees: Reservations are accepted. Sites are $28 per night, plus $1 per person per night for more than two people. Open year-round.

Directions: From Grants Pass, drive north on I-5 for three miles to Exit 61 and bear right to a stop sign and Highland Avenue. Turn left and drive a very short distance to the campground on the right.

Contact: Grants Pass Overniters, 541/479-7289.

150 RIVER PARK RV RESORT

Scenic rating: 6

on the Rogue River
See map page 383

This park has a quiet, serene riverfront setting, yet it is close to all the conveniences of a small city. Highlights here include 700 feet of Rogue River frontage for trout fishing and swimming. It's one of several parks in the immediate area.

RV sites, facilities: There are three tent sites and 47 sites with full or partial hookups (50 amps) for RVs up to 40 feet. Picnic tables are provided. Cable TV, restrooms with showers, a dump station, a public phone, a coin laundry, and ice are available. Leashed pets are permitted.

Reservations, fees: Reservations are accepted at 800/677-8857. Sites are $20–35.50 per night, $2.50 per person per night for more than two people, and $2 per night for an additional vehicle if not towed. Some credit cards are accepted. Open year-round.

Directions: In Grants Pass on I-5, take Exit 55 west to Highway 199. Drive west on Highway 199 for two miles to Parkdale. Turn left on Parkdale and drive one block to Highway 99. Turn left on Highway 99 and drive two miles to the park on the left.

Contact: River Park RV Resort, 541/479-0046 or 800/677-8857.

151 CHINOOK WINDS RV PARK

Scenic rating: 6

on the Rogue River
See map page 383

This campground along the Rogue River is close to chartered boat trips down the Rogue and a golf course. Fishing and swimming access are available from the campground. No tents are permitted. This park was previously known as Circle W RV Park.

RV sites, facilities: There are 25 sites with full or partial hookups (30 and 50 amps) for RVs of any length; some are pull-through sites. Picnic

OREGON

tables and cable TV are provided. Restrooms have flush toilets and showers. A dump station, a coin laundry, and ice are available. A boat dock is nearby. Leashed pets are permitted.

Reservations, fees: Reservations are accepted. Sites are $27.50–30 per night, plus $1.50 per person per night for more than two people. Some credit cards are accepted. Open year-round.

Directions: From Grants Pass, drive south on I-5 for 10 miles to Exit 48 at Rogue River. Take that exit west (over the bridge) to Highway 99. Turn right and drive west one mile to the park on the right.

Contact: Chinook Winds RV Park, 541/582-1686.

152 VALLEY OF THE ROGUE STATE PARK

Scenic rating: 7

on the Rogue River

See map page 383

With easy highway access, this popular campground along the banks of the Rogue River often fills to near capacity during the summer. Recreation options include fishing and boating. This spot makes a good base camp for taking in the Rogue Valley and surrounding attractions: Ashland's Shakespeare Festival, the Britt Music Festival, Crater Lake National Park, historic Jacksonville, and Oregon Caves National Monument.

RV sites, facilities: There are 147 sites for tents or RVs of any length with full or partial hookups (30 and 50 amps) and 21 sites for tents; some are pull-through sites. Three group tent areas for up to 25 people each and six yurts are available. Picnic tables and fire grills are provided. Restrooms have flush toilets and showers. Drinking water, garbage bins, a dump station, firewood, a coin laundry, a meeting hall, and playgrounds are available. A restaurant is nearby. Some facilities are wheelchair accessible. Boat-launching facilities are nearby. Leashed pets are permitted.

Reservations, fees: Reservations are accepted at 800/452-5687 or www.oregonstateparks.org ($6 reservation fee). Sites are $12–20 per night. Group areas are $40–60 per night, yurts are $27 per night, and extra vehicles are $5 per night. Some credit cards are accepted. Open year-round.

Directions: From Grants Pass, drive south on I-5 for 12 miles to Exit 45B/Valley of the Rogue State Park. Take that exit, turn right, and drive a short distance to the park on the right.

Contact: Valley of the Rogue State Park, 541/582-1118; Oregon State Parks, 800/551-6949, www.oregonstateparks.org.

153 KOA GOLD N' ROGUE

Scenic rating: 6

on the Rogue River

See map page 383

This campground is 0.5 mile from the Rogue River, with bike paths, a golf course, and the Oregon Vortex (the house of mystery) in the vicinity. It's one of the many campgrounds between Gold Hill and Grants Pass.

RV sites, facilities: There are 64 sites with full hookups (50 amps) for RVs of any length, 12 tent sites, and four cabins. Some sites are pull-through. Picnic tables are provided, and tent sites have fire rings. Restrooms have flush toilets and showers. Modem access, propane gas, a dump station, firewood, a convenience store, a coin laundry, ice, a playground, and a seasonal swimming pool are available. A café is within one mile, and boat-launching facilities are within five miles. Leashed pets are permitted, with certain restrictions.

Reservations, fees: Reservations are accepted at 800/562-7608. Sites are $24–35 per night, plus $2 per person per night for more than two people. Some credit cards are accepted. Open year-round.

Directions: From Medford, drive north on I-5 for 10 miles to South Gold Hill and Exit 40. Take that exit, turn right, and drive 0.25 mile to Blackwell Road. Turn right (on a paved road) and drive 0.25 mile to the park.

Contact: KOA Gold n' Rogue, 541/855-7710, www.koa.com.

154 MEDFORD OAKS RV PARK

Scenic rating: 6

near Eagle Point
See map page 383

This park is in a quiet, rural setting among the trees. Just a short hop off I-5, it's an excellent choice for travelers heading to or from California. The campground is along the shore of a pond that provides good fishing. Most sites are filled with monthly renters.

RV sites, facilities: There are 10 sites for tents and 47 sites with full or partial hookups (30 and 50 amps) for RVs of any length; most sites are pull-through. There are also three cabins. Restrooms have coin showers. A dump station, modem access, a coin laundry, limited groceries, ice, RV supplies, and propane gas are available. Recreational facilities include a seasonal, heated swimming pool, movies, horseshoe pits, table tennis, a recreation field for baseball and volleyball, and a playground. Leashed pets are allowed with certain restrictions.

Reservations, fees: Reservations are recommended. Sites are $17–33 per night, $3 per person per night for more than two people. Group rates are available. Some credit cards are accepted. Open year-round.

Directions: From Medford, drive northeast on Highway 62 for five miles to Exit 30 and Highway 140. Turn east on Highway 140 and drive 6.8 miles to the park on the left.

Contact: Medford Oaks RV Park, 541/826-5103, fax 541/826-5984, www.medfordoaks.com.

155 WILLOW LAKE RESORT

Scenic rating: 9

on Willow Lake
See map page 383

This campground sits on the shore of Willow Lake. Located at the base of Mount McLough-
lin at an elevation of 3,200 feet, it encompasses 927 wooded acres. The lake has fishing opportunities for bass, crappie, and trout. A hiking trail starts near camp.

RV sites, facilities: There are 54 sites for tents or RVs with full or partial hookups (30 amps), 29 sites for tents or RVs (no hookups), and a group area with 11 sites. There are also four cabins. Picnic tables and fire rings are provided. Restrooms have flush toilets and coin showers. A dump station and firewood are available. Some facilities are wheelchair accessible. Leashed pets are permitted.

Reservations, fees: Reservations are accepted for groups and cabins only at 541/560-3900. Sites are $14–18 per night, $6 per night for an additional vehicle, plus $1 per pet per night. The group area is $150 per night. Open April–October.

Directions: From Medford, drive northeast on Highway 62 for 15 miles to Butte Falls Highway. Turn east and drive 25 miles to Willow Lake Road. Turn right (south) and drive two miles to the campground.

Contact: Jackson County Parks, 541/774-8183, fax 541/774-6320, www.jacksoncounty parks.com.

156 FOURMILE LAKE

Scenic rating: 8

at Fourmile Lake in Winema National Forest
See map page 383

This beautiful spot is the only camp on the shore of Fourmile Lake. Several nearby trails provide access to the Sky Lakes Wilderness. The Pacific Crest Trail passes about two miles from camp. Primitive and with lots of solitude, it attracts a calm and quiet crowd. Afternoon winds can be a problem, and in the evening, if the wind isn't blowing, the mosquitoes often arrive. Although this campground is near the foot of Mount McLoughlin (9,495 feet), there is no view of the mountain from here. Go to the east side of the lake for a good view.

RV sites, facilities: There are 25 sites for tents

OREGON

OREGON

or RVs up to 22 feet (no hookups). Picnic tables, garbage bins, and fire grills are provided. Drinking water and vault toilets are available. Leashed pets are permitted.

Reservations, fees: Reservations are not accepted. Sites are $11 per night, plus $5.50 per night per additional vehicle. Open June–late September, weather permitting.

Directions: From Medford, drive northeast on Highway 62 for five miles to Exit 30 and Highway 140. Turn east on Highway 140 and drive approximately 40 miles to Forest Road 3661. Turn left (north) and drive six miles to the campground.

Contact: Fremont-Winema National Forests, Klamath Ranger District, 541/885-3400, fax 541/885-3452.

157 FISH LAKE

Scenic rating: 8

on Fish Lake in Rogue River National Forest
See map page 383

Bicycling, boating, fishing, and hiking are among the recreation options at this campground on the north shore of Fish Lake. Easy, one-mile access to the Pacific Crest Trail is also available. If this campground is full, Doe Point and Fish Lake Resort are nearby.

RV sites, facilities: There are 19 sites for tents or RVs up to 32 feet and two walk-in tent sites. Picnic tables, fire grills, and garbage bins are provided. Drinking water, vault toilets, a reservable picnic shelter, a store, a café, firewood, and ice are available. A camp host is on-site. Boat docks, launching facilities, boat rentals, a coin laundry, a dump station, and coin showers are nearby. Some facilities are wheelchair accessible. Leashed pets are permitted.

Reservations, fees: Reservations are not accepted for camping. Reservations are required for the picnic shelter at 541/560-3900. Sites are $15 per night, plus $7 per night per additional vehicle. Open mid-May–mid-October, weather permitting.

Directions: From Medford, drive northeast on

Highway 62 for five miles to Exit 30 and Highway 140. Turn east on Highway 140 and drive 30 miles to the campground on the right.

Contact: Rogue River National Forest, Ashland Ranger District, 541/552-2900, fax 541/552-2922.

158 DOE POINT

Scenic rating: 8

on Fish Lake in Rogue River National Forest
See map page 383

This campground (at 4,600 feet elevation) sits along the north shore of Fish Lake, nearly adjacent to Fish Lake Campground. Doe Point is slightly preferable because of its dense vegetation, offering shaded, quiet, well-screened sites. Privacy, rare at many campgrounds, can be found here. Recreation options include biking, boating, fishing, and hiking, plus an easy, one-mile access trail to the Pacific Crest Trail.

RV sites, facilities: There are five walk-in tent sites and 25 sites for tents or RVs up to 32 feet (no hookups). Picnic tables and fire grills are provided. Drinking water, garbage service, flush toilets, a store, a café, firewood, and ice are available. Boat docks, launching facilities, boat rentals, showers, and a dump station are nearby. Leashed pets are permitted.

Reservations, fees: Reservations are not accepted. Sites are $15 per night, plus $7 per night per additional vehicle. Open mid-May–late September, weather permitting.

Directions: From Medford, drive northeast on Highway 62 for five miles to Exit 30 and Highway 140. Turn east on Highway 140 and drive 30 miles to the campground on the right.

Contact: Rogue River National Forest, Ashland Ranger District, 541/552-2900, fax 541/552-2922.

159 FISH LAKE RESORT

Scenic rating: 7

on Fish Lake
See map page 383

This resort along Fish Lake is privately operated under permit by the U.S. Forest Service and offers a resort-type feel, catering primarily to families. This is the largest and most developed of the three camps at Fish Lake. Bicycling, boating, fishing, and hiking are some of the activities here. Cozy cabins are available for rent. Boat speed on the lake is limited to 10 mph.

RV sites, facilities: There are 45 sites with full hookups (30 amps) for RVs up to 38 feet, plus 11 cabins and 12 tent sites. Some sites are pull-through. Picnic tables, fire rings, drinking water, and garbage bins are provided. Restrooms have flush toilets and coin showers. Propane gas, a dump station, a recreation hall, a convenience store, a café, a coin laundry, ice, boat docks, boat rentals, and launching facilities are available. Leashed pets are permitted.

Reservations, fees: Reservations are accepted at 541/949-8500. Tent sites are $17–22 per night, and RV sites are $30–32 per night. Some credit cards are accepted. Open year-round, weather permitting, with limited winter facilities.

Directions: From Medford, drive northeast on Highway 62 for five miles to Exit 30 and Highway 140. Turn east on Highway 140 and drive 30 miles to Fish Lake Road. Turn right (south) and drive 0.5 mile to the resort on the left.

Contact: Fish Lake Resort, 541/949-8500, www.fishlakeresort.net.

160 ROCKY POINT RESORT

Scenic rating: 7

on Upper Klamath Lake
See map page 383

Rocky Point Resort, at the Upper Klamath Wildlife Refuge, boasts 10 miles of canoe trails, along with opportunities for motorized boating and fishing.

RV sites, facilities: There are 28 sites with partial or full hookups (50 amps) for RVs of any length, four tent sites, four cabins, and motel rooms. Some sites are pull-through. Picnic tables and fire rings are provided. Restrooms have flush toilets and showers. Drinking water, firewood, a convenience store, modem access, a coin laundry, ice, a marina with boat gas, and boat and canoe rentals are available. There is a free boat launch and game area. A restaurant and lounge overlook the lake. Leashed pets are permitted.

Reservations, fees: Reservations are accepted. Sites are $16–23 per night, $2 per person per night for more than two people, and $2 per pet per night. Some credit cards are accepted. Open April–November.

Directions: From Klamath Falls, drive northeast on Highway 140 for about 25 miles to Rocky Point Road. Turn right (north) and drive three miles to the resort on the right.

Contact: Rocky Point Resort, 541/356-2287, fax 541/356-2222, www.rockypointoregon.com.

161 LAKE OF THE WOODS RESORT

Scenic rating: 9

on Lake of the Woods
See map page 383

On beautiful Lake of the Woods, this resort offers fishing (four kinds of trout, catfish, and bass) and boating in a secluded forest setting. It's on one of the most beautiful lakes in the Cascade Mountains, surrounded by tall pine trees. A family-oriented campground, it has all the amenities. In the winter, snowmobiling and cross-country skiing are popular. Attractions in the area include the Mountain Lakes Wilderness and the Pacific Crest Trail.

RV sites, facilities: There are 27 sites for tents or RVs up to 35 feet with full or partial hookups (30 amps) and 28 cabins. Picnic tables and fire rings are provided. Restrooms have showers. A dump station, a coin laundry, ice, snacks, a restaurant, a lounge, and propane gas are available. Other amenities include a boat

OREGON

ramp, a dock, a marina, boat and mountain bike rentals, and a barbecue area. Leashed pets are permitted.

Reservations, fees: Reservations are accepted at 866/201-4194. Sites are $25–32 per night, $6 per night per additional vehicle, and $5 per pet per stay. Some credit cards are accepted. Open during summer season; call for winter schedule.

Directions: In Medford on I-5, take Exit 14 to Highway 66. Drive east for less than a mile to Dead Indian Memorial Road. Turn left (east) and drive 40 miles to Lake of the Woods Road. Turn left (north) and drive less than 0.5 mile to the resort.

Contact: Lake of the Woods Resort, 541/949-8300, fax 541/949-8229, www.lakeofthewoods resort.com.

162 ASPEN POINT

Scenic rating: 8

on Lake of the Woods in Winema National Forest

See map page 383

This campground (at 5,000 feet elevation) is near the north shore of Lake of the Woods, adjacent to Lake of the Woods Resort. It's heavily timbered with old-growth fir and has a great view of Mount McLoughlin (9,495 feet). A hiking trail just north of camp leads north for several miles, meandering around Fourmile Lake and extending into the Sky Lakes Wilderness. Other trails nearby head into the Mountain Lakes Wilderness. Boating, fishing, swimming, and waterskiing are among the activities here. Note that of the 60 campsites, 20 are available by reservation, while the rest are first-come, first-served.

RV sites, facilities: There are 60 sites for tents or RVs up to 55 feet (no hookups). Picnic tables, garbage bins, and fire grills are provided. Drinking water, a dump station, and flush toilets are available. Boat docks, launching facilities, and rentals are nearby. Leashed pets are permitted.

Reservations, fees: Reservations are accepted

at 877/444-6777 or www.ReserveUSA.com ($9 reservation fee). Sites are $14 per night, plus $7 per night per additional vehicle. Open late May–early September, weather permitting.

Directions: In Ashland on I-5, take Exit 14 to Highway 66. Drive east for less than a mile to Dead Indian Memorial Road. Turn left (east) and drive 40 miles to Lake of the Woods. Continue along the east shore to the campground turnoff on the left.

Contact: Fremont-Winema National Forests, Klamath Ranger District, 541/885-3400, fax 541/885-3452.

163 SUNSET

Scenic rating: 8

near Lake of the Woods in Winema National Forest

See map page 383

This campground (at 5,000 feet elevation) near the eastern shore of Lake of the Woods is fully developed and offers myriad recreation options. It's popular for both fishing and boating. Of the 67 sites, 20 are available by reservation.

RV sites, facilities: There are 67 sites for tents or RVs up to 50 feet (no hookups). Picnic tables, garbage bins, and fire grills are provided. Drinking water and flush toilets are available. Some facilities are wheelchair accessible. Boat docks, launching facilities, and rentals are nearby. Leashed pets are permitted.

Reservations, fees: Reservations are accepted at 877/444-6777 or www.ReserveUSA.com ($9 reservation fee). Sites are $14 per night, plus $7 per night per additional vehicle. Open late May–early September.

Directions: In Ashland on I-5, take Exit 14 to Highway 66. Drive east for less than a mile to Dead Indian Memorial Road. Turn left (east) and drive 40 miles to Lake of the Woods. Continue along the east shore to Forest Road 3738. Turn left (west) and drive 0.5 mile to the camp.

Contact: Fremont-Winema National Forests, Klamath Ranger District, 541/885-3400, fax 541/885-3452.

OREGON

164 AGENCY LAKE RESORT

Scenic rating: 5

on Agency Lake

See map page 383

This campground sits along Agency Lake in an open, grassy area with some shaded sites. Some sites are filled with monthly renters. It has more than 700 feet of lakefront property, offering world-class trout fishing. Look across the lake and watch the sun set on the Cascades. (See the *Rocky Point Resort* listing in this chapter for more information.)

RV sites, facilities: There are 25 sites for tents or RVs of any length with full or partial hookups (30 and 50 amps), 15 tent sites, three cabins, and one rental trailer. Drinking water and picnic tables are provided. Restrooms have flush toilets and showers. A general store, ice, boat docks, launching facilities, and marine gas are available. Leashed pets are permitted.

Reservations, fees: Reservations are accepted. Sites are $12–20 per night. Some credit cards are accepted. Open year-round, weather permitting.

Directions: From Klamath Falls, drive north on U.S. 97 for 17 miles to Modoc Point Road. Turn left (north) and drive about 10 miles to the resort on the left.

Contact: Agency Lake Resort, 541/783-2489, www.agencylakeresort.com.

165 OREGON 8 MOTEL AND RV PARK

Scenic rating: 6

on Upper Klamath Lake

See map page 383

This campground, surrounded by mountains, big rocks, and trees, is near Hanks Marsh on the southeast shore of Upper Klamath Lake. It's within 50 miles of Crater Lake. Nearby recreation options include bike paths, a golf course, and a marina.

RV sites, facilities: There are 30 pull-through sites with full hookups (30 amps) for RVs of any length and 10 tent sites. A motel is also available. Drinking water, cable TV, and picnic tables are provided. Restrooms have flush toilets and showers. Modem access, a recreation hall, a coin laundry, a community picnic area, ice, and a seasonal heated swimming pool are available. Propane gas and a café are within one mile. Leashed pets are permitted.

Reservations, fees: Reservations are accepted. Tent sites are $15 per night, RV sites are $29.90 per night, and it's $3 per person per night for more than two people. Some credit cards are accepted. Open year-round.

Directions: From Klamath Falls, drive north on U.S. 97 for 3.5 miles to the campground on the right.

Contact: Oregon 8 Motel and RV Park, 541/883-3431.

166 LAKE SELMAC

Scenic rating: 9

on Lake Selmac

See map page 383

Nestled in a wooded, mountainous area, this 300-acre park offers boating, hiking, sailing, swimming, and good trophy bass fishing on beautiful, 160-acre Lake Selmac. Horse trails are also available. There are seasonal hosts and an assistant park ranger on-site.

RV sites, facilities: There are 91 sites for tents or RVs up to 40 feet; some sites have full or partial hookups (50 amps). There are also seven horse camps with corrals and two yurts. Drinking water, fire pits, and picnic tables are provided. Restrooms have coin showers. A dump station, a convenience store, a picnic area, horseshoe pits, a playground, ball fields, two boat ramps, and a dock are available. Some facilities are wheelchair accessible. Leashed pets are permitted.

Reservations, fees: Reservations are accepted at 800/452-5687 or www.reserveamerica.com ($6 reservation fee). Sites are $15–20 per night, $15 per night for a horse site, $5 per night for an additional vehicle, and $26–28 per night for a yurt. Open year-round.

Directions: In Grants Pass on I-5, take the U.S. 199 exit. Turn south on U.S. 199 and drive

OREGON

for 23 miles to Selma. Continue 0.5 mile to the Lake Selmac exit (Lakeshore Drive). Turn left (east) and drive 2.3 miles to the lake and the campground entrance.

Contact: Josephine County Parks, 541/474-5285, fax 541/474-5288, www.co.josephine.or.us.

167 LAKE SELMAC RESORT

Scenic rating: 7

on Lake Selmac
See map page 383

This resort borders the shore of Lake Selmac, a 160-acre lake. Fishing is great for largemouth bass (the state record has been set here three times). Bluegill, catfish, crappie, and trout are also catchable here. Fishing derbies are held during the summer. There is a 5-mph speed limit on the lake. Watch for waterfowl, including eagles, geese, osprey, and swans. A trail circles the lake, and bikers, hikers, and horses are welcome. A disc golf course is 1.5 miles away at the county park, and a golf course is about six miles away. Oregon Caves National Monument, about 30 miles away, makes a good side trip.

RV sites, facilities: There are 29 sites for tents or RVs of any length with partial hookups (30 and 50 amps); most sites are pull-through. Drinking water, fire rings, and picnic tables are provided. Restrooms have flush toilets and showers. Firewood, a general store, a café, a coin laundry, Wi-Fi, ice, propane, bait and tackle, miniature golf, and a playground are available. Boat docks and launching facilities are nearby, and rentals are on-site. Leashed pets are permitted.

Reservations, fees: Reservations are accepted. Sites are $20–30 per night, plus $2 per night per additional vehicle. Some credit cards are accepted. Open year-round, with limited winter facilities.

Directions: In Grants Pass on I-5, take the U.S. 199 exit. Turn southwest on U.S. 199 and drive 23 miles to Selma and the Lake Selmac exit (Lakeshore Drive). Turn left (east) and drive 2.5 miles to the lake and the resort on the left.

Contact: Lake Selmac Resort, 541/597-2277, www.lakeselmacresort.com.

168 MOUNTAIN MAN RV PARK

Scenic rating: 7

on the Illinois River
See map page 383

This park on the Illinois River provides good opportunities for swimming and boating (no motors are permitted). And yes, there is a mountain man here who often shows up in costume in the evening when camp groups build a fire. Great Cats World Park, a wildlife park, is 1.5 miles away. Other nearby side trips include Oregon Caves National Monument (21 miles) and Grants Pass (31 miles). Crescent City is 50 miles away. Note that a majority of the campground is taken by monthly rentals, with the remainder available for overnighters. This park was previously known as Town and Country RV Park.

RV sites, facilities: There are 51 sites for RVs of any length with full hookups (30 amps); some sites are pull-through. Picnic tables are provided and some sites have fire rings. Cable TV, restrooms with showers, a coin laundry, a community fire ring, and ice are available. Horseshoe pits and a clubhouse are also available. Leashed pets are permitted.

Reservations, fees: Reservations are accepted. Sites are $15–20 per night, plus $3 per night per person for more than two people. Monthly rates are available. Open year-round.

Directions: In Grants Pass on I-5, take Exit 55 for U.S. 199. Bear southwest on U.S. 199 and drive 30 miles to Cave Junction and continue for two miles to the park on the right.

Contact: Mountain Man RV Park, tel./fax 541/592-2656.

169 COUNTRY HILLS RESORT

Scenic rating: 7

near Oregon Caves National Monument
See map page 383

Lots of sites at this wooded camp border Sucker Creek, a popular spot for swimming. Several wineries are within two miles. Lake Selmac and Oregon Caves National Monument provide nearby side-trip options.

RV sites, facilities: There are 20 sites with partial hookups (20, 30, and 50 amps) for RVs of any length and 12 tent sites; some are pull-through sites. There are also six cabins and a five-unit motel. Picnic tables and fire rings are provided. Restrooms have flush toilets and coin showers. A dump station, modem access, drinking water, firewood, a convenience store, a coin laundry, a motel, a seasonal ice cream parlor, a seasonal café, and ice are available. Leashed pets are permitted.

Reservations, fees: Reservations are accepted. Sites are $16–21 per night, plus $3 per night per additional vehicle. Some credit cards are accepted. Open year-round.

Directions: In Grants Pass on I-5, take Exit 55 for U.S. 199. Bear southwest on U.S. 199 and drive for 28 miles to Cave Junction and Highway 46/Oregon Caves. Turn left (east) on Highway 46 and drive eight miles to the resort on the right.

Contact: Country Hills Resort, tel./fax 541/ 592-3406.

170 GRAYBACK

Scenic rating: 7

near Oregon Caves National Monument in Siskiyou National Forest

See map page 383

This wooded campground (2,000 feet elevation) along the banks of Sucker Creek has sites with ample shade. It's a good choice if you're planning to visit Oregon Caves National Monument, about 10 miles away. The camp, set in a grove of old-growth firs, is also a prime place for bird-watching. A 0.5-mile trail cuts through the camp.

RV sites, facilities: There are 39 sites for tents or RVs up to 22 feet (no hookups). Picnic tables, garbage bins, and fire grills are provided. Flush toilets and drinking water are available. Some facilities are wheelchair accessible, including a 0.5-mile trail. Leashed pets are permitted.

Reservations, fees: Reservations are not ac-

cepted. Sites are $10 per night, plus $5 per night per additional vehicle. Open May–October, weather permitting.

Directions: In Grants Pass on I-5, take Exit 55 for U.S. 199. Bear southwest on U.S. 199 for 30 miles to Cave Junction and Highway 46. Turn east on Highway 46 and drive 12 miles to the campground on the right.

Contact: Siskiyou National Forest, Illinois Valley Ranger District, 541/592-4000, fax 541/592-4010.

171 CAVE CREEK

Scenic rating: 7

near Oregon Caves National Monument in Siskiyou National Forest

See map page 383

No campground is closer to Oregon Caves National Monument than this U.S. Forest Service camp, a mere four miles away. There is even a two-mile trail out of camp that leads directly to the caves. The camp, at an elevation of 2,500 feet, lies in a grove of old-growth timber along the banks of Cave Creek, a small stream with some trout fishing opportunities (catch-and-release only). The sites are shaded, and an abundance of wildlife can be spotted in the area. Hiking opportunities abound.

RV sites, facilities: There are 18 sites for tents or RVs up to 16 feet (no hookups). Drinking water, garbage bins, vault toilets, and picnic tables are provided. Showers are within eight miles. Leashed pets are permitted.

Reservations, fees: Reservations are not accepted. Sites are $10 per night, plus $4 per night per additional vehicle. Open mid-May–mid-September, weather permitting.

Directions: In Grants Pass on I-5, take Exit 55 for U.S. 199. Bear southwest on U.S. 199 for 30 miles to Cave Junction and Highway 46. Turn east on Highway 46 and drive 16 miles to the campground on the right.

Contact: Siskiyou National Forest, Illinois Valley Ranger District, 541/592-4000, fax 541/592-4010.

172 CANTRALL-BUCKLEY PARK AND GROUP CAMP

Scenic rating: 8

on the Applegate River
See map page 383

This county park outside of Medford offers pleasant, shady sites in a wooded setting. Encompassing 88 acres of land, the camp has 1.75 miles of frontage along the Applegate River, which has good trout fishing.

RV sites, facilities: There are 25 sites for tents or RVs up to 25 feet (no hookups) and one group area for 60–100 people. Picnic tables and fire pits are provided. Drinking water, restrooms with flush toilets and coin showers, a reservable picnic area, and a public phone are available. Recreational facilities include horseshoes, a playground, and a recreation field. Some facilities are wheelchair accessible. Leashed pets are permitted.

Reservations, fees: Reservations are required for the group site at 541/774-8183 but are not accepted for single sites. Sites are $10 per night, plus $1 per pet per night, and it's $65 for the first night for the group site and $50 per night thereafter. Some credit cards are accepted for reservations. Open mid-April–mid-October.

Directions: In Medford on I-5, take the Jacksonville exit to the Jacksonville Highway. Drive west on the Jacksonville Highway (Highway 238) for seven miles to Jacksonsville. Bear left on Highway 238 and drive to Hamilton Road. Turn left (south) on Hamilton Road and drive approximately 0.4 mile to Cantrall Road. Turn right on Cantrall and drive approximately 0.5 mile to the campground.

Contact: Jackson County Parks, 541/774-8183, fax 541/774-6320, www.jacksoncounty parks.com.

173 THE WELLSPRINGS

Scenic rating: 5

near Ashland
See map page 383

This wooded campground has mineral hot springs that empty into a swimming pool. Hot mineral baths are available in private rooms. Massages, sauna use, and swimming are also available for a fee. This is an old Native American birthing ground. Nearby recreation options include a bike path, a golf course, hiking trails, and tennis courts. Boating, fishing, and water-skiing are within 10 miles.

RV sites, facilities: There is a large grassy area for tents, 28 sites with full hookups (30 amps) for RVs of any length, and three tepees. Some sites are pull-through. Picnic tables and fire rings are provided. Restrooms have flush toilets and showers. A coin laundry, ice, volleyball, massage therapists, a soaking pool, a swimming pool, and a sauna are available. Propane gas is within one mile. Leashed pets are permitted with deposit.

Reservations, fees: Reservations are accepted. Tent sites are $15 per night, RV sites are $20 per night, plus $3–6 per person per night for more than two people, and tepees are $25 per night. Some credit cards are accepted. Open year-round.

Directions: From Ashland, drive north on I-5 to Exit 19. Take that exit and drive west for 0.25 mile to the stoplight at Highway 99. Turn right and drive 500 feet to the campground on the left.

Contact: The WellSprings, 541/482-3776, www.jacksonwellsprings.com.

174 GLENYAN CAMPGROUND OF ASHLAND

Scenic rating: 7

near Emigrant Lake
See map page 383

This campground, within seven miles of Ashland and less than one mile from Emigrant

Lake, offers shady sites. Recreation options in the area include a golf course and tennis courts. It's an easy jump from I-5 at Ashland.

RV sites, facilities: There are 46 sites for tents or RVs of any length with full or partial hookups (30 amps) and 22 tent sites. Drinking water, fire rings, and picnic tables are provided. Restrooms have flush toilets and showers. Propane gas, a dump station, wireless Internet service, firewood, a recreation hall, a convenience store, a coin laundry, ice, a playground, and a seasonal heated swimming pool are available. Leashed pets are permitted.

Reservations, fees: Reservations are accepted at 877/453-6926. Sites are $25–27 per night, plus $2 per person per night for more than two people. Some credit cards are accepted. Open year-round.

Directions: From Ashland, drive east on Highway 66 for 3.5 miles to the campground on the right.

Contact: Glenyan Campground of Ashland, 541/488-1785, www.glenyancampground.com.

175 HOWARD PRAIRIE LAKE RESORT

Scenic rating: 7

on Howard Prairie Lake

See map page 383

This wooded campground is along the shore of Howard Prairie Lake, where boating, fishing, hiking, and swimming are among the recreation options. This is one of the largest campgrounds in more than 100 miles.

RV sites, facilities: There are 300 sites for RVs of any length with full hookups (30 amps) and 20 furnished RV rentals. Some sites are pull-through. Picnic tables and fire rings are provided. Restrooms have flush toilets and showers. Propane gas, a dump station, firewood, 24-hour security, a convenience store, a café, a coin laundry, boat docks, boat rentals, moorage, and launching facilities are available. Leashed pets are permitted.

Reservations, fees: Reservations are not ac-

cepted. Sites are $23–25 per night, plus $5 per person per night for more than two people. Some credit cards are accepted. Open mid-April–October.

Directions: In Ashland on I-5, take Exit 14 to Highway 66 and drive east for less than a mile to Dead Indian Memorial Road. Turn left (east) and drive 17 miles to Howard Prairie Road. Turn right (south) and drive two miles to the resort.

Contact: Howard Prairie Lake Resort, 541/482-1979, fax 541/488-7485, www.hplake.com.

176 HOWARD PRAIRIE LAKE RECREATIONAL AREA: LILY GLEN

Scenic rating: 6

near Howard Prairie Lake

See map page 383

Set along the shore of Howard Prairie Lake, this horse camp is a secluded, primitive getaway. The elevation is 4,500 feet. Trout fishing is available. Tubb Springs Wayside State Park and the nearby Rogue River National Forest are possible side trips. There is also nearby access to the Pacific Crest Trail.

RV sites, facilities: There are 26 sites for tents or RVs (no hookups) and two group sites for up to 75 people. Picnic tables and fire grills are provided. Drinking water, vault toilets, individual corrals, and a large barn are available. Some facilities are wheelchair accessible. Leashed pets are permitted.

Reservations, fees: Reservations are accepted for group sites at 541/774-8183 but are not accepted for family sites. Sites are $14–16 per night, $1 per pet per night, and $1 per horse per night for more than two horses; group sites are $50–125 per night. Some credit cards are accepted for reservations. Open mid-April–October.

Directions: In Ashland on I-5, take Exit 14 to Highway 66. Drive east for less than a mile to Dead Indian Memorial Road. Turn left (east) and drive 21 miles to the campground on the right.

OREGON

OREGON

Contact: Jackson County Parks, 541/774-8183, fax 541/774-6320, www.jacksoncounty parks.com.

177 HOWARD PRAIRIE LAKE RECREATIONAL AREA: WILLOW POINT

Scenic rating: 7

near Howard Prairie Lake

See map page 383

Willow Point is the most popular of the three county campgrounds on Howard Prairie Lake. Similar to Grizzly, it offers flat tent sites in an area well covered by trees. The lake is stocked with about 100,000 trout annually.

RV sites, facilities: There are 40 sites for tents or RVs (no hookups). Picnic tables and fire rings are provided. Drinking water, vault toilets, and garbage bins are available. Some facilities are wheelchair accessible. A boat ramp is nearby. A store, a café, laundry facilities, and boat rentals are available within four miles. Leashed pets are permitted.

Reservations, fees: Reservations are not accepted. Sites are $14 per night, $1 per pet per night. Open mid-April–October.

Directions: In Ashland on I-5, take Exit 14 to Highway 66. Drive east for less than a mile to Dead Indian Memorial Road. Turn left (east) and drive 17 miles to Howard Prairie Road. Turn right (south) and drive three miles to the reservoir.

Contact: Jackson County Parks, 541/774-8183, fax 541/774-6320, www.jacksoncounty parks.com.

178 HOWARD PRAIRIE LAKE RECREATIONAL AREA: KLUM LANDING AND SUGAR PINE GROUP CAMP

Scenic rating: 7

near Howard Prairie Lake

See map page 383

Klum Landing is one of three county campgrounds on Howard Prairie Lake. A bonus at this one is that coin-operated showers are available. Sugar Pine Group Camp is more primitive and is situated away from the lake.

RV sites, facilities: At Klum Landing, there are 30 sites for tents or RVs (no hookups). Picnic tables and fire rings are provided. Drinking water, garbage bins, and restrooms with flush toilets and coin showers are available. Some facilities are wheelchair accessible. Sugar Pine can accommodate up to 150 people in tents or self-contained RVs. Vault toilets are available; the facilities are not wheelchair accessible. A boat ramp is nearby. A store, a café, laundry facilities, and boat rentals are available at Howard Prairie Lake Resort. Leashed pets are permitted.

Reservations, fees: Reservations are not accepted for Klum Landing. Sites are $16 per night, plus $1 per pet per night. Reservations are accepted for Sugar Pine Group at 541/774-8183. The group camp is $100–125 per night. Open mid-April–October.

Directions: In Ashland on I-5, take Exit 14 to Highway 66. Drive east for less than a mile to Dead Indian Memorial Road. Turn left (east) and drive 17 miles to Howard Prairie Road. Turn right (south) and drive eight miles to Howard Prairie Dam Road. Turn left (east) and drive 0.25 mile to Sugar Pine Group Camp on the right. Continue 0.75 mile to reach Klum Landing.

Contact: Jackson County Parks, 541/774-8183, fax 541/774-6320, www.jacksoncounty parks.com.

179 EMIGRANT CAMPGROUND

Scenic rating: 8

on Emigrant Lake

See map page 383

This camp is nestled among the trees above Emigrant Lake, a well-known recreational area. Activities at this park include boating, fishing, hiking, swimming, and waterskiing. There are two 280-foot water slides. The park has its own swimming cove (unsupervised). Side-trip possibilities include exploring nearby Mount

Ashland, where a ski area operates in the winter, as well as visiting Ashland's world-renowned Shakespeare Festival, the Britt Music Festival, and historic Jacksonville.

RV sites, facilities: There are 42 sites for tents or RVs (no hookups), 32 sites with full hookups (50 amps) for RVs of any length, an overflow area, and one group camp area for up to 75 people. Restrooms have coin showers. A dump station, snacks in summer, and a barbecue are available. A reservable group picnic and day-use area is also available. Recreational facilities include horseshoe pits, volleyball, and a recreation field. Two boat ramps are provided. Some facilities are wheelchair accessible. Laundry and food facilities are within six miles. Leashed pets are permitted in designated areas only.

Reservations, fees: Reservations are accepted for RV sites and the group site at 541/774-8183. Sites are $16–20 per night, plus $1 per pet per night. The group site is $70–100 per night. Some credit cards are accepted for reservations. Open mid-March–mid-October.

Directions: From Ashland, drive east on Highway 66 for five miles to the campground on the left.

Contact: Jackson County Parks, 541/774-8183, fax 541/774-6320, www.jacksoncounty parks.com.

180 HYATT LAKE

🛶🎣🚤🐕🥾♿🚐⛺

Scenic rating: 8

on Hyatt Lake

See map page 383

This campground is on the south end of Hyatt Reservoir, which has six miles of shoreline. Fishing is good for brook and rainbow trout and smallmouth bass. The boat speed limit here is 10 mph. The Pacific Crest Trail runs next to the campground. Another campground option is Wildcat, about two miles north, with 12 semiprimitive sites.

RV sites, facilities: There are 47 sites for tents or RVs up to 40 feet (no hookups), five horse campsites, one group site for up to 40 people,

and seven walk-in tent sites. Picnic tables and fire grills are provided. Drinking water, restrooms with flush toilets and showers, garbage service, a dump station, a group kitchen, a fish-cleaning station, a day-use area, softball fields, volleyball, a playground, horseshoe pits, and two boat ramps are available. Some facilities are wheelchair accessible. Leashed pets are permitted.

Reservations, fees: Reservations are not accepted. Sites are $12–15 per night, plus $3 per night per additional vehicle, with a 14-day stay limit. Campsites with horse facilities are $10 per night and $5 per night for an additional vehicle; the group site is $95 per night. Sites at nearby primitive Wildcat Campground are $7 per night. Pacific Crest Trail hikers pay $2 per person per night for camping. Open late April–October, weather permitting.

Directions: From Ashland, drive east on Highway 66 for 17 miles to East Hyatt Lake Road. Turn north and drive three miles to the campground entrance on the left.

Contact: Bureau of Land Management, Medford District, 541/618-2200, fax 541/618-2400.

181 HYATT LAKE RESORT

🥾🛶🎣🐕🚐⛺

Scenic rating: 7

on Hyatt Lake

See map page 383

This resort borders Hyatt Lake, just west of the dam, where hiking and fishing are some of the recreation options. This is a scaled-down alternative to the resort at adjacent Howard Prairie Lake. The lake speed limit is 10 mph. The Pacific Crest Trail is just 0.5 mile away.

RV sites, facilities: There are 23 sites with full hookups (30 and 50 amps) for RVs of any length, including three pull-through sites, and 12 sites for tents or RVs (no hookups). There are also four cabins with no kitchen facilities. Drinking water, picnic tables, and fire pits are provided. Restrooms have flush toilets and showers. A dump station, a convenience store, a coin laundry, and ice are available. Boat docks,

OREGON

launching facilities, and rentals are on the resort property. Leashed pets are permitted.

Reservations, fees: Reservations are accepted. Sites are $15–23 per night, plus $5 per night per additional tent. Cabins are $75.75 per night. Some credit cards are accepted. Open April–October.

Directions: From Ashland, drive east on Highway 66 for 17 miles to East Hyatt Lake Road. Turn left (north) and drive three miles to Hyatt Prairie Road. Turn left and drive one mile to the resort on the right.

Contact: Hyatt Lake Resort, 541/482-3331.

182 TOPSY

Scenic rating: 7

on the Upper Klamath River

See map page 383

This campground is on Boyle Reservoir near the Upper Klamath River, a good spot for trout fishing. Swimming is not recommended because of the murky water. This is a top river for rafters (experts only, or nonexperts with professional, licensed guides). There are Class IV and V rapids about four miles southwest at Caldera, Hells Corner, and Satan's Gate. I flipped at Caldera and ended up swimming for it, finally getting out at an eddy. Luckily, I was wearing a dry suit and the best life-jacket available, perfect fitting, which saved my butt.

RV sites, facilities: There are 14 sites with no hookups for RVs up to 40 feet. Picnic tables and fire grills are provided. Drinking water, vault toilets, garbage service, and a dump station are available. Some facilities are wheelchair accessible. Boat-launching facilities are nearby. A camp host is on-site. Leashed pets are permitted.

Reservations, fees: Reservations are not accepted. Sites are $7 per night, plus $4 per night per additional vehicle, with a 14-day stay limit. Open mid-May–mid-September.

Directions: From Klamath Falls, drive west on Highway 66 for 20 miles to Topsy Road. Turn south on Topsy Road and drive 1.5 miles to the campground on the right.

Contact: Bureau of Land Management, Klamath Falls Resource Area, 541/883-6916, fax 541/884-2097.

SOUTHEASTERN OREGON

☾ BEST RV PARKS AND CAMPGROUNDS

☾ Wildlife-Viewing
Chukar Park, page 461.
Adel Store and RV Park, page 472.

☾ Prettiest Rivers
Rome Launch, page 468.

OREGON

Some people think that southeastern Oregon is one big chunk of nothing. They are only half right. True, this high-desert region is dry and foreboding, with many miles between camps in several areas. However, because this part of Oregon is so undervisited, often you'll have vast areas of great land all to yourself.

Among the southeast's highlights is the Newberry Volcanic Monument, with East and Paulina Lakes set within its craters; Paulina is one of the best lakes for a chance to catch big brown trout in the western United States. Here as well is the launch point for one of the best canoe trips, the Owyhee River. This watershed is like nothing most have ever seen. It looks like a miniature Grand Canyon, with steep, orange walls and the river cutting a circuitous route through the desert. I have paddled a canoe through most of it, from remote stretches below the Jarbidge Mountains in Nevada through Idaho and then into Oregon.

Be aware, though, if you tour this area of Oregon, to keep an eye on your gas tank and be alert about how far you are from the coming night's campground. You can cover a hellacious number of miles between a chance for gas and a camp.

Includes:

- Blitzen River
- Campbell Lake
- Chewaucan River
- Chickahominy Reservoir
- Cottonwood Meadow Lake
- Cottonwood Recreation Area
- Dead Horse Lake
- Deep Creek
- Delintment Lake
- Dog Lake
- Fish Lake
- Fremont National Forest
- Goose Lake State Park
- Hart Mountain National Antelope Refuge
- Lake Owyhee State Park
- Lofton Reservoir
- Malheur National Forest
- Malheur National Wildlife Refuge
- Mann Lake
- Mud Creek
- Owyhee Lake
- Steens Mountain Wilderness
- Yellowjacket Lake

OREGON

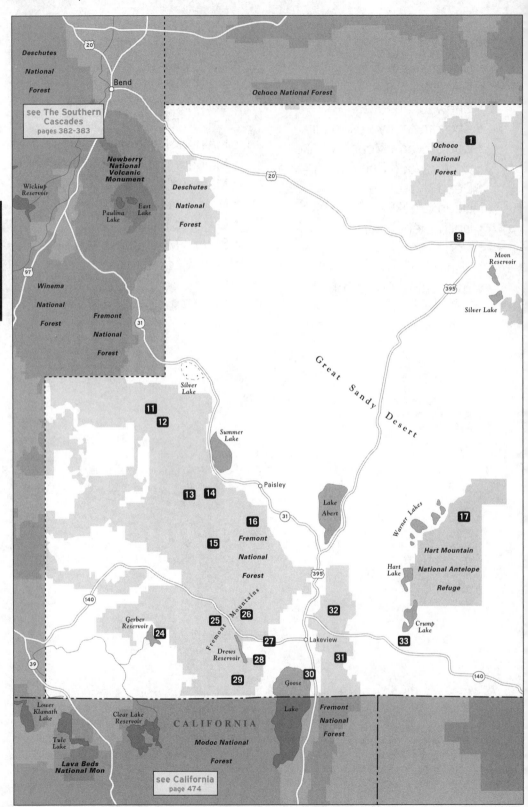

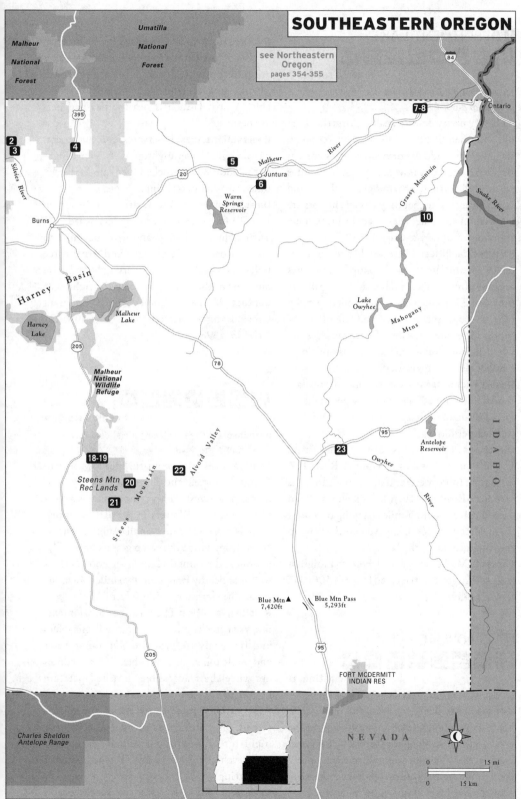

SOUTHEASTERN OREGON

see Northeastern
Oregon
pages 354-355

Malheur

National

Forest

Umatilla

National

Forest

84

Ontario

395

2

3

4

5

7-8

Malheur   River

20   Juntura

6

Warm
Springs
Reservoir

Grassy Mountain

Snake River

Silvies River

10

Burns

Lake
Owyhee

Mahogany
Mtns

Harney   Basin

205

Malheur
Lake

Harney
Lake

Malheur
National
Wildlife
Refuge

78

95

Antelope
Reservoir

23

Owyhee

I D A H O

18-19

Steens Mtn
Rec Lands

20

21

22

Alvord Valley

Steens   Mountain

River

Steens

Blue Mtn ▲
7,420ft

Blue Mtn Pass
5,293ft

95

205

FORT MCDERMITT
INDIAN RES

Charles Sheldon
Antelope Range

N E V A D A

OREGON

0   15 mi

0   15 km

OREGON

1 DELINTMENT LAKE

Scenic rating: 7

on Delintment Lake in Malheur National Forest

See map page 458

This very pretty, forested camp skirts the shore of Delintment Lake. Originally a beaver pond, the lake was gradually developed to its current size of 62 acres. It is now pretty and blue and is stocked with trout, providing good bank and boat fishing. Note that only electric motors are allowed on the lake. Here's an insider's note: Rainbow trout here average 12–18 inches.

RV sites, facilities: There are 29 sites for tents or RVs of any length (no hookups); some sites are pull-through. Picnic tables and fire grills are provided. Drinking water, vault toilets, a camp host, a group picnic area, and boat-launching facilities are available. Some facilities are wheelchair accessible, including a fishing dock. Leashed pets are permitted.

Reservations, fees: Reservations are not accepted. Sites are $8 per night, $4 per night for an additional vehicle. Open May–October, weather permitting.

Directions: From Burns, drive southwest on U.S. 20 for three miles to County Road 127. Turn right (northwest) and drive about 18 miles to Forest Road 41. Turn left on Forest Road 41 and drive about 35 miles (staying on Forest Road 41 at all junctions, paved all the way) to the campground at the lake.

Contact: Malheur National Forest, Emigrant Creek Ranger District, 541/573-4300, fax 541/573-4398.

2 YELLOWJACKET

Scenic rating: 8

on Yellowjacket Lake in Malheur National Forest

See map page 459

This campground (elevation 4,800 feet) in the ponderosa pines is along the shore of Yellowjacket Lake, where fishing for rainbow trout can be very good in the summer. Boats without motors are allowed. The camp is quiet and uncrowded.

RV sites, facilities: There are 20 sites for tents or RVs of any length (no hookups); some sites are pull-through. Picnic tables are provided. Drinking water and vault toilets are available. A boat launch is nearby. Leashed pets are permitted.

Reservations, fees: Reservations are not accepted. Sites are $7 per night, plus $3.50 per night for an additional vehicle. Open late May–October, weather permitting.

Directions: From Burns, drive southwest on U.S. 20 for three miles to County Road 127. Turn right (northwest) and drive 32 miles to Forest Road 37. Turn right and drive three miles to Forest Road 3745. Turn right and drive one mile to the campground on the right.

Contact: Malheur National Forest, Emigrant Creek Ranger District, 541/573-4300, fax 541/573-4398.

3 FALLS

Scenic rating: 5

near Emigrant Creek in Malheur National Forest

See map page 459

Falls camp is in a beautiful meadow next to Emigrant Creek and is surrounded by ponderosa pine forests. This campground is a great place to see wildflowers in the early summer. A short trail leads to a small waterfall on the creek, from which the camp gets its name. Fly-fishing and mountain biking are good here, as well as at nearby Emigrant, two miles down the road. The elevation is 5,200 feet.

RV sites, facilities: There are four sites for tents or RVs of any length (no hookups). Picnic tables and fire grills are provided. Drinking water and vault toilets are available. Some facilities are wheelchair accessible. Leashed pets are permitted.

Reservations, fees: Reservations are not accepted. Sites are $7 per night, plus $3.50 per night for an additional vehicle, except for towed vehicles. Open May–October, weather permitting.

Directions: From Burns, drive southwest on

U.S. 20 for three miles to County Road 127. Turn right (northwest) and drive 25 miles (passing Forest Road 41 on the left) to Forest Road 43 and the junction for Allison Guard Station, Delintment Lake, and Paulina. Turn left on Forest Road 43 and drive eight miles to the campground on the left.

Contact: Malheur National Forest, Emigrant Creek Ranger District, 541/573-4300, fax 541/573-4398.

❹ IDLEWILD

Scenic rating: 8

in Devine Canyon in Malheur National Forest

See map page 459

This campground sits at an elevation of 5,300 feet in Devine Canyon, a designated winter Sno-Park that's popular with locals for snowmobiling and cross-country skiing. Several hiking and biking trailheads start here, including the Divine Summit Interpretive Loop Trail and the Idlewild Loop Trail. Since it provides easy access and a pretty setting, it's also a popular spot for visitors traveling up U.S. 395 and in need of a stopover. Bird-watching for white-headed woodpeckers and goshawks is popular. Expect to hear some highway noise. But the ponderosa pine forest and area trails are so beautiful that this area can feel divine, even if Devine Canyon and neighboring Devine Ridge were named back in the good old days when nobody worried about spelling.

RV sites, facilities: There are 26 sites for tents or RVs of any length (no hookups); some sites are pull-through. Picnic tables and fire grills are provided. Drinking water, a reservable group shelter, picnic areas, and vault toilets are available. Some facilities are wheelchair accessible. Leashed pets are permitted.

Reservations, fees: Reservations are not accepted. Sites are $7 per night, plus $3.50 per night for an additional vehicle, except for towed vehicles. Open late May–mid-October, weather permitting.

Directions: From Burns, drive north on

U.S. 395 for 17 miles to the campground on the right.

Contact: Malheur National Forest, Emigrant Creek Ranger District, 541/573-4300, fax 541/573-4398.

❺ CHUKAR PARK

Scenic rating: 7

near the North Fork of the Malheur River

See map page 459   BEST (

This campground hugs the banks of the North Fork of the Malheur River. The general area provides habitat for chukar, an upland game bird species. Hunting can be good in season during the fall but requires much hiking in rugged terrain. Trout fishing is also popular here. Firewood is not available. The BLM asks that visitors please respect the surrounding private property.

RV sites, facilities: There are 17 sites for tents or RVs up to 36 feet (no hookups). Picnic tables, fire grills, and garbage services are provided. Drinking water (May–October only) and vault toilets are available. Leashed pets are permitted.

Reservations, fees: Reservations are not accepted. Sites are $5 per night per vehicle, with a 14-day stay limit. Open year-round, with limited winter facilities.

Directions: From Burns, drive north on U.S. 395 for three miles to U.S. 20. Take U.S. 20 east and drive 55 miles to Juntura and Beulah Reservoir Road. Turn northwest and drive six miles to the campground.

Contact: Bureau of Land Management, Vale District, 541/473-3144, fax 541/473-6213.

❻ OASIS MOTEL & RV PARK

Scenic rating: 6

in Juntura

See map page 459

One of the few camps in the area, this well-maintained RV park is close to Chukar Park.

OREGON

(See the *Chukar Park* listing in this chapter for more details.)

RV sites, facilities: There are 22 sites with full hookups (20, 30, and 50 amps) for RVs of any length, one cabin, and nine motel rooms. Some sites are pull-through. Picnic tables are provided. Restrooms have flush toilets and showers. A café and ice are available. Leashed pets are permitted.

Reservations, fees: Reservations are not accepted. Sites are $16 per night and $5 per night per pet. Some credit cards are accepted. Open year-round.

Directions: From Burns, drive north on U.S. 395 for three miles to U.S. 20. Turn east and drive 55 miles to Juntura (a very small town). The park is on the left along U.S. 20.

Contact: Oasis Motel & RV Park, 541/277-3605, fax 541/277-3312.

⑦ PROSPECTOR RV PARK

Scenic rating: 5

in Vale

See map page 459

Prospector is one of two RV parks (Westerner RV Park is the other) for travelers in the Vale area. For tents, this one is more comfortable, featuring a specifically designated wooded and grassy area. It claims to be a fishing and hunting paradise, and it even has a game bird–cleaning room. It lies on the historic Oregon Trail.

RV sites, facilities: There are 28 pull-through sites with full hookups (20, 30, and 50 amps) for RVs of any length, plus a separate area for tents. Picnic tables are provided. Restrooms have flush toilets and showers. Propane gas, a dump station, a coin laundry, and ice are available. A store, café, and seasonal heated swimming pool are within one mile. Leashed pets are permitted.

Reservations, fees: Reservations are accepted. Tent sites are $8 per person per night. RV sites are $20–22 per night per RV and $2–5 per person per night for more than two people. Some credit cards are accepted. Open year-round.

Directions: From Ontario (near the Oregon-

Idaho border), drive west on U.S. 20/26 for 12 miles to Vale and U.S. 26. Turn right (north) on U.S. 26 and drive 0.5 mile to Hope Street. Turn right and drive one block east to the park on the left.

Contact: Prospector RV Park, 541/473-3879, fax 541/473-2338.

⑧ WESTERNER MOTEL & RV PARK

Scenic rating: 5

on the Malheur River

See map page 459

This campground on the banks of the Malheur River provides a good layover spot for travelers heading to or from Idaho on U.S. 20/26. (See the *Prospector RV Park* listing in this chapter for more information.)

RV sites, facilities: There are 10 pull-through sites for tents or RVs of any length with full hookups and 14 motel rooms. Drinking water, cable TV, and picnic tables are provided. Propane gas, a store, a café, ice, and a seasonal heated swimming pool are within two blocks. Leashed pets are permitted.

Reservations, fees: Reservations are accepted. Sites are $15 per night, plus $1 per person per night for more than two people. Some credit cards are accepted. Open year-round.

Directions: From Ontario (near the Oregon-Idaho border), drive west on U.S. 20/26 for 12 miles to Vale and the junction of U.S. 26. The campground is on the left at the junction of U.S. 20 and U.S. 26.

Contact: Westerner Motel & RV Park, 541/473-3947.

⑨ CHICKAHOMINY RESERVOIR

Scenic rating: 4

on Chickahominy Reservoir

See map page 458

While a good spot for group camping, this camp is in the high desert with no shade. Weather conditions can be extreme, so come prepared.

The camp is used primarily as an overnight stop for travelers driving through the area. Boats with motors are allowed on the reservoir. There is an access road on the northwest side of the reservoir for day use. The nearest services are five miles east (via U.S. 20) in Riley.

RV sites, facilities: There are 28 sites for tents or RVs up to 35 feet (no hookups). Picnic tables, garbage bins, and fire grills are provided. Drinking water (summer season only) and vault toilets are available. A fish-cleaning station is available nearby. Some facilities are wheelchair accessible. Leashed pets are permitted.

Reservations, fees: Reservations are not accepted. Sites are $8 per night per vehicle, with a stay limit of 14 days. Open year-round, with limited winter facilities.

Directions: From Burns, drive west on U.S. 20 for 30 miles to the campground on the right.

Contact: Bureau of Land Management, Burns District, 541/573-4400, fax 541/573-4411.

10 LAKE OWYHEE STATE PARK

Scenic rating: 7

on Owyhee Lake

See map page 459

There are two campgrounds here, McCormack and Indian Creek, which are 1.5 miles apart. This state park is along the shore of 53-mile-long Owyhee Lake, a good lake for waterskiing in the day and fishing for warm-water species in the morning and evening. Owyhee is famous for its superb bass fishing. The place even has floating restrooms. Other highlights at the park include views of unusual geological formations and huge rock pinnacles. Bighorn sheep, coyotes, golden eagles, mountain lions, mule deer, pronghorn antelope, and wild horses live around here.

RV sites, facilities: McCormack has 31 sites for tents or RVs of any length with partial hookups (30 amps), eight tent sites, and two tepees. Indian Creek has 27 sites for tents or RVs up to 50 feet with full or partial hookups (50 amps). Drinking water, picnic tables, and fire grills are provided. Vault toilets, garbage bins, firewood, a dump station, and a picnic area are available. Restrooms with flush toilets and showers are available at McCormack. A convenience store, gasoline, and propane are available at Indian Creek. Boat docks, launching facilities, fuel, and ice are available nearby. Some facilities are wheelchair accessible. Leashed pets are permitted.

Reservations, fees: Reservations are accepted for tepees only ($6 reservation fee) at 800/452-5687 or www.oregonstateparks.org. Sites are $10–16 per night or $8 per night for overflow sites at Indian Creek; tepees are $27 per night; and it's $5 per night for an additional vehicle. Some credit cards are accepted. Open April–October.

Directions: From Ontario (near the Oregon-Idaho border), drive south on U.S. 20/26 for six miles to the Nyssa exit. Turn south and drive eight miles to Nyssa and Highway 201. Turn left (southeast) on Highway 201 and drive eight miles to Owyhee. Turn east and drive about 20 miles to road's end and the entrance to the park, approximately 33 miles from Nyssa.

Contact: Lake Owyhee State Park, 541/339-2331; Oregon State Parks, 800/551-6949, www.oregonstateparks.org.

11 THOMPSON RESERVOIR

Scenic rating: 3

on Thompson Reservoir in Fremont National Forest

See map page 458

Located on the north shore of Thompson Reservoir among black-bark ponderosa pines the height of telephone poles, this simple and pretty camp features shaded sites close to the water. The area is popular for fishing and boating. Water in the reservoir fluctuates and sometimes nearly dries up altogether in late summer.

RV sites, facilities: There are 19 sites for tents or RVs up to 22 feet (no hookups), plus a separate group camping area. Picnic tables and fire grills are provided. Drinking water and

OREGON

vault toilets are available. Garbage must be packed out. Boat-launching facilities are nearby. Leashed pets are permitted.

Reservations, fees: Reservations are not accepted. There is no fee for camping. Open May–mid-November, weather permitting, with a 14-day stay limit.

Directions: From Bend, drive south on U.S. 97 for 32 miles to Highway 31. Turn southeast on Highway 31 and drive 48 miles to County Road 4-11 (one mile west of the town of Silver Lake). Turn right and drive six miles (the road becomes Forest Road 27) and continue south for nine miles to the campground entrance road. Turn left and drive one mile to the camp.

Contact: Fremont-Winema National Forests, Silver Lake Ranger District, 541/576-2107, fax 541/576-7587.

12 EAST BAY

Scenic rating: 3

on Thompson Reservoir in Fremont National Forest
See map page 458

This campground on the east shore of Thompson Reservoir has paved roads, but it's still a long way from home, so be sure to bring all of your supplies with you. A day-use area is adjacent to the camp. Silver Creek Marsh Campground provides an even more primitive setting along a stream.

RV sites, facilities: There are 17 sites for tents or RVs up to 50 feet (no hookups). Picnic tables and fire grills are provided. Drinking water, garbage bins, vault toilets, and a fishing pier are available. Some facilities are wheelchair accessible. Boat-launching facilities are nearby. Leashed pets are permitted.

Reservations, fees: Reservations are not accepted. Sites are $8 per night. Open May–mid-November, weather permitting.

Directions: From Bend, drive south on U.S. 97 for 32 miles to Highway 31. Turn southeast on Highway 31 and drive 49 miles to Silver Lake. Continue east a short distance on Highway 31 to Forest Road 28. Turn right on Forest Road

28 and drive 13 miles to Forest Road 014. Turn right on Forest Road 014 and drive two miles to the campground.

Contact: Fremont-Winema National Forests, Silver Lake Ranger District, 541/576-2107, fax 541/576-7587.

13 DEAD HORSE LAKE

Scenic rating: 9

on Dead Horse Lake in Fremont National Forest
See map page 458

The shore of Dead Horse Lake is home to this camp (at 7,372 feet elevation). It generally fills on most weekends and holidays. A hiking trail winds around the perimeter of the lake, hooking up with other trails along the way. One original Civilian Conservation Corps canoe, a relic of the 1930s, remains in the lake. Nearby Fremont National Forest provides good side trips. (See the *Campbell Lake* listing in this chapter for more information.)

RV sites, facilities: There are nine sites for tents or RVs up to 25 feet (no hookups) and a separate group area for up to 40 people. Picnic tables and fire grills are provided. Drinking water and vault toilets are available, but garbage must be packed out. A boat launch and day-use area are nearby. Boats with electric motors are permitted, but gas motors are prohibited. Leashed pets are permitted.

Reservations, fees: Reservations are not accepted. There is no fee for camping. Open July–October, weather permitting.

Directions: From Lakeview, drive north on U.S. 395 for 23 miles to Highway 31. Turn northwest and drive 22 miles to Paisley. Continue on Highway 31 for 0.5 mile to Mill Street. Turn west on Mill Street and drive 20 miles (the road becomes Forest Road 033); continue to the T intersection with Forest Road 28. Turn right and drive 11 miles (watch for the turn to Campbell-Dead Horse Lakes) to Forest Road 033. Turn left and drive three miles (gravel road) to the campground.

Contact: Fremont-Winema National Forests,

Paisley Ranger District, 541/943-3114, fax 541/943-4479.

14 CAMPBELL LAKE

Scenic rating: 9

on Campbell Lake in Fremont National Forest

See map page 458

This campground on the pebbled shore of Campbell Lake is near Dead Horse Lake Campground. These high-elevation, crystal-clear lakes were formed during the glacier period, evidence of which can be found on the nearby Lakes Trail system. Both camps are very busy, filling most weekends in July and August. No gas motors are permitted on Campbell Lake. Good side trips are available in Fremont National Forest. A U.S. Forest Service map details the back roads.

RV sites, facilities: There are 16 sites for tents or RVs up to 25 feet (no hookups). Picnic tables and fire grills are provided. Drinking water and vault toilets are available. A boat launch and day-use area are adjacent to the camp. Boats with electric motors are permitted, but gas motors are prohibited. Garbage must be packed out. Leashed pets are permitted.

Reservations, fees: Reservations are not accepted. There is no fee for camping. Open July–late October, weather permitting.

Directions: From Lakeview, drive north on U.S. 395 for 23 miles to Highway 31. Turn northwest and drive 22 miles to Paisley. Continue on Highway 31 for 0.5 mile to Mill Street. Turn west on Mill Street and drive 20 miles (the road becomes Forest Road 33) and continue to the T intersection with Forest Road 28. Turn right and drive eight miles to Forest Road 033. Turn left and drive two miles to the campground.

Contact: Fremont-Winema National Forests, Paisley Ranger District, 541/943-3114, fax 541/943-4479.

15 DAIRY POINT

Scenic rating: 6

on Dairy Creek in Fremont National Forest

See map page 458

This campground, elevation 5,200 feet, is next to the Dairy Creek Bridge in a stand of ponderosa pine and white fir at the edge of a large and open meadow. The setting is beautiful and peaceful, with a towering backdrop of mountains. In the spring, wildflowers are a sight to behold; bird-watching can also be excellent this time of year. Fishing and inner tubing are popular activities at Dairy Creek. Warning: This campground is suitable for large groups and is often full on holidays and most weekends.

RV sites, facilities: There are five sites for tents or RVs up to 25 feet (no hookups). Picnic tables and fire grills are provided. A vault toilet and drinking water are provided. Garbage must be packed out. Leashed pets are permitted.

Reservations, fees: Reservations are not accepted. There is no fee for camping. Open mid-May–October, weather permitting.

Directions: From Lakeview, drive north on U.S. 395 for 23 miles to Highway 31. Turn northwest and drive 22 miles to Paisley. Continue on Highway 31 for 0.5 mile to Mill Street. Turn west on Mill Street and drive 20 miles (the road becomes Forest Road 33); continue to the T intersection with Forest Road 28. Turn left and drive two miles (crossing the Dairy Creek Bridge) to Forest Road 3428. Turn left and drive to the campground (just past the intersection on the left).

Contact: Fremont-Winema National Forests, Paisley Ranger District, 541/943-3114, fax 541/943-4479.

16 MARSTER SPRING

Scenic rating: 6

on the Chewaucan River in Fremont National Forest

See map page 458

This pretty campground (4,845 feet elevation) is on the banks of the Chewaucan River, a good

OREGON

OREGON

fishing area. The largest of several popular camps in this river corridor, Marster Spring sits right on the river among ponderosa pine trees, yet is close to the town of Paisley. The Fremont National Recreation Trail is accessible at the Chewaucan Crossing Trailhead, 0.25 mile to the south.

RV sites, facilities: There are 10 sites for tents or RVs up to 22 feet (no hookups). Picnic tables and fire grills are provided. Drinking water and vault toilets are available. Leashed pets are permitted.

Reservations, fees: Reservations are not accepted. There is no fee for camping. Open May–October, weather permitting.

Directions: From Lakeview, drive north on U.S. 395 for 23 miles to Highway 31. Turn northwest and drive 22 miles to Paisley. Continue on Highway 31 for 0.5 mile to Mill Street. Turn west on Mill Street and drive 7.5 miles (the road becomes Forest Road 33) to the campground on the left.

Contact: Fremont-Winema National Forests, Paisley Ranger District, 541/943-3114, fax 541/943-4479.

17 HART MOUNTAIN NATIONAL ANTELOPE REFUGE/ HOT SPRINGS

Scenic rating: 6

near Adel

See map page 458

One of the few campgrounds managed by the U.S. Fish and Wildlife Service, this unusual refuge features canyons and hot springs in a high-desert area. The hot springs get the highest use in the summer. There is no drinking water at the campground, but it can be obtained at the headquarters, which you pass on the way in. Some of Oregon's largest antelope herds roam this large area. This campground is popular with hunters in the fall. The nearest place for supplies is in the town of Plush.

Campsites, facilities: There are 30 sites for tents or RVs up to 20 feet (no hookups). Some sites have fire rings. Pit toilets are provided, but there is no drinking water. Garbage must be packed

out. Camp host is usually on-site during the summer season. Some facilities are wheelchair accessible. Leashed pets are permitted.

Reservations, fees: Reservations are not accepted. There is no fee for camping. Open year-round, weather permitting, with a 14-day stay limit.

Directions: From Lakeview, drive north on U.S. 395 for five miles to Highway 140. Turn east on Highway 140 and drive 28 miles to Adel and the Plush-Hart Mountain Cutoff. Turn left (signed for Hart Antelope Refuge) and drive north for 43 miles (first paved, then gravel) to the refuge headquarters. Continue four miles to the campground (the road is often impassable in the winter).

Contact: Hart Mountain National Antelope Refuge, 541/947-3315 or 541/947-2731, fax 541/947-4414, www.fws.gov/sheldonhartmtn.

18 STEENS MOUNTAIN RESORT

Scenic rating: 9

on the Blitzen River

See map page 459

The self-proclaimed "gateway to the Steens Mountain," this resort is bordered by the Malheur National Wildlife Refuge on three sides, and it has great views. The mile-high mountain and surrounding gorges make an excellent photo opportunity. Hiking and hunting are other possibilities. Fishing is available on the Blitzen River, with easy access from the camp.

RV sites, facilities: There are 45 pull-through sites for RVs of any length with full hookups (30 amps), 25 tent sites, plus nine cabins and one rental home. Picnic tables and fire pits are provided. Drinking water, restrooms with showers, a dump station, a coin laundry, limited groceries and fishing supplies, and ice are available. Leashed pets are permitted.

Reservations, fees: Reservations are accepted at 800/542-3765. Sites are $15–23 per night and $5 per person per night for more than two people. Some credit cards are accepted. Open year-round.

Directions: From Burns, drive east on Highway 78 for two miles to Highway 205. Turn right (south) on Highway 205 and drive 59 miles to Frenchglen and Steens Mountain Road. Turn left (east) and drive three miles to the resort on the right.

Contact: Steens Mountain Resort, 541/493-2415, www.steensmountainresort.com.

19 PAGE SPRINGS

Scenic rating: 7

near Malheur National Wildlife Refuge
See map page 459

This campground is adjacent to the Malheur National Wildlife Refuge. The Frenchglen Hotel (three miles away) is administered by the state parks department and offers overnight accommodations and meals. Activities include hiking on the area trails, plus bird-watching, fishing, hunting, and sightseeing.

RV sites, facilities: There are 36 sites for tents or RVs up to 34 feet (no hookups). Picnic tables and fire grills are provided. Drinking water, vault toilets, a day-use area with a shelter, and garbage bins are available. Some facilities are wheelchair accessible. Leashed pets are permitted.

Reservations, fees: Reservations are not accepted. Sites are $8 per vehicle per night, with a 14-day stay limit. Open year-round.

Directions: From Burns, drive east on Highway 78 for two miles to Highway 205. Turn south on Highway 205 and drive 60 miles to Frenchglen and Steens Mountain Loop Road. Turn left (east) and drive three miles to the campground.

Contact: Bureau of Land Management, Burns District, 541/573-4400, fax 541/573-4411.

20 FISH LAKE

Scenic rating: 8

on Fish Lake
See map page 459

The shore of Fish Lake is the setting for this primitive but pretty camp. Set among the aspens

at 7,400 feet elevation, it can make an excellent weekend-getaway spot for sightseeing. Trout fishing is an option, made easier by the boat ramp near camp.

RV sites, facilities: There are 23 sites for tents or RVs up to 30 feet (no hookups). Picnic tables and fire grills are provided. Drinking water, garbage bins, and vault toilets are available. Boat-launching facilities are nearby (nonmotorized boats only). Some facilities are wheelchair accessible. Leashed pets are permitted.

Reservations, fees: Reservations are not accepted. Sites are $8 per vehicle per night, with a 14-day stay limit. Open June–October, weather permitting.

Directions: From Burns, drive east on Highway 78 for two miles to Highway 205. Turn south on Highway 205 and drive 60 miles to Frenchglen and Steens Mountain Loop Road. Turn left (east) and drive 17 miles to the campground.

Contact: Bureau of Land Management, Burns District, 541/573-4400, fax 541/573-4411.

21 SOUTH STEENS

Scenic rating: 6

near Steens Mountain Wilderness
See map page 459

This campground hugs the edge of the Steens Mountain Wilderness. The area features deep, glacier-carved gorges, volcanic uplifts, stunning scenery, and a rare chance to see elk and bighorn sheep. Redband trout fishing is a mile away at Donner und Blitzen Wild and Scenic River and its tributaries, a designated reserve. This campground is also good for horse campers, providing them with a separate area from the other campers. Trails are accessible from the campground.

RV sites, facilities: There are 36 sites for tents or RVs up to 35 feet (no hookups); 15 of the sites are designated for horse campers. Picnic tables, corrals, hitching posts, and fire grills are provided. Drinking water and vault toilets are available. Some facilities are wheelchair accessible. Leashed pets are permitted.

OREGON

Reservations, fees: Reservations are not accepted. There is a 14-day stay limit. Sites are $6 per vehicle per night. Open May–October, weather permitting.

Directions: From Burns, drive east on Highway 78 for two miles to Highway 205. Turn south on Highway 205 and drive 60 miles to Frenchglen. Continue south on Highway 205 for 10 miles to Steens South Loop Road. Turn left (east) and drive 18 miles to the campground on the right.

Contact: Bureau of Land Management, Burns District, 541/573-4400, fax 541/573-4411.

22 MANN LAKE

Scenic rating: 8

on Mann Lake

See map page 459

Mann Lake has two small boat ramps and a 10-horsepower limit on motors. Fishing, including wintertime ice fishing, and wildlife-viewing are popular here. Weather can be extreme. The campground sits at the base of Steens Mountain and is open, with sagebrush and no trees. The scenic, high-desert camp is mainly used as a fishing camp; please respect private property on parcels of land next to the lake. Fishing can be very good for cutthroat trout. Nearby Alvord Desert is also an attraction.

RV sites, facilities: There are dispersed sites for tents or RVs up to 35 feet, as well as open areas on each side of the lake. Vault toilets are available. No drinking water is available. Some facilities are wheelchair accessible. Garbage must be packed out. Leashed pets are permitted.

Reservations, fees: Reservations are not accepted. There is no fee for camping. Open year-round.

Directions: From Burns, drive southeast on Highway 78 for 65 miles to East Steens Road. Turn right (south) and drive 22 miles to the campground at Mann Lake.

Contact: Bureau of Land Management, Burns District, 541/573-4400, fax 541/573-4411.

23 ROME LAUNCH

Scenic rating: 6

on the Owyhee River

See map page 459   BEST (

This campground is used mainly by people rafting the Owyhee River and overnighters passing through. A few cottonwood trees and sagebrush dot this campground. There are some farms and ranches in the area. Campsites are adjacent to the Owyhee River. I have canoed most of the Owyhee from the headwaters in Nevada below the Jarbidge Mountains all the way through Idaho and into Oregon, and I would rate this river as one of the top canoeing destinations in North America. The Owyhee Canyon is quite dramatic, like a miniature Grand Canyon. Rome Launch is also a good wildlife-viewing area; mountain lions and bobcats have been spotted. Note: No motorized boats are allowed on the river.

RV sites, facilities: There are five sites for tents or small RVs (no hookups). Picnic tables and fire rings are provided. Drinking water, vault toilets, and a boat launch are available. No firewood is available, and all garbage must be packed out. Leashed pets are permitted.

Reservations, fees: Reservations are not accepted. There is no fee for camping. Open March–October, weather permitting.

Directions: From Burns Junction, drive east on U.S. 95 for 15 miles to Jordan Valley and the signed turnoff for the Owyhee River and BLM-Rome boat launch. Turn south and drive 0.25 mile to the campground.

Contact: Bureau of Land Management, Vale District, 541/473-3144, fax 541/473-6213.

24 GERBER RESERVOIR

Scenic rating: 6

on Gerber Reservoir

See map page 458

This camp can be found at an elevation of 4,800 feet alongside the west shore of Gerber Reservoir. Off the beaten path, Gerber attracts mainly locals. Recreation options include boating (10-mph speed limit), fishing, and hiking. Swimming is not popular here because the water is murky with algae.

RV sites, facilities: There are 50 sites for tents or RVs up to 30 feet (no hookups) and a primitive group area for up to 20 people. Picnic tables and fire grills are provided. Drinking water, a dump station, vault toilets, a boat ramp, a boat dock, launching facilities, and two fish-cleaning stations are available. Some facilities are wheelchair accessible. Leashed pets are permitted.

Reservations, fees: Reservations are not accepted. Sites are $7 per night, plus $4 per night for an additional vehicle. Open year-round, with drinking water and services available May–mid-September.

Directions: From Klamath Falls, drive east on Highway 140 for 16 miles to Dairy and Highway 70. Turn right (south) on Highway 70 and drive seven miles to Bonanza and East Langell Valley Road. Turn left (east) on East Langell Valley Road and drive 11 miles to Gerber Road. Turn left on Gerber Road and drive eight miles to the campground on the right.

Contact: Bureau of Land Management, Klamath Falls Resource Area, 541/883-6916, fax 541/884-2097.

25 LOFTON RESERVOIR

Scenic rating: 6

on Lofton Reservoir in Fremont National Forest

See map page 458

This remote campground sits on the shore of Lofton Reservoir, a small lake that can provide the best trout fishing in this region. Other nearby lakes are accessible by forest roads. This area marks the beginning of the Great Basin, a high-desert area that extends to Idaho. A large fire burned much of the surrounding forest about 20 years ago, making this campground an oasis of sorts.

RV sites, facilities: There are 26 sites for tents or RVs up to 22 feet (no hookups). Picnic tables and fire grills are provided. Vault toilets are available. No drinking water is available. Garbage must be packed out. Boat docks and launching facilities are nearby. Some facilities are wheelchair accessible, including a fishing pier. Leashed pets are permitted.

Reservations, fees: Reservations are not accepted. There is no fee for camping. Open mid-May–late October, weather permitting.

Directions: From Klamath Falls, drive east on Highway 140 for 54 miles to Bly. Continue east on Highway 140 for 13 miles to Forest Road 3715. Turn right and drive seven miles to Forest Road 013. Turn left on Forest Road 013 and drive one mile to the campground.

Contact: Fremont-Winema National Forests, Bly Ranger District, 541/353-2427, fax 541/353-2750.

OREGON

26 COTTONWOOD RECREATION AREA

Scenic rating: 6

on Cottonwood Meadow Lake in Fremont National Forest

See map page 458

This campground along the upper shore of Cottonwood Meadow Lake is one of the better spots in the vicinity for fishing and hiking. Boats with electric motors are allowed on the lake, but gas motors are prohibited. Three hiking trails wind around the lake, and facilities for horses include hitching posts, feeders, water, and corrals. The camp is at an elevation of 6,130 feet in a forested setting with aspen and many huge ponderosa pines.

RV sites, facilities: There are 12 sites for tents or RVs up to 28 feet (no hookups) and nine walk-in tent sites. Picnic tables and fire grills are provided. Drinking water and vault toilets are available, but garbage must be packed out. A camp host is on-site. Two boat ramps are nearby. No gasoline motors are allowed on the lake. The boating speed limit is 5 mph. Leashed pets are permitted.

Reservations, fees: Reservations are not accepted.

There is no fee for camping. Open early June– mid-October, weather permitting.

Directions: From Lakeview, drive west on Highway 140 for 21 miles to Forest Road 3870. Turn right and drive about 10 miles to the campground.

Contact: Fremont-Winema National Forests, Lakeview Ranger District, 541/947-3334, fax 541/947-6375.

27 JUNIPERS RESERVOIR RV RESORT

Scenic rating: 6

on Junipers Reservoir

See map page 458

This resort on an 8,000-acre cattle ranch is in a designated Oregon Wildlife Viewing Area, and campers may catch glimpses of seldom-seen species. Many nature-walking trails meander through the park, and guests can also take driving tours. Fishing for catfish and trout can be good, and because it is a private lake no fishing license is required. The summer climate is mild and pleasant. Antelope and elk can be spotted in this area.

RV sites, facilities: There is a grassy area for tents and 40 pull-through sites with full or partial hookups (20, 30, and 50 amps) for RVs of any length. Picnic tables are provided. Drinking water, restrooms with showers, a dump station, Wi-Fi and computer modem access, a coin laundry, a community fire pit, and ice are available. Recreational facilities include a recreation hall, a volleyball court, and horseshoe pits. Some of the facilities are wheelchair accessible. Leashed pets are permitted.

Reservations, fees: Reservations are recommended. Tent sites are $22.50 per night, and RV sites are $25.50 per night. Weekly rates available. Open May–mid-October.

Directions: From Lakeview, drive west on Highway 140 for 10 miles to the resort (at Milepost 86.5) on the right.

Contact: Junipers Reservoir RV Resort, 541/947-2050, www.junipersrv.com.

28 DREWS CREEK

Scenic rating: 9

near Lakeview in Fremont National Forest

See map page 458

This is an exceptionally beautiful campground, set along Drews Creek at 4,900 feet elevation. Gorgeous, wild roses grow near the creek, and several unmarked trails lead to nearby hills where campers can enjoy scenic views. A great spot for a family trip, Drews Creek features horseshoe pits, an area for baseball, and a large group barbecue, making it equally popular with group campers. Fishing is available in nearby Dog Lake, which also provides facilities for boating. Waterskiing is another option at Drews Reservoir, two miles to the west.

RV sites, facilities: There are five sites for tents or RVs up to 30 feet (no hookups). Picnic tables, fire grills, vault toilets, and drinking water are provided. Garbage must be packed out. Leashed pets are permitted.

Reservations, fees: Reservations are not accepted. There is no fee for camping. Open early June–mid-October, weather permitting.

Directions: From Lakeview, drive west on Highway 140 for 10 miles to County Road 1-13. Turn left and drive four miles to County Road 1-11D. Turn right and drive six miles (the road will become Forest Road 4017) to the bridge that provides access to the campground.

Contact: Fremont-Winema National Forests, Lakeview Ranger District, 541/947-3334, fax 541/947-6375.

29 DOG LAKE

Scenic rating: 5

on Dog Lake in Fremont National Forest

See map page 458

This campground is on the west shore of Dog Lake at an elevation of 5,100 feet. Fishing and boats with motors are permitted, though speeds are limited to 5 mph. Dog Lake provides a popular fishery for bass, crappie, and perch. Native Americans named the lake for its resemblance in shape to the hind leg of a dog. Prospects for seeing waterfowl and eagles are good.

RV sites, facilities: There are 12 sites for tents or RVs up to 16 feet (no hookups). Drinking water, picnic tables, and fire grills are provided. Vault toilets are available. Garbage must be packed out. A boat launch is nearby. Leashed pets are permitted.

Reservations, fees: Reservations are not accepted. There is no fee for camping. Open mid-April–mid-October, weather permitting.

Directions: From Lakeview, drive west on Highway 140 for seven miles to County Road 1-13. Turn left on County Road 1-13 and drive four miles to County Road 1-11D (Dog Lake Road). Turn right and drive four miles (the road becomes Forest Road 4017) into national forest. Continue on Forest Road 4017 for 12 miles (two miles past Drew Reservoir) to Dog Lake and the campground entrance on the left.

Contact: Fremont-Winema National Forests, Lakeview Ranger District, 541/947-3334, fax 541/947-6375.

30 GOOSE LAKE STATE PARK

Scenic rating: 7

on Goose Lake
See map page 458

This park is on the east shore of unusual Goose Lake, which lies half in Oregon and half in California. The fishing at the lake is poor, but better fishing is available in nearby streams. Waterfowl from the Pacific Flyway frequent this out-of-the-way spot. It is home to many species of birds and other wildlife, including a large herd of mule deer that spends much of the time in the campground.

RV sites, facilities: There are 47 sites for tents or RVs up to 40 feet with partial hookups (20 amps). Picnic tables, fire grills, garbage bins, and drinking water are provided. A camp host is on-site. Restrooms have flush toilets and show-

ers. A dump station and firewood are available. Leashed pets are permitted.

Reservations, fees: Reservations are not accepted. Sites are $12–16 per night, plus $5 per night for an additional vehicle. Open mid-April–mid-October.

Directions: From Lakeview, drive south on U.S. 395 for 14 miles to the California border and Stateline Road. Turn right (west) and drive one mile to the campground.

Contact: Goose Lake State Park, 541/947-3111; Oregon State Parks, 800/551-6949, www.oregon stateparks.org.

31 DEEP CREEK

Scenic rating: 8

on Deep Creek in Fremont National Forest
See map page 458

Shaded by huge ponderosa pines and cottonwoods and nestled on the banks of Deep Creek, this pretty, little-used campground is the place if you're after privacy. Deep Creek is a good fishing stream. Magnificent spring wildflowers are a highlight here. The camp sits at an elevation of 5,600 feet.

RV sites, facilities: There are six sites for tents or RVs up to 22 feet (no hookups). Picnic tables and fire grills are provided. Vault toilets are available. There is no drinking water, and garbage must be packed out. Leashed pets are permitted.

Reservations, fees: Reservations are not accepted. There is no fee for camping. Open June–mid-October, weather permitting.

Directions: From Lakeview, drive five miles north on U.S. 395 to Highway 140. Turn right (east) on Highway 140 and drive six miles to Forest Road 3915. Turn right on Forest Road 3915 and drive 14 miles to Deep Creek and the campground entrance road on the right (Forest Road 4015). Turn right and drive one mile to the campground on the right.

Contact: Fremont-Winema National Forests, Lakeview Ranger District, 541/947-3334, fax 541/947-6375.

OREGON

32 MUD CREEK

Scenic rating: 4

on Mud Creek in Fremont National Forest

See map page 458

This remote and quiet camp (at 6,600 feet elevation) sits in an isolated stand of lodgepole pines along the banks of Mud Creek. Drake Peak (8,405 feet elevation) is nearby. There are no other camps in the immediate vicinity. Fishing in Mud Creek is surprisingly good.

RV sites, facilities: There are seven sites for tents or RVs up to 16 feet (no hookups). Picnic tables and fire grills are provided. Drinking water and vault toilets are available. Garbage must be packed out. Leashed pets are permitted.

Reservations, fees: Reservations are not accepted. There is no fee for camping. Open June–mid-October, weather permitting.

Directions: From Lakeview, drive five miles north on U.S. 395 to Highway 140. Turn right on Highway 140 and drive eight miles to Forest Road 3615. Turn left and drive seven miles to the campground.

Contact: Fremont-Winema National Forests, Lakeview Ranger District, 541/947-3334, fax 541/947-6375.

33 ADEL STORE AND RV PARK

Scenic rating: 5

in Adel

See map page 458   BEST (

This remote park is the only game in town, so you'd better grab it while you can. Recreation options in the area include hang gliding, rockhounding, and visiting hot springs at the Hart Mountain National Antelope Refuge, 40 miles north of Adel.

RV sites, facilities: There are seven sites for RVs of any length with full hookups (30 amps). Barbecues are provided. A store, a small café, gasoline, and ice are available. Leashed pets are permitted.

Reservations, fees: Reservations are accepted. Tent sites are $10 per night, and RV sites are $15 per night. Some credit cards are accepted but not for the purchase of gasoline. Open year-round.

Directions: From Lakeview, drive five miles north on U.S. 395 to Highway 140. Turn right (east) on Highway 140 and drive 28 miles to Adel (a very small town). The RV park is in town along Highway 140 on the right.

Contact: Adel Store and RV Park, 541/947-3850.

California

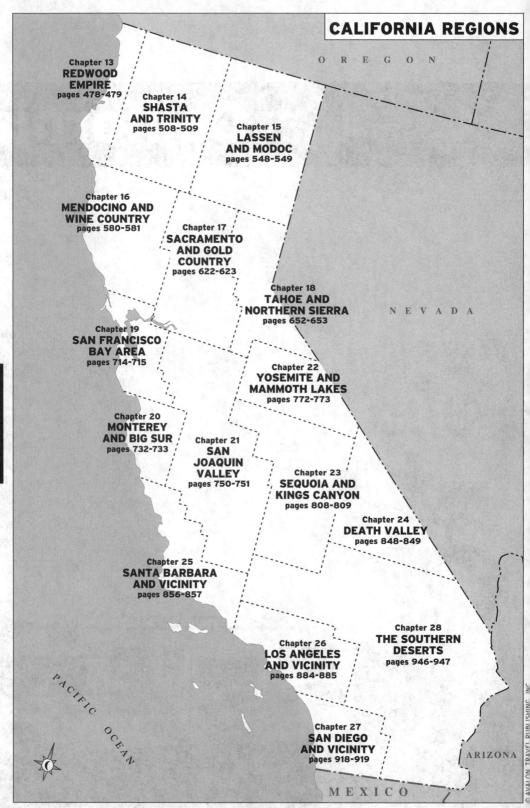

CALIFORNIA

CALIFORNIA REGIONS

O R E G O N

Chapter 13
REDWOOD EMPIRE
pages 478-479

Chapter 14
SHASTA AND TRINITY
pages 508-509

Chapter 15
LASSEN AND MODOC
pages 548-549

Chapter 16
MENDOCINO AND WINE COUNTRY
pages 580-581

Chapter 17
SACRAMENTO AND GOLD COUNTRY
pages 622-623

Chapter 18
TAHOE AND NORTHERN SIERRA
pages 652-653

N E V A D A

Chapter 19
SAN FRANCISCO BAY AREA
pages 714-715

Chapter 22
YOSEMITE AND MAMMOTH LAKES
pages 772-773

Chapter 20
MONTEREY AND BIG SUR
pages 732-733

Chapter 21
SAN JOAQUIN VALLEY
pages 750-751

Chapter 23
SEQUOIA AND KINGS CANYON
pages 808-809

Chapter 24
DEATH VALLEY
pages 848-849

Chapter 25
SANTA BARBARA AND VICINITY
pages 856-857

Chapter 28
THE SOUTHERN DESERTS
pages 946-947

Chapter 26
LOS ANGELES AND VICINITY
pages 884-885

P A C I F I C   O C E A N

Chapter 27
SAN DIEGO AND VICINITY
pages 918-919

A R I Z O N A

M E X I C O

© AVALON TRAVEL PUBLISHING, INC.

REDWOOD EMPIRE

☾ BEST RV PARKS AND CAMPGROUNDS

Visitors come from around the world to the Redwood

Empire for one reason: to see the groves of giant redwoods, the tallest trees in the world. On a perfect day in the redwoods here, refracted sunlight beams through the forest canopy, creating a solemn, cathedral-like effect. It feels as if you are standing in the center of the earth's pure magic.

But the redwood forests are only one of the attractions in this area. The Smith River canyon, Del Norte and Humboldt Coasts, and the remote edge of the Siskiyou Wilderness in Six Rivers National Forest all make this region like none other in the world.

On sunny days in late summer, some visitors are incredulous that so few people live in the Redwood Empire. The reason is the same one that explains why the trees grow so tall: rain in the winter – often for weeks at a time – and fog in the summer. If the sun does manage to appear, it's an event almost worthy of calling the police to say you've spotted a large, yellow Unidentified Flying Object. So most folks are content to just visit.

Three stellar areas should be on your must-see list for outstanding days of adventure here: the redwood parks from Trinidad to Klamath River, the Smith River National Recreation Area, and the Lost Coast.

I've hiked every trailhead from Trinidad to Crescent City, and the hikes here feature some of the best adventuring day trips in Northern California. A good place to start is Prairie Creek Redwoods State Park, where you can see fantastic herds of Roosevelt elk. Then head over to the beach by hiking Fern Canyon, where you walk for 20 minutes at the bottom of a canyon adjacent to vertical walls covered with ferns, and then continue north on the Coastal Trail, where you'll pass through pristine woodlands and fantastic expanses of untouched beaches. All the trails through the redwoods north of the Klamath River are winners; it's just a matter of matching your level of ambition to the right hike.

The Smith River National Recreation Area is equally gorgeous. The Smith is one of the last major free-flowing rivers in America. Wild, pristine, and beautiful, it's set in a series of gorges and bordered by national forest. The centerpiece is Jedediah Smith Redwoods State Park and its grove of monster-sized redwoods. South Fork Road provides an extended tour into Six Rivers National Forest along the South Fork Smith River, with the option of visiting many of the largest trees in Jedediah Smith Redwoods State Park. The turnoff is on U.S. 199 just northeast of the town of Hiouchi. Turn right, cross two bridges, and you will arrive at a fork in the road. Turning left at the fork will take you along the South Fork Smith River and deep into Six Rivers National Forest. Turning right at the fork will take you to a series of trailheads for hikes into redwoods. Of these, the best is the Boy Scout Tree Trail.

The Lost Coast is often overlooked by visitors because of the difficulty in reaching it; your only access is via a slow, curvy road through the Mattole River Valley, past Petrolia, and out to a piece of coast. The experience is like being in suspended animation – your surroundings are peaceful and pristine, with a striking lack of people. One of the best ways to capture the sensation is to drive out near the mouth of the Mattole, then hike south on the Coastal Trail long enough to get a feel for the area.

Compared to other regions in California, this corner of the state is somewhat one-dimensional. The emphasis is primarily on exploring the redwoods and the coast, and to some extent, the Smith River. Most of the campgrounds here are designed with that in mind.

Many private campgrounds are on U.S. 101 as well as near the mouths of the Smith and Klamath Rivers. These make fine base camps for fishing trips when the salmon are running. The state and national park campgrounds in the redwoods are in high demand, and reservations are often necessary in the peak vacation season. On the opposite end of the spectrum are primitive and remote settings in Six Rivers National Forest, the Lost Coast, and even a few surprise nuggets in Redwood National Park.

CALIFORNIA

Includes:

- Benbow Lake State Recreation Area
- Del Norte Coast Redwoods State Park
- Eel River
- Gold Bluff Beach
- Grizzly Creek Redwoods State Park
- Humboldt Bay
- Humboldt Redwoods State Park
- Jedediah Smith Redwoods State Park
- Klamath River
- Mattole River
- Patrick's Point State Park
- Prairie Creek Redwoods State Park
- Richardson Grove State Park
- Six Rivers National Forest
- Smith River
- Van Duzen River

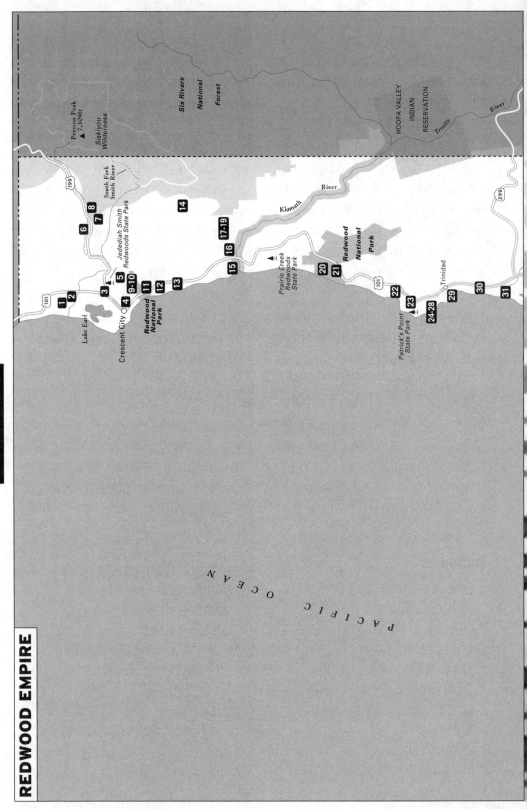

CALIFORNIA

REDWOOD EMPIRE

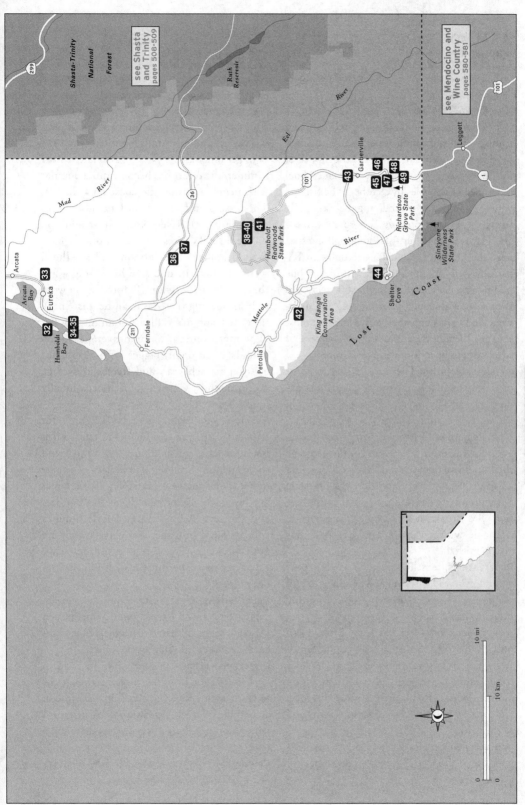

see Shasta and Trinity pages 508-509

see Mendocino and Wine Country pages 580-581

Shasta-Trinity National Forest

Ruth Reservoir

Eel River

299

101

Leggett

1

Garberville

43

46

45 47 48

49

Richardson Grove State Park

Mad River

36

38-40

41

Humboldt Redwoods State Park

River

Sinkyone Wilderness State Park

Arcata

33

Eureka

Arcata Bay

211

Ferndale

37

Mattole

42

King Range Conservation Area

Shelter Cove

44

Lost Coast

32

34-35

Humboldt Bay

Petrolia

CALIFORNIA

10 mi

10 km

0   0

© AVALON TRAVEL PUBLISHING, INC.

CALIFORNIA

❶ SALMON HARBOR RV RESORT

Scenic rating: 6

on the Smith River

See map page 478

If location is everything, this privately operated campground rates high for salmon and steelhead fishing in the fall. It is near the mouth of the Smith River, where salmon enter and school in the deep river holes in October. The fish are big, often in the 20-pound range, occasionally surpassing even 40 pounds. Year-round this is a good layover for RV cruisers looking for a spot near the Oregon border. It is actually an RV parking area with hookups, set within a mobile home park. Salmon Harbor Resort overlooks the ocean, with good beachcombing and driftwood and agate hunting nearby. Note that most sites are filled for the entire summer, but several sites are kept open for overnight campers.

RV sites, facilities: There are 93 sites for tents or RVs up to 40 feet; most sites have full hookups (30 and 50 amps) and are pull-through. Picnic tables and fire grills are provided. Drinking water, restrooms with flush toilets and showers, cable TV, a coin laundry, storage sheds, modem hookups, and a recreation room are available. A grocery store, ice, gas, propane, a restaurant, a boat ramp, a fish-cleaning station, RV storage, a snack bar, and a bar are available within three miles. Leashed pets are permitted.

Reservations, fees: Reservations are accepted at 800/332-6139. Sites are $28 per night, $1.50 per person for more than two people. Monthly rates are available. Open year-round.

Directions: From Crescent City, drive north on U.S. 101 for 13 miles to the town of Smith River. Continue three miles north on U.S. 101 to the Salmon Harbor Road exit. Turn left on Salmon Harbor Road, drive a short distance, and look for Salmon Harbor Resort at the end of the road.

Contact: Salmon Harbor RV Resort, 707/487-3341 or 800/332-6139, www.salmonharbor rvresort.com.

❷ SHIP ASHORE RESORT

Scenic rating: 7

on the Smith River

See map page 478

This is a famous spot for Smith River anglers in late fall and all through winter, when the tales get taller as the evening gets late. In the summer, the resort has become quite popular with people cruising the coast on U.S. 101. The park is on five acres of land adjacent to the lower Smith River. Note that in addition to the 120 RV sites, another 80 sites have mobile homes. The salmon and steelhead seem to come in one size here—big—but they can be as elusive as Bigfoot. If you want to hear how big these fish can be, just check into the Captain's Galley restaurant any fall or winter evening. Salmon average 15–25 pounds, occasionally bigger, with 50-pounders caught each year, and steelhead average 10–14 pounds, with bigger fish occasionally hooked as well.

RV sites, facilities: There are 120 sites for RVs and a separate area for 10–15 tents. Most RV sites have full hookups (30 amps), and some are pull-through. Two houses and some motel rooms are also available. Picnic tables are provided. Restrooms have flush toilets and showers. A boat dock, a boat ramp, a coin laundry, propane, and a restaurant are available. A grocery store is two miles away. Leashed pets are permitted, with a maximum of two pets.

Reservations, fees: Reservations are not accepted. Sites are $9–16 per night, $1 per person per night for more than two people. Some credit cards are accepted. Open year-round.

Directions: From Crescent City, drive north on U.S. 101 for 16 miles, three miles past the town of Smith River, to the Ship Ashore sign at Chinook Street. At Chinook Street, turn left and drive a short distance (less than half a block) to the motel lobby to register.

Contact: Ship Ashore Resort, 707/487-3141, fax 707/487-7070, www.ship-ashore.com.

3 CRESCENT CITY REDWOODS KOA

Scenic rating: 6

five miles north of Crescent City

See map page 478

This KOA camp is on the edge of a recreation wonderland, a perfect jump-off spot for a vacation. The park covers 17 acres, with 11 acres of redwood forest. A few farm animals live here, and guests are allowed to feed them. In addition, there are three golf courses nearby. The camp is only two miles from Redwood National Park, Jedediah Smith Redwoods State Park, and the Smith River National Recreation Area. It is only a 10-minute drive to the beach, to Tolowa Dunes Wildlife Area to the east, and to Crescent City Harbor to the south.

RV sites, facilities: There are 30 sites with full hookups (30 and 50 amps) for RVs of any length and 44 tent sites. Seventeen cabins and one cottage are also available. Picnic tables and fire grills are provided. A dump station, restrooms with flush toilets and showers, a coin laundry, free Wi-Fi, a playground, propane, a convenience store, ice, firewood, recreation room, pool table, table tennis, horseshoes, go-carts, and volleyball are available. Leashed pets are permitted.

Reservations, fees: Reservations are accepted at 800/562-5754. Sites are $20–39 per night, $2.50–3.50 per person per night for more than two people. Some credit cards accepted. Open year-round.

Directions: From Crescent City, take U.S. 101 north for five miles to the campground entrance on the right (east) side of the road.

Contact: Crescent City Redwoods KOA, 707/464-5744, www.crescentcitykoa.com.

4 BAYSIDE RV PARK

Scenic rating: 6

in Crescent City

See map page 478

If you are towing a boat, you just found your personal heaven: This RV park is directly adjacent to the boat docking area in Crescent City Harbor. There are several walks in the immediate area, including exploring the harbor and ocean frontage. For a quick change of scenery, it is only a 15-minute drive to Redwood National Park and Jedediah Smith Redwoods State Park along U.S. 199 to the north. Note that about 20 sites are filled with long-term renters, and most of the spaces book up for the entire season.

RV sites, facilities: There are 110 sites for RVs up to 34 feet. Most sites have full hookups (30 amps) and/or are pull-through. No tents. Picnic tables are provided. Restrooms have flush toilets and showers. Cable TV, Wi-Fi, and a coin laundry are available. A restaurant is adjacent to the park. Leashed pets are permitted.

Reservations, fees: Reservations are accepted at 800/446-9482. Sites are $18–22 per night, $3 per person per night for more than two people. Open year-round.

Directions: From U.S. 101 at the southern end of Crescent City, drive to Citizen Dock Road and continue one-half block south to the park office.

Contact: Bayside RV Park, 707/464-9482.

5 HIOUCHI HAMLET RV RESORT

Scenic rating: 7

near the Smith River

See map page 478

This park is out of the wind and fog you get on the coast and set instead in the heart of the forest country. It makes a good base camp for a steelhead trip in winter. Insiders know that the fried chicken at the Hamlet's market right next door is always good for a quick hit. An excellent side trip is to drive just east of Hiouchi on U.S. 199, turn right, and cross over two bridges, where you will reach a fork in the road. Turn left for a great scenic drive along the South Fork Smith River or turn right to get backdoor access to Jedediah Smith Redwoods State Park and three great trailheads for hiking in the redwoods. My favorite of the latter is the Boy Scout Tree Trail. Note that about one-fourth of the RV sites are filled with long-term renters, and many other sites fill up quickly with summer vacationers.

RV sites, facilities: There are 120 sites with full hookups (30 and 50 amps) for RVs of any length and six tent sites. Some sites are pull-through. Two park-model cabins and six furnished apartments are also available. Restrooms have flush toilets and showers. A dump station, a coin laundry, Wi-Fi, high-speed modem hookups, cable TV, recreation room, horseshoe pits, a grocery store, propane, and deli are available. A motel and café are nearby. A golf course is available within four miles. Some facilities are wheelchair accessible. Leashed pets are permitted.

Reservations, fees: Reservations are accepted at 800/722-9468. Sites are $26.70–28.90 per night, plus $2 per person per night for more than two people. Some credit cards accepted. Open year-round.

Directions: From Crescent City, drive five miles north on U.S. 101 to U.S. 199. Turn east (right) on U.S. 199 and drive about five miles (just past the entrance to Jedediah Smith Redwoods State Park) to the town of Hiouchi. In Hiouchi, turn left at the well-signed campground entrance.

Contact: Hiouchi Hamlet RV Resort, 707/458-3321, fax 707/458-3521.

6 PANTHER FLAT

Scenic rating: 8

on the Smith River in Six Rivers National Forest
See map page 478   BEST (

This is an ideal alternative to the often-crowded Jedediah Smith Redwoods State Park. The park provides easy road access since it is right along U.S. 199, the two-laner that runs beside the Smith River. This is the largest and one of the feature campgrounds in the Smith River National Recreation Area, with excellent prospects for salmon and steelhead fishing in the fall and winter, respectively, and outstanding hiking and backpacking in the summer. A 0.25-mile interpretive trail and viewing area is one

mile north of the campground, off U.S. 199. A great nearby hike is Stony Creek Trail, an easy walk along the North Fork Smith River; the trailhead is in nearby Gasquet on Stoney Creek Road. Redwood National Park is a short drive to the west. The Siskiyou Wilderness is a short drive to the southeast via forest roads detailed on Forest Service maps. The wild and scenic Smith River system provides fishing, swimming, sunbathing, kayaking for experts, and beautiful scenery.

RV sites, facilities: There are 39 sites for tents or RVs up to 40 feet (no hookups). Picnic tables and fire grills are provided. Drinking water and restrooms with flush toilets and coin showers are available. Propane gas, groceries, and coin laundry are available nearby. Some facilities are wheelchair accessible. Leashed pets are permitted.

Reservations, fees: Reservations are accepted ($9 reservation fee) at 877/444-6777 or www.ReserveUSA.com. Sites are $15 per night, $5 per night for an additional vehicle. Open year-round.

Directions: From Crescent City, drive north on U.S. 101 for three miles to the junction with U.S. 199. At U.S. 199, turn east and drive 14.5 miles to Gasquet. From Gasquet, continue for 2.3 miles east on U.S. 199 and look for the entrance to the campground on the left side of the highway.

Contact: Smith River National Recreation Area, Six Rivers National Forest, 707/457-3131, fax 707/457-3794.

7 GRASSY FLAT

Scenic rating: 4

on the Smith River in Six Rivers National Forest
See map page 478   BEST (

This is one in a series of three easy-to-reach Forest Service camps set near U.S. 199 along the beautiful middle fork of the Smith River. It's a classic wild river, popular in the summer with kayakers, and the steelhead come huge in the winter for the crafty few. The camp itself sits directly across from a CalTrans waste area, and if you hit it when the crews are working, it can be noisy here. Most of the time, however, it is peaceful and quiet.

RV sites, facilities: There are 15 sites for tents or RVs up to 30 feet (no hookups) and four walk-in tent sites. Picnic tables and fire grills are provided. Drinking water and vault toilets are available. Propane gas and groceries are available nearby. Some facilities are wheelchair accessible. Leashed pets are permitted.

Reservations, fees: Reservations are accepted ($9 reservation fee) at 877/444-6777 or www.ReserveUSA.com. Sites are $10 per night, $5 per night for an additional vehicle. Open late May–mid-September.

Directions: From Crescent City, drive north on U.S. 101 for three miles to the junction with U.S. 199. Turn east on U.S. 199 and drive 14.5 miles to Gasquet. From Gasquet, continue east on U.S. 199 for 4.4 miles and look for the campground entrance on the right side of the road.

Contact: Smith River National Recreation Area, Six Rivers National Forest, 707/457-3131, fax 707/457-3794.

8 PATRICK CREEK

Scenic rating: 8

in Six Rivers National Forest

See map page 478

This is one of the prettiest spots along U.S. 199, where Patrick Creek enters the upper Smith River. It is also a historic California Conservation Corps site that was built in the 1930s. This section of the Smith looks something like a large trout stream, rolling green past a boulder-lined shore, complete with forest canopy. There are small cutthroat trout and salmon and steelhead in the fall and winter. A big plus for this camp is its nearby access to excellent hiking in the Siskiyou Wilderness, especially the great day hike to Buck Lake. It is essential to have a map of Six Rivers National Forest, both for driving directions to the trailhead and for the hiking route. You can buy maps

at the information center for the Smith River National Recreation Area on the north side of U.S. 199 in Gasquet. An option at this camp is Patrick Creek Lodge, on the opposite side of the highway from the campground, which has a restaurant and bar. A paved trail connects the campground to Patrick Creek Lodge.

RV sites, facilities: There are 13 sites for tents or RVs up to 35 feet (no hookups). Picnic tables and fire grills are provided. Drinking water and flush toilets are available. Some facilities are wheelchair accessible, including a fishing area. Leashed pets are permitted.

Reservations, fees: Reservations are accepted ($9 reservation fee) at 877/444-6777 or www.ReserveUSA.com. Sites are $14 per night, $5 per night for an additional vehicle. Open May–early September.

Directions: From Crescent City, drive north on U.S. 101 for three miles to the junction with U.S. 199. Turn east on U.S. 199 and drive 14.5 miles to Gasquet. From Gasquet, continue east on U.S. 199 for 7.5 miles and look for the campground entrance on the right side of the road.

Contact: Smith River National Recreation Area, Six Rivers National Forest, 707/457-3131, fax 707/457-3794.

9 VILLAGE CAMPER INN RV PARK

Scenic rating: 7

in Crescent City

See map page 478

Woods and water, that's what attracts visitors to California's north coast. Village Camper Inn provides nearby access to big woods and big water. This RV park is on 20 acres of wooded land, with the giant redwoods along U.S. 199 about a 10-minute drive away. In addition, you find some premium beachcombing for driftwood and agates a mile away on the spectacular rocky beaches just west of town. Note that about half of the sites fill up for the entire summer season.

RV sites, facilities: There are 135 sites for RVs of any length in addition to a separate area for tents. Most RV sites have full hookups (30 and 50 amps), and some are pull-through. Picnic tables are provided. Drinking water, a dump station, restrooms with flush toilets and showers, a coin laundry, modem access, and cable TV are available. Leashed pets are permitted, with certain restrictions.

Reservations, fees: Reservations are accepted. Sites are $22.50 per night, $2 per person per night for more than two people. Some credit cards accepted. Open year-round.

Directions: On U.S. 101, driving north in Crescent City: Drive north on U.S. 101 to the Parkway Drive exit. Take that exit and drive 0.5 mile to the campground on the right.

On U.S. 101, driving south in Crescent City: Drive south on U.S. 101 to the Washington Boulevard exit. Turn left on Washington Boulevard and drive one block to Parkway Drive. Turn left on Parkway and drive one block to the campground on the right.

Contact: Village Camper Inn RV Park, 707/464-3544.

10 SUNSET HARBOR RV PARK

Scenic rating: 4

in Crescent City

See map page 478

People camp here with their RVs to be close to the action in Crescent City and to the nearby harbor and beach frontage. For starters, drive a few minutes to the northwest side of town, where the sea is sprinkled with gigantic rocks and boulders, for dramatic ocean views and spectacular sunsets. For finishers, go down to the west side of town for great walks along the ocean parkway or south to the harbor and adjacent beach, which is long and expansive. About half of the sites are filled with long-term renters.

RV sites, facilities: There are 69 sites with full hookups (30 and 50 amps) for RVs up to 40 feet. No tents. Picnic tables are provided at some sites. Restrooms have flush toilets and showers. Cable TV, a coin laundry, and a recreation room are available. A grocery store is available nearby. Some facilities are wheelchair accessible. Leashed pets are permitted.

Reservations, fees: Reservations are accepted. Sites are $26 per night, $2 per person per night for more than two people. Monthly rates are available. Some credit cards accepted. Open year-round.

Directions: In Crescent City on U.S. 101, drive to King Street. At King Street, turn east and drive one block to the park entrance at the end of the road.

Contact: Sunset Harbor RV Park, 707/464-3423.

11 JEDEDIAH SMITH REDWOODS STATE PARK

Scenic rating: 10

on the Smith River

See map page 478

This is a beautiful park set along the Smith River, where the campsites are sprinkled amid a grove of old-growth redwoods. Reservations are usually a necessity during the summer. This park covers 10,000 acres on both sides of the Smith River, a jewel, the last major free-flowing river in California. There are 20 miles of hiking and nature trails, river access, a visitors center with exhibits, and a nature store. The park has hiking trails that lead right out of the campground; one is routed along the beautiful Smith River, and another heads through forest, across U.S. 199, and hooks up with the Simpson-Reed Interpretive Trail. In the summer, interpretive programs are available. There is also a good put-in spot at the park for river access in a drift boat, canoe, or raft. The fishing is best for steelhead from mid-January through March. In the summer, a seasonal footbridge connects the campground with more extensive trails. The best hikes are on the south side of the Smith River, accessible via Howland Hill Road, including the Boy Scout Tree Trail and Stout Grove (for access, see the listing in this chapter for *Hiouchi Hamlet RV Resort*). Note that in winter, 100 inches of cumulative rainfall is common.

RV sites, facilities: There are 106 sites for tents or RVs up to 36 feet and trailers up to 31 feet, five hike-in/bike-in sites, and one group site for up to 15 vehicles and 50 people. No hookups. Picnic tables, fire grills, and food lockers are provided. Drinking water, flush toilets, and a dump station are available. Propane gas and groceries are available within one mile. Some facilities are wheelchair accessible. Leashed pets are permitted only in the campground and on roads.

Reservations, fees: Reservations are accepted ($7.50 reservation fee) at 800/444-PARK (800/444-7275) or www.reserveamerica.com. Sites are $15–20 per night, $6 per night for an additional vehicle, $100 per night for the group site, and $3 per person per night for hike-in/bike-in sites. Open year-round.

Directions: From Crescent City, drive north on U.S. 101 for four miles to the junction with U.S. 199. Turn east at U.S. 199 and drive five miles. Turn right at the well-signed entrance station.

Contact: Redwood National and State Parks, 707/464-6101, fax 707/464-1812, www.parks.ca.gov.

12 DEL NORTE COAST REDWOODS STATE PARK

🚶 🚴 🐕 ♿ 🚐 ⛺

Scenic rating: 8

near Crescent City
See map page 478

The campsites are set in a series of loops in the forest, so while there are a lot of camps, you still feel a sense of privacy. In addition to redwoods, there are also good stands of alders, along with a rambling stream fed by several creeks. It makes for a very pretty setting, with four loop trails available right out of the camp. This park covers 6,400 acres, featuring 50 percent old-growth coastal redwoods and eight miles of wild coastline. Topography is fairly steep, with elevations ranging from sea level to 1,277 feet. This range is oriented in a north–south direction, with steep cliffs adjacent to the ocean. That makes most of the rocky seacoast generally inaccessible except by Damnation Trail and Footsteps Rock Trail. The best coastal access is at Wilson Beach or False Klamath Cove, where there is a half mile of sandy beach bordered by excellent tide pools. The forest interior is dense, with both redwoods and tanoaks, madrones, red alder, big leaf maple, and California bay. One reason for the lush growth is what rangers call the "nurturing" coastal climate. Nurturing, in this case, means rain like you wouldn't believe in the winter, often more than 100 inches in a season, and lots of fog in the summer. Interpretive programs are conducted here.

RV sites, facilities: There are 107 sites for tents or RVs up to 31 feet (no hookups) and 38 tent sites. Hike-in/bike-in sites are also available. Picnic tables, fire pits, and food lockers are provided. Drinking water, a dump station, and restrooms with flush toilets and coin showers are available. Some facilities are wheelchair accessible. Leashed pets are permitted only in the campground.

Reservations, fees: Reservations are accepted ($7.50 reservation fee) at 800/444-PARK (800/444-7275) or www.reserveamerica.com. Sites are $15–20 per night, $4 per night for an additional vehicle, $3 per person per night for hike-in/bike-in sites. Open May–mid-September.

Directions: From Crescent City, drive seven miles south on U.S. 101 to a signed access road for Del Norte Coast Redwoods State Park. Turn left at the park entrance.

Contact: Redwood National and State Parks, 1111 2nd Street, Crescent City, CA 95531, 707/464-6101, fax 707/464-1812, www.nps.gov/redw.

13 MYSTIC FOREST RV PARK

🚶 🏊 🐕 🎣 ♿ 🚐 ⛺

Scenic rating: 6

near the Klamath River
See map page 478

The park features gravel roads, redwood trees, and grassy sites amid a 50-acre park designed primarily for RVs with a separate area for tents.

CALIFORNIA

A bonus here is the 18-hole miniature golf course. The Trees of Mystery attraction is less than a mile away and features a nearly 50-foot-tall Paul Bunyan. The park is about 1.5 miles away from the ocean and 3.5 miles from the Klamath River. Jet-boat tours are available on the Klamath River.

RV sites, facilities: There are 30 sites with full hookups (30 amps) for RVs of any length and 14 tent sites. Some of the RV sites are pull-through. Picnic tables and fire rings are provided. Drinking water, restrooms with flush toilets and showers, a playground, a recreation room, horseshoes, miniature golf, a coin laundry, modem access, a convenience store and gift shop, group facilities, and firewood are available. Some facilities are wheelchair accessible. Leashed pets are permitted.

Reservations, fees: Reservations are accepted. Sites are $16–24 per night, $3 per person per night for more than two people. Group rates available. Some credit cards accepted. Open year-round.

Directions: From Eureka, drive north on U.S. 101 to Klamath and continue north for four miles. Look for the entrance sign on the left side of the road. If you reach the Trees of Mystery, you have gone a mile too far north.

Contact: Mystic Forest RV Park, 707/482-4901, fax 707/482-0704, www.mysticforestrv.com.

14 BIG FLAT

Scenic rating: 7

on Hurdygurdy Creek in Six Rivers National Forest
See map page 478

This camp provides an ideal setting for those who know of it, which is why it gets quite a bit of use for a relatively remote camp. Set along Hurdygurdy Creek, near where the creek enters the South Fork of the Smith River, it provides nearby access to South Kelsey Trail, an outstanding hiking route whether you are walking for a few hours or backpacking for days. In the summer, it is a good layover for rafters or kayakers paddling the South Fork of the Smith River.

RV sites, facilities: There are 25 sites for tents or RVs up to 22 feet (no hookups). Picnic tables and fire grills are provided. Vault toilets and food lockers are available. There is no drinking water, and garbage must be packed out. Some facilities are wheelchair accessible. Leashed pets are permitted.

Reservations, fees: Reservations are not accepted. Sites are $8 per night, plus $5 per night for an additional vehicle. Open May–early September.

Directions: From Crescent City, drive north on U.S. 101 for three miles to the junction with U.S. 199. Turn east on U.S. 199 and drive five miles to Hiouchi. Continue just past Hiouchi to South Fork Road. Turn right and cross two bridges. At the Y, turn left on South Fork Road and drive about 14 miles to Big Flat Road/County Road 405. Turn left and drive 0.25 mile to the campground entrance road (Forest Road 15N59) on the left. Turn left and drive a short distance to the camp on the left.

Contact: Smith River National Recreation Area, Six Rivers National Forest, 707/457-3131, fax 707/457-3794.

15 CHINOOK RV RESORT

Scenic rating: 7

on the Klamath River
See map page 478

The camping area at this park consists of grassy RV sites that overlook the Klamath River. Chinook RV Resort is another of the more well-known parks on the lower Klamath. A boat ramp and fishing supplies are available.

RV sites, facilities: There are 70 sites with full hookups (30 and 50 amps) for RVs of any length and a grassy area for tents. Some RV sites are pull-through. An apartment is also available. Picnic tables and fire grills are provided. Restrooms have flush toilets and showers. Cable television, modem access, a coin laundry, a recreation room, propane, a convenience store, RV supplies, a boat ramp, boat rentals, and a tackle shop are available. Leashed pets are permitted.

Reservations, fees: Reservations are accepted.

RV sites are $25–27 per night, tents are $16 per night, and it's $2 per person per night for more than two people. Some credit cards accepted. Open year-round.

Directions: From Eureka, drive north on U.S. 101 to Klamath. After crossing the bridge at the Klamath River, continue north on U.S. 101 for a mile to the campground on the left.

Contact: Chinook RV Resort, 707/482-3511, fax 707/482-0493, www.chinookrvresort.com.

16 CAMP MARIGOLD

Scenic rating: 7

near the Klamath River
See map page 478

Camp Marigold is surrounded by wonder: Redwood National Park, towering redwoods, Pacific Ocean beaches, driftwood, agates, fossilized rocks, blackberries, Fern Canyon, Lagoon Creek Park, and the Trees of Mystery. Fishing is available nearby, in season, for several species, including king salmon, steelhead, red tail perch, and candlefish. The camp has 3.5 acres of landscaped gardens with hiking trails… get the idea? Well, there's more: It is only two miles to the Klamath River, in case you can't find enough to do already. A few sites are filled with long-term renters.

RV sites, facilities: There are 40 sites for RVs up to 35 feet with full hookups (30 amps). Twelve park-model cabins are also available. Picnic tables and barbecues are provided. Restrooms have showers. Cable TV, group facilities, and a coin laundry are available. Small leashed pets are permitted.

Reservations, fees: Reservations are recommended. Sites are $10–15 per night, $5 per night per person for more than two people. Monthly rates available. Some credit cards are accepted. Open year-round.

Directions: From Eureka, drive 60 miles north on U.S. 101 to the campground at 16101 U.S. 101, four miles north of the Klamath River Bridge, on the right side of the road. The camp is a mile south of the Trees of Mystery.

Contact: Camp Marigold, 707/482-3585 or 800/621-8513.

17 KLAMATH'S CAMPER CORRAL

Scenic rating: 6

on the Klamath River
See map page 478

This 50-acre resort offers 3,000 feet of Klamath River frontage, grassy tent sites, berry picking, access to the ocean, and hiking trails nearby. And, of course, in the fall it has salmon and steelhead, the main attraction on the lower Klamath. A boat launch is about 1.5 miles from the resort. Nature trails are on the property, and there is room for bike riding. River swimming is popular in summer. A nightly campfire is usually available. Organized recreation is available in summer. A free pancake breakfast is offered to campers on Sundays.

RV sites, facilities: There are 140 sites for RVs of any length and 60 tent sites. Many RV sites have full or partial hookups (30 amps) and are pull-through. Picnic tables and fire rings are provided at the tent sites. Drinking water, restrooms with flush toilets and showers, a seasonal heated swimming pool, a recreation hall, a general store, a playground, a dump station, a coin laundry, cable TV, ice, firewood, bait and tackle, a fish-cleaning station, fishing-guide service, group facilities, an arcade, basketball, volleyball, badminton, shuffleboard, horseshoes, table tennis, croquet, and tetherball are available. Leashed pets are permitted.

Reservations, fees: Reservations are accepted at 800/701-7275. Sites are $16–29.95 per night, $2 per night for each additional vehicle, and $2 per person per night for more than two people. Weekly and monthly rates are available. Some credit cards accepted. Open April–October.

Directions: From Eureka, drive north on U.S. 101 to Klamath. Just after crossing the Klamath River/Golden Bear Bridge, take the Terwer Valley/Highway 169 exit. At the stop sign, turn left, drive under the highway and continue a short distance west to the campground.

Contact: Klamath's Camper Corral, 707/482-5741, www.campercorral.net.

CALIFORNIA

18 STEELHEAD LODGE

Scenic rating: 6

on the Klamath River
See map page 478

Many anglers use this park as headquarters when the salmon and steelhead get going in August. The park has grassy sites near the Klamath River.

RV sites, facilities: There are 24 sites with full hookups (30 amps) for RVs of any length or tents; some are pull-through. Picnic tables are provided. Drinking water, restrooms with flush toilets and showers, and ice are available. A bar, restaurant, and motel are also available. Some facilities are wheelchair accessible. Leashed pets are permitted.

Reservations, fees: Reservations are required. RV sites are $20 per night, and tent sites are $10 per night. Some credit cards accepted. Open year-round.

Directions: From Eureka, drive north on U.S. 101 to Klamath and the junction with Highway 169. Turn east on Highway 169 and drive 3.2 miles to Terwer Riffle Road. Turn right (south) on Terwer Riffle Road and drive one block to Steelhead Lodge on the right.

Contact: Steelhead Lodge, 707/482-8145.

19 TERWER PARK

Scenic rating: 7

on the Klamath River
See map page 478

This RV park is near the Terwer Riffle, one of the better shore-fishing spots for steelhead and salmon on the lower Klamath River. You get grassy sites, river access, and some fair trails along the Klamath. When the salmon arrive in late August and September, Terwer Riffle can be loaded with fish, as well as boaters and shore anglers—a wild scene. Note that at this park, tent campers are separated from the RV park, with tent camping at a grassy area near the river. Some sites are taken by monthly renters.

RV sites, facilities: There are 35 sites with full hookups (30 amps) for RVs up to 34 feet as well as a separate tent area. Several sites are pull-through. Five cabins are available. Picnic tables are provided. Restrooms with flush toilets and showers are available. A pulley boat launch is nearby. Leashed pets are permitted.

Reservations, fees: Reservations are accepted. Sites are $17–20 per night and $5 per night for an additional vehicle. Weekly and monthly rates are available. Open April–October.

Directions: From Eureka, drive north on U.S. 101 to Klamath and the junction with Highway 169. Turn east on Highway 169 and drive 3.5 miles to Terwer Riffle Road. Turn right on Terwer Riffle Road and drive two blocks, then bear right on Terwer Riffle Road and continue five blocks (about 0.5 mile) to the park at the end of the road (641 Terwer Riffle Road).

Contact: Terwer Park, 707/482-3855.

20 PRAIRIE CREEK REDWOODS STATE PARK: GOLD BLUFF BEACH

Scenic rating: 8

in Prairie Creek Redwoods State Park
See map page 478   BEST (

The campsites here sit in a sandy, exposed area with man-made windbreaks. A huge, expansive beach is on one side and a backdrop of 100- to 200-foot cliffs marks the other side. You can walk for miles at this beach, often without seeing another soul, and there is a great trail routed north through forest, with many hidden little waterfalls. In addition, Fern Canyon Trail, one of the best 30-minute hikes in California, is at the end of Davison Road. Hikers walk along a stream in a narrow canyon, its vertical walls covered with magnificent ferns. There are some herds of elk in the area, often right along the access road. These camps are rarely used in the winter because of the region's heavy rain and winds. The expanse of beach here is awesome, covering 10 miles of huge, pristine ocean frontage. (See the *Elk Prairie* listing in this chapter for more information about Prairie Creek Redwoods.)

RV sites, facilities: There are 26 sites for tents or RVs up to 24 feet (no hookups). No trailers or vehicles wider than eight feet are allowed. Fire grills, food lockers, and picnic tables are provided. Drinking water and restrooms with flush toilets and cold showers are available. Leashed pets are permitted.

Reservations, fees: Reservations are not accepted. Sites are $14–15 per night, $6 per night for an additional vehicle. Open year-round, weather permitting.

Directions: From Eureka, drive north on U.S. 101 for 45 miles to Orick. At Orick, continue north on U.S. 101 for three miles to Davison Road. Turn left (west) on Davison Road and drive six miles to the campground on the left. Note: No vehicles more than 24 feet long or more than eight feet wide are permitted on Davison Road (gravel road), which is narrow and very bumpy.

Contact: Prairie Creek Redwoods State Park, 707/464-6101, ext. 5301 or 5300 (visitors center), www.parks.ca.gov.

21 PRAIRIE CREEK REDWOODS STATE PARK: ELK PRAIRIE

🚶 🚴 🐾 ♿ 🚐 ⛺

Scenic rating: 9

in Prairie Creek Redwoods State Park

See map page 478   BEST (

A small herd of Roosevelt elk wander free in this remarkable 14,000-acre park. Great opportunities for photographs abound, with a group of about five elk often found right along the highway and access roads. Where there are meadows, there are elk; it's about that simple. An elky here, an elky there, making this one of the best places to see wildlife in California. Remember that these are wild animals, they are huge, and they can be unpredictable; in other words, enjoy them, but don't harass them or get too close. This park consists of old-growth coastal redwoods, prairie lands, and 10 miles of scenic, open beach (Gold Bluff Beach). The interior of the park can be reached by 75 miles of hiking, biking, and nature trails, including a trailhead for a great bike ride at the visitors

center. There are many additional trailheads and a beautiful tour of giant redwoods along the Drury Scenic Parkway. A visitors center, summer interpretive programs with guided walks, and junior ranger programs are available. Because of the prevalent coastal fog, the understory of the forest is very dense. Western azalea and rhododendron bloom in May and June, and the Rhododendron Trail is a favorite for seeing this display. November–May, always bring your rain gear. Summer temperatures range 40–75°F; winter temperatures range 35–55°F.

RV sites, facilities: There are 76 sites for tents or RVs up to 27 feet (no hookups), and one hike-in/bike-in site. Picnic tables, fire rings, and bearproof food lockers are provided. Drinking water and restrooms with flush toilets and coin showers are available. Some facilities are wheelchair accessible. Leashed pets are permitted.

Reservations, fees: Reservations are accepted during the summer ($7.50 reservation fee) at 800/444-PARK (800/444-7275) or www.reserveamerica.com. Sites are $15–20 per night, $6 per night for an additional vehicle, and $3 per person per night for hike-in/bike-in site. Open year-round.

Directions: From Eureka, drive 45 miles north on U.S. 101 to Orick. At Orick, continue north on U.S. 101 for five miles to the Newton B. Drury Scenic Parkway. Take the exit for the Newton B. Drury Scenic Parkway and drive north for a mile to the park. Turn left at the park entrance.

Contact: Prairie Creek Redwoods State Park, 707/464-6101; Elk Prairie Campground, 707/465-7347; Visitors Center, 707/465-7354, www.parks.ca.gov.

22 BIG LAGOON COUNTY PARK

🏊 🎣 🚤 🏠 ♿ 🚐 ⛺

Scenic rating: 7

overlooking the Pacific Ocean

See map page 478

This is a remarkable, huge lagoon that borders the Pacific Ocean. It provides good boating, excellent exploring, fair fishing, and good duck hunting in the winter. It's a good spot to paddle a canoe around on a calm day. A lot of out-of-towners cruise by, note the lagoon's proximity to the ocean, and figure it must be salt water. Wrong! Not only is it freshwater, but it provides a long shot for anglers trying for rainbow trout. One reason not many RV drivers stop here is that most of them are drawn farther north (another eight miles) to Freshwater Lagoon.

RV sites, facilities: There are 25 sites for tents or RVs of any length (no hookups). Picnic tables and fire grills are provided. Drinking water and restrooms with flush toilets and coin showers are available. A boat ramp is also available. Some facilities are wheelchair accessible. Leashed pets are permitted.

Reservations, fees: Reservations are not accepted. Sites are $15 per night per vehicle, $3 per person per night for hike-in/bike-in, $3 per night for a second vehicle, and $1 per pet per night. Open year-round.

Directions: From Eureka, drive 22 miles north on U.S. 101 to Trinidad. At Trinidad, continue north on U.S. 101 for eight miles to Big Lagoon Park Road. Turn left (west) at Big Lagoon Park Road and drive two miles to the park.

Contact: Humboldt County Public Works, 707/445-7651; Humboldt Lagoons State Park, Visitors Center, 707/488-2041, www.co .humboldt.ca.us.

23 PATRICK'S POINT STATE PARK

Scenic rating: 9

near Trinidad
See map page 478

This pretty park covers 640 acres of coastal headlands, and it is filled with Sitka spruce, dramatic ocean lookouts, and several beautiful beaches, including one with agates, one with tidepools, and another with an expansive stretch of beachfront leading to a lagoon. You can best see it on the Rim Trail, which has many little cut-off routes to the lookouts and down to the beaches. The campground is sheltered in the forest, and while it is often foggy and damp in the summer, it is always beautiful. A Native

American village, constructed by the Yurok tribe, is also here. At the north end of the park, a short hike to see the bizarre "Octopus Trees" is a good side trip, with trees that are growing atop downed logs, their root systems exposed like octopus tentacles; the trail here loops through a grove of old-growth Sitka spruce. In addition, there are several miles of pristine beach to the north extending to the lagoons. Interpretive programs are available. The forest here is dense, with spruce, hemlock, pine, fir, and red alder covering an ocean headland. Night and morning fog are common almost year-round, and there are periods when it doesn't lift for days. This area gets 60 inches of rain per year on the average. For camping, plan on making reservations.

RV sites, facilities: There are 85 sites for tents or RVs, 39 sites for RVs up to 31 feet, and one group site for up to 100 people. No hookups. Fire grills, storage lockers, and picnic tables are provided. Drinking water and restrooms with flush toilets and coin showers are available. Some facilities are wheelchair accessible. Leashed pets are permitted at campsites but not on trails or beaches.

Reservations, fees: Reservations are accepted ($7.50 reservation fee) at 800/444-PARK (800/444-7275) or www.reserveamerica.com. Sites are $15–20 per night, plus $6 per night for an additional vehicle, and $200 per night for the group site. Open year-round.

Directions: From Eureka, drive north on U.S. 101 for 22 miles to Trinidad. At Trinidad, continue north on U.S. 101 for 5.5 miles to Patrick's Point Drive. Take that exit; at the stop sign, turn left and drive 0.5 mile to the park entrance.

Contact: Patrick's Point State Park, 707/677-3570, www.parks.ca.gov.

24 SOUNDS OF THE SEA RV PARK

Scenic rating: 6

in Trinidad
See map page 478

The Trinidad area, about 20 miles north of Eureka, is one of the great places on this planet.

Nearby Patrick's Point State Park is one of the highlights, with a Sitka spruce forest, beautiful coastal lookouts, a great easy hike on the Rim Trail, and access to several secluded beaches. To the nearby south at Trinidad Head is a small harbor and dock, with deep-sea and salmon fishing trips available. A breezy beach is to the immediate north of the Seascape Restaurant. A bonus at this privately operated RV park is good berry picking in season.

RV sites, facilities: There are 70 sites with full hookups (30 and 50 amps) for RVs; some sites are pull-through. No tents. Four park-model cabins are also available. Picnic tables and fire rings are provided at most sites. Restrooms have showers. Cable TV, Wi-Fi, an exercise room and indoor spa (fee), bicycle rentals, a dump station, a coin laundry, a convenience store, a gift shop, propane, firewood, and ice are available. Leashed pets are permitted.

Reservations, fees: Reservations are accepted at 877/489-6360. Sites are $18–38 per night, plus $3–5 per person per night for more than two people. Some credit cards accepted. Open year-round.

Directions: From Eureka, drive north on U.S. 101 for 28 miles to Trinidad. In Trinidad, continue north on U.S. 101 for five miles to the Patrick's Point exit. Take the Patrick's Point exit, turn left, and drive 0.5 mile to the park.

Contact: Sounds of the Sea RV Park, 707/677-3271.

25 SYLVAN HARBOR RV PARK AND CABINS

Scenic rating: 8

in Trinidad

See map page 478

This park is designed as an RV park and fish camp, with cleaning tables and canning facilities available on-site. It is a short distance from the boat hoist at Trinidad Pier. Beauty surrounds Sylvan Harbor on all sides for miles. Visitors come to enjoy the various beaches, go agate hunting, or look for driftwood on the beach. Nearby Patrick's Point State Park is an excellent getaway side trip. This is one of several privately operated parks in the Trinidad area, offering a choice of shaded or open sites. (For more information about recreation options nearby, see the listing in this chapter for *Sounds of the Sea RV Park*.)

RV sites, facilities: There are 73 sites with full hookups (30 amps) for RVs up to 35 feet. No tents. A storage shed and cable TV are provided. Three cabins are available. Restrooms have showers. Fish-cleaning stations, fish smokers, canning facilities, a coin laundry, and propane are available. Leashed pets are permitted.

Reservations, fees: Reservations are accepted for cabins only. Sites are $22 per night, $2 per person per night for more than two people. Monthly rates are available during the summer. Open year-round.

Directions: From Eureka, drive north on U.S. 101 for 28 miles to the Trinidad exit. Take that exit to Main Street. Turn left on Main Street and drive 0.1 mile under the freeway to Patrick's Point Drive. Turn right on Patrick's Point Drive and drive one mile to the campground on the right at 875 Patrick's Point Drive.

Contact: Sylvan Harbor RV Park and Cabins, 707/677-9988, www.sylvanharbor.com.

26 VIEW CREST LODGE, COTTAGES, AND CAMPGROUND

Scenic rating: 8

in Trinidad

See map page 478

View Crest Campground is one of the premium spots in Trinidad, with pretty cottages available as well as campsites for RVs and tents. A bonus here is the remarkable flights of swallows, many of which have nests at the cottages. Nearby recreation options include deep-sea and salmon fishing at Trinidad Harbor to the south and outstanding easy hiking at Patrick's Point State Park to the north.

RV sites, facilities: There are 36 sites with full hookups (20 and 30 amps) for RVs of any length and a separate area for tents. Some sites are pull-through. Twelve cottages are also available. Picnic tables and fire rings are provided. Restrooms have showers. Cable TV, a coin laundry, and firewood are available. Leashed pets are permitted only in the campground.

Reservations, fees: Reservations are accepted. Sites are $16–25 per night, $1 per person per night for more than two people. Monthly rates available. Some credit cards accepted. Open year-round.

Directions: From Eureka, drive north on U.S. 101 for 28 miles to Trinidad. Continue north for five miles and take the Patrick's Point State Park exit to Patrick's Point Drive. Turn left and drive 0.9 mile to the lodge on the left.

Contact: View Crest Lodge, Cottages, and Campground, 707/677-3393, www.viewcrestlodge.com.

27 MIDWAY RV PARK

Scenic rating: 6

in Trinidad

See map page 478

This is one of several privately developed campgrounds in Trinidad. In the summer, salmon fishing can be excellent just off Trinidad Head. In the fall, rock fishing is the way to go, and in winter, crabbing is tops. Patrick's Point State Park provides a nearby side-trip option to the north. Note that some sites have long-term renters, and most of the remaining sites fill up for the entire summer season. It can be difficult to get a space here for overnight camping during the summer.

RV sites, facilities: There are 73 sites with full hookups (30 amps) for RVs up to 40 feet. No tents. Picnic tables are provided. Restrooms have showers. Cable TV, a club room, propane, a coin laundry, and a fish-cleaning station are available. Some facilities are wheelchair accessible. Leashed pets are permitted.

Reservations, fees: Reservations are recom-

mended in the summer. Sites are $25–28 per night. Some credit cards accepted. Open year-round.

Directions: From Eureka, drive north on U.S. 101 for 28 miles to the Trinidad exit. Take that exit to Main Street. Turn left on Main Street and drive 0.1 mile under the freeway to Patrick's Point Drive. Turn right on Patrick's Point Drive and drive 0.5 mile to Midway Drive. Turn right and drive 0.1 mile to the campground at 51 Midway Drive.

Contact: Midway RV Park, tel./fax 707/677-3934.

28 EMERALD FOREST

Scenic rating: 5

in Trinidad

See map page 478

This campground is on 12 acres of redwoods, often dark and wet, with the ocean at Trinidad Head only about a five-minute drive away. The campground owners emphasize that it is a vacation and overnight park only, not a mobile home or long-term park.

RV sites, facilities: There are 45 sites with full or partial hookups (30 amps) for RVs up to 45 feet, plus 30 tent sites. Some sites are pull-through. There are also 19 cabins. Picnic tables, fire rings, and barbecues are provided. Restrooms, showers, free cable TV in RV sites, a playground, a convenience store, ice, firewood, a coin laundry, group facilities, a fish-cleaning station, a dump station, propane, telephone and modem hookups, Wi-Fi, volleyball, horseshoes, badminton, and video arcade are available. Leashed pets are permitted, except in the tent sites and cabins.

Reservations, fees: Reservations are recommended in the summer. Sites are $26–38 per night, $2.50–3 per person per night for more than two people. Winter rates available. Some credit cards accepted. Open year-round.

Directions: From Eureka, drive north on U.S. 101 for 28 miles to the Trinidad exit. Take that exit to Main Street. Turn left on Main

CALIFORNIA

Street and drive 0.1 mile under the freeway to Patrick's Point Drive. Turn right on Patrick's Point Drive and drive 0.9 mile north to the campground at 753 Patrick's Point Drive.

Contact: Emerald Forest, 707/677-3554, fax 707/677-0963, www.rvintheredwoods.com.

29 HIDDEN CREEK RV PARK

Scenic rating: 5

in Trinidad

See map page 478

To tell you the truth, there really isn't much hidden about this RV park, but you might be hard-pressed to find year-round Parker Creek. Regardless, it is still in a pretty location in Trinidad, with the Trinidad pier, adjacent harbor, restaurants, and beach all within a drive of just a minute or two. Deep-sea fishing for salmon, lingcod, and rockfish is available on boats out of Trinidad Harbor. Crab and albacore tuna are also caught here, and there's beachcombing for agates and driftwood on the beach to the immediate north. Note that half of the sites are filled with long-term renters.

RV sites, facilities: There are 56 sites with full or partial hookups (30 and 50 amps) for RVs up to 40 feet, as well as a grassy area for tents. Six park-model cabins are also available. Picnic tables are provided. Cable TV, restrooms with showers, a fish-cleaning station, ice, a picnic area, and a dump station are available. Leashed pets are permitted.

Reservations, fees: Reservations are recommended in the summer. Sites are $14–29 per night, $2 per person per night for more than two people. Long-term rates available. Open year-round.

Directions: From Eureka, drive north on U.S. 101 for 28 miles to Trinidad. Take the Trinidad exit to the stop sign. Turn right at Westhaven Drive and drive a short distance to the RV park on the left at 199 North Westhaven.

Contact: Hidden Creek RV Park, 707/677-3775.

30 CLAM BEACH COUNTY PARK

Scenic rating: 7

near McKinleyville

See map page 478

Here awaits a beach that seems to stretch on forever, one of the great places to bring a lover, dog, children, or, hey, all three. While the campsites are a bit exposed, making winds out of the north a problem in the spring, the direct beach access largely makes up for it. The park gets its name from the fair clamming that is available, but you must come equipped with a clam gun or special clam shovel, and then be out when minus low tides arrive at daybreak. Most people just enjoy playing tag with the waves, taking long romantic walks, or throwing sticks for the dog.

RV sites, facilities: There are 12 sites for tents and a parking lot for 15 RVs of any length. No hookups. Picnic tables and fire rings are provided. Drinking water and vault toilets are available. Propane gas, a grocery store, and a coin laundry are available in McKinleyville. Leashed pets are permitted.

Reservations, fees: Reservations are not accepted. Sites are $10 per night per vehicle, $3 per person per night for hike-in/bike-in, and $1 per pet per night. Open year-round.

Directions: From Eureka, drive north on U.S. 101 to McKinleyville. Continue past McKinleyville to the Clam Beach Park exit. Take that exit and turn west at the sign for Clam Beach. Drive two blocks to the campground, which is adjacent to Little River State Beach.

Contact: Humboldt County Public Works, 707/445-7651, www.co.humboldt.ca.us.

31 MAD RIVER RAPIDS RV PARK

Scenic rating: 7

in Arcata

See map page 478

This park is near the farmlands on the outskirts of town, in a pastoral, quiet setting. There is a great bike ride nearby on a trail routed along the

CALIFORNIA

Mad River, and it is also excellent for taking a dog for a walk. Nearby Arcata is a unique town, a bit of the old and a bit of the new, and the Arcata Marsh at the north end of Humboldt Bay provides a scenic and easy bicycle trip, as well as an excellent destination for hiking, sightseeing, and bird-watching. About half of the sites are filled with long-term renters.

RV sites, facilities: There are 92 sites with full hookups (30 and 50 amps) for RVs of any length; some are pull-through. No tents. Picnic tables are provided. Fire grills are provided at two sites. Restrooms have showers. Cable TV, Wi-Fi, a dump station, a recreation room, tennis courts, a fitness room, a playground, basketball courts, a jogging trail, an arcade, table tennis, horseshoe pits, a heated swimming pool, a spa, group facilities, a restaurant and bar, a convenience store, RV supplies, and a coin laundry are available. A motel is adjacent to the park. Some facilities are wheelchair accessible. Leashed pets are permitted.

Reservations, fees: Reservations are accepted at 800/822-7776. Sites are $33 per night. Some credit cards accepted. Weekly and monthly rates available. Open year-round.

Directions: From the junction of U.S. 101 and Highway 299 in Arcata, drive 0.25 mile north on U.S. 101 to the Guintoli Lane/Janes Road exit. Take that exit and turn left (west) on Janes Road and drive two blocks to the park on the left.

Contact: Mad River Rapids RV Park, 707/822-7275, www.madriverrv.com.

32 SAMOA BOAT LAUNCH COUNTY PARK

Scenic rating: 7

on Humboldt Bay

See map page 479

The nearby vicinity of the boat ramp, with access to Humboldt Bay and the Pacific Ocean, makes this a star attraction for campers towing their fishing boats. Near the campground you get good beachcombing and clamming at

low tides and a chance to see a huge variety of seabirds, highlighted by egrets and herons. There's a reason: Directly across the bay is the Humboldt Bay National Wildlife Refuge. Adjacent to the park is the Samoa Dunes Recreation Area, which is popular with ATV enthusiasts who are allowed to ride on the beach. This park is near the famed all-you-can-eat, logger-style Samoa Cookhouse. The park is on the bay, not on the ocean.

RV sites, facilities: There are 20 sites for tents or RVs of any length (no hookups). Overflow camping is available in a parking lot for tents or RVs of any length. Picnic tables and fire grills are provided. Drinking water and restrooms with flush toilets and coin showers are available. A boat ramp, a grocery store, propane, and a coin laundry are available in Eureka (about five miles away). Leashed pets are permitted.

Reservations, fees: Reservations are not accepted. Sites are $14 per night per vehicle, $3 per person per night for hike-in/bike-in, $3 per night for an additional vehicle, and $1 per pet per night. Open year-round.

Directions: From U.S. 101 in Eureka, turn west on Highway 255 and drive two miles until it dead-ends at New Navy Base Road. At New Navy Base Road, turn left and drive five miles to the end of the Samoa Peninsula and the campground entrance.

Contact: Humboldt County Public Works, 707/445-7651, www.co.humboldt.ca.us.

33 EUREKA KOA

Scenic rating: 2

in Eureka

See map page 479

This is a year-round KOA camp for U.S. 101 cruisers looking for a layover spot in Eureka. A bonus here is a few of those little KOA Kamping Kabins, the log-style jobs that win on cuteness alone. The closest significant recreation option is the Arcata Marsh on Humboldt Bay, a richly diverse spot with good trails for biking and hiking or just parking and looking at the water. Another option is excellent salmon fishing in June, July, and August.

RV sites, facilities: There are 140 sites with full or partial hookups (30 and 50 amps) for RVs of any length, 26 tent sites, and eight hike-in/bike-in sites. Most RV sites are pull-through. Ten camping cabins and two cottages are also available. Picnic tables and fire pits are provided. Drinking water, restrooms with flush toilets and showers, cable TV, a playground, a recreation room, a heated swimming pool, two spas, a convenience store, a coin laundry, a dump station, propane, ice, firewood, a fax machine, and Wi-Fi are available. Some facilities are wheelchair accessible. Leashed pets are permitted.

Reservations, fees: Reservations are accepted at 800/562-3136. Sites are $26–45 per night, $3 per person per night for more than two people, $20 per night for hike-in/bike-in sites, $2 per pet per night, and $2 per night for an additional vehicle. Some credit cards accepted. Open year-round.

Directions: From Eureka, drive north on U.S. 101 for four miles to KOA Drive (well signed on the east side of the highway). Turn right on KOA Drive and drive a short distance to the end of the road.

Contact: Eureka KOA, 707/822-4243, fax 707/822-0126, www.koa.com.

34 E-Z LANDING RV PARK AND MARINA

Scenic rating: 6

on Humboldt Bay

See map page 479

This is a good base camp for salmon trips in July and August when big schools of king salmon often teem just west of the entrance of Humboldt Bay. A nearby boat ramp with access to Humboldt Bay is a bonus. It's not the prettiest camp in the world, with quite a bit of asphalt, but most people use this camp as a simple parking spot for sleeping and getting down to the business of the day: fishing. This spot is ideal for ocean fishing, clamming,

beachcombing, and boating. There are a few long-term and seasonal renters.

RV sites, facilities: There are 45 sites with full hookups (30 amps) for RVs; some are pull-through. Tent camping is allowed in vacant RV sites. Restrooms have flush toilets and showers. Marine gas, ice, a coin laundry, bait, and boat slips are available. Some facilities are wheelchair accessible. Leashed pets are permitted.

Reservations, fees: Reservations are accepted. RV sites are $20 per night, $15 per night for tents. Some credit cards accepted. Open year-round.

Directions: From Eureka, drive 3.5 miles south on U.S. 101 to King Salmon Avenue. Turn west (right) on King Salmon Avenue (it becomes Buhne Drive) and drive for 0.5 mile to where the road turns. Turn left (south) on Buhne Drive and go 0.5 mile to the park on the left (1875 Buhne Drive).

Contact: E-Z Landing RV Park and Marina, 707/442-1118, fax 707/442-1999.

35 JOHNNY'S MARINA AND RV PARK

Scenic rating: 5

on Humboldt Bay

See map page 479

This is a good base camp for salmon fishing during the peak season—always call, since the season changes each year as set by the Department of Fish and Game. Mooring for private boats is available, a nice plus for campers trailering boats. Other recreation activities include beachcombing, clamming, and perch fishing from shore. The owners have run this place since 1948. Note that a number of sites are filled with long-term renters.

RV sites, facilities: There are 53 sites with full hookups (30 and 50 amps) for RVs up to 38 feet. No tents. Flush toilets and a dump station are available; there are no showers. A coin laundry and boat dock are available. Leashed pets are permitted.

Reservations, fees: Reservations are accepted.

CALIFORNIA

Sites are $23 per night, plus $1 per person per night for more than two people. Open year-round.

Directions: From Eureka, drive 3.5 miles south on U.S. 101 to King Salmon Avenue. Turn west (right) on King Salmon Avenue (it becomes Buhne Drive). Continue about 0.5 mile to the park on the left (1821 Buhne Drive).

Contact: Johnny's Marina and RV Park, 707/442-2284, fax 707/443-4608.

36 VAN DUZEN COUNTY PARK: SWIMMER'S DELIGHT

Scenic rating: 6

on the Van Duzen River
See map page 479

This campground is near the headwaters of the Van Duzen River, one of the Eel River's major tributaries. The river is subject to tremendous fluctuations in flows and height, so low in the fall that it is often temporarily closed to fishing by the Department of Fish and Game, so high in the winter that only fools would stick their toes in. For a short period in late spring, it provides a benign run for rafting and canoeing, putting in at Grizzly Creek and taking out at Van Duzen. In October, you'll find an excellent salmon fishing spot where the Van Duzen enters the Eel.

RV sites, facilities: There are 30 sites for tents or RVs of any length; some sites have partial hookups (30 amps). Picnic tables and fire grills are provided. Drinking water and restrooms with flush toilets and coin showers are available. A grocery store and coin laundry are available nearby. Some facilities are wheelchair accessible. Leashed pets are permitted in the campground but not on the beach.

Reservations, fees: Reservations are not accepted. Sites are $15–20 per night, $3 per person per night for hike-in/bike-in, $3 per night for an additional vehicle, and $1 per pet per night. Open year-round.

Directions: From Eureka, drive south on U.S. 101 to the junction of Highway 36 at

Alton. Turn east on Highway 36 and drive 12 miles to the campground.

Contact: Humboldt County Public Works, 707/445-7651, www.co.humboldt.ca.us.

37 GRIZZLY CREEK REDWOODS STATE PARK

Scenic rating: 8

near Bridgeville
See map page 479

Most summer vacationers hit the campgrounds on the Redwood Highway; that is, U.S. 101. However, this camp is just far enough off the beaten path to provide some semblance of seclusion. It nestles in redwoods, quite beautiful, with fair hiking and good access to the adjacent Van Duzen River. The park encompasses only a few acres, yet it is very intimate. There are 4.5 miles of hiking trails, a visitors center with exhibits, and a bookstore. The Cheatham Grove in this park is an exceptional stand of coast redwoods. Fishing is catch-and-release only with barbless hooks. Nearby attractions include the Victorian village of Ferndale and Fort Humboldt to the north, Humboldt Redwoods State Park to the south, and Ruth Lake to the more distant east. Insider's tip: Half of the park borders Highway 36, and you can hear highway noise from some campsites.

RV sites, facilities: There are nine sites for tents or small RVs, 11 sites for RVs up to 30 feet or trailers up to 24 feet, 10 tent sites, and one hike-in/bike-in site. No hookups. Picnic tables, food lockers, and fire grills are provided. Drinking water and restrooms with flush toilets and showers are available. A grocery store is within 3.5 miles. Some facilities are wheelchair accessible. Leashed pets are permitted in the campground but not on trails or the beach area.

Reservations, fees: Reservations are accepted ($7.50 reservation fee) at 800/444-PARK (800/444-7275) or www.reserveamerica.com. Sites are $20 per night, $6 per night for an additional vehicle, and $3 per person per night for the hike-in/bike-in site. Open year-round.

Directions: From Eureka, drive south on U.S. 101 to the junction of Highway 36 at Alton. Turn east on Highway 36 and drive about 17 miles to the campground on the right.

Contact: Grizzly Creek Redwoods State Park, 707/777-3683, www.parks.ca.gov.

38 HUMBOLDT REDWOODS STATE PARK: ALBEE CREEK

🏕 🏊 🎣 🐕 ♿ 🚐 ⛺

Scenic rating: 8

in Humboldt Redwoods State Park

See map page 479

Humboldt Redwoods State Park is a massive sprawl of forest that is known for some unusual giant trees in the Federation Grove and Big Tree Area. The park covers nearly 53,000 acres, including more than 17,000 acres of old-growth coast redwoods. It has 100 miles of hiking trails, many excellent, both short and long. The camp sits in a redwood grove, and the smell of these trees has a special magic. Nearby Albee Creek, a benign trickle most of the year, can flood in the winter after heavy rains. Seasonal interpretive programs, campfire talks, nature walks, and junior ranger programs are available.

RV sites, facilities: There are 40 sites for tents or RVs up to 33 feet (no hookups) and trailers up to 24 feet. Picnic tables, fire grills, and food lockers are provided. Drinking water, restrooms with flush toilets and showers, and firewood are available. Some facilities are wheelchair accessible. Leashed pets are permitted.

Reservations, fees: Reservations are accepted ($7.50 reservation fee) at 800/444-PARK (800/444-7275) or www.reserveamerica.com. Sites are $20 per night, $3 per person per night for hike-in/bike-in, and $6 per night for an additional vehicle. Open Memorial Day weekend–mid-October.

Directions: From Eureka, drive south on U.S. 101 about 11 miles to the Honeydew exit (if you reach Weott, you have gone two miles too far). At Mattole Road, turn west and drive five miles to the campground on the right.

Contact: Humboldt Redwoods State Park,

707/946-2472 or 707/946-2409, fax 707/946-2326, www.parks.ca.gov.

39 HUMBOLDT REDWOODS STATE PARK: BURLINGTON

🏕 🏊 🎣 🐕 ♿ 🚐 ⛺

Scenic rating: 7

in Humboldt Redwoods State Park

See map page 479

This camp is one of the centerpieces of Humboldt Redwoods State Park. This park is California's largest redwood state park. It includes the Rockefeller Forest, the largest remaining contiguous old-growth coast redwood forest in the world. The trees here are thousands of years old and have never been logged; they are as pristine now as 200 years ago. This camp is often at capacity during the tourist months. You get shady campsites with big redwood stumps that kids can play on. There's good hiking on trails routed through the redwoods, and in winter, steelhead fishing is often good on the nearby Eel River. The park has 100 miles of trails, but it is little half-mile Founders Grove Nature Trail that has the quickest payoff and requires the least effort. The average rainfall here is 65 inches per year, with most occurring between October and May. Morning and evening fog in the summer keeps the temperature cool in the river basin.

RV sites, facilities: There are 57 sites for tents or RVs up to 33 feet or trailers up to 24 feet (no hookups) and three hike-in/bike-in sites. Picnic tables, fire grills, and food lockers are provided. Drinking water, restrooms with flush toilets and showers, and firewood are available. Some facilities are wheelchair accessible. Leashed pets are permitted.

Reservations, fees: Reservations are accepted ($7.50 reservation fee) at 800/444-PARK (800/444-7275) or www.reserveamerica.com. Sites are $20 per night, $6 per night for an additional vehicle, and $3 per person per night for hike-in/bike-in sites. Open year-round.

Directions: From Eureka, drive south on U.S. 101 for 45 miles to the Weott/Newton Road exit. Turn right on Newton Road and

CALIFORNIA

continue to the T junction where Newton Road meets the Avenue of the Giants. Turn left on the Avenue of the Giants and drive two miles to the campground entrance on the left.

Contact: Humboldt Redwoods State Park, 707/946-1811 or 707/946-2409, fax 707/946-2326, www.parks.ca.gov.

40 HUMBOLDT REDWOODS STATE PARK: HIDDEN SPRINGS

Scenic rating: 7

in Humboldt Redwoods State Park

See map page 479

This camp gets heavy use May–September, but the campsites have been situated in a way that offers relative seclusion. Side trips include good hiking on trails routed through redwoods and a touring drive on Avenue of the Giants. The park has more than 100 miles of hiking trails, many of them amid spectacular giant redwoods, including Bull Creek Flats Trail and Founders Grove Nature Trail. Bears are occasionally spotted by mountain bikers on rides out to the park's outskirts. In winter, nearby High Rock on the Eel River is one of the better shoreline fishing spots for steelhead. (For more information on Humboldt Redwoods, see listings in this chapter for *Albee Creek* and *Burlington* campgrounds.)

RV sites, facilities: There are 154 sites for tents or RVs up to 33 feet or trailers up to 24 feet (no hookups). Picnic tables, fire grills, and food lockers are provided. Drinking water, restrooms with flush toilets and showers, and firewood are available. A grocery store and coin laundry are available within one mile in Myers Flat. Leashed pets are permitted.

Reservations, fees: Reservations are accepted ($7.50 reservation fee) at 800/444-PARK (800/444-7275) or www.reserveamerica.com. Sites are $20 per night and $6 per night for an additional vehicle. Open mid-April–Labor Day weekend.

Directions: From Eureka, drive south 50 miles on U.S. 101 to the Myers Flat/Avenue of the Gi-

ants exit. Continue south and drive less than a mile to the campground entrance on the left.

Contact: Humboldt Redwoods State Park, 707/943-3177 or 707/946-2409, fax 707/946-2326, www.parks.ca.gov.

41 GIANT REDWOODS RV AND CAMP

Scenic rating: 8

on the Eel River

See map page 479

This privately operated park is set in a grove of redwoods and covers 23 acres, much of it fronting the Eel River. Trip options include the scenic drive on Avenue of the Giants.

RV sites, facilities: There are 57 sites for RVs of any length and 26 tent sites. Many of the RV sites have full or partial hookups (30 amps) and are pull-through. Picnic tables and fire rings are provided. Restrooms have showers. Modem hookups, a convenience store, ice, a coin laundry, a playground, a dog "freedom area," and a recreation room are available. Leashed pets are permitted.

Reservations, fees: Reservations are recommended in the summer. Sites are $25.30–37.40 per night, $3 per person per night for more than two people, and $2 per pet per night. Seventh night free. Some credit cards accepted. Open year-round, with limited facilities in winter.

Directions: From Eureka, drive south 50 miles on U.S. 101 to the Myers Flat/Avenue of the Giants exit. Turn right on Avenue of the Giants and make a quick left onto Myers Avenue. Drive 0.25 mile on Myers Avenue to the campground entrance.

Contact: Giant Redwoods RV and Camp, 707/943-3198, www.giantredwoodsrvcamp.com.

42 A. W. WAY COUNTY PARK

Scenic rating: 8

on the Mattole River

See map page 479

This secluded camp provides a home for visitors to the "Lost Coast," the beautiful coastal stretch of California far from any semblance of urban life. The highlight here is the Mattole River, a great steelhead stream when flows are suitable between January and mid-March. Nearby is excellent hiking in the King Range National Conservation Area. For the great hike out to the abandoned Punta Gorda Lighthouse, drive to the trailhead on the left side of Lighthouse Road and head south. It's a level walk, and at low tide, there's a chance to observe tidepool life. Note that this area is typically bombarded with monsoon-level rains in winter.

RV sites, facilities: There are 35 sites for tents or RVs of any length (no hookups). Overflow camping is also available. Picnic tables and fire grills are provided. Drinking water, restrooms with flush toilets, and cold showers are available. A grocery store, a coin laundry, and propane gas are available nearby. Leashed pets are permitted.

Reservations, fees: Reservations are not accepted. Sites are $15 per night per vehicle, $3 per person per night for hike-in/bike-in, $3 per night for an additional vehicle, and $1 per pet per night. Open year-round.

Directions: From Garberville, drive north on U.S. 101 to the South Fork-Honeydew exit. Turn west on South Fork-Honeydew Road and drive 31 miles (the road changes between pavement, gravel, and dirt, and it's steep and curvy) to the park entrance on the left side of the road. The park is 7.5 miles east of the town of Petrolia. (South Fork–Honeydew Road can be difficult for larger vehicles.)

Contact: Humboldt County Public Works, 707/445-7651, www.co.humboldt.ca.us.

43 DEAN CREEK RESORT

Scenic rating: 7

on the South Fork of the Eel River

See map page 479

This year-round RV park is on the South Fork of the Eel River. This is a very family-oriented resort. In the summer, it makes a good base camp for a redwood park adventure, with Humboldt Redwoods State Park (well north of here) providing 100 miles of hiking trails, many routed through awesome stands of giant trees. In the winter heavy rains feed the South Fork Eel, inspiring steelhead upstream on their annual winter journey. Fishing is good in this area, best by shore at nearby High Rock. Bank access is good at several other spots. Note that there is catch-and-release fishing only; check fishing regulations. Contact information for fishing guides is available at the resort, and they offer winter steelhead fishing specials. An excellent side trip is to drive three miles south to the Avenue of the Giants, a tour through giant redwood trees. The campground also offers volleyball, shuffleboard, badminton, and horseshoes. You get the idea.

RV sites, facilities: There are 64 sites for tents or RVs of any length with full or partial hookups (30 and 50 amps); some sites are pull-through. Picnic tables and fire grills are provided. Restrooms have showers. A recreation room, a coin laundry, a motel, a convenience store, modem and Wi-Fi access, RV supplies, firewood, ice, a giant spa, a sauna, a seasonal heated swimming pool, a dump station, an amphitheater, group facilities, an arcade, basketball, tetherball, shuffleboard, volleyball, mini golf, and a playground are available. Some facilities are wheelchair accessible. Leashed pets are permitted.

Reservations, fees: Reservations are recommended in the summer at 877/923-2555. Sites are $26–36 per night, $3.50 per person per night for more than two people, $1.50 per pet per night, $1.50 per night for an additional vehicle. Some credit cards accepted. Open year-round.

Directions: From Eureka, drive 60 miles south on U.S. 101 to the Redwood Drive exit. Exit onto Redwood Drive and continue about one-half block to the motel/campground entrance on the right; check in at the motel.

Contact: Dean Creek Resort, 707/923-2555, www.deancreekresort.com.

CALIFORNIA

44 SHELTER COVE CAMPGROUND AND DELI

Scenic rating: 9

overlooking the Pacific Ocean

See map page 479

This is a prime oceanside spot to set up a base camp for deep-sea fishing, whale-watching, tidepool gazing, beachcombing, and hiking. While this is a prime recreation area, the campground itself is rather uninspiring. Long-term renters occupy some of the campsites. A wide boat ramp makes it perfect for campers who have trailered boats and don't mind the long drive. Reservations are strongly advised here. The park's backdrop is the King Range National Conservation Area, offering spectacular views. The deli is well known for its fish-and-chips. The salmon, halibut, and rockfish fishing is quite good here in the summer; always call first for current regulations and seasons, which change every year. Clamming is best during winter's low tides, and hiking in the King Mountain Range is great during the summer. Seasonal abalone diving and shore fishing for redtail perch are also available. There is heavy rain in winter. Insider's tip: Two miles north is one of the only black-sand beaches in the continental United States.

RV sites, facilities: There are 103 sites for tents or RVs; many have full hookups (30 amps) and some are pull-through. Picnic tables and fire rings are provided. Restrooms have showers. A dump station, a coin laundry, a grocery store, a deli, propane, ice, and RV supplies are available. A boat ramp and marina is across the street. Leashed pets are permitted.

Reservations, fees: Reservations are recommended. Sites are $26–37 per night, $5 per person per night for more than two people, $1 per pet per night. Some credit cards accepted. Open year-round.

Directions: From Eureka, drive 60 miles south on U.S. 101 to the Redway/Shelter Cove exit. Take that exit and drive 2.5 miles north on Redwood Road to Briceland-Thorne Road (which will become Shelter Cove Road). Turn right (west) and drive 18 miles (following the truck/RV route signs) to Upper Pacific Drive. Turn left (south) on Upper Pacific Drive and proceed (it becomes Machi Road) 0.5 mile to the park on the right.

Contact: Shelter Cove Campground and Deli, 707/986-7474, fax 707/986-7101.

45 BENBOW LAKE STATE RECREATION AREA

Scenic rating: 7

on the Eel River

See map page 479

This camp is along the South Fork of the Eel River, with easy access from U.S. 101. It gets heavy use in the summer. In theory, Benbow Lake is created each summer when the river is dammed on a temporary basis, creating a 26-acre lake for swimming and light boating (no motors). This seasonal dam is projected to be installed in mid-June and kept in place until mid-September. However, there is no guarantee this will occur. If you're making a vacation planned around lake recreation, always call first. In the winter, this stretch of river can be quite good for catch-and-release steelhead fishing. Warning: Blue-green algae warnings are sometimes posted here in late summer; the algae can be dangerous to dogs.

RV sites, facilities: There are 77 sites for tents or RVs up to 30 feet; two sites have full hookups (30 amps). Picnic tables, food lockers, and fire grills are provided. Drinking water and restrooms with flush toilets and coin showers are available. A boat ramp (no motors) and seasonal boat rentals are available nearby. There is a dump station at the park entrance. Supplies and a coin laundry are available in Garberville. Leashed pets are permitted at campsites only.

Reservations, fees: Reservations are accepted ($7.50 reservation fee) at 800/444-PARK (800/444-7275) or www.reserveamerica.com. Sites are $20–28 per night, $6 per night for an additional vehicle. Open May–September, weather permitting.

CALIFORNIA

Directions: From the junction of U.S. 101 and Highway 1 in Leggett, drive north on U.S. 101 past Richardson Grove State Park to the Benbow Drive exit (two miles south of Garberville). Take that exit and drive 2.7 miles to the park entrance.

Contact: Benbow Lake State Recreation Area, 707/923-3238; Richardson Grove State Park, 707/247-3318, www.parks.ca.gov.

46 BENBOW VALLEY RV RESORT AND GOLF COURSE

Scenic rating: 7

on the Eel River

See map page 479

This is an RV park set along U.S. 101 and the South Fork Eel River, with both a pretty nine-hole regulation golf course and little Benbow Lake providing nearby recreation. It takes on a dramatically different character in the winter, when the highway is largely abandoned, the river comes up, and steelhead migrate upstream to the stretch of water here. Cooks Valley and Benbow provide good shore-fishing access. Note that fishing restrictions for steelhead are extremely severe and subject to constant change; always check with the Department of Fish and Game before fishing for steelhead. (See the *Benbow Lake State Recreation Area* listing in this chapter for a note on the status of Benbow Lake.)

RV sites, facilities: There are 112 sites with full hookups (30 and 50 amps), including four "VIP" sites, for RVs of any length. Many sites are pull-through. No tents. Cottages, park-model cabins, and trailer rentals are also available. Picnic tables and cable TV are provided. Restrooms have showers. A coin laundry, a convenience store, a snack bar, a playground, a recreation room, a seasonal heated swimming pool, a seasonal spa, Wi-Fi, modem access, fax and copy services, group facilities, organized activities, shuffleboard, table tennis, horseshoes, a game room, RV supplies, and a nine-hole golf course are available. A boat dock and boat rent-als (in summer) are available within 100 feet at Benbow Lake. Leashed pets are permitted. A doggy playground and pet wash are available.

Reservations, fees: Reservations are accepted at 866/236-2697. Sites are $42–47 per night, $4 per person per night for more than two people, $4 per night for an additional vehicle, $3 per pet per night. Some credit cards accepted. Open year-round.

Directions: From the junction of U.S. 101 and Highway 1 in Leggett, drive north on U.S. 101 past Richardson Grove State Park to the Benbow Drive exit (two miles south of Garberville). Take that exit and turn right at the stop sign. Drive a short distance to the end of the road and Benbow Drive. Bear left on Benbow Drive and continue a short distance to the resort on the left.

Contact: Benbow Valley RV Resort and Golf Course, 707/923-2777, www.benbowrv.com.

47 RICHARDSON GROVE STATE PARK: MADRONE AND HUCKLEBERRY

Scenic rating: 8

in Richardson Grove State Park

See map page 479

The highway cuts a swath right through Richardson Grove State Park, and everyone slows to gawk at the tallest trees in the world, one of the most impressive groves of redwoods you can drive through in California. To explore further, there are several campgrounds available at the park, as well as a network of outstanding hiking trails. The best of these are short Redwood Exhibit Trail, Settlers Loop, and Toumey Trail. The park is one of the prettiest and most popular state parks, making reservations a necessity from Memorial Day through Labor Day weekend. When arriving from points south on U.S. 101, this is the first park in the Redwood Empire where you will encounter significant old-growth redwood. There are nine miles of hiking trails, fishing in the winter for steelhead, and several trees of significant note.

CALIFORNIA

RV sites, facilities: At Madrone Camp, there are 40 sites for tents or RVs up to 30 feet. At Huckleberry, there are 36 sites for tents or RVs up to 30 feet. No hookups. Picnic tables, food lockers, and fire grills are provided. Drinking water and restrooms with flush toilets and coin showers are available. A minimart and dump station (three miles away) are available nearby. Some facilities are wheelchair accessible. Leashed pets are permitted at campsites only.

Reservations, fees: Reservations are accepted ($7.50 reservation fee) at 800/444-PARK (800/444-7275) or www.reserveamerica.com. Sites are $15–20 per night, $6 per night for an additional vehicle. Open year-round, but subject to occasional winter closures.

Directions: From the junction of U.S. 101 and Highway 1 in Leggett, drive north on U.S. 101 for 16 miles (past Piercy) to the park entrance along the left (west) side of the road (Garberville is eight miles north on U.S. 101).

Contact: Richardson Grove State Park, 707/247-3318, www.parks.ca.gov.

48 RICHARDSON GROVE STATE PARK: OAK FLAT

Scenic rating: 8

in Richardson Grove State Park
See map page 479

Oak Flat is on the eastern side of the Eel River in the shade of forest and provides easy access to the river. The campground is open only in the summer. (For side-trip information, see the *Madrone and Huckleberry* listing in this chapter.)

RV sites, facilities: There are 100 sites for tents or RVs up to 24 feet (no hookups) and trailers up to 18 feet. Picnic tables, food lockers, and fire grills are provided. Drinking water, restrooms with flush toilets and coin showers, and Wi-Fi are available. A grocery store and propane gas are available nearby. Leashed pets are permitted.

Reservations, fees: Reservations are accepted ($7.50 reservation fee) at 800/444-PARK (800/444-7275) or www.reserveamerica.com.

Sites are $15–20 per night, $6 per night for an additional vehicle. Open mid-June–mid-September, weather permitting.

Directions: From the junction of U.S. 101 and Highway 1 in Leggett, drive north on U.S. 101 for 16 miles (past Piercy) to the park entrance on the left (west) side of the road (eight miles south of Garberville).

Contact: Richardson Grove State Park, 707/247-3318, www.parks.ca.gov.

49 RICHARDSON GROVE CAMPGROUND AND RV PARK

Scenic rating: 7

on the Eel River
See map page 479

This private camp provides a nearby alternative to Richardson Grove State Park, complete with log cabin rentals. The state park, with its grove of giant redwoods and excellent hiking, is the primary attraction. The RV park is family-oriented, with volleyball and basketball courts and horseshoe pits. The adjacent South Fork Eel River may look like a trickle in the summer, but there are some good swimming holes. It also provides good steelhead fishing in January and February, with especially good shore fishing access here as well as to the south in Cooks Valley (check Department of Fish and Game regulations before fishing). This campground is owned and operated by the Northern California/Nevada District Assemblies of God. Because of their nonprofit status, several cabins and a dorm are no longer available for rent.

RV sites, facilities: There are 98 sites for tents or RVs; some are pull-through, and many have full or partial hookups (30 amps). Two log cabins are also available. Picnic tables and fire rings are provided. Restrooms have showers. A dump station, Wi-Fi, modem access, a playground, a coin laundry, a convenience store, group facilities, propane, and ice are available. Leashed pets are permitted.

Reservations, fees: Reservations are recom-

CALIFORNIA

mended in the summer. Sites are $17–25 per night. Weekly, winter, and group rates are available. Some credit cards accepted. Open year-round.

Directions: From the junction of U.S. 101 and Highway 1 in Leggett, drive north on U.S. 101 for 15 miles (one mile before reaching Richardson Grove State Park) to the camp entrance on the west side (left) of the road.

Contact: Richardson Grove Campground and RV Park, 707/247-3380, fax 707/247-9806, www.redwoodfamilycamp.com.

SHASTA AND TRINITY

☾ BEST RV PARKS AND CAMPGROUNDS

At 14,162 feet, Mount Shasta rises like a diamond in a field of coal. Its sphere of influence spans a radius of 125 miles, and its shadow is felt everywhere in the region. This area has much to offer, with giant Shasta Lake, the Sacramento River above and below the lake, the McCloud River, and the wonderful Trinity Divide country with dozens of pretty backcountry lakes and several wilderness areas. This is one of the best regions anywhere for an outdoor adventure – especially hiking, fishing, powerboating, rafting, and exploring.

In this area you can find campgrounds that are truly remote, set near quiet wilderness, and that offer the potential for unlimited adventures. It's easy to find a campground in a secluded setting near great recreation opportunities. That is the main reason people visit.

There are hundreds of destinations, but the most popular are Shasta Lake, the Trinity Alps and its surrounding lakes and streams, and the Klamath Mountains, known as "Bigfoot Country" by the locals.

Shasta Lake is one of America's top recreation lakes. It is the one destination that is big enough to handle all who love it. The massive reservoir boasts 370 miles of shoreline; more than a dozen each of campgrounds, boat launches, and marinas; lakeshore lodging; and 400 houseboat rentals and cabin rentals. A remarkable 22 species of fish live in the lake. Many of the campgrounds feature lake views. In addition, getting here is easy – a straight shot off I-5.

At the charmed center of this beautiful region are the Trinity Alps, where lakes are sprinkled everywhere. It's also home to the headwaters for feeder streams to the Trinity River, Klamath River, New River, Wooley Creek, and others. Trinity Lake provides outstanding boating and fishing, and just downstream, smaller Lewiston Lake offers a quiet alternative. One advantage to Lewiston Lake is that it is always full of water, even all summer long, making for a very pretty scene. Downstream of Lewiston, the Trinity River provides low-cost rafting and outstanding shoreline access along Highway 299 for fishing for salmon and steelhead.

The neighboring Klamath Mountains are well known as Bigfoot Country. If you drive up the Forest Service road at Bluff Creek, just off Highway 96 upstream of Weitchpec, you can even find the spot where the famous Bigfoot home film footage was shot in the 1960s. Well, I haven't seen Bigfoot, but I have discovered tons of outdoor recreation. This remote

CALIFORNIA

region features miles of the Klamath and Salmon Rivers, as well as the Marble Mountain Wilderness. Options include canoeing, rafting, and fishing for steelhead on the Klamath River, or hiking to your choice of more than 100 wilderness lakes.

Includes:

- Castle Crags State Park
- Klamath National Forest
- Klamath River
- Lewiston Lake
- Little Shasta River
- Mount Shasta
- Ruth Lake
- Sacramento River
- Salmon River
- Scott River
- Shasta Lake
- Shasta-Trinity National Forest
- Six Rivers National Forest
- Trinity Lake
- Trinity River
- Whiskeytown Lake

CALIFORNIA

SHASTA AND TRINITY

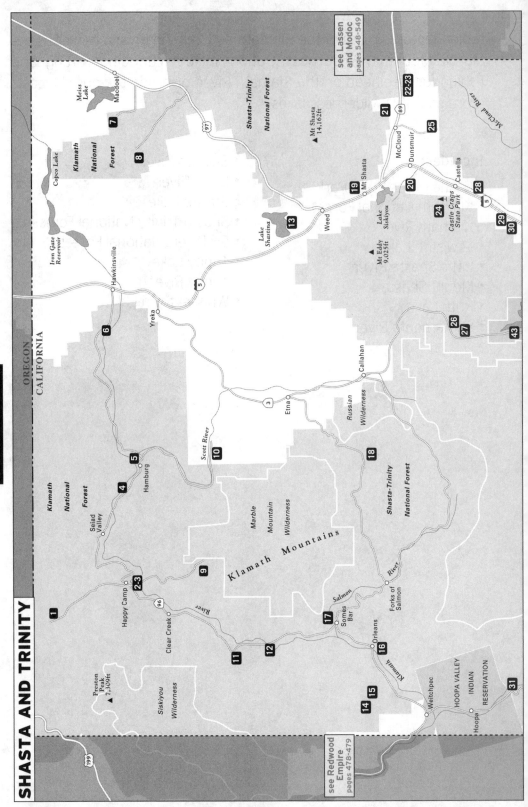

see Lassen and Modoc
pages 548-549

see Redwood Empire
pages 478-479

OREGON
CALIFORNIA

CALIFORNIA

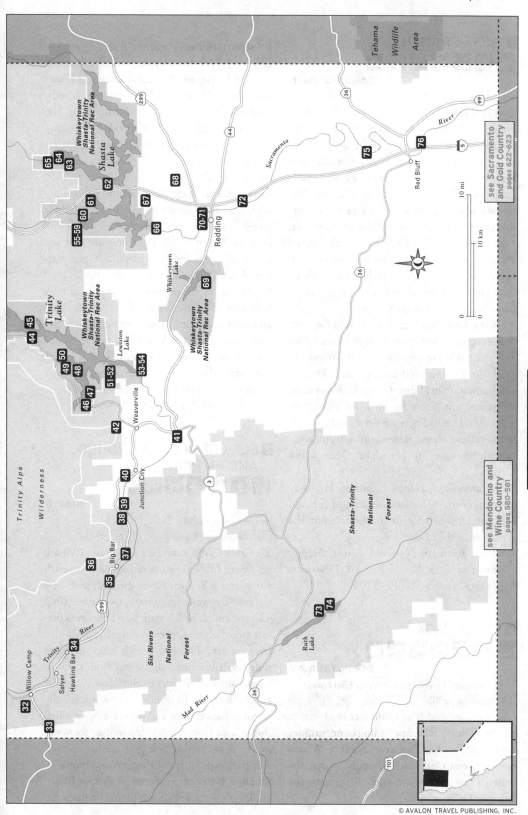

© AVALON TRAVEL PUBLISHING, INC.

CALIFORNIA

1 WEST BRANCH

Scenic rating: 6

in Klamath National Forest

See map page 508

Note: At the time of publication, this campground was closed because of road damage; check current status. This is a virtually unknown, low-charge camp, set in a canyon near Indian Creek. This is deep in Klamath National Forest at 2,200 feet in elevation. The best side trip here is the winding four-mile drive on a bumpy dirt road to Kelly Lake, little known and little used. A remote Forest Service station is on the opposite side of Indian Creek Road from the campground. It is a 20-minute drive from the town of Happy Camp.

RV sites, facilities: There are 12 sites for tents or RVs up to 25 feet (no hookups). Picnic tables and fire grills are provided. Vault toilets are available. There is no drinking water. There is a dump station in Happy Camp. Garbage must be packed out. Some facilities are wheelchair accessible. Leashed pets are permitted.

Reservations, fees: Reservations are not accepted. Sites are $10 per night. Open May–October.

Directions: From Happy Camp on Highway 96, turn north on Indian Creek Road (a paved road) and drive 14.5 miles to the camp on the right side of the road.

Contact: Klamath National Forest, Happy Camp and Oak Knoll Ranger Districts, 530/493-2243, fax 530/493-1794.

2 CURLY JACK

Scenic rating: 7

on the Klamath River in Klamath National Forest

See map page 508

This campground is at 1,000 feet in elevation on the Klamath River, providing opportunities for fishing, light rafting, and kayaking. What's special about Curly Jack, though, is that the water is generally warm enough through the summer for swimming.

RV sites, facilities: There are 16 sites for tents or RVs up to 22 feet, with some specially designed sites for RVs up to 45 feet and three group sites for tents or RVs up to 22 feet that can accommodate up to 30 people each. No hookups. Fire grills and picnic tables are provided. Drinking water and vault toilets are available. Some facilities are wheelchair accessible. Leashed pets are permitted.

Reservations, fees: Reservations are not accepted for individual sites but are required for group sites ($9 reservation fee) at 877/444-6777 or www.ReserveUSA.com. Sites are $10 per night, $30 per night for a group site. Open year-round, with limited winter facilities.

Directions: From the town of Happy Camp on Highway 96, turn south on Elk Creek Road and drive about one mile. Turn right on Curly Jack Road and drive one block to the campground entrance on the right.

Contact: Klamath National Forest, Happy Camp and Oak Knoll Ranger Districts, 530/493-2243, fax 530/493-1794.

3 ELK CREEK CAMPGROUND AND RV PARK

Scenic rating: 8

on the Klamath River

See map page 508

Elk Creek Campground is a year-round RV park set where Elk Creek pours into the Klamath River. It is a beautiful campground, with sites right on the water in a pretty, wooded setting. The section of the Klamath River nearby is perfect for inflatable kayaking and rafting. Guided trips are available, with a wide scope of white water available, rated all the way from the easy Class I stuff all the way to the Class V to-hell-and-back rapids. In addition, the water is quite warm in the summer, and flows are maintained throughout the year, making it ideal for water sports. A swimming hole gets use in summer. The park is popular with anglers and hunters.

RV sites, facilities: There are 34 sites for RVs of any length, some with full or partial hookups (30 and 50 amps), and some are pull-through. There is a separate area for tents. Three cabins and three rental trailers are available. Picnic tables and fire grills are provided. Restrooms have showers. Cable TV, Wi-Fi, a recreation room with billiards and table tennis, horseshoes, a beach, a coin laundry, a dump station, propane, and firewood are available. Leashed pets are permitted.

Reservations, fees: Reservations are recommended. Sites are $20–24 per night, $15 per night for tent sites. Weekly, monthly, and group rates are available. Some credit cards accepted. Open year-round.

Directions: From Highway 96 in the town of Happy Camp, turn south on Elk Creek Road and drive 0.75 mile to the campground on the right.

Contact: Elk Creek Campground and RV Park, 530/493-2208, fax 530/493-2029, www.elkcreekcampground.com.

4 O'NEIL CREEK

Scenic rating: 7

in Klamath National Forest

See map page 508

This camp is near O'Neil Creek at 1,500 feet in elevation, and though it's not far from the Klamath River, access to the river is not easy. To fish or raft, most people will use this as a base camp, then drive out for recreation during the day. That creates a predicament for RV owners, who lose their campsites every time they drive off. During the fall hunting season, this is a good base camp for hunters branching out into the surrounding national forest. There are also historic mining sites nearby.

RV sites, facilities: There are 11 sites for tents or RVs up to 22 feet (no hookups). Picnic tables and fire grills are provided. Drinking water and vault toilets are available. Garbage must be packed out. Supplies can be obtained in Seiad Valley. Leashed pets are permitted.

Reservations, fees: Reservations are not accepted. Sites are $10 per night. Open May–October.

Directions: From Yreka drive north on I-5 to the junction with Highway 96. Turn west on Highway 96 and drive past Hamburg, continuing west for three miles to the campground.

Contact: Klamath National Forest, Happy Camp and Oak Knoll Ranger Districts, 530/493-2243, fax 530/493-1794.

5 SARAH TOTTEN

Scenic rating: 7

on the Klamath River in Klamath National Forest

See map page 508

This is one of the more popular Forest Service camps on the Klamath River, and it's no mystery why. In the summer, its placement is perfect for rafters (Class II+ and III), who camp here and use it as a put-in spot. In fall and winter, anglers arrive for the steelhead run. It's in the "banana belt," or good-weather area of the Klamath, in a pretty grove of oak trees. Fishing is often good here for salmon in early October and for steelhead from November through spring, providing there are fishable water flows.

RV sites, facilities: There are eight sites for tents or RVs up to 22 feet (no hookups). Two group sites for tents or RVs up to 22 feet can accommodate up to 30 people each. No hookups. Picnic tables and fire grills are provided. Drinking water and vault toilets are available. A small grocery store is nearby. Some facilities are wheelchair accessible. Leashed pets are permitted.

Reservations, fees: Reservations are not accepted for individual sites but are required for the group sites ($9 reservation fee) at 877/444-6777 or www.ReserveUSA.com. Sites are $10 for per night, $30 per night for group sites. Open May–October.

Directions: From Yreka, drive north on I-5 to the junction with Highway 96. At Highway 96, turn west and drive to Horse Creek, continuing west for five miles to the campground on the right side of the road. If you reach the town of Hamburg, you have gone 0.5 mile too far.

Contact: Klamath National Forest, Happy Camp and Oak Knoll Ranger Districts, 530/493-2243, fax 530/493-1794.

CALIFORNIA

CALIFORNIA

6 TREE OF HEAVEN

Scenic rating: 7

in Klamath National Forest

See map page 508

This outstanding riverside campground provides excellent access to the Klamath River for fishing, rafting, and hiking. The best deal is to put in your raft, canoe, or drift boat upstream at the ramp below Iron Gate Reservoir, then make the all-day run down to the takeout at Tree of Heaven. This section of river is an easy paddle (Class II, II+, and III) and also provides excellent steelhead fishing in the winter. A 0.25-mile paved interpretive trail is near the camp. On the drive in from the highway, you can watch the landscape turn from high chaparral to forest.

RV sites, facilities: There are 20 sites for tents or RVs up to 35 feet (no hookups). Picnic tables and fire grills are provided. Drinking water and vault toilets are available. A river access spot for put-in and takeout for rafts and drift boats is available. Some facilities are wheelchair accessible. Leashed pets are permitted.

Reservations, fees: Reservations are accepted ($9 reservation fee) at 877/444-6777 or www.ReserveUSA.com. Sites are $10 per night. Open year-round.

Directions: From Yreka, drive north on I-5 to Highway 96. Turn west on Highway 96 and drive seven miles to the campground entrance on the left side of the road.

Contact: Klamath National Forest, Happy Camp and Oak Knoll Ranger Districts, 530/493-2243, fax 530/493-1796.

7 JUANITA LAKE

Scenic rating: 7

in Klamath National Forest

See map page 508

Small and relatively unknown, this camp is along the shore of Juanita Lake at 5,100 feet. Swimming is not recommended because the water is cold and mucky, and mosquitoes can be abundant as well. It is stocked with rainbow

trout, brown trout, bass, and catfish, but a problem with golden shiners has cut into the lake's fishing productivity. It's a small lake and forested, set near the Butte Valley Wildlife Area in the plateau country just five miles to the northeast. The latter provides an opportunity to see waterfowl and, in the winter, bald eagles. Campers will discover a network of Forest Service roads in the area, providing an opportunity for mountain biking. There are designated fishing areas and a paved trail around the lake that is wheelchair-accessible and spans approximately 1.25 miles.

RV sites, facilities: There are 23 sites for tents or RVs up to 32 feet (no hookups), and a group tent site can accommodate up to 50 people. Picnic tables and fire grills are provided. Drinking water and vault toilets are available. Boating is allowed, but no motors are permitted on the lake. Many facilities are wheelchair accessible. Leashed pets are permitted.

Reservations, fees: Reservations are not accepted for individual sites but are required for the group site at 530/398-4391. Sites are $10 per night, and the group site is $30 per night. Open late May to mid-October, weather permitting.

Directions: From Weed and I-5, turn north on U.S. 97 (Klamath Falls exit) and drive approximately 37 miles to Ball Mountain Road. Turn left on Ball Mountain Road, drive 2.5 miles, veer right at the fork, and continue to the campground entrance at the lake.

Contact: Klamath National Forest, Goosenest Ranger District, 530/398-4391, fax 530/398-5749.

8 MARTINS DAIRY

Scenic rating: 8

on the Little Shasta River in Klamath National Forest

See map page 508

This camp is at 6,000 feet, where the deer get big and the country seems wide open. Across the road from this remote camp is a large meadow with fantastic wildflower displays in late spring.

In the fall, this is one of the prettiest camps around, with dramatic color from aspens, elderberries, and willows. It also makes a good base camp for hunters in the fall. Before heading into the surrounding backcountry, buy a map of Klamath National Forest at the Goosenest Ranger Station on Highway 97, on your way in to camp.

RV sites, facilities: There are eight sites for tents or RVs up to 30 feet (no hookups) and a horse campsite. Picnic tables and fire grills are provided. Drinking water and vault toilets are available. Leashed pets are permitted.

Reservations, fees: Reservations are not accepted. Sites are $8 per night. Open late May to early October, weather permitting.

Directions: From Weed and I-5, turn north on U.S. 97 (Klamath Falls exit) and drive to Grass Lake. Continue about seven miles to Forest Road 70/46N10 (if you reach Hebron Summit, you have driven about a mile too far). Turn left, drive about 10 miles to a Y, take the left fork, and drive three miles (including a very sharp right turn) to the campground on the right side of the road. A map of Klamath National Forest is advised.

Contact: Klamath National Forest, Goosenest Ranger District, 530/398-4391, fax 530/398-5749.

9 NORCROSS

Scenic rating: 7

near Happy Camp in Klamath National Forest
See map page 508

Set at 2,400 feet in elevation, this camp serves as a staging area for various trails that provide access into the Marble Mountain Wilderness. There is also access to the popular Kelsey Trail and to swimming and fishing activities.

RV sites, facilities: There are six sites for tents or RVs up to 25 feet (no hookups). Picnic tables and fire pits are provided. Vault toilets, a horse corral, stock water, and a loading ramp are available. No drinking water is available. Garbage must be packed out. Some facilities are wheelchair accessible. Leashed pets are permitted.

Reservations, fees: Reservations are not accepted. There is no fee for camping. Open May–October.

Directions: From Yreka on I-5, drive west on Highway 96 to the town of Happy Camp. In Happy Camp, turn south onto Elk Creek Road and drive 16 miles to the campground.

Contact: Klamath National Forest, Happy Camp and Oak Knoll Ranger Districts, 530/493-2243, fax 530/493-1794.

10 INDIAN SCOTTY

Scenic rating: 7

on the Scott River in Klamath National Forest
See map page 508

This popular camp provides direct access to the adjacent Scott River. Because it is easy to reach (no gravel roads) and shaded, it gets a lot of use. The camp is at 2,400 feet. The levels, forces, and temperatures on the Scott River fluctuate greatly from spring to fall. In the spring, it can be a raging cauldron, but cold from snowmelt. Come summer it quiets, with some deep pools providing swimming holes. By fall, it can be reduced to a trickle. Keep your expectations flexible according to the season.

RV sites, facilities: There are 28 sites and a group site (parking lot) for tents or RVs up to 38 feet. No hookups. Picnic tables and fire grills are provided. Drinking water and vault toilets are available. There is a playground in the group-use area. Leashed pets are permitted.

Reservations, fees: Reservations are not accepted for individual sites but are required for the group site ($9 reservation fee) at 800/444-6777 or www.ReserveUSA.com. Sites are $10 per night, and the group site is $30 per night. Open May–October.

Directions: From Redding, drive north on I-5 to Yreka. In Yreka, turn southwest on Highway 3 and drive 16.5 miles to Fort Jones. In Fort Jones, turn right on Scott River Road and drive 14 miles to a concrete bridge and the adjacent signed campground entrance on the left.

Contact: Klamath National Forest, Scott River

CALIFORNIA

and Salmon River Ranger Districts, 530/468-5351, fax 530/468-1290.

11 DILLON CREEK

Scenic rating: 7

on the Klamath River in Klamath National Forest
See map page 508

This is a prime base camp for rafting or a steelhead fishing trip. A put-in spot for rafting is adjacent to the camp, with an excellent river run available from here on down past Presido Bar to the takeout at Ti-Bar. If you choose to go on, make absolutely certain to pull out at Green Riffle river access and takeout, or risk death at Ishi Pishi Falls. The water is warm here in the summer, and there are many excellent swimming holes in the area. In addition, this is a good stretch of water for steelhead fishing from September to February, best in early winter from Dillon Beach to Ti-Bar. The elevation is 800 feet.

RV sites, facilities: There are 21 sites for tents or RVs up to 30 feet (no hookups). Picnic tables, food lockers, and fire grills are provided. Drinking water and vault toilets are available. There is a dump station in Happy Camp 25 miles north of the campground and at Aikens Creek nine miles west of the town of Orleans. Some facilities are wheelchair accessible. Leashed pets are permitted.

Reservations, fees: Reservations are not accepted. Sites are $10 per night, $5 per night for an additional vehicle. Open mid-May to early November.

Directions: From Yreka drive north on I-5 to the junction with Highway 96. At Highway 96, turn west and drive to the town of Happy Camp. Continue west from Happy Camp for 35 miles and look for the campground on the right side of the road.

Coming from the west, from Somes Bar, drive 15 miles north on Highway 96.

Contact: Six Rivers National Forest, Orleans Ranger District, 530/627-3291, fax 530/627-3401.

12 MARBLE MOUNTAIN RANCH

Scenic rating: 6

near the Klamath River
See map page 508

The lodge is just across the road from the Klamath River, an ideal location as headquarters for a rafting trip in the summer or a steelhead fishing trip in the fall. This ranch is considered a vacation destination, with most people staying for a week. The majority of people staying at the ranch are on a package deal with cabin lodging, but campers can participate in meals and organized activities if they make reservations. Commercial rafting or kayaking trips on the Klamath River and Trinity River are available here, with guided trips offered by the ranch. This piece of river is beautiful and fresh with lots of wildlife and birds, yet not dangerous. However, be absolutely certain to take out at Green Riffle boat access before reaching Ishi Pishi Falls, which cannot be run. There's a full pack station at the ranch for guided trail rides lasting from one hour to overnight. Riding lessons are available. Wilderness pack trips, salmon and steelhead drift-boat fishing, and nature walks are also available. In addition, there is a sporting clays trap course. Hiking trails and swimming holes are available on the property. This is a popular ranch for family reunions, conferences, and weddings.

RV sites, facilities: There are 10 sites with full hookups (30 amps) for RVs of any length and 30 tent sites; some sites are pull-through. Eleven housekeeping cabins and two houses are also available. Picnic tables and fire grills are provided. Restrooms have showers. Drinking water, a coin laundry, ice, firewood, a recreation room, a swimming pool, a spa, a fitness room, a deli and gift shop, a swimming and fishing pond, a petting zoo, a playground, horseshoe pits, and volleyball and basketball courts are available.

Reservations, fees: Reservations are recommended. RV sites are $20 per night, it's $5 per person per night for tent sites, and it's $2 per person per night for more than two people.

CALIFORNIA

Some credit cards are accepted. Open year-round, weather permitting.

Directions: From the junction of U.S. 101 and Highway 299 near Arcata, turn east on Highway 299 and drive to Willow Creek. In Willow Creek, turn north (left) on Highway 96 east and drive to Somes Bar. At Somes Bar, continue for 7.5 miles to Mile Marker 7.6 and Marble Mountain Ranch on the right.

Contact: Marble Mountain Ranch, 530/469-3322 or 800/KLAMATH (800/552-6284), fax 530/469-3321, www.marblemountain ranch.com.

13 LAKE SHASTINA

Scenic rating: 7

near Klamath National Forest and Weed
See map page 508

Lake Shastina is at the northern foot of Mount Shasta at 3,000 feet in elevation. It offers spectacular views, good swimming on hot summer days, waterskiing, and all water sports. There is fishing for catfish and bass in the spring and summer, an occasional opportunity for crappie, and good fishing for trout in late winter and spring. One reason the views of Mount Shasta are so good is that this is largely high sagebrush country with few trees. As such, it can get very dusty, windy, and, in the winter, nasty cold. When the lake is full, the wind is down, and the weather is good, there are few complaints. But that is only rarely the case. The lake level is often low, with the water drained for hay farmers to the north. This is one of the few lakes in Northern California that has property with lakeside housing. Lake Shastina Golf Course is nearby.

RV sites, facilities: There is a small primitive area (no hookups) for tents or RVs of any length. There is one faucet, but you should bring your own water just in case. A vault toilet is available and a boat launch is nearby; the boat ramp is nonfunctional when the lake level drops below the concrete ramp. Garbage service is available May–September only. There

is a 14-day limit for camping. Supplies can be obtained five miles away in Weed. Leashed pets are permitted.

Reservations, fees: Reservations are not accepted. There is no fee for camping. Open May–September.

Directions: From Weed and I-5, turn north on U.S. 97 (Klamath Falls exit) and drive about five miles to Big Springs Road. Turn left (west) on Big Springs Road and drive about two miles to Jackson Ranch Road. Turn left (west) on Jackson Ranch Road and drive 0.5 mile to Emerald Isle Road (watch for the signed turnoff). Turn right and drive one mile to the campground.

Contact: Siskiyou County Public Works, 530/842-8250.

14 FISH LAKE

Scenic rating: 8

in Six Rivers National Forest
See map page 508

This pretty little lake provides good fishing for stocked rainbow trout from the season opener on Memorial Day weekend through July. The camp gets little pressure in other months. It's in the heart of Bigfoot country, with numerous Bigfoot sightings reported near Bluff Creek. No powerboats are permitted on the lake, but it's too small for that anyway, being better suited for a canoe, float tube, raft, or pram. The elevation is 1,800 feet. The presence here of Port-Orford-cedar root disease, spread by spores in the mud, forces closure October–May in some years; call for current status.

RV sites, facilities: There are 24 sites for tents or RVs up to 20 feet (no hookups). Picnic tables and fire grills are provided. Drinking water and vault toilets are available. Some facilities are wheelchair accessible. Leashed pets are permitted.

Reservations, fees: Reservations are not accepted. Sites are $10 per night, plus $5 per night for an additional vehicle. Open late May–early October, weather permitting.

Directions: From I-5 in Redding, turn west on

Highway 299 and drive to Willow Creek. At Willow Creek, turn north (left) on Highway 96 east and drive to Weitchpec, continuing seven miles north on Highway 96 to Fish Lake Road/Bluff Creek Road. Turn left on Fish Lake Road/Bluff Creek Road and drive five miles (stay to the right at the Y) to Fish Lake.

Contact: Six Rivers National Forest, Orleans Ranger District, 530/627-3291, fax 530/627-3401.

15 E-NE-NUCK

Scenic rating: 7

in Six Rivers National Forest
See map page 508

The campground gets its name from a Karuk Indian chief who lived in the area in the late 1800s. It's a popular spot for anglers; Bluff Creek and the Klamath are within walking distance and Fish Lake is eight miles to the west. Lucky anglers can also take advantage of a smoke house, a unique feature at this campground. Bluff Creek is the legendary site where the Bigfoot film of the 1960s was shot. While it was finally admitted that the film was a phony, it still has put Bluff Creek on the map.

RV sites, facilities: There are 11 sites for tents or RVs up to 30 feet (no hookups). Picnic tables, fire rings, and cast-iron firebox stoves are provided. Drinking water, vault toilets, and a smoke house are available. Some facilities are wheelchair accessible. Leashed pets are permitted.

Reservations, fees: Reservations are not accepted. Sites are $10 per night, plus $5 per additional vehicle. Open late June–October.

Directions: From the junction of U.S. 101 and Highway 299 near Arcata, turn east on Highway 299 and drive to Willow Creek. In Willow Creek, turn north (left) on Highway 96 east and drive to Weitchpec, continuing on Highway 96 for about five miles to the campground. E-Ne-Nuck is just beyond Aikens Creek West campground.

Contact: Six Rivers National Forest, Or-

leans Ranger District, 530/627-3291, fax 530/627-3401.

16 KLAMATH RIVERSIDE RV PARK AND CAMPGROUND

Scenic rating: 8

on the Klamath River
See map page 508

Klamath Riverside RV Park and Campground is an option for RV cruisers touring Highway 96—designated the Bigfoot Scenic Byway—and looking for a place in Orleans. The camp has large grassy sites set amid pine trees, right on the river. There are spectacular views of Mount Orleans and the surrounding hills. A 12-foot Bigfoot statue is on the property. Through the years, we've seen many changes at this park. It has been transformed from a dusty fishing spot to a park more resembling a rural resort that attracts hikers, cyclists, gold panners, river enthusiasts, anglers, and hunters. One big plus is that the park offers guided trips during the season for fishing.

RV sites, facilities: There are 45 sites with full hookups (30 and 50 amps) for RVs of any length and 12 tent sites; some are pull-through. Two cabins and six rental trailers are also available. Picnic tables and fire rings are provided. Restrooms have showers. A seasonal swimming pool, a spa, a group pavilion, a fish-cleaning station, a coin laundry, horseshoes, a playground, modem access, a pay phone, and RV storage are available. Guided drift-boat fishing in season is available. Leashed pets are permitted.

Reservations, fees: Reservations are accepted. Sites are $18–24 per night, plus $5 per person per night for more than two people. Group, weekly, and monthly rates are available. Open year-round.

Directions: From the junction of U.S. 101 and Highway 299 near Arcata, drive east on Highway 299 to Willow Creek, turn north (left) on Highway 96 east, and drive past Weitchpec to Orleans. This campground is at the west end of the town of Orleans on Highway 96 on the right.

Contact: Klamath Riverside RV Park and Campground, 530/627-3239 or 800/627-9779, fax 530/627-3755, www.klamathriverside rvpark.com.

17 OAK BOTTOM ON THE SALMON RIVER

Scenic rating: 7

in Klamath National Forest

See map page 508

This camp is just far enough off Highway 96 that it gets missed by zillions of out-of-towners every year. It is across the road from the lower Salmon River, a pretty, clean, and cold stream that pours out of the surrounding wilderness high country. Swimming is very good in river holes, though the water is cold, especially when nearby Wooley Creek is full of snowmelt pouring out of the Marble Mountains to the north. In the fall, there is good shoreline fishing for steelhead, though the canyon bottom is shaded almost all day and gets very cold.

RV sites, facilities: There are 26 sites for tents or RVs up to 25 feet (no hookups). Picnic tables and fire grills are provided. Drinking water and vault toilets are available. There is a dump station at the Elk Creek Campground in Happy Camp and at Aikens Creek, 13 miles southwest of the town of Orleans. Supplies are available in Somes Bar. Some facilities are wheelchair accessible. Leashed pets are permitted.

Reservations, fees: Reservations are not accepted. Sites are $10 per night, $5 per night for an additional vehicle. Open April to mid-October, weather permitting.

Directions: From the junction of U.S. 101 and Highway 299 near Arcata, turn east on Highway 299 and drive to Willow Creek and Highway 96. Turn north (left) on Highway 96 east and drive to Somes Bar-Etna Road (0.25 mile before Somes Bar). Turn right on Somes

Bar-Etna Road and drive two miles to the campground on the left side of the road.

Contact: Six Rivers National Forest, Orleans Ranger District, 530/627-3291, fax 530/627-3401.

18 IDLEWILD

Scenic rating: 8

on the North Fork of the Salmon River in Klamath National Forest

See map page 508

This is one of the prettiest drive-to camps in the region, set on the North Fork of the Salmon River, a beautiful, cold, clear stream and a major tributary to the Klamath River. Most campers use the camp for its nearby trailhead (two miles north on a dirt Forest Service road out of camp). The hike here is routed to the north, climbing alongside the Salmon River for miles into the Marble Mountain Wilderness (wilderness permits are required). It's a rugged 10-mile, all-day climb to Lake of the Island with several other lakes (highlighted by Hancock Lake) to the nearby west, accessible on weeklong trips. The elevation is 2,600 feet.

RV sites, facilities: There are 18 sites for tents or RVs up to 22 feet (no hookups). Picnic tables and fire grills are provided. Drinking water and vault toilets are available, with limited winter facilities. Leashed pets are permitted.

Reservations, fees: Reservations are not accepted. Sites are $10 per night, with no fee during the winter. Open year-round.

Directions: From Yreka, turn southwest on Highway 3 and drive to Etna. In Etna, turn west on Etna-Somes Bar Road (Main Street in town) and drive about 16 miles to the campground on the right side of the road. Note: A shorter, more scenic, and more complex route is available from Gazelle (north of Weed on Old Highway 99). Take Gazelle-Callahan Road west over the summit and continue north to Etna.

Contact: Klamath National Forest, Salmon River and Scott River Ranger Districts, 530/468-5351, fax 530/468-1290.

CALIFORNIA

CALIFORNIA

19 KOA MOUNT SHASTA

Scenic rating: 7

in Mount Shasta City

See map page 508

Despite this KOA camp's relative proximity to the town of Mount Shasta, the extended driveway, wooded grounds, and view of Mount Shasta offer some feeling of seclusion. There are many excellent side trips. The best is driving up Everitt Memorial Highway, which rises up the slopes of Mount Shasta to the tree line at Bunny Flat, where you can take outstanding, short day hikes with great views to the south of the Sacramento River Canyon and Castle Crags. In the winter, you can play in the snow, including heading up to Bunny Flat for snow play or to the Mount Shasta Board and Ski Park for developed downhill and cross-country skiing. An ice skating rink is in Mount Shasta. One of the biggest events of the year in Mount Shasta is the Fourth of July Run For Fun (billed as the largest small-town footrace anywhere) and associated parade and fireworks display at nearby Lake Siskiyou.

RV sites, facilities: There are 47 sites with full or partial hookups (20, 30, and 50 amps) for RVs of any length, 50 additional sites for tents or RVs with partial hookups, and four camping cabins. All sites are pull-through. Picnic tables are provided, and fire grills are provided at tent sites only. Restrooms have showers. A playground, propane gas, a convenience store, a recreation room with arcade, a horseshoe pit, shuffleboard, a seasonal swimming pool, high-speed modem access and Wi-Fi, and coin laundry are available. Leashed pets are permitted.

Reservations, fees: Reservations are accepted at 800/562-3617. Sites are $20–38 per night, plus $3–4 per person per night for more than two people. Some credit cards accepted. Open year-round.

Directions: From Redding, drive north on I-5 to the town of Mount Shasta. Continue past the first Mount Shasta exit and take the Central Mount Shasta exit. At the stop sign, turn right (east) on Lake Street and drive 0.6 mile to Mount Shasta Boulevard. Turn left and drive 0.5 mile to East Hinckley Boulevard. Turn right (signed KOA) on East Hinckley, drive a very short distance, then turn left at the entrance to the extended driveway for KOA Mount Shasta.

Contact: KOA Mount Shasta, 530/926-4029, www.koa.com.

20 LAKE SISKIYOU CAMP-RESORT

Scenic rating: 9

near Mount Shasta

See map page 508

This is a true gem of a lake, a jewel set at the foot of Mount Shasta at 3,181 feet. The lake is almost always full (because it was built for recreation, not water storage) and offers a variety of quality recreation options, with great swimming, low-speed boating, and fishing. The campground complexes are huge, yet they are tucked into the forest so visitors don't get their styles cramped. The water in this 435-acre lake is clean and fresh. There is an excellent beach and swimming area, the latter protected by a buoy line. In spring, the fishing is good for trout, and then as the water warms, for smallmouth bass. A good boat ramp and boat rentals are available, and a 10-mph speed limit is strictly enforced, keeping the lake pristine and quiet. The City of Mount Shasta holds its July 4 fireworks display above the lake.

RV sites, facilities: There are 150 sites with full or partial hookups (30 and 50 amps) for RVs of any length, including some pull-through sites, and 225 additional sites for tents, seven of which are group areas. There are also 20 cabins and 10 park-model cabins. Picnic tables and fire grills are provided. Drinking water, restrooms with flush toilets and showers, a playground, propane, a convenience store, a gift shop, deli, a coin laundry, and a dump station are available. Other amenities include a marina, boat rentals (canoes, kayaks, pedal boats, motorized boats), free boat launching, a fishing dock, a fish-cleaning station, boat slips, a swimming beach, horseshoes, volleyball, group facilities, and a recreation room. A free movie plays every night in the summer. Some facilities are wheelchair accessible. Leashed pets are permitted at the campground only.

Reservations, fees: Reservations are accepted. Sites are $20–29 per night, $3 per person per night for more than two people, $5 per night for an additional vehicle, $2 per pet per night. Some credit cards are accepted. Open April–October, weather permitting.

Directions: From the town of Mount Shasta on I-5, take the Central Mount Shasta exit and drive to the stop sign. Turn west and drive less than a mile to Old Stage Road. Turn left and drive 0.25 mile to a Y intersection at W. A. Barr Road. Bear right on W. A. Barr Road and drive past Box Canyon Dam. Two miles farther, turn right at the entrance road for Lake Siskiyou Campground and Marina and drive a short distance to the entrance station.

Contact: Lake Siskiyou Camp-Resort, 530/926-2618 or 888/926-2618, www.lakesis.com.

21 McCLOUD DANCE COUNTRY RV PARK

🏞️ 🎣 ❄️ 🐾 ♿ 🚐 ⛺

Scenic rating: 6

in McCloud

See map page 508

McCloud Dance Country RV Park is very popular with square dancers in the summer. The town of McCloud is the home of McCloud Dance Country Hall, a large dance hall dedicated to square and round dancing. The park used to be affiliated with the dance hall, but now the park is open to the public. The park is sprinkled with old-growth pine trees and bordered by Squaw Valley Creek, a pretty stream. The RV sites are grassy and manicured, many shaded. McCloud River's three waterfalls are accessible from the McCloud River Loop, five miles south of the park on Highway 89. Mount Shasta Board and Ski Park also offers summer activities such as biking, a rock-climbing structure, and chairlift rides to great views of the surrounding forests.

The ski park access road is six miles west of McCloud off Highway 89 at Snowman's Hill Summit. The McCloud River Railroad runs an excursion and a dinner train on summer weekends out of McCloud; reservations are available in town. If you're lucky you might see "Old Engine No. 25," one of the few remaining steam engines in service. (For more information, see the *Fowler's Camp* listing in this chapter.)

RV sites, facilities: There are 136 sites with full or partial hookups (30 and 50 amps) for RVs of any length, a grassy area for dispersed tent camping, and seven cabins. There are a few long-term rentals. Picnic tables are provided. Drinking water, restrooms with hot showers (heated bathhouse), a central barbecue and campfire area, cable TV, a pay telephone, a coin laundry, a dump station, propane, horseshoes, a fish-cleaning station, and two pet walks are available. Some facilities are wheelchair accessible. Large groups are welcome. Leashed pets are permitted, except in cabins.

Reservations, fees: Reservations are recommended. Sites are $15.74–25 per night, $1.50–3 per person per night for more than two people. Some credit cards accepted. Open year-round.

Directions: From Redding, drive north on I-5 and continue just past Dunsmuir to the junction with Highway 89. Turn east on Highway 89 and drive nine miles to McCloud and Squaw Valley Road. Turn right on Squaw Valley Road and then turn immediately left into the park entrance.

Contact: McCloud Dance Country RV Park, 530/964-2252, www.mccloudrvpark.com.

22 FOWLER'S CAMP

🏞️ 🌊 🎣 🏠 ♿ 🚐 ⛺

Scenic rating: 10

on the McCloud River in Shasta-Trinity National Forest

See map page 508   BEST (

This campground lies beside the beautiful Mc-Cloud River at 3,400 feet, providing the chance for an easy hike to two waterfalls, including one of the most dramatic in Northern California. From the camp, the trail is routed upstream

CALIFORNIA

through forest, a near-level walk for only 15 minutes, then arrives at awesome Middle Falls, a wide-sweeping and powerful cascade best viewed in April. By summer, the flows subside and warm to the point that some people will swim in the pool at the base of the falls. The trail is also routed from camp downstream to Lower Falls, an outstanding swimming hole in midsummer. Fishing the McCloud River here is fair, with trout stocks made from Lakim Dam on downstream to the camp. If this camp is full, Cattle Camp offers an overflow area.

RV sites, facilities: There are 38 sites and one double site for tents or RVs up to 30 feet. No hookups. Picnic tables and fire grills are provided. Drinking water and vault toilets are available. Some facilities are wheelchair accessible. Leashed pets are permitted.

Reservations, fees: Reservations are not accepted. Sites are $12 per night. Open late April–October.

Directions: From Redding, drive north on I-5 and continue just past Dunsmuir to the junction with Highway 89. Turn east on Highway 89 and drive 12 miles to McCloud. From McCloud, continue driving on Highway 89 for five miles to the campground entrance road on the right. Turn right and drive a short distance to a Y intersection, then turn left at the Y to the campground.

Contact: Shasta-Trinity National Forest, McCloud Ranger District, 530/964-2184, fax 530/964-2938.

23 CATTLE CAMP

Scenic rating: 5

on the McCloud River in Shasta-Trinity National Forest

See map page 508

This campground, at 3,700 feet, is ideal for RV campers who want a rustic setting, or as an overflow area if the more attractive Fowler's Camp is filled. A small swimming hole in the McCloud River is near the camp, although the water is typically cold. There are several good side trips in the area, including fishing on the nearby McCloud River, visiting the three waterfalls near Fowler's Camp, and exploring the north slopes of Mount Shasta (a map of Shasta-Trinity National Forest details the back roads).

RV sites, facilities: There are 19 individual sites and four double sites for tents or RVs up to 32 feet. No hookups. Picnic tables and fire grills are provided. Drinking water and vault toilets are available. Some facilities are wheelchair accessible. Leashed pets are permitted.

Reservations, fees: Reservations are not accepted. Sites are $12 per night. Open late April–October, weather permitting.

Directions: From Redding, drive north on I-5 and continue just past Dunsmuir to the junction with Highway 89. Turn east on Highway 89 and drive to McCloud. From McCloud, continue driving on Highway 89 for 11 miles to the campground entrance road on the right. Turn right and drive 0.5 mile to the campground on the left side of the road.

Contact: Shasta-Trinity National Forest, McCloud Ranger District, 530/964-2184, fax 530/964-2938.

24 CASTLE CRAGS STATE PARK

Scenic rating: 9

on the Sacramento River

See map page 508

This park is named for the awesome granite spires that tower 6,000 feet above the park. Beyond to the north is giant Mount Shasta (14,162 feet), making for a spectacular natural setting. The campsites are set in forest, shaded, very pretty, and sprinkled along a paved access road. But not a year goes by when people don't write in complaining of the highway noise from I-5 echoing in the Sacramento River Canyon, as well as of the occasional passing freight trains in the night. Pristine quiet, this campground is not. At the end of the access road is a parking area for the two-minute walk to the Crags Lookout, a beautiful view. Nearby is the trailhead (at 2,500 feet elevation) for hikes up the crags, featuring a 5.4-mile round-trip that rises to the base of Castle Dome at 4,800 feet, the leading spire on the crags' ridge. Again, road noise echoing up the canyon provides a background once you clear the tree line. Trout fishing is good in the nearby Sacramento River but requires driving, walking, and exploring to find the best spots. There are also some good swimming holes, but the water is cold. This is a popular state park, with reservations often required in summer, but with your choice of any campsite even in late spring.

RV sites, facilities: There are 52 sites for tents only, three sites for RVs up to 27 feet, an overflow area with 12 sites and limited facilities, six walk-in environmental sites (100-yard walk required) with limited facilities, and a hike-in/bike-in site. No hookups. Picnic tables, food lockers, and fire grills or fire rings are provided. Drinking water, restrooms with flush toilets and showers, and firewood are available. Leashed pets are permitted at campsites only.

Reservations, fees: Reservations are accepted ($7.50 reservation fee) at 800/444-PARK (800/444-7275) or www.reserveamerica.com. Sites are $13–20 per night, $9 per night for walk-in environmental sites, and $6 per night for an additional vehicle. The hike-in/bike-in site is $3 per person per night. Open year-round.

Directions: From Redding, drive north on I-5 for 45 miles to the Castle Crags State Park exit. Take that exit, turn west, and drive a short distance to the well-signed park entrance on the right side of the road.

Contact: Castle Crags State Park, 530/235-2684, fax 530/235-1965, www.parks.ca.gov.

25 FRIDAY'S RV RETREAT AND McCLOUD FLY FISHING RANCH

Scenic rating: 7

near McCloud

See map page 508

Friday's offers great recreation opportunities for every member of the family. The property features a small private fishing lake, two casting ponds, 1.5 miles of Squaw Valley Creek frontage, and five miles of hiking trails. The ranch specializes in fly-fishing packages, with both lodging and fly-fishing for one price. However, campers are welcome to stay here. In addition, the McCloud River's wild trout section is a 45-minute drive to the south, the beautiful McCloud Golf Course (nine holes) is within a five-minute drive, and a trailhead for the Pacific Crest Trail is also only five minutes away. Lake McCloud is three miles away and offers fishing and water-sports options. The park covers 400 wooded and grassy acres. Owner Bob Friday is quite a character, and he figured out that if he planted giant rainbow trout in the ponds for catch-and-release fishing, fly fishers would stop to catch a monster and take a photograph, and then tell people they caught the fish on the McCloud River, where they are smaller and elusive. Also available is the dinner and excursion train that runs out of McCloud on summer weekends. (See the listing in this chapter for *McCloud Dance Country RV Park* for other information and side-trip options.)

RV sites, facilities: There are 30 sites with full hookups (30 and 50 amps) for RVs of any length, a large, grassy area for dispersed tent camping, and two cabins. Most RV sites are pull-through. Picnic tables and fire pits are provided. Drinking water, restrooms with showers and flush toilets, a coin laundry, a pay phone, propane gas, and a recreation room are available. A fly-fishing school is available by arrangement. Some facilities are wheelchair accessible. Leashed pets are permitted.

Reservations, fees: Reservations are recommended. Sites are $16–24 per night, $3.50 per person per night for more than two people. Monthly rates available. Open early May–September.

Directions: From Redding, drive north on I-5 and continue just past Dunsmuir to the junction with Highway 89. Bear right on Highway 89 and drive nine miles to McCloud and Squaw Valley Road. Turn right at Squaw Valley Road and drive six miles to the park entrance on the right.

Contact: Friday's RV Retreat, 530/964-2878.

26 EAGLE CREEK

Scenic rating: 7

in Shasta-Trinity National Forest
See map page 508

This campground is set where little Eagle Creek enters the north Trinity River. Some campers use it as a base camp for a fishing trip, with the rainbow trout often abundant but predictably small in this stretch of water. The elevation is 2,800 feet.

RV sites, facilities: There are 17 sites for tents or RVs up to 35 feet (no hookups). Picnic tables and fire grills are provided. Drinking water and vault toilets are available. Leashed pets are permitted.

Reservations, fees: Reservations are not accepted. Sites are $9 per night. Open mid-May–October.

Directions: From Redding, drive west on Highway 299 to Weaverville and Highway 3. Turn right (north) on Highway 3 and drive to Trinity Center at the north end of Trinity Lake. From Trinity Center, continue north on Highway 3 for 16.5 miles to the campground on the left side of the road.

Contact: Shasta-Trinity National Forest, Weaverville Ranger Station, 530/623-2121, fax 530/623-6010.

27 TRINITY RIVER

Scenic rating: 7

in Shasta-Trinity National Forest
See map page 508

This camp offers easy access off Highway 3, yet it is fairly secluded and provides streamside access to the upper Trinity River. It's a good base camp for a fishing trip when the upper Trinity is loaded with small trout. The elevation is 2,500 feet.

RV sites, facilities: There are seven sites for tents or RVs up to 35 feet (no hookups). Picnic tables and fire grills are provided. Drinking water and vault toilets are available. Leashed pets are permitted.

Reservations, fees: Reservations are not accepted. Sites are $9 per night. Open May–October.

Directions: From Redding, drive west on Highway 299 to Weaverville and Highway 3. Turn right (north) on Highway 3 and drive to Trinity Center at the north end of Trinity Lake. From Trinity Center, continue north on Highway 3 for 9.5 miles to the campground on the left side of the road.

Contact: Shasta-Trinity National Forest, Weaverville Ranger Station, 530/623-2121, fax 530/623-6010.

28 RAILROAD PARK RV AND CAMPGROUND

Scenic rating: 7

south of Dunsmuir
See map page 508

The resort adjacent to the RV park and campground was designed in the spirit of the railroad, when steam trains ruled the rails. The property features old stage cars (available for overnight lodging) and a steam locomotive. The railroad theme does not extend to the campground, however. What you'll find at the park is a classic campground set amid tall trees. There is a swimming hole in Little Castle Creek alongside the park. Many good side trips are available in the area, including excellent hiking and sightseeing at Castle Crags State Park (where there is a series of awesome granite spires) and outstanding trout fishing on the upper Sacramento River. At night, the sound of occasional passing trains soothes some, wakes others.

RV sites, facilities: There are 31 sites for tents or RVs (no hookups) and 21 sites with full or partial hookups (30 amps) for RVs of any length. Some sites are pull-through. Cabins and a motel are next door at the resort. Picnic tables and fire rings are provided. Restrooms have showers. Ice, a coin laundry, a group barbecue pit, a game room, and horseshoes are available. A restaurant and lounge are within walking distance. Some facilities are wheelchair accessible. Leashed pets are permitted.

CALIFORNIA

Reservations, fees: Reservations are accepted. Sites are $20–27 per night, $3 per person per night for more than two people, and $3 per night for an additional vehicle. Some credit cards accepted. Open April–November, weather permitting.

Directions: From Redding, drive north on I-5 for 45 miles to Exit 728 for Cragview Drive/Railroad Park Road. Take that exit and drive to the stop sign and Railroad Park Road. Turn left and drive under the freeway and continue to the campground on the left.

Contact: Railroad Park RV and Campground, 530/235-0420 or 530/235-4440, www.rrpark.com.

29 SIMS FLAT

Scenic rating: 7

on the Sacramento River
See map page 508

The upper Sacramento River is again becoming one of the best trout streams in the West with easy and direct access off an interstate highway. This camp is a good example. Sitting beside the upper Sacramento River at an elevation of 1,600 feet, it provides access to some of the better spots for trout fishing, particularly late April–July. The trout population has recovered since the devastating spill from a train derailment that occurred in 1991, and there's good trout fishing in this area. There is a wheelchair-accessible interpretive trail. If you want to literally get away from it all, there is a trailhead about three miles east on Sims Flat Road that climbs along South Fork, including a terrible, steep, one-mile section near the top, eventually popping out at Tombstone Mountain. The noise from passing trains can be a shock for newcomers.

RV sites, facilities: There are 20 sites for tents or RVs up to 24 feet (no hookups). Picnic tables and fire grills are provided. Drinking water and flush and vault toilets are available. A nearby seasonal grocery store is open intermittently. Supplies are available to the north in Castella

and Dunsmuir. Some facilities are wheelchair accessible. Leashed pets are permitted.

Reservations, fees: Reservations are not accepted. Sites are $12 per night. Open late April–October.

Directions: From Redding, drive north on I-5 for about 40 miles to the Sims Road exit. Take the Sims Road exit (on the east side of the highway) and drive south for a mile (crossing the railroad tracks and a bridge) to the campground on the right.

Contact: Shasta-Trinity National Forest, Mount Shasta Ranger District, 530/926-4511, fax 530/926-5120.

30 BEST IN THE WEST RESORT

Scenic rating: 3

near Dunsmuir
See map page 508

This is a good layover spot for RV cruisers looking to take a break. The proximity to Castle Crags State Park, the Sacramento River, and Mount Shasta makes the location a winner. Meers Creek runs through the property, and the local area has outstanding swimming holes on the Sacramento River. Trains make regular runs every night in the Sacramento River Canyon and the noise is a problem for some visitors.

RV sites, facilities: There are 12 sites with full hookups (30 and 50 amps) for RVs, a separate grassy area for dispersed tent camping, eight cabins, and a lodge. Picnic tables are provided. Restrooms have showers. Cable TV, a coin laundry, and a playground are available. Leashed pets are permitted.

Reservations, fees: Reservations are accepted. Sites are $17–21 per night. Monthly rates available. Open year-round.

Directions: From Redding, drive north on I-5 for about 40 miles to the Sims Road exit. Take the Sims Road exit and drive one block west on Sims Road to the resort on the left.

Contact: Best in the West Resort, 530/235-2603, http://eggerbestwest.com.

CALIFORNIA

31 TISH TANG

Scenic rating: 8

in Six Rivers National Forest
See map page 508

This campground is adjacent to one of the best swimming holes in all of Northern California. By late July the adjacent Trinity River is warm and slow, perfect for tubing, a quick dunk, and paddling a canoe. There is a large gravel beach, and some people will bring along their shorty lawn chairs and just take a seat on the edge of the river in a few inches of water. Though Tish Tang is a good put-in spot for rafting in the late spring and early summer, the flows are too slow and quiet for most rafters to even ruffle a feather during the summer. The elevation is 300 feet.

RV sites, facilities: There are 40 sites for tents or RVs up to 22 feet (no hookups). Picnic tables and fire grills are provided. Drinking water and vault toilets are available, and there is a camp host. Leashed pets are permitted.

Reservations, fees: Reservations are accepted at 530/625-4284. Sites are $10 per night, $3 per night for an additional vehicle, $15 per night for double sites. Open late May–September.

Directions: From the junction of U.S. 101 and Highway 299 near Arcata, turn east on Highway 299 and drive to Willow Creek. In Willow Creek, turn north (left) on Highway 96 east and drive eight miles north to the campground entrance on the right side of the road.

Contact: Hoopa Valley Tribal Council, Forestry Department, 530/625-4284, fax 530/625-4230.

32 BOISE CREEK

Scenic rating: 7

in Six Rivers National Forest
See map page 509

This camp features a quarter-mile-long trail down to Willow Creek and nearby access to the Trinity River. If you have ever wanted to see Bigfoot, you can do it while camping here because there's a giant wooden Bigfoot on dis-play in nearby Willow Creek. After your Bigfoot experience, your best bet during summer is to head north on nearby Highway 96 (turn north in Willow Creek) to the campground at Tish Tang, where there is excellent river access, swimming, and rafting in the late summer's warm flows. The Trinity River also provides good salmon and steelhead fishing during fall and winter, respectively. Note that fishing is prohibited in nearby Willow Creek.

RV sites, facilities: There are 17 sites for tents or RVs up to 35 feet (no hookups). Picnic tables and fire grills are provided. No drinking water. Vault toilets are available, and a camp host is on-site. A grocery store, gas station, a restaurant, and propane gas are available nearby. Some facilities are wheelchair accessible. Leashed pets are permitted.

Reservations, fees: Reservations are not accepted. Sites are $10 per night, $5 per night for an additional vehicle. Open year-round.

Directions: From the intersection of U.S. 101 and Highway 299 near Arcata, drive 38 miles east on Highway 299 and look for the campground entrance on the left side of the road. If you reach the town of Willow Creek, you have gone 1.5 miles too far.

Contact: Six Rivers National Forest, Lower Trinity Ranger District, 530/629-2118, fax 530/629-2102.

33 EAST FORK WILLOW CREEK

Scenic rating: 9

on Willow Creek
See map page 509

This is a beautiful spot along Willow Creek. Set at a 2,000-foot elevation, it's one of the prettiest campgrounds in the area. While you can dunk into the cold creek, it's not really a good swimming area. Fishing is prohibited.

RV sites, facilities: There are 10 sites for tents or RVs up to 20 feet (no hookups). Picnic tables and fire rings are provided. Vault toilets are available. No drinking water is available. Leashed pets are permitted.

CALIFORNIA

Reservations, fees: Reservations are not accepted. Sites are $8 per night, $5 per night for an additional vehicle. Open late May–September, weather permitting.

Directions: From the junction of U.S. 101 and Highway 299 near Arcata, turn east on Highway 299 and drive 32 miles (six miles west of Willow Creek) and look for the camp's entrance road (well signed) on the right (south) side of the road.

Contact: Six Rivers National Forest, Lower Trinity Ranger District, 530/629-2118, fax 530/629-2102.

34 BURNT RANCH

Scenic rating: 7

on the Trinity River in Shasta-Trinity National Forest

See map page 509

This campground sits on a bluff above the Trinity River and is one of its most compelling spots. This section of river is very pretty, with deep, dramatic canyons nearby. The elevation is 1,000 feet. Note that the trail to Burnt Ranch Falls is not maintained and is partially on private land where the landowners will not take kindly to anyone trespassing.

RV sites, facilities: There are 16 sites for tents or RVs up to 25 feet (no hookups). Picnic tables and fire grills are provided. Drinking water and vault toilets are available. Garbage must be packed out. Supplies can be obtained in Hawkins Bar about one hour away. Leashed pets are permitted.

Reservations, fees: Reservations are not accepted. Sites are $8 per night. Open year-round, weather permitting.

Directions: From Redding, take Highway 299 west and drive past Weaverville to Burnt Ranch. In Burnt Ranch, continue 0.5 mile and look for the campground entrance on the right side of the road.

Contact: Shasta-Trinity National Forest, Big Bar Ranger Station, 530/623-6106, fax 530/623-6123; Trinity River Rafting Company, 530/623-3033.

35 DEL LOMA RV PARK AND CAMPGROUND

Scenic rating: 7

on the Trinity River

See map page 509

RV cruisers looking for a layover spot near the Trinity River will find just that at Del Loma. Shady sites and sandy beaches are available here along the Trinity. Rafting and tubing trips are popular in this area during the summer. Salmon fishing is best in the fall, steelhead fishing in the winter. This camp is popular for family reunions and groups. Salmon fishing can be sensational on the Trinity in the fall, and some anglers will book a year in advance to make certain they get a spot. About two-thirds of the sites are rented for extended periods.

RV sites, facilities: There are 41 sites for tents or RVs with full hookups (50 amps), including two pull-through sites. There are also five park-model cabins and two apartments. Picnic tables and fire grills are provided. Restrooms have flush toilets and showers. A dump station, a convenience store, a clubhouse, a heated pool, a deli, Wi-Fi, RV supplies, firewood, a coin laundry, a recreation room, volleyball, tetherball, 18-hole mini golf, and horseshoe pits are available. Leashed pets are permitted.

Reservations, fees: Reservations are accepted at 800/839-0194. Sites are $23 per night, plus $2 per person per night for more than two people. Group and monthly rates available. Some credit cards accepted. Open year-round.

Directions: From the junction of U.S. 101 and Highway 299 in Arcata, turn east on Highway 299 and drive to Burnt Ranch. From Burnt Ranch, continue 10 miles east on Highway 299 to the town of Del Loma and look for the campground entrance on the right.

Contact: Del Loma RV Park and Campground, 530/623-2834 or 800/839-0194, www.dellomarv.com.

CALIFORNIA

CALIFORNIA

36 HAYDEN FLAT/GROUP

Scenic rating: 7

on the Trinity River in Shasta-Trinity National Forest
See map page 509

This campground is split into two pieces, with most of the sites grouped in a large, shaded area across the road from the river and a few on the river side. A beach is available along the river; it is a good spot for swimming as well as a popular put-in and takeout for rafters. The elevation is 1,200 feet.

RV sites, facilities: There are 36 sites for tents or RVs up to 25 feet (no hookups); it can also be used as a group camp with a three-site minimum. Picnic tables and fire grills are provided. Drinking water and vault toilets are available. Some facilities are wheelchair accessible. Leashed pets are permitted.

Reservations, fees: Reservations are not accepted for individual sites but are required for group sites at 530/623-6106. Sites are $10 per night, $30 minimum per night for groups. Open year-round.

Directions: From the junction of U.S. 101 and Highway 299 in Arcata, head east on Highway 299 and drive to Burnt Ranch. From Burnt Ranch, continue 10 miles east on Highway 299 and look for the campground entrance. If you reach the town of Del Loma, you have gone 0.5 mile too far.

Contact: Shasta-Trinity National Forest, Big Bar Ranger Station, 530/623-6106, fax 530/623-6123.

37 BIG FLAT

Scenic rating: 6

on the Trinity River in Shasta-Trinity National Forest
See map page 509

This level campground is off Highway 299, just across the road from the Trinity River. The sites are close together, and it can be hot and dusty in midsummer. No problem. That is when you will be on the Trinity River, taking a rafting or kayaking trip—as low as $35 to rent an inflatable kayak from Trinity River Rafting in nearby Big Bar. It's fun, exciting, and easy (newcomers are welcome).

RV sites, facilities: There are 10 sites for tents or RVs up to 22 feet (no hookups). Picnic tables and fire grills are provided. Drinking water and vault toilets are available. Some facilities are wheelchair accessible. Leashed pets are permitted.

Reservations, fees: Reservations are not accepted. Sites are $8 per night. Open year-round.

Directions: From Redding, turn on Highway 299 westbound, drive west past Weaverville, Junction City, and Helena, and continue for about seven miles. Look for the campground entrance on the right side of the road. If you reach the town of Big Bar, you have gone three miles too far.

Contact: Shasta-Trinity National Forest, Big Bar Ranger Station, 530/623-6106, fax 530/623-6123; Trinity River Rafting Company, 530/623-3033, www.trinityriverrafting.com.

38 PIGEON POINT AND GROUP

Scenic rating: 7

on the Trinity River in Shasta-Trinity National Forest
See map page 509

In the good old days, huge flocks of bandtail pigeons flew the Trinity River Canyon, swooping and diving in dramatic shows. Nowadays you don't see too many pigeons, but this camp still keeps its namesake. It is better known for its access to the Trinity River, with a large beach for swimming. The elevation is 1,100 feet.

RV sites, facilities: There are 10 sites for tents or RVs up to 22 feet and one group site for tents or RVs up to 16 feet that can accommodate up to 50 people. No hookups. Picnic tables and fire grills are provided. Vault toilets are available. No drinking water is available. Supplies can be obtained within 10 miles in Big Bar or Junction City. Some facilities are wheelchair accessible. Leashed pets are permitted.

Reservations, fees: Reservations are not accepted for individual sites but are required for the group site at 530/623-6106. Sites are $12 per night, and it's $50 per night for the group site. Open year-round.

Directions: From Redding, turn on Highway 299 westbound and drive west to Weaverville. Continue west on Highway 299 to Helena and continue 0.5 mile to the campground on the left (south) side of the road.

Contact: Shasta-Trinity National Forest, Big Bar Ranger Station, 530/623-6106, fax 530/623-6123.

39 BIGFOOT CAMPGROUND AND RV PARK

Scenic rating: 8

on the Trinity River

See map page 509   BEST (

This private RV park is along the Trinity River and has become one of the most popular spots on the Trinity River. Rafting and fishing trips are a feature, along with cabin rentals. It is also a popular layover for Highway 299 cruisers but provides the option for longer stays with rafting, gold panning, and, in the fall and winter, fishing for salmon and steelhead, respectively. RV sites are exceptionally large, and a bonus is that a storage area is available. A three-acre site for tent camping is along the river.

RV sites, facilities: There are 46 sites with full or partial hookups (30 and 50 amps) for RVs of any length, a separate area for tent camping, and four cabins. Tent camping is not allowed during the winter. Picnic tables and barbecues are provided. Restrooms have flush toilets and coin showers. A coin laundry, a convenience store, a dump station, propane gas, a solar-heated swimming pool (summer only), and horseshoe pits are available. Modem hookups, television hookups, fishing licenses, and a tackle shop are also available. Some facilities are wheelchair accessible. Leashed pets are permitted.

Reservations, fees: Reservations are recommended June–October. Sites are $18–24 per night, plus $2 per night per person for more than two people. Some credit cards accepted. Open year-round.

Directions: From Redding, turn on Highway 299 west and drive west to Junction City. Continue west on Highway 299 for three miles to the camp on the left.

Contact: Bigfoot Campground and RV Park, 530/623-6088 or 800/422-5219, www.bigfootr vcabins.com.

40 JUNCTION CITY

Scenic rating: 7

on the Trinity River

See map page 509

Some of the Trinity River's best fall salmon fishing is in this area in September and early October, with steelhead following from mid-October into the winter. That makes it an ideal base camp for a fishing or camping trip.

RV sites, facilities: There are 22 sites for tents or RVs up to 40 feet (no hookups). Picnic tables, fire grills, and bearproof food lockers are provided. Drinking water and vault toilets are available. Groceries and propane gas are available within two miles in Junction City. Some facilities are wheelchair accessible. Leashed pets are permitted.

Reservations, fees: Reservations are not accepted. Sites are $10 per night per vehicle. Open May–November.

Directions: From Redding, turn on Highway 299 west and drive west to Junction City. At Junction City, continue west on Highway 299 for 1.5 miles to the camp on the right.

Contact: Bureau of Land Management, Redding Field Office, 530/224-2100, fax 530/224-2172.

41 DOUGLAS CITY AND STEINER FLAT

Scenic rating: 7

on the Trinity River

See map page 509

If you want to camp along this stretch of the main Trinity River, these camps are your best

CALIFORNIA

bet (they're along the river about two miles from each other). They are set off the main road, near the river, with good bank fishing access (the prime season is from mid-August through winter for salmon and steelhead). Douglas City Campground has paved parking and two beaches. Steiner Flat, a more primitive camp, provides better access for fishing. This can be a good base camp for an off-season fishing trip on the Trinity River or a lounging spot during the summer. The elevation is 1,700 feet.

RV sites, facilities: There are 20 sites for tents or RVs up to 28 feet at Douglas City with dispersed camping at Steiner Flat. No hookups. At Douglas City, picnic tables and fire grills are provided. Drinking water and restrooms with flush toilets and sinks are available. At Steiner Flat, drinking water and toilets are not available. Supplies are available within one mile in Douglas City. Leashed pets are permitted.

Reservations, fees: Reservations are not accepted. Sites are $10 per night at Douglas City; there's no fee at Steiner Flat. Open mid-April–November.

Directions: From Redding, turn on Highway 299 westbound and drive west (toward Weaverville). Continue over the bridge at the Trinity River near Douglas City to Steiner Flat Road. Turn left on Steiner Flat Road and drive 0.5 mile to Douglas City campground on the left. To reach Steiner Flat, continue two more miles and look for the campground on the left.

Contact: Bureau of Land Management, Redding Field Office, 530/224-2100, fax 530/224-2172.

42 EAST WEAVER

Scenic rating: 6

on the east branch of Weaver Creek in Shasta-Trinity National Forest

See map page 509

This camp is along East Weaver Creek. Another mile to the west on East Weaver Road, the road dead-ends at a trailhead, a good side trip. From here, the hiking trail is routed four miles, a significant climb, to tiny East Weaver Lake, set to the southwest of Monument Peak (7,771 feet elevation). The elevation at East Weaver is 2,700 feet.

RV sites, facilities: There are 11 sites for tents or RVs up to 25 feet (no hookups). Picnic tables and fire grills are provided. Drinking water and vault toilets are available. Supplies and a coin laundry are available in Weaverville. Leashed pets are permitted.

Reservations, fees: Reservations are not accepted. Sites are $10 per night, $6 per night in the winter. Open year-round.

Directions: From Redding, drive west on Highway 299 to Weaverville. In Weaverville, turn right (north) on Highway 3 and drive about two miles to East Weaver Road. Turn left on East Weaver Road and drive 3.5 miles to the campground.

Contact: Shasta-Trinity National Forest, Weaverville Ranger Station, 530/623-2121, fax 530/623-6010.

43 TRINITY LAKE KOA

Scenic rating: 8

on Trinity Lake

See map page 508

This huge resort is an ideal family vacation destination, and some people may remember this as the former Wyntoon Resort. Set in a wooded area covering 90 acres on the north shore of Trinity Lake, it provides opportunities for fishing, boating, swimming, and waterskiing, with access within walking distance. The lake boasts a wide variety of fish, including smallmouth bass and rainbow trout. The tent sites are spread out on 20 forested acres. The lake sits at the base of the dramatic Trinity Alps, one of the most beautiful regions in the state.

RV sites, facilities: There are 136 sites with full hookups (30 and 50 amps) for RVs of any length, 77 tent sites, and 19 cottages. Some RV sites are pull-through. Picnic tables and fire rings are provided. Drinking water, restrooms with showers, a coin laundry, a playground, a seasonal heated pool, a dump station, gasoline, a convenience store, ice, a snack bar, a fish-cleaning area, boat rentals, and boat slips are available. Some facilities are wheelchair accessible. Leashed pets are permitted, with certain restrictions.

Reservations, fees: Reservations are accepted. Sites are $28–35 per night, plus $3–5 per person per night for more than two people. Some credit cards accepted. Open year-round.

Directions: From Redding, drive west on Highway 299 to Weaverville and Highway 3. Turn right (north) on Highway 3 and drive approximately 30 miles to Trinity Lake. At Trinity Center, continue 0.5 mile north on Highway 3 to the resort on the right.

Contact: Trinity Lake KOA, 530/266-3337 or 800/715-3337, www.koa.com.

44 PREACHER MEADOW

Scenic rating: 7

in Shasta-Trinity National Forest
See map page 509

The view of the Trinity Alps can be excellent here from the right vantage point. Otherwise, compared to all the other camps in the area so close to Trinity Lake, it has trouble matching up in the quality department. If the lakeside camps are full, this camp provides an overflow option. The winter of 2000 was one of the strangest on record, when a localized wind storm knocked down 66 trees at this campground.

RV sites, facilities: There are 45 sites for tents or RVs up to 40 feet (no hookups). Picnic tables and fire grills are provided. Drinking water and vault toilets are available. Supplies, a coin laundry, and a small airport are available nearby. Leashed pets are permitted.

Reservations, fees: Reservations are not accepted. Sites are $11 per night. Open mid-May–October.

Directions: From Redding, drive west on Highway 299 to Weaverville at Highway 3. Turn

right (north) on Highway 3 and drive to Trinity Lake. Continue toward Trinity Center and look for the campground entrance on the left side of the road (if you reach Trinity Center you have gone two miles too far).

Contact: Shasta-Trinity National Forest, Weaverville Ranger Station, 530/623-2121, fax 530/623-6010.

45 JACKASS SPRINGS

Scenic rating: 6

on Trinity Lake in Shasta-Trinity National Forest
See map page 509

If you're poking around for a more secluded campsite on this end of the lake, halt your search and pick the best spot you can find at this campground, since it's the only one in this area of Trinity Lake. The campground is one-half mile from Trinity Lake, but you can't see the lake from the camp. It is most popular in the fall as a base camp for deer hunters. The elevation is 2,500 feet.

RV sites, facilities: There are 21 sites for tents or RVs up to 32 feet (no hookups). Picnic tables and fire grills are provided. Vault toilets are available. No drinking water is available. Garbage must be packed out. Leashed pets are permitted.

Reservations, fees: Reservations are not accepted. There is no fee for camping. Open year-round, weather permitting.

Directions: From Redding, drive west on Highway 299 to Weaverville and the junction with Highway 3. Turn right (north) on Highway 3 and drive 29 miles to Trinity Center. Continue five miles past Trinity Center to County Road 106. Turn right on County Road 106 and drive 12 miles to the Jackass Springs/County Road 119 turnoff. Turn right on County Road 119 and drive five miles to the campground near the end of the road.

Contact: Shasta-Trinity National Forest, Weaverville Ranger Station, 530/623-2121, fax 530/623-6010.

CALIFORNIA

46 PINEWOOD COVE RESORT

Scenic rating: 7

on Trinity Lake

See map page 509

This is a privately operated camp with full boating facilities at Trinity Lake. If you don't have a boat but want to get on Trinity Lake, this can be a good starting point. A reservation is advised during the peak summer season. The elevation is 2,300 feet.

RV sites, facilities: There are 50 sites with full or partial hookups (30 and 50 amps) for RVs up to 40 feet, including 10 RV sites rented for the entire season and wait-listed, and 28 tent sites. There are also 15 park-model cabins. Picnic tables and fire grills are provided. Restrooms have showers. A coin laundry, a dump station, RV supplies, a seasonal heated swimming pool, a playground, a children's treehouse, volleyball, badminton, free movies three nights a week in summer, modem access, video rentals, a recreation room with billiards and video arcade, a convenience store, ice, fishing tackle, a library, a boat dock with 32 slips, a beach, and canoe and kayak rentals are available. Some facilities are wheelchair accessible. Leashed pets are permitted.

Reservations, fees: Reservations are recommended in the summer. Sites are $27.50–37.50 per night, $4 per person per night for more than two people, and $4 per pet per night. Some credit cards accepted. Open mid-April–October.

Directions: From Redding, drive west on Highway 299 to Weaverville. In Weaverville, turn north (right) on Highway 3 and drive 14 miles to the campground entrance on the right.

Contact: Pinewood Cove Resort, 530/286-2201 or 800/988-5253, www.pinewoodcove.com.

47 TANNERY GULCH

Scenic rating: 8

on Trinity Lake in Shasta-Trinity National Forest

See map page 509

This is one of the more popular Forest Service camps on the southwest shore of huge Trinity Lake. There's a nice beach near the campground, provided the infamous Bureau of Reclamation hasn't drawn the lake level down too far. It can be quite low in the fall. The elevation is 2,400 feet. A side note is that this campground was named by the tannery that once operated in the area; bark from local trees was used in the tanning process.

RV sites, facilities: There are 72 sites and four double sites for tents or RVs up to 40 feet (no hookups). Picnic tables and fire grills are provided. Drinking water, flush and vault toilets, and a boat ramp are available. Leashed pets are permitted.

Reservations, fees: Reservations are accepted ($9 reservation fee) at 877/444-6777 or www.ReserveUSA.com. Sites are $16–22 per night, $5 per night for an additional vehicle. Open early May to late September.

Directions: From Redding, drive west on Highway 299 to Weaverville. In Weaverville, turn right (north) on Highway 3 and drive 13.5 miles north to County Road 172. Turn right on County Road 172 and drive 1.5 miles to the campground entrance.

Contact: Shasta-Trinity National Forest, Weaverville Ranger Station, 530/623-2121, fax 530/623-6010.

48 MINERSVILLE

Scenic rating: 7

on Trinity Lake in Shasta-Trinity National Forest

See map page 509

The setting is near lakeside, quite beautiful when Trinity Lake is fullest in the spring and early summer. This is a good camp for boaters, with a boat ramp in the cove a short distance to the north. But note that the boat ramp is not always functional. When the lake level drops to 65 feet below full, the ramp is not usable. The elevation is 2,400 feet.

RV sites, facilities: There are 14 sites for tents or RVs up to 36 feet (no hookups). Picnic tables and fire grills are provided. Drinking water, flush toilets, and a low-water boat ramp are provided. Leashed pets are permitted.

Reservations, fees: Reservations are not accepted. Sites are $15–24 per night, $7.50–12 per night during the winter season. Open year-round, with limited winter services.

Directions: From Redding, drive west on Highway 299 to Weaverville. Turn right (north) on Highway 3 and drive about 18 miles (if you reach the Mule Creek Ranger Station, you have gone 0.5 mile too far). Turn right at the signed campground access road and drive 0.5 mile to the camp.

Contact: Shasta-Trinity National Forest, Weaverville Ranger Station, 530/623-2121, fax 530/623-6010.

49 HAYWARD FLAT

Scenic rating: 7

on Trinity Lake in Shasta-Trinity National Forest
See map page 509

When giant Trinity Lake is full of water, Hayward Flat is one of the prettiest places you could ask for. The camp has become one of the most popular Forest Service campgrounds on Trinity Lake because it sits right along the shore and offers a beach. The elevation is 2,400 feet.

RV sites, facilities: There are 98 sites for tents or RVs up to 40 feet and four double sites. No hookups. Picnic tables and fire grills are provided. Drinking water and flush toilets are available, and there is usually a camp host. Supplies and a boat ramp are available nearby. Some facilities are wheelchair accessible. Leashed pets are permitted.

Reservations, fees: Reservations are accepted ($9 reservation fee) at 877/444-6777 or www.ReserveUSA.com. Sites are $16–22 per night, $5 per night for an additional vehicle. Open mid-May–mid-September.

Directions: From Redding, drive west on Highway 299 to Weaverville. In Weaverville, turn right (north) on Highway 3 and drive 19.5 miles, approximately three miles past the Mule Creek Ranger Station. Turn right at the signed access road for Hayward Flat and drive about three miles to the campground at the end of the road.

Contact: Shasta-Trinity National Forest,

Weaverville Ranger Station, 530/623-2121, fax 530/623-6010.

50 ALPINE VIEW

Scenic rating: 9

on Trinity Lake in Shasta-Trinity National Forest
See map page 509

This is an attractive area, on the shore of Trinity Lake at a creek inlet. The boat ramp nearby provides a bonus. It's a very pretty spot, with views to the west across the lake arm and to the Trinity Alps, featuring Granite Peak. The Forest Service occasionally runs tours from the campground to historic Bowerman Barn, which was built in 1894. The elevation is 2,400 feet.

RV sites, facilities: There are 53 sites for tents or RVs up to 32 feet (no hookups). Picnic tables and fire grills are provided. Drinking water and flush toilets are available. Some facilities are wheelchair accessible. The Bowerman boat ramp is nearby. Leashed pets are permitted.

Reservations, fees: Reservations are not accepted. Sites are $16–22 per night, $5 per night for an additional vehicle. Open mid-May–mid-September.

Directions: From Redding, drive west on Highway 299 to Weaverville. In Weaverville, turn right (north) on Highway 3 and drive 22.5 miles to Covington Mill (south of Trinity Center). Turn right (south) on Guy Covington Drive and drive three miles to the camp (one mile past Bowerman boat ramp) on the right side of the road.

Contact: Shasta-Trinity National Forest, Weaverville Ranger Station, 530/623-2121, fax 530/623-6010.

51 LAKEVIEW TERRACE RESORT

Scenic rating: 8

on Lewiston Lake
See map page 509

This might be your Golden Pond. It's a terraced RV park—with cabin rentals also available—

that overlooks Lewiston Lake, one of the prettiest drive-to lakes in the region. Fishing for trout is excellent from Lakeview Terrace on upstream toward the dam. Lewiston Lake is perfect for fishing, with a 10-mph speed limit in effect (all the hot boats go to nearby Trinity Lake), along with excellent prospects for rainbow and brown trout. Other fish species include brook trout and kokanee salmon. The topper is that Lewiston Lake is always full to the brim, just the opposite of the up-and-down nightmare of its neighboring big brother, Trinity.

RV sites, facilities: There are 40 sites with full hookups (50 amps) for RVs up to 40 feet; some sites are pull-through. No tents. Cabins are also available. Picnic tables and barbecues are provided. Restrooms have showers. A coin laundry, a seasonal heated pool, propane gas, ice, horseshoes, a playground, bait, and boat and patio boat rentals are available. Supplies are available within five miles. Leashed pets are permitted.

Reservations, fees: Reservations are recommended. Sites are $24 per night, plus $3 per person per night for more than two people. Some credit cards accepted. Open year-round.

Directions: From Redding, turn on Highway 299 westbound and drive west over Buckhorn Summit; continue for five miles to Trinity Dam Boulevard. Turn right on Trinity Dam Boulevard and drive 10 miles (five miles past Lewiston) to the resort on the left side of the road.

Contact: Lakeview Terrace Resort, 530/778-3803, fax 530/778-3960, www.lakeviewterraceresort.com.

52 ACKERMAN

Scenic rating: 7

on Lewiston Lake in Shasta-Trinity National Forest
See map page 509

Of the camps and parks at Lewiston Lake, Ackerman is closest to the lake's headwaters. This stretch of water below Trinity Dam is the best area for trout fishing on Lewiston Lake. Nearby Pine Cove boat ramp, two miles south of the camp, offers the only boat launch on Lewiston

Lake with docks and a fish-cleaning station—a popular spot for anglers. When the Trinity powerhouse is running, trout fishing is excellent in this area. The elevation is 2,000 feet.

RV sites, facilities: There are 66 sites for tents or RVs up to 40 feet (no hookups). Picnic tables and fire grills are provided. Drinking water, flush toilets, and a dump station are available. Leashed pets are permitted.

Reservations, fees: Reservations are not accepted. Sites are $12 per night in summer, $6 per night during the winter. Open year-round.

Directions: From Redding, turn on Highway 299 westbound and drive west over Buckhorn Summit; continue for five miles to Trinity Dam Boulevard. Turn right on Trinity Dam Boulevard and drive four miles to Lewiston. Continue north on Trinity Dam Boulevard for eight miles to the campground.

Contact: Shasta-Trinity National Forest, Weaverville Ranger Station, 530/623-2121, fax 530/623-6010.

53 OLD LEWISTON BRIDGE RV RESORT

Scenic rating: 7

on the Trinity River
See map page 509

This is a popular spot for calm-water kayaking, rafting, and fishing. Though much of the water from Trinity and Lewiston Lakes is diverted via tunnel to Whiskeytown Lake (en route to the valley and points south), enough escapes downstream to provide a viable stream here near the town of Lewiston. This upstream section below Lewiston Lake is prime in the early summer for trout, particularly the chance for a huge brown trout (special regulations in effect). A fishing shuttle service is available. The campground is in a hilly area but has level sites, with nearby Lewiston Lake also a major attraction. Some sites are occupied by long-term renters.

RV sites, facilities: There are 52 sites with full hookups (30 amps) for RVs up to 45 feet, a separate area for tents, and five rental trailers. Picnic tables are provided. Restrooms have showers. A coin laundry, a grocery store, modem access, ice, bait and tackle, and propane gas refills are available. A group picnic area is available by reservation. A restaurant is within 0.5 mile. Leashed pets are permitted.

Reservations, fees: Reservations are accepted by phone or website. Sites are $26 per night for RVs, $14 per night per vehicle for tent campers, and $2 per person per night for more than two people. Monthly rates available. Some credit cards accepted. Open year-round.

Directions: From Redding, turn on Highway 299 and drive west over Buckhorn Summit; continue for five miles to Trinity Dam Boulevard. Turn right on Trinity Dam Boulevard and drive four miles to Lewiston, then continue north to Rush Creek Road. Turn left (west) on Rush Creek Road and drive 0.25 mile to the resort on the left.

Contact: Old Lewiston Bridge RV Resort, 800/922-1924 or tel./fax 530/778-3894, www.lewistonbridgerv.com.

54 TRINITY RIVER LODGE RV RESORT

Scenic rating: 7

on the Trinity River

See map page 509

For many, this privately operated park has an ideal location. You get level, grassy sites with shade trees along the Trinity River, yet it is just a short drive north to Lewiston Lake or a bit farther to giant Trinity Lake. Lake or river, take your pick. The resort covers nearly 14 acres, and about half the sites are rented for the entire summer.

RV sites, facilities: There are 60 sites with full hookups (30 and 50 amps) for RVs up to 40 feet, five tent sites, and one cottage. Restrooms have showers. A coin laundry, cable TV, modem access, a recreation room, a lending library, a clubhouse, an athletic field, propane gas, a camp store, ice, firewood, boat and trailer storage, horseshoes, and a picnic area are avail-

able. Some facilities are wheelchair accessible. Leashed pets are permitted.

Reservations, fees: Reservations are recommended. Tent sites are $14.70 per night, and RV sites are $24 per night. Some credit cards accepted. Open year-round.

Directions: From Redding, turn on Highway 299 westbound and drive west over Buckhorn Summit; continue for five miles to Trinity Dam Boulevard. Turn right on Trinity Dam Boulevard and drive four miles to Lewiston. Continue on Trinity Dam Boulevard to Rush Creek Road. Turn left on Rush Creek Road and drive 2.3 miles to the campground on the left.

Contact: Trinity River Lodge RV Resort, 530/778-3791 or 800/761-2769, www.trinityriverresort.com.

55 LAKESHORE VILLA RV PARK

Scenic rating: 7

on Shasta Lake

See map page 509

This is a large campground with level, shaded sites for RVs, set near the northern Sacramento River arm of giant Shasta Lake. Most of the campers visiting here are boaters coming for the water sports, waterskiing, wakeboarding, or tubing. The sites are level and graveled.

RV sites, facilities: There are 92 sites with full or partial hookups (20, 30, and 50 amps) for RVs up to 45 feet; some sites are pull-through. There are also two RV rentals. No tents. Restrooms have showers. Ice, a dump station, cable TV, modem access, a playground, group facilities, and a boat dock are available. A boat ramp, store, a restaurant, and bar are nearby. Some facilities are wheelchair accessible. Leashed pets are permitted.

Reservations, fees: Reservations are accepted. Sites are $25 per night. A few long-term rentals available. Some credit cards are accepted. Open May–September.

Directions: From Redding, drive north on I-5 for 24 miles to Exit 702 for Lakeshore Drive/Antlers Road in Lakehead. Take that exit, turn

CALIFORNIA

left at the stop sign, and drive under the freeway to Lakeshore Drive. Turn left on Lakeshore Drive and drive 0.5 mile to the campground on the right.

Contact: Lakeshore Villa RV Park, 530/238-8688, www.american-rvresorts.com.

56 LAKESHORE INN & RV

Scenic rating: 7

on Shasta Lake

See map page 509

Shasta Lake is a boater's paradise and an ideal spot for campers with boats. The nearest marina is 2.75 miles away. It is on the Sacramento River arm of Shasta Lake. Shasta Lake Caverns are 10 miles away, and Shasta Dam tours are available about 20 miles away.

RV sites, facilities: There are 40 sites for tents or RVs of any length with full or partial hookups (30 and 50 amps); some are pull-through. Ten cabins are also available. Picnic tables are provided. Restrooms have showers. Cable TV, a dump station, a seasonal swimming pool, a playground, a video arcade, a coin laundry, a seasonal bar and restaurant, and a small seasonal convenience store are available. Family barbecues are held on Sunday in season, 5–9 P.M. Live music is scheduled most Friday and Saturday nights. Some facilities are wheelchair accessible. Leashed pets are permitted in the campground only.

Reservations, fees: Reservations are recommended at 530/238-2003. Sites are $25–29 per night, $2 per person per night for more than two people, and $1 per pet per night. Some credit cards accepted. Open year-round, with limited winter facilities.

Directions: From Redding, drive north on I-5 for 24 miles to Exit 702 for Lakeshore Drive/Antlers Road in Lakehead. Take that exit, turn left at the stop sign, and drive under the freeway to Lakeshore Drive. Turn left on Lakeshore Drive and drive one mile to the campground.

Contact: Lakeshore Inn & RV, 530/238-2003, www.shastacamping.com.

57 SHASTA LAKE RV RESORT AND CAMPGROUND

Scenic rating: 7

on Shasta Lake

See map page 509

Shasta Lake RV Resort and Campground is one of a series on the upper end of Shasta Lake with easy access off I-5 by car, then easy access by boat to premium trout or bass fishing as well as waterskiing and water sports.

RV sites, facilities: There are 53 sites with full hookups (30 amps) for RVs up to 40 feet, 21 tent sites, one trailer rental, and three cabins. Some sites are pull-through. Picnic tables, barbecues, and fire rings are provided. Restrooms have showers. A seasonal convenience store, firewood, bait, a coin laundry, a playground, table tennis, horseshoes, trailer and boat storage, modem access, and a seasonal swimming pool are available. There is also a private dock with 36 boat slips. Leashed pets are permitted.

Reservations, fees: Reservations are accepted at 800/374-2782. Sites are $20–29 per night, plus $1 per pet per night. Some credit cards accepted. Open year-round.

Directions: From Redding, drive north on I-5 for 24 miles to the Lakeshore Drive/Antlers Road exit in Lakehead. Take that exit, turn left at the stop sign, and drive under the freeway to Lakeshore Drive. Turn left on Lakeshore Drive and drive 1.5 miles to the campground on the right.

Contact: Shasta Lake RV Resort and Campground, 530/238-2370, www.shasta lakerv.com.

58 ANTLERS RV PARK AND CAMPGROUND

Scenic rating: 7

on Shasta Lake

See map page 509

Antlers Park is along the Sacramento River arm of Shasta Lake at 1,215 feet. The park is on 20 acres and has shady sites. This is a full-service spot for campers, boaters, and anglers, with access to the beautiful Sacramento River arm. The camp often fills in summer, including on weekdays.

RV sites, facilities: There are 70 sites with full hookups (30 and 50 amps) for RVs of any length (several are pull-through), 40 sites for tents, and several rental trailers. Picnic tables and fire rings or fire grills are provided. Tent sites also have food lockers. Restrooms have showers. Amenities include a seasonal convenience store and snack bar, ice, a coin laundry, Sunday pancake breakfasts, video games, a playground, volleyball, table tennis, horseshoes, basketball, and a seasonal swimming pool. Boat rentals, houseboats, moorage, and a complete marina with recreation room are available adjacent to the park. Some facilities are wheelchair accessible. Leashed pets are permitted, with a limit of two.

Reservations, fees: Reservations are accepted. Sites are $22.50–33.50 per night, $4 per person per night for more than two people, and $3 per pet per night. Some credit cards accepted. Open year-round.

Directions: From Redding, drive north on I-5 for 24 miles to the Lakeshore Drive/Antlers Road exit in Lakehead. Take that exit, turn right at the stop sign, and drive a short distance to Antlers Road. At Antlers Road, turn right and drive 1.5 miles south to the campground on the left.

Contact: Antlers RV Park and Campground, 530/238-2322 or 800/642-6849, www.antlersrvpark.com.

59 ANTLERS

Scenic rating: 7

on Shasta Lake in Shasta-Trinity National Forest
See map page 509

This spot is on the primary Sacramento River inlet of giant Shasta Lake. Antlers is a well-known spot that attracts returning campers and boaters year after year. It is the farthest upstream marina/camp on the lake. Because of that, lake levels can fluctuate greatly from spring through fall, and the operators will move their docks to compensate. Easy access off I-5 is a big plus for boaters.

RV sites, facilities: There are 41 individual sites and 18 double sites for tents or RVs up to 30 feet. No hookups. Picnic tables, food lockers, and fire grills are provided. Drinking water and flush and vault toilets are available. A boat ramp, an amphitheater with summer interpretive programs, a grocery store, and a coin laundry are available nearby. Some facilities are wheelchair accessible. Leashed pets are permitted.

Reservations, fees: Reservations are accepted ($9 reservation fee) at 877/444-6777 or www.ReserveUSA.com. Sites are $18 per night, $30 per night for a double site, $5 per night for an additional vehicle. Open year-round.

Directions: From Redding, drive north on I-5 for 24 miles to the Lakeshore Drive/Antlers Road exit in Lakehead. Take that exit, turn right at the stop sign, and drive a short distance to Antlers Road. At Antlers Road, turn right and drive one mile south to the campground.

Contact: Shasta-Trinity National Forest, Shasta Lake Ranger District, 530/275-1587, fax 530/275-1512; Shasta Lake Visitor Center, 530/275-1589; Shasta Recreation Company, 530/275-8113.

60 LAKESHORE EAST

Scenic rating: 7

on Shasta Lake in Shasta-Trinity National Forest
See map page 509

Lakeshore East is near the full-service community of Lakehead and is on the Sacramento arm of Shasta Lake. It's a nice spot, with a good boat ramp and marina nearby at Antlers or Sugarloaf.

RV sites, facilities: There are 20 individual sites and six double sites for tents or RVs up to 30 feet. No hookups. Picnic tables and fire grills are provided. Drinking water and flush toilets are available. A boat ramp, a grocery store, and coin laundry are available nearby. Some facilities are wheelchair accessible. Leashed pets are permitted.

Reservations, fees: Reservations are accepted ($9 reservation fee) at 877/444-6777 or www.ReserveUSA.com. Sites are $18 per night for a single site, $30 for a double site, $5 per night for an additional vehicle. Open year-round.

Directions: From Redding, drive north on I-5 for 24 miles to the Lakeshore Drive/Antlers Road exit at Lakehead. Take the Antlers exit, turn left at the stop sign, and drive under the freeway to Lakeshore Drive. Turn left on Lakeshore Drive and drive three miles. Look for the campground entrance on the left side of the road.

Contact: Shasta-Trinity National Forest, Shasta Lake Ranger District, 530/275-1587, fax 530/275-1512; Shasta Lake Visitor Center, 530/275-1589; Shasta Recreation Company, 530/275-8113.

61 TRAIL IN RV PARK AND CAMPGROUND

Scenic rating: 7

near Shasta Lake
See map page 509

This is a privately operated campground near the Salt Creek arm of giant Shasta Lake. Open, level sites are available. Many of the sites are filled with long-term renters. The nearest boat launch is one mile away and the lake offers fishing, boating, and swimming. Its proximity to I-5 makes this a popular spot, fast and easy to reach, which is extremely attractive for drivers of RVs and trailers who want to avoid the many twisty roads surrounding Shasta Lake.

RV sites, facilities: There are 39 sites with full hookups (30 and 50 amps) for RVs of any length and four tent sites; some sites are pull-through. Picnic tables and fire grills are provided. Restrooms have showers. Satellite TV hookups, a seasonal heated swimming pool, a playground, a convenience store, ice, firewood, and a coin laundry are available. Leashed pets are permitted.

Reservations, fees: Reservations are accepted. Sites are $28 per night for RV camping, $17 per night for tent camping, $2 per person per night for more than two people, and $1 per pet per night. Monthly rates available. Some credit cards accepted. Open year-round.

Directions: From Redding, drive 22 miles north on I-5 to Exit 698/the Gilman Road/Salt Creek Road exit. Take that exit, turn left on Salt Creek Road, and drive a short distance to Gregory Creek Road. Turn right and drive 0.25 mile to the campground on the right.

Contact: Trail In RV Park and Campground, tel./fax 530/238-8533.

62 HOLIDAY HARBOR RESORT

Scenic rating: 7

on Shasta Lake
See map page 509

This camp is one of the more popular family-oriented, all-service resorts on Shasta Lake, which has the second largest dam in the United States. It is on the lower McCloud arm of the lake, which is extremely beautiful with a limestone mountain ridge off to the east. It is an ideal jump-off for all water sports, especially houseboating, boating, all water sports, and fishing. A good boat ramp, boat rentals, and a store with all the goodies are bonuses. The place is full service and even offers boat-launching service. Campers staying here get a 15 percent discount on boat rentals. Another plus is the nearby side trip to Shasta Caverns, a privately guided adventure (fee charged) into limestone caves. This camp often fills in summer, even on weekdays.

RV sites, facilities: There are 28 sites with full hookups (50 amps) for RVs up to 40 feet, with tents allowed in several sites. Picnic tables and barbecues are provided. Restrooms have showers. A general store, a seasonal café, a gift shop, a coin laundry, a marina, marine repair service, boat moorage, a swim area, a playground, propane gas, and houseboat, boat, and personal watercraft rentals are available. Some facilities are wheelchair accessible. Leashed pets are permitted.

Reservations, fees: Reservations are recommended. Sites are $21.50–34.25 per night, $5.25–7.25 per person per night for more than two people, $4–6 per night for an additional vehicle, and $7.50–9.50 per night for boat moorage. Some credit cards accepted. Open April–October.

Directions: From Redding, drive 18 miles north on I-5 to Exit 695 and the O'Brien Road/Shasta Caverns Road exit. Turn right (east) at Shasta Caverns Road and drive one mile to the resort entrance on the right; check in at the store at 20061 Shasta Caverns Road.

Contact: Holiday Harbor Resort, 530/238-2383 or 800/776-2628, www.lakeshasta.com.

63 HIRZ BAY

Scenic rating: 8

on Shasta Lake in Shasta-Trinity National Forest
See map page 509

This is one of two camps in the immediate area (the other is Hirz Bay Group Camp) that provide nearby access to a boat ramp (a half mile down the road) and the McCloud River arm of Shasta Lake. The camp is on a point at the entrance of Hirz Bay. This is an excellent spot to make a base camp for a fishing trip, with great trolling for trout in this stretch of the lake.

RV sites, facilities: There are 37 individual sites and 10 double sites for tents or RVs up to 40 feet. No hookups. Picnic tables and fire grills are provided. Drinking water and flush and vault toilets are available. A camp host is usually available in the summer. A boat ramp is nearby. Some facilities are wheelchair accessible. Leashed pets are permitted.

Reservations, fees: Reservations are accepted ($9 reservation fee) at 877/444-6777 or www.ReserveUSA.com. Sites are $18 per night, $30 per night for a double site, $5 per night for an additional vehicle. Open year-round.

Directions: From Redding, drive north on I-5

for about 20 miles to the Salt Creek/Gilman exit. Turn right on Gilman Road/County Road 7H009 and drive northeast for 10 miles to the campground/boat launch access road. Turn right and drive 0.5 mile to the camp on the left side of the road.

Contact: Shasta-Trinity National Forest, Shasta Lake Ranger District, 530/275-1587, fax 530/275-1512; Shasta Lake Visitor Center, 530/275-1589; Shasta Recreation Company, 530/275-8113.

64 ELLERY CREEK

Scenic rating: 7

on Shasta Lake in Shasta-Trinity National Forest
See map page 509

This camp sits at a pretty spot where Ellery Creek empties into the upper McCloud arm of Shasta Lake. Several sites are set on the pavement with an unobstructed view of the beautiful McCloud arm. This stretch of water is excellent for trout fishing in the summer, with bank-fishing access available two miles upstream at the McCloud Bridge. In the spring, there are tons of small spotted bass along the shore from the camp on upstream to the inlet of the McCloud River. Boat-launching facilities are available five miles south at Hirz Bay.

RV sites, facilities: There are 19 sites for tents or RVs up to 25 feet (no hookups). Picnic tables, food lockers, and fire grills are provided. Drinking water and vault toilets are available. Leashed pets are permitted.

Reservations, fees: Reservations are accepted ($9 reservation fee) at 877/444-6777 or www.ReserveUSA.com. Sites are $14 per night, plus $5 per night for an additional vehicle. Open early May–September.

Directions: From Redding, drive north on I-5 for about 20 miles to the Salt Creek/Gilman exit. Turn right on Gilman Road/County Road 7H009 and drive northeast for 15 miles to the campground on the right side of the road.

Contact: Shasta-Trinity National Forest,

Shasta Lake Ranger District, 530/275-1587, fax 530/275-1512; Shasta Lake Visitor Center, 530/275-1589; Shasta Recreation Company, 530/275-8113.

65 PINE POINT AND GROUP CAMP

Scenic rating: 7

on Shasta Lake in Shasta-Trinity National Forest

See map page 509

Pine Point is a pretty little camp, set on a ridge above the McCloud arm of Shasta Lake amid oak trees and scattered ponderosa pines. The view is best in spring, when lake levels are generally highest. Boat-launching facilities are available at Hirz Bay; boaters park their boats on shore below the camp while the rest of their party arrives at the camp by car. That provides a chance not only for camping, but also for boating, swimming, waterskiing, and fishing. Note: July–September, this campground can be reserved as a group site only. It is also used as a summer overflow camping area on weekends and holidays.

RV sites, facilities: There are 14 sites for tents or RVs up to 24 feet (no hookups), which can also be used as a group camp for up to 100 people. Picnic tables, food lockers, and fire rings are provided. Drinking water and vault toilets are available. Leashed pets are permitted.

Reservations, fees: Reservations are required ($9 reservation fee) for the group site at 877/444-6777 or www.ReserveUSA.com. Sites are $14 per night, plus $5 per night for an additional vehicle, and it's $110 per night for the group site. Open May to early September.

Directions: From Redding, drive north on I-5 for about 20 miles to the Salt Creek/Gilman exit. Turn right on Gilman Road/County Road 7H009 and drive northeast for 17 miles to the campground entrance road on the right.

Contact: Shasta-Trinity National Forest, Shasta Lake Ranger District, 530/275-1587, fax 530/275-1512; Shasta Lake Visitor Center,

530/275-1589; Shasta Recreation Company, 530/275-8113.

66 SHASTA

Scenic rating: 6

on the Sacramento River in Shasta-Trinity National Forest

See map page 509

Because campers must drive across Shasta Dam to reach this campground, general access was closed in 2002 for national security reasons. Call at least one week in advance (Bureau of Reclamation, Security Office, 530/275-4253) to get approval to cross the dam and make arrangements before planning a visit. The closed road also provides access to an adjacent OHV area, one of the few in the north state. When open, this place is thus for quads and dirt bikes, loud and wild, and hey, it's a perfect spot for them. It's barren, with almost no shade, because of past mining in the area, but the views of the river and Shasta Dam are incredible. Nearby dam tours are unique and memorable.

RV sites, facilities: There are 22 sites for tents or RVs up to 30 feet (no hookups). Picnic tables and fire rings are provided. Drinking water and vault toilets are available. A boat ramp is nearby. Groceries and bait are available in Shasta Lake City. Leashed pets are permitted.

Reservations, fees: Reservations are not accepted. Sites are $10 per night, $5 per night for an additional vehicle. Open year-round.

Directions: From I-5 in Redding, drive north for three miles to the exit for the town of Shasta Lake City and Shasta Dam Boulevard. Take that exit and bear west on Shasta Dam Boulevard and drive three miles to Lake Boulevard. Turn right on Lake Boulevard and drive two miles. Cross Shasta Dam and continue four miles to the signed campground.

Contact: Bureau of Reclamation, Shasta Dam Visitor Center, 530/275-4463; Shasta-Trinity National Forest, Shasta Lake Ranger District, 530/275-1587, fax 530/275-1512; Shasta Lake Visitor Center, 530/275-1589.

67 FAWNDALE OAKS RV PARK

Scenic rating: 5

near Shasta Lake

See map page 509

This park is midway between Shasta Lake and Redding, so it's close to many recreational activities. Toward Redding, the options include Turtle Bay Exploration Park, WaterWorks Park, public golf courses, and Sacramento River trails, which are paved, making them accessible for wheelchairs and bicycles. Toward Shasta Lake, there are tours of Shasta Caverns, via a short drive to Holiday Harbor. The RV park is on 40 acres and has shaded sites.

RV sites, facilities: There are 15 sites with full hookups (30 and 50 amps) and cable TV for RVs up to 45 feet. Some sites are pull-through. There are also 10 tent sites and a cabin and trailer are available for rent. Picnic tables are provided, and some sites have barbecues. Phone/modem hookups, a coin laundry, boat and RV storage, a general store, a picnic area, a playground, a seasonal swimming pool, a club room, a game room, propane, and group facilities are available. Some facilities are wheelchair accessible. Leashed pets are permitted.

Reservations, fees: Reservations are accepted by telephone or website. RV sites are $23.50–27.50 per night for two people, tent sites are $17 per night for a family of four, plus $2 per person per night for additional people, $1 per pet per night, $1 per night for an additional vehicle, and $2 per night for a phone/modem hookup. Weekly and monthly rates are available. Some credit cards accepted. Open year-round.

Directions: From Redding, drive north on I-5 for nine miles to the Fawndale Road exit (Exit 689). Take that exit and turn right (east) on Fawndale Road. Drive 0.5 mile to the second RV park at the end of the road at 15015 Fawndale Road.

Contact: Fawndale Oaks RV Park, 530/275-0764 or 888/838-2159, www.fawndaleoaksrv.com.

68 BEAR MOUNTAIN RV RESORT AND CAMPGROUND

Scenic rating: 5

near Shasta Lake

See map page 509

This is a privately operated park in the remote Jones Valley area five miles from Shasta Lake. It is on 52 acres. A hiking trail leaves from the campground, rises up a hill, and provides a great view of Redding. The resort emphasizes that there is no train noise here, as there often is at campgrounds closer to Shasta Lake.

RV sites, facilities: There are 70 sites with full or partial hookups (30 amps) for RVs up to 40 feet, 24 tent sites, and four park-model cabins. Some RV sites are pull-through. Picnic tables and fire rings are provided. Drinking water, restrooms with flush toilets and coin showers, a coin laundry, modem access, a convenience store, a dump station, a seasonal swimming pool, a recreation hall, an arcade, table tennis, two playgrounds, volleyball, and a horseshoe pit are available. Some facilities are wheelchair accessible. A boat ramp is within three miles. Leashed pets are permitted.

Reservations, fees: Reservations are accepted at 800/952-0551. Tent sites are $14 per night, RV sites are $16–20 per night, plus $2 per person per night for more than two people $2 per night for an additional vehicle. Weekly and monthly rates available. Some credit cards accepted. Open year-round.

Directions: From Redding, drive north on I-5 for three miles to Exit 682 for Oasis Road. Take that exit and drive to Oasis Road. Turn right on Oasis Road and drive 3.5 miles to Bear Mountain Road. Turn right on Bear Mountain Road and drive 3.5 miles to the campground on the left.

Contact: Bear Mountain RV Resort and Campground, 530/275-4728, www.campshasta.com.

CALIFORNIA

69 BRANDY CREEK

Scenic rating: 7

on Whiskeytown Lake
See map page 509

For campers with boats, this is the best place to stay at Whiskeytown Lake, with a boat ramp less than a quarter mile away. Whiskeytown is popular for sailing and sailboarding, as it gets a lot more wind than other lakes in the region. Personal watercraft have been banned from this lake. Fishing for kokanee salmon is good in the early morning before the wind comes up; trout fishing is pretty good as well. The lake has 36 miles of shoreline.

RV sites, facilities: There are 37 sites with no hookups for RVs up to 35 feet. No tents. Drinking water and a dump station are available. Leashed pets are permitted.

Reservations, fees: Reservations are not accepted. Sites are $14 per night, $7 per night during off-season, plus a park use permit of $5 per day or $10 per week. Open year-round.

Directions: From Redding, drive west on Highway 299 for eight miles to the visitors center and Kennedy Memorial Drive. Turn left at the visitors center (Kennedy Memorial Drive) and drive five miles to the campground entrance road on the right. Turn right and drive a short distance to the camp.

Contact: Whiskeytown National Recreation Area, 530/242-3400, fax 530/246-5154; Whiskeytown Visitor Center, 530/246-1225, www.nps.gov/whis.

70 PREMIER RV RESORT

Scenic rating: 2

in Redding
See map page 509

If you're stuck with no place to go, this large park could be your savior. Nearby recreation options include a water slide park and the Turtle Bay Museum and Exploration Park on the Sacramento River. The newest attraction is Sundial Bridge, with its glass walkway that allows users to look down into the river, a stunning feat of architecture—where the experience simulates walking on air. In addition, Whiskeytown Lake is nearby to the west and Shasta Lake to the north. A casino and several golf courses are nearby.

RV sites, facilities: There are 111 sites with full or partial hookups (30 and 50 amps) for RVs of any length and two yurts. No tents. Picnic tables and fire grills are provided. Drinking water, restrooms with flush toilets and showers, a playground, a seasonal swimming pool, a coin laundry, a dump station, satellite TV hookups, modem access, a convenience store, propane gas, and a recreation room are available. Some facilities are wheelchair accessible. Leashed pets are permitted.

Reservations, fees: Reservations are accepted. Sites are $39 per night, plus $3 per person per night for more than two people. Some credit cards accepted. Open year-round.

Directions: In Redding, drive north on I-5 to the Lake Boulevard/Burney-Alturas exit. Turn west (left) on Lake Boulevard and drive 0.25 mile to North Boulder Drive. Turn right (north) on North Boulder Drive and drive one block to the resort on the left.

Contact: Premier RV Resort, 530/246-0101 or 888/710-8450.

71 MARINA RV PARK

Scenic rating: 6

on the Sacramento River
See map page 509 **BEST (**

The riverside setting is a highlight here, with the Sacramento River providing relief from the dog days of summer. An easy, paved walking and bike trail is available nearby at the Sacramento River Parkway, providing river views and sometimes a needed breeze on hot summer evenings. It is two miles away from the Turtle Bay Museum and close to a movie theater. A golf driving range is nearby. This park includes an area with long-term RV renters.

RV sites, facilities: There are 42 sites with full or partial hookups (30 amps) for RVs up to 40 feet. Picnic tables, restrooms with showers, a coin laundry, a small store, modem access, a seasonal swimming pool, a spa, a boat ramp, and a dump station are available. Leashed pets are permitted.

Reservations, fees: Reservations are accepted. Sites are $29.70 per night, $2 per person per night for more than two people. Weekly and monthly rates available. Open year-round.

Directions: In Redding, turn west on Highway 44 and drive 1.5 miles to the exit for Convention Center/Marina Park Drive. Take that exit, turn left, and drive over the highway to a stoplight and Marina Park Drive. Turn left (south) on Marina Park Drive and drive 0.8 mile to the park on the left.

Contact: Marina RV Park, 530/241-4396.

72 SACRAMENTO RIVER RV RESORT

Scenic rating: 7

south of Redding

See map page 509   BEST (

This makes a good headquarters for a fall fishing trip on the Sacramento River, where the salmon come big August–October. In the summer trout fishing is very good from this area as well, but a boat is a must. No problem; there's a boat ramp at the park. In addition, you can hire fishing guides who launch from here daily. The park is open year-round, and if you want to stay close to home, a three-acre pond with bass, bluegill, and perch is also available at the resort. You also get great long-distance views of Mount Shasta and Mount Lassen.

RV sites, facilities: There are 140 sites with full hookups (30 and 50 amps) for RVs of any length and 10 sites for tents in a shaded grassy area. Some RV sites are pull-through. Picnic tables, restrooms with showers, a coin laundry, a dump station, cable TV, modem access, bait, a boat launch, a playground, two tennis courts, a golf driving range, and a large seasonal swimming pool are available. A clubhouse is available by reservation. Some facilities are wheelchair accessible. Leashed pets are permitted.

Reservations, fees: Reservations are accepted. Sites are $16.50–27.40 per night. Some credit cards accepted. Open year-round.

Directions: From Redding, drive south on I-5 for five miles to the Knighton Road exit. Turn west (right) and drive a short distance to Riverland Drive. Turn left on Riverland Drive and drive two miles to the park at the end of the road.

Contact: Sacramento River RV Resort, 530/365-6402, fax 530/365-2601, www.sacramento riverrvresort.com.

73 FIR COVE

Scenic rating: 7

on Ruth Lake in Six Rivers National Forest

See map page 509

This spot is along Ruth Lake adjacent to Bailey Cove. The elevation is 2,600 feet, and the lake covers 1,200 acres. Swimming and all water sports are allowed on Ruth Lake, and there are three boat ramps. In the summer the warm water makes this an ideal place for families to spend some time swimming. Fishing is decent for rainbow trout in the spring and for bass in the summer.

RV sites, facilities: There are 19 sites for tents or RVs up to 22 feet (no hookups). Picnic tables and fire grills are provided. Drinking water and vault toilets are available. Some facilities are wheelchair accessible. Leashed pets are permitted.

Reservations, fees: Reservations are not accepted. Sites are $12 per night, plus $5 per night for an additional vehicle. Open late May–mid-September.

Directions: From Eureka, drive south on U.S. 101 to Alton and the junction with Highway 36. Turn east on Highway 36 and drive about 50 miles to the town of Mad River. Turn right at the sign for Ruth Lake/Lower Mad River Road and drive 12 miles to the campground on the right side of the road.

Contact: Six Rivers National Forest, Mad River Ranger District, 707/574-6233, fax 707/574-6273.

CALIFORNIA

74 BAILEY CANYON

Scenic rating: 7

on Ruth Lake in Six Rivers National Forest

See map page 509

Ruth Lake is the only major lake within a reasonable driving distance of U.S. 101, although some people might argue with you over how reasonable this twisty drive is. Regardless, you end up at a camp along the east shore of Ruth Lake, where fishing for trout or bass and waterskiing are popular. What really wins out is that it is hot and sunny all summer, the exact opposite of the fogged-in Humboldt coast. The elevation is 2,600 feet.

RV sites, facilities: There are 25 sites for tents or RVs up to 22 feet (no hookups). Picnic tables and fire grills are provided. Drinking water and vault toilets are available. A boat ramp and small marina are nearby. Some facilities are wheelchair accessible. Leashed pets are permitted.

Reservations, fees: Reservations are not accepted. Sites are $12 per night, plus $5 per night for an additional vehicle. Open late May–mid-September.

Directions: From Eureka, drive south on U.S. 101 to Alton and the junction with Highway 36. Turn east on Highway 36 and drive about 50 miles to the town of Mad River. Turn right at the sign for Ruth Lake/Lower Mad River Road and drive 13 miles to the campground on the right side of the road.

Contact: Six Rivers National Forest, Mad River Ranger District, 707/574-6233, fax 707/574-6273.

75 BEND RV PARK AND FISHING RESORT

Scenic rating: 7

on the Sacramento River

See map page 509

Here's a spot for RV cruisers to rest their rigs for a while. Bend RV Park and Fishing Resort beside the Sacramento River is open year-round. The salmon average 15–25 pounds in this area, and anglers typically have the best results mid-August–October. In recent years, the gates of the Red Bluff Diversion Dam have been raised in early September. When that occurs, huge numbers of salmon charge upstream from Red Bluff to Anderson, holding in each deep river hole. Expect very hot weather in July and August.

RV sites, facilities: There are 14 sites with full or partial hookups (30 amps) for RVs up to 40 feet. There is a separate area for tents only. Picnic tables are provided. Drinking water, restrooms with showers and flush toilets, a convenience store, bait and tackle, a boat ramp, a boat dock, a coin laundry, and a dump station are available. Leashed pets are permitted.

Reservations, fees: Reservations are accepted. Sites are $21.50–24 per night, plus $3.50 per person per night for more than two people. Open year-round.

Directions: From I-5 in Red Bluff, drive four miles north on I-5 to the Jelly's Ferry Road exit. Take that exit and turn northeast on Jelly's Ferry Road; drive 2.5 miles to the resort at 21795 Bend Ferry Road.

Contact: Bend RV Park and Fishing Resort, 530/527-6289.

76 LAKE RED BLUFF

Scenic rating: 6

on the Sacramento River near Red Bluff

See map page 509

Lake Red Bluff is created by the Red Bluff Diversion Dam on the Sacramento River, and waterskiing, bird-watching, hiking, and fishing are the most popular activities. A three-mile-long paved trail parallels the river, and cycling and skating are allowed on the trail. It has become a backyard swimming hole for local residents in the summer when the temperatures reach the high 90s and low 100s almost every day. In early September, the Bureau of Reclamation raises the gates at the diversion dam to allow migrating salmon an easier course on the upstream journey, and in the process,

CALIFORNIA

Lake Red Bluff reverts to its former self as the Sacramento River.

RV sites, facilities: There are 30 sites for tents or RVs up to 35 feet (no hookups) at Sycamore Camp. There is also a group camp (Camp Discovery) for tents only that also has 11 screened cabins and can accommodate up to 100 people. Drinking water, restrooms with coin showers and flush toilets, vault toilets, picnic areas, a visitors center, two boat ramps, and a fish-viewing plaza are available. There are two large barbecues, electrical outlets, lockable storage, five large picnic tables, restrooms with showers and sinks, and an amphitheater in the group camp area. Some facilities are wheelchair accessible. Leashed pets are permitted.

Reservations, fees: Reservations are not accepted for individual sites but are required for the group camp at 530/527-1196. Individual sites are $12–24 per night, and the group camp is $150 per night. Open April–October.

Directions: From I-5 at Red Bluff, turn east on Highway 36 and drive 100 yards to the first turnoff at Sale Lane. Turn right (south) on Sale Lane and drive 2.5 miles to the campground at the end of the road.

Contact: Mendocino National Forest, Red Bluff Recreation Area, 530/527-2813, fax 530/527-1312; Discovery Center, 530/527-1196.

CALIFORNIA

LASSEN AND MODOC

(BEST RV PARKS AND CAMPGROUNDS

(Wildlife-Viewing
Indian Well, page 550.

Mount Lassen and its awesome volcanic past seem to cast a shadow everywhere you go in this region. At 10,457 feet, the mountain's domed summit is visible for more than 100 miles in all directions. It blew its top in 1914, with continuing eruptions through 1918. Although it's now dormant, volcanic geology dominates the landscape everywhere you look.

Of all the areas of California covered in this book, this region has the least number of romantic getaway spots. It caters instead primarily to outdoors enthusiasts. And Lassen Volcanic National Park is one of the best places to lace up the hiking boots or spool new line on a reel. It's often off the radar scope of vacationers, making it one of the few national parks where you can enjoy the wilderness in relative solitude. Unique features of the region include its pumice boulders, volcanic rock, and spring-fed streams from the underground lava tubes.

The national park is easily explored along the main route, the Lassen Park Highway. Along the way, you can pick a few trails for adventure. The best hikes are the Summit Climb (moderate to challenging), best done first thing in the morning, and Bumpass Hell (easy and great for kids), to see the sulfur vents and boiling mud pots. Another favorite for classic alpine beauty is the Shadow Lake Trail.

Nearby is McArthur – Burney Falls Memorial State Park, along with the Pit River and Lake Britton, which together make up one of Northern California's best recreation destinations for families. This is also one of the best areas for fly-fishing, especially at Hat Creek, Pit River, Burney Creek, and Manzanita Lake. For more beautiful settings, you can visit Lake Almanor and Eagle Lake, both of which provide lakeside campgrounds and excellent fishing and boating recreation.

And there's more. In remote Modoc County, you'll find Lava Beds National Monument and the South Warner Wilderness. Lava Beds is a stark, pretty, and often lonely place. It's sprinkled with small lakes full of trout, is home to large-antlered deer that migrate in after the first snow (and after the hunting season has closed), and features a unique volcanic habitat with huge flows of obsidian (dark, smooth, natural glass formed by the cooling of molten lava) and dacite (gray, craggy volcanic flow). Lava Beds National Monument boasts about 500 caves and lava tubes, including the 6,000-foot Catacomb tunnel. Nearby is pretty

Medicine Lake, formed in a caldera, which provides good trout fishing, hiking, and exploring.

It seems no matter where you go, there are so many campgrounds that you can always find a match for what you desire.

Includes:

- Antelope Lake
- Battle Creek Reservoir
- Butt Valley Reservoir
- Duncan Reservoir
- Eagle Lake
- Feather River
- Hat Creek
- Iron Canyon Reservoir
- Klamath National Forest
- Lake Almanor
- Lake Britton
- Lassen National Forest
- Lassen Volcanic National Park
- Lava Beds National Monument
- McArthur – Burney Falls Memorial State Park
- Medicine Lake
- Modoc National Forest
- Pit River
- Shasta-Trinity National Forest
- Silver Lake

CALIFORNIA

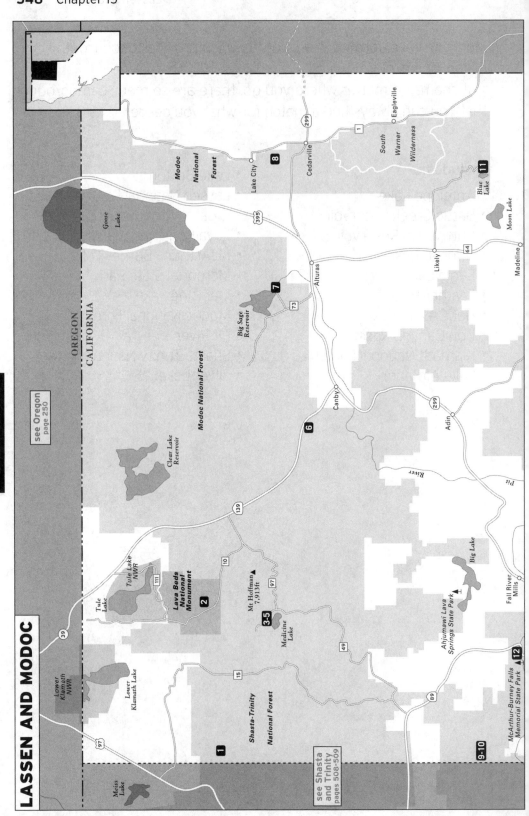

LASSEN AND MODOC

CALIFORNIA

see Oregon page 250

OREGON
CALIFORNIA

Meiss Lake

Lower Klamath NWR

Tule Lake NWR

Tule Lake

Lava Beds National Monument

Clear Lake Reservoir

Goose Lake

Modoc National Forest

Lake City

Cedarville

Eagleville

South Warner Wilderness

8

11

Blue Lake

Moon Lake

Likely

Madeline

Alturas

Big Sage Reservoir

7

Canby

Adin

Pit River

Lower Klamath Lake

Mt Hoffman 7,913ft

Medicine Lake

2

3-5

6

Big Lake

Ahjumawi Lava Springs State Park

Fall River Mills

1

Shasta-Trinity National Forest

see Shasta and Trinity pages 508-509

9-10

12

McArthur-Burney Falls Memorial State Park

Modoc National Forest

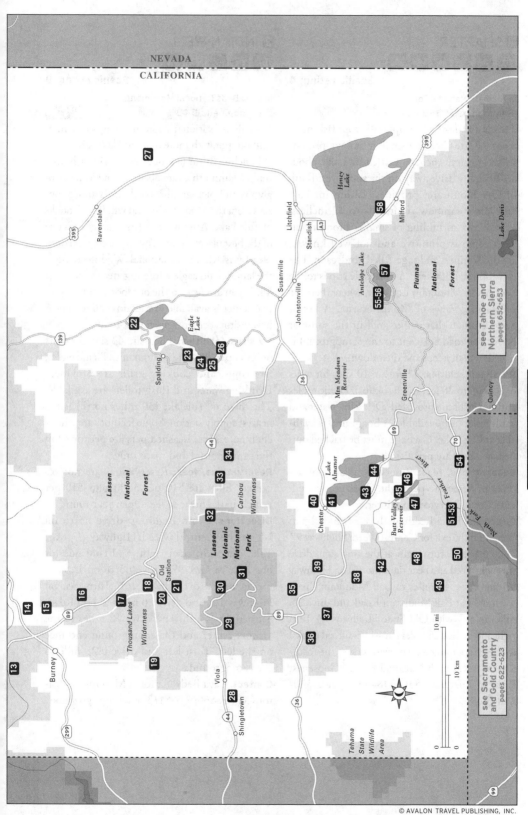

NEVADA
CALIFORNIA

CALIFORNIA

27

Honey Lake

395

Litchfield

58

Milford

Standish

A3

Susanville

Johnstonville

Ravendale

395

Antelope Lake

57

55-56

Plumas National Forest

Lake Davis

22

Eagle Lake

26

23

24 25

Spalding

139

36

Mtn Meadows Reservoir

Greenville

Quincy

see Tahoe and Northern Sierra pages 652-653

44

34

33

Caribou Wilderness

Lake Almanor

44

46

89

70

54

Feather River

43

45

32

Lassen National Forest

Lassen Volcanic National Park

40 41

Chester

47

51-53

Butt Valley Reservoir

North Fork

50

31

30

39

42

48

14 15

16

17

18

Old Station

21

20

29

35

37

38

49

89

13

Thousand Lakes Wilderness

19

Burney

89

Viola

36

28

Shingletown

44

299

10 mi

10 km

see Sacramento and Gold Country pages 622-623

Tehama State Wildlife Area

99

1 SHAFTER

🏃 🏞 🎣 🏕 🚐 ⛺

Scenic rating: 4

in Klamath National Forest
See map page 548

This is a little-used camp with trout fishing at nearby Butte Creek for small rainbows, primarily six- to eight-inchers. Little Orr Lake, about a 10-minute drive away on the southwest flank of Orr Mountain, provides fishing for bass and larger rainbow trout, 10- to 12-inchers, as well as a sprinkling of smaller brook trout. This camp is primitive and not well known, set in a juniper- and sage-filled landscape. The elevation is 4,300 feet. A great side trip is to the nearby Orr Mountain Lookout, where there are spectacular views of Mount Shasta. A Forest Service touch that is like gold in the summer is that the road adjacent to the campground is paved, which keeps the dust down.

RV sites, facilities: There are 10 sites for tents or RVs up to 28 feet (no hookups). Picnic tables and fire grills are provided. Drinking water and vault toilets are available. A boat ramp is available at Orr Lake. Garbage must be packed out. Leashed pets are permitted.

Reservations, fees: Reservations are not accepted. Sites are $6 per night. Open year-round, with limited services in winter.

Directions: From Redding, drive north on I-5 to Weed and the exit for Central Weed/Highway 97. Take that exit, turn right at the stop sign, drive through Weed and bear right (north) on Highway 97, and drive 40 miles to Ball Mountain Road. Turn right at Ball Mountain Road and drive 2.5 miles to a T with Old State Highway 97. Turn right and drive 4.25 miles (crossing railroad tracks) to the campground on the right side of the road.

Contact: Klamath National Forest, Goosenest Ranger District, 530/398-4391, fax 530/398-5749.

2 INDIAN WELL

🏃 🐕 ♿ 🚐 ⛺

Scenic rating: 9

in Lava Beds National Monument
See map page 548   **BEST (**

Lava Beds National Monument is a one-in-a-million spot with more than 500 lava tube caves, Schonchin Butte (a cinder cone with a hiking trail), Mammoth Crater, Native American petroglyphs and pictographs, battlefields and campsites from the Modoc War, and wildlife overlooks of Tule Lake. After winter's first snow, this is one of the best places in the West to photograph deer. Nearby is Klamath National Wildlife Refuge, the largest bald eagle wintering area in the lower 48. If you are new to the outdoors, an interpretive center is available to explain it all to you. A new visitors center is open year-round.

RV sites, facilities: There are 43 sites for tents or RVs up to 30 feet (no hookups). Picnic tables, fire rings, and cooking grills are provided. Drinking water and flush toilets are available. The town of Tulelake (30 miles north) is the nearest supply station. Some facilities are wheelchair accessible. Leashed pets are permitted in the campground and roads only.

Reservations, fees: Reservations are not accepted. Sites are $10 per night plus $10 per vehicle park entrance fee. Open year-round.

Directions: From Redding, drive north on I-5 to the Central Weed/Highway 97 exit. Take that exit, turn right, and continue for one mile to U.S. 97. Drive north on U.S. 97 for 54 miles to Highway 161. Turn east on Highway 161 and drive 20 miles to Hill Road. Turn right (south) and drive 18 miles to the visitors center and the campground entrance on the left. Turn left and drive 0.25 mile to the campground.

Contact: Lava Beds National Monument Visitor Center, 530/667-8113, www.nps.gov/labe.

3 HARRIS SPRINGS

Scenic rating: 3

in Shasta-Trinity National Forest

See map page 548

This camp is a hidden spot in remote Shasta-Trinity National Forest, nestled in the long, mountainous ridge that runs east from Mount Shasta to the Lava Beds National Monument. The camp is at 4,800 feet, with a part-time fire station within a quarter mile on the opposite side of the access road. The area is best explored by four-wheel drive, venturing to a series of small buttes, mountaintops, and lookouts in the immediate area. A map of Shasta-Trinity National Forest is a must.

RV sites, facilities: There are 15 sites for tents or RVs up to 32 feet (no hookups). Picnic tables and fire grills are provided. There is no drinking water. Vault toilets are available. Garbage must be packed out. Leashed pets are permitted.

Reservations, fees: Reservations are not accepted. There is no fee for camping. Open late May–early October, weather permitting.

Directions: From Redding, drive north on I-5 past Dunsmuir to the junction with Highway 89. Turn east on Highway 89 and drive 28 miles (just past Bartle) to Forest Road 15/Harris Springs Road. Bear left on Forest Road 15 and drive five miles to the Y intersection with Harris Springs Road and Medicine Lake Road/Forest Road 49. Bear left at the Y, staying on Harris Springs Road/Forest Road 15, and drive 12 miles to a junction with a forest road signed for the Harris Springs Ranger Station. Turn right and drive a short distance, and look for the campground entrance on the right side of the road.

Contact: Shasta-Trinity National Forest, Mc-Cloud Ranger District, 530/964-2184, fax 530/964-2938.

4 MEDICINE

Scenic rating: 7

on Medicine Lake in Modoc National Forest

See map page 548

Lakeside campsites tucked away in conifers make this camp a winner. Medicine Lake, at 640 acres, was formed in the crater of an old volcano and is surrounded by lodgepole pine and fir trees. The lake is stocked with rainbow and brook trout in the summer, gets quite cold in the fall, and freezes over in winter. All water sports are permitted. Many side trips are possible, including nearby Bullseye and Blanche Lakes and Ice Caves (both signed and off the access road) and Lava Beds National Monument just 15 miles north. At 6,700 feet, temperatures can drop in summer and the season is short.

RV sites, facilities: There are 22 sites for tents or RVs up to 30 feet (no hookups). Picnic tables and fire grills are provided. Drinking water and vault toilets are available. Ranger-guided cave tours, walks, and talks are available during the summer. A boat ramp is available nearby. A café and bar are available in Bartle; otherwise, no supplies are available within an hour's drive. Some facilities are wheelchair accessible. Leashed pets are permitted.

Reservations, fees: Reservations are not accepted. Sites are $7 per vehicle per night. Open late May–early October, weather permitting.

Directions: From Redding, drive north on I-5 past Dunsmuir to Highway 89. Turn east on Highway 89 and drive 28 miles (just past Bartle) to Forest Road 15/Harris Springs Road. Turn left on Forest Road 15 and drive approximately five miles to the Y intersection with Forest Road 49/Medicine Lake Road. Turn right on Forest Road 49 and drive approximately 26 miles to the lake and campground access road.

Contact: Modoc National Forest, Double-head Ranger District, 530/667-2246, fax 530/667-8609.

CALIFORNIA

⑤ A. H. HOGUE

Scenic rating: 7

on Medicine Lake in Modoc National Forest

See map page 548

This camp was created in 1990 when the original Medicine Lake Campground was divided in half. (For more information, see the *Medicine* listing in this chapter.)

RV sites, facilities: There are 24 sites for tents or RVs up to 30 feet (no hookups). Picnic tables and fire grills are provided. Drinking water and vault toilets are available. A boat ramp is available nearby. A café and bar is in Bartle; otherwise, no supplies are available within an hour's drive. Some facilities are wheelchair accessible. Leashed pets are permitted.

Reservations, fees: Reservations are not accepted. Sites are $7 per vehicle per night. Open late May–early October, weather permitting.

Directions: From Redding, drive north on I-5 past Dunsmuir to Highway 89. Turn east on Highway 89 and drive 28 miles (just past Bartle) to Forest Road 15/Harris Springs Road. Turn left on Forest Road 15 and drive approximately five miles to the Y intersection with Forest Road 49/Medicine Lake Road. Turn right on Forest Road 49 and drive approximately 26 miles to the lake and campground access road.

Contact: Modoc National Forest, Double-head Ranger District, 530/667-2246, fax 530/667-8609.

⑥ HOWARD'S GULCH

Scenic rating: 6

near Duncan Reservoir in Modoc National Forest

See map page 548

This is the nearest campground to Duncan Reservoir, three miles to the north and stocked with trout each year by the Department of Fish and Game. The camp is in the typically sparse woods of Modoc National Forest, but a beautiful grove of aspen is three miles west on Highway 139, on the left side of the road. By the way, Highway 139 isn't much of a highway

at all, but it is paved and will get you there. The elevation is 4,700 feet.

RV sites, facilities: There are 11 sites for tents or RVs up to 22 feet (no hookups). Picnic tables and fire grills are provided. Drinking water and vault toilets are available. Supplies are available within five miles in Canby. Some facilities are wheelchair accessible. Leashed pets are permitted.

Reservations, fees: Reservations are not accepted. Sites are $6 per night. Open May–October, weather permitting.

Directions: From Redding, drive east on Highway 299 for about 100 miles to Adin. Continue on Highway 299 for about 25 miles to Highway 139. Turn left (northwest) on Highway 139 and drive six miles to the campground on the left side of the road.

Contact: Modoc National Forest, Devil's Garden Ranger District, 530/233-5811, fax 530/233-8709.

⑦ BIG SAGE RESERVOIR

Scenic rating: 5

in Modoc National Forest

See map page 548

This is a do-it-yourself camp; that is, pick your own spot, bring your own water, and don't expect to see anybody else. This camp is along Big Sage Reservoir—that's right, sagebrush country at 5,100 feet elevation. It is a big lake, covering 5,000 surface acres, and a boat ramp is adjacent to the campground. This is one of the better bass lakes in Modoc County. Catfish and crappie are also here. Water sports are allowed, except for personal watercraft. Swimming is not recommended because of algae growth in midsummer, murky water, and the muddy shoreline. Water levels can fluctuate greatly.

RV sites, facilities: There are six sites for tents or RVs up to 22 feet (no hookups). Picnic tables and fire grills are provided. Vault toilets are available. There is no drinking water. Garbage must be packed out. A boat ramp is available nearby. Supplies can be obtained in Alturas, about eight miles away. Some facilities are wheelchair accessible. Leashed pets are permitted.

Reservations, fees: Reservations are not accepted. There is no fee for camping. Open May–September.

Directions: From Alturas, drive west on Highway 299 for three miles to Crowder Flat Road/County Road 73. Turn right on Crowder Flat Road and drive about five miles to County Road 180. Turn right on County Road 180 and drive four miles. Turn left at the access road for the campground and boat ramp and drive a short distance to the camp on the left side of the road.

Contact: Modoc National Forest, Doublehead Ranger District, 530/667-2246, fax 530/667-8309.

8 STOUGH RESERVOIR

Scenic rating: 8

in Modoc National Forest

See map page 548

Stough Reservoir looks like a large country pond where cattle might drink. You know why? Because it once actually was a cattle pond on a family ranch that has since been converted to Forest Service property. It is in the north Warner Mountains (not to be confused with the South Warner Wilderness), which feature many back roads and remote four-wheel-drive routes. The camp is at an elevation of 6,200 feet. Note that you may find this campground named "Stowe Reservoir" on some maps. The name is now officially spelled "Stough Reservoir," after the family that originally owned the property.

RV sites, facilities: There are 14 sites for tents or RVs up to 22 feet (no hookups). Picnic tables and fire grills are provided. Drinking water and vault toilets are available. Garbage must be packed out. Leashed pets are permitted. Supplies can be obtained in Cedarville, six miles away.

Reservations, fees: Reservations are not accepted. There is no fee for camping. Open late May–early October, weather permitting.

Directions: From Redding, drive east on Highway 299 to Alturas. In Alturas, continue north on Highway 299/U.S. 395 for five miles to the split-off for Highway 299. Turn right on Highway 299 and drive about 12 miles (just past Cedar Pass). Look for the signed entrance road on the left side of the road. Turn left and drive one mile to the campground on the left side of the road.

Contact: Modoc National Forest, Warner Mountain Ranger District, 530/279-6116, fax 530/279-8309.

9 DEADLUN

Scenic rating: 7

on Iron Canyon Reservoir in Shasta-Trinity National Forest

See map page 548

Deadlun is a pretty campground set in the forest, shaded and quiet, with a five-minute walk or one-minute drive to the Deadlun Creek arm of Iron Canyon Reservoir. Drive? If you have a canoe to launch or fishing equipment to carry, driving is the choice. Trout fishing is good here, both in April and May, then again in October and early November. One downer is that the shoreline is often very muddy in March and early April. Because of an engineering error with the dam, the lake never fills completely, causing the lakeshore to be strewn with stumps and quite muddy after spring rains and snowmelt. There are hot springs in the town of Big Bend.

RV sites, facilities: There are 25 sites for tents or RVs up to 24 feet (no hookups). Picnic tables and fire grills are provided. Vault toilets are available. No drinking water is available. A small boat ramp is available one mile from the camp. Garbage must be packed out. Leashed pets are permitted.

Reservations, fees: Reservations are not accepted. There is no fee for camping. Open year-round.

Directions: From Redding, drive east on Highway 299 for 37 miles to Big Bend Road/County Road 7M01. Turn left and drive 17 miles to the

CALIFORNIA

town of Big Bend. Continue for five miles to the lake, bearing right at the T intersection, and continue for two miles (past the boat-launch turnoff) to the campground turnoff on the left side of the road. Turn left and drive one mile to the campground.

Contact: Shasta-Trinity National Forest, Shasta Lake Ranger District, 530/275-1587, fax 530/275-1512; Shasta Lake Visitor Center, 530/275-1589.

10 HAWKINS LANDING

Scenic rating: 7

on Iron Canyon Reservoir
See map page 548

The adjacent boat ramp makes Hawkins Landing the better of the two camps at Iron Canyon Reservoir for campers with trailered boats (though Deadlun is far more secluded). Iron Canyon, with 15 miles of shoreline, provides good fishing for trout, has a resident bald eagle or two, and also has nearby hot springs in the town of Big Bend. One problem with this lake is the annual drawdown in late fall, which causes the shoreline to be extremely muddy in the spring. For this reason, swimming is lousy because there is no beach and lots of debris in the water. The lake usually rises high enough to make the boat ramp functional by mid-April. This camp is at an elevation of 2,700 feet.

RV sites, facilities: There are 10 sites for tents or RVs up to 30 feet (no hookups). Picnic tables and fire grills are provided. Drinking water, vault toilets, and a small boat ramp are available. Supplies can be obtained in Big Bend. Leashed pets are permitted.

Reservations, fees: Reservations are not accepted. Sites are $10 per night, $1 per pet per night, $3 per night for an additional vehicle, and $7 per night for an additional RV. Open mid-May–Labor Day weekend, weather permitting.

Directions: From Redding, drive east on Highway 299 for 37 miles to Big Bend Road. At Big Bend Road turn left and drive 15.2 miles

to the town of Big Bend. Continue for 2.1 miles to Forest Road 38N11. Turn left and drive 3.3 miles to the Iron Canyon Reservoir Spillway. Turn right and drive 1.1 miles to a dirt road. Turn left and drive 0.3 mile to the campground.

Contact: PG&E Land Projects, 916/386-5164, www.pge.com/recreation.

11 BLUE LAKE

Scenic rating: 6

in Modoc National Forest
See map page 548

You won't believe this: A few years ago, the Blue Fire burned 35,000 acres in this area, including the east and west slopes adjoining Blue Lake, yet this campground was untouched. It is a strange scene, a somewhat wooded campground (with some level campsites) near the shore of Blue Lake. The lake covers 160 acres and provides fishing for large brown trout and rainbow trout. A 5-mph speed limit assures quiet water for small boats and canoes. A trail circles the lake and takes less than an hour to hike. The elevation is 6,000 feet. Bald eagles have been spotted here. While their presence negates year-round use of six campsites otherwise available, the trade-off is an unprecedented opportunity to view the national bird.

RV sites, facilities: There are 48 sites for tents or RVs up to 22 feet (no hookups). Picnic tables and fire grills are provided. Drinking water and vault toilets are available. Some facilities are wheelchair accessible, including a paved boat launch and fishing pier. Supplies are available in Likely. Leashed pets are permitted.

Reservations, fees: Reservations are not accepted. Sites are $7 per night. Open June–October, weather permitting.

Directions: From Alturas, drive south on U.S. 395 for seven miles to the town of Likely, where you'll come to Jess Valley Road. Turn left on Jess Valley Road/County Road 64 and drive nine miles to the fork. At the fork, bear right on Forest Road 64 and drive seven miles to Forest Road 38N30. Turn right on Forest Road 38N30 and drive two miles to the campground.

Contact: Modoc National Forest, Warner Mountain Ranger District, 530/279-6116, fax 530/279-8309.

12 NORTHSHORE

Scenic rating: 8

on Lake Britton

See map page 548

This peaceful campground is among the woodlands near the shore of Lake Britton, directly across the lake from McArthur–Burney Falls Memorial State Park. Boating and fishing are popular here, and once the water warms up in midsummer, swimming is also a winner. Boat rentals are available near the boat ramp. The lake has fair prospects for trout and is sometimes excellent for crappie. For side trips, the best trout fishing in the area is on the Pit River near Powerhouse Number Three. A hot spring is available in Big Bend, about a 30-minute drive from camp. The elevation is 2,800 feet. Note: This is a bald eagle nesting area, and the area is subject to closure to protect the raptors.

RV sites, facilities: There are 30 sites for tents or RVs up to 30 feet (no hookups). Picnic tables and fire grills are provided. Drinking water and vault toilets are available. An unimproved boat ramp is available near the camp, and an improved boat ramp is available in McArthur–Burney Falls Memorial State Park (about four miles away). Supplies can be obtained in Fall River Mills or Burney. Leashed pets are permitted.

Reservations, fees: Reservations are not accepted. Sites are $16 per night, $3 per night for an additional vehicle, and $1 per pet per night. Open mid-May–mid-September, weather permitting.

Directions: From Redding, drive east on Highway 299 to Burney and then continue for five miles to Highway 89. Turn left (north) and drive 9.7 miles (past the state park entrance and over the Lake Britton Bridge) to Clark Creek

Road. Turn left (west) and drive about a mile to the camp access road. Turn left and drive one mile to the camp.

Contact: PG&E Land Projects, 916/386-5164, www.pge.com/recreation.

13 BURNEY FALLS MEMORIAL STATE PARK AND HORSE CAMP

Scenic rating: 9

in McArthur–Burney Falls Memorial State Park

See map page 549

Burney Falls is a 129-foot waterfall, a beautiful cascade split at the top by a little grove of trees, with small trickles oozing and falling out of the adjacent moss-lined wall. Since it is fed primarily by a spring, it runs strong and glorious most of the year, producing 100 million gallons of water every day. The Headwaters Trail provides an outstanding hike, both to see the waterfall and Burney Creek, as well as for an easy adventure and fishing access to the stream. An excellent fly-fishing section of the Pit River is available below the dam. There are other stellar recreation options at this state park. At the end of the campground access road is a boat ramp for Lake Britton, with rentals available for canoes and pedal boats. This is a beautiful lake, with pretty canyon walls on its upper end, and good smallmouth bass (at rock piles) and crappie fishing (near the train trestle). There is also a good swimming beach. The Pacific Crest Trail is routed right through the park and provides an additional opportunity for a day hike, best explored downstream from the dam. Reservations for sites are essential during the summer. This park features 910 acres of forest and five miles of stream and lake shore. The park's landscape was created by volcanic activity, as well as erosion from weather and stream action.

RV sites, facilities: There are 128 sites for tents or RVs up to 32 feet, six horse camp sites, and one hike-in/bike-in site. No hookups. Picnic tables, food lockers, and fire grills are provided. Drinking water, restrooms with flush toilets and

CALIFORNIA

showers, and a dump station are available. Vault toilets and a small horse corral are available at the horse camp. A grocery/gift store and boat rentals are available in the summer. Some facilities are wheelchair accessible. Leashed pets are permitted, except on the trails and the beach.

Reservations, fees: Reservations are accepted ($7.50 reservation fee) at 800/444-PARK (800/444-7275) or www.reserveamerica.com. Sites are $15–20 per night, $6 per night for an additional vehicle, and $3 per person per night for the hike-in/bike-in site. The horse camp is $9 per night and $2 per night per horse. Boat launching is $8 per day. Open year-round.

Directions: From Redding, drive east on Highway 299 to Burney and then continue for five miles to the junction with Highway 89. At Highway 89, turn north (left) and drive six miles to the campground entrance on the left side of the road.

Contact: McArthur–Burney Falls Memorial State Park, 530/335-2777, www.parks.ca.gov.

14 PIT RIVER

Scenic rating: 6

on the Pit River

See map page 549

Very few out-of-towners know about this hidden campground set along the Pit River. It can provide a good base camp for a fishing trip adventure. The best stretch of trout water on the Pit is near Powerhouse Number Three. In addition to fishing there are many other recreation options. A parking area and trail along Hat Creek are available where the Highway 299 bridge crosses Hat Creek. Baum Lake, Crystal Lake, and the Cassel section of Hat Creek are all within five miles of this camp.

RV sites, facilities: There are seven sites for tents or RVs up to 32 feet (no hookups) and one double site for up to eight people. Picnic tables and fire rings are provided. Vault toilets, a wheelchair-accessible fishing pier, and small-craft launch ramp are available. No drinking water is available. Garbage must be packed

out. There are supplies and a coin laundry in Fall River Mills. Some facilities are wheelchair accessible. Leashed pets are permitted.

Reservations, fees: Reservations are not accepted. Sites are $8 per night, and it's $12 per night for the double site. Open mid-April–mid-November.

Directions: From Redding, drive east on Highway 299 to Burney and continue for five miles to the junction with Highway 89. At the junction, continue straight on Highway 299, cross the Pit River Bridge, and drive about three miles to Pit One Powerhouse Road. Turn right and drive down the hill to the Pit River Lodge. Turn right and drive 0.5 mile to the campground.

Contact: Bureau of Land Management, Alturas Field Office, 530/233-4666, fax 530/233-5696.

15 CASSEL

Scenic rating: 8

on Hat Creek

See map page 549

This camp is at 3,200 feet in the beautiful Hat Creek Valley. It is an outstanding location for a fishing trip base camp, with nearby Crystal Lake, Baum Lake, and Hat Creek (all set in the Hat Creek Valley) providing trout fishing. This section of Hat Creek is well known for its challenging fly-fishing. A good source of fishing information is Vaughn's Sporting Goods in Burney. Baum Lake is ideal for car-top boats with electric motors.

RV sites, facilities: There are 27 sites for tents or RVs up to 30 feet (no hookups). Picnic tables and fire grills are provided. Drinking water and vault toilets are available. Some facilities are wheelchair accessible. Leashed pets are permitted.

Reservations, fees: Reservations are not accepted. Sites are $16 per night, $3 per night for an additional vehicle, and $1 per pet per night. Open mid-April–mid-November, weather permitting.

Directions: From Redding, drive east on Highway 299 to Burney and continue for five miles to the junction with Highway 89. At the junction, continue straight on Highway 299 for two miles to Cassel Road. At Cassel Road, turn right and drive 3.6 miles to the campground entrance on the left.

Contact: PG&E Land Projects, 916/386-5164, www.pge.com/recreation.

16 HAT CREEK HEREFORD RANCH RV PARK AND CAMPGROUND

Scenic rating: 8

near Hat Creek

See map page 549

This privately operated campground is set in a working cattle ranch. Campers are not allowed near the cattle pasture or cattle. Fishing is available in Hat Creek or in the nearby stocked trout pond. Swimming is also allowed in the pond. Sightseeing is excellent with Burney Falls, Lassen Volcanic National Park, and Subway Caves all within 30 miles.

RV sites, facilities: There are 40 RV sites with full or partial hookups (30 amps) and 40 tent sites; some are pull-through. Picnic tables and fireplaces are provided. Restrooms have showers. A dump station, a coin laundry, a playground, modem hookups, wireless Internet access, and a convenience store are available. Some facilities are wheelchair accessible. Leashed pets are permitted.

Reservations, fees: Reservations are recommended and can be made by telephone or website. Sites are $21.90–25.75 per night, $2 per night for more than two people, and $1 per night per pet. Some credit cards accepted. Open April–October.

Directions: From Redding, drive east on Highway 299 to Burney and continue for five miles to the junction with Highway 89. Turn right (south) on Highway 89 and drive 12 miles to the second Doty Road Loop exit. Turn left and drive 0.5 mile to the park entrance on the right.

Contact: Hat Creek Hereford Ranch RV Park and Campground, 530/335-7171 or 877/459-9532, www.hatcreekrv.com.

17 BRIDGE CAMP

Scenic rating: 7

on Hat Creek in Lassen National Forest

See map page 549

This camp is one of four along Highway 89 in the area along Hat Creek. It is at 4,000 feet elevation, with shaded sites and the stream within very short walking distance. Trout are stocked on this stretch of the creek, with fishing access available out of camp, as well as at Rocky (tent camping only) and Cave Camps to the south and Honn (tent camping only) to the north. In one weekend, anglers might hit all four.

RV sites, facilities: There are 25 sites for tents or RVs up to 22 feet (no hookups). Picnic tables and fire grills are provided. There is no drinking water. Vault toilets are available. A grocery store and propane gas are available nearby. Leashed pets are permitted.

Reservations, fees: Reservations are not accepted. Sites are $10 per night, $5 per night for an additional vehicle. Open late April–October, weather permitting.

Directions: From Redding, drive east on Highway 299 to Burney and continue for five miles to the junction with Highway 89. Turn right (south) on Highway 89 and drive 19 miles to the campground entrance on the right side of the road. If you reach Old Station, you have gone five miles too far.

Contact: Lassen National Forest, Hat Creek Ranger District, 530/336-5521, fax 530/336-5758; Department of Fish and Game fishing information, 530/225-2146.

18 CAVE CAMP

Scenic rating: 7

on Hat Creek in Lassen National Forest

See map page 549

Cave Camp is right along Hat Creek, with both easy access off Highway 89 and an anglers' trail available along the stream. This stretch of Hat Creek is planted with rainbow trout twice per month by the Department of Fish and Game,

CALIFORNIA

starting with the opening of trout season on the last Saturday of April. Nearby side trips include Lassen Volcanic National Park, about a 15-minute drive south on Highway 89, and Subway Caves (turn left at the junction just across the road from the campground). A rare bonus at this camp is that wheelchair-accessible fishing is available.

RV sites, facilities: There are 46 sites for tents or RVs up to 22 feet (no hookups). Picnic tables and fire grills are provided. Drinking water and flush and vault toilets are available. Supplies can be obtained in Old Station. Some facilities are wheelchair accessible. Leashed pets are permitted.

Reservations, fees: Reservations are not accepted. Sites are $16 per night, plus $5 per night for an additional vehicle. Open late April–October, weather permitting.

Directions: From Redding, drive east on Highway 299 to Burney and continue for five miles to the junction with Highway 89. Turn right (south) on Highway 89 and drive 23 miles to the campground entrance on the right side of the road. If you reach Old Station, you have gone one mile too far.

Contact: Lassen National Forest, Hat Creek Ranger District, 530/336-5521, fax 530/336-5758; Department of Fish and Game fishing information, 530/225-2146.

19 NORTH BATTLE CREEK RESERVOIR

Scenic rating: 7

on Battle Creek Reservoir
See map page 549

This little-known lake is at 5,600 feet in elevation, largely surrounded by Lassen National Forest. No gas engines are permitted on the lake, making it ideal for canoes, rafts, and car-top aluminum boats equipped with electric motors. When the lake level is up in early summer, it is a pretty setting with good trout fishing.

RV sites, facilities: There are 10 sites for tents or RVs up to 30 feet (no hookups) and five walk-in tent sites. Picnic tables and fire grills

are provided. Drinking water and vault toilets are available. A car-top boat launch is available nearby. Leashed pets are permitted.

Reservations, fees: Reservations are not accepted. Sites are $13 per night, $3 per night for an additional vehicle, and $1 per pet per night. Open mid-May–mid-September, weather permitting.

Directions: From Redding, drive east on Highway 44 to Viola. From Viola, continue east for 3.5 miles to Forest Road 32N17. Turn left on Forest Road 32N17 and drive five miles to Forest Road 32N31. Turn left and drive four miles to Forest Road 32N18. Turn right and drive 0.5 mile to the reservoir and the campground on the right side of the road.

Contact: PG&E Land Projects, 916/386-5164, www.pge.com/recreation.

20 HAT CREEK

Scenic rating: 7

on Hat Creek in Lassen National Forest
See map page 549

This is one in a series of Forest Service camps set beside beautiful Hat Creek, a good trout stream stocked regularly by the Department of Fish and Game. The elevation is 4,300 feet. The proximity to Lassen Volcanic National Park to the south is a big plus. Supplies are available in the little town of Old Station one mile to the north.

RV sites, facilities: There are 75 sites for tents or RVs up to 30 feet, and three group camps for tents or RVs up to 30 feet can accommodate up to 50 people each. No hookups. Picnic tables and fire grills are provided. Drinking water and vault toilets are available. A grocery store, a dump station, a coin laundry, and propane gas are available nearby. Leashed pets are permitted.

Reservations, fees: Reservations are accepted for individual sites and required ($9 reservation fee) for group camps at 877/444-6777 or www.ReserveUSA.com. Sites are $17 per night, $5 per night for an additional vehicle, $85 per night for group camps. Open late April–October, weather permitting.

Directions: From Redding, drive east on Highway 44 to the junction with Highway 89 (near the entrance to Lassen Volcanic National Park). Turn left (north) on Highway 89 and drive about 12 miles to the campground entrance on the left side of the road. Turn left and drive a short distance to the campground.

Contact: Lassen National Forest, Hat Creek Ranger District, 530/336-5521, fax 530/336-5758; Department of Fish and Game fishing information, 530/225-2146.

21 BIG PINE CAMP

Scenic rating: 7

on Hat Creek in Lassen National Forest

See map page 549

This campground is on the headwaters of Hat Creek, a pretty spot amid ponderosa pines. A dirt road out of camp parallels Hat Creek, providing access for trout fishing. A great vista point is on the highway, a mile south of the campground entrance road. It is only a 10-minute drive south to the Highway 44 entrance station for Lassen Volcanic National Park. The elevation is 4,500 feet.

RV sites, facilities: There are 19 sites for tents or RVs up to 22 feet (no hookups). Picnic tables and fire grills are provided. Drinking water (at two hand pumps) and vault toilets are available. A dump station, a grocery store, and propane gas are available nearby. Leashed pets are permitted.

Reservations, fees: Reservations are not accepted. Sites are $12 per night, plus $5 per night for an additional vehicle. Open late April–October, weather permitting.

Directions: From Redding, drive east on Highway 44 to the junction with Highway 89 (near the entrance to Lassen Volcanic National Park). Turn left (north) on Highway 89 and drive about eight miles (one mile past the vista point) to the campground entrance on the right side of the road. Turn right and drive 0.5 mile to the campground.

Contact: Lassen National Forest, Hat Creek

Ranger District, 530/336-5521, fax 530/336-5758; Department of Fish and Game fishing information, 530/225-2146.

22 NORTH EAGLE LAKE

Scenic rating: 7

on Eagle Lake

See map page 549

This camp provides direct access in the fall to the best fishing area of huge Eagle Lake. When the weather turns cold, the population of big Eagle Lake trout migrates to its favorite haunts just outside the tules, often in water only 5–8 feet deep. A boat ramp is about 1.5 miles to the southwest on Stone Road. In the summer this area is quite exposed and the lake can be hammered by west winds, which can howl from midday to sunset. The elevation is 5,100 feet.

RV sites, facilities: There are 20 sites for tents or RVs up to 35 feet (no hookups). Picnic tables and fire grills are provided. Drinking water and vault toilets are available. A private dump station and boat ramp are available within 1.5 miles. Leashed pets are permitted.

Reservations, fees: Reservations are not accepted. Sites are $8 per night. Open Memorial Day–mid-November, weather permitting.

Directions: From Red Bluff, drive east on Highway 36 to Susanville. In Susanville, turn left (north) on Highway 139 and drive 29 miles to County Road A1. Turn left at County Road A1 and drive 0.5 mile to the campground on the right.

Contact: Bureau of Land Management, Eagle Lake Field Office, 530/257-0456, fax 530/257-4831.

23 EAGLE LAKE RV PARK

Scenic rating: 7

near Susanville

See map page 549

Eagle Lake RV Park has become something of a headquarters for anglers in pursuit of Eagle

CALIFORNIA

Lake trout, which typically range 18–22 inches. A nearby boat ramp provides access to Pelican Point and Eagle Point, where the fishing is often best in the summer. In the fall, the north end of the lake provides better prospects (see listing in this chapter for *North Eagle Lake* campground). This RV park has all the amenities, including a small store. That means no special trips into town, just vacation time, lounging beside Eagle Lake, maybe catching a big trout now and then. One downer: The wind typically howls most summer afternoons. When the whitecaps are too big to deal with and surface conditions become choppy, get off the water; it can be dangerous. Resident deer can be like pets here on late summer evenings, including bucks with spectacular racks.

RV sites, facilities: There are 69 RV sites with full hookups (30 amps), including some pull-through sites; a separate grassy area for tents only; and cabin and RV rentals. Picnic tables and fire grills are provided. Restrooms have showers. A coin laundry, satellite TV hookups, a dump station, a convenience store, propane gas, diesel, bait and tackle, video rentals, RV supplies, firewood, and a recreation room are available. A boat ramp, dock, and boat slips are nearby. Some facilities are wheelchair accessible. Leashed pets are permitted.

Reservations, fees: Reservations are recommended. Sites are $25–32.50 per night, plus $1 per pet per night. Some credit cards accepted. Open late May–early November, weather permitting.

Directions: From Red Bluff, drive east on Highway 36 toward Susanville. Just before reaching Susanville, turn left on County Road A1 and drive approximately 25 miles to County Road 518 near Spalding Tract. Turn right on County Road 518 and drive through a small neighborhood to The Strand (the lake frontage road). Turn right on The Strand and drive about eight blocks to Palmetto Way and the entrance to the store and the park entrance at 687-125 Palmetto Way. Register at the store.

Contact: Eagle Lake RV Park, 530/825-3133, www.eaglelakeandrv.com.

24 CHRISTIE

Scenic rating: 7

on Eagle Lake in Lassen National Forest

See map page 549

This camp is along the southern shore of Eagle Lake at 5,100 feet. Eagle Lake, with 100 miles of shoreline, is well known for its big trout (yea) and big winds (boo). The camp offers some protection from the north winds. Its location is also good for seeing osprey with the Osprey Management Area, which covers a six-mile stretch of shoreline, just two miles to the north above Wildcat Point. A nearby resort is a bonus. The nearest boat ramp is at Gallatin Marina. A five-mile-long paved trail runs from Christie to Aspen Grove Campground, perfect for hiking, cycling, and horseback riding.

RV sites, facilities: There are 69 individual sites and 10 double sites for tents or RVs up to 50 feet. No hookups. Picnic tables and fire grills are provided. Drinking water and flush toilets are available. A grocery store is nearby. A dump station is 2.5 miles away at Merrill Campground. Some facilities are wheelchair accessible. Leashed pets are permitted.

Reservations, fees: Reservations are accepted ($9 reservation fee) at 877/444-6777 or www.ReserveUSA.com. Sites are $18 per night, $30 per night for double sites, and $5 per night for an additional vehicle. Open May–October, weather permitting.

Directions: From Red Bluff, drive east on Highway 36 toward Susanville. Three miles before Susanville turn left on Eagle Lake Road/County Road A1 and drive 19.5 miles to the campground on the right side of the road.

Contact: Lassen National Forest, Eagle Lake Ranger District, 530/257-4188, fax 530/252-5803.

25 MERRILL

Scenic rating: 8

on Eagle Lake in Lassen National Forest
See map page 549

This is one of the largest, most developed Forest Service campgrounds in the entire county. It sits along the southern shore of huge Eagle Lake at 5,100 feet. The nearest boat launch is at Gallatin Marina, where there is a developed swim beach.

RV sites, facilities: There are 173 individual and two double sites for tents or RVs up to 50 feet with full or partial hookups (30 and 50 amps). Picnic tables and fire grills are provided. Drinking water and flush toilets are available. A dump station, a grocery store, and a boat ramp are nearby. Some facilities are wheelchair accessible. Leashed pets are permitted.

Reservations, fees: Reservations are accepted ($9 reservation fee) at 877/444-6777 or www.ReserveUSA.com. RV sites are $29–33 per night, double sites are $56 per night, and tent sites are $18–19 per night. Open May–October, weather permitting.

Directions: From Red Bluff, drive east on Highway 36 toward Susanville. Three miles before Susanville, turn left on Eagle Lake Road/ County Road A1 and drive 17.5 miles to the campground on the right side of the road.

Contact: Lassen National Forest, Eagle Lake Ranger District, 530/257-4188, fax 530/252-5803.

26 EAGLE

Scenic rating: 9

on Eagle Lake in Lassen National Forest
See map page 549

Eagle is just up the road from Aspen Grove Campground; the latter is more popular because of the boat ramp nearby, but there are no RV sites. The elevation is 5,100 feet. Eagle Lake is one of the great trout lakes in California, producing the fast-growing and often huge Eagle Lake rainbow trout. All water sports are allowed, and with a huge lake and 100 miles of shoreline, there's plenty of room for everyone. Just be prepared for cold lake water. The one problem with Eagle Lake is the wind, which can whip the huge but shallow lake into a froth in the early summer. It is imperative that anglers/boaters get on the water early and then get back to camp early, with the fishing for the day often done by 10:30 A.M. A bonus is a good chance to see bald eagles and osprey.

RV sites, facilities: There are 50 individual and two double sites for tents or RVs up to 32 feet (no hookups). Picnic tables and fire grills are provided. Drinking water and flush toilets are available. There is a boat launch nearby at Gallatin Marina. Some facilities are wheelchair accessible. Leashed pets are permitted.

Reservations, fees: Reservations are accepted ($9 reservation fee) at 877/444-6777 or www.ReserveUSA.com. Sites are $18 per night, double sites are $30 per night, and it's $5 per night for an additional vehicle. Open May–October, weather permitting.

Directions: From Red Bluff, drive east on Highway 36 toward Susanville. Three miles before Susanville, turn left on Eagle Lake Road/County Road A1 and drive 15.5 miles to County Road 231. Turn right and drive 0.5 mile to the campground on the left side of the road.

Contact: Lassen National Forest, Eagle Lake Ranger District, 530/257-4188, fax 530/252-5803.

27 RAMHORN SPRINGS

Scenic rating: 3

south of Ravendale
See map page 549

This camp is not even three miles off the biggest state highway in northeastern California, yet it feels remote and is little known. It is way out in Nowhere Land, near the flank of Shinn Peak (7,562 feet). There are large numbers of antelope in the area, along with a sprinkling of large mule deer. Hunters lucky enough to get a deer tag can use this camp for their base in the fall. It is also popular for upland game hunters in search of sage grouse and chukar.

RV sites, facilities: There are 12 sites for tents or RVs up to 35 feet (no hookups). Picnic tables and fire grills are provided. Vault toilets and a horse corral are available. There is no drinking water, although spring water, which can be filtered, is available. Leashed pets are permitted.

Reservations, fees: Reservations are not accepted. There is no fee for camping, but donations are encouraged. Open year-round, weather permitting.

Directions: From Red Bluff, drive east on Highway 36 to Susanville. In Susanville, turn north on U.S. 395 and drive 45 miles to Post Camp Road. Turn right on Post Camp Road (unmarked except for small recreation sign) and drive 2.5 miles east to the campground.

Contact: Bureau of Land Management, Eagle Lake Field Office, 530/257-0456, fax 530/257-4831.

28 MOUNT LASSEN/ SHINGLETOWN KOA

Scenic rating: 6

near Lassen Volcanic National Park

See map page 549

This popular KOA camp is 14 miles from the entrance of Lassen Volcanic National Park and has pretty, wooded sites. Location is always the critical factor on vacations, and this park is set up perfectly for launching trips to the nearby east. Hat Creek provides trout fishing along Highway 89, and just inside the Highway 44 entrance station at Lassen Park is Manzanita Lake, providing good fishing and hiking.

RV sites, facilities: There are 46 sites for tents or RVs up to 40 feet with full or partial hookups (30 and 50 amps) including some pull-through sites, and five cabins. Picnic tables and fire grills are provided. Restrooms have flush toilets and showers. A playground, a heated pool (summer only), a dump station, a convenience store, ice, firewood, a coin laundry, a video arcade and recreation room, a dog run,

and propane gas are available. Leashed pets are permitted.

Reservations, fees: Reservations are accepted with a deposit at 800/562-3403. Sites are $25–45 per night, $3–5 per person per night for more than two people. Some credit cards accepted. Open mid-March–November.

Directions: From Redding, turn east on Highway 44 and drive to Shingletown. In Shingletown, continue east for four miles and look for the park entrance on the right (signed for KOA).

Contact: Mount Lassen/Shingletown KOA, 530/474-3133, www.koa.com.

29 MANZANITA LAKE

Scenic rating: 9

in Lassen Volcanic National Park

See map page 549

Manzanita Lake, set at 5,890 feet, is one of the prettiest lakes in Lassen Volcanic National Park, and it has good catch-and-release trout fishing for experienced fly fishers in prams and other nonpowered boats. This is no place for a dad, mom, and a youngster to fish from shore with Power Bait because of the fishing regulations. Swimming is permitted, but there are few takers. Because of the great natural beauty of the lake, the campground is often crowded. Evening walks around the lake are beautiful. A museum, visitors center, and small store are available nearby. Ranger programs are offered in the summer.

RV sites, facilities: There are 179 sites for tents or RVs up to 35 feet (no hookups). Picnic tables, fire grills, and bearproof food lockers are provided. Drinking water and flush toilets are available. Propane gas, groceries, coin showers, a dump station, and a coin laundry are available nearby. A boat launch is also nearby (no motors are permitted on boats at Manzanita Lake). Some facilities are wheelchair accessible. Leashed pets are permitted at campsites only.

Reservations, fees: Reservations are accepted at 877/444-6777 ($9 reservation fee) or www.ReserveUSA.com. Sites are $16 per night, and there's a $10 per vehicle park entrance fee. Some credit cards accepted. Open late May–late September, weather permitting (during the fall, it's open without drinking water until the camp is closed by snow).

Directions: From Redding, drive east on Highway 44 to the junction with Highway 89. Turn right (south) on Highway 89 and drive one mile to the entrance station to Lassen Volcanic National Park (the state highway becomes Lassen Park Highway/Main Park Road). Continue a short distance on Lassen Park Highway/Main Park Road to the campground entrance road. Turn right and drive 0.5 mile to the campground.

Contact: Lassen Volcanic National Park, 530/595-4444, fax 530/595-3262, www.nps .gov/lavo.

30 CRAGS

Scenic rating: 8

in Lassen Volcanic National Park
See map page 549

Crags is sometimes overlooked as a prime spot at Lassen Volcanic National Park because there is no lake nearby. No problem, because even though this campground is small compared to the giant complex at Manzanita Lake, the campsites are more spacious, they do not fill up as quickly, and many are backed by forest. In addition, Emigrant Trail runs out of camp, routing east and meeting pretty Lost Creek after a little more than a mile, a great short hike. Directly across from Crags are the towering Chaos Crags, topping out at 8,503 feet. The elevation here is 5,720 feet.

RV sites, facilities: There are 45 sites for tents or RVs up to 35 feet (no hookups). Picnic tables, fire rings, and bearproof food lockers are provided. Drinking water and vault toilets are available. Leashed pets are permitted in campground and on paved roads only.

Reservations, fees: Reservations are not accepted. Sites are $11 per night, and there's a $10 per vehicle park entrance fee. Open late June–early September.

Directions: From Redding, drive east on Highway 44 for 42 miles to the junction with Highway 89. Turn right and drive one mile to the entrance station at Lassen Volcanic National Park (the state highway becomes Lassen Park Highway/Main Park Road). Continue on Lassen Park Highway/Main Park Road for about five miles to the campground on the left side of the road.

Contact: Lassen Volcanic National Park, 530/595-4444, fax 530/595-3262, www.nps .gov/lavo.

31 SUMMIT LAKE, NORTH, SOUTH, AND EQUESTRIAN

Scenic rating: 9

in Lassen Volcanic National Park
See map page 549

Summit Lake is a beautiful spot where deer often visit each evening on the adjacent meadow just east of the campground. The lake is small, just 15 acres, and since trout plants were suspended, it has been just about fished out. Summit Lake is the most popular lake for swimming in the park. Evening walks around the lake are perfect for families. A more ambitious trail is routed out of camp and leads past lavish wildflower displays in early summer to a series of wilderness lakes. The campgrounds are set at an elevation of 6,695 feet.

RV sites, facilities: There are 46 sites for tents or RVs up to 35 feet at North Summit, 48 sites for tents or RVs up to 30 feet at South Summit, and one equestrian site for tents or RVs up to 35 feet that can accommodate up to 10 people and eight horses. No hookups. Picnic tables, fire rings, and bearproof food lockers are provided. Drinking water and toilets (flush toilets on the north side, pit toilets on the south side, and vault toilets at the equestrian site) are available. Ranger programs are sometimes available in summer. Some facilities are wheelchair accessible. Leashed pets are permitted at campsites only.

Reservations, fees: Reservations are accepted for individual sites at 877/444-6777 ($9 reservation fee) or www.ReserveUSA.com. Reservations are

CALIFORNIA

required for equestrian sites at 530/335-7029. Sites are $14 (South) to $16 (North) per night, $14 per night plus $4 per horse per night at the equestrian site, and there's a $10 per vehicle park entrance fee. Some credit cards accepted. Open late June–mid-September, weather permitting.

Directions: From Redding, drive east on Highway 44 to the junction with Highway 89. Turn south on Highway 89 and drive one mile to the entrance station to Lassen Volcanic National Park (where the state highway becomes Lassen Park Highway/Main Park Road). Continue on Lassen Park Highway/Main Park Road for 12 miles to the campground entrance on the left side of the road; the equestrian camp is on the right side of the road.

Contact: Lassen Volcanic National Park, 530/595-4444, fax 530/595-3262, www.nps.gov/lavo.

32 BUTTE LAKE

Scenic rating: 9

in Lassen Volcanic National Park

See map page 549

Butte Lake campground is in an open, volcanic setting with a sprinkling of lodgepole pine. The contrast of the volcanics against the emerald greens of the lake is beautiful and memorable. Cinder Cone Trail can provide an even better look. The trailhead is near the boat launch area, and it's a strenuous hike involving a climb of 800 feet over the course of two miles to the top of the Cinder Cone. The footing is often loose because of volcanic pebbles. At the rim, you can peer inside the Cinder Cone, as well as be rewarded with lake views and a long-distance vista. Trout fishing is poor at Butte Lake, as at nearly all the lakes at this national park, because trout have not been planted for years. The elevation is 6,100 feet, and the lake covers 212 acres.

RV sites, facilities: There are 101 sites for tents or RVs up to 35 feet, one equestrian site, and six group tent sites that can accommodate 10–25 people each. No hookups. Some sites are pull-through. Picnic tables, fire rings, and bearproof food lockers are provided. Drinking water and

flush and vault toilets are available. A boat ramp is nearby. No motors are permitted on the lake. Some facilities are wheelchair accessible. Leashed pets are permitted at campsites only.

Reservations, fees: Reservations are accepted for individual sites ($9 reservation fee) at 877/444-6777 or www.ReserveUSA.com. Reservations are required for equestrian and group sites at 530/335-7029. Sites are $14 per night, equestrian sites are $14 per night plus $4 per horse per night, group sites are $50 per night, and there's a $10 per vehicle park entrance fee. Open mid-June–mid-September, weather permitting.

Directions: From Redding, drive east on Highway 44 to the junction with Highway 89. Bear north on Highway 89/44 and drive 13 miles to Old Station. Just past Old Station, turn right (east) on Highway 44 and drive 10 miles to Forest Road 32N21/Butte Lake Road. Turn right and drive six miles to the campground.

Contact: Lassen Volcanic National Park, 530/595-4444, fax 530/595-3262, www.nps.gov/lavo.

33 SILVER BOWL

Scenic rating: 7

on Silver Lake in Lassen National Forest

See map page 549

Silver Lake is a pretty lake set at 6,400 feet elevation at the edge of the Caribou Wilderness. There is an unimproved boat ramp at the southern end of the lake. It is occasionally planted by the Department of Fish and Game with Eagle Lake trout and brown trout, which provides a summer fishery for campers. A trailhead from adjacent Caribou Lake is routed west into the wilderness, with routes available to Emerald Lake to the northwest and Betty, Trail, and Shotoverin Lakes nearby to the southeast.

RV sites, facilities: There are 18 sites for tents or RVs up to 25 feet (no hookups). Picnic tables and fire grills are provided. Drinking water and vault toilets are available. Leashed pets are permitted.

Reservations, fees: Reservations are not accepted. Sites are $12 per night, $5 per night for

an additional vehicle. Open late May–October, weather permitting.

Directions: From Red Bluff, drive east on Highway 36 to the junction with Highway 89. Continue east on Highway 36 past Lake Almanor to Westwood. In Westwood, turn left on County Road A21 and drive 12.5 miles to Silver Lake Road. Turn left on Silver Lake Road/County Road 110 and drive 8.5 miles north to Silver Lake. At Silver Lake, turn right and drive 0.75 mile to the campground.

Contact: Lassen National Forest, Almanor Ranger District, 530/258-2141, fax 530/258-5194.

34 ROCKY KNOLL

Scenic rating: 7

on Silver Lake in Lassen National Forest

See map page 549

This is one of two camps at pretty Silver Lake, set at 6,400 feet elevation at the edge of the Caribou Wilderness. The other camp is Silver Bowl to the nearby north, which is larger and provides better access for hikers. This camp, however, is closer to the boat ramp, which is at the south end of the lake. Silver Lake provides a good summer fishery for campers.

RV sites, facilities: There are 18 sites for tents or RVs up to 27 feet (no hookups). Picnic tables and fire grills are provided. Drinking water and vault toilets are available. Leashed pets are permitted.

Reservations, fees: Reservations are not accepted. Sites are $12 per night, plus $5 per night for an additional vehicle. Open late May–early November, weather permitting.

Directions: From Red Bluff, drive east on Highway 36 to the junction with Highway 89. Continue east on Highway 36 past Lake Almanor to Westwood. In Westwood, turn left on County Road A21 and drive 12.5 miles to Silver Lake Road. Turn left (west) on Silver Lake Road/ County Road 110 and drive 8.5 miles to Silver Lake. At Silver Lake, turn left and drive 300 yards to the campground.

Contact: Lassen National Forest, Al-

manor Ranger District, 530/258-2141, fax 530/258-5194.

35 CHILDS MEADOW RESORT

Scenic rating: 7

near Mill Creek

See map page 549

Childs Meadow Resort is an 18-acre resort set at 5,000 feet elevation. It features many recreation options, including catch-and-release fishing one mile away at Mill Creek. There are also trails nearby for horseback riding. The trailhead for Spencer Meadow Trail is just east of the resort along Highway 36. The trail provides a 12-mile route (one-way) to Spencer Meadow and an effervescent spring that is the source of Mill Creek.

RV sites, facilities: There are eight tent sites and 24 sites with full hookups (50 amps) for RVs of any length; most are pull-through. Cabins, park-model cabins, and a motel are also available. Picnic tables and fire rings are provided. Drinking water and restrooms with flush toilets and showers are available. A coin laundry, store, a restaurant, group picnic area, meeting room, and horseshoes are on-site. Groups can be accommodated. Leashed pets are permitted.

Reservations, fees: Reservations are accepted at 888/595-3383. Sites are $15–25 per night, plus $5 per pet per night. Some credit cards accepted. Open mid-May–October, weather permitting.

Directions: From Red Bluff, drive east on Highway 36 for 43 miles to the town of Mineral. Continue east on Highway 36 for 10 miles to the resort on the left.

Contact: Childs Meadow Resort, 530/595-3383, www.childsmeadowresort.com.

36 BATTLE CREEK

Scenic rating: 7

on Battle Creek in Lassen National Forest

See map page 549

This pretty spot offers easy access and streamside camping along Battle Creek. The trout fishing can be good in May, June, and early July, when the creek is stocked with trout by the Department of Fish and Game. Many people drive right by without knowing there is a stream here and that the fishing can be good. The elevation is 4,800 feet.

RV sites, facilities: There are 50 sites for tents or RVs up to 30 feet (no hookups). Picnic tables and fire grills are provided. Drinking water, flush and vault toilets, and a day-use picnic area are available. Supplies can be obtained in the town of Mineral. Leashed pets are permitted.

Reservations, fees: Reservations are not accepted. Sites are $18 per night, $5 per night for an additional vehicle. Open late April–early November, weather permitting.

Directions: From Red Bluff, turn east on Highway 36 and drive 39 miles to the campground (if you reach Mineral, you have gone two miles too far).

Contact: Lassen National Forest, Almanor Ranger District, 530/258-2141, fax 530/258-5194; Department of Fish and Game fishing information, 530/225-2146.

37 MILL CREEK RESORT

Scenic rating: 7

on Mill Creek near Lassen National Forest
See map page 549

This is a great area, surrounded by Lassen National Forest and within close range of the southern Highway 89 entrance to Lassen Volcanic National Park. It is at 4,800 feet along oft-bypassed Highway 172. A highlight here is Mill Creek (to reach it, turn south on the Forest Service road in town and drive to a parking area at the end of the road along the stream), where there is a great easy walk along the stream and fair trout fishing. Note that about half the campsites are taken by long-term renters.

RV sites, facilities: There are 14 sites for tents or RVs up to 35 feet, eight with full hookups (30 amps). Nine one- and two-bedroom cabins are also available. Picnic tables and fire rings are provided. Drinking water, vault toilets, seasonal showers, a seasonal coin laundry, a playground, a small grocery store, and a restaurant are also available. Some facilities are wheelchair accessible. Leashed pets are permitted.

Reservations, fees: Reservations are accepted. Sites are $15–25 per night. Campsites are open May–October. Cabins are available year-round.

Directions: From Red Bluff, drive 43 miles east on Highway 36 to the town of Mineral and the junction with Highway 172. Turn right and drive six miles to the town of Mill Creek. In Mill Creek, look for the sign for Mill Creek Resort on the right side of the road.

Contact: Mill Creek Resort, 530/595-4449 or 888/595-4449, www.millcreekresort.net.

38 ELAM

Scenic rating: 7

on Deer Creek in Lassen National Forest
See map page 549

Of the campgrounds set on Deer Creek along Highway 32, Elam gets the most use. It is the first stopping point visitors arrive at while heading west on narrow, curvy Highway 32, and it has an excellent day-use picnic area available. The stream here is stocked with rainbow trout in late spring and early summer, with good access for fishing. It is a pretty area, set where Elam Creek enters Deer Creek. A Forest Service Information Center is nearby in Chester. If the camp has too many people to suit your style, consider other more distant and primitive camps downstream on Deer Creek. The elevation here is 4,600 feet.

RV sites, facilities: There are 11 sites for tents or RVs up to 30 feet (no hookups). Picnic tables and fire grills are provided. Drinking water and vault toilets are available. Leashed pets are permitted.

Reservations, fees: Reservations are not accepted. Sites are $14 per night, plus $5 per night for an additional vehicle. Open mid-April–October, weather permitting.

Directions: From Red Bluff, take Highway 36 east for 44 miles to the junction with Highway 89. Continue east on Highway 36/89 to the junction with Highway 32. Turn south on Highway 32 and drive three miles to the campground on the right side of the road. Trailers are not recommended.

Contact: Lassen National Forest, Almanor Ranger District, 530/258-2141, fax 530/258-5194.

39 GURNSEY CREEK

Scenic rating: 7

in Lassen National Forest
See map page 549

This camp is at 5,000 feet in Lassen National Forest, with extremely easy access off Highway 36. The camp is on the headwaters of little Gurnsey Creek, a highlight of the surrounding Lost Creek Plateau. Gurnsey Creek runs downstream and pours into Deer Creek, a good trout stream with access along narrow, winding Highway 32 to the nearby south.

RV sites, facilities: There are 30 sites for tents or RVs up to 30 feet (no hookups). Picnic tables and fire grills are provided. Drinking water and vault toilets are available. Supplies are available in Mineral. Leashed pets are permitted.

Reservations, fees: Reservations are not accepted. Sites are $14 per night. Open May–early November, weather permitting.

Directions: From Red Bluff, drive east on Highway 36 for 55 miles (five miles east of Childs Meadow). Turn left at the campground entrance road and drive a short distance to the campground.

Contact: Lassen National Forest, Almanor Ranger District, 530/258-2141, fax 530/258-5194.

40 LAST CHANCE CREEK

Scenic rating: 7

near Lake Almanor
See map page 549

This secluded camp is at 4,500 feet, adjacent to where Last Chance Creek empties into the north end of Lake Almanor. It is an unpublicized PG&E camp that is known primarily by locals and gets missed almost every time by out-of-towners. The adjacent lake area is a breeding ground in the spring for white pelicans, and the beauty of these birds in large flocks can be extraordinary.

RV sites, facilities: There are 12 sites for tents or RVs up to 30 feet, and three group camps can accommodate up to 100 people. No hookups. Picnic tables and fire grills are provided. Drinking water and vault toilets are available. Leashed pets are permitted.

Reservations, fees: Reservations are not accepted for individual sites but are required for the group camps at 916/386-5164. Sites are $16 per night for individual sites, $3 per night for an additional vehicle, $60–120 per night for group sites, and $1 per pet per night. Group sites require a two-night minimum stay and a three-night stay on holidays. Open mid-May–September, weather permitting.

Directions: From Red Bluff, take Highway 36 east to Chester and continue for two miles over the causeway (at the north end of Lake Almanor). About 0.25 mile after crossing the causeway, turn left on the campground access road and drive 3.5 miles to the campground.

Contact: PG&E Land Projects, 916/386-5164, www.pge.com/recreation.

41 NORTH SHORE CAMPGROUND

Scenic rating: 7

on Lake Almanor
See map page 549

This is a large, privately developed park on the northern shoreline of beautiful Lake Almanor. The park has 37 acres and a mile of shoreline. The camp is amid pine tree cover, and most of the sites are lakefront or lakeview. About half of the sites are filled with seasonal renters. The lending library was once the original Chester jail, built in 1925. Alas, the jail itself busted out during a storm a few years ago and was found washed ashore at this campground, which converted it to its new use.

RV sites, facilities: There are 94 sites with partial hookups (30 amps) for RVs up to 40 feet and 34 tent sites; a few sites are pull-through. Two log cabins are also available. Picnic tables and fire rings are provided. Drinking water, restrooms with showers and flush toilets, a coin laundry, a general store, a playground, lending library, modem access, Wi-Fi, propane, a dump station, a fish-cleaning station, horseshoes, a boat ramp, boat dock, boat slips, and boat rentals are available. Leashed pets are permitted.

Reservations, fees: Reservations are accepted. Sites are $29–41 per night, $5 per person per night for more than two people (children under age 12 are free), and $2 per pet per night. Monthly and seasonal rates available. Some credit cards accepted. Open April–October.

Directions: From Red Bluff, take Highway 36 east for 44 miles to the junction with Highway 89. Drive east on Highway 36/89; the camp is two miles past Chester on the right.

Contact: North Shore Campground, 530/258-3376, fax 530/258-2838, www.northshorecampground.com.

42 POTATO PATCH

Scenic rating: 7

on Deer Creek in Lassen National Forest
See map page 549

You get good hiking and fishing at this camp. It is beside Deer Creek at 3,400 feet elevation, with good access for trout fishing. This is a wild trout stream in this area, and the use of artificials with a single barbless hook and catch-and-release are required along most of the river; check Department of Fish and Game regulations. An excellent angler's/swimmer's trail is available along the river.

RV sites, facilities: There are 32 sites for tents or RVs up to 27 feet (no hookups). Picnic tables and fire grills are provided. Drinking water and vault toilets are available. Leashed pets are permitted.

Reservations, fees: Reservations are not accepted. Sites are $14 per night, plus $5 per night for an additional vehicle. Open early April–early November, weather permitting.

Directions: From Red Bluff, take Highway 36 east for 44 miles to the junction with Highway 89. Continue east on Highway 36/89 to the junction with Highway 32. Turn south on Highway 32 and drive 11 miles to the campground on the right side of the road.

Contact: Lassen National Forest, Almanor Ranger District, 530/258-2141, fax 530/258-5194; Department of Fish and Game, 530/225-2146.

43 ROCKY POINT CAMPGROUND

Scenic rating: 7

on Lake Almanor
See map page 549

What you get here is a series of four campgrounds along the southwest shore of Lake Almanor provided by PG&E as mitigation for its hydroelectric activities on the Feather River system. The camps are set upstream from the dam, with boat ramps available on each side of the dam. This is a pretty spot, with giant Almanor ringed by lodgepole pine and firs. The lake is usually full, or close to it, well into summer, with Mount Lassen in the distance to the north—bring your camera. The lake is 13 miles long, and all water sports are permitted. The lake level remains full most of the year, and much of the shoreline is wooded. Though it can take a day or two to find the fish, once that effort is made, fishing is good for large trout and salmon in the spring and fall and for smallmouth bass in the summer.

RV sites, facilities: There are 131 sites for tents or RVs up to 30 feet (no hookups). Picnic tables and fire grills are provided. Drinking water, vault toilets, and a dump station are available. Some facilities are wheelchair accessible. Leashed pets are permitted.

Reservations, fees: Reservations are not accepted. Sites are $18 per night, $3 per night for

an additional vehicle, and $1 per pet per night. Open May–September.

Directions: From Red Bluff, take Highway 36 east for 44 miles to the junction with Highway 89. Continue east on Highway 36/89 to Lake Almanor and the next junction with Highway 89 (two miles before reaching Chester). Turn right on Highway 89 and drive eight miles to the southwest end of Lake Almanor. Turn left at your choice of four campground entrances.

Contact: PG&E Land Projects, 916/386-5164, www.pge.com/recreation.

44 ALMANOR NORTH AND SOUTH

Scenic rating: 8

on Lake Almanor in Lassen National Forest

See map page 549

This is one of Lake Almanor's best-known and most popular Forest Service campgrounds. It is along the western shore of beautiful Almanor at 4,550 feet elevation, directly across from the beautiful Almanor Peninsula. There is an excellent view of Mount Lassen to the north, along with gorgeous sunrises. A 10-mile recreation trail runs right through the campground and is excellent for biking or hiking. This section of the lake provides good fishing for smallmouth bass in the summer. Fishing in this lake is also good for rainbow trout, brown trout, and lake-raised salmon. There are two linked campgrounds, named North and South.

RV sites, facilities: There are 104 sites for tents or RVs up to 40 feet, and a group camp for tents or RVs up to 40 feet can accommodate up to 100 people. No hookups. Picnic tables and fire grills are provided. Drinking water and vault toilets are available. A boat ramp and beach area are nearby. Some facilities are wheelchair accessible. Leashed pets are permitted.

Reservations, fees: Reservations are accepted for individual sites and required for the group camp ($9 reservation fee) at 877/444-6777 or www.ReserveUSA.com. Sites are $18 per

night, $5 per night for an additional vehicle, and $100 per night for the group camp. Open May–October, weather permitting.

Directions: From Red Bluff, take Highway 36 east for 44 miles to the junction with Highway 89. Continue east on Highway 36/89 to Lake Almanor and the next junction with Highway 89 (two miles before reaching Chester). Turn right on Highway 89 and drive six miles to County Road 310. Turn left on County Road 310 and drive 0.25 mile to the campground.

Contact: Lassen National Forest, Almanor Ranger District, 530/258-2141, fax 530/258-5194.

45 PONDEROSA FLAT

Scenic rating: 7

on Butt Valley Reservoir

See map page 549

This camp is at the north end of Butt Valley Reservoir (more commonly called Butt Lake), the little brother to nearby Lake Almanor. It is a fairly popular camp, with the boat ramp a prime attraction, allowing campers/anglers a lakeside spot with easy access. Technically, Butt is the "afterbay" for Almanor, fed by a four-mile-long pipe with water from Almanor. What occurs is that pond smelt from Almanor get ground up in the Butt Lake powerhouse, providing a huge amount of feed for trout at the head of the lake; that's why the trout often get huge at Butt Lake. The one downer is that lake drawdowns are common, exposing tree stumps.

RV sites, facilities: There are 63 sites for tents or RVs up to 30 feet and an overflow camping area. No hookups. Picnic tables and fire grills are provided. Drinking water, vault toilets, and a boat ramp are available. Some facilities are wheelchair accessible. Leashed pets are permitted.

Reservations, fees: Reservations are not accepted. Sites are $18 per night, $3 per night for an additional vehicle, and $1 per pet per night. Open May–October, weather permitting.

Directions: From Red Bluff, take Highway 36 east for 44 miles to the junction with Highway 89. Continue east on Highway 36/89 to Lake Almanor and the next junction with Highway 89 (two miles before reaching Chester). Turn right on Highway 89 and drive about seven miles to Butt Valley Road. Turn right on Butt Valley Road and drive 3.2 miles to the campground on the right side of the road.

Contact: PG&E Land Projects, 916/386-5164, www.pge.com/recreation.

46 COOL SPRINGS

Scenic rating: 7

on Butt Valley Reservoir
See map page 549

One of two camps at Butt Lake (officially known as Butt Valley Reservoir), Cool Springs is about midway down the lake on its eastern shore, 2.5 miles south of Ponderosa Flat. Cool Springs Creek enters the lake near the camp. (For more information about Butt Lake, see the listing in this chapter for *Ponderosa Flat*.)

RV sites, facilities: There are 25 sites for tents or RVs up to 30 feet (no hookups) and five walk-in tent sites. Picnic tables and fire grills are provided. Drinking water, vault toilets, and a boat ramp are available. Some facilities are wheelchair accessible. Leashed pets are permitted.

Reservations, fees: Reservations are not accepted. Sites are $16 per night, $3 per night for an additional vehicle, and $1 per pet per night. Open May–October, weather permitting.

Directions: From Red Bluff, take Highway 36 east for 44 miles to the junction with Highway 89. Continue east on Highway 36/89 to Lake Almanor and the next junction with Highway 89 (two miles before reaching Chester). Turn right on Highway 89 and drive about seven miles to Butt Valley Road. Turn right on Butt Valley Road and drive 5.7 miles to the campground on the right side of the road.

Contact: PG&E Land Projects, 916/386-5164, www.pge.com/recreation.

47 YELLOW CREEK

Scenic rating: 8

in Humbug Valley
See map page 549

Yellow Creek is one of Cal Trout's pet projects. It's a beautiful stream for fly fishers, demanding the best from skilled anglers. This camp is at 4,400 feet in Humbug Valley and provides access to this stretch of water. An option is to fish Butt Creek, much easier fishing for small, planted rainbow trout, with access available along the road on the way in.

RV sites, facilities: There are 10 sites for tents or RVs up to 30 feet (no hookups). Picnic tables and fire grills are provided. Drinking water and vault toilets are available. Leashed pets are permitted.

Reservations, fees: Reservations are not accepted. Sites are $16 per night, $3 per night for an additional vehicle, and $1 per pet per night. Open May–September.

Directions: From Red Bluff, take Highway 36 east for 44 miles to the junction with Highway 89. Continue east on Highway 36/89 for eight miles to Humbug Road. Turn right and drive 0.6 mile and bear left to stay on Humbug Road. Continue for 1.2 miles and bear right (signed for Longville) to stay on Humbug Road. Continue for 5.4 miles to Humbug Valley and an intersection. Turn left to stay on Humbug Road and drive 1.2 miles (passing the Soda Springs Historic Site) to a fork. Bear right to stay on Humbug Road and drive 0.3 mile to the campground.

Contact: PG&E Land Projects, 916/386-5164, www.pge.com/recreation.

48 CHERRY HILL

Scenic rating: 7

on Butte Creek in Lassen National Forest
See map page 549

The camp is along little Butte Creek at the foot of Cherry Hill, just downstream from the confluence of Colby Creek and Butte Creek. It is also on the western edge of the alpine zone in Lassen National Forest. A four-mile drive to the north, much of it along Colby Creek, will take visitors to the Colby Mountain Lookout at 6,002 feet for a dramatic view of the Ishi Wilderness to the west. Nearby to the south is Philbrook Reservoir.

RV sites, facilities: There are six walk-in tent sites and 13 sites for tents or RVs up to 25 feet (no hookups). Picnic tables and fire grills are provided. Drinking water and vault toilets are available. Supplies are available in the town of Butte Meadows. Leashed pets are permitted.

Reservations, fees: Reservations are not accepted. Sites are $13 per night, $5 per night for an additional vehicle. Open late April–early November, weather permitting.

Directions: From Chico, drive northeast on Highway 32 for approximately 24 miles to the junction with Humboldt Road (well past the town of Forest Ranch). Turn right and drive five miles to Butte Meadows. Continue on Humboldt Road for three miles to the campground on the right side of the road.

Contact: Lassen National Forest, Almanor Ranger District, 530/258-2141, fax 530/258-5194.

49 BUTTE MEADOWS

Scenic rating: 6

on Butte Creek in Lassen National Forest
See map page 549

On hot summer days, when a cold stream sounds even better than a cold drink, Butte Meadows provides a hideout in the national forest east of Chico. This is a summer camp along Butte Creek, which is stocked with rainbow trout by the Department of Fish and Game. Nearby Doe Mill Ridge and the surrounding Lassen National Forest can provide a good side-trip adventure. The camp elevation is 4,600 feet.

RV sites, facilities: There are 13 sites for tents or RVs up to 25 feet (no hookups). Fire grills and picnic tables are provided. Drinking water and vault toilets are available. Supplies are available in Butte Meadows. Leashed pets are permitted.

Reservations, fees: Reservations are not accepted. Sites are $12 per night, plus $5 per night for an additional vehicle. Open late April–early November, weather permitting.

Directions: From Chico, drive about 15 miles northeast on Highway 32 to the town of Forest Ranch. Continue on Highway 32 for another nine miles. Turn right on Humboldt Road and drive five miles to Butte Meadows.

Contact: Lassen National Forest, Almanor Ranger District, 530/258-2141, fax 530/258-5194; Department of Fish and Game fishing information, 530/225-2146.

50 PHILBROOK RESERVOIR

Scenic rating: 7

in Lassen National Forest
See map page 549

Philbrook Reservoir is at 5,600 feet on the western mountain slopes above Chico, on the southwest edge of Lassen National Forest. It is a pretty lake, though subject to late-season drawdowns, with a scenic lookout a short distance from camp. Swimming beaches and a picnic area are bonuses. The lake is loaded with small trout—a dink here, a dink there, a dink everywhere.

RV sites, facilities: There are 20 sites for tents or RVs up to 30 feet (no hookups) and an overflow camping area. Picnic tables and fire grills are provided. Drinking water and vault toilets are available. Trailer and car-top boat launches are available. Some facilities are wheelchair accessible. Leashed pets are permitted.

Reservations, fees: Reservations are not accepted. Sites are $16 per night, $3 per night for an additional vehicle, and $1 per pet per night. Open May–September.

Directions: At Orland on I-5, take the Highway 32/Chico exit and drive to Chico and the junction with Highway 99. Turn south on Highway 99 and drive to Skyway Road/Paradise (in south Chico). Turn east on Skyway Road, drive through Paradise, and continue for 27 miles to Humbug Summit Road. Turn right and drive two miles to Philbrook Road. Turn right and drive 3.1 miles to the campground entrance road. Turn right and drive 0.5 mile to the campground. Note: Access roads are unpaved and often rough.

Contact: PG&E Land Projects, 916/386-5164, www.pge.com/recreation.

51 QUEEN LILY

Scenic rating: 7

on the North Fork of the Feather River in Plumas National Forest

See map page 549

The North Fork Feather River is a prime destination for camping and trout fishing, especially for families. This is one of three camps along the river on Caribou Road. This stretch of river is well stocked. Insider's note: The first 150 yards of river below the dam at Caribou typically have large but elusive trout.

RV sites, facilities: There are 12 sites for tents or RVs up to 30 feet (no hookups). Picnic tables and fire grills are provided. Drinking water and vault toilets are available. A grocery store and coin laundry are available within three miles. Leashed pets are permitted.

Reservations, fees: Reservations are not accepted. Sites are $18 per night. Open May–September.

Directions: From Oroville, drive north on Highway 70 to Caribou Road (two miles past Belden). Turn left on Caribou Road and drive about three miles to the campground on the left side of the road.

Contact: Plumas National Forest, Mount Hough Ranger District, 530/283-0555, fax 530/283-1821; Northwest Park Management, 530/283-5559.

52 NORTH FORK

Scenic rating: 7

on the North Fork of the Feather River in Plumas National Forest

See map page 549

This camp is between Queen Lily to the nearby north and Gansner Bar camp to the nearby south, all three set on the North Fork Feather River. The elevation is 2,600 feet. Fishing access is good and trout plants are decent, making for a good fishing/camping trip. Note: All three camps are extremely popular on summer weekends.

RV sites, facilities: There are 20 sites for tents or RVs up to 32 feet (no hookups). Picnic tables and fire grills are provided. Drinking water and vault toilets are available. A grocery store and coin laundry are available within three miles. Leashed pets are permitted.

Reservations, fees: Reservations are not accepted. Sites are $18 per night. Open May–September.

Directions: From Oroville, drive north on Highway 70 to Caribou Road (two miles past Belden at Gansner Ranch Ranger Station). Turn left on Caribou Road and drive about two miles to the campground on the left side of the road.

Contact: Plumas National Forest, Mount Hough Ranger District, 530/283-0555, fax 530/283-1821; Northwest Park Management, 530/283-5559.

53 GANSNER BAR

Scenic rating: 7

on the North Fork of the Feather River in Plumas National Forest

See map page 549

Gansner Bar is the first of three camps along Caribou Road, which runs parallel to the North Fork Feather River. Of the three, this one receives the highest trout stocks of rainbow trout in the 10- to 12-inch class. Caribou Road runs upstream to Caribou Dam, with stream and fishing access along almost all of it. The camps often fill on summer weekends.

RV sites, facilities: There are 14 sites for tents or RVs up to 30 feet (no hookups). Picnic tables and fire grills are provided. Drinking water and vault toilets are available. A grocery store and coin laundry are available within one mile. Some facilities are wheelchair accessible. Leashed pets are permitted.

CALIFORNIA

Reservations, fees: Reservations are not accepted. Sites are $18 per night. Open April–October.

Directions: From Oroville, drive northeast on Highway 70 to Caribou Road (two miles past Belden). Turn left on Caribou Road and drive a short distance to the campground on the left side of the road.

Contact: Plumas National Forest, Mount Hough Ranger District, 530/283-0555, fax 530/283-1821; Northwest Park Management, 530/283-5559.

54 HALLSTED

Scenic rating: 7

on the North Fork of the Feather River in Plumas National Forest

See map page 549

Easy highway access and a pretty trout stream right alongside have made this an extremely popular campground. It typically fills on summer weekends. Hallsted is on the East Branch North Fork Feather River at 2,800 feet elevation. The river is stocked with trout by the Department of Fish and Game.

RV sites, facilities: There are 20 sites for tents or RVs up to 30 feet (no hookups). Picnic tables and fire grills are provided. Drinking water and vault toilets are available. A grocery store is available within a quarter mile. Some facilities are wheelchair accessible. Leashed pets are permitted.

Reservations, fees: Reservations are accepted ($9 reservation fee) at 877/444-6777 or www.ReserveUSA.com. Sites are $18 per night. Open May–September.

Directions: From Oroville, drive northeast on Highway 70 to Belden. Continue past Belden for about 12 miles to the campground entrance on the right side of the road. Turn right and drive 0.25 mile to the campground.

Contact: Plumas National Forest, Mount Hough Ranger District, 530/283-0555, fax 530/283-1821; Northwest Park Management, 530/283-5559.

55 BOULDER CREEK

Scenic rating: 7

at Antelope Lake in Plumas National Forest

See map page 549

Antelope Lake is a pretty mountain lake circled by conifers with nice campsites and good trout fishing. It is at 5,000 feet in remote eastern Plumas National Forest, far enough away so the marginally inclined never make the trip. Campgrounds are at each end of the lake (this one is just north of Lone Rock at the north end), with a boat ramp at Lost Cove on the east side of the lake. All water sports are permitted, and swimming is best near the campgrounds. The lake isn't huge, but it is big enough, with 15 miles of shoreline and little islands, coves, and peninsulas to give it an intimate feel.

RV sites, facilities: There are 70 sites for tents or RVs up to 40 feet (no hookups). Picnic tables and fire grills are provided. Drinking water and vault toilets are available. A dump station, a boat ramp, and a grocery store are nearby. Some facilities are wheelchair accessible. Leashed pets are permitted.

Reservations, fees: Reservations are accepted ($9 reservation fee) at 877/444-6777 or www.ReserveUSA.com. Sites are $18–20 per night, double sites are $35 per night, plus $5 per night for an additional vehicle. Open May–early September.

Directions: From Red Bluff, drive east on Highway 36 to Susanville and U.S. 395. Turn south on U.S. 395 and drive about 10 miles (one mile past Janesville) to County Road 208. Turn right on County Road 208 (signed for Antelope Lake) and drive about 15 miles to a Y (one mile before Antelope Lake). Turn left at the Y and drive four miles to the campground entrance on the right side of the road (on the northwest end of the lake).

Contact: Plumas National Forest, Mount Hough Ranger District, 530/283-0555, fax 530/283-1821; Northwest Park Management, 530/283-5559.

CALIFORNIA

56 LONE ROCK

Scenic rating: 9

at Antelope Lake in Plumas National Forest

See map page 549

This camp provides an option to nearby Boulder Creek, to the immediate north at the northwest shore of Antelope Lake. (For more information, see the listing in this chapter for *Boulder Creek*.) The elevation is 5,000 feet. Campfire programs are offered in the summer at the on-site amphitheater.

RV sites, facilities: There are 87 sites for tents or RVs up to 40 feet (no hookups). Picnic tables and fire grills are provided. Drinking water and vault toilets are available. A dump station, a boat ramp, and grocery store are nearby. Some facilities are wheelchair accessible. Leashed pets are permitted.

Reservations, fees: Reservations are accepted ($9 reservation fee) at 877/444-6777 or www.ReserveUSA.com. Sites are $18–20 per night. Open May–October.

Directions: From Red Bluff, drive east on Highway 36 to Susanville and U.S. 395. Go south on U.S. 395 and drive about 10 miles (one mile past Janesville) to County Road 208. Turn right on County Road 208 (signed Antelope Lake) and drive about 15 miles to a Y (one mile before Antelope Lake). Turn left at the Y and drive three miles to the campground entrance on the right side of the road (on the northwest end of the lake).

Contact: Plumas National Forest, Mount Hough Ranger District, 530/283-0555, fax 530/283-1821; Northwest Park Management, 530/283-5559.

57 LONG POINT FAMILY AND GROUP CAMP

Scenic rating: 7

at Antelope Lake in Plumas National Forest

See map page 549

Long Point is a pretty camp set on a peninsula that extends well into Antelope Lake, facing Lost Cove. The lake's boat ramp is at Lost Cove, a three-mile drive around the northeast shore. Trout fishing is often good here for both rainbow and brown trout, and there is a nature trail. A group campground is within this campground.

RV sites, facilities: There are 38 sites for tents or RVs up to 30 feet, and four group sites for tents or RVs up to 35 feet can accommodate up to 25 people each. No hookups. Picnic tables and fire grills are provided. Drinking water and vault toilets are available. A grocery store, a boat ramp, and dump stations are nearby. Leashed pets are permitted.

Reservations, fees: Reservations are accepted for individual sites and required for the group sites ($9 reservation fee) at 877/444-6777 or www.ReserveUSA.com. Sites are $16–18 per night, double sites are $35 per night, and it's $50 per night for group sites. Open May–October.

Directions: From Red Bluff, drive east on Highway 36 to Susanville and U.S. 395. Go south on U.S. 395 and drive about 10 miles (one mile past Janesville) to County Road 208. Turn right on County Road 208 (signed for Antelope Lake) and drive about 15 miles to a Y (one mile before Antelope Lake). Turn right at the Y and drive one mile to the campground entrance on the left side of the road.

Contact: Plumas National Forest, Mount Hough Ranger District, 530/283-0555, fax 530/283-1821; Northwest Park Management, 530/283-5559.

58 HONEY LAKE CAMPGROUND

Scenic rating: 4

near Milford

See map page 549

For newcomers, Honey Lake is a strange-looking place—a vast, shallow lake set on the edge of the desert of the Great Basin. The campground is at 4,385 feet and covers 30 acres, most of it overlooking the lake. There are a few pine trees in the campground, and a waterfowl management area is along the north shore of the lake. This campground is popular with hunters. Equestrian facilities, including a corral and exercise ring, are available. Fishing for Eagle Lake trout is good here. The lake is 26 miles across, and on rare flat calm evenings, the sunsets are spectacular.

RV sites, facilities: There are 63 pull-through sites for tents or RVs of any length, most with full or partial hookups (30 amps), plus 25 mobile homes and trailers available. Picnic tables are provided. Restrooms have showers. A coin laundry, a dump station, propane gas, a restaurant, a gift and grocery store, a playground, ice, video rentals, and a recreation room are available. Some facilities are wheelchair accessible. Leashed pets are permitted.

Reservations, fees: Reservations are not accepted. Sites are $14.50–29.95 per night, plus $3.50 per person per night for more than two people. Long-term rentals available. Some credit cards accepted. Open year-round.

Directions: From Susanville on U.S. 395, drive 17 miles south (if you reach Milford, you have gone two miles too far) to the campground on the west side of the highway. It is 65 miles north of Reno.

Contact: Honey Lake Campground, 530/253-2508.

CALIFORNIA

MENDOCINO AND WINE COUNTRY

(BEST RV PARKS AND CAMPGROUNDS

(Fishing
Doran Regional Park, page 616.
Westside Regional Park, page 616.

(Wildlife-Viewing
MacKerricher State Park, page 586.
Caspar Beach RV Park, page 591.
Ocean Cove Campground, page 607.

For many people, this region offers the best possible combination of geography, weather, and outdoor activities around. The Mendocino coast is dramatic and remote, with several stellar state parks for hiking, while Sonoma Valley, in the heart of wine country, produces some of the most popular wines in the world. Add in the self-indulgent options of mud baths and hot springs at Calistoga and a dash of mainstream recreation at Clear Lake, Lake Berryessa, or any other lake, and you have a capsule summary of why the Mendocino coast and the wine country have turned into getaway favorites.

But it's like two worlds, and the twain do not meet.

For many, this area is where people go for romance, fine cuisine, great wine, mineral springs, and anything else that comes to mind spur-of-the-moment. Such is a vacation in the Napa-Sonoma wine country, or on the beautiful Sonoma and Mendocino coasts.

This region wouldn't be the best of both worlds if there weren't options on the other end of the spectrum. Campgrounds set up primarily for family recreation are available at Clear Lake, Lake Berryessa, and Blue Lakes. If the shoe fits – and for many, it does – you can have a great time fishing, boating, and waterskiing.

The coast features a series of romantic hideaways and excellent adventuring and hiking. The Fort Bragg area alone has three state parks, all with outstanding recreation options, including several easy hikes, many amid redwoods and along pretty streams. Reservations are always required here far in advance for a chance at getting a campsite at a state park on a summer weekend. Fort Bragg also offers excellent fishing out of Noyo Harbor.

The driving tour of Highway 1 along the coast here is the fantasy of many, and it can live up to that fantasy if you don't mind the twists and turns of the road. Along the way, there are dozens of hidden beaches and stretches of untouched coastline where you can stop and explore and maybe play tag with the waves. The prize spots are MacKerricher State Park, Salt Point State Park, and Anchor Bay.

CALIFORNIA

Includes:

- Black Butte Lake
- Bodega Bay
- Boggs Mountain Demonstration State Forest
- Clear Lake State Park
- Eel River
- Fort Ross State Historic Park
- Hendy Woods State Park
- Jackson Demonstration State Forest
- Lake Berryessa
- Lake Mendocino
- Lake Pillsbury
- Letts Lake
- MacKerricher State Park
- Manchester State Beach
- Mendocino National Forest
- Napa Valley State Park
- Navarro River Redwoods State Park
- Russian Gulch State Park
- Russian River
- Salt Point State Park
- Sonoma Coast State Beach
- Standish-Hickey State Recreation Area
- Sugarloaf Ridge State Park
- Upper Blue Lake
- Van Damme State Park
- Westport-Union Landing State Beach

CALIFORNIA

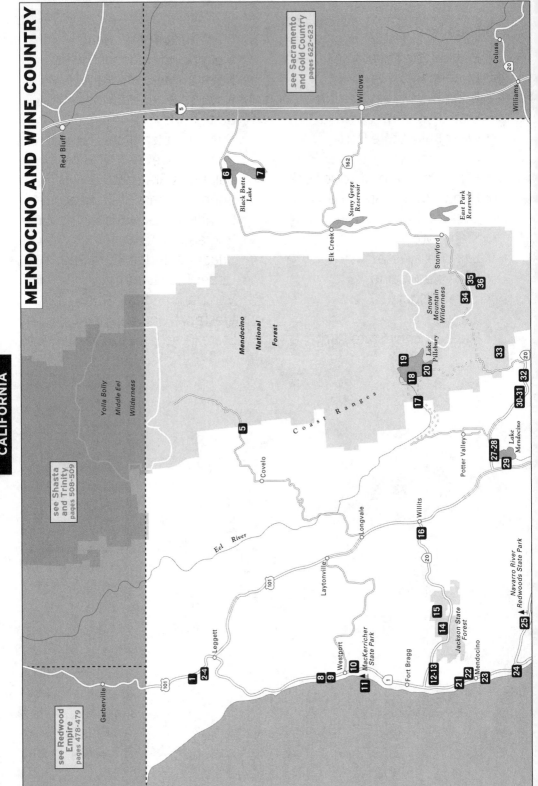

MENDOCINO AND WINE COUNTRY

CALIFORNIA

see Shasta and Trinity
pages 508-509

see Redwood Empire
pages 478-479

see Sacramento and Gold Country
pages 622-623

Red Bluff

Garberville

Colusa

Williams

Willows

Black Butte Lake

Stony Gorge Reservoir

East Park Reservoir

Elk Creek

Stonyford

Snow Mountain Wilderness

Mendocino National Forest

Yolla Bolly Middle Eel Wilderness

Lake Pillsbury

Coast Ranges

Covelo

Potter Valley

Lake Mendocino

Eel River

Longvale

Willits

Laytonville

Leggett

Westport

MacKerricher State Park

Fort Bragg

Jackson State Forest

Mendocino

Navarro River Redwoods State Park

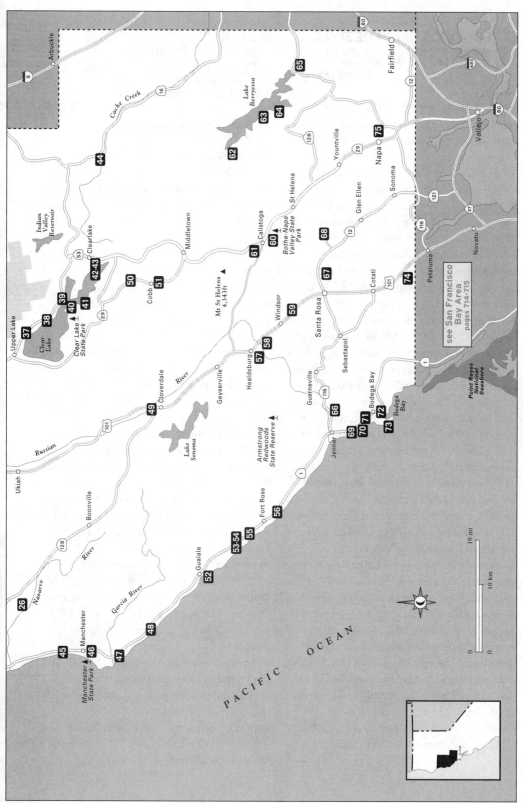

1 REDWOODS RIVER RESORT

🚶‍♀️ 🚣 ⛵ 🐕 🎣 ♿ 🚐 ⛺

Scenic rating: 8

on the Eel River

See map page 580

This resort is in a 21-acre grove of redwoods on U.S. 101 and features 1,500 feet of river access, including a sandy beach and two swimming holes. Many of the campsites are shaded. A hiking trail leads from the resort to the Eel River, a walk of just over a quarter mile. This is one in a series of both public and private campgrounds along the highway between Leggett and Garberville. Steelhead and salmon fishing are popular here in the winter, and the resort provides nearby access to state parks. The elevation is 700 feet.

RV sites, facilities: There are 27 sites with full hookups (30 amps) for RVs of any length and 14 tent sites; some sites are pull-through. Eight cabins and eight lodge rooms are also available. At campsites, picnic tables and fire rings are provided. Restrooms have showers. A seasonal heated swimming pool, a playground, a recreation room, modem access, a minimart, a coin laundry, a group kitchen, a dump station, table tennis, basketball, volleyball, badminton, horseshoes, shuffleboard, group facilities, seasonal organized activities, and a seasonal evening campfire are available. Some facilities are wheelchair accessible. Leashed pets are permitted, except in buildings.

Reservations, fees: Reservations are recommended in the summer. Sites are $22–35 per night, $3.75 per person per night for more than two people, and $1.50 per pet per night. Off-season discounts available. Some credit cards accepted. Open year-round.

Directions: From the junction of U.S. 101 and Highway 1 in Leggett, drive north on U.S. 101 for seven miles to the campground entrance on the left.

Contact: Redwoods River Resort, 707/925-6249, www.redwoodriverresort.com.

2 STANDISH-HICKEY STATE RECREATION AREA: REDWOOD CAMPGROUND

🚶‍♀️ 🚣 ⛵ 🐕 ♿ 🚐 ⛺

Scenic rating: 8

on the Eel River in Standish-Hickey State Recreation Area

See map page 580

This is one of three camps in Standish-Hickey State Recreation Area, and it is by far the most unusual. To reach Redwood Campground requires driving over a temporary "summer bridge," which provides access to a pretty spot along the South Fork Eel River. In early September, out comes the bridge and up comes the river. The elevation is 800 feet. Standish-Hickey is the gateway to the tall trees country. It covers 1,012 acres in an inland river canyon. The South Fork Eel provides two miles of river frontage. One of the few virgin stands of redwoods in this area can be seen on the Grove Trail. Note that two other campgrounds are available at this park, and that this camp is open only in summer.

RV sites, facilities: There are 63 sites for tents or RVs up to 18 feet (no hookups). No trailers, including pop-up tent trailers, are permitted. Picnic tables, food lockers, and fire rings are provided. Drinking water and restrooms with coin showers and flush toilets are available. Some facilities are wheelchair accessible. Leashed pets are permitted.

Reservations, fees: Reservations are accepted ($7.50 reservation fee) at 800/444-PARK (800/444-7275) or www.reserveamerica.com. Sites are $20 per night, $6 per night for an additional vehicle. Open July–Labor Day weekend.

Directions: From the junction of U.S. 101 and Highway 1 in Leggett, drive north on U.S. 101 for one mile to the park entrance on the left (west) side of the road.

Contact: Standish-Hickey State Recreation Area, 707/925-6482, fax 707/925-6402, www.parks.ca.gov.

❸ STANDISH-HICKEY STATE RECREATION AREA: ROCK CREEK

Scenic rating: 8

on the Eel River in Standish-Hickey State Recreation Area

See map page 580

This is one of two main campgrounds set in a mixed redwood grove at Standish-Hickey State Recreation Area (the other is Hickey). It is the classic state park camp, with numbered sites, flat tent spaces, picnic tables, and food lockers. There are 12 miles of hiking trails in the park. Hiking is only fair, but most people enjoy the short tromp down to the nearby South Fork Eel River. In the winter, steelhead migrate through the area. (See the listing in this chapter for *Redwood Campground* for more details on this park.)

RV sites, facilities: There are 65 sites for tents or RVs up to 27 feet (no hookups) and trailers up to 24 feet, along with one hike-in/bike-in site. Picnic tables, food lockers, and fire rings are provided. Drinking water and restrooms with coin showers and flush toilets are available. Some facilities are wheelchair accessible. Leashed pets are permitted.

Reservations, fees: Reservations are accepted ($7.50 reservation fee) at 800/444-PARK (800/444-7275) or www.reserveamerica.com. Sites are $20 per night, $6 per night for an additional vehicle; it's $3 per person per night for the hike-in/bike-in site. Open year-round.

Directions: From the junction of U.S. 101 and Highway 1 in Leggett, drive north on U.S. 101 for one mile to the park entrance on the left (west) side of the road.

Contact: Standish-Hickey State Recreation Area, 707/925-6482, fax 707/925-6402, www.parks.ca.gov.

❹ STANDISH-HICKEY STATE RECREATION AREA: HICKEY

Scenic rating: 8

on the Eel River in Standish-Hickey State Recreation Area

See map page 580

This is an ideal layover for U.S. 101 cruisers yearning to spend a night in the redwoods. The park is best known for its campsites set amid redwoods and for the nearby South Fork Eel River with its steelhead fishing in the winter. The elevation is 800 feet. Insider's tip: There's a great swimming hole here in the summer. (See details about Standish-Hickey State Recreation Area in the listing for *Redwood Campground* in this chapter.)

RV sites, facilities: There are 65 sites for tents or RVs up to 27 feet (no hookups) and trailers up to 24 feet. Picnic tables, food lockers, and fire rings are provided. Drinking water and restrooms with showers and flush toilets are available. A grocery store is nearby. Some facilities are wheelchair accessible. Leashed pets are permitted.

Reservations, fees: Reservations are accepted ($7.50 reservation fee) at 800/444-PARK (800/444-7275) or www.reserveamerica.com. Sites are $20 per night, plus $6 per night for an additional vehicle. Open year-round.

Directions: From the junction of U.S. 101 and Highway 1 in Leggett, drive north on U.S. 101 for one mile to the park entrance on the left (west) side of the road.

Contact: Standish-Hickey State Recreation Area, 707/925-6482, fax 707/925-6402, www.parks.ca.gov.

❺ EEL RIVER

Scenic rating: 8

in Mendocino National Forest

See map page 580

This is a little-known spot, set in oak woodlands at the confluence of the Middle Fork of the Eel River and Black Butte River. The

CALIFORNIA

elevation is 1,500 feet, and it's often extremely hot in summer. Eel River is an ancient Native American campsite and a major archaeological site. For this reason restoration has been limited and at times the camp is overgrown and weedy. Who cares, though? After all, you're camping.

RV sites, facilities: There are 15 sites for tents or RVs up to 21 feet (no hookups). Picnic tables and fire grills are provided. Drinking water and vault toilets are available. Garbage must be packed out. Leashed pets are permitted.

Reservations, fees: Reservations are not accepted. Sites are $6 per night. Open April–December.

Directions: From Willits, drive north on U.S. 101 for 13 miles to Longvale and the junction with Highway 162. Turn northeast on Highway 162 and drive to Covelo. Continue east on Highway 162 for 13 miles to the campground.

Contact: Mendocino National Forest, Covelo Ranger District, 707/983-6118, fax 707/983-8004.

6 BUCKHORN

Scenic rating: 7

on Black Butte Lake

See map page 580

Black Butte Lake is in the foothills of the north Sacramento Valley at 500 feet. It is one of the 10 best lakes in Northern California for crappie, best in spring. There can also be good fishing for largemouth, smallmouth, and spotted bass, channel catfish, bluegill, and sunfish. Recreation options include powerboating, sailboating, and sailboarding. A one-mile-long interpretive trail is available.

RV sites, facilities: There are 65 sites for tents or RVs up to 35 feet (no hookups). Picnic tables and fire grills are provided. Drinking water, restrooms with flush toilets and showers, a dump station, a fish-cleaning station, and a playground are available. A boat ramp is nearby. Some facilities are wheelchair accessible. Leashed pets are permitted.

Reservations, fees: Reservations are accepted at 877/444-6777 or www.ReserveUSA.com. Sites are $15 per night, $10 per night November–March. Open year-round.

Directions: From I-5 in Orland, take the Black Butte Lake exit. Drive about 15 miles west on Road 200/Newville Road to Buckhorn Road. Turn left and drive a short distance to the campground on the north shore of the lake.

Contact: Black Butte Lake, U.S. Army Corps of Engineers, 530/865-4781, fax 530/865-5283.

7 ORLAND BUTTES

Scenic rating: 7

on Black Butte Lake

See map page 580

Black Butte Lake isn't far from I-5, but a lot of campers zoom right by it. The lake has 40 miles of shoreline at 500 feet in elevation. All water sports are allowed. The prime time to visit is in late spring and early summer, when the bass and crappie fishing can be quite good. Three self-guided nature trails are in the immediate area, including Paul Thomas Trail, a short quarter-mile walk to an overlook. (See the listing in this chapter for *Buckhorn* for more information.) Note: In late winter and early spring, this area is delightful as spring arrives, but from mid-June through August, expect very hot, dry weather.

RV sites, facilities: There are 35 sites for tents or RVs up to 35 feet (no hookups). Picnic tables and fire grills are provided. Drinking water, restrooms with showers, a boat ramp, a fish-cleaning station, and a dump station are available. Leashed pets are permitted.

Reservations, fees: Reservations are accepted at 877/444-6777 or www.ReserveUSA.com. Sites are $15 per night. Open April–early September.

Directions: From I-5 in Orland, take the Black Butte Lake exit. Drive west on Road 200/Newville Road for six miles to Road 206. Turn left and drive three miles to the camp entrance on the right.

Contact: Black Butte Lake, U.S. Army Corps of Engineers, 530/865-4781, fax 530/865-5283.

8 WESTPORT-UNION LANDING STATE BEACH

Scenic rating: 8

overlooking the Pacific Ocean

See map page 580

The northern Mendocino coast is remote, beautiful, and gets far less people pressure than the Fort Bragg area. That is the key to its appeal. The campsites are on an ocean bluff. It can get windy here, but the reward is the view. This park covers more than three miles of rugged and scenic coastline. There are magnificent views, sunsets, and tree-covered mountains that can provide great opportunities for photos. Several small sandy beaches, and one large beach at the mouth of Howard Creek, provide some good spots for surf fishing. Several species of rockfish and abalone can be taken when tides and ocean conditions are right. But note that the surf here can surge, discouraging all but the hardy. The park was named for two early-day communities, Westport and Union Landing, settlements famous for supply lumber and rail ties. This state beach formerly had 100 campsites, but some were closed to protect an endangered species, the Point Arena mountain beaver, and other sites are temporarily closed because a section of the state beach road eroded and fell into the ocean.

RV sites, facilities: There are 46 sites for tents or RVs of any length (no hookups); eight people maximum per site. Picnic tables and fire rings are provided. Drinking water and chemical flush toilets are available. A grocery store is nearby. Leashed pets are permitted.

Reservations, fees: Reservations are not accepted. Sites are $15 per night, $6 per night for an additional vehicle. Open year-round.

Directions: From Fort Bragg, drive north on Highway 1 to Westport. In Westport, continue north on Highway 1 for three miles to the campground entrance on the west side of the road.

Contact: California State Parks, Mendocino District, 707/937-5804, fax 707/937-2953, www.parks.ca.gov.

9 WESTPORT BEACH RV AND CAMPING

Scenic rating: 8

overlooking the Pacific Ocean

See map page 580

Westport Beach RV and Camping is above the beach near the mouth of Wages Creek, with both creekside sites and beach sites available. The 30-acre campground has a quarter mile of beach frontage. You will notice as you venture north from Fort Bragg that the number of vacationers in the area falls way off, providing a chance for quiet beaches and serene moments. The best nearby hiking is to the north out of the trailhead for the Sinkyone Wilderness.

RV sites, facilities: There are 75 sites with full hookups (20, 30, and 50 amps) for RVs of any length, 24 sites with no hookups for RVs of any length, 47 sites for tents only, and six group sites for tents or RVs (no hookups) that can accommodate 12–50 people each. Some RV sites are pull-through. A two-bedroom house is also available. Picnic tables and fire rings are provided at most sites. Drinking water, restrooms with coin showers and flush toilets, a convenience store, a coin laundry, telephone/modem access, a playground, volleyball, shuffleboard, horseshoes, firewood, and ice are available. Some facilities are wheelchair accessible. Leashed pets are permitted.

Reservations, fees: Reservations are accepted. Sites are $32–36 per night for RV sites, $22 per night per vehicle for tent and RV sites (including group sites) with no hookups, $3–5 per night per person for more than two people, and $1 per pet per night. Monthly rates available. Some credit cards accepted. Open year-round.

Directions: From Fort Bragg, drive north on Highway 1 to Westport. In Westport, continue north on Highway 1 for 0.5 mile to the campground entrance on the west side of the highway.

Contact: Westport Beach RV and Camping, 707/964-2964, fax 707/964-8185, www.westportbeachrv.com.

CALIFORNIA

10 CREEKSIDE CABINS AND RV RESORT

Scenic rating: 5

north of Willits

See map page 580

The privately operated park is in a pretty valley, primarily oak/bay woodlands with a sprinkling of conifers. It was previously known as Hidden Valley Campground. The most popular nearby recreation option is taking the Skunk Train in Willits for the ride out to the coast at Fort Bragg. There are also two golf courses within six miles. Note that about half of the sites are occupied by long-term renters.

RV sites, facilities: There are 50 sites, including 35 with full or partial hookups (20 and 30 amps), for tents or RVs up to 38 feet. Picnic tables and fire grills are provided, and some sites provide satellite TV and telephone and Wi-Fi access. Restrooms have showers. Ice, a coin laundry, and a dump station are available. Leashed pets are permitted.

Reservations, fees: Reservations are accepted. Sites are $18–33 per night, $3 per person per night for more than two people. Open year-round.

Directions: From Willits on U.S. 101, drive north for 6.5 miles on U.S. 101 to the campground on the east side (right) of the road at 29801 North Highway 101.

Contact: Creekside Cabins and RV Resort, 707/459-2521.

11 MacKERRICHER STATE PARK

Scenic rating: 9

overlooking the Pacific Ocean

See map page 580   BEST (

MacKerricher is a beautiful park on the Mendocino coast, a great destination for adventure and exploration. The camps are set in a coastal forest, with gorgeous walk-in sites. Nearby is a small beach, great tidepools, a rocky point where harbor seals hang out in the sun, a small lake (Cleone) with trout fishing, a great bike trail, and outstanding short hikes. The short jaunt around little Cleone Lake has many romantic spots, often tunneling through vegetation, then emerging for lake views. The coastal walk to the point to see seals and tidepools is equally captivating. For wheelchair users, there is a wheelchair-accessible trail to Laguna Point and also a route on a raised boardwalk that runs halfway around Cleone Lake, a former tidal lagoon. This park covers more than 1,530 acres of beach, bluff, headlands, dune, forest, and wetlands. That diverse landscape provides habitat for more than 90 species of birds, most in the vicinity of Cleone Lake. In winter and spring, the headland provides a good lookout for whale-watching.

RV sites, facilities: There are 142 sites for tents or RVs up to 35 feet, 10 walk-in sites, and two group sites for up to 40–60 people each. No hookups. Picnic tables, fire rings, and food lockers are provided. Drinking water, restrooms with flush toilets and coin showers, a picnic area, Wi-Fi, and a dump station are available. A seasonal junior ranger program with nature walks, campfire programs, and exhibits is also available. Some facilities are wheelchair accessible. Leashed pets are permitted.

Reservations, fees: Reservations are accepted ($7.50 reservation fee) at 800/444-PARK (800/444-7275) or www.reserveamerica.com. Sites are $25 per night, $6 per night for an additional vehicle. Group sites are $120–180 per night. Open year-round.

Directions: From Fort Bragg, drive north on Highway 1 for three miles to the campground entrance on the left side of the road.

Contact: MacKerricher State Park, 707/964-9112; Mendocino District, 707/937-5804, fax 707/937-2953, www.parks.ca.gov.

12 FORT BRAGG LEISURE TIME RV PARK

Scenic rating: 5

in Fort Bragg

See map page 580

This privately operated park adjoins Jackson State Forest, with easy access for hiking and

CALIFORNIA

cycling trails. The park offers horseshoes, badminton, and a covered group picnic area. The drive from Willits to Fort Bragg on Highway 20 is always a favorite, a curving two-laner through redwoods, not too slow, not too fast, best seen from the saddle of a Harley-Davidson. At the end of it is the coast, and just three miles inland is this campground in the sunbelt, said to be out of the fog by breakfast. Within short drives are Noyo Harbor in Fort Bragg, Russian Gulch State Park, Mendocino to the south, and MacKerricher State Park to the north. In fact, there's so much in the area, you could explore for days. Note that about 10 percent of the sites are filled with permanent or long-term renters.

RV sites, facilities: There are 70 pull-through sites, many with full or partial hookups (30 amps), for tents or RVs up to 40 feet. Picnic tables and fire rings are provided. Restrooms have coin showers. Satellite TV, modem access, a dump station, a fish-cleaning station, horseshoes, RV storage, and a coin laundry are available. Some facilities are wheelchair accessible. Leashed pets are permitted.

Reservations, fees: Reservations are accepted at 800/700-8542. Sites are $21.50–32 per night, $1 per night for an additional vehicle, $2 per night for the first pet, and $1 per night for an additional pet. Monthly and seasonal rates available. Some credit cards accepted. Open year-round.

Directions: In Fort Bragg at the junction of Highway 1 and Highway 20, turn east on Highway 20 and drive 2.5 miles to the campground entrance on the right side of the road at 30801 Highway 20.

Contact: Fort Bragg Leisure Time RV Park, 707/964-5994.

13 POMO RV PARK AND CAMPGROUND

Scenic rating: 7

in Fort Bragg

See map page 580

This park covers 17 acres of lush, native vegetation, including rhododendrons, near the ocean. It is one of several camps on the Fort Bragg and Mendocino coast, and groups are welcome. Nearby Noyo Harbor offers busy restaurants, deep-sea fishing, a boat ramp, a harbor, and a nice walk out to the Noyo Harbor jetty. Huckleberry picking is also an option. Many of the RV spaces are quite wide at this park.

RV sites, facilities: There are 94 sites with full or partial hookups (30 and 50 amps) for RVs of any length, as well as 30 sites for tents. Some sites are pull-through. Picnic tables and fire rings are provided. Restrooms have coin showers. Cable TV hookups, Wi-Fi, a convenience store, firewood, ice, RV supplies, propane gas, a coin laundry, a dump station, a fish-cleaning table, horseshoe pits, and a large grass playing field are available. Some facilities are wheelchair accessible. Leashed pets are permitted.

Reservations, fees: Reservations are recommended in the summer. Sites are $24–35 per night, $3–5 per person per night for more than two people, $1 per pet per night. Open year-round.

Directions: In Fort Bragg at the junction of Highway 1 and Highway 20, drive south on Highway 1 for one mile to Tregoning Lane. Turn left (east) and drive a short distance to the park at the end of the road (17999 Tregoning Lane).

Contact: Pomo RV Park and Campground, 707/964-3373.

14 JACKSON DEMONSTRATION STATE FOREST, CAMP 1

Scenic rating: 7

near Fort Bragg

See map page 580

Primitive campsites set in a vast forest of redwoods and Douglas fir are the prime attraction at Jackson Demonstration State Forest. Even though Highway 20 is a major connecting link to the coast in the summer, these camps get bypassed because they are primitive and largely unknown. Why? Because reaching them requires driving on dirt roads sometimes frequented by logging trucks, and there are few campground signs along the highway. This camp features lots of tree cover, with oaks, redwoods, and madrones. Most of the campsites are adjacent to the South Fork of the North Fork of the Noyo River, well-known among locals but completely missed by most others. A one-mile trail circles the campground, and the trailhead is at the day-use area. A Department of Fish and Game hatchery is next to the campground, but note that no fishing is permitted in the river.

RV sites, facilities: There are 32 sites for tents or RVs up to 27 feet (no hookups), and one group site for tents or RVs up to 45 feet can accommodate up to 150 people. Picnic tables and fire pits are provided. Vault toilets are available. No drinking water is available. Leashed pets are permitted.

Reservations, fees: Reservations are accepted only for the group site at 707/964-5674. There is no fee for camping. A camping permit is required and a campground map is needed. Both can be obtained from the State Department of Forestry and Fire Protection office at 802 North Main Street (Highway 1) in Fort Bragg. Open late May–September.

Directions: From Willits on U.S. 101, turn west on Highway 20 and drive 27 miles to Forest Road 350 (at the 5.9 mile marker). Turn right (north) and drive 1.3 miles to the campground.

Contact: Jackson Demonstration State Forest, 707/964-5674.

15 JACKSON DEMONSTRATION STATE FOREST, DUNLAP

Scenic rating: 6

near Fort Bragg

See map page 580

A highlight of Jackson Demonstration Forest is a 50-foot waterfall on Chamberlain Creek. Set in a steep canyon at the east end of the forest, amid giant firs and redwoods, it can be reached with a 10-minute walk. Extensive logging roads are good yet challenging for mountain biking. What to do first? Get a map from the State Forestry Department. For driving, the roads are extremely dusty in summer and muddy in winter.

RV sites, facilities: There are 30 sites for tents or RVs up to 27 feet (no hookups), including eight equestrian sites across the road at Big River Camp. Picnic tables and fire rings are provided. Vault toilets are available. No drinking water is available. Leashed pets are permitted.

Reservations, fees: Reservations are not accepted for individual sites but are required for equestrian sites at 707/964-5674. There is no fee for camping. A camping permit is required, and a campground map is needed. Both can be obtained from the State Department of Forestry and Fire Protection office at 802 North Main Street (Highway 1) in Fort Bragg. Open late May–September.

Directions: From Willits on U.S. 101, turn west on Highway 20 and drive 17 miles. At the 16.9-mile marker (just past the Chamberlain Bridge) continue driving for about 0.25 mile to the Dunlap camp entrance on the left.

Contact: Jackson Demonstration State Forest, 707/964-5674, fax 707/964-0941.

16 WILLITS-UKIAH KOA

Scenic rating: 3

near Willits

See map page 580

This is an ideal spot to park your RV if you plan on taking the Skunk Train west to Fort Bragg. A depot for the train is within walking distance of the campground, and tickets are available at KOA. The campground, which has a western theme, also offers nightly entertainment in summer. The elevation is 1,377 feet.

RV sites, facilities: There are 21 sites for tents and 50 sites with full or partial hookups (30 and 50 amps) for RVs of any length. Many sites are pull-through. Twelve cabins and two lodges are also available. Groups can be accommodated. Picnic tables and fire rings are provided. Drinking water, restrooms with flush toilets and showers, Wi-Fi, a playground, a seasonal heated swimming pool, hay rides, mini golf, basketball, volleyball, a fishing pond, a convenience store, RV supplies, a coin laundry, and a dump station are available. Some facilities are wheelchair accessible. Leashed pets are permitted, with certain restrictions.

Reservations, fees: Reservations are accepted at 800/562-8542. RV sites are $37–50 per night, tent sites are $33–37 per night, plus $3–4 per person per night for more than two people. Some credit cards accepted. Open year-round.

Directions: From Willits at the junction of U.S. 101 and Highway 20, turn west on Highway 20 and drive 1.5 miles to the campground on the right at 1600 Highway 20.

Contact: Willits-Ukiah KOA, 707/459-6179, fax 707/459-1489, www.koa.com.

17 POGIE POINT

Scenic rating: 7

on Lake Pillsbury in Mendocino National Forest
See map page 580

This camp sits beside Lake Pillsbury in Mendocino National Forest, in the back of a cove at the lake's northwest corner. When the lake is full, this spot is quite pretty. A boat ramp is about a quarter mile to the south, a bonus. The elevation is 1,900 feet. (For more information about Lake Pillsbury, see the listing for *Fuller Grove* in this chapter.)

RV sites, facilities: There are 50 sites for tents or RVs up to 16 feet (no hookups). Picnic tables and fire grills are provided. Drinking water and vault toilets are available. Some facilities are wheelchair accessible. Leashed pets are permitted.

Reservations, fees: Reservations are not accepted. Sites are $13 per night, $3 per night for an additional vehicle, $1 per pet per night. Open May–October.

Directions: From Ukiah on U.S. 101, drive north to the junction with Highway 20. Turn east (right) on Highway 20 and drive five miles. Turn northwest on East Potter Valley Road toward Lake Pillsbury. Drive 5.9 miles to the town of Potter Valley. Continue on east Potter Valley Road to Eel River Road. Turn right and

drive 15 miles to the Eel River Information Kiosk at Lake Pillsbury. Continue for two miles to the campground access road. Turn right and drive a short distance to the campground.

Contact: Mendocino National Forest, Upper Lake Ranger District, 707/275-2361, fax 707/275-0676; PG&E Land Services, 916/386-5164, www.pge.com/recreation.

18 FULLER GROVE AND FULLER GROVE GROUP CAMP

Scenic rating: 7

on Lake Pillsbury in Mendocino National Forest
See map page 580

This is one of several campgrounds bordering Lake Pillsbury, which at 2,000 acres is by far the largest lake in Mendocino National Forest. Set at an elevation of 1,800 feet, Pillsbury is big and pretty when full, with 65 miles of shoreline. It has lakeside camping and good boat ramps. In the spring, fishing is good for trout, and in the warmer months bass is the catch. This camp is along the northwest shore of the lake, with a boat ramp about a quarter mile away to the north. There are numerous backcountry roads in the area, which provide access to a state game refuge to the north and the Snow Mountain Wilderness to the east.

RV sites, facilities: There are 30 sites for tents or RVs up to 16 feet and a group tent area for up to 60 people. No hookups. Picnic tables and fire grills are provided. Drinking water and vault toilets are available. A boat ramp is nearby. Leashed pets are permitted.

Reservations, fees: Reservations are not accepted for individual sites but are required for the group site at 916/386-5164. Sites are $13 per night for individual sites, $3 per night for an additional vehicle, $1 per pet per night, and $100 per night for the group site (two-night minimum for the group site). Open May–October.

Directions: From Ukiah on U.S. 101, drive north to the junction with Highway 20. Turn east (right) on Highway 20 and drive five miles to East Potter Valley Road. Turn northwest

CALIFORNIA

on East Potter Valley Road toward Lake Pillsbury and drive 5.9 miles to the town of Potter Valley. Continue on East Potter Valley Road to Eel River Road. Turn right and drive 15 miles to the Eel River Information Kiosk at Lake Pillsbury. Continue for 2.2 miles to the campground access road. Turn right and drive 0.25 mile to the campground; the group camp is adjacent to the boat ramp.

Contact: Mendocino National Forest, Upper Lake Ranger District, 707/275-2361, fax 707/275-0676; PG&E Land Services, 916/386-5164, www.pge.com.

19 SUNSET CAMPGROUND

Scenic rating: 7

on Lake Pillsbury in Mendocino National Forest

See map page 580

This camp is on the northeast corner of Lake Pillsbury, and Pillsbury Pines boat launch and picnic area is less than a quarter mile to the south. Lakeshore Trail, an adjacent designated nature trail along the shore of the lake, is accessible to hikers, equestrians, and bicyclists. However, a section of the trail is covered with water when the lake is full. The surrounding national forest offers side-trip possibilities.

RV sites, facilities: There are 54 sites for tents or RVs up to 16 feet (no hookups). Picnic tables and fire grills are provided. Drinking water and vault toilets are available. A boat ramp is nearby. Leashed pets are permitted.

Reservations, fees: Reservations are not accepted. Sites are $13 per night, $3 per night for an additional vehicle, $1 per pet per night. Open May–October.

Directions: From Ukiah on U.S. 101, drive north to the junction with Highway 20. Turn east (right) on Highway 20 and drive five miles. Turn northwest on East Potter Valley Road toward Lake Pillsbury. Drive 5.9 miles to the town of Potter Valley. Continue on East Potter Valley Road to Eel River Road. Turn right and drive 15 miles to the Eel River Information Kiosk at Lake Pillsbury. Continue east for 4.1

miles to Lake Pillsbury and the junction with Hall Mountain Road. Turn right and drive three miles to the camp entrance.

Contact: Mendocino National Forest, Upper Lake Ranger District, 707/275-2361, fax 707/275-0676; PG&E Land Services, 916/386-5164, www.pge.com.

20 LAKE PILLSBURY RESORT

Scenic rating: 6

on Lake Pillsbury

See map page 580

This is a pretty spot beside the shore of Lake Pillsbury in the heart of Mendocino National Forest. It can be headquarters for a vacation involving boating, fishing, waterskiing, or exploring the surrounding national forest. A boat ramp, small marina, and full facilities make this place a prime attraction in a relatively remote location. This is the only resort on the lake that accepts reservations, and it has some lakefront sites.

RV sites, facilities: There are 25 sites for tents or RVs up to 30 feet (no hookups) and two sites with full hookups (30 amps). Eight cabins are also available. Picnic tables and fire pits are provided. Drinking water, restrooms with flush toilets and coin showers, a playground, boat rentals, fuel, a boat dock, fishing supplies, and a small marina are available. Leashed pets are permitted.

Reservations, fees: Reservations are recommended. Sites are $22.75–30.25 per night, $7 per pet per night. Boat launching is $6 per day. Weekly rates available. Some credit cards accepted. Open May–October.

Directions: From Ukiah on U.S. 101, drive north to the junction with Highway 20. Turn east (right) on Highway 20 and drive five miles to East Potter Valley Road (toward Lake Pillsbury). Turn left (northwest) on East Potter Valley Road and drive 5.9 miles to the town of Potter Valley. Continue on East Potter Valley Road to Eel River Road. Turn right and drive 11 miles (unpaved road) to the stop sign. Turn right (still Eel River Road) and drive 0.2 mile

to Kapranos Road. Turn left and drive about 1.5 miles to the resort at 2756 Kapranos Road.
Contact: Lake Pillsbury Resort, 707/743-9935, www.lprandm.com.

21 CASPAR BEACH RV PARK

Scenic rating: 8

near Mendocino

See map page 580   **BEST (**

This privately operated park has opportunities for beachcombing, kayaking, fishing, abalone and scuba diving, and whale-watching from lookouts. The park is across the road from the ocean and somewhat wooded, with a small, year-round creek running behind it. The park is about midway between Fort Bragg and Mendocino, with Fort Bragg five miles north. Note that some of the sites are filled with long-term renters.

RV sites, facilities: There are 59 sites with full or partial hookups (30 amps) for RVs up to 50 feet, 30 tent sites, and two group tent sites that can accommodate up to 20 people each. Some sites are pull-through. Picnic tables and fire rings are provided. Cable TV, Wi-Fi, restrooms with flush toilets and coin showers, a dump station, a convenience store, firewood, a playground, a video arcade, video rentals, and a coin laundry are available. Some facilities are wheelchair accessible. Leashed pets are permitted.

Reservations, fees: Reservations are accepted. Sites are $25–35 per night, $3–5 per person per night for more than two people, $2 per pet per night. Group tent sites are $60 per night and $3–5 per person per night for more than six people. Monthly rates available. Some credit cards accepted. Open year-round.

Directions: From Mendocino on Highway 1, drive north for 3.5 miles to the Point Cabrillo exit. Turn west on Point Cabrillo Drive and continue 0.75 mile to the campground on the left at 14441 Point Cabrillo Drive.

From Fort Bragg on Highway 1, drive south for 4.5 miles to Point Cabrillo Drive (Mile Marker 54.6). Turn right and continue 0.75 mile to the campground.

Contact: Caspar Beach RV Park, 707/964-3306, fax 707/964-0526, www.casparbeach rvpark.com.

22 RUSSIAN GULCH STATE PARK

Scenic rating: 9

near the Pacific Ocean

See map page 580

Russian Gulch State Park is near some of California's most beautiful coastline, but the camp speaks to the woods, not the water, with the campsites set in a wooded canyon. They include some of the prettiest and most secluded drive-in sites available on the Mendocino coast. There is a great hike here, an easy hourlong walk to Russian Gulch Falls, a wispy 36-foot waterfall that falls into a rock basin. While it's always pretty, it's awesome in late winter. Much of the route is accessible by bicycle, with a bicycle rack available where the trail narrows and turns to dirt. The park covers more than 1,100 acres with about 1.5 miles of ocean frontage, with its rugged headlands thrusting into the Pacific. It rivals Point Lobos for coastal beauty. And yet the park is better known for its heavily forested canyon, Russian Gulch Creek Canyon, and a headland that features the Devil's Punchbowl. The latter is a large collapsed sea cave with churning water that acts as a blowhole. It was created by the pounding of waves against the coastal headlands, gouging a 200-foot tunnel that ends where the earth caved away. That forms a hole 100 feet across and 60 feet deep, where one can look right in and watch the surge. A beach offers tidepool exploring, swimming, diving, and rock fishing. In addition, there are many more miles of hiking trails and a few miles of trails for cycling.

RV sites, facilities: There are 30 sites for tents or RVs up to 24 feet, one hike-in/bike-in site, four equestrian sites, and one group site for up to 40 people. No hookups. Picnic tables, fire grills, and food lockers are provided. Drinking water, coin showers, and flush toilets are available. A seasonal junior ranger program with

CALIFORNIA

nature walks, campfire programs, and exhibits is also available. A day-use picnic area, beach access, and recreation hall are available nearby. Some facilities are wheelchair accessible. Leashed pets are permitted in the campground and on some trails.

Reservations, fees: Reservations are accepted ($7.50 reservation fee) at 800/444-PARK (800/444-7275) or www.reserveamerica.com. Equestrian sites can be reserved at 707/937-5804. Sites are $25 per night for individual and equestrian sites, $6 per night for an additional vehicle, $90 per night for the group site, and $3 per night per person for hike-in/bike-in site. Open mid-March–October, weather permitting, with a two-night maximum stay for hike-in/bike-in campers.

Directions: From Mendocino, drive two miles north on Highway 1 to the campground entrance on the west side of the highway.

Contact: Russian Gulch State Park, 707/937-4296; Mendocino District, 707/937-5804, fax 707/937-2953, www.parks.ca.gov.

23 VAN DAMME STATE PARK

🥾 🚴 🏊 🎣 🛶 🐕 ♿ 🚐 ⛺

Scenic rating: 10

near Mendocino

See map page 580

The campsites at Van Damme are extremely popular, usually requiring reservations, but with a bit of planning your reward is a base of operations in a beautiful park with redwoods and a remarkable fern understory. The Fern Canyon Trail, which is located in the park, is one of the most popular hikes in the Mendocino area, with the trail crossing the Little River several times and weaving among old trees. Just across from the entrance of the park is a small but beautiful coastal bay with a pretty beach, ideal for launching sea kayaks. The park covers 1,831 acres. A sidelight is the Pygmy Forest, where mature cone-bearing cypress and pine trees are only six inches to eight feet tall. Another favorite is the Bog Trail, where skunk cabbage grows in abundance, most striking when seen in May and June. The park has 10 miles of trails along the fern-carpeted canyon along the Little River. A paved road is used by joggers and bicyclists. The beach is popular with abalone divers. Kayak tours may be available at the beach parking lot in the summer.

RV sites, facilities: There are 74 sites for tents or RVs up to 35 feet and one group campsite for up to 50 people. No hookups. Picnic tables, food lockers, and fire grills are provided. Drinking water, restrooms with flush toilets and coin showers, Wi-Fi, and a dump station are available. A seasonal junior ranger program with nature walks, campfire programs, and exhibits is also available. A grocery store and propane gas are available nearby. Some facilities are wheelchair accessible. Leashed pets are permitted at campsites but not in environmental sites.

Reservations, fees: Reservations are accepted ($7.50 reservation fee) at 800/444-PARK (800/444-7275) or www.reserveamerica.com. Sites are $25 per night, $6 per night for an additional vehicle, $15 per night for environmental sites, $111 per night for the group site, $3 per night per person for the hike-in/bike-in site. Open year-round.

Directions: From Mendocino on Highway 1, drive south for three miles to the town of Little River and the park entrance road on the left (east) side of the road.

Contact: Mendocino District, State Parks, 707/937-5804, fax 707/937-2953, www.parks.ca.gov.

24 NAVARRO RIVER REDWOODS STATE PARK: NAVARRO BEACH CAMPGROUND

🥾 🦌 🚐 ⛺

Scenic rating: 6

near the mouth of the Navarro River

See map page 580

Navarro Beach is a primitive campground that can bail out drivers stuck for a night without a spot. It is small and open, with no tree cover, set near the ocean and the Navarro River. The camps are just south of the Navarro River Bridge.

RV sites, facilities: There 10 sites for tents or RVs up to 35 feet (no hookups). Picnic tables and fire grills are provided. No drinking water. Pit toilets are available. Leashed pets are permitted.

Reservations, fees: Reservations are not accepted. Sites are $15 per night, $6 per night for an additional vehicle. Open year-round.

Directions: Drive on U.S. 101 to the turnoff for Highway 128 (two miles north of Cloverdale). Turn west on Highway 128 and drive 55 miles to Highway 1. Turn south on Highway 1 and, almost immediately, take the exit for Navarro Bluffs Road. Drive a short distance on Navarro Bluffs Road to the campground (on the south side of the Navarro River Bridge).

Contact: Navarro River Redwoods State Park, c/o Hendy Woods, 707/895-3141; Mendocino District, 707/937-5804, fax 707/937-2953, www.parks.ca.gov.

25 NAVARRO RIVER REDWOODS STATE PARK: PAUL M. DIMMICK CAMPGROUND

Scenic rating: 7

on the Navarro River in Navarro River Redwoods State Park

See map page 580

A pretty grove of second-growth redwood trees and the nearby Navarro River are the highlights of this campground at Navarro River Redwoods State Park. It's a nice spot but, alas, lacks any significant hiking trails that could make it an overall spectacular destination; all the trailheads along Highway 128 turn out to be just little spur routes from the road to the river. That is because the park consists of an 11-mile "redwood tunnel" along the Navarro River in its course to the ocean. The river provides swimming in summer but is better suited for easy kayaking and canoeing in later winter and early spring.

RV sites, facilities: There are 25 sites for tents or RVs up to 30 feet (no hookups) and trailers up to 24 feet. Picnic tables and fire grills are provided. Drinking water (summer only) and

vault (summer) and pit (winter) toilets are available. Leashed pets are permitted.

Reservations, fees: Reservations are not accepted. Sites are $15 per night, $6 per night for an additional vehicle. Open year-round, weather permitting.

Directions: From Cloverdale on U.S. 101, drive north for two miles to Highway 128. Turn west on Highway 128 and drive approximately 50 miles. Look for the signed campground entrance on the left side of the road at Mile Marker 8.

Contact: Navarro River Redwoods State Park, c/o Hendy Woods State Park, 707/895-3141; Mendocino District, 707/987-5804, fax 707/937-2953, www.parks.ca.gov.

26 HENDY WOODS STATE PARK

Scenic rating: 7

near Boonville

See map page 581

This is a remarkable setting where the flora changes from open valley grasslands and oaks to a cloaked redwood forest with old growth, as if you had waved a magic wand. The campsites are set in the forest, with a great trail routed amid the old redwoods and up to the Hermit Hut (a fallen redwood stump covered with branches), where a hobo lived for 18 years. No, it wasn't me. The park features two virgin redwood groves, Big Hendy (80 acres with a self-guided discovery trail available) and Little Hendy (20 acres). The Navarro River runs through the length of the park, but note fishing is forbidden in the park and that catch-and-release fishing is the law from the bridge at the park entrance on downstream; check regulations. The park is in the middle of the Anderson Valley wine district, which will at first seem an unlikely place to find an 845-acre redwood park, far warmer and less foggy than the redwood parks along the coast.

RV sites, facilities: There are 92 sites for tents or RVs up to 35 feet (no hookups), two hike-in/bike-in sites, and four cabins. Picnic tables, food lockers, and fire grills are provided. Drinking water, flush toilets, coin showers, and a dump station are available. A seasonal junior ranger program with nature walks, campfire programs, and exhibits is also available. A grocery store and propane gas station are available nearby. Some facilities are wheelchair accessible. Leashed pets are permitted.

Reservations, fees: Reservations are accepted ($7.50 reservation fee) at 800/444-PARK (800/444-7275) or www.reserveamerica.com. Sites are $25 per night, $6 per night for an additional vehicle, $3 per person per night for hike-in/bike-in sites. Open year-round.

Directions: From Cloverdale on U.S. 101, turn northwest on Highway 128 and drive about 35 miles to Philo Greenwood Road. Turn left on Philo Greenwood Road and drive 0.5 mile to the park entrance on the left.

Contact: Hendy Woods State Park, 707/895-3141; Mendocino District, 707/937-5804, fax 707/937-2953, www.parks.ca.gov.

27 BU-SHAY

Scenic rating: 7

at Lake Mendocino

See map page 580

Bu-Shay, on the northeast end of Lake Mendocino, sits on a point that provides a pretty southern exposure when the lake is full. The lake is five miles long and one mile wide. It offers fishing for striped bass, largemouth bass, smallmouth bass, crappie, catfish, and bluegill, as well as waterskiing and powerboating. A nearby visitors center features exhibits of local Native American history. The elevation is 750 feet, and the lake covers 1,750 acres and has 15 miles of shoreline. (For more information about Lake Mendocino, see the listing in this chapter for *Che-Ka-Ka*.)

RV sites, facilities: There are 164 sites for tents or RVs up to 35 feet. There are three group sites for up to 120 people each. No hookups. Picnic tables, fire rings, and lantern holders are provided. Drinking water, restrooms with showers, a playground (in the adjacent day-use

area), group facilities, and a dump station are available. The boat ramp is two miles from camp near Ky-En Campground. Some facilities are wheelchair accessible. Leashed pets are permitted.

Reservations, fees: Reservations are accepted (no reservation fee) at 877/444-6777 or www.ReserveUSA.com. Sites are $20–25 per night, group sites are $140–200 per night. Boat launching is free with a camping pass. Open year-round, with limited winter facilities.

Directions: From Ukiah, drive north on U.S. 101 for five miles to the Highway 20 turnoff. Drive five miles east on Highway 20. Just after crossing the Russian River bridge, turn left (Inlet Road) and drive approximately one mile to the campground.

Contact: U.S. Army Corps of Engineers, Lake Mendocino, 707/462-7581, fax 707/462-3372.

28 KY-EN

Scenic rating: 7

at Lake Mendocino

See map page 580

This camp is on the north shore of Lake Mendocino. With the access road off Highway 20 instead of U.S. 101 (as with Che-Ka-Ka), it can be overlooked by newcomers. A nearby boat ramp makes it especially attractive. (For more information, see the listings in this chapter for *Che-Ka-Ka* and *Bu-Shay*.)

RV sites, facilities: There are 101 sites for tents or RVs up to 30 feet (no hookups). Picnic tables, fire grills, and lantern holders are provided. Restrooms have showers. A playground (in the adjacent day-use area), a dump station, and a boat ramp are available. Some facilities are wheelchair accessible. Leashed pets are permitted, except in some day-use areas.

Reservations, fees: Reservations are accepted (no reservation fee) at 877/444-6777 or www.ReserveUSA.com. Sites are $20 per night. Boat launching is free with a camping pass. Open April–mid-October.

Directions: From Ukiah, drive north on

U.S. 101 for five miles to the Highway 20 turnoff. Drive east on Highway 20 to Marina Drive. Turn right and drive 200 yards (past the boat ramp) to the campground.

Contact: U.S. Army Corps of Engineers, Lake Mendocino, 707/462-7581, fax 707/462-3372.

29 CHE-KA-KA

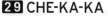

Scenic rating: 7

at Lake Mendocino

See map page 580

Lake Mendocino is known for good striped bass fishing, waterskiing, and boating. Nearby, upstream of the lake, is Potter Valley and the East Fork Russian River (also called Cold Creek), which provides trout fishing in the summer. A boat ramp adjacent to the dam is a bonus. The elevation is 750 feet. This campground sits beside the dam at the south end of Lake Mendocino, and the Kaweyo trailhead is nearby. Insider's tip: A newly installed 18-hole frisbee golf course is at the Che-Ka-Ka overlook.

RV sites, facilities: There are 21 sites for tents or RVs up to 35 feet (no hookups). Picnic tables, lantern hangers, and fire grills are provided. Drinking water, vault toilets, and a playground are available. A boat ramp is nearby. Leashed pets are permitted.

Reservations, fees: Reservations are accepted (no reservation fee) at 877/444-6777 or www.ReserveUSA.com. Sites are $16 per night. Boat launching is free with a camping pass. Open early April–September.

Directions: From Ukiah, drive north on U.S. 101 to Lake Mendocino Drive. Exit right on Lake Mendocino Drive and continue to the first stoplight. Turn left on North State Street and drive to the next stoplight. Turn right (which will put you back on Lake Mendocino Drive) and drive about two miles to the signed entrance to the campground at Coyote Dam.

Contact: U.S. Army Corps of Engineers, Lake Mendocino, 707/462-7581, fax 707/462-3372.

30 PINE ACRES BLUE LAKES RESORT

Scenic rating: 8

on Upper Blue Lake

See map page 580

Because of their proximity to Clear Lake, the Blue Lakes are often overlooked. Lake frontage sites are available, and other bonuses are a sandy beach and swim area. These lovely lakes offer good fishing for trout, especially in spring and early summer on Upper Blue Lake. Other fish species are bass, crappie, catfish, and bluegill. With a speed limit (5 mph) in place, quiet boating is the rule. Swimming is good here. For tent camping, a lawn area is available. Note that the RV sites are spaced very close together.

RV sites, facilities: There are 30 sites with full or partial hookups (30 amps) for RVs up to 40 feet, a lawn area for dispersed tent camping, six cabins, and four lodge rooms. Two sites are pull-through. Picnic tables and barbecues are provided. Restrooms have flush toilets and coin showers. A dump station, group facilities, boat rentals, boat launching, moorings, a boat ramp, a fish-cleaning station, horseshoes, a convenience store, fishing supplies, and lake frontage sites are available. Leashed pets are permitted, with certain restrictions.

Reservations, fees: Reservations are accepted for RV sites, cabins, and lodge rooms, but not for tent camping. Sites are $23–28 per night, $2 per person per night for more than two people, $3.50 per night for an additional vehicle, $5 per pet per night. Boat launching is free for campers. Some credit cards accepted. Open year-round.

Directions: From Ukiah, drive north on U.S. 101 for five miles to the junction with Highway 20. Turn east on Highway 20 and drive about 13 miles to Irvine Avenue. Turn right on Irvine Avenue and drive one block to the end of the road and Blue Lakes Road. Turn right and drive a short distance to the resort on the right at 5328 Blue Lakes Road.

Contact: Pine Acres Blue Lakes Resort, 707/275-2811, www.bluelakepineacres.com.

CALIFORNIA

CALIFORNIA

31 NARROWS LODGE RESORT

Scenic rating: 8

on Upper Blue Lake

See map page 580

This is one of several campgrounds in the immediate vicinity at Blue Lakes. This campground is a good fish camp with boat docks and a fish-cleaning station. The Blue Lakes are often overlooked because of their proximity to Clear Lake, but they are a quiet and pretty alternative, with good trout fishing in the spring and early summer, and decent prospects year-round. The lakes are long and narrow with a primarily forested shoreline, and the elevation is 1,400 feet.

RV sites, facilities: There are 48 sites for tents or RVs of any length with full or partial hook-ups (50 amps), three park-model cabins, two cabins, and 14 motel rooms. Picnic tables are provided. Restrooms have flush toilets and showers. A dump station, modem access, recreation room, boat rentals, pier, a boat ramp, boat slips, fishing supplies, a picnic area, and ice are available. Leashed pets are allowed.

Reservations, fees: Reservations are accepted at 800/476-2776. Sites are $23–25 per night, $3–4 per person per night for more than two people, $3 per pet per night. Some credit cards accepted. Open year-round.

Directions: From Ukiah, drive north on U.S. 101 for five miles to the junction with Highway 20. Turn east on Highway 20 and drive about 13 miles to Blue Lakes Road. Turn right and drive one mile to the resort (5690 Blue Lakes Road).

Contact: Narrows Lodge Resort, 707/275-2718 or 800/476-2776, www.thenarrowsresort.com.

32 KELLY'S FAMILY KAMPGROUND AND RV PARK

Scenic rating: 6

on Scotts Creek near Clear Lake

See map page 580

This privately operated park is beside Scotts Creek, within short driving range of Blue Lakes to the north on Highway 20 and the north end of Clear Lake to the south. The staff is friendly here, and the owner has been running the place for more than 30 years. A bonus is a 1.5-acre pond that can be used for swimming. Fishing is available 1.5 miles away at Blue Lakes.

RV sites, facilities: There are 75 sites for tents or RVs up to 40 feet, many with partial hook-ups (30 amps). Picnic tables, fire pits, and barbecues are provided. Restrooms have flush toilets and coin showers. A dump station, a coin laundry, ice, volleyball, basketball, horseshoes, and a small camp store are available. Leashed pets are permitted.

Reservations, fees: Reservations are accepted. Sites are $22–26 per night, $2 per night for an additional vehicle, $1 per pet per night. Open April–October.

Directions: From Ukiah on U.S. 101, drive north to the junction with Highway 20. Turn east and drive 14 miles (five miles from Upper Lake) to Scotts Valley Road. Turn right (south) and drive 1.5 miles to the park on the left (at 8220 Scotts Valley Road).

Contact: Kelly's Family Kampground and RV Park, 707/263-5754.

33 MIDDLE CREEK CAMPGROUND

Scenic rating: 6

in Mendocino National Forest

See map page 580

This camp is not widely known, but it's known well enough as an off-highway-vehicle staging area. Some call it "CC Camp." It is at 2,000 feet at the confluence of the West and East Forks of Middle Creek. An easy track for beginners on dirt bikes and OHVs is here.

RV sites, facilities: There are 23 sites for tents or RVs up to 30 feet (no hookups). Picnic tables and fire grills are provided. Drinking water and vault toilets are available. Leashed pets are permitted.

Reservations, fees: Reservations are not accepted. Sites are $4 per night, $8 per night for

a double site, $2 per night for an additional vehicle. Open year-round.

Directions: From Ukiah on U.S. 101, drive north to the junction with Highway 20. Turn east on Highway 20 and drive to the town of Upper Lake and Mendenhall Avenue. Turn left on Mendenhall Avenue (which becomes Forest Road M1) and drive eight miles to the camp on the right side of the road.

Contact: Mendocino National Forest, Upper Lake Ranger District, 707/275-2361, fax 707/275-0676.

34 DAVIS FLAT

Scenic rating: 1

in Mendocino National Forest
See map page 580

This camp was a victim to the forest fire that swept through this area in August 2001. It is across the road from Fouts and South Fork campgrounds. All three are in a designated off-highway-vehicle area, so expect OHVers, especially in the winter; campers are allowed to ride their OHVs from the campground. This isn't the quietest camp around, but there is some good hiking in the area to the immediate west in the Snow Mountain Wilderness. The elevation is 1,700 feet.

RV sites, facilities: There are 60 dispersed sites for tents or RVs of any length (no hookups). Picnic tables and fire grills are provided. Drinking water and vault toilets are available. Garbage must be packed out. Some facilities are wheelchair accessible. Leashed pets are permitted.

Reservations, fees: Reservations are not accepted. There is no fee for camping. Open year-round, weather permitting.

Directions: From I-5 at Maxwell, turn west on Maxwell-Sites Road and drive to Sites. Turn left on Sites-Lodoga Road and continue to Lodoga. Turn right on Lodoga-Stonyford Road and loop around East Park Reservoir to reach Stonyford. From Stonyford, turn west on Fouts Springs Road/County Road M10 and drive

about nine miles to Forest Road 18N03. Turn right and drive one mile to the campground on your left.

Contact: Mendocino National Forest, Grindstone Ranger District, Stonyford Work Center, 530/963-3128, fax 530/963-3173.

35 MILL VALLEY

Scenic rating: 5

near Letts Lake in Mendocino National Forest
See map page 580

This camp is beside Lily Pond, a little, teeny guy, with larger Letts Lake just a mile away. Since Lily Pond does not have trout and Letts Lake does, this camp gets far less traffic than its counterpart. The area is crisscrossed with numerous creeks, OHV routes, and Forest Service roads, making it a great adventure for owners of four-wheel drives who are allowed to drive their OHVs from the campground. The elevation is 4,200 feet.

RV sites, facilities: There are 15 sites for tents or RVs up to 18 feet (no hookups). Picnic tables and fire stoves are provided. Vault toilets and drinking water are available. Leashed pets are permitted.

Reservations, fees: Reservations are not accepted. Sites are $8 per night. Open mid-April–October, weather permitting.

Directions: From I-5 at Maxwell, turn west on Maxwell-Sites Road and drive to Sites and Sites-Lodoga Road. Turn left on Sites-Lodoga Road and continue to Lodoga and Lodoga-Stonyford Road. Turn right on Lodoga-Stonyford Road and loop around East Park Reservoir to reach Stonyford and Fouts Spring Road. Turn west on Fouts Springs Road/County Road M10 and drive about 16 miles into national forest (where the road becomes Forest Service 17N02) to the camp access road on the left. Turn left and drive 0.25 mile to the camp.

Contact: Mendocino National Forest, Grindstone Ranger District, Stonyford Work Center, 530/963-3128, fax 530/963-3173.

CALIFORNIA

CALIFORNIA

36 LETTS LAKE COMPLEX

Scenic rating: 9

in Mendocino National Forest
See map page 580

An increasingly popular spot is Letts Lake, a 35-acre, spring-fed lake set in a mixed conifer forest at 4,500 feet just south of the Snow Mountain Wilderness. There are four main loops, each with a separate campground: Main, Stirrup, Saddle, and Spillway. The complex is on the east side of the lake. No motors are allowed at Letts Lake, making it ideal for canoes, rafts, and float tubes. Swimming is allowed, although the shoreline is rocky. This lake is stocked with rainbow trout in the early summer and is known also for black bass. It's a designated historical landmark, the site where the homesteaders known as the Letts brothers were murdered. While that may not impress you, the views to the north of the Snow Mountain Wilderness will. In addition, there are several natural springs that can be fun to hunt up. By the way, after such a long drive to get here, don't let your eagerness cause you to stop at Lily Pond (on the left, one mile before reaching Letts Lake), because there are no trout in it.

RV sites, facilities: There are four campgrounds with 44 sites for tents or RVs up to 20 feet (no hookups). Picnic tables and fire rings are provided. Drinking water and vault toilets are available. A picnic area is nearby. Some facilities are wheelchair accessible, including a fishing pier. Leashed pets are permitted.

Reservations, fees: Reservations are not accepted. Sites are $10 per night, and there is a 14-day limit. Open May–October.

Directions: From I-5 at Maxwell, turn west on Maxwell-Sites Road and drive to Sites and Sites-Lodoga Road. Turn left on Sites-Lodoga Road and continue to Lodoga and Lodoga-Stonyford Road. Turn right on Lodoga-Stonyford Road and loop around East Park Reservoir to reach Stonyford and Fouts Spring Road. Turn west on Fouts Springs Road/County Road M10 and drive about 18 miles into national forest (where the road becomes Forest Service 17N02) to the campground on the east side of Letts Lake.

Contact: Mendocino National Forest, Grindstone Ranger District, Stonyford Work Center, 530/963-3128, fax 530/963-3173.

37 NICE HOLIDAY HARBOR RV PARK AND MARINA

Scenic rating: 7

on Clear Lake
See map page 581

This is one of the most popular resorts at the north end of Clear Lake. It is ideal for boaters, with a marina, gas, and a major docking complex. Fishing for bass is good in this area, along old docks and submerged pilings. Waterskiing just offshore is also good, with the north end of the lake often more calm than the water to points south. The elevation is about 2,000 feet. Unlike in several privately owned campgrounds in this area, no long-term rentals are permitted, a plus for vacationers. Note: At the time of publication, this resort was being sold; check current status.

RV sites, facilities: There are 30 sites with full or partial hookups (30 amps) for RVs of any length; some are pull-through. No tents. Picnic tables are provided. Restrooms have coin showers. A recreation room, modem access, a dump station, a coin laundry, and ice are available. An enclosed marina with 150 boat slips, a boat ramp, and an adjacent beach are also available. Leashed pets are permitted.

Reservations, fees: Reservations are accepted. Sites are $22 per night, $3 per person per night for more than two people. Open year-round.

Directions: From north of Ukiah on U.S. 101, drive north to the junction with Highway 20. Turn east on Highway 20 and drive to the town of Nice and Howard Avenue. Turn right on Howard Avenue and drive 200 feet to the park at the end of the road at 3605 Lakeshore Boulevard.

Contact: Nice Holiday Harbor RV Park and Marina, 707/274-1136, www.niceholiday harbor.com.

38 FANTASY COTTAGES BED AND BREAKFAST AND RV RESORT

Scenic rating: 6

on Clear Lake

See map page 581

Lucerne is known for its harbor and its long stretch of well-kept public beaches along the shore of Clear Lake. The town offers a shopping district, restaurants, and cafés. In summer, crappie fishing is good at night from the boat docks.

RV sites, facilities: There are 16 sites with full hookups (30 amps) for RVs up to 45 feet and an area for tents. One RV site is pull-through. Two cottages are also available. Picnic tables and barbecues are provided. Restrooms have showers. A dump station, a coin laundry, pier, moorings, bait and tackle, a fish-cleaning station, a boat ramp, a convenience store, wine-tasting room, a picnic area, and ice are available. Leashed pets are permitted.

Reservations, fees: Reservations are accepted. Sites are $13–25 per night. Weekly and monthly rates available. Open year-round.

Directions: From north of Ukiah on U.S. 101 (or from Williams on I-5), turn on Highway 20 and drive to the east side of the town of Lucerne to the resort at 6720 East Highway 20.

Contact: Fantasy Cottages Bed and Breakfast and RV Resort, 707/274-7715, www.fantasycottages resort.com.

39 GLENHAVEN BEACH CAMP AND MARINA

Scenic rating: 6

on Clear Lake

See map page 581

This makes a good base camp for all boaters, water-skiers, and anglers. It is on a peninsula on the eastern shore of Clear Lake, with nearby Indian Beach providing a good recreation and water-play spot. In addition, it is a short boat ride out to Anderson Island, Weekend Island, and Buckingham Point, where bass fishing can be excellent along shaded tules. Note that in addition to the campsites listed, there are another 22 sites occupied by long-term or permanent renters.

RV sites, facilities: There are 23 sites with full or partial hookups (30 amps) for RVs up to 35 feet and tents. Picnic tables and fire rings are provided. Drinking water, restrooms with showers and flush toilets, a marina with gas, a pier, mooring, a convenience store, bait and tackle, a boat ramp, boat and personal watercraft rentals, and a recreation room are available. A boat ramp and boat rentals are available nearby. Leashed pets are permitted.

Reservations, fees: Reservations are accepted. Sites are $18–20 per night, $2 per person per night for more than two people. Some credit cards accepted. Open year-round.

Directions: From north of Ukiah on U.S. 101 (or I-5 at Williams), turn on Highway 20 and drive to Clear Lake and the town of Glenhaven (four miles northwest of Clearlake Oaks). In Glenhaven, continue on Highway 20 to the camp (lakeside) at 9625 East Highway 20.

Contact: Glenhaven Beach Camp and Marina, 707/998-3406.

40 CLEAR LAKE STATE PARK

Scenic rating: 9

in Kelseyville at Clear Lake

See map page 581

If you have fallen in love with Clear Lake and its surrounding oak woodlands, it is difficult to find a better spot than at Clear Lake State Park. It sits on the western shore of Clear Lake, and though the oak woodlands flora means you can seem quite close to your camping neighbors, the proximity to quality boating, water sports, and fishing makes the lack of privacy worth it. Reservations are a necessity in summer. That stands to reason, with excellent bass fishing from boats beside a tule-lined shoreline near the park and good catfishing in the sloughs that run through the park. Some campsites have water frontage. The elevation is 1,500 feet.

CALIFORNIA

Clear Lake is California's largest natural freshwater lake within state borders, and it has 150 miles of shoreline. Despite its name, the lake is not clear but green and, in late summer, rather soupy with algae and water grass in certain areas. The high nutrients in the lake give rise to a flourishing aquatic food chain. With that comes the highest number of large bass of any lake in Northern California. A few short hiking trails are also available at the park. The self-guided Indian Nature Trail passes through the site of what was once a Pomo village. Rangers here are friendly, helpful, and provide reliable fishing information. Junior ranger programs and guided walks for bird and flower identification are also available.

RV sites, facilities: There are 147 sites for tents or RVs up to 35 feet, two group sites for up to 40 people each, and two hike-in/bike-in sites. No hookups. Picnic tables and fire rings are provided. Drinking water, restrooms with coin showers and flush toilets, and a dump station are available. A boat ramp, dock, fish-cleaning stations, a boat battery charging station, a visitors center, Wi-Fi, and a swimming beach are available nearby. A grocery store, a coin laundry, propane gas, a restaurant, and a gas station are within three miles. Some facilities are wheelchair accessible, including the boat ramp. Leashed pets are permitted in the campgrounds.

Reservations, fees: Reservations are accepted ($7.50 reservation fee) at 800/444-PARK (800/444-7275) or www.reserveamerica.com. Sites are $20–30 per night, $6 per night for an additional vehicle, $66 per night for a group site, $3 per person per night for hike-in/bike-in sites. Boat launching is $8 per day. Open year-round.

Directions: From Vallejo, drive north on Highway 29 to Lower Lake. Turn left on Highway 29 and drive seven miles to Soda Bay Road. Turn right on Soda Bay Road and drive 11 miles to the park entrance on the right side of the road.

From Kelseyville on Highway 29, take the Kelseyville exit and turn north on Main Street. Drive a short distance to State Street. Turn right and drive 0.25 mile to Gaddy Lane. Turn right

on Gaddy Lane and drive about two miles to Soda Bay Road. Turn right and drive one mile to the park entrance on the left.

Contact: Clear Lake State Park, 707/279-4293, www.parks.ca.gov.

41 EDGEWATER RESORT AND RV PARK

Scenic rating: 7

on Clear Lake

See map page 581

Soda Bay is one of Clear Lake's prettiest and most intimate spots, and this camp provides excellent access. It also provides friendly, professional service. Both waterskiing and fishing for bass and bluegill are excellent in this part of the lake. The resort has 600 feet of lake frontage, including 300 feet of swimming beach and a 230-foot fishing pier. This resort specializes in groups and family reunions. Wine tasting, casinos, and golfing are nearby. Insider's tip: This park is very pet friendly and has occasional doggie socials.

RV sites, facilities: There are 61 sites with full hookups (20, 30, and 50 amps) for tents or RVs of any length, along with eight cabins. Picnic tables and fire grills are provided. Restrooms have showers. Cable TV, modem access, a clubhouse, group facilities, a general store, a coin laundry, a seasonal heated swimming pool, horseshoes, volleyball, and table tennis are available. A seasonal swimming beach, a pet station, a dog run, bait and tackle, a boat ramp, a fishing pier, boat docking, a fish-cleaning station, and watercraft rentals are available on the premises. Firewood is available for purchase. Leashed pets are permitted.

Reservations, fees: Reservations are accepted at 800/396-6224. Sites are $30–40 per night, $5 per person per night for more than two people, $2.50 per pet per night. Boat launching is $5 per day. Winter discounts and weekly rates are available. Some credit cards accepted. Open year-round.

Directions: In Kelseyville on Highway 29, take the Merritt Road exit and drive on Merritt Road for two miles (it becomes Gaddy Lane) to Soda

Bay Road. Turn right on Soda Bay Road and drive three miles to the campground entrance on the left at 6420 Soda Bay Road.

Contact: Edgewater Resort and RV Park, 707/279-0208, www.edgewaterresort.net.

42 SHAW'S SHADY ACRES

Scenic rating: 7

on Cache Creek

See map page 581

Shaw's Shady Acres is beside Cache Creek, just south of Clear Lake. Canoeing and kayaking are popular. The fishing for catfish is often quite good on summer nights in Cache Creek, a deep green, slow-moving water that looks more like a slough in a Mississippi bayou than a creek. Waterfront campsites with scattered walnut, ash, and oak trees are available. Clear Lake (the lake, not the town) is a short drive north, and a state park is across the creek. Besides the campsites mentioned, there are an additional 36 long-term or permanent sites. Note: At the time of publication, this campground was in the process of a sale; check for current status.

RV sites, facilities: There are 13 sites, six with full hookups (30 amps) and seven with partial hookups, for RVs up to 38 feet and tents. Picnic tables and barbecues are provided. Restrooms have showers. A dump station, fishing dock, fishing boat rentals, a boat ramp, a coin laundry, swimming pool (seasonal), recreation patio, fishing supplies, and a convenience store are available. Leashed pets are allowed, with certain restrictions.

Reservations, fees: Reservations are recommended. Sites are $22 per night, $3 per person per night for more than two people, $0.50 per pet per night. Boat launching is $1–3 per day. Open year-round.

Directions: From the town of Lower Lake, drive north on Highway 53 for 1.3 miles to Old Highway 53. Turn left on Old Highway 53 and then almost immediately you will arrive at Cache Creek Way. Turn left and drive 0.25 mile to the park entrance at 7805 Cache Creek Way.

Contact: Shaw's Shady Acres, 707/994-2236.

43 FUNTIME RV PARK AND WATERSPORTS

Scenic rating: 7

on Clear Lake

See map page 581

This is one of several privately operated parks near the mouth of Cache Creek at the southern end of Clear Lake. Anderson Marsh State Park is nearby. Note that a mobile-home park is adjacent to the campground.

RV sites, facilities: There are 80 sites with full hookups (30 and 50 amps) for tents or RVs of any length, four park-model cabins, and two cabins. Most sites are pull-through. Picnic tables and barbecues are provided. Restrooms have flush toilets and showers. Cable TV, modem access, boat rentals, a pier, a boat ramp, a fish-cleaning station, a seasonal swimming pool, a wading pool, fishing supplies, a coin laundry, an arcade, and a convenience store are available. Some facilities are wheelchair accessible. Leashed pets are permitted.

Reservations, fees: Reservations are accepted. Sites are $17–30 per night, $3 per person per night for more than two people. Some credit cards accepted. Open year-round.

Directions: From the town of Lower Lake, drive north on Highway 53 for 1.3 miles to Old Highway 53. Turn left on Old Highway 53 and drive 1.2 miles to the resort entrance on the left.

Contact: Funtime RV Park, 707/994-6267, www.funtimervparks.com.

44 CACHE CREEK CANYON REGIONAL PARK

Scenic rating: 7

near Rumsey

See map page 581

This is the best campground in Yolo County, yet it's known by few out-of-towners. It is at 1,300 feet beside Cache Creek, which is the closest river to the Bay Area that provides whitewater rafting opportunities. This section of river features primarily Class I and II water, ideal for inflatable kayaks and overnight trips. One rapid, Big Mother, is sometimes considered Class III, though that might be a stretch. Occasionally, huge catfish are caught in this area.

RV sites, facilities: There are 45 sites for tents or RVs up to 42 feet (no hookups), and three group sites can accommodate 20–30 people each. Picnic tables, barbecue pits, and fire rings are provided. Drinking water, restrooms with flush toilets, and a dump station are available. Some facilities are wheelchair accessible. Leashed pets are permitted.

Reservations, fees: Reservations are accepted only for group sites at 530/666-8115. Sites are $19 per night, $5 per night per additional vehicle, $2 per pet per night. Group sites are $165 per night. Off-season discounts available. Discount for Yolo County residents. Open year-round.

Directions: From Vacaville on I-80, turn north on I-505 and drive 21 miles to Madison and the junction with Highway 16 west. Turn northwest on Highway 16 and drive northwest for about 35 miles to the town of Rumsey. From Rumsey, continue west on Highway 16 for five miles to the park entrance on the left at 1475 State Highway 16.

Contact: Cache Creek Canyon Regional Park, Yolo County, 530/666-8115, fax 530/666-8837, www.yolocounty.org/prm/default/htm.

are also two cottages and 27 cabins. Picnic tables, barbecues, and fire rings are provided. Drinking water, restrooms with flush toilets and showers, Wi-Fi and modem access, a heated seasonal pool, a spa, a recreation room, a playground, a dump station, a convenience store, group facilities, ice, firewood, a coin laundry, and propane gas are available. Some facilities are wheelchair accessible. Leashed pets are permitted, with certain breeds prohibited; call for details.

Reservations, fees: Reservations are accepted at 800/562-4188. Sites are $27–49 per night, $3–5 per person per night for more than two people. Some credit cards accepted. Open year-round.

Directions: From U.S. 101 in Petaluma, take the Washington Street exit to Washington Street. Turn west on Washington Street and drive through Petaluma (Washington Street becomes Bodega Highway) and continue for 17 miles to Highway 1. Continue straight (west) on Highway 1 for eight miles to Bodega Bay. Turn north on Highway 1 and drive 66 miles to Point Arena. Continue north on Highway 1 for about six miles to Kinney Road. Turn west (toward the ocean) and drive one mile to the campground at 44330 Kinney Road.

Contact: Manchester Beach KOA, 707/882-2375, fax 707/882-3104, www.manchester beachkoa.com.

45 MANCHESTER BEACH KOA

Scenic rating: 7

north of Point Arena at Manchester State Beach
See map page 581

This is a privately operated KOA park beside Highway 1 and near the beautiful Manchester State Beach. Cute little log cabins, a great plus, come complete with electric heat. They can provide a great sense of privacy, and after a good sleep, campers are ready to explore the adjacent state park.

RV sites, facilities: There are 43 sites for tents or RVs of any length with full or partial hookups (30 and 50 amps) and 57 tent sites. There

46 MANCHESTER STATE PARK

Scenic rating: 8

near Point Arena
See map page 581

Manchester State Park is a beautiful park on the Sonoma coast, set near the Garcia River with the town of Point Arena to the nearby north providing a supply point. If you hit it during one of the rare times when the skies are clear and the wind is down, the entire area will seem aglow in magical sunbeams. The park features 760 acres of beach, sand dunes, and grasslands, with 18,000 feet of ocean frontage and five miles of gentle sandy beach stretching southward toward the Point Arena Lighthouse. The beach curves to form a catch basin for sea debris, which explains the high volume of driftwood here. Alder Creek Trail is a great hike, routed north along beachfront to the mouth of Alder Creek and its beautiful coastal lagoon. This is where the San Andreas Fault heads off from land and into the sea. In winter, the main attraction is steelhead fishing in the Garcia River. In spring and early summer, coastal wildflowers abound, including sea pinks, poppies, lupines, baby blue eyes, and blue iris. The park provides habitat for tundra swans. The region near the park is grazing land for sheep and cattle. Sixteen campsites were closed in 2004 to protect an endangered species, the Point Arena mountain beaver.

RV sites, facilities: There are 18 sites for tents or RVs up to 32 feet, 10 environmental sites (a one-mile walk in), and one group site for up to 40 people and RVs up to 21 feet. No hookups. Picnic tables and fire grills are provided. Drinking water, vault toilets, and a dump station are available. The environmental sites have pit toilets, picnic tables, and fire rings but no drinking water, and garbage must be packed out. Leashed pets are permitted. No dogs are allowed in environmental sites.

Reservations, fees: Reservations are accepted only for the group site ($7.50 reservation fee) at 800/444-PARK (800/444-7275) or www.reserveamerica.com. Sites are $15 per night, $6 per night for an additional vehicle, $15 per night for environmental sites, $90 per night for group site. Open year-round.

Directions: On U.S. 101 north of Santa Rosa, turn west on River Road and drive 16 miles to Guerneville and Highway 116. Continue west on Highway 116 and drive about 20 miles to Highway 1 at Jenner. Turn north on Highway 1 and drive 55 miles to Point Arena. From Point Arena, continue north about five miles to Kinney Lane. Turn left and drive one mile to the campground entrance on the right.

Contact: Manchester State Beach, 707/882-2463; Mendocino District, 707/937-5804, fax 707/937-2953, www.parks.ca.gov.

47 ROLLERVILLE JUNCTION

Scenic rating: 7

near Point Arena

See map page 581

The location makes Rollerview Junction an attractive spot, with the beautiful Manchester State Beach, Alder Creek, and Garcia River all available nearby on one of California's most attractive stretches of coastline. Point Arena Lighthouse and a fishing pier are also nearby. The elevation of the camp is 220 feet. Insider's tip: More than 1,100 acres of public land across the road from this campground are available for exploring; this is prime ocean frontage property bought from private owners.

RV sites, facilities: There are 34 sites with full hookups (30 and 50 amps) for RVs of any length, 10 tent sites, five sleeping cabins, and two park-model cabins. Some sites are pull-through. Picnic tables and fire rings are provided. Drinking water, restrooms with flush toilets and showers, a spa, a seasonal heated swimming pool, cable TV hookups, modem access, a dump station, a coin laundry, a seasonal café, a convenience store, and propane gas are available. Some facilities are wheelchair accessible. Leashed pets are permitted.

Reservations, fees: Reservations are accepted by telephone at 800/910-4317. Sites are $30–40 per night, $3–5 per person per night for more than two people. Some credit cards accepted. Open year-round.

Directions: On U.S. 101 north of Santa Rosa, turn west on River Road and drive 16 miles to Guerneville and Highway 116. Continue west on Highway 116 and drive about 20 miles to Highway 1 at Jenner. Turn north on Highway 1 and drive 55 miles to Point Arena. From Point Arena, continue north for 1.5 miles to Point Arena Lighthouse Road and the campground on the left (west side) at 22990 North Highway 1.

Contact: Rollerville Junction, 707/882-2440, fax 707/882-3049.

CALIFORNIA

CALIFORNIA

48 ANCHOR BAY CAMPGROUND

Scenic rating: 8

near Gualala

See map page 581

This is a quiet and beautiful stretch of California coast. The six-acre campground is on the ocean side of Highway 1 north of Gualala, with sites set at ocean level as well as amid trees—take your pick. Nearby Gualala Regional Park, six miles to the south, provides an excellent easy hike, the headlands-to-beach loop with coastal views, a lookout of the Gualala River, and many giant cypress trees. In winter, the nearby Gualala River attracts large but elusive steelhead.

RV sites, facilities: There are 37 sites for tents or RVs up to 40 feet; 12 sites have partial hookups (15 amps). Picnic tables and fire pits are provided. Drinking water, restrooms with flush toilets and coin showers, Wi-Fi, a fish-cleaning room, a dive gear washroom, a picnic area, and a dump station are available. Leashed pets are permitted, with certain restrictions, including a maximum of two per site.

Reservations, fees: Reservations are accepted ($10 reservation fee). Sites are $38–42 per night, $3–5 per person per night for more than two people, $20 per night for an additional vehicle, $3 per pet per stay. Boat launching is $5 per day. Some credit cards accepted. Open year-round.

Directions: On U.S. 101 north of Santa Rosa, turn west on River Road and drive 16 miles to Guerneville and Highway 116. Continue west on Highway 116 and drive about 13.1 miles to Highway 1 at Jenner. Turn north on Highway 1 and drive 38 miles to Gualala. Continue four miles north on Highway 1 to the campground on the left (west) side of the road.

Contact: Anchor Bay Campground, 707/884-4222, www.abcamp.com.

49 CLOVERDALE KOA

Scenic rating: 7

near the Russian River

See map page 581

This KOA campground is just above the Russian River in the Alexander Valley wine country, just south of Cloverdale. The park is both rustic and tidy. The hillside pool has a nice view. In addition, a fishing pond is stocked with largemouth bass, bluegill, and catfish. On moonless nights, this is a great place for stargazing. Bird-watching is another pastime in this area. The nearby Russian River is an excellent beginner's route in an inflatable kayak or canoe. The nearby winery in Asti makes for a popular side trip.

RV sites, facilities: There are 89 sites with full hookups (30 and 50 amps) for RVs of any length, 49 sites for tents, 18 cabins, and five lodges. Some sites are pull-through. Picnic tables and fire grills are provided. Restrooms have flush toilets and showers. Wi-Fi, a solar-heated swimming pool, a playground, a dump station, a coin laundry, a recreation room, mini golf, nature trails, a catch-and-release fishpond, weekend entertainment in the summer, and a convenience and gift store are available. Some facilities are wheelchair accessible. Leashed pets are permitted, with certain restrictions.

Reservations, fees: Reservations are accepted at 800/562-4042. Sites are $35–50 per night, $8 per person per night for more than two people, $8 per night for an additional vehicle. Some credit cards accepted. Open year-round.

Directions: From Cloverdale on U.S. 101, take the Central Cloverdale exit, which puts you on Asti Road. Drive straight on Asti Road to 1st Street. Turn right (east) and drive a short distance to River Road. Turn right (south) and drive four miles to Asti Ridge Road. Turn left and drive to the campground entrance.

In summer/fall: South of Cloverdale on U.S. 101, take the Asti exit to Asti Road. Turn right (south) on Asti Road and drive 1.5 miles to Washington School Road. Turn left (east) and drive 1.5 miles to Asti Ridge Road. Turn right and drive to the campground entrance. (Note:

This route is usually open Memorial Day weekend to late November, when a seasonal bridge is in place.) Both routes are well signed.

Contact: Cloverdale KOA, 707/894-3337, www.winecountrykoa.com.

50 BOGGS MOUNTAIN DEMONSTRATION STATE FOREST

Scenic rating: 5

near Middletown

See map page 581

This overlooked spot is in a state forest that covers 3,500 acres of pine and Douglas fir. Two campgrounds adjoin here. This is a popular destination for the region's equestrians. There are numerous trails for horses, hikers, and bikers. Remember: Equestrians have the right of way over hikers and bikers, and hikers have the right of way over bikers. Got it? The International Mountain Biking Association has chosen this as one of the top 10 riding areas in the country. There is a 14-mile trail system available that started as a series of hand-built fire lines. Note that in early fall, this area is open to deer hunting. Boggs is one of nine state forests managed with the purpose of demonstrating economical forest management, which means there is logging along with compatible recreation.

RV sites, facilities: There are 22 sites for tents or RVs up to 22 feet (no hookups). No drinking water is available. Picnic tables and fire pits are provided. Vault toilets are available. Garbage must be packed out. A coin laundry, pizza parlor, and gas station are within two miles. Horses are permitted. Leashed pets are permitted.

Reservations, fees: Reservations are not accepted. There is no fee for camping. Self-registration required. Open year-round.

Directions: From Vallejo, drive north on Highway 29 past Calistoga to Middletown and the junction with Highway 175. Turn left (north) on Highway 175 and drive seven miles (through the town of Cobb) to Forestry Road. Turn right and drive one mile to the campgrounds on the left.

Contact: Boggs Mountain Demonstration State Forest, 707/928-4378.

51 JELLYSTONE RV PARK

Scenic rating: 7

near Cobb Mountain

See map page 581

This camp has a trout creek, a pond with canoe and kayak rentals in summer, plus plenty of hiking and bird-watching opportunities. Kelsey Creek runs through the campground. In addition, horseback riding and hot-air balloon rides are available nearby. This camp is near Highway 175 between Middletown and Clear Lake, and while there is a parade of vacation traffic on Highway 29, relatively few people take the longer route on Highway 175. Cobb Mountain looms nearby. Golf courses are in the vicinity. This park was formerly called Beaver Creek RV Park.

RV sites, facilities: There are 97 sites with full hookups (30 and 50 amps) for RVs up to 40 feet, 10 tent sites, and four cabins. Most sites are pull-through. Picnic tables and fire rings are provided. Drinking water, restrooms with showers, group facilities, a coin laundry, Wi-Fi and modem access, a seasonal swimming pool, kayak and pedal boat rentals, boating pond, a playground, horseshoes, miniature golf, a recreation hall, a picnic area, an athletic field, basketball, volleyball, horseshoes, firewood, ice, propane, and a camp store are available. Some facilities are wheelchair accessible. Leashed pets are permitted.

Reservations, fees: Reservations are accepted. Sites are $25–35 per night, $3–5 per person per night for more than two people. Some credit cards accepted. Open year-round.

Directions: From Vallejo, drive north on Highway 29 past Calistoga to Middletown and the junction with Highway 175. Turn north on Highway 175 (to Cobb) and drive 12 miles to Bottle Rock Road. Turn left and drive three miles to the campground entrance on the left side of the road at 14117 Bottle Rock Road.

Contact: Jellystone RV Park, 707/928-4322, www.jellystonecobbmtn.com.

CALIFORNIA

52 GUALALA POINT REGIONAL PARK

Scenic rating: 8

at Sonoma County Regional Park

See map page 581

This is a dramatic spot near the ocean, close to the mouth of the Gualala River. The campground is on the east side of the highway, about 0.3 mile from the ocean. A trail along the bluff provides an easy hiking adventure; on the west side of the highway other trails to the beach are available.

RV sites, facilities: There are 19 sites for tents or RVs up to 25 feet (no hookups), six walk-in tent sites, and one hike-in/bike-in site. Picnic tables and fire rings are provided. Drinking water, restrooms with flush toilets and coin showers, a dump station, and firewood are available. Some facilities are wheelchair accessible. Leashed pets are permitted with a valid rabies certificate.

Reservations, fees: Reservations are accepted ($7 reservation fee) on weekdays at 707/565-2267. Sites are $17 per night, $5 per person per night for hike-in/bike-in site, $6 per night for an additional vehicle, $1 per pet per night. Open year-round.

Directions: On U.S. 101 north of Santa Rosa, turn west on River Road and drive 16 miles to Guerneville and Highway 116. Continue west on Highway 116 and drive about 20 miles to Highway 1 at Jenner. Turn north on Highway 1 and drive 38 miles to Gualala. Turn right at the park entrance (a day-use area is on the west side of the highway).

Contact: Gualala Point Regional Park, 707/785-2377, www.sonoma-county.org/parks.

53 SALT POINT STATE PARK

Scenic rating: 9

near Fort Ross

See map page 581

This is a gorgeous piece of Sonoma coast, highlighted by Fisk Mill Cove, inshore kelp beds, outstanding short hikes, and abalone diving. In fact, this is one of the finest diving areas for red abalone in the state. There is also an underwater reserve for divers, which is a protected area. Unfortunately, there are also diving accidents that are due to the occasional large surf, strong currents, and rocky shoreline. There are two campgrounds here, Gerstle Cove Campground and the much larger Woodside Campground. Great hikes include Bluff Trail and Stump Beach Trail (great views). During abalone season, this is one of the best and most popular spots on the Northern California coast. The Kruse Rhododendron Reserve is within the park and definitely worth the stroll. This is a 317-acre conservation reserve that features second-growth redwoods, Douglas firs, tan oak, and many rhododendrons, with five miles of hiking trails. After the fall rains, this area is popular for mushroom hunters (the Kruse Rhododendron Reserve is closed to mushroom picking). Mushroom hunters must park in the area open to picking and be limited to five pounds per day. Of course, this can be a dangerous hobby; only eat mushrooms you can identify as safe. But you knew that, right?

RV sites, facilities: At Gerstle Cove Campground, there are 30 sites for tents or RVs up to 31 feet. At Woodside Campground, there are 79 sites for tents or RVs up to 31 feet, 20 walk-in tent sites (about a 300-yard walk), 10 hike-in/bike-in sites, a group site that can accommodate up to 40 people, and a primitive overflow area for self-contained vehicles. No hookups. Picnic tables and fire rings are provided. Drinking water and flush toilets are available. Summer interpretive programs are also available; firewood is available for purchase. The picnic area and one hiking trail are wheelchair accessible. Leashed pets are permitted, except on trails.

Reservations, fees: Reservations are accepted ($7.50 reservation fee) at 800/444-PARK (800/444-7275) or www.reserveamerica.com. Sites are $25 per night, $6 per night for an additional vehicle, $15 per night for walk-in and overflow sites, $3 per person per night for hike-in/bike-in sites, $150 for the group site. Open year-round.

Directions: On U.S. 101 north of Santa Rosa, turn west on River Road and drive 16 miles to Guerneville and Highway 116. Continue west on Highway 116 and drive 13.1 miles to Highway 1 at Jenner. Turn north on Highway 1 and drive about 20 miles to the park entrance; Woodside Campground is on the right and Gerstle Cove is on the left.

Contact: Salt Point State Park, 707/847-3221; Russian River District, 707/865-2391, fax 707/865-2046, www.parks.ca.gov.

54 OCEAN COVE CAMPGROUND

Scenic rating: 8

on the ocean five miles north of Fort Ross

See map page 581   BEST (

The highlights here are the campsites on a bluff overlooking the ocean. Alas, it can be foggy during the summer. A good side trip is to Fort Ross, with a stellar easy hike available on the Fort Ross Trail, which features a walk through an old colonial fort as well as great coastal views, excellent for whale-watching. There is also excellent hiking at Stillwater Cove Regional Park, just a mile south off Highway 1.

RV sites, facilities: There are 125 pull-through sites for tents or RVs of any length (no hookups). Picnic tables and fire grills are provided. Drinking water, chemical toilets, and coin showers are available. A boat launch, a grocery store, fishing supplies, and diving gear sales are available nearby. Leashed pets are permitted.

Reservations, fees: Reservations are not accepted. Sites are $17 per night per vehicle, $2 per pet per night, $8 per day for boat launching. Some credit cards accepted. Open April–November.

Directions: On U.S. 101 north of Santa Rosa, turn west on River Road and drive 16 miles to Guerneville and Highway 116. Continue west on Highway 116 and drive about 13 miles to Highway 1 at Jenner. Turn north on Highway 1 and drive 17 miles north on Highway 1 (five miles north of Fort Ross) to the campground entrance on the left.

Contact: Ocean Cove Campground, 707/847-3422, www.oceancove.org.

55 STILLWATER COVE REGIONAL PARK

Scenic rating: 8

near Fort Ross

See map page 581

Stillwater Cove has a dramatic rock-strewn cove and sits on a classic chunk of Sonoma coast. The campground is sometimes overlooked, since it is a county-operated park and not on the state park reservation system. One of the region's great hikes is available here: Stockoff Creek Loop, with the trailhead at the day-use parking lot. In a little more than a mile, the trail is routed through forest with both firs and redwoods, and then along a pretty stream. To get beach access, you need to cross Highway 1 and then drop to the cove.

RV sites, facilities: There are 23 sites for tents or RVs up to 30 feet (no hookups), as well as a hike-in/bike-in site. Picnic tables and fire rings are provided. Drinking water, restrooms with flush toilets and coin showers, firewood, and a dump station are available. Supplies can be obtained in Ocean Cove (one mile north) and Fort Ross. Some facilities are wheelchair accessible. Leashed pets are permitted with a valid rabies certificate.

Reservations, fees: Reservations are accepted ($7 reservation fee) at 707/565-2267 on weekdays. Sites are $17 per night, $6 per night for each additional vehicle, $5 per person per night for the hike-in/bike-in site, and $1 per pet per night. Open year-round.

Directions: On U.S. 101 north of Santa Rosa, turn west on River Road and drive 16 miles to Guerneville and Highway 116. Continue west on Highway 116 and drive about 13 miles to Highway 1 at Jenner. Turn north on Highway 1 and drive 16 miles north on Highway 1 (four miles north of Fort Ross) to the park entrance.

Contact: Stillwater Cove Regional Park, Sonoma County, 707/847-3245; Sonoma

County Regional Parks, 707/565-2041, www .sonoma-county.org/parks.

56 FORT ROSS REEF

Scenic rating: 8

at Fort Ross State Historic Park
See map page 581

Fort Ross is just as its name announces: an old fort, in this case, an old Russian fort from 1812. The campground is two miles south of the north entrance station, less than a quarter mile from the ocean. Some redwoods and pines provide cover, and some sites are open. The privacy and beauty of the campsites vary as much as in any state park camp in California. The sites at the end of the road fill up very quickly. Though the weather is relatively benign, tents are needed for protection against moisture from fog. From camp, a trail leads down to a beach, more rocky than sandy, and a one-mile trail leads to the fort. As a destination site, Fort Ross is known as a popular abalone diving spot, with the best areas below the campground and also at nearby Reef Terrace. It also provides good, easy hikes amid its 3,386 acres. The park features a museum in the visitors center, which is always a must-see for campers making the tour up Highway 1. Note: Mushroom picking is prohibited in this park.

RV sites, facilities: There are 20 sites for tents or RVs up to 18 feet (no hookups). Picnic tables, food lockers, and fire rings are provided. Drinking water and flush toilets are available. Supplies can be obtained nearby. A visitors center and guided tours and programs are available. Some facilities are wheelchair accessible. Leashed pets are permitted.

Reservations, fees: Reservations are not accepted. Sites are $15 per night, $6 per night for an additional vehicle. Open April–November, weather permitting.

Directions: On U.S. 101 north of Santa Rosa, turn west on River Road and drive 16 miles to Guerneville and Highway 116. Continue west on Highway 116 and drive about 13 miles to Highway 1 at Jenner. Turn north on Highway 1 and drive 10 miles to the (Fort Ross Reef) campground entrance. To reach the main state park entrance, drive north for two miles.

Contact: Fort Ross State Historic Park, 707/847-3286 or 707/847-3708.

57 HILTON PARK FAMILY CAMPGROUND

Scenic rating: 6

on the Russian River
See map page 581

This lush, wooded park is on the banks of the Russian River, with a choice of open or secluded sites. The highlight of the campground is a large, beautiful beach that offers access for swimming, fishing, and canoeing. You get a choice of many recreation options in the area.

RV sites, facilities: There are 37 tent sites, five sites with partial hookups (30 amps) for RVs up to 35 feet, and eight camping cottages. Picnic tables and fire rings are provided. Restrooms have coin showers. A dishwashing area, an arcade, a playground, a coin laundry, a camp store, firewood, and ice are available. A beach is available nearby. Boat rentals are available within three miles. Leashed pets are permitted, with certain restrictions.

Reservations, fees: Reservations are recommended. Sites are $32–42 per night, $10 per person per night for more than two people, $5 per night for an additional vehicle, $5 per night per pet. Some credit cards are accepted. Open May–October.

Directions: From U.S. 101 north of Santa Rosa, take the River Road/Guerneville exit. Drive west on River Road for 11.5 miles (one mile after the metal bridge) to the campground on the left side of the road (just before the Russian River Pub) at 10750 River Road.

Contact: Hilton Park Family Campground, 707/887-9206, www.hiltonparkcampground .com.

CALIFORNIA

58 SCHOOLHOUSE CANYON CAMPGROUND

Scenic rating: 8

in the Russian River Valley

See map page 581

This campground comprises 200 acres and river access along the Russian River, campsites in a grove of large redwoods, and a parklike setting on land originally homesteaded in the 1850s. A scenic hiking trail, two miles round-trip, is routed up to a ridge for some nice views of the countryside. This overlooks Korbel Winery and vineyards, with long-distance views of several counties. Touring the adjacent Korbel Winery is a popular side trip.

RV sites, facilities: There are 45 sites for tents or RVs up to 25 feet; some sites have partial hookups. Picnic tables and fire grills are provided. Drinking water, restrooms with flush toilets and coin showers, and firewood are available. Some facilities are wheelchair accessible. Leashed pets are permitted.

Reservations, fees: Reservations are not accepted. Call for current prices. Open May–September.

Directions: From Santa Rosa, drive north on U.S. 101 about 2.5 miles and take the River Road/Guerneville exit. Drive to the stop sign, turn left on River Road, and drive 12.5 miles to the campground entrance (next to Korbel Winery) on the right.

Contact: Schoolhouse Canyon Campground, 707/869-2311.

59 WINDSORLAND RV PARK

Scenic rating: 3

near Santa Rosa

See map page 581

This developed park is close to the Russian River, the wine country to the east, redwoods to the west, and Lake Sonoma to the northwest. But with a swimming pool, playground, and recreation room, many visitors are content to stay right here, spend the night, then head out on their vacation. Note that some sites are long-term rentals.

RV sites, facilities: There are 55 sites with full hookups (30 amps) for RVs up to 35 feet, plus a separate area for tents. Restrooms have flush toilets and showers. A seasonal heated swimming pool, dump station, coin laundry, recreation room, picnic area, dog run, and playground are available. Leashed pets are permitted.

Reservations, fees: Reservations are accepted at 800/864-3407. Sites are $27–30 per night. Monthly rates available. Open year-round.

Directions: From Santa Rosa on U.S. 101, drive north for nine miles to Windsor. Take the Windsor exit, turn left on Old Redwood Highway, and drive under the freeway to the stoplight. Turn right (still on Old Redwood Highway) and drive 0.25 mile to the park on the right (9290 Old Redwood Highway).

Contact: Windsorland RV Park, 707/838-4882.

60 NAPA VALLEY STATE PARK

Scenic rating: 7

near Calistoga

See map page 581

It's always a stunner for newcomers to discover this beautiful park with redwoods and a pretty stream so close to the Napa Valley wine and spa country. Though the campsites are relatively exposed, they are set beneath a pretty oak/bay/madrone forest, with trailheads for hiking nearby. One trail is routed south from the day-use parking lot for 1.8 mile to the restored Bale Grist Mill, a giant restored waterwheel on a pretty creek. Weekend tours of the Bale Grist Mill are available in summer. Another, more scenic route, the Redwood Trail, heads up Ritchey Canyon, amid redwoods and towering Douglas fir, and along Ritchey Creek, all of it beautiful and intimate. The park covers 2,000 acres. Most of it is rugged, with elevations ranging 300–2,000 feet. In summer, temperatures can reach the 100s, which is why finding a redwood grove can be stunning. The park has more than 10 miles of trails. Those who explore will find that the forests are on the north-facing slopes while the south-facing slopes tend to be brushy. The geology here is primarily volcanic, yet the vegetation hides most of it. Bird-watchers will note that this is one of the few places where you can see six species of woodpeckers, including the star of the show, the pileated woodpecker (the size of a crow).

RV sites, facilities: There are 37 sites for tents or RVs up to 31 feet and trailers up to 24 feet, nine walk-in (up to 50 feet) tent sites, one hike-in/bike-in site, and one group tent site for up to 30 people. No hookups. Picnic tables and fire grills are provided. Drinking water, restrooms with flush toilets and coin showers, and a seasonal swimming pool are available. Supplies can be obtained four miles away in Calistoga. Some facilities are wheelchair accessible. Leashed pets are permitted, but not on trails.

Reservations, fees: Reservations are accepted ($7.50 reservation fee) at 800/444-PARK (800/444-7275) or www.reserveamerica.com. Sites are $20–25 per night, plus $6 per night for an additional vehicle; it's $2 per person per night for the hike-in/bike-in site; the fee is $66 per night for the group site, and there's a $1–3 pool fee (free for children five and under). Open year-round.

Directions: From Napa on Highway 29, drive north to St. Helena and continue north for five miles (one mile past the entrance to Bale Grist Mill State Park) to the park entrance road on the left.

Contact: Bothe–Napa Valley State Park, 707/942-4575, www.parks.ca.gov.

61 NAPA COUNTY FAIRGROUNDS

Scenic rating: 3

in Calistoga

See map page 581

What this really is, folks, is just the county fairgrounds, converted to an RV park. It is open year-round, except when the county fair is in progress. Who knows, maybe you can win a stuffed animal. What is more likely, of course, is that you have come here for the health spas, with great natural hot springs, mud baths, and assorted goodies at the health resorts in Calistoga. The downtown is within walking distance. Nearby parks for hiking include Bothe–Napa Valley and Robert Louis Stevenson State Parks. Cycling, wine tasting, and hot-air balloon rides are also popular.

RV sites, facilities: There are 78 sites with partial or full hookups (30 and 50 amps) for RVs and a lawn area for tents. Some sites are pull-through. Group sites are available by reservation only with a 10-vehicle minimum. Restrooms have flush toilets and showers. A picnic area and a dump station are available. No fires are permitted. A nine-hole golf course is adjacent to the campground area. Some facilities are wheelchair accessible. Leashed pets are permitted.

Reservations, fees: Reservations are accepted and required for groups at 707/942-5221 or by website. Sites are $10–27 per night. Some credit cards accepted. Open year-round.

Directions: From Napa on Highway 29, drive north to Calistoga, turn right on Lincoln Avenue, and drive four blocks to Fairway. Turn left and drive about four blocks to the end of the road to the campground.

Contact: Napa County Fairgrounds, 707/942-5111, fax 707/942-5125, www.napacounty fairgrounds.com.

62 PUTAH CREEK RESORT

Scenic rating: 7

on Lake Berryessa

See map page 581

This campground is at 400 feet elevation on the northern end of Lake Berryessa. The lake is well known for powerboats and water sports. The Putah Creek arm provides very good bass fishing in the spring and trout trolling in the summer. In the fall, the trout come to the surface and provide excellent fishing at the mouth of Pope Creek or Putah Creek. The resort has a small, rustic motel. There is a two-week camping limit in season. Also, there is an area within this resort filled with long-term RV sites.

RV sites, facilities: There are 125 sites for tents and 55 sites with full or partial hookups (30 and 50 amps) for RVs of any length; some sites are pull-through. Picnic tables and barbecues are provided. Vault toilets, a dump station, a coin laundry, two boat ramps, a seasonal snack bar, motel, cocktail lounge, a restaurant, propane gas, ice, and a convenience store are available. Leashed pets are permitted, with some restrictions.

Reservations, fees: Reservations are accepted at 707/966-0794. Sites are $23–28 per vehicle per night, $2 per pet per night. Some credit cards accepted. Open year-round.

Directions: From Vallejo, drive eastbound on I-80 to the Suisun Valley Road exit. Take Suisun Valley Road and drive north to Highway 121. Turn north on Highway 121 and drive five miles to Highway 128. Turn left on Highway 128 and drive five miles to Berryessa-Knoxville Road. Turn right and continue 13 miles to 7600 Knoxville Road.

Contact: Putah Creek Resort, 707/966-0775; store, 707/966-2116.

63 LAKE BERRYESSA MARINA RESORT

Scenic rating: 7

on Lake Berryessa
See map page 581

With 165 miles of shoreline, Lake Berryessa is the Bay Area's backyard water recreation headquarters, the number-one lake (in the greater Bay Area) for waterskiing, loafing, and fishing. All water sports are permitted, but the focus is on powerboating, wakeboarding, waterskiing, and tubing. This resort lies on the west shore of the main lake, one of several resorts at the lake. The addition of park-model cabins is a great plus here.

RV sites, facilities: There are 50 sites with full hookups (30 amps) for RVs up to 40 feet, an open area for tents, and 15 park-model cabins.

Picnic tables are provided, and fire grills are also provided at the tent sites. Restrooms have flush toilets and showers. A dump station, a coin laundry, a full-service marina, watercraft and houseboat rentals, and a convenience store are available. Leashed pets are permitted at RV sites but prohibited at tent sites and cabins.

Reservations, fees: Reservations are recommended. Sites are $25–30 per night, $4 per person per night for more than two people, $1 per pet per night. Boat launching is $5 per day. Some credit cards accepted. Open year-round.

Directions: From Vallejo, drive west on I-80 to the Suisun Valley Road exit. Take Suisun Valley Road and drive north to Highway 121. Turn north on Highway 121 and drive five miles to Highway 128. Turn left on Highway 128 and drive five miles to Berryessa-Knoxville Road. Turn right and continue nine miles to 5800 Knoxville Road.

Contact: Lake Berryessa Marina Resort, 707/966-2161, www.lakeberryessa.com.

64 SPANISH FLAT RESORT

Scenic rating: 7

on Lake Berryessa
See map page 581

This is one of several lakeside camps at Lake Berryessa. As at Lake Berryessa Marina Resort, the addition of park-model cabins has given this resort a nice touch. This is one of the most popular because many of the sites are on the waterfront. That makes it a natural gathering place for water-skiers and powerboaters, and on summer weekends, particularly holidays, it can get rowdy here. In fact, I have received notes from campers that they have had poor family experiences here. Berryessa, considered the Bay Area's backyard fishing hole, is the third-largest man-made lake in Northern California (Lakes Shasta and Oroville are larger). Trout fishing is good, and there are also bass and salmon. The elevation is approximately 500 feet. Note that an additional 180 RV sites are filled with seasonal renters.

RV sites, facilities: There are 120 sites for tents or RVs up to 37 feet, two yurts, and 16 park-model cabins. Some sites have partial hookups (30 amps). Picnic tables and fire grills are provided. Restrooms have flush toilets and showers. Drinking water, a dump station, boat storage, a picnic area, an ATM, a boat launch, a full-service marina, boat rentals, and a convenience store are available. A snack bar is open on summer weekends. A coin laundry, restaurant, and bar are available within one mile. Some facilities are wheelchair accessible. Leashed pets are permitted.

Reservations, fees: Reservations are accepted ($4 reservation fee). Sites are $25 per night, yurts cost $50 per night, boat launching fee is $5 per day, and it's $2 per pet per night. Some credit cards accepted. Open year-round.

Directions: From Vallejo, drive north on I-80 to the Suisun Valley Road exit. Take that exit and turn left onto Suisun Valley Road and drive north for approximately 17 miles to Highway 121. Turn north (right) on Highway 121 and drive seven miles to Highway 128. Turn north (left) on Highway 128 and drive five miles to Berryessa-Knoxville Road. Turn right on Berryessa-Knoxville Road and continue 4.5 miles to 4290 Knoxville Road.

Contact: Spanish Flat Resort, 707/966-7700, www.spanishflatresort.com; Spanish Flat Marina, 707/966-7708.

65 LAKE SOLANO COUNTY PARK

Scenic rating: 6

near Lake Berryessa

See map page 581

Lake Solano provides a low-pressure option to nearby Lake Berryessa. It is a long, narrow lake set below the outlet at Monticello Dam at Lake Berryessa, technically called the afterbay. Compared to Berryessa, life here moves at a much slower pace and some people prefer it. The water temperature at Lake Solano is also much cooler than at Berryessa. The lake has fair trout fishing in the spring, and it is known among Bay Area anglers as the closest fly-fishing spot for trout in the region. No motors, including electric motors, are permitted on boats at the lake. The park covers 177 acres along the river. A swimming pond is available in summer, and a children's fishing pond (trout and bass) is open year-round. The gate closes at night; check in before dusk.

RV sites, facilities: There are 50 sites for tents or RVs (no hookups) and 41 sites with full or partial hookups (30 amps) for tents or RVs up to 38 feet; some sites are pull-through. Picnic tables and fire grills are provided. Drinking water, restrooms with flush toilets and showers, two dump stations, a picnic area, a boat ramp (summer weekends only), and boat rentals are available. A grocery store is within walking distance, and firewood and ice are sold on the premises. Some facilities are wheelchair accessible. Leashed pets are permitted in the campground only.

Reservations, fees: Reservations are recommended. Sites are $15–33 per night, $7 per night for an additional vehicle, $1 per pet per night. Holiday rates are higher. Some credit cards accepted. Open year-round.

Directions: In Vacaville, turn north on I-505 and drive 11 miles to the junction of Highway 128. Turn west on Highway 128 and drive about five miles (past Winters) to Pleasant Valley Road. Turn left on Pleasant Valley Road and drive to the park at 8685 Pleasant Valley Road (well signed).

Contact: Lake Solano County Park, 530/795-2990, fax 530/795-1408, www.solanocounty.com.

66 CASINI RANCH FAMILY CAMPGROUND

Scenic rating: 8

on the Russian River

See map page 581

Woods and water—this campground has both, with sites set near the Russian River in both sun-filled and shaded areas. Its location on the lower river makes a side trip to the coast easy, with the Sonoma Coast State Beach about a 15-minute drive to the nearby west. No long-term rentals are available.

RV sites, facilities: There are 225 sites for tents or RVs of any length; many have full or partial hookups (30 amps) and some are pull-through. Picnic tables and fire grills are provided. Restrooms have flush toilets and showers. A playground, a dump station, a coin laundry, cable TV, Wi-Fi, a game arcade, boat and canoe rentals, propane gas, group facilities, seasonal activities, and a convenience store are available. Some facilities are wheelchair accessible. Leashed pets are permitted.

Reservations, fees: Reservations are accepted at 800/451-8400. Sites are $26–34 per night, $3 per person per night for more than two people, $1 per pet per night. Weekly and monthly rates available. Some credit cards accepted. Open year-round.

Directions: On U.S. 101 north of Santa Rosa, turn west on River Road and drive 16 miles to Guerneville and Highway 116. Continue west on Highway 116 and drive eight miles to Duncan Mills and Moscow Road. Turn left (southeast) on Moscow Road and drive 0.6 mile to the campground on the left.

Contact: Casini Ranch Family Campground Store, 707/865-2255, www.casiniranch.com.

67 SPRING LAKE REGIONAL PARK

🥾 🎣 🚣 🐕 ♿ 🚐 ⛺

Scenic rating: 6

at Spring Lake near Santa Rosa

See map page 581

Spring Lake is one of the few lakes in the greater Bay Area that provide lakeside camping. No gas-powered boats are permitted on this small, pretty lake, which keeps things fun and quiet for everybody. An easy trail along the west shore of the lake to the dam, then into adjoining Howarth Park, provides a pleasant evening stroll. This little lake is where a 24-pound world-record bass was reportedly caught, a story taken as a hoax by nearly all anglers.

RV sites, facilities: There are 31 sites for tents or RVs up to 40 feet and one group site for up to 75 people and 15 vehicles. No hookups. Several sites are pull-through. Picnic tables and fire grills are provided. Drinking water, restrooms with flush toilets and showers, a dump station, a boat ramp (no gas-powered motorboats), and boat rentals (in summer) are available. A grocery store, a coin laundry, firewood, and propane gas are available within five minutes. Some facilities are wheelchair accessible. Leashed pets are permitted.

Reservations, fees: Reservations are accepted (with a $7 reservation fee and $30–50 reservation fee for the group site) at 707/565-2267. Sites are $18 per night, $6 per night for an additional vehicle; the group site is $3 per person per night with a $50 minimum; it's $1 per pet per night. There is a 10-day camping limit. Open daily May–September and on weekends and holidays only during off-season.

Directions: From Santa Rosa on U.S. 101, turn east on Highway 12 and drive two miles to the junction with Hoen Avenue. Continue straight (east) onto Hoen Avenue and drive one mile (crossing Summerfield Road) to Newanga Avenue. Turn left and drive 0.5 mile to the park entrance at 5585 Newanga Avenue.

Contact: Spring Lake Regional Park, 707/539-8092; Sonoma County Parks, 707/565-2041, www.sonoma-county.org/parks.

68 SUGARLOAF RIDGE STATE PARK

🥾 🚲 🐕 🚐 ⛺

Scenic rating: 5

near Santa Rosa

See map page 581

Sugarloaf Ridge State Park is a perfect example of a place that you can't make a final judgment about from your first glance. Your first glance will lead you to believe that this is just hot foothill country, with old ranch roads set in oak woodlands for horseback riding and sweaty hiking or biking. A little discovery here, however, is that a half-mile walk off the Canyon Trail will

CALIFORNIA

lead you to a 25-foot waterfall, beautifully set in a canyon, complete with a redwood canopy. A shortcut to this waterfall is available off the south side of the park's entrance road. Otherwise, it can be a long, hot, and challenging hike. In all, there are 25 miles of trail here for hikers and equestrians. Hikers planning for a day of it should leave early, wear a hat, and bring plenty of water. Rangers report that some unprepared hikers have suffered heat stroke in summer, and many others have just plain suffered. In the off-season, when the air is cool and clear, the views from the ridge are eye-popping—visitors can see the Sierra Nevada, Golden Gate, and a thousand other points of scenic beauty from the top of Bald Mountain at 2,769 feet. For the less ambitious, a self-guided nature trail along Sonoma Creek begins at the campground.

RV sites, facilities: There are 47 sites for tents or RVs up to 27 feet and one group site for tents only for up to 50 people. No hookups. Picnic tables, food lockers, and fire grills are provided. Drinking water and flush toilets are available. Leashed pets are permitted in campsites only.

Reservations, fees: Reservations are recommended ($7.50 reservation fee) at 800/444-PARK (800/444-7275) or www.reserveamerica.com. Sites are $20 per night, $6 per night for an additional vehicle, $111 per night for the group site. Open year-round.

Directions: From Santa Rosa on U.S. 101, turn east on Highway 12 and drive seven miles to Adobe Canyon Road. Turn left and drive 3.5 miles to the park entrance at the end of the road.

Contact: Sugarloaf Ridge State Park, 707/833-5712, www.parks.ca.gov.

69 SONOMA COAST STATE BEACH: WRIGHTS BEACH

Scenic rating: 8

in Sonoma Coast State Beach

See map page 581

This park provides for more than its share of heaven and hell. This state park campground is at the north end of a beach that stretches south for about a mile, yet to the north it is steep and rocky. The campsites are considered a premium because of their location next to the beach. Because the campsites are often full, a key plus is an overflow area available for self-contained vehicles. The beach actually consists of a series of beaches that are separated by rock bluffs and headlands, and it extends for 17 miles from Bodega Head to Vista Trail (four miles north of Jenner). You can reach the beach from more than a dozen points along the highway. There are many excellent side trips. The best is to the north, where you can explore dramatic Shell Beach (the turnoff is on the west side of Highway 1) or take Pomo Trail (the trailhead is on the east side of the highway, across from Shell Beach) up the adjacent foothills for sweeping views of the coast. That's the heaven. Now for the hell: Dozens of people have drowned here. Wrights Beach is not for swimming because of rip currents, heavy surf, and surprise rogue waves that can make even surf play dangerous. Many rescues are made each year. The bluffs and coastal rocks can also be unstable and unsafe for climbing. Got it? 1. Stay clear of the water. 2. Don't climb the bluffs. Now it's up to you to get it right.

RV sites, facilities: There are 27 sites for tents or RVs up to 27 feet, with a limit of eight people per site, and an overflow area for self-contained vehicles. No hookups. Picnic tables, food lockers, and fire rings are provided. Drinking water and flush toilets are available. Showers are available at nearby Bodega Dunes Campground. Leashed pets are permitted in the campground and on the beach.

Reservations, fees: Reservations are recommended ($7.50 reservation fee) at 800/444-PARK (800/444-7275) or www.reserveamerica.com. Sites are $25–35 per night, $6 per night for an additional vehicle. Open year-round, weather permitting.

Directions: In Petaluma on U.S. 101, take the East Washington exit and turn west (this street becomes Bodega Avenue). Drive west through Petaluma and continue for 17 miles to Highway 1. Turn right (north) on Highway 1 and drive nine miles to Bodega Bay. From Bodega Bay, continue north for six miles to the campground entrance.

Contact: Sonoma Coast State Beach, 707/875-3483, www.parks.ca.gov.

70 BODEGA BAY RV PARK

Scenic rating: 8

in Bodega Bay

See map page 581

Bodega Bay RV Park is one of the oldest RV parks in the state, and there are few north-state coastal destinations better than Bodega Bay. Excellent seafood restaurants are available within five minutes, and some of the best deep-sea fishing is available out of Bodega Bay Sportfishing. In addition, there is a great view of the ocean at nearby Bodega Head to the west. It is a 35-minute walk from the park to the beach.

RV sites, facilities: There are 85 sites, most with full hookups (30 and 50 amps), for RVs of any length; some are pull-through. No tents. Picnic tables are provided. Drinking water and restrooms with flush toilets and showers are available. A coin laundry, a restaurant, group facilities, horseshoes, a video arcade, boccie ball, Wi-Fi, and cable TV are available. Some facilities are wheelchair accessible. Leashed pets are permitted.

Reservations, fees: Reservations are recommended at 800/201-6864. Sites are $35–39 per night, $3 per person per night for more than two people. Some credit cards accepted. Open year-round.

Directions: In Petaluma on U.S. 101, take the East Washington exit and turn west (this street becomes Bodega Avenue). Drive west through Petaluma and continue for 17 miles to Highway 1. Turn right (north) on Highway 1 and drive nine miles to Bodega Bay. In Bodega Bay, continue north for two miles to the RV park on the left at 2001 Highway 1.

Contact: Bodega Bay RV Park, 707/875-3701, www.bodegabayrvpark.com.

71 SONOMA COAST STATE BEACH: BODEGA DUNES

Scenic rating: 8

in Sonoma Coast State Beach

See map page 581

Sonoma Coast State Beach features several great campgrounds, and if you like the beach, this one rates high. It is at the end of Salmon Creek Beach, which stretches for miles, providing stellar beach walks and excellent beach-combing during low tides. For some campers, a foghorn sounding repeatedly through the night can make sleep difficult. The quietest sites here are among the dunes. A day-use area includes a wheelchair-accessible boardwalk that leads out to a sandy beach. In summer, camp-fire programs and junior ranger programs are often available. To the nearby south is Bodega Bay, including a major deep-sea sportfishing operation, crowned by often excellent salmon fishing; check current fishing regulations. The town of Bodega Bay offers a full marina and restaurants. The nearest beach, Salmon Creek Beach, is far safer than Wrights Beach, which is about five miles away. (See the *Wrights Beach* listing in this chapter for details about Sonoma Coast State Beach.)

RV sites, facilities: There are 98 sites for tents or RVs up to 31 feet (no hookups) and one hike-in/bike-in site. Picnic tables, food lockers, and fire grills are provided. Drinking water, restrooms with flush toilets and free showers, and a dump station are available. Laundry facilities, supplies, and horse rentals are available within one mile. Some facilities are wheelchair accessible. Leashed pets are permitted at the campsites only.

Reservations, fees: Reservations are accepted ($7.50 reservation fee) at 800/444-PARK (800/444-7275) or www.reserveamerica.com. Sites are $25 per night, $6 per night for an additional vehicle, $3 per person per night for the hike-in/bike-in site. Open year-round.

Directions: In Santa Rosa on U.S. 101, turn west on Highway 12 and drive 10 miles to Sebastopol (Highway 12 becomes Bodega

Highway). Continue straight (west) for 10 miles to Bodega. Continue for 0.5 mile to Highway 1. Turn right (north) on Highway 1 and drive five miles to Bodega Bay. Continue 0.5 mile north to the campground entrance on the left (west).

Contact: Sonoma Coast State Beach, 707/875-3483, www.parks.ca.gov.

72 DORAN REGIONAL PARK

Scenic rating: 7

on Bodega Bay

See map page 581   BEST (

This campground is beside Doran Beach on Bodega Bay, which offers complete fishing and marina facilities. In season, it's also a popular clamming and crabbing spot. This park has a wide, somewhat sheltered sandy beach. Salmon fishing is often excellent during the summer at the Whistle Buoy offshore from Bodega Head, and rock fishing is good year-round offshore. Fishing is also available off the rock jetty in the park.

RV sites, facilities: There are 10 sites for tents and 128 sites for tents or RVs of any length, one group tent site for up to 50 people, and one hike-in/bike-in site. No hookups. Picnic tables and fire grills are provided. Drinking water, restrooms with flush toilets and coin showers, dump stations, a fish-cleaning station, and a boat ramp are available. Supplies can be obtained in Bodega Bay. Some facilities are wheelchair accessible. Leashed pets are permitted with a valid rabies certificate.

Reservations, fees: Reservations are accepted ($7 reservation fee and $30–50 reservation fee for the group site) on weekdays at 707/565-2267. Sites are $18 per night, $6 per night for an additional vehicle, $5 per person per night for the hike-in/bike-in site, $1 per pet per night. The group site is $3 per person per night with a minimum of $72 and a maximum of 15 vehicles. Open year-round.

Directions: In Petaluma on U.S. 101, take the East Washington exit and turn west (this street becomes Bodega Avenue). Drive west through Petaluma and continue for 17 miles to Highway 1. Merge right (north) on Highway 1 and drive toward Bodega Bay and Doran Park Road. Turn left onto the campground entrance road. If you reach the town of Bodega Bay, you have gone a mile too far.

Contact: Sonoma County Parks Department, 707/875-3540 or 707/565-2041, www.sonoma-county.org/parks.

73 WESTSIDE REGIONAL PARK

Scenic rating: 7

on Bodega Bay

See map page 581   BEST (

This campground is on the west shore of Bodega Bay. One of the greatest boat launches on the coast is adjacent to the park on the south, providing access to prime fishing waters. Salmon fishing is excellent from mid-June through August; check current fishing regulations. A small, protected beach (for kids to dig in the sand and wade) is available at the end of the road beyond the campground. Hiking trails can be found at the state beach nearby.

RV sites, facilities: There are 47 sites for tents or RVs of any length (no hookups); most sites are pull-through. Picnic tables and fire grills are provided. Drinking water, restrooms with flush toilets and coin showers, a fish-cleaning station, firewood, and a boat ramp are available. A dump station is available at Doran Regional Park. Supplies can be obtained in Bodega Bay. Some facilities are wheelchair accessible. Leashed pets are permitted with a valid rabies certificate.

Reservations, fees: Reservations are accepted ($7 reservation fee) on weekdays at 707/565-2267. Sites are $18 per night, $6 per night for each additional vehicle, $1 per pet per night. Open year-round.

Directions: In Petaluma on U.S. 101, take the East Washington exit and turn west (this street becomes Bodega Avenue). Drive west through Petaluma and continue for 17 miles to

Highway 1 north. Merge right onto Highway 1 and drive north nine miles to Bodega Bay. In Bodega Bay, continue north to Eastshore Road. Turn left and drive one block to Bay Flat Road. Turn right and drive (Bay Flat Road becomes Westshore Road) two miles to the park on the left, 0.5 mile past Spud Point Marina.

Contact: Westside Regional Parks, Sonoma County Parks Department, 707/875-3540 or 707/565-2041, www.sonoma-county.org/parks.

74 SAN FRANCISCO NORTH/ PETALUMA KOA

Scenic rating: 3

near Petaluma

See map page 581

This campground is less than a mile from U.S. 101, yet it has a rural feel in a 60-acre farm setting. It's a good base camp for folks who require some quiet mental preparation before heading south to the Bay Area or to the nearby wineries, redwoods, and the Russian River. There are recreation activities and live music on Saturdays in summer. During October, a pumpkin patch and corn maze are open across the street from the park.

RV sites, facilities: There are 272 sites, most with full or partial hookups (30 and 50 amps) for RVs or tents, 34 cabins, and a lodge. Most sites are pull-through. Picnic tables and fire pits are provided. Restrooms have flush toilets and showers. Cable TV hookups, modem access and free Wi-Fi, a dump station, a playground, recreation rooms, basketball, volleyball, a heated seasonal swimming pool, a spa, a petting farm, shuffleboard, a coin laundry, propane gas, and a convenience store are available. Some facilities are wheelchair accessible. Leashed pets are permitted, with certain restrictions.

Reservations, fees: Reservations are accepted at 800/562-1233 or by website. Sites are $29.95–56 per night, $5–7 per person per night for more than two people. Some credit cards accepted. Open year-round.

Directions: From Petaluma on U.S. 101 north, take the Penngrove exit and drive west for 0.25 mile on Petaluma Boulevard to Stony Point Road. Turn right (north) on Stony Point Road and drive 0.25 mile to Rainsville Road. Turn left (west) on Rainsville Road and drive a short distance to the park entrance at 20 Rainsville Road.

Contact: San Francisco North/Petaluma KOA, 707/763-1492, www.koa.com.

75 NAPA VALLEY EXPOSITION RV PARK

Scenic rating: 2

in Napa

See map page 581

This RV park is directly adjacent to the Napa Valley Exposition. When the fair is in operation in late July and early August, the RV park is closed. The rest of the year it is simply an RV parking area, and it can come in handy.

RV sites, facilities: There are 45 sites with partial hookups (30 and 50 amps) for RVs of any length and a grassy area for at least 100 self-contained RVs. Some sites are pull-through. Picnic tables, restrooms with showers, a coin laundry, and a dump station are available. A camp host is on-site. A grocery store and a restaurant are within walking distance. Some facilities are wheelchair accessible. Leashed pets are permitted.

Reservations, fees: Reservations are not accepted for individual sites but are required for groups at 707/253-4900, ext. 102. Sites are $20 per night. Open year-round, except during the fair.

Directions: From Napa on Highway 29, drive to the Napa/Lake Berryessa exit. Take that exit and turn right (east) and drive about one mile to Silverado/Highway 121. Turn right and drive less than one mile to the fairgrounds entrance on the left.

Contact: Napa Valley Exposition, 707/253-4900, fax 707/253-4943, www.napavalleyexpo.com.

CALIFORNIA

SACRAMENTO AND GOLD COUNTRY

BEST RV PARKS AND CAMPGROUNDS

(**Fishing**
Lundborg Landing, page 644.

(**Prettiest Rivers**
Moonshine Campground, page 630.

From a distance, this section of the Sacramento Valley looks like flat farmland extending into infinity, with a sprinkling of cities and towns interrupting the view. But a closer look reveals a landscape filled with Northern California's most significant rivers – the Sacramento, Feather, Yuba, American, and Mokelumne. All of these provide water recreation, in both lakes and rivers, as well as serve as the lifeblood for a series of wildlife refuges.

The highlight of the foothill country for lake recreation is the series of great lakes for water sports and fishing. These include Camanche, Rollins, Oroville, and many others. Note that the mapping I use for this region extends up to Bucks Lake, which is high in Plumas National Forest, the northern start to the Gold Country.

Timing is everything in love and the great outdoors, and so it is in the Central Valley and the nearby foothills. Spring and fall are gorgeous here, along with many summer evenings. But there are always periods of 100-plus temperatures in the summer.

But that's what gives the lakes and rivers such appeal, and in turn, why they are treasured. Take your pick: Lake Oroville in the northern Sierra, Folsom Lake outside Sacramento... the list goes on. On a hot day, jumping into a cool lake makes water more valuable than gold, a cold drink on ice worth more than silver. These have become top sites for boating-based recreation and fantastic areas for water sports and fishing.

In the Mother Lode country, three other lakes – Camanche, Amador, and Pardee – are outstanding for fishing. Three of this chapter's lakes rank among the top 10 lakes for fishing in the state – Lake Oroville and Lake Camanche make the list for bass and Lake Amador makes it for bluegill and catfish – no small feat considering the 300-plus other lakes they were up against.

For touring, the state capital and nearby Old Sacramento are favorites. Others prefer reliving the gold-mining history of California's past or exploring the foothill country, where you'll find Malakoff Diggins State Historic Park nearby.

Includes:

- American River
- Brannan Island State Recreation Area
- Bucks Lake
- Bullards Bar Reservoir
- Collins Lake Recreation Area
- Cosumnes River
- Folsom Lake State Recreation Area
- Indian Grinding Rock State Historic Park
- Jenkinson Lake
- Lake Amador Recreation Area
- Lake Camanche
- Lake Oroville
- New Hogan Reservoir
- Pardee Reservoir
- Plumas National Forest
- Rancho Seco Recreation Area
- Sacramento River
- Sacramento River State Recreation Area
- Sly Park Recreation Area
- Woodson Bridge State Recreation Area
- Yuba River

CALIFORNIA

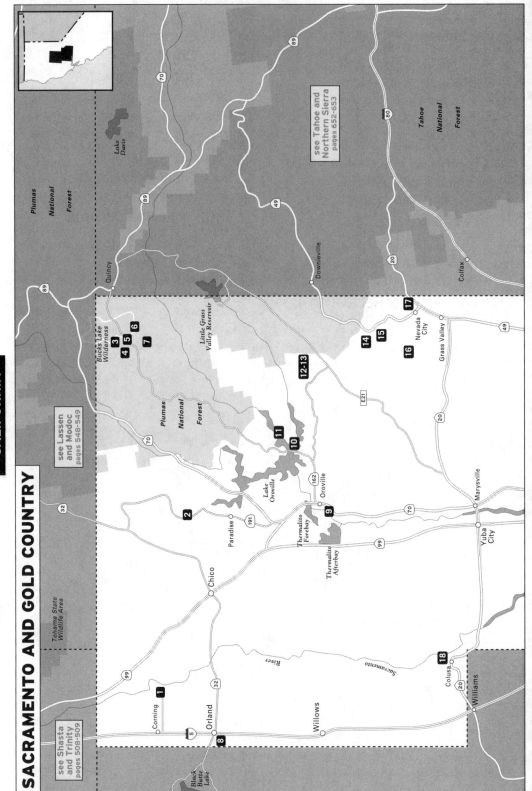

SACRAMENTO AND GOLD COUNTRY

CALIFORNIA

see Lassen
and Modoc
pages 548-549

see Tahoe and
Northern Sierra
pages 652-653

see Shasta
and Trinity
pages 508-509

*Plumas
National
Forest*

*Tahoe
National
Forest*

*Tehama State
Wildlife Area*

*Bucks Lake
Wilderness*

*Plumas
National
Forest*

*Little Grass
Valley Reservoir*

*Lake
Davis*

*Lake
Oroville*

*Black
Butte
Lake*

*Thermalito
Forebay*

*Thermalito
Afterbay*

Sacramento River

Quincy
Paradise
Chico
Corning
Orland
Willows
Williams
Colusa
Yuba City
Marysville
Oroville
Nevada City
Grass Valley
Downieville
Colfax

89
70
89
89
70
32
99
99
32
5
191
162
70
99
20
49
80
49
E21
E20
20

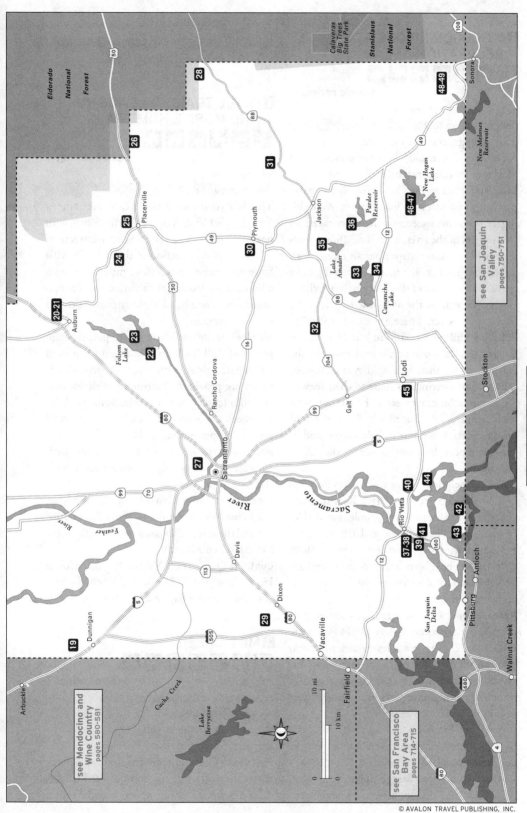

CALIFORNIA

see San Joaquin Valley pages 750-751

see Mendocino and Wine Country pages 580-581

see San Francisco Bay Area pages 714-715

Eldorado National Forest

Calaveras Big Trees State Park

Stanislaus National Forest

New Melones Reservoir

New Hogan Lake

Pardee Reservoir

Camanche Lake

Lake Amador

Folsom Lake

Feather River

Sacramento River

San Joaquin Delta

Cache Creek

Lake Berryessa

Sonora

Sacramento

Placerville

Plymouth

Jackson

Lodi

Stockton

Galt

Rancho Cordova

Auburn

Davis

Dixon

Vacaville

Fairfield

Arbuckle

Dunnigan

Rio Vista

Antioch

Pittsburg

Walnut Creek

© AVALON TRAVEL PUBLISHING, INC.

■ WOODSON BRIDGE STATE RECREATION AREA

Scenic rating: 7

on the Sacramento River

See map page 622

This campground features direct access to the Sacramento River, and a boat ramp makes it an ideal spot for campers with trailered boats. The boat ramp is across the road in the county park, providing easy access for water sports. Waterskiing and personal watercraft are discouraged on this section of the river. This is a 328-acre preserve with a dense, native riparian forest, with a sand and gravel beach nearby. The junglelike grove displays some of the last remaining virgin riparian habitat on the 400-mile length of the Sacramento River. There are about two miles of hiking trails in the park. In June, the nearby Tehama Riffle is one of the best spots on the entire river for shad fishing. By mid-August, salmon start arriving, en route to their spawning grounds. Summer weather here is hot, with high temperatures commonly 85–100°F and up. In winter, it is home to bald eagles, and in summer it provides a nesting site for the yellow bill cuckoo.

RV sites, facilities: There are 37 sites for tents or RVs up to 31 feet and five boat-in sites. One group site for up to 40 people is available. No hookups. Picnic tables and fire grills are provided. Drinking water, coin showers, flush toilets, and a boat launch (across the street) are available, and there is a camp host. Leashed pets are permitted.

Reservations, fees: Reservations are accepted ($7.50 reservation fee) at 800/444-PARK (800/444-7275) or www.reserveamerica.com. Sites are $11–14 per night, $6 per night for an additional vehicle, $6 per night for boat-in sites, $90 per night for the group camp. Open year-round.

Directions: From I-5 in Corning, take the South Avenue exit and drive six miles east to the campground on the left.

Contact: Woodson Bridge State Recreation Area, 530/839-2112, www.parks.ca.gov; North

Buttes District, 530/538-2200; Bidwell Mansion Visitor Center, 530/895-6144.

■ QUAIL TRAILS VILLAGE RV AND MOBILE HOME PARK

Scenic rating: 4

near Paradise

See map page 622

This is a rural motor home campground, set near the west branch of the Feather River, with nearby Lake Oroville as the feature attraction. The Lime Saddle section of the Lake Oroville State Recreation Area is three miles away, with a beach, boat-launching facilities, and concessions. About one-third of the sites are taken by long-term rentals.

RV sites, facilities: There are 20 pull-through sites with full hookups (30 amps) for RVs of any length, along with five tent sites. Picnic tables are provided. Restrooms with showers and coin laundry are available. Some facilities are wheelchair accessible. Leashed pets up to 30 pounds are permitted.

Reservations, fees: Reservations are accepted. Sites are $15–25 per night. Weekly rates available. Open year-round.

Directions: From Oroville, drive north on Highway 70 for six miles to Pentz Road. Turn left and drive six miles south to the park on the left (5110 Pentz Road).

Contact: Quail Trails Village RV and Mobile Home Park, 530/877-6581, fax 530/876-0516, www.quailtrailsvillage.com.

■ MILL CREEK

Scenic rating: 7

at Bucks Lake in Plumas National Forest

See map page 622

When Bucks Lake is full, this is one of the prettiest spots on the lake. The camp is deep in Mill Creek Cove, adjacent to where Mill Creek enters the northernmost point of Bucks Lake. A boat ramp is a half mile away to the south, providing boat access to one of the better trout fishing spots at the lake. Unfortunately, when the lake level falls, this camp is left high and dry, some distance from the water. All water sports are permitted on this 1,800-acre lake. The elevation is 5,200 feet.

RV sites, facilities: There are 10 sites for tents or RVs up to 27 feet and two walk-in tent sites. No hookups. Picnic tables and fire grills are provided. Drinking water and vault toilets are available. Groceries are available within five miles. Leashed pets are permitted.

Reservations, fees: Reservations are not accepted. Sites are $18–20 per night. Open mid-May–September, weather permitting.

Directions: From Oroville, drive north on Highway 70 to the junction with Highway 89. Turn south on Highway 89/70 and drive 11 miles to Quincy. In Quincy, turn right at Bucks Lake Road and drive 17 miles to Bucks Lake and the junction with Bucks Lake Dam Road/Forest Road 33. Turn right, drive around the lake, cross over the dam, and continue for about three miles to the campground.

Contact: Plumas National Forest, Mount Hough Ranger District, 530/283-0555, fax 530/283-1821; Northwest Park Management, 530/283-5559.

4 SUNDEW

Scenic rating: 7

on Bucks Lake in Plumas National Forest

See map page 622

Sundew camp sits on the northern shore of Bucks Lake, just north of Bucks Lake Dam. A boat ramp is about two miles north at Sandy Point Day Use Area at the Mill Creek Cove, providing access to one of the better trout spots on the lake. You want fish? At Bucks Lake you can get fish—it's one of the state's top mountain trout lakes. Fish species include rainbow, brown, and Mackinaw trout. Sunrises are often spectacular from this camp, with the light glowing on the lake's surface.

RV sites, facilities: There are 19 sites for tents

or RVs up to 35 feet (no hookups). Picnic tables and fire grills are provided. Drinking water and vault toilets are available. Leashed pets are permitted. There is a boat ramp two miles north of the camp.

Reservations, fees: Reservations are not accepted. Sites are $18–20 per night. Open mid-May–September, weather permitting.

Directions: From Oroville, drive north on Highway 70 to the junction with Highway 89. Turn south on Highway 89/70 and drive 11 miles to Quincy. In Quincy, turn right at Bucks Lake Road and drive 17 miles to Bucks Lake and the junction with Bucks Lake Dam Road/Forest Road 33. Turn right, drive around the lake, cross over the dam, continue for 0.5 mile, and turn right at the campground access road.

Contact: Plumas National Forest, Mount Hough Ranger District, 530/283-0555, fax 530/283-1821; Northwest Park Management, 530/283-5559.

5 HASKINS VALLEY

Scenic rating: 7

on Bucks Lake

See map page 622

This is the biggest and most popular of the campgrounds at Bucks Lake, a pretty alpine lake with excellent trout fishing and clean campgrounds. A boat ramp is available to the nearby north, along with Bucks Lodge. This camp is deep in a cove at the extreme south end of the lake, where the water is quiet and sheltered from north winds. Bucks Lake, 5,200 feet elevation, is well documented for excellent fishing for rainbow and Mackinaw trout, with high catch rates of rainbow trout and lake records in the 16-pound class. Insider's tip: This is the best lake in the region for sailboarding.

RV sites, facilities: There are 65 sites for tents or RVs up to 30 feet (no hookups). Picnic tables and fire grills are provided. Drinking water and vault toilets are available. A dump station and boat ramp are available nearby. Some facilities are wheelchair accessible. Leashed pets are permitted.

Reservations, fees: Reservations are not accepted. Sites are $18 per night, $3 per night for an additional vehicle, $1 per pet per night. Open May–early October, weather permitting.

Directions: From Oroville, drive north on Highway 70 to the junction with Highway 89. Turn south on Highway 89/70 and drive 11 miles to Quincy. In Quincy, turn right at Bucks Lake Road and drive 16.5 miles to the campground entrance on the right side of the road.

Contact: PG&E Land Services, 916/386-5164, www.pge.com/recreation.

6 WHITEHORSE

Scenic rating: 7

near Bucks Lake in Plumas National Forest

See map page 622

This campground is along Bucks Creek, about two miles from the boat ramps and south shore concessions at Bucks Lake. The trout fishing can be quite good at Bucks Lake. The elevation is 5,200 feet. (For more information, see the listing in this chapter for *Haskins Valley*.)

RV sites, facilities: There are 20 sites for tents or RVs up to 27 feet (no hookups). Picnic tables and fire grills are provided. Drinking water and vault toilets are available. A grocery store and coin laundry are available within five miles. Leashed pets are permitted.

Reservations, fees: Reservations are not accepted. Sites are $16 per night. Open June–September.

Directions: From Oroville, drive north on Highway 70 to the junction with Highway 89. Turn south on Highway 89/70 and drive 11 miles to Quincy and Bucks Lake Road. Turn right at Bucks Lake Road and drive 14.5 miles to the campground entrance on the right side of the road.

Contact: Plumas National Forest, Mount Hough Ranger District, 530/283-0555, fax 530/283-1821; Northwest Park Management, 530/283-5559.

7 GRIZZLY CREEK

Scenic rating: 4

near Bucks Lake in Plumas National Forest

See map page 622

This is an alternative to the more developed, more crowded campgrounds at Bucks Lake. It is a small, primitive camp set near Grizzly Creek at 5,400 feet in elevation. Nearby Bucks Lake provides good trout fishing, resorts, and boat rentals.

RV sites, facilities: There are eight sites for tents or RVs up to 35 feet (no hookups). Picnic tables and fire grills are provided. Drinking water and vault toilets are available. A boat ramp is available at Bucks Lake. A grocery store and coin laundry are available within five miles. Leashed pets are permitted.

Reservations, fees: Reservations are not accepted. Sites are $18 per night. Open June–October.

Directions: From Oroville, drive north on Highway 70 to the junction with Highway 89. Turn south on Highway 89/70 and drive 11 miles to Quincy and Bucks Lake Road. Turn right at Bucks Lake Road and drive 17 miles to Bucks Lake and the junction with Bucks Lake Dam Road/Forest Road 33. Turn right and drive one mile to the junction with Oroville-Quincy Road/Forest Road 36. Bear left and drive one mile to the campground on the right side of the road.

Contact: Plumas National Forest, Mount Hough Ranger District, 530/283-0555, fax 530/283-1821; Northwest Park Management, 530/283-5559.

8 OLD ORCHARD RV PARK

Scenic rating: 4

near Orland

See map page 622

Most folks use this as a layover spot while on long trips up or down I-5 in the Central Valley. If you're staying longer than a night, there are two side trips that have appeal for anglers.

Nearby Black Butte Lake to the west, with crappie in the early summer, and the Sacramento River to the east, with salmon in the late summer and early fall, can add some spice to your trip. The elevation is 250 feet. Some sites are filled with long-term renters.

RV sites, facilities: There are 52 pull-through sites with partial or full hookups (30 and 50 amps) for RVs of any length and six tent sites. Restrooms have showers. A dump station, a coin laundry, and modem access are available. Some facilities are wheelchair accessible. Leashed pets are permitted.

Reservations, fees: Reservations are accepted. Sites are $15–24 per night, $2 per person per night for more than two people. Some credit cards accepted. Open year-round.

Directions: From I-5 at Orland, take the Chico/Highway 32 exit west (Exit 619). Drive west one block to County Road HH. Turn right on County Road HH and drive north one block to the park on the right at 4490 County Road HH.

Contact: Old Orchard RV Park, 877/481-9282, tel./fax 530/865-5335.

⑨ DINGERVILLE USA

Scenic rating: 3

near Oroville

See map page 622

You're right, they thought of this name all by themselves, needed no help. It is an RV park set in the Oroville foothill country—hot and dry in the summer, but with side trips available. It is adjacent to a wildlife area and the Feather River and within short range of Lake Oroville and the Thermalito Afterbay for boating, water sports, and fishing. The RV park is a clean, quiet campground with easy access from the highway. Some of the sites are occupied by long-term renters.

RV sites, facilities: There are 29 pull-through sites with full hookups (30 and 50 amps) for RVs of any length. No tents. Picnic tables are provided. Restrooms have showers. Modem

access, cable TV, a seasonal swimming pool, a coin laundry, a horseshoe pit, and a nine-hole executive golf course are available. Some facilities are wheelchair accessible. Leashed pets are permitted.

Reservations, fees: Reservations are recommended. Sites are $27 per night. Some credit cards accepted. Open year-round.

Directions: From Oroville, drive south on Highway 70 to the second Pacific Heights Road turnoff. Turn right at Pacific Heights Road and drive less than one mile to the campground on the left.

From Marysville, drive north on Highway 70 to Palermo-Welsh Road. Turn left on Palermo-Welsh Road and drive to Pacific Heights Road. Turn left (north) on Pacific Heights Road and drive 0.5 mile to the campground entrance on the right.

Contact: Dingerville USA, 530/533-9343.

⑩ BIDWELL CANYON

Scenic rating: 7

on Lake Oroville

See map page 622

Bidwell Canyon is a major destination at giant Lake Oroville as the campground is near a major marina and boat ramp. It is along the southern shore of the lake, on a point directly adjacent to the massive Oroville Dam to the west. Many campers use this spot for boating headquarters. Lake Oroville is created from the tallest earth-filled dam in the country, rising 770 feet above the streambed of the Feather River. It creates a huge reservoir when full. It is popular for waterskiing, as the water is warm enough in the summer for all water sports, and there is enough room for both anglers and water-skiers. Fishing is excellent for spotted bass. What a lake—there are even floating toilets here (imagine that!). It is very hot in midsummer, with high temperatures ranging from the mid-80s to the low 100s. The area has four distinct seasons—spring is quite beautiful with many wildflowers and greenery.

A must-see is the view from the 47-foot tower using the high-powered telescopes, where there is a panoramic view of the lake, Sierra Nevada, valley, foothills, and the Sutter Buttes. The Feather River Hatchery is nearby.

RV sites, facilities: There are 75 sites for RVs up to 40 feet with full hookups (30 amps) and trailers up to 31 feet (including boat trailers). Picnic tables and fire grills are provided. Drinking water, flush toilets, and coin showers are available. Boat rentals are available on the lake. A grocery store, a boat ramp, a marina with fuel and a boat pumping station, a snack bar, and propane gas are available within two miles. Leashed pets are permitted, except on trails or beaches.

Reservations, fees: Reservations are accepted ($7.50 reservation fee) at 800/444-PARK (800/444-7275) or www.reserveamerica.com. Sites are $19–24 per night, $4 per night for an additional vehicle. Open year-round.

Directions: From Oroville, drive east on Oroville Dam Boulevard/Highway 162 (it becomes the Olive Highway) for 6.8 miles to Kelly Ridge Road. Turn left (north) on Kelly Ridge Road and drive 1.5 miles to Arroyo Drive. Turn right and drive 0.25 mile to the campground.

Contact: Lake Oroville State Recreation Area, 530/538-2200; Lake Oroville Visitor Center, 530/538-2219, www.parks.ca.gov.

11 LOAFER CREEK FAMILY, GROUP, AND EQUESTRIAN CAMPS

Scenic rating: 7

on Lake Oroville

See map page 622

These are three different campground areas that are linked, designed for individual use, groups, and equestrians, respectively. The camps are just across the water at Lake Oroville from Bidwell Canyon, but campers come here for more spacious sites. It's also a primary option for campers with boats, with the Loafer Creek boat ramp one mile away. So hey, this spot is no

secret. A bonus is an extensive equestrian trail system right out of camp.

RV sites, facilities: There are 137 sites for tents or RVs up to 40 feet and trailers up to 31 feet (including boat trailers), 15 equestrian sites with a two-horse limit per site, and six group sites for up to 25 people each. No hookups. Picnic tables and fire grills are provided. Drinking water, restrooms with flush toilets and coin showers, laundry tubs, Wi-Fi, and a dump station are available. A tethering and feeding station is near each site for horses, and a horse-washing station is provided. Propane, groceries, boat rentals, and a boat ramp are available nearby. Some facilities are wheelchair accessible. Leashed pets are permitted, but not on trails or beaches.

Reservations, fees: Reservations are accepted ($7.50 reservation fee) at 800/444-PARK (800/444-7275) or www.reserveamerica.com. Sites are $13–18 per night for single sites, $4 per night for an additional vehicle, $60 per night for group sites, $30 per night for equestrian sites. Open year-round.

Directions: From Oroville, drive east on Oroville Dam Boulevard/Highway 162 (becomes the Olive Highway) for approximately eight miles to the signed campground entrance on the left.

Contact: Lake Oroville State Recreation Area, 530/538-2200; Lake Oroville Visitor Center, 530/538-2219, www.parks.ca.gov.

12 SLY CREEK

Scenic rating: 7

on Sly Creek Reservoir in Plumas National Forest

See map page 622

Sly Creek Camp is on Sly Creek Reservoir's southwestern shore near Lewis Flat, with a boat ramp about a mile to the north. Both camps at this lake are well situated for campers/anglers. This camp provides direct access to the lake's main body, with good trout fishing well upstream on the main lake arm. You get quiet water and decent fishing. The elevation is 3,530 feet.

RV sites, facilities: There are 26 sites for tents or RVs up to 40 feet (no hookups). Five walk-in tent cabins are also available. Picnic tables and fire grills are provided. Drinking water and vault toilets are available. A car-top boat launch and fish-cleaning stations are available on Sly Creek Reservoir. Some facilities are wheelchair accessible. Leashed pets are permitted.

Reservations, fees: Reservations are not accepted. Sites are $18 per night. Open late April–mid-October, weather permitting.

Directions: From Oroville, drive east on Highway 162/Oroville Dam Boulevard for about eight miles (it becomes the Olive Highway) to Forbestown Road. Turn right and drive through Forbestown to Challenge and LaPorte Road. Turn left on LaPorte Road and drive 15 miles to Forest Road 16 (signed for Sly Creek Reservoir). Turn left on Forest Road 16 and drive 4.5 miles to the campground on the eastern end of the lake.

Contact: Plumas National Forest, Feather River Ranger District, 530/534-6500, fax 530/532-1210; Northwest Park Management, 530/283-5559.

13 STRAWBERRY

Scenic rating: 7

on Sly Creek Reservoir in Plumas National Forest

See map page 622

Sly Creek Reservoir is a long, narrow lake in western Plumas National Forest. There are two campgrounds on opposite ends of the lake, with different directions to each. This camp nestles in the back of a cove on the lake's eastern arm at an elevation of 3,530 feet, with a nearby boat ramp available. This is a popular lake for trout fishing in the summer. The water source (such as at the fish-cleaning station) has a high mineral content and strong smell; campers must bring their own drinking water.

RV sites, facilities: There are 27 sites for tents or RVs up to 40 feet (no hookups). Picnic tables and fire grills are provided. There is no drinking water. Vault toilets are available. A car-top boat launch and fish-cleaning station are available on Sly Creek Reservoir. Leashed pets are permitted.

Reservations, fees: Reservations are not accepted. Sites are $18 per night. Open late April–mid-October, weather permitting.

Directions: From Oroville, drive east on Highway 162/Oroville Dam Boulevard for about eight miles (it becomes the Olive Highway) to Forbestown Road. Turn right and drive through Forbestown to Challenge and LaPorte Road. Turn left on LaPorte Road and drive 15 miles to Forest Road 16 (signed for Sly Creek Reservoir). Turn left on Forest Road 16 and drive two miles to the campground on the eastern end of the lake.

Contact: Plumas National Forest, Feather River Ranger District, 530/534-6500, fax 530/532-1210; Northwest Park Management, 530/283-5559.

14 SCHOOLHOUSE

Scenic rating: 7

on Bullards Bar Reservoir

See map page 622

Bullards Bar Reservoir is one of the better lakes in the Sierra Nevada for camping, primarily because the lake levels tend to be higher here than at many other lakes. The camp is on the southeast shore, with a trail available out of the camp to a beautiful lookout of the lake. Bullards Bar is known for good fishing for trout and kokanee salmon, waterskiing, and all water sports. A concrete boat ramp is to the south at Cottage Creek. Boaters should consider the special boat-in camps at the lake. The elevation is 2,200 feet.

RV sites, facilities: There are 56 sites with no hookups (one triple, 11 double, and 44 single sites) for tents or RVs of any length. Single sites accommodate six people, double sites accommodate 12, and triple sites hold up to 18 people. Picnic tables and fire rings are provided. Drinking water and flush and vault toilets are available. A boat ramp and boat rentals are nearby. Supplies are available in North San Juan, Camptonville, Dobbins, and at the marina. Some facilities are wheelchair accessible. Leashed pets are permitted.

Reservations, fees: Reservations and a camping permit are required ($7.50 reservation fee) from Emerald Cove Marina at 530/692-3200. Sites are $17 per night, $34 per night for a double site, and $51 per night for a triple site. Open mid-April–mid-October.

Directions: From Marysville, drive east on Highway 20 for 12 miles to Marysville Road (signed for Bullards Bar Reservoir). Turn left on Marysville Road and drive 12 miles to Old Marysville Road. Turn right on Old Marysville Road and drive 14 miles to the dam, then continue three miles to the campground entrance road on the left.

Contact: Emerald Cove Marina, 530/692-3200; Tahoe National Forest, Yuba River Ranger District, North, 530/288-3231, fax 530/288-0727, www.bullardsbar.com.

15 MOONSHINE CAMPGROUND

Scenic rating: 7

near the Yuba River and Bullards Bar Reservoir

See map page 622   **BEST (**

This campground features shaded sites and a swimming hole on the nearby Middle Fork Yuba River. Both are needed, with the weather hot here in the summer, at 1,430 feet in the Sierra foothills. Gold panning is an option. It's a seven-mile drive to a three-lane boat ramp at Dark Day Picnic Area at Bullards Bar Reservoir, the feature side trip. Malakoff Diggins State Historic Park is 15 miles away. A few of the sites are occupied by seasonal renters.

RV sites, facilities: There are 25 sites for tents or RVs up to 30 feet with partial hookups (30 amps). Picnic tables and fire rings are provided. Drinking water, vault toilets, ice, and firewood are available. A grocery store, café, deli, and propane gas are available about three miles away in North San Juan. Some facilities are wheelchair accessible. Leashed pets are permitted.

Reservations, fees: Reservations are required. Sites are $25–30 per night, $3 per night for air-conditioning. Open May–early October, weather permitting.

Directions: From Auburn, drive north on Highway 49 to Nevada City and the exit for Downieville/Highway 49. Turn left and drive for 17 miles through the town of North San Juan. Continue on Highway 49 and cross a bridge over the Middle Fork Yuba River to Moonshine Road (immediately after bridge crossing). Turn left on Moonshine Road and drive 0.75 mile to the campground on the left.

Contact: Moonshine Campground, 530/288-3585, www.moonshinecampground.com.

16 COLLINS LAKE RECREATION AREA

Scenic rating: 8

near Marysville on Collins Lake

See map page 622

Collins Lake is in the foothill country east of Marysville at 1,200 feet in elevation, ideal for the camper, boater, and angler. I counted 45 campsites set near the lakefront. This lake is becoming known as an outstanding destination for trophy-sized trout, especially in late spring through early summer, though fishing is often good year-round for know-hows. Other fish species are bass, crappie, bluegill, and catfish. The lake has 12 miles of shoreline and is quite pretty. In summer, warm water makes the lake exceptional for waterskiing (permitted May–mid-October). There is a marina adjacent to the campground, and farther south is a 60-foot-wide swimming beach and boat ramp. Bonuses for anglers: No personal watercraft are allowed on the lake, and a weekly fishing report is available at the camp's website. Insider's tip: Lakefront sites fill quickly; book early.

RV sites, facilities: There are 150 sites with full or partial hookups (30 amps) for RVs or tents, 60 sites with no hookups, five group tent sites, one RV group site, and a large overflow camping area. Some sites are pull-through.

Four rental trailers and five cabins are also available. Picnic tables and barbecues are provided. Restrooms have flush toilets and coin showers. Drinking water, portable toilets, a dump station, a playground, a marina, a boat ramp, boat rentals, berths, a sandy swimming beach, beach volleyball, three group picnic areas, a convenience store, a coin laundry, firewood, ice, and propane gas are available. Some facilities are wheelchair accessible. Leashed pets are permitted.

Reservations, fees: Reservations are accepted up to one year in advance with an $8 reservation fee. Sites are $22–40 per night, $7 per night for an additional vehicle, $2 per pet per night. Group tent sites are $8 per person per night with a $75–150 per night minimum, and group RV sites are $10 per person per night with a $200 minimum per night. Boat launching is $6 per day. Weekly and monthly rates available. Some credit cards accepted. Open year-round.

Directions: From Marysville, drive east on Highway 20 for about 12 miles to Marysville Road/Road E-21. Turn left (north) and drive approximately 10 miles to the recreation area entrance road on the right. Turn right, drive 0.3 mile to the entrance station and store, and then continue to the campground. (For detailed directions from other areas, log on to the website.)

Contact: Collins Lake Recreation Area, 530/692-1600 or 800/286-0576, www.collins lake.com.

17 NEVADA COUNTY FAIRGROUNDS

Scenic rating: 6

at the fairgrounds near Grass Valley

See map page 622

The motto here is "California's Most Beautiful Fairgrounds," and that's right. The area is at 2,300 feet in the Sierra foothills, with a good number of pines sprinkled about. The park is adjacent to the fairgrounds, and even though the fair runs for a week every August, the park is open year-round. However, check status be-fore planning a trip because the campground is sometimes closed for scheduled activities. A caretaker at the park is available to answer any questions. Kids can fish at a small lake nearby. The Draft Horse Classic is held here every September, and a country Christmas Faire is held Thanksgiving weekend.

RV sites, facilities: There are 130 sites with full or partial hookups (50 amps) for RVs of any length, and a open dirt and grassy area with no hookups is available as an overflow area. No tents. Two dump stations, drinking water, restrooms with showers and flush toilets, and group facilities are available. Some facilities are wheelchair accessible. Leashed pets are permitted.

Reservations, fees: Reservations are accepted. Sites are $21–26 per night. A seven-day limit is enforced. Some credit cards accepted. Open year-round.

Directions: From Auburn, drive north on Highway 49 to Grass Valley and the McKnight Way exit. Take that exit and turn left on McKnight Way and drive over the freeway to Freeman Lane (just past the shopping center on the left). Turn right on Freeman Lane and drive to the second stop sign and McCourtney Road. Continue straight on McCourtney Road and drive two blocks to the fairgrounds on the right. Continue to Gate 4.

Contact: Nevada County Fairgrounds, 530/273-6217, fax 530/273-1146, www.nevadacounty fair.com.

18 SACRAMENTO RIVER STATE RECREATION AREA

Scenic rating: 5

near Colusa

See map page 622

This region of the Sacramento Valley is well known as a high-quality habitat for birds. This park covers 67 acres and features great bird-watching opportunities. Nearby Delevan and Colusa National Wildlife Refuges are outstanding destinations for wildlife-viewing as well, and they provide good duck hunting in December. The nearby Sacramento River is a bonus with shad fishing in June and July, salmon fishing August–October, sturgeon fishing in the winter, and striped bass fishing in the spring. The landscape here features cottonwoods and willows along the Sacramento River.

RV sites, facilities: There are 10 sites for tents, four sites for tents or RVs up to 30 feet, and one group site for 10–40 people. No hookups. Picnic tables and barbecues are provided. Drinking water, restrooms with flush toilets and coin showers, a boat ramp, Wi-Fi, and a dump station are available. A grocery store, a restaurant, a gas station, a tackle shop, and a coin laundry are nearby (within three blocks). Some facilities are wheelchair accessible. Leashed pets are permitted.

Reservations, fees: Reservations for individual sites are accepted ($7.50 reservation fee) at 800/444-PARK (800/444-7275) or www.reserveamerica.com. Group reservations are accepted at 530/458-4927. Sites are $12–15 per night, $6 per night for an additional vehicle, $90 per night for the group site. Open year-round.

Directions: In Williams, at the junction of I-5 and Highway 20, drive east on Highway 20 for nine miles to the town of Colusa. Turn north (straight ahead) on 10th Street and drive two blocks, just over the levee, to the park.

Contact: Colusa–Sacramento River State Recreation Area, 530/458-4927, fax 530/458-8033; North Buttes District, 530/538-2200, www.parks.ca.gov.

19 CAMPERS INN RV PARK AND GOLF COURSE

Scenic rating: 1

near Dunnigan

See map page 623

This private park has a rural valley atmosphere and provides a layover for drivers cruising I-5. The park has a par-three golf course (nine holes), and it specializes in golf tournaments and group outings. The Sacramento River to the east is the closest body of water, but this section of river is hardly a premium side-trip destination. There are no nearby lakes.

RV sites, facilities: There are three tent sites and 72 sites with full or partial hookups (30 and 50 amps) for RVs of any length. Many sites are pull-through. Picnic tables are provided. Restrooms have flush toilets and showers. Modem access, a seasonal swimming pool, two clubhouses/meeting rooms, horseshoes, a nine-hole golf course, a coin laundry, propane gas, ice, and a general store are available. Some facilities are wheelchair accessible. Leashed pets are permitted.

Reservations, fees: Reservations are accepted. Sites are $18–29.50 per night. Some credit cards accepted. Open year-round.

Directions: From I-5 in Dunnigan, take the Dunnigan exit (just north of the I-505 cutoff). Drive west on County Road E4/Road 6 for a mile to County Road 88. Turn right and drive for 1.5 miles to the park.

Contact: Campers Inn RV Park and Golf Course, 530/724-3350 or 800/79-GOLF3 (800/794-6533), www.campersinnrv.com.

20 AUBURN GOLD COUNTRY RV PARK

Scenic rating: 4

near Auburn

See map page 623

This year-round park is at 1,250 feet and has all the amenities. Hey, a swimming pool is always a bonus in Auburn. Some may remember that this park was once a KOA campground. An 18-hole golf course is within one-half mile. The American River and Auburn State Recreation Area, which includes Clementine Lake, are nearby.

RV sites, facilities: There are 66 sites with full and partial hookups (30 and 50 amps) for RVs up to 40 feet, plus 10 tent sites. Some sites are pull-through. Two cabins are available. Picnic tables and fire rings are provided. Restrooms have flush toilets and showers. Drinking water, a dump station, a playground, a seasonal heated swimming pool, a spa, a recreation room, a fishing pond, basketball, horseshoes, a convenience store, a coin laundry, and propane gas are available. Some facilities are wheelchair accessible. Leashed pets are permitted, with certain restrictions.

Reservations, fees: Reservations are accepted at 866/822-8362. Sites are $27–45 per night, $2.50–4.50 per person per night for more than two people. Some credit cards accepted. Open year-round.

Directions: From Auburn, drive north on Highway 49 for 3.5 miles to Rock Creek Road (one block past Bell Road). Turn right on Rock Creek Road and drive a short distance to the entrance on the left.

Contact: Auburn Gold Country RV Park, 530/885-0990.

21 AUBURN STATE RECREATION AREA: MINERAL BAR

Scenic rating: 8

near Colfax

See map page 623

Mineral Bar camp is in the Auburn State Recreation Area, near the American River. This state park is a jewel in the valley foothill country, covering more than 42,000 acres along 40 miles of the North and Middle Forks of the American River. This area once teemed with thousands of gold miners, but it is now a natural area offering a wide variety of recreational opportunities and wildlife. The Auburn SRA is actually made up of land set aside for the Auburn Dam, consisting of 40 miles along two forks of the American River. There is one boat-in campground at Clementine Lake. The lake is 3.5 miles long and very narrow. All water sports are allowed on the lake. The American River runs through the park, offering visitors opportunities to fish, boat, kayak, and raft. In addition, there are more than 100 miles of hiking, biking, and horseback-riding trails. Clementine Lake offers fishing (not stocked) and waterskiing, with

a boat limit of 25 boats per day; the quota is reached every day on summer weekends. White-water rafting is extremely popular, with more than 30 private outfitters licensed for trips in sections of river through the park.

RV sites, facilities: There are 17 sites for tents or RVs up to 24 feet (no hookups). Picnic tables and fire grills are provided. Chemical toilets are available. No drinking water is available. Garbage must be packed out. Leashed pets are permitted.

Reservations, fees: Reservations are not accepted. Sites are $15 per night, $5 per night for an additional vehicle. Open year-round, with limited winter facilities.

Directions: From I-80 in Auburn, drive east for 15 miles to Colfax and the Canyon Way/Placer Hills Drive exit. Take that exit, turn left on Canyon Way, and drive one mile to Iowa Hill Road. Turn right and drive three miles on a narrow paved road to the campground.

Contact: Auburn State Recreation Area, 530/885-4527, fax 530/885-2798, www.parks.ca.gov.

22 BEAL'S POINT

Scenic rating: 6

in Folsom Lake State Recreation Area

See map page 623

Folsom Lake State Recreation Area is Sacramento's backyard vacation spot, a huge lake covering about 18,000 acres with 75 miles of shoreline, which means plenty of room for boating, waterskiing, fishing, and suntanning. This camp is on the lake's southwest side, just north of the dam, with a boat ramp nearby at Granite Bay. The lake has a productive trout fishery in the spring, a fast-growing population of kokanee salmon, and good prospects for bass in late spring and early summer. By summer wakeboarders and water-skiers usually take over the lake each day by about 10 A.M. One problem with this lake is that a minor water drawdown can cause major amounts of shoreline to become exposed on its upper

CALIFORNIA

arms. There are opportunities for hiking, biking, running, picnics, and horseback riding. A 32-mile-long trail connects Folsom Lake with many Sacramento County parks before reaching Old Sacramento. This trail is outstanding for family biking and roller-blading. Summers are hot and dry.

RV sites, facilities: There are 69 sites for tents or RVs up to 31 feet; some sites have full hookups (30 and 50 amps). Picnic tables and fire grills are provided. Drinking water, restrooms with flush toilets and showers, Wi-Fi, and a dump station are available. A bike path and horseback-riding facilities are nearby. There are boat rentals, moorings, a summer snack bar, ice, and bait and tackle available at the Folsom Lake Marina. Some facilities are wheelchair accessible. Leashed pets are permitted.

Reservations, fees: Reservations are accepted April–September ($7.50 reservation fee) at 800/444-PARK (800/444-7275) or www.reserveamerica.com. Sites are $15–20 per night, $5–7 per night for an additional vehicle. Open year-round.

Directions: From Sacramento, drive east on U.S. 50 to the Folsom Boulevard exit. Take that exit to the stop sign and Folsom Boulevard. Turn left and continue north on Folsom Boulevard for 3.5 miles (the road changes names to Folsom-Auburn Road) to the park entrance on the right.

Contact: Folsom Lake State Recreation Area, 916/988-0205, fax 916/988-9062; Beal's Point Campground, 916/791-1531, www.parks.ca.gov.

23 PENINSULA

Scenic rating: 6

in Folsom Lake State Recreation Area
See map page 623

This is one of the big camps at Folsom Lake, but it is also more remote than the other camps, requiring a circuitous drive. It is on the peninsula on the northeast shore, right where the North Fork American River arm of the lake enters the main lake area. A nearby boat ramp, a marina, and boat rentals make this a great weekend spot. Fishing for bass and trout is often quite good in spring and early summer, and other species include catfish and perch. Waterskiing and wakeboarding are popular in the hot summer, and all water sports are allowed.

RV sites, facilities: There are 100 sites for tents or RVs up to 32 feet (no hookups). Picnic tables and fire grills are provided. Drinking water and restrooms with flush toilets are available. A bike path is nearby. Boat rentals, moorings, a snack bar, ice, and bait and tackle are available at the Folsom Lake Marina. Leashed pets are permitted.

Reservations, fees: Reservations are accepted ($7.50 reservation fee) at 800/444-PARK (800/444-7275) or www.reserveamerica.com. Sites are $15–20 per night, $5–7 per night for an additional vehicle. Open year-round.

Directions: From Placerville, drive east on U.S. 50 to the Spring Street/Highway 49 exit. Turn north on Highway 49 (toward the town of Coloma) and continue 8.3 miles into the town of Pilot Hill and Rattlesnake Bar Road. Turn left on Rattlesnake Bar Road and drive nine miles to the end of the road and the park entrance.

Contact: Folsom Lake State Recreation Area, 916/988-0205, fax 916/988-9062, www.parks.ca.gov.

24 CAMP LOTUS

Scenic rating: 7

on the American River near Coloma
See map page 623

This is a great area with a half mile of frontage on the South Fork of the American River. During spring and summer you'll see plenty of white-water rafters and kayakers here because this is a popular place for outfitters to put in and take out. Several swimming holes are in the immediate vicinity. The camp is on 23 acres at 700 feet in elevation. Trees at Camp Lotus include pines, oaks, willows, and cottonwoods. Coloma, two miles away, is where you'll find the Marshall Gold Discovery Site. Gold was discovered there in 1848, and the site features displays and exhibits on gold rush–era mining methods and the history of the California gold rush. Wineries are nearby, and gold panning, hiking, and fishing are also popular.

RV sites, facilities: There are 10 sites for tents or RVs of any length with partial hookups (20 and 30 amps) and 26 tent sites. A cabin and three lodge rooms are also available for rent. Picnic tables and fire grills are provided. Drinking water, restrooms with showers, Wi-Fi, a general store with deli, volleyball, horseshoes, and raft and kayak put-in and take-out areas are available. Groups can be accommodated. Limited supplies are available in Coloma. Some facilities are wheelchair accessible. Dogs are not permitted.

Reservations, fees: Reservations are accepted and required for weekends. Sites are $7–9 per person per night with a minimum campsite fee of $21–27 per night. Some credit cards accepted. Open March–October.

Directions: From Sacramento, drive east on Highway 50 for approximately 30 miles (past Cameron Park) to Exit 37, the Ponderosa Road exit. Take that exit and drive north over the freeway to North Shingle Road. Turn right and drive 10 miles (the road becomes Lotus Road) to Bassi Road. Turn left and drive one mile to the campground entrance on the right.

Contact: Camp Lotus, 530/622-8672, www .camplotus.com.

25 PLACERVILLE KOA

Scenic rating: 5

near Placerville

See map page 623

This is a classic KOA campground, complete with the cute little log cabins KOA calls "Kamping Kabins." The location of this camp is ideal for many, set near U.S. 50 in the Sierra foothills, the main route up to South Lake Tahoe. Nearby is Apple Hill, where from September to November it is a popular tourist attraction, when the local ranches and orchards

sell produce and crafts, often with live music. In addition, the Marshall Gold Discovery Site is 10 miles north, where gold was discovered in 1848, setting off the 1849 gold rush. White-water rafting and gold panning are popular on the nearby American River.

RV sites, facilities: There are 70 sites with full or partial hookups (30 and 50 amps) for RVs of any length, 14 tent sites, including eight with electricity, 20 sites for tents or RVs, and eight cabins. Some sites are pull-through. Picnic tables and barbecues are provided. Restrooms have flush toilets and showers. Drinking water, a dump station, a pay phone, cable TV, modem access, Wi-Fi, a recreation room, a seasonal swimming pool, a spa (some restrictions apply), a playground, a video arcade, basketball courts, an 18-hole miniature golf course, a convenience store, a snack bar, a dog run, a petting zoo, a fishing pond, bike rentals, pavilion cooking facilities, a volleyball court, and horseshoe pits are available. Some facilities are wheelchair accessible. Leashed pets are permitted, with certain restrictions.

Reservations, fees: Reservations are accepted at 800/562-4197. Sites are $28–48 for RV sites, $25–30 for tent sites, $4 per person per night for more than two people. Some credit cards accepted. Open year-round.

Directions: From U.S. 50 west of Placerville, take the exit for Shingle Springs Drive/Exit 39 (and not the Shingle Springs/Ponderosa Road exit). Drive one block to Rock Barn Road. Turn left and drive 0.5 mile to the campground at the end of the road.

Contact: Placerville KOA, 530/676-2267, www.koa.com or www.koa-placerville.com.

26 SLY PARK RECREATION AREA

Scenic rating: 7

on Jenkinson Lake

See map page 623

Jenkinson Lake is at 3,500 feet in elevation in the lower reaches of Eldorado National Forest, with a climate that is perfect for waterskiing, wakeboarding, and fishing. The lake covers 640

CALIFORNIA

CALIFORNIA

acres and features eight miles of forested shoreline. Participants of these sports get along, with most water-skiers/wakeboarders motoring around the lake's main body, while anglers head upstream into the Hazel Creek arm of the lake for trout (in the spring) and bass (in the summer). Good news for anglers: Personal watercraft are not permitted. More good news: This is one of the better lakes in the Sierra for brown trout. There is a boat ramp at the campground, and another one is on the southwest end of the lake. The area also has several hiking trails, and the lake is good for swimming. There are nine miles of trails available for hiking, biking, and equestrians; an equestrian trail also circles the lake. A group camp is available for visitors with horses, complete with riding trails, hitching posts, and corrals. Note: No pets or babies with diapers are allowed in the lake.

RV sites, facilities: There are 164 sites for tents or RVs up to 40 feet. There are five group sites that can accommodate 50–100 people and an equestrian camp called Black Oak, which has 12 sites and two youth-group areas. No hookups. Picnic tables, fire rings, and barbecues are provided. Drinking water, vault toilets, boat rentals, and firewood are available. Two boat ramps are available nearby. A grocery store, a snack bar, a dump station, bait, and propane gas are available nearby. Some facilities are wheelchair accessible. Leashed pets are permitted.

Reservations, fees: Reservations are accepted at least seven days in advance ($8 reservation fee) at 530/644-2792. Sites are $20–25 per night, $200 per night for a group site, $100 per night for a youth group site, $10 per night for an additional vehicle. Boat launching is $6 per day. Reduced rates available in winter. Some credit cards accepted during the summer season. Open year-round.

Directions: From Sacramento, drive east on U.S. 50 to Pollock Pines and take the exit for Sly Park Road. Drive south for 4.5 miles to Jenkinson Lake and the campground entrance.

Contact: Sly Park Recreation Area, El Dorado Irrigation District, 530/644-2545, www.eid.org.

27 SACRAMENTO WEST/ OLD TOWN KOA

Scenic rating: 2

west Sacramento

See map page 623

This is the choice of car and RV campers touring California's capital and looking for a layover spot. It is in West Sacramento not far from the Capitol building, the railroad museum, Sutter's Fort, Old Sacramento, Crocker Museum, and shopping.

RV sites, facilities: There are 95 pull-through sites with full or partial hookups (30 and 50 amps) for RVs up to 40 feet, as well as 27 tent sites. Twelve cabins are also available. Restrooms have flush toilets and showers. Wi-Fi, cable TV, a playground, a fishing pond, a seasonal swimming pool, a coin laundry, propane gas, and a convenience store are available. Some facilities are wheelchair accessible. Leashed pets are permitted, with certain restrictions.

Reservations, fees: Reservations are accepted at 800/562-2747. Sites are $30–45 per night. Some credit cards accepted. Open year-round.

Directions: From Sacramento, drive west on I-80 about four miles to the West Capitol Avenue exit. Exit and turn left onto West Capitol Avenue, going under the freeway to the second stoplight and the intersection with Lake Road. Turn left onto Lake Road and continue a half block to the camp on the right at 3951 Lake Road.

Contact: Sacramento West/Old Town KOA, 916/371-6771 or 800/545-KAMP (800/545-5267), www.koa.com.

28 PIPI

Scenic rating: 7

on the Middle Fork of the Cosumnes River in Eldorado National Forest

See map page 623

This place is far enough out of the way to get missed by most campers. It is beside the Middle Fork of the Cosumnes River at 4,100 feet. There are some good swimming holes in the area, but the water is cold and swift in early summer (after all, it's snowmelt). A trail/boardwalk along the river is wheelchair accessible. Several sites border a pretty meadow in the back of the camp. This is also a gateway to a vast network of Forest Service roads to the north in Eldorado National Forest.

RV sites, facilities: There are 51 sites for tents or RVs up to 45 feet (no hookups), including two double sites. Picnic tables and fire grills are provided. Drinking water and vault toilets are available. Some facilities are wheelchair accessible. Leashed pets are permitted.

Reservations, fees: Reservations are accepted ($9 reservation fee) at 877/444-6777 or www.ReserveUSA.com. Sites are $18 per night, $36 per night for a double site, $5 per night for an additional vehicle. Open May–mid-November, weather permitting.

Directions: From Jackson, drive east on Highway 88 to Pioneer and continue for nine miles to Omo Ranch Road. Turn left and drive 0.8 mile to North-South Road/Forest Road 6. Turn right and drive 5.9 miles to the campground on the right side of the road.

Contact: Eldorado National Forest, Amador Ranger District, 209/295-4251, fax 209/295-5998.

29 VINEYARD RV PARK

Scenic rating: 2

in Vacaville

See map page 623

This is one of two privately operated parks in the area set up primarily for RVs. It is in a eucalyptus grove, with clean, well-kept sites. If you are heading to the Bay Area, it is late in the day, and you don't have your destination set, this spot offers a chance to hole up for the night and formulate your travel plans. Note that about half of the sites are long-term rentals.

RV sites, facilities: There are 110 sites with full hookups (30 and 50 amps) for RVs of any length. No tents. Some sites are pull-through. Picnic tables are provided. Restrooms have flush toilets and showers. Wi-Fi, a seasonal swimming pool, a coin laundry, a putting green, an enclosed dog walk, and ice are available. Some facilities are wheelchair accessible. Leashed pets are permitted, with certain restrictions.

Reservations, fees: Reservations are recommended at 866/447-8797. Sites are $44–48 per night, $2 per person per night for more than two people, $1 per pet per night. Some credit cards accepted. Open year-round.

Directions: From Vacaville on I-80, turn north on I-505 and drive three miles to Midway Road. Turn right (east) on Midway Road and drive 0.5 mile to the second campground on the left at 4985 Midway Road.

Contact: Vineyard RV Park, 707/447-8797, www.vineyardrvpark.com.

30 FAR HORIZONS 49ER VILLAGE RV RESORT

Scenic rating: 4

in Plymouth

See map page 623

This is the granddaddy of RV parks, set on 23 acres in the heart of the gold country 40 miles east of Stockton and Sacramento. It is rarely crowded and offers warm pools and a huge spa. A bonus is the year-round heated, covered swimming pool. This resort is pet-friendly, and dogs receive a free milk bone at check-in. About one-fourth of the sites are occupied by annual renters. Wineries are nearby.

RV sites, facilities: There are 329 sites with full hookups (30 and 50 amps) for RVs up to 40 feet; some are pull-through. Eleven park-model cabins and an RV rental are also available. Restrooms have flush toilets and showers. Cable TV, a dump station, a playground, two heated swimming pools, an indoor spa, a recreation room, a TV lounge, a recreation complex, modem access, Wi-Fi, business services, organized activities, a café, a gift shop, a coin laundry, propane gas, and a general store are available. Some facilities are wheelchair accessible. Leashed pets are permitted.

Reservations, fees: Reservations are recommended at 800/339-6981. Sites are $46–56 per night, $2 per night for an additional vehicle. Winter discounts are available. Some credit cards accepted. Open year-round.

Directions: From Sacramento, drive east on U.S. 50 to Watt Avenue. Turn south on Watt Avenue and drive to Highway 16. Turn left (east) on Highway 16/Jackson Road and drive approximately 30 miles to Highway 49 north/Jackson Road. Merge north on Highway 49 and drive two miles to the resort on the left side of the road at 18265 Highway 49. Note: This is a mile south of Main Street in Plymouth.

Contact: Far Horizons 49er Village RV Resort, 209/245-6981, www.49ervillage.com.

31 INDIAN GRINDING ROCK STATE HISTORIC PARK

Scenic rating: 7

near Jackson

See map page 623

Visiting this park is like entering a time machine. It offers a reconstructed Miwok village with petroglyphs, bedrock mortars, a museum, a two-mile nature trail, and interpretive talks for groups, by reservation. Campers get free access to the museum. One unique element is that you will discover *Chaw-fe* (grinding rock) signs about the park. The camp is at 2,500 feet in the Sierra foothills, about 12 miles from Jackson. It covers 135 acres and is nestled in a small valley with open meadows and large valley oaks. There is a large outcropping of marbleized limestone with 1,185 mortar holes, the largest collection of bedrock mortars in North America. Ceremonies are scheduled several times a year by local Native Americans, including the Acorn Harvest Thanksgiving in September. Summers are warm and dry, with temperatures often exceeding 90°F. Spring and fall are ideal, with winters cool, often right on the edge of snow (a few times) and rain (mostly) during most storms.

RV sites, facilities: There are 23 sites for tents or RVs up to 27 feet, and a group camp for up to 44 people includes bark houses. No hookups. Picnic tables, fire grills, and food lockers

are provided. Drinking water and restrooms with flush toilets and coin showers are available. Some facilities are wheelchair accessible. Leashed pets are permitted.

Reservations, fees: Reservations are accepted for the group camp only ($10 reservation fee), which includes bark houses. Sites are $18–20 per night, $6 per night for an additional vehicle, $75 per night for the group camp. Open year-round.

Directions: From Jackson, drive east on Highway 88 for 11 miles to Pine Grove-Volcano Road. Turn left on Pine Grove-Volcano Road and drive 1.75 miles to the campground on the left.

Contact: Indian Grinding Rock State Historic Park, 209/296-7488, www.parks.ca.gov.

32 RANCHO SECO RECREATION AREA

Scenic rating: 6

near Sacramento

See map page 623

There is a shortage of campgrounds close to Sacramento, so this one about 35 miles from the state capital comes in handy. This public facility has a 160-acre lake that is surrounded by 400 acres of open space and includes trails for walking and bicycling. In 2006, a seven-mile loop nature trail opened next to the lake. The centerpiece of this facility is the lake, which is especially popular for fishing and sailboarding. The lake is stocked with rainbow trout, and fishing derbies are held during the winter. Other fish species include bass, bluegill, redear sunfish, crappie, and catfish. Live bait is prohibited and only electric motors are allowed. A bonus is that the lake level remains constant year-round, and since the lake is fed by the Folsom South Canal, the water is warm in summer. Swimming is popular, and there is a large sandy beach with summer lifeguard service. Pedal boats and kayaks can also be rented on weekends in summer. Tent sites are situated along the lake. The Amanda Blake Memorial

Wildlife Refuge is here, and visitors can observe exotic captive wildlife that has been rescued from circuses and other performing groups. Migratory birds, including bald eagles, winter at the lake. What are those two large towers? They're remnants of the now-closed Rancho Seco nuclear power-generating station.

RV sites, facilities: There are 18 sites with partial hookups (30 amps) for RVs of any length, 20 tent sites, and two group tent sites that can accommodate up to 200 people each. A couple of sites are pull-through. Picnic tables and fire grills are provided. Drinking water, restrooms with coin showers, a dump station, swimming beach, six fishing piers, picnic areas, a coin laundry, a fish-cleaning station, a horseshoe pit, a recreation room, a seasonal general store, weekend boat rentals, and a boat launch are available. Supplies are available in Galt. Some facilities are wheelchair accessible, including some fishing piers. Leashed pets are permitted.

Reservations, fees: Reservations are accepted at 916/732-4913. Sites are $10–15 per night, and the group tent site is $45 per night for the first 20 people, plus $1.50 per person per night for additional campers. There is a 14-day maximum stay. Open year-round.

Directions: From Sacramento, drive south on Highway 99 for approximately 25 miles to the Twin Cities Road/Highway 104 exit. Take that exit and drive east for 13 miles, past the two towers, to the Rancho Seco Park exit. Turn right and continue to the lake and campground.

Contact: Rancho Seco Recreation Area, 209/748-2318, www.smud.org/about/recreation/rancho.html.

will beckon you for water sports and is excellent for boat owners and all water sports, with a full-service marina available. The warm, clean waters make for good waterskiing and wakeboarding (in specified areas), as well as fishing for trout in spring, for bass in early summer, and for crappie, bluegill, and catfish in summer. There are five miles of hiking and equestrian trails.

RV sites, facilities: There are 219 sites for tents or RVs of any length and four group sites for 12–72 people. No hookups. Nine cottages, four triplexes, and motel rooms are also available. Picnic tables and fire grills are provided. Restrooms have showers. Drinking water, a dump station, a boat ramp, boat rentals, a coin laundry, a convenience store, café, and a playground are available. Some facilities are wheelchair accessible. Leashed pets are permitted.

Reservations, fees: Reservations are accepted ($8.25 reservation fee) at 866/763-5121. Sites are $24 per night, $10 per night for an additional vehicle, $50–212 per night for a group site, $3 per pet per night. Boat launching is $6.50 per day. Group rates are available. Some credit cards accepted. Open year-round.

Directions: From Stockton, drive east on Highway 88/Waterloo Road for 17 miles to Clements. One mile east of Clements, bear left on Highway 88 and drive six miles to Liberty Road/North Camanche Parkway. Turn right and drive six miles to Camanche Road. Turn right and drive to the Camanche North Shore entrance gate.

Contact: Lake Camanche North, 209/763-5121, fax 209/763-5789, www.camanchecreation.com.

33 LAKE CAMANCHE NORTH

Scenic rating: 7

on Camanche Lake

See map page 623

The sites at North Shore feature grassy spots with picnic tables set above the lake, and though there are few trees and the sites seem largely exposed, the lake view is quite pretty. The lake

34 LAKE CAMANCHE SOUTH AND EQUESTRIAN CAMP

Scenic rating: 7

on Lake Camanche

See map page 623

Lake Camanche is a huge, multifaceted facility, covering 7,700 acres with 53 miles of shoreline, set in the foothills east of Lodi at 325 feet in elevation. It is the number-one recreation lake for waterskiing, wakeboarding, and personal watercraft (in specified areas), as well as swimming. In the spring and summer, it provides outstanding fishing for bass, trout, crappie, bluegill, and catfish. There are two campgrounds at the lake, and both have boat ramps nearby and full facilities. A new equestrian campground is open, and it's about one mile from the main campground area. This one at South Shore has a large but exposed overflow area for camping, a way to keep from getting stuck for a spot on popular weekends.

RV sites, facilities: There are 297 sites for tents or RVs of any length (no hookups), 99 sites with full hookups (30 and 50 amps) for RVs of any length, 25 double sites, five triple sites, two quad sites, seven equestrian sites, and one group site for 16–64 people. Seven cottages are also available. Additionally, Miners Camp has 108 RV sites with full hookups (30 and 50 amps), 63 of which are long-term rentals. Picnic tables and fire grills are provided. Drinking water, restrooms with flush toilets and showers, chemical toilets, a dump station, a trout pond, a marina, a boat ramp, boat rentals, a coin laundry, an amphitheater with seasonal movies, basketball, tennis courts, and a convenience store are available. Some facilities are wheelchair accessible. Leashed pets are permitted.

Reservations, fees: Reservations are accepted ($8.25 reservation fee) at 866/763-5178. Sites are $36 per night, $35–106 per night for equestrian sites, $190 per night for the group site, $10 per night for an additional vehicle, $3 per pet per night. The boat-launch fee is $6.50 per day. Monthly rates available, with a six-month limit. Some credit cards accepted. Open year-round.

Directions: From Stockton, drive east on Highway 88/Waterloo Road for 17 miles to Clements. One mile east of Clements continue east on Highway 12 and drive six miles to South Camanche Parkway at Wallace. Continue straight and drive five miles to the entrance gate.

Contact: Lake Camanche South, 209/763-5178, www.camancherecreation.com.

35 LAKE AMADOR RECREATION AREA

Scenic rating: 7

near Stockton

See map page 623

Lake Amador is in the foothill country east of Stockton at an elevation of 485 feet, covering 400 acres with 13 miles of shoreline. Everything here is set up for fishing, with large trout stocks from winter through late spring and the chance for huge bass. The lake record bass weighed 17 pounds, 1.25 ounces. The Carson Creek arm and Jackson Creek arm are the top spots. Night fishing is available. Waterskiing and personal watercraft are prohibited, and the speed limit is 5 mph. A bonus is a swimming pond. About half of the sites are lakefront with full hookups.

RV sites, facilities: There are 150 sites for tents or RVs of any length and 13 group sites for 5–30 vehicles each; some sites have full hookups (30 and 50 amps). Picnic tables and fire grills are provided. Drinking water, restrooms with showers, a dump station, a boat ramp, boat rentals, fishing supplies (including bait and tackle), a café, a convenience store, propane gas, a swimming pond, and a playground are available. Some facilities are wheelchair accessible. Leashed pets are permitted.

Reservations, fees: Reservations are accepted ($5 reservation fee) in the summer. Sites are $22–30 per night per vehicle, $3 per night for electricity. Boat launching is $6 per day and fishing is $8 per day. Winter rates are available. Some credit cards accepted. Open year-round.

Directions: From Stockton, turn east on Highway 88 and drive 24 miles to Clements. Just east of Clements, bear left on Highway 88 and drive nine miles to Jackson Valley Road. Turn right (well signed) and drive five miles to Lake Amador Drive. Turn right and drive over the dam to the campground office.

Contact: Lake Amador Recreation Area, 209/274-4739, www.lakeamador.com.

36 LAKE PARDEE MARINA

Scenic rating: 7

on Pardee Reservoir

See map page 623

Many people think that Pardee is the prettiest lake in the Mother Lode country; it's a big lake covering 2,257 acres with 37 miles of shoreline. It is a beautiful sight in the spring when the lake is full and the surrounding hills are green and glowing. Waterskiing, personal watercraft, swimming, and all water/body contact are prohibited at the lake; it is set up expressly for fishing, with high catch rates for rainbow trout and kokanee salmon. During hot weather, attention turns to bass, both smallmouth and largemouth, as well as catfish and sunfish. The lake speed limit is 25 mph.

RV sites, facilities: There are 14 sites for tents or RVs up to 32 feet (no hookups) and 12 sites with full hookups (50 amps) for RVs. Picnic tables and fire grills are provided. Drinking water, restrooms with showers (in the hookup section), chemical toilets (in the no-hookup campground), a dump station, a full-service marina, a fish-cleaning station, a boat ramp, boat rentals, a coin laundry, a café, a gas station, a convenience store, propane gas, RV and boat storage, a wading pool, and a seasonal swimming pool are available. Some facilities are wheelchair accessible. Leashed pets are permitted.

Reservations, fees: Reservations are accepted. Sites are $19 per night, $10 per night for an additional vehicle, $2 per pet per night. Boat launching is $6.50 per day. Monthly and seasonal rates available. A fishing fee is charged. Some credit cards accepted. Open February–October.

Directions: From Stockton, drive east on Highway 88/Waterloo Road for 17 miles to the town of Clements. One mile east of Clements, bear left on Highway 88 and drive 11 miles to Jackson Valley Road. Turn right and drive 3.4 miles to a four-way stop sign at Buena Vista. Turn right and drive 3.1 miles to Stony Creek Road. Turn left and drive a mile to the campground on the right. (Driving directions from other areas are available on the marina's website.)

Contact: Lake Pardee Marina, 209/772-1472, fax 209/772-0985, www.pardeelakerecreation.com.

37 SANDY BEACH REGIONAL PARK

Scenic rating: 6

on the Sacramento River

See map page 623

This is a surprisingly little-known park, especially considering it provides beach access to the Sacramento River. It is a popular spot for sunbathers in hot summer months, and the park has a sandy beach stretching for more than a half mile. Note that swimming is not allowed, however, because there is no lifeguard; wading is permitted. Sailboarding and sailing are possible here. In winter, it is one of the few viable spots where you can fish from the shore for sturgeon; check fishing regulations. It also provides outstanding boating access to the Sacramento River, including one of the best fishing spots for striped bass in the fall, the Rio Vista Bridge.

RV sites, facilities: There are 42 sites for tents or RVs of any length with partial hookups (30 amps). Picnic tables and fire pits are provided. Drinking water, restrooms with flush toilets and showers, a dump station, picnic areas, volleyball, horseshoes, firewood, and a boat ramp are available. A camp host is on-site. Supplies can be obtained nearby (within 1 mile). Some facilities are wheelchair accessible. Leashed pets are permitted in the campground only.

Reservations, fees: Reservations are accepted. Sites are $21 per night, $7 per night for an additional vehicle, $1 per pet per night. Some credit cards accepted. Open year-round.

Directions: From I-80 in Fairfield, take the Highway 12 exit and drive southeast for 14 miles to Rio Vista and the intersection with Main Street. Turn right on Main Street and drive a short distance to 2nd Street. Turn right

CALIFORNIA

and drive 0.5 mile to Beach Drive. Turn left (west) and drive 0.5 mile to the park.

Contact: Sandy Beach Regional Park, 707/374-2097, fax 707/374-4972, www.solanocounty.com.

38 DELTA MARINA YACHT HARBOR AND RV

Scenic rating: 6

on the Sacramento River Delta
See map page 623

This is a prime spot for boat campers. Summers are hot and breezy, and waterskiing is popular on the nearby Sacramento River. From November to March, the striped bass fishing is quite good, often as close as just a half mile upriver at the Rio Vista Bridge. The boat launch at the harbor is a bonus, especially with night lighting. Some campsites have river frontage, and some sites are filled with long-term renters.

RV sites, facilities: There are 25 sites with full hookups (30 and 50 amps) for RVs up to 40 feet. No tents. Picnic tables and fire grills are provided. Restrooms have showers. Cable TV, a coin laundry, a playground, a boat ramp, a fishing pier, marine repair service, a pet restroom, a restaurant, marine supplies and gift store, ice, and propane gas are available. Fuel is available 24 hours. Free boat launching for RV guests. Some facilities are wheelchair accessible. Leashed pets are permitted.

Reservations, fees: Reservations are accepted. Sites are $25–35 per night, with a two-week maximum stay in summer. Some credit cards accepted. Open year-round.

Directions: From Fairfield on I-80, take the Highway 12 exit and drive southeast for 14 miles to Rio Vista and the intersection with Main Street. Take the Main Street exit and drive a short distance to 2nd Street. Turn right on 2nd Street and drive to Marina Drive. Turn left on Marina Drive and continue a short distance to the harbor.

Contact: Delta Marina Yacht Harbor and RV, 707/374-2315, fax 707/374-6471, www.deltamarina.com.

39 BRANNAN ISLAND STATE RECREATION AREA

Scenic rating: 7

on the Sacramento River
See map page 623

This state park is perfectly designed for boaters, set in the heart of the Delta's vast waterways. You get year-round adventure: Waterskiing, wakeboarding, and fishing for catfish are popular in the summer, and in the winter the immediate area is often good for striped bass fishing. The proximity of the campgrounds to the boat launch deserves a medal. What many people do is tow a boat here, launch it, keep it docked, and then return to their site and set up; this allows them to come and go as they please, boating, fishing, and exploring in the Delta. There is a six-lane boat ramp that provides access to a maze of waterways amid many islands, marshes, sloughs, and rivers. Day-use areas include the Windy Cove sailboarding area. Though striped bass in winter and catfish in summer are the most favored fish here, sturgeon, bluegill, perch, bullhead, and bass are also caught. Some sections of the San Joaquin Delta are among the best bass fishing spots in California. A hiking/biking trail circles the park.

RV sites, facilities: There are 102 sites for tents or RVs up to 36 feet, eight walk-in sites, and six group sites for up to 30 people each. No hookups. Picnic tables and fire grills are provided. Drinking water, restrooms with coin showers (at campground and boat launch), boat berths, a dump station, Wi-Fi, and a boat launch are available. Supplies can be obtained three miles away in Rio Vista. Some facilities are wheelchair accessible. Leashed pets are permitted.

Reservations, fees: Reservations are accepted at 800/444-PARK (800/444-7275) or www.reserveamerica.com ($7.50 reservation fee). Sites are $15–20 per night, $5 per night for an additional vehicle, $66 per night for

CALIFORNIA

group sites. Boat launching is $5 per day. Open year-round.

Directions: In Fairfield on I-80, take the Highway 12 exit, drive southeast 14 miles to Rio Vista, and continue to Highway 160. Turn right on Highway 160 and drive three miles to the park entrance on the left.

Contact: Brannan Island State Recreation Area, 916/777-6671; Entrance Kiosk, 916/777-7701; Goldfield District Office, 916/988-0205, www.parks.ca.gov.

40 WESTGATE LANDING COUNTY PARK

Scenic rating: 6

in the San Joaquin River Delta near Stockton

See map page 623

Summer temperatures typically reach the high 90s and low 100s here, and this county park provides a little shade and boating access to the South Fork Mokelumne River. On hot summer nights, some campers will stay up late and night fish for catfish. Between storms in winter, the area typically gets smothered in dense fog. For RV drivers, the sites are not pull-through but semicircles, which work nearly as well.

RV sites, facilities: There are 14 sites for tents or RVs up to 32 feet (no hookups). Picnic tables and barbecues are provided. Drinking water and flush toilets are available. Groceries and propane gas are nearby. A fishing pier, 24 boat slips, and boat docking are available. Some facilities are wheelchair accessible. Leashed pets are permitted, with a limit of two.

Reservations, fees: Reservations are accepted ($10 reservation fee) two weeks or more in advance. Otherwise, sites are first-come, first-served. Sites are $15 per night, $5 per night for an additional vehicle, boat slips $15 per day, $1 per pet per night. Open year-round.

Directions: On I-5, drive to Lodi and Highway 12. Take Highway 12 west and drive about five miles to Glasscock Road. Turn right and drive about a mile to the park.

Contact: San Joaquin County Parks De-partment, 209/953-8800 or 209/331-7400, www.co.san-joaquin.ca.us/parks.

41 SNUG HARBOR RESORT

Scenic rating: 7

near Rio Vista

See map page 623

This year-round resort is an ideal resting place for families who enjoy waterskiing, wakeboarding, boating, biking, swimming, and fishing. After the ferry ride, it is only a few minutes to Snug Harbor, a gated marina resort on eight acres with a campground, RV hookups, and a separate area with cabins and cottages. Some say that the waterfront sites with docks give the place the feel of a Louisiana bayou, yet everything is clean and orderly, including a full-service marina, a store, and all facilities—an excellent location to explore the boating paradise of the Delta. Anglers will find good prospects for striped bass, black bass, blue gill, steelhead, sturgeon, and catfish. The waterfront sites with docks are a bonus.

RV sites, facilities: There are 38 waterfront sites with docks and full hookups (30 and 50 amps) for RVs of any length, 15 water-view sites with full hookups for RVs, six group sites for RVs, four tent trailers, and 20 park-model cabins. Barbecues or burn barrels are provided. Restrooms have showers. A dump station, Wi-Fi, a convenience store, a swimming beach, a children's play area, volleyball, croquet, boccie ball, badminton, horseshoes, a boat launch, propane gas, and a full-service marina are available. Some facilities are wheelchair accessible.

Reservations, fees: Reservations by website are recommended. Sites are $32–45 per night, $7.50 per night for an additional vehicle, $60–90 per night for group sites, $2 per pet per night. Boat launching is $10 per day. Call or check the website for tent trailer and cabin prices. Some credit cards accepted. Open year-round.

Directions: From the Bay Area, take I-80 to Fairfield and Highway 12. Turn east on Highway 12 and drive to Rio Vista and Front Street. Turn left on Front Street (before crossing the

CALIFORNIA

bridge) and drive under the bridge to River Road. Turn right on River Road and drive two miles to the Rio Vista/Real McCoy Ferry (signed Ryer Island). Take the ferry (free) across the Sacramento River to Ryer Island and Levee Road. Turn right on Levee Road and drive 4.5 miles to the Snug Harbor entrance on the right. For recorded directions from other areas, including Sacramento, call 916/775-1594.

Contact: Snug Harbor Resort, 916/775-1455, fax 916/775-1594, www.snugharbor.net.

42 LUNDBORG LANDING

Scenic rating: 6

on the San Joaquin River Delta

See map page 623   BEST (

This park is on Bethel Island in the heart of the California Delta. The boat ramp provides immediate access to an excellent area for water-skiing, and it turns into a playland on hot summer days. In the fall and winter, the area often provides good striper fishing at nearby Frank's Tract, False River, and the San Joaquin River. The fishing for largemouth bass at Frank's Tract is rated among the best in North America. Catfishing in surrounding slough areas is also good year-round. The Delta Sportsman Shop at Bethel Island has reliable fishing information. Live web camera pictures of Frank's Tract are available on the website. Note that some sites are occupied by long-term tenants.

RV sites, facilities: There are 70 sites with full hookups (30 and 50 amps) for RVs; some are pull-through and some sites allow tents. A large overflow area can handle up to 300 RVs and many tents. Several cabins are also available. Restrooms have showers. A coin laundry, a dump station, propane gas, modem access, a playground, a boat ramp, fishing pier, berthing, boat storage, a fish-cleaning station, and a full restaurant and bar are available. Some facilities are wheelchair accessible. Leashed pets are permitted.

Reservations, fees: Reservations are accepted. Sites are $16–24 per night. Long-term rates available. Open year-round.

Directions: From Antioch, turn east on Highway 4 and drive to Oakley and East Cypress Road. Turn left on East Cypress Road, drive over the Bethel Island Bridge, and continue 0.5 mile to Gateway Road. Turn right on Gateway Road and drive two miles to the park entrance on the left (signed well, next to the tugboat).

Contact: Lundborg Landing, 925/684-9351, www.lundborglanding.com.

43 EDDOS HARBOR AND RV PARK

Scenic rating: 6

on the San Joaquin River Delta

See map page 623

This is an ideal spot for campers with boats. Eddos is set on the San Joaquin River and Gallagher Slough, upstream of the Antioch Bridge, in an outstanding region for fishing, powerboating, wakeboarding, and waterskiing. In summer, boaters have access to 1,000 miles of Delta waterways, with the best of them in a nearby spiderweb of rivers and sloughs off the San Joaquin to False River, Frank's Tract, and Old River. Hot weather and sheltered sloughs make this ideal for waterskiing. In the winter, a nearby fishing spot, as well as the mouth of the False River, attract striped bass. Many of the sites here are occupied by seasonal renters; plan well ahead for the summer.

RV sites, facilities: There are 44 sites with full hookups (15 amps) for RVs up to 40 feet. Picnic tables are provided. Restrooms have flush toilets and showers. A launch ramp, boat storage, a fuel dock, Wi-Fi, a coin laundry, and a small grocery store are available. Some facilities are wheelchair accessible. Leashed pets are permitted.

Reservations, fees: Reservations are recommended. Sites are $25 per night and $1 per pet per night. Monthly rates available. Some credit cards accepted. Open year-round.

Directions: In Fairfield on I-80, take the Highway 12 exit, drive 14 miles southeast to Rio Vista, and continue three miles to Highway 160 (at the signal just after the bridge). Turn right on Highway 160 and drive three miles to Sherman Island/East Levee Road, at the end of the drawbridge. Turn left on East Levee Road and drive 5.5 miles to the campground along the San Joaquin River. Note: If arriving by boat, the camp is adjacent to Light 21.

Contact: Eddos Harbor and RV Park, 925/757-5314.

44 STOCKTON DELTA KOA

Scenic rating: 6

near Stockton

See map page 623

Some people may remember this campground by its previous name: Tower Park Resort. This huge resort is ideal for boat-in campers who desire a full-facility marina. The camp is on Little Potato Slough near the Mokelumne River. In the summer, this is a popular waterskiing area. Some hot weekends are like a continuous party. Note that tents are now allowed here.

RV sites, facilities: There are 300 sites with full hookups (30 amps) for RVs up to 45 feet, 20 tent sites, and five park-model cabins. Picnic tables are provided. Restrooms have showers. A dump station, a pavilion, a banquet room, boat rentals, overnight boat slips, boat storage, double boat launch, a playground, a swimming pool, a spa, horseshoes, a gas station, a restaurant, a coin laundry, a gift shop, a store, ice, and propane gas are available. Some facilities are wheelchair accessible. Leashed pets are permitted, with certain restrictions.

Reservations, fees: Reservations are available, with a three-night minimum on summer holidays. Sites are $30–54 per night, maximum six people per site. Some credit cards accepted. Open year-round.

Directions: On I-5, drive to Lodi and Highway 12. Take Highway 12 west and drive about five miles to Tower Park Way (before the first bridge). Turn left and drive a short distance to the park.

Contact: Stockton Delta KOA, 209/369-1041, fax 209/369-1301, www.koa.com or www.stocktondeltakoa.com.

45 STOCKTON/LODI RV PARK

Scenic rating: 3

in Lodi

See map page 623

This former KOA camp is in the heart of the San Joaquin Valley. The proximity to I-5 and Highway 99 makes it work for long-distance vacationers looking for a spot to park the rig for the night. The San Joaquin Delta is 15 miles to the west, with best access provided off Highway 12 to Isleton and Rio Vista; it's also a pretty drive.

RV sites, facilities: There are 102 sites, most pull-through and many with full hookups (30 and 50 amps), for RVs of any length; 13 tent sites; and two cabins. Picnic tables are provided. Restrooms have showers. A dump station, a convenience store, propane gas, a coin laundry, modem access, a recreation room, a seasonal swimming pool, bicycle rentals, and a playground are available. Some facilities are wheelchair accessible. Leashed pets are permitted at campsites, with certain restrictions, but not in cabins.

Reservations, fees: Reservations are accepted at 800/562-1229. Sites are $26–34 per night, $2–4 per night for more than two people. Some credit cards accepted. Open year-round.

Directions: On I-5, drive to Eight Mile Road (five miles north of Stockton). Turn east and drive five miles to the campground at 2851 East Eight Mile Road.

Contact: Stockton/Lodi RV Park, tel./fax 209/941-2573 or 209/334-0309 (from Lodi), www.stknlodirv.com.

46 OAK KNOLL

Scenic rating: 7

at New Hogan Reservoir

See map page 623

This is one of two camps at New Hogan. The reservoir was created by an Army Corps of Engineers dam project on the Calaveras River. (See the listing in this chapter for *Acorn Campground* for more information.)

RV sites, facilities: There are 50 sites for tents

CALIFORNIA

or RVs of any length, and a group site for tents or RVs of any length can accommodate up to 50 people. No hookups. Fire grills and picnic tables are provided. Drinking water and vault toilets are available. A dump station and a four-lane boat ramp (at Fiddleneck) are available nearby. A grocery store and propane gas are available within five miles. Leashed pets are permitted.

Reservations, fees: Reservations are accepted at 877/444-6777 or www.ReserveUSA.com. Sites are $10 per night, and the group site is $100 per night. Open May–early September.

Directions: From Stockton, drive east on Highway 26 for about 30 miles to Valley Springs and Hogan Dam Road. Turn right and drive 1.5 miles to Hogan Parkway. Turn left and drive one mile to South Petersburg Road. Turn left and drive 0.5 mile to the campground on the right (adjacent to Acorn Campground).

Contact: U.S. Army Corps of Engineers, Sacramento District, 209/772-1343, fax 209/772-9352.

47 ACORN CAMPGROUND

Scenic rating: 7

at New Hogan Reservoir

See map page 623

New Hogan is a big lake in the foothill country east of Stockton, at an elevation of 680 feet and covering 4,000 acres with 50 miles of shoreline. Acorn is on the lake and operated by the Army Corps of Engineers. Boaters might also consider boat-in sites near Deer Flat on the eastern shore, and there is a group camp at Coyote Point. Boating and waterskiing are popular here, and all water sports are allowed. It's a decent lake for fishing with a unique opportunity for striped bass, and it's OK for largemouth bass. Other species are crappie, bluegill, and catfish. There are bicycle trails and an eight-mile equestrian trail. An interpretive trail below the dam is worth checking out. Insider's tip: This is a wintering area for bald eagles.

RV sites, facilities: There are 127 sites for tents or RVs of any length (no hookups) and

30 boat-in sites. Fire pits and picnic tables are provided. Drinking water, restrooms with flush toilets and coin showers, pay telephones, a fish-cleaning station, an amphitheater, and a dump station are available. A two-lane, paved boat ramp is nearby. Nature walks and ranger programs are sometimes available. Groceries, a restaurant, and propane gas are available within two miles. Leashed pets are permitted.

Reservations, fees: Reservations are accepted at 877/444-6777 or www.ReserveUSA.com. Sites are $12–16 per night, and boat-in sites are $10 per night. Some credit cards accepted. Open year-round, with a reduced number of sites in winter; boat-in sites are open May–September.

Directions: From Stockton, drive east on Highway 26 for about 30 miles to Valley Springs and Hogan Dam Road. Turn right and drive 1.5 miles to Hogan Parkway. Turn left and drive one mile to South Petersburg Road. Turn left and drive 0.25 mile to the campground on the right.

Contact: U.S. Army Corps of Engineers, Sacramento District, 209/772-1343, fax 209/772-9352.

48 49ER RV RANCH

Scenic rating: 6

near Columbia

See map page 623

This historic ranch/campground was originally built in 1852 as a dairy farm. Several original barns are still standing. The place has been brought up to date, of course, with a small store on the property providing last-minute supplies. Location is a plus, with the Columbia State Historic Park only a half mile away and the Stanislaus River arm of New Melones Lake within a five-minute drive. Live theater and wineries are nearby. The elevation is 2,100 feet. Note that there is a separate mobile home park on the premises.

RV sites, facilities: There are 42 sites with full hookups (30 and 50 amps) for trailers and RVs up to 40 feet. No tents. Picnic tables and cable

TV are provided. Restrooms have showers. Drinking water, a coin laundry, a convenience store, a dump station, modem access, Wi-Fi, propane gas, and a large barn for group or club activities are available. Some facilities are wheelchair accessible. Leashed pets are permitted.

Reservations, fees: Reservations are accepted by phone or website. Sites are $35.90 per night, $2.50 per person per night for more than two people, $3 per night for an additional vehicle. Seasonal rates and group rates available. Open year-round.

Directions: From Sonora, turn north on Highway 49 and drive for 2.5 miles to Parrotts Ferry Road. Turn right and drive 1.7 miles to Columbia Street. Turn right and drive 0.4 mile to Pacific Street. Turn left and drive a block to Italian Bar Road. Turn right and drive 0.5 mile to the campground on the right.

Contact: 49er RV Ranch, tel./fax 209/532-4978, www.49rv.com.

49 MARBLE QUARRY RV PARK

Scenic rating: 6

near Columbia

See map page 623

This is a family-oriented RV park set at 2,100 feet in the Mother Lode country, within nearby range of several adventures. A quarter-mile trail leads directly to Columbia State Historic Park, and the Stanislaus River arm of New Melones Lake is only five miles away.

RV sites, facilities: There are 85 sites with full or partial hookups (30 and 50 amps) for RVs of any length, a small area for tents, and three sleeping cabins. A few sites are pull-through. Picnic tables are provided. Restrooms have showers. Satellite TV, a seasonal swimming pool, a coin laundry, modem access, a convenience store, a dump station, a playground, two clubhouses, a reading/TV room, group facilities, and propane gas are available. Some facilities are wheelchair accessible. Leashed pets are permitted.

Reservations, fees: Reservations are accepted. Sites are $33.50–36.50 per night for RV sites, $24 per night for tent sites, $3 per person per night for more than two people. Some credit cards accepted. Open year-round.

Directions: From Sonora, turn north on Highway 49 and drive 2.5 miles to Parrotts Ferry Road (stop sign). Bear right on Parrotts Ferry Road and drive 1.5 miles to Columbia Street. Turn right and drive a short distance to Jackson Street. Turn right on Jackson Street and drive 0.25 mile (becomes Yankee Hill Road) to the campground on the right (at 11551 Yankee Hill Road).

Contact: Marble Quarry RV Park, 866/677-8464 or 209/532-9539, www.marblequarry.com.

CALIFORNIA

TAHOE AND NORTHERN SIERRA

☾ BEST RV PARKS AND CAMPGROUNDS

Mount Tallac affords a view across Lake Tahoe like

no other: a cobalt blue expanse of water bordered by mountains that span miles of Sierra wildlands. The beauty is stunning. Lake Tahoe is one of the few places on earth where people feel an emotional response just by looking at it. Yosemite Valley, the giant sequoias, the Grand Canyon, a perfect sunset on the Pacific Ocean... these are a few other sights that occasionally can evoke the same response. But Tahoe often seems to strike the deepest chord. It can resonate inside you for weeks, even after a short visit.

This area has the widest range and number of campgrounds in California. "What about all the people?" you ask. It's true that people come here in droves. But I found many spots that I shared only with the chipmunks. You can enjoy these spots, too, if you read my books, hunt a bit, and most important, time your trip to span Monday through Thursday.

Tahoe and the northern Sierra feature hundreds of lakes, including dozens you can drive to. The best for scenic beauty are Echo Lakes, Donner, Fallen Leaf, Sardine, Caples, Loon, Union Valley... well, I could go on and on. It is one of the most beautiful regions anywhere on earth.

The north end of the North Sierra starts near Bucks Lake, a great lake for trout fishing, and extends to Bear River Canyon (and Caples Lake, Silver Lake, and Bear River Reservoir). In between are the Lakes Basin Recreation Area (containing Gold, Sardine, Packer, and other lakes) in southern Plumas County, the Crystal Basin (featuring Union Valley Reservoir and Loon Lake, among others) in the Sierra foothills west of Tahoe, Lake Davis (with the highest catch rates for trout) near Portola, and the Carson River Canyon and Hope Valley south of Tahoe.

You could spend weeks exploring any of these places, having the time of your life, and still not get to Tahoe's magic. But it is Tahoe where the adventure starts for many, especially in the surrounding Tahoe National Forest and Desolation Wilderness.

One of California's greatest day trips from Tahoe is to Echo Lakes, where you can take a hiker's shuttle boat across the two lakes to the Pacific Crest Trail, then hike a few miles into Desolation Wilderness and Aloha Lakes. Yet with so many wonderful ways to spend a day in this area, this day trip is hardly a blip on the radar scope.

With so many places and so little time, this region offers what can be the ultimate adventureland.

Includes:

- American River
- Bear River
- Big Reservoir
- Calaveras Big Trees State Park
- Carson River
- D. L. Bliss State Park
- Donner Lake
- Donner Memorial State Park
- Eldorado National Forest
- Emerald Bay State Park and Boat-In
- Feather River
- Frenchman Lake
- Grover Hot Springs State Park
- Hell Hole Reservoir
- Humboldt-Toiyabe National Forest
- Indian Creek Recreation Area
- Lake Alpine
- Lake Davis
- Lake Tahoe
- Little Truckee River
- Malakoff Diggins State Historic Park
- Packer Lake
- Peninsula Recreation Area
- Plumas National Forest
- Plumas-Eureka State Park
- Rollins Lake
- Scotts Flat Lake Recreation Area
- Silver Lake
- Stampede Lake
- Stanislaus National Forest
- Stanislaus River
- Stumpy Meadows Lake
- Sugar Pine Point State Park
- Tahoe National Forest
- Tahoe State Recreation Area
- Topaz Lake
- Truckee River
- Walker River
- Yuba River

CALIFORNIA

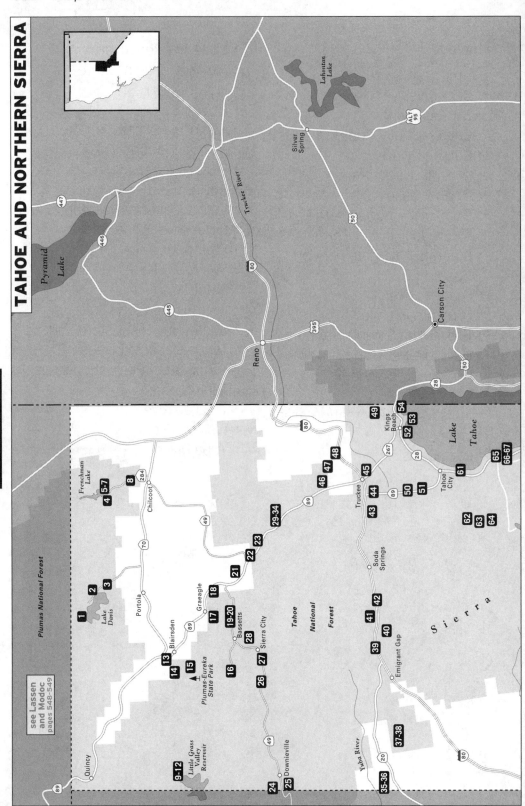

TAHOE AND NORTHERN SIERRA

CALIFORNIA

see Lassen
and Modoc
pages 548-549

Pyramid
Lake

Frenchman
Lake

Lahontan
Lake

Silver
Spring

Truckee River

Carson City

Reno

Plumas National Forest

Lake
Davis

Little Grass
Valley
Reservoir

Chilcoot

Portola

Graeagle

Blairsden

Bassetts

Sierra City

Plumas-Eureka
State Park

Quincy

Downieville

Yuba River

Emigrant Gap

Soda
Springs

Tahoe
National
Forest

Truckee

Tahoe City

Lake
Tahoe

Kings
Beach

Sierra

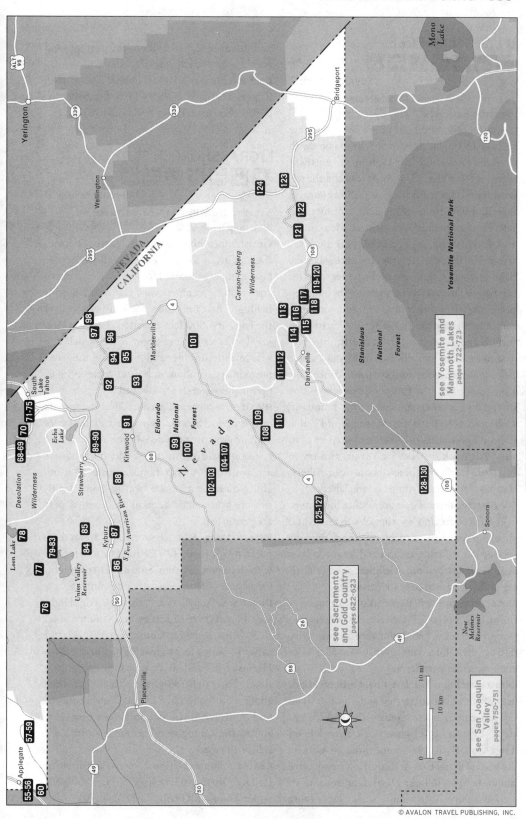

CALIFORNIA

Mono Lake

Bridgeport

Yosemite National Park

see Yosemite and Mammoth Lakes
pages 722-723

Yerington

Wellington

NEVADA
CALIFORNIA

Carson-Iceberg
Wilderness

Stanislaus National Forest

Markleeville

Dardanelle

South Lake Tahoe

Echo Lake

Eldorado National Forest

N e v a d a

Sonora

Desolation Wilderness

Strawberry

Kirkwood

Kyburz

S Fork American River

Loon Lake

Union Valley Reservoir

New Melones Reservoir

Placerville

see Sacramento
and Gold Country
pages 622-623

Applegate

see San Joaquin
Valley
pages 750-751

10 mi

10 km

© AVALON TRAVEL PUBLISHING, INC.

1 LIGHTNING TREE

Scenic rating: 7

on Lake Davis in Plumas National Forest

See map page 652

Lightning Tree campground is near the shore of Lake Davis. Davis is a good-sized lake, with 32 miles of shoreline, set high in the northern Sierra at 5,775 feet. Lake Davis is one of the top mountain lakes for fishing in California, with large rainbow trout in the early summer and fall. This camp is perfectly situated for a fishing trip. It is at Lightning Tree Point on the lake's remote northeast shore, directly across the lake from Freeman Creek, one of the better spots for big trout. This lake is famous for the botched poisoning job (an attempt to wipe out nonnative northern pike) in the 1990s by the Department of Fish and Game, and then, in turn, the biggest trout plants in California history at a single lake: more than one million trout! Since pike have reappeared, the future of this lake is one of the biggest environmental time bombs in California. The Department of Fish and Game plans on poisoning this lake again. After that, they will stock the lake with trout and try to establish Davis as a blue-ribbon trout fishery. There are three boat ramps on the lake.

RV sites, facilities: There are 40 sites for tents or RVs up to 50 feet (no hookups). Vault toilets and drinking water are available. Garbage must be packed out. A dump station and a car-top boat launch are nearby. Some facilities are wheelchair accessible. Leashed pets are permitted.

Reservations, fees: Reservations are accepted at 877/444-6777 ($9 reservation fee) or www.ReserveUSA.com. Sites are $9 per night, $16 per night for a double site. Open May–October, weather permitting.

Directions: From Truckee, turn north on Highway 89 and drive to Sattley and County Road A23. Turn right on County Road A23 and drive 13 miles to Highway 70. Turn left on Highway 70 and drive one mile to Grizzly Road. Turn right on Grizzly Road and drive about six miles to Lake Davis. Continue north on Lake Davis Road along the lake's east shore and drive about five miles to the campground entrance on the left side of the road.

Contact: Plumas National Forest, Beckwourth Ranger District, 530/836-2575, fax 530/836-0493; Thousand Trails, 530/832-1076.

2 GRASSHOPPER FLAT

Scenic rating: 7

on Lake Davis in Plumas National Forest

See map page 652

Grasshopper Flat provides a nearby alternative to Grizzly at Lake Davis, with the nearby boat ramp at adjacent Honker Cove a primary attraction for campers with trailered boats for fishing. The camp is on the southeast end of the lake, at 5,800 feet elevation. Lake Davis is known for its large rainbow trout, which bite best in early summer and fall. Swimming and powerboats are allowed, but no waterskiing or personal watercraft are allowed.

RV sites, facilities: There are 70 sites for tents or RVs up to 35 feet (no hookups). Picnic tables and fire grills are provided. Drinking water and restrooms with flush toilets and coin showers are available. A boat ramp, a grocery store, and a dump station are nearby. Some facilities are wheelchair accessible. Leashed pets are permitted.

Reservations, fees: Reservations are accepted at 877/444-6777 ($9 reservation fee) or www.ReserveUSA.com. Sites are $16 per night. Open May–October, weather permitting.

Directions: From Truckee, turn north on Highway 89 and drive to Sattley and County Road A23. Turn right on County Road A23 and drive 13 miles to Highway 70. Turn left on Highway 70 and drive one mile to Grizzly Road. Turn right on Grizzly Road and drive about six miles to Lake Davis. Continue north on Lake Davis Road for a mile (just past Grizzly) to the campground entrance on the left side of the road.

Contact: Plumas National Forest, Beckwourth Ranger District, 530/836-2575, fax 530/836-0493; Thousand Trails, 530/832-1076.

CALIFORNIA

3 GRIZZLY

Scenic rating: 7

on Lake Davis in Plumas National Forest

See map page 652

This is one of the better developed campgrounds at Lake Davis and is a popular spot for camping anglers. Its proximity to the Grizzly Store, just over the dam to the south, makes getting last-minute supplies a snap. In addition, a boat ramp is to the north in Honker Cove, providing access to the southern reaches of the lake, including the island area, where trout trolling is good in early summer and fall. The elevation is 5,800 feet.

RV sites, facilities: There are 55 sites for tents or RVs up to 35 feet (no hookups). Picnic tables and fire grills are provided. Drinking water and flush toilets are available. A boat ramp, a grocery store, and a dump station are nearby. Some facilities are wheelchair accessible. Leashed pets are permitted.

Reservations, fees: Reservations are accepted at 877/444-6777 ($9 reservation fee) or www.ReserveUSA.com. Sites are $16 per night. Open May–October, weather permitting.

Directions: From Truckee, turn north on Highway 89 and drive to Sattley and County Road A23. Turn right on County Road A23 and drive 13 miles to Highway 70. Turn left on Highway 70 and drive one mile to Grizzly Road. Turn right on Grizzly Road and drive about six miles to Lake Davis. Continue north on Lake Davis Road for less than a mile to the campground entrance on the left side of the road.

Contact: Plumas National Forest, Beckwourth Ranger District, 530/836-2575, fax 530/836-0493; Thousand Trails, 530/832-1076.

4 COTTONWOOD SPRINGS

Scenic rating: 7

near Frenchman Lake in Plumas National Forest

See map page 652

Cottonwood Springs, elevation 5,800 feet, is largely an overflow camp at Frenchman Lake.

It is the only camp at the lake with a group site. The more popular Frenchman, Big Cove, and Spring Creek camps are along the southeast shore of the lake near a boat ramp.

RV sites, facilities: There are 20 sites for tents or RVs up to 50 feet (no hookups) and two group sites for tents or RVs up to 35 feet that can accommodate 25–50 people each. Picnic tables and fire rings are provided. Drinking water and flush toilets are available. A boat ramp and dump station are nearby. Some facilities are wheelchair accessible. Leashed pets are permitted.

Reservations, fees: Reservations are accepted for individual sites and are required for group sites at 877/444-6777 ($9 reservation fee) or www.ReserveUSA.com. Sites are $16 per night, $50–90 per night for groups. Open May–October, weather permitting.

Directions: From Reno, drive north on U.S. 395 to the junction with Highway 70. Turn west on Highway 70 and drive to Chilcoot and the junction with Frenchman Lake Road. Turn right on Frenchman Lake Road and drive nine miles to the lake and to a Y. At the Y, turn left and drive 1.5 miles to the campground on the right side of the road.

Contact: Plumas National Forest, Beckwourth Ranger District, 530/836-2575, fax 530/836-0493; Thousand Trails, 530/832-1076.

5 BIG COVE

Scenic rating: 7

at Frenchman Lake in Plumas National Forest

See map page 652

Big Cove is one of four camps at the southeastern end of Frenchman Lake, with a boat ramp available about a mile away near the Frenchman and Spring Creek camps. The elevation is 5,800 feet. (See the listing in this chapter for *Frenchman* for more information.) A trail from the campground leads to the lakeshore. Another trail connects to the Spring Creek Campground, a walk of a half mile.

RV sites, facilities: There are 38 sites for tents

or RVs up to 50 feet (no hookups). Picnic tables and fire rings are provided. Drinking water and flush toilets are available. A boat ramp and dump station are nearby. A grocery store and propane gas are available seven miles away. Some facilities are wheelchair accessible. Leashed pets are permitted.

Reservations, fees: Reservations are accepted at 877/444-6777 ($9 reservation fee) or www.ReserveUSA.com. Sites are $16–32 per night. Open May–October, weather permitting.

Directions: From Reno, drive north on U.S. 395 to the junction with Highway 70. Turn west on Highway 70 and drive to Chilcoot and the junction with Frenchman Lake Road. Turn right on Frenchman Lake Road and drive nine miles to the lake and to a Y. At the Y, turn right and drive two miles to Forest Road 24N01. Turn left and drive a short distance to the campground entrance on the left side of the road (on the east side of the lake).

Contact: Plumas National Forest, Beckwourth Ranger District, 530/836-2575, fax 530/836-0493; Thousand Trails, 530/832-1076.

6 SPRING CREEK

Scenic rating: 7

on Frenchman Lake in Plumas National Forest

See map page 652

Frenchman Lake is at 5,800 feet elevation, on the edge of high desert to the east and forest to the west. The lake is surrounded by a mix of sage and pines, and it has 21 miles of shoreline. All water sports are allowed. This camp is on the southeast end of the lake, where there are three other campgrounds, including a group camp and a boat ramp. The lake provides good fishing for stocked rainbow trout, best in the cove near the campgrounds. Trails lead out from the campground, one heading a quarter mile to the Frenchman Campground, the other routed a half mile to Big Cove Campground.

RV sites, facilities: There are 35 sites for tents or RVs up to 35 feet (no hookups). Picnic tables and

fire grills are provided. Drinking water and vault toilets are available. A boat ramp and dump station are nearby. Some facilities are wheelchair accessible. Leashed pets are permitted.

Reservations, fees: Reservations are accepted at 877/444-6777 ($9 reservation fee) or www.ReserveUSA.com. Sites are $16 per night. Open May–October, weather permitting.

Directions: From Reno, drive north on U.S. 395 to the junction with Highway 70. Turn west on Highway 70 and drive to Chilcoot and the junction with Frenchman Lake Road. Turn right on Frenchman Lake Road and drive nine miles to the lake and to a Y. At the Y, turn right and drive two miles to the campground on the left side of the road.

Contact: Plumas National Forest, Beckwourth Ranger District, 530/836-2575, fax 530/836-0493; Thousand Trails, 530/832-1076.

7 FRENCHMAN

Scenic rating: 7

on Frenchman Lake in Plumas National Forest

See map page 652

This camp is on the southeast end of the lake, where there are three other campgrounds, including a group camp and a boat ramp. The best trout fishing is in the cove near the campgrounds and the two inlets, one along the west shore and one at the head of the lake. The proximity to Reno, only 35 miles away, keeps gambling in the back of the minds of many anglers. Because of water demands downstream, the lake often drops significantly by the end of summer. A trail from camp is routed a quarter mile to the Spring Creek Campground.

RV sites, facilities: There are 38 sites for tents or RVs up to 35 feet (no hookups). Picnic tables and fire grills are provided. Drinking water and vault toilets are available. A dump station and boat ramp are nearby. Leashed pets are permitted.

Reservations, fees: Reservations are accepted at 877/444-6777 ($9 reservation fee) or www.ReserveUSA.com. Sites are $16 per night. Open May–October, weather permitting.

Directions: From Reno, drive north on U.S. 395 to the junction with Highway 70. Turn west on Highway 70 and drive to Chilcoot and the junction with Frenchman Lake Road. Turn right on Frenchman Lake Road and drive nine miles to the lake and to a Y. At the Y, turn right and drive 1.5 miles to the campground on the left side of the road.

Contact: Plumas National Forest, Beckwourth Ranger District, 530/836-2575, fax 530/836-0493; Thousand Trails, 530/832-1076.

8 CHILCOOT

Scenic rating: 7

on Little Last Chance Creek in Plumas National Forest

See map page 652

This small camp is along Little Last Chance Creek at 5,400 feet in elevation, about three miles downstream from Frenchman Lake. The stream provides good trout fishing, but access can be difficult at some spots because of brush.

RV sites, facilities: There are 120 sites for tents or RVs up to 40 feet (no hookups), along with five walk-in sites for tents only. Picnic tables and fire rings are provided. Drinking water and flush toilets are available. A boat ramp, a grocery store, and a dump station are nearby. Some facilities are wheelchair accessible. Leashed pets are permitted.

Reservations, fees: Reservations are accepted at 877/444-6777 ($9 reservation fee) or www.ReserveUSA.com. Sites are $16 per night. Open May–October, weather permitting.

Directions: From Reno, drive north on U.S. 395 to the junction with Highway 70. Turn west on Highway 70 and drive to Chilcoot and the junction with Frenchman Lake Road. Turn right on Frenchman Lake Road and drive six miles to the campground on the left side of the road.

Contact: Plumas National Forest, Beckwourth Ranger District, 530/836-2575, fax 530/836-0493; Thousand Trails, 530/832-1076.

9 RUNNING DEER

Scenic rating: 7

on Little Grass Valley Reservoir in Plumas National Forest

See map page 652

Little Grass Valley Reservoir is a pretty mountain lake at 5,060 feet in Plumas National Forest, providing lakeside camping, boating, and fishing for rainbow trout and kokanee salmon. Looking straight north from the camp is a spectacular view, gazing across the water and up at Bald Mountain, 6,255 feet in elevation. One of seven campgrounds on the eastern shore, this one is on the far northeastern end of the lake. A trailhead for the Pacific Crest Trail is available nearby at little Fowler Lake about four miles north of Little Grass Valley Reservoir. Note that while no fish-cleaning station is available at Running Deer, there is one available nearby at Little Beaver.

RV sites, facilities: There are 40 sites for tents or RVs up to 40 feet (no hookups). Picnic tables and fire rings are provided. Drinking water, flush toilets, and a nearby fish-cleaning station are available. A boat ramp, a grocery store, and a dump station are nearby. Leashed pets are permitted.

Reservations, fees: Reservations are accepted ($9 reservation fee) at 877/444-6777 or www.ReserveUSA.com. Sites are $18–20 per night. Open late May–September.

Directions: From Oroville, drive east on Highway 162/Oroville Dam Boulevard for about eight miles (it becomes the Olive Highway) to Forbestown Road. Turn right and drive through Forbestown to Challenge and LaPorte Road. Turn left on LaPorte Road and drive to LaPorte. Continue on County Road 512 (which becomes County Road 514/Little Grass Valley Road) for three miles to Forest Road 22N57. Turn right and drive three miles to the campground on the left.

Contact: Plumas National Forest, Feather River Ranger District, 530/534-6500, fax 530/532-1210; Northwest Management, 530/283-5559.

CALIFORNIA

10 WYANDOTTE

Scenic rating: 8

on Little Grass Valley Reservoir in Plumas National Forest

See map page 652

Of the eight camps on Little Grass Valley Reservoir, this is the favorite. It is on a small peninsula at 5,100 foot elevation that extends well into the lake, with a boat ramp nearby. All water sports are allowed. (For more information, see the listing in this chapter for *Running Deer.*)

RV sites, facilities: There are 28 individual sites and two double sites for tents or RVs up to 40 feet. No hookups. Picnic tables and fire rings are provided. Drinking water and flush toilets are available. A dump station, a boat ramp, a fish-cleaning station, and a grocery store are nearby. Leashed pets are permitted.

Reservations, fees: Reservations are not accepted. Sites are $18–20 per night, $30 per night for a double site. Open late May–mid-October, weather permitting.

Directions: From Oroville, drive east on Highway 162/Oroville Dam Boulevard for about eight miles (it becomes the Olive Highway) to Forbestown Road. Turn right and drive through Forbestown to Challenge and LaPorte Road. Turn left on LaPorte Road and drive to LaPorte. Continue two miles past LaPorte to the junction with County Road 514/Little Grass Valley Road. Turn left and drive one mile to a junction. Turn left and drive one mile to the campground entrance road on the right.

Contact: Plumas National Forest, Feather River Ranger District, 530/534-6500, fax 530/532-1210; Northwest Management, 530/283-5559.

11 LITTLE BEAVER

Scenic rating: 7

on Little Grass Valley Reservoir in Plumas National Forest

See map page 652

This is one of eight campgrounds on Little Grass Valley Reservoir, set at 5,060 feet. Take

your pick. (For more information, see the listing in this chapter for *Running Deer.*)

RV sites, facilities: There are 120 sites for tents or RVs up to 40 feet (no hookups). Picnic tables and fire rings are provided. Drinking water and flush toilets are available. A grocery store, a dump station, a fish-cleaning station, and a boat ramp are nearby. Some facilities are wheelchair accessible. Leashed pets are permitted.

Reservations, fees: Reservations are not accepted. Sites are $18–20 per night. Open June–mid-September, weather permitting.

Directions: From Oroville, drive east on Highway 162/Oroville Dam Boulevard for about eight miles (it becomes the Olive Highway) to Forbestown Road. Turn right and drive through Forbestown to Challenge and LaPorte Road. Turn left on LaPorte Road and drive to LaPorte. Continue two miles past LaPorte to the junction with County Road 514/Little Grass Valley Road. Turn left and drive one mile to a junction. Turn right and drive two miles to the campground entrance road on the left.

Contact: Plumas National Forest, Feather River Ranger District, 530/534-6500, fax 530/532-1210; Northwest Management, 530/283-5559.

12 RED FEATHER CAMP

Scenic rating: 7

on Little Grass Valley Reservoir in Plumas National Forest

See map page 652

This camp is well developed and popular, set on the eastern shore of Little Grass Valley Reservoir, just south of Running Deer and just north of Little Beaver. Bears frequent this area, so be sure to properly store your food and avoid scented products. (For more information, see the listing in this chapter for *Running Deer.*)

RV sites, facilities: There are 60 sites for tents or RVs up to 40 feet (no hookups). Picnic tables and fire rings are provided. Drinking water and flush toilets are available. A dump station, a boat ramp, a fish-cleaning station, and a grocery store are nearby. Leashed pets are permitted.

Reservations, fees: Reservations are accepted ($9 reservation fee) at 877/444-6777 or www.ReserveUSA.com. Sites are $18–20 per night. Open late June–September, weather permitting.

Directions: From Oroville, drive east on Highway 162/Oroville Dam Boulevard for about eight miles (it becomes the Olive Highway) to Forbestown Road. Turn right and drive through Forbestown to Challenge and LaPorte Road. Turn left on LaPorte Road and drive to LaPorte. Continue two miles past LaPorte to the junction with County Road 514/Little Grass Valley Road. Turn left and drive one mile to a junction. Turn right and drive three miles to the campground entrance road on the left.

Contact: Plumas National Forest, Feather River Ranger District, 530/534-6500, fax 530/532-1210; Northwest Management, 530/283-5559.

13 MOVIN' WEST RV PARK

Scenic rating: 5

in Graeagle

See map page 652

This RV park began life as a mobile home park. This has become a very popular park for golfers, and about half of the sites are rented for the full summer. A nine-hole golf course is across the road, and five other golf courses are within five miles. The elevation is 4,300 feet.

RV sites, facilities: There are 51 sites with full or partial hookups (30 amps) for RVs of any length, three tent sites, and two cabins. Some sites are pull-through. Picnic tables and fire rings are provided. Drinking water, restrooms with flush toilets and showers, a pay phone, cable TV, modem access, and a coin laundry are available. Propane gas, a nine-hole golf course, a swimming pond, a horse stable, and mini golf are nearby. Leashed pets are permitted.

Reservations, fees: Reservations are recom-

mended. Sites are $22.71–26.61 per night, $3–5 per person per night for more than two people. Open May–October.

Directions: From Truckee, drive northwest on Highway 89 about 50 miles to Graeagle. Continue just past Graeagle to County Road A14 (Graeagle-Johnsville Road). Turn left and drive 0.25 mile northwest to the campground on the left.

Contact: Movin' West RV Park, 530/836-2614.

14 LITTLE BEAR RV PARK

Scenic rating: 7

on the Feather River

See map page 652

This is a privately operated RV park near the Feather River. Nearby destinations include Plumas-Eureka State Park and the Lakes Basin Recreation Area. The elevation is 4,300 feet. About half of the sites are taken by full-season rentals.

RV sites, facilities: There are 97 sites with full or partial hookups (20 and 30 amps) for RVs of any length, as well as 10 sleeping cabins. No tents are allowed. Picnic tables and fire rings are provided. Drinking water, restrooms with showers and flush toilets, a coin laundry, a convenience store, satellite TV, modem access, RV storage, propane, and ice are available. A dump station, clubhouse, table tennis, shuffleboard, and horseshoes are also available. Leashed pets are permitted.

Reservations, fees: Reservations are recommended. Sites are $24–26 per night, $4–8 per person per night for more than two people, $1 per pet per night. Weekly and monthly rates available. Open mid-April–late October.

Directions: In Truckee, drive north on Highway 89 to Graeagle. Continue north on Highway 89 for one mile to Little Bear Road. Turn left on Little Bear Road and drive a short distance to the campground on the right.

Contact: Little Bear RV Park, tel./fax 530/836-2774, www.littlebearrvpark.com.

15 PLUMAS-EUREKA STATE PARK

🚶 🎣 🐕 🏕 ♿ 🚐 ⛺

Scenic rating: 9

near Graeagle

See map page 652

Plumas-Eureka State Park is a beautiful chunk of parkland, featuring great hiking, a pretty lake, and this well-maintained campground. For newcomers to the area, Jamison Camp at the southern end of the park makes for an excellent first stop. So does the nearby hike to Grass Lake, a first-class tromp that takes about two hours and features a streamside walk along Little Jamison Creek, with the chance to take a five-minute cutoff to see 40-foot Jamison Falls. A historic mine, park museum, blacksmith shop, stable, and stamp mill are also here, with campers provided free admission to the museum. Other must-see destinations in the park include Eureka Lake, and from there, the 1,100-foot climb to Eureka Peak (formerly known as Gold Mountain), 7,447 feet, for a dramatic view of all the famous peaks in this region. Camp elevation is 5,200 feet. The park covers 5,500 acres. Fishing opportunities feature Madora and Eureka Lakes and Jamison Creek, best in May and June. The visitors center was originally constructed as a bunkhouse for miners. More than $8 million of gold was mined here.

RV sites, facilities: There are 67 sites for tents or RVs up to 30 feet (no hookups) and one group tent site for up to 50 people. Picnic tables, food lockers, and fire rings are provided. Drinking water and restrooms with flush toilets and free showers are available. A dump station is available nearby. A grocery store, a coin laundry, and propane gas are available within five miles. Some facilities are wheelchair accessible. Leashed pets are permitted.

Reservations, fees: Reservations are accepted for the group site only. Sites are $20 per night, $6 per night for an additional vehicle, $200 per night for the group site. Open mid-May–mid-October, weather permitting.

Directions: In Truckee, drive north on Highway 89 to Graeagle. Just after passing Graeagle (one mile from the junction of Highway 70) turn left on County Road A14/Graeagle-Johnsville Road and drive west for about five miles to the park entrance on the left.

Contact: Plumas-Eureka State Park, 530/836-2380, fax 530/836-0498, www.parks.ca.gov.

16 PACKSADDLE

🚶 🐕 ♿ 🚐 ⛺

Scenic rating: 6

near Packer Lake in Tahoe National Forest

See map page 652

Packsaddle is a Forest Service site about a half mile from Packer Lake, with an additional 15 lakes within a five-mile radius and one of America's truly great hiking trails nearby. The trail to the Sierra Buttes features a climb of 2,369 feet over the course of five miles. It is highlighted by a stairway with 176 steps that literally juts into open space and crowned by an astounding view for hundreds of miles in all directions. Packer Lake, 6,218 feet, is at the foot of the dramatic Sierra Buttes and has lakefront log cabins, good trout fishing, and low-speed boating The campground elevation is 6,000 feet.

RV sites, facilities: There are 15 sites for tents or RVs up to 35 feet (no hookups). Vault toilets and drinking water are available. Pack and saddle animals are permitted, and corrals and hitching rails are available. Supplies are available in Bassetts and Sierra City. Some facilities are wheelchair accessible. Leashed pets are permitted.

Reservations, fees: Reservations are not accepted. Sites are $18 per night, $5 per night for an additional vehicle. Open late May–September, weather permitting.

Directions: From Truckee, turn north on Highway 89 and drive 20 miles to Sierraville. At Sierraville, turn left on Highway 49 and drive about 10 miles to the Bassetts Store. Turn right on Gold Lake Road and drive 1.5 miles to Packer Lake Road. Turn left, drive a short distance, bear right at the fork, and drive 2.5 miles to the campground on the left.

Contact: Tahoe National Forest, Yuba River Ranger District, North, 530/288-3231, fax 530/288-0727; California Land Management, 650/322-1181.

CALIFORNIA

17 LAKES BASIN

Scenic rating: 8

in Plumas National Forest
See map page 652

This camp is a great location for a base camp to explore the surrounding Lakes Basin Recreation Area. From nearby Gold Lake or Elwell Lodge, there are many short hikes to small pristine lakes. A must-do trip is the easy hike to Frazier Falls, only a mile round-trip to see the spectacular 176-foot waterfall, though the trail is crowded during the middle of the day. The trail to this waterfall is paved and is wheelchair-accessible. The camp elevation is 6,400 feet.

RV sites, facilities: There are 23 sites for tents or RVs up to 30 feet (no hookups). Picnic tables and fire grills are provided. Drinking water and vault toilets are available. Some facilities are wheelchair accessible. Supplies are available in Graeagle. Leashed pets are permitted.

Reservations, fees: Reservations are accepted at 877/444-6777 ($9 reservation fee) or www.ReserveUSA.com. Sites are $16 per night and double sites are $32 per night. Open June–October, weather permitting.

Directions: From Truckee, drive north on Highway 89 toward Graeagle to the Gold Lake Highway (one mile before reaching Graeagle). Turn left on the Gold Lake Highway and drive about seven miles to the campground.

Contact: Plumas National Forest, Beckwourth Ranger District, 530/836-2575, fax 530/836-0493; Thousand Trails, 530/832-1076.

18 CLIO'S RIVER'S EDGE RV PARK

Scenic rating: 7

on the Feather River
See map page 652

This is a giant RV park adjacent to a pretty and easily accessible stretch of the Feather River. There are many possible side-trip destinations, including Plumas-Eureka State Park, Lakes Basin Recreation Area, several nearby golf courses, and a horseback-riding facility. The elevation is about 4,500 feet. Many of the sites are rented for the entire summer season.

RV sites, facilities: There are 220 sites with full hookups (50 amps) for RVs of any length. Some sites are pull-through. No tents are allowed. Picnic tables are provided. Drinking water, restrooms with flush toilets and coin showers, a coin laundry, modem access, and cable TV are available. A grocery store is within three miles. Some facilities are wheelchair accessible. Leashed pets are permitted, with certain restrictions.

Reservations, fees: Reservations are accepted. Sites are $27–32 per night, $5 per person per night for more than two people, $1 per night for an additional vehicle not towed. Weekly and monthly rates available. Some credit cards accepted. Open mid-April–October.

Directions: From Truckee, drive north on Highway 89 toward Graeagle and Blairsden. Near Clio (4.5 miles south of Highway 70 at Blairsden), look for the campground entrance on the right (0.2 mile south of Graeagle).

Contact: Clio's River's Edge RV Park, tel./fax 530/836-2375, fax 530/836-2378, www.riversedgervpark.net.

19 SALMON CREEK

Scenic rating: 9

in Tahoe National Forest
See map page 652

This campground is at the confluence of Packer and Salmon Creeks, 5,800 feet in elevation, with easy access off the Gold Lakes Highway. It is near the Lakes Basin Recreation Area, with literally dozens of small lakes within five miles, plus great hiking, fishing, and low-speed boating.

RV sites, facilities: There are 31 sites for tents or RVs up to 30 feet (no hookups). Picnic tables and fire grills are provided. Drinking water and vault toilets are available. Supplies and a coin laundry are available in Sierra City. Leashed pets are permitted.

Reservations, fees: Reservations are not accepted. Sites are $18 per night, $5 per night for an additional vehicle. Open June–October.

CALIFORNIA

Directions: From Truckee, turn north on Highway 89 and drive 20 miles to Sierraville and Highway 49. Turn left on Highway 49 and drive about 10 miles to the Bassetts Store and Gold Lake Road. Turn right on Gold Lake Road and drive two miles to the campground on the left side of the road.

Contact: Tahoe National Forest, Yuba River Ranger District, North, 530/288-3231, fax 530/288-0727; California Land Management, 650/322-1181.

20 SARDINE LAKE

Scenic rating: 8

in Tahoe National Forest

See map page 652   **BEST (**

Lower Sardine Lake is a jewel set below the Sierra Buttes, one of the prettiest settings in California. The campground is actually about a mile east of the lake. Nearby is beautiful Sand Pond Interpretive Trail. A great hike is routed along the shore of Lower Sardine Lake to a hidden waterfall (in spring) that feeds the lake, and ambitious hikers can explore beyond and discover Upper Sardine Lake. Trout fishing is excellent in Lower Sardine Lake, with a primitive boat ramp available for small boats. The speed limit and small size of the lake keeps boaters slow and quiet. A small marina and boat rentals are available.

RV sites, facilities: There are 29 sites for tents or RVs up to 22 feet (no hookups). Picnic tables and fire grills are provided. Drinking water and vault toilets are available. Limited supplies are available at the Sardine Lake Lodge or in Bassetts. Some facilities are wheelchair accessible. Leashed pets are permitted.

Reservations, fees: Reservations are not accepted. Sites are $18 per night, $5 per night for an additional vehicle. Open June–October, weather permitting.

Directions: From Truckee, drive north on Highway 89 for 20 miles to Sierraville. Turn left on Highway 49 and drive about 10 miles to the Bassetts Store. Turn right on Gold Lake Road and drive 1.5 miles to Packer Lake Road.

Turn left, drive a short distance, then bear left at the fork (signed) and drive 0.5 mile to the campground on the left.

Contact: Tahoe National Forest, Yuba River Ranger District, North, 530/288-3231, fax 530/288-0727.

21 CHAPMAN CREEK

Scenic rating: 8

on the North Yuba River in Tahoe National Forest

See map page 652

This campground is along Chapman Creek at 6,000 feet, just across the highway from where it enters the North Yuba River. A good side trip is to hike Chapman Creek Trail, which leads out of camp to Beartrap Meadow or to Haskell Peak (8,107 feet).

RV sites, facilities: There are 29 sites for tents or RVs up to 22 feet (no hookups). Picnic tables and fire grills are provided. Drinking water and vault toilets are available. Supplies are available in Bassetts. Leashed pets are permitted.

Reservations, fees: Reservations are not accepted. Sites are $18 per night, $5 per night for an additional vehicle. Open June–October, weather permitting.

Directions: From Truckee, turn north on Highway 89 and drive 20 miles to Sierraville. At Sierraville, turn left on Highway 49, drive over Yuba Pass, and continue for four miles to the campground on the right.

Contact: Tahoe National Forest, Yuba River Ranger District, North, 530/288-3231, fax 530/288-0727; California Land Management, 650/322-1181.

22 YUBA PASS

Scenic rating: 6

in Tahoe National Forest

See map page 652

This camp is right at Yuba Pass at an elevation of 6,700 feet. In the winter, the surrounding area is a Sno-Park, which gives it an unusual look in summer. Yuba Pass is a popular bird-watching area in the summer.

RV sites, facilities: There are 20 sites for tents or RVs up to 22 feet (no hookups). Picnic tables and fire grills are provided. Vault toilets are available. There is no drinking water. Supplies are available at Bassetts. Leashed pets are permitted.

Reservations, fees: Reservations are not accepted. Sites are $18 per night, $5 per night for an additional vehicle. Open late June–October, weather permitting.

Directions: From Truckee, drive north on Highway 89 past Sattley to the junction with Highway 49. Turn west on Highway 49 and drive about six miles to the campground on the left side of the road.

Contact: Tahoe National Forest, Yuba River Ranger District, North, 530/288-3231, fax 530/288-0727; California Land Management, 650/322-1181.

23 COTTONWOOD CREEK

Scenic rating: 7

in Tahoe National Forest
See map page 652

This camp sits beside Cottonwood Creek at 5,800 feet elevation. An interpretive trail starts at the upper camp and makes a short loop, and there are several nearby side-trip options, including trout fishing on the Little Truckee River to the nearby south, visiting the Sierra Hot Springs out of Sierraville to the nearby north, or venturing into the surrounding Tahoe National Forest.

RV sites, facilities: There are 46 sites for tents or RVs up to 22 feet (no hookups). Picnic tables and fire rings are provided. Drinking water and vault toilets are available. Supplies are available in Sierraville. Some facilities are wheelchair accessible. Leashed pets are permitted.

Reservations, fees: Reservations are accepted at 877/444-6777 ($9 reservation fee) or www.ReserveUSA.com. Sites are $15 per night, $3 per night for an additional vehicle. Open mid-May–early October, weather permitting.

Directions: From Truckee, drive north on Highway 89 for about 20 miles to the campground entrance road on the right (0.5 mile past Cold Creek Camp).

Contact: Tahoe National Forest, Sierraville Ranger District, 530/994-3401, fax 530/994-3143; California Land Management, 650/322-1181.

24 INDIAN VALLEY

Scenic rating: 7

on the North Yuba River in Tahoe National Forest
See map page 652

This is an easy-to-reach spot set at 2,200 feet beside the North Yuba River. Highway 49 runs adjacent to the Yuba River for miles eastward, providing easy access to the river in many areas. There are several other campgrounds in the immediate area (see the listing in this chapter for *Carlton/Cal-Ida,* within a mile).

RV sites, facilities: There are 17 sites for tents or RVs up to 22 feet (no hookups). Picnic tables and fire grills are provided. Drinking water and vault toilets are available. Limited supplies are available nearby at the Indian Valley Outpost. Some facilities are wheelchair accessible. Leashed pets are permitted.

Reservations, fees: Reservations are not accepted. Sites are $18 per night, $5 per night for an additional vehicle. Open year-round.

Directions: From Auburn, take Highway 49 north to Nevada City and continue on Highway 49 (the road jogs left, then narrows) to Camptonville. Drive 10 miles to the camp entrance on the right.

Contact: Tahoe National Forest, Yuba River Ranger District, North, 530/288-3231, fax 530/288-0727; California Land Management, 650/322-1181.

CALIFORNIA

25 CARLTON/CAL-IDA

Scenic rating: 7

on the North Yuba River in Tahoe National Forest

See map page 652

Carlton is on the North Yuba River, and Cal-Ida is across the road. This is a beautiful river, one of the prettiest to flow westward out of the Sierra Nevada, with deep pools and miniature waterfalls. It is popular for rafting out of Goodyears Bar, and if you can stand the cold water, there are many good swimming holes along Highway 49. It's set at 2,200 feet.

RV sites, facilities: There are 30 sites at Carlton and 20 sites at Cal-Ida for tents or RVs up to 28 feet. No hookups. Picnic tables and fire grills are provided. Drinking water and vault toilets are available. Some supplies are available at the Indian Valley Outpost nearby. Some facilities are wheelchair accessible. Leashed pets are permitted.

Reservations, fees: Reservations are not accepted. Sites are $18 per night. Open mid-April–November, weather permitting.

Directions: From Auburn, take Highway 49 north to Nevada City and continue on Highway 49 (the road jogs left, then narrows) to Camptonville. Continue northeast for nine miles to the campground entrance. The camping area at Carlton is one mile northeast of the Highway 49 bridge at Indian Valley. The camping area at Cal-Ida is just east of the Indian Valley Outpost on the Cal-Ida Road.

Contact: Tahoe National Forest, Yuba River Ranger District, North, 530/288-3231, fax 530/288-0727; California Land Management, 650/322-1181.

26 UNION FLAT

Scenic rating: 8

on the North Yuba River in Tahoe National Forest

See map page 652

Of all the campgrounds on the North Yuba River along Highway 49, this one has the best swimming. The camp has a nice swimming hole next to it, and the water is cold. Recreational mining is also an attraction here. The elevation is 3,400 feet.

RV sites, facilities: There are 11 sites for tents or RVs up to 35 feet (no hookups). Picnic tables and fire grills are provided. Drinking water and vault toilets are available. Supplies are available in Downieville. Some facilities are wheelchair accessible. Leashed pets are permitted.

Reservations, fees: Reservations are not accepted. Sites are $18 per night, $5 per night for an additional vehicle. Open May–October, weather permitting.

Directions: From Auburn, take Highway 49 north to Nevada City and continue (the road jogs left, then narrows) to Downieville. Drive six miles east to the campground entrance on the right.

Contact: Tahoe National Forest, Yuba River Ranger District, North, 530/288-3231, fax 530/288-0727; California Land Management, 650/322-1181.

27 LOGANVILLE

Scenic rating: 8

on the North Yuba River in Tahoe National Forest

See map page 652

Nearby Sierra City is only two miles away, meaning you can make a quick getaway for a prepared meal or any food or drink you may need to add to your camp. Loganville is on the North Yuba River, elevation 4,200 feet. It offers a good stretch of water in this region for trout fishing, with many pools set below miniature waterfalls.

RV sites, facilities: There are 20 sites for tents or RVs up to 22 feet (no hookups). Picnic tables and fire grills are provided. Drinking water and vault toilets are available. Supplies and a coin laundry are available in Sierra City. Leashed pets are permitted.

Reservations, fees: Reservations are not accepted. Sites are $18 per night, $5 per night

CALIFORNIA

for an additional vehicle. Open May–October, weather permitting.

Directions: From Auburn, take Highway 49 north to Nevada City and continue on Highway 49 (the road jogs left, then narrows) to Downieville. Drive 12 miles east to the campground entrance on the right (two miles west of Sierra City).

Contact: Tahoe National Forest, Yuba River Ranger District, North, 530/288-3231, fax 530/288-0727; California Land Management, 650/322-1181.

28 WILD PLUM

Scenic rating: 8

on Haypress Creek in Tahoe National Forest

See map page 652

This popular Forest Service campground is on Haypress Creek at 4,400 feet. There are several hidden waterfalls in the area, which makes this a popular camp for the people who know of them. There's a scenic hike up Haypress Trail, which goes past a waterfall to Haypress Valley. Two other nearby waterfalls are Loves Falls (on the North Yuba on Highway 49 two miles east of Sierra City) and Hackmans Falls (remote, set in a ravine one mile south of Sierra City; no road access).

RV sites, facilities: There are 44 sites for tents or RVs up to 22 feet (no hookups). Picnic tables, food lockers, and fire grills are provided. Drinking water and vault toilets are available. Supplies and a coin laundry are available in Sierra City. Leashed pets are permitted.

Reservations, fees: Reservations are not accepted. Sites are $18 per night, $5 per night for an additional vehicle. Open May–October, weather permitting.

Directions: From Auburn, take Highway 49 north to Nevada City and continue (the road jogs left, then narrows) past Downieville to Sierra City at Wild Plum Road. Turn right on Wild Plum Road and drive two miles to the campground entrance road on the right.

Contact: Tahoe National Forest, Yuba River Ranger District, North, 530/288-3231, fax 530/288-0727; California Land Management, 650/322-1181.

29 WOODCAMP

Scenic rating: 7

at Jackson Meadow Reservoir in Tahoe National Forest

See map page 652

Woodcamp and Pass Creek are the best camps for boaters at Jackson Meadow Reservoir because each is directly adjacent to a boat ramp. That is critical because fishing is far better by boat here than from shore, with a good mix of both rainbow and brown trout. The camp is at 6,700 feet along the lake's southwest shore, in a pretty spot with a swimming beach and short interpretive hiking trail nearby. All water sports are allowed. This is a beautiful lake in the Sierra Nevada, complete with pine forest and a classic granite backdrop.

RV sites, facilities: There are 20 sites for tents or RVs up to 22 feet (no hookups). Picnic tables and fire rings are provided. Drinking water, flush and vault toilets, food lockers, and firewood (fee) are available. Supplies are available in Truckee or Sierraville. A boat ramp is adjacent to the camp and a dump station is nearby. Leashed pets are permitted.

Reservations, fees: Reservations are accepted at 877/444-6777 ($9 reservation fee) or www.ReserveUSA.com. Sites are $18 per night, $5 per night for an additional vehicle. Open June–October, weather permitting.

Directions: From Truckee, drive north on Highway 89 for 17 miles to Forest Road 7. Turn left on Forest Road 7 and drive 16 miles to Jackson Meadow Reservoir. At the lake, continue across the dam around the west shoreline and then turn left at the campground access road. The entrance is on the right just before the Woodcamp boat ramp.

Contact: Tahoe National Forest, Sierraville Ranger District, 530/994-3401, fax 530/994-3143; California Land Management, 650/322-1181.

CALIFORNIA

30 FINDLEY

Scenic rating: 7

at Jackson Meadow Reservoir in Tahoe
National Forest

See map page 652

Findley is near Woodcamp Creek, a quarter
mile from where it pours into Jackson Meadow
Reservoir. Though it is not a lakeside camp, it
is quite pretty just the same, and within a mile
of the boat ramp near Woodcamp. It is at 6,300
feet. This is one of several camps at the lake.

RV sites, facilities: There are 14 sites for tents
or RVs up to 22 feet (no hookups). Picnic tables
and fire rings are provided. Drinking water, flush
and vault toilets, and food lockers are available.
Supplies are available in Truckee or Sierraville.
A boat ramp is nearby. Some facilities are wheelchair accessible. Leashed pets are permitted.

Reservations, fees: Reservations are accepted at 877/444-6777 ($9 reservation fee) or
www.ReserveUSA.com. Sites are $18 per night,
$5 per night for an additional vehicle. Open
May–October.

Directions: From Truckee, drive north on
Highway 89 for 17 miles to Forest Road 7.
Turn left on Forest Road 7 and drive 16 miles
to Jackson Meadow Reservoir. Continue across
the dam around the lake to the west side. Turn
left at the campground access road and drive
about 0.25 mile to the entrance on the left.

Contact: Tahoe National Forest, Sierraville Ranger District, 530/994-3401, fax
530/994-3143; California Land Management,
650/322-1181.

31 PASS CREEK

Scenic rating: 7

at Jackson Meadow Reservoir in Tahoe
National Forest

See map page 652

This is the premium campground at Jackson Meadow Reservoir, a developed site with
water, a concrete boat ramp, a swimming beach
nearby at Aspen Creek Picnic Area, and access
to the Pacific Crest Trail a half mile to the
east (you'll pass it on the way in). This lake
has the trademark look of the high Sierra,
and the bonus here is that lake levels are often
kept higher than at other reservoirs on the
western slopes of the Sierra Nevada. Trout
stocks are excellent, with rainbow and brown
trout planted each summer after ice-out. The
elevation is 6,100 feet.

RV sites, facilities: There are 30 sites for tents
or RVs up to 22 feet (no hookups). Picnic
tables and fire rings are provided. Drinking
water, flush and vault toilets, and food lockers are available. A dump station is nearby.
A boat ramp is nearby. Supplies are available in Truckee or Sierraville. Leashed pets
are permitted.

Reservations, fees: Reservations are accepted at 877/444-6777 ($9 reservation fee) or
www.ReserveUSA.com. Sites are $18 per night,
$5 per night for an additional vehicle. Open
May–October, weather permitting.

Directions: From Truckee, drive north on Highway 89 for 17 miles to Forest Road 7. Turn left
on Forest Road 7 and drive 16 miles to Jackson
Meadow Reservoir; the campground is on the
left at the north end of the lake.

Contact: Tahoe National Forest, Sierraville Ranger District, 530/994-3401, fax
530/994-3143; California Land Management,
650/322-1181.

32 EAST MEADOW

Scenic rating: 7

at Jackson Meadow Reservoir in Tahoe
National Forest

See map page 652

This camp is in a beautiful setting on the northeast side of Jackson Meadow Reservoir, on the
edge of a sheltered cove. The Pacific Crest Trail
(PCT) passes right by camp, providing access
for a day trip, though no stellar destinations are
on this stretch of the PCT. The nearest boat
ramp is at Pass Creek, two miles away. The
elevation is 6,200 feet.

RV sites, facilities: There are 46 sites for tents or RVs up to 40 feet (no hookups). Picnic tables and fire rings are provided. Drinking water, flush and vault toilets, food lockers, and firewood (fee) are available. A dump station and boat ramp are available near Pass Creek. Supplies are available in Truckee or Sierraville. Some facilities are wheelchair accessible. Leashed pets are permitted.

Reservations, fees: Reservations are accepted at 877/444-6777 ($9 reservation fee) or www.ReserveUSA.com. The fee is $18 per night, $5 per night for an additional vehicle. Open May–October, weather permitting.

Directions: From Truckee, drive north on Highway 89 for 17 miles to Forest Road 7. Turn left on Forest Road 7 and drive 15 miles to the campground entrance road on the left (if you reach Pass Creek, you have gone too far). Turn left and drive a mile to the campground on the right.

Contact: Tahoe National Forest, Sierraville Ranger District, 530/994-3401, fax 530/994-3143; California Land Management, 650/322-1181.

33 UPPER LITTLE TRUCKEE

Scenic rating: 7

on the Little Truckee River in Tahoe National Forest
See map page 652

This camp is along the Little Truckee River at 6,100 feet. The Little Truckee is a pretty trout stream, with easy access not only from this campground, but also from another three miles northward along Highway 89, then from another seven miles to the west along Forest Road 7, the route to Webber Lake. It is only about a 10-minute drive from this camp to reach Stampede Lake to the east.

RV sites, facilities: There are 26 sites for tents or RVs up to 30 feet (no hookups). Picnic tables and fire rings are provided. Drinking water and vault toilets are available. Supplies are available in Sierraville. Leashed pets are permitted.

Reservations, fees: Reservations are accepted at 877/444-6777 ($9 reservation fee) or www.ReserveUSA.com. Sites are $15 per night, $5 per night for an additional vehicle. Open mid-May–October, weather permitting.

Directions: From Truckee, drive north on Highway 89 for about 11 miles to the campground on the left, a short distance beyond Lower Little Truckee Camp.

Contact: Tahoe National Forest, Sierraville Ranger District, 530/994-3401, fax 530/994-3143; California Land Management, 650/322-1181.

34 LOWER LITTLE TRUCKEE

Scenic rating: 7

on the Little Truckee River in Tahoe National Forest
See map page 652

This pretty camp is along Highway 89 and the Little Truckee River at 6,200 feet. (For more information, see the listing in this chapter for *Upper Little Truckee*.)

RV sites, facilities: There are 15 sites for tents or RVs up to 20 feet (no hookups). Picnic tables and fire grills are provided. Drinking water and vault toilets are available. Supplies are available in Sierraville or Truckee. Leashed pets are permitted.

Reservations, fees: Reservations are accepted at 877/444-6777 ($9 reservation fee) or www.ReserveUSA.com. Sites are $15 per night, $5 per night for an additional vehicle. Open May–October, weather permitting.

Directions: From Truckee, drive north on Highway 89 for about 12 miles to the campground on the left. If you reach Upper Little Truckee Camp, you have gone 0.5 mile too far.

Contact: Tahoe National Forest, Sierraville Ranger District, 530/994-3401, fax 530/994-3143; California Land Management, 650/322-1181.

CALIFORNIA

35 MALAKOFF DIGGINS STATE HISTORIC PARK

Scenic rating: 7

near Nevada City

See map page 652

This camp is near a small lake in the park, but the main attraction of the area is the gold-mining history. Tours of the numerous historic sites are available during the summer. The elevation is 3,400 feet. A trip here is like a walk through history. Malakoff Diggins State Historic Park is the site of California's largest "hydraulic" mine (which is not open to the public for viewing). Huge cliffs have been carved by mighty streams of water, a gold-mining technique involving the washing away of entire mountains to find the precious metal. This practice began in the 1850s and continued for many years. Several major gold-mining operations combined hydraulic mining with giant sluice boxes. Hydraulic mining was a scourge to the land, of course, and legal battles between mine owners and downstream farmers eventually ended this method of mining.

The park also contains a 7,847-foot bedrock tunnel that served as a drain. Although this tunnel is not open to the public, a shorter tunnel is available for viewing. The visitors center has exhibits on life in the old mining town of North Bloomfield. Tours of the numerous historic sites are available during the summer.

RV sites, facilities: There are 30 sites for tents or RVs up to 24 feet (no hookups), three cabins, and one group tent site for up to 50 people. Picnic tables and fire grills are provided. Drinking water and flush toilets (except mid-November through February) are available. Leashed pets are permitted.

Reservations, fees: Reservations are accepted Memorial Day–Labor Day ($7.50 reservation fee) at 800/444-PARK (800/444-7275) or www.reserveamerica.com. Sites are $11–15 per night, $6 per night for an additional vehicle, $111 per night for the group site. The cabins are $35 per night. Open year-round.

Directions: From Auburn, drive north on High-way 49 to Nevada City and continue 11 miles to the junction of Tyler Foote Crossing Road. Turn right and drive approximately 11 miles (in the process the road changes names to Cruzon Grade and Back Bone Road) to Der Bec Road. Turn right on Der Bec Road and drive one mile to North Bloomfield Road. Turn right and drive two miles to the entrance on the right. The route is well-signed; the last two miles are quite steep.

Contact: California State Parks, Goldrush District, tel./fax 530/265-2740, www.parks.ca.gov.

36 SOUTH YUBA

Scenic rating: 7

near the Yuba River

See map page 652

This little-known BLM camp is next to where little Kenebee Creek enters the Yuba River. The Yuba is about a mile away, with some great swimming holes and evening trout fishing spots to explore. A good side trip is to nearby Malakoff Diggins State Historic Park and the town of North Bloomfield (about a 10-minute drive to the northeast on North Bloomfield Road), which is being completely restored to its 1850s character. Twelve-mile-long South Yuba Trail begins at the state park and features outstanding spring wildflower blooms. The elevation is 2,600 feet.

RV sites, facilities: There are 16 sites for tents or RVs up to 27 feet (no hookups). Picnic tables and fire grills are provided. Drinking water and vault toilets are available. Some facilities are wheelchair accessible. Leashed pets are permitted.

Reservations, fees: Reservations are not accepted. Sites are $5 per night. Open April–October, weather permitting.

Directions: From Auburn turn north on Highway 49 to Nevada City and continue on Highway 49 (the highway jogs left in town) to Tyler Foote Crossing Road. Turn right and drive to Grizzly Hills Road (just past North Columbia). Turn right and drive two miles to North Bloomfield Road. Bear right on North Bloomfield Road and drive 0.5 mile to the campground on the left.

Contact: The Bureau of Land Management, Folsom Field Office, 916/985-4474, fax 916/985-3259.

37 WHITE CLOUD

Scenic rating: 5

in Tahoe National Forest
See map page 652

This camp is along historic Pioneer Trail, which has turned into one of the top mountain-bike routes in the Sierra Nevada, easy and fast. The trail traces the route of the first wagon road opened by emigrants and gold seekers in 1850. It is best suited for mountain biking, with a lot of bikers taking the one-way downhill ride (with an extra car for a shuttle ride) from Bear Valley to Lone Grave. The Omega Overlook is the highlight, with dramatic views of granite cliffs and the Yuba River. The elevation is 4,200 feet.

RV sites, facilities: There are 46 sites for tents or RVs of any length (no hookups). Picnic tables and fire grills are provided. Drinking water, flush toilets, and vault toilets are available. Some facilities are wheelchair accessible. Leashed pets are permitted.

Reservations, fees: Reservations are accepted ($9 reservation fee) at 877/444-6777 or www.ReserveUSA.com. Sites are $18 per night, $5 per night for an additional vehicle. Open May–October, weather permitting.

Directions: From Sacramento, drive east on I-80 to Emigrant Gap. Take the off-ramp and then head north on the short connector road to Highway 20. Turn west on Highway 20 and drive about 15 miles to the campground entrance on the left.

Contact: Tahoe National Forest, Yuba River Ranger District, South, 530/265-4531, fax 530/478-6109; Big Bend Visitor's Center, 530/426-3609, fax 530/426-1744.

38 SCOTTS FLAT LAKE RECREATION AREA

Scenic rating: 8

near Grass Valley
See map page 652

Scotts Flat Lake (at 3,100 feet in elevation) is shaped like a large teardrop and is one of the prettier lakes in the Sierra foothills, with 7.5 miles of shoreline circled by forest. Rules prohibiting personal watercraft keep the place sane. The camp is on the lake's north shore, largely protected from spring winds and within short range of the marina and one of the lake's two boat launches. Trout fishing is good here in the spring and early summer. When the lake heats up, waterskiing and powerboating become more popular. Sailing and sailboarding are also good during afternoon winds.

RV sites, facilities: There are 187 sites for tents or RVs up to 35 feet (no hookups). Picnic tables and fire pits are provided. Restrooms have flush toilets and coin showers. A coin laundry and a dump station are provided. A general store, bait and tackle, boat rentals, a boat ramp, and a playground are also available. Groups can be accommodated. Some facilities are wheelchair accessible. Leashed pets are permitted.

Reservations, fees: Reservations are recommended in the summer at 530/265-5302. Sites are $23–28 per night, $6.25 per night for an additional vehicle, $3 per pet per night, with a 14-day maximum stay. Some credit cards accepted. Open year-round, weather permitting.

Directions: From Auburn, drive north on Highway 49 to Nevada City and the junction with Highway 20. Continue straight onto Highway 20 and drive five miles (east) to Scotts Flat Road. Turn right and drive four miles to the camp entrance road on the right (on the north shore of the lake).

Contact: Scotts Flat Lake Recreation Area, 530/265-5302 or 530/265-8861.

CALIFORNIA

39 LAKE SPAULDING

Scenic rating: 8

near Emigrant Gap

See map page 652

Lake Spaulding is at 5,000 feet in the Sierra Nevada, complete with huge boulders and a sprinkling of conifers. Its clear, pure, very cold water has startling effects on swimmers. The 772-acre lake is extremely pretty, with the Sierra granite backdrop looking as if it has been cut, chiseled, and smoothed. Just one problem. There's not much of a lake view from the campground, although there are a few sites with filtered views. In fact, the lake is about a quarter mile from the campground. The drive here is nearly a straight shot up I-80, so there will be plenty of company at the campground. All water sports are allowed, except personal watercraft. Fishing for kokanee salmon and rainbow trout is often good, as well as fishing for trout at the nearby South Fork Yuba River. There are many other lakes set in the mountain country to the immediate north that can make for excellent side trips, including Bowman, Weaver, and Faucherie Lakes.

RV sites, facilities: There are 25 sites (13 are walk-in) for tents or RVs up to 30 feet and an overflow area. No hookups. Picnic tables and fire grills are provided. Drinking water, vault toilets, and picnic areas are available. A boat ramp is available nearby. Supplies are available in Nevada City. Some facilities are wheelchair accessible. Leashed pets are permitted.

Reservations, fees: Reservations are not accepted. Sites are $18 per night, $5 per night for an additional vehicle, $1 per pet per night, $7 per day for boat launching. Open mid-May–September, weather permitting.

Directions: From Sacramento, drive east on I-80 past Emigrant Gap to Highway 20. Drive west on Highway 20 for 2.3 miles to Lake Spaulding Road. Turn right on Lake Spaulding Road and drive 0.5 mile to the campground.

Contact: PG&E Land Projects, 916/386-5164; Big Bend Visitor's Center, 530/426-3609, fax 530/426-1744, www.pge.com/recreation.

40 LODGEPOLE

Scenic rating: 8

on Lake Valley Reservoir in Tahoe National Forest

See map page 652

Lake Valley Reservoir is at 5,786 feet and covers 300 acres. It is gorgeous when full, its shoreline sprinkled with conifers and boulders. The lake provides decent results for anglers, who have the best luck while trolling. A 15-mph speed limit prohibits waterskiing and personal watercraft, and that keeps the place quiet and peaceful. The camp is about a quarter mile from the lake's southwest shore and two miles from the boat ramp on the north shore. A trailhead from camp leads south up Monumental Ridge and to Monumental Creek (three miles, one-way) on the northwestern flank of Quartz Mountain (6,931 feet).

RV sites, facilities: There are 35 sites for tents or RVs up to 30 feet (no hookups). Picnic tables and fire grills are provided. Drinking water and vault toilets are available. A boat ramp is available nearby. Supplies can be obtained off I-80. Some facilities are wheelchair accessible. Leashed pets are permitted.

Reservations, fees: Reservations are not accepted. Sites are $18 per night, $5 per night for an additional vehicle, $1 per pet per night. Open late May–September, weather permitting.

Directions: From I-80, take the Yuba Gap exit and drive south for 0.4 mile to Lake Valley Road. Turn right on Lake Valley Road and drive for 1.2 miles until the road forks. Bear right and continue for 1.5 miles to the campground entrance road to the right on another fork.

Contact: PG&E Land Projects, 916/386-5164, www.pge.com/recreation.

41 INDIAN SPRINGS

Scenic rating: 7

near the Yuba River in Tahoe National Forest

See map page 652   **BEST (**

The camp is easy to reach from I-80 yet is in a beautiful setting at 5,600 feet along the South Fork Yuba River. This is a gorgeous stream, running deep blue-green and pure through a granite setting, complete with giant boulders and beautiful pools. Trout fishing is fair. There is a small beach nearby where you can go swimming, though the water is cold. There are also several lakes in the vicinity.

RV sites, facilities: There are 35 sites for tents or RVs up to 26 feet (no hookups). Picnic tables and fire grills are provided. Drinking water and vault toilets are available. A grocery store and propane gas are available nearby. Some facilities are wheelchair accessible. Leashed pets are permitted.

Reservations, fees: Reservations are not accepted. Sites are $18 per night, $5 per night for an additional vehicle. Open June–September, weather permitting.

Directions: From Sacramento, drive east on I-80 to Yuba Gap and continue for about three miles to the Eagle Lakes exit. Head north on Eagle Lakes Road for a mile to the campground on the left side of the road.

Contact: Tahoe National Forest, Yuba River Ranger District, South, 530/265-4531, fax 530/478-6109; Big Bend Visitor's Center, 530/426-3609, fax 530/426-1744.

42 HAMPSHIRE ROCKS

Scenic rating: 8

on the Yuba River in Tahoe National Forest

See map page 652

This camp sits along the South Fork of the Yuba River at 5,800 feet in elevation, with easy access off I-80 and a nearby Forest Service visitor information center. Fishing for trout is fair. There are some swimming holes, but the water is often very cold. Nearby lakes that can provide side trips include Sterling and Fordyce Lakes (drive-to) to the north, and the Loch Leven Lakes (hike-to) to the south.

RV sites, facilities: There are 31 sites for tents or RVs up to 22 feet (no hookups) and four walk-in tent sites. Picnic tables and fire grills are provided. Drinking water and vault toilets are available. A convenience store, a restaurant, and propane gas are available nearby. Some

facilities are wheelchair accessible. Leashed pets are permitted.

Reservations, fees: Reservations are accepted at 877/444-6777 ($9 reservation fee) or www.ReserveUSA.com. Sites are $18 per night, $5 per night for an additional vehicle. Open June–September, weather permitting.

Directions: From Sacramento, drive east on I-80 to Cisco Grove and continue for a mile to the Big Bend exit. Take that exit (remaining just south of the highway), then turn left on the frontage road and drive east for two miles to the campground on the right.

Contact: Tahoe National Forest, Yuba River Ranger District, South, 530/265-4531, fax 530/478-6109; Big Bend Visitor's Center, 530/426-3609, fax 530/426-1744.

43 DONNER MEMORIAL STATE PARK

Scenic rating: 9

on Donner Lake

See map page 652   BEST (

The remarkable beauty of Donner Lake often evokes a deep, heartfelt response. Nearly everybody passing by from nearby I-80 has looked down and seen it. The lake is big, three miles long and three-quarters of a mile wide, gemlike blue, and set near the Sierra crest at 5,900 feet. The area is well developed, with a number of cabins and access roads, and this state park is the feature destination. Along the southeastern end of the lake, it is extremely pretty, but the campsites are set in forest, not along the lake. Fishing is good here (typically only in the early morning), trolling for kokanee salmon or rainbow trout, with big Mackinaw and brown trout providing wild cards. The park features more than three miles of frontage of Donner Creek and Donner Lake, with 2.5 miles of hiking trails. Donner Lake itself has 7.5 miles of shoreline. The lake is open to all water sports, and there is no boat launch at the park; a public ramp is available in the northwest corner of the lake. Campers get free admission to Emigrant Trail Museum.

CALIFORNIA

RV sites, facilities: There are 150 sites for tents or RVs up to 28 feet (no hookups) and trailers up to 24 feet, plus two hike-in/bike-in sites. Picnic tables and fire pits are provided. Drinking water, coin showers, vault toilets, a picnic area, and an interpretive trail are available. Supplies are available about one mile away in Truckee. Some facilities are wheelchair accessible. Leashed pets are permitted.

Reservations, fees: Reservations are accepted at 800/444-PARK (800/444-7275) or www.reserveamerica.com ($7.50 reservation fee). Sites are $25 per night, $6 per night for an additional vehicle, $3 per person per night for hike-in/bike-in sites. Open late May–mid-September, weather permitting.

Directions: From Auburn, drive east on I-80 just past Donner Lake to the Donner State Park exit. Take that exit and turn south (right) on Donner Pass Road and drive 0.5 mile to the park entrance on the left at the southeast end of the lake.

Contact: Donner Memorial State Park, 530/582-7892 or 530/582-7894. For boat-launching info, call 530/582-7720, www.parks.ca.gov.

44 GRANITE FLAT

Scenic rating: 6

on the Truckee River in Tahoe National Forest
See map page 652

This camp is along the Truckee River at 5,800 feet, in an area known for a ton of traffic on adjacent Highway 89, as well as decent trout fishing and, in the spring and early summer, rafting. It is about a 15-minute drive to Squaw Valley or Lake Tahoe. A bike route extends along the Truckee River out of Tahoe City.

RV sites, facilities: There are 68 sites for tents or RVs up to 40 feet (no hookups) and seven walk-in tent sites. Picnic tables and fire grills are provided. Drinking water and vault toilets are available. Some facilities are wheelchair accessible. Leashed pets are permitted.

Reservations, fees: Reservations are accepted at 877/444-6777 ($9 reservation fee) or www.ReserveUSA.com. Sites are $15 per night,

$5 per night for an additional vehicle. Open May–October, weather permitting.

Directions: From Truckee, drive south on Highway 89 for 1.5 miles to the campground entrance on the left.

Contact: Tahoe National Forest, Truckee Ranger District, 530/587-3558, fax 530/587-6914; California Land Management, 530/544-0426.

45 COACHLAND RV PARK

Scenic rating: 6

in Truckee
See map page 652

Truckee is the gateway to recreation at North Tahoe. Within minutes are Donner Lake, Prosser Creek Reservoir, Boca Reservoir, Stampede Lake, the Truckee River, and ski resorts. Squaw Valley is a short distance to the south off Highway 89, and Northstar is just off Highway 267. The park is in a wooded area near I-80, providing easy access. The downtown Truckee area (with restaurants) is a half mile away. This is one of the few parks in the area that is open year-round. The elevation is 6,000 feet. One problem: Only 25 of the 131 sites are available for overnighters, with the rest taken by long-term rentals.

RV sites, facilities: There are 131 pull-through sites with full hookups (30 and 50 amps) for trailers or RVs up to 40 feet. No tents. Picnic tables are provided. Restrooms have showers. A coin laundry, cable TV, modem access, Wi-Fi, a playground, horseshoes, an athletic field, tetherball, a clubhouse, and propane are available. Some facilities are wheelchair accessible. Leashed pets are permitted.

Reservations, fees: Reservations are recommended. Sites are $39 per night, $1.50–3 per person per night for more than two people, $2 per night for an additional vehicle. Monthly rates available. Major credit cards accepted. Open year-round.

Directions: From eastbound I-80 in Truckee, take the 188A exit to Donner Pass Road. Turn north on Donner Pass Road and drive one block to Pioneer Trail. Turn left and drive a short distance to the park at 10100 Pioneer Trail on the left side of the road.

From westbound I-80 in Truckee, take the 188 exit to Highway 89. Turn right on Highway 89 and drive north one block to Donner Pass Road. Turn left and drive one block to Pioneer Trail. Turn right and continue to the park.

Contact: Coachland RV Park, 530/587-3071, fax 530/587-6976, www.coachlandrvpark.com.

46 LAKESIDE

Scenic rating: 7

on Prosser Creek Reservoir in Tahoe National Forest

See map page 652

This primitive camp is in a deep cove in the northwestern end of Prosser Creek Reservoir, near the lake's headwaters. It is a gorgeous lake, set at 5,741 feet, and a 10-mph speed limit keeps the fast boats out. The adjacent shore is decent for hand-launched, car-top boats, providing the lake level is up, and a concrete boat ramp is a mile down the road. Lots of trout are stocked here every year. The trout fishing is often quite good after the ice breaks up in late spring. Sound perfect? Unfortunately for many, the Prosser OHV Park is nearby and can be noisy.

RV sites, facilities: There are 30 sites for tents or RVs up to 33 feet (no hookups). Drinking water and vault toilets are available. A boat ramp is nearby. Leashed pets are permitted.

Reservations, fees: Reservations are accepted at 877/444-6777 ($9 reservation fee) or www.ReserveUSA.com. Sites are $13 per night, $5 per night for an additional vehicle. Open June–October, weather permitting.

Directions: From Truckee, drive north on Highway 89 for three miles to the campground entrance road on the right. Turn right and drive less than a mile to the campground.

Contact: Tahoe National Forest, Truckee Ranger District, 530/587-3558, fax 530/587-6914; California Land Management, 530/544-0426.

47 LOGGER

Scenic rating: 7

at Stampede Lake in Tahoe National Forest

See map page 652

Covering 3,400 acres and with 25 miles of shoreline, Stampede Lake is a huge lake by Sierra standards—the largest in the region after Lake Tahoe. It is at 6,000 feet, surrounded by Sierra granite mountains and pines, and on days when the wind is down, it's quite beautiful. The campground is also huge, set along the lake's southern shore, a few minutes' drive from the Captain Roberts boat ramp. This camp is ideal for campers, boaters, and anglers. The lake is becoming one of the top fishing lakes in California for kokanee salmon (which can be caught only by trolling), and it also has some large Mackinaw trout and a sprinkling of planter-sized rainbow trout. All water sports are allowed. One problem at Stampede is receding water levels from midsummer through fall, a real pain that puts the campsites some distance from the lake. Even when the lake is full, there are only a few "lakeside" campsites. However, the boat ramp has been extended to assist boaters during drawdowns.

RV sites, facilities: There are 252 sites for tents or RVs up to 32 feet (no hookups). Picnic tables and fire rings are provided. Drinking water, vault toilets, and a dump station are available. A concrete boat ramp is available one mile from camp. Some facilities are wheelchair accessible. Leashed pets are permitted.

Reservations, fees: Reservations are accepted at 877/444-6777 ($9 reservation fee) or www.ReserveUSA.com. Sites are $16 per night, $5 per night for an additional vehicle. Open May–October.

Directions: From Truckee, drive east on I-80 for seven miles to the Boca-Hirschdale/County Road 270 exit. Take that exit and drive north on County Road 270 for about seven miles (past Boca Reservoir) to the junction with County Road S261 on the left. Turn left and drive 1.5 miles to the campground on the right.

Contact: Tahoe National Forest, Truckee Ranger

CALIFORNIA

District, 530/587-3558, fax 530/587-6914; California Land Management, 530/544-0426.

48 BOCA REST CAMPGROUND

Scenic rating: 7

on Boca Reservoir in Tahoe National Forest

See map page 652

The Boca Dam faces I-80, so the reservoir is out of sight of the zillions of highway travelers who would otherwise certainly stop here. Those who do stop find that the lake is very pretty, set at 5,700 feet in elevation and covering 1,000 acres with deep, blue water and 14 miles of shoreline. All water sports are allowed. Boca Reservoir is known as a "big fish factory," with some huge but rare brown trout and rainbow trout sprinkled among a growing fishery for kokanee salmon. While the surrounding landscape is not in the drop-dead beautiful class, the lake can still seem a Sierra gem on a windless dawn, out on a boat. This camp is on the lake's northeastern shore, not far from the inlet to the Little Truckee River. The boat ramp is some distance away.

RV sites, facilities: There are 31 sites for tents or RVs up to 22 feet (no hookups). Picnic tables and fire grills are provided. Drinking water and vault toilets are available. A hand-launch boat ramp is also available. A concrete boat ramp is three miles away on the southwest shore of Boca Reservoir. Leashed pets are permitted.

Reservations, fees: Reservations are accepted at 877/444-6777 ($9 reservation fee) or www.ReserveUSA.com. Sites are $14 per night, $5 per night for an additional vehicle. Open May–October, weather permitting.

Directions: From Truckee, drive east on I-80 for seven miles to the Boca-Hirschdale exit. Take that exit and drive north on County Road 270 for about 2.5 miles to the campground on the left side of the road.

Contact: Tahoe National Forest, Truckee Ranger District, 530/587-3558, fax 530/587-6914; California Land Management, 530/544-0426.

49 MARTIS CREEK LAKE

Scenic rating: 7

near Truckee

See map page 652

If only this lake weren't so often windy in the afternoon, it would be heaven to fly fishers in float tubes. To some it's heaven anyway, with Lahontan cutthroat trout growing to 25 inches. This is a special catch-and-release fishery where anglers are permitted to use only artificial lures with single, barbless hooks. The setting is somewhat sparse and open—a small lake, 70 acres, on the eastern edge of the Martis Valley. No motors are permitted at the lake, making it ideal (when the wind is down) for float tubes or prams. Sailing, sailboarding, and swimming are permitted. There is no boat launch, but small boats can be hand launched. The lake level can fluctuate daily, which, along with the wind, can be frustrating for those who show up expecting automatic perfection; that just isn't the way it is out there. At times, the lake level can be very low. The elevation is 5,800 feet.

RV sites, facilities: There are 25 sites for tents or RVs up to 30 feet (no hookups). Some sites are pull-through. Picnic tables and fire grills are provided. Drinking water, vault toilets, tent pads, and pay phones are available. Supplies are available six minutes away in Truckee. Some facilities are wheelchair accessible. Leashed pets are permitted.

Reservations, fees: Reservations are accepted only for the wheelchair-accessible sites at 530/587-8113. Sites are $12 per night. Open May–mid-November, weather permitting.

Directions: From Truckee, drive south on Highway 267 for about three miles (past the airport) to the lake entrance road on the left. Turn left and drive another 2.5 miles to the campground at the end of the road.

Contact: U.S. Army Corps of Engineers, Sacramento District, 530/587-8113, fax 530/432-6418.

50 GOOSE MEADOWS

Scenic rating: 6

on the Truckee River in Tahoe National Forest

See map page 652

There are three campgrounds along the Truckee River off Highway 89 between Truckee and Tahoe City. Goose Meadows provides good fishing access with decent prospects, despite the high number of vehicles roaring past on the adjacent highway. This stretch of river is also popular for rafting. The elevation is 5,800 feet.

RV sites, facilities: There are 24 sites for tents or RVs up to 30 feet (no hookups). Picnic tables and fire grills are provided. Drinking water and vault toilets are available. Supplies are available in Truckee and Tahoe City. Some facilities are wheelchair accessible. Leashed pets are permitted.

Reservations, fees: Reservations are accepted at 877/444-6777 ($9 reservation fee) or www.ReserveUSA.com. Sites are $13 per night, $5 per night for an additional vehicle. Open May–October, weather permitting.

Directions: From Truckee, drive south on Highway 89 for four miles to the campground entrance on the left (river) side of the highway.

Contact: Tahoe National Forest, Truckee Ranger District, 530/587-3558, fax 530/587-6914; California Land Management, 530/544-0426.

51 SILVER CREEK

Scenic rating: 8

on the Truckee River in Tahoe National Forest

See map page 652

This pretty campground is near where Silver Creek enters the Truckee River. The trout fishing is often good in this area. This is one of three campgrounds along Highway 89 and the Truckee River, between Truckee and Tahoe City. The elevation is 6,000 feet.

RV sites, facilities: There are 21 sites for tents or RVs up to 40 feet (no hookups) and seven walk-in tent sites. Picnic tables and fire grills are provided. Drinking water and vault toilets

are available. Supplies are available in Truckee and Tahoe City. Some facilities are wheelchair accessible. Leashed pets are permitted.

Reservations, fees: Reservations are accepted at 877/444-6777 ($9 reservation fee) or www.ReserveUSA.com. Sites are $13 per night, $5 per night for an additional vehicle. Open June–September, weather permitting.

Directions: From Truckee, drive south on Highway 89 for six miles to the campground entrance on the river side of the highway.

Contact: Tahoe National Forest, Truckee Ranger District, 530/587-3558, fax 530/587-6914; California Land Management, 530/544-0426.

52 LAKE FOREST CAMPGROUND

Scenic rating: 8

on Lake Tahoe

See map page 652

The north shore of Lake Tahoe provides beautiful lookouts and excellent boating access. The latter is a highlight of this camp, with a boat ramp nearby. From here it is a short cruise to Dollar Point and around the corner north to Carnelian Bay, one of the better stretches of water for trout fishing. The elevation is 6,200 feet. There is a 10-day camping limit.

RV sites, facilities: There are 20 sites for tents or RVs up to 20 feet (no hookups). Picnic tables and fire grills are provided. Drinking water and vault toilets are available. A grocery store, a coin laundry, and propane gas are available within four miles. Some facilities are wheelchair accessible. Leashed pets are permitted.

Reservations, fees: Reservations are not accepted. Sites are $15 per night. Open April–October, weather permitting.

Directions: From Truckee, drive south on Highway 89 through Tahoe City to Highway 28. Bear north on Highway 28 and drive four miles to the campground entrance road (Lake Forest Road) on the right.

Contact: Tahoe City Public Utility District, Parks and Recreation, 530/583-3796, ext. 7, fax 530/583-8452.

CALIFORNIA

53 TAHOE STATE RECREATION AREA

Scenic rating: 9

on Lake Tahoe

See map page 652

This is a popular summer-only campground at the north shore of Lake Tahoe. The Tahoe State Recreation Area covers a large area just west of Highway 28 near Tahoe City. There are opportunities for hiking and horseback riding nearby (though not right at the park). It is also near shopping, restaurants, and, unfortunately, traffic jams in Tahoe City. A boat ramp is two miles to the northwest at nearby Lake Forest, and bike rentals are available in Tahoe City for rides along Highway 89 near the shore of the lake. For a more secluded site nearby at Tahoe, see the listing in this chapter for *Sugar Pine Point State Park,* 11 miles south on Highway 89.

RV sites, facilities: There are 100 sites for tents or RVs up to 40 feet (no hookups) and trailers up to 24 feet. Picnic tables, food lockers, barbecues, and fire pits are provided. Drinking water, vault toilets, and coin showers are available. Firewood, other supplies, and a coin laundry are available within walking distance. Leashed pets are permitted.

Reservations, fees: Reservations are accepted at 800/444-PARK (800/444-7275) or www.reserveamerica.com ($7.50 reservation fee). Sites are $25 per night, $6 per night for an additional vehicle. Open May–October, weather permitting.

Directions: From Truckee, drive south on Highway 89 through Tahoe City. Turn north on Highway 28 and drive 0.9 mile to the campground entrance on the right side of the road.

Contact: Tahoe State Recreation Area, 530/583-3074; Sierra District, 530/525-7232, www.parks.ca.gov.

54 SANDY BEACH CAMPGROUND

Scenic rating: 8

on Lake Tahoe

See map page 652

Sandy Beach Campground is at 6,200 feet near the northwest shore of Lake Tahoe. A nearby boat ramp provides access to one of the better fishing areas of the lake for Mackinaw trout. A public beach is across the road. But the water in Tahoe is always cold, and though a lot of people will get suntans on beaches next to the lake, swimmers need to be members of the Polar Bear Club. A short drive to the east will take you past the town of Kings Beach and into Nevada, where there are some small casinos near the shore of Crystal Bay. Note that some sites fill up for the summer season.

RV sites, facilities: There are 27 sites for tents or RVs up to 40 feet with full or partial hookups (30 amps). Some sites are pull-through. Picnic tables, barbecues, and fire rings are provided. Drinking water, restrooms with showers and flush toilets, a dump station, and a coin laundry are available. A free public boat ramp is half a block away. A grocery store and propane gas are available nearby. Leashed pets are permitted, with a two-dog limit per site.

Reservations, fees: Reservations are recommended. Sites are $20–25 per night for up to six people with two vehicles. For weeklong stays, the seventh night is free. Some credit cards accepted. Open May–October.

Directions: From Truckee, drive south on Highway 267 to Highway 28. Turn right and drive one mile to the park on the right side of the road (entrance well signed).

Contact: Sandy Beach Campground, 530/546-7682.

55 ORCHARD SPRINGS RESORT

Scenic rating: 7

on Rollins Lake

See map page 653

Orchard Springs Resort is on the shore of Rollins Lake in the Sierra Nevada foothills among

CALIFORNIA

pine, oak, and cedar trees. The summer heat makes the lake excellent for waterskiing, boating, and swimming, and the spring and fall are great for trout and bass fishing.

RV sites, facilities: There are 13 sites for RVs up to 40 feet with full hookups (30 amps) and 90 tent sites. Two sites are pull-through. Two cabins and four camping cabins are also available. Picnic tables, fire rings, and barbecues are provided. Drinking water, restrooms with flush toilets and showers, a launch ramp, boat rentals, slips, bait and tackle, a swimming beach, a group picnic area, a lakeview restaurant, and a convenience store are available. Some facilities are wheelchair accessible. Leashed pets are permitted.

Reservations, fees: Reservations are accepted. Sites are $29–39 per night, $15 per night for an additional vehicle unless towed, $5.75 per boat per night, $3 per pet per night. Some credit cards accepted. Open year-round.

Directions: From Auburn, drive northeast on I-80 for about 20 miles to the Colfax/Grass Valley exit. Take that exit and loop back over the freeway to the stop sign. Turn right and drive a short distance to Highway 174. Turn right and drive north on Highway 174 (a winding, two-lane road) for 3.7 miles (bear left at Giovanni's Restaurant) to Orchard Springs Road. Turn right on Orchard Springs Road and drive 0.5 mile to the road's end. Turn right at the gatehouse and continue to the campground.

Contact: Orchard Springs Resort, 866/624-7497 or 530/346-2212, www.osresort.com.

56 PENINSULA CAMPING AND BOATING RESORT

Scenic rating: 8

on Rollins Lake
See map page 653

Peninsula Campground is on a point that extends into Rollins Lake, flanked on each side by two sprawling lake arms. The resort has 280 acres and 1.5 miles of lake frontage. A bonus is that you can boat directly from some of the lakefront sites. If you like boating, waterskiing,

or swimming, you'll definitely like this place in the summer. All water sports are allowed. This is a family-oriented campground with lots of youngsters on summer vacation. Fishing is available for rainbow and brown trout, small- and largemouth bass, perch, crappie, and catfish.

RV sites, facilities: There are 78 sites for tents or RVs up to 40 feet and three group sites for 16–40 people. No hookups. Three cabins are also available. Picnic tables and fire pits are provided. Restrooms have flush toilets and showers. Drinking water, modem access, Wi-Fi, a dump station, boat rentals (fishing boats, patio boats, canoes, and kayaks), a boat ramp, boat storage, limited fishing licenses, a fish-cleaning station, a swimming beach, horseshoes, volleyball, and a convenience store are available. Marine gas is available on the lake. Leashed pets are permitted, but call for current status.

Reservations, fees: Reservations are accepted by phone or website. Sites are $26–30 per night, $10 per night for an additional vehicle, $65–150 per night for a group site, $3 per pet per night. Maximum 14-day stay. Some credit cards accepted. Open mid-April–September.

Directions: From Auburn, drive northeast on I-80 for about 20 miles to the Colfax/Grass Valley exit. Take that exit and loop back over the freeway to the stop sign. Turn right and drive a short distance to Highway 174. Turn right and drive north on Highway 174 (a winding, two-lane road) for eight miles to You Bet Road. Turn right, drive 4.3 miles (turning right again to stay on You Bet Road), and continue another 3.1 miles to the campground entrance at the end of the road.

Contact: Peninsula Camping and Boating Resort, 866/4MY-CAMP (866/469-2267) or 530/477-9413, www.penresort.com.

57 GIANT GAP

Scenic rating: 7

on Sugar Pine Reservoir in Tahoe National Forest
See map page 653

This is a lakeside spot along the western shore of Sugar Pine Reservoir at 4,000 feet in elevation in Tahoe National Forest. For boaters, there is a ramp on the south shore. Note that a 10-mph speed limit is the law, making this lake ideal for anglers in search of quiet water. Other recreation notes: There's a little less than a mile of paved trail, which goes through the day-use area. Big Reservoir (also known as Morning Star Lake), five miles to the east, is the only other lake in the region and also has a campground. The trout and bass fishing at Sugar Pine are fair, not usually great, not usually bad. Swimming is allowed, and kayaking and canoeing are popular.

RV sites, facilities: There are 30 sites for tents or RVs of any length (no hookups). Picnic tables and fire grills are provided. Drinking water and vault toilets are available. A dump station and boat ramp are available on the south shore. Supplies can be obtained in Foresthill. Some facilities are wheelchair accessible. Leashed pets are permitted.

Reservations, fees: Reservations are accepted ($9 reservation fee) at 877/444-6777 or www.ReserveUSA.com. Sites are $16 per night, $32 per night for a double site, and $48 per night for a triple site. Open May–mid-October, weather permitting.

Directions: From Sacramento, drive east on I-80 to the north end of Auburn and the Foresthill Road exit. Take that exit and drive east for 20 miles to Foresthill. Drive through Foresthill (road changes to Foresthill Divide Road) and continue for eight miles to Sugar Pine Road. Turn left and drive five miles to a fork. Turn right and drive one mile to the campground.

Contact: Tahoe National Forest, American River Ranger District, Foresthill Ranger Station, 530/367-2224, fax 530/367-2992.

58 SHIRTTAIL CREEK

Scenic rating: 7

on Sugar Pine Reservoir in Tahoe National Forest
See map page 653

This camp is near the little creek that feeds into the north end of Sugar Pine Reservoir. The boat ramp is all the way around the south side

of the lake, near Forbes Creek Group Camp. (For recreation information, see the listing in this chapter for *Giant Gap*.)

RV sites, facilities: There are 30 sites for tents or RVs of any length (no hookups) (double and triple sites are available). Picnic tables and fire grills are provided. Drinking water and vault toilets are available. A dump station and boat ramp are available on the south shore. Supplies can be obtained in Foresthill. Some facilities are wheelchair accessible. Leashed pets are permitted.

Reservations, fees: Reservations are accepted ($9 reservation fee) at 877/444-6777 or www.ReserveUSA.com. Sites are $16 for single sites, $32 for double sites, $48 for a triple site, per night. Open May–mid-October, weather permitting.

Directions: From Sacramento, drive east on I-80 to the north end of Auburn and the Foresthill Road exit. Take that exit and drive east for 20 miles to Foresthill. Drive through Foresthill (the road changes to Foresthill Divide Road) and continue for eight miles to Sugar Pine Road. Turn left and drive five miles to the campground access road. Turn right (signed) and drive to the campground.

Contact: Tahoe National Forest, American River Ranger District, Foresthill Ranger Station, 530/367-2224, fax 530/367-2992.

59 BIG RESERVOIR/ MORNING STAR LAKE

Scenic rating: 7

on Big Reservoir in Tahoe National Forest
See map page 653

Here's a quiet lake where only electric boat motors are allowed; no gas motors are permitted. That makes it ideal for canoeists, rowboaters, and tube floaters who don't like the idea of having to dodge water-skiers. The lake is stocked with rainbow trout; free fishing permits are required and can be obtained at the lake. Big Reservoir (also known as Morning Star Lake) is quite pretty and has a nice beach and some lakefront campsites. The elevation is 4,000 feet.

RV sites, facilities: There are 100 sites for tents or RVs up to 40 feet (no hookups). Picnic tables and fire grills are provided. Drinking water, vault toilets, free showers, a dump station, and firewood (fee) are available. There is a small store near the campground, and supplies are also available in Foresthill. Some facilities are wheelchair accessible. Leashed pets are permitted.

Reservations, fees: Reservations are accepted at 530/367-2129. Sites are $18–20 per night. Fishing fees are charged. Open May–October, weather permitting.

Directions: From Sacramento, drive east on I-80 to the north end of Auburn and the Foresthill Road exit. Take that exit and drive east for 20 miles to Foresthill. Drive through Foresthill (the road changes to Foresthill Divide Road) and continue for eight miles to Sugar Pine Road. Turn left and drive about three miles to Forest Road 24 (signed Big Reservoir). Continue straight onto Forest Road 24 and drive about three miles to the campground entrance road on the right.

Contact: Tahoe National Forest, American River Ranger District, Foresthill Ranger Station, 530/367-2224, fax 530/367-2992; concessionaire, DeAnza Placer Gold Mining Company, 530/367-2129.

60 BEAR RIVER CAMPGROUND
🚶 🏊 🛶 🎣 🐕 🚐 ⛺

Scenic rating: 7

near Colfax on Bear River

See map page 653

This RV park is in the Sierra foothills at 1,800 feet, near Bear River, featuring riverfront campsites. The park covers 200 acres, offers five miles of hiking trails, and is right on the Placer and Nevada County lines. It fills up on weekends and is popular with both locals and out-of-towners. In the spring, when everything is green, it can be a gorgeous landscape. Fishing is OK for rainbow and brown trout, smallmouth bass, and bluegill. Noncommercial gold panning is permitted, and some rafting is popular on the river. A 14-day maximum stay is enforced.

RV sites, facilities: There are 25 sites for tents or RVs up to 40 feet, and two group sites for tents or RVs up to 35 feet can accommodate 50–100 people. No hookups. Picnic tables and fire rings are provided. Pit toilets are available. There is no drinking water. Supplies are available within five miles in Colfax or Bowman. Leashed pets are permitted.

Reservations, fees: Reservations are accepted ($5 reservation fee) only for the group site at 530/886-4900. Sites are $10 per night, $2 per night for an additional vehicle, $1 per pet per night, and $40–75 per night for group sites. Open March–September.

Directions: From Sacramento, drive east on I-80 east of Auburn to West Weimar Cross Road exit. Take that exit onto Weimar Cross Road and drive north for 1.5 miles to Placer Hills Road. Turn right and drive 2.5 miles to Plum Tree Road. Turn left and drive one mile to the campground on the left. The access road is steep and narrow.

Contact: Bear River Campground, Placer County Facilities Services, 530/889-4900, fax 530/886-6809, www.placer.ca.gov.

61 WILLIAM KENT
🏊 🎣 🐕 🦽 🚐 ⛺

Scenic rating: 8

near Lake Tahoe in the Lake Tahoe Basin

See map page 652

William Kent camp is a little pocket of peace set near the busy traffic of Highway 89 on the western shore corridor. It is on the west side of the highway, meaning visitors have to cross the highway to get lakeside access. The elevation is 6,300 feet, and the camp is wooded with primarily lodgepole pines. The drive here is awesome or ominous, depending on how you look at it, with the view of incredible Lake Tahoe to the east, the third-deepest blue in North America and the 10th-deepest lake in the world. But you often have a lot of time to look at it, since traffic rarely moves quickly.

RV sites, facilities: There are 36 sites with no hookups for RVs up to 40 feet and 55 tent sites.

Picnic tables, food lockers, and fire grills are provided. Drinking water, flush toilets, and a dump station are available. A grocery store, a coin laundry, and propane gas are available nearby. Some facilities are wheelchair accessible. Leashed pets are permitted.

Reservations, fees: Reservations are accepted at 877/444-6777 ($9 reservation fee) or www.ReserveUSA.com. Sites are $16 per night, $5 per night for an additional vehicle. Open late May–mid-October, weather permitting.

Directions: From Truckee, drive south on Highway 89 to Tahoe City. Turn south on Highway 89 and drive three miles to the campground entrance on the right side of the road.

Contact: Lake Tahoe Basin Management Unit, 530/543-2600, fax 530/543-2693; Taylor Creek Visitor Center, 530/543-2674; California Land Management, 530/583-3642.

62 FRENCH MEADOWS

Scenic rating: 7

on French Meadows Reservoir in Tahoe National Forest

See map page 652

The nearby boat launch makes this the choice for boating campers. The camp is on French Meadows Reservoir at 5,300 feet. It is on the lake's southern shore, with the boat ramp about a mile to the south (you'll see the entrance road on the way in). This is a big lake set in remote Tahoe National Forest in the North Fork American River Canyon with good trout fishing. All water sports are allowed. The lake level often drops in late summer, and then a lot of stumps and boulders start poking through the lake surface. This creates navigational hazards for boaters and water-skiers, but it also makes it easier for the anglers to know where to find the fish. If the fish don't bite here, boaters should make the nearby side trip to pretty Hell Hole Reservoir to the south.

RV sites, facilities: There are 75 sites for tents or RVs up to 45 feet (no hookups). Picnic tables and fire grills are provided. Drinking water and vault toilets are available. A concrete boat ramp is nearby. Supplies are available in Foresthill. Some facilities are wheelchair accessible. Leashed pets are permitted.

Reservations, fees: Reservations are available at 877/444-6777 ($9 reservation fee) or www.ReserveUSA.com. Sites are $16 per night, $5 per night for an additional vehicle. Open late May–October, weather permitting.

Directions: From Sacramento, drive east on I-80 to the north end of Auburn and the Foresthill Road exit. Take that exit and drive east to Foresthill and Mosquito Ridge Road (Forest Road 96). Turn right (east) and drive 40 miles (curvy) to Anderson Dam and to a junction. Turn left (still Mosquito Ridge Road) and then continue along the southern shoreline of French Meadows Reservoir for four miles to the campground.

Contact: Tahoe National Forest, American River Ranger District, Foresthill Ranger Station, 530/367-2224, fax 530/367-2992.

63 LEWIS

Scenic rating: 7

on French Meadows Reservoir in Tahoe National Forest

See map page 652

This camp is not right at lakeside but is just across the road from French Meadows Reservoir. It is still quite pretty, set along a feeder creek near the lake's northwest shore. A boat ramp is available only a half mile to the south, and the adjacent McGuire boat ramp area has a trailhead that is routed along the lake's northern shoreline. This lake is big (2,000 acres) and pretty, created by a dam on the Middle Fork American River, with good fishing for rainbow trout.

RV sites, facilities: There are 40 sites for tents or RVs up to 45 feet (no hookups). Picnic tables and fire grills are provided. Drinking water and vault toilets are available. A concrete boat ramp is nearby. Supplies are available in Foresthill. Some facilities are wheelchair accessible. Leashed pets are permitted.

Reservations, fees: Reservations are accepted at 877/444-6777 ($9 reservation fee) or www.ReserveUSA.com. Sites are $16 per night, $5 per night for an additional vehicle. Open mid-May–early September.

Directions: From Sacramento, drive east on I-80 to the north end of Auburn and the Foresthill Road exit. Take that exit and drive east to Foresthill and Mosquito Ridge Road (Forest Road 96). Turn right (east) and drive 40 miles (curvy) to Anderson Dam and to a junction. Turn left (still Mosquito Ridge Road) and then continue along the southern shoreline of French Meadows Reservoir for five miles to a fork at the head of the lake. Bear left at the fork and drive 0.5 mile to the camp on the right side of the road.

Contact: Tahoe National Forest, American River Ranger District, Foresthill Ranger Station, 530/367-2224, fax 530/367-2992.

64 BIG MEADOWS

Scenic rating: 7

near Hell Hole Reservoir in Eldorado National Forest

See map page 652

This camp sits on a meadow near the ridge above Hell Hole Reservoir (which is about two miles away). The reservoir is a mountain temple with sapphire-blue water. All water sports are allowed, and the reservoir has 15 miles of shoreline. Fishing is available for Mackinaw trout, kokanee salmon, brown trout, and a sprinkling of rainbow trout.

RV sites, facilities: There are 54 sites for tents or RVs of any length (no hookups). Picnic tables are provided. Drinking water and flush and vault toilets are available. Leashed pets are permitted.

Reservations, fees: Reservations are not accepted. Sites are $10 per night, $5 per night for an additional vehicle. Open mid-May–early November, weather permitting.

Directions: From Sacramento, drive east on I-80 to the north end of Auburn. Take the Elm Avenue exit and turn left at the first stoplight onto Elm Avenue. Drive 0.1 mile, turn left on High Street, and continue through the signal where High Street merges with Highway 49. Continue on Highway 49 for about 3.5 miles, turn right over the bridge, and drive about 2.5 miles into the town of Cool. Turn left on Georgetown Road/Highway 193 and drive about 14 miles into Georgetown. At the four-way stop turn left on Main Street (which becomes Wentworth Springs/Forest Road 1) and drive about 25 miles. Turn left on Forest Road 2 and drive 21 miles to the campground on the left.

Contact: Eldorado National Forest, Georgetown Ranger District, 530/333-4312, fax 530/333-5522.

65 SUGAR PINE POINT STATE PARK

Scenic rating: 10

on Lake Tahoe

See map page 652

This is one of three beautiful and popular state parks on the west shore of Lake Tahoe. It is just north of Meeks Bay on General Creek, with almost two miles of lake frontage available, though the campground is on the opposite side of Highway 89. General Creek, a feeder stream to Lake Tahoe here, is one of the clearest streams imaginable. A pretty trail is routed seven miles along the creek up to Lost Lake, just outside the northern boundary of the Desolation Wilderness. This stream also provides trout fishing from mid-July to mid-September. This park contains one of the finest remaining natural areas at Lake Tahoe. The park features dense forests of pine, fir, aspen, and junipers, covering more than 2,000 acres of beautiful landscape. There are many hiking trails, a swimming beach, and, in winter, 20 kilometers of cross-country skiing trails and a heated restroom. There is also evidence of occupation by Washoe Indians, with bedrock mortars, or grinding rocks, near the Ehrman Mansion. The elevation is 6,200 feet.

RV sites, facilities: There are 175 sites for tents or RVs up to 32 feet and trailers up to 26 feet. There are also 10 group sites for up to 40 people each. No hookups. Picnic tables and fire rings are provided. Drinking water, restrooms with flush toilets and coin showers (except in winter), a dump station, a day-use area, and a nature center with a bird display are available. A grocery store, a coin laundry, and propane gas are available nearby. Some facilities are wheelchair accessible. Leashed pets are permitted.

Reservations, fees: Reservations are accepted at 800/444-PARK (800/444-7275) or www.reserveamerica.com ($7.50 reservation fee). Sites are $15–20 per night, $6 per night for an additional vehicle, $111 per night for a group site. Open year-round.

Directions: From Truckee, drive south on Highway 89 through Tahoe City. Continue south on Highway 89 and drive 9.3 miles to the campground (signed) on the right (west) side of the road.

Contact: Sugar Pine Point State Park, 530/525-7982; Sierra District, 530/525-7232, www.parks.ca.gov.

66 MEEKS BAY

Scenic rating: 9

on Lake Tahoe

See map page 652

Meeks Bay is a beautiful spot along the western shore of Lake Tahoe. A bicycle trail is available nearby and is routed along the lake's shore, but it requires occasionally crossing busy Highway 89.

RV sites, facilities: There are 40 sites for tents or RVs up to 20 feet (no hookups). Picnic tables, food lockers, and fire grills are provided. Drinking water and flush toilets are available. A coin laundry and groceries are available nearby. Leashed pets are permitted.

Reservations, fees: Reservations are accepted at 877/444-6777 ($9 reservation fee) or www.ReserveUSA.com. Sites are $17 per night, $5 per night for an additional vehicle. Open mid-May–mid-October, weather permitting.

Directions: In South Lake Tahoe at the junction of Highway 89 and U.S. 50, turn north on Highway 89 and drive 17 miles to the campground (signed) on the east side of Highway 89.

Contact: Lake Tahoe Basin Management Unit, 530/543-2600, fax 530/543-2693; Taylor Creek Visitor Center, 530/543-2674; California Land Management, 530/544-0426.

67 MEEKS BAY RESORT & MARINA

Scenic rating: 7

on Lake Tahoe

See map page 652

Prime access for boating makes this a camp of choice for the boater/camper at Lake Tahoe. This campground is extremely popular and often booked well ahead of time for July and August. A boat launch is not only on the premises, but access to Rubicon Bay and beyond to breathtaking Emerald Bay is possible, a six-mile trip one-way for boats. The resort is adjacent to a 20-mile paved bike trail, with a swimming beach also nearby. A 14-day stay limit is enforced.

RV sites, facilities: There are 10 sites with full hookups (50 amps) for RVs of any length and 24 sites for tents. Some sites are pull-through. Lodge rooms, cabins, and a house are also available. Picnic tables and fire grills are provided. Restrooms have showers and flush toilets. A coin laundry, snack bar, gift shop, and convenience store are available. A boat ramp, boat rentals (kayaks, canoes, and pedal boats), and boat slips are also available. No pets are allowed.

Reservations, fees: Reservations are accepted at 866/589-3411. Sites are $25–30 per night; boat slips cost $25 per night. Some credit cards accepted. Open May–September.

Directions: In South Lake Tahoe at the junction of Highway 89 and U.S. 50, turn north on Highway 89 and drive 17 miles to the campground on the right at 7941 Emerald Bay Road.

Contact: Meeks Bay Resort & Marina, 530/525-6946, www.meeksbayresort.com.

68 D. L. BLISS STATE PARK

Scenic rating: 10

on Lake Tahoe
See map page 653   BEST (

D. L. Bliss State Park is on one of Lake Tahoe's most beautiful stretches of shoreline, from Emerald Point at the mouth of Emerald Bay on northward to Rubicon Point, spanning about three miles. The camp is at the north end of the park, the sites nestled amid pine trees, with 80 percent of the campsites within a half mile to mile of the beach. The grandeur of this park and landscape is the result of successive upheavals of the mountain-building process that raised the Sierra Nevada range. The park is named for a pioneering lumberman, railroad owner, and banker of the region, whose family donated this 744-acre parcel to California in 1929. There are two great easy hiking trails. Rubicon Trail is one of Tahoe's most popular easy hikes, a meandering path just above the southwest shore of Lake Tahoe, wandering through pine, cedars, and firs, with breaks for fantastic panoramas of the lake, as well as spots where you can see nearly 100 feet into the lake. Don't be surprised if you are joined by a chipmunk circus, many begging, sitting upright, hoping for their nut for the day. While this trail is beautiful and solitary at dawn, by noon it can be crowded by hikers and chipmunks alike. Another trail, a great hike for youngsters, is Balancing Rock Trail, just a half-mile romp, where after about 40 yards you arrive at this 130-ton, oblong granite boulder that is set on a tiny perch, and the whole thing seems to defy gravity. Some day it has to fall, right? Not yet. Rubicon Trail runs all the way past Emerald Point to Emerald Bay.

RV sites, facilities: There are 165 sites for tents or RVs up to 18 feet and trailers up to 15 feet, one hike-in or bike-in site, and a group site for up to 50 people. No hookups. Picnic tables, fire grills, and food lockers are provided. Restrooms with coin showers and flush toilets are available. All water must sometimes be pump-filtered or boiled before use, depending on current water conditions. Some facilities are wheelchair accessible. Leashed pets are permitted at campsites only.

Reservations, fees: Reservations are accepted at 800/444-PARK (800/444-7275) or www.reserveamerica.com ($7.50 reservation fee). Sites are $25–35 per night, $6 per night for an additional vehicle, $111 per night for the group site, $6 per night for the hike-in/bike-in site. Open late May–late September, weather permitting.

Directions: In South Lake Tahoe at the junction of Highway 89 and U.S. 50, turn north on Highway 89 and drive 10.5 miles to the state park turnoff on the right side of the road. Turn right (east) and drive to the park entrance. (If arriving from the north, drive from Tahoe City south on Highway 89 for 17 miles to the park entrance road.)

Contact: D. L. Bliss State Park, 530/525-7277; Sierra District, 530/525-7232, www.parks.ca.gov.

69 EMERALD BAY STATE PARK AND BOAT-IN

Scenic rating: 10

on Lake Tahoe
See map page 653   BEST (

This is one of the most beautiful and popular state parks on the planet. The campground is at Eagle Point, near the mouth of Emerald Bay on Lake Tahoe, a place of rare, divine beauty. Although the large crowds at Lake Tahoe, and at this park in particular, present inevitable problems, there is a remarkable solution: 20 boat-in sites. There may be no more beautiful place anywhere to run a boat than in Emerald Bay, with its deep cobalt-blue waters, awesome surrounding ridgelines, glimpses of Lake Tahoe out the mouth of the bay, and even a little island. The park also has several short hiking trails. Emerald Bay is a designated underwater park. It features Fanette Island, Tahoe's only island. The park also features Vikingsholm, one of the finest examples of Scandinavian architecture in North America; tours are available and very popular, and the hike here features a two-mile round-trip with 500-foot drop in elevation to the "castle." The boat-in camps are

CALIFORNIA

on the northern side of Emerald Bay at the site of the old Emerald Bay Resort.

RV sites, facilities: There are 100 sites for tents or RVs up to 21 feet and trailers up to 18 feet, one hike-in/bike-in site, and 22 boat-in sites. No hookups. Picnic tables and fire grills are provided. Drinking water and restrooms with flush toilets and coin showers are available. At boat-in sites, drinking water and vault toilets are available. Some facilities are wheelchair accessible. Leashed pets are permitted in the campground and on asphalt, but not on trails.

Reservations, fees: Reservations are accepted at 800/444-PARK (800/444-7275) or www.reserveamerica.com ($7.50 reservation fee). Sites are $25 per night, $6 per night for an additional vehicle, $20 per night for boat-in sites, $6 per person per night for hike-in/bike-in sites. Open early June–mid-September, weather permitting.

Directions: In South Lake Tahoe at the junction of Highway 89 and U.S. 50, turn north on Highway 89 and drive 6.5 miles to the state park entrance turnoff on the right side of the road.

Contact: Emerald Bay State Park, 530/541-3030; D. L. Bliss State Park, 530/525-7277, www.parks.ca.gov.

70 HISTORIC CAMP RICHARDSON RESORT

Scenic rating: 7

on Lake Tahoe

See map page 653

Camp Richardson Resort is within minutes of boating, biking, gambling and, in the winter (lodging only), skiing and snowboarding. It's a take-your-pick deal. With cabins, a restaurant, and live music (often nightly in summer) also on the property, this is a place that offers one big package. The campsites are set in the woods, not on the lake itself. From here you can gain access to an excellent bike route that runs for three miles, then loops around by the lake for another three miles, most of it flat and easy, all of it beautiful. Expect company. The elevation is 6,300 feet.

RV sites, facilities: There are 223 sites for tents and 112 sites with full or partial hookups (30 amps) for RVs up to 35 feet. Some sites are pull-through. Cabins, duplex units, inn rooms, and hotel rooms are also available. Picnic tables and fire pits are provided. Restrooms have showers and flush toilets. Drinking water, a dump station, group facilities, and a playground are available. A full-service marina, a boat ramp, boat rentals, a swimming beach, bike rentals, a general store, a restaurant, an ice cream parlor, and propane gas are available nearby. Some facilities are wheelchair accessible.

Reservations, fees: Reservations are accepted at 800/544-1801. Sites are $20–35 per night, $5 per night for an additional vehicle. Some credit cards accepted. Open June–October, with lodging available year-round.

Directions: In South Lake Tahoe at the junction of Highway 89 and U.S. 50, turn north on Highway 89 and drive 2.5 miles to the resort on the right side of the road.

Contact: Historic Camp Richardson Resort, 530/541-1801, www.camprichardson.com.

71 CAMP SHELLEY

Scenic rating: 7

near Lake Tahoe in the Lake Tahoe Basin

See map page 653

This campground is near South Lake Tahoe within close range of an outstanding bicycle trail. The camp is in the woods, with campfire programs available on Saturday night in summer. Nearby to the west is the drive to Inspiration Point and the incredible lookout of Emerald Bay, as well as the parking area for the short hike to Eagle Falls. Nearby to the east are Fallen Leaf Lake and the south shore of Lake Tahoe.

RV sites, facilities: There are 26 sites for tents or RVs up to 24 feet (no hookups) and 10.5 feet high. Picnic tables and fire grills are provided. Drinking water, restrooms with free showers and flush toilets, horseshoes, table tennis, volleyball, and basketball are available. A boat ramp, groceries, and propane gas are available nearby at Camp Richardson. Some facilities are wheelchair accessible. Leashed pets are permitted.

Reservations, fees: Reservations can be made in person, 9 A.M.–4 P.M. Monday–Friday, at the Robert Livermore Community Center, 4444 East Avenue, Livermore, CA 94550. Reservations can also be made by mail, by fax, or at the campground office, which is intermittently staffed during the season. A reservation form can be downloaded from the website. Sites are $20–25 per night, ($12–18 for Livermore residents), $5 per night for an additional vehicle. Open mid-June–Labor Day weekend.

Directions: In South Lake Tahoe at the junction of U.S. 50 and Highway 89, turn north on Highway 89, drive 2.5 miles to Camp Richardson, and then continue for 1.3 miles to the sign for Mount Tallac. Turn left at the sign for Mount Tallac Trailhead/Camp Shelly and drive to the campground on the right.

Contact: Camp Shelly, 530/541-6985; Livermore Area Recreation and Park District, 925/373-5700, fax 925/447-2754, www.larpd.dst.ca.us.

72 FALLEN LEAF CAMPGROUND

Scenic rating: 7

in the Lake Tahoe Basin

See map page 653

This is a large camp near the north shore of Fallen Leaf Lake, set at 6,337 feet. The lake is almost as deep blue as nearby Lake Tahoe. It's a big lake, three miles long, and also quite deep, 430 feet at its deepest point. The campground is operated by the concessionaire. There are a variety of recreational opportunities, including boat rentals at the marina and horseback-riding rentals at Camp Richardson Resort. Fishing is best in the fall for kokanee salmon. Because Fallen Leaf Lake is circled by forest and much of it is private property, you will need a boat to fish or explore the lake. A visitors center is north of the Fallen Leaf Lake turnoff on Highway 89.

RV sites, facilities: There are 75 sites for tents and 130 sites for tents or RVs up to 40 feet.

No hookups. Picnic tables, food lockers, and fire grills are provided. Drinking water, vault toilets, and coin showers are available. A boat ramp, a coin laundry, and supplies are available nearby. Some facilities are wheelchair accessible. Leashed pets are permitted.

Reservations, fees: Reservations are accepted at 877/444-6777 ($9 reservation fee) or www.ReserveUSA.com. Sites are $20 per night, $5 per night for an additional vehicle. Open mid-May–mid-October, weather permitting.

Directions: In South Lake Tahoe at the junction of U.S. 50 and Highway 89, turn north on Highway 89 and drive two miles to the Fallen Leaf Lake turnoff. Turn left and drive 1.5 miles to the campground.

Contact: Lake Tahoe Basin Management Unit, 530/543-2600, fax 530/543-2693; Taylor Creek Visitor Center, 530/543-2674; California Land Management, 530/544-0426; Fallen Leaf Lake Marina, 530/544-0787.

73 TAHOE VALLEY CAMPGROUND

Scenic rating: 5

near Lake Tahoe

See map page 653

This is a massive, privately operated park near South Lake Tahoe. The nearby attractions include five golf courses, horseback riding, casinos, and, of course, "The Lake." Note that about half of the sites are filled with seasonal renters.

RV sites, facilities: There are 305 sites with full or partial hookups (30 and 50 amps) for RVs of any length and 77 sites for tents. Some sites are pull-through. Picnic tables and fire grills are provided. Restrooms have showers. Cable TV, Wi-Fi, modem access, a dump station, a coin laundry, a seasonal heated swimming pool, a playground, tennis courts, a grocery store, RV supplies, propane gas, ice, firewood, and a recreation room are available. Some facilities are wheelchair accessible. Leashed pets are permitted.

Reservations, fees: Reservations are recommended. Sites are $36–46 per night. Monthly rates available. Some credit cards accepted. Open year-round.

Directions: Entering South Lake Tahoe on U.S. 50, drive east on U.S. 50 to Meyers. Continue on U.S. 50 about five miles beyond Meyers to the signed entrance on the right. Turn right on C Street and drive 1.5 blocks to the campground.

Contact: Tahoe Valley Campground, 530/541-2222, fax 530/541-1825.

7.4 CAMPGROUND BY THE LAKE

Scenic rating: 5

near Lake Tahoe
See map page 653

This city-operated campground provides an option at South Lake Tahoe. It is at 6,200 feet, across the road from the lake, with pine trees and views of the lake.

RV sites, facilities: There are 175 sites for tents or RVs up to 40 feet and one group site for 30–50 people. Some sites have partial hookups (30 and 50 amps) and/or are pull-through. One cabin is also available. Picnic tables, barbecues, and fire grills are provided. Drinking water, restrooms with flush toilets and showers, a dump station, a playground, and a boat ramp (check current status) are available. An indoor ice-skating rink and a public indoor heated pool are nearby (fee for access). Supplies and a coin laundry are nearby. Some facilities are wheelchair accessible. Leashed pets are permitted.

Reservations, fees: Reservations are accepted ($3.50 reservation fee) at 530/542-6055. Sites are $22.50–30.50 per night, $4 per night for an additional vehicle, $150–250 per night for the group site, $1 per pet per night. Weekly rates available. Some credit cards accepted. Open April–October, with a 14-day maximum stay.

Directions: If entering South Lake Tahoe on U.S. 50, drive east on U.S. 50 to Rufus Allen Boulevard. Turn right and drive 0.25 mile to the campground on the right side of the road.

Contact: Campground by the Lake, 530/542-6096; City of South Lake Tahoe, Parks and Recreation Department, 530/542-6055, www.recreationintahoe.com.

7.5 KOA SOUTH LAKE TAHOE

Scenic rating: 5

near Lake Tahoe
See map page 653

Like so many KOA camps, this one is on the outskirts of a major destination area—in this case, South Lake Tahoe. It is within close range of gambling, fishing, hiking, and bike rentals. The camp is at 6,300 feet.

RV sites, facilities: There are 40 sites with full hookups (30 amps) for RVs up to 36 feet and 16 sites for tents or RVs (no hookups). Some sites are pull-through. A lodge is also available. Picnic tables and fire grills are provided. Restrooms have showers. Cable TV, Wi-Fi, a dump station, a recreation room, a seasonal heated swimming pool, a playground, a coin laundry, a convenience store, RV supplies, horseshoes, firewood, ice, and propane gas are available. Leashed pets are permitted.

Reservations, fees: Reservations are recommended at 800/562-3477. Sites are $36–53 per night, $4 per person per night for more than two people, $4 per night for an additional vehicle, $10–15 per boat per night, $4 per pet per night. Weekly and monthly rates available. Holiday rates are higher. Some credit cards accepted. Open April–mid-October.

Directions: From Sacramento, take U.S. 50 and drive east over the Sierra Nevada past Echo Summit to Meyers. As you enter Meyers, it will be the first campground on the right. Turn right and enter the campground.

Contact: KOA South Lake Tahoe, 530/577-3693, www.laketahoekoa.com.

76 STUMPY MEADOWS

Scenic rating: 7

on Stumpy Meadows Lake in Eldorado
National Forest

See map page 653

This is the camp of choice for visitors to Stumpy
Meadows Lake. The first thing visitors notice is
the huge ponderosa pine trees, noted for their
distinctive mosaic-like bark. The lake is at
4,400 feet in Eldorado National Forest and covers 320 acres with water that is cold and clear.
The lake has both rainbow and brown trout,
and in the fall fishing is good for big browns
(they move up into the head of the lake, near
where Pilot Creek enters).

RV sites, facilities: There are 40 sites for tents
or RVs of any length (no hookups). Two of the
sites are double units. Picnic tables and fire
grills are provided. Drinking water and vault
toilets are available. A boat ramp is nearby.
Leashed pets are permitted.

Reservations, fees: Reservations are accepted at 877/444-6777 ($9 reservation fee) or
www.ReserveUSA.com. Sites are $16 per night,
$28 per night for double-unit sites, $5 per
night for an additional vehicle. Boat launching
is $8 per day. Open April–October, weather
permitting.

Directions: From Sacramento on I-80, drive
east to the north end of Auburn. Turn left on
Elm Avenue and drive about 0.1 mile. Turn left
on High Street and drive through the signal
that marks the continuation of High Street as
Highway 49. Drive 3.5 miles on Highway 49,
turn right over the bridge, and drive 2.5 miles
into the town of Cool. Turn left on Georgetown
Road/Highway 193 and drive 14 miles into
Georgetown. At the four-way stop, turn left
on Main Street, which becomes Georgetown-
Wentworth Springs Road/Forest Road 1. Drive
about 18 miles to Stumpy Meadows Lake. Continue about a mile and turn right into Stumpy
Meadows campground.

Contact: Eldorado National Forest, Georgetown Ranger District, 530/333-4312, fax
530/333-5522.

77 GERLE CREEK

Scenic rating: 7

on Gerle Creek Reservoir in Eldorado
National Forest

See map page 653

This is a small, pretty, but limited spot set along
the northern shore of little Gerle Creek Reservoir at 5,231 feet in elevation. The lake is ideal
for canoes or other small boats because no motors are permitted and no boat ramp is available.
That makes for quiet water. It is in the Gerle
Creek Canyon, which feeds into the South
Fork Rubicon River. No trout plants are made
at this lake, and fishing can be correspondingly
poor. A wild brown trout population lives here,
though. A network of Forest Service roads to
the north can provide great exploring. A map
of Eldorado National Forest is a must.

RV sites, facilities: There are 50 sites for tents
or RVs up to 25 feet (no hookups). Picnic tables
and fire grills are provided. Drinking water and
vault toilets are available. Wheelchair-accessible
trails and a fishing pier are available nearby.
Leashed pets are permitted.

Reservations, fees: Reservations accepted at 877/444-6777 ($9 reservation fee) or
www.ReserveUSA.com. Sites are $18 per night,
$5 per night for an additional vehicle. Open
mid-May–mid-October, weather permitting.

Directions: From Placerville, drive east on
U.S. 50 for 23 miles to Riverton and the junction with Ice House Road/Forest Road 3. Turn
north and drive 27 miles (past Union Valley
Reservoir) to a fork with Forest Road 30. Turn
left, drive two miles, bear left on the campground entrance road, and drive a mile to the
campground.

Contact: Eldorado National Forest, Pacific Ranger District, 530/644-2349, fax
530/647-5405.

CALIFORNIA

78 LOON LAKE

Scenic rating: 9

in Eldorado National Forest

See map page 653

Loon Lake is near the Sierra crest at 6,400 feet, covering 600 acres with depths up to 130 feet. This is the lake's primary campground, and it is easy to see why, with a picnic area, beach (includes a small unit to change your clothes in), and boat ramp adjacent to the camp. The lake provides good trout fishing, and once the access road is clear of snow, the lake is stocked on a regular basis. Afternoon winds drive anglers off the lake but are cheered by sailboarders. An excellent trail is also available here, with the hike routed along the lake's eastern shore to Pleasant Hike-In/Boat-In, where there's a trailhead for the Desolation Wilderness.

RV sites, facilities: There are 53 sites for tents or RVs up to 40 feet, nine sites for equestrians, and one group equestrian site for tents or RVs up to 40 feet that can accommodate up to 25 people. No hookups. Picnic tables and fire grills are provided. Drinking water and vault toilets are available. Tie lines are available for horses. A boat ramp and swimming beach are nearby. Some facilities are wheelchair accessible. Leashed pets are permitted.

Reservations, fees: Reservations are accepted at 877/444-6777 ($9 reservation fee) or www.ReserveUSA.com. Sites are $18 per night, $34 per night for a double site, $5 per night for an additional vehicle. Open June–mid-October, weather permitting.

Directions: From Placerville, drive east on U.S. 50 for 23 miles to Riverton and the junction with Ice House Road/Forest Road 3. Turn left and drive 34 miles to a fork at the foot of Loon Lake. Turn right and drive one mile to the Loon Lake Picnic Area or boat ramp.

Contact: Eldorado National Forest, Pacific Ranger District, 530/644-2349, fax 530/644-5405.

79 WOLF CREEK AND WOLF CREEK GROUP

Scenic rating: 9

on Union Valley Reservoir in Eldorado National Forest

See map page 653

Wolf Creek Camp is on the north shore of Union Valley Reservoir. Listen up. Notice that it's quieter? Yep. That's because there are not as many water-skiers in the vicinity. Why? There's no boat ramp in the immediate area; it is three miles away. The view of the Crystal Range from the campground is drop-dead gorgeous. The elevation is 4,900 feet.

RV sites, facilities: There are 42 sites for tents or RVs up to 40 feet, and three group sites for tents or RVs up to 40 feet can accommodate up to 50 people each. No hookups. Picnic tables and fire grills are provided. Drinking water and vault toilets are available. A boat ramp is three miles away at the campground at Yellowjacket. Some facilities are wheelchair accessible. Leashed pets are permitted.

Reservations, fees: Reservations are accepted for individual sites and required for group sites at 877/444-6777 ($9 reservation fee) or www.ReserveUSA.com. Sites are $18 per night for a single site, $34 per night for a double site, $5 per night for an additional vehicle. Group sites are $100–150 per night. Open mid-May–mid-October, weather permitting.

Directions: From Placerville, drive east on U.S. 50 for 23 miles to Riverton and the junction with Ice House Road/Forest Road 3. Turn left (north) and drive 19 miles to Forest Road 12N78/Union Valley Road (at the head of Union Valley Reservoir). Turn left (west) and drive two miles to the campground.

Contact: Eldorado National Forest, Pacific Ranger District, 530/644-2349, fax 530/647-5405.

80 CAMINO COVE

Scenic rating: 10

on Union Valley Reservoir in Eldorado
National Forest

See map page 653

Camino Cove Camp is the nicest spot at Union Valley Reservoir, a slam dunk. It is at the north end of the lake on a peninsula, absolutely beautiful, a tree-covered landscape and yet with sweeping views of the Crystal Basin. The nearest boat ramp is 1.5 miles to the west at West Point. If this camp is full, there is a small camp at West Point, with just eight sites. The elevation is 4,900 feet.

RV sites, facilities: There are 32 sites for tents or RVs up to 30 feet (no hookups). Fire rings are provided. Vault toilets are available. No drinking water is available. Garbage must be packed out. A swimming beach is nearby and a boat ramp is 1.5 miles away at the campground at West Point. Some facilities are wheelchair accessible. Leashed pets are permitted.

Reservations, fees: Reservations are not accepted. There is no fee for camping. Open early May–October, weather permitting.

Directions: From Placerville, drive east on U.S. 50 for 23 miles to Riverton and the junction with Ice House Road/Forest Road 3. Turn north on Ice House Road and drive seven miles to Peavine Ridge Road. Turn left and drive three miles to Bryant Springs Road. Turn right and drive five miles north past the West Point boat ramp, and continue 1.5 miles east to the campground entrance on the right.

Contact: Eldorado National Forest, Pacific Ranger District, 530/644-2349, fax 530/647-5405.

81 YELLOWJACKET

Scenic rating: 8

on Union Valley Reservoir in Eldorado
National Forest

See map page 653

The camp is at 4,900 feet on the north shore of gorgeous Union Valley Reservoir. A boat launch adjacent to the camp makes this an ideal destination for trout-angling campers with boats. Union Valley Reservoir, a popular weekend destination for campers from the Central Valley, is stocked with brook trout and rainbow trout by the Department of Fish and Game.

RV sites, facilities: There are 40 sites for tents or RVs up to 30 feet (no hookups). Picnic tables and fire rings are provided. Drinking water and vault toilets are available. A boat ramp and dump station are nearby. Leashed pets are permitted.

Reservations, fees: Reservations are accepted at 877/444-6777 ($9 reservation fee) or www.ReserveUSA.com. Sites are $18 per night, $5 per night for an additional vehicle. Open mid-May–mid-October, weather permitting.

Directions: From Placerville, drive east on U.S. 50 for 23 miles to Riverton and the junction with Ice House Road/Forest Road 3. Turn left (north) and drive 19 miles to Forest Road 12N78/Union Valley Road (at the head of Union Valley Reservoir). Turn left (west) and drive one mile to Forest Road 12N33. Turn left (south) and drive 0.5 mile to the campground.

Contact: Eldorado National Forest, Pacific Ranger District, 530/644-2349, fax 530/647-5405.

82 WENCH CREEK AND WENCH CREEK GROUP

Scenic rating: 7

on Union Valley Reservoir in Eldorado
National Forest

See map page 653

The Crystal Basin Recreation Area is the most popular backcountry region for campers from the Sacramento area, and Union Valley Reservoir is the centerpiece. The area gets its name from the prominent granite Sierra ridge, which looks like crystal when it is covered with frozen snow. Wench Creek is on the northeast shore of the reservoir. This is a big lake, set at 4,900 feet in elevation, with numerous lakeside campgrounds; three boat ramps provide access. (For

CALIFORNIA

more information, see the listing in this chapter for *Peninsula Recreation Area*.)

RV sites, facilities: There are 100 sites for tents or RVs up to 30 feet (no hookups) and two group tent sites for up to 50 people each. Picnic tables and fire grills are provided. Drinking water and vault toilets are available. A boat ramp is three miles away at the campground at Yellowjacket. Leashed pets are permitted.

Reservations, fees: Reservations are not accepted for individual sites but are accepted for group sites at 877/444-6777 ($9 reservation fee) or www.ReserveUSA.com. Sites are $18 per night, $5 per night for an additional vehicle. The group sites are $100 per night. Open mid-May–September.

Directions: From Placerville, drive east on U.S. 50 for 23 miles to Riverton and the junction with Ice House Road/Forest Road 3. Turn left and drive 15 miles to the campground entrance road (four miles past the turnoff for Sunset Camp). Turn left and drive a mile to the campground at the end of the road.

Contact: Eldorado National Forest, Pacific Ranger District, 530/644-2349, fax 530/647-5405.

83 PENINSULA RECREATION AREA

Scenic rating: 8

on Union Valley Reservoir in Eldorado National Forest

See map page 653

The two campgrounds here, Sunset and Fashoda, are the prettiest of all the camps at Union Valley Reservoir, set at the eastern tip of the peninsula that juts into the lake at the mouth of Jones Fork. A nearby boat ramp (you'll see it on the left on the way in) is a big plus, along with a picnic area and beach. All water sports are allowed. The lake has decent trout fishing, with brook trout, brown trout, rainbow trout, Mackinaw, kokanee salmon, and smallmouth bass. The place is gorgeous, set at 4,900 feet in the Sierra Nevada.

RV sites, facilities: There are 131 sites for tents or RVs up to 50 feet at Sunset Camp and 30 walk-in tent sites at Fashoda Camp. No hookups. Picnic tables, fire rings, and fire grills are provided. Drinking water, coin showers (at Fashoda), vault toilets, a boat ramp, and a dump station are available. Some facilities are wheelchair accessible. Leashed pets are permitted.

Reservations, fees: Reservations are accepted and required for the walk-in sites at 877/444-6777 ($9 reservation fee) or www.ReserveUSA.com. Sites are $18 per night, $34 per night for a double site, $5 per night for an additional vehicle. Open late May–early September, weather permitting.

Directions: From Placerville, drive east on U.S. 50 for 23 miles to Riverton and the junction with Ice House Road/Forest Road 3. Turn left and drive 14 miles to the campground entrance road (a mile past the turnoff for Jones Fork Camp). Turn left and drive 1.5 miles to the campground at the end of the road.

Contact: Eldorado National Forest, Pacific Ranger District, 530/644-2349, fax 530/647-5405.

84 ICE HOUSE UPPER AND LOWER

Scenic rating: 8

on Ice House Reservoir in Eldorado National Forest

See map page 653

Along with Loon Lake and Union Valley Reservoir, Ice House Reservoir is a feature destination in the Crystal Basin Recreation Area. Ice House gets most of the anglers and Union Valley gets most of the campers. All water sports are allowed at Ice House, though. The camp here is on the lake's northwestern shore, 5,500 feet in elevation, just up from the dam and adjacent to the lake's boat ramp. The lake was created by a dam on South Fork Silver Creek and covers 650 acres, with the deepest spot about 130 feet deep. It is stocked with rainbow trout, brook trout, and brown trout. A 2.5-mile bike trail connects Ice House to Northwind and Strawberry Point campgrounds.

RV sites, facilities: There are 83 sites for tents or RVs up to 30 feet (no hookups). Picnic tables and fire grills are provided. Drinking water, vault toilets, a boat ramp, and a dump station are available. Some facilities are wheelchair accessible. Leashed pets are permitted.

Reservations, fees: Reservations are accepted at 877/444-6777 ($9 reservation fee) or www.ReserveUSA.com. Sites are $18 per night, $34 per night for a double site, $5 per night for an additional vehicle. Open mid-June–mid-October, weather permitting.

Directions: From Placerville, drive east on U.S. 50 for 23 miles to Riverton and the junction with Ice House Road/Forest Road 3. Turn left (north) and drive 11 miles to Forest Road 32/Ice House/Wrights Tie Road. Turn right (east) and drive 1.5 miles to the campground access road on the right.

Contact: Eldorado National Forest, Pacific Ranger District, 530/644-2349, fax 530/647-5405.

85 WRIGHTS LAKE

Scenic rating: 9

in Eldorado National Forest

See map page 653

This high mountain lake (7,000 feet) has shoreline picnicking and good fishing and hiking. There is no boat ramp, and the rules do not permit motors, so it is ideal for canoes, rafts, prams, and people who like quiet. Swimming is allowed. Fishing is fair for both rainbow trout and brown trout. It is a classic alpine lake, though small (65 acres), with a trailhead for the Desolation Wilderness at its north end. From here it is only a three-mile hike to the beautiful Twin Lakes and Island Lake, set on the western flank of Mount Price (9,975 feet).

RV sites, facilities: There are 68 sites for tents or RVs up to 50 feet (no hookups). Picnic tables and fire grills are provided. Drinking water and vault toilets are available. Some facilities are wheelchair accessible, including a boat dock. Leashed pets are permitted.

Reservations, fees: Reservations are accepted at 877/444-6777 ($9 reservation fee) or www.ReserveUSA.com. Sites are $18 per night, $36 per night for a double site, $5 per night for an additional vehicle. Open late June–mid-October, weather permitting.

Directions: From Placerville, drive east on U.S. 50 for 23 miles to Riverton and the junction with Ice House Road/Forest Road 3. Turn left (north) and drive 11 miles to Forest Road 32/Ice House/Wrights Tie Road. Turn right (east) and drive nine miles to Forest Road 4/Wrights Lake Road. Turn left (north) and drive two miles to the campground on the right side of the road.

Contact: Eldorado National Forest, Pacific Ranger District, 530/644-2349, fax 530/644-5405.

86 SAND FLAT

Scenic rating: 7

on the South Fork of the American River in Eldorado National Forest

See map page 653

This first-come, first-served campground often gets filled up by U.S. 50 travelers. And why not? You get easy access, a well-signed exit, and a nice setting on the South Fork of the American River. The elevation is 3,900 feet. The river is very pretty here, but fishing is often poor. In winter, the snow level usually starts just a few miles uphill.

RV sites, facilities: There are 23 sites for tents or RVs of any length (no hookups) and six walk-in tent sites. Picnic tables and fire grills are provided. Drinking water and vault toilets are available. Groceries, a restaurant, and gas are available nearby. Some facilities are wheelchair accessible. Leashed pets are permitted.

Reservations, fees: Reservations are not accepted. Sites are $14 per night, $28 per night for a double site, $5 per night for an additional vehicle. Open May–late October, weather permitting.

Directions: From Sacramento, drive east on U.S. 50 to Placerville and continue 28 miles to the campground on the right. (If you reach

CALIFORNIA

the Kyburz store, you have driven about one mile too far.)

Contact: Eldorado National Forest, Placerville Ranger District, 530/644-2324, fax 530/647-5315.

87 CHINA FLAT

Scenic rating: 7

on the Silver Fork of the American River in Eldorado National Forest

See map page 653

China Flat sits across the road from the Silver Fork American River, with a nearby access road that is routed along the river for a mile. This provides access for fishing, swimming, gold panning, and exploring. The elevation is 4,800 feet. The camp feels far off the beaten path, even though it is only five minutes from that parade of traffic on U.S. 50.

RV sites, facilities: There are 18 sites for tents or RVs of any length (no hookups). Picnic tables and fire grills are provided. Drinking water and vault toilets are available. Some facilities are wheelchair accessible. Leashed pets are permitted.

Reservations, fees: Reservations are not accepted. Sites are $14 per night, $28 per night for double sites, $5 per night for an additional vehicle. Open May–October, weather permitting.

Directions: From Sacramento, drive east on U.S. 50 to Kyburz and Silver Fork Road. Turn right and drive three miles to the campground on the right side of the road.

Contact: Eldorado National Forest, Placerville Ranger District, 530/644-2324, fax 530/647-5315.

88 SILVER FORK

Scenic rating: 7

on the Silver Fork of the American River in Eldorado National Forest

See map page 653

The tons of vacationers driving U.S. 50 along the South Fork American River always get frustrated when they try to fish or camp, because there are precious few opportunities for either, with about zero trout and camps alike. But, just 20 minutes off the highway, you can find both at Silver Fork Camp. The access road provides many fishing opportunities, and the stream is stocked with rainbow trout by the state. The camp is right along the river, at 5,500 feet in elevation, in Eldorado National Forest.

RV sites, facilities: There are 35 sites for tents or RVs of any length and four double sites. No hookups. Picnic tables and fire grills are provided. Drinking water and vault toilets are available. Some of the facilities are wheelchair accessible. Leashed pets are permitted.

Reservations, fees: Reservations are not accepted. Sites are $14 per night, $28 per night for double sites, $5 per night for an additional vehicle. Open May–October, weather permitting.

Directions: From Sacramento, drive east on U.S. 50 to Kyburz and Silver Fork Road. Turn right and drive eight miles to the campground on the right side of the road.

Contact: Eldorado National Forest, Placerville Ranger District, 530/644-6048, fax 530/647-5315.

89 SILVER LAKE WEST

Scenic rating: 9

on Silver Lake in Eldorado National Forest

See map page 653

The Highway 88 corridor provides access to three excellent lakes: Lower Bear River Reservoir, Silver Lake, and Caples Lake. Silver Lake is difficult to pass by, with cabin rentals, pretty campsites, decent trout fishing, and excellent hiking. The lake is at 7,200 feet in a classic granite cirque just below the Sierra ridge. This camp is on the west side of Highway 88, across the road from the lake. A great hike starts at the trailhead on the east side of the lake, a two-mile tromp to little Hidden Lake, one of several nice hikes in the area. In addition, horseback-riding rentals are available nearby at Plasse's Resort. Note that bears frequent this campground, so store food properly and avoid scented products.

RV sites, facilities: There are 42 sites for tents or RVs up to 30 feet (no hookups). Picnic tables, food lockers, and fire pits are provided. Vault toilets and drinking water are available. A boat ramp and boat rentals are nearby. Leashed pets are permitted. There's a maximum of six people and two pets per site.

Reservations, fees: Reservations are not accepted. Sites are $16 per night, $3 per night for an additional vehicle, $1 per pet per night. Open Memorial Day weekend–October, weather permitting.

Directions: From Jackson, drive east on Highway 88 for 50 miles (to the north end of Silver Lake) to the campground entrance road on the left.

Contact: Eldorado Irrigation District, 530/644-1960, fax 530/647-5155.

90 SILVER LAKE EAST

Scenic rating: 7

in Eldorado National Forest

See map page 653

Silver Lake is an easy-to-reach alpine lake at 7,200 feet, which provides a beautiful setting, good trout fishing, and hiking. This camp is on the northeast side of the lake, with a boat ramp nearby. (See the listing in this chapter for *Silver Lake West* for more information.)

RV sites, facilities: There are 62 sites for tents or RVs up to 40 feet (no hookups). Picnic tables and fire grills are provided. Drinking water and vault toilets are available. A grocery store, boat rentals, a boat ramp, and propane gas are nearby. Leashed pets are permitted.

Reservations, fees: Reservations are accepted at 877/444-6777 ($9 reservation fee) or www.ReserveUSA.com. Sites are $19 per night, $5 per night for an additional vehicle, $38 per night for a double site. Open June–mid-October, weather permitting.

Directions: From Jackson, drive east on Highway 88 for 50 miles (to the north end of Silver Lake) to the campground entrance road on the right.

Contact: Eldorado National Forest, Amador Ranger District, 209/295-4257, fax 209/295-5998; Silver Lake Resort, 209/258-8598.

91 CAPLES LAKE

Scenic rating: 8

in Eldorado National Forest

See map page 653

Caples Lake, here in the high country at 7,800 feet, is a pretty lake right along Highway 88. It covers 600 acres, has a 5-mph speed limit, and provides good trout fishing and excellent hiking terrain. Swimming is allowed. The camp is across the highway (a little two-laner) from the lake, with the Caples Lake Resort and boat rentals nearby. There is a parking area at the west end of the lake, and from here you can begin a great 3.5-mile hike to Emigrant Lake, in the Mokelumne Wilderness on the western flank of Mount Round Top (10,310 feet).

RV sites, facilities: There are 30 sites for tents or RVs up to 35 feet (no hookups), plus six walk-in tent sites requiring a 200-foot walk. Picnic tables and fire grills are provided. Drinking water and vault toilets are available. Groceries, propane gas, a boat ramp, and boat rentals are nearby. Some facilities are wheelchair accessible. Leashed pets are permitted.

Reservations, fees: Reservations are not accepted. Sites are $20 per night, $5 per night for an additional vehicle, $40 per night for a double site. Open June–mid-October, weather permitting.

Directions: From Jackson, drive east on Highway 88 for 63 miles (one mile past the entrance road to Kirkwood Ski Area) to the camp entrance road on the left.

Contact: Eldorado National Forest, Amador Ranger District, 209/295-4251, fax 209/295-5998; Caples Lake Resort, 209/258-8888.

CALIFORNIA

92 HOPE VALLEY

Scenic rating: 7

near the Carson River in Humboldt-Toiyabe National Forest

See map page 653

The West Fork of the Carson River runs right through Hope Valley, a pretty trout stream with a choice of four streamside campgrounds. Trout stocks are made near the campgrounds during summer. The campground at Hope Valley is just east of Carson Pass, at 7,300 feet in elevation, in a very pretty area. A trailhead for the Pacific Crest Trail is three miles south of the campground. The primary nearby destination is Blue Lakes, about a 10-minute drive away. An insider's note is that little Tamarack Lake, set just beyond the turnoff for Lower Blue Lake, is excellent for swimming.

RV sites, facilities: There are 20 sites for tents or RVs up to 22 feet and a group site for tents or RVs up to 22 feet that can accommodate up to 16 people. No hookups. Picnic tables and fire grills are provided. Drinking water and vault toilets are available. Leashed pets are permitted.

Reservations, fees: Reservations are accepted for individual sites and are required for the group site at 877/444-6777 ($9 reservation fee) or www.ReserveUSA.com. Sites are $13 per night, $25 per night for the group camp. Open June–September.

Directions: From Sacramento, drive east on U.S. 50 to the junction with Highway 89. Turn south on Highway 89 and drive over Luther Pass to the junction with Highway 88. Turn right (west) and drive two miles to Blue Lakes Road. Turn left (south) and drive 1.5 miles to the campground on the right side of the road.

From Jackson, drive east on Highway 88 over Carson Pass and continue east for five miles to Blue Lakes Road. Turn right (south) and drive 1.5 miles to the campground on the right side of the road.

Contact: Humboldt-Toiyabe National Forest, Carson Ranger District, 775/882-2766, fax 775/884-8199.

93 LOWER BLUE LAKE

Scenic rating: 7

near Carson Pass

See map page 653

This is the high country, 8,400 feet, where the terrain is stark and steep and edged by volcanic ridgelines, and where the deep blue-green hue of lake water brightens the landscape. Lower Blue Lake provides a popular trout fishery, with rainbow trout, brook trout, and cutthroat trout all stocked regularly. The boat ramp is adjacent to the campground. The access road crosses the Pacific Crest Trail, providing a route to a series of small, pretty, hike-to lakes just outside the edge of the Mokelumne Wilderness.

RV sites, facilities: There are 17 sites for tents or RVs up to 25 feet (no hookups). Picnic tables and fire grills are provided. Drinking water and vault toilets are available. Leashed pets are permitted.

Reservations, fees: Reservations are not accepted. Sites are $16 per night, $5 per night for an additional vehicle, $1 per pet per night; there's a 14-day occupancy limit. Open June–September, weather permitting.

Directions: From Sacramento, drive east on U.S. 50 to the junction with Highway 89. Turn south on Highway 89 and drive over Luther Pass to the junction with Highway 88. Turn right and drive 2.5 miles to Blue Lakes Road. Turn left and drive 12 miles to a junction at the south end of Lower Blue Lake. Turn right and drive a short distance to the campground on the left side of the road.

From Jackson, drive east on Highway 88 over Carson Pass and continue east for five miles to Blue Lakes Road. Turn right (south) and drive 12 miles to a junction at the south end of Lower Blue Lake. Turn right and drive a short distance to the campground on the left.

Contact: PG&E Land Projects, 916/386-5164, www.pge.com/recreation.

CALIFORNIA

94 CRYSTAL SPRINGS

Scenic rating: 8

on the West Fork of the Carson River in
Humboldt-Toiyabe National Forest

See map page 653

For many people, this camp is an ideal choice.
It is at an elevation of 6,000 feet, right alongside
the West Fork of the Carson River. This stretch
of water is stocked with trout by the Department of Fish and Game. Crystal Springs is easy
to reach, just off Highway 88, and supplies can
be obtained in nearby Woodfords or Markleeville. Grover Hot Springs State Park makes a
good side-trip destination.

RV sites, facilities: There are 20 sites for tents
or RVs up to 22 feet (no hookups). Picnic
tables and fire grills are provided. Drinking
water and vault toilets are available. Some facilities are wheelchair accessible. Leashed pets
are permitted.

Reservations, fees: Reservations are not accepted. Sites are $12 per night. Open late
April–early October, weather permitting.

Directions: From Sacramento, drive east on
U.S. 50 to the junction with Highway 89. Turn
south on Highway 89 and drive over Luther
Pass to the junction with Highway 88. Turn left
(east) and drive 4.5 miles to the campground
on the right side of the road.

From Jackson, drive east on Highway 88 over
Carson Pass to the junction with Highway 89
and continue for 4.5 miles to the campground
on the right side of the road.

Contact: Humboldt-Toiyabe National Forest,
Carson Ranger District, 775/882-2766, fax
775/884-8199.

95 GROVER HOT SPRINGS STATE PARK

Scenic rating: 8

near Markleeville

See map page 653

This is a famous spot for folks who like the rejuvenating powers of a hot spring. Some say they feel a glow about them for weeks. When touring the South Tahoe/Carson Pass area, many
vacationers take part of a day to make the trip to
the hot springs. This park is in alpine meadow
at 5,900 feet on the east side of the Sierra at the
edge of the Great Basin, and it is surrounded
by peaks that top 10,000 feet. The hot springs
are green because of the mineral deposits at the
bottom of the pools. The landscape is primarily
pine forest and sagebrush. It is well known for
the great fluctuations in weather, from major
blizzards to dry scorchers, from warm, clear
nights to awesome rim-rattling thunderstorms.
High winds are occasional but legendary. During thunderstorms, the hot springs pools close
because of the chance of lightning strikes. Yet
they remain open in snow, even blizzards, when
it can be a euphoric experience to sit in the
steaming water. Note that the pools are closed
for maintenance for two weeks in September.
A forest fire near here remains in evidence.
A 2.4-mile round-trip hike starts from the
campground and continues to a series of small
waterfalls. Side-trip options include a nature
trail in the park and driving to the Carson
River (where the water is a mite cooler) and
fishing for trout.

RV sites, facilities: There are 28 sites for tents
or RVs up to 34 feet (no hookups) or trailers up
to 24 feet and 26 sites for tents. Picnic tables,
fire grills, and food lockers are provided. Restrooms have flush toilets and coin showers (summer only). Drinking water, a hot springs pool
with wheelchair access, and a heated swimming
pool are available. A grocery store is four miles
away, and a coin laundry is within 10 miles.
Leashed pets are permitted.

Reservations, fees: Reservations are accepted at 800/444-PARK (800/444-7275) or
www.reserveamerica.com ($7.50 reservation
fee). Sites are $20–25 per night, $6 per night
for an additional vehicle; pool fees are $2–5 per
person per day. Open year-round, with reduced
facilities in winter.

Directions: From Sacramento, drive east on
U.S. 50 to the junction with Highway 89. Turn
south on Highway 89 and drive over Luther

Pass to the junction with Highway 88. Turn left and drive to Woodfords and the junction with Highway 89. Turn right (south) and drive six miles to Markleeville and the junction with Hot Springs Road. Turn right and drive four miles to the park entrance.

Contact: Grover Hot Springs State Park, 530/694-2248; Sierra District, 530/525-7232, www.parks.ca.gov.

96 TURTLE ROCK PARK

Scenic rating: 5

near Woodfords

See map page 653

This pretty, wooded campground, set at 6,000 feet, gets missed by a lot of folks—but not by mountain bikers. It gets missed by vacationers because it is administered at the county level and also because most vacationers want the more pristine beauty of the nearby camps along the Carson River. (If it snows, it closes, so call ahead if you're planning an autumn visit.) But it doesn't get missed by mountain bikers, who travel here for the "Death Ride," an event held in July each year, a wild ride over several mountain passes. This camp always fills for this riding event. Nearby side trips include Grover Hot Springs and the hot springs in Markleeville.

RV sites, facilities: There are 28 sites for tents or RVs up to 34 feet (no hookups). Picnic tables and fire grills are provided. Drinking water, vault toilets, and showers are available. A recreation building is available for rent. A camp host is on-site. A coin laundry, groceries, and propane gas are available within two miles. Some facilities are wheelchair accessible. Leashed pets are permitted.

Reservations, fees: Reservations are not accepted. Sites are $10 per night, $3 per night for an additional vehicle. Monthly rates available. Open May–mid-October, weather permitting.

Directions: From Sacramento, drive east on U.S. 50 to the junction with Highway 89. Turn south on Highway 89 and drive over Luther

Pass to the junction with Highway 88. Turn left (east) and drive to Woodfords and the junction with Highway 89. Turn south on Highway 89 and drive 4.5 miles to the park entrance on the right side of the road.

Contact: Alpine County Public Works, 530/694-2140.

97 INDIAN CREEK RECREATION AREA

Scenic rating: 10

near Indian Creek Reservoir and Markleeville

See map page 653

This beautiful campground is amid sparse pines near Indian Creek Reservoir, elevation 5,600 feet. The campground is popular and often fills to capacity. There is little shade in the group camp during the summer. This is an excellent lake for trout fishing, and the nearby Carson River is managed as a trophy trout fishery. The lake covers 160 acres, with a maximum speed for boats on the lake set at 5 mph. Sailing, sailboarding, and swimming are allowed. There are several good hikes in the vicinity; the best is a short trek, a one-mile climb to Summit Lake, with scenic views of the Indian Creek area. Summers are dry and warm, with high temperatures typically in the 80s, and nights are cool and comfortable. Bears occasionally visit. The lake freezes over in winter. It is about 35 miles to Carson City, Nevada, and two miles to Markleeville.

RV sites, facilities: There are 19 sites for tents or RVs up to 30 feet, 10 walk-in sites for tents only, and a group tent site for up to 40 people. No hookups. Picnic tables and fire grills are provided. Drinking water and restrooms with flush toilets and showers are available. A boat ramp is nearby. Some facilities are wheelchair accessible. Leashed pets are permitted.

Reservations, fees: Reservations are not accepted for individual sites but are required for the group tent site at 775/885-6000. Sites are $20 per night, double sites are $32 per night, plus $5 per night for an additional vehicle; it's $14–20 per night for walk-in sites and $50 per night for the group site. Open late April–mid-October, weather permitting.

Directions: From Sacramento, drive east on U.S. 50 over Echo Summit to Meyers and Highway 89. Turn south on Highway 89 and drive to Highway 88. Turn left (east) on Highway 88/89 and drive six miles to Woodfords and Highway 89. Turn right (south) on Highway 89 and drive about four miles to Airport Road. Turn left on Airport Road and drive four miles to Indian Creek Reservoir. At the fork, bear left and drive to the campground on the west side of the lake.

From Markleeville, drive north on Highway 89 for about four miles to Airport Road. Turn right on Airport Road and drive about four miles to Indian Creek Reservoir. At the fork, bear left and drive to the campground on the west side of the lake.

Contact: Bureau of Land Management, Carson City Field Office, 775/885-6000, fax 775/885-6147.

98 TOPAZ LAKE RV PARK

Scenic rating: 6

on Topaz Lake, near Markleeville

See map page 653

Topaz Lake, set at 5,000 feet, is one of the hidden surprises for California anglers. The surprise is the size of the rainbow trout, with one of the highest rates of 15- to 18-inch trout of any lake in the mountain country. All water sports are allowed on this 2,400-acre lake, and there is a swimming area. The campground itself is attractive with a number of shade trees. The setting is on the edge of barren high desert, which also serves as the border between California and Nevada. Wind is a problem for small boats, especially in the early summer. Some of the sites here are rented for the entire season.

RV sites, facilities: There are 54 sites with full hookups (30 amps) for RVs up to 40 feet. Some sites are pull-through. Tents are allowed with RVs only. Picnic tables and cable TV are provided. Restrooms have coin showers.

A coin laundry, propane gas, a small grocery store, a fish-cleaning station, and modem access are available. A 40-boat marina with courtesy launch and boat trailer storage is available at lakeside. Some facilities are wheelchair accessible. Leashed pets are permitted.

Reservations, fees: Reservations are accepted. Sites are $24–26 per night, $2 per person for more than two people. Monthly rates available. Some credit cards accepted. Open March–early October, weather permitting.

Directions: From Carson City, drive south on U.S. 395 for 45 miles to Topaz Lake and the campground on the left side of the road.

From Bridgeport, drive north on U.S. 395 for 45 miles to the campground on the right side of the road (0.3 mile south of the California-Nevada border).

Contact: Topaz Lake RV Park, 530/495-2357, fax 530/495-2118.

99 UPPER BLUE LAKE DAM AND EXPANSION

Scenic rating: 7

near Carson Pass

See map page 653

These two camps are across the road from each other along Upper Blue Lake and are two of five camps in the area. The trout fishing is usually quite good here in early summer. (See the listing in this chapter for *Lower Blue Lake* for more information.) These camps are three miles past the Lower Blue Lake Campground. The elevation is 8,400 feet.

RV sites, facilities: There are 10 sites at Upper Blue Lake Dam and 15 sites at the expansion area for tents or RVs up to 25 feet. Picnic tables and fire grills are provided at Upper Blue Lake Dam only. Drinking water and vault toilets are available. Some facilities are wheelchair accessible. Leashed pets are permitted.

Reservations, fees: Reservations are not accepted. Sites are $16 per night, $5 per night for an additional vehicle, $1 per pet per night. Open June–mid-September, weather permitting.

Directions: From Sacramento, drive east on U.S. 50 to the junction with Highway 89. Turn south on Highway 89 and drive over Luther Pass to the junction with Highway 88. Turn right and drive 2.5 miles to Blue Lakes Road. Turn left and drive 12 miles to a junction at the south end of Lower Blue Lake. Turn right and drive three miles to the Upper Blue Lake Dam campground on the left side of the road and Upper Blue Lake Dam Expansion on the right.

From Jackson, drive east on Highway 88 over Carson Pass and continue east for five miles to Blue Lakes Road. Turn right (south) and drive 12 miles to a junction at the south end of Lower Blue Lake. Turn right and drive three miles to the Upper Blue Lake Dam campground on the left side of the road and Upper Blue Lake Dam Expansion on the right.

Contact: PG&E Land Projects, 916/386-5164, www.pge.com/recreation.

100 MIDDLE CREEK AND EXPANSION

Scenic rating: 7

near Carson Pass and Blue Lakes

See map page 653

This is a tiny, captivating spot set along the creek that connects Upper and Lower Blue Lakes, providing a take-your-pick deal for anglers. PG&E has expanded this facility and now offers a larger camping area about 200 yards from the original campground. (See the listing in this chapter for *Lower Blue Lake* for more information.) The elevation is 8,200 feet.

RV sites, facilities: There are five sites for tents or RVs up to 30 feet at Middle Creek and 25 sites for tents or RVs up to 45 feet at the expansion area. No hookups. Picnic tables and fire grills are provided. Drinking water and vault toilets are available at the expansion area. Some facilities are wheelchair accessible. Leashed pets are permitted.

Reservations, fees: Reservations are not accepted. Sites are $16 per night, $5 per night

for an additional vehicle, $1 per pet per night. Open June–September, weather permitting.

Directions: From Sacramento, drive east on U.S. 50 to the junction with Highway 89. Turn south on Highway 89 and drive over Luther Pass to the junction with Highway 88. Turn right and drive 2.5 miles to Blue Lakes Road. Turn left and drive 12 miles to a junction at the south end of Lower Blue Lake. Turn right and drive 1.5 miles to the Middle Creek campground on the left side of the road and continue another 200 yards to reach the expansion area.

From Jackson, drive east on Highway 88 over Carson Pass and continue east for five miles to Blue Lakes Road. Turn right (south) and drive 12 miles (road becomes dirt) to a junction at the south end of Lower Blue Lake. Turn right and drive 1.5 miles to the Middle Creek campground on the left side of the road and continue another 200 yards to reach the expansion area.

Contact: PG&E Land Projects, 916/386-5164, www.pge.com/recreation.

101 SILVER CREEK

Scenic rating: 6

in Humboldt-Toiyabe National Forest

See map page 653

This pretty spot, near Silver Creek, has easy access from Highway 4 and, in years without washouts, good fishing in early summer for small trout. It is in the remote high Sierra, east of Ebbetts Pass. A side trip to Ebbetts Pass features Kinney Lake, Pacific Crest Trail access, and a trailhead at the north end of the lake (on the west side of Highway 4) for a mile hike to Lower Kinney Lake. No bikes are permitted on the trails. The elevation is 6,800 feet.

RV sites, facilities: There are 22 sites for tents or RVs up to 22 feet (no hookups). Picnic tables and fire grills are provided. Drinking water and vault toilets are available. Some facilities are wheelchair accessible. Leashed pets are permitted.

Reservations, fees: Reservations are accepted at 877/444-6777 ($9 reservation fee) or www.ReserveUSA.com. Sites are $13 per night. Open late May–early September, weather permitting.

Directions: From Angels Camp, drive east on Highway 4 all the way over Ebbetts Pass and continue for about six miles to the campground.

From Markleeville, drive south on Highway 89 to the junction with Highway 4. Turn west on Highway 4 (steep and winding) and drive about five miles to the campground.

Contact: Humboldt-Toiyabe National Forest, Carson Ranger District, 775/882-2766, fax 775/884-8199.

102 SOUTH SHORE

Scenic rating: 7

on Bear River Reservoir in Eldorado National Forest

See map page 653

Bear River Reservoir is at 5,900 feet, which means it becomes ice-free earlier in the spring than its uphill neighbors to the east, Silver Lake and Caples Lake. It is a good-sized lake—725 acres—and cold and deep, too. All water sports are allowed. It gets double-barreled trout stocks, receiving fish from the state and from the operator of the lake's marina and lodge. This campground is on the lake's southern shore, just east of the dam. Explorers can drive south for five miles to Salt Springs Reservoir, which has a trailhead and parking area on the north side of the dam for a great day hike along the lake.

RV sites, facilities: There are 22 sites for tents or RVs up to 35 feet (no hookups). Picnic tables and fire grills are provided. Drinking water and vault toilets are available. A boat ramp, a grocery store, boat rentals, and propane gas are available at nearby Bear River Lake Resort. Some facilities are wheelchair accessible. Leashed pets are permitted.

Reservations, fees: Reservations are accepted at 877/444-6777 ($9 reservation fee) or www.ReserveUSA.com. Sites are $20 per night, $40 per night for a double site. Open mid-May–mid-October, weather permitting.

Directions: From Stockton, drive east on Highway 88 for about 80 miles to the lake entrance on the right side of the road (well signed). Turn right and drive four miles (past the dam) to the campground entrance on the right side of the road.

Contact: Eldorado National Forest, Amador Ranger District, 209/295-4251, fax 209/295-5998.

103 BEAR RIVER LAKE RESORT

Scenic rating: 8

on Bear River Reservoir

See map page 653

Bear River Lake Resort is a complete vacation service lodge, with everything you could ask for. A lot of people have been asking in recent years, making this a popular spot that often requires a reservation. The resort also sponsors fishing derbies in the summer and sweetens the pot considerably by stocking exceptionally large rainbow trout. Other fish species include brown trout and Mackinaw trout. The resort is at 6,000 feet. The lake freezes over in the winter. (For more information about Bear River Reservoir, see the listing in this chapter for *South Shore*.)

RV sites, facilities: There are 150 sites for tents or RVs up to 35 feet with partial hookups (15 amps), a group site for up to 60 people, and eight rental trailers. Picnic tables and fire pits are provided. Vault toilets, coin showers, drinking water, a dump station, a boat ramp, boat rentals, berthing, bait and tackle, fishing licenses, a video arcade, a playground, firewood, ice, propane gas, a coin laundry, a pay phone, a restaurant and cocktail lounge, and a grocery store are available. Some facilities are wheelchair accessible. Leashed pets are permitted at campsites but not in lodging units.

Reservations, fees: Reservations are recommended. Sites are $29 per night, $5 per night for an additional vehicle, $240 per night for the group site, plus a $5 one-time pet fee. Some credit cards accepted. Open April–October.

Directions: From Stockton, drive east on Highway 88 for about 80 miles to the lake entrance

CALIFORNIA

on the right side of the road, 42 miles east of Jackson. Turn right and drive 2.5 miles to a junction (if you pass the dam, you have gone 0.25 mile too far). Turn left and drive 0.5 mile to the campground entrance on the right side.

Contact: Bear River Lake Resort, 209/295-4868.

104 PINE MARTEN

Scenic rating: 8

near Lake Alpine in Stanislaus National Forest

See map page 653

Lake Alpine is a beautiful Sierra lake surrounded by granite and pines at 7,320 feet, just above where the snowplows stop in winter. This camp is on the northeast side, about a quarter mile from the shore. Fishing for rainbow trout is good in May and early June, before the summer crush. Despite the long drive to get here, the lake is becoming better known for its beauty, camping, and hiking. Lake Alpine has 180 surface acres and a 10-mph speed limit. A trailhead out of nearby Silver Valley Camp provides a two-mile hike to pretty Duck Lake and beyond into the Carson-Iceberg Wilderness.

RV sites, facilities: There are 32 sites for tents or RVs up to 27 feet (no hookups). Picnic tables and fire grills are provided. Drinking water and restrooms with flush toilets are available. A boat ramp is nearby. A grocery store, propane gas, and coin laundry are nearby. Some facilities are wheelchair accessible. Leashed pets are permitted.

Reservations, fees: Reservations are not accepted. Sites are $18 per night, $5 per night for an additional vehicle. Open June–early October, weather permitting.

Directions: From Angels Camp, drive east on Highway 4 to Arnold and continue for 29 miles to Lake Alpine. Drive to the northeast end of the lake to the campground entrance on the right side of the road.

Contact: Stanislaus National Forest, Calaveras Ranger District, 209/795-1381, fax 209/795-6849.

105 SILVER VALLEY

Scenic rating: 8

on Lake Alpine in Stanislaus National Forest

See map page 653

This is one of four camps at Lake Alpine. Silver Valley is on the northeast end of the lake at 7,400 feet in elevation, with a trailhead nearby that provides access to the Carson-Iceberg Wilderness. (For recreation information, see the listing in this chapter for *Pine Marten.*)

RV sites, facilities: There are 21 sites for tents or RVs up to 16 feet (no hookups). Picnic tables and fire grills are provided. Drinking water and vault toilets are available. A boat launch, a grocery store, and coin laundry are nearby. Some facilities are wheelchair accessible. Leashed pets are permitted.

Reservations, fees: Reservations are not accepted. Sites are $18 per night. A free campfire permit is required. Open June–October, weather permitting.

Directions: From Angels Camp, drive east on Highway 4 to Arnold and continue for 29 miles to Lake Alpine. Drive to the northeast end of the lake to the campground entrance on the right side of the road. Turn right and drive 0.5 mile to the campground.

Contact: Stanislaus National Forest, Calaveras Ranger District, 209/795-1381, fax 209/795-6849.

106 LAKE ALPINE CAMPGROUND

Scenic rating: 8

on Lake Alpine in Stanislaus National Forest

See map page 653

This is the campground that is in the greatest demand at Lake Alpine, and it is easy to see why. It is very small, a boat ramp is adjacent to the camp, you can get supplies at a small grocery store within walking distance, and during the evening rise you can often see the jumping trout from your campsite. Lake Alpine is one of the prettiest lakes you can drive to, set at 7,303 feet amid pines and Sierra granite. A trailhead out of nearby Silver Valley Camp provides a two-mile hike to pretty Duck Lake and beyond into the Carson-Iceberg Wilderness.

RV sites, facilities: There are 25 sites for tents or RVs up to 27 feet (no hookups). Picnic tables and fire grills are provided. Drinking water, flush and vault toilets, and a boat launch are available. A grocery store, a restaurant, coin showers, and a coin laundry are nearby. Some facilities are wheelchair accessible. Leashed pets are permitted.

Reservations, fees: Reservations are not accepted. Sites are $18 per night. Open June–October, weather permitting.

Directions: From Angels Camp, drive east on Highway 4 to Arnold and continue for 29 miles to Lake Alpine. Just before reaching the lake turn right and drive 0.25 mile to the campground on the left.

Contact: Stanislaus National Forest, Calaveras Ranger District, 209/795-1381, fax 209/795-6849.

107 SILVER TIP

Scenic rating: 6

near Lake Alpine in Stanislaus National Forest

See map page 653

This camp is just over a half mile from the shore of Lake Alpine at an elevation of 7,350 feet. Why then would anyone camp here when there are campgrounds right at the lake? Two reasons: One, those lakeside camps are often full on summer weekends. Two, Highway 4 is snowplowed to this campground entrance, but not beyond. So in big snow years when the road is still closed in late spring and early summer, you can park your rig here to camp, then hike in to the lake. In the fall, it also makes for a base camp for hunters. (See the listing in this chapter for *Lake Alpine Campground* for more information.)

RV sites, facilities: There are 23 sites for tents or RVs up to 27 feet (no hookups). Picnic tables and fire grills are provided. Drinking water and flush toilets are available. A boat launch is about a mile away. A grocery store, a coin laundry, and coin

showers are nearby. Some facilities are wheelchair accessible. Leashed pets are permitted.

Reservations, fees: Reservations are not accepted. Sites are $18 per night. Open June–early October, weather permitting.

Directions: From Angels Camp, drive east on Highway 4 to Arnold and continue for 29 miles to Lake Alpine. A mile before reaching the lake (adjacent to the Bear Valley/Mount Reba turn-off), turn right at the campground entrance on the right side of the road.

Contact: Stanislaus National Forest, Calaveras Ranger District, 209/795-1381, fax 209/795-6849.

108 WA KA LUU HEP YOO

Scenic rating: 8

on the Stanislaus River in Stanislaus National Forest

See map page 653

This is a riverside Forest Service campground that provides good trout fishing on the Stanislaus River and a put-in for white-water rafting. The highlight for most is the fishing, one of the best spots on the Stanislaus, stocked by Fish and Game, and good for rainbow, brook, and brown trout. It is four miles downstream of Dorrington and was first opened in 1999 as part of the Sourgrass Recreation Complex. There are cultural sites and preserved artifacts, such as grinding rocks. It is a pretty streamside spot, with ponderosa pine and black oak providing good screening. A wheelchair-accessible trail is available along the stream. The camp sits at an elevation of 3,900 feet, but it feels higher. By the way, I was told that the name of the campground means "wild river."

RV sites, facilities: There are 49 sites for tents or RVs up to 50 feet and four walk-in tent sites. No hookups. Picnic tables and fire grills are provided. Drinking water and restrooms with flush and vault toilets are available. Some facilities are wheelchair accessible. Leashed pets are permitted.

Reservations, fees: Reservations are not accepted. Sites are $16 per night, $5 per night for

an additional vehicle. Free campfire permits are required. Open Memorial Day weekend–October, weather permitting.

Directions: From Angels Camp, drive east on Highway 4, past Arnold to Dorrington and Boards Crossing Road. Turn right and drive four miles to the campground on the left (just before the bridge that crosses the Stanislaus River).

Contact: Stanislaus National Forest, Calaveras Ranger District, 209/795-1381, fax 209/795-6849.

109 BIG MEADOW AND BIG MEADOW GROUP CAMP

Scenic rating: 5

in Stanislaus National Forest
See map page 653

Big Meadow is at 6,460 feet on the western slopes of the Sierra Nevada. Of the many recreation attractions nearby, the most prominent is the North Fork Stanislaus River two miles south in national forest, with access available from a four-wheel-drive road just east of camp or on Spicer Reservoir Road (see the *Stanislaus River* listing in this chapter). Lake Alpine, a pretty, popular lake for trout fishing, is nine miles east on Highway 4. Three mountain reservoirs, Spicer, Utica, and Union, are all within a 15-minute drive. Big Meadow is also a good base camp for hunting.

RV sites, facilities: There are 68 sites for tents or RVs up to 27 feet, and one group tent site (requires a walk-in of 100 feet) can accommodate up to 25 people. No hookups. Picnic tables and fire grills are provided. Drinking water and vault toilets are available. Groceries, a coin laundry, and propane gas are within five miles. Leashed pets are permitted.

Reservations, fees: Reservations are accepted for individual sites and required for the group camp at 877/444-6777 ($9 reservation fee) or www.ReserveUSA.com. Sites are $15 per night, $5 per night for an additional vehicle, $65 per night for the group camp. Open June–October, weather permitting.

Directions: From Angels Camp on Highway 49, turn east on Highway 4 and drive about 30 miles (three miles past Ganns Meadows) to the campground on the right.

Contact: Stanislaus National Forest, Calaveras Ranger District, 209/795-1381, fax 209/795-6849.

110 STANISLAUS RIVER

Scenic rating: 8

in Stanislaus National Forest
See map page 653

As you might figure from its name, this camp provides excellent access to the adjacent North Fork Stanislaus River. The elevation is 6,200 feet, with timbered sites and the river just south of camp.

RV sites, facilities: There are 25 sites for tents or RVs up to 35 feet (no hookups). Fire grills and picnic tables are provided. Drinking water and vault toilets are available. Supplies are available in Bear Valley. Leashed pets are permitted.

Reservations, fees: Reservations are not accepted. Sites are $8 per night. Open June–October, weather permitting.

Directions: From Angels Camp on Highway 49, turn east on Highway 4 and drive about 44 miles to Spicer Reservoir Road. Turn right and drive four miles to the campground on the right side of the road.

Contact: Stanislaus National Forest, Calaveras Ranger District, 209/795-1381, fax 209/795-6849.

111 SPICER RESERVOIR

Scenic rating: 8

near Spicer Reservoir in Stanislaus National Forest
See map page 653

Spicer Reservoir, at 6,200 feet, isn't big by reservoir standards, covering 227 acres, but it is surrounded by canyon walls and is quite pretty from a boat. The beauty is added to by good trout fishing, even awesome. A boat ramp is available near the campground, and the lake speed limit is 10 mph. Trails along much of the lake provide a day-hiking option. A trail links the east end of Spicer Reservoir to the Summit Lake trailhead, with the route bordering the north side of the reservoir. Note: This area can really get hammered with snow in big winters, so in the spring and early summer, always check for access conditions before planning a trip.

RV sites, facilities: There are 60 sites for tents or RVs up to 50 feet (no hookups). Picnic tables and fire grills are provided. Drinking water and vault toilets are available. A boat ramp is nearby. Some facilities are wheelchair accessible. Leashed pets are permitted.

Reservations, fees: Reservations are not accepted. Sites are $16 per night. Open June–October, weather permitting.

Directions: From Angels Camp, drive east on Highway 4 for about 32 miles to Spicer Reservoir Road/Forest Road 7N01. Turn right, drive seven miles, bear right at a fork with a sharp right turn, and drive a mile to the campground at the west end of the lake.

Contact: Stanislaus National Forest, Calaveras Ranger District, 209/795-1381, fax 209/795-6849.

112 CLARK FORK AND CLARK FORK HORSE

Scenic rating: 8

on the Clark Fork of the Stanislaus River in Stanislaus National Forest

See map page 653

Clark Fork borders the Clark Fork of the Stanislaus River and is used by both drive-in vacationers and backpackers. A trailhead for hikers is a quarter mile away on the north side of Clark Fork Road (a parking area is available here). From here the trail is routed up along Arnot Creek, skirting between Iceberg Peak on the left and Lightning Mountain on the right, for eight miles to Wolf Creek Pass and the junction with the Pacific Crest Trail. (For another nearby trailhead, see the listing in this chapter for *Sand Flat*.)

RV sites, facilities: There are 88 sites for tents or RVs up to 40 feet and, at an adjacent area, 14 equestrian sites for tents or RVs up to 22 feet. No hookups. Picnic tables and fire grills are provided. Drinking water and flush toilets are available. At the equestrian site, no drinking water is available, but there are water troughs. Supplies are available in Dardanelle. Some facilities are wheelchair accessible. Leashed pets are permitted.

Reservations, fees: Reservations are not accepted. Sites are $12–13 per night, the horse camp fee is $7 per night, and it's $5 per night for an additional vehicle. Open May–October, weather permitting.

Directions: From Sonora, drive east on Highway 108 past the town of Strawberry to Clark Fork Road. Turn left, drive five miles, turn right again, and drive 0.5 mile to the campground entrance on the right side of the road.

Contact: Stanislaus National Forest, Summit Ranger District, 209/965-3434, fax 209/965-3372.

113 SAND FLAT

Scenic rating: 7

on the Clark Fork of the Stanislaus River in Stanislaus National Forest

See map page 653

Sand Flat Campground, at 6,200 feet, is only three miles (by vehicle on Clark Fork Road) from an outstanding trailhead for the Carson-Iceberg Wilderness. The camp is used primarily by late-arriving backpackers who camp for the night, get their gear in order, then head off on the trail. The trail is routed out of Iceberg Meadow, with a choice of heading north to Paradise Valley (unbelievably green and loaded with corn lilies along a creek) and onward to the Pacific Crest Trail, or east to Clark Fork and upstream to Clark Fork Meadow below Sonora Peak. Two choices, both winners.

RV sites, facilities: There are 53 sites for tents or RVs up to 40 feet (no hookups) and 15 walk-in tent sites. Picnic tables and fire grills are provided. Drinking water and vault toilets are available. You can buy supplies in Dardanelle. Some facilities are wheelchair accessible. Leashed pets are permitted.

Reservations, fees: Reservations are not accepted. Sites are $9 per night per vehicle. Open May–early October, weather permitting.

Directions: From Sonora, drive east on Highway 108 past the town of Strawberry to Clark Fork Road. Turn left on Clark Fork Road and drive six miles to the campground entrance on the right side of the road.

Contact: Stanislaus National Forest, Summit Ranger District, 209/965-3434, fax 209/965-3372.

114 FENCE CREEK

Scenic rating: 4

near the Middle Fork of the Stanislaus River in Stanislaus National Forest

See map page 653

Fence Creek is a feeder stream to Clark Fork, which runs a mile downstream and joins with the Middle Fork Stanislaus River en route to Donnells Reservoir. The camp sits along little Fence Creek, 5,600 feet in elevation. Fence Creek Road continues east for another nine miles to an outstanding trailhead at Iceberg Meadow on the edge of the Carson-Iceberg Wilderness.

RV sites, facilities: There are 38 sites for tents or RVs up to 22 feet (no hookups). Picnic tables and fire grills are provided. Vault toilets are available. No drinking water is available. You can buy supplies in Pinecrest about 10 miles away. Leashed pets are permitted.

Reservations, fees: Reservations are not accepted. Sites are $8 per night. Open May–mid-October, weather permitting.

Directions: From Sonora, drive east on Highway 108 about 50 miles to Clark Ford Road. Turn left and drive a mile to Forest Road 6N06. Turn left again and drive 0.5 mile to the campground on the right.

Contact: Stanislaus National Forest, Sum-

mit Ranger District, 209/965-3434, fax 209/965-3372.

115 BOULDER FLAT

Scenic rating: 7

near the Middle Fork of the Stanislaus River in Stanislaus National Forest

See map page 653

You want camping on the Stanislaus River? As you drive east on Highway 108, this is the first in a series of campgrounds along the Middle Fork Stanislaus. Boulder Flat is at 5,600 feet and offers easy access off the highway. Here's another bonus: This stretch of river is stocked with trout.

RV sites, facilities: There are 21 sites for tents or RVs up to 22 feet (no hookups). Picnic tables and fire grills are provided. Drinking water and vault toilets are available. You can buy supplies in Dardanelle. Some facilities are wheelchair accessible. Leashed pets are permitted.

Reservations, fees: Reservations are not accepted. Sites are $15–17 per night, $5 per night for an additional vehicle. Open May–October, weather permitting.

Directions: From Sonora, drive east on Highway 108 past the town of Strawberry to Clark Fork Road. At Clark Fork Road, continue east on Highway 108 for a mile to the campground on the left side of the road.

Contact: Stanislaus National Forest, Summit Ranger District, 209/965-3434, fax 209/965-3372.

116 BRIGHTMAN FLAT

Scenic rating: 7

on the Middle Fork of the Stanislaus River in Stanislaus National Forest

See map page 653

This camp is on the Middle Fork of the Stanislaus River at 5,700 feet elevation, a mile east of Boulder Flat and two miles west of Dardanelle. The trout are small here and get fished hard. About 3.5 miles east on Highway 108 is the short trail to Columns of the Giants, a rare example of columnar hexagonal rock, similar to the phenomenon at Devils Postpile near Mammoth Lakes.

RV sites, facilities: There are 33 sites for tents or RVs up to 22 feet (no hookups). Picnic tables and fire grills are provided. Vault toilets and drinking water are available. You can buy supplies in Dardanelle. Some facilities are wheelchair accessible. Leashed pets are permitted.

Reservations, fees: Reservations are not accepted. Sites are $12 per night, $5 per night for an additional vehicle. Open May–October, weather permitting.

Directions: From Sonora, drive east on Highway 108 past the town of Strawberry to Clark Fork Road. At Clark Fork Road continue east on Highway 108 for two miles to the campground entrance on the left side of the road.

Contact: Stanislaus National Forest, Summit Ranger District, 209/965-3434, fax 209/965-3372.

117 EUREKA VALLEY

Scenic rating: 8

on the Middle Fork of the Stanislaus River in Stanislaus National Forest

See map page 653

There are about a half dozen campgrounds on this stretch of the Middle Fork Stanislaus River near Dardanelle, at 6,100 feet in elevation. The river runs along two sides of this campground, making it quite pretty. This stretch of river is planted with trout by the Department of Fish and Game, but it is hit pretty hard despite its relatively isolated location. A good short and easy hike is to Columns of the Giants, accessible on a quarter-mile-long trail out of Pigeon Flat, a mile west.

RV sites, facilities: There are 28 sites for tents or RVs up to 22 feet (no hookups). Picnic tables and fire grills are provided. Drinking water and

vault toilets are available. You can buy supplies in Dardanelle. Leashed pets are permitted.

Reservations, fees: Reservations are not accepted. Sites are $15 per night, $5 per night for an additional vehicle. Open May–October, weather permitting.

Directions: From Sonora, drive east on Highway 108 past the town of Strawberry to Dardanelle. Continue three miles east to the campground on the right.

Contact: Stanislaus National Forest, Summit Ranger District, 209/965-3434, fax 209/965-3372.

118 DARDANELLE

Scenic rating: 7

on the Middle Fork of the Stanislaus River in Stanislaus National Forest

See map page 653

This Forest Service camp is within walking distance of supplies in Dardanelle and is also right alongside the Middle Fork Stanislaus River. This section of river is stocked with trout by the Department of Fish and Game. The trail to see Columns of the Giants is just 1.5 miles east out of Pigeon Flat.

RV sites, facilities: There are 28 sites for tents or RVs up to 28 feet (no hookups). Picnic tables and fire grills are provided. Drinking water and vault toilets are available. You can buy supplies in Dardanelle. Some facilities are wheelchair accessible. Leashed pets are permitted.

Reservations, fees: Reservations are not accepted. Sites are $17–21 per night, $5 per night for an additional vehicle. Open May–October, weather permitting.

Directions: From Sonora, drive east on Highway 108 past Strawberry to Dardanelle and the campground on the left side of the road.

Contact: Stanislaus National Forest, Summit Ranger District, 209/965-3434, fax 209/965-3372.

CALIFORNIA

119 BAKER

🚶 🏊 🎣 🐕 ♿ 🚐 ⛺

Scenic rating: 7

on the Middle Fork of the Stanislaus River in Stanislaus National Forest

See map page 653

Baker lies at the turnoff for the well-known and popular Kennedy Meadow trailhead for the Emigrant Wilderness. The camp sits along the Middle Fork Stanislaus River, 6,200 feet elevation, downstream a short way from the confluence with Deadman Creek. The trailhead, with a nearby horse corral, is another two miles farther on the Kennedy Meadow access road. From here it is a 1.5-mile hike to a fork in the trail; right will take you two miles to Relief Reservoir, 7,226 feet, and left will route you up Kennedy Creek for five miles to pretty Kennedy Lake, just north of Kennedy Peak (10,716 feet).

RV sites, facilities: There are 44 sites for tents or RVs up to 22 feet (no hookups). Picnic tables and fire grills are provided. Drinking water and vault toilets are available. You can buy supplies in Dardanelle. Some facilities are wheelchair accessible. Leashed pets are permitted.

Reservations, fees: Reservations are not accepted. Sites are $15 per night, $5 per night for an additional vehicle. Open May–mid-October, weather permitting.

Directions: From Sonora, drive east on Highway 108 past Strawberry to Dardanelle. From Dardanelle, continue 5.5 miles east to the campground on the right side of the road at the turnoff for Kennedy Meadow.

Contact: Stanislaus National Forest, Summit Ranger District, 209/965-3434, fax 209/965-3372.

120 DEADMAN

🚶 🏊 🎣 🐕 ♿ 🚐 ⛺

Scenic rating: 7

on the Middle Fork of the Stanislaus River in Stanislaus National Forest

See map page 653

This is a popular trailhead camp and an ideal jump-off point for backpackers heading into the adjacent Emigrant Wilderness. The elevation is 6,200 feet. The camp is a short distance from Baker (see the listing in this chapter for *Baker* for hiking destinations).

RV sites, facilities: There are 17 sites for tents or RVs up to 22 feet (no hookups). Picnic tables and fire grills are provided. Drinking water and vault toilets are available. You can buy supplies in Dardanelle. Some facilities are wheelchair accessible. Leashed pets are permitted.

Reservations, fees: Reservations are not accepted. Sites are $15 per night, $5 per night for an additional vehicle. Open May–early October, weather permitting.

Directions: From Sonora, drive east on Highway 108 past the town of Strawberry to Dardanelle. From Dardanelle, continue 5.5 miles east to the Kennedy Meadow turnoff. Drive a mile on Kennedy Meadow Road to the campground, which is opposite the parking area for Kennedy Meadow Trail.

Contact: Stanislaus National Forest, Summit Ranger District, 209/965-3434, fax 209/965-3372.

121 LEAVITT MEADOWS

🚶 🎣 🐕 🚐 ⛺

Scenic rating: 9

on the Walker River in Humboldt-Toiyabe National Forest

See map page 653

While Leavitt Meadows sits right aside Highway 108, a little winding two-laner, there are several nearby off-pavement destinations that make this camp a winner. The camp is in the high eastern Sierra, east of Sonora Pass at 7,000 feet in elevation, where Leavitt Creek and Brownie Creek enter the West Walker River. There is a pack station for horseback riding nearby. For four-wheel-drive owners, the most popular side trip is driving four miles west on Highway 108, then turning south and driving four miles to Leavitt Lake, where the trout fishing is sometimes spectacular, if you're trolling a gold Cripplure.

RV sites, facilities: There are 16 sites for tents

CALIFORNIA

or RVs up to 30 feet (no hookups). Picnic tables, food lockers, and fire grills are provided. Drinking water and vault toilets are available. Leashed pets are permitted.

Reservations, fees: Reservations are not accepted. Sites are $13 per night, $5 per night for an additional vehicle. Open April–October, weather permitting.

Directions: From the junction of Highway 108 and U.S. 395 north of Bridgeport, turn west on Highway 108 and drive approximately seven miles to the campground on the left side of the road.

Contact: Humboldt-Toiyabe National Forest, Bridgeport Ranger District, 760/932-7070, fax 760/932-5899.

122 SONORA BRIDGE

Scenic rating: 7

near the Walker River in Humboldt-Toiyabe National Forest

See map page 653

The West Walker River is a pretty stream, flowing over boulders and into pools, and each year this stretch of river is well stocked with rainbow trout by the Department of Fish and Game. One of several campgrounds near the West Walker, Sonora Bridge is at 6,800 feet, about a half mile from the river. The setting is in the transition zone from high mountains to high desert on the eastern edge of the Sierra Nevada.

RV sites, facilities: There are 23 sites for tents or RVs up to 35 feet (no hookups). Picnic tables and fire grills are provided. Drinking water and vault toilets are available. Leashed pets are permitted.

Reservations, fees: Reservations are not accepted. Sites are $13 per night, $5 per night for an additional vehicle. Open May–October, weather permitting.

Directions: From north of Bridgeport, at the junction of U.S. 395 and Highway 108, turn west on Highway 108 and drive one mile to the campground on the left.

Contact: Humboldt-Toiyabe National Forest,

Bridgeport Ranger District, 760/932-7070, fax 760/932-5899.

123 CHRIS FLAT

Scenic rating: 7

on the Walker River in Humboldt-Toiyabe National Forest

See map page 653

This is one of two campgrounds set along U.S. 395 next to the West Walker River, a pretty trout stream with easy access and good stocks of rainbow trout. The plants are usually made at two campgrounds, resulting in good prospects here at Chris Flat and west on Highway 108 at Sonora Bridge. The elevation is 6,600 feet.

RV sites, facilities: There are 15 sites for tents or RVs up to 30 feet (no hookups). Picnic tables and fire grills are provided. Drinking water (shut off during freezing temperatures) and vault toilets are available. Leashed pets are permitted.

Reservations, fees: Reservations are not accepted. Sites are $15 per night, $5 per night for an additional vehicle. Open April–early November, weather permitting.

Directions: From Carson City, drive south on U.S. 395 to Coleville and then continue south for 15 miles to the campground on the east side of the road (four miles north of the junction of U.S. 395 and Highway 108).

Contact: Humboldt-Toiyabe National Forest, Bridgeport Ranger District, 760/932-7070, fax 760/932-5899.

124 BOOTLEG
![icons]

Scenic rating: 6

on the Walker River in Humboldt-Toiyabe National Forest

See map page 653

Location is always a key, and easy access off U.S. 395, the adjacent West Walker River, and good trout stocks in summer make this a popular spot. (See the listings in this chapter for *Chris Flat* and *Sonora Bridge* for more information.) Note that this camp is on the west side of the highway, and that anglers will have to cross the road to gain fishing access. The elevation is 6,600 feet.

RV sites, facilities: There are 63 sites for tents or RVs up to 35 feet (no hookups). Picnic tables and fire grills are provided. Drinking water and flush toilets are available. Leashed pets are permitted.

Reservations, fees: Reservations are not accepted. Sites are $15 per night, $5 per night for an additional vehicle. Open early May–mid-September, weather permitting.

Directions: From Carson City, drive south on U.S. 395 to Coleville and then continue south for 13 miles to the campground on the west side of the highway (six miles north of the junction of U.S. 395 and Highway 108).

Contact: Humboldt-Toiyabe National Forest, Bridgeport Ranger District, 760/932-7070, fax 760/932-5899.

125 GOLDEN PINES RV RESORT AND CAMPGROUND

Scenic rating: 6

near Arnold

See map page 653

This is a privately operated park set at 5,800 feet on the slopes of the Sierra Nevada. The resort is surrounded by 400 acres of forest and has a self-guided nature trail. Nearby destinations include Stanislaus National Forest, the North Stanislaus River, and Calaveras Big Trees State Park (two miles away). The latter features 150 giant sequoias, along with the biggest stump you can imagine, and two easy hikes, one routed through the North Grove, another through the South Grove. The BearValley/Mount Reba ski resort is nearby. Note that about half the sites are long-term vacation leases.

RV sites, facilities: There are 33 sites with full or partial hookups (30 amps) for RVs up to 42 feet, along with 40 tent sites. Picnic tables,

fire pits, and barbecues are provided. Drinking water, restrooms with showers, a seasonal heated swimming pool, a playground, horseshoes, table tennis, volleyball, group facilities, a pay phone, a coin laundry, and propane gas are available. Some facilities are wheelchair accessible. Leashed pets are permitted.

Reservations, fees: Reservations are recommended. Sites are $20–35 per night, $2.50 per night for an additional vehicle, $2.50 one-time charge per pet. Some credit cards accepted. Open year-round.

Directions: From Angels Camp, turn northeast on Highway 4 and drive 22 miles to Arnold. Continue for seven miles to the campground entrance on the left.

Contact: Golden Pines RV Resort and Campground, 209/795-2820, www.goldenpinesrvresort.com.

126 NORTH GROVE

Scenic rating: 7

in Calaveras Big Trees State Park

See map page 653

This is one of two campgrounds at Calaveras Big Trees State Park, the state park known for its two groves of giant sequoias (Sierra redwoods). The park covers 6,500 acres, preserving the extraordinary North Grove of giant sequoias. The grove includes the Discovery Tree. Through the years, additional acreage surrounding the grove has been added, providing a mixed conifer forest as a buffer around the giant sequoias. The trailhead for a hike on North Grove Loop is here; it's an easy 1.5-mile walk that is routed among 150 sequoias, where the sweet fragrance of the huge trees fills the air. These trees are known for their massive diameter, not for their height, as is the case with coastal redwoods. Another hike, a five-miler, is in the South Grove, where the park's two largest sequoias (the Agassiz Tree and the Palace Hotel Tree) can be seen on a spur trail. A visitors center is open during peak periods, offering exhibits on the giant sequoia and natural history. The North Fork Stanislaus River runs near Highway 4, providing trout-fishing access. The Stanislaus (near the bridge) and Beaver Creek (about 10 miles away) are stocked with trout in late spring and early summer. In the winter this is a popular spot for cross-country skiing and snowshoeing. The elevation is 4,800 feet.

RV sites, facilities: There are 51 sites for tents, 48 sites for RVs up to 30 feet, five hike-in environmental sites, and two group sites for 40–60 people each. No hookups. Fire grills, food lockers, and picnic tables are provided. Drinking water, restrooms with flush toilets and coin showers, firewood, and a dump station are available. Some facilities are wheelchair accessible, including a nature trail and exhibits. No bicycles are allowed on the paths, but they are permitted on fire roads and paved roads. Leashed pets are permitted but not on trails.

Reservations, fees: Reservations are accepted ($7.50 reservation fee) at 800/444-PARK (800/444-7275) or www.reserveamerica.com. Sites are $25 per night, $6 per night for an additional vehicle, $90–135 per night for group sites, and $15 per night for environmental sites. Open year-round, with 12 sites available in winter.

Directions: From Angels Camp, drive east on Highway 4 for 23 miles to Arnold and then continue another four miles to the park entrance on the right.

Contact: Calaveras Big Trees State Park, 209/795-2334; Columbia State Park, 209/532-0150, www.parks.ca.gov.

127 OAK HOLLOW

Scenic rating: 7

in Calaveras Big Trees State Park
See map page 653

This is one of two campgrounds at Calaveras Big Trees State Park. (See the listing in this chapter for *North Grove* for recreation information.)

RV sites, facilities: There are 23 sites for tents only and 18 sites with no hookups for RVs up to 30 feet. Picnic tables, fire rings, and food lockers are provided. Drinking water and

restrooms with flush toilets and coin showers are available. A dump station is available four miles away at North Grove. You can buy supplies in Dorrington or Arnold. Some facilities are wheelchair accessible, including a nature trail and exhibits. Leashed pets are permitted in the campground but not on trails.

Reservations, fees: Reservations are accepted ($7.50 reservation fee) at 800/444-PARK (800/444-7275) or www.reserveamerica.com. Sites are $25 per night, $6 per night for an additional vehicle. Open March–November.

Directions: From Angels Camp, drive east on Highway 4 for 23 miles to Arnold and then continue four miles to the park entrance on the right. Continue another four miles to the campground on the right.

Contact: Calaveras Big Trees State Park, 209/795-2334; Columbia State Park, 209/532-0150, www.parks.ca.gov.

128 BEARDSLEY

Scenic rating: 6

at Beardsley Reservoir in Stanislaus National Forest
See map page 653

This lake lies in a deep canyon with a paved ramp, nice picnic area, and a fair beach. It is often an outstanding fishery early in the season for brown trout, and then once planted, good for limits of hatchery fish during the evening bite. In winter and spring, as soon as the gate is opened to the boat ramp access road, the fishing is best when the wind blows. This lake also allows powerboats and all water sports. The water is generally warm enough for swimmers by midsummer. The camp is at 3,400 feet, but because it is near the bottom of the lake canyon, it actually feels much higher in elevation. Since the lake is a reservoir, it is subject to severe drawdowns. Bonus: There is more fishing nearby on the Middle Fork of the Stanislaus.

RV sites, facilities: There are 16 sites for tents or RVs up to 22 feet (no hookups). Fire rings are provided. Vault toilets are available. No drinking water is available. Garbage must be packed out. Leashed pets are permitted.

Reservations, fees: Reservations are not accepted. There is no fee for camping. Open May–October, weather permitting (the road is often gated at the top of the canyon, when the boat ramp road at lake level is iced over).

Directions: From Sonora, drive east on Highway 108 for about 25 miles to Strawberry and the turnoff for Beardsley Reservoir/Forest Road 52. Turn left and drive seven miles to Beardsley Dam. Continue for 0.25 mile past the dam to the campground.

Contact: Stanislaus National Forest, Summit Ranger District, 209/965-3434, fax 209/965-3372.

129 FRASER FLAT

Scenic rating: 7

on the South Fork of the Stanislaus River in Stanislaus National Forest

See map page 653

This camp is along the South Fork of the Stanislaus River at 4,800 feet in elevation. If the fish aren't biting, a short side trip via Forest Service roads will route you north into the main canyon of the Middle Fork Stanislaus. A map of Stanislaus National Forest is required for this adventure.

RV sites, facilities: There are 38 sites for tents or RVs up to 30 feet (no hookups). Picnic tables and fire grills are provided. Drinking water, vault toilets, and a wheelchair-accessible fishing pier are available. A grocery store and propane gas are nearby. Some facilities are wheelchair accessible. Leashed pets are permitted.

Reservations, fees: Reservations are not accepted. Sites are $15 per night, $5 per night for an additional vehicle. Open May–October, weather permitting.

Directions: From Sonora, drive east on High-

way 108 to Long Barn. Continue east for six miles to Spring Gap Road/Forest Road 4N01. Turn left and drive three miles to the campground on the left side of the road.

Contact: Stanislaus National Forest, Mi-Wok Ranger District, 209/586-3234, fax 209/586-0643.

130 SUGARPINE RV PARK

Scenic rating: 5

in Twain Harte

See map page 653

Twain Harte is a beautiful little town, right at the edge of the snow line in winter, and right where pines take over the alpine landscape. This park is at the threshold of mountain country, with Pinecrest, Dodge Ridge, and Beardsley Reservoir nearby. It sits on 15 acres and features several walking paths. Note that only 17 of the RV sites are available for overnight campers; the other sites are rented as annual vacation leases. RVs and mobile homes are also for sale at the park.

RV sites, facilities: There are 78 sites with full hookups (20, 30, and 50 amps) for RVs up to 40 feet, 15 tent sites, and three park-model cabins. Picnic tables are provided. Restrooms have showers. Cable TV, modem access, a playground, a seasonal swimming pool, horseshoes, volleyball, badminton, tetherball, basketball, a coin laundry, group facilities, and a convenience store are available. Some facilities are wheelchair accessible. Leashed pets are permitted.

Reservations, fees: Reservations are accepted. Sites are $20–32 per night, $1 per pet per night, $3 per night for an additional vehicle, except for towed vehicles. Some credit cards accepted. Open year-round.

Directions: From Sonora, drive east on Highway 108 for 17 miles to the park on the right side of the road, three miles east of Twain Harte.

Contact: Sugarpine RV Park, 209/586-4631.

CALIFORNIA

SAN FRANCISCO BAY AREA

☾ BEST RV PARKS AND CAMPGROUNDS

☾ Coastal Sites
San Francisco RV Resort, page 719.

☾ Wildlife-Viewing
Olema Ranch Campground, page 716.

It's ironic that many people who have chosen to live in the Bay Area are often the ones who complain the most about it. I've even heard some say, "Some day I'm going to get out of here and start having a good time."

I wish I could take anyone who has ever had these thoughts on a little trip in my airplane and circle the Bay Area at 3,000 feet. What you see is that despite strips of roadways and pockets of cities where people are jammed together, most of the region is wild, unsettled, and beautiful. There is no metropolitan area in the world that offers better and more diverse recreation and open space so close to so many.

The Bay Area has 150 significant parks (including 12 with redwoods), 7,500 miles of hiking and biking trails, 45 lakes, 25 waterfalls, 100 miles of coast, mountains with incredible lookouts, bays with islands, and in all, 1.2 million acres of greenbelt with hundreds of acres being added each year with land bought by money earmarked from property taxes. The land has no limit. Enjoy it.

Alongside the unique recreation possibilities remain traditional drive-in sites for RVers at state, county, and regional parks throughout the region.

Note that proximity to a metropolitan area means that the demand is higher. So plan ahead. One shocker is that in spring and fall, there is a huge drop-off in use on weekdays, Sunday–Thursday. And on weekends, Friday evenings through Sunday, the parks get nearly 85 percent of their use.

There are many world-class landmarks to see while staying in the Bay Area. In San Francisco alone, sights include the Golden Gate Bridge, Fisherman's Wharf, Alcatraz, Ghirardelli Square, Chinatown, SBC ballpark, the Crissy Field waterfront, cable cars, Fort Point, the Cliff House and Ocean Beach, and Fort Funston.

CALIFORNIA

Includes:

- Anthony Chabot Regional Park
- Big Basin Redwoods State Park
- Butano State Park
- Del Valle Regional Park
- Half Moon Bay
- Half Moon Bay State Beach
- Henry Cowell Redwoods State Park
- Henry W. Coe State Park
- Mount Diablo State Park
- Portola Redwoods State Park
- Samuel P. Taylor State Park
- Skyline Ridge

CALIFORNIA

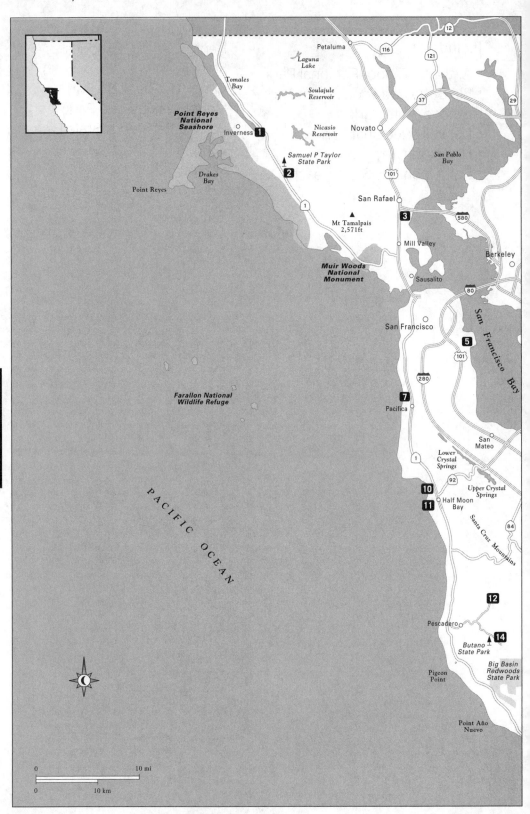

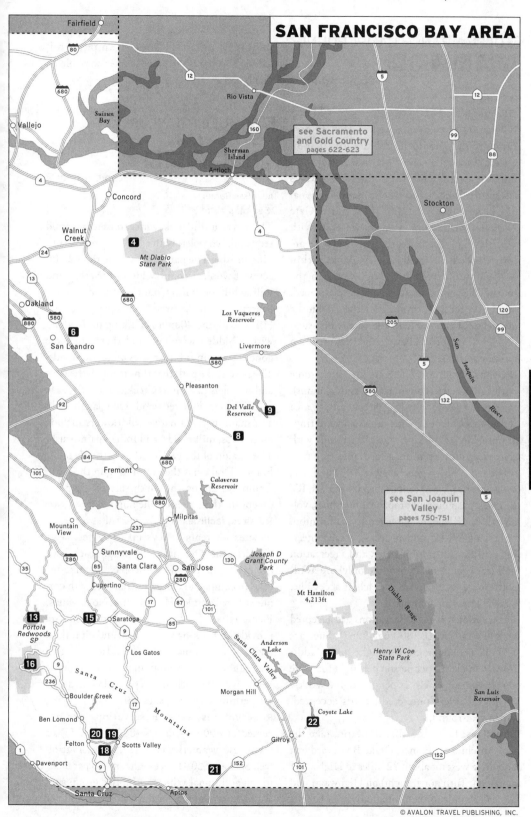

CALIFORNIA

◼ OLEMA RANCH CAMPGROUND

Scenic rating: 4

in Olema

See map page 714 | BEST (

If location is everything, then this 32-acre campground should be rated a 10. It is in Olema, in a valley amid Marin's coastal foothills, an ideal jump-off spot for a Point Reyes adventure. It borders the Point Reyes National Seashore to the west and the Golden Gate National Recreation Area to the east, with Tomales Bay to the nearby north. There are several excellent trailheads available within a 10-minute drive along Highway 1 to the south. The campsites are small, tightly placed, and I have received complaint letters about the ambience of the place. In the past, when such problems are noted, I have found they are often quickly addressed.

RV sites, facilities: There are 203 sites, some with full or partial hookups (20 and 30 amps), for tents or RVs of any length, and a large area for up to 175 tents. Picnic tables and fire rings are provided. Drinking water, restrooms with showers, a dump station, a coin laundry, a post office, an ATM, a general store, firewood, ice, a playground, video rentals, bicycle rentals, RV supplies, gasoline and propane, horseshoes, volleyball, shuffleboard, table tennis, badminton, tetherball, Wi-Fi, modem access, arcade, meeting facilities, an amphitheater, and a recreation hall (for groups of 25 or more only) are available. Some facilities are wheelchair accessible. Leashed pets are permitted.

Reservations, fees: Reservations are accepted at 800/655-CAMP (800/655-2267). Sites are $25–38 per night, $2 per night for an additional vehicle, $3 per person per night for more than two people, $1 per pet per night. Weekly rates available. Some credit cards accepted. Open year-round.

Directions: From U.S. 101 in Marin, take the San Anselmo/Sir Francis Drake Boulevard exit and drive west for about 22 miles to Highway 1 at Olema. Turn north (right) on Highway 1 and drive 0.25 mile to the campground on the left.

Contact: Olema Ranch Campground, 415/663-8001, fax 415/663-8832, www.olema ranch.com.

◼ SAMUEL P. TAYLOR STATE PARK

Scenic rating: 9

near San Rafael

See map page 714

This is a beautiful park, with campsites set amid redwoods, complete with a babbling brook running nearby. The park covers more than 2,700 acres of wooded countryside in the steep and rolling hills of Marin County, featuring unique contrasts of coast redwoods and open grassland. Hikers will find 20 miles of hiking trails, along with a hidden waterfall, and there are some good mountain-biking routes on service roads. The paved bike path that runs through the park and parallels Lagunitas Creek is a terrific, easy ride. Trees include redwood, Douglas fir, oak, and madrone, and native wildflowers include buttercups, milkmaids, and Indian paintbrush. The section of the park on the north side of Sir Francis Drake has the best hiking in the park. Campsites are on the south side of the park, except for three sites on the north side.

RV sites, facilities: There are 25 sites for tents, 35 sites for tents or RVs up to 27 feet, two primitive sites for up to 10 people each, two group sites for 25 and 50 people, one hike-in/bike-in camp, and one equestrian site with corrals at Devil's Gulch Horse Camp. No hookups. Picnic tables, food lockers, and fire grills are provided. Drinking water, flush and pit toilets, and Wi-Fi are available. You'll find a small store and café two miles away in Lagunitas. Some facilities are wheelchair accessible. Leashed pets are permitted in campsites only.

Reservations, fees: Reservations are accepted at 800/444-PARK (800/444-7275) or www.reserveamerica.com ($7.50 reservation fee). Sites are $20–25 per night and $6 per night for an additional vehicle, primitive group sites are $23 per night, group sites are $75–150 per night, the equestrian camp costs $50 per night, and it's $3 per person per night for the hike-in/bike-in site. Open year-round.

Directions: From U.S. 101 in Marin, take the Sir Francis Drake Boulevard exit and drive west for about 15 miles to the park entrance on the left side of the road.

Contact: Samuel P. Taylor State Park, 415/488-9897, fax 415/488-4315; California State Parks, Marin Sector, 415/898-4362, www.parks.ca.gov.

3 MARIN RV PARK

Scenic rating: 2

in Greenbrae

See map page 714

This can make an ideal RV base camp for Marin County adventures. To the west are Mount Tamalpais State Park, Muir Woods National Monument, Samuel P. Taylor State Park, and Point Reyes National Seashore. To the nearby east is the Loch Lomond Marina on San Pablo Bay, where fishing trips can be arranged for striped bass and sturgeon; phone Loch Lomond Bait Shop, 415/456-0321. The park offers complete sightseeing information and easy access to buses and ferry service to San Francisco.

RV sites, facilities: There are 89 sites for tents or RVs with full hookups (30 and 50 amps). Restrooms have showers. A coin laundry, modem access, a swimming pool, a dump station, and RV supplies are available. Some facilities are wheelchair accessible. Leashed pets are permitted.

Reservations, fees: Reservations are recommended. Sites are $40 per night, $2 per person per night for more than two people. Six people maximum per site. Weekly and monthly rates available. Some credit cards accepted. Open year-round.

Directions: From the south: From the Golden Gate Bridge, drive north on U.S. 101 for 10 miles to Lucky Drive (south of San Rafael). Exit and turn left on Redwood Highway (no

sign) and drive three blocks north to the park entrance on the right.

From the north: From San Rafael, drive south on U.S. 101 to the Lucky Drive exit (450A). Take that exit to the first light at Tamal Vista. Turn left and drive to the next stoplight and Wornum Avenue. Turn left at Wornum Avenue and drive under the freeway to Redwood Highway (frontage road). Turn left and drive four blocks north to the park entrance.

Contact: Marin RV Park, 415/461-5199 or 888/461-5199, fax 415/925-1584, www.marinrvpark.com.

4 MOUNT DIABLO STATE PARK

Scenic rating: 6

east of Oakland

See map page 715

Mount Diablo, elevation 3,849 feet, provides one of the most all-encompassing lookouts anywhere in America, an awesome 360 degrees on clear mornings. On crystal-clear days you can see the Sierra Nevada and its white, snowbound crest. Some claim to have seen Half Dome in Yosemite with binoculars. The drive to the summit is a must-do trip, and the weekend interpretive center right on top of the mountain is one of the best in the Bay Area. The camps at Mount Diablo are set in foothill/oak grassland country, with some shaded sites. Winter and spring are good times to visit, when the weather is still cool enough for good hiking trips. Most of the trails require long hikes, often including significant elevation gains and losses. No alcohol is permitted in the park. The park offers extensive but challenging hiking, biking, and horseback riding. A combination museum, visitors center, and gift shop perches on the Diablo summit. Summers are hot and dry, and in late summer the park can be closed because of fire danger. In winter, snow occasionally falls on the peak; according to my logbook, it happens during the first full moon in February.

RV sites, facilities: There are 64 sites for tents or RVs up to 20 feet (in three campgrounds), five group sites for 20–50 people, and one group site that is accessible for equestrian use with hitching posts and a water trough. No hookups. Picnic tables and fire grills are provided. Drinking water and flush and vault toilets are available. Showers are available at Juniper and Live Oak campgrounds. Leashed pets are permitted in campgrounds and picnic areas.

Reservations, fees: Reservations are accepted at 800/444-PARK (800/444-7275) or www.reserveamerica.com ($7.50 reservation fee). Sites are $14–19 per night, $6 per night for an additional vehicle; group sites are $55–111 per night. Open year-round.

Directions: From Danville on I-680, take the Diablo Road exit. Turn east on Diablo Road and drive three miles to Mount Diablo Scenic Boulevard. Turn left and continue 3.5 miles (the road becomes South Gate Road) to the park entrance station. Register at the kiosk, obtain a park map, and drive to the designated campground.

Contact: Mount Diablo State Park, 925/837-2525 or 925/837-0904; Diablo Vista District, 707/769-5652, www.mdia.org or www.parks .ca.gov.

5 CANDLESTICK RV PARK

Scenic rating: 6

in San Francisco

See map page 714

This RV park is adjacent to the old stadium that everybody calls Candlestick Park; the name is now officially Monster Park, however. It is five miles from downtown San Francisco and an ideal destination for out-of-towners who want to explore the city without having to drive, because the park offers tours and inexpensive shuttles to the downtown area. In addition, there are good hiking opportunities along the shoreline of the bay. On summer afternoons, when the wind howls at 20 to 30 mph here, sailboarders rip by. Rates are higher, much higher, on 49er game days, and the stadium is usually packed with 60,000 or more people.

RV sites, facilities: There are 165 sites with full hookups (30 and 50 amps) for trailers or RVs up to 42 feet, plus 24 tent sites. Some sites are pull-through. Restrooms have showers. A coin laundry, modem access, a grocery store, game room, motor home washing, and propane are available. Shuttles and bus tours are also available. A security officer is posted at the entry station at night. Some facilities are wheelchair accessible. Small leashed pets are permitted.

Reservations, fees: Reservations are recommended at 800/888-CAMP (800/888-2267). Sites are $55–58 per night, $10 per night for an additional vehicle, $3 per person per night for more than two people. Rates are higher on 49er game days. Some credit cards accepted. Open year-round.

Directions: From San Francisco on U.S. 101, take the Monster Park exit to Gilman Road. Turn east on the stadium entrance road/Gilman Road and drive around the parking lot to the far end of the stadium (Gate 4).

Contact: Candlestick RV Park, 415/822-2299, fax 415/822-7638, www.sanfranciscorvpark.com.

6 ANTHONY CHABOT REGIONAL PARK

Scenic rating: 7

near Castro Valley

See map page 715

The campground at Chabot Regional Park is on a hilltop sheltered by eucalyptus, with good views and trails available. The best campsites are the walk-in units, requiring a walk of only a minute or so. Several provide views of Lake Chabot to the south a half mile away. The 315-acre lake provides good trout fishing in the winter and spring, and a chance for huge but elusive largemouth bass. Huckleberry Trail is routed down from the campground (near walk-in site 20) to the lake at Honker Bay, a good fishing area. There is also a good 12-mile bike ride around the lake. In all, this 5,000-acre park includes 31 miles of hiking, biking, and riding trails. East Bay Skyline Trail runs the length of the park. Boat rentals are available, but no swimming or water-body contact is permitted. A weekend marksmanship range is available at the park, and a golf course is nearby.

RV sites, facilities: There are 53 sites for tents and small RVs, 12 sites with full hookups (30 amps) for RVs, and 10 walk-in sites for tents only. Picnic tables and fire grills are provided. Restrooms have flush toilets and showers. Drinking water, a dump station, an amphitheater, a small marina, boat rentals, a snack bar, a picnic area, bait and tackle, and naturalist-led campfire programs are available. There's no boat launch, and gas motors and inflatables are prohibited. Leashed pets are permitted.

Reservations, fees: Reservations are accepted at 510/562-2267 ($7 reservation fee). Sites are $18–25 per night, $6 per night for an additional vehicle, $2 per pet per night. Some credit cards accepted. Open year-round.

Directions: From I-580 in the Oakland hills, drive to the 35th Avenue exit. Take that exit, and at the stop sign, turn east on 35th Avenue and drive up the hill and straight across Skyline Boulevard, where 35th Avenue becomes Redwood Road. Continue on Redwood Road for eight miles to the park and Marciel Road (campground entrance road) on the right.

Contact: Regional Park Headquarters, 510/635-0135, ext. 2200, fax 510/569-4319; Anthony Chabot Regional Park, 510/639-4751; Chabot Equestrian Center, 510/569-4428, www.ebpark.org/parks.htm.

7 SAN FRANCISCO RV RESORT

Scenic rating: 8

in Pacifica

See map page 714   BEST

This is one of the best RV parks in the Bay Area. It is on the bluffs just above the Pacific Ocean in Pacifica, complete with beach access, a nearby fishing pier, and sometimes excellent surf fishing. There is also a nearby golf course and the chance for dramatic ocean sunsets. The park is kept clean and in good shape, and though there is too much asphalt, the proximity to the beach overcomes that downfall. It is only 20 minutes from San Francisco.

RV sites, facilities: There are 182 sites with full hookups (50 amps) for RVs up to 45 feet. No tents. Restrooms have showers. A heated swimming pool, a year-round spa, a playground, a game room, group facilities, cable TV, Wi-Fi, modem access, a convenience store, a coin laundry, and propane gas are available. Some facilities are wheelchair accessible. Leashed pets are permitted, with some exceptions.

Reservations, fees: Reservations are recommended at 650/355-7093. Sites are $40–60 per night. Some credit cards accepted. Open year-round.

Directions: From San Francisco, drive south on Highway 280 to Highway 1. Bear west on Highway 1 and drive into Pacifica to the Palmetto Drive exit. Take that exit and drive south to the stop sign (you will be on the west side of the highway). Continue straight ahead (the road becomes Palmetto Avenue) for about two blocks and look for the entrance to the park on the right side of the road at 700 Palmetto.

From the south, drive north on Highway 1 into Pacifica. Take the Manor Drive exit. At the stop sign, turn left on Oceana Avenue (you will be on the east side of the highway) and drive a block to another stop sign at Manor Drive. Turn left, drive a short distance over the highway to a stop sign at Palmetto Avenue. Turn left and drive about two blocks to the park on the right.

Contact: San Francisco RV Resort, 650/355-7093, fax 650/355-7102, www.san franciscorvresort.com.

8 JOSEPH D. GRANT COUNTY PARK

Scenic rating: 7

near San Jose

See map page 715

Grant Ranch is a great, wild playland covering more than 9,000 acres in the foothills of nearby Mount Hamilton to the east. It features

CALIFORNIA

52 miles of hiking trails (horses permitted), 20 miles of old ranch roads that are perfect for mountain biking, a pretty lake (Grant Lake), and miles of foothills, canyons, oaks, and grasslands. The campground is amid oak grasslands, is shaded, and can be used as a base camp for planning the day's recreation. The best hikes are to Halls Valley, especially in the winter and spring when there are many secret little creeks and miniature waterfalls in hidden canyons; Hotel Trail; and Ca-ada de Pala Trail, which drops to San Felipe Creek, the prettiest stream in the park. Warm-water fishing is available in the lake and several smaller ponds. A great side trip is the slow, curvy drive east to Lick Observatory for great views of the Santa Clara Valley. Wood fires are often banned in summer.

RV sites, facilities: There are 40 sites for tents or RVs up to 31 feet (no hookups). Picnic tables, food lockers, and fire pits are provided. Drinking water, restrooms with flush toilets and free showers, and a dump station are available. Some facilities are wheelchair accessible. Leashed pets are permitted.

Reservations, fees: Reservations are recommended ($6 reservation fee) at 408/355-2201. Sites are $9–18 per night. Check-in required before sunset; gates are locked at dusk. Open year-round.

Directions: In San Jose at the junction of I-680 and U.S. 101, take I-680 north to the Alum Rock Avenue exit. Turn east and drive four miles to Mount Hamilton Road. Turn right and drive eight miles to the park headquarters entrance on the right side of the road.

Contact: Joseph D. Grant County Park, 408/274-6121, fax 408/270-4808, www.parkhere.org.

⑨ DEL VALLE REGIONAL PARK

Scenic rating: 7

near Livermore

See map page 715

Of the 65 parks in the East Bay Regional Park District, it is Del Valle that provides the great-est variety of recreation at the highest quality. Del Valle Reservoir is the centerpiece, a five-mile-long narrow lake that fills a canyon with 16 miles of shoreline, providing a good boat launch for powerboating (10-mph speed limit) and good fishing for trout (stocked), striped bass, panfish, and catfish. Two swimming beaches are popular in summer. The park offers boat tours of the natural history and lake ecology of the area. The sites are somewhat exposed because of the grassland habitat, but they fill anyway on most weekends and three-day holidays. A trailhead south of the lake provides access to Ohlone Wilderness Trail, and for the well conditioned, there is the 5.5-mile butt-kicker of a climb to Murietta Falls, gaining 1,600 feet in 1.5 miles. Murietta Falls is the Bay Area's highest waterfall, 100 feet tall, though its thin, silvery wisp is difficult to view directly and rarely evokes much emotional response after such an intense climb. Riding trails are also available in this 4,000-acre park.

RV sites, facilities: There are 150 sites for tents or RVs of any length, including 21 with water and sewer hookups, and two walk-in group areas for up to 75 people each. Group camps require a walk of a quarter mile to one mile. Picnic tables and fire grills are provided. Drinking water, restrooms with flush toilets and showers, a dump station, full marina, boat and sailboard rentals, seasonal campfire programs, swimming beaches, and a boat launch are available. Some facilities are wheelchair accessible. Leashed pets are permitted.

Reservations, fees: Reservations are required with a $7 reservation fee at 510/636-1684. Sites are $18–25 per night, $6 per night per additional vehicle, $2 per pet per night. The boat-launch fee is $2–3 per day. Some credit cards accepted. Open year-round.

Directions: From I-580 east at Livermore, take the North Livermore Avenue exit and turn south (right if driving from San Francisco). Drive south and proceed through Livermore (the road becomes South Livermore Avenue). Continue for 1.5 miles (the road then becomes Tesla Road) to Mines Road. Turn right on

Mines Road and drive 3.5 miles to Del Valle Road. Continue straight on Del Valle Road for four miles to the park entrance.

Contact: Del Valle Regional Park, 925/373-0332; East Bay Regional Park District, 510/635-0135, www.ebparks.org/parks.htm.

10 HALF MOON BAY STATE BEACH

Scenic rating: 7

at Half Moon Bay

See map page 714

In summer, this park often fills to capacity with campers touring Highway 1. The campground has level, grassy sites for tents, a clean parking area for RVs, and a state beach available just a short walk away. The feature here is four miles of broad, sandy beaches with three access points with parking. A visitors center is available. Side trips include Princeton and Pillar Point Marina, seven miles north on Highway 1, where fishing and whale-watching trips are possible. Typical weather is fog in summer, clear days in spring and fall, and wet and windy in the winter—yet occasionally there are drop-dead beautiful days in winter between storms: warm, clear, and windless. Temperatures range from lows in the mid-40s in winter to highs in the mid-60s in fall. One frustrating point: The weekend traffic on Highway 1 up and down the coast here is often jammed, with absolute gridlock during festivals.

RV sites, facilities: There are 52 sites for tents or RVs up to 40 feet, four hike-in/bike-in sites, and one group site (for up to 50 people) two miles north of the main campground. No hookups. Picnic tables, food lockers, and fire grills are provided. Restrooms have flush toilets and coin showers. Drinking water, Wi-Fi, pay telephone, and a dump station are available. Some facilities are wheelchair accessible. Leashed pets are permitted, except on the beach.

Reservations, fees: Reservations are required at 800/444-PARK (800/444-7275) or www.reserveamerica.com ($7.50 reservation

fee). Sites are $25 per night, $111 per night for group site, $3 per person per night for hike-in/bike-in sites, $6 per night for an additional vehicle. Open year-round.

Directions: Drive to Half Moon Bay to the junction of Highway 1 and Highway 92. Turn south on Highway 1 and drive two blocks to Kelly Avenue. Turn right on Kelly Avenue and drive 0.5 mile to the park entrance at the end of the road.

Contact: Half Moon Bay State Beach, 650/726-8820 or 650/726-8819; Santa Cruz District, 831/335-6318, www.parks.ca.gov.

11 PELICAN POINT RV PARK

Scenic rating: 7

in Half Moon Bay

See map page 714

This park is in a rural setting on the southern outskirts of the town of Half Moon Bay, set on an extended bluff near the ocean. The sites consist of cement slabs with picnic tables. Half of the RV sites are monthly rentals. All facilities are available nearby, with restaurants available in Half Moon Bay and 10 miles north in Princeton at Pillar Point Harbor. The harbor has an excellent boat launch, a fish-cleaning station, party boat trips for salmon and rockfish, and, in the winter, whale-watching trips.

RV sites, facilities: There are 75 sites with full hookups (30 and 50 amps) for RVs up to 40 feet. No tents. Picnic tables are provided. Restrooms have showers. A coin laundry, propane gas, a small store, clubhouse, and a dump station are available. Leashed pets are permitted.

Reservations, fees: Reservations are accepted. Sites are $40–45 per night, $2 per night for an additional vehicle, $3.30 per person per night for more than two people, $1 per pet per night. Some credit cards accepted. Open year-round.

Directions: In Half Moon Bay, at the junction of Highway 1 and Highway 92, turn south on Highway 1 and drive 2.5 miles to Miramontes Point Road. Turn right and drive a short distance to the park entrance on the left.

CALIFORNIA

Contact: Pelican Point RV Park, 650/726-9100.

12 MEMORIAL COUNTY PARK

Scenic rating: 8

near La Honda

See map page 714

This beautiful 500-acre redwood park is on the western slopes of the Santa Cruz Mountains, tucked in a pocket between the tiny towns of La Honda and Loma Mar. The park is known for its family camping areas and Tan Oak and Mount Ellen nature trails. The campground features access to a nearby network of 50 miles of trails, with the best hike along the headwaters of Pescadero Creek. In late winter, it is sometimes possible to see steelhead spawn (no fishing permitted, of course). The trails link with others in nearby Portola State Park and Sam McDonald County Park, providing access to a vast recreation land. A swimming hole on Pescadero Creek next to the campground is popular during the summer. The camp is often filled on summer weekends, but the sites are spaced so it won't cramp your style.

RV sites, facilities: There are 156 sites for tents or RVs up to 35 feet, two group sites for tents or RVs up to 35 feet that can accommodate up to 75 people each, and six youth group areas for up to 50 people each. No hookups. Picnic tables, food lockers, and fire grills are provided. Drinking water, restrooms with coin showers and flush toilets, an amphitheater, a picnic area, a summer convenience store, a visitors center, summer campfire programs, and firewood are available. A dump station operates May–October. No pets are allowed.

Reservations, fees: Reservations are accepted for groups only at 650/363-4021. Sites are $19 per vehicle per night, $8 per night for an additional vehicle. Group sites are $130 per night, plus $5 per vehicle per stay. Open year-round.

Directions: From Half Moon Bay at the junction of Highway 1 and Highway 92, drive south on Highway 1 for 18 miles to the Pescadero Road exit. Turn left (east) on Pescadero Road and drive about 10.5 miles to the park entrance on the right.

Contact: Memorial County Park, 650/879-0212 or 650/879-0238; San Mateo County Parks and Recreation, 650/363-4021, www.sanmateocountyparks.org.

13 PORTOLA REDWOODS STATE PARK

Scenic rating: 9

near Skyline Ridge

See map page 715

Portola Redwoods State Park is very secluded, since visitors are required to travel on an extremely slow and winding series of roads to reach it. The park features redwoods and a mixed evergreen and hardwood forest on the western slopes of the Santa Cruz Mountains, the headwaters of Pescadero Creek, and 18 miles of hiking trails. A literal highlight is a 300-foot-high redwood, one of the tallest trees in the Santa Cruz Mountains. In addition to redwoods, there are Douglas firs and live oaks, as well as a riparian zone along the stream. A four-mile hike links up to nearby Pescadero Creek County Park (which, in turn, borders Memorial County Park). At times in the summer, a low fog will move in along the San Mateo coast, and from lookouts near Skyline, visitors can peer to the west at what seems like a pearlescent sea with little islands (hilltops) poking through (this view is available from the access road, not from campsites). Wild pigs are occasionally spotted here, with larger numbers at neighboring Pescadero Creek County Park.

RV sites, facilities: There are 52 sites for tents or RVs up to 24 feet, four hike-in/bike-in sites, four walk-in sites, six hike-in backpack sites (three-mile hike), and four group sites for 25–50 people each. No hookups. Picnic tables, storage lockers, and fire grills are provided. Drinking water, restrooms with flush toilets and coin showers, and firewood are available. There are nature hikes and campfire programs scheduled on weekends from Memorial Day through Labor Day. The nearest gas is 13 miles away. Leashed pets are permitted on paved surfaces only.

Reservations, fees: Reservations are accepted at 800/444-PARK (800/444-7275) or www.reserveamerica.com ($7.50 reservation fee). Sites are $25 per night, $6 per night for an additional vehicle, $3 per person per night for hike-in/bike-in sites, $10 per person per night for walk-in sites and hike-in backpack sites, $111–224 per night for group sites. Open April–November.

Directions: From Palo Alto on I-280, turn west on Page Mill Road and drive (slow and twisty) to Skyline Boulevard/Highway 35. Cross Skyline and continue west on Alpine Road (very twisty) for about three miles to Portola State Park Road. Turn left on Portola State Park Road and drive about three miles to the park entrance at the end of the road.

Contact: Portola Redwoods State Park, 650/948-9098; Santa Cruz District, 831/335-6318, www.parks.ca.gov.

14 BUTANO STATE PARK

Scenic rating: 9

near Pescadero
See map page 714

The campground at Butano is in a canyon filled with a redwood forest, so pretty and with such good hiking that it has become popular enough to make reservations a must. The reason for its popularity is a series of exceptional hikes, including one to the Año Nuevo Lookout (well, the lookout is now blocked by trees, but there are glimpses of the ocean elsewhere along the way), Mill Ox Loop, and, for the ambitious, 11-mile Butano Rim Loop. The latter has a backpack camp with seven trail campsites (primitive with pit toilets available) requiring a 5.5-mile hike in the park's most remote area, where no drinking water is available. Creek water is within a half mile of the campsites; bring a water purifier.

RV sites, facilities: There are 20 sites for tents or RVs up to 24 feet (no hookups), 18 walk-in sites, and seven hike-in sites (5.5 miles, with pit toilets available). No hookups. Picnic tables, food lockers, and fire grills are provided. Drinking water and restrooms with flush toilets are available. Leashed pets are permitted in campsites, picnic areas, and on paved roads.

Reservations, fees: Reservations are accepted at 800/444-PARK (800/444-7275) or www.reserveamerica.com ($7.50 reservation fee). Sites are $25 per night, $10 per night for walk-in sites and hike-in trail sites, $6 per night for an additional vehicle. Note: Reservations are not available for hike-in trail sites and are available in summer only for walk-in sites. Open year-round.

Directions: Drive to Half Moon Bay and the junction of Highway 1 and Highway 92. Drive south on Highway 1 for 18 miles to the Pescadero Road exit and Pescadero Road. Turn left on Pescadero Road and drive three miles past the town of Pescadero to Cloverdale Road. Turn right and drive 4.5 miles to the park entrance on the left.

Contact: Butano State Park, 650/879-2040, fax 650/879-2173; California State Parks, Santa Cruz District, 831/335-6318, www.parks. ca.gov.

15 SANBORN-SKYLINE COUNTY PARK

Scenic rating: 8

near Saratoga
See map page 715

This is a pretty camp set in redwood forest, semiprimitive, but like a world in a different orbit compared to the asphalt of San Jose and the rest of the Santa Clara Valley. These campgrounds get heavy use on summer weekends, of course. This is headquarters for a 3,688-acre park that stretches from the foothills of Saratoga up to the Skyline Ridge in the Santa Cruz Mountains. Many hiking trails are available, including a trailhead at camp, in all 15 miles of trails. Most explore lush wooded slopes, with

CALIFORNIA

redwoods and tan oak. Dogs are prohibited from walk-in sites. Dogs are permitted, however, at the RV sites, the main park's grassy area, and day-use areas.

RV sites, facilities: There are 15 sites with full hookups (20 and 30 amps) for RVs up to 30 feet, a separate walk-in campground with 33 sites for tents, and a youth group area for up to 35 people. Picnic tables, food lockers, and fire pits are provided. Drinking water, restrooms with flush toilets and coin showers, a dump station, a seasonal youth science center, and a one-mile nature trail are available. Some facilities are wheelchair accessible. Leashed pets are permitted in the RV campground and picnic areas only.

Reservations, fees: Reservations are required ($6 reservation fee) at 408/355-2201. Sites are $25 per night for RV sites, $10 per night for walk-in, $25 for the youth group area for up to 35 people for the first night and then $10 per night. Check-in before sunset is required; gates are locked at dusk. Some credit cards accepted. RV sites open year-round, walk-in sites open April–mid-October.

Directions: From Highway 17 in San Jose, drive south for six miles to Highway 9/Saratoga Avenue. Turn west and drive to Saratoga, then continue on Highway 9 for two miles to Sanborn Road. Turn left and drive one mile to the park on the right. Walk-in sites require a 0.1- to 0.5-mile walk from the parking area.

Contact: Sanborn-Skyline County Park, 408/867-9959, www.parkhere.org.

16 BIG BASIN REDWOODS STATE PARK

Scenic rating: 10

near Santa Cruz

See map page 715

Big Basin is one of the best state parks in California, featuring giant redwoods near the park headquarters, secluded campsites set in forest, and rare opportunities to stay in a tent cabin or a backpacking trail site. The park covers more than 18,000 acres of redwoods, much of it old-growth, including forest behemoths more than 1,000 years old. It is a great park for hikers, with four waterfalls, making for stellar destinations. Sempervirens Falls, a long, narrow, silvery stream, is an easy 1.5-hour round-trip on Sequoia Trail. The famous Berry Creek Falls, a spectacular 70-foot cascade in a beautiful canyon, is framed by redwoods. For hikers in good condition, figure two hours (4.7 miles) to reach Berry Creek Falls, five hours for the round-trip in and out, and six hours for the complete loop (12 miles) that extends into the park's most remote areas. Other waterfalls include Silver Falls and Golden Falls. An easy nature loop trail near the park headquarters in the valley floor winds past several mammoth redwoods. This is California's oldest state park, established in 1902. It is home to the largest continuous stand of ancient coast redwoods south of Humboldt State Park in far Northern California. There are more than 80 miles of trails with elevations varying from 2,000 feet at the eastern Big Basin Rim on down to sea level. Rainfall averages 60 inches per year, most arriving December–mid-March.

RV sites, facilities: There are 31 sites for tents or RVs up to 27 feet or trailers up to 24 feet, 69 sites for tents only, 38 walk-in sites, 36 tent cabins (reservations required), two hike-in/bike-in sites, 52 hike-in campsites, and four group sites for 40–50 people. No hookups. Picnic tables, food lockers, and fire grills are provided. Drinking water, restrooms with flush toilets and coin showers, a dump station, firewood, and groceries are available. Some facilities are wheelchair accessible. Leashed pets are allowed in campsites and on paved roads only.

Reservations, fees: Reservations are accepted at 800/444-PARK (800/444-7275) or www.reserveamerica.com ($7.50 reservation fee). Sites are $25 per night for individual sites and walk-in sites, $6 per night for an additional vehicle, $10 per person for hike-in sites, $3 per person per night for hike-in/bike-in sites, $180–224 per night for group sites. Reserve tent cabins at 800/874-8368. Open year-round.

Directions: From Santa Cruz, turn north on Highway 9 and drive 12 miles to Boulder Creek and Highway 236 (signed Big Basin). Turn west on Highway 236 and drive nine miles to the park headquarters.

Contact: Big Basin Redwoods State Park, 831/338-8860 or 831/338-8861; Santa Cruz District, 831/335-6318, www.santacruzstateparks.org or www.parks.ca.gov.

17 HENRY W. COE STATE PARK

Scenic rating: 8

near Gilroy

See map page 715

This is the Bay Area's backyard wilderness, with 87,000 acres of wildlands, including a 23,300-acre wilderness area. There are more than 100 miles of ranch roads and 300 miles of hiking trails, a remarkable network that provides access to 140 ponds and small lakes, hidden streams, and a habitat that is paradise for fish, wildlife, and wild flora. The best camping introduction is at drive-in campsites at park headquarters, set at a hilltop at 2,600 feet that is ideal for stargazing and watching meteor showers. That provides a taste. If you like it, then come back for the full meal. It is the wilderness hike-in and bike-in sites where you will get the full flavor of the park. Before setting out for the outback, always consult with the rangers here—the ambitious plans of many hikers cause them to suffer dehydration and heatstroke. For wilderness trips, the best jump-off point is Coyote Creek or Hunting Hollow trailheads upstream of Coyote Reservoir near Gilroy. The park has excellent pond-style fishing but requires extremely long hikes (typically 10- to 25-mile round-trips) to reach the best lakes, including Mustang Pond, Jackrabbit Lake, Coit Lake, and Mississippi Lake. Expect hot weather in the summer; spring and early summer are the prime times. Even though the park may appear to be 120 square miles of oak foothills, the terrain is often steep, and making ridges often involves climbs of 1,500 feet. There are many great secrets to be discovered here, including Rooster Comb and Coyote Creek. At times on spring days, wild pigs seem to be everywhere. Golden eagles are also abundant. Bring a water purifier for hikes because there is no drinking water in the outback.

RV sites, facilities: There are 10 sites for tents and 10 sites for tents or RVs up to 24 feet. There are also eight equestrian campsites, 82 hike-in/bike-in sites, and 10 group sites for 10–50 people. No hookups. At the drive-in site at park headquarters, picnic tables and fire grills are provided. Drinking water and vault toilets are available. Leashed pets are permitted at the drive-in campgrounds only. At the horse camps, corrals and water troughs are available. At hike-in/bike-in sites, vault toilets are provided, but no drinking water is available. Garbage must be packed out at hike-in/bike-in camps.

Reservations, fees: Reservations are accepted at 800/444-PARK (800/444-7275) or www.reserveamerica.com ($7.50 reservation fee). Sites are $12 per night, $5 per night for an additional vehicle, $30 per night for group sites. No reservations are taken for hike-in/bike-in or horse sites; it's $14 per night for horse sites, $3 per person per night for hike-in/bike-in sites. For hike-in/bike-in or horse sites, a wilderness permit is required from park headquarters. Make reservations for group sites ($7.50 reservation fee) at 408/779-2728. Open year-round.

Directions: From Morgan Hill on U.S. 101, take the East Dunne Avenue exit. Turn east and drive 13 miles (including over the bridge at Anderson Lake, then very twisty and narrow) to the park entrance.

Contact: Henry W. Coe State Park, 408/779-2728, www.coepark.org or www.parks.ca.gov.

18 HENRY COWELL REDWOODS STATE PARK

Scenic rating: 8

near Santa Cruz

See map page 715

This is a redwood state park near Santa Cruz with good hiking, good views, and a chance

CALIFORNIA

of fishing in the winter for steelhead. The 1,750-acre park features a grove of old-growth redwoods, estimated at 1,400–1,800 years old, along with 20 miles of trails in the forest. One great easy hike is a 15-minute walk to a great lookout platform over Santa Cruz and the Pacific Ocean; the trailhead is near campsite 49. Another good hike is Eagle Creek Trail, a three-mile walk that heads along Eagle Creek and the San Lorenzo River, running through a classic redwood canyon. In winter, there is limited steelhead fishing in the San Lorenzo River. A side-trip option is taking the Roaring Camp Big Trees Railroad, which is adjacent to camp, 831/335-4400. Insider's tips: Poison oak is prevalent in this park and around the campground, so take precautions. Also, alcohol is prohibited in the campground but not in the day-use area.

RV sites, facilities: There are 111 sites for tents or RVs up to 35 feet (no hookups) and one hike-in/bike-in site. Picnic tables and fire grills are provided. Drinking water, restrooms with flush toilets and coin showers, and Wi-Fi are available. A nature center, bookstore, and picnic area are nearby. Some facilities are wheelchair accessible. Leashed pets are permitted and must be kept inside tents or vehicles at night.

Reservations, fees: Reservations accepted mid-March–October; reserve at 800/444-PARK (800/444-7275) or www.reserveamerica.com ($7.50 reservation fee). Sites are $25 per night (maximum of eight people), $3 per person per night for the hike-in/bike-in site. Open mid-February–November.

Directions: In Scotts Valley on Highway 17, take the Mount Hermon Road exit and drive west toward Felton to Lockwood Lane. Turn left on Lockwood Lane and drive about one mile to Graham Hill Road. Turn left on Graham Hill Road and drive 0.5 mile to the campground on the right.

Contact: Henry Cowell Redwoods State Park, 831/438-2396 or 831/335-4598, www.santacruzstateparks.org ow www.parks.ca.gov.

19 SANTA CRUZ RANCH RV PARK

Scenic rating: 5

near Scotts Valley

See map page 715

This camp is situated on 6.5 acres and is just a short hop from Santa Cruz and the shore of Monterey Bay. There are many side-trip options, making this a prime location for vacationers cruising the California coast. In Santa Cruz there are several quality restaurants, plus fishing trips and boat rentals at Santa Cruz Wharf, as well as the famous Santa Cruz Boardwalk and amusement park. Discount tickets for local attractions are available in the office. Note that most of the sites are filled with long-term renters; a few sites are set aside for overnight vacationers. Note: Some may remember this place as Carbonero Creek Trailer Park.

RV sites, facilities: There are 25 pull-through sites with full hookups (30 amps) for RVs up to 43 feet and five sites for tents. Picnic tables are provided. Restrooms have showers. Cable TV, a dump station, a coin laundry, free Wi-Fi and modem access, a recreation and meeting room, spa, and a seasonal heated swimming pool are available. No open fires. Leashed pets are permitted with approval.

Reservations, fees: Reservations are recommended. RV sites are $34–48 per night, tent sites are $26.10–29 per night, plus $2 per night for an additional vehicle. The first pet is free and a second pet is $1 per night. Weekly, monthly, and group rates are available. Some credit cards accepted. Open year-round.

Directions: From Santa Cruz, at the junction of Highways 1 and 17, turn north on Highway 17 and drive three miles to the Mount Hermon/Big Basin exit. Take that exit north onto Mount Hermon Road and drive 0.5 mile to Scotts Valley Drive. Turn right and drive 0.7 mile to Disc Drive. Turn right and continue to 917 Disc Drive on the left.

Contact: Santa Cruz Ranch RV Park, 831/438-1288 or 800/546-1288, fax 831/438-2877, www.santacruzranchrv.com.

20 COTILLION GARDENS RV PARK

Scenic rating: 6

near Santa Cruz

See map page 715

This is a pretty place with several possible side trips. It is on the edge of the Santa Cruz Mountain redwoods, near Henry Cowell Redwoods State Park and the San Lorenzo River. The Santa Cruz Beach and Boardwalk is only a few minutes' drive from the park, and Monterey is 45 miles away. Other side trips include the steam engine ride along the San Lorenzo River out of Roaring Camp Train Rides in Felton and visiting Loch Lomond Reservoir near Ben Lomond for hiking, boat rentals, or fishing. A golf course is nearby. There is a mix of overnighters and some long-term rentals at this park.

RV sites, facilities: There are 80 sites with full or partial hookups (30 amps) for RVs up to 36 feet, two sites for tents, and five camping cabins. One RV site is pull-through. Picnic tables and fire rings are provided. Restrooms have showers. A dump station, cable TV, modem access, recreation room, heated seasonal swimming pool, and a convenience store are available. Some facilities are wheelchair accessible. Leashed pets are permitted.

Reservations, fees: Reservations are recommended for RV sites but are not accepted for tent sites. RV sites are $41–45 per night, tent sites are $30 per night, plus $3 per person per night for more than two people. Call for cabin prices. Some credit cards accepted. Open year-round.

Directions: From Los Gatos, drive west on Highway 17 for 20 miles toward Santa Cruz to the Mount Hermon Road exit/Scotts Valley (second exit in Scotts Valley). Take the Mount Hermon Road exit to the stoplight at Mount Hermon Road. Turn right on Mount Hermon Road and drive 3.5 miles to Felton and Graham Hill Road (Y intersection). Bear right onto Graham Hill Road, immediately move to the left lane, and drive 50 feet to Highway 9. Turn left on Highway 9 and drive 1.5 miles to the park on the left.

Contact: Cotillion Gardens RV Park, 831/335-7669.

21 MOUNT MADONNA COUNTY PARK

Scenic rating: 7

between Watsonville and Gilroy

See map page 715

It's a twisty son-of-a-gun road to reach the top of Mount Madonna, but the views on clear days of Monterey Bay to the west and Santa Clara Valley to the east always make it worth the trip. In addition, a small herd of white deer are kept protected in a pen near the parking area for a rare chance to see unique wildlife. This 3,688-acre park is dominated by redwood forest, but at the lower slopes of Mount Madonna the landscape changes to oak woodland, dense chaparral, and grassy meadows. Ohlone Indians once lived here. There are many good hiking trails in the park; the best is Bayview Loop. The 20-mile trail system includes a one-mile self-guided nature trail. Elevation in the park reaches 1,896 feet. Free programs are offered at the amphitheater on Saturday evenings during the summer. Insider's notes: Campsite 105 at Valley View is the only pull-through site. While no credit cards are accepted in person, there is a self-pay machine that accepts credit cards, a nice touch. The campsites are dispersed throughout four campgrounds.

RV sites, facilities: There are 118 sites for tents or RVs up to 31 feet with partial hookups (30 amps) and two group areas for up to 240 people. Five youth group areas for 40–50 people each are also available; youth groups must have tax-exempt status. Picnic tables, food lockers, and fire pits are provided. Drinking water, restrooms with coin showers and flush toilets, a dump station, seasonal live music, an archery range, picnic areas, an amphitheater, and a visitors center are available. Some facilities are wheelchair accessible. Leashed pets are permitted.

Reservations, fees: Reservations are accepted ($6 reservation fee) at 408/355-2201. Sites are

$18–25 per night; it's $150–450 per night for group areas and $25 per night for youth group areas. Some credit cards accepted at self-serve machine. Open year-round.

Directions: From U.S. 101 in Gilroy, take the Hecker Pass Highway/Highway 152 exit west. Drive west seven miles to Pole Line Road and the park entrance on the right.

From Highway 1 in Watsonville, turn east onto Highway 152 and drive about 12 miles east to Pole Line Road and the park entrance on the left.

Contact: Mount Madonna County Park, 408/842-2341, fax 408/842-6642, www.park here.org.

22 COYOTE LAKE COUNTY PARK

Scenic rating: 7

near Gilroy

See map page 715

Coyote Lake is a pretty surprise to newcomers, a long, narrow lake set in a canyon just over the ridge east of U.S. 101. It covers 635 acres and is stocked with trout from late winter through spring; the lake also provides the top fishery for bass in the Bay Area. Other species are bluegill and crappie. Both power- and nonpowerboating are allowed, and the boat launch is one mile north of the visitors center. Swimming is prohibited. The campsites are within walking distance of the lake. The campground is nestled in oaks, among 796 acres of parkland,

furnishing some much-needed shade. There are no longer hiking trails along the lakeshore, but more than 13 miles of multi-use trails (horses and mountain bikes are allowed) are available. Note: If you continue east about four miles on the access road that runs past the lake to the Coe State Park Hunting Hollow entrance, you'll come to two outstanding trailheads (one at a parking area, one at the Coyote Creek gate) into that park's wildlands. Wildlife is abundant, including deer and wild turkey.

RV sites, facilities: There are 74 pull-through sites for tents or RVs up to 31 feet (no hookups). Picnic tables, food lockers, and fire pits are provided. Drinking water, flush toilets, and a boat ramp are available. A visitors center is also available. Some facilities are wheelchair accessible. Leashed pets are permitted.

Reservations, fees: Reservations are required ($6 reservation fee) at 408/355-2201. Sites are $10–18 per night, $6 per day for boat launching. Some credit cards accepted. Open year-round.

Directions: Drive on U.S. 101 to Gilroy and Leavesley Road. Take that exit and drive east on Leavesley Road for 1.75 miles to New Avenue. Turn left on New Avenue and drive 0.6 mile to Roop Road. Turn right on Roop Road and drive three miles to Coyote Reservoir Road. Turn left on Coyote Reservoir Road and drive to the campground.

Contact: Coyote Lake County Park, 408/842-7800, fax 408/842-6439, www.park here.org; Coyote Discount Bait and Tackle, 408/463-0711.

MONTEREY AND BIG SUR

☾ **BEST RV PARKS AND CAMPGROUNDS**

❰ **Coastal Sites**
Seacliff State Beach, page 734.

The scenic charm seems to extend to infinity from
the seaside towns of Santa Cruz, Monterey, and Big Sur. The primary
treasure is the coast, which is rock-strewn and sprinkled with inshore
kelp beds, where occasionally you can find sea otters playing Pop Goes
the Weasel. The sea here is a color like no other, often more of a tour-
maline than a straight green or blue.

From Carmel to Lucia alone, touring Big Sur on Highway 1 is one of the
most captivating drives anywhere. The inland strip along Highway 1 provides access to state parks, redwoods, coastal streams, Los Padres National
Forest, and the Ventana Wilderness. As you explore farther south on the
Pacific Coast Highway, you will discover a largely untouched coast.

Most vacations to this region include several must-do trips, often starting in Monterey with a visit to Fisherman's Wharf and its domesticated
sea lions, and then to the nearby Monterey Bay Aquarium.

From there, most head south to Big Sur to take in a few brush strokes
of nature's canvas, easily realizing why this area is beloved around the
world. At first glance, however, it's impossible not to want the whole
painting. That is where the campgrounds come in. They provide both
the ideal getaway and a launch point for adventure.

At Big Sur, the campgrounds are what many expect: small hideaways
in the big redwoods. Most are in a variety of settings, some near Big
Sur River, others in the forest.

Other good opportunities are available in Los Padres National Forest
and the adjacent Ventana Wilderness, which provides outstanding camping and hiking in the off-season, when the Sierra is buried in snow.

One note of caution: The state park campgrounds on Highway 1 are
among the most popular in North America. Reservations far in advance
are required all summer, even on weekdays. They are always the first
to fill on the state's reservation system. So get the game wired to get
your site.

During the summer, only the fog on the coast and the intense heat
just 10 miles inland keep this region from attaining perfection.

CALIFORNIA

Includes:

- Arroyo Seco River
- Big Sur
- Big Sur River
- Carmel River
- Fremont Peak State Park
- Hollister Hills State Vehicular Recreation Area
- Laguna Seca Recreation Area
- Limekiln State Park
- Los Padres National Forest
- McAlpine Lake and Park
- New Brighton State Beach
- Pfeiffer Big Sur State Park
- Pinnacles National Monument
- Pinto Lake Park
- San Juan Bautista
- Seacliff State Beach
- Sunset State Beach

CALIFORNIA

CALIFORNIA

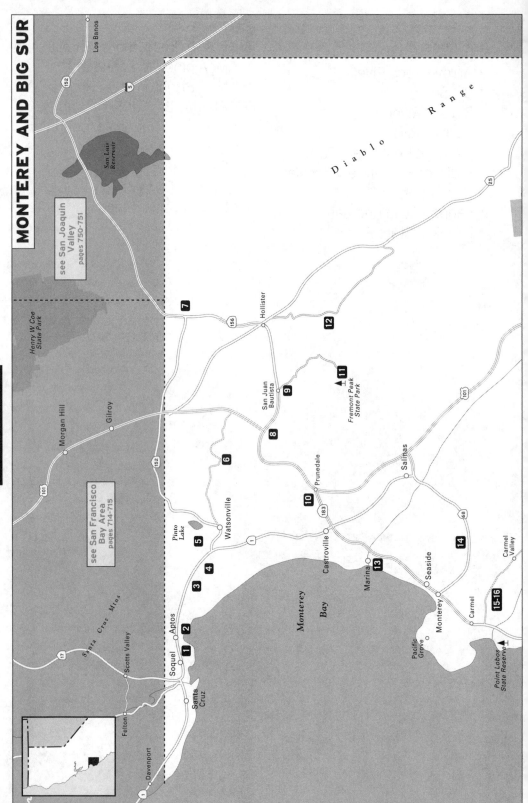

MONTEREY AND BIG SUR

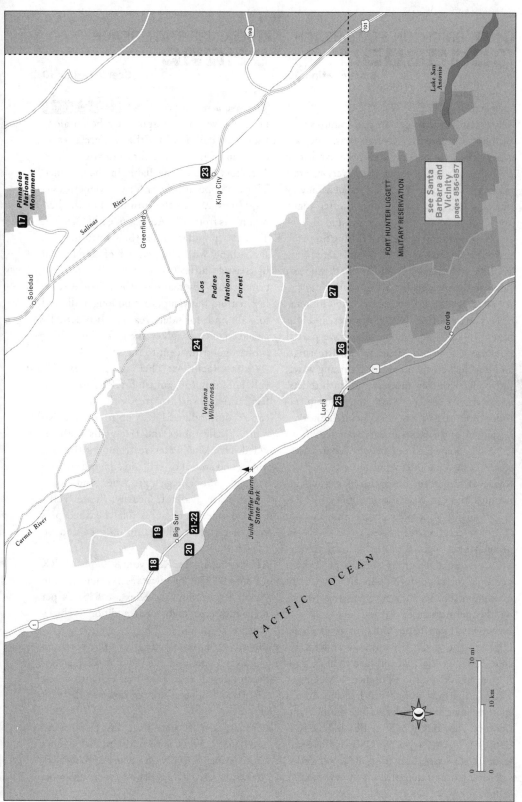

CALIFORNIA

Pinnacles National Monument

17

Salinas River

Soledad

Greenfield

King City **23**

Los Padres National Forest

24

27

26

Ventana Wilderness

Lucia **25**

FORT HUNTER LIGGETT MILITARY RESERVATION

Lake San Antonio

see Santa Barbara and Vicinity pages 856–857

Gorda

1

Carmel River

19 Big Sur

21-22

18 **20**

Julia Pfeiffer Burns State Park

1

PACIFIC OCEAN

10 mi

10 km

0   0

1 NEW BRIGHTON STATE BEACH

Scenic rating: 10

near Capitola

See map page 732

This is one in a series of state park camps set on the bluffs overlooking Monterey Bay. They are among the most popular and in-demand state campgrounds in California. Reservations are a necessity. This camp is near a forest of Monterey pine and live oak. The summer is often foggy and cool, especially in the morning. Beachcombing, swimming, and surf fishing for perch provide recreation options, and skiff rentals are available at the nearby Capitola Wharf. The San Lorenzo River enters the ocean nearby.

RV sites, facilities: There are 111 sites for tents or RVs up to 36 feet, three group sites, and four hike-in/bike-in sites. Some sites have partial hookups (30 amps). Picnic tables, fire rings, and food lockers are provided. Drinking water, restrooms with coin showers and flush toilets, and a visitors center are available. Dump stations, propane gas, groceries, a coin laundry, a restaurant, and a gas station are available within 2.5 miles. Some facilities are wheelchair accessible. Leashed pets are permitted.

Reservations, fees: Reservations are recommended and can be made at 800/444-PARK (800/444-7275) or www.reserveamerica.com ($7.50 reservation fee). Sites are $25–35 per night, $6 per night for an additional vehicle, $125 per night for group site, $5 per person per night for a hike-in/bike-in site. Two-night maximum stay per month. Open year-round, weather permitting.

Directions: From Santa Cruz, drive south on Highway 1 for about five miles to the Park Avenue exit. Take that exit and turn right on Park Avenue and drive a short distance to McGregor Drive (a four-way stop). Turn left and drive a short distance to the park entrance on the right.

Contact: New Brighton State Beach, 831/464-6330 or 831/464-6329; California State Parks, Santa Cruz District, 831/335-6318, www.santacruzstateparks.org or www.parks .ca.gov.

2 SEACLIFF STATE BEACH

Scenic rating: 10

near Santa Cruz

See map page 732

Here is a very pretty spot on a beach along Monterey Bay. Beach walks are great, especially on clear evenings for dramatic sunsets. A visitors center is available in the summer. This is a popular layover for vacationers touring Highway 1 in the summer, but the best weather is from mid-August to early October. This is a popular beach for swimming and sunbathing, with a long stretch of sand backed by coastal bluffs. A structure called the "old cement ship" by many nearby provides some fascination, but visitors are no longer allowed to walk on it for safety reasons. It is actually an old concrete freighter, the *Palo Alto*. Fishing is often good adjacent to the ship.

RV sites, facilities: There are 25 sites with full hookups (30 amps) for RVs up to 40 feet, and an overflow area with no hookups can accommodate 21 RVs up to 34 feet. No tents. Picnic tables and fire grills are provided. Drinking water, restrooms with flush toilets and coin showers, and a picnic area are available. Propane gas, groceries, and a coin laundry are available nearby. Some facilities are wheelchair accessible. Leashed pets are permitted in the camping area and on the beach.

Reservations, fees: Reserve at 800/444-PARK (800/444-7275) or www.reserveamerica.com ($7.50 reservation fee). Sites are $35–44 per night and $6 per night for an additional vehicle. Open year-round.

Directions: From Santa Cruz, drive south on Highway 1 about six miles to State Park Drive/ Seacliff Beach exit. Take that exit, turn west (right), and drive a short distance to the park entrance.

Contact: Seacliff State Beach, 831/685-6442 or 831/685-6500; California State Parks, Santa Cruz District, 831/429-2851, fax 831/429-2876, www.santacruzstateparks.org or www.parks .ca.gov.

CALIFORNIA

3 SANTA CRUZ KOA

Scenic rating: 8

near Watsonville

See map page 732

Bike rentals and nearby access to Manresa State Beach make this KOA campground a winner. The little log cabins are quite cute, and security is first class. It is a popular layover spot and weekend vacation destination. The only downer is the amount of asphalt.

RV sites, facilities: There are 180 sites, including five pull-through, with full or partial hookups (30 and 50 amps) for RVs up to 40 feet, six sites for tents only, 50 camping cabins, and three camping lodges. Picnic tables and fire grills are provided. Restrooms have showers. Two dump stations, free Wi-Fi, modem access, swimming pool, spa, a playground, two recreation rooms, bicycle rentals, miniature golf, a convenience store, and propane gas are available. Some facilities are wheelchair accessible. Leashed pets are permitted.

Reservations, fees: Reservations are advised by calling 800/562-7701. Sites are $51.70–104.50 per night, $3–6 per night per person for more than two people. Some credit cards accepted. Open year-round.

Directions: From Santa Cruz, drive 12 miles southeast on Highway 1. Take the San Andreas Road exit and head southwest for 3.5 miles to 1186 San Andreas Road.

Contact: Santa Cruz KOA, 831/722-0551, fax 831/722-0989, www.santacruzkoa.com or www.koa.com.

4 SUNSET STATE BEACH

Scenic rating: 9

near Watsonville

See map page 732

On clear evenings, the sunsets here look as if they are imported from Hawaii. The camp is on a bluff along Monterey Bay. While there are no ocean views from the campsites, the location makes for easy, short walks down to the beach for beautiful shoreline walks. The beachfront features pine trees, bluffs, and expansive sand dunes. The park is bordered by large agricultural fields. This area was once a good spot for clamming, but they've just about been fished out. The best weather is in late summer and fall. Spring can be windy here, and early summer is often foggy. Reservations are often needed well in advance to secure a spot.

RV sites, facilities: There are 90 sites for tents or RVs up to 31 feet (no hookups), one hike-in/bike-in site, and one group site for up to 50 people. Picnic tables, food lockers, and fire grills are provided. Drinking water, restrooms with flush toilets and coin showers, Wi-Fi, and firewood are available. Some facilities are wheelchair accessible. Leashed pets are permitted, except on the beach.

Reservations, fees: Reserve at 800/444-PARK (800/444-7275) or www.reserveamerica.com ($7.50 reservation fee). Sites are $25 per night, $6 per night for an additional vehicle, $5 per person per night for the hike-in/bike-in site, $224 per night for the group site. Open year-round.

Directions: From Highway 1 near Watsonville, take the Riverside Drive exit toward the ocean to Beach Road. Drive 3.5 miles on Beach Road to the San Andreas Road exit. Turn right on San Andreas Road and drive about three miles to Sunset Beach Road. Turn left and drive a short distance to the park entrance.

Contact: Sunset State Beach, 831/763-7063; California State Parks, Santa Cruz District, 831/335-6318, www.santacruzstateparks.org or www.parks.ca.gov.

5 PINTO LAKE PARK

Scenic rating: 7

near Watsonville

See map page 732

Pinto Lake can be a real find. Of the nine lakes in the nine Bay Area counties that offer camping, it is the only one where the RV campsites are actually near the lake. For the few who

CALIFORNIA

know about it, it's an offer that can't be refused. But note that no tent camping is permitted. The lake is best known as a fishing lake, with trout stocks and a small resident population of crappie and bluegill. Rainbow trout are stocked twice weekly in season. A 5-mph speed limit has been established for boaters, and no swimming or wading is permitted. The leash law for dogs is strictly enforced.

RV sites, facilities: There are 28 sites with full hookups (30 amps) for RVs of any length. No tents. Picnic tables, cable TV, and barbecues are provided. A boat ramp, boat rentals, volleyball, softball field, and horseshoes are available nearby in the summer. Leashed pets are permitted. Most facilities are wheelchair accessible. Open year-round.

Reservations, fees: Reservations are accepted. Sites are $25 per night, $2 per night per person for more than two people (children 12 and under are free), $2 per night for an additional vehicle, $2 per pet per night. Credit cards are not accepted.

Directions: From Santa Cruz, drive 17 miles south on Highway 1 to the exit for Watsonville/Gilroy-Highway 152. Take that exit onto Main Street, then immediately turn left on Green Valley Road and drive 2.7 miles (0.5 mile past Holohan intersection) to the entrance for the lake and campground on the left.

From Monterey, drive north on Highway 1 to the Green Valley Road exit. Take that exit and turn right at the Green Valley Road and drive 2.7 miles (0.5 mile past the Holohan intersection) to the entrance for the lake and campground.

Contact: Pinto Lake Park, City of Watsonville, 831/722-8129, www.pintolake.com.

6 McALPINE LAKE AND PARK

Scenic rating: 5

near San Juan Bautista
See map page 732

This is the only privately operated campground in the immediate region that has any spots for tenters. The camping cabins here look like miniature log cabins, quite cute and comfortable. In addition, the park has a 40-foot-deep lake stocked with trout, bass, bluegill, and catfish; no fishing license is required. The swimming pool was recently transformed into a trout-fishing pond. Other highlights of the park are its proximity to Mission San Juan Bautista and the relatively short drive to the Monterey-Carmel area.

RV sites, facilities: There are 27 sites for tents or RVs with partial hookups (30 amps), 14 sites with full hookups (30 amps) for RVs, 40 sites for tents only, and four cabins. Picnic tables and fire grills are provided. Restrooms have flush toilets and showers. A dump station, banquet facilities, a fishing pond, bait and tackle, gold panning, a coin laundry, propane gas, and groceries are available. Some facilities are wheelchair accessible. Leashed pets are permitted.

Reservations, fees: Reservations are accepted. Sites are $27–35 per night, $3–5 per person per night for more than two people, $5 per night for an additional vehicle. Some credit cards accepted. Open year-round.

Directions: On U.S. 101, drive to the Highway 129 exit. Take Highway 129 west and drive 100 feet to Searle Road (frontage road). Turn left onto Searle Road and drive to the stop sign at Anzar. Turn left again on Anzar and drive under the freeway to the park entrance on the left (900 Anzar Road).

Contact: McAlpine Lake and Park, 831/623-4263, fax 831/623-4559, www.mcalpinelake.com.

7 CASA DE FRUTA RV ORCHARD RESORT

Scenic rating: 3

near Pacheco Pass
See map page 732

This 80-acre RV park has a festival-like atmosphere to it, with country music and dancing every weekend in the summer and barbecues on Sunday. The resort is also busy during the Gilroy Garlic Festival in July and the Hollister

Independence Rally, a motorcycle event held nearby during the Fourth of July weekend. Huge, but sparse, San Luis Reservoir is 20 miles to the east.

RV sites, facilities: There are 300 sites with full hookups (30 amps) for RVs; some are pull-through. Tent sites are also available. Picnic tables are provided. Restrooms have flush toilets and showers. A dump station, satellite TV, a coin laundry, a playground, a swimming pool, a wading pool, an outdoor dance floor, horseshoes, volleyball courts, baseball diamonds, a wine- and cheese-tasting room, a candy factory, a bakery, a fruit stand, a 24-hour restaurant, a motel, a gift shop, a carousel, a narrow-gauge train ride through animal park, and a minimart are available. Some facilities are wheelchair accessible. Leashed pets are permitted.

Reservations, fees: Reservations are accepted at 800/548-3813. Sites are $30–36 per night, $2 per person per night for more than two people, $3 per pet per night. Some credit cards accepted. Open year-round.

Directions: Drive on U.S. 101 to the junction with Highway 152 (near Gilroy). Take Highway 152 east and drive 13 miles to Casa de Fruta Parkway. Take that exit and drive a short distance to the resort.

Contact: Casa de Fruta RV Orchard Resort, 408/842-9316 or 800/548-3813, www.casadefruta.com.

8 MONTEREY VACATION RV PARK

Scenic rating: 4

near San Juan Bautista
See map page 732

This RV park has an ideal location for many vacationers. It's a 10-minute drive to San Juan Bautista, 15 minutes to winery tours, 30 minutes to the Monterey Bay Aquarium, and 40 minutes to Monterey's Fisherman's Wharf and Cannery Row. It's set in an attractive spot with some trees, but the nearby attractions are what make it a clear winner. The park is next to the old stagecoach trail where Joaquin Murrieta,

the famous outlaw, once ambushed travelers. Note that about half of the sites are occupied by long-term renters.

RV sites, facilities: There are 88 sites with full hookups (30 amps) for RVs up to 40 feet; many are pull-through. No tents. Picnic tables and barbecues are provided at some sites. Restrooms have flush toilets and showers. Spa, swimming pool, a coin laundry, recreation halls, modem access (in office), and propane gas are available. Some facilities are wheelchair accessible. Leashed pets up to 40 pounds are permitted, with certain restrictions.

Reservations, fees: Reservations are recommended for three-day holiday weekends. Sites are $27–35 per night, $3 per person per night for more than two people, $1 per pet per night. Some credit cards accepted (except on discounts). Open year-round.

Directions: On U.S. 101, drive toward San Juan Bautista (between Gilroy and Salinas). The park is on U.S. 101 two miles south of the Highway 156/San Juan Bautista exit at 1400 Highway 101.

Contact: Monterey Vacation RV Park, 831/726-9118, fax 831/726-1841.

9 MISSION FARM RV PARK

Scenic rating: 4

near San Juan Bautista
See map page 732

The primary appeal of this RV park is that it is within easy walking distance of San Juan Bautista. The park is beside a walnut orchard. Golfing and fishing are nearby.

RV sites, facilities: There are 144 sites with full hookups (30 amps) for RVs up to 33 feet. No tents. Picnic tables are provided. Restrooms have flush toilets and showers. A barbecue area, cable TV, a coin laundry, and propane gas are available. Leashed pets are permitted; a dog run is available.

Reservations, fees: Reservations are recommended. Sites are $28–31 per night, $7 per person per night for more than two people,

$1–2 per pet per night. Monthly rates available. Some credit cards accepted. Open year-round.
Directions: From U.S. 101 near San Juan Bautista, drive three miles east on U.S. 101/Highway 156. Merge onto Highway 156 eastbound toward San Juan Bautista/Hollister and drive three miles to The Alameda. Turn right at The Alameda and drive one block to San Juan–Hollister Road. Turn left and drive 0.25 mile to the campground at 400 San Juan–Hollister Road.
Contact: Mission Farm RV Park, 831/623-4456.

10 CABANA HOLIDAY RV RESORT

Scenic rating: 3

near Salinas
See map page 732

If Big Sur, Monterey, and Carmel are packed, this spot provides some overflow space. This is the artichoke capital of the world. It's about a half-hour drive from the Monterey area.
RV sites, facilities: There are 79 sites with full or partial hookups (30 and 50 amps) for RVs up to 40 feet; some are pull-through. Limited space for tents is available, and 21 cabins can be rented. Picnic tables are provided. Restrooms have showers. A recreation room, a swimming pool (heated and open mid-May to mid-October), a playground, a clubhouse, a basketball court, and a coin laundry are available. Some facilities are wheelchair accessible. Leashed pets are permitted.
Reservations, fees: Reservations are recommended. RV sites are $45 per night and tent sites are $20 per night. Some credit cards accepted. Open year-round.
Directions: From Salinas, drive north on U.S. 101 for seven miles to Highway 156 westbound. Take the exit for Highway 156 westbound and drive over the overpass 0.2 mile to the Prunedale Road exit. Take that exit to Prunedale North Road. Turn right and drive a short distance to the campground entrance on the left.
Contact: Cabana Holiday RV Resort, 831/663-

2886 or 800/541-0085 (reservations), fax 831/663-1660, www.reynoldsresorts.com.

11 FREMONT PEAK STATE PARK

Scenic rating: 7

near San Juan Bautista
See map page 732

Most vacationers in this region are heading to Monterey Bay and the surrounding environs. That's why Fremont Peak State Park is missed by a lot of folks. It is on a ridge (2,900 feet) with great views of Monterey Bay available on the trail going up Fremont Peak (3,169 feet) in the Gavilan Range. An observatory with a 30-inch telescope at the park is open to the public on specified Saturday evenings. There are views of the San Benito Valley, Salinas Valley, and the Santa Lucia Mountains east of Big Sur. A picnic is held in the park each April to commemorate Captain John C. Fremont, his expeditions, and his raising of the U.S. flag in defiance of the Mexican government. Note: There is no access from this park to the adjacent Hollister Hills State Vehicular Recreation Area.
RV sites, facilities: There are 25 primitive sites for tents or RVs up to 25 feet (no hookups) and one group site for up to 50 people. Picnic tables and fire rings are provided. Drinking water and vault toilets are available. Some facilities are wheelchair accessible. Leashed pets are permitted.
Reservations, fees: Reservations are accepted at 800/444-PARK (800/444-7275) or www.reserveamerica.com ($7.50 reservation fee). Sites are $11–15 per night, $4 per night for an additional vehicle, $75 per night for group site. Open March–November.
Directions: From Highway 156 in San Juan Bautista, drive to San Juan Canyon Road. Turn south on San Juan Canyon Road (unsigned except for state park directional sign) and drive 11 miles (narrow, twisty, not recommended for vehicles longer than 25 feet) to the park.
Contact: Fremont Peak State Park, 831/623-4255; Monterey State Park District, Gavilan

Sector, 831/623-4526; observatory, 831/623-2465, www.parks.ca.gov.

12 HOLLISTER HILLS STATE VEHICULAR RECREATION AREA

Scenic rating: 4

near Hollister

See map page 732

This unique park was designed for off-highway-vehicle enthusiasts. It provides 80 miles of trails for motorcycles and 40 miles of trails for four-wheel-drive vehicles. Some of the trails are accessible directly from the campground. All trails close at sunset. Note that there is no direct access to Fremont Peak State Park, bordering directly to the west. Elevations at the park range 800–2,600 feet. Visitors are advised to always call in advance when planning a trip because the area is sometimes closed for special events. A sidelight is that a 288-acre area is set aside for hiking and mountain biking. In addition, a self-guided natural history walk is routed into Azalea Canyon and along the San Andreas Fault.

RV sites, facilities: There are four campgrounds with a total of 125 sites for tents or RVs of any length (no hookups) and group sites for up to 300 people. Picnic tables and fire rings are provided. Drinking water, restrooms with flush toilets and showers, and a camp store are available. Leashed pets are permitted.

Reservations, fees: Reservations are not accepted. Sites are $10 per night per vehicle. Call for group rates. Open year-round.

Directions: From Highway 156 west of Hollister, drive east to Union Road. Turn right (south) on Union Road and drive three miles to Cienega Road. Turn right (south) on Cienega Road and drive five miles to the park on the right.

Contact: Hollister Hills State Vehicular Recreation Area, 831/637-3874, District Office, 831/637-8186; Pit Stop, park store, 831/637-3138, www.parks.ca.gov.

13 MARINA DUNES RV PARK

Scenic rating: 4

near Monterey Bay

See map page 732

This is a popular park for RV cruisers who are touring Highway 1 and want a layover spot near Monterey. This place fills the bill, open all year and in Marina, just a short drive from the many side-trip opportunities available in Monterey and Carmel. It is set in the sand dunes, about 300 yards from the ocean. Horseback riding, boat rentals, and golfing are nearby.

RV sites, facilities: There are 65 sites for RVs of any length, most with full hookups (30 and 50 amps), and 10 sites for tents. Picnic tables and barbecue grills are provided, and some sites have fireplaces. Restrooms have showers. Drinking water, a coin laundry, cable TV, Wi-Fi, modem access, a recreation room, a playground, a meeting room, a picnic area, RV supplies, a gift shop, and propane are available. Some facilities are wheelchair accessible. Leashed pets are permitted.

Reservations, fees: Reservations are recommended. Sites are $45–65 per night, $5 per night for an additional vehicle. Some credit cards accepted. Open year-round.

Directions: From Highway 1 in Marina, drive to the Reservation Road exit. Take that exit and drive west a short distance to Dunes Drive. Turn right on Dunes Drive and drive to the end of the road and the park entrance on the right.

Contact: Marina Dunes RV Park, 831/384-6914, fax 831/384-0285, www.marinadunesrv.com.

14 LAGUNA SECA RECREATION AREA

Scenic rating: 5

near Monterey

See map page 732

This campground is just minutes away from the sights in Monterey and Carmel. It is situated in oak woodlands overlooking the world-famous Laguna Seca Raceway. There are three separate camping areas.

RV sites, facilities: There are 172 sites for tents or RV up to 40 feet; most sites have partial hookups (30 amps). A large overflow area is also available for RVs and tents. Picnic tables and fire pits are provided. Restrooms have showers. A dump station, pond, rifle and pistol range, clubhouse, and group camping and meeting facilities are available. Some facilities are wheelchair accessible. Leashed pets are permitted.

Reservations, fees: Reservations are accepted at 831/755-4895 or 888/588-2267 ($5 reservation fee). Sites are $22–30 per night, $10 per night for an additional vehicle, $2 per pet per night. Some credit cards accepted. Open year-round.

Directions: From Monterey and Highway 101, drive east on Highway 68 for 6.5 miles to the park entrance on the left.

Contact: Laguna Seca Recreation Area, 831/758-3604, fax 831/758-6818, www.co.monterey.ca.us/parks.

15 CARMEL BY THE RIVER RV PARK

Scenic rating: 8

on the Carmel River
See map page 732

Location, location, location. That's what vacationers want. Well, this park is on the Carmel River, minutes away from Carmel, Cannery Row, the Monterey Bay Aquarium, golf courses, and the beach. Each RV site is separated by hedges and flowers.

RV sites, facilities: There are 35 sites with full hookups (50 amps) for RVs of any length. No tents. Restrooms have showers. Cable TV, Wi-Fi, modem access (in office), a recreational cabana, a game room with pool tables, a barbecue area, and river access are available. A convenience store, a coin laundry, and propane gas are nearby. Some facilities are wheelchair accessible. Leashed pets are permitted.

Reservations, fees: Reservations are accepted for two or more nights. Sites are $56 per night, $2–3 per person per night for more than two people, $3 per night for an additional vehicle, $3 per pet per night. Open year-round.

Directions: In Carmel on Highway 1 drive to Carmel Valley Road. Take Carmel Valley Road southeast and drive 4.5 miles to Schulte Road. Turn right and drive to the end of the road (27680 Schulte Road in Carmel).

Contact: Carmel by the River RV Park, 831/624-9329, fax 831/624-8416, www.carmelrv.com.

16 SADDLE MOUNTAIN RV PARK AND CAMPGROUND

Scenic rating: 6

near the Carmel River
See map page 732

This pretty park is about 100 yards from the Carmel River amid a grove of oak trees. The park offers hiking trails, and if you want to make a buyer's swing into Carmel, it's only a five-mile drive. Note: The Carmel River is reduced to a trickle most of the year.

RV sites, facilities: There are 25 sites with full hookups (30 amps) for RVs up to 40 feet and 25 tent sites. Picnic tables, food lockers, cable TV, Wi-Fi, and fire grills are provided. Restrooms have flush toilets and showers. A seasonal swimming pool, a playground, horseshoe pits, a basketball court, and a game room are nearby. Some facilities are wheelchair accessible. Leashed pets are permitted in the RV area only; check for current status of pet policy for campground.

Reservations, fees: Reservations are accepted for weekends only. Sites are $30–50 per night, $5 per person per night for more than two people, $5 per night for an additional vehicle. Group rates available. Open year-round.

Directions: In Carmel on Highway 1 drive to Carmel Valley Road. Take Carmel Valley Road southeast and drive 4.5 miles to Schulte Road. Turn right and drive to the park at the end of the road.

Contact: Saddle Mountain RV Park and Campground, 831/624-1617, www.saddlemountaincamping.com.

17 PINNACLES CAMPGROUND

Scenic rating: 7

near Pinnacles National Monument

See map page 733

This is the only camp at the Pinnacles National Monument, where there are more than 30 miles of hiking trails and two sets of talus caves. The jagged pinnacles for which the park was named were formed by the erosion of an ancient volcanic eruption and are popular for rock climbing. The Pinnacles National Monument is like a different planet, and condors can sometimes be seen flying in the monument and over the campground. It's a 24,000-acre park with volcanic clusters and strange caves, all great for exploring. This is a popular place for astronomy buffs, and ranger-led dark sky viewings are available occasionally. Campfire programs are held in the amphitheater most of the year. If you are planning to stay a weekend in the spring, arrive early on Friday evening to be sure you get a campsite. In the summer, beware of temperatures in the 90s and 100s. Also note that caves can be closed to access; always check with rangers. Note that a ban on wood fires is in effect. Duraflame logs are permitted as a substitute.

RV sites, facilities: There are 103 sites for tents, 36 sites with partial hookups (30 amps) for RVs, and 13 group sites. Picnic tables and fire grills are provided. Drinking water, restrooms with flush toilets and coin showers, a dump station, an amphitheater, a convenience store, and a swimming pool are available. Some facilities are wheelchair accessible. Although discouraged, leashed pets are permitted, except on trails.

Reservations, fees: Reservations ($7 reservation fee) are available by phone (limited hours and days) and by website; they're required for group sites. RV sites are $15–40 per person per night, tent sites are $10–35 per night, plus $5 per night for an additional vehicle and $3 per pet per stay. It's $7.50 per person per night with a $75 minimum for a group site. Some credit cards accepted. Open year-round, weather permitting.

Directions: From Hollister, drive south on Highway 25 for 32 miles to Highway 146 west (signed for Pinnacles). Take Highway 146 and drive 2.5 miles to the campground.

Contact: Pinnacles Campground, 831/389-4462, www.pinncamp.com.

18 BIG SUR CAMPGROUND AND CABINS

Scenic rating: 8

on the Big Sur River

See map page 733

This camp is in the redwoods near the Big Sur River. Campers can stay in the redwoods, hike on great trails through the forest at nearby state parks, or explore nearby Pfeiffer Beach. Nearby Los Padres National Forest and Ventana Wilderness in the mountains to the east provide access to remote hiking trails with ridge-top vistas. Cruising Highway 1 south to Lucia and back offers endless views of breathtaking coastal scenery.

RV sites, facilities: There are 40 sites with partial hookups (20 and 30 amps) for RVs up to 36 feet, 40 sites for tents or RVs (no hookups), 15 cabins, and four tent cabins. Picnic tables and fire grills are provided. Restrooms have flush toilets and showers. Drinking water, a dump station, a playground, basketball, inner tube rentals, a convenience store, and a coin laundry are available. Some facilities are wheelchair accessible. Leashed pets are permitted at campsites. No pets in cabins.

Reservations, fees: Reservations are recommended. Sites are $30 per night, $4 per night for RV hookups, $4 per person per night for more than two people, $8 per night for an additional vehicle, $4 per pet per night. Some credit cards accepted. Open year-round.

Directions: From Carmel, drive 25 miles south on Highway 1 to the campground on the right side of the road (two miles north of the state park).

Contact: Big Sur Campground and Cabins, 831/667-2322.

CALIFORNIA

19 PFEIFFER BIG SUR STATE PARK

Scenic rating: 10

in Big Sur

See map page 733

This stretch of coast is one of the most beautiful anywhere. Pfeiffer Big Sur is one of the most popular state parks in California, and it's easy to see why. You can have it all: fantastic coastal vistas along Highway 1, redwood forests and waterfalls in the Julia Pfeiffer Burns State Park (11.5 miles to the south), expansive beaches with elusive sea otters playing on the edge of kelp beds in the Andrew Molera State Park (4.5 miles north), great restaurants such as Ventana Inn (a few miles south), and private, patrolled sites. Reservations are a necessity. Some campsites in this park are along the Big Sur River. The park features 800 acres of redwoods, conifers, oaks, sycamores, cottonwoods, maples, alders, and willows, plus open meadows—just about everything, in other words. Wildlife includes raccoons, skunk, deer, squirrels, occasional bobcats and mountain lions, and many birds, among them water ouzels and belted kingfishers. Wild boars are spotted infrequently. A number of loop trails provide spectacular views of the Pacific Ocean and the Big Sur Gorge. Big Sur Lodge is within the park.

RV sites, facilities: There are 218 sites for tents or RVs up to 32 feet and trailers up to 27 feet, two hike-in or bike-in sites, and two group sites for up to 35 people. Picnic tables and fire grills are provided. Restrooms have flush toilets and showers. Wi-Fi and drinking water are available. Groceries, a café, and propane gas are available nearby. Some facilities are wheelchair accessible. Leashed pets are permitted in the campground only.

Reservations, fees: Reservations are accepted at 800/444-PARK (800/444-7275) or www.reserveamerica.com ($7.50 reservation fee). Sites are $20–35 per night, $8 per night for an additional vehicle, $75 per night for group sites, $3 per person per night for hike-in/bike-in sites. Open year-round.

Directions: From Carmel, drive 26 miles south on Highway 1 to the park on the left (east side of highway).

Contact: Pfeiffer Big Sur State Park, 831/667-2315, fax 831/667-2886; California State Parks, Monterey District, 831/649-2836, www.parks.ca.gov.

20 RIVERSIDE CAMPGROUND AND CABINS

Scenic rating: 8

on the Big Sur River

See map page 733

This is one in a series of privately operated camps designed for Highway 1 cruisers touring the Big Sur area. This camp is set amid redwoods. Side trips include expansive beaches with sea otters playing on the edge of kelp beds (Andrew Molera State Park), redwood forests and waterfalls (Julia Pfeiffer Burns State Park), and several quality restaurants, including Nepenthe for those on a budget and the Ventana Inn for those who can light cigars with $100 bills.

RV sites, facilities: There are 45 sites for tents or RVs up to 40 feet; 14 sites have partial hookups (20 amps). Cabins are also available. Picnic tables and fire pits are provided. Restrooms have coin showers. A coin laundry and firewood are available. A store is nearby. Leashed pets are permitted at campsites.

Reservations, fees: Reservations are recommended. Sites are $30 per night, $5 per person per night for more than two people, $10 per night for an additional vehicle, $5 per pet per night. Some credit cards accepted. Open April–October.

Directions: From Carmel, drive 22 miles south on Highway 1 to the campground on the right.

Contact: Riverside Campground and Cabins, tel./fax 831/667-2414, www.riverside campground.com.

21 FERNWOOD PARK

Scenic rating: 7

on the Big Sur River
See map page 733

This RV park is on the banks of the Big Sur River in the redwoods of the beautiful Big Sur coast. Many of the sites are set along the river. There also are eight tent cabins. A highlight is that there is live music on Saturday nights in season. You can crown your trip with a dinner at the Ventana Inn (first-class—bring your bank with you). The park is adjacent to Pfeiffer Big Sur State Park.

RV sites, facilities: There are 13 sites for tents only, 31 sites with partial hookups (30 amps) for RVs up to 36 feet, 11 tent cabins, and a motel. Fire grills and picnic tables are provided. Restrooms have showers. A grocery store, a restaurant, and a bar are available. Leashed pets are permitted.

Reservations, fees: Reservations are accepted. Sites are $27–30 per night, $5 per person per night for more than two people (maximum of six), $5 per night for an additional vehicle, $5 per pet per night. Tent cabins are $60 per night, plus $10 per person per night for more than two people. Discounts available in off-season. Some credit cards accepted. Open year-round.

Directions: From Carmel, drive 26 miles south on Highway 1 to the campground on the right.

Contact: Fernwood Park, 831/667-2422, fax 831/667-2663, www.fernwoodbigsur.com.

22 VENTANA CAMPGROUND

Scenic rating: 10

in Big Sur
See map page 733

This rustic camp has wooded sites and is in an ideal location for many. The campsites are private and extremely beautiful, set in the redwoods with a small creek running through camp, with a few small waterfalls nearby. Premium side trips are available, highlighted by the beautiful beach at Andrew Molera State Park (a one-mile hike is necessary), the majestic redwoods, a creek hike, and a bluff-top waterfall in Julia Pfeiffer Burns State Park.

RV sites, facilities: There are 20 sites for tents or RVs up to 22 feet (no hookups) and 60 tent sites. Picnic tables and fire rings are provided. A restroom with showers and flush toilets is available. A small store is nearby with firewood and ice. Some facilities are wheelchair accessible. Leashed pets are permitted.

Reservations, fees: Reservations are accepted by telephone or website. Sites are $29–35 per night, $5 per person per night for more than two people, $5 per night for an additional vehicle, $5 per pet per night. A three-day minimum stay is required on holidays. Some credit cards accepted. Open March–October.

Directions: From Carmel, drive 30 miles south on Highway 1 to Big Sur and the campground entrance on the left, 0.5 mile past the post office.

Contact: Ventana Campground, 831/667-2712, www.ventanacampground.com.

23 SAN LORENZO COUNTY PARK

Scenic rating: 3

in King City
See map page 733

A lot of folks cruising up and down the state on U.S. 101 can underestimate their travel time and find themselves caught out near King City, a small city about midpoint between Northern and Southern California. Well, don't sweat it, because San Lorenzo County Park offers a spot to overnight. It's set near the Salinas River, which isn't exactly the Mississippi, but it'll do. A museum complex captures the rural agricultural life of the valley. The park covers 200 acres, featuring playgrounds and ball fields.

RV sites, facilities: There are 99 sites for tents or RVs of any length with full or partial hookups (30 amps); some sites are pull-through. Picnic tables and fire pits are provided. A dump station, restrooms with flush toilets and showers, a picnic area, a coin laundry, meeting facilities,

CALIFORNIA

playgrounds, horseshoes, volleyball, softball fields, a walking trail, and computer kiosks are available. Some facilities are wheelchair accessible. Leashed pets are permitted.

Reservations, fees: Reservations are accepted ($5 reservation fee) at 831/385-5964. Sites are $18–27 per night, $10 per night for an additional vehicle, $2 per pet per night. Off-season and group rates available. Open year-round.

Directions: From King City on U.S. 101, take the Broadway exit, turn onto Broadway, and drive to the park at 1160 Broadway.

Contact: San Lorenzo County Park, 831/385-5964, www.co.monterey.ca.us/parks.

24 ARROYO SECO

Scenic rating: 8

along Arroyo Seco River in Los Padres National Forest

See map page 733

This pretty spot near Arroyo Seco River is just outside the northern border of the Ventana Wilderness. The elevation is 900 feet. Arroyo Seco Group Camp is available to keep the pressure off this campground.

RV sites, facilities: There are 49 sites for tents or RVs up to 26 feet, plus a group site for 25–50 people. Picnic tables and fire grills are provided. Drinking water, restrooms with flush toilets and coin showers, and a dump station are available. Leashed pets are permitted.

Reservations, fees: Reservations are accepted for individual sites and required for group sites at 877/444-6777 ($9 reservation fee) or www.ReserveUSA.com. Sites are $20 per night, $5 per night for an additional vehicle, $50 per night for the group site. Open year-round.

Directions: Drive on U.S. 101 to the town of Greenfield and the Arroyo Seco Road/Elm Avenue exit. Turn west on Elm Avenue/Road G16 and drive six miles to Arroyo Seco Road. Turn left and drive 6.5 miles to Carmel Valley Road. Turn right and drive 3.5 miles to the campground.

Contact: Los Padres National Forest, Monterey

Ranger District, 831/385-5434, fax 831/385-0628; Rocky Mountain Recreation Company, 831/674-5726.

25 KIRK CREEK

Scenic rating: 8

near the Pacific Ocean in Los Padres National Forest

See map page 733

This pretty camp is along Kirk Creek as it empties into the Pacific Ocean. There is beach access through a footpath. Another trail from camp branches north through the Ventana Wilderness, which is sprinkled with little-used, hike-in, backcountry campsites. For gorgeous scenery without all the work, a quaint little café in Lucia provides open-air dining on a cliff-top deck, with a dramatic sweeping lookout over the coast.

RV sites, facilities: There are 33 sites for tents or RVs up to 30 feet (no hookups). Picnic tables and fire grills are provided. Drinking water and flush toilets are available. Leashed pets are permitted.

Reservations, fees: Reservations are not accepted. Sites are $20 per night. Open year-round.

Directions: From Monterey, drive south on Highway 1 to Lucia. From Lucia, continue south on Highway 1 for four miles to the campground on the right.

Contact: Parks Management Company, 805/434-1996, fax 805/434-1986; Los Padres National Forest, Monterey Ranger District, 831/385-5434, fax 831/385-0628.

26 LIMEKILN STATE PARK

Scenic rating: 9

south of Big Sur on the Pacific Ocean

See map page 733

Limekiln State Park provides breathtaking views of the Big Sur Coast. This camp provides a great layover spot in the Big Sur area of Highway 1, with drive-in campsites set up both near the beach and the redwoods—take your pick. Several hiking trails are nearby, including one that is routed past some historic lime kilns, which were used in the late 1800s to make cement and bricks. Want more? A short rock hop on a spur trail (just off the main trail) leads to dramatic 100-foot Limekiln Falls, a gorgeous waterfall. This camp was originally called Limekiln Beach Redwoods and was privately operated. It became a state park in 1995. One remaining problem: Parking is limited.

RV sites, facilities: There are 18 sites for tents or RVs up to 24 feet (no hookups) and trailers up to 15 feet, plus 10 sites for tents. Picnic tables and fire grills are provided. Drinking water, restrooms with showers and flush toilets, and firewood are available. Leashed pets are allowed, except on trails.

Reservations, fees: Reservations are accepted ($7.50 reservation fee) at 800/444-PARK (800/444-7275) or www.reserveamerica.com. Sites are $20–25 per night, $6 per night for an additional vehicle. Some credit cards are accepted for reservations but not at the park. Open year-round, weather and road conditions permitting.

Directions: From Big Sur, drive south on Highway 1 for 32 miles (past Lucia) to the park on the left.

Contact: Limekiln State Park, 831/667-2403; California State Parks, Monterey District, 831/649-2836, www.parks.ca.gov.

27 PONDEROSA

Scenic rating: 4

in Los Padres National Forest

See map page 733

As soon as you turn off Highway 1, you leave behind the crowds and enter a land that is largely unknown to people. This camp is at 1,500 feet elevation in Los Padres National Forest, not far from the border of the Ventana Wilderness (good hiking and backpacking) and the Hunter Liggett Military Reservation (wild-pig hunting is allowed there with a permit). It is one in a series of small camps on Nacimiento-Ferguson Road.

RV sites, facilities: There are 23 sites for tents or RVs up to 35 feet. Picnic tables and fire grills are provided. Vault toilets and drinking water are available. Leashed pets are permitted.

Reservations, fees: Reservations are not accepted. Sites are $15 per night. Open year-round.

Directions: From Monterey, drive south on Highway 1 to Lucia. From Lucia, continue south on Highway 1 for four miles to Nacimiento-Ferguson Road. Turn left on Nacimiento-Ferguson Road and drive about 12 miles to the campground on the right.

Contact: Parks Management Company, 805/434-1996, fax 805/434-1986, www.campone.com; Los Padres National Forest, Monterey Ranger District, 831/385-5434, fax 831/385-0628.

CALIFORNIA

SAN JOAQUIN VALLEY

The San Joaquin Valley is noted for its searing

weather all summer long. But that is also when the lakes in the foothills become something like a Garden of Eden for boating and water-sports enthusiasts. The region also offers many settings in the Sierra foothills, which can serve as launch points for short drives into the alpine beauty of Yosemite, Sequoia, and Kings Canyon National Parks.

Most of the campgrounds in this region are family oriented. Many of them are on access roads to Yosemite. A bonus is that most have lower prices than their counterparts in the park, and as I said, are more hospitable to children.

The lakes are the primary recreation attraction, with the refreshing, clean water revered as a tonic against the valley heat all summer long. When viewed from the air, the closeness of these lakes to the Sierra Nevada mountain range is surprising to many. Their proximity to the high country results in cool, high-quality water – the product of snowmelt sent down river canyons on the western slope. Some of these lakes are among the best around for waterskiing and powerboat recreation, including Lake Don Pedro east of Modesto and Lake McClure near Merced.

In addition, Lake Don Pedro, Pine Flat Reservoir, and Lake Kaweah are among the best fishing lakes in the entire Central Valley; some anglers rate Don Pedro as the number-one all-around fishing lake in the state. The nearby Sierra rivers that feed these lakes (and others) also offer the opportunity to fly-fish for trout. In particular, the Kaweah and Kings Rivers boast many miles of ideal pocket water for fly fishers. Although the trout on these streams are only occasionally large, the catch rates are often high, and the rock-strewn beauty of the river canyons is exceptional.

CALIFORNIA

Includes:

- Bagby Recreation Area
- Barrett Cove Recreation Area
- Buena Vista Aquatic Recreation Area
- Caswell Memorial State Park
- Codorniz Recreation Area
- Colonel Allensworth State Historic Park
- Eastman Lake
- Hensley Lake
- Kern National Wildlife Refuge
- Lake Don Pedro
- Lake McClure
- Lake McSwain Recreation Area
- Lake Tulloch
- McClure Point Recreation Area
- McConnell State Recreation Area
- McSwain Dam
- Merced River
- Millerton Lake State Recreation Area
- San Joaquin River
- Stanislaus National Forest
- Stanislaus River
- Turlock Lake State Recreation Area

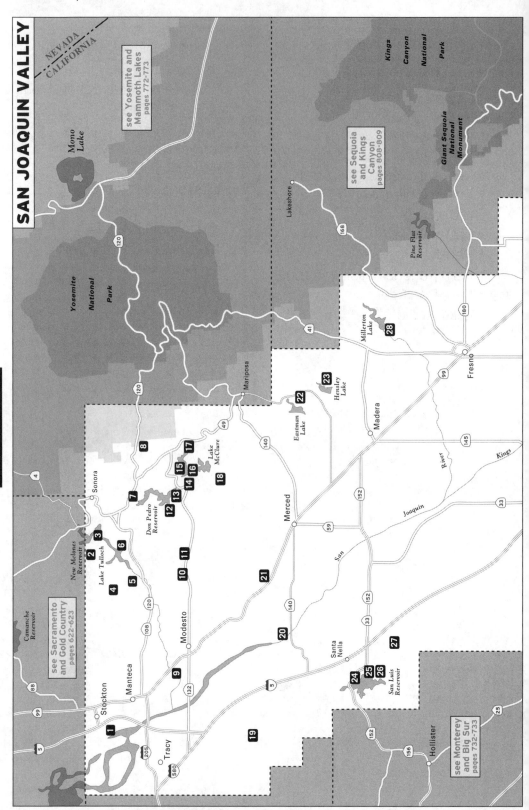

CALIFORNIA

SAN JOAQUIN VALLEY

NEVADA
CALIFORNIA

see Yosemite and Mammoth Lakes
pages 772-773

Kings Canyon National Park

see Sequoia and Kings Canyon
pages 808-809

Giant Sequoia National Monument

Mono Lake

120

Yosemite National Park

Lakeshore

168

Pine Flat Reservoir

180

Millerton Lake
28

41

Fresno

99

120

Mariposa

8

17
15 **16**
14
13
12
7

49

Lake McClure

18

140

22

Eastman Lake

23

Hensley Lake

Madera

145

Sonora

4

New Melones Reservoir

Lake Tulloch

2 **3**
6

4 **5**

Don Pedro Reservoir

120

108

11
10

59

Merced

Kings River

33

San Joaquin

152

Comanche Reservoir

see Sacramento and Gold Country
pages 622-623

Manteca

Modesto

132

9

88

99

Stockton

1

5

205

Tracy

580

20

21

140

152

33

Santa Nella

27

24 **25**
26

San Luis Reservoir

19

152

156

Hollister

25

see Monterey and Big Sur
pages 732-733

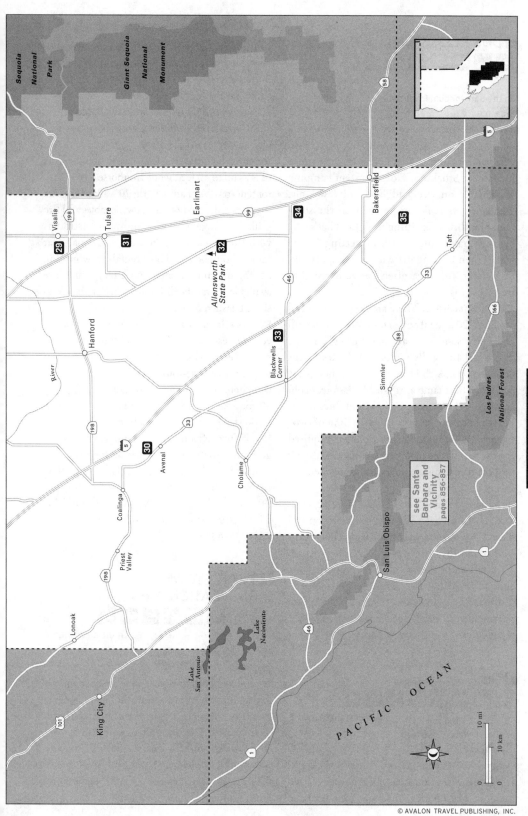

Sequoia National Park

Giant Sequoia National Monument

CALIFORNIA

58
5

Earlimart
Tulare
Visalia
198
99
34
Bakersfield
35

29
31
32
46
Taft
33

Allensworth State Park

Hanford

33
Blackwells Corner
58
Simmler
166

River

Los Padres National Forest

198
30
Avenal
33
Cholame

5

Coalinga

see Santa Barbara and Vicinity pages 856-857

Priest Valley
198
San Luis Obispo
1

Lonoak

Lake Nacimiento
46

Lake San Antonio

King City
101

PACIFIC OCEAN

1

10 mi
10 km
0
0

© AVALON TRAVEL PUBLISHING, INC.

CALIFORNIA

1 DOS REIS COUNTY PARK

Scenic rating: 6

on the San Joaquin River near Stockton

See map page 750

This is a nine-acre county park that has a quarter mile of San Joaquin River frontage, a boat ramp, and nearby access to the eastern Delta near Stockton. Note that tent camping is available on weekends and holidays only. The sun gets scalding hot here in the summer, branding everything in sight. That's why boaters make quick work of getting in the water, then cooling off with water sports. In the winter, this area often has zero visibility from tule fog.

RV sites, facilities: There are 26 sites with full hookups (20 and 30 amps) for RVs of any length and tents; some sites are pull-through. Picnic tables and fire grills are provided. Restrooms have showers. A children's play area, horseshoe pits, and a boat ramp are available. A store, a coin laundry, and propane gas are within three miles. Leashed pets are permitted with a limit of two.

Reservations, fees: Reservations are required at least two weeks in advance. Sites are $20 per night, $10 per night for an additional vehicle, $1 per pet per night. Open year-round.

Directions: From I-5 and Stockton, drive south to the Lathrop exit. Turn west on Lathrop and drive 1.5 blocks to Manthy Road. Turn north (right) and drive 0.5 mile to Dos Reis Road. Turn left and drive to the campground at the end of the road.

Contact: San Joaquin County Parks Department, 209/953-8800 or 209/331-7400, www.co.san-joaquin.ca.us/parks.

2 GLORY HOLE

Scenic rating: 7

at New Melones Reservoir

See map page 750

Glory Hole encompasses both Big Oak and Ironhorse campgrounds. This is one of two major recreation areas on New Melones Lake in the Sierra Nevada foothills, a popular spot with a boat ramp nearby for access to outstanding waterskiing and fishing. (See the listing in this chapter for *Tuttletown Recreation Area*.) Campfire programs are often available at the amphitheater in summer. Camps hosts are usually on-site year-round.

RV sites, facilities: Big Oak has 55 sites for tents or RVs up to 40 feet, while Ironhorse has 89 sites for tents or RVs of any length; 20 walk-in sites are for tents only. No hookups. Picnic tables and fire grills are provided. Drinking water, restrooms with flush toilets and showers, a marina, boat ramps, houseboat and boat rentals, a swimming beach, an amphitheater, and a playground are available. Some facilities are wheelchair accessible. Leashed pets are permitted.

Reservations, fees: Reservations are accepted (no reservation fee) at 877/444-6777 or www.ReserveUSA.com. Sites are $12–16 per night. Open year-round.

Directions: From Sonora, drive north on Highway 49 for about 15 miles (Glory Hole Market will be on the left side of the road) to Whittle Ranch Road. Turn left and drive five miles to the campground, with sites on both sides of the road.

Contact: U.S. Bureau of Reclamation, New Melones Visitor Center, 209/536-9094, fax 209/536-9652; New Melones Lake Marina, 209/785-3300; Glory Hole Sports, 209/736-4333.

3 TUTTLETOWN RECREATION AREA

Scenic rating: 7

at New Melones Reservoir

See map page 750

Here is a mammoth camping area set on the giant New Melones Lake in the Sierra Nevada foothills, a beautiful sight when the lake is full. The lake is set in the valley foothills between the historic mining towns of Angels Camp and Sonora. New Melones is established as one of California's top recreation lakes. All water sports are permitted. Waterskiing and houseboating are particularly popular. Tuttletown encompasses three campgrounds (Acorn, Manzanita, and Chamise) and two group camping areas (Oak Knoll and Fiddleneck). New Melones is a huge reservoir that covers 12,500 acres and offers more than 100 miles of shoreline and good fishing. The elevation is 1,085 feet. A boat ramp is near camp. Although the lake's main body is huge, the better fishing is well up the lake's Stanislaus River arm (for trout) and in its coves (for bass and bluegill), where there are submerged trees providing perfect aquatic habitat. Trolling for kokanee salmon also has become popular. The lake level often drops dramatically in the fall.

RV sites, facilities: At Acorn there are 69 sites for tents or RVs of any length and at Manzanita there are 55 sites for tents or RVs of any length and 13 walk-in tent sites. The Oak Knoll group site holds up to 80 people; Fiddleneck group site holds up to 48 people. No hookups. Picnic tables and fire grills are provided. Drinking water, restrooms with flush toilets and showers, a dump station, a playground, and a boat ramp are available. Some facilities are wheelchair accessible. Leashed pets are permitted.

Reservations, fees: Reservations are accepted (no reservation fee) at 877/444-6777 or www.ReserveUSA.com. Sites are $12–16 per night, and the group fee is $128–160 per night. Open year-round.

Directions: From Sonora, drive north on Highway 49 to Reynolds Ferry Road. Turn left and drive about two miles to the entrance road to the campgrounds.

Contact: U.S. Bureau of Reclamation, New Melones Visitor Center, 209/536-9094, fax 209/536-9652.

▣ WOODWARD RESERVOIR COUNTY PARK

Scenic rating: 7

near Oakdale

See map page 750

This is one of the best sailing lakes in Northern California. Regattas are held throughout the year, and it is also very popular for sailboarding. Woodward's nickname, in fact, is "Windward Reservoir." Woodward Reservoir is a large lake covering 2,900 acres with 23 miles of shoreline, set in the rolling foothills just north of Oakdale. It is a good lake for both waterskiing and fishing, with minimal conflict between the two sports. All boating is allowed, and the speedboats have the main lake body to let her rip. Trout fishing has improved and they are stocked here in winter. Bass fishing has been slow the past several years. Note that because this is one of the largest reservoirs near Modesto and Stockton, it gets lots of local traffic, especially on summer weekends. There are equestrian facilities at this park, and horse camping is permitted in undeveloped sites only.

RV sites, facilities: There are 155 sites for RVs or tents, 114 with partial hookups and four with full hookups (30 amps). Picnic tables and fire grills are provided. Drinking water is available intermittently; check for current status. Restrooms have flush toilets and showers. A dump station, picnic shelter, three boat ramps, dry boat storage, and some equestrian facilities are available. Some facilities are wheelchair accessible. Leashed pets are permitted.

Reservations, fees: Reservations are not accepted. Sites are $15–23 per night per vehicle, $3 per pet per night, $2 per horse per night. There's a $7 per day boat-launch fee. Holiday rates are higher. Open year-round.

Directions: Drive on Highway 120 to Oakdale (the road becomes Highway 108/120) and the junction with County Road J14/26 Mile Road. Turn left on 26 Mile Road and drive four miles to the park entrance at Woodward Reservoir (14528 26 Mile Road).

Contact: Woodward Reservoir County Park, 209/847-3304; Stanislaus County Parks, 209/525-6750, www.co.stanislaus.ca.us/ER/PARKS/Parks.htm; Woodward Marina, 209/847-3129.

CALIFORNIA

CALIFORNIA

5 THE RIVER'S EDGE

Scenic rating: 7

on the Stanislaus River

See map page 750

New owners bought this place and changed the name from Knights Ferry Resort. This is a privately run campground in the small historic town of Knights Ferry. The campground has a good number of trees. A nice touch is a restaurant overlooking the Stanislaus River. Side trips include tours of the covered bridge ("the longest west of the Mississippi") and several historic buildings and homes, all within walking distance of the park. River access and hiking trails are available at the east end of town. Two runs are available: the Goodwin Canyon Run, which is exciting, even scary and challenging, and the Knights Ferry Run, an easy float. Raft and canoe rentals are also available nearby. This resort is popular with rafters and canoeists.

RV sites, facilities: There are 14 sites for tents or RVs up to 40 feet with partial hookups (30 amps). A community fire pit, restrooms with showers, and a restaurant are available. No pets permitted.

Reservations, fees: Reservations are required with a deposit. Sites are $35 per night. Some credit cards accepted. Open April–October.

Directions: From Oakdale, drive east on Highway 108 for approximately 12 miles to Knight's Ferry and Kennedy Road. Turn left and drive to a bridge, cross the bridge, and continue a short distance to Sonora Road/Main Street. Turn left and drive to the campground entrance at the River's Edge Restaurant.

Contact: The River's Edge, 209/881-3349.

6 LAKE TULLOCH RV CAMPGROUND AND MARINA

Scenic rating: 7

on the south shore of Lake Tulloch

See map page 750

This camp features tons of waterfront on Lake Tulloch, a dispersed tent area, and cabins with direct beach access. Unlike so many reservoirs in the foothill country, this one is nearly always full of water. In addition, it is a place where anglers and water-skiers live in harmony. That is because of the many coves and a six-mile-long arm with an enforced 5-mph speed limit. It's a big lake, shaped like a giant X with extended lake arms adding up to 55 miles of shoreline. The campground features mature oak trees that provide shade to most of the developed sites. A secret at Tulloch is that fishing is also good for crawdads. The elevation is 500 feet.

RV sites, facilities: There are 130 sites, including 31 boat sites and 72 with full or partial hookups (30 and 50 amps) for tents or RVs up to 40 feet, a large area for lakefront tent camping and self-contained RVs, and 10 waterfront cabins. Picnic tables and fire grills are provided. Drinking water, restrooms with flush toilets and showers, a coin laundry, a convenience store, a dump station, a playground, a restaurant, volleyball, horseshoes, tetherball, table tennis, swimming beach, a marina, boat rentals, boat slips, fuel dock, and a boat launch are available. Some facilities are wheelchair accessible. Leashed pets are permitted.

Reservations, fees: Reservations are accepted. The fee is $20–30 per night, $12 per night for an additional vehicle, and $1 per pet per night. Group rates are available. Boat launch fee is $5 per day. Some credit cards accepted. Open year-round.

Directions: From Manteca, drive east on Highway 120 (it becomes Highway 108/120) to Oakdale. Continue east for 13 miles to Tulloch Road on the left. Turn left and drive 4.6 miles to the campground entrance and gatehouse at the south shore of Lake Tulloch.

Contact: Lake Tulloch RV Campground and Marina, 209/881-0107 or 800/894-2267, www .laketullochcampground.com.

7 MOCCASIN POINT

Scenic rating: 7

at Lake Don Pedro

See map page 750

This camp is at the northeastern end of Lake Don Pedro, adjacent to a boat ramp. Moccasin Point juts well into the lake, directly across from where the major Tuolumne River arm enters the lake. Don Pedro is a giant lake, with extended lake arms and nearly 13,000 surface acres and 160 miles of shoreline. It is one of the best boating and recreation lakes in California, but it's subject to drawdowns from midsummer through early fall. At different times, fishing is excellent for salmon, trout, or bass. Other species are redear sunfish, catfish, crappie, and bluegill. Houseboating and boat-in camping (bring sunscreen) provide options. The elevation is 800 feet.

RV sites, facilities: There are 50 sites for tents, 18 sites with full hookups (20 and 30 amps) for RVs of any length, and an overflow camping area. Some sites are pull-through. Picnic tables, food lockers, and barbecue units are provided at all sites. Drinking water, restrooms with showers, a dump station, group picnic area, a fish-cleaning station, propane gas, ice, a small store, a boat ramp, motorboat and houseboat rentals, fuel, moorings, and bait and tackle are available. Ground fires are prohibited. Some facilities are wheelchair accessible.

Reservations, fees: Reservations are accepted for a minimum of two nights, or three nights on holidays. Reservations can be made with a $6 reservation fee by telephone or website. Sites are $19–26 per night, $6 per night for an additional vehicle. Boat launching is $6 per day. Some credit cards accepted. Open year-round.

Directions: From Manteca, drive east on Highway 120 (it becomes Highway 108/120) for 30 miles to the Highway 120/Yosemite exit. Bear right on Highway 120 and drive 11 miles to Jacksonville Road. Turn left on Jacksonville Road and drive a short distance to the campground on the right.

Contact: Don Pedro Recreation Agency, 209/852-2396; Moccasin Point Marina, 209/989-2206, www.donpedrolake.com.

8 THE PINES

Scenic rating: 4

in Stanislaus National Forest

See map page 750

The Pines camp is at 3,200 feet in elevation on the western edge of Stanislaus National Forest, only a half mile from the Groveland District Office and about five miles from the Tuolumne River. A Forest Service road is routed south of camp for two miles, climbing to Smith Peak Lookout (3,877 feet) and providing sweeping views to the west of the San Joaquin Valley foothills.

RV sites, facilities: There are 11 sites for tents or RVs up to 22 feet (no hookups), along with two group sites for up to 50 people each. Picnic tables and fire grills are provided. Drinking water and vault toilets are available. A convenience store is nearby. Leashed pets are permitted.

Reservations, fees: Reservations are required for the group sites only at 877/444-6777 ($9 reservation fee) or www.ReserveUSA.com. Sites are $12 per night, $65 per night for group site. Open late April–October, weather permitting.

Directions: From Groveland, drive east on Highway 120 for nine miles (about a mile past the County Road J132 turnoff) to the signed campground entrance road on the right. Turn right onto the campground entrance road and drive a short distance to the camp.

Contact: Stanislaus National Forest, Groveland Ranger District, 209/962-7825, fax 209/962-7412.

9 CASWELL MEMORIAL STATE PARK

Scenic rating: 7

on the Stanislaus River near Stockton

See map page 750

Caswell Memorial State Park features shoreline frontage along the Stanislaus River, along with an additional 250 acres of parkland. The Stanislaus provides shoreline fishing for catfish

CALIFORNIA

on summer nights. Bass and crappie are also occasionally caught. Other recreation options include an interpretive nature trail and swimming. Bird-watching is popular; look for red-shouldered and red-tail hawks. During warm months, bring mosquito repellent.

RV sites, facilities: There are 64 sites for tents or RVs up to 24 feet and one group site for up to 50 people. No hookups. Picnic tables, food lockers, and fire grills are provided. Drinking water, flush toilets, showers, firewood, a swimming beach, and nature trails are available. Weekend interpretive programs and junior ranger programs are available in the summer. Some facilities are wheelchair accessible. Leashed pets are permitted.

Reservations, fees: Reservations are accepted for the summer with a $7.50 reservation fee at 800/444-PARK (800/444-7275) or www.reserveamerica.com. Sites are $20 per night plus $6 per night for an additional vehicle; groups with up to 12 vehicles pay $110 per night. Open year-round.

Directions: Drive on Highway 99 to Austin Road (1.5 miles south of Manteca). Turn south on Austin Road and drive four miles to the park entrance at the end of the road.

Contact: Caswell Memorial State Park, 209/599-3810; California State Parks, Four Rivers Sector, 209/826-1197, fax 209/826-0284, www.parks.ca.gov.

10 MODESTO RESERVOIR REGIONAL PARK

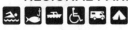

Scenic rating: 7

on Modesto Reservoir

See map page 750

Modesto Reservoir is a big lake, at 2,800 acres with 31 miles of shoreline, set in the hot foothill country. That's good because it is a popular place in the summer. Waterskiing is excellent in the main lake body. Sandy swimming beaches are available, and swimming is popular. Anglers head to the southern shore of the lake, which is loaded with submerged trees and coves and

is also protected by a 5-mph speed limit. Fishing for bass is good, though the fish are often small. Wildlife-viewing is good, and waterfowl hunting is available in season. The elevation is 200 feet.

RV sites, facilities: There are 145 sites for RVs up to 36 feet with full hookups (30 amps) and 36 tent sites. Picnic tables and fire grills are provided. Drinking water, restrooms with flush toilets and showers, a dump station, two boat ramps, a store, a snack bar, propane, gas, an archery range, and a radio-controlled glider field are available. No gas cans are permitted. Some facilities are wheelchair accessible.

Reservations, fees: Reservations are not accepted. Sites are $15–23 per night, $2 surcharge per vehicle on holidays. Boat launching is $7 per day. Open year-round.

Directions: From Modesto, drive east on Highway 132 for 16 miles past Waterford to Reservoir Road. Turn left and drive to the campground at 18143 Reservoir Road.

Contact: Modesto Reservoir Regional Park, 209/525-6750, fax 209/525-6773; Modesto Marina, 209/874-1340, www.co.stanislaus.ca.us/ER/PARKS/Parks.htm.

11 TURLOCK LAKE STATE RECREATION AREA

Scenic rating: 6

east of Modesto

See map page 750

This campground is on the shady south shore of the Tuolumne River, about one mile from Turlock Lake. Turlock Lake warms to 65–74°F in the summer, cooler than many Central Valley reservoirs, since the water entering this lake is released from the bottom of Don Pedro Reservoir. It often seems just right for boating and all water sports on hot summer days. The lake covers 3,500 surface acres and offers 26 miles of shoreline. A boat ramp is available near the camp, making it ideal for boaters/campers. Bass fishing is fair in the summer. In the late winter and spring, the lake is quite cold, fed by snowmelt from the Tuolumne River. Trout fishing is good year-round as a result. The elevation is 250 feet. The park is bordered by ranches, orchards, and mining tailings along the river.

RV sites, facilities: There are 48 sites for tents or RVs up to 27 feet (no hookups), 15 sites for tents, and one hike-in/bike-in site. Picnic tables, fire grills, and food lockers are provided. Drinking water and restrooms with flush toilets and coin showers are available. A swimming beach and boat ramp are nearby. The boat facilities are wheelchair accessible. Leashed pets are permitted.

Reservations, fees: Reservations are accepted ($7.50 reservation fee) at 800/444-PARK (800/444-7275) or www.reserveamerica.com. Sites are $20 per night, $6 per night for an additional vehicle, $5 per person per night for the hike-in/bike-in site. Boat launching is $6 per day. Open year-round.

Directions: From Modesto, drive east on Highway 132 for 14 miles to Waterford, then continue eight miles on Highway 132 to Roberts Ferry Road. Turn right (south) and drive one mile to Lake Road. Turn left and drive two miles to the campground on the left.

Contact: Turlock Lake State Recreation Area, 209/874-2056 or 209/874-2008, www.parks.ca.gov.

12 BLUE OAKS

Scenic rating: 7

at Lake Don Pedro

See map page 750

Blue Oaks is between the dam at Lake Don Pedro and Fleming Meadows. The on-site boat ramp to the east is a big plus. (See the listings in this chapter for *Fleming Meadows* and *Moccasin Point* for more information.)

RV sites, facilities: There are 195 sites for tents or RVs of any length; some sites have partial hookups (20 and 30 amps), and one is pull-through. Group camping is available. Picnic tables, food lockers, and barbecue units are provided. Drinking water, restrooms with

flush toilets and showers, a boat launch, fish-cleaning stations, and a dump station are available. A store, a coin laundry, and propane gas are nearby at Fleming Meadows Marina. No ground fires are permitted. Some facilities are wheelchair accessible.

Reservations, fees: Reservations are accepted ($6 reservation fee) by telephone or website (there's two-night minimum; it's three nights on holidays). Sites are $19–23 per night, $6 per night for an additional vehicle; the group fee is $200 per night. Boat launching is $6 per day. Some credit cards accepted. Open Memorial Day weekend–Labor Day weekend.

Directions: From Manteca, take Highway 120 east to Oakdale (the road becomes Highway 120/108). Continue east on Highway 108 for 20 miles to La Grange Road/J59 (signed for Don Pedro Reservoir). Turn right on La Grange Road and drive 10 miles to Bonds Flat Road. Turn left on Bonds Flat Road and drive 0.5 mile to the campground on the left.

Contact: Don Pedro Recreation Area, 209/852-2396, www.donpedrolake.com.

13 FLEMING MEADOWS

Scenic rating: 7

on Lake Don Pedro

See map page 750

Fleming Meadows is on the shore of Lake Don Pedro, just east of the dam. A boat ramp is available in the campground on the southeast side of the dam. A sandy beach and concession stand are here. This is a big camp at the foot of a giant lake, where hot weather, warm water, waterskiing, and bass fishing make for weekend vacations. Don Pedro has many extended lake arms, providing 160 miles of shoreline and nearly 13,000 surface acres when full. (See the listing in this chapter for *Moccasin Point* for more information.)

RV sites, facilities: There are 172 sites for tents or RVs of any length, including 50 walk-in sites for tents, and 90 sites with full hookups (20 and 30 amps) for RVs. A few sites are pull-through.

CALIFORNIA

Picnic tables, food lockers, and barbecues are provided. Drinking water, restrooms with flush toilets and showers, and a dump station are available. A coin laundry, store, ice, a snack bar, group picnic areas, a restaurant, a swimming lagoon, an amphitheater, a softball field, volleyball, bait and tackle, motorboat and houseboat rentals, a boat ramp, mooring, boat storage, engine repairs, and propane gas are nearby. Ground fires are prohibited. Some facilities are wheelchair accessible.

Reservations, fees: Reservations are accepted ($6 reservation fee) with a two-night minimum (a three-night minimum on holidays). Sites are $19–26 per night, $6 per night for an additional vehicle. Boat launching is $6 per day. Some credit cards accepted. Open year-round.

Directions: From Manteca, take Highway 120 east to Oakdale (the road becomes Highway 120/108). Continue east on Highway 108 for 20 miles to La Grange Road/J59 (signed Don Pedro Reservoir). Turn right on La Grange Road and drive 10 miles to Bonds Flat Road. Turn left on Bonds Flat Road and drive 2.5 miles to the campground on the left.

Contact: Don Pedro Recreation Area, 209/852-2396; Lake Don Pedro Marina, 209/852-2369, www.donpedrolake.com.

14 BARRETT COVE RECREATION AREA

Scenic rating: 7

on Lake McClure

See map page 750

Lake McClure is shaped like a giant horseshoe, with its lake arms providing 82 miles of shoreline. The lake is popular for water sports, including skiing, wakeboarding, houseboating, and fishing. Although swimming is not prohibited in the lake, you'll rarely see people swimming or playing along the shore, mainly because of the typically steep dropoffs. This camp is on the left side of the horseshoe; that is, on the western shore, within a park that provides a good boat ramp. This is the largest

in a series of camps on Lake McClure. (See the listings in this chapter for *Lake McClure/Horseshoe Bend Recreation Area, McClure Point Recreation Area,* and *Bagby Recreation Area* for more information.)

RV sites, facilities: There are 275 sites for tents or RVs of any length, including 89 with full hookups (30 amps). Picnic tables and barbecues are provided. Restrooms have showers. Boat ramps, a dump station, a swimming lagoon, and a playground are available. A convenience store, a coin laundry, a marina, picnic areas, fish-cleaning stations, boat and houseboat rentals, and propane gas are also available on-site. Some facilities are wheelchair accessible. Leashed pets are permitted.

Reservations, fees: Reservations are accepted ($6 reservation fee) at 800/468-8889. Sites are $16–25 per night, $6–19 per night for an additional vehicle, $3 per pet per night. Boat launching is $6 per day. Some credit cards accepted. Open year-round.

Directions: From Modesto, drive east on Highway 132 for 31 miles to La Grange and then continue for about eight miles (toward Coulterville) to Merced Falls Road. Turn right and drive three miles to the campground entrance on the left. Turn left and drive a mile to the campground on the left side of the road.

Contact: Barrett Cove Recreation Area, 209/378-2611; Merced Irrigation District, 209/378-2521, fax 209/378-2519, www.lakemcclure.com.

15 LAKE McCLURE/HORSESHOE BEND RECREATION AREA

Scenic rating: 7

on Lake McClure

See map page 750

Lake McClure is a unique, horseshoe-shaped lake in the foothill country west of Yosemite. It adjoins smaller Lake McSwain, connected by the Merced River. McClure is shaped like a giant horseshoe, with its lake arms providing 82 miles of shoreline, warm water for waterskiing, and fishing for bass (on the left or west half of the horseshoe near Cotton Creek) and for trout (on the right or east half of the horseshoe). There is a boat launch adjacent to the campground. It's one of four lakes in the immediate area; the others are Don Pedro Reservoir to the north and Modesto Reservoir and Turlock Lake to the west. The elevation is 900 feet.

RV sites, facilities: There are 110 sites for tents or RVs of any length, including 35 with partial hookups (30 amps). Picnic tables and barbecues are provided. Restrooms have showers. A dump station, a boat ramp, fish-cleaning stations, picnic areas, a swimming lagoon, a store, and a coin laundry are available. Some facilities are wheelchair accessible. Leashed pets are permitted.

Reservations, fees: Reservations are accepted ($6 reservation fee) at 800/468-8889. Sites are $16–25 per night, $6–19 per night for an additional vehicle, $3 per pet per night. Boat launching is $6 per day. Some credit cards accepted. Open year-round.

Directions: From Modesto, drive east on Highway 132 for 31 miles to La Grange and then continue for about 17 miles (toward Coulterville) to the north end of Lake McClure and the campground entrance road on the right side of the road. Turn right and drive 0.5 mile to the campground.

Contact: Horseshoe Bend Recreation Area, 209/878-3452; Merced Irrigation District, 209/378-2521, www.lakemcclure.com.

16 McCLURE POINT RECREATION AREA

Scenic rating: 7

on Lake McClure

See map page 750

McClure Point Recreation Area is the campground of choice for campers/boaters coming from the Turlock and Merced areas. It is a well-developed facility with an excellent boat ramp that provides access to the main body of Lake McClure. This is the best spot on the lake for waterskiing.

RV sites, facilities: There are 100 sites for tents or RVs up to 40 feet; 52 sites have partial hookups (30 amps). Picnic tables and barbecues are provided. Restrooms have showers. Boat ramps, boat rentals, a marina, fish-cleaning stations, picnic areas, a swimming lagoon, and a coin laundry are available. A store is nearby. Leashed pets are permitted.

Reservations, fees: Reservations are accepted ($6 reservation fee) at 800/468-8889. Sites are $19–25 per night, $3 per pet per night. Boat launching is $6 per day. Open year-round.

Directions: From Turlock, drive east on County Road J16 for 19 miles to the junction with Highway 59. Continue east on Highway 59/County Road J16 for 4.5 miles to Snelling and bear right at Lake McClure Road. Drive approximately two miles to Lake McSwain Dam and continue for seven miles to the campground at the end of the road.

Contact: McClure Point and Bagby Recreation Area, 209/378-2521, fax 209/378-2519, www.lakemcclure.com.

17 BAGBY RECREATION AREA

Scenic rating: 7

on upper Lake McClure

See map page 750

This is the most distant and secluded camp on Lake McClure. It is near the Merced River as it enters the lake, way up adjacent to the Highway 49 Bridge, nearly an hour's drive from the dam. Trout fishing is good in the area, and it makes sense; when the lake heats up in summer, the trout naturally congregate near the cool incoming flows of the Merced River.

RV sites, facilities: There are 30 sites for tents or RVs of any length, including 10 with partial hookups (30 amps). Drinking water, restrooms with flush toilets and coin showers, picnic areas, fish-cleaning stations, and a boat ramp are available. Leashed pets are permitted.

Reservations, fees: Reservations are accepted ($6 reservation fee) at 800/468-8889. Sites are $19–25 per night, $6–19 per night for an

CALIFORNIA

additional vehicle, $3 per pet per night. Boat launching is $6 per day. Open year-round.

Directions: From Turlock, drive east on County Road J16 for 19 miles to the junction with Highway 59. Continue east on Highway 59/ County Road J16 for 4.5 miles to Snelling and Merced Falls Road (continue straight, well signed). Drive 0.5 mile to Hornitos Road. Turn right and drive eight miles (drive over the bridge) to Hornitos to a Y. Bear left at the Y in Hornitos (signed to Highway 49) and drive 10 miles to Highway 49. Turn left on Highway 49 and drive eight miles to the Bagby Bridge and entrance kiosk on the right.

Contact: McClure Point and Bagby Recreation Area, 209/378-2521, fax 209/378-2519, www.lakemcclure.com.

18 LAKE McSWAIN RECREATION AREA

Scenic rating: 7

near McSwain Dam on the Merced River

See map page 750

Lake McSwain is actually the afterbay for adjacent Lake McClure, and this camp is near the McSwain Dam on the Merced River. Even though McClure and McSwain sit beside each other, each has its own identity. McSwain is low-key with a 10-mph speed limit. If you have a canoe or car-top boat, this lake is preferable to Lake McClure because waterskiing is not allowed. In terms of size, McSwain is like a puddle compared to the giant McClure, but unlike McClure, the water levels are kept up almost year-round at McSwain. The water is cold, and trout stocks are good in the spring. The lake is used primarily by anglers, and several fishing derbies are held here each year. The shoreline is favorable for swimming, and there is even a good sandy beach. Note: The best access sites for large RVs are the pull-through sites in the G Loop.

RV sites, facilities: There are 99 sites for tents or RVs up to 40 feet, including 65 with partial hookups (30 amps). Picnic tables, barbecues,

and electrical connections are provided. Drinking water, a dump station, restrooms with showers, a boat ramp, boat rentals, a coin laundry, and a playground are available. A convenience store, a marina, a snack bar, fish-cleaning stations, a picnic area, and propane gas are available nearby. Leashed pets are permitted.

Reservations, fees: Reservations are accepted with a $6 reservation fee at 800/468-8889. Sites are $19–25 per night, $3 per pet per night. Boat launching is $6 per day. Open year-round.

Directions: From Turlock, drive east on County Road J16 for 19 miles to the junction with Highway 59. Continue east on Highway 59/ County Road J16 for 4.5 miles to Snelling. Continue straight ahead to Lake McClure Road and drive seven miles to the campground turn-off on the right.

Contact: Lake McSwain Recreation Area, 209/378-2521, fax 209/378-2519; Lake Mc-Swain Marina, 209/378-2534, www.lake mcclure.com.

19 FRANK RAINES REGIONAL PARK

Scenic rating: 4

near Modesto

See map page 750

This park is primarily a riding area for folks with dirt bikes, all-terrain vehicles, and dune buggies who take advantage of the rough-terrain riding course available here. About 1,500 acres of the 2,000-acre park are reserved for off-highway-vehicle (OHV) use. Deer and pig hunting in season are possibilities. A side-trip option is to visit Minniear Park, directly to the east, which is a day-use wilderness park with hiking trails and a creek. This area is very pretty in the spring when the foothills are still green and many wildflowers are blooming.

RV sites, facilities: There are 34 sites for tents or RVs with full hookups (50 amps) and 20 sites for tents or RVs (no hookups). Some sites are pull-through. Fire grills and picnic tables are provided. Restrooms have showers. Drinking water, a picnic area, a baseball diamond, group facilities, nature trails, and a recreation hall are available. Some facilities are wheelchair accessible. Leashed pets are permitted.

Reservations, fees: Reservations are not accepted. Sites are $15–23 per night, $5 per night for an additional vehicle, $3 per pet per night, and there's an extra fee for use of OHV area. Open year-round.

Directions: On I-5, drive to the Patterson exit (south of the junction of I-5 and I-580). Turn west on the Patterson exit and drive onto Diablo Grande Parkway. Continue a short distance under the freeway to Del Puerto Canyon Road. Turn west (right) and drive 16 miles to the park and the campground on the right.

Contact: Stanislaus County Parks and Recreation Department, 866/648-7275 or 209/525-6750, www.co.stanislaus.ca.us/ER/PARKS/Parks.htm.

20 FISHERMAN'S BEND RIVER CAMPGROUND

Scenic rating: 5

on the San Joaquin River

See map page 750

This small, privately operated campground is set along the San Joaquin River on the southern outskirts of the San Joaquin Delta country. The park offers shaded sites and direct river access for boaters. This section of river provides fishing for catfish on hot summer nights. Although many of the sites are rented seasonally or longer, about 10 sites are usually available for overnight campers.

RV sites, facilities: There are 38 pull-through sites with full hookups (30 amps) for RVs of any length, along with 20 sites for tents only. Picnic tables are provided. Drinking water, restrooms with showers, a dump station, a coin laundry, a boat ramp, a fish-cleaning station, a seasonal swimming pool, a playground, and modem access are available. Some facilities are wheelchair accessible. Leashed pets are permitted, with certain restrictions.

Reservations, fees: Reservations are accepted at 800/862-3731. Sites are $17–30 per night, $3 per person per night for more than three people. Monthly rates available. Some credit cards accepted. Open year-round.

Directions: Drive on I-5 to the exit for Newman/Stuhr Road (south of the junction of I-5 and I-580). Take that exit and turn east on County Road J18/Stuhr Road and drive 6.5 miles to Hills Ferry Road. Turn left and drive a mile to River Road. Turn left on River Road and drive to 26836 River Road on the right.

Contact: Fisherman's Bend River Campground, 209/862-3731.

21 McCONNELL STATE RECREATION AREA

Scenic rating: 6

on the Merced River

See map page 750

The weather gets scorching hot around these parts in the summer, and a lot of out-of-towners would pay a bunch for a little shade and a river to sit next to. That's what this park provides, with the Merced River flowing past, along with occasional mermaids on the beach. The park covers 70 acres and has many trees. Fishing is popular for catfish, black bass, and panfish. In high-water years the Merced River attracts salmon (in the fall); check current fishing regulations.

RV sites, facilities: There are 20 sites for tents or RVs up to 30 feet (no hookups); two group sites for tents only hold 25–50 people. Picnic tables, fire grills, and food lockers are provided. Drinking water, restrooms with flush toilets and coin showers, and a swimming beach are available. Group sites have an electrical hookup (20 amps). Firewood is available for purchase. Supplies can be obtained in Delhi, five miles away. Leashed pets are permitted.

Reservations, fees: Reservations are accepted with a $7.50 reservation fee at 800/444-PARK (800/444-7275) or www.reserveamerica.com. Sites are $15–20 per night, $6 per night for an

CALIFORNIA

additional vehicle, $53–111 per night for group sites. Open year-round.

Directions: From Modesto, drive south on Highway 99 to Delhi. Continue south for five miles to the South Avenue exit. Take that exit and turn east on South Avenue and drive 2.7 miles to Pepper Street. Turn right and drive one mile to McConnell Road. Turn right and drive a short distance to the park entrance at the end of the road.

Contact: McConnell State Recreation Area, 209/394-7755; Four Rivers Sector, 209/826-1197, fax 209/826-0284, www.parks.ca.gov.

22 CODORNIZ RECREATION AREA

Scenic rating: 6

on Eastman Lake

See map page 750

Eastman Lake provides relief on your typical 90–100°F summer day out here. It is tucked in the foothills of the San Joaquin Valley at an elevation of 650 feet and covers 1,800 surface acres. Shade shelters have been added at 12 of the more exposed campsites, a big plus. The warm water in summer makes it a good spot for a dip, and it is thus a favorite for waterskiing, swimming, and, in the spring, for fishing. Swimming is best at the large beach on the west side. The Department of Fish and Game has established a trophy bass program here, and fishing can be good in the appropriate season for rainbow trout, catfish, bluegill, and redear sunfish. Check fishing regulations, posted on all bulletin boards. The lake is also a designated "Watchable Wildlife" site with 163 species of birds, and it is home to a nesting pair of bald eagles. A small area near the upper end of the lake is closed to boating to protect a bald eagle nest site. Some may remember the problem that Eastman Lake had with hydrilla, an invasive weed. The problem has been largely solved, and a buoy line has been placed at the mouth. No water activities are allowed upstream of this line. Mild winter temperatures are a tremendous plus at this lake.

RV sites, facilities: There are 62 sites for tents or RVs of any length (some have full hookups—50 amp—and one is pull-through), three group sites for up to 200 people, three equestrian sites, and one group equestrian site. Picnic tables and fire grills are provided. Drinking water, flush toilets with showers, a dump station, a playground, a volleyball court, a Frisbee golf course, and a boat ramp are available. An equestrian staging area is available for overnight use, and there are seven miles of hiking, biking, and equestrian trails. Leashed pets are permitted.

Reservations, fees: Reservations are accepted at 877/444-6777 or www.ReserveUSA.com. Sites are $14–22 per night, $55–75 per night for group sites, and $8–25 per night for equestrian sites. Open year-round.

Directions: Drive on Highway 99 to Chowchilla and the Avenue 26 exit. Take that exit and drive east for 17 miles to County Road 29. Turn left (north) on County Road 29 and drive eight miles to the lake.

Contact: U.S. Army Corps of Engineers, Sacramento District, Eastman Lake, 559/689-3255, fax 559/689-3408.

23 HIDDEN VIEW

Scenic rating: 5

north of Fresno on Hensley Lake

See map page 750

Hensley Lake is popular with water-skiers and personal watercraft users in spring and summer, and it has good prospects for bass fishing as well. Hensley covers 1,500 surface acres with 24 miles of shoreline, and as long as water levels are maintained, it makes for a wonderful water playland. Swimming is good, with the best spot at Buck Ridge on the east side of the lake, where there are picnic tables and trees for shade. The reservoir was created by a dam on the Fresno River. A nature trail is also here. The elevation is 540 feet.

RV sites, facilities: There are 55 sites for tents or RVs of any length, some with electric hookups (30 amps), and two group sites for 25–100 people. Picnic tables and fire grills are provided. Restrooms have flush toilets and showers. Drinking water, a dump station, a playground, and a boat ramp are available. Some facilities are wheelchair accessible. Leashed pets are permitted.

Reservations, fees: Reservations are accepted at 877/444-6777 or www.ReserveUSA.com. Sites are $14–20 per night, $50 per night for group sites. Boat launching is free for campers. Open year-round.

Directions: From Madera, drive northeast on Highway 145 for about six miles to County Road 400. Bear left on County Road 400 and drive to County Road 603 below the dam. Turn left and drive about two miles on County Road 603 to County Road 407. Turn right on County Road 407 and drive a half mile to the campground.

Contact: U.S. Army Corps of Engineers, Sacramento District, Hensley Lake, 559/673-5151, fax 559/673-2044.

24 SAN LUIS CREEK

Scenic rating: 5

on San Luis Reservoir

See map page 750

San Luis Creek Campground is near San Luis Reservoir. It is one in a series of camps operated by the state in the San Luis Reservoir State Recreation Area, adjacent to the reservoir and O'Neill Forebay, home of many of the biggest striped bass in California, including the world record for landlocked stripers.

RV sites, facilities: There are 53 sites for tents or RVs up to 35 feet with partial hookups (20 and 30 amps), as well as two group sites for up to 30–60 people. Picnic tables and fire pits are provided. Drinking water, pit toilets, and a dump station are available. A boat ramp is nearby. Leashed pets are permitted.

Reservations, fees: Reservations are accepted with a $7.50 reservation fee at 800/444-PARK (800/444-7275) or www.reserveamerica.com. Sites are $20–25 per night, $6 per night for an

additional vehicle, $66–135 per night for group sites. Open year-round.

Directions: Drive on Highway 152 to San Luis Reservoir (12 miles west of Los Banos) and the signed campground entrance road (15 miles west of Los Banos). Turn north and drive two miles to the campground on the left.

Contact: San Luis Reservoir State Recreation Area, 209/826-1196; Four Rivers Sector, 209/826-1197, fax 209/826-0284, www.parks .ca.gov.

25 MEDEIROS

Scenic rating: 5

on O'Neill Forebay near Santa Nella

See map page 750

This is a vast, primitive campground set on the stark expanse of foothill country on O'Neill Forebay near Santa Nella and San Luis Reservoir. Some of the biggest striped bass in California history have been caught here at the forebay. It is best known for wind in the spring, hot weather in the summer, and low water levels in the fall. Striped bass fishing is best in the fall when the wind is down and stripers will corral schools of bait fish near the lake surface. There's a large, developed, swimming beach on O'Neill Forebay, and boats can be launched four miles west of the campground at San Luis Creek. There used to be another boat ramp at Medeiros, but it's been closed since 9/11 and will not reopen. In addition to security concerns, there were problems with launching in low-water conditions. Sailboarding is decent. The forebay can get congested on weekends and holidays. The reservoir is less crowded. The campground elevation is 225 feet. (See the listing in this chapter for *Basalt* campground for more information about San Luis.)

RV sites, facilities: There are 350 primitive sites for tents or RVs of any length. Some shaded ramadas with fire grills and picnic tables are available. Drinking water and chemical toilets are available. A boat ramp is four miles away. Leashed pets are permitted.

CALIFORNIA

Reservations, fees: Reservations are not accepted. Sites are $10 per night, and an additional vehicle is $6 per night. Boat launching is $6 per day. Open year-round.

Directions: Drive on Highway 152 to Highway 33 (about 10 miles west of Los Banos). Turn north (right) on Highway 33 and drive 0.25 mile to the campground entrance on the left.

Contact: San Luis Reservoir State Recreation Area, 209/826-1196; Four Rivers Sector, 209/826-1197, fax 209/826-0284, www.parks .ca.gov.

26 BASALT

Scenic rating: 5

on San Luis Reservoir

See map page 750

San Luis Reservoir is a huge, man-made lake, covering 13,800 acres with 65 miles of shoreline, developed among stark foothills to provide a storage facility along the California Aqueduct. It fills by late winter and is used primarily by anglers, water-skiers, and sailboarders. When the Sacramento River Delta water pumps take the water, they also take the fish, filling this lake up with both. Striped bass fishing is best in the fall when the stripers chase schools of bait fish on the lake surface. Spring and early summer can be quite windy, but that makes for good sailboarding. The adjacent O'Neill Forebay is the best recreation bet because of the boat launch and often good fishing. There is a visitors center at the Romero Overlook. The elevation is 575 feet. Summer temperatures can occasionally exceed 100°F, but evenings are usually pleasant. During winter, tule fog is common. Note that in spring and early summer, it can turn windy very quickly. Warning lights mark several spots at the reservoir and forebay.

RV sites, facilities: There are 79 sites for tents or RVs up to 30 feet (no hookups). Picnic tables and fire grills are provided. Drinking water, restrooms with flush toilets and coin showers, a dump station, picnic areas, and a boat ramp are

available. A store, a coin laundry, a gas station, a restaurant, and propane gas are nearby (about 1.5 miles away). Some facilities are wheelchair accessible. Leashed pets are permitted.

Reservations, fees: Reservations are accepted with a $7.50 reservation fee at 800/444-PARK (800/444-7275) or www.reserveamerica.com. Sites are $15–20 per night, $6 per night for an additional vehicle. Boat launching is $6 per day. Open year-round.

Directions: Drive on Highway 152 to San Luis Reservoir (12 miles west of Los Banos) and the Basalt Campground entrance road. Turn south on Basalt Road and drive 2.5 miles to the campground on the left.

Contact: San Luis Reservoir State Recreation Area, 209/826-1196; Four Rivers Sector, 209/826-1197, fax 209/826-0284, www.parks .ca.gov.

27 LOS BANOS CREEK RESERVOIR

Scenic rating: 6

near Los Banos

See map page 750

Los Banos Creek Reservoir is in a long, narrow valley, covering 410 surface acres with 12 miles of shoreline. It provides a smaller, more low-key setting (a 5-mph speed limit is enforced) compared to the nearby giant, San Luis Reservoir. In spring, it can be quite windy and is a popular spot for sailboarding and sailing. It is also stocked with trout in late winter and spring, and some large bass have been caught here. The elevation is 330 feet. Although drinking water is available, campers are advised to bring their own water, as the water supply is limited.

RV sites, facilities: There are 15 sites for tents or RVs up to 30 feet (no hookups). Picnic tables, drinking water, and fire grills are provided. Chemical toilets and picnic areas are available. A boat ramp is available nearby. Leashed pets are permitted.

Reservations, fees: Reservations are not accepted. Sites are $10 per night, plus $6 per night for an additional vehicle. Boat launching is $6 per day. Open year-round, weather permitting.

Directions: Drive on Highway 152 to Volta Road (five miles west of Los Banos). Turn south on Volta Road and drive about a mile to Pioneer Road. Turn left on Pioneer Road and drive a mile to Canyon Road. Turn south (right) onto Canyon Road and drive about five miles to the park.

Contact: San Luis Reservoir State Recreation Area, 209/826-1196; Four Rivers Sector, 209/826-1197, fax 209/826-0284, www.parks .ca.gov.

28 MILLERTON LAKE STATE RECREATION AREA

Scenic rating: 6

near Madera

See map page 750

As the temperature gauge goes up in the summer, the value of Millerton Lake increases at the same rate. The lake is at 578 feet in the foothills of the San Joaquin Valley, and the water is like gold here. The campground and recreation area are set on a peninsula along the north shore of the lake; there are sandy beach areas on both sides of the lake with boat ramps available near the campgrounds. It's a big lake, with 43 miles of shoreline, from a narrow lake inlet extending to an expansive main lake body. The irony at Millerton is that when the lake is filled to the brim, the beaches are covered, so ideal conditions are actually when the lake level is down a bit, typically from early summer on. Fishing can be good here in spring for bass. Catfish are popular for shoreliners on summer evenings. Waterskiing is very popular in summer, of course. Anglers head upstream, water-skiers downstream. The lake's south side has a huge day-use area. During winter, boat tours are available to view bald eagles. A note of history: The original Millerton County Court-house, built in 1867, is in the park.

RV sites, facilities: There are 148 sites, 26 with full hookups, for tents or RVs up to 36 feet; three boat-in sites; and two group sites for 45–75 people. Picnic tables and fire grills are provided. Drinking water, restrooms with flush toilets and coin showers, a dump station, picnic areas, a full-service marina, a snack bar, boat rentals, and boat ramps are available. Supplies are available in Friant. Some facilities are wheelchair accessible. Leashed pets are permitted.

Reservations, fees: Reservations are accepted ($7.50 reservation fee) at 800/444-7275 or www.reserveamerica.com. Sites are $25–34 per night, $7 per night for an additional vehicle, $11 for boat-in sites, $90–168 per night for group sites. Boat launching is $7 per day. Open year-round.

Directions: Drive on Highway 99 to Madera at the exit for Highway 145 eastbound. Take that exit east and drive on Highway 145 for 22 miles (six miles past the intersection with Highway 41) to the park entrance on the right.

Contact: Millerton Lake State Recreation Area, 559/822-2332, fax 559/822-2319, www.parks .ca.gov.

29 VISALIA/FRESNO SOUTH KOA

Scenic rating: 3

west of Visalia

See map page 751

This is a layover spot for Highway 99 cruisers. If you're looking for a spot to park your rig for the night, you can't get too picky around these parts. Most campers here are on their way to or from Sequoia and Kings Canyon National Parks. The swimming pool is a great bonus during the summer. Grassy shaded sites are available. Golf and tennis are nearby. Note that a few of the sites are occupied by monthly renters.

RV sites, facilities: There are 48 pull-through sites with full or partial hookups (30 and 50 amps), 20 sites for tents or RVs (no hookups), 20 sites for tents only, and eight cabins. Restrooms have showers. A seasonal heated swimming pool, laundry facilities, a playground, a recreation room, free Wi-Fi, a dog walk, a store, a gift shop, a dump station, and propane gas are available. Leashed pets are permitted, with certain restrictions.

Reservations, fees: Reservations are accepted at 800/562-0544. Sites are $25.75–39.75 per night, $5 per person per night for more than two people. Some credit cards accepted. Open year-round.

Directions: From Highway 99 near Visalia, take the Goshen Avenue exit and drive 0.2 mile to Betty Drive/County Road 332. Turn left and drive 0.5 mile to County Road 76. Turn left and drive 0.5 mile (becomes Avenue 308) to the campground.

Contact: Visalia/Fresno KOA, 559/651-0544, www.koa.com.

30 TRAVELER'S RV PARK

Scenic rating: 2

near Kettleman City
See map page 751

Being stuck in Kings County looking for a place to park an RV is no picnic. Unless, that is, you are lucky enough to know about Traveler's RV Park. The spaces are wide open with long-distance views of the Sierra. It's literally the "only game in town." Visitors will find access to miles of open paths and roads for hiking or running. The restaurant is open 24 hours a day, and campers get a 10 percent discount. Some may remember this park as Kettleman City RV Park.

RV sites, facilities: There are 46 pull-through sites with full hookups (30 and 50 amps) for RVs up to 36 feet, plus two tent sites. Picnic tables are provided. Restrooms have showers. A coin laundry, playgrounds, a swimming pool, a dump station, a dog run, tire and RV repair, and propane gas are available. A restaurant and snack bar are nearby. Some facilities are wheelchair accessible. Leashed pets are permitted.

Reservations, fees: Reservations are accepted. Sites are $27–29 per night, $5 per night for an additional vehicle. Weekly and monthly rates available. Some credit cards accepted. Open year-round.

Directions: Drive on I-5 to the junction with Highway 41 (Kettleman Junction). Take Highway 41 north and drive 0.5 mile to Hubert Way. Turn left on Hubert Way and drive a short distance to Cyril Place. Turn right on Cyril Place and continue to the park entrance (30000 Cyril Place).

Contact: Traveler's RV Park, 559/386-0583.

31 SUN AND FUN RV PARK

Scenic rating: 2

near Tulare
See map page 751

This RV park is just off Highway 99, exactly halfway between San Francisco and Los Angeles. Are you having fun yet? Anybody making the long drive up or down the state on Highway 99 will learn what a dry piece of life the San Joaquin Valley can seem in summer. That's why the swimming pool at this RV park can be a lifesaver. The park has a number of mature trees, providing an opportunity for shade. Note that most of the sites are filled with long-term renters, but a few spaces are reserved for overnight campers.

RV sites, facilities: There are 53 sites with full hookups (30 and 50 amps) for RVs of any length. No tents. Picnic tables and barbecues are provided at some sites. Restrooms have showers. Drinking water, cable TV, modem access, a dump station, a playground, a swimming pool, a spa, a coin laundry, dog runs, and a recreation room are available. A golf course, a restaurant, and a store are nearby. Some facilities are wheelchair accessible. Leashed pets are permitted.

Reservations, fees: Reservations are accepted. Sites are $26 per night. Monthly rates available. Open year-round.

Directions: From Tulare, drive south on Highway 99 for three miles to the Avenue 200 exit. Take Avenue 200 west and drive a short distance to the park (1000 Avenue 200).

Contact: Sun and Fun RV Park, 559/686-5779.

32 COLONEL ALLENSWORTH STATE HISTORIC PARK

Scenic rating: 2

near Earlimart

See map page 751

What you have here is the old town of Allensworth, which has been restored as a historical park dedicated to the African-American pioneers who founded it with Colonel Allen Allensworth. He was the highest-ranking army chaplain of his time. Allensworth is the only town in California to be founded, funded, and governed by African Americans. One museum is at the school here and another is at the colonel's house with a 30-minute movie on the history of Allensworth. Tours are available by appointment. One frustrating element is that railroad tracks run alongside the park and it can be disruptive. There can be other problems, such as very hot weather in the summer, and since it is an open area, the wind can blow dust and sand. Are we having fun yet? One nice touch is the addition of shade ramadas at some campsites. A history note: This small farming community was founded in 1908, but a drop in the water table led to its demise.

RV sites, facilities: There are 15 sites for tents or RVs up to 35 feet (no hookups). Picnic tables and fire grills are provided. Restrooms have flush toilets and coin showers. Drinking water, a dump station, a visitors center, and a picnic area are available. A store and coin laundry are 12 miles away in Delano. Some facilities are wheelchair accessible. Leashed pets are permitted.

Reservations, fees: Reservations are not accepted. Sites are $10 per night, and it's $5 per night for an additional vehicle. Open year-round.

Directions: From Fresno, drive south on Highway 99 about 60 miles to Earlimart and the Avenue 56 exit. Turn right (west) on Avenue 56 and drive seven miles to the Highway 43 turnoff. Turn left (south) on Highway 43 and drive two miles to Palmer Avenue. Turn right (and drive over the railroad tracks) to the park entrance.

Contact: Colonel Allensworth State Historic Park, 661/849-3433 or 661/634-3795, www.parks.ca.gov.

33 LOST HILLS RV PARK

Scenic rating: 2

near Kern National Wildlife Refuge

See map page 751

The pickings can get slim around these parts when you're cruising north on I-5, so if it's late, you'll likely be happy to find this camp, which was formerly known as Lost Hills KOA. The cabin that sleeps four is a nice plus. The nearby Kern National Wildlife Refuge, about a 15-minute drive away, offers a side-trip possibility. It's a reserve that attracts ducks, geese, and other waterfowl in the fall and winter. An 18-hole golf course is within 15 miles.

RV sites, facilities: There are 79 sites, all pull-through, with full hookups (30 and 50 amps) for RVs, nine sites for tents only, an overflow area with 20 sites for tents and self-contained RVs, and one cabin. Picnic tables are provided. Restrooms have showers. Drinking water, a swimming pool, a coin laundry, a store, modem access, and propane gas are available. Restaurants are nearby. Some facilities are wheelchair accessible. Leashed pets are permitted, with certain restrictions.

Reservations, fees: Reservations are accepted at 661/797-2719. Sites are $28–31 per night, $3 per person per night for more than two people. Some credit cards accepted. Open year-round.

Directions: Drive on I-5 to the junction with Highway 46 (41 miles south of Avenal near Lost Hills). Turn west on Highway 46 and drive a short distance to the park entrance on the south side of the road (near the Carl's Jr.).

Contact: Lost Hills RV Park, 661/797-2719.

34 BAKERSFIELD KOA

Scenic rating: 2

north of Bakersfield

See map page 751

If you're stuck in the southern valley and the temperature makes you feel as if you're sitting in a cauldron, well, this spot provides a layover for the night near the town of Shafter. The closest golf course is eight miles away.

RV sites, facilities: There are 35 RV sites with full or partial hookups (30 and 50 amps), 20 tent sites, and two cabins. Picnic tables are provided. Restrooms have showers. Drinking water, a seasonal swimming pool, a coin laundry, a convenience store, a dump station, and propane gas are available. Some facilities are wheelchair accessible. Leashed pets are permitted.

Reservations, fees: Reservations are accepted at 800/562-1633. Sites are $28–35 per night, $2 per person per night for more than two people. Some credit cards accepted. Open year-round.

Directions: From Bakersfield, drive north on Highway 99 for 12 miles to the Shafter-Lerdo Highway exit. Take that exit and drive a mile west on Lerdo Highway to the park (5101 East Lerdo Highway in Shafter).

Contact: Bakersfield KOA, 661/399-3107, fax 661/399-8981, www.koa.com.

35 BUENA VISTA AQUATIC RECREATION AREA

Scenic rating: 6

near Bakersfield

See map page 751

This is the showpiece of Kern County recreation. Buena Vista is actually two connected lakes fed by the West Side Canal: little Lake Evans to the west and larger Lake Webb to the east. Be certain to know the difference between the two: Lake Webb (875 acres) is open to all boating including personal watercraft, and fast boats towing skiers are a common sight in designated ski areas. The speed limit is 45 mph. Lake Evans (85 acres) is small, quiet, and has a strictly enforced 5-mph speed limit, an ideal lake for family water play and fishing. Swimming is prohibited at both lakes but is allowed in the lagoons. Lake Webb is a catfish lake, while Lake Evans is stocked in season with trout, and also has bass, bluegill, catfish, and crappie. The elevation is 330 feet on the outskirts of Bakersfield.

RV sites, facilities: There are 112 sites for RVs or tents, some with full hookups (30 and 50 amps), and an overflow camping area. Picnic tables and fire grills are provided. Restrooms have flush toilets and showers. Drinking water, a playground, four boat ramps, a store, a dump station, and picnic shelters are available. Two swimming lagoons, a marina, a snack bar, fishing supplies, and groceries are available nearby. A PGA-rated golf course is two miles west. Some facilities are wheelchair accessible. Leashed pets are permitted.

Reservations, fees: Reservations are accepted at 661/868-7050 Monday–Friday. Sites are $26–39 per night, $7–15 per night for an additional vehicle, $4 per night per pet. Some credit cards accepted. Open year-round.

Directions: From I-5 just south of Bakersfield, take Highway 119 west and drive two miles to Highway 43. Turn south (left) on Highway 43 and drive two miles to the campground at road's end.

Contact: Buena Vista Aquatic Recreation Area, Kern County Parks, 661/868-7000; Buena Vista concession, 661/763-1770, www.co.kern.ca.us/parks/index.htm.

YOSEMITE AND MAMMOTH LAKES

☾ BEST RV PARKS AND CAMPGROUNDS

☾ Wildlife-Viewing
White Wolf, page 775.
Tuolumne Meadows, page 775.

☾ Prettiest Lakes
Porcupine Flat, page 776.

Some of nature's most perfect artwork has been
created in Yosemite and the adjoining eastern Sierra near Mammoth Lakes,
as well as some of the most profound natural phenomena imaginable.

Yosemite Valley is the world's greatest showpiece. It is also among
the most highly visited and well-known destinations on earth. Many of
the campgrounds listed in this section are within close driving proximity
of Yosemite National Park.

Anything in Yosemite, or in its sphere of influence, is going to be in
high demand almost year-round, and the same is true near Mammoth
Mountain.

Many family recreation opportunities exist at lake-based settings,
including at Lake Alpine, Pinecrest Lake on the western slopes of the
Sierra, and at June Lake, Silver Lake, Lake Mary, Twin Lakes, Convict
Lake, and Rock Creek Lake on the eastern Sierra. I noticed that the
demand for campgrounds is fairly high in the vicinity of Highway 4 and
Calaveras Big Trees, as well as Highway 108 and Pinecrest. That's what
happens when you're competing with Yosemite.

Of course, most visits to this region start with a tour of Yosemite
Valley. It is framed by El Capitan, the Goliath of Yosemite, on one side
and the three-spired Cathedral Rocks on the other. As you enter the
valley, Bridalveil Falls comes into view, a perfect freefall over the south
canyon rim, then across a meadow. To your left you'll see the two-tiered
Yosemite Falls, and finally, Half Dome, the single most awesome piece
of rock in the world.

The irony is that this is all most people ever see of the region, even
though it represents but a fraction of this fantastic land of wonder, adventure, and unparalleled natural beauty. Though 24,000 people jam
into five square miles of Yosemite Valley each summer day, the park is
actually 90 percent wilderness. Other landmark areas you can reach
by car include the Wawona Grove of Giant Sequoias, Tenaya Lake, Tuolumne Meadows, and Hetch Hetchy.

But that's still only scratching the surface. For those who hike, another
world will open up: Yosemite has 318 lakes, dozens of pristine streams,
the Grand Canyon of the Tuolumne River, Matterhorn Peak, Benson
Lake (with the largest white-sand beach in the Sierra), and dozens of
spectacular waterfalls.

CALIFORNIA

If you explore beyond the park boundaries, the adventures just keep getting better. Over Tioga Pass, outside the park and just off Highway 120, are Tioga Lake, Ellery Lake, and Saddlebag Lake (10,087 feet), the latter of which is the highest lake in California accessible by car. To the east is Mono Lake and its weird tufa spires, which create a stark moonscape.

The nearby June Lake Loop and Mammoth Lakes area is a launch point to another orbit. Both have small lakes with on-site cabin rentals, excellent fishing, great hiking and mountain biking for all levels, and phenomenal skiing and winter sports. In addition, just east of Mammoth Lakes airport is a series of hot springs, including a famous spot on Hot Creek, something of a legend in these parts.

More hiking and fishing opportunities abound at Devils Postpile National Monument, where you can hike to Rainbow Falls. At nearby Agnew Meadows, a trail hugs the pristine San Joaquin River up to Thousand Island Lake and leads to the beautiful view from Banner and Ritter Peaks in the Ansel Adams Wilderness. Horseback riding is also popular in this area, with pack trips available from Red's Meadow.

If you didn't already know, this region is home to many of California's best lakes for catching giant rainbow and brown trout. They include Bridgeport Reservoir, Twin Lakes, June Lake, Convict Lake, and Crowley Lake in the eastern Sierra, and Beardsley and Spicer Meadows in the western Sierra.

This region has it all: beauty, variety, and a chance at the hike or fish of a lifetime. There is nothing else like it.

CALIFORNIA

Includes:

- Cherry Lake
- Convict Lake
- Crowley Lake
- Devils Postpile National Monument
- Humboldt-Toiyabe National Forest
- Inyo National Forest
- June Lake
- Lake Mary
- Mammoth Lakes
- Merced River
- Pinecrest Lake
- San Joaquin River
- Sierra National Forest
- Stanislaus National Forest
- Tuolumne River
- Twin Lakes
- Yosemite National Park

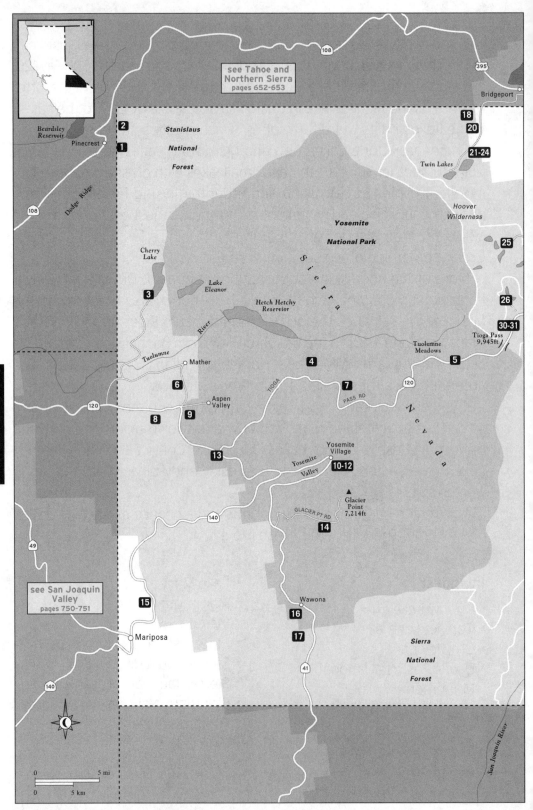

CALIFORNIA

see Tahoe and
Northern Sierra
pages 652-653

Bridgeport

2

18
20
21-24

Beardsley
Reservoir

Pinecrest

1

Stanislaus

National

Forest

Twin Lakes

108

Dodge Ridge

108

*Cherry
Lake*

*Lake
Eleanor*

*Hetch Hetchy
Reservoir*

3

Tuolumne

River

Yosemite

National Park

Sierra

*Hoover
Wilderness*

25

26

30-31

*Tioga Pass
9,945ft*

*Tuolumne
Meadows*

5

Mather

6

4

7

TIOGA

PASS RD

120

Nevada

120

Aspen
Valley

8   **9**

13

Yosemite

Valley

Yosemite
Village

10-12

▲
*Glacier
Point
7,214ft*

140

GLACIER PT RD

14

see San Joaquin
Valley
pages 750-751

49

15

Mariposa

Wawona

16

17

Sierra

National

Forest

140

41

San Joaquin River

0   5 mi
0   5 km

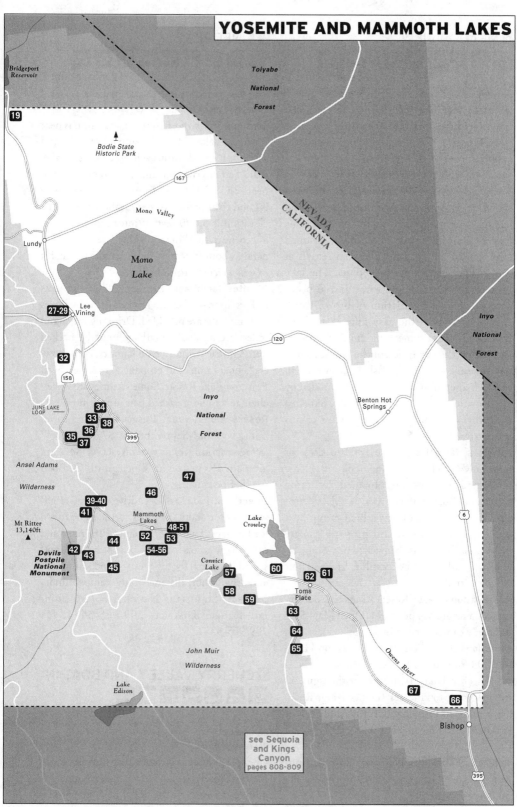

YOSEMITE AND MAMMOTH LAKES

Bridgeport
Reservoir

Toiyabe

National

Forest

19

Bodie State
Historic Park

167

NEVADA
CALIFORNIA

Mono Valley

Lundy

Mono
Lake

Inyo

National

Forest

27-29 Lee
Vining

120

32

158

Benton Hot
Springs

JUNE LAKE
LOOP

34

33 **38**

36

35

37

395

Inyo

National

Forest

Ansel Adams

Wilderness

47

6

46

Mt Ritter
13,140ft

39-40

41

Mammoth
Lakes

Lake
Crowley

**Devils
Postpile
National
Monument**

42 **43**

44

52

45

48-51

53

54-56

Convict
Lake

57

58

59

60

62 **61**

Toms
Place

63

John Muir

Wilderness

64

65

Owens River

Lake
Edison

67

66

Bishop

see Sequoia
and Kings
Canyon
pages 808-809

395

CALIFORNIA

CALIFORNIA

1 MEADOWVIEW

Scenic rating: 7

near Pinecrest Lake in Stanislaus National Forest

See map page 772

No secret here, folks. This camp is one mile from Pinecrest Lake, a popular weekend vacation area (and there's a trail that connects the camp with the town). Pinecrest Lake is at 5,621 feet, covers 300 acres and 2.5 miles of shoreline, has a sandy swimming beach, and has a 20-mph speed limit for boaters. The lake is the centerpiece of a fully developed family vacation area, and the boat rentals at the small marina are a big bonus. The lake is stocked with rainbow trout and also has a small resident population of brown trout. A popular walk is the easy hike around the lake. If you want something more ambitious, a cutoff on the north side of the lake is routed one mile up to little Catfish Lake, which in reality is a set of shallow ponds surrounded by old-growth forest. The Dodge Ridge Ski Area is nearby, with many privately owned cabins in the area.

RV sites, facilities: There are 100 sites for tents or RVs up to 22 feet (no hookups). Picnic tables and fire grills are provided. Drinking water and flush toilets are available. A grocery store, a coin laundry, a boat ramp, boat rentals, coin showers, and propane gas are nearby. Garbage must be packed out. Some facilities are wheelchair accessible. Leashed pets are permitted.

Reservations, fees: Reservations are not accepted. Sites are $14 per night. Open May–September, weather permitting.

Directions: From Sonora, drive east on Highway 108 for about 30 miles to the signed road for Pinecrest Lake. Turn right at the sign and drive 0.5 mile to Pinecrest/Dodge Ridge Road. Turn right and drive about 200 yards to the campground entrance on the right side of the road.

Contact: Stanislaus National Forest, Summit Ranger District, 209/965-3434, fax 209/965-3372.

2 PINECREST

Scenic rating: 7

near Pinecrest Lake in Stanislaus National Forest

See map page 772

This monster-sized Forest Service camp is near Pinecrest Lake. A launch ramp is available, and a 20-mph speed limit is enforced on the lake. A trail circles the lake and also branches off to nearby Catfish Lake. In early summer, there is good fishing for stocked rainbow trout. The elevation is 5,600 feet. Winter camping is allowed near the Pinecrest Day-Use Area. (For details about Pinecrest Lake, see the listing for *Meadowview* in this chapter.)

RV sites, facilities: There are 200 sites for tents or RVs up to 40 feet (no hookups). Picnic tables and fire grills are provided. Drinking water and toilets are available. Garbage must be packed out. A grocery store, a coin laundry, coin showers, a boat ramp, and propane gas are nearby at Pinecrest Lake Resort. Some facilities are wheelchair accessible. Leashed pets are permitted.

Reservations, fees: Reservations required mid-May–mid-September at 877/444-6777 ($9 reservation fee) or www.ReserveUSA.com. Sites are $19 per night. Open April–October, weather permitting.

Directions: From Sonora, drive east on Highway 108 for about 30 miles to the signed turn for Pinecrest Lake on the right. Turn right and drive to the access road (0.7 mile past the turnoff signed Pinecrest) for the campground. Turn right and drive a short distance to the campground.

Contact: Stanislaus National Forest, Summit Ranger District, 209/965-3434, fax 209/965-3372.

3 CHERRY VALLEY AND BOAT-IN

Scenic rating: 8

on Cherry Lake in Stanislaus National Forest

See map page 772

Cherry Lake is a mountain lake surrounded by national forest at 4,700 feet in elevation, just outside the western boundary of Yosemite National Park. It is much larger than most people anticipate and provides much better trout fishing than anything in Yosemite. The camp is on the southwest shore of the lake, a very pretty spot, about a mile ride to the boat launch on the west side of the Cherry Valley Dam. A bonus is that dispersed boat-in camping is allowed on the lake's east side. All water sports are allowed, yet because it takes a considerable drive to reach the lake, you won't find nearly the waterskiing traffic as at other regional lakes. Water levels can fluctuate here. The lake is bordered to the east by Kibbie Ridge; just on the other side are Yosemite Park and Lake Eleanor. Insider's tip: During periods of campfire restrictions, which is often most of the summer in this national forest, this campground is the only one in the area where campfires are permitted. A fire permit is required from the Forest Service.

RV sites, facilities: There are 45 sites for tents or RVs up to 22 feet (no hookups). Primitive boat-in camping is permitted on the lake's east side. Picnic tables and fire grills are provided. Drinking water and vault toilets are available. A boat ramp is nearby. Leashed pets are permitted.

Reservations, fees: Reservations are not accepted. Sites are $15 per night, $30 per night for double sites. There is no camping fee for boat-in sites. Open April–October, weather permitting.

Directions: From Groveland, drive east on Highway 120 for about 15 miles to Forest Road 1N07/Cherry Lake Road. Turn left and drive 20 miles to Cottonwood Road/Forest Road 1N04. Turn left and drive one mile to the campground entrance road. Turn right and drive one mile to the campground.

Contact: Stanislaus National Forest, Groveland Ranger District, 209/962-7825, fax 209/962-7412.

▣ WHITE WOLF

Scenic rating: 8

in Yosemite National Park

See map page 772 BEST (

This is one of Yosemite National Park's prime mountain camps for people who like to hike,

either for great day hikes in the immediate area and beyond, or for overnight backpacking trips. The day hike to Lukens Lake is an easy two-mile trip, the payoff being this pretty little alpine lake set amid a meadow, pines, and granite. Just about everybody who camps at White Wolf makes the trip. Backpackers (wilderness permit required) can make the overnight trip into the Ten Lakes Basin, set below Grand Mountain and Colby Mountain. Bears are common at this camp, and it is required that you secure your food in the bearproof lockers. The elevation is 8,000 feet.

RV sites, facilities: There are 74 sites for tents or RVs up to 27 feet (no hookups). Tent cabins are also available. Picnic tables, food lockers, and fire grills are provided. Drinking water and flush toilets are available. Evening ranger programs are occasionally available. A small store with a walk-up window and limited items is nearby. Leashed pets are permitted in the campground, but not on trails.

Reservations, fees: Reservations are not accepted. Sites are $14 per night, plus a $20 park entrance fee per vehicle. Open July–early September, weather permitting.

Directions: From Merced, drive east on Highway 140 to the Arch Rock entrance station. Continue east to the Big Oak Flat Road junction (0.5 mile before entering Yosemite Valley). Turn left and drive 14 miles to Tioga Road. Turn right and drive 15 miles to White Wolf Road on the left. Turn left and drive a mile to the campground entrance road on the right.

Contact: Yosemite National Park, 209/372-0200 for a touch-tone menu of recorded information, www.nps.gov/yose.

▣ TUOLUMNE MEADOWS

Scenic rating: 8

in Yosemite National Park

See map page 772 BEST (

This is Yosemite's biggest camp, and for the variety of nearby adventures, it might also be the best. It is in the high country, at 8,600 feet, and can be used as a base camp for fishing, hiking, and horseback riding, or as a start-up point for a backpacking trip (wilderness permits required). This is one of the top trailheads in North America. There are two outstanding and easy day hikes from here, one heading north on the Pacific Crest Trail for the near-level walk to Tuolumne Falls and Glen Aulin, the other heading south up Lyell Fork (toward Donohue Pass), with good fishing for small brook trout. With a backpack (wilderness permit required), either route can be extended for as long as desired into remote and beautiful country. The campground is huge, and neighbors are guaranteed, but it is well wooded and feels somewhat secluded even with all the RVs and tents. There are lots of food-raiding bears in the area, so use of the food lockers is required.

RV sites, facilities: There are 36 sites for tents or RVs up to 22 feet (no hookups), four horse camps, and seven group sites that can accommodate 30 people each. Additionally, 25 hike-in sites are available for backpackers (no parking is available for backpacker campsites, often reserved for those hiking the Pacific Crest Trail, for which a wilderness permit is required). Picnic tables, fire grills, and food lockers are provided. Drinking water, flush toilets, and a dump station are available. Showers and groceries are nearby. Leashed pets are permitted, except in group sites, horse camps, and backpacker sites.

Reservations, fees: Reservations are accepted at 800/436-PARK (800/436-7275) or http://reservations.nps.gov; half of the sites are available through reservations, while the other half are first-come, first-served. Sites are $20 per night for individual sites, $5 per night per person for walk-in (backpack) sites, $25 per night for a horse camp, and $40 per night for group sites, plus a $20 per vehicle park entrance fee. Open July–mid-September, weather permitting.

Directions: From Merced, drive east on Highway 140 to the Arch Rock entrance station. Continue east to the Big Oak Flat Road junction (0.5 mile before entering Yosemite Valley). Turn left and drive 14 miles to Tioga Road.

Turn right and drive 46 miles to the campground on the right side of the road.

From just south of Lee Vining at the junction of U.S. 395 and Highway 120, turn west and drive to the Tioga Pass entrance station for Yosemite National Park. Continue for about eight miles to the campground entrance on the left. **Contact:** Yosemite National Park, 209/372-0200 for a touch-tone menu of recorded information, www.nps.gov/yose.

⬚ DIMOND "O"

Scenic rating: 7

in Stanislaus National Forest
See map page 772

Dimond "O" is at 4,400 feet in elevation on the eastern side of Stanislaus National Forest—just two miles from the western border of Yosemite National Park.

RV sites, facilities: There are 36 sites for tents or RVs up to 22 feet (no hookups). Picnic tables and fire grills are provided. Drinking water and vault toilets are available. Some facilities are wheelchair accessible. Leashed pets are permitted.

Reservations, fees: Reservations are accepted at 877/444-6777 ($9 reservation fee) or www.ReserveUSA.com. Sites are $16 per night. Open April–October, weather permitting.

Directions: From Groveland, drive east on Highway 120 for 25 miles to Evergreen Road/Forest Road 12. Turn left on Evergreen Road and drive six miles to the campground.

Contact: Stanislaus National Forest, Groveland Ranger District, 209/962-7825, fax 209/962-7412.

⬚ PORCUPINE FLAT

Scenic rating: 6

near Yosemite Creek in Yosemite National Park
See map page 772   **BEST (**

Porcupine Flat, at 8,100 feet, is southwest of Mount Hoffman, one of the prominent nearby peaks along Tioga Road in Yosemite National

Park. The trailhead for a hike to May Lake, set just below Mount Hoffman, is about five miles away on a signed turnoff on the north side of the road. There are several little peaks above the lake where hikers can gain great views, including one of the back side of Half Dome.

RV sites, facilities: There are 52 sites for tents or RVs up to 35 feet (no hookups). There is limited RV space. Picnic tables, fire rings, and food lockers (mandatory use) are provided. Pit toilets are available. No drinking water is available. No pets are allowed.

Reservations, fees: Reservations are not accepted. Sites are $10 per night, plus a $20 park entrance fee per vehicle. Open July–mid-October, weather permitting.

Directions: From Merced, drive east on Highway 140 to the Arch Rock entrance station. Continue east to the Big Oak Flat Road junction (0.5 mile before entering Yosemite Valley). Turn left and drive 14 miles to Tioga Road. Turn right and drive about 25 miles to the campground on the left side of the road (16 miles west from Tuolumne Meadows).

Contact: Yosemite National Park, 209/372-0200 for a touch-tone menu of recorded information, www.nps.gov/yose.

8 YOSEMITE LAKES

Scenic rating: 7

on Tuolumne River at Groveland
See map page 772

This is a 400-acre park set at 3,600 feet along the South Fork Tuolumne River in the Sierra foothills near Groveland. Its proximity to Yosemite National Park, just five miles from the west entrance station, makes it ideal for many. The park is an affiliate of Thousand Trails, whose facilities usually are open only to members, but in this rare case, it is open to the general public. It is a family-oriented park with a large variety of recreation options and seasonal organized activities. Fishing and swimming are popular, and the river is stocked with trout. A plus is 24-hour security.

RV sites, facilities: There are 20 sites with full hookups (30 amps) for RVs of any length and 25 sites for tents available to the public (more sites are available to Thousand Trails members only), as well as cabins, yurts, and a hostel. Picnic tables and fire rings are provided. Restrooms, drinking water, showers, flush toilets, a fish-cleaning station, and coin laundry are available. A store, gas station, propane, and firewood are available. Kayak rentals, pedal boats, inner tubes, and bicycles are available for rent. Leashed pets are permitted.

Reservations, fees: Reservations are accepted at 800/533-1001. Sites are $37–39.50 per night for RVs, $29.50–32 per night for tents. Some credit cards accepted. Open year-round, weather permitting.

Directions: Drive east on Highway 120 to Groveland. From Groveland, continue east for 18 miles to the entrance road (signed) for Yosemite Lakes on the right. Turn right and drive a short distance to the park.

Contact: Yosemite Lakes, 209/962-0121, www.stayatyosemite.com.

9 HODGDON MEADOW

Scenic rating: 7

in Yosemite National Park
See map page 772

Hodgdon Meadow is on the outskirts of Yosemite, just inside the park's borders at the Big Oak Flat (Highway 120) entrance station, at 4,900 feet in elevation. It is near a small feeder creek to the South Fork Tuolumne River. It is about a 20-minute drive on Highway 120 to a major junction, where a left turn takes you on Tioga Road and to Yosemite's high country, including Tuolumne Meadows, and where staying on Big Flat Road routes you toward Yosemite Valley (25 miles from the camp). Because of the presence of bears, use of food lockers is required.

RV sites, facilities: There are 105 sites for tents or RVs up to 35 feet (no hookups) and four group sites for 13–30 people each. Picnic tables, fire rings, and food lockers are provided. Drinking water and flush toilets are available.

CALIFORNIA

Leashed pets are permitted in the campground but not in group camps or on trails.

Reservations, fees: Reservations are accepted at 800/436-PARK (800/436-7275) or http://reservations.nps.gov. Reservations are required April–mid-October. Sites are $20 per night May–October, $14 the remainder of the year, and a group campsite costs $40 per night, plus a $20 park entrance fee per vehicle. Open year-round, except for group sites.

Directions: From Groveland, drive east on Highway 120 to the Big Oak Flat entrance station for Yosemite National Park. Just after passing the entrance station, turn left and drive a short distance to the campground on the right.

Contact: Yosemite National Park, 209/372-0200 for a touch-tone menu of recorded information, www.nps.gov/yose.

10 LOWER PINES

Scenic rating: 9

in Yosemite Valley in Yosemite National Park

See map page 772

Lower Pines sits right along the Merced River, quite pretty, in the center of Yosemite Valley. Of course, the tents and RVs are jammed in quite close together. Within walking distance is the trail to Mirror Lake (a zoo on parade), as well as the trailhead at Happy Isles for the hike up to Vernal Fall and Nevada Fall. The park's shuttle bus picks up riders near the camp entrance.

RV sites, facilities: There are 60 sites for tents or RVs up to 40 feet, one double site for tents or RVs up to 40 feet, and two group camps. No hookups. Fire rings, picnic tables, and food lockers (mandatory use) are provided. Drinking water and flush toilets are available. A grocery store, a coin laundry, propane gas, a recycling center, and horse and bike rentals are available nearby. Leashed pets are allowed.

Reservations, fees: Reservations are required at 800/436-PARK (800/436-7275) or http://reservations.nps.gov. Sites are $20 per night, $30 per night for double or group sites, plus a $20 park entrance fee per vehicle. There is a

seven-day limit during the summer. Open late March–October, weather permitting.

Directions: From Merced, drive east on Highway 140 to the Arch Rock entrance station. Continue east to the Big Oak Flat Road junction (0.5 mile before entering Yosemite Valley). Continue into Yosemite Valley and drive past Curry Village (on the right) to the campground entrance on the left side of the road (just before Clarks Bridge).

Contact: Yosemite National Park, 209/372-0200 for a touch-tone menu of recorded information, www.nps.gov/yose.

11 UPPER PINES

Scenic rating: 9

in Yosemite Valley in Yosemite National Park

See map page 772

Of the campgrounds in Yosemite Valley, Upper Pines is the closest trailhead to paradise, providing you can get a campsite at the far south end of the camp. From here it is a short walk to Happy Isles trailhead and with it the chance to hike to Vernal Fall on Mist Trail (steep) or beyond to Nevada Fall (very steep) at the foot of Liberty Cap. But crowded this camp is, and you'd better expect it. People come from all over the world to camp here. Sometimes it appears as if they are from other worlds as well. The elevation is 4,000 feet.

RV sites, facilities: There are 238 sites for tents or RVs up to 35 feet (no hookups), 39 sites for tents or RVs up to 35 feet with partial hookups (30 amps), and 50 walk-in sites. Fire rings, picnic tables, and food lockers (mandatory use) are provided. Drinking water, flush toilets, and a dump station are available. A grocery store, a coin laundry, propane gas, a recycling center, and horse and bike rentals are available nearby. Leashed pets are permitted in the campgrounds but not on trails.

Reservations, fees: Reservations are required at 800/436-PARK (800/436-7275) or http://reservations.nps.gov. Sites are $20 per night, plus a $20 park entrance fee per vehicle. There is a seven-day limit during the summer. Open year-round.

Directions: From Merced, drive east on High-

CALIFORNIA

way 140 to the Arch Rock entrance station. Continue east to the Big Oak Flat Road junction (0.5 mile before entering Yosemite Valley). Continue into Yosemite Valley, driving past Curry Village (on the right) to the campground entrance on the right side of the road (just before Clarks Bridge).

Contact: Yosemite National Park, 209/372-0200 for a touch-tone menu of recorded information, www.nps.gov/yose.

12 NORTH PINES

Scenic rating: 9

in Yosemite Valley in Yosemite National Park

See map page 772

North Pines is along the Merced River. A trail out of camp heads east and links with the paved road/trail to Mirror Lake, a virtual parade of people. If you continue hiking past Mirror Lake you will get astounding views of Half Dome and then leave the masses behind as you enter Tenaya Canyon. The elevation is 4,000 feet.

RV sites, facilities: There are 81 sites for tents or RVs up to 40 feet (no hookups). Picnic tables, fire grills, and food lockers (mandatory use) are provided. Drinking water and flush toilets are available. A grocery store, a coin laundry, a recycling center, propane gas, and horse and bike rentals are available nearby. Leashed pets are allowed.

Reservations, fees: Reservations are required at 800/436-PARK (800/436-7275) or http:// reservations.nps.gov. Sites are $20 per night, plus a $20 park entrance fee per vehicle. Open April–September, weather permitting.

Directions: From Merced, drive east on Highway 140 to the Arch Rock entrance station. Continue east to the Big Oak Flat Road junction (0.5 mile before entering Yosemite Valley). Continue into Yosemite Valley, drive past Curry Village (on the right), continue past Upper and Lower Pines Campgrounds, and drive over Clarks Bridge to a junction at the horse stables. Turn left at the horse stables and drive a short distance to the campground on the right.

Contact: Yosemite National Park, 209/372-0200

for a touch-tone menu of recorded information, www.nps.gov/yose.

13 CRANE FLAT

Scenic rating: 6

near Tuolumne Grove of Big Trees in Yosemite National Park

See map page 772

Crane Flat is within a five-minute drive of the Tuolumne Grove of Big Trees and Merced Grove to the nearby west. This is the feature attraction in this part of Yosemite National Park, set near the western border in close proximity to the Big Oak Flat entrance station (Highway 120). The elevation is 6,200 feet. Yosemite Valley is about a 25-minute drive away.

RV sites, facilities: There are 166 sites for tents or RVs up to 35 feet (no hookups). Picnic tables, fire rings, and food lockers are provided. Drinking water and flush toilets are available. Groceries, propane gas, and a gas station are nearby. Leashed pets are allowed in the campground.

Reservations, fees: Reservations are required at 800/436-PARK (800/436-7275) or http:// reservations.nps.gov. Sites are $20 per night, plus a $20 park entrance fee per vehicle. Open June–September, weather permitting.

Directions: From Groveland, drive east on Highway 120 to the Big Oak Flat entrance station for Yosemite National Park. After passing through the entrance station, drive about 10 miles to the campground entrance road on the right. Turn right and drive 0.5 mile to the campground.

Contact: Yosemite National Park, 209/372-0200 for a touch-tone menu of recorded information, www.nps.gov/yose.

14 BRIDALVEIL CREEK

Scenic rating: 10

near Glacier Point in Yosemite National Park

See map page 772

There may be no better view in the world than the one from Glacier Point, looking down into

Yosemite Valley, where Half Dome stands like nature's perfect sculpture. Then there are the perfect views of Yosemite Falls, Nevada Fall, Vernal Fall, and several hundred square miles of Yosemite's wilderness backcountry. This is the closest camp to Glacier Point's drive-to vantage point, but it is also the closest camp to the best day hikes in the entire park. Along Glacier Point Road are trailheads to Sentinel Dome (incredible view of Yosemite Falls) and Taft Point (breathtaking drop, incredible view of El Capitan), and to McGurk Meadow (one of the most pristine spots on earth). At 7,200 feet, the camp is more than 3,000 feet higher than Yosemite Valley. A good day hike out of camp leads you to Ostrander Lake, just below Horse Ridge.

RV sites, facilities: There are 110 sites for tents or RVs up to 35 feet, three equestrian sites, and two group sites for 13–30 people each. No hookups. Picnic tables, fire grills, and food lockers (mandatory use) are provided. Drinking water and flush toilets are available. Leashed pets are permitted, except in group sites.

Reservations, fees: Reservations are not accepted for individual sites, but they are required for equestrian sites and group sites at 800/436-PARK (800/436-7275) or http://reservations. nps.gov. Sites are $14 per night, $25 per night for an equestrian site, and $40 per night for a group site, plus a $20 park entrance fee per vehicle. A 14-day stay limit is enforced. Open July–early September, weather permitting.

Directions: From Merced, drive east on Highway 140 to the Arch Rock entrance station. Continue east (past Big Oak Flat Road junction) to the junction with Wawona Road/Highway 41 (just before Yosemite Valley). Turn right on Highway 41/Wawona Road and drive about 10 miles to Glacier Point Road. Turn left on Glacier Point Road and drive about five miles (a few miles past Badger Pass Ski Area) to Peregoy Meadow and the campground access road on the right. Turn right and drive a short distance to the campground.

Contact: Yosemite National Park, 209/372-0200 for a touch-tone menu of recorded information, www.nps.gov/yose.

15 YOSEMITE-MARIPOSA KOA

Scenic rating: 7

near Mariposa

See map page 772

A little duck pond, a swimming pool, and proximity to Yosemite National Park make this one a winner. A shuttle bus service (fee) to the national park is a great bonus. The RV sites are lined up along the entrance road. A 10 P.M. "quiet time" helps ensure a good night's sleep. It's a one-hour drive to Yosemite Valley, and your best bet is to get there early to enjoy the spectacular beauty before the park is packed with people.

RV sites, facilities: There are 49 sites with full or partial hookups (30 and 50 amps) for RVs up to 40 feet, 26 tent sites, 12 cabins, and three lodges. Picnic tables and barbecues are provided; no wood fires. Restrooms have showers. A dump station, Wi-Fi, telephone/modem access, a coin laundry, a convenience store, propane gas, recreation room, seasonal swimming pool, peewee golf, a train caboose with arcade, and a playground are available. Some facilities are wheelchair accessible. Leashed pets are permitted in RV and tent sites only, with certain restrictions.

Reservations, fees: Reservations are accepted at 800/562-9391. Sites are $30–55 per night, $6 per person per night for more than two people, $5 per night for an additional vehicle, $2 per pet per night. Call for cabin and lodge prices. Some credit cards accepted. Open year-round.

Directions: From Merced, drive east on Highway 140 to Mariposa. Continue on Highway 140 for seven miles to Midpines and the campground entrance on the left at 6323 Highway 140.

Contact: Yosemite-Mariposa KOA, 209/966-2201, www.koa.com.

CALIFORNIA

16 WAWONA

Scenic rating: 9

on the South Fork of the Merced River in Yosemite
National Park

See map page 772

Wawona Camp is an attractive alternative to
the packed camps in Yosemite Valley, providing
you don't mind the relatively long drives to the
best destinations. The camp is pretty, set along
the South Fork of the Merced River, with the
sites more spacious than at most other drive-to
camps in the park. The nearest attraction is the
Mariposa Grove of Giant Sequoias, but get your
visit in by 9 A.M., because after that it turns
into a zoo, complete with shuttle train. The
best nearby hike is a strenuous 10-mile round-
trip to Chilnualna Falls, the prettiest sight in
the southern region of the park; the trailhead
is at the east end of Chilnualna Road in North
Wawona. It's a 45-minute drive to either Glacier
Point or Yosemite Valley.

RV sites, facilities: There are 93 sites for tents
or RVs up to 35 feet, two group tent sites for
13–30 people each, and two horse camps.
No hookups. Picnic tables, fire grills, and
food lockers (mandatory use) are provided.
Drinking water and flush toilets are available.
Leashed pets are permitted but not in group
sites, horse camps, or on trails. There are also
some stock-handling facilities for camping
with pack animals; call for further information. A grocery store, a dump station, propane
gas, a gas station, a post office, a restaurant,
and seasonal horseback-riding facilities are
available nearby.

Reservations, fees: Reservations are required
May–September. Reserve by calling 800/436-
PARK (800/436-7275) or http://reservations.
nps.gov. Sites are $20 per night, $25 per
night for horse camps, $40 per night for
group tent sites, plus a $20 park entrance
fee per vehicle. No reservations are taken
October–April, and rates are reduced to $14
per night for individual sites. A seven-day
camping limit is enforced during the summer.
Open year-round.

Directions: From Oakhurst, drive north on
Highway 41 to the Wawona entrance of Yosemite National Park. Continue north on Highway
41 past Wawona (golf course on the left) and
drive one mile to the campground entrance on
the left.

Contact: Yosemite National Park, 209/372-
0200 for a touch-tone menu of recorded information, www.nps.gov/yose.

17 SUMMERDALE

Scenic rating: 7

on the South Fork of the Merced River in Sierra
National Forest

See map page 772

You can't get much closer to Yosemite National
Park. This camp is within a mile of the Wawona
entrance to Yosemite, about a five-minute drive
to the Mariposa Grove. If you don't mind its
proximity to the highway, this is a pretty spot
in its own right, set along Big Creek, a feeder
stream to the South Fork Merced River. Some
good swimming holes are in this area. The
elevation is 5,000 feet.

RV sites, facilities: There are 30 sites for tents
or RVs up to 24 feet (no hookups). Picnic
tables and fire grills are provided. Drinking
water and vault toilets are available. A grocery
store is nearby (within one mile). Some facilities are wheelchair accessible. Leashed pets
are permitted.

Reservations, fees: Reservations are accepted at 877/444-6777 ($9 reservation fee) or
www.ReserveUSA.com. Sites are $17 per night,
$5 per night per additional vehicle. Open May–
October, weather permitting.

Directions: From Oakhurst, drive north on
Highway 41 to Fish Camp and continue for
one mile to the campground entrance on the
left side of the road.

Contact: Sierra National Forest, Bass Lake Ranger District, 559/877-2218, fax 559/877-3108.

18 BUCKEYE

Scenic rating: 8

near Buckeye Creek in Humboldt-Toiyabe
National Forest

See map page 772

Here's a little secret: A two-mile hike out of camp heads to the undeveloped Buckeye Hot Springs. That is what inspires campers to bypass the fishing at nearby Robinson Creek (three miles away) and Twin Lakes (six miles away). The camp feels remote and primitive, set at 7,000 feet on the eastern slope of the Sierra near Buckeye Creek. Another secret is that rainbow trout are planted at the little bridge that crosses Buckeye Creek near the campground. A trail that starts near camp is routed through Buckeye Canyon and into the Hoover Wilderness.

RV sites, facilities: There are 65 paved sites for tents or RVs up to 35 feet (no hookups). Picnic tables and fire grills are provided. Drinking water and vault and flush toilets are available. Some facilities are wheelchair accessible. Leashed pets are permitted.

Reservations, fees: Reservations are not accepted. Sites are $13 per night, $5 per night for each additional vehicle. Open May–October, weather permitting.

Directions: On U.S. 395, drive to Bridgeport and the junction with Twin Lakes Road. Turn west and drive seven miles to Buckeye Road. Turn right (north) on Buckeye Road (dirt, often impassable when wet) and drive 3.5 miles to the campground.

Contact: Humboldt-Toiyabe National Forest, Bridgeport Ranger District, 760/932-7070, fax 760/932-5899; American Land and Leisure, 760/932-9888.

19 WILLOW SPRINGS RV PARK

Scenic rating: 6

near Bridgeport

See map page 773

Willow Springs RV Park is at 6,800 feet along U.S. 395, which runs along the eastern Sierra

from Carson City south to Bishop and beyond to Lone Pine. The park is one mile from the turnoff to Bodie ghost town. A nice touch to the place is a central campfire that has been in place for more than 50 years. The country is stark here on the edge of the high Nevada desert, but there are many side trips that give the area life. The most popular destinations are to the nearby south: Mono Lake, with its tufa towers and incredible populations of breeding gulls and waterfowl, and the Bodie ghost town. For trout fishing, there's Bridgeport Reservoir to the north (good trolling) and downstream to the East Walker River (fly-fishing), both excellent destinations, as well as Twin Lakes to the west (huge brown trout).

RV sites, facilities: There are 25 sites with full hookups (30 amps) for RVs of any length. No tents. A motel is also available. Picnic tables are provided. Restrooms have showers. A coin laundry and nightly campfires are available. A restaurant is within walking distance. Leashed pets are permitted.

Reservations, fees: Reservations are accepted. Sites are $28 per night, $4 per person per night for more than two people. Open May–October.

Directions: From Bridgeport on U.S. 395, drive five miles south to the park, which is on the east side of the highway.

Contact: Willow Springs RV Park, 760/932-7725.

20 HONEYMOON FLAT

Scenic rating: 8

on Robinson Creek in Humboldt-Toiyabe
National Forest

See map page 772

The camp is beside Robinson Creek at 7,000 feet in elevation, in the transition zone between the Sierra Nevada range to the west and the high desert to the east. It is easy to reach on the access road to Twin Lakes, only three miles farther. The lake is famous for occasional huge brown trout. However, the fishing at Robinson Creek is also often quite good, thanks to large numbers of trout planted each year.

CALIFORNIA

RV sites, facilities: There are 35 sites for tents or RVs up to 35 feet (no hookups). Picnic tables and fire grills are provided. Drinking water, food lockers, and vault toilets are available. Some facilities are wheelchair accessible. Leashed pets are permitted.

Reservations, fees: Reservations are accepted at 877/444-6777 ($9 reservation fee) or www.ReserveUSA.com. Sites are $13 per night, $5 per night for each additional vehicle. Open mid-April–October.

Directions: On U.S. 395, drive to Bridgeport and the junction with Twin Lakes Road. Turn west and drive eight miles to the campground.

Contact: Humboldt-Toiyabe National Forest, Bridgeport Ranger District, 760/932-7070, fax 760/932-5899; American Land and Leisure, 760/932-9888.

21 PAHA

Scenic rating: 8

near Twin Lakes in Humboldt-Toiyabe National Forest

See map page 772

This is one in a series of camps near Robinson Creek and within close range of Twin Lakes. The elevation at the camp is 7,000 feet. (See the listings in this chapter for *Lower Twin Lake* and *Honeymoon Flat* for more information.)

RV sites, facilities: There are 22 sites for tents or RVs up to 35 feet (no hookups). Picnic tables and fire grills are provided. Drinking water, flush toilets, and food lockers are available. Two boat launches, a store, coin showers, and a coin laundry are available nearby at Twin Lakes Resort. Leashed pets are permitted.

Reservations, fees: Reservations are accepted at 877/444-6777 ($9 reservation fee) or www.ReserveUSA.com. Sites are $15 per night, $5 per night for each additional vehicle. Open May–October, weather permitting.

Directions: On U.S. 395, drive to Bridgeport and the junction with Twin Lakes Road. Turn west and drive 10 miles to the campground.

Contact: Humboldt-Toiyabe National Forest,

Bridgeport Ranger District, 760/932-7070, fax 760/932-5899; American Land and Leisure, 760/932-9888.

22 ROBINSON CREEK

Scenic rating: 9

near Twin Lakes in Humboldt-Toiyabe National Forest

See map page 772

This campground, one of a series in the area, is at 7,000 feet on Robinson Creek, not far from Twin Lakes. The campground is divided into two areas. (For recreation options, see the listings in this chapter for *Lower Twin Lake* and *Honeymoon Flat*.)

RV sites, facilities: There are 54 paved sites for tents or RVs up to 35 feet (no hookups). Picnic tables, food lockers, and fire grills are provided. Drinking water and flush and vault toilets are available. An amphitheater is nearby. Boat launches, a store, a coin laundry, and coin showers are nearby at Twin Lakes Resort. Some facilities are wheelchair accessible. Leashed pets are permitted.

Reservations, fees: Reservations are accepted at 877/444-6777 ($9 reservation fee) or www.ReserveUSA.com. Sites are $15 per night, $5 per night for each additional vehicle. Open mid-April–October, weather permitting.

Directions: On U.S. 395, drive to Bridgeport and the junction with Twin Lakes Road. Turn west and drive 10 miles to the campground.

Contact: Humboldt-Toiyabe National Forest, Bridgeport Ranger District, 760/932-7070, fax 760/932-5899; American Land and Leisure, 760/932-9888.

23 CRAGS CAMPGROUND

Scenic rating: 8

on Robinson Creek in Humboldt-Toiyabe National Forest

See map page 772

Crags Camp is at 7,100 feet in the Sierra, one of a series of campgrounds along Robinson Creek

CALIFORNIA

CALIFORNIA

near Lower Twin Lake. While this camp does not offer direct access to Lower Twin, home of giant brown trout, it is very close. (See the listings in this chapter for *Lower Twin Lake* and *Honeymoon Flat*.)

RV sites, facilities: There are 52 sites for tents or RVs up to 45 feet (no hookups). Picnic tables, food lockers, and fire grills are provided. Drinking water and flush toilets are available. A boat launch (at Lower Twin Lake), store, coin laundry, and coin showers are within a half mile. Some facilities are wheelchair accessible. Leashed pets are permitted.

Reservations, fees: Reservations are accepted at 877/444-6777 ($9 reservation fee) or www.ReserveUSA.com. Sites are $15 per night, $5 per night for each additional vehicle. Open April–October, weather permitting.

Directions: On U.S. 395, drive to Bridgeport and the junction with Twin Lakes Road. Turn west and drive 11 miles to South Twin Road (just before reaching Lower Twin Lake). Turn left and drive over the bridge at Robinson Creek to another road on the left. Turn left and drive a short distance to the campground.

Contact: Humboldt-Toiyabe National Forest, Bridgeport Ranger District, 760/932-7070, fax 760/932-5899; American Land and Leisure, 760/932-9888.

24 LOWER TWIN LAKE

Scenic rating: 9

in Humboldt-Toiyabe National Forest
See map page 772

The Twin Lakes are actually two lakes, set high in the eastern Sierra at 7,000 feet. Each lake is unique. Lower Twin, known as the fishing lake, with a 5-mph speed limit, has a full resort, a marina, a boat ramp, and some of the biggest brown trout in the West. The state record brown was caught here in 1985, 26.5 pounds. Of course, most of the trout are your typical 10- to 12-inch planted rainbow trout, but nobody seems to mind, with the chance of a true monster-sized fish always in the back of

the minds of anglers. Upper Twin Lake, with a resort and marina, is a primary destination for boaters, personal watercraft, water-skiers, swimmers, and sailboarders. These lakes are very popular in summer. An option for campers is an excellent trailhead for hiking near Mono Village at the head of Upper Twin Lake. Here you will find Barney Lake Trail, which is routed up the headwaters of Robinson Creek, steeply at times, to Barney Lake, an excellent day hike.

RV sites, facilities: There are 15 paved sites for tents or RVs up to 35 feet (no hookups). Picnic tables and fire grills are provided. Drinking water, flush toilets, and food lockers are available. A boat launch, store, coin showers, and a coin laundry are available nearby. Leashed pets are permitted.

Reservations, fees: Reservations are accepted at 877/444-6777 ($9 reservation fee) or www.ReserveUSA.com. Sites are $15 per night, $5 per night for each additional vehicle. Open early May–mid-October, weather permitting.

Directions: On U.S. 395, drive to Bridgeport and the junction with Twin Lakes Road. Turn west and drive 11 miles to South Twin Road (just before reaching Lower Twin Lake). Turn left and drive over the bridge at Robinson Creek and to the campground entrance road on the right.

Contact: Humboldt-Toiyabe National Forest, Bridgeport Ranger District, 760/932-7070, fax 760/932-5899; American Land and Leisure, 760/932-9888.

25 TRUMBULL LAKE

Scenic rating: 8

in Humboldt-Toiyabe National Forest
See map page 772

This is a high-mountain camp (9,500 feet) at the gateway to a beautiful Sierra basin. Little Trumbull Lake is the first lake on the north side of Virginia Lakes Road, with Virginia Lakes nearby, along with the Hoover Wilderness and access to many other small lakes by trail. A trail meanders just north of Blue Lake, and then it leads west to Frog Lake, Summit Lake, and beyond into a remote area of Yosemite National Park. If you don't want to rough it, cabins, boat rentals, and a restaurant are available at Virginia Lakes Resort. Gas motors, swimming, and water/body contact are prohibited at Virginia Lakes.

RV sites, facilities: There are 45 sites for tents or RVs up to 35 feet (no hookups). Picnic tables and fire grills are provided. Drinking water and vault toilets are available. A store is nearby at the resort. Some facilities are wheelchair accessible. Leashed pets are permitted.

Reservations, fees: Reservations are accepted at 877/444-6777 ($9 reservation fee) or www.ReserveUSA.com. Sites are $13 per night, $5 per night for each additional vehicle. Open June–September, weather permitting.

Directions: From Bridgeport, drive south on U.S. 395 for 13.5 miles to Virginia Lakes Road. Turn right on Virginia Lakes Road and drive 6.5 miles to the campground entrance road.

Contact: Humboldt-Toiyabe National Forest, Bridgeport Ranger District, 760/932-7070, fax 760/932-5899; American Land and Leisure, 760/932-9888.

26 SADDLEBAG LAKE

Scenic rating: 10

in Inyo National Forest

See map page 772

This camp is in spectacular high country above the tree line, the highest drive-to camp and lake in California; Saddlebag Lake sits at 10,087 feet. The camp is about a quarter mile from the lake, within walking range of the little store, boat rentals, and a one-minute drive for launching a boat at the ramp. The scenery is stark; everything is granite, ice, or water, with only a few lodgepole pines managing precarious toeholds, sprinkled across the landscape on the access road. An excellent trailhead is available for hiking, with the best hike routed out past little Hummingbird Lake to Lundy Pass. A hiker's shuttle boat, which will ferry you across the lake, is a nice plus. Note that with the el-

evation and the high mountain pass, it can be windy and cold here, and some people find it difficult to catch their breath on simple hikes. In addition, RV users should note that level sites are extremely hard to come by.

RV sites, facilities: There are 20 sites for tents or RVs up to 30 feet (no hookups) and one group tent site for up to 25 people. Drinking water, fire grills, and picnic tables are provided. Vault toilets, boat rentals, and a primitive boat launch are available. A grocery store is nearby. Some facilities are wheelchair accessible. Leashed pets are permitted.

Reservations, fees: Reservations are not accepted for individual sites but are required for the group site at 877/444-6777 ($9 reservation fee) or www.ReserveUSA.com. Sites are $17 per night, $56 per night for the group site. Open early June–mid-October, weather permitting.

Directions: On U.S. 395, drive 0.5 mile south of Lee Vining and the junction with Highway 120. Turn west and drive about 11 miles to Saddlebag Lake Road. Turn right and drive 2.5 miles to the campground on the right.

From Merced, drive east on Highway 140 to the Arch Rock entrance station. Continue east to the Big Oak Flat Road junction (0.5 mile before entering Yosemite Valley). Turn left and drive 14 miles to Tioga Road. Turn right and drive about 65 miles (past Tuolumne Meadows) and through the Tioga Pass entrance station. Continue two miles to Saddlebag Lake Road. Turn left and drive 2.5 miles (rough road) to the campground on the right.

Contact: Inyo National Forest, Mono Basin Scenic Area Ranger Station and Visitor Center, 760/647-3044, fax 760/647-3046.

27 LOWER LEE VINING CAMP

Scenic rating: 7

near Lee Vining

See map page 773

This former Mono County camp and its neighboring camps—Cattleguard, Moraine, Aspen, Big Bend, and Boulder—can be a godsend for

CALIFORNIA

vacationers who show up at Yosemite National Park and make the discovery that there are no sites left, a terrible experience for some late-night arrivals. But these Forest Service campgrounds provide a great safety valve, even if they are extremely primitive, on the edge of timber. Lee Vining Creek is the highlight, flowing right past the campgrounds along Highway 120, bound for Mono Lake to the east. It is stocked regularly during the fishing season. A must-do side trip is venturing to the south shore of Mono Lake to walk amid the bizarre yet beautiful tufa towers. There is good rock-climbing and hiking. Although sunshine is the norm, be prepared for all kinds of weather: It can snow every month of the year here. Short but lively thunderstorms are common in early summer. Other nearby trips are available to Mammoth Lakes, June Lake, and Bodie State Park.

RV sites, facilities: There are 59 sites for tents or RVs up to 40 feet (no hookups). Picnic tables and fire rings are provided. Portable toilets are available. No drinking water is available. You can buy supplies in Lee Vining (about two miles away). Leashed pets are permitted.

Reservations, fees: Reservations are not accepted. Sites are $14 per night. Open May–October, weather permitting.

Directions: On U.S. 395, drive to just south of Lee Vining and the junction with Highway 120. Turn west on Highway 120 and drive about 2.5 miles. Turn left into the campground entrance.

Contact: Inyo National Forest, Mono Basin Scenic Area Ranger Station and Visitor Center, 760/647-3044, fax 760/647-3046.

28 BIG BEND

Scenic rating: 8

on Lee Vining Creek in Inyo National Forest
See map page 773

This camp is in sparse but beautiful country along Lee Vining Creek at 7,800 feet elevation. Ancient pine trees are on-site. It is an excellent bet for an overflow camp if Tuolumne Meadows in nearby Yosemite is packed. The view from the camp to the north features Mono Dome (10,614 feet) and Lee Vining Peak (11,691 feet).

RV sites, facilities: There are 17 sites for tents or RVs up to 30 feet (no hookups). Picnic tables and fire grills are provided. Drinking water and vault toilets are available. Some facilities are wheelchair accessible. Leashed pets are permitted.

Reservations, fees: Reservations are not accepted. Sites are $17 per night. Open late April–mid-October, weather permitting.

Directions: On U.S. 395, drive to just south of Lee Vining and the junction with Highway 120. Turn west on Highway 120 and drive about 3.5 miles to Poole Power Plant Road and the signed campground access road on the right. Turn right and drive a short distance to the camp.

Contact: Inyo National Forest, Mono Basin Scenic Area Ranger Station and Visitor Center, 760/647-3044, fax 760/647-3046.

29 ASPEN

Scenic rating: 8

on Lee Vining Creek
See map page 773

This high-country, primitive camp is along Lee Vining Creek at 7,500 feet, on the eastern slopes of the Sierra just east of Yosemite National Park. Take the side trip to moonlike Mono Lake, best seen at the south shore's Tufa State Reserve.

RV sites, facilities: There are 58 sites for tents or RVs up to 40 feet (no hookups). Picnic tables and fire rings are provided. Portable toilets are available. Drinking water is available. You can buy supplies in Lee Vining. Leashed pets are permitted.

Reservations, fees: Reservations are not accepted. Sites are $14 per night. Open May–October, weather permitting.

Directions: On U.S. 395, drive to just south of Lee Vining and the junction with Highway 120. Turn west on Highway 120 and drive about 3.5 miles. Exit onto Poole Power Plant Road. Turn left and drive about four miles west to the campground on the left.

CALIFORNIA

Contact: Inyo National Forest, Mono Basin Scenic Area Ranger Station and Visitor Center, 760/647-3044, fax 760/647-3046.

Contact: Inyo National Forest, Mono Basin Scenic Area Ranger Station and Visitor Center, 760/647-3044, fax 760/647-3046.

30 ELLERY LAKE

Scenic rating: 9

in Inyo National Forest

See map page 772

Ellery Lake offers all the spectacular beauty of Yosemite but is two miles outside park borders. That means it is stocked with trout by the Department of Fish and Game (no lakes in Yosemite are planted, hence the lousy fishing). Just like neighboring Tioga Lake, here are deep-blue waters set in rock in the 9,500-foot elevation range, one of the most pristine highway-access lake settings anywhere. Although there is no boat ramp, boats with small motors are allowed and can be hand-launched. Nearby Saddlebag Lake is a common side trip, the highest drive-to lake in California. Whenever Tuolumne Meadows fills in Yosemite, this camp fills shortly thereafter. Camp elevation is 9,500 feet.

RV sites, facilities: There are 12 sites for tents or RVs up to 30 feet (no hookups). Picnic tables and fire grills are provided. Drinking water and vault toilets are available. A grocery store is nearby. Some facilities are wheelchair accessible. Leashed pets are permitted.

Reservations, fees: Reservations are not accepted. Sites are $15 per night. Open early June–mid-October, weather permitting.

Directions: On U.S. 395, drive to just south of Lee Vining and the junction with Highway 120. Turn west on Highway 120 and drive about 10 miles to the campground on the left side of the road.

From Merced, drive east on Highway 140 to the Arch Rock entrance station. Continue east to the Big Oak Flat Road junction (0.5 mile before entering Yosemite Valley). Turn left and drive 14 miles to Tioga Road. Turn right and drive about 65 miles, past Tuolumne Meadows and through the Tioga Pass entrance station. Continue four miles to the campground entrance road on the right.

31 TIOGA LAKE

Scenic rating: 9

in Inyo National Forest

See map page 772

Tioga Lake is a dramatic sight, with gemlike blue waters encircled by Sierra granite at 9,700 feet in elevation. Tioga and adjacent Ellery Lake make a pair of gorgeous waters with near-lake camping, trout fishing (stocked with rainbow trout), and access to Yosemite National Park and Saddlebag Lake. Conditions here are much like those at neighboring Ellery. The only downers: It can get windy here (no foolin'!) and the camps fill quickly from the overflow crowds at Tuolumne Meadows. (See the listing in this chapter for *Ellery Lake* for more information.)

RV sites, facilities: There are 13 sites for tents or RVs up to 30 feet (no hookups). Picnic tables and fire grills are provided. Drinking water and vault toilets are available. Some facilities are wheelchair accessible. Leashed pets are permitted.

Reservations, fees: Reservations are not accepted. Sites are $17 per night. Open early June–mid-October, weather permitting.

Directions: On U.S. 395, drive to just south of Lee Vining and the junction with Highway 120. Turn west on Highway 120 and drive about 11 miles (just past Ellery Lake) to the campground on the left side of the road.

From Merced, drive east on Highway 140 to the Arch Rock entrance station. Continue east to the Big Oak Flat Road junction (0.5 mile before entering Yosemite Valley). Turn left and drive 14 miles to Tioga Road. Turn right and drive about 65 miles, past Tuolumne Meadows and through the Tioga Pass entrance station. Continue one mile to the campground entrance road on the right side of the road.

Contact: Inyo National Forest, Mono Basin Scenic Area Ranger Station and Visitor Center, 760/647-3044, fax 760/647-3046.

CALIFORNIA

32 SILVER LAKE

Scenic rating: 9

in Inyo National Forest

See map page 773

Silver Lake is at 7,200 feet, an 80-acre lake in the June Lake Loop with Carson Peak looming in the background. Boat rentals, fishing for trout at the lake, a beautiful trout stream (Rush Creek) next to the camp, and a nearby trailhead for wilderness hiking and horseback riding (rentals available) are the highlights. The camp is largely exposed and vulnerable to winds, the only downer. Within walking distance to the south is Silver Lake, always a pretty sight, especially when afternoon winds cause the lake surface to sparkle in crackling silver. The lake speed limit is 10 mph. Swimming is not recommended because of the rocky shoreline. Just across the road from the camp is a great trailhead for the Ansel Adams Wilderness, with a two-hour hike available that climbs to pretty Agnew Lake overlooking the June Lake basin; a wilderness permit is required for overnight use.

RV sites, facilities: There are 63 sites for tents or RVs up to 32 feet (no hookups). Picnic tables and fire grills are provided. Drinking water, flush toilets, and horseback-riding facilities are available. A grocery store, a coin laundry, motorboat rentals, a boat ramp, bait, a café, boat fuel, and propane gas are available nearby. Some facilities are wheelchair accessible. Leashed pets are permitted.

Reservations, fees: Reservations are accepted at 877/444-6777 ($9 reservation fee) or www.ReserveUSA.com. Sites are $15 per night, $4 per night for each additional vehicle. Open late April–early November, weather permitting.

Directions: From Lee Vining on U.S. 395, drive south for six miles to the first Highway 158 north/June Lake Loop turnoff. Turn west (right) and drive nine miles (past Grant Lake) to Silver Lake. Just as you arrive at Silver Lake (a small store is on the right), turn left at the campground entrance.

Contact: Inyo National Forest, Mono Basin Scenic Area Ranger Station and Visitor Center, 760/647-3044, fax 760/647-3046.

33 OH! RIDGE

Scenic rating: 8

on June Lake in Inyo National Forest

See map page 773

This is the largest of the campgrounds on June Lake. However, it is not the most popular since it is not right on the lakeshore, but back about a quarter mile or so from the north end of the lake. Regardless, it has the best views of the lake, with the ridge of the high Sierra providing a backdrop. The lake is a good one for trout fishing. The elevation is 7,600 feet.

RV sites, facilities: There are 148 sites for tents or RVs up to 40 feet (no hookups). Picnic tables and fire grills are provided. Drinking water, flush toilets, and a swimming beach are available. A grocery store, a coin laundry, a boat ramp, boat and tackle rentals, moorings, and propane gas are available nearby. Some facilities are wheelchair accessible. Leashed pets are permitted.

Reservations, fees: Reservations are accepted at 877/444-6777 ($9 reservation fee) or www.ReserveUSA.com. Sites are $15 per night, $4 per night for each additional vehicle. Open late April–early November, weather permitting.

Directions: From Lee Vining, drive south on U.S. 395 (past the first Highway 158/June Lake Loop turnoff) to June Lake Junction (a gas station/store is on the west side of the road) and Highway 158 south. Turn west on Highway 158 south and drive two miles to Oh! Ridge Road. Turn right and drive a mile to the campground access road (signed). Turn left and drive to the campground.

Contact: Inyo National Forest, Mono Basin Scenic Area Ranger Station and Visitor Center, 760/647-3044, fax 760/647-3046.

34 PINE CLIFF RESORT

Scenic rating: 7

at June Lake

See map page 773

You found "kid heaven" at Pine Cliff Resort. This camp is in a pretty setting along the north shore of June Lake (7,600 feet in elevation), the feature lake among four in the June Lake Loop. The campsites are nestled in pine trees, designed so each site accommodates different-sized rigs and families, and the campground is about a quarter mile from June Lake. This is the only camp at June Lake Loop that has a swimming beach. The landscape is a pretty one, with the lake below snowcapped peaks. The bonus is that June Lake gets large numbers of trout plants each summer, making it extremely popular with anglers. Of the lakes in the June Lake Loop, this is the one that has the most of everything—the most beauty, the most fish, the most developed accommodations, and, alas, the most people. This resort has been operated as a family business for more than 50 years.

RV sites, facilities: There are 154 sites with full hookups (20 and 30 amps) for RVs, 17 sites for tents or RVs with partial hookups (20 and 30 amps), and 55 sites for tents; a few sites are pull-through. There are also 14 rental trailers. Picnic tables and fire rings are provided. Restrooms have flush toilets and showers. Drinking water, a coin laundry, basketball, volleyball, tetherball, horseshoes, a convenience store, and propane gas are available. A primitive boat ramp, fish-cleaning facilities, and fuel are available nearby. Some facilities are wheelchair accessible. Leashed pets are permitted, with a maximum of two pets per site.

Reservations, fees: Reservations are recommended. Sites are $14–24 per night, $5 per night for an additional vehicle. The first pet is free, and the second pet is $1 per night. Open mid-April–October.

Directions: From Lee Vining, drive south on U.S. 395 (passing the first Highway 158 north/June Lake Loop turnoff) to June Lake Junction (a sign is posted for June Lake Village) and Highway 158 south. Turn right (west) on Highway 158 south and drive two miles to North Shore Drive (a sign is nearby for Pine Cliff Resort). Turn right and drive 0.5 mile to Pine Cliff Road. Turn left and drive 0.5 mile to the resort store on the right (route is well signed).

Contact: Pine Cliff Resort, 760/648-7558.

35 GULL LAKE

Scenic rating: 8

in Inyo National Forest

See map page 773

Little Gull Lake, just 64 acres, is the smallest of the lakes on the June Lake Loop, but to many it is the prettiest. It is at 7,600 feet, just west of June Lake, and with Carson Peak looming on the Sierra crest to the west, it is a dramatic and intimate setting. The lake is stocked with trout each summer, providing good fishing. A boat ramp is on the lake's southwest corner. Insider's tip: A rope swing at Gull Lake appeals to youngsters.

RV sites, facilities: There are 11 sites for tents or RVs up to 30 feet (no hookups). Drinking water, fire grills, and picnic tables are provided, and flush toilets are available. A grocery store, a coin laundry, a boat ramp, and propane gas are available nearby. Some facilities are wheelchair accessible. Leashed pets are permitted.

Reservations, fees: Reservations are not accepted. Sites are $15 per night, $4 per night for each additional vehicle. Open late April–early November, weather permitting.

Directions: From Lee Vining, drive south on U.S. 395 (past the first Highway 158/June Lake Loop turnoff) to June Lake Junction (a gas station/store is on the west side of the road) and Highway 158. Turn west on Highway 158 and drive three miles to the campground entrance on the right side of the road.

Contact: Inyo National Forest, Mono Basin Scenic Area Ranger Station and Visitor Center, 760/647-3044, fax 760/647-3046.

36 REVERSED CREEK

Scenic rating: 6

in Inyo National Forest

See map page 773

This camp is at 7,600 feet near pretty Reversed Creek, the only stream in the region that flows toward the mountains, not away from them. It is a small, tree-lined stream that provides decent

CALIFORNIA

trout fishing. The campsites are sheltered and set in a grove of aspen, but close enough to the road so you can still hear highway traffic. There are also cabins available for rent near here. Directly opposite the camp, on the other side of the road, is Gull Lake and the boat ramp. Two miles to the west, on the west side of the road, is the trailhead for the hike to Fern Lake on the edge of the Ansel Adams Wilderness, a little butt-kicker of a climb.

RV sites, facilities: There are 17 sites for tents or RVs up to 30 feet (no hookups). Picnic tables and fire grills are provided. Drinking water and flush toilets are available. A grocery store, a coin laundry, and propane gas are nearby. Boating is available at nearby Silver Lake, two miles away. Some facilities are wheelchair accessible. Leashed pets are permitted.

Reservations, fees: Reservations are not accepted. Sites are $15 per night, $4 per night for each additional vehicle. Open mid-May–October, weather permitting.

Directions: From Lee Vining, drive south on U.S. 395 (past the first Highway 158/June Lake Loop turnoff) to June Lake Junction (a gas station/store is on the west side of the road) and Highway 158 south. Turn right (west) on Highway 158 south and drive three miles to the campground on the left side of the road (across from Gull Lake).

Contact: Inyo National Forest, Mono Basin Scenic Area Ranger Station and Visitor Center, 760/647-3044, fax 760/647-3046.

37 JUNE LAKE

Scenic rating: 9

in Inyo National Forest
See map page 773

June Lake gets the highest use of all the lakes in the June Lakes Loop, and it has the best swimming, best fishing, and best sailboarding. There are three campgrounds at pretty June Lake; this is one of the two operated by the Forest Service (the other is Oh! Ridge). This one is on the northeast shore of the lake at 7,600 feet in eleva-

tion, a pretty spot with all supplies available just two miles to the south in the town of June Lake. The nearest boat launch is north of town. This is a good lake for trout fishing, receiving high numbers of stocked trout per year. A 10-mph speed limit is enforced.

RV sites, facilities: There are 28 sites for tents or RVs up to 32 feet (no hookups). Picnic tables and fire grills are provided. Drinking water, restrooms with flush toilets and coin showers, and a boat ramp are available. A grocery store, a coin laundry, boat and tackle rentals, moorings, and propane gas are available nearby. Leashed pets are permitted.

Reservations, fees: Reservations are accepted at 877/444-6777 ($9 reservation fee) or www.ReserveUSA.com. Sites are $15 per night, $4 per night for each additional vehicle. Open late April–early November, weather permitting.

Directions: From Lee Vining, drive south on U.S. 395 for 20 miles (six miles past Highway 158 north) to June Lake Junction (a sign is posted for June Lake Village) and Highway 158 south. Turn west (right) on Highway 158 south and drive two miles to June Lake. Turn right (signed) and drive a short distance to the campground.

Contact: Inyo National Forest, Mono Basin Scenic Area Ranger Station and Visitor Center, 760/647-3044, fax 760/647-3046.

38 HARTLEY SPRINGS

Scenic rating: 8

in Inyo National Forest
See map page 773

Even though this camp is only a five-minute drive from U.S. 395, those five minutes will take you into another orbit. It is in a forest of Jeffrey pine and has the feel of a remote, primitive camp, set in a high-mountain environment at an elevation of 8,400 feet. About two miles to the immediate north at elevation 8,611 feet is Obsidian Dome "Glass Flow," a craggy geologic formation that some people enjoy scrambling around and exploring; pick your access point carefully.

RV sites, facilities: There are 20 sites for tents or RVs up to 40 feet (no hookups). Picnic tables and fire grills are provided. Vault toilets are available. No drinking water is available. Garbage must be packed out. Leashed pets are permitted.

Reservations, fees: Reservations are not accepted. There is no fee for camping. Open late May–early November, weather permitting.

Directions: From Lee Vining, drive south on U.S. 395 (passing the first Highway 158/June Lake Loop turnoff) for 10 miles to June Lake Junction. Continue south on U.S. 395 for six miles to Glass Creek Road (a dirt road on the west side of the highway). Turn west (right) and drive two miles to the campground entrance road on the left.

Contact: Inyo National Forest, Mono Basin Scenic Area Ranger Station and Visitor Center, 760/647-3044, fax 760/647-3046.

39 AGNEW MEADOWS

Scenic rating: 9

in Inyo National Forest

See map page 773

This is a perfect camp to use as a launching pad for a backpacking trip or day of fly-fishing for trout. It is along the Upper San Joaquin River at 8,400 feet, with a trailhead for the Pacific Crest Trail available near the camp. From here you can hike seven miles to the gorgeous Thousand Island Lake, a beautiful lake sprinkled with islands set below Banner and Ritter Peaks in the spectacular Minarets. For day hikes, another choice is walking River Trail, which ventures from Agnew Meadows along the San Joaquin, providing excellent fishing, though the trout are small.

RV sites, facilities: There are 21 sites for tents or RVs up to 45 feet, and four group sites for tents or RVs can accommodate 10–20 people each. No hookups. Picnic tables and fire grills are provided. Drinking water, vault toilets, and horseback-riding facilities are available (three family sites have hitching racks where horse camping is permitted). Supplies can be obtained at Red's Meadow store. Leashed pets are permitted.

Reservations, fees: Reservations are not accepted for individual sites but are required for equestrian sites and group sites at 877/444-6777 ($9 reservation fee) or www.ReserveUSA.com. Sites are $16–20 per night for individual sites, $30–50 per night for equestrian and group sites, plus a $4–7 per person Red's Meadow/Agnew Meadows access fee. Open mid-June–mid-September, weather permitting.

Directions: On U.S. 395, drive to Mammoth Junction/Highway 203. Turn west on Highway 203 and drive four miles, through the town of Mammoth Lakes to Minaret Road (still Highway 203). Turn right and drive five miles to Minaret Station (past the Mammoth Mountain Ski Area). Continue for 2.6 miles to the campground entrance road on the right. Turn right and drive just under a mile to the campground. Note: The access road to the group sites is steep and narrow.

Access note: Noncampers are required to use a shuttle bus (fee) from the shuttle bus terminal at Mammoth Mountain Main Lodge Gondola Station 7 A.M.–7:30 P.M. Space is available for leashed dogs, bikes, and backpacks.

Contact: Inyo National Forest, Mammoth Ranger Station and Visitor Center, 760/924-5500, fax 760/924-5547.

40 PUMICE FLAT

Scenic rating: 8

on the San Joaquin River in Inyo National Forest

See map page 773

Pumice Flat (7,700 feet in elevation) provides roadside camping within short range of several adventures. A trail out of camp links with the Pacific Crest Trail, where you can hike along the Upper San Joaquin River for miles, providing excellent access for fly-fishing, and head north into the Ansel Adams Wilderness. Devils Postpile National Monument is just two miles south, along with the trailhead for Rainbow Falls.

RV sites, facilities: There are 17 sites for tents or RVs up to 45 feet (no hookups). Picnic tables

and fire grills are provided. Drinking water, vault toilets, and horseback-riding facilities are available. Limited supplies are available at a small store, or buy full supplies in Mammoth Lakes. Leashed pets are permitted.

Reservations, fees: Reservations are not accepted. Sites are $16 per night, plus a $4–7 per person Red's Meadow/Agnew Meadows access fee. Open mid-June–mid-September, weather permitting.

Directions: On U.S. 395, drive to Mammoth Junction/Highway 203. Turn west on Highway 203 and drive four miles, through the town of Mammoth Lakes to Minaret Road (still Highway 203). Turn right and drive five miles to Minaret Station (past the Mammoth Mountain Ski Area). Continue for 5.1 miles to the campground on the right.

Access note: Noncampers are required to use a shuttle bus (fee) from the shuttle bus terminal at Mammoth Mountain Main Lodge Gondola Station 7 A.M.–7:30 P.M. Space available for leashed dogs, bikes, and backpacks.

Contact: Inyo National Forest, Mammoth Ranger Station and Visitor Center, 760/924-5500, fax 760/924-5547.

41 UPPER SODA SPRINGS

Scenic rating: 8

on the San Joaquin River in Inyo National Forest
See map page 773

This is a premium location within earshot of the Upper San Joaquin River and within minutes of many first-class recreation options. The river is stocked with trout at this camp, with several good pools within short walking distance. Farther upstream, accessible by an excellent trail, are smaller wild trout that provide good fly-fishing prospects. Devils Postpile National Monument, a massive formation of ancient columnar jointed rock, is only three miles to the south. The Pacific Crest Trail passes right by the camp, providing a trailhead for access to numerous lakes in the Ansel Adams Wilderness. The elevation is 7,700 feet.

RV sites, facilities: There are 28 sites for tents or RVs up to 47 feet (no hookups) and four group sites for tents or RVs up to 45 feet (no hookups) than can accommodate 20–50 people each. Picnic tables and fire grills are provided. Drinking water, flush toilets, and horseback-riding facilities are available. Limited supplies can be obtained at Red's Meadow store. Leashed pets are permitted.

Reservations, fees: Reservations are not accepted. Sites are $16 per night, plus a $4–7 per person Red's Meadow/Agnew Meadows access fee. Open mid-June–mid-September, weather permitting.

Directions: On U.S. 395, drive to Mammoth Junction/Highway 203. Turn west on Highway 203 and drive four miles, through the town of Mammoth Lakes to Minaret Road (still Highway 203). Turn right and drive five miles to Minaret Station (past the Mammoth Mountain Ski Area). Continue for 5.1 miles to the campground entrance road on the right. Turn right and drive 0.25 mile to the campground.

Access note: Noncampers are required to use a shuttle bus (fee) from the shuttle bus terminal at Mammoth Mountain Main Lodge Gondola Station 7 A.M.–7:30 P.M. Space is available for leashed dogs, bikes, and backpacks.

Contact: Inyo National Forest, Mammoth Ranger Station and Visitor Center, 760/924-5500, fax 760/924-5547.

42 MINARET FALLS

Scenic rating: 8

on the San Joaquin River in Inyo National Forest
See map page 773

This camp has one of the prettiest settings of the series of camps along the Upper San Joaquin River and near Devils Postpile National Monument. It is at 7,600 feet near Minaret Creek, across from where beautiful Minaret Falls pours into the San Joaquin River. Devils Postpile National Monument, one of the best examples in the world of hexagonal, columnar jointed rock, is less than a mile from camp, where there is also a trail to awesome Rainbow Falls. The Pacific Crest Trail runs right through this area as well, and if you hike to the south, there is excellent streamside fishing access.

RV sites, facilities: There are 28 sites for tents or RVs up to 47 feet (no hookups). Picnic tables and fire grills are provided. Drinking water and vault toilets are available. Horseback-riding facilities are nearby. You can buy limited supplies at Red's Meadow store, or all supplies in Mammoth Lakes. Some facilities are wheelchair accessible. Leashed pets are permitted.

Reservations, fees: Reservations are not accepted. Sites are $16 per night, plus a $4–7 per person Red's Meadow/Agnew Meadows access fee. Open mid-June–mid-September, weather permitting.

Directions: On U.S. 395, drive to Mammoth Junction/Highway 203. Turn west on Highway 203 and drive four miles, through the town of Mammoth Lakes to Minaret Road (still Highway 203). Turn right and drive five miles to Minaret Station (past the Mammoth Mountain Ski Area). Continue for six miles to the campground entrance road on the right. Turn right and drive 0.25 mile to the campground.

Access note: Noncampers are required to use a shuttle bus from the shuttle bus terminal at Mammoth Mountain Main Lodge Gondola Station 7 A.M.–7:30 P.M. Space is available for leashed dogs, bikes, and backpacks.

Contact: Inyo National Forest, Mammoth Ranger Station and Visitor Center, 760/924-5500, fax 760/924-5547.

43 DEVILS POSTPILE NATIONAL MONUMENT

Scenic rating: 9

near the San Joaquin River

See map page 773

Devils Postpile is a spectacular and rare example of hexagonal, columnar jointed rock that looks like posts, hence the name. The camp is at 7,600 feet in elevation and provides nearby access for the easy hike to the Postpile. Guided walks are offered during the summer; call for details. If you keep walking, it is a 2.5-mile walk to Rainbow Falls, a breathtaking 101-foot cascade that produces rainbows in its floating mist, seen only from the trail alongside the waterfall looking downstream. The camp is adjacent to the Middle Fork San Joaquin River and the Pacific Crest Trail.

RV sites, facilities: There are 21 sites for tents or RVs up to 25 feet (no hookups). Picnic tables, food lockers, and fire grills are provided. Drinking water and flush toilets are available. Some facilities are wheelchair accessible. Leashed pets are permitted.

Reservations, fees: Reservations are not accepted. Sites are $14 per night, plus a $4–7 per person Red's Meadow/Devils Postpile access fee. Open mid-June–mid-October, weather permitting, with a two-week maximum stay. Note: The National Parks Pass and the Golden Passport are not accepted.

Directions: On U.S. 395, drive to Mammoth Junction/Highway 203. Turn west on Highway 203 and drive four miles, through the town of Mammoth Lakes to Minaret Road (still Highway 203). Turn right and drive five miles to Minaret Station (past the Mammoth Mountain Ski Area). Continue for nine miles to the campground entrance road on the right.

Access note: Noncampers are required to use a shuttle bus from the shuttle bus terminal at Mammoth Mountain Main Lodge Gondola Station 7 A.M.–7:30 P.M. Space is available for leashed dogs, bikes, and backpacks.

Contact: Devil Postpile National Monument, 760/934-2289, www.nps.gov/depo.

44 RED'S MEADOW

Scenic rating: 6

in Inyo National Forest

See map page 773

Red's Meadow has long been established as one of the best outfitters for horseback-riding trips. To get the feel of it, three-mile round-trip rides are available to Rainbow Falls. Multiday trips into the Ansel Adams Wilderness on the Pacific Crest Trail are also available. A small restaurant is a bonus here, always a must-stop for long-distance hikers getting a shot to chomp their first hamburger in weeks, something like a bear finding a candy bar, quite a sight for the drive-in campers. The nearby Devils Postpile National Monument, Rainbow Falls, Minaret Falls, and San Joaquin River provide recreation options. The elevation is 7,600 feet.

RV sites, facilities: There are 56 sites for tents or RVs up to 30 feet (no hookups). Picnic tables, food lockers, and fire grills are provided. Drinking water, flush toilets, horseback riding, and natural hot springs are available. You can buy limited supplies at a small store. Leashed pets are permitted.

Reservations, fees: Reservations are not accepted. Sites are $16 per night, plus a $4–7 per person Red's Meadow/Agnew Meadows access fee. Open mid-June–mid-September, weather permitting.

Directions: On U.S. 395, drive to Mammoth Junction/Highway 203. Turn west on Highway 203 and drive four miles, through the town of Mammoth Lakes to Minaret Road (still Highway 203). Turn right and drive five miles to Minaret Station (past the Mammoth Mountain Ski Area). Continue for 7.4 miles to the campground entrance on the left.

Access note: Noncampers are required to use a shuttle bus from the shuttle bus terminal at Mammoth Mountain Main Lodge Gondola Station 7 A.M.–7:30 P.M. Space is available for leashed dogs, bikes, and backpacks.

Contact: Inyo National Forest, Mammoth Ranger Station and Visitor Center, 760/924-5500, fax 760/924-5547.

45 LAKE GEORGE

Scenic rating: 8

in Inyo National Forest
See map page 773

The sites here have views of Lake George, a beautiful lake in a rock basin set below the spectacular Crystal Crag. Lake George is at 9,000 feet in elevation, a small lake fed by creeks coming from both Crystal Lake and TJ Lake. Both of the latter make excellent short hiking trips; TJ Lake is only about a 20-minute walk from the campground, and Crystal Lake is about a 45-minute romp. Trout fishing at Lake George is decent—not great, not bad, but decent. Swimming is not allowed, but boats with small motors are permitted.

RV sites, facilities: There are 16 sites for tents or RVs up to 25 feet (no hookups). Picnic tables and fire grills are provided. Drinking water and flush toilets are available. A grocery store, a coin laundry, coin showers, a primitive boat launch, and propane gas are available nearby. Leashed pets are permitted.

Reservations, fees: Reservations are not accepted. Sites are $16 per night with a seven-day limit. Open mid-June–mid-September, weather permitting.

Directions: From Lee Vining on U.S. 395, drive south for 25 miles to Mammoth Junction and Highway 203/Minaret Summit Road. Turn west on Highway 203 and drive four miles to Lake Mary Road. Continue straight through the intersection and drive four miles to Lake Mary Loop Drive. Turn left and drive 0.3 mile to Lake George Road. Turn right and drive 0.5 mile to the campground.

Contact: Inyo National Forest, Mammoth Ranger Station and Visitor Center, 760/924-5500, fax 760/924-5547.

46 GLASS CREEK

Scenic rating: 5

in Inyo National Forest
See map page 773

This camp is along Glass Creek at 7,600 feet, about a mile from Obsidian Dome to the nearby west. A trail follows Glass Creek past the southern edge of the dome, a craggy, volcanic formation that tops out at 8,611 feet in elevation. That trail continues along Glass Creek, climbing to the foot of San Joaquin Mountain for a great view of the high desert to the east. Insider's tip: The Department of Fish and Game stocks Glass Creek with trout just once each June, right at the camp.

RV sites, facilities: There are 50 sites for tents or RVs up to 40 feet (no hookups). Picnic tables and fire grills are provided. Vault toilets are available. No drinking water is available. Some facilities are wheelchair accessible. Leashed pets are permitted.

Reservations, fees: Reservations are not accepted. There is no fee for camping. Open late April–early November, weather permitting.

Directions: From Lee Vining, drive south on U.S. 395 (past the first Highway 158/June Lake Loop turnoff) for 11 miles to June Lake Junction. Continue south on U.S. 395 for six miles to a Forest Service road (Glass Creek Road). Turn west (right) and drive 0.25 mile to the camp access road on the right. Turn right and continue 0.5 mile to the main camp at the end of the road. Two notes: 1. A primitive area with large RV sites can be used as an overflow area on the right side of the access road. 2. If arriving from the south on U.S. 395, a direct left turn to Glass Creek Road is impossible. Heading north you will pass the CalTrans Crestview Maintenance Station on the right. Continue north, make a U-turn when possible, and follow the above directions.

Contact: Inyo National Forest, Mono Basin Scenic Area Ranger Station and Visitor Center, 760/647-3044, fax 760/647-3046.

47 BIG SPRINGS

Scenic rating: 5

on Deadman Creek in Inyo National Forest

See map page 773

Big Springs, at 7,300 feet, is on the edge of the high desert on the east side of U.S. 395. The main attractions are Deadman Creek, which runs right by the camp, and Big Springs, which is just on the opposite side of the river. There are several hot springs in the area, best reached by driving south on U.S. 395 to the Mammoth

Lakes Airport and turning left on Hot Creek Road; check for current status. As with all hot springs, use at your own risk.

RV sites, facilities: There are 26 sites for tents or RVs up to 40 feet (no hookups). Picnic tables and fire grills are provided. Vault toilets are available. No drinking water is available. Leashed pets are permitted.

Reservations, fees: Reservations are not accepted. There is no fee for camping. Open late April–early November, weather permitting.

Directions: From Lee Vining, drive south on U.S. 395 (past the first Highway 158/June Lake Loop turnoff) to June Lake Junction. Continue south for about seven miles to Owens River Road. Turn east (left) and drive two miles to a fork. Bear left at the fork and drive 0.25 mile to the camp on the left side of the road.

Contact: Inyo National Forest, Mono Basin Scenic Area Ranger Station and Visitor Center, 760/647-3044, fax 760/647-3046.

48 PINE GLEN

Scenic rating: 6

in Inyo National Forest

See map page 773

This is a well-situated base camp for several side trips. The most popular is the trip to Devils Postpile National Monument, with a shuttle ride from the Mammoth Ski Area. Other nearby trips include exploring Inyo Craters, Mammoth Lakes, and the hot springs at Hot Creek east of Mammoth Lakes Airport. The elevation is 7,800 feet.

RV sites, facilities: There are 11 sites (used as overflow from Old Shady Rest and New Shady Rest campgrounds) and five group sites for tents or RVs up to 55 feet that can accommodate 25–30 people each. No hookups. Picnic tables and fire grills are provided. Drinking water, flush toilets, and a dump station are available. A grocery store, a coin laundry, propane gas, and horseback-riding facilities are nearby in Mammoth Lakes. Leashed pets are permitted.

Reservations, fees: Reservations are not accepted for individual sites but are required for group sites at 877/444-6777 ($9 reservation fee) or www.ReserveUSA.com. Sites are $15 per night, and group sites are $35–50 per night. Open late May–September, weather permitting.

Directions: From Lee Vining on U.S. 395, drive south for 25 miles to Mammoth Junction and Highway 203/Minaret Summit Road. Turn west on Highway 203 and drive about three miles to the Mammoth Lakes Visitor Center. Just past the visitor center, turn right on Old Sawmill Road and drive a short distance to the campground on the right.

Contact: Inyo National Forest, Mammoth Ranger Station and Visitor Center, 760/924-5500, fax 760/924-5547.

49 NEW SHADY REST

Scenic rating: 6

in Inyo National Forest

See map page 773

This easy-to-reach camp is at 7,800 feet, not far from the Mammoth Mountain Ski Area. The surrounding Inyo National Forest provides many side-trip opportunities, including Devils Postpile National Monument by shuttle available from near the Mammoth Mountain Ski Area, Upper San Joaquin River, and the Inyo National Forest backcountry trails, streams, and lakes.

RV sites, facilities: There are 95 sites for tents or RVs up to 38 feet (no hookups). Picnic tables and fire grills are provided. Drinking water and flush toilets are available. A dump station, a playground, a grocery store, a coin laundry, and propane gas are available nearby. Leashed pets are permitted.

Reservations, fees: Reservations are accepted at 877/444-6777 ($9 reservation fee) or www.ReserveUSA.com. Sites are $15 per night with a 14-day limit. Open mid-May–October, weather permitting.

Directions: From Lee Vining on U.S. 395, drive south for 25 miles to Mammoth Junction and Highway 203/Minaret Summit Road. Turn west on Highway 203 and drive about three miles to the Mammoth Lakes Visitor Center. Just past the visitor center, turn right on Old Sawmill Road and drive a short distance to the campground on the right.

Contact: Inyo National Forest, Mammoth Ranger Station and Visitor Center, 760/924-5500, fax 760/924-5547.

50 OLD SHADY REST

Scenic rating: 6

in Inyo National Forest

See map page 773

Names such as "Old Shady Rest" are usually reserved for mom-and-pop RV parks. The Forest Service respected tradition in officially naming this park what the locals have called it all along. Like New Shady Rest, this camp is near the Mammoth Lakes Visitor Center, with the same side trips available. It is one of three camps in the immediate vicinity. The elevation is 7,800 feet.

RV sites, facilities: There are 51 sites for tents or RVs up to 55 feet (no hookups). Picnic tables and fire grills are provided. Drinking water and flush toilets are available. A dump station, a playground, a grocery store, a coin laundry, and propane gas are available nearby. Leashed pets are permitted.

Reservations, fees: Reservations are accepted at 877/444-6777 ($9 reservation fee) or www.ReserveUSA.com. Sites are $15 per night with a 14-day limit. Open mid-June–early September, weather permitting.

Directions: From Lee Vining on U.S. 395, drive south for 25 miles to Mammoth Junction and Highway 203/Minaret Summit Road. Turn west on Highway 203 and drive about three miles to the Forest Service Visitor Center. Just past the visitors center, turn right and drive 0.3 mile to the campground on the left.

Contact: Inyo National Forest, Mammoth Ranger Station and Visitor Center, 760/924-5500, fax 760/924-5547.

51 MAMMOTH MOUNTAIN RV PARK

Scenic rating: 6

near Mammoth Lakes

See map page 773

This RV park is just across the street from the Forest Service Visitor Center. Got a question? Someone there has got an answer. This camp is open year-round, making it a great place to stay for a ski trip.

RV sites, facilities: There are 185 sites, some with full hookups (50 amps), for tents or RVs up to 45 feet. Two cabins are also available. Picnic tables are provided. Fire pits are provided at some sites. Restrooms have showers. Drinking water, cable TV, modem access, a dump station, a coin laundry, a heated year-round swimming pool, a seasonal recreation room, a playground, RV supplies, and a spa are available. Supplies can be obtained in Mammoth Lakes, a quarter mile away. Some facilities are wheelchair accessible. Leashed pets are permitted, with certain restrictions.

Reservations, fees: Reservations are accepted at 800/582-4603. Sites are $21–40 per night, $3 per person per night for more than two people, $2 per night for an additional vehicle, $3 per pet per night. Some credit cards accepted. Open year-round.

Directions: From Lee Vining on U.S. 395, drive south for 25 miles to Mammoth Junction and Highway 203. Turn west on Highway 203 and drive three miles to the park on the left.

From Bishop, drive 40 miles north on Highway 395 to Mammoth Lakes exit. Turn west on Highway 203, go under the overpass, and drive three miles to the park on the left.

Contact: Mammoth Mountain RV Park, 760/934-3822, fax 760/934-1896, www.mammothrv.com.

52 TWIN LAKES

Scenic rating: 8

in Inyo National Forest

See map page 773

From Twin Lakes, you can look southwest and see pretty Twin Falls, a wide cascade that runs into the head of upper Twin Lake. There are two camps here, one on each side of the access road, at 8,600 feet. Lower Twin Lake is a favorite for fly fishers in float tubes. Powerboats, swimming, and sailboarding are not permitted. Use is heavy at the campground. Often there will be people lined up waiting for another family's weeklong vacation to end so theirs can start. Excellent hiking trails are in the area.

RV sites, facilities: There are 94 sites for tents or RVs up to 40 feet (no hookups). Picnic tables and fire grills are provided. Drinking water, flush toilets, and a boat launch are available. A grocery store, a coin laundry, coin showers, and propane gas are available nearby. Some facilities are wheelchair accessible. Leashed pets are permitted.

Reservations, fees: Reservations are accepted at 877/444-6777 ($9 reservation fee) or www.ReserveUSA.com. Sites are $14 per night. Open mid-May–late October, weather permitting.

Directions: From Lee Vining on U.S. 395, drive south for 25 miles to Mammoth Junction and Highway 203/Minaret Summit Road. Turn west on Highway 203 and drive four miles to Lake Mary Road. Continue straight through the intersection and drive 2.3 miles to Twin Lakes Loop Road. Turn right and drive 0.5 mile to the campground.

Contact: Inyo National Forest, Mammoth Ranger Station and Visitor Center, 760/924-5500, fax 760/924-5547.

53 SHERWIN CREEK

Scenic rating: 7

in Inyo National Forest

See map page 773

This camp is along little Sherwin Creek, at 7,600 feet in elevation, a short distance from the

CALIFORNIA

town of Mammoth Lakes. If you drive a mile east on Sherwin Creek Road, then turn right at the short spur road, you will find a trailhead for a hike that is routed up six miles to Valentine Lake in the John Muir Wilderness, set on the northwest flank of Bloody Mountain.

RV sites, facilities: There are 87 sites for tents or RVs up to 34 feet (no hookups) and 15 walk-in sites for tents only. Picnic tables and fire grills are provided. Drinking water and flush toilets are available. Leashed pets are permitted.

Reservations, fees: Reservations are accepted at 877/444-6777 ($9 reservation fee) or www.ReserveUSA.com. Sites are $15 per night. Open early May–mid-September, weather permitting.

Directions: From Lee Vining on U.S. 395, drive south for 25 miles to Mammoth Junction and Highway 203/Minaret Summit Road. Turn west on Highway 203 and drive about three miles to the Mammoth Lakes Visitor Center and continue a short distance to Old Mammoth Road. Turn left and drive about a mile to Sherwin Creek. Turn south and drive two miles on largely unpaved road to the campground on the left side of the road.

Contact: Inyo National Forest, Mammoth Lakes Visitor Center, 760/924-5500, fax 760/924-5547.

54 LAKE MARY

Scenic rating: 9

in Inyo National Forest

See map page 773

Lake Mary is the star of the Mammoth Lakes region. Of the 11 lakes in the area, this is the largest and most developed. It provides a resort, a boat ramp, and boat rentals, and it receives the highest number of trout stocks. No water/body contact, including swimming, is allowed, and the speed limit is 10 mph. It is at 8,900 feet in a place of incredible natural beauty, one of the few spots that literally has it all. Of course, that often includes quite a few other people. If there are too many for you, an excellent trailhead is available at nearby Coldwater camp that takes you up to Emerald Lake.

RV sites, facilities: There are 48 sites for tents or RVs up to 30 feet (no hookups). Picnic tables, food lockers, and fire grills are provided. Drinking water and flush toilets are available. A grocery store, a coin laundry, and propane gas are nearby. Leashed pets are permitted.

Reservations, fees: Reservations are not accepted. Sites are $16 per night with a 14-day limit. Open early June–mid-September, weather permitting.

Directions: Take U.S. 395 to Mammoth Junction and Highway 203. Turn west on Highway 203 and drive through the town of Mammoth Lakes to the junction of Minaret Road/Highway 203 and Lake Mary Road. Continue straight through the intersection and drive 3.6 miles to Lake Mary Loop Drive. Turn right and drive 0.5 mile to the campground entrance.

Contact: Inyo National Forest, Mammoth Ranger Station and Visitor Center, 760/924-5500, fax 760/924-5547.

55 PINE CITY

Scenic rating: 7

near Lake Mary in Inyo National Forest

See map page 773

This camp is at the edge of Lake Mary at an elevation of 8,900 feet. This camp is popular for both families and fly fishers with float tubes. Swimming is not permitted.

RV sites, facilities: There are 10 sites for tents or RVs up to 40 feet (no hookups). Picnic tables and fire grills are provided. Drinking water and flush toilets are available. A grocery store, a coin laundry, boat launch, boat rentals, and propane gas are available nearby. Some facilities are wheelchair accessible. Leashed pets are permitted.

Reservations, fees: Reservations are not accepted. Sites are $16 per night. Open early June–mid-September.

Directions: Take U.S. 395 to Mammoth Junction and Highway 203. Turn west on Highway 203 and drive through the town of Mammoth Lakes to the junction of Minaret Road/ Highway 203 and Lake Mary Road. Continue straight through the intersection and drive 3.6 miles to Lake Mary Loop Drive. Turn left and drive 0.25 mile to the campground.

Contact: Inyo National Forest, Mammoth Ranger Station and Visitor Center, 760/924-5500, fax 760/924-5547.

56 COLDWATER

Scenic rating: 7

on Coldwater Creek in Inyo National Forest
See map page 773

While this camp is not the first choice of many simply because there is no lake view, it has a special attraction all its own. First, it is a two-minute drive from the campground to Lake Mary, which has a boat ramp, rentals, and good trout fishing. Second, at the end of the campground access road is a trailhead for two outstanding hikes. From the Y at the trailhead, if you head right, you will be routed up Coldwater Creek to Emerald Lake, a great little hike. If you head to the left, you will have a more ambitious trip to Arrowhead, Skelton, and Red Lakes, all within three miles. The elevation is 8,900 feet.

RV sites, facilities: There are 78 sites for tents or RVs up to 50 feet (no hookups). Picnic tables and fire grills are provided. Drinking water, flush toilets, and horse facilities are available. You can buy supplies in Mammoth Lakes. Leashed pets are permitted.

Reservations, fees: Reservations are accepted at 877/444-6777 ($9 reservation fee) or www.ReserveUSA.com. Sites are $16 per night, with a 14-day limit. Open mid-June–mid-September.

Directions: From Lee Vining on U.S. 395, drive south for 25 miles to Mammoth Junction and Highway 203/Minaret Summit Road. Turn west on Highway 203 and drive four miles to Lake Mary Road. Continue straight through the intersection and drive 3.6 miles to Lake Mary Loop Drive. Turn left and drive 0.6 mile to the camp entrance road.

Contact: Inyo National Forest, Mammoth Ranger Station and Visitor Center, 760/924-5500, fax 760/924-5547.

57 CONVICT LAKE

Scenic rating: 7

in Inyo National Forest
See map page 773

After driving in the stark desert on U.S. 395 to get here, it is always astonishing to clear the rise and see Convict Lake (7,583 feet) and its gemlike waters set in a mountain bowl beneath a back wall of high, jagged wilderness peaks. The camp is right beside Convict Creek, about a quarter mile from Convict Lake. Both provide very good trout fishing, including some rare monster-sized brown trout below the Convict Lake outlet. Fishing is often outstanding in Convict Lake, with a chance of hooking a 10- or 15-pound trout. The lake speed limit is 10 mph, and although swimming is allowed, it is not popular because of the cold, often choppy water. A trail circles the lake, providing a nice day hike. A bonus is an outstanding resort with a boat launch, boat rentals, cabin rentals, a small store, a restaurant, and bar. Horseback rides and hiking are also available, with a trail passing along the north side of the lake, then along upper Convict Creek (a stream crossing is required about three miles in) and into the John Muir Wilderness. This is the most popular camp in the Mammoth area, and it is frequently full. While the lake rates a 10 for scenic beauty, the camp itself is in a stark desert setting, out of sight of the lake, plus it can get windy and cold here because of the exposed sites.

RV sites, facilities: There are 88 sites for tents or RVs up to 40 feet (no hookups). Rental cabins are also available through the Convict Lake Resort. Picnic tables and fire grills are provided. Drinking water and flush toilets are available. A dump station, a boat ramp, a store, a restaurant, and horseback-riding facilities are nearby. Some facilities are wheelchair accessible. Leashed pets are permitted.

CALIFORNIA

Reservations, fees: Reservations are accepted at 877/444-6777 ($9 reservation fee) or www.ReserveUSA.com. Sites are $16 per night. For cabin reservations, phone 760/934-3880 or 800/992-2260. Open mid-April–October, weather permitting; cabins are open year-round.

Directions: From Lee Vining on U.S. 395, drive south for 31 miles (five miles past Mammoth Junction) to Convict Lake Road (adjacent to Mammoth Lakes Airport). Turn west (right) on Convict Lake Road and drive three miles to Convict Lake. Cross the dam and drive a short distance to the campground entrance road on the left. Turn left and drive 0.25 mile to the campground.

From Bishop, drive north on U.S. 395 for 35 miles to Convict Lake Road. Turn west (left) and drive three miles to the lake and campground.

Contact: Inyo National Forest, Mammoth Ranger Station and Visitor Center, 760/924-5500, fax 760/924-5547; Convict Lake Resort and Cabins, 800/992-2260.

58 McGEE CREEK RV PARK

Scenic rating: 6

near Crowley Lake

See map page 773

This is a popular layover spot for folks visiting giant Crowley Lake. Crowley Lake is still one of the better lakes in the Sierra for trout fishing, with good prospects for large rainbow trout and brown trout, though the 20-pound brown trout that once made this lake famous are now mainly a legend. McGee Creek runs through the campground, and trout fishing is popular. Several trout ponds are available; call for fees. Beautiful Convict Lake provides a nearby side-trip option. It is also about nine miles to Rock Creek Lake, a beautiful high-mountain destination. The elevation is 7,000 feet.

RV sites, facilities: There are 40 sites with full, partial, or no hookups (50 amps) for tents or RVs up to 40 feet; some are pull-through. Picnic

tables and fire pits are provided. Drinking water and restrooms with showers and flush toilets are available. Leashed pets are permitted.

Reservations, fees: Reservations are accepted. Sites are $19–29 per night, $3 per person per night for more than two people. Weekly and monthly rates available. Open late April–September, weather permitting.

Directions: From the junction of U.S. 395 and Highway 203 (the Mammoth Lakes turnoff), drive south on U.S. 395 for eight miles to the turnoff for McGee Creek Road. Take that exit and look for the park entrance on the left.

Contact: McGee Creek RV Park, 760/935-4233.

59 McGEE CREEK

Scenic rating: 7

in Inyo National Forest

See map page 773

This is a Forest Service camp at an elevation of 7,600 feet, set along little McGee Creek, a good location for fishing and hiking. There are few trees here. The stream is stocked with trout, and a trailhead is just up the road. From here you can hike along upper McGee Creek and into the John Muir Wilderness.

RV sites, facilities: There are 28 sites for tents or RVs up to 25 feet (no hookups). Picnic tables and fire grills are provided. Drinking water, flush toilets, and shade structures are available. Horseback-riding facilities are available nearby. Some facilities are wheelchair accessible. Leashed pets are permitted.

Reservations, fees: Reservations are accepted at 877/444-6777 ($9 reservation fee) or www.ReserveUSA.com. Sites are $17 per night, $5 per night for an additional vehicle. Open mid-May–mid-October, weather permitting.

Directions: From Mammoth Lakes at the junction of U.S. 395 and Highway 203, drive south on U.S. 395 for 8.5 miles to McGee Creek Road (signed). Turn right (toward the Sierra) and drive 1.5 miles on a narrow, windy road to the campground.

Contact: Inyo National Forest, White Mountain Ranger District, 760/873-2500, fax 760/873-2563; McGee Creek Pack Station, 760/935-4324.

60 CROWLEY LAKE

Scenic rating: 5

near Crowley Lake
See map page 773

This large BLM camp is across U.S. 395 from the south shore of Crowley Lake. For many, Crowley is the trout-fishing capital of the eastern Sierra, with the annual opener (the last Saturday in April) a great celebration. Though the trout fishing can go through a lull in midsummer, it can become excellent again in the fall when the lake's population of big brown trout heads up to the top of the lake and the mouth of the Owens River. This is a large lake with 45 miles of shoreline. In the summer, water sports include swimming, waterskiing, wakeboarding, personal watercraft riding, and sailboarding. The surroundings are fairly stark; the elevation is 6,800 feet.

RV sites, facilities: There are 47 sites for tents or RVs of any length (no hookups). Picnic tables and fire grills are provided. Vault toilets are available. No drinking water is available. A grocery store, a boat ramp, boat rentals, and horseback-riding facilities are nearby. Floating chemical toilets are available on the lake. Leashed pets are permitted.

Reservations, fees: Reservations are not accepted. Sites are $5 per night, and season passes are available for $300. Open late April–October, weather permitting.

Directions: Drive on U.S. 395 to the Crowley Lake Road exit (30 miles north of Bishop). Take that exit west (toward the Sierra) to Crowley Lake Road. Turn right on Crowley Lake Road and drive northwest for three miles to the campground entrance on the left (well signed).

Contact: Bureau of Land Management, Bishop Field Office, 760/872-4881, fax 760/872-5050; McGee Creek Pack Station, 760/935-4324.

61 TUFF

Scenic rating: 5

near Crowley Lake in Inyo National Forest
See map page 773

Easy access off U.S. 395 makes this camp a winner, though it is not nearly as pretty as those up Rock Creek Road to the west of Tom's Place. The fact that you can get in and out of here quickly makes it ideal for campers planning fishing trips to nearby Crowley Lake. The elevation is 7,000 feet.

RV sites, facilities: There are 34 sites for tents or RVs up to 45 feet (no hookups). Picnic tables and fire grills are provided. Drinking water and flush toilets are available. Some facilities are wheelchair accessible. Leashed pets are permitted.

Reservations, fees: Reservations are accepted at 877/444-6777 ($9 reservation fee) or www.ReserveUSA.com. Sites are $17 per night, $5 per night for an additional vehicle. Open late April–mid-October, weather permitting.

Directions: From Mammoth Lakes at the junction of U.S. 395 and Highway 203, drive south on U.S. 395 for 15.5 miles (one mile north of Tom's Place) to Rock Creek Road. Turn left (east) on Rock Creek Road and drive 0.5 mile to the campground.

Contact: Inyo National Forest, White Mountain Ranger District, 760/873-2500, fax 760/873-2563.

62 FRENCH CAMP

Scenic rating: 5

on Rock Creek near Crowley Lake in Inyo National Forest
See map page 773

French Camp is just a short hop from U.S. 395 and Tom's Place, right where the high Sierra turns into high plateau country. Side-trip opportunities include boating and fishing on giant Crowley Lake and, to the west on Rock Creek Road, visiting little Rock Creek Lake 10 miles away. The elevation is 7,500 feet.

RV sites, facilities: There are 86 sites for tents

CALIFORNIA

or RVs up to 35 feet (no hookups). Picnic tables and fire grills are provided. Drinking water, flush toilets, and a dump station are available. Leashed pets are permitted.

Reservations, fees: Reservations are accepted at 877/444-6777 ($9 reservation fee) or www.ReserveUSA.com. Sites are $17 per night, $5 per night for an additional vehicle. Open late April–October, weather permitting.

Directions: From Mammoth Lakes at the junction of U.S. 395 and Highway 203, drive south on U.S. 395 for 15 miles to Tom's Place and Rock Creek Road. Turn right (toward the Sierra) at Rock Creek Road and drive 0.25 mile to the campground on the right.

Contact: Inyo National Forest, White Mountain Ranger District, 760/873-2500, fax 760/873-2563.

63 IRIS MEADOW

Scenic rating: 5

near Crowley Lake in Inyo National Forest

See map page 773

Iris Meadow, at 8,300 feet elevation on the flank of Red Mountain (11,472 feet), is the first in a series of five Forest Service camps set near Rock Creek Canyon on the road leading from Tom's Place up to pretty Rock Creek Lake. A bonus is that some of the campsites are next to the creek. Rock Creek is stocked with trout, and nearby Rock Creek Lake also provides fishing and boating for hand-launched boats. This camp also has access to a great trailhead for wilderness exploration.

RV sites, facilities: There are 14 sites for tents or RVs up to 30 feet (no hookups). Picnic tables and fire grills are provided. Drinking water and flush toilets are available. Limited supplies are available in Tom's Place, three miles away. Some facilities are wheelchair accessible. Leashed pets are permitted.

Reservations, fees: Reservations are not accepted. Sites are $18 per night, $5 per night for an additional vehicle. Open late May–mid-September, weather permitting.

Directions: From Mammoth Lakes at the junction of U.S. 395 and Highway 203, drive south on U.S. 395 for 15 miles to Tom's Place and Rock Creek Road. Turn right (toward the Sierra) at Rock Creek Road and drive three miles to the campground.

Contact: Inyo National Forest, White Mountain Ranger District, 760/873-2500, fax 760/873-2563.

64 EAST FORK

Scenic rating: 8

near Crowley Lake in Inyo National Forest

See map page 773

This is a beautiful, popular campground set along East Fork Rock Creek at 9,000 feet elevation. The camp is only three miles from Rock Creek Lake, where there's an excellent trailhead. Mountain biking is popular in this area, and Lower Rock Creek and Sand Canyon have two of the most difficult and desirable trails around; they're suggested for experienced riders only.

RV sites, facilities: There are 133 sites for tents or RVs up to 35 feet (no hookups). Picnic tables and fire grills are provided. Drinking water and flush toilets are available. Limited supplies are available in Tom's Place and at Rock Creek Lakes Resort. Leashed pets are permitted.

Reservations, fees: Reservations are accepted at 877/444-6777 ($9 reservation fee) or www.ReserveUSA.com. Sites are $17 per night, $5 per night for an additional vehicle. Open mid-May–October.

Directions: From Mammoth Lakes at the junction of U.S. 395 and Highway 203, drive south on U.S. 395 for 15 miles south to Tom's Place and Rock Creek Road. Turn right (toward the Sierra) at Rock Creek Road and drive five miles to the campground access road on the left.

Contact: Inyo National Forest, White Mountain Ranger District, 760/873-2500, fax 760/873-2563.

65 ROCK CREEK LAKE

Scenic rating: 9

in Inyo National Forest

See map page 773

Rock Creek Lake, at an elevation of 9,600 feet, is a small but beautiful lake that features cool, clear water, small trout, and a great trailhead for access to the adjacent John Muir Wilderness, with 50 other lakes within a two-hour hike. The setting is drop-dead beautiful, hence the high rating for scenic beauty, but note that the campsites are set close together, side by side, in a paved parking area. This 63-acre lake has a 5-mph speed limit and swimming is allowed. The lake is stocked with Alpers trout, and they are joined by resident brown trout in the 10- to 16-pound class. At times, especially afternoons in late spring, winds out of the west can be cold and pesky at the lake. Insider's tip: Rock Creek Lakes Resort has mouthwatering homemade pie in the café.

RV sites, facilities: There are 26 sites for tents or RVs up to 22 feet (no hookups) and one group tent site for up to 50 people; some of the sites require a short walk-in. Picnic tables and fire grills are provided. Drinking water, flush toilets, an unimproved boat launch, and boat rentals are available. Horseback-riding facilities and a café are nearby. Limited supplies can be obtained in Tom's Place and at Rock Creek Lakes Resort. Leashed pets are permitted.

Reservations, fees: Reservations are accepted for individual sites and required for group sites at 877/444-6777 ($9 reservation fee) or www.ReserveUSA.com. Sites are $18 per night, $5 per night for an additional vehicle, $55 per night for a group site. Open mid-May–October, weather permitting.

Directions: From the junction of U.S. 395 and Highway 203 (the Mammoth Lakes turnoff), drive 15 miles south on U.S. 395 to Tom's Place. Turn right (toward the Sierra) at Rock Creek Road and drive seven miles to the campground.

Contact: Inyo National Forest, White Mountain Ranger District, 760/873-2500, fax 760/873-2563; Rock Creek Pack Station, 760/935-4493.

66 PLEASANT VALLEY

Scenic rating: 7

near Pleasant Valley Reservoir

See map page 773

Pleasant Valley County Campground is near long, narrow Pleasant Valley Reservoir, created by the Owens River. A 15-minute walk from camp will take you to the lake. It is east of the Sierra range in the high desert plateau country; the elevation is 4,200 feet. That makes it available for year-round fishing, and trout are stocked. The Owens River passes through the park, providing wild trout fishing, with most anglers practicing catch-and-release fly-fishing. This is also near a major jump-off point for hiking, rock-climbing, and wilderness fishing at the Bishop Pass area to the west.

RV sites, facilities: There are 200 sites for tents or RVs of any length (no hookups). Picnic tables and fire grills are provided. Drinking water (hand-pumped well water) and vault toilets are available. Groups can be accommodated. Some facilities are wheelchair accessible. Leashed pets are permitted.

Reservations, fees: Reservations are not accepted. Sites are $10 per night per vehicle. Open year-round.

Directions: Drive on U.S. 395 to Pleasant Valley Road (seven miles north of Bishop) on the east side of the road. Turn northeast and drive one mile to the park entrance.

Contact: Inyo County Parks Department, 760/878-0272 or 760/873-5577, www.395.com/inyo/campgrounds.

67 HIGHLANDS RV PARK

Scenic rating: 3

near Bishop

See map page 773

This is a privately operated RV park near Bishop that is set up for U.S. 395 cruisers. There is a Native American casino in town. A great side trip is up two-lane Highway 168

CALIFORNIA

to Lake Sabrina. The elevation is 4,300 feet. Note that a few sites are occupied by long-term renters.

RV sites, facilities: There are 103 sites with full hookups (30 and 50 amps) for RVs of any length; many sites are pull-through. No tents. Picnic tables and cable TV are provided. Drinking water, restrooms with flush toilets and showers, a dump station, a social room with pool table, modem access (in office), propane gas, ice, a fish-cleaning station, and a coin laundry are available. You can buy groceries nearby (about three blocks away). Leashed pets are permitted.

Reservations, fees: Reservations are recommended. Sites are $33 per night, $1 per person per night for more than two people. Weekly and monthly rates available. Some credit cards are accepted. Open year-round.

Directions: From Bishop, drive two miles north on U.S. 395/North Sierra Highway to the campground on the right (east side of road) at 2275 North Sierra Highway.

Contact: Highlands RV Park, 760/873-7616.

SEQUOIA AND KINGS CANYON

(**Wildlife-Viewing**
Dorst Creek, page 828.

(**Prettiest Lakes**
Sabrina, page 820.

There is no place on earth like the high Sierra, from Mount Whitney north through Sequoia and Kings Canyon National Parks. This is a paradise filled with deep canyons, high peaks, and fantastic natural beauty, sprinkled with groves of the largest living things in history – giant sequoias.

Though the area is primarily known for the national parks, the campgrounds available span a great variety of settings. The most popular spots, though, are in the vicinity of Sequoia and Kings Canyon National Parks, or on the parks' access roads.

Sooner or later, everyone will want to see the biggest tree of them all – the General Sherman Tree, estimated to be 2,300 to 2,700 years old with a circumference of 102.6 feet. It is in the Giant Forest at Sequoia National Park. To stand in front of it is to know true awe. That said, I found Grant Grove and Muir Grove even more enchanting.

These are among the highlights of a driving tour through both parks. A must for most is taking in the view from Moro Rock, parking, and then making the 300-foot walk up a succession of stairs to reach the 6,725-foot summit. Here you can scan a series of mountain rims and granite peaks, highlighted by the Great Western Divide.

The drive out of Sequoia and into Kings Canyon features rim-of-the-world-type views as you first enter the Kings River canyon. You then descend to the bottom of the canyon, right along the Kings River, gaze up at the high glacial-carved canyon walls, and drive all the way out to Cedar Grove, the end of the road. The canyon rises 8,000 feet from the river to Spanish Peak, making it the deepest canyon in the continental United States.

Crystal Cave is another point of fascination. Among the formations are adjoined crystal columns that look like the sound pipes in the giant organ at the Mormon Tabernacle. Lights are placed strategically for perfect viewing.

This is only a start. Bears, marmots, and deer are abundant and are commonly seen in Sequoia, especially at Dorst Creek Campground. If you drive up to Mineral King and take a hike, it can seem like the marmot capital of the world.

But this region also harbors many wonderful secrets having nothing to do with the national parks. One of them, for instance, is the Muir Trail

Ranch near Florence Lake. The ranch is in the John Muir Wilderness and requires a trip by foot, boat, or horse to reach it. Other unique launch points for trips into the wilderness lie nearby.

On the western slopes of the Sierra, pretty lakes with good trout fishing include Edison, Florence, and Hume Lakes. Hidden spots in Sierra National Forest provide continual fortune hunts, especially up the Dinkey Creek drainage above Courtright Reservoir. Powerboat enthusiasts will enjoy Bass Lake near Oakhurst, Pine Flat Lake east of Fresno, and Lake Kaweah near Visalia. On the eastern slopes, small streams offer good vehicle access; here, too, you'll encounter the beautiful Rock Creek Lake, Sabrina and South Lakes (west of Bishop), and great wilderness trailheads at the end of almost every road.

The remote Golden Trout Wilderness on the southwest flank of Mount Whitney is one of the most pristine areas in California. Yet it is lost in the shadow of giant Whitney, elevation 14,497.6 feet, the highest point in the continental United States, where hiking has become so popular that reservations are required at each trailhead for overnight use, and quotas are enforced to ensure an undisturbed experience for each visitor.

In the Kernville area, there is a series of campgrounds along the Kern River. Most choose this canyon for one reason: the outstanding whitewater rafting and kayaking.

Includes:

- Bass Lake
- Dorst Creek
- Florence Lake
- Giant Sequoia National Monument
- Huntington Lake
- Inyo National Forest
- Isabella Lake
- Kaweah River
- Kern River
- Kings Canyon National Park
- Kings River
- Lake Edison
- Lake Kaweah
- Lake Ming
- Lake Sabrina
- Lake Success
- Mountain Home State Forest
- Mount Whitney
- Pacific Crest Trail
- Pine Flat Lake
- San Joaquin River
- Sequoia National Park
- Shaver Lake
- Sierra National Forest
- South Lake

CALIFORNIA

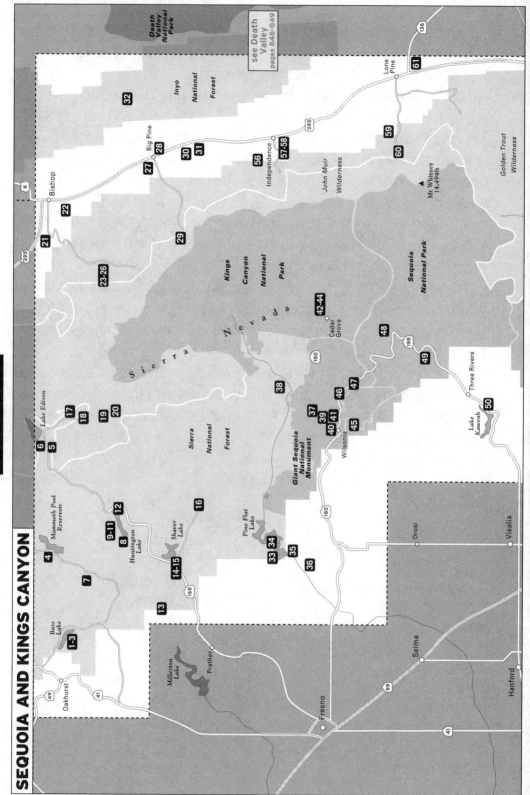

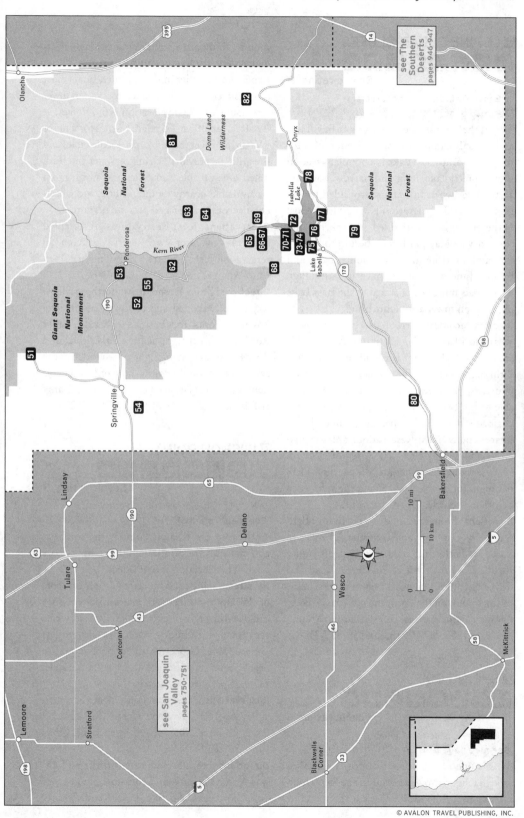

see The
Southern
Deserts
pages 946-947

see San Joaquin
Valley
pages 750-751

CALIFORNIA

© AVALON TRAVEL PUBLISHING, INC.

CALIFORNIA

1 LUPINE-CEDAR BLUFFS

Scenic rating: 8

on Bass Lake in Sierra National Forest
See map page 808

This is the camping headquarters at Bass Lake and the only camp open year-round, except for the group camp. Bass Lake is a popular vacation spot, a pretty lake, long and narrow, covering 1,200 acres when full and surrounded by national forest. The elevation is 3,500 feet. Most of the campgrounds are filled on weekends and three-day holidays. Fishing is best in the spring for rainbow trout and largemouth bass, and by mid-June water-skiers have usually taken over. Boats must be registered at the Bass Lake observation tower after launching.

RV sites, facilities: There are 113 sites for tents or RVs up to 40 feet (no hookups) and several double sites. Picnic tables and fire grills are provided. Drinking water and flush toilets are available. Groceries, coin showers, and a boat ramp are available within two miles. Some facilities are wheelchair accessible. Leashed pets are permitted.

Reservations, fees: Reservations are accepted at 877/444-6777 or www.ReserveUSA.com ($9 reservation fee). Sites are $19 per night, $38 per night for double sites, $5 per night for each additional vehicle. Open year-round.

Directions: From Fresno, drive north on Highway 41 to Oakhurst and continue 2.5 miles to Yosemite Forks and Bass Lake Road/County Road 222. Turn right at Bass Lake Road and drive eight miles (staying right at two forks) to the campground (on the south shore of Bass Lake).

Contact: Sierra National Forest, Bass Lake Ranger District, 559/877-2218, fax 559/877-3108.

2 SPRING COVE

Scenic rating: 8

on Bass Lake in Sierra National Forest
See map page 808

This is one of the several camps beside Bass Lake, a long, narrow reservoir in the Sierra foothill country. A bonus here is that the shoreline is quite sandy nearly all around the lake. That makes for good swimming and sunbathing. Expect hot weather in the summer. Boats must be registered at the Bass Lake observation tower after launching. The elevation is 3,400 feet.

RV sites, facilities: There are 63 sites for tents or RVs up to 35 feet (no hookups). Picnic tables and fire grills are provided. Drinking water and flush toilets are available. Groceries and a boat ramp are available nearby. Some facilities are wheelchair accessible. Leashed pets are permitted.

Reservations, fees: Reservations are accepted at 877/444-6777 or www.ReserveUSA.com ($9 reservation fee). Sites are $19 per night. Open May–August.

Directions: From Fresno, drive north on Highway 41 to Oakhurst and continue 2.5 miles to Yosemite Forks and Bass Lake Road/County Road 222. Turn right at Bass Lake Road and drive 8.5 miles (staying right at two forks) to the campground (on the south shore of Bass Lake).

Contact: Sierra National Forest, Bass Lake Ranger District, 559/877-2218, fax 559/877-3108.

3 WISHON POINT

Scenic rating: 9

on Bass Lake in Sierra National Forest
See map page 808

This camp on Wishon Point is the smallest, and many say the prettiest, of the camps at Bass Lake. The elevation is 3,400 feet.

RV sites, facilities: There are 47 sites for tents or RVs up to 30 feet (no hookups). Some sites are pull-through. Picnic tables and fire grills are provided. Drinking water and flush toilets are available. Groceries and a boat ramp are nearby. Some facilities are wheelchair accessible. Leashed pets are permitted.

Reservations, fees: Reservations are accepted at 877/444-6777 or www.ReserveUSA.com ($9 reservation fee). Sites are $19 per night. Open June–September.

Directions: From Fresno, drive north on Highway 41 to Oakhurst and continue 2.5 miles to Yosemite Forks and Bass Lake Road/County

Road 222. Turn right at Bass Lake Road and drive nine miles (staying right at two forks) to the campground (on the south shore of Bass Lake).

Contact: Sierra National Forest, Bass Lake Ranger District, 559/877-2218, fax 559/877-3108.

4 MAMMOTH POOL

Scenic rating: 7

near Mammoth Pool Reservoir in Sierra
National Forest

See map page 808

Mammoth Pool was created by a dam in the San Joaquin River gorge, a steep canyon, resulting in a long, narrow lake with steep, high walls. The lake seems much higher than its official elevation of 3,330 feet, but that is because of the high ridges. This is the only drive-in camp at the lake, though there is a boat-in camp, China Camp, on the lake's upper reaches. All water sports are allowed. Trout fishing can be good in the spring and early summer, with waterskiing dominant during warm weather. Get this: Water sports are restricted from May 1 to June 15 because of deer migrating across the lake—that's right, swimming—but the campgrounds are still open. Note that the water level can drop significantly by late summer.

RV sites, facilities: There are 47 sites for tents or RVs up to 30 feet (no hookups). Picnic tables and fire grills are provided. Drinking water and vault toilets are available. A store and boat ramp are within a mile. Leashed pets are permitted.

Reservations, fees: Reservations are accepted at 877/444-6777 or www.ReserveUSA.com ($9 reservation fee). Sites are $15 per night, $5 per night for each additional vehicle. Open May–October.

Directions: From Fresno, drive north on Highway 41 for about 25 miles to North Fork Road/County Road 200. Turn right and drive northeast for 17.5 miles to Auberry Road/County Road 222. Turn left (north) and drive one mile to the town of North Fork

and Mammoth Pool Road. Turn right and drive 1.5 miles to County Road 225 (still Mammoth Pool Road). Turn right and drive about 37 miles (the road becomes Minarets Road/Forest Road 81) to a junction. Bear right (still Mammoth Pool Road) and drive three miles to Mammoth Pool Reservoir and the campground. The drive from North Fork takes 1.5–2 hours.

Contact: Sierra National Forest, Bass Lake Ranger District, 559/877-2218, fax 559/877-3108.

5 VERMILLION

Scenic rating: 8

on Lake Edison in Sierra National Forest

See map page 808

Lake Edison is a premium vacation destination. It is a large, high-mountain camp just a few miles from the border of the John Muir Wilderness. The elevation is 7,700 feet. A 15-mph speed limit on the lake guarantees quiet water, and trout fishing is often quite good in early summer, with occasionally huge brown trout hooked. Swimming is allowed. A day-trip option is to hike the trail from the camp out along the north shore of Lake Edison for five miles to Quail Meadows, where it intersects with the Pacific Crest Trail in the John Muir Wilderness. A lodge at the lake provides meals and supplies, with a hiker's boat shuttle available to the head of the lake. Hang out here for long and you are bound to see JMT hikers taking a break. Note that the drive in is long and extremely twisty on a narrow road. Also note that the lake level can drop dramatically here by late summer.

RV sites, facilities: There are 31 sites for tents or RVs up to 16 feet (no hookups). Picnic tables and fire grills are provided. Drinking water and vault toilets are available. A boat ramp, boat rentals, bait and tackle, horseback-riding facilities, a convenience store, and restaurant are nearby. Leashed pets are permitted.

Reservations, fees: Reservations are accepted at 877/444-6777 ($9 reservation fee) or www.ReserveUSA.com. Sites are $16 per night, $5 per night for an additional vehicle. Open June–September.

Directions: From the town of Shaver Lake, drive east on Highway 168 for 21 miles to Kaiser Pass Road. Bear northeast on Kaiser Pass Road/Forest Road 80 (slow and curvy) to Mono Hot Springs (the road becomes Edison Lake Road). Continue on Kaiser Pass/Edison Lake Road for five miles to the campground. It is about 0.25 mile from the west shore of Lake Edison.

Contact: Sierra National Forest, High Sierra Ranger District, 559/855-5355, fax 559/855-5375; California Land Management, 559/893-2111.

6 MONO HOT SPRINGS

Scenic rating: 8

on the San Joaquin River in Sierra National Forest
See map page 808

The campground is in the Sierra at 7,400 feet in elevation along the San Joaquin River directly adjacent to the Mono Hot Springs Resort. The hot springs are typically 104°F, with public pools (everybody wears swimming suits) available just above the river on one side, and the private resort (rock cabins available) with its private baths on the other. A small convenience store and excellent restaurant are available at the lodge. The best swimming lake in the Sierra Nevada, Dorris Lake, is a 15-minute walk past the lodge; the lake is clear, clean, and yet not too cold, with walls on one side for fun jumps into deep water. The one downer: The drive in to the campground is long, slow, and hellacious, with many blind corners in narrow sections.

RV sites, facilities: There are 26 sites for tents or RVs up to 16 feet (no hookups). Picnic tables and fire grills are provided. Vault toilets are available. Drinking water is not available. You can buy supplies in Mono Hot Springs. Leashed pets are permitted.

Reservations, fees: Reservations are accept-

ed at 877/444-6777 ($9 reservation fee) or www.ReserveUSA.com. Sites are $16 per night, $32 per night for a double site, $5 per night for an additional vehicle. Open May–mid-October, weather permitting.

Directions: From the town of Shaver Lake, drive east on Highway 168 for 21 miles to Kaiser Pass Road. Bear northeast on Kaiser Pass Road/Forest Road 80 (slow and curvy) to Mono Hot Springs Campground Road (signed). Turn left and drive a short distance to the campground.

Contact: Sierra National Forest, High Sierra Ranger District, 559/855-5355, fax 559/855-5375; California Land Management, 559/893-2111.

7 ROCK CREEK

Scenic rating: 6

in Sierra National Forest
See map page 808

Drinking water is the big bonus here. It's easier to live with than the no-water situation at Fish Creek, the other camp in the immediate area. It is also why this camp tends to fill up on weekends. A side trip is the primitive road that heads southeast out of camp, switchbacks as its heads east, and drops down the canyon near where pretty Aspen Creek feeds into Rock Creek. The elevation at camp is 4,300 feet. (Note that the best camp in the immediate region is at Mammoth Pool.)

RV sites, facilities: There are 18 sites for tents or RVs up to 32 feet (no hookups). Picnic tables and fire grills are provided. Drinking water and vault toilets are available. Leashed pets are permitted.

Reservations, fees: Reservations are accepted at 877/444-6777 or www.ReserveUSA.com ($9 reservation fee). Sites are $15 per night, $30 per night for a double site. Open April–October, weather permitting.

Directions: From Fresno, drive north on Highway 41 for about 25 miles to North Fork Road/County Road 200. Turn right and drive northeast for 17.5 miles to Auberry Road/County

Road 222. Turn left (north) and drive one mile to the town of North Fork and Mammoth Pool Road. Turn right and drive 1.5 miles to County Road 225 (still Mammoth Pool Road). Turn right and drive about 25 miles (the road becomes Minarets Road/Forest Road 81) to the campground on the right.

Contact: Sierra National Forest, Bass Lake Ranger District, 559/877-2218, fax 559/877-3108.

8 UPPER AND LOWER BILLY CREEK

Scenic rating: 8

on Huntington Lake in Sierra National Forest

See map page 808

Huntington Lake is at an elevation of 7,000 feet in the Sierra Nevada, and this is one of several camps here. These camps are at the west end of the lake along the north shore, where Billy Creek feeds the lake. Of these two adjacent campgrounds, Lower Billy Creek is smaller than Upper Billy and has lakeside sites. The lake is four miles long and a half mile wide, with 14 miles of shoreline, several resorts, boat rentals, and a trailhead for hiking into the Kaiser Wilderness.

RV sites, facilities: Upper Billy has 44 sites for tents or RVs up to 30 feet. Lower Billy has 13 sites for tents or RVs up to 30 feet. No hookups. Picnic tables and fire grills are provided. Drinking water and flush and vault toilets are available at Upper Billy. Drinking water and vault toilets are available at Lower Billy. A small store is nearby. Leashed pets are permitted.

Reservations, fees: Reservations are accepted at 877/444-6777 or www.ReserveUSA.com ($9 reservation fee). Sites are $17 per night, $5 per night for an additional vehicle. Open June–September, weather permitting.

Directions: From Fresno, drive east on Highway 168 to Shaver Lake, then continue 21 miles to Huntington Lake and Huntington Lake Road. Turn left on Huntington Lake Road and drive about five miles to the campgrounds on the left.

Contact: Sierra National Forest, High Sierra Ranger District, 559/855-5355, fax 559/855-5375; California Land Management, 559/893-2111.

9 CATAVEE

Scenic rating: 7

on Huntington Lake in Sierra National Forest

See map page 808

Catavee Camp is one of three camps in the immediate vicinity, set on the north shore at the eastern end of Huntington Lake. The camp sits near where Bear Creek enters the lake. Huntington Lake is a scenic, High Sierra Ranger District lake at 7,000 feet, where visitors can enjoy fishing, hiking, and sailing. Sailboat regattas take place here regularly during the summer. All water sports are allowed. Nearby resorts offer boat rentals and guest docks, and a boat ramp is nearby. Tackle rentals and bait are also available. A trailhead near camp offers access to the Kaiser Wilderness.

RV sites, facilities: There are 23 sites for tents or RVs up to 30 feet (no hookups). Picnic tables and fire grills are provided. Drinking water and flush toilets are available. Horseback-riding facilities and a small store are nearby. Some facilities are wheelchair accessible. Leashed pets are permitted.

Reservations, fees: Reservations are accepted at 877/444-6777 or www.ReserveUSA.com ($9 reservation fee). Sites are $17 per night, $5 per night for an additional vehicle. Open June–October, weather permitting.

Directions: From Fresno, drive east on Highway 168 to Shaver Lake, then continue 21 miles to Huntington Lake and Huntington Lake Road. Turn left on Huntington Lake Road and drive one mile (just past Kinnikinnick) to the campground on the right.

Contact: Sierra National Forest, High Sierra Ranger District, 559/855-5355, fax 559/855-5375; California Land Management, 559/893-2111.

CALIFORNIA

10 KINNIKINNICK

Scenic rating: 7

on Huntington Lake in Sierra National Forest
See map page 808

Flip a coin; there are three camps in the immediate vicinity on the north shore of the east end of Huntington Lake, and with a boat ramp nearby they are all favorites. Kinnikinnick is between Catavee and Deer Creek campgrounds. The elevation is 7,000 feet.

RV sites, facilities: There are 27 sites for tents or RVs up to 40 feet (no hookups). Picnic tables and fire grills are provided. Drinking water and vault toilets are available. Horseback-riding facilities and a store are nearby. Some facilities are wheelchair accessible. Leashed pets are permitted.

Reservations, fees: Reservations are accepted at 877/444-6777 or www.ReserveUSA.com ($9 reservation fee). Sites are $19 per night, $5 per night for an additional vehicle. Open June–October, weather permitting.

Directions: From Fresno, drive east on Highway 168 to Shaver Lake, then continue 21 miles to Huntington Lake and Huntington Lake Road. Turn left on Huntington Lake Road and drive one mile to the campground on the right.

Contact: Sierra National Forest, High Sierra Ranger District, 559/855-5355, fax 559/855-5375; California Land Management, 559/893-2111.

11 DEER CREEK

Scenic rating: 8

on Huntington Lake in Sierra National Forest
See map page 808

This is one of the best camps at Huntington Lake, set near lakeside at Bear Cove with a boat ramp nearby. It is on the north shore of the lake's eastern end. Huntington Lake is four miles long and a half mile wide, with 14 miles of shoreline, several resorts, boat rentals, and a trailhead for hiking into the Kaiser Wilderness. Two other campgrounds are nearby.

RV sites, facilities: There are 28 sites for tents or RVs up to 40 feet (no hookups). Picnic tables and fire grills are provided. Drinking water and flush toilets are available. A store and propane gas are nearby. Some facilities are wheelchair accessible. Leashed pets are permitted.

Reservations, fees: Reservations are accepted at 877/444-6777 or www.ReserveUSA.com ($9 reservation fee). Sites are $19–21 per night, $5 per night for an additional vehicle. Open June–October, weather permitting.

Directions: From Fresno, drive east on Highway 168 to Shaver Lake, then continue 21 miles to Huntington Lake and Huntington Lake Road. Turn left on Huntington Lake Road and drive one mile to the campground entrance road on the left.

Contact: Sierra National Forest, High Sierra Ranger District, 559/855-5355, fax 559/855-5375.

12 RANCHERIA

Scenic rating: 8

on Huntington Lake in Sierra National Forest
See map page 808

This is the granddaddy of the camps at Huntington Lake, also the easiest to reach. It is along the shore of the lake's eastern end. A bonus is nearby Rancheria Falls National Recreation Trail, which provides access to beautiful Rancheria Falls. Another side trip is the 15-minute drive to Bear Butte (the access road is across from the campground entrance) at 8,598 feet, providing a sweeping view of the lake below. The elevation at camp is 7,000 feet.

RV sites, facilities: There are 149 sites for tents or RVs up to 40 feet (no hookups). Picnic tables and fire grills are provided. Drinking water and flush and vault toilets are available. A store and propane gas are available nearby. Leashed pets are permitted.

Reservations, fees: Reservations are accepted at 877/444-6777 or www.ReserveUSA.com ($9 reservation fee). Sites are $17 per night, $5 per night for an additional vehicle. Open year-round, weather permitting.

Directions: From Fresno, drive east on Highway 168 to Shaver Lake, then continue 20 miles to Huntington Lake and the campground on the left.

Contact: Sierra National Forest, High Sierra Ranger District, 559/855-5355, fax 559/855-5375; California Land Management, 559/893-2111.

13 SMALLEY COVE

Scenic rating: 7

on Kerckhoff Reservoir near Madera
See map page 808

Kerckhoff Reservoir can get so hot that it might seem you could fry an egg on the rocks. Campers should be certain to have some kind of tarp they can set up as a sun screen. The lake is small and remote, and the use of boat motors more than five horsepower is prohibited. Most campers bring rafts or canoes, and there is a good swimming beach near the picnic area and campground. Fishing is not so good here. The elevation is 1,000 feet.

RV sites, facilities: There are five sites for tents or RVs up to 30 feet (no hookups). Picnic tables and fire grills are provided. Drinking water and vault toilets are available. Five group picnic sites are available. You can buy supplies in Auberry. Some facilities are wheelchair accessible. Leashed pets are permitted.

Reservations, fees: Reservations are not accepted. Sites are $10 per night, $3 per night for an additional vehicle, $7 per night for additional RV, $1 per pet per night. Open year-round.

Directions: From Fresno, take Highway 41 north for three miles to the exit for Highway 168 east. Take that exit and drive east on Highway 168 for about 22 miles to Auberry Road. Turn left (north) and drive 2.8 miles to Powerhouse Road. Turn left and drive 8.5 miles to the campground.

Contact: PG&E Land Services, 916/386-5164, fax 916/386-5388, www.pge.com/recreation.

14 CAMP EDISON

Scenic rating: 8

on Shaver Lake
See map page 808

Camp Edison is the best camp at Shaver Lake, set on a peninsula along the lake's western shore, with a boat ramp and marina. The lake is at an elevation of 5,370 feet in the Sierra, a pretty area that has become popular for its calm, warm days and cool water. Boat rentals and bait and tackle are available at the marina. Newcomers with youngsters will discover that the best area for swimming and playing in the water is on the east side of the lake. Though more distant, this part of the lake offers sandy beaches rather than rocky drop-offs.

RV sites, facilities: There are 252 sites for RVs or tents; some sites have full or partial hookups (20, 30, and 50 amps). During the summer season, 45 tent trailers also are available. Picnic tables, fire rings, and barbecues are provided. Restrooms have flush toilets and pay showers. Drinking water, cable TV, Wi-Fi, a general store, a dump station, a coin laundry, a marina, a boat ramp, and horseback-riding facilities are available. Some facilities are wheelchair accessible. Leashed pets are permitted.

Reservations, fees: Reservations are recommended. Sites are $24–45 per night, $6 per night for an additional vehicle, $6 per day for boat launching, $5 per pet per night. Tent trailers are $75 per night. Group and long-term rates available. Open year-round with limited winter services.

Directions: From Fresno, take the exit for Highway 41 north and drive north on Highway 41 to the exit for Highway 180 east. Take that exit and drive east on Highway 180 to Highway 168 east. Take that exit and drive east on Highway 168 to the town of Shaver Lake. Continue one mile on Highway 168 to the campground entrance road on the right. Turn right and drive to the campground on the west shore of Shaver Lake.

Contact: Camp Edison, Southern California Edison, 559/841-3134, fax 559/841-3193, www.sce.com/campedison.

CALIFORNIA

CALIFORNIA

15 DORABELLE

Scenic rating: 7

on Shaver Lake in Sierra National Forest
See map page 808

This is one of the few Forest Service camps in the state that is up more for RVers than for tenters. The camp is along a long cove at the southwest corner of the lake, well-protected from winds out of the northwest. Shaver Lake is a popular one for vacationers, and waterskiing and wakeboarding are favorite activities. It is well stocked with trout and kokanee salmon. Boat rentals and bait and tackle are available at the nearby marina. The elevation is 5,400 feet.

RV sites, facilities: There are 68 sites for tents or RVs up to 40 feet (no hookups). Picnic tables and fire grills are provided. Drinking water and vault toilets are available. A store is nearby. Leashed pets are permitted.

Reservations, fees: Reservations are accepted at 877/444-6777 or www.ReserveUSA.com ($9 reservation fee). Sites are $17 per night, $5 per night for an additional vehicle. Open May–September, weather permitting.

Directions: From Fresno, drive east on Highway 168 to Dorabelle Road (on the right just as you enter the town of Shaver Lake). Turn right on Dorabelle Road and drive one mile to the campground at the southwest end of Shaver Lake.

Contact: Sierra National Forest, High Sierra Ranger District, 559/855-5355, fax 559/855-5375; California Land Management, 559/893-2111.

16 DINKEY CREEK

Scenic rating: 7

in Sierra National Forest
See map page 808

This is a huge Forest Service camp set along Dinkey Creek at 5,700 feet, well in the interior of Sierra National Forest. It is a popular camp for anglers who take the trail and hike upstream along the creek for small-trout fishing in a pristine setting. Backpackers occasionally lay

over here before driving on to the Dinkey Lakes Parking Area, for hikes to Mystery Lake, Swede Lake, South Lake, and others in the nearby Dinkey Lakes Wilderness.

RV sites, facilities: There are 128 sites for tents or RVs up to 35 feet, along with one group site for up to 50 people. No hookups. Picnic tables and fire grills are provided. Drinking water, flush and vault toilets, and horseback-riding facilities are available nearby. You can buy supplies in Dinkey Creek. Leashed pets are permitted.

Reservations, fees: Reservations are accepted for individual sites and required for the group site ($9 reservation fee) at 877/444-6777 or www.ReserveUSA.com. Sites are $20 per night, $5 per night for an additional vehicle, $140 per night for the group site. Open May–September, weather permitting.

Directions: From Fresno, drive east on Highway 168 to Dinkey Creek Road (on the right just as you enter the town of Shaver Lake). Turn right and drive 13 miles to the campground. A map of Sierra National Forest is advised.

Contact: Sierra National Forest, High Sierra Ranger District, 559/855-5355, fax 559/855-5375.

17 JACKASS MEADOW

Scenic rating: 7

on Florence Lake in Sierra National Forest
See map page 808

Jackass Meadows is a pretty spot adjacent to Florence Lake, near the Upper San Joaquin River. There are good canoeing, rafting, and float-tubing possibilities, all high-Sierra style, and swimming is allowed. The boat speed limit is 15 mph. The elevation is 7,200 feet. The lake is remote and can be reached only after a long, circuitous drive on a narrow road and many blind turns. A trailhead at the lake offers access to the wilderness and the John Muir Trail. A hiker's water taxi is available.

RV sites, facilities: There are 44 sites for tents or RVs up to 20 feet (no hookups). Picnic tables

and fire grills are provided. Vault toilets are available. There is no drinking water. A boat launch, fishing boat rentals, and wheelchair-accessible fishing pier are nearby. Leashed pets are permitted.

Reservations, fees: Reservations are accepted at 877/444-6777 ($9 reservation fee) or www.ReserveUSA.com. Sites are $16 per night, $32 per night for a double site, $5 per night for an additional vehicle. Open June–mid-October, weather permitting.

Directions: From the town of Shaver Lake, drive east on Highway 168 for 21 miles to Kaiser Pass Road. Bear northeast on Kaiser Pass Road/Forest Road 80 (slow and curvy) to a junction (left goes to Mono Hot Springs and Lake Edison) with Florence Lake Road. Bear right at the junction and drive seven miles to the campground.

Contact: Sierra National Forest, High Sierra Ranger District, 559/855-5355, fax 559/855-5375; California Land Management, 559/893-2111.

18 TRAPPER SPRINGS

Scenic rating: 8

on Courtright Reservoir in Sierra National Forest

See map page 808

Trapper Springs is on the west shore of Courtright Reservoir, set at 8,200 feet on the west slope of the Sierra. Courtright is a great destination, with excellent camping, boating, fishing, and hiking into the nearby John Muir Wilderness. A 15-mph speed limit makes the lake ideal for fishing, canoeing, and rafting. Swimming is allowed, but the water is very cold. The lake level can drop dramatically by late summer. A trailhead a mile north of camp by car heads around the north end of the lake to a fork; to the left it leads into the Dinkey Lakes Wilderness, and to the right it goes to the head of the lake and then follows Dusy Creek in a long climb into spectacular country in the John Muir Wilderness. There are two driving routes to this lake, one from Shaver Lake and the other from Pine Flat Reservoir; both are very long, slow, and twisty drives.

RV sites, facilities: There are 75 sites for tents or RVs up to 35 feet (no hookups). Picnic tables and fire grills are provided. Drinking water and vault toilets are available. A boat ramp is nearby. Some facilities are wheelchair accessible. Leashed pets are permitted.

Reservations, fees: Reservations are not accepted. Sites are $18 per night, $9 per night for an additional RV, $3 per night for an additional vehicle, $1 per pet per night. Open June–October.

Directions: From Fresno, drive east on Highway 168 to Dinkey Creek Road (on the right just as you enter the town of Shaver Lake). Turn right and drive 13 miles to McKinley Grove Road/Forest Road 40. Turn right and drive 14 miles to Courtright Road. Turn left (north) and drive 12 miles to the campground entrance road on the right.

Contact: Sierra National Forest, High Sierra Ranger District, 559/855-5355, fax 559/855-5375; PG&E Land Services, 916/386-5164, fax 916/386-5388, www.pge.com/recreation.

19 WISHON VILLAGE RV RESORT

Scenic rating: 7

near Wishon Reservoir

See map page 808

This privately operated mountain park is near the shore of Wishon Reservoir, about one mile from the dam. Trout stocks often make for good fishing in early summer, and anglers with boats love the 15-mph speed limit, which keeps personal watercraft off the water. Backpackers and hikers can find a great trailhead at the south end of the lake at Coolidge Meadow, where a trail awaits that is routed to the Woodchuck Creek drainage and numerous lakes in the John Muir Wilderness. The elevation is 6,500 feet.

RV sites, facilities: There are 97 sites with full hookups (50 amps) for RVs up to 60 feet and 26 sites for tents. A rental trailer is available. Picnic tables and fire pits are provided. Restrooms have

CALIFORNIA

coin showers. Drinking water and Sunday church service are available. A coin laundry, ice, a boat ramp, motorboat rentals, bait and tackle, boat slips, volleyball, horseshoes, and propane gas are available nearby. Leashed pets are permitted.

Reservations, fees: Reservations are recommended. RV sites are $33 per night, $23 per night for tent sites, $3 per person per night for more than two people, $2 per pet per night. Weekly and monthly rates available. Open May–October.

Directions: From Fresno, drive east on Highway 168 to Dinkey Creek Road (on the right just as you enter the town of Shaver Lake). Turn right and drive 13 miles to McKinley Grove Road (Forest Road 40). Turn right and drive 15 miles to the park (66500 McKinley Grove Road/Forest Road 40).

Contact: Wishon Village RV Resort, 559/865-5361, www.wishonvillage.com.

20 LILY PAD

Scenic rating: 7

near Wishon Reservoir in Sierra National Forest
See map page 808

Wishon Reservoir is a great place for a camping trip. When the lake is full, which is not often enough, the place has great natural beauty, set at 6,400 feet and surrounded by national forest. The fishing is fair enough on summer evenings, and a 15-mph speed limit keeps the lake quiet. Swimming is allowed, but the water is very cold. This is the smallest of the camps at Wishon Reservoir. It is along the southwest shore, about a mile from both the lake and a good boat ramp. The conditions at this lake are similar to those at Courtright Reservoir. There are two driving routes to this lake, one from Shaver Lake and the other from Pine Flat Reservoir; both are very long, slow, and twisty drives.

RV sites, facilities: There are 11 sites for tents or RVs up to 35 feet (no hookups) and four hike-in sites. Picnic tables and fire grills are provided. Drinking water and vault toilets are available. Groceries, boat rentals, a boat ramp,

and propane gas are available nearby. Leashed pets are permitted.

Reservations, fees: Reservations are not accepted. Sites are $16 per night, $7 per night for an additional RV, $3 per night for an additional vehicle, $1 per pet per night. Open May–October, weather permitting.

Directions: From Fresno, drive east on Highway 168 to Dinkey Creek Road (on the right just as you enter the town of Shaver Lake). Turn right and drive 13 miles to McKinley Grove Road (Forest Road 40). Turn right and drive 16 miles to the campground on the right.

Contact: Sierra National Forest, High Sierra Ranger District, 559/855-5355, fax 559/855-5375; PG&E Land Services, 916/386-5164, www.pge.com/recreation.

21 BROWN'S MILLPOND CAMPGROUND

Scenic rating: 6

near Bishop
See map page 808

This privately operated camp is adjacent to the Millpond Recreation Area, which offers ball fields, playgrounds, and a swimming lake. No powerboats are allowed. There is also the opportunity for sailing, archery, tennis courts, horseshoe games, and fishing.

RV sites, facilities: There are 75 sites for tents or RVs of any length; some sites have partial hookups (30 amps). Picnic tables and fire grills are provided. Restrooms have flush toilets and coin showers. Drinking water and a coin laundry are available. Leashed pets are permitted.

Reservations, fees: Reservations are accepted. Sites are $17–20 per vehicle per night. Open March–October.

Directions: Drive on U.S. 395 to a road signed for Millpond/County Park (seven miles north of Bishop). Turn southwest (toward the Sierra) at that road (Ed Powers Road) and drive 0.2 mile to Sawmill Road. Turn right and drive 0.8 mile to Millpond Road. Turn left and drive a short distance to the campground.

Contact: Brown's Millpond Campground, 760/873-5342, www.brownscampgrounds.com/millpond.html.

22 BROWN'S TOWN

Scenic rating: 5

near Bishop

See map page 808

This privately operated campground is one of several in the vicinity of Bishop. It's all shade and grass, and it's next to the golf course.

RV sites, facilities: There are 150 sites for tents or RVs of any length (no hookups) and 44 sites for tents or RVs with partial hookups (30 amps). Some sites are pull-through. Picnic tables are provided, and fire grills are at most sites. Restrooms have flush toilets and coin showers. Drinking water, cable TV at 10 sites, a dump station, a museum, a convenience store, and a snack bar are available. Leashed pets are permitted.

Reservations, fees: Reservations are accepted. Sites are $17–22 per night, $1 per person per night for more than two people. There's a one-vehicle limit per site and a 14-day stay limit per season. Some credit cards accepted. Open March–Thanksgiving, weather permitting.

Directions: Drive on U.S. 395 to Schober Lane (one mile south of Bishop) and the campground entrance. Turn northwest (toward the Sierra) and into the campground.

Contact: Brown's Town, 760/873-8522, www.brownscampgrounds.com/browns.html.

23 BISHOP PARK

Scenic rating: 6

near Lake Sabrina in Inyo National Forest

See map page 808

Bishop Park Camp is one in a series of camps along Bishop Creek. This one is just behind the summer community of Aspendell. It is about two miles from Lake Sabrina, an ideal day trip or jump-off spot for a backpacking expedition into the John Muir Wilderness. The elevation is 8,400 feet.

RV sites, facilities: There are 21 sites for tents or RVs up to 22 feet (no hookups), and a group tent site holds up to 25 people. Picnic tables and fire grills are provided. Drinking water and flush toilets are available. Horseback-riding facilities are available nearby. Supplies are available in Bishop. Some facilities are wheelchair accessible. Leashed pets are permitted.

Reservations, fees: Reservations are not accepted for the family sites but are required for the group site. Reservations are accepted at 877/444-6777 ($9 reservation fee) or www.ReserveUSA.com. Sites are $16 per night, $45 per night for the group site. Open mid-May–mid-October, weather permitting.

Directions: Drive on U.S. 395 to Bishop and Highway 168. Turn west (toward the Sierra) on Highway 168 and drive 15 miles to the campground.

Contact: Inyo National Forest, White Mountain Ranger District, 760/873-2500, fax 760/873-2563; Rainbow Pack Outfitters, 760/872-8803.

24 FOUR JEFFREY

Scenic rating: 8

near South Lake in Inyo National Forest

See map page 808

The camp is on the South Fork of Bishop Creek at 8,100 feet, about four miles from South Lake. If you can arrange a trip in the fall, make sure you visit this camp. The fall colors are spectacular, with the aspen trees exploding in yellows and oranges. It is also the last camp on South Lake Road to be closed in the fall, and though nights are cold, it is well worth the trip. This is by far the largest of the Forest Service camps in the vicinity. There are three lakes in the area: North Lake, Lake Sabrina, and South Lake. South Lake is stocked with trout and has a 5-mph speed limit.

RV sites, facilities: There are 106 sites for tents or RVs up to 25 feet (no hookups). Picnic tables and fire grills are provided. Drinking water, vault toilets, and a dump station are available. Horseback-riding facilities are available nearby.

A café, a small store, and fishing-boat rentals are available at South Lake. Supplies are available in Bishop. Some facilities are wheelchair accessible. Leashed pets are permitted.

Reservations, fees: Reservations are accepted at 877/444-6777 ($9 reservation fee) or www.ReserveUSA.com. Sites are $16 per night. Open mid-April–October, weather permitting.

Directions: Drive on U.S. 395 to Bishop and Highway 168. Turn west (toward the Sierra) on Highway 168 and drive 14 miles to South Lake Road. Turn left and drive 0.5 mile to the campground.

Contact: Inyo National Forest, White Mountain Ranger District, 760/873-2500, fax 760/873-2563; Rainbow Pack Outfitters, 760/872-8803.

25 CREEKSIDE RV PARK

Scenic rating: 7

on the South Fork of Bishop Creek

See map page 808

This privately operated park in the high country is up primarily for RVs. A lot of folks are surprised to find it here. The South Fork of Bishop Creek runs through the park. A bonus is a fishing pond stocked with Alpers trout. North, Sabrina, and South Lakes are in the area. The elevation is 8,300 feet.

RV sites, facilities: There are 45 sites with full or partial hookups (20 and 30 amps) for RVs up to 40 feet, four sites for tents, and 14 rental trailers. Restrooms have flush toilets and coin showers. Drinking water, a convenience store, propane, horseshoes, and fish-cleaning facilities are available. Leashed pets are permitted.

Reservations, fees: Reservations are accepted. Sites are $35 per night, $1 per person per night for more than two people, $5 per night for an additional vehicle, $5 per pet per night. Open May–October. Some credit cards accepted.

Directions: Drive on U.S. 395 to Bishop and Highway 168. Turn west (toward the Sierra) on Highway 168 and drive 14 miles to South Lake Road. Turn left and drive two miles to the

campground entrance on the left (1949 South Lake Road).

Contact: Creekside RV Park, 760/873-4483.

26 SABRINA

Scenic rating: 8

near Lake Sabrina in Inyo National Forest

See map page 808   BEST (

You get the best of both worlds at this camp. It is at 9,000 feet on Bishop Creek, just a half mile from 200-acre Lake Sabrina, a beautiful High Sierra lake. By the way, Sabrina is pronounced "Sa-bry-na," not "Sa-bree-na." A 10-mph boat speed limit is in effect. Sabrina is stocked with trout, including some big Alpers trout. Trails nearby are routed into the high country of the John Muir Wilderness. Take your pick. Whatever your choice, it's a good one.

RV sites, facilities: There are 18 sites for tents or RVs up to 30 feet (no hookups). Picnic tables and fire grills are provided. Drinking water and vault toilets are available. A boat ramp and boat rentals are nearby. Supplies are available in Bishop. Leashed pets are permitted.

Reservations, fees: Reservations are not accepted. Sites are $16 per night. Open mid-May–October, weather permitting.

Directions: Drive on U.S. 395 to Bishop and Highway 168. Turn west (toward the Sierra) on Highway 168 and drive 17 miles (signed for Lake Sabrina at a fork) to the campground.

Contact: Inyo National Forest, White Mountain Ranger District, 760/873-2500, fax 760/873-2563; Bishop Pack Outfitters, 760/873-4785.

27 BAKER CREEK CAMPGROUND

Scenic rating: 4

near Big Pine

See map page 808

Because this is a county-operated RV park, it is overlooked by many who usually consider only camps on reservations systems. That makes this a good option for cruisers touring the eastern

Sierra on U.S. 395. It's ideal for a quick over-nighter, with easy access from Big Pine. The camp is along Baker Creek at 4,000 feet in the high plateau country of the eastern Sierra. An option is fair trout fishing during the evening bite on the creek.

RV sites, facilities: There are 70 sites for tents or RVs up to 40 feet. No hookups. Picnic tables and fire grills are provided. Vault toilets and hand-pumped well water are available. You can buy supplies about 1.5 miles away in Big Pine. Leashed pets are permitted.

Reservations, fees: Reservations are not accepted. The fee is $10 per vehicle per night. Open year-round, weather permitting.

Directions: Drive on U.S. 395 to Big Pine and Baker Creek Road. Turn west (toward the Sierra) on Baker Creek Road and drive a mile to the campground.

Contact: Inyo County Parks Department, 760/878-0272 or 760/763-5577, www.395.com/inyo/campgrounds.

28 GLACIER VIEW

Scenic rating: 4

near Big Pine

See map page 808

This is one of two county camps near the town of Big Pine, providing U.S. 395 cruisers with two options. The camp is along the Big Pine Canal at 3,900 feet. It is owned by the county but operated by a concessionaire. Brown's runs five small campgrounds in the area: Glacier View, Keough Hot Springs, Brown's Millpond, Brown's Owens River, and Brown's Town.

RV sites, facilities: There are 40 sites for tents or RVs of any length; some sites have partial hookups (30 amps) and/or are pull-through. Picnic tables and fire grills are provided. Restrooms have flush toilets and coin showers, and drinking water is available. Supplies are available in Big Pine. Leashed pets are permitted.

Reservations, fees: Reservations are not accepted. Sites are $10–15 per vehicle per night. Open year-round.

Directions: Drive on U.S. 395 to the park entrance (0.5 mile north of Big Pine) on the southeast side of the road. Turn east (away from the Sierra) and enter the park.

Contact: Inyo County Parks Department, 760/872-6911 or 760/873-5577, www.395.com/inyo/campgrounds or www.brownscampgrounds.com.

29 BIG PINE CREEK

Scenic rating: 8

in Inyo National Forest

See map page 808

This is another good spot for backpackers to launch a multiday trip. The camp is along Big Pine Creek at 7,700 feet, with trails near the camp that are routed to the numerous lakes in the high country of the John Muir Wilderness.

RV sites, facilities: There are 36 sites for tents or RVs up to 22 feet (no hookups). Picnic tables and fire grills are provided. Drinking water and vault toilets are available. Some facilities are wheelchair accessible. Leashed pets are permitted.

Reservations, fees: Reservations are not accepted. Sites are $16 per night. Open early May–October, weather permitting.

Directions: Drive on U.S. 395 to Big Pine and Crocker Street/Glacier Lodge Road. Turn west (toward the Sierra) and drive nine miles (the road becomes Glacier Lodge Road) to the campground.

Contact: Inyo National Forest, White Mountain Ranger District, 760/873-2500, fax 760/873-2563.

30 TINEMAHA CAMPGROUND

Scenic rating: 6

near Big Pine

See map page 808

This primitive, little-known (to out-of-towners) county park campground is on Tinnemaha Creek at 4,400 feet. The creek is stocked with

CALIFORNIA

Alpers trout. Horse camping is allowed, but call ahead.

RV sites, facilities: There are 55 sites for tents or RVs of any length (no hookups). Picnic tables and fire grills are provided. Vault toilets are available. Limited drinking water is available. Stream water is available and must be boiled or pump-filtered before use. Leashed pets are permitted.

Reservations, fees: Reservations are not accepted. Sites are $10 per vehicle per night. Open year-round.

Directions: Drive on U.S. 395 to Tinnemaha Creek Road (seven miles south of Big Pine and 19.5 miles north of Independence). Turn west (toward the Sierra) on Fish Springs Road and drive 0.5 mile to Tinnemaha Creek Road. Turn west (left) and drive two miles to the park on the right.

Contact: Inyo County Parks Department, 760/878-0272 or 760/873-5577, www.395.com/inyo/campgrounds.

31 TABOOSE CREEK CAMPGROUND

Scenic rating: 4

near Big Pine
See map page 808

The eastern Sierra is stark country, but this little spot provides a stream (Taboose Creek) and some trees near the campground. There is an opportunity for trout fishing—fair, not spectacular. The easy access off U.S. 395 is a bonus. The elevation is 3,900 feet.

RV sites, facilities: There are 56 sites for tents or RVs up to 40 feet (no hookups). Picnic tables and fire grills are provided. Drinking water (hand-pumped from a well) and vault toilets are available. Supplies are available in Big Pine or Independence. Leashed pets are permitted.

Reservations, fees: Reservations are not accepted. The fee is $10 per vehicle per night. Open year-round.

Directions: Drive on U.S. 395 to Taboose Creek Road (11 miles south of Big Pine and 14 miles north of Independence). Turn west (toward the

Sierra) on Taboose Creek Road and drive 2.5 miles to the campground (straight in).

Contact: Inyo County Parks Department, 760/878-0272 or 760/873-5577, www.395.com/inyo/campgrounds.

32 GRANDVIEW

Scenic rating: 6

near Big Pine in Inyo National Forest
See map page 808

This is a primitive and little-known camp, and the folks who find this area earn their solitude. It is in the White Mountains east of Bishop at 8,600 feet along White Mountain Road. The road borders the Ancient Bristlecone Pine Forest to the east and leads north to jump-off spots for hikers heading up Mount Barcroft (13,023 feet) or White Mountain (14,246 feet, the third-highest mountain in California). A trail out of the camp leads up to an old mining site.

RV sites, facilities: There are 26 sites for tents or RVs up to 22 feet (no hookups). Picnic tables and fire grills are provided. Vault toilets are available. No drinking water is available. Garbage must be packed out. Leashed pets are permitted.

Reservations, fees: Reservations are not accepted. There is no camping fee. Open year-round.

Directions: From Big Pine on U.S. 395, turn east on Highway 168 and drive 13 miles. Turn north on White Mountain/Bristlecone Forest Road (Forest Road 4S01) and drive 5.5 miles to the campground.

Contact: Inyo National Forest, White Mountain Ranger District, 760/873-2500, fax 760/873-2563.

33 ISLAND PARK AND DEER CREEK POINT GROUP

Scenic rating: 7

on Pine Flat Lake
See map page 808

These are two of four Army Corps of Engineer campgrounds available at Pine Flat Lake, a popular lake set in the foothill country east of Fresno. When Pine Flat is full, or close to full, it is very pretty. The lake is 21 miles long with 67 miles of shoreline and 4,270 surface acres. Right—a big lake with unlimited potential. Because the temperatures get warm in spring here, then smoking hot in summer, the lake is like Valhalla for boating and water sports. The fishing for white bass is often excellent in late winter and early spring, and after that, conditions are ideal for water sports. The elevation is 1,000 feet.

RV sites, facilities: There are 52 sites for tents or RVs of any length (no hookups), 60 over-flow sites (at Island Park), and two group sites for 50 people each for tents or RVs up to 45 feet. Picnic tables and fire grills are provided. Restrooms have flush toilets and coin showers. Drinking water, a pay telephone, a boat ramp, a fish-cleaning station, and a dump station are available. There is a seasonal store at the campground entrance. Boat rentals are available within five miles. Some facilities are wheelchair accessible. Leashed pets are permitted.

Reservations, fees: Reservations are accepted and required for the group sites at 877/444-6777 ($9 reservation fee) or www.ReserveUSA.com. Sites are $16 per night, $75 per night for group site. Boat launching is $3 per day. Open year-round.

Directions: From Fresno, drive east on Highway 180 for 17.5 miles to Trimmer Springs Road. Turn left and drive eight miles to the town of Piedra. Continue on Trimmer Springs Road for one mile to Pine Flat Road. Turn right and drive 0.25 mile to the park entrance (signed for Island Park).

Contact: U.S. Army Corps of Engineers, Sacramento District, Pine Flat Field Office, 559/787-2589, fax 559/787-2773.

34 LAKERIDGE CAMPING AND BOATING RESORT

Scenic rating: 7

on Pine Flat Lake

See map page 808

Pine Flat Lake is a 20-mile-long reservoir with seemingly unlimited recreation potential. It is an excellent lake for all water/body contact sports. It is in the foothills east of Fresno at 970 feet elevation, covering 4,912 surface acres with 67 miles of shoreline. The lake's proximity to Fresno has made it a top destination for boating and water sports. Fishing for white bass can be excellent in the spring and early summer. There are also rainbow trout, largemouth bass, smallmouth bass, bluegill, catfish, and black crappie. Note: A downer is that there are only a few sandy beaches, and the lake level can drop to as low as 20 percent full.

RV sites, facilities: There are 107 sites for tents or RVs up to 36 feet with full or partial hookups (30 amps). Picnic tables and barbecue grills are available at some sites. Restrooms have showers. Modem access, a coin laundry, ice, horseshoes, and a pay phone are available. A convenience store and boat and houseboat rentals are nearby. Leashed pets are permitted.

Reservations, fees: Reservations are recommended at 877/787-2260. Sites are $20–25 per night, $2.50 per pet per night. Some credit cards accepted. Open year-round.

Directions: From Fresno, drive east on Highway 180 for 17.5 miles to Trimmer Springs Road. Turn left and drive eight miles to the town of Piedra. Continue on Trimmer Springs Road for four miles to Sunnyslope Road. Turn right and drive one mile to the resort on the right.

Contact: Lakeridge Camping and Boating Resort, 559/787-2260, fax 559/787-2354; marina, 559/787-2506.

35 PINE FLAT RECREATION AREA

Scenic rating: 7

on Pine Flat Lake

See map page 808

This is a county park that is open all year, set below the dam of Pine Flat Lake, actually not on the lake at all. As a county park campground, it is often overlooked by out-of-towners.

RV sites, facilities: There are 52 pull-through sites for tents or RVs of any length (no hookups). Fire grills and picnic tables are provided.

Restrooms have flush toilets. Drinking water, a dump station, and a wheelchair-accessible fishing area are available. A store, a coin laundry, and propane gas are nearby (within a mile). Leashed pets are permitted.

Reservations, fees: Reservations are not accepted. Sites are $11 per night, $5 per night for an additional vehicle. Open year-round.

Directions: From Fresno, drive east on Highway 180 for 17.5 miles to Trimmer Springs Road. Turn left and drive eight miles to the town of Piedra. Continue on Trimmer Springs Road for one mile to Pine Flat Road. Turn right and drive three miles to the campground on the right.

Contact: Fresno County Parks Department, 559/488-3004, fax 559/488-1988.

36 CHOINUMNI

Scenic rating: 7

on lower Kings River

See map page 808

This campground is in the San Joaquin foothills on the Kings River, a pretty area. Since the campground is operated by Fresno County, it is off the radar scope of many visitors. Fishing, rafting, canoeing, and hiking are popular. The elevation is around 1,000 feet, surrounded by a landscape of oak woodlands and grassland foothills. The park is roughly 33 miles east of Fresno.

RV sites, facilities: There are 36 sites for tents or RVs of any length (no hookups) and one group site for up to 75 people. Some sites are pull-through. Picnic tables and fire rings are provided. Drinking water, flush toilets, and a dump station are available. Canoe rentals are available nearby. No facilities within 10 miles. Leashed pets are permitted.

Reservations, fees: No reservations accepted, except for the group site. Sites are $11 per night, $5 per night for an additional vehicle, $80 per night for the group site. Open year-round.

Directions: From Fresno, drive east on Highway 180 for 17.5 miles to Piedra Road. Turn left on Piedra Road and drive eight miles to Trimmer

Springs Road. Turn right on Trimmer Springs Road and drive one mile to Pine Flat Road. Turn right and drive 100 yards to the camp entrance on the right.

Contact: Fresno County Parks Department, 559/488-3004, fax 559/488-1988.

37 PRINCESS

Scenic rating: 7

on Princess Meadow in Giant Sequoia National Monument

See map page 808

This mountain camp is at 5,900 feet. It is popular because of its proximity to both Hume Lake and the star attractions at Kings Canyon National Park. Hume Lake is just four miles from the camp, and the Grant Grove entrance to Kings Canyon National Park is only six miles away to the south, while continuing on Highway 180 to the east will take you into the heart of Kings Canyon.

RV sites, facilities: There are 90 sites for tents or RVs up to 22 feet (no hookups). Picnic tables and fire grills are provided. Drinking water, vault toilets, and a dump station are available. A store is four miles away at Hume Lake. Leashed pets are permitted.

Reservations, fees: Reservations are accepted ($9 reservation fee) at 877/444-6777 or www.ReserveUSA.com. Sites are $15 per night, $30 per night for a double site, $5 per night for an additional vehicle, plus a $20 per vehicle national park entrance fee. Prices are higher on holiday weekends. Open May–September, weather permitting.

Directions: From Fresno, drive east on Highway 180 for 55 miles to the Big Stump entrance station at Sequoia and Kings Canyon National Parks. Continue 1.5 miles to a junction (signed left for Grant Grove). Turn left and drive 1.5 miles to Grant Grove Village, then continue for 4.5 miles to the campground on the right.

Contact: Sequoia National Forest, Hume Lake Ranger District, 559/338-2251, fax 559/338-2131.

38 HUME LAKE

Scenic rating: 8

in Giant Sequoia National Forest
See map page 808

For newcomers, Hume Lake is a surprise: a pretty lake, with great summer camps for teenagers. Canoeing and kayaking are excellent, and so is the trout fishing, especially near the dam. Swimming is allowed. A 5-mph speed limit is in effect on this 85-acre lake, and only electric motors are permitted. Another surprise is the adjacent religious camp center. The nearby entrances to Kings Canyon National Park add a bonus. The elevation is 5,200 feet.

RV sites, facilities: There are 50 sites for tents or RVs up to 22 feet (no hookups) and 60 tent sites. Picnic tables and fire grills are provided. Drinking water and flush toilets are available. A store, café, bicycle rentals, and boat rentals are nearby. Leashed pets are permitted.

Reservations, fees: Reservations are accepted ($9 reservation fee) at 877/444-6777 or www.ReserveUSA.com. Sites are $17 per night, $5 per night for an additional vehicle, plus $20 per vehicle national park entrance fee. Rates are higher on holiday weekends. Open May–early September, weather permitting.

Directions: From Fresno, drive east on Highway 180 for 55 miles to the Big Stump entrance station at Sequoia and Kings Canyon National Parks. Continue 1.5 miles to a junction (signed left for Grant Grove). Turn left and drive six miles to the Hume Lake Road junction. Turn right and drive three miles to Hume Lake and the campground entrance road. Turn right and drive 0.25 mile to the campground on the left.

Contact: Sequoia National Forest, Hume Lake Ranger District, 559/338-2251, fax 559/338-2131.

39 CRYSTAL SPRINGS

Scenic rating: 5

in Kings Canyon National Park
See map page 808

Directly to the south of this camp is the General Grant Grove and its giant sequoias. But continuing on Highway 180 provides access to the interior of Kings Canyon National Park, and this camp makes an ideal jump-off point. From here you can drive east, passing Cedar Grove Village, cruising along the Kings River, and finally coming to a dead-end loop, taking in the drop-dead gorgeous landscape of one of the deepest gorges in North America. One of the best hikes, but also the most demanding, is the 13-mile round-trip to Lookout Peak, out of the Cedar Grove Village area. It involves a 4,000-foot climb to 8,531 feet, and with it, a breathtaking view of Sierra ridges, Cedar Grove far below, and Kings Canyon.

RV sites, facilities: There are 50 sites for tents or RVs up to 22 feet (no hookups). Picnic tables and fire grills are provided. Drinking water and flush toilets are available. Evening ranger programs are often available in the summer. A store and horseback-riding facilities are nearby. Showers are available in Grant Grove Village during the summer season. Some facilities are wheelchair accessible. Leashed pets are permitted, except on trails.

Reservations, fees: Reservations are not accepted. Sites are $18 per night, plus a $20 per vehicle national park entrance fee. Open mid-May–mid-September, weather permitting.

Directions: From Fresno, drive east on Highway 180 for 55 miles to the Big Stump entrance station at Sequoia and Kings Canyon National Parks. Continue 1.5 miles to a junction (signed left for Grant Grove). Turn left and drive 1.5 miles to Grant Grove Village, then continue for 0.7 mile to the campground entrance on the right.

Contact: Sequoia and Kings Canyon National Parks, 559/565-3341; Grant Grove Visitor Center, 559/565-4307, www.nps.gov/seki.

CALIFORNIA

CALIFORNIA

40 AZALEA

Scenic rating: 7

in Kings Canyon National Park

See map page 808

This camp is tucked just inside the western border of Kings Canyon National Park. It is at 6,600 feet near the General Grant Grove of giant sequoias. (For information on several short, spectacular hikes among the giant sequoias, see the listing in this chapter for *Sunset*.) Nearby Sequoia Lake is privately owned; no fishing, no swimming, no trespassing. To see the spectacular Kings Canyon, one of the deepest gorges in North America, reenter the park on Highway 180.

RV sites, facilities: There are 110 sites for tents or RVs up to 30 feet (no hookups). Picnic tables and fire grills are provided. Drinking water and flush toilets are available. Evening ranger programs are often available. A store and horseback-riding facilities are nearby. Showers are available in Grant Grove Village during the summer. Some facilities are wheelchair accessible. Leashed pets are permitted, except on trails.

Reservations, fees: Reservations are not accepted. Sites are $18 per night, plus a $20 per vehicle national park entrance fee. Open year-round.

Directions: From Fresno, drive east on Highway 180 for 55 miles to the Big Stump entrance station at Sequoia and Kings Canyon National Parks. Continue 1.5 miles to a junction (signed left for Grant Grove). Turn left and drive 1.5 miles to Grant Grove Village, then continue for 0.7 mile to the campground entrance on the left.

Contact: Sequoia and Kings Canyon National Parks, 559/565-3341; Grant Grove Visitor Center, 559/565-4307; Grant Grove Horse Stables, 559/335-9292, www.nps.gov/seki.

41 SUNSET

Scenic rating: 7

in Kings Canyon National Park

See map page 808

This is the biggest of the camps that are just inside the Sequoia National Park boundaries at Grant Grove Village, 6,600 feet in elevation. The nearby General Grant Grove of giant sequoias is the main attraction, with many short, easy walks among the sequoias, each breathtakingly beautiful. They include Big Stump Trail, Sunset Trail, North Grove Loop, General Grant Tree, Manzanita and Azalea Loop, and Panoramic Point and Park Ridge Trail. Seeing the General Grant Tree is a rite of passage for newcomers; after a half-hour walk you arrive at a sequoia that is approximately 1,800 years old, 107 feet in circumference, and 267 feet tall.

RV sites, facilities: There are 157 sites for tents or RVs up to 30 feet (no hookups). Picnic tables and fire grills are provided. Drinking water and flush toilets are available. In the summer, evening ranger programs often take place. A store and horseback-riding facilities are nearby. Showers are available in Grant Grove Village during the summer. Some facilities are wheelchair accessible. Leashed pets are permitted, except on trails.

Reservations, fees: Reservations are not accepted. Sites are $18 per night, plus a $20 per vehicle national park entrance fee. Open late May–mid-September, weather permitting.

Directions: From Fresno, drive east on Highway 180 for 55 miles to the Big Stump entrance station at Sequoia and Kings Canyon National Parks. Continue 1.5 miles to a junction (signed left for Grant Grove). Turn left (still Highway 180) and drive one mile to the campground entrance (0.5 mile before reaching Grant Grove Village).

Contact: Sequoia and Kings Canyon National Parks, 559/565-3341; Grant Grove Visitor Center, 559/565-4307, www.nps.gov/seki.

42 SENTINEL

Scenic rating: 8

in Kings Canyon National Park

See map page 808

This camp provides a nearby alternative to Sheep Creek. They both tend to fill up quickly in the summer. It's a short walk to Cedar Grove

Village, the center of activity in the park. The elevation is 4,600 feet. Hiking and trout fishing are excellent in the vicinity. The entrance road provides stunning rim-of-the-world views of Kings Canyon, and then drops to right along the Kings River.

RV sites, facilities: There are 82 sites for tents or RVs up to 30 feet (no hookups). Picnic tables and fire grills are provided. Restrooms have flush toilets, and drinking water is available. A store. Coin showers, a coin laundry, and snack bar are nearby. Some facilities are wheelchair accessible. Leashed pets are permitted.

Reservations, fees: Reservations are not accepted. Sites are $18 per night, plus $20 per vehicle national park entrance fee. Open late April–mid-November, weather permitting.

Directions: From Fresno, drive east on Highway 180 for 55 miles to the Big Stump entrance station at Sequoia and Kings Canyon National Parks. Continue 1.5 miles to a junction (signed left for Grant Grove). Turn left and drive 32 miles to the campground entrance on the left (near Cedar Grove Village).

Contact: Sequoia and Kings Canyon National Parks, 559/565-3341; Cedar Grove Visitor Center, 559/565-3793, www.nps.gov/seki.

43 SHEEP CREEK

Scenic rating: 8

in Kings Canyon National Park

See map page 808

This is one of the camps that always fills up quickly on summer weekends. It's a pretty spot and just a short walk from Cedar Grove Village. The camp is along Sheep Creek at 4,600 feet.

RV sites, facilities: There are 111 sites for tents or RVs up to 30 feet (no hookups). Picnic tables and fire grills are provided. Restrooms have flush toilets, and drinking water is available. A store, a coin laundry, a snack bar, and coin showers are nearby. Leashed pets are permitted.

Reservations, fees: Reservations are not accepted. Sites are $18 per night, plus a $20 per

vehicle national park entrance fee. Open late April–mid-November.

Directions: From Fresno, drive east on Highway 180 for 55 miles to the Big Stump entrance station at Sequoia and Kings Canyon National Parks. Continue 1.5 miles to a junction (signed left for Grant Grove). Turn left and drive 31.5 miles to the campground entrance on the left (near Cedar Grove Village).

Contact: Sequoia and Kings Canyon National Parks, 559/565-3341; Cedar Grove Visitor Center, 559/565-3793, www.nps.gov/seki.

44 MORAINE

Scenic rating: 8

in Kings Canyon National Park

See map page 808

This is one in a series of camps in the Cedar Grove Village area of Kings Canyon National Park. This camp is used only as an overflow area. Hikers should drive past the Cedar Grove Ranger Station to the end of the road at Copper Creek, a prime jump-off point for a spectacular hike. The elevation is 4,600 feet.

RV sites, facilities: There are 120 sites for tents or RVs up to 30 feet (no hookups). Picnic tables and fire grills are provided. Drinking water and flush toilets are available. Coin showers, a store, a snack bar, and a coin laundry are nearby. Leashed pets are permitted.

Reservations, fees: Reservations are not accepted. Sites are $18 per night, plus a $20 per vehicle national park entrance fee. Open June–September, weather permitting.

Directions: From Fresno, drive east on Highway 180 for 55 miles to the Big Stump entrance station at Sequoia and Kings Canyon National Parks. Continue 1.5 miles to a junction (signed left for Grant Grove). Turn left and drive 33 miles to the campground entrance (one mile past the ranger station, near Cedar Village).

Contact: Sequoia and Kings Canyon National Parks, 559/565-3341; Cedar Grove Visitor Center, 559/565-3793, www.nps.gov/seki.

CALIFORNIA

45 ESHOM CREEK

Scenic rating: 7

on Eshom Creek in Giant Sequoia National Monument

See map page 808

The campground at Eshom Creek is just two miles outside the boundaries of Sequoia National Park. It is well hidden and a considerable distance from the crowds and sights in the park interior. It is along Eshom Creek at an elevation of 4,800 feet. Many campers at Eshom Creek hike straight into the national park, with a trailhead at Redwood Saddle (just inside the park boundary) providing a route to see the Redwood Mountain Grove, Fallen Goliath, Hart Tree, and Hart Meadow in a sensational loop hike.

RV sites, facilities: There are 23 sites for tents or RVs up to 22 feet, and five group sites hold up to 12 people each. No hookups. Picnic tables and fire grills are provided. Drinking water and vault toilets are available. Leashed pets are permitted.

Reservations, fees: Reservations are not accepted. Sites are $15 per night, $5 per night for an additional vehicle, $30 per night for a group site. Camping fees are higher on holiday weekends. Open May–early October, weather permitting.

Directions: Drive on Highway 99 to Visalia and the exit for Highway 198 east. Take that exit and drive east on Highway 198 for 11 miles to Highway 245. Turn left (north) on Highway 245 and drive 18 miles to Badger and County Road 465. Turn right and drive eight miles to the campground.

Contact: Sequoia National Forest, Hume Lake Ranger District, 559/338-2251, fax 559/338-2131.

46 STONY CREEK

Scenic rating: 6

in Giant Sequoia National Monument

See map page 808

Stony Creek Camp provides a good option if the national park camps are filled. It is at creek-side at 6,400 feet elevation. Sequoia and Kings Canyon National Parks are nearby.

RV sites, facilities: There are 49 sites for tents or RVs up to 22 feet (no hookups). Picnic tables and fire grills are provided. Drinking water and flush toilets are available. A store and coin laundry are nearby. Leashed pets are permitted.

Reservations, fees: Reservations are accepted ($9 reservation fee) at 877/444-6777 or www.ReserveUSA.com. Sites are $17 per night, $5 per night for an additional vehicle, plus a $20 per vehicle national park entrance fee. Fees are higher on holiday weekends. Open May–early September, weather permitting.

Directions: From Fresno, drive east on Highway 180 for 55 miles to the Big Stump entrance station at Sequoia and Kings Canyon National Parks. Continue 1.5 miles to a junction (signed left for Grant Grove). Turn right at Generals Highway and drive about 13 miles to the campground entrance on the right.

Contact: Sequoia National Forest, Hume Lake Ranger District, 559/338-2251, fax 559/338-2131.

47 DORST CREEK

Scenic rating: 7

on Dorst Creek in Sequoia National Park

See map page 808   BEST (

Things that go bump in the night swing through Dorst all summer long. That's right, Mr. Bear (a whole bunch of them) makes food raids like a UPS driver on a pick-up route. There are so many bears raiding food here that some years rangers keep a running tally posted on the bulletin board. That's why keeping your food in a bearproof locker is not only a must, it's the law. The camp is on Dorst Creek at 6,700 feet, near a trail that is routed into the backcountry and through Muir Grove. It is one in a series of big, popular camps in Sequoia National Park.

RV sites, facilities: There are 204 sites for tents or RVs up to 30 feet and five group sites for 12–50 people each. No hookups. Picnic tables and fire grills are provided. Drinking water, flush toilets, and a dump station are available. A store, coin showers, and a coin laundry are eight miles away. Some facilities are wheelchair accessible. Leashed pets are permitted.

Reservations, fees: Reservations are accepted at 800/365-CAMP (800/365-2267) or http://reservations.nps.gov. Sites are $20 per night (includes reservation fee), or $40–60 per night for group sites, plus a $20 per vehicle national park entrance fee. Open Memorial Day–Labor Day.

Directions: From Fresno, drive east on Highway 180 for 55 miles to the Big Stump entrance station at Sequoia and Kings Canyon National Parks. Continue 1.5 miles to a junction (signed left for Grant Grove). Turn right at Generals Highway and drive about 25.5 miles to the campground entrance on the right.

Contact: Sequoia and Kings Canyon National Parks, 559/565-3341; Lodgepole Visitor Center, 559/565-4436, www.nps.gov/seki.

48 LODGEPOLE

Scenic rating: 8

on the Marble Fork of the Kaweah River in Sequoia National Park

See map page 808

This giant, pretty camp on the Marble Fork of the Kaweah River is typically crowded. A bonus here is an excellent trailhead nearby that leads into the backcountry of Sequoia National Park. The elevation is 6,700 feet. For information on backcountry permits, phone the Mineral King Ranger Station, 559/565-3135.

RV sites, facilities: There are 214 sites for tents or RVs up to 40 feet (no hookups). Picnic tables and fire grills are provided. Restrooms have flush toilets. Drinking water, a dump station, a gift shop, and evening ranger programs are available. A store, deli, coin showers, and a coin laundry are nearby. Leashed pets are permitted.

Reservations, fees: Reservations are accepted at 800/365-CAMP (800/365-2267) or http:// reservations.nps.gov. Sites are $18–20 per night

(includes reservation fee), plus a $20 per vehicle national park entrance fee. Open year-round, with limited winter services.

Directions: From Fresno, drive east on Highway 180 for 55 miles to the Big Stump entrance station at Sequoia and Kings Canyon National Parks. Continue 1.5 miles to a junction (signed left for Grant Grove). Turn right at Generals Highway and drive about 25 miles to Lodgepole Village and the turnoff for Lodgepole Campground. Turn left and drive 0.25 mile (past Lodgepole Village) to the campground.

Contact: Sequoia and Kings Canyon National Parks, 559/565-3341, www.nps.gov/seki.

49 POTWISHA

Scenic rating: 7

on the Marble Fork of the Kaweah River in Sequoia National Park

See map page 808

This pretty spot on the Marble Fork of the Kaweah River is one of Sequoia National Park's smaller drive-to campgrounds. By looking at maps, newcomers may think it is a very short drive farther into the park to see the General Sherman Tree, Giant Forest, and the famous trailhead for the walk up Moro Rock. Nope. It's a slow, twisty drive, but with many pullouts for great views. A few miles east of the camp, visitors can find Buckeye Flat and a trail that is routed along Paradise Creek.

RV sites, facilities: There are 42 sites for tents or RVs up to 30 feet (no hookups). Picnic tables and fire grills are provided. Drinking water, flush toilets, a dump station, and evening ranger programs are available. Some facilities are wheelchair accessible. Leashed pets are permitted.

Reservations, fees: Reservations are not accepted. Sites are $18 per night, plus a $20 per vehicle national park entrance fee. Open year-round.

Directions: From Visalia, drive east on Highway 198 for 36 miles to the Ash Mountain entrance station to Sequoia and Kings Canyon National Parks. Continue into the park (the road becomes

CALIFORNIA

Generals Highway) and drive four miles to the campground on the left. Caution: Vehicles of 22 feet or longer are not advised on Generals Highway from Potwisha to Giant Forest Village and are advised to use Highway 180 through the Big Stump entrance station.

Contact: Sequoia and Kings Canyon National Parks, 559/565-3341, www.nps.gov/seki.

50 HORSE CREEK

Scenic rating: 6

on Lake Kaweah

See map page 808

Lake Kaweah is a big lake, covering nearly 2,000 acres with 22 miles of shoreline. This camp is on the southern shore of the lake. In the spring when the lake is full and the surrounding hills are green, you may even think you have found Valhalla. With such hot weather in the San Joaquin Valley, it's a boater's heaven, ideal for water-skiers. In spring, when the water is still too cool for water sports, anglers can have the lake to themselves with good bass fishing. Other species include trout, catfish, and crappie. By early summer, it's crowded with personal watercraft and ski boats. The lake level fluctuates, and a potential problem is flooding in some years. Another problem is that the water level drops a great deal during late summer, as thirsty farms suck up every drop they can get, killing prospects of developing beaches for swimming and wading. The elevation is 300 feet.

RV sites, facilities: There are 80 sites for tents or RVs up to 30 feet (no hookups). Picnic tables and fire grills are provided. Restrooms have flush toilets and showers. Drinking water, a playground, and a dump station are available. Two paved boat ramps are available at Kaweah Recreation Area and Lemon Hill Recreation Area. A store, a coin laundry, boat and water-ski rentals, ice, a snack bar, a restaurant, gas station, and propane gas are available nearby. Some facilities are wheelchair accessible. Leashed pets are permitted.

Reservations, fees: Reservations are accept-

ed at 877/444-6777 ($9 reservation fee) or www.ReserveUSA.com. Sites are $16 per night. Some credit cards accepted. Open year-round.

Directions: From Visalia, drive east on Highway 198 for 25 miles to Lake Kaweah's south shore and the camp on the left.

Contact: U.S. Army Corps of Engineers, Lake Kaweah, 559/597-2301, fax 559/597-2468.

51 BALCH PARK

Scenic rating: 6

near Mountain Home State Forest

See map page 809

Balch Park is surrounded by Mountain Home State Forest and Giant Sequoia National Monument. A nearby grove of giant sequoias is a featured attraction. The elevation is 6,500 feet. Two stocked fishing ponds are also a feature.

RV sites, facilities: There are 71 sites for tents or RVs up to 40 feet (no hookups); some are pull-through. No hookups. Picnic tables and fire grills are provided. Drinking water and flush toilets and vault toilets are available. Some facilities are wheelchair accessible. Leashed pets are permitted.

Reservations, fees: Reservations are not accepted. Sites are $16 per night, $5 per night for an additional vehicle, $3 per pet per night. Open May–late October.

Directions: From Porterville, drive east on Highway 190 for 19 miles (1 mile past the town of Springville) to Balch Park Road. Turn left (north) at Balch Park Road and drive 40 long and curvy miles to the park.

Contact: Balch Park, Tulare County, 559/733-6291, www.co.tulare.ca.us.

52 COY FLAT

Scenic rating: 4

in Giant Sequoia National Monument

See map page 809

Coy Flat is between Coy Creek and Bear Creek, small forks of the Tule River, at 5,000 feet in elevation. The road out of camp is routed five miles (through Rogers' Camp, which is private property) to the Black Mountain Grove of redwoods, with some giant sequoias set just inside the border of the neighboring Tule River Indian Reservation. From camp, a hiking trail (Forest Trail 31S31) goes east for two miles through the Belknap Camp Grove of sequoias and then turns and heads south for four miles to Slate Mountain, where it intersects with Summit National Recreation Trail, a steep butt-kicker of a hike that tops out at over 9,000 feet.

RV sites, facilities: There are 20 sites for tents or RVs up to 22 feet (no hookups). Picnic tables and fire grills are provided. Drinking water and vault toilets are available. Leashed pets are permitted.

Reservations, fees: Reservations are accepted ($9 reservation fee) at 877/444-6777 or www.ReserveUSA.com. Sites are $15 per night, $5 per night for an additional vehicle. Camping fees are higher for holiday weekends. Open mid-April–mid-November.

Directions: From Porterville, drive east on Highway 190 for 34 miles to Camp Nelson and Coy Flat Road. Turn right on Coy Flat Road and drive one mile to the campground.

Contact: Sequoia National Forest and Giant Sequoia National Monument, Tule River/Hot Springs Ranger District, 559/539-2607, fax 559/539-2067.

of sequoias in four miles. This camp is in the vicinity of the Sequoia National Forest fire, named the McNalley Fire, which burned more than 100,000 acres to the east of this area in the summer of 2002. The fire started in the Kern River Canyon and then burned up the Kern Canyon north to Forks of the Kern and the surrounding environs. While 11 groves of giant sequoias here were saved, much of the surrounding forest several miles east of the camps was burned.

RV sites, facilities: There are 32 sites for tents or RVs up to 24 feet (no hookups). Picnic tables and fire grills are provided. Drinking water and vault toilets are available. A store is nearby. Some facilities are wheelchair accessible. Leashed pets are permitted.

Reservations, fees: Reservations are accepted ($9 reservation fee) at 877/444-6777. Sites are $15 per night, $5 per night for an additional vehicle. Fees are higher on holiday weekends. Open May–mid-November, weather permitting.

Directions: From Porterville, drive east on Highway 190 for 34 miles to Camp Nelson. Continue east on Highway 190 for 11 miles to the campground on the right.

Contact: Sequoia National Forest and Giant Sequoia National Monument, Tule River/Hot Springs Ranger District, 559/539-2607, fax 559/539-2067.

53 QUAKING ASPEN

Scenic rating: 4

in Giant Sequoia National Monument

See map page 809

Quaking Aspen sits at a junction of Forest Service roads at 7,000 feet in elevation, near the headwaters of Freeman Creek. A trailhead for Summit National Recreation Trail runs right through camp; it's a popular trip on horseback, heading deep into Sequoia National Forest. Another trailhead is a half mile away on Forest Road 21S50. This hike is routed east along Freeman Creek and reaches the Freeman Grove

54 TULE

Scenic rating: 7

on Lake Success

See map page 809

Lake Success is a big lake with many arms, providing 30 miles of shoreline and making the place seem like a dreamland for boaters on hot summer days. The lake is in the foothill country, at an elevation of 650 feet, where day after day of 100°F summer temperatures is common. That is why boating, waterskiing, and personal watercraft are so popular—anything to get wet. In the winter and spring, fishing for

CALIFORNIA

trout and bass is good, including the chance for largemouth bass. No beaches are developed for swimming because of fluctuating water levels, though the day-use area has a decent sloped stretch of shore that is good for swimming. Lake Success is much shallower than most reservoirs, and the water can fluctuate from week to week, with major drawdowns during the summer. The wildlife area along the west side of the lake is worth exploring, and there is a nature trail below the dam. The campground is the centerpiece of the Tule Recreation Area.

RV sites, facilities: There are 104 sites for tents or RVs up to 35 feet; some sites have electrical hookups (30 and 50 amps). Picnic tables and fire grills are provided. Restrooms have flush toilets and showers. A dump station, picnic areas, and a playground are available. A store; marina; boat ramp; houseboat, boat, and water-ski rentals; bait and tackle; propane gas; restaurant; and gas station are available nearby. Leashed pets are permitted.

Reservations, fees: Reservations are accepted at 877/444-6777 or www.ReserveUSA.com. Sites are $16–21 per night. Open year-round.

Directions: Drive on Highway 65 to Porterville and the junction with Highway 190. Turn east on Highway 190 and drive eight miles to Lake Success and the campground entrance on the left.

Contact: U.S. Army Corps of Engineers, Sacramento District, 559/784-0215, fax 559/784-5469; Success Marina, 559/781-2078.

55 REDWOOD MEADOW

Scenic rating: 7

near Parker Meadow Creek in Giant Sequoia National Monument

See map page 809

The highlight here is the 1.5-mile Trail of the Hundred Giants, which passes through a grove of giant sequoias and is accessible for wheelchair hikers. This is the site where President Clinton proclaimed the Giant Sequoia National Monument in 2000. The camp is near Parker Meadow Creek at 6,100 feet eleva-

tion. Despite its remoteness, this has become a popular place.

RV sites, facilities: There are 15 sites for tents or RVs up to 16 feet (no hookups). Picnic tables and fire grills are provided. Drinking water and vault toilets are available. Leashed pets are permitted.

Reservations, fees: Reservations are accepted ($9 reservation fee) at 877/444-6777 or www.ReserveUSA.com. Sites are $15 per night, $5 per night for an additional vehicle. Camping fees are higher on holiday weekends. Open June–October, weather permitting.

Directions: Drive on Highway 99 to Earlimart (about eight miles north of Delano) and the exit for Avenue 56/County Road J22. Take that exit east and drive 39 miles to the town of California Hot Springs and Parker Pass Road/County Road M50. Turn left on Parker Pass Road and drive 12 miles to Western Divide Highway/County Road M107. Turn left on Western Divide Highway and drive three miles to the campground entrance.

Contact: Sequoia National Forest and Giant Sequoia National Monument, Tule River/Hot Springs Ranger District, 559/539-2607, fax 559/539-2067.

56 OAK CREEK

Scenic rating: 6

in Inyo National Forest

See map page 808

Oak Creek is in a series of little-known camps west of Independence that provide a jump-off spot for backpackers. This camp is at 5,000 feet, with a trail from camp that is routed west (and up) into the California Bighorn Sheep Zoological Area, a rugged, stark region well above the tree line. Caution: Plan on a terrible, long, butt-kicker of a climb up to the Sierra crest; stay on the trail.

RV sites, facilities: There are 22 sites for tents or RVs up to 28 feet (no hookups). Picnic tables and fire grills are provided. There is no drinking water. Vault toilets are available. Garbage must be packed out. Supplies and a coin laundry are available in Independence. Some facilities are wheelchair accessible. Leashed pets are permitted.

Reservations, fees: Reservations are not accepted. There is no fee for camping, but donations are encouraged. Open year-round, with a 14-day stay limit.

Directions: Drive on U.S. 395 to North Oak Creek Drive (two miles north of Independence). Turn west (toward the Sierra) at North Oak Creek Drive and drive three miles to the campground on the right.

Contact: Inyo National Forest, Mount Whitney Ranger District, 760/876-6200, fax 760/876-6202; Interagency Visitor Center, 760/876-6222.

57 GRAY'S MEADOW

Scenic rating: 6

on Independence Creek in Inyo National Forest

See map page 808

Gray's Meadow is one of two adjacent camps along Independence Creek. The creek is stocked with small trout by the Department of Fish and Game. The highlight in the immediate area is the trailhead at the end of the road at Onion Valley Camp. For U.S. 395 cruisers looking for a spot, this is a pretty alternative to the camps in Bishop.

RV sites, facilities: There are 52 sites for tents or RVs up to 34 feet (no hookups). Picnic tables and fire grills are provided. Drinking water and flush toilets are available. Supplies and a coin laundry are available in Independence. Leashed pets are permitted.

Reservations, fees: Reservations are accepted ($9 reservation fee) at 877/444-6777 or www .ReserveUSA.com. Sites are $12–13 per night. Open March–October, with a 14-day stay limit.

Directions: Drive on U.S. 395 to Independence and Market Street. Turn west (toward the Sierra) at Market Street (becomes Onion Valley Road) and drive five miles to the campground on the right.

Contact: Inyo National Forest, Mount Whitney Ranger District, 760/876-6200, fax

760/876-6202; Interagency Visitor Center, 760/876-6222.

58 INDEPENDENCE CREEK CAMPGROUND

Scenic rating: 4

in Independence

See map page 808

This unpublicized county park is often overlooked among U.S. 395 cruisers. It is at 3,900 feet just outside of Independence, which is spiraling downward into something resembling a ghost town. True to form, maintenance is sometimes lacking here. Independence Creek runs through the campground, and a museum is within walking distance. At the rate it's going, the whole town could be a museum.

RV sites, facilities: There are 25 sites for tents or RVs up to 40 feet (no hookups). Picnic tables and fire grills are provided. Drinking water and vault toilets are available. Supplies and a coin laundry are available in Independence. Some facilities are wheelchair accessible. Leashed pets are permitted.

Reservations, fees: Reservations are not accepted. Sites are $10 per vehicle per night. Open year-round.

Directions: Drive on U.S. 395 to Independence and Market Street. Turn west (toward the Sierra) at Market Street and drive one mile (outside the town limits) to the campground.

Contact: Inyo County Parks Department, 760/878-0272 or 760/873-5577, www.395.com/ inyo/campgrounds.

59 LONE PINE AND LONE PINE GROUP

Scenic rating: 8

near Mount Whitney in Inyo National Forest

See map page 808

This is an alternative for campers preparing to hike Mount Whitney or start the John Muir Trail. It is at 6,000 feet, 2,000 feet below

CALIFORNIA

Whitney Portal (the hiking jump-off spot), providing a lower-elevation location for hikers to acclimate themselves to the altitude. The camp is on Lone Pine Creek, with decent fishing and spectacular views of Mount Whitney. Because of its exposure to the east, there are also beautiful sunrises, especially in fall.

RV sites, facilities: There are 43 sites for tents or RVs up to 35 feet, and one group site holds up to 15 people. No hookups. Picnic tables and fire grills are provided. Drinking water and pit toilets are available. Supplies are available in Lone Pine. Leashed pets are permitted.

Reservations, fees: Reservations are accepted at 877/444-6777 or www.ReserveUSA.com ($9 reservation fee). Sites are $14 per night, $45 per night for the group site. Open year-round, with a 14-day stay limit.

Directions: Drive on U.S. 395 to Lone Pine and Whitney Portal Road. Turn west (toward the Sierra) on Whitney Portal Road and drive six miles to the campground on the left.

Contact: Inyo National Forest, Mount Whitney Ranger District, 760/876-6200, fax 760/876-6202; Interagency Visitor Center, 760/876-6222.

60 WHITNEY PORTAL AND WHITNEY PORTAL GROUP

Scenic rating: 9

near Mount Whitney in Inyo National Forest
See map page 808

This camp is home to a world-class trailhead. It is regarded as the number-one jump-off spot for the hike to the top of Mount Whitney, the highest spot in the continental United States, 14,497.6 feet, as well as the start of the 211-mile John Muir Trail from Mount Whitney to Yosemite Valley. Hikers planning to scale the summit must have a wilderness permit, available by reservation at the Forest Service office in Lone Pine. The camp is at 8,000 feet, and virtually everyone staying here plans to make the trek to the Whitney summit, a climb of 6,500 feet over the course of 10 miles. The trip

includes an ascent over 100 switchbacks (often snow-covered in early summer) to top Wotan's Throne and reach Trail Crest (13,560 feet). Here you turn right and take Summit Trail, where the ridge is cut by huge notch windows providing a view down more than 10,000 feet to the little town of Lone Pine and the Owens Valley. When you sign the logbook on top, don't be surprised if you see my name in the registry. A plus at the campground is watching the JMT hikers arrive who are just finishing the trail from north to south; that is, from Yosemite to Whitney. There is no comparing the happy look of success when they drop their packs for the last time, head into the little store, and pick a favorite refreshment for celebration.

RV sites, facilities: There are 44 sites for tents or RVs up to 30 feet, and three group sites hold up to 15 people each. No hookups. Picnic tables and fire grills are provided. Drinking water and vault toilets are available. Supplies are available in Lone Pine. Some facilities are wheelchair accessible. Leashed pets are permitted.

Reservations, fees: Reservations are accepted ($9 reservation fee) at 877/444-6777 or www.ReserveUSA.com. Sites are $16 per night, $45 per night for a group site. Open late May–mid-October, with a 7-day stay limit.

Directions: Drive on U.S. 395 to Lone Pine and Whitney Portal Road. Turn west (toward the Sierra) on Whitney Portal Road and drive 13 miles to the campground on the left.

Contact: Inyo National Forest, Mount Whitney Ranger District, 760/876-6200, fax 760/876-6202; Interagency Visitor Center, 760/876-2222.

61 DIAZ LAKE

Scenic rating: 6

near Lone Pine
See map page 808

Diaz Lake is at 3,650 feet in the Owens Valley. It is sometimes overlooked by visitors to nearby Mount Whitney. It's a small lake, just 85 acres, and it is popular for trout fishing in the spring, when a speed limit of 15 mph is enforced. The lake is stocked with Alpers trout. May–October, when hot weather takes over and the speed limit is bumped to 35 mph, you can say *adios* to the anglers and *hola* to water-skiers. Diaz Lake is extremely popular for waterskiing and swimming, and it is sunny most of the year. A 20-foot limit is enforced for boats. A nine-hole golf course is nearby.

RV sites, facilities: There are 200 sites for RVs of any length or tents; some have partial hookups. Picnic tables and fire grills are provided. Restrooms have flush toilets and solar showers. Drinking water (from a well), a playground, and a boat ramp are available. Supplies and a coin laundry are available in Lone Pine. Leashed pets are permitted.

Reservations, fees: Group reservations are accepted at 760/876-5656. Sites are $10–14 per vehicle per night. Open year-round.

Directions: Drive on U.S. 395 to the Diaz Lake entrance (three miles south of Lone Pine) on the west side of the road.

Contact: Inyo County Parks Department, 760/878-0272 or 760/873-5577, www.395.com/inyo/campgrounds.

62 FAIRVIEW

Scenic rating: 1

on the Kern River in Sequoia National Forest
See map page 809

Fairview is one of six campgrounds set on the Upper Kern River above Isabella Lake and adjacent to the Kern River, one of the prime rafting and kayaking rivers in California. This camp sits at 3,500 feet. Many of the rapids are rated Class IV and Class V, for experts with guides only. The favored put-in is at the Johnsondale Bridge, and from here it's a 21-mile run to Kernville. The river eventually pours into Isabella Lake. Two sections are unrunnable, Fairview Dam (Mile 2.5) and Salmon Falls (Mile Eight). This campground was one of two burned in the McNalley Fire in the summer of 2002. The first started near Road's End Lodge (which burned

down), 16 miles up the Kern River Highway. Other campgrounds to the south of that were not burned. Even though the canyon has been blackened and left with tree skeletons from the start of the fire on north past Forks of the Kern, the river can still provide an outstanding rafting experience. The sight of the damage from the fire, however, is shocking.

RV sites, facilities: There are 55 sites for tents or RVs up to 45 feet (no hookups). Picnic tables and fire grills are provided. Drinking water and vault toilets are available. Supplies and a coin laundry are available in Kernville. Some facilities are wheelchair accessible. Leashed pets are permitted.

Reservations, fees: Reservations are accepted ($9 reservation fee) at 877/444-6777 or www.ReserveUSA.com. Sites are $15 per night, $5 per night for an additional vehicle. Camping fees are higher on holiday weekends. Open April–October, weather permitting.

Directions: From Bakersfield, drive east on Highway 178 for about 40 miles to the town of Lake Isabella and Highway 155/Burlando Way. Turn left (north) and drive 10 miles to Kernville and the Kern River Highway/Sierra Way. Turn left on the Kern River Highway and drive 18 miles to the town of Fairview. Continue to the north end of town to the campground entrance.

Contact: Sequoia National Forest, Kern River Ranger District, Kernville Office, 760/376-3781, fax 760/376-3795.

63 HORSE MEADOW

Scenic rating: 8

on Salmon Creek in Sequoia National Forest
See map page 809

This is a little-known spot set along Salmon Creek at 7,600 feet. It is a region known for big meadows, forests, backcountry roads, and plenty of horses. It is just west of the Dome Land Wilderness, and there are three public pastures for horses in the area, as well as trails ideal for horseback riding. From camp, one such trail follows along Salmon Creek to the west to Salmon Falls, a favorite for the few who know of it. A more popular overnight trip is to head to a trailhead about five miles east, which provides a route to Manter Meadows in the Dome Lands.

RV sites, facilities: There are 41 sites for tents or RVs up to 22 feet (no hookups). Picnic tables and fire grills are provided. Drinking water and vault toilets are available. Garbage must be packed out. Leashed pets are permitted.

Reservations, fees: Reservations are not accepted. Sites are $10 per night, $5 per night per additional vehicle. Open June–October, weather permitting.

Directions: From Bakersfield, drive east on Highway 178 for about 40 miles to the town of Lake Isabella and Highway 155/Burlando Way. Turn left (north) and drive 10 miles to Kernville and the Kern River Highway/Sierra Way. Turn left on the Kern River Highway for about 20 miles to Sherman Pass Road (signed for Highway 395/Black Rock Ranger Station). Make a sharp right on Sherman Pass Road and drive about 6.5 miles to Cherry Hill Road/Forest Road 22S12 (there is a green gate with a sign that says Horse Meadow/Big Meadow). Turn right and drive about four miles (the road becomes dirt) and continue for another three miles (follow the signs) to the campground entrance road.

Contact: Sequoia National Forest, Kern River Ranger District, Kernville Office, 760/376-3781, fax 760/376-3795.

64 GOLDLEDGE

Scenic rating: 7

on the Kern River in Sequoia National Forest

See map page 809

This is another in the series of camps on the Kern River north of Isabella Lake. This one is at 3,200 feet.

RV sites, facilities: There are 37 sites for tents or RVs up to 30 feet (no hookups). Picnic tables and fire grills are provided. Drinking water and vault toilets are available. Supplies and a coin laundry are available in Kernville. Leashed pets are permitted.

Reservations, fees: Reservations are accepted ($9 reservation fee) at 877/444-6777 or www.ReserveUSA.com. Sites are $15 per night, $5 per night for an additional vehicle. Camping fees are higher on holiday weekends. Open May–August.

Directions: From Bakersfield, drive east on Highway 178 for about 40 miles to the town of Lake Isabella and Highway 155/Burlando Way. Turn left (north) and drive 10 miles to Kernville and the Kern River Highway/Sierra Way. Turn left on the Kern River Highway and drive 10 miles to the campground.

Contact: Sequoia National Forest, Kern River Ranger District, Kernville Office, 760/376-3781, fax 760/376-3795.

65 HOSPITAL FLAT

Scenic rating: 8

on the North Fork of the Kern River in Sequoia National Forest

See map page 809

It's kind of like the old shell game, trying to pick the best of the campgrounds along the North Fork of the Kern River. This one is seven miles north of Isabella Lake. The elevation is 2,800 feet. (For information on rafting on the Kern River, see the listing in this chapter for *Fairview*.)

RV sites, facilities: There are 40 sites for tents or RVs up to 30 feet and one group site for up to 30 people. No hookups. Picnic tables and fire grills are provided. Drinking water and vault toilets are available. Supplies and a coin laundry are available in Kernville. Some facilities are wheelchair accessible. Leashed pets are permitted.

Reservations, fees: Reservations are accepted for individual sites and required for the group site ($9 reservation fee) at 877/444-6777 or www.ReserveUSA.com. Sites are $15 per night, $5 per night for an additional vehicle, $75 per night for the group site. Camping fees are higher on holiday weekends. Open May–August.

Directions: From Bakersfield, drive east on Highway 178 for about 40 miles to the town of Lake Isabella and Highway 155/Burlando Way.

Turn left (north) and drive 10 miles to Kernville and the Kern River Highway/Sierra Way. Turn left on the Kern River Highway and drive 6.5 miles to the campground.

Contact: Sequoia National Forest, Kern River Ranger District, Kernville Office, 760/376-3781, fax 760/376-3795.

66 CAMP 3

Scenic rating: 9

on the North Fork of the Kern River in Sequoia National Forest

See map page 809

This is the second in a series of camps along the Kern River north of Isabella Lake (in this case, five miles north of the lake). If you don't like this spot, Hospital Flat is just two miles upriver and Headquarters is just one mile downriver. The camp elevation is 2,800 feet.

RV sites, facilities: There are 52 sites for tents or RVs up to 30 feet, and two group sites hold up to 30 people. No hookups. Picnic tables and fire grills are provided. Drinking water and vault toilets are available. A store and a coin laundry are available in Kernville. Some facilities are wheelchair accessible. Leashed pets are permitted.

Reservations, fees: Reservations are accepted for individual sites and required for the group sites ($9 reservation fee) at 877/444-6777 or www.ReserveUSA.com. Sites are $15 per night, $5 per night for an additional vehicle, $75 per night for a group site. Camping fees are higher on holiday weekends. Open May–August.

Directions: From Bakersfield, drive east on Highway 178 for about 40 miles to the town of Lake Isabella and Highway 155/Burlando Way. Turn left (north) and drive 10 miles to Kernville and the Kern River Highway/Sierra Way. Turn left on the Kern River Highway and drive five miles to the campground.

Contact: Sequoia National Forest, Kern River Ranger District, Kernville Office, 760/376-3781, fax 760/376-3795.

67 HEADQUARTERS

Scenic rating: 8

on the North Fork of the Kern River in Sequoia National Forest

See map page 809

As you head north from Isabella Lake on Sierra Way, this is the first in a series of Forest Service campgrounds from which to take your pick, all of them set along the North Fork of the Kern River. The North Fork Kern is best known for offering prime white water for rafting and kayaking. The elevation is 2,800 feet.

RV sites, facilities: There are 44 sites for tents or RVs up to 27 feet (no hookups). Picnic tables and fire grills are provided. Drinking water and vault toilets are available. Supplies and a coin laundry are available in Kernville. Some facilities are wheelchair accessible. Leashed pets are permitted.

Reservations, fees: Reservations are accepted ($9 reservation fee) at 877/444-6777 or www.ReserveUSA.com. Sites are $15 per night, $5 per night for an additional vehicle. Camping fees are higher on holiday weekends. Open year-round.

Directions: From Bakersfield, drive east on Highway 178 for about 40 miles to the town of Lake Isabella and Highway 155/Burlando Way. Turn left (north) and drive 10 miles to Kernville and the Kern River Highway/Sierra Way. Turn left on the Kern River Highway and drive three miles to the campground.

Contact: Sequoia National Forest, Kern River Ranger District, Kernville Office, 760/376-3781, fax 760/376-3795.

68 GREENHORN MOUNTAIN PARK

Scenic rating: 7

near Shirley Meadows

See map page 809

This county campground is near the Shirley Meadows Ski Area, a small ski park open on weekends in winter when there is sufficient snow. Greenhorn Mountain Park covers 160 acres, set at 6,000 feet in elevation. The region is filled with a spiderweb network of Forest Service roads, detailed on a map of Sequoia National Forest. Isabella Lake is a 15-minute drive to the east.

RV sites, facilities: There are 70 sites for tents or RVs up to 24 feet (no hookups). Fourteen cabins are also available as a group rental. Picnic tables and fire pits or fire rings are provided. Drinking water is available intermittently; check for current status. Restrooms with flush toilets and showers are available. Leashed pets are permitted.

Reservations, fees: No reservations accepted, except for groups of at least 40 people. Sites are $14 per night. Open spring–fall, weather permitting.

Directions: From Bakersfield, drive east on Highway 178 for about 40 miles to the town of Lake Isabella and Highway 155/Burlando Way. Turn left (north) and drive six miles to Wofford Heights. Turn left (west) on Highway 155 and drive 10 miles to the park on the left.

Contact: Kern County Parks, 661/868-7000, www.co.kern.ca.us/parks/.

69 RIVERNOOK CAMPGROUND

Scenic rating: 7

on the North Fork of the Kern River

See map page 809

This is a large, privately operated park near Isabella Lake a few miles from the head of the lake. Boat rentals are available at one of the nearby marinas. An optional side trip is to visit Keysville, the first town to become established on the Kern River during the gold rush days. The elevation is 2,665 feet.

RV sites, facilities: There are 30 pull-through sites with full hookups (30 and 50 amps) for RVs, 41 sites with partial hookups for RVs, and 59 sites for tents. Picnic tables, fire rings, and drinking water are provided. Restrooms have flush toilets and showers. Three dump stations and cable TV are available. Some facilities are wheelchair accessible. Leashed pets are permitted.

Reservations, fees: Reservations are recommended. Sites are $25–35 per night, $5 per person per night for more than two people. Some credit cards accepted. Open year-round.

Directions: From Bakersfield, drive east on Highway 178 for about 40 miles to the town of Lake Isabella and Highway 155/Burlando Way. Turn left (north) and drive 10 miles to Kernville and the Kern River Highway/Sierra Way. Turn left on Sierra Way and drive 0.5 mile to the park entrance (14001 Sierra Way).

Contact: Rivernook Campground, 760/376-2705, fax 760/376-2595.

70 LIVE OAK NORTH AND SOUTH

Scenic rating: 8

on Isabella Lake

See map page 809

This is one of two camps set in the immediate area on Isabella Lake's northwest side; the other is Tillie Creek. Live Oak is on the west side of the road, Tillie Creek on the eastern, lake side of the road. (For recreation information, see the listing in this chapter for *Tillie Creek*.)

RV sites, facilities: There are 150 sites for tents or RVs up to 30 feet and one group site for up to 100 people. No hookups. Picnic tables and fire grills are provided. Drinking water and restrooms with coin showers and flush toilets are available. Supplies are available in nearby Wofford Heights. Leashed pets are permitted.

Reservations, fees: Reservations are accepted for individual sites and required for the group site at 877/444-6777 ($9 reservation fee) or www.ReserveUSA.com. Sites are $17 per night, $5 per night for an additional vehicle, $250 per night for the group site for up to 100 people. Open May–September.

Directions: From Bakersfield, drive east on Highway 178 for about 40 miles to the town of Lake Isabella and Highway 155. Turn left (north) and drive six miles to the campground entrance road on the left (0.5 mile before reaching Wofford Heights).

Contact: Sequoia National Forest, Kern River Ranger District, Lake Isabella Office, 760/379-5646, fax 760/379-8597.

71 TILLIE CREEK

Scenic rating: 9

on Isabella Lake

See map page 809

This is one of two camps (the other is Live Oak) near where Tillie Creek enters Isabella Lake, set on the northwest shore of the lake near the town of Wofford Heights. Isabella Lake is a large lake, and with it comes a dynamic array of campgrounds, marinas, and facilities. It is at 2,650 feet in the foothills east of Bakersfield, fed by the Kern River and dominated by water sports of all kinds.

RV sites, facilities: There are 159 sites for tents or RVs up to 45 feet, and four group sites for tents or RVs up to 45 feet can accommodate 60–150 people each. No hookups. Picnic tables and fire grills are provided. Drinking water and restrooms with showers and flush toilets are available. A dump station, a playground, an amphitheater, and a fish-cleaning station are available nearby. Supplies are nearby in Wofford Heights. Some facilities are wheelchair accessible. Leashed pets are permitted.

Reservations, fees: Reservations are accepted for individual sites and required for group sites at 877/444-6777 ($9 reservation fee) or www.ReserveUSA.com. Sites are $17 per night, $5 per night for an additional vehicle, $125–220 per night for group sites. Open year-round.

Directions: From Bakersfield, drive east on Highway 178 for about 40 miles to the town of Lake Isabella and Highway 155. Turn left (north) and drive five miles to the campground (0.5 mile before reaching Wofford Heights).

Contact: Sequoia National Forest, Kern River Ranger District, Lake Isabella Office, 760/379-5646, fax 760/379-8597.

72 CAMP 9

Scenic rating: 8

on Isabella Lake

See map page 809

This campground is primitive and sparsely covered, but it has several bonus features. It is along the northeast shore of Isabella Lake, known for good boating, waterskiing in the summer, and fishing in the spring. Other options include great rafting and kayaking waters along the North Fork of the Kern River (north of the lake), a good bird-watching area at the South Fork Wildlife Area (along the east side of the lake), and an off-highway-motorcycle park across the road from this campground. The elevation is 2,650 feet.

RV sites, facilities: There are 109 primitive sites for tents or RVs of any length (no hookups) and two group sites that can accommodate 40 people each. Drinking water, flush and vault toilets, a dump station, a boat launch, and a fish-cleaning station are available. Supplies and a coin laundry are available nearby in Kernville. Some facilities are wheelchair accessible. Leashed pets are permitted.

Reservations, fees: Reservations are not accepted. Sites are $10 per night, $5 per night for an additional vehicle, $60 per night for a group site. Open year-round.

Directions: From Bakersfield, drive east on Highway 178 for about 40 miles to the town of Lake Isabella and Highway 155. Turn right (south) and drive six miles to the campground entrance on the right (on the northeast shore of Isabella Lake). The campground entrance is just south of the small airport at Lake Isabella.

Contact: Sequoia National Forest, Kern River Ranger District, Lake Isabella Office, 760/379-5646, fax 760/379-8597.

73 HUNGRY GULCH

Scenic rating: 9

on Isabella Lake in Sequoia National Forest

See map page 809

Hungry Gulch is on the western side of Isabella Lake but across the road from the shore. Nearby Boulder Gulch, directly across the road, is an option. There are no boat ramps in the immediate area. (For details about Isabella Lake, see the listing in this chapter for *Pioneer Point*.)

CALIFORNIA

RV sites, facilities: There are 78 sites for tents or RVs up to 30 feet (no hookups). Picnic tables and fire grills are provided. Drinking water and restrooms with coin showers and flush toilets are available. A playground is nearby. Supplies and a coin laundry are available in Lake Isabella. Leashed pets are permitted.

Reservations, fees: Reservations are accepted ($9 reservation fee) at 877/444-6777 or www.ReserveUSA.com. Sites are $17 per night, $5 per night for an additional vehicle. Open April–September.

Directions: From Bakersfield, drive east on Highway 178 for about 40 miles to the town of Lake Isabella and Highway 155. Turn left (north) and drive four miles on Highway 155 to the campground.

Contact: Sequoia National Forest, Kern River Ranger District, Lake Isabella Office, 760/379-5646, fax 760/379-8597.

74 BOULDER GULCH

Scenic rating: 8

on Isabella Lake
See map page 809

Boulder Gulch lies fairly near the western shore of Isabella Lake, across the road from Hungry Gulch. Take your pick. Isabella is one of the biggest lakes in Southern California and a prime destination point for Bakersfield-area residents. Fishing for trout and bass is best in the spring. The lake is stocked with trout in winter, and other species are bluegill, catfish, and crappie. By the dog days of summer, when people are bow-wowin' at the heat, water-skiers take over, along with folks just looking to cool off. Like a lot of lakes in the valley, Isabella is subject to drawdowns. The elevation is 2,650 feet. (For more information, see the listing in this chapter for *Pioneer Point*.)

RV sites, facilities: There are 78 sites for tents or RVs up to 45 feet (no hookups). Picnic tables and fire grills are provided. Restrooms have

flush toilets and coin showers. Drinking water, a playground, and a fish-cleaning station are available. Supplies and a coin laundry are available in the town of Lake Isabella. Leashed pets are permitted.

Reservations, fees: Reservations are accepted ($9 reservation fee) at 877/444-6777 or www.ReserveUSA.com. Sites are $17 per night, $5 per night for an additional vehicle. Open April–September.

Directions: From Bakersfield, drive east on Highway 178 for about 40 miles to the town of Lake Isabella and Highway 155. Turn left (north) and drive four miles to the campground entrance.

Contact: Sequoia National Forest, Kern River Ranger District, Lake Isabella Office, 760/379-5646, fax 760/379-8597.

75 PIONEER POINT

Scenic rating: 9

on Isabella Lake in Sequoia National Forest
See map page 809

Isabella Lake is one of the largest freshwater lakes in Southern California, and with it comes a dynamic array of campgrounds, marinas, and facilities. It is at 2,650 feet in the foothills east of Bakersfield, fed by the Kern River and dominated by boating sports of all kinds. This camp is at the lake's southwest corner, between the spillway and the main dam, with a boat ramp available a mile to the east. Another camp is nearby—Main Dam. Isabella is a first-class lake for waterskiing, but in the spring and early summer sailboarding is also excellent, best just east of the Auxiliary Dam. Boat rentals of all kinds are available at several marinas.

RV sites, facilities: There are 78 sites for tents or RVs up to 30 feet (no hookups). Picnic tables and fire grills are provided. Drinking water and restrooms with coin showers and flush toilets are available. A playground and a fish-cleaning station are available nearby. A boat ramp is three miles from camp. Supplies and a coin laundry are available in the town of Lake Isabella. Leashed pets are permitted.

Reservations, fees: Reservations are accepted ($9 reservation fee) at 877/444-6777 or www.ReserveUSA.com. Sites are $17 per night, $5 per night for an additional vehicle. Open year-round.

Directions: From Bakersfield, drive east on Highway 178 for about 40 miles to the town of Lake Isabella and Highway 155. Turn left (north) and drive 2.5 miles north on Highway 155 to the campground.

Contact: Sequoia National Forest, Kern River Ranger District, Lake Isabella Office, 760/379-5646, fax 760/379-8597.

76 MAIN DAM

Scenic rating: 8

on Isabella Lake

See map page 809

This camp is on the south shore of Isabella Lake, just east of Pioneer Point and within a mile of a boat ramp. The elevation is 2,500 feet. This camp is used as an overflow area and is only open on holiday weekends. (For recreation information, see the listing in this chapter for *Pioneer Point.*)

RV sites, facilities: There are 82 sites for tents or RVs up to 45 feet (no hookups). Picnic tables and fire grills are provided. Drinking water and flush and vault toilets are available. A dump station is available nearby. Supplies and a coin laundry are available in the town of Lake Isabella. Leashed pets are permitted.

Reservations, fees: Reservations are not accepted. Sites are $15 per night, $5 per night for an additional vehicle. Open May–September, holiday weekends only.

Directions: From Bakersfield, drive east on Highway 178 for about 40 miles to the town of Lake Isabella and Highway 155. Turn left (north) and drive 1.5 miles to the campground.

Contact: Sequoia National Forest, Kern River Ranger District, Lake Isabella Office, 760/379-5646, fax 760/379-8597.

77 PARADISE COVE

Scenic rating: 6

on Isabella Lake

See map page 809

Paradise Cove is on the southeast shore of Isabella Lake at 2,600 feet in elevation. A boat ramp is about two miles away to the west, near the South Fork Picnic Area. While the camp is not directly at the lakeshore, it does overlook the broadest expanse of the lake. This part of the lake is relatively undeveloped compared to the areas near Wofford Heights and the dam.

RV sites, facilities: There are 58 sites for tents and a primitive area for up to 80 RVs of any length. No hookups. Picnic tables and fire grills are provided at some sites. Drinking water, restrooms with flush toilets and coin showers, and a fish-cleaning station are available. Supplies, a dump station, and a coin laundry are available in Mountain Mesa. Some facilities are wheelchair accessible. Leashed pets are permitted.

Reservations, fees: Reservations are accepted ($9 reservation fee) at 877/444-6777 or www.ReserveUSA.com. Sites are $12–17 per night, $5 per night for an additional vehicle. Open year-round.

Directions: From Bakersfield, drive east on Highway 178 for about 40 miles to the town of Lake Isabella. Continue east on Highway 178 for six miles to the campground entrance.

Contact: Sequoia National Forest, Kern River Ranger District, Lake Isabella Office, 760/379-5646, fax 760/379-8597.

78 KOA LAKE ISABELLA

Scenic rating: 4

on Isabella Lake

See map page 809

This KOA camp provides a good, clean option to the Forest Service camps on the southern end of Isabella Lake, Southern California's largest lake. It is in South Fork Valley (elevation 2,600 feet), east of the lake off Highway 178. The nearest boat ramp is at South Fork Picnic Area (about a five-minute drive to the west), where there is also a good view of the lake.

RV sites, facilities: There are 70 sites for tents or RVs up to 40 feet with full or partial hookups (30 amps); some sites are pull-through. Picnic tables are provided, along with fire rings at some sites. Restrooms have flush toilets and showers. Drinking water, a playground, a seasonal swimming pool, a coin laundry, a recreation room, pub, a convenience store, a dump station, firewood, and propane gas are available. Leashed pets are permitted.

Reservations, fees: Reservations are accepted. Sites are $23–38 per night for RVs, $4 per person per night for more than three people. Some credit cards accepted. Open year-round.

Directions: From Bakersfield, drive east on Highway 178 for about 40 miles to the town of Lake Isabella. Continue east on Highway 178 for 10 miles to the campground entrance on the left (well signed).

Contact: KOA Lake Isabella, 760/378-2001 or 800/562-2085, www.koa.com.

79 HOBO

Scenic rating: 7

on the Kern River in Sequoia National Forest
See map page 809

The secret is out about Hobo: It is adjacent to a mineral hot springs—that is, an open-air springs, with room for about 10 people at once. The camp is also along the lower Kern River, about 10 miles downstream of the dam at Isabella Lake. Rafters sometimes use this camp as a put-in spot for an 18-mile run to the takeout at Democrat Picnic Area, a challenging Class IV run. The elevation is 2,300 feet.

RV sites, facilities: There are 35 sites for tents or RVs up to 24 feet (no hookups). Fire grills and picnic tables are provided. Drinking water, vault toilets, and showers are available. Leashed pets are permitted.

Reservations, fees: Reservations are accepted ($9 reservation fee) at 877/444-6777 or

www.ReserveUSA.com. The fee is $14 per night for the first vehicle, $5 per night for an additional vehicle. Open year-round.

Directions: From Bakersfield, drive east on Highway 178 for 35 miles to Borel Road (five miles from Lake Isabella). Turn right (south) at Borel Road and drive 0.3 mile to Old Kern Road. Turn right and drive two miles to the campground on your right.

Contact: Sequoia National Forest, Kern River Ranger District, Lake Isabella Office, 760/379-5646, fax 760/379-8597.

80 KERN RIVER CAMPGROUND

Scenic rating: 7

at Lake Ming
See map page 809

The campground is at Lake Ming, a small but exciting place. The lake covers just 205 surface acres, and with the weather so hot, the hot jet boats can make it a wild affair here. It's become a popular spot for southern valley residents, only a 15-minute drive from Bakersfield. It is so popular for water sports that every year, beginning in March, the lake is closed to the public one weekend per month for private boat races and waterskiing competitions. The lake is restricted to sailing and sailboarding on the second weekend of every month and on Tuesday and Thursday afternoons. All other boating, including waterskiing, is permitted on the remaining days. All boats are required to have a permit; boaters may buy one at the park. Swimming is not allowed because there is a parasite in the water that has been known to cause "swimmer's itch." Yikes. The lake is stocked with rainbow trout in the winter months, and they join a sprinkling of bluegill, catfish, crappie, and bass. The elevation is 450 feet.

RV sites, facilities: There are 50 sites for tents or RVs up to 28 feet. Picnic tables and fire rings are provided. Restrooms have flush toilets and coin showers. Drinking water, a dump station, a playground, a concession stand, a picnic area, and a boat ramp are available. A store is nearby. Some facilities are wheelchair accessible. Leashed pets are permitted.

Reservations, fees: Reservations are not accepted. Sites are $22 per night, $4 per night per pet. Maximum stay is 10 days. Discounts available in winter. Open year-round.

Directions: From Bakersfield, drive east on Highway 178 for 11 miles to Alfred Harrell Highway. Turn left (north) on Alfred Harrell Highway and drive four miles to Lake Ming Road. Turn right on Lake Ming Road and follow the signs to the campground on the right, one-quarter mile west of the lake.

Contact: Kern County Parks and Recreation Department, 661/868-7000, www.co.kern.ca.us/parks/.

81 KENNEDY MEADOW

Scenic rating: 8

on the South Fork of the Kern River in Sequoia National Forest

See map page 809

This is a pretty Forest Service campground set amid piñon pine and sage country, with the Pacific Crest Trail running by the camp. That makes it a great trailhead camp, as well as a refreshing stopover for PCT through-hikers. A highlight is the nearby South Fork Kern River, which provides fishing for rainbow trout. The camp receives moderate use.

RV sites, facilities: There are 38 sites for tents or RVs up to 30 feet (no hookups). Picnic tables and fire rings are provided. Drinking water (seasonal) and vault toilets are available. Garbage must be packed out. Leashed pets are permitted.

Reservations, fees: Reservations are not accepted. Sites are $10 per night. Open year-round, weather permitting.

Directions: Drive on U.S. 395 to Ninemile Canyon Road (four miles north of the town

of Pearsonville, 48 miles south of Lone Pine). Turn west on Ninemile Canyon Road and drive 21 miles to a small store. Bear right at the store (still Ninemile Canyon Road) and continue for three miles to the campground.

Contact: Sequoia National Forest, Kern River Ranger District, Kernville Office, 760/376-3781, fax 760/376-3795.

82 CHIMNEY CREEK

Scenic rating: 5

on the Pacific Crest Trail

See map page 809

This BLM camp is at 5,900 feet along the headwaters of Chimney Creek, on the southern flank of Chimney Peak (7,990 feet) two miles to the north. This is a trailhead camp for the Pacific Crest Trail, one of its relatively obscure sections. The PCT heads north from camp, and in 10 miles it skirts the eastern border of Dome Land Wilderness.

RV sites, facilities: There are 36 sites for tents or RVs up to 25 feet (no hookups). Picnic tables and fire grills are provided. Vault toilets are available. No drinking water is available. Garbage must be packed out. Leashed pets are permitted.

Reservations, fees: Reservations are not accepted. There is no fee for camping, but donations are encouraged. Open year-round.

Directions: Drive on U.S. 395 to Ninemile Canyon Road (four miles north of the town of Pearsonville, 48 miles south of Lone Pine). Turn west on Ninemile Canyon Road and drive 11 miles to the BLM Work Station and Cane Brake Road. Turn left on Cane Brake Road (the dirt road opposite the BLM station) and drive three miles to the camp on the left.

Contact: Bureau of Land Management, Bakersfield Field Office, 661/391-6000, fax 661/391-6041.

CALIFORNIA

DEATH VALLEY

What good are Death Valley, the Panamint Range, and the nearby desert environs? The answer is that this country is good to look at. On a fall evening, you can take a seat on a ridge, overlooking hundreds of square miles of landscape, and just watch. Every few minutes, you'll find, the view changes. It is like watching the face of someone you care for, one minute joyous, the next pensive, then wondrous, then mysterious.

The desert is like this, always changing the way it looks, just as the sunlight changes. The reason is that as the sun passes through the sky, its azimuth is continuously changing. In turn, that causes a continuous transformation in the way sunlight is refracted through the atmosphere and across the vast landscape. So every few minutes, especially at dawn and dusk in spring and fall, the desert looks different. For those who appreciate this subtlety, the desert calls for them in a way that many others do not understand.

There are other attractions. It is often warm even on the fringe of winter; the wildflowers are small but can be spectacular in spring; and the highways – and everything else – are wide open, at times without another soul for miles in all directions. This region is huge, with Death Valley the largest national park in the lower 48 states, yet there are only six campgrounds suitable for RVs. Because of the sparse nature of the land, campers should arrive self-contained; that is, equipped with everything they need.

Some of the highlights include the lowest point in the United States, 282 feet below sea level, at Badwater in Death Valley National Park. Yet also in the park is Telescope Peak, towering at 11,048 feet. Crazy? Oh yeah.

When viewed from a distance, in between is a terrain that seems devoid of vegetation. The sub-sea-level salt flats can seem indeed like a bunch of nothing. But they are linked to barren, rising mountains, Eureka Dunes, and surrounding vastness everywhere.

Camping is good at the developed campsites, but this is a great place to leave the RV behind and strike out on your own with a tent to create your own site, do-it-yourself style. One key is to never camp at a water source or in the bottom of a ravine. Instead, always camp a good distance from water sources and on shelves or flat spots above ravines.

CALIFORNIA

This is why: 1) If you camp at a water source, you may unintentionally block it from use by wildlife. In their case, it may be life or death, and yet you are in their way – so keep a wide berth from water sources at night. 2) Never camp at the bottom of ravines in the desert because you can drown. What? Yep. Thunderstorms with tremendous short-term rainfall are common in the desert. If the runoff is blocked, the water can back itself up like a small lake and then suddenly break through with the force of a small flood. In turn, if you are camped at the bottom of a ravine, you can find yourself in the path of a surprise torrent of water – right in the middle of the desert, the driest place in the state.

Of course, summer is well known for the blazing temperatures, over 100°F about every day and occasionally hitting 120°F and up.

But that is not when people visit here. They visit in fall, winter, and spring. And if you see somebody sitting on an overlooking ridge at dusk, watching the changing colors of the landscape as if it were created from the palette of an artist, well, don't be surprised. When it comes to beautiful views, the changing colors of the emotion of the land, it doesn't get any better than this.

CALIFORNIA

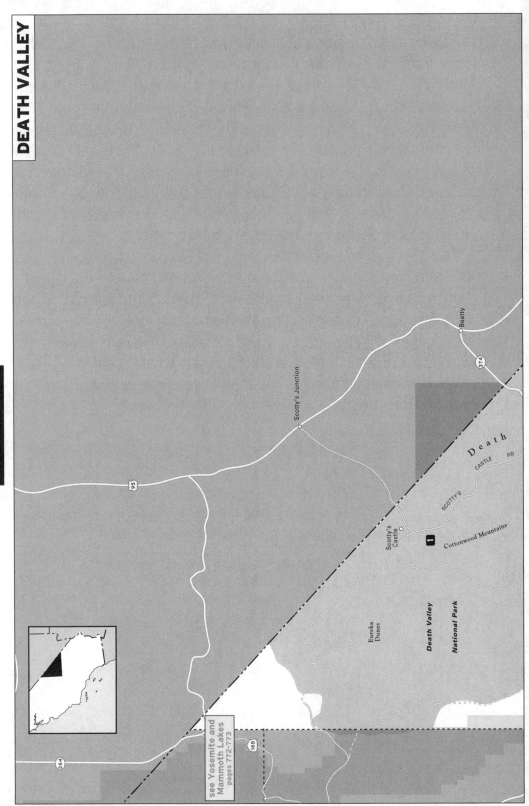

DEATH VALLEY

CALIFORNIA

Beatty

Scotty's Junction

95

Death

CASTLE RD

SCOTTY'S

Scotty's
Castle

1

Cottonwood Mountains

Eureka
Dunes

Death Valley

National Park

264

168

see Yosemite and
Mammoth Lakes
pages 772-773

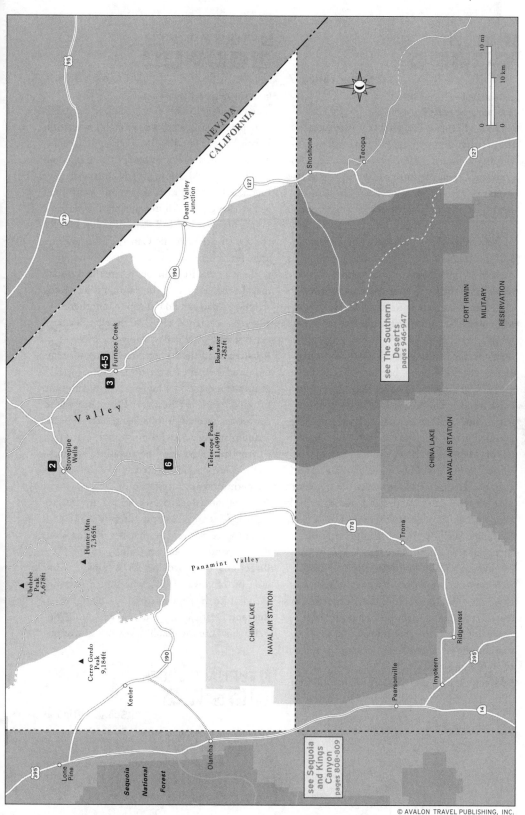

© AVALON TRAVEL PUBLISHING, INC.

1 MESQUITE SPRING

Scenic rating: 7

in Death Valley National Park
See map page 848

Mesquite Spring is the northernmost and often the prettiest campground in Death Valley, providing you time it right. If you are a lover of desert beauty, then you must make this trip in late winter or early spring, when all kinds of tiny wildflowers can bring the stark valley floor to life. The key is soil moisture, courtesy of rains in November and December. The elevation is 1,800 feet. Mesquite Spring Campground is within short range of two side trips. It is five miles (past the Grapevine entrance station) to Ubehebe Crater, a scenic point, and four miles to Scotty's Castle, a historic building, where tours are available.

RV sites, facilities: There are 30 sites for tents or RVs up to 30 feet (no hookups). Picnic tables and fire grills are provided. Drinking water, flush toilets, and a dump station are available. Some facilities are wheelchair accessible. Leashed pets are permitted.

Reservations, fees: Reservations are not accepted. Sites are $12 per night, plus a $20 park entrance fee that is valid for seven days. Visitors may pay the entrance fee and obtain a park brochure at the Furnace Creek, Grapevine, Stovepipe Wells, or Beatty Ranger Station.

Directions: From Furnace Creek Visitor Center, drive north on Highway 190 for 19 miles to Scotty's Castle Road. Turn right (east) and drive 33 miles (just before the Grapevine entrance station and three miles before reaching Scotty's Castle) to the campground entrance road on the left. Turn left and drive two miles to the campground.

Contact: Death Valley National Park, 760/786-3200, fax 760/786-3283, www.nps.gov/deva.

2 STOVEPIPE WELLS

Scenic rating: 4

in Death Valley National Park
See map page 849

Stovepipe Wells is on the major highway through Death Valley. The RV sites consist of an enormous asphalt area with sites simply marked on it. There is no shelter or shade. But note: Get fuel here because prices are usually lower than at Furnace Creek. An unusual trail is available off the highway within a short distance; look for the sign for the Mosaic Canyon Trail parking area. From here you can take the easy one-mile walk up a beautiful canyon, where the walls are marble and seem as if they are polished. Rock scramblers can extend the trip for another mile. The elevation is at sea level on the edge of a large expanse of Death Valley below sea level.

RV sites, facilities: There are 18 sites for tents only and 200 sites with no hookups for RVs of any length. Picnic tables and fire rings are provided at the tent sites. Drinking water, restrooms with flush toilets and coin showers, a dump station, a swimming pool (extra fee), a camp store, and gasoline are available. Some facilities are wheelchair accessible. Leashed pets are permitted at campsites only.

Reservations, fees: Reservations are not accepted. Sites are $12 per night, plus a $20 park entrance fee per vehicle that is valid for seven days. Open mid-October–mid-April.

Directions: In Stovepipe Wells Village, drive west on Highway 190 to the signed entrance (just before the general store) on the right.

Contact: Death Valley National Park, 760/786-3200, fax 760/786-3283, www.nps.gov/deva.

3 FURNACE CREEK

Scenic rating: 5

in Death Valley National Park
See map page 849

This is a well-developed national park site that provides a good base camp for exploring Death Valley, especially for newcomers. The nearby

CALIFORNIA

visitors center includes Death Valley Museum and offers maps and suggestions for hikes and drives in this unique wildland. The elevation is 190 feet below sea level. This camp offers shady sites, a rarity in Death Valley. It's open all year, but keep in mind that the daytime summer temperatures commonly exceed 120°F, making this area virtually uninhabitable in the summer.

RV sites, facilities: There are 136 sites for tents or RVs up to 35 feet (no hookups), and two group sites hold up to 10 vehicles and 40 people each. Picnic tables and fire rings are provided. Drinking water, flush toilets, a dump station, and evening ranger programs are available. Campfires are not permitted during the summer. Some facilities are wheelchair accessible. Leashed pets are permitted at campsites only.

Reservations, fees: Reservations are recommended mid-October through mid-April at 800/365-CAMP (800/365-2267) or at http://reservations.nps.gov. Sites are $18 per night (includes reservation fee), plus a $20 park entrance fee per vehicle that is valid for seven days. Group sites are $50 per night. Open year-round.

Directions: From Furnace Creek Ranch, drive one mile north on Highway 190 to the signed campground entrance on the left.

Contact: Death Valley National Park, 760/786-3200, fax 760/786-3283, www.nps.gov/deva.

4 TEXAS SPRING

Scenic rating: 2

in Death Valley National Park

See map page 849

Although this camp is slightly more protected than Sunset camp, there's limited shade and no shelter. The lower half of the campground is for tents only. It is open only in winter. The upper end of the camp has trails that provide access to the historic springs and a viewing area. The nearby visitors center, which features the Death Valley Museum, offers maps and suggestions for hikes and drives. The lowest point in the United States, Badwater, at 282 feet below sea

level, is to the southwest. This camp has one truly unique feature: bathrooms that are listed on the National Historic Register.

RV sites, facilities: There are 92 sites for tents or RVs of any length (no hookups). Picnic tables and fire rings are provided. Drinking water, flush toilets, and a dump station are available. Campfires are not permitted in the summer. Some facilities are wheelchair accessible. Leashed pets are permitted.

Reservations, fees: No reservations are accepted. Sites are $12 per night, plus a $20 park entrance fee per vehicle that is valid for seven days. Open mid-October–mid-April.

Directions: From Furnace Creek Ranch, drive south on Highway 190 for 0.25 mile to the signed campground entrance on the left.

Contact: Death Valley National Park, 760/786-3200, fax 760/786-3283, www.nps.gov/deva.

5 SUNSET

Scenic rating: 4

in Death Valley National Park

See map page 849

This camp is another enormous section of asphalt where the campsites consist of white lines for borders. Sunset is one of several options for campers in the Furnace Creek area of Death Valley, with an elevation of 190 feet below sea level. It is advisable to make your first stop at the nearby visitors center for maps and suggested hikes (according to your level of fitness) and drives. Don't forget your canteen—and if you're backpacking, never set up a wilderness camp closer than 100 yards to water in Death Valley.

RV sites, facilities: There are 1,000 sites with no hookups for RVs of any length. Drinking water, flush toilets, and a dump station are available. Campfires are not permitted in the summer. Some facilities are wheelchair accessible. Leashed pets are permitted at campsites.

Reservations, fees: No reservations are accepted for individual sites. Sites are $10 per night, plus a $20 park entrance fee per vehicle that is valid for seven days. Open mid-October–mid-April.

Directions: From Furnace Creek Ranch, turn south on Highway 190 and drive 0.25 mile to the signed campground entrance and turn left into the campground.

Contact: Death Valley National Park, 760/786-3200, fax 760/786-3283, www.nps.gov/deva.

6 WILDROSE

Scenic rating: 4

in Death Valley National Park

See map page xxx

Wildrose is on the road that heads out to the primitive country of the awesome Panamint Range, eventually coming within range of Telescope Peak, the highest point in Death Valley National Park (11,049 feet). The elevation at the camp is 4,100 feet.

RV sites, facilities: There are 23 sites for tents or RVs up to 25 feet (no hookups). Picnic tables and fire rings are provided. Drinking water (April–November only) and pit toilets are available. Campfires are not permitted during the summer. Leashed pets are permitted at campsites only.

Reservations, fees: No reservations are accepted, and there is no camping fee; however, there is a $20 park entrance fee per vehicle that is valid for seven days. Open year-round.

Directions: From Stovepipe Wells Village, drive south on Highway 190 for eight miles to Emigrant Canyon Road (just past the Emigrant rest area). Turn left (east) on Emigrant Canyon Road and drive 22 miles to the campground entrance on the left.

Contact: Death Valley National Park, 760/786-3200, fax 760/786-3283, www.nps.gov/deva.

SANTA BARBARA AND VICINITY

☾ BEST RV PARKS AND CAMPGROUNDS

For many, this region of California coast is like a dream, the best place in the world to live. Visitors, picking one or several of the campgrounds in the region, can get a taste of why it is so special. What you will likely find, however, is that a taste will only whet your appetite. That's how it is here. Many keep coming back for more. Some eventually even move here.

The region is a unique mix of sunswept sand beaches that stretch 200 miles and surprise inland coastal forests. The coast offers a series of stunning state beaches, where getting a campsite reservation can feel like winning the lottery. If you have a dream trip in mind in which you cruise the coast highway the entire length, you'd better have the reservation system wired from the start. These campsites go fast and are filled every night of the vacation season. There are many highlights on the coast: San Simeon, Hearst Castle, all the state beaches, the stunning towns of Cambria, Goleta, and Cayucos, and the Coast Highway that provides a route through all of it.

Yet as popular as the coast may seem, just inland lie many remote, hidden campsites and destinations. Los Padres National Forest spans a matrix of canyons with small streams, mountaintop lookouts, and wilderness trailheads. The landscape is a mix of pine, deep canyons, chaparral, and foothills.

Two of California's best recreation lakes also provide major destinations, Lake Nacimiento and San Antonio Reservoir. Nacimiento is one of the top family-oriented lakes for water sports, and it also provides sensational fishing for white bass and largemouth bass in the spring. San Antonio is a great lake for bass, at times even rating as one of the best in America, and tours to see bald eagles are also popular in the winter. Cachuma Lake and Lake Casitas near Santa Barbara have produced some of the largest bass caught in history.

The ocean is dramatic here, the backdrop for every trip on the Coast Highway, and it seems to stretch to forever. Maybe it does. For many visiting here, forever is how long they wish to stay.

CALIFORNIA

Includes:

- Carpinteria State Beach
- El Capitan State Beach
- Emma Wood State Beach
- Gaviota State Park
- Lake Nacimiento
- Lake San Antonio
- Los Padres National Forest
- McGrath State Beach
- Montaña de Oro State Park
- Morro Bay
- Morro Bay State Park
- Morro Strand State Beach
- Oceano Dunes State Vehicular Recreation Area
- Pismo State Beach
- Point Mugu State Park
- Refugio State Beach
- San Luis Obispo Bay
- San Simeon State Park
- Santa Margarita Lake
- Santa Ynez River

CALIFORNIA

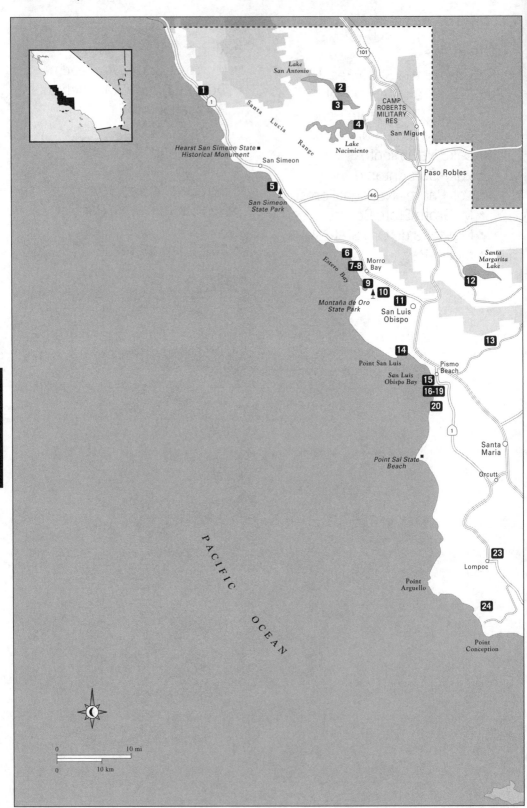

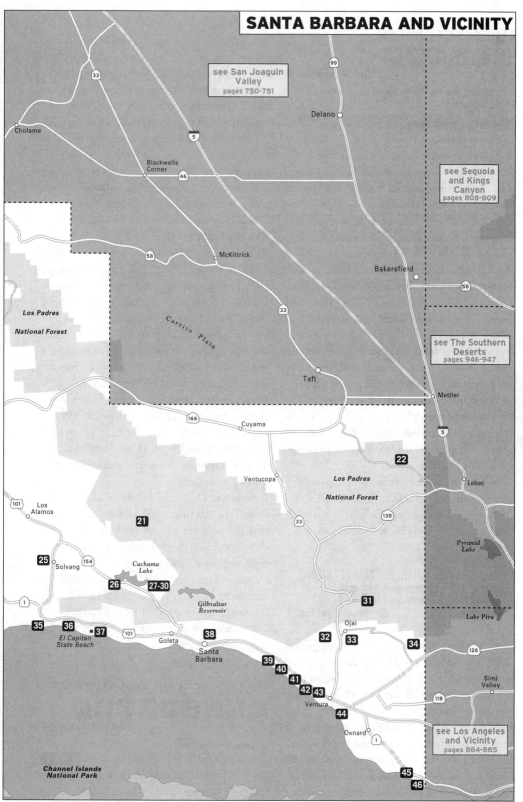

SANTA BARBARA AND VICINITY

see San Joaquin
Valley
pages 750-751

Delano

see Sequoia
and Kings
Canyon
pages 808-809

Cholame

Blackwells
Corner

McKittrick

Bakersfield

58

Carrizo Plain

*Los Padres
National Forest*

see The Southern
Deserts
pages 946-947

Taft

Mettler

CALIFORNIA

166

Cuyama

22

Ventucopa

*Los Padres
National Forest*

Lebec

Los
Alamos

21

*Pyramid
Lake*

25

Solvang

154

*Cachuma
Lake*

26

27-30

*Gilbraltar
Reservoir*

31

Lake Piru

35

36

37

*El Capitan
State Beach*

Goleta

38

Santa
Barbara

Ojai

32

33

34

126

39

40

41

42 **43**

Ventura

44

Simi
Valley

118

Oxnard

1

*Channel Islands
National Park*

45

46

see Los Angeles
and Vicinity
pages 884-885

CALIFORNIA

1 PLASKETT CREEK

Scenic rating: 8

overlooking the Pacific Ocean in Los Padres
National Forest

See map page 856

This is a premium coastal camp for Highway
1 cruisers, at an elevation of just 100 feet along
little Plaskett Creek above the Pacific Ocean.
The campground provides access to Sand Dollar
Beach. It gets overlooked by many for two reasons: It is not listed with a reservation service, and
it is farther south of Big Sur than most are willing
to drive. A little café in Lucia provides open-air
dining with a dramatic lookout over the coast.

RV sites, facilities: There are 45 sites for tents or
RVs up to 30 feet (no hookups). Picnic tables and
fire grills are provided. Drinking water and flush
toilets are available. Leashed pets are permitted.

Reservations, fees: Reservations are not accepted. Sites are $22 per night, $5 per night
per person for bicyclists, $5 per person per extra
vehicle. Open year-round.

Directions: From Monterey, drive south on
Highway 1 to Lucia. From Lucia, continue
south on Highway 1 for 9.5 miles to the campground on the left.

Contact: Los Padres National Forest, Monterey
Ranger District, 831/385-5434, fax 831/385-
0628; Parks Management Company, 805/434-
1996, fax 805/434-1986, www.campone.com.

2 NORTH SHORE SAN ANTONIO

Scenic rating: 7

on Lake San Antonio

See map page 856   **BEST (**

Lake San Antonio makes a great year-round
destination for adventure. It is a big, warm-
water lake, long and narrow, at 780 feet in
the foothills north of Paso Robles. The camp
features four miles of shoreline camping, with
the bonus of primitive sites along Pleyto Points.
The lake is 16 miles long, covers 5,500 surface
acres, and has 60 miles of shoreline and average
summer water temperatures in the 70s, making

it an ideal place for fun in the sun. It is one of
the top lakes in California for bass fishing, best
in spring and early summer. It is also good for
striped bass, catfish, crappie, sunfish, and bluegill. It provides the best wintering habitat in the
region for bald eagles, and eagle-watching tours
are available from the south shore of the lake.
Of course, the size of the lake, along with hot
temperatures all summer, makes waterskiing
and water sports absolutely first-class. Note that
boat rentals are not available here, but at South
Shore. Equestrian trails are also available.

RV sites, facilities: There are 200 sites for tents or
RVs of any length (no hookups), 24 sites for tents
or RVs of any length with full or partial hookups
(30 amps), and up to 1,800 primitive dispersed
sites near the shoreline. Mobile home rentals are
also available. Fire grills and picnic tables are provided. Restrooms have showers. Drinking water,
a dump station, a boat ramp, hitching posts, a
general store, volleyball, and fishing licenses are
available. Leashed pets are permitted.

Reservations, fees: Reservations are not accepted. Sites are $23–25 per night, $15 per
night for an additional vehicle, $2 per pet per
night. Boat launching is $6 per day. Off-season
discounts available. Some credit cards accepted.
Open year-round.

Directions: On U.S. 101, drive to the Jolon
Road/G14 exit (just north of King City). Take
that exit and turn south on Jolon Road and
drive 27 miles to Pleyto Road (curvy road). Turn
right and drive three miles to the North Shore
entrance of the lake. Note: When arriving from
the south or east on U.S. 101 near Paso Robles,
it is faster to take the G18/Jolon Road exit.

Contact: North Shore, 805/472-2311, www.co
.monterey.ca.us/parks.

3 SOUTH SHORE SAN ANTONIO

Scenic rating: 7

on Lake San Antonio

See map page 856   **BEST (**

Harris Creek, Redondo Vista, and Lynch are
the three campgrounds near each other along

the south shore of Lake San Antonio, a 16-mile reservoir that provides good bass fishing in the spring and waterskiing in the summer. There are 26 miles of good biking and hiking trails in the park. The park's administration building holds a museum and visitors center. In the winter, the Monterey County Department of Parks offers a unique eagle-watching program here that includes boat tours. (See the listing in this chapter for *North Shore San Antonio* for more details about the lake.) Note that South Shore has boat rentals, laundry facilities, and a playground.

RV sites, facilities: There are three campgrounds here: Redondo has 173 sites for tents or RVs (no hookups) and 86 sites for tents or RVs with full hookups (30 amps); Lynch has 54 sites for tents or RVs with partial hookups and 52 sites for tents; Harris Creek has 26 sites for tents or RVs with partial hookups and 88 sites for tents. Mobile home rentals are also available. Picnic tables and fire grills are provided. Drinking water and flush toilets are available. Restrooms have showers. A dump station, a marina, a boat ramp, boat rentals, boat slips, bait and tackle, a playground, a recreation room, a coin laundry, a general store, and fishing licenses are available nearby. Leashed pets are permitted.

Reservations, fees: Reservations are accepted for 15 sites only at 888/588-2267. Sites are $27 per night, $15 per night for an additional vehicle, $2 per pet per night. Boat launching is $6 per day. Some credit cards accepted. Off-season discounts available. Group reservations at 805/472-2311. Open year-round.

Directions: From the north, on U.S. 101 (just north of King City), take the Jolon Road/G14 exit. Turn south on Jolon Road and drive 21 miles to Lockwood and Interlake Road (G14). Turn right and drive 18 miles to San Antonio Lake Road. Turn left and drive three miles to the South Shore entrance of the lake.

From the south, drive on U.S. 101 to Paso Robles and the 24th Street exit (G14 west). Take that exit and drive 14 miles to Lake Nacimiento Drive. Turn right and drive across Lake Nacimiento Dam to Interlake Road. Turn left and drive seven miles to Lake San Antonio Road. Turn right and drive three miles to the South Shore entrance.

Contact: South Shore, 805/472-2311, www.lakesanantonio.net or www.co.monterey.ca.us/parks.

▣ LAKE NACIMIENTO RESORT

Scenic rating: 8

at Lake Nacimiento

See map page 856

This is the only game in town at Nacimiento, and the management plays it well. It's an outstanding operation, with headquarters for a great fishing or water sports trip. The fishing for white bass and largemouth bass can be incredible. And the water play is also great, with such a big lake, 70-degree temperatures, and some of the best waterskiing in California. The lake has 165 miles of shoreline with an incredible number of arms, many ideal for bass fishing. Nacimiento hosts about 25 fishing tournaments per year. Not only is bass fishing good, but there are opportunities for trout (in cool months) and bluegill and catfish (in warm months). The resort has a lakeview restaurant open during the summer, and the campsites provide limited tree cover with pines and oaks. Two camps are on the lake's shore, and the rest are set back about three-quarters of a mile from the lake. Lakeview lodging is also available.

RV sites, facilities: There are a series of campgrounds with 297 sites for tents or RVs of any length (no hookups), 40 sites with full hookups for RVs up to 35 feet, and 12 group sites for 15–40 people each. Nineteen lodges, eight trailers, and two mobile homes are also available for rent. Picnic tables and fire grills are provided. Drinking water, restrooms with showers and flush toilets, a dump station, a boat ramp, boat docks, boat rentals, a playground, seasonal swimming pool, seasonal restaurant, a coin laundry, a general store, fishing licenses, swimming beaches, basketball and volleyball courts, and horseshoe pits are available. Leashed pets are permitted.

Reservations, fees: Reservations are accepted. Sites are $30–40 per vehicle per night, $10 per pet per night. Some credit cards accepted. Open year-round.

Directions: On U.S. 101, drive to Paso Robles and the 24th Street/Lake Nacimiento exit. Take that exit, turn west on 24th Street (becomes Lake Nacimiento Drive/G14), and drive for nine miles. Bear right on Lake Nacimiento Drive and continue for seven miles to the resort entrance on the left. Note: If you cross the Lake Nacimiento dam, you've gone too far.

Contact: Lake Nacimiento Resort, 805/238-3256 or 800/323-3839, www.nacimientoresort.com.

⑤ SAN SIMEON STATE PARK

Scenic rating: 9

in San Simeon State Park
See map page 856

Hearst Castle is only five miles northeast, so San Simeon Creek is a natural for visitors planning to take the tour; for a tour reservation, phone 800/444-4445. San Simeon Creek Campground is across the highway from the ocean, with easy access under the highway to the beach. San Simeon Creek, while not exactly the Mississippi, runs through the campground and adds a nice touch. Washburn Campground is an option at this park, and while it provides better views, the sites are exposed and can be windy. It is one mile inland on a plateau overlooking the Pacific Ocean and Santa Lucia Mountains. The best hike in the area is from Leffingwell Landing to Moonstone Beach, featuring sweeping views of the coast from ocean bluffs and a good chance to see passing whales. There are three preserves in the park, including a wintering site for monarch butterfly populations, and it has an archaeological site dating from more than 5,800 years ago. In the summer, junior ranger programs and interpretive programs are available.

RV sites, facilities: At San Simeon Creek Camp,

there are 115 sites for tents or RVs up to 35 feet (no hookups), 10 sites for tents only, and two hike-in/bike-in sites. Picnic tables and fire grills are provided. Drinking water, a dump station, and restrooms with flush toilets and coin showers are available. At Washburn Camp, there are 70 sites for tents or RVs up to 31 feet (no hookups). Picnic tables and fire grills are provided. Drinking water, chemical flush toilets, and firewood are available. A grocery store, a coin laundry, a gas station, restaurants, and propane gas are two miles away in Cambria. Some facilities are wheelchair accessible. Leashed pets are permitted in the campgrounds only.

Reservations, fees: Reservations are accepted at 800/444-PARK (800/444-7275) or www.reserveamerica.com ($7.50 reservation fee). Sites are $20–25 per night at San Simeon Creek, $11–15 per night at Washburn, $3 per night for an additional vehicle, $2 per person per night for hike-in/bike-in sites. Open year-round.

Directions: From Cambria, drive two miles north on Highway 1 to San Simeon Creek Road. Turn east and drive 0.2 mile to the park entrance on the right.

Contact: San Simeon State Park, 805/927-2035, www.parks.ca.gov.

⑥ MORRO STRAND STATE BEACH

Scenic rating: 7

near Morro Bay
See map page 856

A ton of Highway 1 cruisers plan to stay overnight at this state park. It is along the ocean near Morro Bay, right on the beach, a pretty spot year-round. The park features a three-mile stretch of beach that connects the southern and northern entrances to the state beach. Fishing, jogging, sailboarding, and kite flying are popular. Side trips include the Morro Bay Wildlife Refuge, the Museum of Natural History, or an ocean-fishing trip out of Morro Bay. (See the listing in this chapter for *Morro Bay State Park* for more information.)

RV sites, facilities: There are 76 sites for tents

or RVs up to 24 feet (no hookups). Picnic tables and fire grills are provided. Drinking water and flush toilets are available. Cold, outdoor showers are also available. Supplies and a coin laundry are available in Morro Bay. Leashed pets are permitted, but not on the beach.

Reservations, fees: Reservations are accepted at 800/444-PARK (800/444-7275) or www.reserveamerica.com ($7.50 reservation fee). Sites are $20–35 per night, $5 per night for an additional vehicle. Open year-round.

Directions: On Highway 1, drive to Morro Bay. Take the Yerba Buena Street/Morro Strand State Beach exit. Turn west on Yerba Buena Street and drive one block to the campground.

Contact: Morro Strand State Beach, 805/772-8812; Morro Bay State Park, 805/772-7434; San Luis Obispo Coast District, 805/927-2065, www.parks.ca.gov.

7 RANCHO COLINA RV PARK

Scenic rating: 6

in Morro Bay

See map page 856

This privately operated RV park is one of several camping options in the Morro Bay area. Folks who park here typically stroll the boardwalk, exploring the little shops. (For recreation, see the listing for *Morro Bay State Park* in this chapter.) About 20 percent of the sites here are long-term rentals.

RV sites, facilities: There are 57 sites with full hookups (30 amps) for RVs up to 40 feet. No tents. Picnic tables are provided. Restrooms have showers. Laundry facilities and a recreation room are available. You can buy supplies nearby. Leashed pets are permitted.

Reservations, fees: Reservations are accepted. Sites are $30 per night. Monthly rates available. Some credit cards accepted. Open year-round.

Directions: From Morro Bay on Highway 1, drive one mile east on Atascadero Road/Highway 41 to the park at 1045 Atascadero Road.

Contact: Rancho Colina RV Park, 805/772-8420.

8 MORRO DUNES TRAVEL TRAILER PARK AND RESORT CAMPING

Scenic rating: 6

in Morro Bay

See map page 856

A wide array of side-trip possibilities and great natural beauty make Morro Bay an attractive destination. Most visitors will walk the boardwalk, try at least one of the coastal restaurants, and then head to Morro Bay State Park for hiking or sea kayaking. Other folks will head straight to the port for fishing or just explore the area before heading north to San Simeon for the Hearst Castle tour. (See the listing for *Morro Bay State Park* in this chapter for more information.)

RV sites, facilities: There are 178 sites with full or partial hookups (30 amps) for RVs of any length and 48 sites for tents. Some sites are pull-through. Picnic tables and fire grills are provided. Restrooms have showers. Drinking water, cable TV, Wi-Fi, modem access, a coin laundry, a general store, clubhouse, RV storage, RV supplies and repair, a recreation hall, group facilities, horseshoes, basketball, firewood, ice, and a dump station are available. Propane gas, a golf course, a playground, and boat rentals are nearby. Some facilities are wheelchair accessible. Leashed pets are permitted.

Reservations, fees: Reservations are accepted. RV sites are $27.50–31.90 per night, tent sites are $23.10 per night, plus $1 per person per night for more than two people and $1 per pet per night. Weekly and monthly rates are available during the winter. Some credit cards accepted. Open year-round.

Directions: Drive on Highway 1 to Morro Bay and the exit for Highway 41. Take that exit and turn west on Atascadero Road/Highway 41 and drive 0.5 mile to 1700 Embarcadero/Atascadero Road.

Contact: Morro Dunes Travel Trailer Park and Resort Camping, 805/772-2722, fax 805/772-2372, www.morrodunes.com.

❾ MORRO BAY STATE PARK

Scenic rating: 9

in Morro Bay
See map page 856

Reservations are strongly advised at this popular campground. This is one of the premium stopover spots for folks cruising north on Highway 1. The park offers a wide range of activities and exhibits covering the natural and cultural history of the area. The park features lagoon and natural bay habitat. The most prominent feature is Morro Rock. A "morro" is a small volcanic peak, and there are nine of them along the local coast. The top hike at the park climbs one of them, Black Hill, and rewards hikers with sensational coastal views. The park has a marina and golf course, with opportunities for sailing, fishing, and bird-watching. Activities include beach walks, kayaking in Morro Bay, fishing the nearby ocean on a party boat, and touring Hearst Castle.

RV sites, facilities: There are 95 sites for tents or RVs up to 31 feet (no hookups), 27 sites with partial hookups (15 and 30 amps) for RVs up to 35 feet, five hike-in/bike-in sites, and two group sites for 25–35 people. Picnic tables, food lockers, and fire rings are provided. Restrooms have flush toilets and coin showers. Drinking water, a dump station, Wi-Fi, museum exhibits, and nature walks and interpretive programs are available. A coin laundry, a grocery store, propane gas, a boat ramp, mooring, boat rentals, gas stations, and food service are available in Morro Bay. Some facilities are wheelchair accessible. Leashed pets are permitted, but not on the beach.

Reservations, fees: Reservations are accepted at 800/444-PARK (800/444-7275) or www.reserveamerica.com ($7.50 reservation fee). Sites are $20–34 per night, $5 per person per night for hike-in/bike-in sites, $66–111 per night for group sites. Open year-round.

Directions: On Highway 1, drive to Morro Bay and take the exit for Los Osos-Baywood Park/Morro Bay State Park. Turn south and drive one mile to State Park Road. Turn right and drive one mile to the park entrance on the right.

Contact: Morro Bay State Park, 805/772-7434; San Luis Obispo Coast District, 805/927-2065, www.parks.ca.gov.

❿ MONTAÑA DE ORO STATE PARK

Scenic rating: 9

near Morro Bay
See map page 856

This sprawling chunk of primitive land includes coastline, 8,500 acres of foothills, and Valencia Peak at 1,373 feet in elevation. The name means "mountain of gold," named for the golden wildflowers that bloom here in the spring. The camp is perched near a bluff, and while there are no sweeping views from campsites, they await nearby. Bluffs Trail is one of the best easy coastal walks anywhere, offering stunning views of the ocean and cliffs and, in the spring, tons of wildflowers over the course of just 1.5 miles. Another hiking option at the park is to climb Valencia Peak, a little buttkicker of an ascent that tops out at 1,373 feet, providing more panoramic coastal views. These are the two best hikes among 50 miles of trails for horses, mountain bikers, and hikers, with trails accessible right out of the campground.

RV sites, facilities: There are 48 sites for tents or RVs up to 27 feet (no hookups), four walk-in (50–150 yards) environmental sites, four equestrian sites, and two group equestrian sites for up to 50 people and 25 horses. Picnic tables and fire grills are provided, but fires are not allowed at the environmental sites. Vault toilets are available. Drinking water is available only at the main campground; stock water is available at the equestrian campground. There is limited corral space, and single-site equestrian camps have two stalls each. Garbage from equestrian and environmental sites must be packed out. Supplies and a coin laundry are available five miles away in the town of Los Osos. Leashed pets are permitted, except at the environmental sites and on trails.

Reservations, fees: Reservations are accepted at 800/444-PARK (800/444-7275) or www

.reserveamerica.com ($7.50 reservation fee). Sites are $11–15 per night, $25–30 for equestrian sites, $3 per night for an additional vehicle, $75 per night for group sites. Open year-round.

Directions: From Morro Bay, drive two miles south on Highway 1. Turn on South Bay Boulevard and drive four miles to Los Osos. Turn right on Los Osos Valley Road and drive five miles (it becomes Pecho Valley Road) to the park.

Contact: Montaña de Oro State Park, 805/528-0513; San Luis Obispo Coast District, 805/927-2065, www.parks.ca.gov.

11 EL CHORRO REGIONAL PARK

Scenic rating: 6

near San Luis Obispo

See map page 856

North of Morro Bay on the way to San Simeon and Hearst Castle, this can be a prime spot for RV travelers. Note that the campground isn't in the state park reservation system, which means there are times when coastal state parks can be jammed full and this regional park may still have space. Morro Bay, six miles away, provides many possible side trips. The park has full recreational facilities, including a golf course, volleyball, horseshoe pits, softball fields, hiking trails, and botanical gardens. Note that there's a men's prison about four miles away. For some people, this can be a real turnoff.

RV sites, facilities: There are 63 sites for tents or RVs up to 40 feet and some undesignated overflow sites; 44 sites have full hookups and the remaining sites have no hookups. Some primitive sites are pull-through. Fire grills and picnic tables are provided. Restrooms have flush toilets and showers. Drinking water, a playground, a picnic area, an off-leash dog area, and recreational facilities are available. Supplies and a coin laundry are nearby in San Luis Obispo. Leashed pets are permitted.

Reservations, fees: Reservations are accepted for groups only (minimum of six campsites). Sites are $18–27 per night, $9 per night for an additional vehicle, $2 per pet per night. Weekly rates available. Two-week maximum stay. Some credit cards accepted. Open year-round.

Directions: From San Luis Obispo, drive 4.5 miles north on Highway 1 to the park entrance on the right side of the highway.

Contact: El Chorro Regional Park, 805/781-5930, www.slocountyparks.com.

12 SANTA MARGARITA KOA

Scenic rating: 6

near Santa Margarita Lake

See map page 856

Santa Margarita Lake should have a sign at its entrance that proclaims, "Fishing Only!" That's because the rules here do not allow waterskiing or any water contact, including swimming, wading, using float tubes, and sailboarding. The excellent prospects for bass fishing, along with the prohibitive rules, make this lake a favorite among anglers. Santa Margarita Lake covers nearly 800 acres, most of it long and narrow and set in a dammed-up valley in the foothill country at an elevation of 1,300 feet, just below the Santa Lucia Mountains. Horseback riding is available nearby.

RV sites, facilities: There are 54 sites for tents or RVs up to 40 feet; most have full or partial hookups (30 amps), and one is pull-through. Eleven cabins are also available. Picnic tables and fire grills are provided. Restrooms have flush toilets and showers. Drinking water, modem access, a seasonal swimming pool, a playground, a coin laundry, a convenience store, a dump station, and propane gas are available. Leashed pets are permitted.

Reservations, fees: Reservations are accepted at 800/562-5619. Sites are $24–35 per night, $3–4 per person per night for more than two people. Some credit cards accepted. Open year-round.

Directions: From San Luis Obispo, drive north on U.S. 101 for eight miles to the Highway 58/Santa Margarita exit. Take that exit and drive through the town of Santa Margarita to Estrada. Turn right on Estrada and drive eight miles (Estrada becomes Pozo Road) to Santa Margarita Lake Road. Turn left and drive 0.5 mile to the campground on the right.

CALIFORNIA

Contact: Santa Margarita KOA, 805/438-5618, fax 805/438-3576, www.koa.com.

13 LOPEZ LAKE RECREATION AREA

Scenic rating: 7

near Arroyo Grande

See map page 856

Lopez Lake has become an example of how to do something right, with specially marked areas set aside exclusively for waterskiing, personal watercraft, and sailboarding, and the rest of the lake designated for fishing and low-speed boating. There are also full facilities for swimming, with a big swimming beach and two giant water slides, a children's wading pool, and a nice beach area. Scenic boat tours are available on Saturday, and they get plenty of takers. A 25-mile trail system provides opportunities for biking, hiking, and horseback riding. That makes it perfect for just about everyone, and with good bass fishing, the lake has become very popular, especially on spring weekends when the bite is on. Other species include trout, bluegill, crappie, and catfish. Lopez Lake is amid oak woodlands southeast of San Luis Obispo. The lake is shaped something like a horseshoe, has 940 surface acres with 22 miles of shoreline when full, and gets excellent weather most of the year. Features of the park in summer are ranger-led hikes and campfire shows. Many campsites overlook the lake or are nestled among oaks.

RV sites, facilities: There are 143 sites for tents or RVs with full hookups (20 and 30 amps), 211 sites for tents, an overflow site (no hookups) for tents or RVs of any length, and six group sites for 50–100 people each. Picnic tables and fire rings are provided. Restrooms have showers. A playground, children's wading pool, a coin laundry, a convenience store, ice, a snack bar, a marina, a boat ramp, mooring, boat fuel (dry land fueling only), tackle, boat rentals, and water slides are available. Some facilities are wheelchair accessible. Leashed pets are permitted.

Reservations, fees: Reservations are required by phone or website. Sites are $18–27 per night, $9 per night for an additional vehicle, $96–192 per night for a group site, $2 per dog per night. Boat launching is $6 per day. Group rates available. Two-week maximum stay in summer. Some credit cards accepted. Open year-round.

Directions: From Arroyo Grande on U.S. 101, take the Grand Avenue exit. Turn east and drive through Arroyo Grande to Lopez Drive. Turn left (northeast) on Lopez Drive and drive 10 miles to the park.

Contact: Lopez Lake Recreation Area, 805/788-2381; Lopez Lake Marina, 805/489-1006, www.slocountyparks.com.

14 AVILA HOT SPRINGS SPA AND RV PARK

Scenic rating: 6

on San Luis Obispo Bay

See map page 856

The hot mineral pool here is a featured attraction. This is a natural mineral hot springs with an artesian well that produces water directly into the spas at 104°F. A pizza kitchen and snack bar are available as well. Nearby recreation options include Avila State Beach and Pismo State Beach.

RV sites, facilities: There are 21 sites with full hookups for RVs, 17 tent sites in three areas, and 21 cabins. Some sites are pull-through. Picnic tables and fire grills (at some sites) are provided. Restrooms have showers. Cable TV, a heated swimming pool, a hot mineral pool, a spa, a dump station, a recreation room, an arcade, a pizza kitchen, and group barbecue pits are available. An 18-hole golf course is nearby. Some facilities are wheelchair accessible. Leashed pets are permitted.

Reservations, fees: Reservations are accepted at 805/595-2359. Sites are $45 per night, $5 per night for an additional vehicle. Some credit cards accepted. Open year-round.

Directions: From San Luis Obispo, drive south on U.S. 101 for nine miles to the Avila Beach Drive exit. Take that exit and drive a short distance to the park at 250 Avila Beach Drive.

Contact: Avila Hot Springs Spa and RV Park, 805/595-2359, www.avilahotsprings.com.

15 PISMO STATE BEACH: NORTH BEACH

Scenic rating: 7

in Pismo State Beach

See map page 856

Pismo State Beach is nationally renowned for its beaches, dunes, and, in the good old days, clamming. The adjacent tree-lined dunes make for great walks or, for kids, great rolls. The clamming on minus low tides was legendary. The beach is popular with bird-watchers, and the habitat supports the largest wintering colony of monarch butterflies in the United States. Plan on getting a reservation and having plenty of company in summer. This is an exceptionally popular state beach, either as an ultimate destination or as a stopover for folks cruising Highway 1. There are four restaurants and ATV rentals within two blocks. A trolley service provides a shuttle to the surrounding community. Poaching has devastated the clamming here, with no legal clams taken for years.

RV sites, facilities: There are 103 sites for tents or RVs up to 36 feet (no hookups). Fire grills and picnic tables are provided. Restrooms have showers and flush toilets. Drinking water, Wi-Fi, and a dump station are available. Horseback-riding facilities, a grocery store, ATV rentals, restaurants, a coin laundry, and propane gas are nearby. Some facilities are wheelchair accessible. Leashed pets are permitted at the campground and on the beach.

Reservations, fees: Reservations are accepted at 800/444-PARK (800/444-7275) or www.reserveamerica.com ($7.50 reservation fee). Sites are $20–25 per night, and it's $6 per night for an additional vehicle. Open year-round.

Directions: On Highway 1 in Pismo Beach, take the North Beach/State Campground exit (well signed) and drive to the park entrance.

Contact: Pismo State Beach, 805/773-2334, www.parks.ca.gov.

16 PISMO COAST VILLAGE RV RESORT

Scenic rating: 7

in Pismo Beach

See map page 856

This big-time RV park gets a lot of use by Highway 1 cruisers. Set near the ocean, its location is a plus. Pismo Beach is well known for its sand dunes and beautiful coastal frontage.

RV sites, facilities: There are 400 sites with full hookups (30 and 50 amps) for RVs up to 40 feet. No tents. Picnic tables, fire rings, and satellite TV are provided. Restrooms have showers. Modem access, Wi-Fi, playgrounds, a heated swimming pool, a coin laundry, a convenience store, firewood, ice, recreation room, propane gas, seasonal recreation programs, a restaurant, RV supplies and repair, bicycle rentals, and a nine-hole miniature golf course are available. Some facilities are wheelchair accessible. Leashed pets are permitted, with restrictions on certain breeds.

Reservations, fees: Reservations are accepted at 888/RV BEACH (888/782-3224). Sites are $34–47 per night. Group discounts available in the off-season. Some credit cards accepted. Open year-round.

Directions: In Pismo Beach, drive on Highway 1/Pacific Coast Highway to the park at 165 South Dolliver Street/Highway 1.

Contact: Pismo Coast Village, 805/773-1811, fax 805/773-1507, www.pismocoastvillage.com.

17 LE SAGE RIVIERA

Scenic rating: 6

near Pismo State Beach

See map page 856

This is a year-round RV park that can serve as headquarters for folks who are interested in visiting several nearby attractions, including neighboring Pismo State Beach and Lopez Lake, 10 miles to the east. The park is on the ocean side of Highway 1, 250 yards from the beach. Note that many sites are filled with seasonal renters.

RV sites, facilities: There are 60 sites with full

CALIFORNIA

hookups (30 and 50 amps) for RVs up to 55 feet; many are pull-through. No tents. Picnic tables are provided. Restrooms have showers. Drinking water and a coin laundry are available. Stores, restaurants, and golf courses are nearby. Some facilities are wheelchair accessible. Leashed pets are permitted with certain restrictions.

Reservations, fees: Reservations are accepted. Sites are $25–55 per night, $3 per night for an additional vehicle. Holiday rates are higher. Winter discount. Some credit cards accepted. Open year-round.

Directions: In Pismo Beach on Highway 1, drive south on Highway 1 for 0.5 mile to the park on the right (west side) to 319 North Highway 1 (in Grover Beach).

Contact: Le Sage Riviera, 805/489-5506, fax 805/489-2103.

18 OCEANO MEMORIAL PARK AND CAMPGROUND

Scenic rating: 7

in Oceano

See map page 856

This San Luis Obispo county park is extremely busy during the summer and busy the rest of the year. The location is a bonus; it's within a quarter mile of the Pismo State Beach entrance, the site of great sand dunes and wide-open ocean frontage. Oceano has a fishing lagoon.

RV sites, facilities: There are 22 sites for tents or RVs up to 40 feet with full hookups. No pull-through sites. Picnic tables and fire grills are provided. Drinking water, restrooms with coin showers and flush toilets, basketball court, horseshoes, an athletic field, and a picnic area are available. A playground, a coin laundry, a grocery store, and propane gas are available nearby. Leashed pets are permitted.

Reservations, fees: Reservations are not accepted. Sites are $23–27 per night for RVs, $18 per night for tents, $9 per night for an additional vehicle, $2 per pet per night. Weekly rates are available. Four-week maximum stay. Open year-round.

Directions: From Pismo Beach, drive south on U.S. 101 to the Pismo Beach/Grand Avenue exit west to Highway 1. Take that exit and turn south on Highway 1 and drive 1.5 miles to Pier Avenue. Turn right on Pier Avenue and drive a short distance to Norswing. Turn left and drive to the end of the street and Mendel Avenue. Turn right and drive to Air Park Drive. Turn right and drive to the park on the right.

Contact: Oceano Memorial Park and Campground, 805/781-5930, fax 805/781-1102, www.slocountyparks.com.

19 PISMO STATE BEACH: OCEANO

Scenic rating: 6

in Pismo State Beach

See map page 856

This is a prized state beach campground, with Pismo Beach and its sand dunes and coastal frontage a centerpiece for the state park system. Its location on the central coast on Highway 1, as well as its beauty and recreational opportunities, makes it extremely popular. It fills to capacity most nights, and reservations are usually a necessity. (For more information on Pismo State Beach, see the listing in this chapter for *Pismo State Beach: North Beach.*)

RV sites, facilities: There are 40 sites for tents or RVs up to 31 feet (no hookups) and with 42 sites with partial hookups for trailers and RVs up to 36 feet. Picnic tables and fire grills are provided. Drinking water and restrooms with flush toilets and coin showers are available. Horseback-riding facilities, a grocery store, a coin laundry, a dump station, restaurants, and gas stations are nearby. Some facilities are wheelchair accessible, including a fishing overlook at Oceano Lagoon. Leashed pets are permitted at the campground and beach.

Reservations, fees: Reservations are accepted at 800/444-PARK (800/444-7275) or www.reserveamerica.com ($7.50 reservation fee). Sites are $20–34 per night, $5 per night for an additional vehicle. Open year-round.

Directions: From Pismo Beach, drive two miles

south on Highway 1 to Pier Avenue. Turn right and drive 0.2 mile to the campground entrance. **Contact:** Pismo State Beach, 805/473-7220, www.parks.ca.gov.

20 OCEANO DUNES STATE VEHICULAR RECREATION AREA

Scenic rating: 6

south of Pismo Beach

See map page 856

This is "National Headquarters" for all-terrain vehicles (ATVs)—you know, those three- and four-wheeled motorcycles that turn otherwise normal people into lunatics. The camps are along 1–3 miles of beach and 1,500 acres of open sand dunes, and since not many make the walk to the campsites, four-wheel drives or ATVs are needed for access. This is the only California state park where vehicles can be driven on the beach. The area covers 3,600 acres, including 5.5 miles of beach open for vehicles and 1,500 acres of sand dunes available for OHVs (off-highway vehicles). They roam wild on the dunes here; that's the law, so don't go planning a quiet stroll. If you don't like 'em, you are strongly advised to go elsewhere. If this is your game, have fun and try to keep from killing yourself. Each fall, the National Sand Drags are held here. More than one million people visit each year. High tides can limit access. A beach towing service for RVs and trailers is available. Surfing, swimming, surf fishing, horseback riding, bird-watching, and nutcase-watching are also popular.

RV sites, facilities: There are 1,000 sites for tents or RVs of any length (no hookups). Chemical and vault toilets are provided. There is no drinking water at the campsites. Horseback-riding facilities, drinking water, a grocery store, a coin laundry, restaurants, gas stations, Wi-Fi, and a dump station are available nearby. Leashed pets are permitted at the campground and beach.

Reservations, fees: Reservations are accepted at 800/444-PARK (800/444-7275) or www

.reserveamerica.com ($7.50 reservation fee). Sites are $10 per night per vehicle. Open year-round.

Directions: Drive on U.S. 101 to Arroyo Grande and take the Grand Avenue exit. Turn left (toward the beach) on Grand Avenue and drive four miles until the road ends at the North Entrance beach camping area. The South Entrance is one mile south. To get there from Highway 1, take Pier Avenue.

Contact: Oceano Dunes, 805/473-7230, fax 805/473-7234, www.parks.ca.gov.

21 FIGUEROA

Scenic rating: 7

in Los Padres National Forest

See map page 857

This is one of the more attractive camps in Los Padres National Forest. It is at 3,500 feet beneath an unusual stand of oak and huge manzanita trees and offers a view of the Santa Ynez Valley. Nearby attractions include the Pino Alto Picnic Area, 2.5 miles away, offering a panoramic view of the adjacent wildlands with a half-mile, wheelchair-accessible nature trail. An exceptional view is also available from the nearby Figueroa fire lookout. Though it requires a circuitous 10-mile ride around Figueroa Mountain to get there, Nira campground to the east provides the best trailhead for the San Rafael Wilderness in this area.

RV sites, facilities: There are 32 sites for tents or RVs up to 25 feet (no hookups). Picnic tables and fire grills are provided. Drinking water and vault toilets are available. Garbage must be packed out. Leashed pets are permitted.

Reservations, fees: Reservations are not accepted and there is no camping fee. An Adventure Pass ($30 annual fee or $5 daily pass) per parked vehicle is required. Open year-round.

Directions: Drive on Highway 154 to Los Olivos and Figueroa Mountain Road. Turn northeast on Figueroa Mountain Road and drive 12.5 miles to the campground.

Contact: Los Padres National Forest, Santa Lucia Ranger District, 805/925-9538, fax 805/961-5781.

CALIFORNIA

22 McGILL

Scenic rating: 6

near Mount Pinos in Los Padres National Forest
See map page 857

The camp is at 7,400 feet, about four miles from the top of nearby Mount Pinos. Although the road is closed to the top of Mount Pinos, there are numerous hiking and biking trails in the area that provide spectacular views. On clear days, there are vantage points to the high Sierra, the San Joaquin Valley, and Antelope Valley.

RV sites, facilities: There are 73 sites for tents or RVs up to 16 feet (no hookups), and two group sites hold 60–80 people. Picnic tables and fire grills are provided. Pit toilets are available. There is no drinking water. Some facilities are wheelchair accessible. Leashed pets are permitted.

Reservations, fees: Reservations are required for group sites at 877/444-6777 ($9 group reservation fee) or www.ReserveUSA.com. Sites are $14 per night, $75 per night for a group site. Open late May–October, weather permitting.

Directions: Drive on I-5 to just south of Lebec to the Frazier Park exit. Take that exit and drive west on Frazier Mountain Road to the town of Lake of the Woods and Cuddy Valley Road. Continue straight on Cuddy Valley Road and drive about six miles to Mount Pinos Highway. Bear left and drive about five miles to the campground on the right.

Contact: Los Padres National Forest, Mount Pinos Ranger District, 661/245-3731, fax 661/245-1526.

23 RIVER PARK

Scenic rating: 4

in Lompoc
See map page 856

Before checking in here you'd better get a lesson in how to pronounce Lompoc. It's "LOM-poke." If you arrive and say, "Hey, it's great to be in LOM-pock," they might just tell ya to get on back to the other cowpokes. The camp is next to the lower Santa Ynez River, which

looks quite a bit different than it does up in Los Padres National Forest. A small fishing lake within the 45-acre park is stocked with trout and catfish. A camp host and resident ranger are on-site. Side-trip possibilities include the nearby La Purisima Mission State Historic Park and Jalama Beach.

RV sites, facilities: There are 33 sites with full hookups for RVs up to 40 feet, a group camping area for tents or RVs, and an open area for up to five tents. No pull-through sites. Picnic tables and barbecues are provided. Restrooms have flush toilets and coin showers. Drinking water, a dump station, a fishing pond, a fitness trail, sand volleyball, horseshoes, group facilities, and a playground are available. Supplies and a coin laundry are nearby. Leashed pets are permitted with certain restrictions.

Reservations, fees: Reservations are not accepted for family sites but are required for groups at 805/875-8036. Sites are $5–15 per night, $10 per night for an additional vehicle, $5 per night for hike-in/bike-in sites, $1 per pet per night. Group fees are $5 per night per tent, $10 per night per RV, with a $25 minimum. Weekly rates available. Some credit cards accepted. Open year-round.

Directions: In Lompoc, drive to the junction of Highway 246 and Sweeney Road at the southwest edge of town and continue to the park at 401 East Highway 246.

Contact: Lompoc Parks and Recreation Department, 805/875-8100, fax 805/736-5195, www.ci.lompoc.ca.us.

24 JALAMA BEACH COUNTY PARK

Scenic rating: 8

near Lompoc on the Pacific Ocean
See map page 856

This is a pretty spot set where Jalama Creek empties into the ocean, about five miles north of Point Conception and just south of Vandenberg Air Force Base. The area is known for its sunsets and beachcombing. The camp is so popular that a waiting list is common in summer. Activities include surfing, sailboarding, and fishing for perch, cabezon, kelp bass, and halibut.

RV sites, facilities: There are 117 sites for tents or RVs up to 40 feet, and two group sites hold 7–15 vehicles each. Some sites have electrical (30 amps) hookups. Picnic tables and fire pits are provided. Restrooms have flush toilets and showers. Drinking water, a dump station, a general store, a snack bar, bait and tackle, a picnic area, firewood, and ice are available. Note that the nearest gas station is 20 miles away. Some facilities are wheelchair accessible. Leashed pets are permitted, but a vaccination certificate is required.

Reservations, fees: Reservations are not accepted for individual sites. Sites are $18–25 per night, $8 per night for an additional vehicle, $144 per night for a group site, $3 per pet per night. Weekly rates available in the off-season. Some credit cards accepted. Open year-round.

Directions: From Lompoc, drive about five miles south on Highway 1. Turn southwest on Jalama Road and drive 14 miles to the park.

Contact: Jalama Beach County Park, 805/736-6316, fax 805/735-8020 or 805/736-3504, www.santabarbaraparks.org.

25 FLYING FLAGS RV RESORT AND CAMPGROUND

Scenic rating: 3

near Solvang

See map page 857

This is one of the few privately operated parks in the area that welcomes tenters as well as RVers. Nearby side trips include the Santa Ynez Mission, just east of Solvang. The town of Solvang is of interest. It was originally a small Danish settlement that has expanded since the 1920s yet managed to keep its cultural heritage intact through the years. The town is exceptionally clean, an example of how to do something right. Wineries and casinos are nearby.

RV sites, facilities: There are 256 sites with full or partial hookups (30 and 50 amps) for RVs of any length and 100 sites for tents. Most sites

are pull-through. Picnic tables are provided. Restrooms have showers. Cable TV, a playground, a heated swimming pool, a spa, a coin laundry, a convenience store, a dump station, ice, a recreation room, modem access, free Wi-Fi, an arcade, five clubhouses, group facilities, and propane gas are available. A nine-hole golf course, boat launch, and boat rentals are nearby. Some facilities are wheelchair accessible. Leashed pets are permitted with certain restrictions.

Reservations, fees: Reservations are accepted by phone or website. Sites are $21–46 per night, $3 per person per night for more than two people, $5 per night for an additional vehicle, $1 per pet per night for more than two dogs. Holiday rates are higher. Monthly rates available. Open year-round. Some credit cards accepted.

Directions: From Santa Barbara, drive 45 miles north on U.S. 101 to Highway 246. Turn west (left) on Highway 246 and drive about a half mile to Avenue of the Flags (a four-way stop). Turn left on Avenue of the Flags and drive about one block to the campground entrance on the left at 180 Avenue of the Flags.

Contact: Flying Flags RV Resort and Campground, 805/688-3716, fax 805/688-9245, www.flyingflags.com.

26 LAKE CACHUMA RECREATION AREA

Scenic rating: 7

near Santa Barbara

See map page 857

Cachuma has become one of the best lakes in America for fishing big bass, and the ideal climate makes it a winner for camping as well. Cachuma is at 750 feet in the foothills northwest of Santa Barbara, a big, beautiful lake covering 3,200 acres. In low-rain years the drawdowns are so significant that you'd hardly recognize the place. The rules are perfect for fishing: Waterskiing, personal watercraft, swimming, canoeing, kayaking, and sailboarding is prohibited;

CALIFORNIA

for fishing boats there is a 5-mph speed limit in the coves and a 40-mph limit elsewhere. After fishing, picnicking and camping come in a distant second and third in popularity.

RV sites, facilities: There are 420 sites for tents or RVs of any length and nine group areas for 8–30 vehicles. Some sites have full or partial hookups (30 amps) and/or are pull-through. Yurts are also available. Picnic tables and fire pits are provided. Drinking water, restrooms with flush toilets and coin showers, and coin laundry are available. A playground, a general store, propane gas, seasonal swimming pool, full-service marina, fishing piers, bait and tackle, a boat ramp, mooring, boat fuel, boat and water-bike rentals, bicycle rentals, nature cruises, miniature golf, a dump station, group facilities, RV storage, gas station, ice, and a snack bar are available nearby. Watercraft under 10 feet and inflatables under 12 feet are prohibited on the lake. Leashed pets are permitted, but they must be kept at least 50 feet from the lake.

Reservations, fees: Reservations are accepted only for groups and yurts at 805/686-5050. Sites are $18–25 per night, $8 per night for an additional vehicle, $144–540 per night for group sites, $3 per pet per night. Some credit cards accepted. Open year-round.

Directions: From Santa Barbara, drive 18 miles north on Highway 154 to the campground entrance on the right.

Contact: Lake Cachuma Recreation Area, Santa Barbara County, 805/686-5054; Cachuma Marina and Boat Rentals, 805/688-4040; Cachuma Boat Tours, 805/686-5050, www.cachuma.com.

27 FREMONT

Scenic rating: 7

near the Santa Ynez River in Los Padres National Forest

See map page 857

As you travel west to east, Fremont is the first in a series of Forest Service campgrounds near the Santa Ynez River. This one is just inside the boundary of Los Padres National Forest at 900 feet in elevation, nine miles east of Lake Cachuma to the west.

RV sites, facilities: There are 15 sites for tents or RVs up to 22 feet (no hookups). Picnic tables and fire grills are provided. Drinking water and flush toilets are available. Groceries are available within two miles, and propane gas is available at Lake Cachuma nine miles away. Some facilities are wheelchair accessible. Leashed pets are permitted.

Reservations, fees: Reservations are accepted at 877/444-6777 ($9 group reservation fee) or www.ReserveUSA.com. Sites are $15 per night, $5 per night for an additional vehicle. Open early April–late October.

Directions: From Santa Barbara, drive northwest on Highway 154 for about 10 miles to Paradise Road/Forest Road 5N18. Turn right on Paradise Road/Forest Road 5N18 and drive 2.5 miles to the campground on the right.

Contact: Los Padres National Forest, Santa Barbara Ranger District, 805/967-3481, fax 805/967-7312; Rocky Mountain Recreation Company, 805/521-1319.

28 LOS PRIETOS

Scenic rating: 7

near the Santa Ynez River in Los Padres National Forest

See map page 857

Los Prietos is across from the Santa Ynez River at an elevation of 1,000 feet, just upstream from nearby Fremont campground to the west. There are several nice hiking trails nearby; the best starts near the Los Prietos Ranger Station, heading south for two miles to Wellhouse Falls (get specific directions and a map at the ranger station). River access is available a quarter mile away at the White Rock day-use area.

RV sites, facilities: There are 37 sites for tents or RVs up to 22 feet (no hookups). Picnic tables and fire grills are provided. Drinking water and flush toilets are available. Some facilities are wheelchair accessible. Leashed pets are permitted.

Reservations, fees: Reservations are accepted at 877/444-6777 ($9 group reservation fee) or www.ReserveUSA.com. Sites are $15 per night, $5 per night for an additional vehicle. Open early April–late October.

Directions: From Santa Barbara, take Highway 154 and drive 10 miles northeast to Paradise Road/Forest Road 5N18. Turn right on Paradise Road/Forest Road 5N18 and drive 3.8 miles to the campground.

Contact: Los Padres National Forest, Santa Barbara Ranger District, 805/967-3481, fax 805/967-7312.

29 UPPER OSO FAMILY AND EQUESTRIAN CAMP

Scenic rating: 7

near the Santa Ynez River in Los Padres National Forest

See map page 857

This is one of the Forest Service campgrounds in the Santa Ynez Recreation Area. It is in Oso Canyon at 1,100 feet, one mile from the Santa Ynez River. This is a prime spot for equestrians, with horse corrals available at adjacent campsites. Note that at high water this campground can become inaccessible. A mile north of camp is the Santa Cruz trailhead for a hike that is routed north up Oso Canyon for a mile, then three miles up to Happy Hollow, and beyond that to a trail camp just west of Little Pine Mountain, elevation 4,508 feet. A trailhead into the San Rafael Wilderness is nearby, and once on the trail, you'll find many primitive sites in the backcountry.

RV sites, facilities: There are 25 sites for tents or RVs up to 22 feet (no hookups). Picnic tables and fire grills are provided. Drinking water and flush toilets are available. Many sites have horse corrals. Some facilities are wheelchair accessible. Leashed pets are permitted.

Reservations, fees: Reservations are accepted at 877/444-6777 ($9 group reservation fee) or www.ReserveUSA.com. Sites are $15 per night, $20 per night for equestrian sites, $5 per night for an additional vehicle. Open year-round, weather permitting.

Directions: From Santa Barbara, take Highway 154 and drive 10 miles northeast to Paradise Road/Forest Road 5N18. Turn right on Paradise Road/Forest Road 5N18 and drive six miles to Upper Oso Road. Turn left on Upper Oso Road and drive one mile to the campground at the end of the road.

Contact: Los Padres National Forest, Santa Barbara Ranger District, 805/967-3481, fax 805/967-7312.

30 PARADISE

Scenic rating: 7

near the Santa Ynez River in Los Padres National Forest

See map page 857

Here is yet another option among the camps along the Santa Ynez River. As you drive east it is the second camp you will come to, just after Fremont. Trout are usually planted upriver of the campground during the spring. One of the best hiking trailheads nearby is at Upper Oso Camp. Lake Cachuma is six miles to the west.

RV sites, facilities: There are 15 sites for tents or RVs up to 22 feet. Picnic tables and fire grills are provided. Drinking water and flush toilets are available. Groceries are available nearby. Some facilities are wheelchair accessible. Leashed pets are permitted.

Reservations, fees: Reservations are accepted at 877/444-6777 ($9 reservation fee) or www.ReserveUSA.com. Sites are $15 per night, $5 per night for an additional vehicle. Open year-round.

Directions: From Santa Barbara, take Highway 154 and drive 10 miles northeast to Paradise Road/Forest Road 5N18. Turn right on Paradise Road/Forest Road 5N18 and drive three miles to the campground on the right.

Contact: Los Padres National Forest, Santa

CALIFORNIA

Barbara Ranger District, 805/967-3481, fax 805/967-7312.

31 WHEELER GORGE

Scenic rating: 7

on Matilija Creek in Los Padres National Forest

See map page 857

This developed Forest Service camp is at 2,000 feet and is one of the more popular spots in the area. The North Fork of the Matilija runs beside the camp and provides some fair trout fishing in the spring and good swimming holes in early summer. Interpretive programs are also available, a nice plus, and a nature trail is adjacent to the campground.

RV sites, facilities: There are 70 sites for tents or RVs up to 35 feet (no hookups), including six double sites. Picnic tables and fire grills are provided. Pit toilets are available. Drinking water is available intermittently; check for current status. Garbage must be packed out. Some facilities are wheelchair accessible. Leashed pets are permitted.

Reservations, fees: Reservations are accepted at 877/444-6777 ($9 reservation fee) or www.ReserveUSA.com. Sites are $20 per night, $5 per night for an additional vehicle. Open year-round.

Directions: From Ojai, drive northwest on Highway 33 for 8.5 miles to the campground entrance on the left.

Contact: Los Padres National Forest, Ojai Ranger District, 805/646-4348, fax 805/646-0484; Rocky Mountain Recreation, 805/640-1977.

32 LAKE CASITAS RECREATION AREA

Scenic rating: 7

north of Ventura

See map page 857

Lake Casitas is known as one of Southern California's world-class fish factories, with more 10-pound bass produced here than anywhere and including the former state record, a bass that weighed 21 pounds, 3 ounces. Other fish species include catfish, crappie, and sunfish. Fishing at night is permitted on selected weekends. The ideal climate in the foothill country gives the fish a nine-month growing season and provides excellent weather for camping. Casitas is north of Ventura at an elevation of 567 feet in the foothills bordering Los Padres National Forest. The lake has 32 miles of shoreline with a huge number of sheltered coves, covering 2,710 acres. The lake is managed primarily for anglers. Waterskiing, personal watercraft, and swimming are not permitted, and only boats between 11 and 26 feet are allowed on the lake. Canoes and kayaks are allowed. The park holds many special events, including the Ojai Wine Festival and the Ojai Renaissance Festival.

RV sites, facilities: There are 400 sites for tents or RVs of any length and a group site for a minimum of 10 vehicles; some sites have full or partial hookups (30 and 50 amps) and/or are pull-through. Trailer rentals are also available. Picnic tables and fire rings are provided. Restrooms have flush toilets and showers. Drinking water, two dump stations, playgrounds, a general store, picnic areas, propane, ice, a snack bar, water playground, bike rentals, and a full-service marina (including boat ramps, boat rentals, slips, fuel, tackle, and bait) are available. Some facilities are wheelchair accessible. Leashed pets are permitted, except on the lake or boats.

Reservations, fees: Reservations are accepted with a $7.50 reservation fee ($65 fee for group sites) at 805/649-1122. Sites are $19–50 per night, $10 per night for an additional vehicle, $2.50 per pet per night. The fee for the group site is $19 per vehicle per night with a two-night, 10-vehicle minimum. Some credit cards accepted. Open year-round.

Directions: From Ventura, drive north on Highway 33 for 10.5 miles to Highway 150/Baldwin Road. Turn left (west) on Highway 150 and drive three miles to Santa Ana Road. Turn left and drive to the lake and campground entrance at 11311 Santa Ana Road.

Contact: Lake Casitas Recreation Area, 805/649-2233, fax 805/649-4661; Lake Casitas

Marina, 805/649-2043; Nature Cruises, 805/682-4726, ext. 654, www.lakecasitas.info.

33 CAMP COMFORT PARK

Scenic rating: 4

on San Antonio Creek
See map page 857

This Ventura County park gets missed by many. It's set in a residential area in the Ojai Valley foothill country at 1,000 feet. San Antonio Creek runs through the park and there are shade trees. Lake Casitas Recreation Area is 10 miles away.

RV sites, facilities: There are 15 sites for RVs up to 34 feet with full hookups (30 and 50 amps); some sites have electrical hookups. Picnic tables and fire pits are provided. Restrooms have flush toilets and showers. Drinking water, a coin laundry, picnic areas, group facilities, a clubhouse, and a playground are available. Supplies are nearby. Leashed pets are permitted in the campground only.

Reservations, fees: Reservations are accepted with a $20 reservation fee. Sites are $37 per night, $1 per pet per night. Open year-round.

Directions: From Ventura, take Highway 33 north to North Creek Road. Turn right and drive 4.5 miles to the park at 11969 North Creek Road.

Contact: Camp Comfort Park, 805/654-3951, http://gsa.countyofventura.org/parks/.

34 FAR WEST RESORT

Scenic rating: 7

on Santa Paula Creek
See map page 857

Far West Resort is near little Santa Paula Creek in the foothill country adjacent to Steckel County Park. For those who want a well-developed park with a lot of amenities, the shoe fits. Note that at one time the two campgrounds, Far West Resort and Steckel County Park, were linked. No more, and for good reason. Far West Resort is a tight ship where the gates close at 10 P.M.

and quiet time assures campers of a good night's sleep. It is a good place to bring a family. Steckel County Park, on the other hand, has a campground with so many problems that I removed it from the book. Steckel is a beautiful place gone bad, crime-ridden and scary for most visitors, with partying, fights, and loud noise. So what do you do? Go next door to Far West where the inmates aren't running the asylum, and the days are fun and nights are peaceful.

RV sites, facilities: There are 72 sites with full or partial hookups (20, 30, and 50 amps) for RVs of any length, and a tent area holds up to 400 people. Picnic tables and fire rings are provided. Restrooms have flush toilets and showers. Drinking water, a coin laundry, modem access, Wi-Fi, a dump station, a clubhouse, a petting zoo, a video room, RV storage, and horseshoes are available. Supplies are nearby. Leashed pets are permitted.

Reservations, fees: Reservations are accepted for RV sites and required for the tent area. Sites are $26.50 per night for RVs, $16 per night for tents, $3 per night for an additional vehicle, $1 per pet per night, $3 per person per night for group sites. Weekly, monthly, and group rates available. Some credit cards accepted. Open year-round for RVs; tent sites closed in winter.

Directions: From Ventura, drive east on Highway 126 for 14 miles to Highway 150. Turn northwest on Highway 150 and drive five miles to the resort entrance on the right.

Contact: Far West Resort, 805/933-3200.

35 GAVIOTA STATE PARK

Scenic rating: 10

near Santa Barbara
See map page 857

This is the granddaddy, the biggest of the three state beaches along U.S. 101 northwest of Santa Barbara. Spectacular and beautiful, the park covers 2,700 acres, providing trails for hiking and horseback riding, as well as a mile-long stretch of stunning beach frontage. Gaviota means "seagull" and was first named by the soldiers of the Portola Expedition in 1769, who learned why you always wear a hat (or a helmet) when they are passing overhead. The ambitious can hike the beach to get more seclusion. Trails to Gaviota Overlook (1.5 miles) and Gaviota Peak (3.2 miles one-way) provide lookouts with drop-dead gorgeous views of the coast and Channel Islands. Want more? There is also a half-mile trail to the hot springs. This park is known for being windy and for shade being hard to find. Unfortunately, a railroad trestle crosses above the day-use parking lot. You know what that means? Of course you do. It means trains run through here day and night, and with them, noise. This is a popular beach for swimming and surf fishing, as well as boat launching and fishing from the pier.

RV sites, facilities: There are 41 sites for tents or RVs up to 30 feet (no hookups) and an area with hike-in/bike-in sites. Picnic tables and fire grills are provided. Restrooms have flush toilets and coin showers. Drinking water, summer lifeguard service, and a boat hoist (two-ton maximum weight) are available. A convenience store (open summer only) is nearby. Some facilities are wheelchair accessible. Leashed pets are permitted at campsites.

Reservations, fees: Reservations are not accepted. Sites are $20–25 per night, $8 per night for an additional vehicle, $3 per person per night for hike-in/bike-in sites. Boat launching is $8 per day. Stays are restricted to a one-week maximum in summer and two-week maximum in winter. Open year-round.

Directions: From Santa Barbara, drive north on U.S. 101 for 30 miles to the Gaviota State Beach exit. Take that exit and turn west and drive a short distance to the park entrance.

Contact: California State Parks, Channel Coast District, 805/968-1033, www.parks.ca.gov.

Capitan, which also have campgrounds. Palm trees planted close to Refugio Creek provide a unique look to this beach and campground. This is a great spot for family campers with bikes, with a paved two-mile bike trail connecting Refugio campground with El Capitan. Fishing is often good in this area of the coast. As with all state beaches and private camps on the Coast Highway, reservations are strongly advised and often a necessity throughout the vacation season.

RV sites, facilities: There are 174 sites for tents or RVs up to 30 feet (no hookups), one hike-in/bike-in site, and three group sites for tents or RVs that can accommodate up to 80 people and 25 vehicles. Picnic tables and fire grills are provided. Restrooms have flush toilets and coin showers. Drinking water, summer lifeguard service, summer convenience store, and food services are available. Some facilities are wheelchair accessible. Leashed pets are permitted at campsites.

Reservations, fees: Reservations are accepted at 800/444-PARK (800/444-7275) or www.reserveamerica.com ($7.50 reservation fee). Sites are $25–35 per night, $8 per night for an additional vehicle, $3 per night per person for hike-in/bike-in sites, $125–180 per night for the group site. Stays are restricted to a one-week maximum in summer and two-week maximum in winter. Open year-round, weather permitting.

Directions: From Santa Barbara, drive northwest on U.S. 101 for 23 miles to the Refugio State Beach exit. Take that exit and turn west (left) and drive a short distance to the campground entrance.

Contact: Refugio State Beach, 805/968-1711; Channel Coast District, 805/968-1033, www.parks.ca.gov.

36 REFUGIO STATE BEACH

Scenic rating: 9

near Santa Barbara

See map page 857 BEST (

Refugio State Beach is the smallest of the three beautiful state beaches along U.S. 101 north of Santa Barbara. The others are Gaviota and El

37 EL CAPITAN STATE BEACH

Scenic rating: 10

near Santa Barbara

See map page 857 BEST (

This is one in a series of beautiful state beaches along the Santa Barbara coast. The water is warm, the swimming good. A stairway descends from the bluffs to the beach, a beautiful setting. El Capitan has a sandy beach, rocky tidepools, and stands of sycamores and oaks along El Capitan Creek. A paved, two-mile bicycle trail is routed to Refugio State Beach, a great family trip. This is a perfect layover for Coast Highway vacationers, and reservations are usually required to assure a spot. Refugio State Beach to the north is another camping option.

RV sites, facilities: There are 130 sites for tents or RVs up to 40 feet, one hike-in/bike-in site, two group sites for tents or RVs that can accommodate 50–125 people each, and three group sites for tents only that can accommodate 50–125 people each. No hookups. Picnic tables and fire grills are provided. Restrooms have flush toilets and coin showers. Drinking water, summer lifeguard service, and a summer convenience store are available. Some facilities are wheelchair accessible. Leashed pets are permitted in the campgrounds but not on the beach.

Reservations, fees: Reservations are accepted at 800/444-PARK (800/444-7275) or www .reserveamerica.com ($7.50 reservation fee). Sites are $25 per night, $8 per night for an additional vehicle, $3 per person per night for hike-in/bike-in sites, $111–280 per night for group sites. Stays are restricted to a one-week maximum in summer and two-week maximum in winter. Open year-round, weather permitting.

Directions: From Santa Barbara, drive north on U.S. 101 for 20 miles to the El Capitan State Beach exit. Turn west (left) and drive a short distance to the campground entrance.

Contact: Refugio State Beach, 805/968-1711; Channel Coast District, 805/968-1033, www.parks.ca.gov.

38 SANTA BARBARA SUNRISE RV PARK

Scenic rating: 3

in Santa Barbara

See map page 857

Motor-home cruisers get a little of two worlds here. For one thing, the park is close to the beach; for another, the downtown shopping area isn't too far away, either. This is the only RV park in Santa Barbara.

RV sites, facilities: There are 33 sites with full hookups (20, 30, and 50 amps) for RVs of any length. Several sites are pull-through. Restrooms have showers. Cable TV, free Wi-Fi, and a coin laundry are available. A grocery store, golf course, tennis courts, and propane gas are nearby. Leashed pets are permitted.

Reservations, fees: Reservations are recommended. Sites are $45 per night, $5 per person per night for more than two people, $5 per night for an additional vehicle, $5 per pet per night. Some credit cards accepted. Open year-round.

Directions: In Santa Barbara on U.S. 101 northbound, drive to the Salinas Street exit. Take that exit and drive to the park (well signed) at 516 South Salinas Street, near the highway exit.

In Santa Barbara on U.S. 101 southbound, drive to the Milpas Street exit. Take that exit and turn left on Milpas Street. Drive under the freeway to Carpinteria Street. Turn right and drive 0.5 mile to Salinas Street. Turn right and drive 0.5 mile to the park on the right.

Contact: Santa Barbara Sunrise RV Park, 805/966-9954 or 800/345-5018, fax 805/966-7950.

39 CARPINTERIA STATE BEACH

Scenic rating: 8

near Santa Barbara

See map page 857

First, plan on reservations, and then, plan on plenty of neighbors. This state beach is one pretty spot, and a lot of folks cruising up the coast like the idea of taking off their boots here for awhile. This is an urban park; that is, it is within walking distance of downtown, restaurants, and shopping. You can love it or hate it, but this camp is almost always full. It features one mile of beach. Harbor seals can be seen December–May, along with an occasional passing gray whale. Tidepools here are protected and contain starfish, sea anemones, crabs, snails, octopus, and sea urchins. In the summer, the visitors center features a living tidepool exhibit. Other state beaches to the nearby north are El Capitan State Beach and Refugio State Beach, both with campgrounds.

RV sites, facilities: There are 79 sites with full or partial hookups (30 amps) for RVs up to 30 feet, 29 sites with partial hookups for RVs up to 35 feet, 38 sites for RVs up to 21 feet (no hookups), 65 sites for tents, one hike-in/bike-in site, and seven group sites that can accommodate 25 to 65 people each. Picnic tables and fire rings are provided. Drinking water, restrooms with flush toilets and coin showers, and a picnic area are available. A convenience store, a coin laundry, restaurants, and propane gas are nearby in the town of Carpinteria. Some facilities are wheelchair accessible. Leashed pets are permitted, except on the beach.

Reservations, fees: Reservations are accepted at 800/444-PARK (800/444-7275) or www .reserveamerica.com ($7.50 reservation fee). Sites are $25–44 per night, $8 per night for an additional vehicle, $5 per person per night for hike-in/bike-in site, $90–224 per night for group sites. Open year-round, except for group sites.

Directions: From Santa Barbara, drive south on U.S. 101 for 12 miles to Carpinteria and the Casitas Pass Road exit. Take that exit and turn right on Casitas Pass Road and drive about a block to Carpinteria Avenue. Turn right and drive a short distance to Palm Avenue. Turn left and drive about six blocks to the campground at the end of Palm Avenue.

Contact: Carpinteria State Beach, 805/684-2811; Channel Coast District, 805/968-1033, www.parks.ca.gov.

40 HOBSON COUNTY PARK

Scenic rating: 6

on the Pacific Ocean north of Ventura
See map page 857

This county park is at the end of Rincon Parkway, kind of like a crowded cul-de-sac, with easy access to the beach and many side-

trip possibilities. There is a great reef here for exploring at low tides. Emma Wood State Beach, San Buenaventura State Beach, and McGrath State Beach are all within 11 miles of the park.

RV sites, facilities: There are 31 sites for tents or RVs up to 34 feet; some sites have full hookups, including cable TV. Picnic tables and fire pits are provided. Restrooms have flush toilets and coin showers. Drinking water and a snack bar are available. Leashed pets are permitted, but not on the beach.

Reservations, fees: Reservations are not accepted. Sites are $27–40 per night, $1 per pet per night. Open year-round.

Directions: From Ventura, drive northwest on U.S. 101 for three miles to the State Beaches exit. Take that exit and turn north on West Pacific Highway and drive five miles to the campground on the left.

Contact: Ventura County Parks Department, 805/654-3951; http://gsa.countyofventura .org/parks/.

41 FARIA COUNTY PARK

Scenic rating: 7

on the Pacific Ocean north of Ventura
See map page 857

This county park provides a possible base of operations for beach adventures, including surf fishing. It is along the ocean, with Emma Wood State Beach, San Buenaventura State Beach, and McGrath State Beach all within 10 miles of the park.

RV sites, facilities: There are 42 sites for tents or RVs up to 34 feet; some sites have full hookups (30 amps), including cable TV. Picnic tables and fire pits are provided. Restrooms have flush toilets and coin showers. Drinking water and a snack bar are available. Leashed pets are permitted.

Reservations, fees: Reservations are not accepted. Sites are $27–40 per night, $1 per pet per night. Open year-round.

Directions: From Ventura, drive north on

U.S. 101 for three miles to the State Beaches exit. Take that exit, turn north on West Pacific Highway, and drive four miles to the campground.

Contact: Ventura County Parks Department, 805/654-3951; http://gsa.countyofventura.org/parks/.

42 RINCON PARKWAY

Scenic rating: 5

on the Pacific Ocean north of Ventura
See map page 857

This is basically an RV park near the ocean, where the sites are parking end-to-end along old Highway 1. It is not quiet. Passing trains across the highway vie for noise honors with the surf. Emma Wood State Beach, San Buenaventura State Beach, and McGrath State Beach are all within 10 miles. Two activities you can do here are surf fish and watch great sunsets.

RV sites, facilities: There are 127 sites with no hookups for RVs up to 34 feet. No tents. Supplies are available nearby. Leashed pets are allowed, but not on the beach.

Reservations, fees: Reservations are not accepted. Sites are $21 per night per vehicle. Open year-round.

Directions: From Ventura, drive northwest on U.S. 101 for three miles to the State Beaches exit. Take that exit, turn north on West Pacific Highway, and drive 4.5 miles to the campground on the left.

Contact: Ventura County Parks Department, 805/654-3951, http://gsa.countyofventura.org/parks/.

43 EMMA WOOD STATE BEACH

Scenic rating: 8

on the Pacific Ocean north of Ventura
See map page 857

This is more of a parking lot than a campground with individual sites. And oh, what a place to camp: It is along the ocean, a pretty spot with tidepools full of all kinds of little marine critters waiting to be discovered. It is also just a short drive from the town of Ventura and the Mission San Buenaventura. One downer, a big one for many: noise from passing trains. Another downer: no toilets at night, so you must have a self-contained vehicle. The gate closes at 10 P.M. and reopens at 6 A.M.

RV sites, facilities: There are 90 sites with no hookups for RVs up to 40 feet. No tents. Chemical toilets are available for day use only. No drinking water is available. Supplies and a coin laundry are three miles away. Leashed pets are permitted, but not on the beach.

Reservations, fees: Reservations are not accepted. Sites are $20 per night, $8 per night for an additional vehicle. Open year-round, weather and tides permitting.

Directions: From Ventura drive north on U.S. 101 for three miles to the State Beaches exit. Take that exit, drive under the freeway, and continue less than a mile to the park entrance on the left.

Contact: Emma Wood State Beach, 805/648-4807; Ventura Sector, 805/648-4127; Channel Coast District, 805/968-1033, www.parks.ca.gov.

44 McGRATH STATE BEACH

Scenic rating: 9

on the Pacific Ocean south of Ventura
See map page 857

This is a pretty spot just south of Ventura Harbor. Campsites are about 400 yards from the beach. This park features two miles of beach frontage, as well as lush riverbanks and sand dunes along the ocean shore. That gives rise to some of the best bird-watching in California. The north tip of the park borders the Santa Clara River Estuary Natural Preserve, where the McGrath State Beach Nature Trail provides an easy walk (wheelchair-accessible) along the Santa Clara River as it feeds into the

CALIFORNIA

estuary and then into the ocean. Rangers caution all considering swimming here to beware of strong currents and rip tides; they can be deadly. Note that the park and campground can close on short notice during winter because of river floodings; check status before planning a trip here. Ventura Harbor and the Channel Islands National Park Visitor Center are nearby side trips.

RV sites, facilities: There are 174 sites for tents or RVs up to 30 feet (no hookups)—29 of the sites can be used as group sites—and a hike-in/bike-in site. Picnic tables and fire grills are provided. Restrooms have flush toilets and coin showers. Drinking water and a dump station are available. A lifeguard service is provided in summer. Supplies and a coin laundry are nearby. Some facilities are wheelchair accessible. Leashed pets are permitted in campsites only.

Reservations, fees: Reservations are accepted for individual sites at 800/444-PARK (800/444-7275) or www.reserveamerica.com ($7.50 reservation fee). Sites are $20–25 per night, $8 per night for an additional vehicle, $5 per person per night for the hike-in/bike-in site. For group prices and reservations, phone 805/648-3918. Open year-round, weather and river conditions permitting.

Directions: Drive on U.S. 101 to south of Ventura and the Seaward exit. Take that exit and drive to the stoplight and Harbor Boulevard. Turn west on Harbor Boulevard and drive four miles to the park (signed).

Contact: McGrath State Beach, 805/654-4744; Ventura Sector, 805/648-4127; Channel Coast District, 805/968-1033, www.parks.ca.gov.

45 POINT MUGU STATE PARK: THORNHILL BROOME

Scenic rating: 7

in Point Mugu State Park

See map page 857

Point Mugu State Park is known for its rocky bluffs, sandy beaches, rugged hills, and up-

lands. There are two major river canyons and wide grassy valleys sprinkled with sycamores, oaks, and a few native walnut trees. Of the campgrounds at Point Mugu, Thornehill Broome Campground is more attractive than Big Sycamore (see listing in this chapter for *Point Mugu State Park: Big Sycamore Canyon*) for many visitors because it is on the ocean side of the highway (Big Sycamore is on the north side of the highway). The beachfront is pretty and you can always just lie there in the sun and pretend you're a beached whale, but the park's expanse on the east side of the highway in the Santa Monica Mountains provides more recreation options. That includes two stellar hikes, the 9.5-mile Big Sycamore Canyon Loop and the seven-mile La Jolla Valley Loop. In all, the park covers 14,980 acres, far more than the obvious strip of beachfront. The park has more than 70 miles of hiking trails and five miles of ocean shoreline. Swimming, body surfing, and surf fishing are available on the beach.

RV sites, facilities: There are 65 primitive sites with no hookups for RVs up to 31 feet or tents. Picnic tables and fire rings are provided. Drinking water and chemical toilets are available. Supplies can be obtained nearby. Note that nearby Big Sycamore has a restroom with flush toilets and coin-operated showers, an RV dump station, and a nature center. Drinking water, flush toilets, and showers are available at La Jolla Canyon Group Camp. Some facilities are wheelchair accessible. Leashed pets are permitted.

Reservations, fees: Reservations are accepted at 800/444-PARK (800/444-7275) or online at www.reserveamerica.com ($7.50 reservation fee). Sites are $16 per night, $10 per night for an additional vehicle. Open year-round, but subject to closure during inclement weather and the fire season.

Directions: From Oxnard, drive 15 miles south on Highway 1 to the camp entrance on the right.

Contact: Thornhill Broome State Beach, 818/880-0350, fax 818/880-6165.

46 POINT MUGU STATE PARK: BIG SYCAMORE CANYON

Scenic rating: 6

in Point Mugu State Park

See map page 857

While this camp is across the highway from the ocean, it is also part of Point Mugu State Park, which covers 14,980 acres. That gives you plenty of options. One of the best is taking the Big Sycamore Canyon Loop, a long hiking route with great views that starts right at the camp. In all, it's a 9.5-mile loop that climbs to a ridge top and offers beautiful views of nearby canyons and long-distance vistas of the coast. Note: The front gate closes at 10 P.M. and reopens at 7 A.M.

RV sites, facilities: There are 55 sites for tents or RVs up to 31 feet (no hookups) and one hike-in/bike-in site. Picnic tables and fire grills are provided. Restrooms have flush toilets and coin showers. Drinking water and a dump station are available. A weekend nature center is within walking distance. Supplies can be obtained nearby. Some facilities are wheelchair accessible. Leashed pets are permitted at campsites and on the beach but not on trails.

Reservations, fees: Reservations are accepted at 800/444-PARK (800/444-7275) or www.reserveamerica.com ($7.50 reservation fee). Sites are $25 per night, $10 per night for an additional vehicle, $3 per person per night for the hike-in/bike-in site. Open year-round.

Directions: From Oxnard, drive south on Highway 1 for 16 miles to the camp on the left.

Contact: California State Parks, Angeles District, 818/880-0350, www.parks.ca.gov.

CALIFORNIA

LOS ANGELES AND VICINITY

The stereotypical image of the region you see on

TV – the blonde in a convertible, the surfer with the movie-star jaw-line – is so flawed as to be ridiculous, pathetic, and laughable. And while there is some classic beach, lifeguards and all, the surrounding area for recreation spans some of the best opportunities in California.

In fact, there are approximately 60 campgrounds for RVs in this region, more than in many other of California's 16 geographic regions. It stuns some to learn that Los Angeles and its nearby forests provide this many camping opportunities, even for RVers.

But for those of us who know this landscape, it does not come as a surprise. The area has a tremendous range of national forests, canyons, mountains, lakes, coast, and islands. In fact, there are so many hidden gems that it is like a giant scavenger hunt for those who love the outdoors.

While most people first think of the coast, the highways, and the beaches when envisioning this region, it is the opportunities for camping and hiking in the national forests that surprise most. Angeles National Forest and San Bernardino National Forest provide more than one million acres and a thousand miles of trails.

The mountaintop views are incredible, probably best from Mount Baldy (10,064 feet), Mount San Jacinto (10,834 feet), and Mount San Gorgonio (11,490 feet). Great campgrounds nestle on the flanks of all three of these destinations. It is only a start.

Even more famous is the region's top recreation lake, Big Bear, for fishing and boating. Though the region is known for its high population, and Big Bear is no exception on weekends, the relatively few people on weekdays, especially Monday to Thursday mornings, can be stunning to discover. Other top lakes include Arrowhead, Castaic, and several smaller reservoirs.

Yet this is not even the best of it. Look over the opportunities and take your pick. People? What people?

Includes:

- Angeles National Forest
- Big Bear Lake
- Bolsa Chica State Beach
- Cleveland National Forest
- Disneyland
- Green Valley Lake
- Huntington Beach
- Jackson Lake
- Jenks Lake
- Lake Arrowhead
- Lake Elsinore
- Lake Gregory
- Lake Hemet
- Lake Perris
- Lake Piru
- Lake Skinner
- Leo Carrillo State Park
- Malibu Creek State Park
- Manhattan Beach
- Mount Baldy
- Mount San Jacinto State Park
- Prado Park Lake
- Puddingstone Lake
- San Bernardino National Forest
- San Gabriel Wilderness
- San Gorgonio Wilderness
- Santa Ana Mountains
- Santa Ana River
- Silverwood Lake

CALIFORNIA

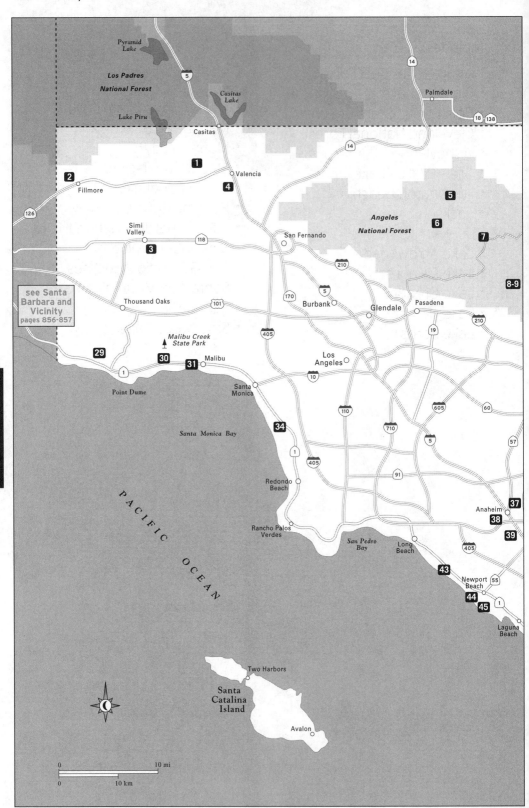

CALIFORNIA

Pyramid Lake

Los Padres National Forest

Casitas Lake

Lake Piru

14

Palmdale

18 138

Casitas

14

1

2
Fillmore

Valencia

4

126

5

Angeles National Forest

6

7

Simi Valley

118

San Fernando

3

210

8-9

see Santa Barbara and Vicinity pages 856-857

Thousand Oaks

101

170

5

Burbank

Glendale

Pasadena

210

19

Malibu Creek State Park

29

30

31 Malibu

Point Dume

405

Los Angeles

10

Santa Monica

34

Santa Monica Bay

1

110

710

605

60

405

5

57

91

Redondo Beach

Anaheim

37

38

39

Rancho Palos Verdes

San Pedro Bay

Long Beach

405

43

PACIFIC OCEAN

Newport Beach

55

44

45

1

Laguna Beach

Two Harbors

Santa Catalina Island

Avalon

0   10 mi

0   10 km

LOS ANGELES AND VICINITY

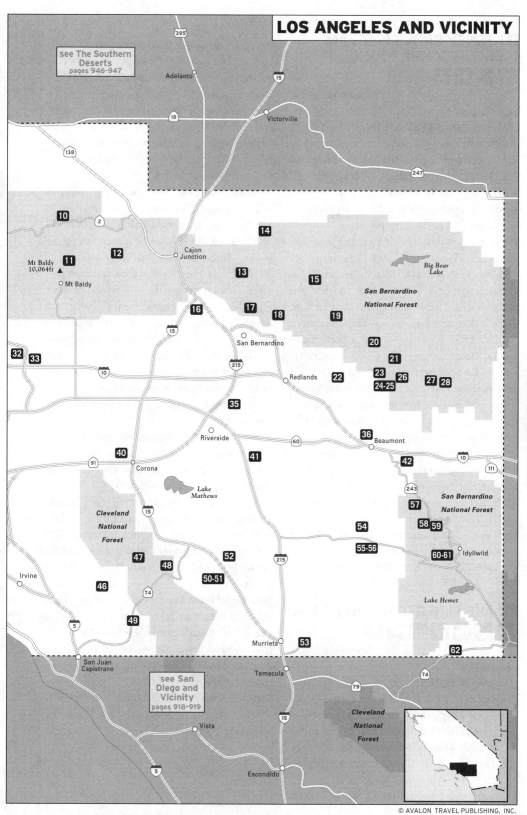

see The Southern
Deserts
pages 946-947

Adelanto

Victorville

395

15

18

247

138

10

2

12

Cajon
Junction

14

Mt Baldy
10,064ft 11

Mt Baldy

13

15

Big Bear
Lake

San Bernardino

National Forest

16

15

17

18

19

San Bernardino

20

32

33

215

21

10

Redlands

22

23

24-25 26

27 28

35

Riverside

36 Beaumont

40

60

41

42

91

Corona

111

10

Lake
Mathews

243

57

Cleveland

National

Forest

54

58 59

47

55-56

60-61 Idyllwild

Irvine

48

52

50-51

Lake Hemet

46

74

215

49

5

Murrieta 53

62

San Juan
Capistrano

see San
Diego and
Vicinity
pages 918-919

Temecula

79

74

Vista

15

Cleveland

National

Forest

5

Escondido

CALIFORNIA

1 KENNEY GROVE PARK AND GROUP CAMPGROUND

Scenic rating: 4

near Fillmore

See map page 884

A lot of folks miss this spot, a park tucked away among orchards, coastal live oaks, and eucalyptus groves, with several group campgrounds. This is a privately leased facility on Ventura County property. It's just far enough off the highway to allow for some privacy.

RV sites, facilities: This is a group camp with 33 sites with partial hookups (30 amps) for RVs up to 40 feet and 18 sites for tents. No pull-through sites. Picnic tables and fire pits are provided. Drinking water, restrooms with flush toilets and showers, an amphitheater, a softball field, horseshoes, and a playground are available. Supplies and a coin laundry are nearby. Leashed pets are permitted.

Reservations, fees: Reservations are required, and a minimum of five sites must be reserved. Sites are $17 per night for tents, $20 per night for RVs, $1 per pet per night. Open year-round.

Directions: From Ventura, drive east on Highway 126 for 22 miles to Old Telegraph Road (before the town of Fillmore). Turn left on Old Telegraph Road and drive 0.6 mile to 7th Street. Turn left (northwest) and drive 0.3 mile to North Oak Avenue. Turn right and drive 0.5 mile to the park on the left.

Contact: Kenney Grove, tel./fax 805/524-0750.

2 LAKE PIRU RECREATION AREA

Scenic rating: 7

on Lake Piru

See map page 884

Things can get crazy at Lake Piru, but it's usually a happy crazy, not an insane crazy. Lake Piru is shaped like a teardrop and covers 1,200 acres when full. Elevation is 1,055 feet. This is a lake set up for waterskiing, with lots of fast boats. All others be forewarned: The rules prohibit boats under 12 feet or over 26 feet, as well as personal watercraft. Canoes and kayaks over eight feet are permitted in a special-use area. Bass and trout fishing can be quite good in the spring before the waterskiers take over. From Memorial Day weekend–Labor Day weekend, there is a designated swimming area, safe from the boats. The tent sites here consist of roughly 40-by-40-foot areas amid trees.

RV sites, facilities: There are 235 sites for tents or RVs up to 40 feet with partial hookups (30 and 50 amps), seven sites with full hookups (30 and 50 amps) for RVs, and one group camp (no hookups) for tents or RVs that can accommodate 4–12 vehicles. Fire pits and picnic tables are provided. Restrooms have flush toilets and showers. Drinking water, a dump station, a convenience store, a coin laundry, a picnic area, boat storage, propane, a fish-cleaning station, seasonal snack bar, ice, full-service marina, a boat ramp, temporary mooring, boat rentals, and bait and tackle are available. Some facilities are wheelchair accessible. Leashed pets are permitted, but not in the lake.

Reservations, fees: Reservations are accepted ($7 reservation fee) for individual sites and required for group sites ($20 reservation fee and $50 key charge) at 805/521-1572. Sites are $19–42 per night, $2 per pet per night. Group sites are $96 minimum per night for up to four vehicles (with a two-night minimum), $24 per night per additional vehicle. Holiday rates are higher. Some credit cards accepted. Open year-round.

Directions: From Ventura, drive east on Highway 126 for about 30 miles to the Lake Piru Recreation Area/Piru Canyon Road exit. Take that exit and drive northeast on Piru Canyon Road for about six miles to the campground at the end of the road.

Contact: Lake Piru Recreation Area, 805/521-1500; Lake Piru Marina, 805/521-1231, www.lake-piru.org.

3 OAK PARK

Scenic rating: 3

in Simi Valley near Moorpark

See map page 884

One of the frustrations of trying to find a camp for the night is that so many state and national park campgrounds are full from reservations, especially at the state beaches. The county parks often provide a safety valve, and Oak Park certainly applies. But not always, and that's the catch. This is an oft-overlooked county park set in the foothill country of Simi Valley. The park has many trails offering good hiking possibilities. The camp is somewhat secluded, more so than many expect. The catch? Sometimes the entire campground is rented to a single group. Note: Gates close at dusk and reopen at 8 A.M.

RV sites, facilities: There are 16 sites with partial hookups (20 and 30 amps) for RVs, a group area for up to 13 RVs, and a large tent area with no hookups that can accommodate up to 140 people. Picnic tables and fire pits are provided. Restrooms have flush toilets. Drinking water, group facilities, a clubhouse, and a dump station are available. Horseshoe pits, a playground, and basketball and volleyball courts are available nearby. Supplies and a coin laundry are within two miles. Leashed pets are permitted.

Reservations, fees: Reservations are accepted. Sites are $10 per night for tents, $12–25 per night for RVs, $5 per person per night for more than two people, $17–20 per night per vehicle for the group RV site, $1 per pet per night. Open year-round, except Christmas Day.

Directions: From Ventura, drive south on U.S. 101 to Highway 23. Turn north on Highway 23 (which becomes Highway 123 eastbound) and drive about three miles to the Collins Street exit. Continue straight through the intersection (it becomes Old Los Angeles Avenue) and drive 1.5 miles to the park entrance on the left.

Contact: Oak Park, 805/527-6886, www.ventura.org/gsa/parks.

4 VALENCIA TRAVEL VILLAGE

Scenic rating: 6

in Valencia

See map page 884

This huge RV park is in the scenic San Fernando foothills, just five minutes from Six Flags Magic Mountain. Lake Piru and Lake Castaic are only 15 minutes away. The camp was built on a 65-acre horse ranch.

RV sites, facilities: There are 379 sites with full or partial hookups (30 and 50 amps) for RVs; most are pull-through. No tents. Picnic tables and fire pits (some sites) are provided. A market, two heated swimming pools, a spa, a lounge, a video and games arcade, a playground, shuffleboard, horseshoes, volleyball courts, a coin laundry, Wi-Fi, modem access, propane, and a dump station are available. Some facilities are wheelchair accessible. Leashed pets are permitted.

Reservations, fees: Reservations are recommended at 888/LUV-TORV (888/588-8678). Sites are $49 per night, $2 per person per night for more than two people. Weekly and monthly rates are available. Some credit cards accepted. Open year-round.

Directions: Drive on I-5 to Santa Clarita and Highway 126 westbound/Henry Mayo Road. Take that exit and drive west on Highway 126 for one mile to the camp on the left.

Contact: Valencia Travel Village, 661/257-3333.

5 CHILAO

Scenic rating: 6

near the San Gabriel Wilderness in Angeles National Forest

See map page 884

This popular trailhead camp gets a lot of use. And it's easy to see why, with the Chilao Visitor Center nearby (have any questions?—here's where you ask them) and a national recreation trail running right by the camp. Access to the Pacific Crest Trail is three miles north at Three Points (five miles if hiking the Silver Moccasin Trail), and parking is available there. An Adventure Pass is required to park at all trailheads. The elevation is 5,300 feet. Note: There is frequent bear activity, so use precautions.

RV sites, facilities: There are 84 sites for tents or RVs up to 28 feet (no hookups), with one site for RVs up to 36 feet. Picnic tables and fire rings are provided. Drinking water and vault toilets are available. Some facilities are wheelchair accessible. Leashed pets are permitted.

Reservations, fees: Reservations are not accepted. Sites are $12 per night. Open April–mid-November, weather permitting.

Directions: From Pasadena, drive north on I-210 for four miles to the exit for Highway 2/Angeles Crest Highway. Take that exit and drive northeast on Highway 2 for 27 miles to the campground entrance road (signed) on the left.

Contact: Angeles National Forest, Los Angeles River Ranger District, 818/899-1900, fax 818/896-6727; Chilao Visitor Center, 626/796-5541.

6 MONTE CRISTO

🥾 🎣 🐕 ♿ 🚐 ⛺

Scenic rating: 7

on Mill Creek in Angeles National Forest
See map page 884

This is a Forest Service camp on Mill Creek at 3,600 feet, just west of Iron Mountain. The camp is situated under sycamore trees, which provide great color in the fall. In most years Mill Creek flows six months out of the year.

RV sites, facilities: There are 19 sites for tents or RVs up to 30 feet (no hookups). Picnic tables and fire grills are provided. Vault toilets are available. There is no drinking water. Some facilities are wheelchair accessible. Leashed pets are permitted.

Reservations, fees: Reservations are not accepted. Sites are $8 per night. Open year-round.

Directions: From Pasadena, drive north on I-210 for four miles to the exit for Highway 2/Angeles Crest Highway. Take that exit and

drive northeast on Highway 2 for nine miles to Angeles Forest Highway/County Road N3. Turn left on Angeles Forest Highway and drive about 10 miles to the campground on the right.

Contact: Angeles National Forest, Los Angeles River Ranger District, 818/899-1900, fax 818/896-6727.

7 BUCKHORN

🥾 🐕 🚐 ⛺

Scenic rating: 9

near Snowcrest Ridge in Angeles National Forest
See map page 884

This is a prime jump-off spot for backpackers in Angeles National Forest. The camp is at 6,300 feet among huge pine and cedar trees, along a small creek near Mount Waterman (8,038 feet). A great day hike begins here, a tromp down to Cooper Canyon and the PCT; hikers will be rewarded by beautiful Cooper Falls on this three-hour round-trip. Want a weekend trip? Got it: The Burkhart National Recreational Trail descends into Caruthers Canyon, where hikers can access the High Desert National Recreational Trail and head east to Devil's Punchbowl County Park to Vincent's Gap and the Pacific Crest Trail.

RV sites, facilities: There are 38 sites for tents or RVs up to 18 feet (no hookups). Picnic tables and fire pits are provided. Drinking water and vault toilets are available. Leashed pets are permitted.

Reservations, fees: Reservations are not accepted. Sites are $12 per night. Open April–mid-November, weather permitting.

Directions: From Pasadena, drive north on I-210 for four miles to the exit for Highway 2/Angeles Crest Highway. Take that exit and drive northeast on Highway 2 for 35 miles to the signed campground entrance.

Contact: Angeles National Forest, Los Angeles River Ranger District, 818/899-1900, fax 818/896-6727.

CALIFORNIA

8 MOUNTAIN OAK

Scenic rating: 4

near Jackson Lake in Angeles National Forest
See map page 884

This is one of four camps within a mile of little Jackson Lake on Big Pines Highway. The others are Lake, Peavine, and Apple Tree. This camp is about a quarter mile northwest of the lake. The elevation is 6,200 feet.

RV sites, facilities: There are 17 sites for tents or RVs up to 18 feet (no hookups). Picnic tables and fire pits are provided. Vault and flush toilets are available. There is no drinking water. Groceries and propane gas are nearby. Leashed pets are permitted.

Reservations, fees: Reservations are accepted at 877/444-6777 or www.ReserveUSA.com ($9 reservation fee). Sites are $12 per night. Open May–November, weather permitting.

Directions: Drive on I-15 to Cajon Junction (north of San Bernardino) and the exit for Highway 138 west. Take that exit and drive west on Highway 138 to Angeles Crest Highway/Highway 2. Turn west on Angeles Crest Highway and drive five miles to Wrightwood, and then continue for three miles to Big Pines and Big Pines Highway/County Road N4. Bear right on Big Pines Highway and drive three miles to the campground.

Contact: Angeles National Forest, Santa Clara/Mojave Rivers Ranger District, 661/296-9710, fax 661/296-5847.

9 LAKE

Scenic rating: 8

on Jackson Lake in Angeles National Forest
See map page 884

This is a pretty setting on the southeast shore of little Jackson Lake. Of the four camps within a mile, this is the only one right beside the lake. The elevation is 6,100 feet.

RV sites, facilities: There are eight sites for tents or RVs up to 18 feet (no hookups). Picnic tables and fire pits are provided. Vault toilets

are available. There is no drinking water. Some facilities are wheelchair accessible. Leashed pets are permitted.

Reservations, fees: Reservations are accepted at 877/444-6777 or www.ReserveUSA.com ($9 reservation fee). Sites are $12 per night. Open May–November, weather permitting.

Directions: Drive on I-15 to Cajon Junction (north of San Bernardino) and the exit for Highway 138 west. Take that exit and drive west on Highway 138 to Angeles Crest Highway/Highway 2. Turn west on Angeles Crest Highway and drive five miles to Wrightwood, and then continue for three miles to Big Pines and Big Pines Highway/County Road N4. Bear right on Big Pines Highway and drive 2.5 miles to the campground.

Contact: Angeles National Forest, Santa Clara/Mojave Rivers Ranger District, 661/296-9710, fax 661/296-5847.

10 TABLE MOUNTAIN

Scenic rating: 6

in Angeles National Forest
See map page 885

This is a family campground that accommodates both tents and RVs. The road leading in is a paved two-lane county road, easily accessible by any vehicle. The nearby Big Pines Visitor Information Center, one mile to the south, can provide maps and information on road conditions. The camp elevation is 7,200 feet. A rough road for four-wheel-drive rigs leads north out of camp along the Table Mountain Ridge.

RV sites, facilities: There are 115 sites for tents or RVs up to 32 feet (no hookups). Picnic tables and fire pits are provided. Drinking water, vault toilets, and a reservable amphitheater are available. Leashed pets are permitted.

Reservations, fees: Reservations are accepted at 877/444-6777 or www.ReserveUSA.com ($9 reservation fee). Sites are $13 per night. Open May–November, weather permitting.

Directions: Drive on I-15 to Cajon Junction (north of San Bernardino) and the exit for Highway

CALIFORNIA

138 west. Take that exit and drive west on Highway 138 to Angeles Crest Highway/Highway 2. Turn west on Angeles Crest Highway and drive five miles to Wrightwood, then continue for three miles to Big Pines and Table Mountain Road. Turn right on Table Mountain Road and drive one mile to the campground.

Contact: Angeles National Forest, Santa Clara/Mojave Rivers Ranger District, 661/296-9710, fax 661/296-5847; Big Pines Visitor Center, 760/249-3504.

11 MANKER FLATS

Scenic rating: 7

near Mount Baldy in Angeles National Forest
See map page 885

This camp is best known for its proximity to Mount Baldy and the nearby trailhead to reach San Antonio Falls. The trail to San Antonio Falls starts at an elevation of 6,160 feet, 0.3 mile up the road on the left. From here, it's a 1.5-mile saunter on a ski park maintenance road to the waterfall, a pretty 80-footer. The wild and ambitious can continue six more miles and climb to the top of Mount Baldy (10,064 feet) for breathtaking 360-degree views. Making this all-day butt-kicker is like a baptism for Southern California hikers.

RV sites, facilities: There are 21 sites for tents or RVs up to 16 feet (no hookups). Picnic tables and fire grills are provided. Drinking water and flush toilets are available. Leashed pets are permitted. There is no drinking water in dry years.

Reservations, fees: Reservations are not accepted. Sites are $12 per night, $5 per night for an additional vehicle. Open May–September.

Directions: Drive on I-10 to Ontario and the exit for Highway 83. Take that exit and drive north on Highway 83 to Mount Baldy Road. Continue north on Mount Baldy Road for nine miles to the campground.

Contact: Angeles National Forest, San Gabriel River Ranger District, 626/335-1251, fax 626/914-3790.

12 APPLE WHITE

Scenic rating: 5

near Lytle Creek in San Bernardino National Forest
See map page 885

Nothing like a little insider's know-how, especially at this camp, set at 3,300 feet near Lytle Creek. You can reach the Middle Fork of Lytle Creek by driving north from Fontana via Serra Avenue to the Lytle Creek area. To get to the stretch of water that is stocked with trout by the Department of Fish and Game, turn west on Middle Fork Road, which is 1.5 miles before the campground at Apple White. The first mile upstream is stocked repeatedly every other week in spring and early summer.

RV sites, facilities: There are 44 sites for tents or RVs up to 30 feet (no hookups). Picnic tables and fire grills are provided. Restrooms have flush toilets, and drinking water is available. A store is nearby. Some facilities are wheelchair accessible. Leashed pets are permitted.

Reservations, fees: Reservations are not accepted. Sites are $10 per night, double sites are $15 per night, $3 per night for an additional vehicle. Open year-round.

Directions: Drive to Ontario and the junction of I-10 and I-15. Take I-15 north and drive 11 miles to the Sierra Avenue exit. Take that exit and turn left, go under the freeway, and continue north (into the national forest) for about nine miles to the campground on the right.

Contact: San Bernardino National Forest, Front Country Ranger District, Lytle Creek Ranger Station, 909/382-2850, fax 909/887-8197.

13 SILVERWOOD LAKE STATE RECREATION AREA: MESA

Scenic rating: 6

on Silverwood Lake
See map page 885

The Old Fire did extensive damage to this park in 2003. The prettiest part of the recreation area was destroyed by fire, along with damage to a section of this campground. Sites

1–13 were burned and there is no shade, so bring your own. This state park campground is on the west side of Silverwood Lake at 3,355 feet in elevation, bordered by San Bernardino National Forest to the south and high desert to the north. The hot weather and proximity to San Bernardino make it a winner with boaters, who have 1,000 surface acres of water and 13 miles of shoreline to explore. All water sports are allowed. It's a great lake for waterskiing (35-mph speed limit), water sports (5-mph speed limit in major coves), and sailboarding, with afternoon winds usually strong in the spring and early summer. Note that the quota on boats is enforced, with a maximum of 166 boats per day, and that boat-launch reservations are required on summer weekends and holidays. There are also designated areas for boating, waterskiing, and fishing to reduce conflicts. Fishing varies dramatically according to season, with trout planted in the cool months and largemouth bass, bluegill, striped bass, catfish, and crappie caught the rest of the year. A large sandy swimming beach is available on the lake's southeast side at the Sawpit Recreation Area. The park also has a modest trail system with both nature and bike trails. Note that because of the 2003 wildfire, Miller Canyon is accessible only by foot. It is off-limits during bald eagle nesting season. A bonus is that there are also some hike-in/bike-in campsites.

RV sites, facilities: There are 131 sites for tents or RVs up to 34 feet (no hookups), a few for RVs of any length, and four hike-in/bike-in sites. Some sites are pull-through. Picnic tables and fire rings (fire restriction may be in effect) are provided. Restrooms have flush toilets and coin showers. Drinking water, Wi-Fi, a dump station, a boat ramp, a marina, boat rentals, and a small store are available. Some facilities are wheelchair accessible. Leashed pets are permitted.

Reservations, fees: Reservations are accepted at 800/444-PARK (800/444-7275) or www.reserveamerica.com ($7.50 reservation fee). Sites are $20–25 per night, $8 per night for an additional vehicle, $2 per night per person for hike-in/bike-in sites. Open year-round.

Directions: Drive on I-15 to Cajon Junction (north of San Bernardino) and the exit for Highway 138 east. Take that exit and drive east on Highway 138 for 12 miles to the park entrance on the right.

Contact: Silverwood Lake State Recreation Area, 760/389-2303 or 760/389-2281; Silverwood Lake Marina, 760/389-2299, www.parks .ca.gov.

14 MOJAVE RIVER FORKS REGIONAL PARK

Scenic rating: 5

near Silverwood Lake

See map page 885

The bonuses here are for RV drivers, with the full hookups for RVs and the park's proximity to Silverwood Lake—which is only 15 minutes away but does not have any sites with hookups. The sites are well spaced, but the nearby "river" is usually dry. The elevation is 3,000 feet.

RV sites, facilities: There are 25 sites, seven drive-through, with full hookups (30 amps) for RVs; 25 sites for RVs or tents; 30 sites for tents only; and four group sites. Picnic tables and fire grills are provided. Restrooms, drinking water, flush toilets, showers, limited cell phone reception, and an RV dump station are available. An ATM is within 10 miles. Leashed pets are permitted.

Reservations, fees: Reservations are accepted. The fees are $10 per night for tent sites and $15 per night for RV sites with hookups, plus $5 per night for each additional vehicle and $1 per pet per night. Open year-round.

Directions: Drive on I-15 to Cajon Junction (north of San Bernardino) and the exit for Highway 138 (Silverwood). Take that exit east and drive nine miles to a fork with Highway 173. Bear left at the fork on Highway 173 and drive six miles to the park on the right.

Contact: Mojave River Forks Regional Park, 760/389-2322.

CALIFORNIA

15 NORTH SHORE

Scenic rating: 8

on Lake Arrowhead in San Bernardino
National Forest

See map page 885

Of the two camps at Lake Arrowhead, this
one is preferable. It is at 5,300 feet near the
northeastern shore of the lake, which provides
decent trout fishing in the spring and early
summer from a boat. Note that this is a private
lake, and there is no shore access. To the nearby
north, Deep Creek in San Bernardino National
Forest is well worth exploring; a hike along the
stream to fish for small trout (catch-and-release
only) or see a unique set of small waterfalls is
highly recommended.

RV sites, facilities: There are 27 sites for tents
or RVs up to 22 feet (no hookups). Picnic tables
and fire rings are provided. Drinking water
and flush toilets are available. A store is nearby. Some facilities are wheelchair accessible.
Leashed pets are permitted.

Reservations, fees: Reservations are accepted at 877/444-6777 ($9 reservation fee) or
www.ReserveUSA.com. Sites are $16 per night,
$5 per night for an additional vehicle. Open
May–September.

Directions: Drive on Highway 30 to San Bernardino and the Waterman exit. Take that
exit and drive north on Waterman Avenue
until it becomes Highway 18. Continue on
Highway 18/Rim of the World Highway and
drive 17 miles to Highway 173. Turn left on
Highway 173 and drive north for 1.6 miles
to the stop sign. Turn right (still on Highway
173) and drive 2.9 miles to Hospital Road.
Turn right and continue 0.1 mile to the top
of the small hill. Turn left just past the hospital entrance and continue a short distance to
the campground.

Contact: San Bernardino National Forest, Mountaintop Ranger District, Arrowhead Ranger Station, 909/382-2782, fax
909/337-1104.

16 GLEN HELEN REGIONAL PARK

Scenic rating: 4

near Cajon Pass

See map page 885

The centerpieces of Glen Helen Regional Park
are two lakes. The San Bernardino County
park covers 1,340 acres in the rolling hills at
the mouth of Cajon Pass. Hiking trails are
nearby. The ponds are stocked with trout in
winter and with catfish in summer, and bass are
also occasionally caught. Both lakes are set up
for shore-fishing, with no boats allowed on the
lakes, except for those little pedal boats, and no
swimming or water contact is permitted. Two
350-foot water slides, a lagoon pool, and sandy
beaches are a great bonus. A major obtrusive
problem is the location of the campground, just
across the street from the park, near both the
freeway and the railroad tracks. That's right,
drivers in passing cars can actually see you,
and at night, passing trains make it feel and
sound like the world is ending. The Hyundai
Pavilion is within the park, and it is the largest
outdoor amphitheater in the United States and
can accommodate up to 65,000 people at major
events. A OHV (off-highway vehicle) park is
also four miles away.

RV sites, facilities: There are 47 sites for tents
or RVs of any length and two group sites for
50–200 people. Some sites are pull-through,
and one site has partial hookups. Picnic tables
and fire rings are provided. Restrooms have
flush toilets and showers. Drinking water and
a dump station are on-site. A swimming lagoon,
water park, a picnic area with shelters, bait and
tackle, pedal boat rentals, volleyball, and horseshoes are available in the park. A snack bar is
available on weekends. A store and gas station
are a half mile away. Some facilities are wheelchair accessible. Leashed pets are permitted.

Reservations, fees: Reservations are accepted
at 909/887-7540. Sites are $13–18 per night,
$5 per night for an additional vehicle, $1 per
pet per night. A fee is charged for fishing.
Youth group rates available. Must show proof
of vehicle registration, insurance, and driver's

CALIFORNIA

license. Maximum 14-day stay in any 30-day period. Group sites are $3 per person per night ($10 reservation fee). Open year-round.

Directions: From San Bernardino, drive north on I-215 for nine miles to the exit for Devore Road. Take that exit, turn west on Devore Road, and drive one mile (crossing the railroad tracks) to the campground and the park (adjacent to the interchange for I-15 and I-215).

Contact: Glen Helen Regional Park, 909/887-7540, fax 909/887-1359; Hyundai Pavilion, 909/880-6500 or 909/88-MUSIC (909/886-8742), www.co.san-bernardino.ca.us/parks.

17 CAMP SWITZERLAND
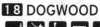

Scenic rating: 7

near Lake Gregory

See map page 885

Well, it really doesn't look much like Switzerland, but this camp is in a wooded canyon at 4,500 feet below the dam at little Lake Gregory. Since it is well below the dam, there are no lake views or even much of a sense that the lake is nearby. Yet it is only a short distance away. Lake Gregory covers just 120 acres, and while no privately owned boats are permitted here, boats can be rented at the marina. No gas motors are permitted at the lake, but electric motors are allowed. Trout and steelhead are stocked. It is surrounded by the San Bernardino National Forest. A large swimming beach is available on the south shore (about three-quarters of a mile away) with a water slide and dressing rooms.

RV sites, facilities: There are 40 sites for tents or RVs up to 25 feet with full or partial hookups (30 amps) and a few sites for RVs of any length. Some sites are pull-through. Two cabins are also available. Picnic tables are provided. Restrooms have flush toilets and coin showers, and drinking water is available. Campfires are now allowed. A store and propane gas are nearby. Leashed pets are permitted, with some restrictions.

Reservations, fees: Reservations are accepted. Sites are $27–32 per night, $3–5 per night for more than two people, $5 per night for an

additional vehicle, $6 per pet per night. Open year-round, weather permitting.

Directions: Drive on Highway 30 to San Bernardino and the Waterman Avenue exit. Take that exit and drive north on Waterman Avenue until it becomes Highway 18. Continue on Highway 18 (two miles east of the junction of Highway 30 and Highway 259). Turn north on Highway 18/Rim of the World Highway and drive 14 miles to Crestline/Highway 138. Turn north (left) on Highway 138 and drive two miles to Lake Drive. Continue straight and drive three miles to the campground entrance (signed, just past the fire station, below the dam at the north end of Lake Gregory).

Contact: Camp Switzerland, 909/338-2731.

18 DOGWOOD

Scenic rating: 6

near Lake Arrowhead in San Bernardino National Forest

See map page 885

So close, but yet so far—that's the paradox between Lake Arrowhead and Dogwood. The lake is just a mile away, but there is no public access. The lake is ringed by gated trophy homes. The elevation is 5,600 feet. Any questions? The rangers at the Arrowhead Ranger Station, about 1.5 miles down the road to the east, can answer them.

RV sites, facilities: There are 38 sites for tents or RVs up to 22 feet (no hookups); some sites have partial hookups (30 amps). Picnic tables and fire grills are provided. Drinking water, restrooms with flush toilets and coin showers, and a dump station are available. A store is nearby. Some facilities are wheelchair accessible. Leashed pets are permitted.

Reservations, fees: Reservations are accepted at 877/444-6777 or www.ReserveUSA.com ($9 reservation fee). Sites are $24–29 per night, $5 per night for an additional vehicle. Open mid-May–October.

Directions: Drive on Highway 30 to San Bernardino and Highway 18 (two miles east of the junction of Highway 30 and Highway 215). Turn north on Highway 18 and drive 15 miles to Rim of the World Highway. Continue on Highway 18 for 0.3 mile to the road immediately after Daley Canyon Road. Turn left and make an immediate right on the Daley Canyon access road. Drive a short distance to the campground entrance on the left.

Contact: San Bernardino National Forest, Mountaintop Ranger District, Arrowhead Ranger Station, 909/382-2782, fax 909/337-1104.

19 GREEN VALLEY

Scenic rating: 7

near Green Valley Lake in San Bernardino National Forest

See map page 885

This camp sits along pretty Green Valley Creek at an elevation of 7,000 feet. Little Green Valley Lake is a mile to the west; it is privately owned, but public access is allowed. It's quiet and intimate at this lake, and kayaks and rowboats can be rented. The lake is stocked with trout by the Department of Fish and Game, and it is also a good spot to take a flying leap and belly flop when water levels are high enough.

RV sites, facilities: There are 38 sites for tents or RVs up to 22 feet (no hookups). Picnic tables and fire grills are provided. Drinking water and flush toilets are available. A store and coin laundry are nearby. Leashed pets are permitted.

Reservations, fees: Reservations are accepted at 877/444-6777 ($9 reservation fee) or www.ReserveUSA.com. Sites are $16 per night, $5 per night for an additional vehicle. Open May–October.

Directions: From San Bernardino, take Highway 30 east to the junction with Highway 330 (east of San Bernardino near Highland). Take Highway 330 north (signed for Mountain Resorts) and drive to Running Springs and the junction with Highway 18. Turn east on Highway 18 and drive to Green Valley Lake Road. Turn left on Green Valley Lake Road and drive

five miles to the campground (one mile past the town of Green Valley Lake).

Contact: San Bernardino National Forest, Mountaintop Ranger District, Arrowhead Ranger Station, 909/382-2782, fax 909/337-1104.

20 HANNA FLAT

Scenic rating: 8

near Big Bear Lake in San Bernardino National Forest

See map page 885

This is one of the largest, best maintained, and most popular of the Forest Service camps in the Big Bear Lake District (Serrano Campground is the most popular). All the trees and vegetation provide seclusion for individual sites. There is great forest scenery with many hardwood trees, including oak and mountain mahogany. The camp is at 7,000 feet on the slopes on the north side of Big Bear Lake, just under three miles from the lake. Big Bear is a beautiful mountain lake covering more than 3,000 acres, with 22 miles of shoreline and often excellent trout fishing and waterskiing. A trailhead for the Pacific Crest Trail is a mile by road north of the camp.

RV sites, facilities: There are 88 sites for tents or RVs up to 32 feet (no hookups). Picnic tables and fire grills are provided. Drinking water and flush toilets are available. Some facilities are wheelchair accessible. Leashed pets are permitted.

Reservations, fees: Reservations are accepted at 877/444-6777 or www.ReserveUSA.com ($9 reservation fee). Sites are $20 per night, $5 per night for an additional vehicle. Open May–September.

Directions: Drive on Highway 30 to the junction with Highway 330 (east of San Bernardino near Highland). Take Highway 330 north (signed for Mountain Resorts) and drive 28 miles (Highway 330 becomes Highway 18/Rim of the World Highway) to the Big Bear Lake Dam and a fork with Highway 38 and Highway 18. Continue straight on Highway 38 and drive approximately four miles to the town of Fawnskin and Rim of the World Highway. Turn left and drive three miles (after a half mile, it becomes Forest Road 3N14, a dirt road) to the campground on the left.

Contact: San Bernardino National Forest, Mountaintop Ranger District, Big Bear Ranger Station/Discovery Center, 909/382-2790, fax 909/866-1781.

21 SERRANO

Scenic rating: 8

on Big Bear Lake in San Bernardino National Forest

See map page 885

This campground opened in the 1990s and became the first National Forest campground to offer state-of-the-art restrooms and hot showers. That is why it costs more to camp here. Regardless, it has since become the most popular campground in the region. Location is also a big plus, as this is one of the few camps at Big Bear within walking distance of the lakeshore. It covers 60 acres. Another bonus is a paved trail that is wheelchair-accessible. Want more? Big Bear is the jewel of Southern California lakes, the Lake Tahoe of the south, with outstanding trout fishing and waterskiing. All water sports are allowed. The lake is stocked with trout and catfish, and it also has large- and smallmouth bass, crappie, bluegill, and sunfish. Swimming is excellent at this lake with large, sandy beaches around the shoreline. However, the water is cold. A trailhead for the Pacific Crest Trail is nearby, and Canada is only 2,200 miles away. The elevation is 6,800 feet.

RV sites, facilities: There are 132 sites for tents or RVs up to 35 feet; some sites have full hookups (30 amps). Picnic tables and fire rings are provided. Restrooms have flush toilets and coin showers. Drinking water and a dump station are available. A store is nearby. Some facilities are wheelchair accessible. Leashed pets are permitted.

Reservations, fees: Reservations are accepted at 877/444-6777 or www.ReserveUSA.com ($9 reservation fee). Sites are $24–34 per night, $48 per night for double sites. Open April–November.

Directions: Drive on Highway 30 to the junction with Highway 330 (east of San Bernardino near Highland). Take Highway 330 north (signed for Mountain Resorts) and drive 28 miles (Highway 330 becomes Highway 18/Rim of the World Highway) to the Big Bear Lake Dam and a fork with Highway 38 and Highway 18. Continue straight on Highway 38 and drive about 2.5 miles to Fawnskin and North Shore Lane (signed for Serrano Campground). Turn right on North Shore Lane and drive to the campground entrance.

Contact: San Bernardino National Forest, Mountaintop Ranger District, Big Bear Ranger Station/Discovery Center, 909/382-2790, fax 909/866-1781.

22 YUCAIPA REGIONAL PARK

Scenic rating: 7

near Redlands

See map page 885

This is a great family-oriented county park, complete with water slides and pedal boats for the kids, fishing access and hiking trails for adults. Three lakes are stocked weekly with catfish in the summer and trout in the winter, the closest thing around to an insurance policy for anglers. Spectacular scenic views of the Yucaipa Valley, the San Bernardino Mountains, and Mount San Gorgonio are possible from the park. The park covers 885 acres in the foothills of the San Bernardino Mountains. A one-acre swimming lagoon and two water slides make this a favorite for youngsters. The Yucaipa Adobe and the Mousley Museum of Natural History are nearby.

RV sites, facilities: There are 26 sites for RVs of any length and nine sites for tents. All sites have full hookups (20, 30, and 50 amps) and/or are pull-through. Picnic tables and fire rings are provided at most sites. Drinking water and restrooms with flush toilets and showers are available, and shade ramadas are available at tent

CALIFORNIA

sites. A seasonal swimming lagoon and water slides, fishing ponds, seasonal pedal boat and aquacycle rentals, a pay phone, seasonal snack bar, picnic shelters, a playground, volleyball (bring net), horseshoes, group facilities, bait shop, and a dump station are available nearby. The water slide is open Memorial Day weekend–Labor Day weekend. Some facilities are wheelchair accessible. Leashed pets are permitted.

Reservations, fees: Reservations are accepted ($2 reservation fee). Sites are $18 per night for tent sites, $27 per night per vehicle for RV sites, $1 per pet per night. Weekly and youth group rates available. Some credit cards accepted. Additional charges apply for fishing, swimming, and use of the water slide. Proof of vehicle registration is required for campers. Maximum 14-day stay in any 30-day period. Open year-round.

Directions: Drive on I-10 to Redlands and the exit for Yucaipa Boulevard. Take that exit and drive east on Yucaipa Boulevard to Oak Glen Road. Turn left and continue two miles to the park on the left.

Contact: Yucaipa Regional Park, 909/790-3127, fax 909/790-3121, www.co.san-bernardino.ca.us/parks.

23 HOLLOWAY'S MARINA AND RV PARK

Scenic rating: 6

on Big Bear Lake
See map page 885

This privately operated RV park (no tent sites) is a good choice at Big Bear Lake, with boat rentals, a ramp, and a full marina available. Big Bear is the jewel of Southern California's lakes, covering more than 3,000 surface acres with 22 miles of shoreline. Its cool waters make for excellent trout fishing, and yet, by summer, it has heated up enough to make for superb waterskiing. A bonus in the summer is that a breeze off the lake keeps the temperature in the mid-80s. Note that about one-third of the sites are occupied by long-term renters. (For details

about the lake, see the listing in this chapter for *Serrano*.)

RV sites, facilities: There are 116 sites with full hookups (30 and 50 amps) for RVs up to 40 feet. No tents. Picnic tables and fire grills are provided. Restrooms have flush toilets and showers. Drinking water, a dump station, cable TV, a convenience store, ice, propane gas, a coin laundry, a playground, and a full marina with boat rentals are on the premises. Leashed pets are permitted.

Reservations, fees: Reservations are accepted at 800/448-5335. Sites are $45–55 per night, $5 per night for an additional vehicle. Monthly rates available. Some credit cards accepted. Open year-round, weather permitting.

Directions: Drive on Highway 30 to the junction with Highway 330 (east of San Bernardino near Highland). Take Highway 330 north (signed for Mountain Resorts) and drive 28 miles (Highway 330 becomes Highway 18/Rim of the World Highway) to the Big Bear Lake Dam and a fork with Highway 38 and Highway 18. Turn left on Highway 18 and drive three miles to Edgemoor Road. Turn left at Edgemoor Road and drive 0.25 mile to the park entrance on the left.

Contact: Holloway's Marina and RV Park, 909/866-5706 or 800/448-5335, fax 909/866-5436, www.800bigbearboating.com.

24 BARTON FLATS

Scenic rating: 7

near Jenks Lake in San Bernardino National Forest
See map page 885

This is one of the more developed Forest Service camps in San Bernardino National Forest. The camp is at 6,500 feet, about two miles from Jenks Lake, a small, pretty lake with good hiking and a picnic area. Barton Creek, a small stream, runs nearby although it may be waterless in late summer. The San Gorgonio Wilderness, one mile to the south, is accessible via Forest Service roads to the wilderness area trailhead. Permits are required for overnight camping within the wilderness boundaries and are available at Forest Service ranger stations. Those driving in on Highway 38 should stop at the Mill Creek Ranger Station in Redlands.

RV sites, facilities: There are 52 sites for tents or RVs of any length (no hookups). Picnic tables and fire grills are provided. Drinking water and restrooms with coin showers and flush toilets are available. Some facilities are wheelchair accessible. Leashed pets are permitted.

Reservations, fees: Reservations are accepted at 877/444-6777 or www.ReserveUSA.com ($9 reservation fee). Sites are $20 per night, $40 per night for multifamily sites, $5 per night for an additional vehicle. Open May–mid-November.

Directions: Drive on I-10 to Redlands and Highway 38. Take Highway 38 northeast and drive 27.5 miles to the campground on the left.

Contact: San Bernardino National Forest, Mountaintop Ranger District, Big Bear Ranger Station/Discovery Center, 909/382-2790, fax 909/866-1781.

25 SAN GORGONIO

Scenic rating: 7

near the San Gorgonio Wilderness in San Bernardino National Forest

See map page 885

San Gorgonio is one in a series of Forest Service camps along Highway 38 and about 2.5 miles from Jenks Lake. (See the listing in this chapter for *Barton Flats* for details.) The elevation is 6,500 feet.

RV sites, facilities: There are 53 sites for tents or RVs of any length (no hookups). Picnic tables and fire grills are provided. Drinking water and restrooms with flush toilets and coin showers are available. Some facilities are wheelchair accessible. Leashed pets are permitted.

Reservations, fees: Reservations are accepted at 877/444-6777 or www.ReserveUSA.com ($9 reservation fee). Sites are $20 per night, $40 per night for multifamily sites, $5 per night for an additional vehicle. Open mid-May–mid-October.

Directions: Drive on I-10 to Redlands and Highway 38. Take Highway 38 northeast and drive 28 miles to the campground.

Contact: San Bernardino National Forest, Mountaintop Ranger District, Big Bear Ranger Station/Discovery Center, 909/382-2790, fax 909/866-1781.

26 PINEKNOT

Scenic rating: 6

near Big Bear Lake in San Bernardino National Forest

See map page 885

This popular, developed Forest Service camp is just east of Big Bear Lake Village (on the southern shore of the lake) about two miles from the lake. It is a popular spot for mountain biking, with several ideal routes available. Of the camps at Big Bear, this is the closest to supplies. The elevation is 7,000 feet. (For details about the lake, see the listing for *Serrano* in this chapter.)

RV sites, facilities: There are 52 sites for tents or RVs up to 35 feet (no hookups). Picnic tables and fire grills are provided. Drinking water and flush toilets are available. A store and coin laundry are nearby. Some facilities are wheelchair accessible. Leashed pets are permitted.

Reservations, fees: Reservations are accepted at 877/444-6777 or www.ReserveUSA.com ($9 reservation fee). Sites are $19 per night. Open May–mid-October.

Directions: Drive on Highway 30 to the junction with Highway 330 (east of San Bernardino near Highland). Take Highway 330 north (signed for Mountain Resorts) and drive 28 miles (Highway 330 becomes Highway 18/ Rim of the World Highway) to the Big Bear Lake Dam and a fork with Highway 38 and Highway 18. Turn right at Highway 18 and drive about six miles to Summit Boulevard. Turn right and drive through the parking area to the road on the left (just before the gate to the ski area). Turn left and drive 0.25 mile to the campground on the right.

CALIFORNIA

Contact: San Bernardino National Forest, Mountaintop Ranger District, Big Bear Ranger Station/Discovery Center, 909/382-2790, fax 909/866-1781.

27 SOUTH FORK

Scenic rating: 7

near the Santa Ana River in San Bernardino National Forest

See map page 885

This is an easy-access Forest Service camp just off Highway 38, set at 6,400 feet near the headwaters of two rivers, the South Fork River and the Santa Ana River. It is part of the series of camps in the immediate area, just north of the San Gorgonio Wilderness. This one is a four-mile drive from little Jenks Lake. (See the listing for *Barton Flats* in this chapter for more details.)

RV sites, facilities: There are 24 sites for tents or RVs up to 25 feet (no hookups). Picnic tables and fire rings are provided. Drinking water and vault toilets are available. Leashed pets are permitted.

Reservations, fees: Reservations are accepted at 877/444-6777 or www.ReserveUSA.com ($9 reservation fee). Sites are $15 per night, $5 per night for an additional vehicle. Open mid-May–September.

Directions: Drive on I-10 to Redlands and Highway 38. Take Highway 38 northeast and drive 29.5 miles to the campground entrance road.

Contact: San Bernardino National Forest, Mountaintop Ranger District, Big Bear Ranger Station/Discovery Center, 909/382-2790, fax 909/866-1781.

28 HEART BAR FAMILY CAMP

Scenic rating: 4

in San Bernardino National Forest

See map page 885

It's a good thing there is drinking water at this camp. Why? Because Heart Bar Creek often isn't much more than a trickle and can't be relied on for water. The camp is at 6,900 feet near

Big Meadows, the location of the Heart Bar Fire Station. A challenging butt-kicker of a hike has a trailhead about a half mile away to the north off a spur road, midway between the camp and the fire station. The trail here is routed along Wildhorse Creek to Sugarloaf Mountain (9,952 feet, about eight or nine miles one-way to the top). Insider's note: Just past the midway point on the trail to Sugarloaf Mountain is a trail camp on Wildhorse Creek.

RV sites, facilities: There are 95 sites for tents or RVs up to 40 feet and one group tent site for up to 25 people. No hookups. Picnic tables and fire grills are provided. Drinking water and vault toilets are available. Some facilities are wheelchair accessible. Leashed pets are permitted.

Reservations, fees: Reservations are accepted for individual sites and required for the group site at 877/444-6777 or www.ReserveUSA.com ($9 reservation fee). Sites are $15 per night, $30 per night for multifamily sites, $70 per night for the group site. Open mid-May–early October.

Directions: Drive on I-10 to Redlands and Highway 38. Take Highway 38 northeast and drive 33.5 miles to Forest Road 1N02. Turn right and drive one mile to the campground.

Contact: San Bernardino National Forest, Mountaintop Ranger District, Big Bear Ranger Station/Discovery Center, 909/382-2790, fax 909/866-1781.

29 LEO CARRILLO STATE PARK

Scenic rating: 8

north of Malibu

See map page 884

The camping area at this state park is in a canyon, and reservations are essential during the summer and on weekends the remainder of the year. Giant sycamores shade the campsites. The Nicholas Flat Trail is an excellent hike to the Willow Creek Overlook for beautiful views of the beach. In addition, a pedestrian tunnel accesses a wonderful coastal spot with sea caves, tunnels, tidepools, and patches of beach. This park features 1.5 miles of beach for swimming, surfing, and surf fishing. In the summer, lifeguards are posted at the beach. Many will remember a beach camp that was once popular here. Well, that sucker is gone, wiped out by a storm.

RV sites, facilities: There are 127 sites for tents or RVs up to 31 feet (no hookups), one hike-in/bike-in area for up to 24 people, and one group tent site for up to 50 people. Picnic tables and fire rings are provided. Front gates close at 10 P.M. and reopen at 7 A.M. Restrooms have flush toilets and coin showers. Drinking water, a dump station, a seasonal visitors center, Wi-Fi, summer programs, and a summer convenience store are available. Some facilities are wheelchair accessible. Leashed pets are permitted.

Reservations, fees: Reservations are recommended at 800/444-PARK (800/444-7275) or www.reserveamerica.com ($7.50 reservation fee). Sites are $20–25 per night, $10 per night for an additional vehicle, $3 per person per night for the hike-in/bike-in site, and $120 per night for the group tent site. Open year-round.

Directions: From Santa Monica, drive north on Highway 1 for 28 miles to the park entrance (signed) on the right.

From Oxnard, drive south on Highway 1 for 20 miles to the park entrance (signed) on the left.

Contact: California State Parks, Angeles District, 818/880-0350, fax 818/880-6165, www.parks.ca.gov.

30 MALIBU CREEK STATE PARK

🚶 🚴 🏊 🎣 🐕 ♿ 🚐 ⛺

Scenic rating: 9

near Malibu

See map page 884

If you plan on staying here, be sure to get your reservation in early. This 6,600-acre state park is just a few miles out of Malibu between Highway 1 and U.S. 101, two major thoroughfares for vacationers. Despite its popularity, the park manages to retain a natural setting, with miles of trails for hiking, biking, and horseback rid-

ing, together with inspiring scenic views. The park offers 15 miles of streamside trail through oak and sycamore woodlands and also some chaparral-covered slopes. It is an ideal spot for a break on a coastal road trip. This park was once used as a setting for the filming of some movies and TV shows, including *Planet of the Apes* and *M*A*S*H*.

RV sites, facilities: There are 62 sites for tents or RVs up to 30 feet (no hookups) and a group tent site for up to 60 people. Picnic tables are provided. No wood fires are permitted in the summer, but propane or charcoal barbecues are allowed. Drinking water and restrooms with flush toilets and coin showers are available. Some facilities are wheelchair accessible. Leashed pets are permitted, but only in the campground area.

Reservations, fees: Reservations are accepted at 800/444-PARK (800/444-7275) or www.reserveamerica.com ($7.50 reservation fee). Sites are $25 per night, $8 per night for an additional vehicle, $120 per night for the group site. Open year-round.

Directions: From U.S. 101: Drive on U.S. 101 to the exit for Las Virgenes Canyon Road (on the western border of Calabasas). Take that exit south and drive on Las Virgenes Canyon Road/County Road N1 for four miles to the park entrance on the right.

From Highway 1: Drive on Highway 1 to Malibu and Malibu Canyon Road. Turn north on Malibu Canyon Road and drive north for 5.5 miles (the road becomes Las Virgenes Canyon Road/County Road N1) to the park entrance on the left.

Contact: Malibu Creek State Park, 818/880-0367, fax 818/706-3869, www.parks.ca.gov.

31 MALIBU BEACH RV PARK

🏊 🎣 🐕 🛶 ♿ 🚐 ⛺

Scenic rating: 7

in Malibu

See map page 884

This is one of the few privately developed RV parks in the region that provide some sites for

CALIFORNIA

CALIFORNIA

tent campers. It's one of the nicer spots in the area, set on a bluff overlooking the Pacific Ocean, near both Malibu Pier (for fishing) and Paradise Cove. Each site has a view of either the ocean or adjacent mountains. Sites with ocean views are charged a small premium. Whale-watching is best in March and April, and then again in October and November. Dolphin-watching is popular year-round.

RV sites, facilities: There are 35 sites for tents and 140 sites with full or partial hookups (30 and 50 amps) for RVs; some sites are pull-through. Picnic tables and barbecue grills are provided. Restrooms have showers. A spa, a recreation room, a playground, a coin laundry, Wi-Fi, modem access, a dog-walk area, propane gas, ice, cable TV, a dump station, and a convenience store are available. Some facilities are wheelchair accessible. Leashed pets are permitted, except in the tent area, and certain breeds are prohibited.

Reservations, fees: Reservations are recommended at 800/622-6052. Sites are $29.12–77.28 for RV sites, $5 per person per night for tent sites (four-person maximum per site), $10 per night for an additional vehicle, $5 per person per night for more than two people, $3 per night per pet. Some credit cards accepted. Open year-round.

Directions: Drive on Pacific Coast Highway/Highway 1 to the Malibu area. The park is two miles north of the intersection of Highway 1 and Malibu Canyon Road on the east side of the road.

Contact: Malibu Beach RV Park, 310/456-6052, www.maliburv.com.

32 LOS ANGELES-POMONA-FAIRPLEX KOA

Scenic rating: 4

in Pomona

See map page 885

This is what you might call an urban RV park. Then again, the L.A. County Fairgrounds are right across the street, and there's something

going on there every weekend. Frank G. Bonnelli Regional Park, which includes Puddingstone Lake, is only 15 minutes away.

RV sites, facilities: There are 159 pull-through sites with full hookups (50 amps) for RVs, 27 sites with partial hookups for RVs, and 11 tent sites. Two cabins are also available. Restrooms have showers. A heated pool and spa, convenience store, dump station, dog walk, and coin laundry are available. Some facilities are wheelchair accessible. Leashed pets are permitted, with certain restrictions.

Reservations, fees: Reservations are accepted. Sites are $34–37.50 per night, $25 per night for tent sites, $3 per night for an additional vehicle, $4 per person per night for more than two people. Some credit cards accepted. Open year-round.

Directions: Drive on I-10 to the exit for Fairplex Drive (five miles west of Pomona). Take that exit north (toward the mountain) and drive two miles to McKinley Avenue. Turn right on McKinley Avenue and drive one mile to White Avenue. Turn left and drive about a half mile (0.2 mile south of Arrow Street) to the park on the right (2200 North White Avenue).

Contact: Los Angeles-Pomona-Fairplex KOA, 909/593-8915, www.koa.com.

33 EAST SHORE RV PARK

Scenic rating: 7

at Puddingstone Lake

See map page 885

Considering how close Puddingstone Lake is to so many people, the quality of fishing and waterskiing might be a surprise to newcomers. The lake covers 250 acres and is an excellent recreation facility. For the most part, rules permit waterskiing and personal watercraft between 10 A.M. and sunset, making it an excellent lake for fishing for bass and trout (in season) during the morning and evening. All water sports are allowed here with specific days and hours for powerboating and personal watercraft. A ski beach is available on the north shore, and there is a large, sandy swimming beach on the southwest shore about a mile away. The lake is just south of Raging Waters in San Dimas and is bordered to the south by Bonnelli Regional Park; a golf course and equestrian facilities are adjacent to the park.

RV sites, facilities: There are 519 sites with full hookups (20, 30, and 50 amps) for RVs of any length, 25 walk-in sites for tents, and three group tent sites. Some sites are pull-through. Restrooms have showers. Cable TV, modem access, a recreation room, swimming pools, a general store, a playground, basketball, volleyball, horseshoes, propane gas delivery, 24-hour ranger service, and a coin laundry are available. A hot-tub facility is nearby. Some facilities are wheelchair accessible. Leashed pets are permitted at RV sites, but not at tent sites.

Reservations, fees: Reservations are accepted. Sites are $37–44 per night for RV sites for up to two people, $24 per night for up to three people at tent sites, $2 per person per night for additional people, $8 per person per night for the group tent sites, $2 per pet per night. Monthly and seasonal rates available. Some credit cards accepted. Open year-round.

Directions: Drive on I-10 to the exit for Fairplex Drive (five miles west of Pomona). Take that exit north to Via Verde (the first traffic light). Turn left on Via Verde and drive to the first stop sign at Campers View. Turn right on Campers View and drive into the park.

Contact: East Shore RV Park, 909/599-8355 or 800/809-3778, www.eastshorervpark.com.

34 DOCKWEILER BEACH RV PARK

Scenic rating: 6

on the Pacific Ocean near Manhattan Beach
See map page 884

This layover spot for coast cruisers is just a hop from the beach and the Pacific Ocean. There is access to a 26-mile-long coastal bike path.

RV sites, facilities: There are 117 sites with full hookups (20, 30, and 50 amps) for RVs up to 37 feet. No tents. Picnic tables and barbecue grills

are provided. Restrooms have flush toilets and showers. A dump station and coin laundry are available. Supplies are available nearby. Some facilities are wheelchair accessible. Leashed pets are permitted, with a two-dog limit.

Reservations, fees: Reservations are accepted ($7 reservation fee) at 310/322-4951 or 800/950-7275. Sites are $24–32 per night, $2 per pet per night. Open year-round. Some credit cards accepted.

Directions: From Santa Monica and the junction of I-405 and I-10, take I-405 south and drive 12 miles to the exit for Imperial Highway west. Take that exit and drive west on Imperial Highway for four miles to the park (signed) on the left.

Contact: Dockweiler Beach RV Park, Los Angeles County, 310/322-7036.

35 RANCHO JURUPA PARK

Scenic rating: 4

near Riverside
See map page 885

Lord, it gets hot in the summertime, but there is shade and grass here at this 200-acre park. The setting is along the Santa Ana River, amid cottonwood trees and meadows. This Riverside County park stocks trout and catfish in a three-acre fishing lake. Hiking, cycling, and equestrian trails are also available in the park. Shaded picnic sites are a plus. Summer visitors will find that the nearest lake for swimming and water sports is Lake Perris, about a 20-minute drive away. The elevation is 780 feet.

RV sites, facilities: There are 67 sites for tents or RVs of any length with full or partial hookups (30 and 50 amps). Picnic tables and fire grills are provided. Drinking water, flush toilets with showers, and a dump station are available. Some facilities are wheelchair accessible. Leashed pets are permitted.

Reservations, fees: Reservations are accepted ($6.50 reservation fee) for the individual sites and required ($12 reservation fee) for the group camp at 800/234-7275. Sites are $18–20 per

CALIFORNIA

night, $144 per night for the group camp, $1 per pet per night. Weekly rates available. A fishing fee is charged. Some credit cards accepted. Open year-round, with a maximum 14-day stay in a 28-day period.

Directions: Drive on I-215 to Riverside and Highway 60. Take Highway 60 east and drive seven miles to Rubidoux Boulevard. Turn left on Rubidoux Boulevard and drive 0.5 mile to Mission Boulevard. Turn left on Mission Boulevard and drive about one mile to Crestmore Road. Turn right and drive 1.5 miles to the park gate on the left (4800 Crestmore Road).

Contact: Rancho Jurupa Park, 951/684-7032, fax 951/955-4305, www.riversidecounty parks.org.

36 BOGART PARK

Scenic rating: 4

in Cherry Valley

See map page 885

This county park is overlooked by many vacationers on I-10, and it is as pretty as it gets for this area. There are two miles of horse trails and some hiking trails for a recreation option during the cooler months. It covers 414 acres of Riverside County foothills set at the north end of Cherry Valley. The elevation is 2,800 feet. Bears frequent this area, so store your food properly and avoid scented products.

RV sites, facilities: There are 26 sites for tents or RVs up to 40 feet, a group campground for tents that can accommodate up to 100 people, and a group equestrian campground. No hookups. Fire grills and picnic tables are provided. Drinking water and flush toilets are available. The equestrian camp has corrals and water troughs. Supplies are available in Beaumont. Some facilities are wheelchair accessible. Leashed pets are permitted.

Reservations, fees: Reservations are accepted and required for group sites ($6.50–12 reservation fee) at 800/234-7275. Sites are $12 per night, $120 per night for the group equestrian camp, $144 per night for the group camp, $1

per night per pet or horse. Open year-round, but closed on Tuesday and Wednesday.

Directions: Drive on I-10 to Beaumont and the exit for Beaumont Avenue. Take that exit north and drive four miles to Brookside. Turn right and drive 0.5 mile to Cherry Avenue. Turn left at Cherry Avenue and drive to the park on the right (9600 Cherry Avenue).

Contact: Bogart Park, 951/845-3818; Riverside County Parks, 800/234-7275, www.riversidecountyparks.org.

37 ORANGELAND RV PARK

Scenic rating: 1

near Disneyland

See map page 884

This park is about three miles east of Disneyland. If the other RV parks near Disneyland are filled, this is a useful alternative. Note that about half of the sites are filled with long-term renters.

RV sites, facilities: There are 203 sites with full hookups for RVs of any length; some are pull-through. No tents. Picnic tables and fire grills are provided. Restrooms have showers. A playground, heated swimming pool, spa, exercise room, coin laundry, convenience store, modem access, Wi-Fi Internet access, a car wash, shuffleboard court, billiards, a dump station, ice, and a recreation room are available. Some facilities are wheelchair accessible. Leashed pets are permitted, with certain restrictions.

Reservations, fees: Reservations are recommended. Sites are $55–75 per night, $1 per pet per night. Monthly rates available. Some credit cards accepted. Open year-round.

Directions: Drive on I-5 to Anaheim and the exit for Katella Avenue. Take that exit east for Katella Avenue and drive two miles (passing Anaheim Stadium and the Santa Ana River) to Struck Avenue. Turn right and drive 200 yards to the park on the right (1600 West Struck Avenue).

Contact: Orangeland RV Park, 714/633-0414, fax 714/633-9012, www.orangeland.com.

38 TRAVELERS WORLD RV PARK

Scenic rating: 1

near Disneyland

See map page 884

This is one of the most popular RV parks for visitors to Disneyland and other nearby attractions. It is easy to see why, with the park just a half mile from Disneyland. A shuttle service is available to Disneyland for a fee.

RV sites, facilities: There are 335 sites for tents or RVs up to 40 feet with full hookups (20, 30, and 50 amps); some sites are pull-through. Picnic tables and fire grills are provided. Restrooms have showers. Cable TV, modem access, a playground, an adult lounge/game room, a heated swimming pool, a coin laundry, a convenience store, a dump station, ice, a recreation room, an RV wash rack, and propane gas are available. Some facilities are wheelchair accessible. Leashed pets are permitted.

Reservations, fees: Reservations are recommended. Sites are $32–38 per night, $3 per person per night for more than two people, $3 per night for an additional vehicle, $2 per pet per night. Some credit cards accepted. Open year-round.

Directions: Drive on I-5 to Anaheim and the exit for Ball Road. Take that exit and drive on Ball Road for about one block to the park on the left at 333 West Ball Road.

Contact: Travelers World RV Park, 714/991-0100, fax 714/991-4939.

39 C. C. CAMPERLAND

Scenic rating: 1

near Disneyland

See map page 884

Camperland is nine blocks south of Disneyland, and that right there is the number-one appeal. The Crystal Cathedral is one mile away, and Knott's Berry Farm is also close by. An outdoor sink for washing dishes and a pet restroom are bonuses.

RV sites, facilities: There are 70 sites for RVs up to 40 feet with full hookups (30 and 50 amps). No pull-through sites. Picnic tables are provided. Restrooms have showers. A swimming pool, a coin laundry, a dump station, and ice are available. Leashed pets are permitted with certain restrictions, except in the tent area.

Reservations, fees: Reservations are accepted. Sites are $36–56 per night for RVs, $28–34 per night for tents, $3 per person per night for more than two people, $3 per night for an additional vehicle, $3 per pet per night. Some credit cards accepted. Open year-round.

Directions: Drive on I-5 to Garden Grove and the exit for Harbor Boulevard/Anaheim south. Take that exit and drive south on Harbor Boulevard for 1.5 miles to the park on the left (12262 Harbor Boulevard).

Contact: C. C. Camperland, 714/750-6747, www.cccamperland.com.

40 PRADO REGIONAL PARK

Scenic rating: 6

on Prado Park Lake near Corona

See map page 885

Prado Park Lake is the centerpiece of a 2,280-acre recreation-oriented park that features hiking trails, an equestrian center, athletic fields, a shooting range, a dog-training facility, and a 36-hole golf course. The lake is small and used primarily for paddling small boats and fishing, which is best in the winter and early spring when trout are planted, and then in early summer for catfish and bass. Gas motors, inflatables, sailboarding, swimming, and water/body contact are not permitted. The shooting facility is outstanding, the site of the 1984 Olympic shooting venue.

RV sites, facilities: There are 75 sites with full hookups (30 and 50 amps) for RVs of any length, 15 tent sites, and nine group sites. Most sites are pull-through. Picnic tables and fire rings are provided. Restrooms have showers. A coin laundry, a pay phone, a snack bar, a picnic area, a playground, group facilities, a boat ramp, and bait shop are available. A playing field with

CALIFORNIA

softball, soccer, and horseshoes is on-site. Some facilities are wheelchair accessible. Leashed pets are permitted.

Reservations, fees: Reservations accepted with a $2 reservation fee or a $10 reservation fee for group sites. Sites are $22 per night, $5 per night for an additional vehicle, $1 per pet per night. Group sites are $3 per person per night for up to 50 people and $2 per person per night for more than 50 people. Weekly rates available. A fee is charged for fishing. Campers must show proof of vehicle registration and insurance. Some credit cards accepted. Open year-round, with a maximum 14-day stay in a 30-day period.

Directions: Drive on Highway 91 to Highway 71 (west of Norco and Riverside). Take Highway 71 north and drive four miles to Highway 83/Euclid Avenue. Turn right on Euclid Avenue and drive one mile to the park entrance on the right.

Contact: Prado Regional Park, 909/597-4260, fax 909/393-8428, www.co.san-bernardino.ca.us/parks.

41 LAKE PERRIS STATE RECREATION AREA

Scenic rating: 7

on Lake Perris

See map page 885

Lake Perris is a great recreation lake with first-class fishing for spotted bass, and many fishing records have been set here. In the summer, it's an excellent destination for boating and water sports. It is at 1,500 feet in Moreno Valley, just southwest of the Badlands foothills. The lake has a roundish shape, covering 2,200 acres, with an island that provides a unique boat-in picnic site. There are large ski beaches on the northeast and southeast shores and a designated sailing cove on the northwest side, an ideal spot for various water sports; inflatables are not permitted. Swimming is also excellent, but it's allowed only at the developed beaches a short distance from the campground. The recreation area covers 8,300 acres and includes 10 miles of paved bike trails, including a great route that

circles the lake; 15 miles of equestrian trails; and five miles of hiking trails. Summer campfire and junior ranger programs are available. There is also a special area for scuba diving, and a rock-climbing area is just south of the dam.

RV sites, facilities: There are 254 sites for tents or RVs up to 31 feet with partial hookups (30 amps), 177 sites for tents only, seven primitive horse camps with corrals and water troughs, and six group sites with no hookups for 25–100 people each. Picnic tables and fire grills are available. Restrooms have flush toilets and coin showers. Drinking water, Wi-Fi, a dump station, a playground, a convenience store, two swimming beaches, a boat launch, and fishing boat rentals are available. Some facilities are wheelchair accessible. Leashed pets are permitted, with certain restrictions, except at the beach or in the water.

Reservations, fees: Reservations are accepted for individual sites at 800/444-PARK (800/444-7275) or www.reserveamerica.com ($7.50 reservation fee). Sites are $15–28 per night, $21 per night for equestrian sites, $8 per night for an additional vehicle, $120 per night for group sites. Reserve group sites at 951/940-5611 and equestrian sites at 951/940-5600. Open year-round.

Directions: From Riverside, drive southeast on Highway 215/60 for about five miles to the Highway 215/60 split. Bear south on Highway 215 at the split and drive six miles to Ramona Expressway. Turn left (east) and drive 3.5 miles to Lake Perris Drive. Turn left and drive 0.75 mile to the park entrance.

Contact: Lake Perris State Recreation Area, 951/657-0676, or Lake Perris Marina, 951/657-2179, www.parks.ca.gov.

42 PINE RANCH RV PARK

Scenic rating: 2

in Banning

See map page 885

Banning may not seem like a hotbed of civilization at first glance, but this clean, comfortable park is a good spot to make camp while exploring some of the area's hidden attractions, including Agua Caliente Indian Canyons and the Lincoln Shrine. It is at 2,400 feet, 22 miles from Palm Springs. A good side trip is to head south on curving "Highway" 240 up to Vista Point in the San Bernardino National Forest.

RV sites, facilities: There are 106 sites with full hookups (30 and 50 amps) for RVs; many sites are pull-through. No tents. Picnic tables and fire grills are provided. Restrooms have showers. Cable TV, a playground, a heated swimming pool, a coin laundry, Wi-Fi, a dump station, ice, horseshoes, and propane gas are available. Leashed pets are permitted, with certain restrictions.

Reservations, fees: Reservations are accepted for groups only. Sites are $29 per night, $2 per person per night for more than two people, $1 per night for an additional vehicle. Some credit cards accepted. Open year-round.

Directions: Drive on I-10 to Banning and the exit for Highway 243. Take that exit south and take 8th Street south for one block to Lincoln. Turn left on Lincoln and drive two blocks to San Gorgonio. Turn right and drive one mile to the park (1455 South San Gorgonio Avenue).

Contact: Pine Ranch RV Park, 951/849-7513, fax 951/849-7998.

43 BOLSA CHICA STATE BEACH

Scenic rating: 7

near Huntington Beach

See map page 884

This state beach extends three miles from Seal Beach to Huntington Beach City Pier. A bikeway connects it with Huntington State Beach, seven miles to the south. Across the road from Bolsa Chica is the 1,000-acre Bolsa Chica Ecological Preserve, managed by the Department of Fish and Game. The campground consists of basically a beachfront parking lot, but a popular one at that. A great little walk is available at the adjacent Bolsa Chica State Reserve, a 1.5-mile loop that provides an escape from the parking

lot and entry into the 530-acre nature reserve, complete with egrets, pelicans, and many shorebirds. Lifeguard service is available during the summer. This camp has a seven-day maximum stay during the summer and a 14-day maximum stay during the winter. Surf fishing is popular here for perch, cabezon, small sharks, and croaker. There are also occasional runs of grunion, a small fish that spawns in hordes on the sandy beaches of Southern California.

RV sites, facilities: There are 56 sites with full hookups (30 and 50 amps) available in a parking lot configuration for RVs up to 48 feet. No tents. Fire rings are provided. Restrooms have flush toilets and coin showers. Drinking water, Wi-Fi, a dump station, picnic areas, a bicycle trail, volleyball, basketball, and food service (seasonal) are available. Some facilities are wheelchair accessible, including a paved ramp for wheelchair access to the beach. Leashed pets are permitted at campsites.

Reservations, fees: Reservations are accepted at 800/444-PARK (800/444-7275) or www.reserveamerica.com ($7.50 reservation fee). Sites are $29–39 per night, plus $10 per night for an additional vehicle. Open year-round.

Directions: Drive on Highway 1 to the park entrance (1.5 miles north of Huntington Beach).

Contact: Bolsa Chica State Beach, 714/846-3460; Huntington State Beach, 714/536-1454, www.parks.ca.gov.

44 HUNTINGTON CITY BEACH

Scenic rating: 7

in Huntington Beach

See map page 884

This RV park is operated by the city of Huntington Beach. This park is a helpful layover for Highway 1 cruisers. Bolsa Chica State Beach provides an alternative spot to park an RV. The best nearby adventure is the short loop walk at Bolsa Chica State Reserve (see the listing for *Bolsa Chica State Beach* in this chapter for more information).

RV sites, facilities: There are 46 sites with

CALIFORNIA

partial hookups (30 and 50 amps) for RVs up to 40 feet. Fire rings are provided. Drinking water, outdoor cold showers, flush toilets, and a dump station are available. Supplies are available within a mile. Leashed pets are allowed.

Reservations, fees: Reservations are accepted by mail or in person. Sites are $45 per night. Some credit cards accepted. Open October–May.

Directions: Drive on I-405 to Huntington Beach and the exit for Beach Boulevard. Take that exit west and drive on Beach Boulevard to Highway 1/Pacific Coast Highway. Turn right (north) and drive approximately one mile to 1st Street. Turn left and drive a short distance to the park entrance.

Contact: Huntington Beach, Parks Department, 714/536-5286.

45 NEWPORT DUNES WATERFRONT RESORT

Scenic rating: 9

in Newport Beach

See map page 884

This five-star resort is in a pretty spot on the bay, with a beach, a boat ramp, and storage area providing bonuses. The resort received the "Mega Park of the Year Award 2003" from the California Travel Parks Association. It is on 100 acres of Newport Bay beach, beautiful and private, without public access. It features one mile of beach and a swimming lagoon, beachfront sites, and 24-hour security. A one-mile promenade circles the resort and is popular for cycling and roller blading. Nearby to the west is Corona del Mar State Beach, and to the south is Crystal Cove State Park. The park is five minutes' walking distance from Balboa Island and is next to the largest estuary in California, the Upper Newport Bay Ecological Reserve.

RV sites, facilities: There are 382 sites for RVs up to 50 feet with full hookups (30 and 50 amps). Cottages are also available. Picnic tables are provided. Restrooms have showers. A heated swimming pool and spa, waveless

saltwater lagoon, 440-slip marina, satellite TV, Wi-Fi, organized activities, beach volleyball, a coin laundry, a market, a waterfront restaurant, a café, a fitness center, a game room/video arcade, group facilities, a dog run, a playground, RV and boat storage, RV and boat wash, and a marina with boat launch ramp are available. Boat, kayak, sailboard, and bicycle rentals are available, along with lessons for various water sports. Some facilities are wheelchair accessible. Leashed pets are permitted, with some restrictions, but not in the cottages.

Reservations, fees: Reservations are accepted up to two years in advance (except for July 4) at 800/765-7661. Tent sites are $69–70 per night, RV sites are $89–220 per night, plus $8 per night for an additional vehicle, $2 per pet per night. Monthly rates available. Some credit cards accepted. Open year-round.

Directions: Drive on I-405 to the exit for Highway 55. Take that exit south and drive on Highway 55 to Highway 73. Turn south on Highway 73 and drive three miles to the Jamboree Road exit. Take that exit, turn right, and drive south on Jamboree Road for five miles to Back Bay Drive. Turn right and drive a short distance to the resort on the left.

Contact: Newport Dunes Waterfront Resort, 949/729-3863, fax 949/729-1133, www.newportdunes.com.

46 O'NEILL REGIONAL PARK

Scenic rating: 6

near Cleveland National Forest

See map page 885

This Orange County park is just far enough off the main drag to get missed by most of the RV cruisers on I-5. It is near Trabuco Canyon, adjacent to Cleveland National Forest to the east. About 70 percent of the campsites are under a canopy of sycamore and oak, and in general, the park is heavily wooded. The park covers 3,800 acres and features 18 miles of trails, including those accessible by equestrians. Several roads near this park lead to trailheads into Cleveland

National Forest. Occasional mountain lion warnings are posted by rangers. The elevation is 1,000 feet.

RV sites, facilities: There are 79 sites for tents or RVs of any length (no hookups), six equestrian sites for up to two horses per site, and two group camping areas for 20–130 people each. A few sites are pull-through. Picnic tables and fire rings are provided. Restrooms have flush toilets and showers. Drinking water, a playground, a picnic area, an amphitheater, horseshoes, firewood, and a dump station are available. Horse corral, water faucets, and an arena are available at equestrian sites. An interpretive center is open on weekends. A store is nearby. Some facilities are wheelchair accessible. Leashed pets are permitted.

Reservations, fees: Reservations are not accepted for equestrian sites. Reservations are accepted with a $12 reservation fee for individual sites and required with a $25 reservation fee for group sites. Sites are $15 per night, $5 per night for an additional vehicle, $2 per pet per night, $3 per night per horse. The group site is $15 per vehicle per night, plus a $12 processing fee. Some credit cards accepted. Open year-round.

Directions: From I-5 in Laguna Hills, take the County Road S18/El Toro Road exit and drive east (past El Toro) for 7.5 miles. Turn right onto Live Oak Canyon Road/County Road S19 and drive about three miles to the park on the right.

Contact: O'Neill Regional Park, 949/923-2260 or 949/923-2256, www.ocparks.com.

47 BLUE JAY

Scenic rating: 4

in the Santa Ana Mountains in Cleveland
National Forest

See map page 885

The few hikers who know of this spot like it and keep coming back, provided they time their hikes when temperatures are cool. The trailheads to San Juan Trail and Chiquito Trail (which is accessed from the San Juan Trail), both of which lead into the backcountry and the Santa Ana Mountains, are adjacent to the camp. A Forest Service map is strongly advised. The elevation is 3,400 feet.

RV sites, facilities: There are 50 sites for tents or RVs up to 20 feet (no hookups). Picnic tables and fire rings are provided. Drinking water and vault toilets are available. A store is within five miles. Leashed pets are permitted.

Reservations, fees: Reservations are not accepted. Sites are $15 per night. Open year-round, weather permitting.

Directions: Drive on I-15 to Lake Elsinore and the Central exit to Highway 74 west. Take that exit and drive west on Highway 74 for 12 miles (the road becomes Grand Avenue for a couple of miles in Lake Elsinore, then bears right) to Forest Road 6S05 (Long Canyon Road). Turn right and drive approximately four miles to Falcon Group Camp on the left.

Contact: Cleveland National Forest, Trabuco Ranger District, 951/736-1811, fax 951/736-3002.

48 EL CARISO NORTH CAMPGROUND

Scenic rating: 5

near Lake Elsinore in Cleveland National Forest

See map page 885

This pretty, shaded spot at 2,600 feet is just inside the border of Cleveland National Forest with Lake Elsinore to the east. On the drive in there are great views to the east, looking down at Lake Elsinore and across the desert country. Hikers should head west to the Upper San Juan Campground.

RV sites, facilities: There are 18 sites for tents or RVs up to 32 feet (no hookups). Picnic tables and fire rings are provided. Drinking water and vault toilets are available. Leashed pets are permitted.

Reservations, fees: Reservations are not accepted. Sites are $15 per night. Open year-round, weather permitting.

Directions: Drive on I-15 to Lake Elsinore and the Central exit to Highway 74 west. Take that exit and drive west on Highway 74 for 12 miles (the road becomes Grand Avenue for a couple of miles in Lake Elsinore, then bears right) to the campground on the right.

Drive on I-5 to San Juan Capistrano and Highway 74/Ortega Highway. Turn east on the Ortega Highway and drive 24 miles northeast (into national forest) to the campground.

Contact: Cleveland National Forest, Trabuco Ranger District, 951/736-1811, fax 951/736-3002.

49 CASPERS WILDERNESS PARK

Scenic rating: 6

on the San Juan Creek

See map page 885

This is an 8,500-acre protected wilderness preserve that is best known for coastal stands of live oak and magnificent stands of California sycamore. Highway 74 provides access to this regional park. It is a popular spot for picnics, day hikes, horseback riding, and cycling. Since the campground is not listed with any of the computer-based reservation services, it is overlooked by most out-of-town travelers. A highlight is 30 miles of trails. Much of the land is pristine and protected in its native state. It is bordered to the south by the San Juan Creek and to the east by the Cleveland National Forest and the San Mateo Canyon Wilderness, adding to its protection.

RV sites, facilities: There are 42 sites for tents or RVs of any length with partial hookups (no electrical), 23 equestrian sites, six group sites for 40–60 people each, and 13 sites in an overflow area for tents and RVs. Picnic tables, fire pits, and barbecues are provided. Drinking water, restrooms with flush toilets and showers, a dump station, corrals, stables, an amphitheater, a museum with interpretive programs, and a playground are available. Some facilities are wheelchair accessible.

Reservations, fees: Reservations are required at

800/600-1600. Sites are $13–15 per night, $3 per night per horse. Some credit cards accepted. Open year-round.

Directions: Drive on I-5 to San Juan Capistrano and Highway 74/Ortega Highway. Turn east on Ortega Highway and drive 7.5 miles northeast to the signed park entrance on the left.

Contact: Caspers Wilderness Park, Orange County, 949/923-2210, fax 949/728-0346, www.ocparks.com.

50 LAKE ELSINORE WEST MARINA & RV RESORT

Scenic rating: 7

on Lake Elsinore

See map page 885

This privately operated RV park has 1,000 feet of lake frontage and boat rentals are nearby. Note that about a third of the sites are occupied by long-term renters. (For information about Lake Elsinore, see the listing in this chapter for *Lake Elsinore Campground and Recreation Area.*)

RV sites, facilities: There are 195 sites with full hookups (50 amps) for RVs up to 40 feet. No tents. Picnic tables and cable TV are provided. Restrooms have showers. A dump station, a horseshoe pit, a clubhouse, modem access, a convenience store, group facilities, propane, and a boat ramp are available. Some facilities are wheelchair accessible. Leashed pets are permitted, with some restrictions.

Reservations, fees: Reservations are accepted at 800/328-6844. Sites are $40 per night, $3–5 per person per night for more than two people, $1 per pet per night. Some credit cards accepted. Open year-round.

Directions: Drive to the junction of I-15 and Highway 74. At that junction, take Highway 74 west/Central Avenue and drive west for four miles to the entrance to the park on the left (32700 Riverside Drive).

Contact: Lake Elsinore West Marina, 951/678-1300 or 800/328-6844, fax 951/678-6377, www.lakeelsinoremarina.com.

51 LAKE ELSINORE CAMPGROUND AND RECREATION AREA

Scenic rating: 7

on Lake Elsinore
See map page 885

The weather is hot and dry enough in this region to make the water in Lake Elsinore more valuable than gold. Elsinore is a huge, wide lake, where water-skiers, personal watercraft riders, and sailboarders can find a slice of heaven. This camp is along the north shore, where there are also several trails for hiking, biking, and horseback riding. There is a designated area near the campground for swimming and water play, with a gently sloping lake bottom a big plus. Fishing has improved greatly in recent years, and the lake is stocked with trout and striped bass. Other fish species include channel catfish, crappie, and bluegill. Night fishing is available. Anglers have a chance to fish for Whiskers, a very special catfish. It is a hybrid channel catfish that was stocked in 2000. It is a genetic cross between a blue and channel catfish, meaning that Whiskers could grow to more than 100 pounds. If you catch Whiskers, it's worth $200 in prize money; call the 24-hour hotline at 909/245-9976. If you like thrill sports, hang gliding and parachuting are also available at the lake; as you scan across the water, you can often look up and see these daredevils soaring overhead. The recreation area covers 3,300 acres and has 15 miles of shoreline. The elevation is 1,239 feet. While the lake is huge when full, in low-rain years Elsinore's water level can be subject to extreme and erratic fluctuations. Boaters planning to visit this lake should call first to get the latest on water levels and quality.

RV sites, facilities: There are nine primitive sites and 185 sites for tents or RVs up to 40 feet; several sites have full hookups (30 amps). Fire pits are provided. Picnic tables are provided at some sites. Restrooms have flush toilets and showers. Drinking water, a picnic area, and a dump station are available. Supplies and a coin laundry are nearby. Some facilities are wheelchair accessible. Leashed pets are permitted.

Reservations, fees: Reservations are accepted at 800/416-6992. Sites are $25–30 per night, $5 per pet per night. Some credit cards accepted. Open year-round.

Directions: Drive to the junction of I-15 and Highway 74. At that junction, take Highway 74 west/Central Avenue. Drive a short distance on Central Avenue to Collier. Turn right on Collier and drive 0.25 mile to Riverside Drive. Turn left and drive approximately 1.5 miles to the campground on the left.

Contact: Lake Elsinore Campground and Recreation Area, 951/471-1212; City of Lake Elsinore, 951/674-3124, fax 951/245-9308.

52 PALM VIEW RV PARK

Scenic rating: 5

near Lake Elsinore
See map page 885

This privately operated RV park is in a quiet valley at 700 feet elevation and has a duck pond. The sites are fairly rustic, with some shade trees. The park's recreation area offers basketball, volleyball, horseshoes, tetherball, and a playground. For you wonderful goofballs, bungee jumping and parachuting are available in the town of Perris. Note that most of the sites are occupied by long-term renters.

RV sites, facilities: There are 41 sites with full hookups (30 amps) for RVs, nine tent sites, and a group tent area that can accommodate up to 200 people. Some sites are pull-through. Picnic tables and fire rings are provided. Restrooms, a dump station, a recreation area, modem access, a seasonal swimming pool, a coin laundry, a playground, a convenience store, ice, and firewood are available. Leashed pets are permitted.

Reservations, fees: Reservations are accepted. Sites are $25–28 per night. The group area is $5 per person per night. Monthly rates available. Open year-round.

CALIFORNIA

Directions: Drive to the junction of I-15 and Highway 74. At that junction, take Highway 74/Central Avenue and drive east on Highway 74 for 4.5 miles to River Road. Turn right (south) and drive one mile to the park on the left (22200 River Road).

Contact: Palm View RV Park, 951/657-7791, fax 951/657-7673.

53 LAKE SKINNER RECREATION AREA

Scenic rating: 7

on Lake Skinner

See map page 885

Lake Skinner is within a Riverside County park at an elevation of 1,470 feet in sparse foothill country, where the water can sparkle, and it covers 1,200 surface acres. There is a speed limit of 10 mph, and only four-stroke engines are allowed. Unlike nearby Lake Elsinore, which is dominated by fast boats and water-skiers, no water contact sports are permitted here; hence no waterskiing, no swimming, no sailboarding. However, a one-half acre swimming pool is available in the summer. Afternoon winds make for great sailing, and you can count on consistent midday breezes. The fishing can be good. Many fish are stocked at this lake, including trophy-sized bass and trout, along with catfish and bluegill. The fishing records here include a 39.5-pound striped bass, 33-pound catfish, and 14-pound, 8-ounce largemouth bass. The recreation area also provides hiking trails.

RV sites, facilities: There are 213 sites for tents or RVs of any length, an overflow area, and three group camping areas; many sites have full or partial hookups (50 amps) and/or are pull-through. Picnic tables and fire grills are provided. Restrooms have flush toilets and coin showers. Drinking water, a playground, a convenience store, a picnic area, group facilities, ice, bait, a dump station, a swimming pool (in the summer), a boat ramp, a marina, mooring, boat rentals, and propane gas are

available. Some facilities are wheelchair accessible. Leashed pets are permitted.

Reservations, fees: Reservations are accepted with a $6.50 reservation fee at 800/234-7275. Sites are $17–20 per night, $12 per night for overflow area, $192–216 per night for group sites, $1 per pet per night. Open year-round. Some credit cards accepted.

Directions: Drive on I-15 to Temecula and the exit for Rancho California. Take that exit and drive northeast 9.5 miles to the park entrance on the right.

Contact: Lake Skinner Recreation Area, 951/926-1541, www.riversidecountyparks.org.

54 GOLDEN VILLAGE PALMS RV RESORT

Scenic rating: 5

in Hemet

See map page 885

This RV resort is for those ages 55 and over. It is the biggest RV park in Southern California. The grounds are lush, with gravel pads for RVs. It is near Diamond Valley Lake, about 10 miles south, a new lake that is the largest reservoir in Southern California. A golf course is nearby, Lake Hemet is 20 miles east, and winery tours are available in Temecula, a 30-minute drive. About 250 of the 1,019 sites are rented on a year-round basis.

RV sites, facilities: There are 1,019 sites with full hookups (50 amps) for RVs up to 45 feet; some sites are pull-through. No tent sites. Restrooms have flush toilets and showers. Drinking water, cable TV, modem access, Wi-Fi, business services, three heated swimming pools, three spas, a recreation room, a fitness center, a billiard room, a coin laundry, a large clubhouse, banquet and meeting rooms, organized activities, a pavilion, church services, a library, a ballroom, shuffleboard, a nine-hole putting green, volleyball courts, and horseshoe pits are available. A day-use area with propane barbecues is also available. Leashed pets are permitted.

Reservations, fees: Reservations are accepted at 800/323-9610. Sites are $36–50 per night, $10 per person per night for more than two people. Weekly, monthly, and annual rates available. Open year-round.

Directions: Drive to the junction of I-215 and Highway 74 (near Perris). At that junction, take Highway 74 east and drive 14 miles to Hemet (the highway becomes Florida Avenue in Hemet) and continue to the resort on the left.

Contact: Golden Village Palms RV Resort, 951/925-2518, www.goldenvillagepalms.com.

55 CASA DEL SOL RV RESORT

Scenic rating: 3

in Hemet

See map page 885

Hemet is a retirement town, so if you want excitement, the four lakes in the area are the best place to look for it: Lake Perris to the northwest, Diamond Valley Lake and Lake Skinner to the south, and Lake Hemet to the east. The elevation at this 20-acre resort is 1,575 feet. Note that many of the sites are taken by year-round or long-term rentals.

RV sites, facilities: There are 358 sites with full hookups (30 and 50 amps) for RVs up to 40 feet. No tents. Restrooms have flush toilets and showers. Drinking water, cable TV, telephone and modem access, ice, a library, a heated swimming pool, a spa, a recreation room, an exercise room, a billiard room, shuffleboard courts, a golf driving cage, dog runs, and a coin laundry are available. Leashed pets are permitted.

Reservations, fees: Reservations are accepted at 888/925-2516. Sites are $32 per night, $2.50 per person per night for more than two people. Weekly and monthly rates available. Some credit cards accepted. Open year-round.

Directions: Drive to the junction of I-215 and Highway 74 (near Perris). At that junction, take Highway 74 east and drive 15 miles to Hemet (the highway becomes Florida

Avenue in Hemet) and drive to Kirby Avenue. Turn right (south) on Kirby Avenue and drive a half block to the resort (2750 West Acacia Avenue).

Contact: Casa del Sol RV Resort, 951/925-2515, www.casadelsolrvpark.com.

56 MOUNTAIN VALLEY RV PARK

Scenic rating: 3

in Hemet

See map page 885

This is one of three RV parks in the Hemet area. Four lakes in the area provide side-trip possibilities: Lake Perris to the northwest, Lake Skinner and Diamond Valley Lake to the south, and Lake Hemet to the east. Golf courses are nearby.

RV sites, facilities: There are 170 sites with full hookups (30 and 50 amps) for RVs up to 40 feet. No tents or campers. Restrooms have flush toilets and showers. Cable TV, drinking water, a fireside room, a heated swimming pool, an enclosed spa, a fitness center, a golf driving cage, card-access laundry, a billiard room, a meeting room, group facilities, computer kiosk, Wi-Fi, and telephone hookups are available. A store and propane gas are nearby. Some facilities are wheelchair accessible. Leashed pets are permitted, with some breeds prohibited.

Reservations, fees: Reservations are accepted at 800/926-5593. Sites are $33 per night, $5 per person per night for more than two people, $2 per pet per night. Weekly, monthly, and annual rates available. Some credit cards accepted. Open year-round.

Directions: Drive to the junction of I-215 and Highway 74 (near Perris). At that junction, take Highway 74 east and drive 15 miles to Hemet (the highway becomes Florida Avenue in Hemet) and continue to South Lyon Avenue. Turn right on South Lyon Avenue and drive to the park at the corner of Lyon and South Acacia (235 South Lyon).

Contact: Mountain Valley RV Park, 951/925-5812, www.mountainvalleyrvp.com.

CALIFORNIA

57 MOUNT SAN JACINTO STATE PARK: STONE CREEK

Scenic rating: 7

in Mount San Jacinto State Park

See map page 885

This is a wooded camp in Mount San Jacinto State Park, a quarter mile off the main road along Stone Creek, just outside the national forest boundary. The elevation is 5,900 feet. It is less than a mile from Fern Basin and less than three miles from Dark Canyon. The best trailhead in the immediate area is Seven Pines Trail out of Marion Mountain Camp, one-half mile from this camp.

RV sites, facilities: There are 26 sites for tents and 21 sites for tents or RVs up to 24 feet. No hookups. Picnic tables and fire rings are provided. Drinking water and vault toilets are available. Supplies and a coin laundry are three miles away in Pine Cove. Some facilities are wheelchair accessible. Leashed pets are permitted.

Reservations, fees: Reservations are accepted at 800/444-PARK (800/444-7275) or www.reserveamerica.com ($7.50 reservation fee). Sites are $11–15 per night, $5 per night for an additional vehicle. Open year-round.

Directions: Drive on I-10 to Banning and Highway 243/Idyllwild Panoramic Highway. Turn south on Idyllwild Panoramic Highway and drive about 13 miles south to the park entrance on the left.

Contact: Mount San Jacinto State Park, 951/659-2607, www.parks.ca.gov; Inland Empire District, 951/443-2423.

58 IDYLLWILD COUNTY PARK

Scenic rating: 6

near San Bernardino National Forest

See map page 885

This Riverside County park covers 202 acres surrounded by Mount San Jacinto State Park, San Jacinto Wilderness, and the San Bernardino National Forest lands. That provides plenty of options for visitors. The park, elevation 5,300 feet, has equestrian trails and an interpretive trail. The top hike in the region is the ambitious climb up the western slopes to the top of Mount San Jacinto (10,804 feet), a terrible challenge of a butt-kicker that provides one of the most astounding views in all the land. (The best route, however, is out of Palm Springs, taking the aerial tramway, which will get you to 8,516 feet in elevation before you hike out the rest.)

RV sites, facilities: There are 83 sites for tents or RVs up to 40 feet (no hookups). Fire grills and picnic tables are provided. Drinking water and restrooms with flush toilets and coin showers are available, but there is no drinking water in dry years. A store, a coin laundry, and propane gas are nearby. Some facilities are wheelchair accessible. Leashed pets are permitted.

Reservations, fees: Reservations are accepted at 800/234-PARK (800/234-7275) ($6.50 reservation fee). Sites are $17 per night, $1 per pet per night. Some credit cards accepted. Open year-round.

Directions: Drive on I-10 to Banning and Highway 243/Idyllwild Panoramic Highway. Turn south on Idyllwild Panoramic Highway and drive to Idyllwild and Riverside County Playground Road. Turn west on Riverside County Playground Road and drive 0.5 mile (follow the signs) to the park entrance on the right.

Contact: Idyllwild County Park, 951/659-2656, www.riversidecountyparks.org.

59 MOUNT SAN JACINTO STATE PARK: IDYLLWILD

Scenic rating: 8

in Mount San Jacinto State Park

See map page 885

This is a prime spot for hikers and one of the better jump-off points for trekking in the area. There are no trails from this campground, set at 5,400 feet, but a half-mile north is Deer Spring Trail, which is connected with the Pacific Crest Trail and then climbs on to Mount San Jacinto (10,834 feet) and its astounding lookout.

RV sites, facilities: There are 11 sites for tents

only, 10 sites for tents or RVs up to 18 feet, eight sites for RVs only up to 24 feet, and three hike-in/bike-in sites. Two of the sites have full hookups. Fire grills and picnic tables are provided. Drinking water, restrooms with flush toilets and coin showers, and Wi-Fi are available. Supplies and coin laundry (100 yards) are nearby. Some facilities are wheelchair accessible. Leashed pets are permitted.

Reservations, fees: Reservations are accepted at 800/444-PARK (800/444-7275) or www .reserveamerica.com ($7.50 reservation fee). Sites are $15–29 per night, $5 per night for an additional vehicle, $3 per person per night for the hike-in/bike-in sites. Open year-round.

Directions: In Idyllwild, drive to the north end of town on Highway 243 to the park entrance on the left (next to the fire station).

From I-10 in Banning, take the A Street exit onto Highway 243. Drive south on Highway 243 for 23.8 miles to the campground on the right, just before the town of Idyllwild.

Contact: Mount San Jacinto State Park, 951/659-2607, www.parks.ca.gov; Inland Empire District, 951/443-2423.

60 LAKE HEMET
🎣 🚤 🐕 👫 ♿ 🚐 ⛺

Scenic rating: 7

near Hemet
See map page 885

Lake Hemet covers 420 acres, is at 4,340 feet, and sits near San Bernardino National Forest just west of Garner Valley. Many campsites have lake views. It provides a good camping/fishing destination, with large stocks of trout each year, and yep, catch rates are good. The lake also has bass, bluegill, and catfish. Boating rules prohibit boats under 10 feet, canoes, sailboats, inflatables, and swimming—no swimming or wading at Lake Hemet. The boat speed limit is 10 mph.

RV sites, facilities: There are 275 sites for RVs up to 40 feet, and two group sites for tents or RVs can accommodate up to 100 people each. Some sites have full hookups (20 amps) or are pull-through. Picnic tables and fire rings are provided. Restrooms have flush toilets and coin showers. Drinking water, a dump station, a playground, a boat ramp, boat rentals, a convenience store, a coin laundry, and propane gas are available. Some facilities are wheelchair accessible. Leashed pets are permitted.

Reservations, fees: Reservations are accepted for groups only. Sites are $17–21 per vehicle per night, $1–2.50 per person per night for more than two people, $1 per pet per night. Some credit cards accepted. Open year-round.

Directions: From Palm Desert, drive southwest on Highway 74 for 33 miles (near Lake Hemet) to the campground entrance on the left. For directions if arriving from the west (several options), phone 951/659-2680, ext. 2.

Contact: Lake Hemet, 951/659-2680, www.lake hemet.org.

61 HURKEY CREEK PARK
🏃 🎣 🐕 👫 ♿ 🚐 ⛺

Scenic rating: 5

near Lake Hemet
See map page 885

This large Riverside County park is just east (across the road) of Lake Hemet, beside Hurkey Creek (which runs in winter and spring). The highlight, of course, is the nearby lake, known for good fishing in the spring. No swimming is permitted. The camp elevation is 4,800 feet. The park covers 59 acres.

RV sites, facilities: There are 130 sites and five group sites for tents or RVs up to 40 feet that can accommodate up to 100 people each. No hookups. Fire grills and picnic tables are provided. Drinking water, restrooms with flush toilets and coin showers, a playground, and picnic areas are available. A dump station is at nearby Lake Hemet. Some facilities are wheelchair accessible. Leashed pets are permitted.

Reservations, fees: Reservations are accepted for individual sites and required for the group areas ($6.50–12 reservation fee) at 800/234-PARK (800/234-7275). Sites are $17 per night, $1 per pet per night. Group sites are $160 per night for up to 40 people, plus $4 per person per night for more than 40 people. Some credit cards accepted. Open year-round.

Directions: From Palm Desert, drive southwest on Highway 74 for 32 miles (near Lake Hemet) to the campground entrance on the right.

Contact: Hurkey Creek Park, 951/659-2050, www.riversidecountyparks.org.

62 ANZA RV RESORT

Scenic rating: 4

near Anza

See map page 885

This is a year-round RV park set at 4,100 feet, with many nearby recreation options. Lake Hemet is 16 miles away, with hiking, motorbiking, and jeep trails nearby in San Bernardino National Forest. Pacific Crest Trail hikers are welcome to clean up and to arrange for food and mail pick-up. Note that most sites are filled with long-term renters.

RV sites, facilities: There are 116 sites for tents or RVs; many sites have full hookups (30 and 50 amps), and some are pull-through. Picnic tables are provided. Restrooms have showers. A catch-and-release fishing pond, horseshoe pits, a coin laundry, a convenience store, a dump station, ice, a recreation room, modem access, and propane gas are available. Leashed pets are permitted, with certain restrictions.

Reservations, fees: Reservations are accepted. Sites are $18–20 per night, $1 per person per night for more than two people. Open year-round.

Directions: From Palm Desert, drive west on Highway 74 for 24 miles to Highway 371. Turn left on Highway 371 and drive west to the town of Anza and Kirby Road. Turn left on Kirby Road and drive 3.5 miles to the campground on the left at Terwilliger Road (look for the covered wagon out front).

Contact: Anza RV Resort, 951/763-4819, fax 951/763-0619.

SAN DIEGO AND VICINITY

BEST RV PARKS AND CAMPGROUNDS

《 Coastal Sites
South Carlsbad State Beach, **page 928.**

《 Fishing
Campland on the Bay, **page 931.**

San Diego was picked as one of the best regions of America to live in according to an unofficial vote at a national conference for the Outdoor Writers Association of America.

It is easy to understand why: the weather, the ocean and beaches, the lakes and the fishing, Cleveland National Forest, the state parks, the Palomar Mountains, the hiking, biking, and water sports. What more could anyone ask for? For many, the answer is you don't ask for more, because it does not get any better than this.

The weather is near perfect. It fits a warm coastal environment with an azure-tinted sea that borders foothills and mountains. In a relatively small geographic spread, you get it all.

The ocean here is warm and beautiful, with 70 miles of beaches and often sensational fishing offshore for albacore, yellowtail, and marlin. The foothills provide canyon settings for many lakes, including Lower Otay, Morena, Barrett, El Capitan, Cuyamaca, San Vicente, Hodges, Henshaw, and several more – with some of the biggest lake-record bass ever caught in the world.

Cleveland National Forest provides a surprise for many – remote mountains with canyons, hidden streams, small campgrounds, and a terrain with a forest of fir, cedar, and hardwoods such as oak. A landmark is Palomar Mountain, with several campgrounds at Palomar State Park and nearby in national forest. This is a great family destination. Long-distance views, stargazing, and watching meteor showers are all among the best anywhere in the state from the 5,000-foot ridges and lookouts on the edge of Anza-Borrego Desert to the nearby east.

For more urban pursuits, San Diego's Mission Bay Park offers a fantastic network of recreation, with trails for biking and rollerblading, plus beaches and boating access.

Everywhere you go, you will find campgrounds and parks, from primitive to deluxe, including developed RV parks that cost as much as fine hotel rooms in other parts of the state – and they're worth it, like silver dollars in a sea of pennies. The region is one of the few that provide year-round recreation at a stellar level.

If you could live anywhere in America, where would it be? Well, that's what makes it so special to explore and visit, camping along the way.

CALIFORNIA

Includes:

- Agua Tibia Wilderness
- Anza-Borrego Desert State Park
- Cleveland National Forest
- Cuyamaca Rancho State Park
- Doheny State Beach
- Lake Henshaw
- Lake Jennings
- McCain Valley Recreation Area
- Ocotillo Wells State Vehicle Recreation Area
- Palomar Mountain State Park
- San Clemente State Beach
- San Elijo State Beach
- Santee Lakes Recreation Preserve
- South Carlsbad State Beach
- Sweetwater Reservoir
- Sweetwater Summit Regional Park

CALIFORNIA

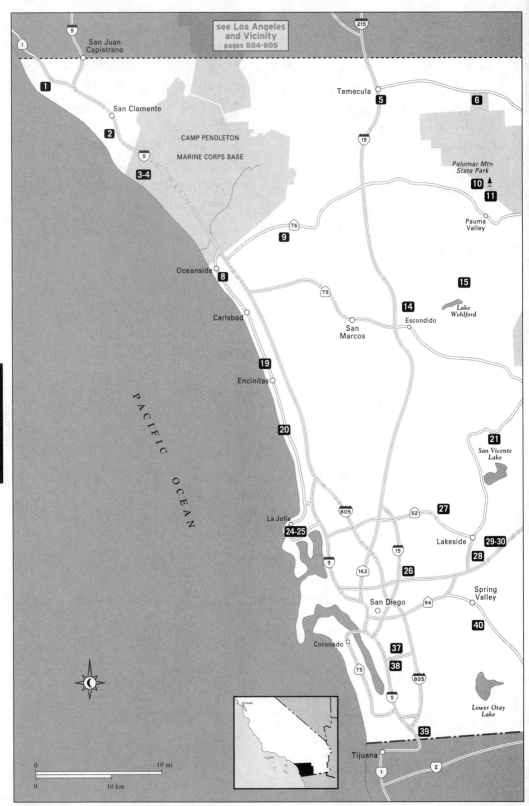

see Los Angeles
and Vicinity
pages 884-885

San Juan
Capistrano

San Clemente

CAMP PENDLETON
MARINE CORPS BASE

Temecula

Palomar Mtn
State Park

Pauma
Valley

Oceanside

Carlsbad

San
Marcos

Escondido

Lake
Wohlford

PACIFIC OCEAN

Encinitas

San Vicente
Lake

La Jolla

Lakeside

Spring
Valley

San Diego

Coronado

Lower Otay
Lake

Tijuana

CALIFORNIA

0   10 mi

0   10 km

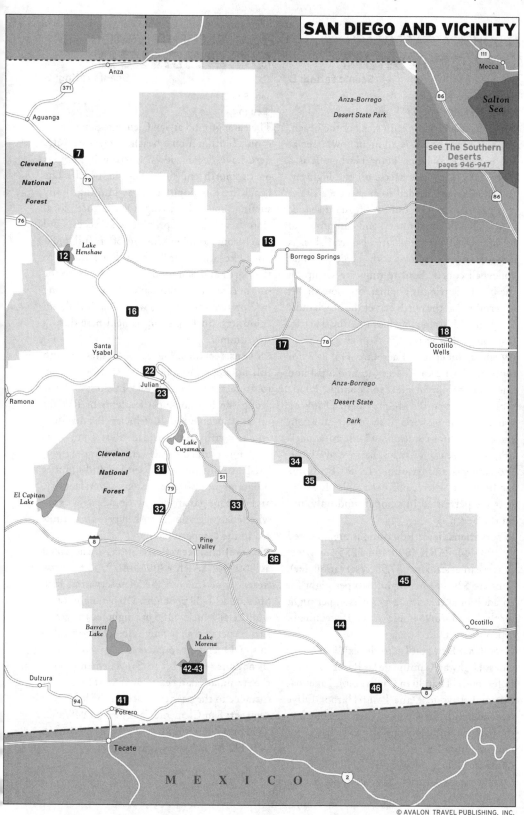

SAN DIEGO AND VICINITY

111

Mecca

Anza-Borrego
Desert State Park

86

*Salton
Sea*

see The Southern
Deserts
pages 946-947

86

371

Anza

Aguanga

7

79

Cleveland

National

Forest

76

Lake
Henshaw

12

16

13

Borrego Springs

Santa
Ysabel

22

Julian

23

Ramona

17

78

18

Ocotillo
Wells

Anza-Borrego

Desert State

Park

Lake
Cuyamaca

31

34

51

35

Cleveland

National

Forest

79

33

El Capitan
Lake

32

Pine
Valley

36

45

*Barrett
Lake*

8

44

*Lake
Morena*

42-43

Dulzura

94

41

Potrero

46

8

Ocotillo

Tecate

M E X I C O

2

CALIFORNIA

1 DOHENY STATE BEACH

Scenic rating: 8

on Dana Point Harbor

See map page 918

Some campsites are within steps of the beach. Yet this state beach is right in town, set at the entrance to Dana Point Harbor. It is a pretty spot with easy access off the highway. Reservations are needed to guarantee a site at this popular campground. A lifeguard service is available in the summer, and campfire and junior ranger programs are also available. A day-use area has a lawn with picnic area and volleyball courts. Bonfire rings are set up on the beach. Surfing is popular, but note that it is permitted at the north end of the beach only. San Juan Capistrano provides a nearby side trip, just three miles away.

RV sites, facilities: There are 115 sites for tents or RVs up to 35 feet (no hookups) and one hike-in/bike-in site. No hookups. Picnic tables and fire grills are provided. Drinking water, restrooms with flush toilets and coin showers, a dump station, Wi-Fi, an aquarium, and a seasonal snack bar are available. Propane gas and gasoline are nearby. Some facilities are wheelchair accessible. Leashed pets are permitted in campground only, not on the beach.

Reservations, fees: Reservations are accepted at 800/444-PARK (800/444-7275) or www .reserveamerica.com ($7.50 reservation fee). Sites are $20–40 per night, $10 per night for an additional vehicle, $3 per person per night for the hike-in/bike-in site (photo ID required). Open year-round.

Directions: Drive on I-5 to the exit for Pacific Coast Highway/Camino de las Ramblas (three miles south of San Juan Capistrano). Take that exit and drive to Dana Point/Harbor Drive (second light). Turn left and drive one block to the park entrance. Doheny State Beach is about one mile from I-5.

Contact: Doheny State Beach, 949/496-6172; Orange Coast District, San Clemente Sector, 949/492-0802, www.parks.ca.gov.

2 SAN CLEMENTE STATE BEACH

Scenic rating: 8

near San Clemente

See map page 918

The campground at San Clemente State Beach is on a bluff, not on a beach. A few campsites here have ocean views. Surfing is popular on the north end of a one-mile beach. The beach here is popular for swimming, body surfing, and skin diving. Of the three local state beaches that provide easy access and beachfront camping, this one offers full hookups. The others are Doheny State Beach to the north and San Onofre State Beach to the south. A feature at this park is a two-mile long interpretive trail, along with hike-in/bike-in campsites. Surfing camp is held here during the summer.

RV sites, facilities: There are 160 sites, 56 with full hookups (30 amps) for tents or RVs up to 40 feet; two hike-in/bike-in sites; and one group site (no hookups) for tents or RVs for up to 50 people and 20 vehicles. Picnic tables and fire grills are provided. Restrooms have flush toilets and coin showers. A dump station, Wi-Fi, summer lifeguard service, and summer programs are available. A store, a coin laundry, and propane gas are nearby. Some facilities are wheelchair accessible. Leashed pets are permitted in the campground only.

Reservations, fees: Reservations are accepted at 800/444-PARK (800/444-7275) or www .reserveamerica.com ($7.50 reservation fee). Sites are $20–39 per night, $10 per night for an additional vehicle, $186 per night for the group site, $3 per person per night for a hike-in/bike-in site. Open year-round.

Directions: From I-5 in San Clemente, take the Avenida Calafia exit. Drive west for a short distance to the park entrance on the left.

Contact: San Clemente State Beach, 949/492-3156 or 949/492-3281; Orange Coast District, 949/492-0802, www.parks.ca.gov.

CALIFORNIA

3 SAN ONOFRE STATE BEACH: BLUFF AREA

Scenic rating: 7

near San Clemente

See map page 918

This camp may appear perfect at first glance, but nope, it is very noisy. Both the highway and the train tracks are within very close range; you can practically feel the ground rumble, and that's not all. With Camp Pendleton just on the other side of the freeway, there is considerable noise from helicopters and other operations. Too bad. This is one of three parks along the beach near San Clemente, just off the busy Coast Highway. The campground is on top of a 90-foot bluff. This state beach covers more than 3,000 acres, featuring 3.5 miles of sandy beaches and access trails on the neighboring bluffs. This area is one of the most popular in California for surfing, with this state beach also good for swimming. The shadow of the San Onofre Nuclear Power Plant is nearby. Other state beaches in the area are San Clemente State Beach and Doheny State Beach, both to the north.

RV sites, facilities: There are 176 sites for tents or RVs up to 30 feet and one group site for up to 50 people. No hookups. Picnic tables and fire rings are provided. Drinking water, flush toilets, and cold outdoor showers are available. A store, a coin laundry, and propane gas are available within about five miles. Some facilities are wheelchair accessible. Leashed pets are permitted at the campground and beach but must stay on designated trails to access the beach.

Reservations, fees: Reservations are accepted at 800/444-PARK (800/444-7275) or www.reserveamerica.com ($7.50 reservation fee). Sites are $20–25 per night, $10 per night for an additional vehicle, $175 per night for the group site. Open March–October, weather permitting.

Directions: From San Clemente, drive south on I-5 for three miles to the Basilone Road exit. Take that exit and drive south on Basilone Road for two miles to the park.

Contact: San Onofre State Beach, 949/492-4872; Orange Coast District Office, 949/492-0802 or 909/366-8500, www.parks.ca.gov.

4 SAN ONOFRE STATE BEACH: SAN MATEO

Scenic rating: 9

near San Clemente

See map page 918

This state beach is considered one of the best surf breaks in the United States—it's well known as the outstanding Trestles Surfing Area. The camp is inland and includes a nature trail, featuring a marshy area where San Mateo Creek meets the shoreline. Although this is a state beach, the camp is relatively far from the ocean; it is a 1.5-mile walk to the beach. But it sure is a lot quieter than the nearby option, Bluff Area Campground.

RV sites, facilities: There are 159 sites for tents or RVs up to 35 feet; 67 sites have partial hookups (30 amps). Picnic tables and fire grills are provided. A dump station and restrooms with coin showers and flush toilets are available. A store, propane gas, and a coin laundry are nearby. Some facilities are wheelchair accessible. Leashed pets are permitted.

Reservations, fees: Reservations are accepted at 800/444-PARK (800/444-7275) or www.reserveamerica.com ($7.50 reservation fee). Sites are $20–39 per night, $10 per night for an additional vehicle. Open year-round.

Directions: Drive on I-5 to the southern end of San Clemente and the Cristianitos Road exit. Take that exit and drive east on Cristianitos Road for 1.5 miles to the park entrance on the right.

Contact: San Onofre State Beach, 949/492-4872; Orange Coast District Office, 949/492-0802 or 909/366-8500, www.parks.ca.gov.

CALIFORNIA

⑤ INDIAN OAKS TRAILER RANCH

Scenic rating: 5

near Temecula

See map page 918

This campground is on 21 acres in the Temecula Valley. The highlight of the ranch is a spring-fed lake with swimming beach and pedal boat rentals. Catch-and-release fishing is allowed at no charge, and no fishing license is required. The lake is stocked with catfish, bluegill, and largemouth bass. Shaded campsites are available and there is plenty of open space. Horseback-riding facilities are across the road from the campground. Nearby attractions are golf courses, hot-air balloon rides, wineries, a casino, and Old Town Temecula.

RV sites, facilities: There are 17 sites with full or partial hookups (30 amps) for RVs up to 40 feet and 29 tent sites. One site is pull-through. Picnic tables and fire pits are provided at the tent sites and some of the RV sites. Drinking water, a coin laundry, a snack bar, a dump station, a picnic area, propane, a playground, group facilities, pedal boat rentals, horseshoes, shuffleboard, billiards, and organized activities are available. Some facilities are wheelchair accessible. Leashed pets are permitted.

Reservations, fees: Reservations are recommended. Sites are $20 per night for a tent site and $25–35 per night for an RV site. Weekly and monthly rates are available. Some credit cards accepted. Open year-round.

Directions: From Temecula, drive north on I-15 to the exit for Rancho California Road. Take that exit and drive east on Rancho California Road for 15 miles to East Benton Road. Turn right and drive three miles to the ranch on the right.

Contact: Indian Oaks Trailer Ranch, 951/302-5399.

⑥ DRIPPING SPRINGS

Scenic rating: 7

near the Agua Tibia Wilderness in Cleveland National Forest

See map page 918

This is one of the premium Forest Service camps available, set just inside the national forest border near Vail Lake and adjacent to the Agua Tibia Wilderness. Dripping Springs Trail is routed south out of camp, starting at 1,600 feet and climbing near the peak of Agua Tibia Mountain, 4,779 feet.

RV sites, facilities: There are 33 sites for tents or RVs up to 22 feet (no hookups). Equestrian sites are available. Picnic tables and fire rings are provided. There is no drinking water. Vault toilets are available. Supplies are available nearby in Temecula. Leashed pets are permitted.

Reservations, fees: Reservations are not accepted. Sites are $12 per night. Open June–February. Closed March–May for protection of an endangered species, the arroyo southwestern toad.

Directions: From I-15 in Temecula, drive 11 miles southeast on Highway 79 to the campground.

Contact: Cleveland National Forest, Palomar Ranger District, 760/788-0250, fax 760/788-6130.

⑦ OAK GROVE

Scenic rating: 4

near Temecula Creek in Cleveland National Forest

See map page 919

Oak Grove camp is on the northeastern fringe of Cleveland National Forest at 2,800 feet. Easy access from Highway 79 makes this a popular camp. The Palomar Observatory is five miles up the mountain to the west, but there is no direct way to reach it from the campground, and it cannot be viewed from camp. Lake Henshaw is about a half-hour drive to the south. A boat ramp and boat rentals are available there.

RV sites, facilities: There are 81 sites for tents or RVs up to 27 feet (no hookups). Picnic tables

CALIFORNIA

and fire grills are provided. Drinking water and flush toilets are available. Propane gas and groceries are nearby. Leashed pets are permitted.

Reservations, fees: Reservations are not accepted. Sites are $15–23 per night. Open year-round.

Directions: Drive on I-15 to the Highway 79 exit. Take that exit and drive south on Highway 79 to Aguanga. Continue southeast on Highway 79 for 6.5 miles to the camp entrance.

Contact: Cleveland National Forest, Palomar Ranger District, 760/788-0250, fax 760/788-6130.

8 PARADISE BY THE SEA RV RESORT

Scenic rating: 7

in Oceanside

See map page 918

This is a classic oceanfront RV resort, but no tenters need apply. It's an easy walk to the beach. Note that the main coastal rail line runs adjacent to the resort, so expect some train noise. For boaters, Oceanside Marina to the immediate north is the place to go. Oceanside is an excellent headquarters for deep-sea fishing, with charter trips available; contact Helgren's Sportfishing, 760/722-2133, to arrange charters. Legoland is four miles from the resort, and The Wave Water Park and Mission San Luis Rey are seven miles away. Camp Pendleton, a huge Marine Corps training complex, is to the north.

RV sites, facilities: There are 102 sites with full hookups (30 amps) for RVs up to 40 feet; a few sites are pull-through. No tents. Picnic tables are provided. Restrooms, flush toilets, showers, cable TV, Wi-Fi Internet access, a heated swimming pool, a spa, a clubhouse, a banquet room, a coin laundry, RV supplies, and a convenience store are available. Boat rentals are nearby. Leashed pets are permitted, with certain breeds prohibited.

Reservations, fees: Reservations are recommended. Sites are $39–50 per night, $3 per

person per night for more than two people, $15 per night for each additional vehicle, $1.50 per pet per night. Ninety-day limit per stay. Some credit cards accepted. Open year-round.

Directions: Drive on I-5 to Oceanside and the Oceanside Boulevard exit. Take that exit and drive west on Oceanside Boulevard for 0.5 mile to South Coast Highway. Turn left on South Coast Highway and drive to the park on the right (1537 South Coast Highway).

Contact: Paradise by the Sea RV Resort, 760/439-1376, fax 760/439-1919, www.paradisebythesearvresort.com.

9 GUAJOME COUNTY PARK

Scenic rating: 5

in Oceanside

See map page 918

Guajome means "home of the frog" and, yep, so it is with little Guajome Lake and the adjacent marsh, both of which can be explored with a delightful two-mile hike. The lake provides a bit of fishing for warm-water species, mainly sunfish and catfish. Swimming is prohibited. Because of the wetlands, a huge variety of birds will stop here on their migratory journeys, making this a favorite area for bird-watching. A historic adobe house in the park is a must-see. The park covers 557 acres and features several miles of trails for hiking and horseback riding. A nearby museum exhibits antique gas and steam engines and farm engines.

RV sites, facilities: There are 35 sites with full hookups (30 amps) for tents or RVs up to 45 feet; a few sites are pull-through. Picnic tables and fire grills are provided. Drinking water, restrooms with flush toilets and showers, a dump station, and a playground are available. An enclosed pavilion and gazebo can be reserved for groups. A store and propane gas are nearby. Leashed pets are permitted.

Reservations, fees: Reservations are accepted ($3 reservation fee) at 858/565-3600. Sites are $16 per night, $1 per pet per night. Some credit cards accepted. Open year-round.

Directions: From Oceanside, drive east on Highway 76/Mission Avenue for seven miles to Guajome Lakes Road. Turn right (south) on Guajome Lakes Road and drive to the entrance.

Contact: San Diego County Parks Department, Guajome County Park, 760/724-4489, fax 760/945-5152, www.sdparks.org.

10 PALOMAR MOUNTAIN STATE PARK

Scenic rating: 8

near the Palomar Observatory

See map page 918

This is one of the best state parks in Southern California for hiking. It is also one of the friendliest. In fact, in 2004 Reserve America named Palomar as one of the top 100 family campgrounds in the United States. It features 14 miles of trails, including several loop trails, often featuring long-distance views. Yet forest covers much of this park, one of the few sites in this Southern California region with a Sierra Nevada–like feel to it. This camp offers hiking trails and some fishing in Doane Pond (state fishing laws are in effect here—great for youngsters learning to fish). There are numerous excellent hikes, including Boucher Trail (four miles) and Lower Doane Valley Trail (three miles). The view from Boucher Lookout is stunning, at 5,438 feet looking out over the valley below. This developed state park is a short drive from the Palomar Observatory. Four other campgrounds in the immediate area are a short distance from the observatory. At the Palomar Observatory (not part of the park) you'll find the 200-inch Hale telescope, America's largest telescope. This is a private, working telescope, run by the California Institute of Technology. Observatory tours are available, and the telescope can be viewed (but not used) by the public. The elevation is 4,700 feet.

RV sites, facilities: There are 65 sites for tents or RVs up to 25 feet (no hookups) and trailers up to 24 feet, three group sites for 15–25 people, and one hike-in/bike-in site. Picnic tables, fire grills, and food lockers are provided. Drinking water and restrooms with flush toilets and coin showers are available. Some facilities are wheelchair accessible. Leashed pets are permitted in the campground but not on trails.

Reservations, fees: Reservations are accepted at 800/444-PARK (800/444-7275) or www .reserveamerica.com ($7.50 reservation fee). Sites are $15–20 per night, $6 per night for an additional vehicle, $3 per person per night for the hike-in/bike-in site, $60–90 per night for group sites. A fishing license is required for the fishing pond; buy before arrival. Open year-round.

Directions: Drive on I-15 to the Highway 76 exit (east of Oceanside). Take that exit and drive east on Highway 76 for approximately 25 miles to County Road S6 (which brings you to the top of Palomar Mountain). At the top of the mountain, turn left and drive about 50 feet to State Park Road/County Road S7. Turn left on State Park Road/County Road S7 and drive about 3.5 miles to the park entrance.

Contact: Palomar Mountain State Park, 760/742-3462; Colorado Desert District, 760/767-5311, www.parks.ca.gov; Palomar Observatory, 760/742-2119.

11 OAK KNOLL CAMPGROUND

Scenic rating: 5

near the Palomar Observatory

See map page 918

The camp is at 3,000 feet in San Diego County foothill country among giant old California oaks. It is at the western base of Palomar Mountain, and to visit the Palomar Observatory and its awesome 200-inch telescope requires a remarkably twisty 10-mile drive up the mountain (the telescope is not open to the public, but the observatory is open). The campground managers suggest you bring your telescope or borrow one of theirs for nighttime stargazing. A good side trip is driving to the Boucher Lookout in Palomar Mountain State Park. Trailheads for excellent hikes on Palomar Mountain include Observatory Trail (starting at Observatory) and Doane Valley Loop (starting in Palomar Mountain State Park).

RV sites, facilities: There are 46 sites for tents or RVs up to 30 feet; many sites have full or partial hookups (30 amps). Picnic tables and fire barrels are provided. Drinking water, restrooms with flush toilets and coin showers, a dump station, a library, a video arcade, Wi-Fi, a recreation hall, a pavilion, seasonal activities, a playground, a swimming pool, a baseball diamond, horseshoes, a basketball court, a coin laundry, propane gas, and a convenience store are available. Leashed pets are permitted, with certain restrictions.

Reservations, fees: Reservations are accepted. Sites are $25–35 per night, $5 per person per night for more than two people, $3 per night for an additional vehicle, $2 per pet per night. Monthly rates available. Open year-round.

Directions: Drive on I-15 to the Highway 76 exit (east of Oceanside). Take that exit and drive east on Highway 76 for 21 miles to South Grade Road/County Road S6. Turn left and drive a short distance to the campground on the left.

Contact: Oak Knoll Campground, 760/742-3437, www.oakknoll.net.

12 LAKE HENSHAW RESORT

Scenic rating: 7

near Santa Ysabel

See map page 919

Lake Henshaw is the biggest lake in San Diego County, with 25 miles of shoreline, yet it has only one camp. It's a good one, with the cabin rentals a big plus. The camp is on the southern corner of the lake, at 2,727 feet near Cleveland National Forest. Swimming, water/body contact, canoes, and rafts are not permitted, and a 10-mph speed limit is in effect. The fishing is best for catfish, especially in the summer, and at times decent for bass, with the lake-record bass weighing 14 pounds, 4 ounces. Other fish species are trout, bluegill, and crappie. Like many reservoirs, Lake Henshaw is sometimes plagued by low water levels. A mobile home park is also on the premises.

RV sites, facilities: There are 139 sites for tents or RVs of any length (no hookups) and 25 sites for RVs of any length with full hookups (20 amps). Picnic tables and fire pits are provided. Restrooms have flush toilets and showers. Cabins, a swimming pool, a spa, a picnic area, a clubhouse, a playground, a dump station, a coin laundry, propane gas, boat and motor rentals, a boat launch, bait and tackle, a café, and a convenience store are available. A golf course is 10 miles away. Some facilities are wheelchair accessible. Leashed pets are permitted.

Reservations, fees: Reservations are not accepted. Sites are $18–23 per night, $2 per pet per night, and $7.50 per person per day for lake use. Boat launching is $5 per day. Some credit cards accepted. Open year-round.

Directions: From Santa Ysabel, drive seven miles north on Highway 79 to Highway 76. Turn east on Highway 76 and drive four miles to the campground on the left.

Contact: Lake Henshaw Resort, 760/782-3487 or 760/782-3501.

13 BORREGO PALM CANYON

Scenic rating: 4

in Anza-Borrego Desert State Park

See map page 919

This is one of the best camps in Anza-Borrego Desert State Park; it offers two excellent hikes. The short hike into Borrego Palm Canyon is like being transported to another world, from the desert to the tropics, complete with a small waterfall, a rare sight in these parts. Panorama Overlook Trail also starts here. An excellent visitors center displays an array of exhibits and a slide show. The elevation is 760 feet. Anza-Borrego Desert State Park is one of the largest state parks in the continental United States, covering more than 600,000 acres and with 500 miles of dirt roads. "Borrego" means bighorn sheep, appropriately named for the desert bighorn sheep that live in the mountains of this park.

RV sites, facilities: There are 65 sites for tents or RVs up to 25 feet (no hookups), 52 sites with full hookups (30 amps) for RVs up to 35 feet,

CALIFORNIA

and five group tent sites for up to 24 people each. Picnic tables and fire grills are provided. Drinking water, restrooms with flush toilets and showers, and a dump station are available. A store, a coin laundry, and propane gas are nearby. Some facilities are wheelchair accessible. Leashed pets are permitted.

Reservations, fees: Reservations are accepted at 800/444-PARK (800/444-7275) or www.reserveamerica.com ($7.50 reservation fee). Sites are $12–26 per night, $53 per night for group sites. Open year-round.

Directions: From Julian, at the junction of Highway 78 and Highway 79, drive east on Highway 78 (steep and curvy) for 19.5 miles to Yaqui Pass Road/County Road S3. Turn left (north) and drive eight miles to Borrego Springs and Palm Canyon Drive. Turn left (west) and drive 4.5 miles to the campground entrance road on the right.

Contact: Anza-Borrego Desert State Park, 760/767-4205; Colorado Desert District, 760/767-5311, fax 760/767-3427, www.parks.ca.gov.

14 DIXON LAKE RECREATION AREA

Scenic rating: 7

near Escondido

See map page 918

Little Dixon Lake is the centerpiece of a regional park in the Escondido foothills. The camp is at an elevation of 1,405 feet, about 400 feet above the lake's shoreline. No private boats or swimming is permitted, and a 5-mph speed limit for rental boats keeps things quiet. The water is clear, with fair bass fishing (a 25-pound, 1-ounce bass was caught in 2006) in the spring and trout fishing in the winter and early spring. Catfish are stocked in the summer, trout in winter and spring. In the summer, the lake is open at night for fishing for catfish. A pretty and easy hike is Jack Creek Nature Trail, a one-mile walk to a seasonal 20-foot waterfall. Note that no wood fires are permitted, but charcoal and gas are allowed.

RV sites, facilities: There are 45 sites for tents or RVs up to 35 feet; 11 sites have full hookups (30 amps). A cabin is also available. Picnic tables, fire grills, and food lockers are provided. Drinking water, restrooms with flush toilets and showers, picnic shelters, boat rentals, bait, ice, a snack bar, and a playground are available. Some facilities are wheelchair accessible. No pets are allowed.

Reservations, fees: Reservations are accepted ($5 reservation fee) at 760/741-3328. Sites are $20–25 per night. Groups can be accommodated. Some credit cards accepted. Open year-round.

Directions: Drive on I-15 to the exit for El Norte Parkway (four miles north of Escondido). Take that exit northeast and drive four miles to La Honda Drive. Turn left and drive about one mile to Dixon Lake.

Contact: Dixon Lake Recreation Area, City of Escondido, 760/839-4680, www.dixonlake.com.

15 WOODS VALLEY KAMPGROUND

Scenic rating: 5

near Lake Wohlford

See map page 918

This privately operated park is on 20 acres and is popular with families. Lake Wohlford is about 10 miles to the south and has a lake speed limit of 5 mph. The lake is stocked with rainbow trout, brown trout, steelhead, channel catfish, and blue catfish. Insider's tip: A bald eagle winters at Lake Wohlford.

RV sites, facilities: There are 59 sites for RVs of any length and 30 sites for tents. Many of the RV sites have partial hookups, and some have full hookups (30 amps). Picnic tables and fire barrels are provided. Drinking water, restrooms with flush toilets and showers, a dump station, a coin laundry, swimming pool, catch-and-release fishing pond, small animal farm, playground, volleyball, horseshoes, a recreation hall, group facilities, and supplies are available. Leashed pets are permitted, with some dogs prohibited.

CALIFORNIA

Reservations, fees: Reservations are accepted. Sites are $31–45 per night, $3 per night for an additional vehicle, $3 per pet per night. Monthly rates available. Open year-round.

Directions: From San Diego, drive north on I-15 to the Escondido area and take the Via Rancho Parkway exit and continue to Via Rancho Parkway. Turn right (name changes to Bear Valley Parkway) and drive approximately nine miles to a T intersection and Valley Parkway. Turn right on Valley Parkway and drive approximately six miles (name changes to Valley Center Road) to Woods Valley Road. Turn right and drive 2.2 miles to the park on the left.

Contact: Woods Valley Kampground, 760/749-2905, www.woodsvalley.com.

16 STAGECOACH TRAILS RV PARK

Scenic rating: 6

near Julian

See map page 919

You want space? You got space. That includes 600,000 acres of public lands bordering this RV campground, making Stagecoach Trails Resort ideal for those who love horseback riding and hiking. Ninety corrals and two round pens at the campground let you know right away that this camp is very horse-friendly. It is more than a horse camp, however, with amenities for various types of campers. The resort provides the perfect jumping-off place for trips into neighboring Anza-Borrego Desert State Park and the Pacific Crest Trail, which is 2.5 miles away. The resort's name comes from its proximity to the old Wells Fargo Butterfield Stage Route. While the scenic rating merits a 6, if the rating were based purely on cleanliness, professionalism, and friendliness, this resort would rate a 10.

RV sites, facilities: There are 250 sites with full hookups (30 amps) for RVs of any length and a large dispersed camping area for tents. Most RV sites are pull-through. Picnic tables and fire rings are provided. Drinking water, restrooms with flush toilets and showers, a heated pool, 90 horse corrals, a roping area, guided horseback riding, a convenience store, an ATM, a coin laundry, group facilities, horseshoe pits, shuffleboard, 24-hour security, and propane gas are available. Some facilities are wheelchair accessible. Leashed pets are permitted.

Reservations, fees: Reservations are accepted at 877/896-2267 (877/TWO-CAMP). Sites are $30 per night, $5 per person per night for more than two people, $5 per night per horse. Some credit cards accepted. Open year-round.

Directions: From Santa Ysabel, turn north on Highway 79 and drive 14 miles to County Road S2/San Felipe Road. Turn right and drive 17 miles to Highway 78. Turn right (west, toward Julian) and drive 0.3 mile to County Road S2 (Great Southern Overland Stage Route). Turn left and drive four miles to the resort on the right (at Mile Marker 21 on Road S2). Note that Highway 78, just east and west of Julian, is not recommended for RVs because of steep, curvy grades. (Call the resort for driving details.)

Contact: Stagecoach Trails RV Park, 760/765-2197, www.stagecoachtrails.com.

17 TAMARISK GROVE

Scenic rating: 5

in Anza-Borrego Desert State Park

See map page 919

This is the number one campground in Anza-Borrego Desert State Park, and it is easy to see why: Big tamarisk trees offer shade, and the park provides limited drinking water (it's recommended that you bring your own water as a backup). It is one of three camps in the immediate area, so if this camp is full, primitive Yaqui Well to the immediate west and Yaqui Pass to the north on Yaqui Pass Road provide alternatives for small RVs. Cactus Loop Trail, with the trailhead just north of camp, is a hiking option. This 1.5-mile loop passes seven varieties of cacti, some as tall as people. The elevation is 1,400 feet at this campground.

CALIFORNIA

RV sites, facilities: There are 27 sites for tents or RVs up to 21 feet (no hookups). Picnic tables and fire grills are provided. Restrooms have flush toilets and coin showers. Limited drinking water is available. Some facilities are wheelchair accessible. Leashed pets are permitted in the campground but not on trails or in wilderness.

Reservations, fees: Reservations are accepted at 800/444-PARK (800/444-7275) or www.reserveamerica.com ($7.50 reservation fee). Sites are $12–17 per night, $6 per night for an additional vehicle. Open October–May.

Directions: From Julian, at the junction of Highway 78 and Highway 79, drive east on Highway 78 (steep and curvy) for 19.5 miles to Yaqui Pass Road/County Road S3. Turn left (north) and drive 0.5 mile to the campground on the right.

Contact: Anza-Borrego Desert State Park, 760/767-4205; Colorado Desert District, 760/767-5311, fax 760/767-3427, www.parks.ca.gov.

18 OCOTILLO WELLS STATE VEHICLE RECREATION AREA

Scenic rating: 4

in Ocotillo Wells

See map page 919

This can be a wild place, a giant off-highway-vehicle (OHV) camp where the population of Ocotillo Wells can go from 100 to 5,000 overnight, no kidding. Yet if you arrive when there is no off-road event, it can also be a lonely, extremely remote destination. Some locals call the OHV crowd "escapees" and watch stunned as they arrive every February for two or three weeks. OHV events are held here occasionally. Mountain bikers also use these trails. One great side note is that annually there is "Desert Cleanup Day," when OHV users will clean up the place; the date changes every year. The non-OHV crowd can still use this camp, but most come in the winter on weekdays, when activity is lower. The landscape is barren desert, dry as an iguana's back. A few shade ramadas are provided on-site. The area covers 72,000 acres, ranging from below sea level to an elevation of 400 feet. It is adjacent to Anza-Borrego Desert State Park, another 600,000 acres of wildlands. The wash-and-ridge terrain includes a butte with dunes, a sand bowl, a blow sand dune, and springs. After wet winters, the blooms of wildflowers can be excellent. While this area is well-known as a wild play area for the OHV crowd, it is also a place where on most days you can literally disappear and see no one. All drivers should watch for soft ground. Many vehicles get stuck here and have to be towed out. Also, dispersed camping is allowed in most of these state park lands.

RV sites, facilities: There are 60 dispersed primitive sites for tents or RVs of any length (no hookups). Picnic tables and fire rings are provided. Chemical toilets and shade ramadas are available. There is no drinking water. A coin-shower building is available near the ranger station, and another is 3.5 miles east at Holmes Camp. A store, restaurants, propane, and auto supplies are available four miles away in Ocotillo Wells. A gas station is seven miles from the ranger station. Leashed pets are permitted.

Reservations, fees: No reservations are accepted and there is no fee, with a 30-day maximum stay per year. Open year-round.

Directions: From Julian, at the junction of Highway 78 and Highway 79, drive east on Highway 78 for 31.5 miles to Ranger Station Road. Turn left and drive 0.25 mile to the ranger station. (Note: For an alternative route, advisable for big rigs, that avoids curvy sections of Highway 78, see the detour route detailed in the listing for *Stagecoach Trails RV Park* in this chapter.)

Contact: Ocotillo Wells SVRA, 760/767-5391, fax 760/767-4951, www.parks.ca.gov.

19 SOUTH CARLSBAD STATE BEACH

Scenic rating: 9

near Carlsbad

See map page 918   BEST (

No reservation? Then likely you can forget about staying here. This is a beautiful state beach and, as big as it is, the sites go fast to the coastal cruisers who reserved a spot. The campground is on a bluff, with half the sites overlooking the ocean. The nearby beach is accessible by a series of stairs. This is a phenomenal place for scuba diving and snorkeling, with a nearby reef available. It is also a popular spot for surfing and body surfing. Legoland is one mile away.

RV sites, facilities: There are 222 sites for tents or RVs up to 35 feet (no hookups). Picnic tables and fire rings are provided. Drinking water, restrooms with flush toilets and coin showers, Wi-Fi, and a dump station are available. A lifeguard service is provided in summer. Supplies and a coin laundry are available in Carlsbad. Some facilities are wheelchair accessible. Leashed pets are permitted, but not on the beach.

Reservations, fees: Reservations are accepted at 800/444-PARK (800/444-7275) or www.reserveamerica.com ($7.50 reservation fee). Sites are $25–35 per night, $10 per night for an additional vehicle. Open year-round, with limited facilities in the winter.

Directions: Drive on I-5 to Carlsbad and the exit for Palomar Airport Road. Take that exit and drive west for 0.3 mile to Carlsbad Boulevard South. Turn south on Carlsbad Boulevard South and drive three miles to Poinsettia Avenue and the park entrance on the right.

Contact: South Carlsbad State Beach, 760/438-3143; San Diego Coast District, 619/688-3260, www.parks.ca.gov.

20 SAN ELIJO STATE BEACH

Scenic rating: 9

in Cardiff by the Sea

See map page 918

As with South Carlsbad State Beach, about half the sites overlook the ocean; that is, these are bluff-top campgrounds. Swimming and surfing are good. The narrow bluff-backed stretch of sandy beach has a nearby reef that is popular for snorkeling and diving. What more could you ask for? Well, for one thing, how about not so many trains? Yep, train tracks run nearby, and the

trains roll by several times a day. So much for a chance at tranquility. Regardless, it is a beautiful beach just north of the small town of Cardiff by the Sea. As at all state beaches, reservations are usually required to get a spot between Memorial Day weekend and Labor Day weekend. Nearby San Elijo Lagoon at Solana Beach is an ecological preserve. Though this is near a developed area, there are numerous white egrets, as well as occasional herons and other marine birds.

RV sites, facilities: There are 73 sites for tents or RVs up to 50 feet (no hookups), 26 sites with full hookups for RVs up to 24 feet or tents, and one hike-in/bike-in site. Picnic tables and fire rings are provided. Drinking water, restrooms with flush toilets and coin showers, Wi-Fi, a coin laundry, a dump station, and a small store are available. A lifeguard service is available in the summer. Some facilities are wheelchair accessible. Leashed pets are permitted, but not on the beach.

Reservations, fees: Reservations are accepted at 800/444-PARK (800/444-7275) or www.reserveamerica.com ($7.50 reservation fee). Sites are $25–44 per night, $10 per night for an additional vehicle, $3 per person per night for hike-in/bike-in site. Open year-round.

Directions: Drive on I-5 to Encinitas and the Encinitas Boulevard exit. Take that exit and drive west on Encinitas Boulevard for one mile to U.S. 101 (South Coast Highway). Turn south (left) on U.S. 101 and drive two miles to the park on the right.

Contact: San Elijo State Beach, 760/753-5091; San Diego Coast District, 619/688-3260 or 760/720-7005, www.parks.ca.gov.

21 DOS PICOS COUNTY PARK

Scenic rating: 6

near Ramona

See map page 918

Dos Picos means "two peaks" and is the highlight of a landscape featuring old groves of oaks and steep, boulder-strewn mountain slopes. Some of the oaks are 300 years old. The park covers 78 acres and has a nature trail. As a county park, this camp is often missed. It is quite picturesque, with plenty of shade trees and a small pond. Fishing is allowed in the pond, but swimming is prohibited. Several nearby recreation options include Lake Poway and Lake Sutherland. The elevation is 1,500 feet. Note that this park was partially damaged by the Cedar Fire of 2003, although the campground is intact.

RV sites, facilities: There are two sites with full hookups (30 amps), 61 sites with partial hookups, 11 sites with no hookups, one youth group area for up to 25 people, and a caravan area for tents or RVs. Picnic tables and fire grills are provided. Restrooms have flush toilets and showers. Drinking water, a dump station, a playground, horseshoes, and a soccer field are available. Supplies and a coin laundry are one mile away in Ramona. Leashed pets are permitted.

Reservations, fees: Reservations are accepted with a $3 reservation fee at 858/565-3600. Sites are $12–16 per night, $25 per night for the group area, $225 per night for the caravan area, $1 per pet per night. Some credit cards accepted. Open year-round.

Directions: Drive on I-8 to El Cajon and the exit for Highway 67. Take that exit and drive north on Highway 67 for 22 miles to Mussey Grade Road. Turn right (a sharp turn) on Mussey Grade Road and drive two miles to the park.

Contact: San Diego County Parks Department, Dos Picos County Park, 760/789-2220, fax 760/789-8435, www.sdparks.org.

22 PINEZANITA RV PARK AND CAMPGROUND

Scenic rating: 6

near Julian

See map page 919

Set at an elevation of 4,680 feet in dense pine and oak, this camp has had the same owners, the Stanley family, for more than 30 years. The fishing pond is a great attraction for kids (no license is required); no swimming allowed. The pond is stocked with bluegill and catfish, some of which are 12 inches or longer. Two possible side trips include Lake Cuyamaca, five miles to the south, and William Heise County Park, about 10 miles to the north as the crow flies. Note that while the 2003 wildfires burned the area adjacent to the park, Pinezanita itself sustained no damage.

RV sites, facilities: There are 210 sites with full or partial hookups (30 and 50 amps) for RVs, 32 sites for tents, and three cottages. Picnic tables and fire rings are provided. Restrooms have flush toilets and showers. Drinking water, a general store, ice, propane, bait and tackle, a fishing pond, and a dump station are available. Leashed pets are permitted, but not in the cottages.

Reservations, fees: Reservations are accepted. Sites are $24 per night per vehicle, $2 per night per person for more than two people, $4–6 per night for hookups, and $2 per night per pet. Some credit cards accepted. Open year-round.

Directions: From El Cajon, drive east on I-8 to Highway 79 (near Descanso Junction). Turn north on Highway 79 and drive 20 miles to Julian and the campground on the left.

Contact: Pinezanita RV Park and Campground, 760/765-0429, www.pinezanita.com.

23 WILLIAMHEISE COUNTY PARK

Scenic rating: 6

near Julian

See map page 919

This is a beautiful county park, set at 4,200 feet, that offers hiking trails and a playground, all amid pretty woodlands with a mix of oak and pine. A great hike starts right at camp (at the tent camping area), signed as Nature Trail. It joins Canyon Oak Trail and, after little more than a mile, links with Desert View Trail. Here you will reach an overlook with a beautiful view of the Anza-Borrego Desert and the Salton Sea. The park features more than 900 acres of mountain forests of oak, pine, and cedar. A popular equestrian trail is

Kelly Ditch Trail, which is linked to Cuyamaca Rancho State Park and Lake Cuyamaca. The vast Anza-Borrego Desert State Park lies to the east, and the historic mining town of Julian is five miles away. Julian is known for its Apple Day Festival each fall. Note: The wildfires of 2003 damaged some of this area, and several trails were still closed at the time of publication; check for current status.

RV sites, facilities: There are 37 sites for tents or RVs up to 40 feet with full hookups, 20 sites for tents or RVs up to 40 feet with partial hookups (30 amps), 42 sites for tents only, two group sites for up to 30 people each, and four cabins. Picnic tables and fire grills are provided. Restrooms have flush toilets and showers. Drinking water, a coin laundry, a dump station, picnic areas, and a playground are available. Supplies are available five miles away in Julian. Leashed pets are permitted.

Reservations, fees: Reservations are accepted with a $3 reservation fee at 858/565-3600. Sites are $12–18 per night, group sites are $25–50 per night, plus $1 per pet per night. Some credit cards accepted. Open year-round.

Directions: From El Cajon, drive east on I-8 to Highway 79 (near Descanso Junction). Turn north on Highway 79 and drive to Julian and Highway 78. Turn west (left) on Highway 78 and drive to Pine Hills Road. Turn left (south) on Pine Hills Road and drive two miles to Frisius Drive. Turn left (south) on Frisius Drive and drive two miles to the park.

Contact: San Diego County Parks Department, 760/765-0650, www.sdparks.org.

24 CAMPLAND ON THE BAY

Scenic rating: 6

on Mission Bay

See map page 918   BEST (

No kidding, this is one of the biggest campgrounds on this side of the galaxy. I used to get numerous complaints about poor communications and customer service support as well as a shortage of staff and safety issues. These problems appear to have been addressed by management, and the situation has improved. The place has a prime location, overlooks Kendall Frost Wildlife Preserve and on Mission Bay, a beautiful spot and a boater's paradise; it includes a private beach. Waterskiing, sailboarding, and ocean access for deep-sea fishing are preeminent. Sea World, just north of San Diego, offers a premium side trip.

RV sites, facilities: There are more than 558 sites, most with full or partial hookups (30 and 50 amps) for tents or RVs up to 45 feet. Picnic tables and fire pits are provided. Restrooms have flush toilets and showers. Drinking water, cable TV, phone and modem access, Wi-Fi, swimming pools, a spa, a recreation hall, an arcade, a playground, a café, a dump station, a coin laundry, a grocery store, an amphitheater, RV and boat storage, RV supplies, propane gas, a boat ramp, a marina, boat docks, water toy rentals, boat and bike rentals, and organized activities and events are available. Leashed pets are permitted, with certain restrictions.

Reservations, fees: Reservations are accepted up to two years in advance at 800/422-9386 ($25 site guarantee fee). Tent sites are $39–84 per night, RV sites are $46–249.90 per night, plus $7 per night for an additional vehicle or boats and trailers, and $3 per night per pet. Weekly rates are available during the winter. Some credit cards accepted. Open year-round.

Directions: Drive on I-5 south to San Diego and the Balboa-Garnet exit. Take that exit to Mission Bay Drive and drive to Grand Avenue. Turn right and drive one mile to Olney Street. Turn left on Olney Street and drive to Pacific Beach Drive. Turn left and drive a short distance to the campground entrance.

From northbound I-5 in San Diego, take the Grand-Garnet exit. Stay in the left lane to Grand Avenue. Turn left on Grand Avenue and drive to Olney Street. Turn left on Olney Street and continue as above.

Contact: Campland on the Bay, 800/422-9386, administration office 858/581-4200, www.campland.com.

25 SANTA FE PARK RV RESORT

Scenic rating: 3

in San Diego

See map page 918

This resort is a short drive from a variety of side trips, including the San Diego Zoo, Sea World, the historic San Diego Mission and Presidio Park, golf courses, beaches, sportfishing, and Tijuana.

RV sites, facilities: There are 129 sites with full hookups (20 and 30 amps) for RVs up to 40 feet. No tent camping is allowed. Picnic tables and barbecues are provided. Restrooms have flush toilets and showers. Drinking water, a playground, a heated swimming pool, a spa, a dump station, satellite TV, Wi-Fi, a recreation room, a mini theater, a fitness center, and coin laundry are available. Some facilities are wheelchair accessible. Leashed pets under 25 pounds are permitted, with some restrictions.

Reservations, fees: Reservations are accepted by website or at 800/959-3787. Sites are $41–59 per night, $2 per pet per night. Weekly and monthly rates available. Some credit cards accepted. Open year-round.

Directions: Drive on I-5 south to San Diego and Exit 23 for Balboa-Garnet. Take that exit, get in the left lane, and drive a short distance to the second stoplight and Damon Street. Turn left and drive 0.25 mile to Santa Fe Street. Turn left and drive 1.4 miles to the resort on the right (5707 Santa Fe Street).

On northbound I-5, drive to Exit 23 for Grand-Garnet. Take that exit and continue as it feeds to East Mission Bay Drive. Continue through four traffic signals to Damon Street. Turn right and drive 0.25 mile to Santa Fe Street. Turn left and drive 1.4 miles to the resort on the right (5707 Santa Fe Street). Note: Disregard the "Not a through street" sign on Santa Fe.

Contact: Santa Fe Park RV Resort, 858/272-4051 or 800/959-3787, fax 858/272-2845, www.santafeparkrvresort.com.

26 MISSION TRAILS REGIONAL PARK

Scenic rating: 7

in San Diego

See map page 918

Kumeyaay Lake and its campground are the centerpiece of this more than 6,000-acre park, which is only eight miles northeast of downtown San Diego. The park includes chaparral, oak woodland, mountains, and grasslands. Fishing is permitted for bass, bluegill, crappie, catfish, and carp; catch-and-release fishing is recommended. There are more than 40 miles of trails for hiking, biking, and horseback riding. Bird-watching is good in this park. Interpretive programs and organized activities are available.

RV sites, facilities: There are 46 sites for tents or RVs up to 40 feet (no hookups). Picnic tables, tent pads, and fire boxes are provided. Restrooms have flush toilets and solar-heated showers. A dump station, an amphitheater, a picnic area, and firewood are available. Alcoholic beverages are prohibited. Some facilities are wheelchair accessible. Leashed pets are permitted.

Reservations, fees: Reservations are accepted at www.mtrp.org/campground. Sites are $14 per night, $4 per night for an additional vehicle, $3 per pet per night. Open year-round Friday–Monday; campground is closed Tuesday–Thursday.

Directions: From I-8 in San Diego, take the Mission Gorge/Fairmount exit. Turn north on Mission Gorge Road and drive 6.5 miles to the northern (Kumeyaay Lake) entrance and Father Junipero Serra Trail. Turn left on Father Junipero Serra Trail and drive 0.2 mile to the lake and campground on the right.

Contact: Mission Trails Regional Park, City of San Diego, 619/668-2748; visitors center 619/668-3281, www.sandiego.gov.

27 SANTEE LAKES RECREATION PRESERVE

Scenic rating: 6

near Santee

See map page 918

This is a 190-acre park built around a complex of seven lakes. Some campsites are lakefront, and the park is best known for its fishing. The lakes are stocked with large numbers of trout and catfish, with fantastic lake records including a 39-pound catfish, 13-pound rainbow trout, 13.9-pound largemouth bass, and 2.5-pound bluegill. Rowboats, pedal boats, kayaks, and canoes are available for rent. So how many lakes can you boat on? Answer: Only one, Lake 5. Fishing is now allowed on all lakes, and float tubing is permitted on four lakes for campers only. No swimming or water/body contact is allowed here, and no private motorized boats are permitted. This small regional park is 20 miles east of San Diego. It receives more than 100,000 visitors per year. The camp is at 400 feet. The Carlton Oaks Country Club is a half mile away and open to the public.

RV sites, facilities: There are 300 sites with full hookups (50 amps) for RVs of any length, and tents are allowed at some sites. Some sites are pull-through. Picnic tables are provided, and some sites have barbecue grills. Restrooms have flush toilets and showers. Drinking water, a dump station, boat rentals, a playground, seasonal swimming pool, a general store, a picnic area, an amphitheater, RV storage, a recreation center, Wi-Fi, a pay phone, propane, and a coin laundry are available. Some facilities are wheelchair accessible. Leashed pets are permitted in the campground.

Reservations, fees: Reservations are accepted by website or at 619/596-3141. Sites are $32–42 per night, $2 per night for an additional vehicle, $1 per pet per night. Weekly and monthly rates available. Some credit cards accepted. Open year-round.

Directions: Drive on I-8 to El Cajon and Highway 67. Take the Highway 67 exit north (toward Santee) and drive one mile to Bradley Avenue. Take that exit and drive a short distance to Bradley Avenue. Turn left and drive one mile to Cuyamaca Street. Turn right and drive 1.6 miles to Mission Gorge Road. Turn left (west) and drive 0.3 mile to Fanita Parkway. Turn right and drive a short distance to the campground entrance on the left at 9310 Fanita Parkway.

Contact: Santee Lakes Recreation Preserve, Padre Dam Municipal Water District, 619/596-3141, www.santeelakes.com.

28 VACATIONER RV RESORT

Scenic rating: 2

near El Cajon

See map page 918

This well-maintained resort is 25 minutes from San Diego, 40 minutes from Mexico. Discount tickets to area attractions such as the San Diego Zoo, Sea World, and the Wild Animal Park are available. There is the very real chance of getting highway noise if you have a site at the back of the park. The RV sites are on asphalt and gravel, and there are many shade trees. The elevation is 260 feet.

RV sites, facilities: There are 150 sites with full hookups (30 and 50 amps) for RVs up to 40 feet, including 20 pull-through sites. No tent camping is allowed. Restrooms have flush toilets and showers. Drinking water, a coin laundry, recreation room, horseshoe pits, telephone and modem access, Wi-Fi, a heated swimming pool, a spa, satellite TV, a free video library, RV storage, and a picnic area with barbecues are available. A store is nearby. Some facilities are wheelchair accessible. Leashed pets up to 20 pounds are permitted, with certain restrictions.

Reservations, fees: Reservations are accepted at 866/490-5844. Sites are $40 per night, $2 per person per night for more than two people, $5 per night per additional vehicle, $2 per pet per night. Some credit cards accepted. Open year-round.

Directions: From El Cajon, drive east on I-8 for

CALIFORNIA

three miles to the Greenfield Drive exit. Take that exit, turn north, and drive 100 feet to East Main Street. Turn left (west) and drive 0.5 mile to the park on the left.

Contact: Vacationer RV Resort, 866/490-5844 or 619/442-0904, fax 619/442-4378.

29 RANCHO LOS COCHES RV PARK

Scenic rating: 2

near Lake Jennings
See map page 918

This is not your typical RV park. This place has plenty of charm and a private setting. There is an abundance of history here, too. The park land was once the smallest Mexican land grant of the 19th century. The former ranch was also once a station for the Jackass Mail and Butterfield Stage routes. Windmill House, built in 1925, is featured prominently on the property and is a local historic landmark. Nearby Lake Jennings provides an option for boaters and anglers and also has a less developed camp on its northeast shore. Vista Point on the southeastern side of the lake provides a side trip. (For more information, see the listing in this chapter for *Lake Jennings County Park*.) Casinos are nearby.

RV sites, facilities: There are 142 sites with full hookups (30 and 50 amps) for RVs up to 45 feet and four tent areas. Restrooms have flush toilets and showers. Drinking water, cable TV, a dump station, a heated swimming pool, a spa, a recreation hall, horseshoes, table tennis, Wi-Fi, and coin laundry are available. A store and gas station are one mile away. Leashed pets are permitted.

Reservations, fees: Reservations are accepted by website or at 800/630-0448. Sites are $39 per night for RVs, $25 per night for tents, $3 per person per night for more than two people. Weekly and monthly rates available. Open year-round.

Directions: From El Cajon, drive east on I-8 to the Los Coches Road exit. Take that exit and

drive under the freeway to Highway 8 Business Route. Turn right on Highway 8 Business Route and drive 0.25 mile to the park entrance on the left (13468 Highway 8 Business).

Contact: Rancho Los Coches RV Park, 619/443-2025, fax 619/443-8440, www.rancholos cochesrv.com.

30 LAKE JENNINGS COUNTY PARK

Scenic rating: 6

on Lake Jennings
See map page 918

Lake Jennings, at 108 acres, is a nice little backyard fishing hole and recreation area set at 700 feet, with easy access from I-8. Most people come here for the fishing; the lake is stocked with trout and catfish. It has quality prospects for giant catfish, as well as largemouth bass, bluegill, and, in cool months, rainbow trout. The lake record blue catfish is 60 pounds. Note that while shore fishing is available on a daily basis, boats are permitted on the lake November–August, Friday–Sunday. Night fishing is allowed on weekends during the summer. A fishing permit is required. The highlights here are evening picnics, summer catfishing, and a boat ramp and rentals. Swimming and water/body contact are prohibited. Miles of hiking trails are routed through chaparral-covered hills. Only one camp is available right at the lake, and this is it. Note that some of this park was damaged in the Cedar Fire of 2003; the campground was unaffected.

RV sites, facilities: There are 30 sites with full hookups (30 amps) for RVs up to 35 feet, 35 sites with partial hookups (20 amps) for RVs up to 25 feet, 25 tent sites, and a youth group area for up to 35 people. Some sites are pull-through. Picnic tables and fire grills are provided. Restrooms have flush toilets and showers. Drinking water, a nature trail, a clubhouse, horseshoes, and a dump station are available. A store is nearby. Leashed pets are permitted.

Reservations, fees: Reservations are accepted

at 858/565-3600. Sites are $14–18 per night, $25 per night for the group area, $1 per pet per night. Open year-round.

Directions: From San Diego, drive east on I-8 for 21 miles to Lake Jennings Park Road. Turn north (left) on Lake Jennings Park Road and drive one mile to the park entrance.

Contact: San Diego County Parks Department, 858/694-3049, fax 858/495-5841; Lake Jennings entrance station, 619/443-2004; boat rentals, 619/443-9503; http://sdparks.org.

31 CUYAMACA RANCHO STATE PARK: PASO PICACHO

🥾 🚴 🎣 🏕 ♿ 🚐 ⛺

Scenic rating: 2

in Cuyamaca Rancho State Park

See map page 919

This camp is at 4,900 feet in Cuyamaca Rancho State Park, best known for Cuyamaca Peak, 6,512 feet. Stonewall Peak Trail is accessible from across the street. This is a five-mile (sun-exposed) round-trip, featuring the climb to the summit at 5,730 feet. There are long-distance views from here, highlighted by the Salton Sea and the Anza-Borrego State Desert. It's the most popular hike in the park, a fair to moderate grade, and completed by a lot of families. Another, more ambitious hike is the trail up to Cuyamaca Peak, starting at the southern end of the campground, a 6.5-mile round-trip tromp (alas, on a paved road; at least it's closed to traffic) with a climb of 1,600 feet in the process. The view from the top is breathtaking, with the Pacific Ocean and Mexico visible to the west and south, respectively. Cuyamaca means "the rain beyond."

RV sites, facilities: There are 85 sites for tents or RVs up to 30 feet (no hookups) and 10 feet tall, five cabins, a nature den cabin, four wood cabins, two group tent sites for up to 60 people each, and one hike-in/bike-in site. Fire grills and picnic tables are provided. Restrooms have flush toilets and coin showers. Drinking water, Wi-Fi, and a dump station are available. Supplies are available nearby in Cuyamaca. Leashed pets are permitted.

Reservations, fees: Reservations are accepted at 800/444-PARK (800/444-7275) or www.reserveamerica.com ($7.50 reservation fee). Sites are $15–20 per night, $350 per night for group sites, $50 per night for the nature den cabin, $45 per night for cabins, $3 per person per night for the hike-in/bike-in site. Open year-round.

Directions: From El Cajon, drive east on I-8 to Highway 79 (near Descanso Junction). Turn north (left) and drive 13.5 miles to the park entrance on the left.

Contact: Cuyamaca Rancho State Park, 760/765-0755, fax 760/765-3021, www.parks.ca.gov.

32 CUYAMACA RANCHO STATE PARK: GREEN VALLEY

🥾 🚴 🎣 🏕 ♿ 🚐 ⛺

Scenic rating: 3

in Cuyamaca Rancho State Park

See map page 919

Green Valley is the southernmost camp in Cuyamaca Rancho State Park, which was 98 percent burned in the Cedar Fire of 2003; parts of the park are still closed because of fire damage. It is at 3,900 feet, with Cuyamaca Peak (6,512 feet) looming overhead to the northwest. A trailhead is available (look for the picnic area) at the camp for an easy five-minute walk to Green Valley Falls, and it can be continued out to the Sweetwater River in a 1.5-mile round-trip. The park covers 25,000 acres with trails for hiking, mountain biking, and horseback riding.

RV sites, facilities: There are 81 sites for tents or RVs up to 30 feet (no hookups) and 10 feet tall, along with one hike-in/bike-in site. Picnic tables and fire grills are provided. Restrooms have flush toilets and coin showers. Drinking water, Wi-Fi, and a dump station are available. A store and propane gas are nearby. Some facilities are wheelchair accessible. Leashed pets are permitted.

Reservations, fees: Reservations are accepted at 800/444-PARK (800/444-7275) or www.reserveamerica.com ($7.50 reservation

CALIFORNIA

fee). Sites are $15–20 per night, $6 per night for an additional vehicle, $3 per person per night for the hike-in/bike-in site. Open year-round.

Directions: From El Cajon, drive east on I-8 to Highway 79 (near Descanso Junction). Turn north (left) on Highway 79 and drive seven miles to the campground entrance on the left (near Mile Marker 4).

Contact: Cuyamaca Rancho State Park, 760/765-0755, fax 760/765-3021, www.parks .ca.gov.

33 LAGUNA

Scenic rating: 4

near Little Laguna Lake in Cleveland National Forest

See map page 919

Laguna is on Little Laguna Lake, one of the few lakes in America where "Little" is part of its official name. That's because for years everybody always referred to it as "Little Laguna Lake," and it became official. Yep, it's a "little" lake all right, a relative speck, and the lake can occasionally dry up. The camp is on its eastern side at an elevation of 5,550 feet. A trailhead for the Pacific Crest Trail is a mile north on the Sunrise Highway. Big Laguna Lake, which is actually a pretty small lake, is one mile to the west.

RV sites, facilities: There are 73 sites for tents or RVs up to 50 feet (no hookups) and 103 sites for tents. Picnic tables and fire grills are provided. Drinking water and restrooms with flush toilets and coin showers are available. A store and propane gas are available nearby. Some facilities are wheelchair accessible. Leashed pets are permitted.

Reservations, fees: Reservations are accepted at 877/444-6777 ($9 reservation fee) or www.ReserveUSA.com. Sites are $15 per night. Open year-round.

Directions: From San Diego, drive east on I-8 about 50 miles to the Laguna Junction exit for the Sunrise Highway. Turn north on the Sunrise Highway and drive 11 miles to the town of Mount Laguna. Continue north on Sunrise Highway for 2.5 miles to the campground entrance road on the left.

Contact: Cleveland National Forest, Descanso Ranger District, 619/445-6235, fax 619/445-1753; Laguna Mountain Visitor Center, 619/473-8547.

34 VALLECITO COUNTY PARK

Scenic rating: 3

near Anza-Borrego Desert State Park

See map page 919

This county park in the desert gets little attention in the face of the other nearby attractions. It is a 71-acre park built around a sod reconstruction of the historic Vallecito Stage Station. It was part of the Butterfield Overland Stage from 1858 to 1861. The route carried mail and passengers from Missouri to San Francisco in 25 days, covering 2,800 miles. Vallecito means "little valley." It provides a quiet alternative to some of the busier campgrounds in the desert. One bonus is that it is usually 10° cooler here than at Agua Caliente. A covered picnic area is a big plus. Other nearby destinations include Agua Caliente Hot Springs, Anza-Borrego Desert State Park to the east, and Lake Cuyamaca and Cuyamaca Rancho State Park about 35 miles away. The elevation is 1,500 feet.

RV sites, facilities: There are 44 sites for tents or RVs up to 40 feet (no hookups), one group area for up to 15 RVs, and one youth camping area for up to 35 people. Picnic tables, fire rings, and barbecues are provided. Drinking water, flush toilets, and a playground are available. Leashed pets are permitted.

Reservations, fees: Reservations are available with a $3 reservation fee at 858/565-3600. Sites are $12 per night, $75 per night for the group area, $25 per night for the youth group area, $1 per pet per night. Some credit cards accepted. Open Labor Day weekend–Memorial Day weekend; closed June, July, and August.

Directions: From El Cajon, drive east on I-8 for about 75 miles to the town of Ocotillo (the first town after crossing from San Diego County to Imperial County) and County Road S2/Imperial Highway. Turn north (left) on County Road S2/Imperial Highway and drive 30 miles to the park entrance.

Contact: San Diego County Parks Department, 858/694-3049, fax 858/495-5841, www.sdparks.org.

35 AGUA CALIENTE COUNTY PARK

Scenic rating: 3

near Anza-Borrego Desert State Park

See map page 919

This is a popular park in winter. It has two naturally fed pools: A large outdoor thermal pool is kept at its natural 90°F, and an indoor pool is heated to 102°F and outfitted with jets. Everything is hot here. The weather is hot, the coffee is hot, and the water is hot. And hey, that's what Agua Caliente means—"hot water," named after the nearby hot springs. Anza-Borrego Desert State Park is also nearby. If you would like to see some cold water, Lake Cuyamaca and Cuyamaca Rancho State Park are about 35 miles away. The elevation is 1,350 feet. The park covers 910 acres with several miles of hiking trails.

RV sites, facilities: There are 106 sites with full or partial hookups (30 amps) for RVs up to 40 feet, 35 sites for tents or RVs (no hookups), and a group area for up to 100 people. Picnic tables and fire grills are provided. Restrooms have flush toilets and showers. Drinking water, outdoor and indoor pools, a picnic area, and a playground with horseshoes and shuffleboard are available. Groceries and propane gas are nearby. Some facilities are wheelchair accessible. No pets are allowed.

Reservations, fees: Reservations are accepted with a $3 reservation fee at 858/565-3600. Sites are $14–18 per night, and the group area is $75 per night. Some credit cards accepted. Open

Labor Day weekend–Memorial Day weekend; closed June, July, and August.

Directions: From El Cajon, drive east on I-8 about 75 miles to the town of Ocotillo (the first town after crossing from San Diego County to Imperial County) and County Road S2/Imperial Highway. Turn north (left) on County Road S2/Imperial Highway and drive 25 miles to the park entrance.

From Julian, take Highway 78 east and drive 12 miles to County Road S2/San Felipe Road. Turn right on County Road S2/San Felipe Road and drive 21 miles south to the park entrance.

Contact: San Diego County Parks Department, 858/694-3049, fax 858/495-5841, www.sdparks.org.

36 BURNT RANCHERIA

Scenic rating: 6

near the Pacific Crest Trail in Cleveland National Forest

See map page 919

Burnt Rancheria is high on the slopes of Mount Laguna in Cleveland National Forest, at an elevation of 6,000 feet. The Pacific Crest Trail is approximately one mile from camp. It is quiet and private with large, roomy sites and was remodeled in 2005. Desert View Picnic Area, a mile to the north, provides a good side trip. Wooded Hill Group Campground is less than one mile away.

RV sites, facilities: There are 58 sites for tents or RVs up to 50 feet (no hookups) and 51 sites for tents only. Picnic tables and fire grills are provided. Vault and flush toilets and coin showers are available. Drinking water is available. Some facilities are wheelchair accessible. Supplies are nearby in Mount Laguna. Leashed pets are permitted.

Reservations, fees: Reservations are accepted at 877/444-6777 ($9 reservation fee) or www.ReserveUSA.com. Sites are $15 per night. Open May–October, weather permitting.

Directions: From San Diego, drive east on I-8 about 50 miles to the Laguna Junction exit for

CALIFORNIA

the Sunrise Highway. Turn north on the Sunrise Highway and drive about 10 miles north to the campground entrance road on the right.

Contact: Cleveland National Forest, Descanso Ranger District, 619/445-6235, fax 619/445-1753.

37 SAN DIEGO METROPOLITAN KOA

Scenic rating: 2

in Chula Vista

See map page 918

This is one in a series of parks set up primarily for RVs cruising I-5. Chula Vista is between Mexico and San Diego, allowing visitors to make side trips east to Lower Otay Lake, north to the San Diego attractions, south to Tijuana, or "around the corner" on Highway 75 to Silver Strand State Beach. Nearby San Diego Bay is beautiful with excellent waterskiing (in designated areas), sailboarding, and a great swimming beach.

RV sites, facilities: There are 208 sites with full hookups for RVs of any length, 48 sites for tents, and 27 cabins. Many sites are pull-through. Picnic tables and barbecue grills are provided. Restrooms have flush toilets and showers. Drinking water, modem access, Wi-Fi, a playground, a dump station, a coin laundry, a heated swimming pool, a spa, bike rentals, propane gas, seasonal organized activities, and a convenience store are available. Some facilities are wheelchair accessible. Leashed pets are permitted.

Reservations, fees: Reservations are accepted at 800/762-KAMP (800/762-5267). Sites are $30–49 per night for tents, $38–67 per night for RVs, $5 per night for an additional vehicle, $4 per person per night for more than two people. Some credit cards accepted. Open year-round.

Directions: Drive on I-5 to Chula Vista and the exit for E Street. Take that exit and drive east on E Street for three miles to 2nd Avenue. Turn left (north) on 2nd Avenue and drive

0.75 mile to the park on the right (111 North 2nd Avenue).

Contact: San Diego Metropolitan KOA, 619/427-3601, fax 619/427-3622, www.koa.com.

38 CHULA VISTA RV RESORT

Scenic rating: 6

in Chula Vista

See map page 918

This RV park is about 50 yards from San Diego Bay, a beautiful, calm piece of water where waterskiing is permitted in designated areas. An excellent swimming beach is available, and conditions in the afternoon for sailboarding are also excellent. Bike paths are nearby.

RV sites, facilities: There are 237 sites with full hookups (30 and 50 amps) for RVs. Some sites are pull-through. No tents. Picnic tables and cable TV are provided. Restrooms have flush toilets and showers. Drinking water, Wi-Fi Internet access, modem access, fitness center, playgrounds, a heated swimming pool and spa, a game room, two waterfront restaurants, a marina, a fishing pier, free boat launch, a coin laundry, propane gas, bicycle rentals, car rentals, a picnic area, meeting rooms, and a general store are available. Some facilities are wheelchair accessible. Leashed pets up to 20 pounds are permitted, with certain restrictions.

Reservations, fees: Reservations are accepted by website at 800/770-2878. Sites are $41.50–54.50 per night, $3 per night per additional person for more than two people, $3 per night for an additional vehicle, $1 per pet per night. Boat slips are $16–20 per day. Weekly and monthly rates are available. Some credit cards accepted. Open year-round.

Directions: Drive on I-5 to Chula Vista and the exit for J Street/Marina Parkway. Take that exit, turn left, and drive 0.5 mile west to Sandpiper Way. Turn left and drive a short distance to the park on the left (460 Sandpiper Way).

Contact: Chula Vista RV Resort, 619/422-0111, fax 619/422-8872, www.chulavistarv.com.

39 LA PACIFICA RV RESORT

Scenic rating: 1

in San Ysidro

See map page 918

This RV park is less than two miles from the Mexican border. Note that many sites are filled with long-term renters, but some sites are available for overnight use.

RV sites, facilities: There are 177 sites with full hookups (30 and 50 amps) for RVs up to 40 feet. No tents. Many sites are pull-through. Picnic tables are provided at most sites. Restrooms have flush toilets and showers. A heated swimming pool, a whirlpool, a clubhouse, a video and book library, cable TV, phone and modem hookups, Wi-Fi, a recreation room, a dump station, a coin laundry, and propane gas are available. All facilities are wheelchair accessible. Leashed pets under 20 pounds are permitted.

Reservations, fees: Reservations are accepted at 888/786-6997. Sites are $40 per night. Weekly and monthly rates available. Some credit cards accepted. Open year-round.

Directions: From the San Diego area, drive south on I-5 to San Ysidro and the exit for Dairymart Road. Take that exit east to Dairymart Road and drive a short distance to San Ysidro Boulevard. Turn left and drive to the park on the left (1010 San Ysidro Boulevard).

Contact: La Pacifica RV Resort, 619/428-4411, fax 619/428-4413.

40 SWEETWATER SUMMIT REGIONAL PARK

Scenic rating: 7

near Sweetwater Reservoir in Bonita

See map page 918

This regional park overlooks the Sweetwater Reservoir in Bonita. The campground is right on the summit, overlooking the Sweetwater Valley. This camp has equestrian sites with corrals for the horses. There are 15 miles of trails for hiking, mountain biking, and horseback riding in the park. There are several golf courses nearby, and it is 15 minutes from Tijuana. The Chula Vista Nature Center is nearby on the shore of south San Diego Bay.

RV sites, facilities: There are 46 sites for tents or RVs up to 45 feet with partial hookups (20 amps), including 15 equestrian sites with corrals. Picnic tables and fire grills are provided. Restrooms have flush toilets and showers. Drinking water, a covered pavilion, and a dump station are available. Leashed pets are permitted.

Reservations, fees: Reservations are accepted ($3 reservation fee) at 858/565-3600 or 877/565-3600. Sites are $16 per night, $2 per horse per night, $1 per pet per night. Open year-round.

Directions: From San Diego, drive south on I-805 for 10 miles to Bonita Road. Turn east on Bonita Road and drive to San Miguel Road. Bear right on San Miguel Road and drive two miles to the park entrance on the left.

Contact: San Diego County Parks Department, Sweetwater Summit Regional Park, 619/472-7572, fax 619/472-7571, www.sdparks.org.

41 POTRERO COUNTY PARK

Scenic rating: 3

near the Mexican border

See map page 919

If you are looking for a spot to hole up for the night before getting through customs, this is the place. This park covers 115 acres, at an elevation of 2,300 feet. It is a broad valley peppered with coastal live oaks amid grassy meadows and rocky foothills. The average summer high temperature is in the 90°F range, and the average winter low is 34°F. There is occasional light snowfall in the winter. Potrero means "pasturing place." Some of the summer grazers are rattlesnakes, occasionally spotted here. Side trips include the railroad museum and century-old historic stone store in Campo and the Mexican community of Tecate. In fact, it is just a heartbeat away from the customs inspection station in Tecate. A good side trip is to the

CALIFORNIA

nearby Tecate Mission Chapel, where you can pray that the guards do not rip your vehicle up in the search for contraband. Insider's tip: In the spring you may hear the evening call of the Pacific tree frog.

RV sites, facilities: There are 39 sites with partial hookups (20, 30, and 50 amps) for RVs up to 45 feet, 10 tent sites, and a group site for up to 45 people. Picnic tables and fire grills are provided. Restrooms have flush toilets and showers. Drinking water, a playground, and a dump station are available. Picnic areas, ball fields, and a dance pavilion are available. You can buy supplies in Potrero. Leashed pets are permitted.

Reservations, fees: Reservations are accepted ($3 reservation fee) at 858/565-3600 or 877/565-3600. Sites are $10–12 per night, $25–50 per night for the group site, $1 per pet per night. Open year-round.

Directions: From El Cajon, drive east on Highway 94 for 42 miles (near the junction of Highway 188) to Potrero Valley Road. Turn north on Potrero Valley Road and drive one mile to Potrero Park Road. Turn right (east) on Potrero Park Road and drive one mile to the park entrance.

Contact: San Diego County Parks Department, 619/478-5212, fax 619/478-2060, www.sdparks .org.

42 LAKE MORENA COUNTY PARK

Scenic rating: 7

near Campo

See map page 919

Lake Morena is like a silver dollar in a field of pennies if you like to fish, but there is no swimming or powerboating allowed. Yes, Lake Morena is out in the boondocks, but it's well worth the trip. If you like to fish for bass, don't miss it. The county park camp is on the southern shore at an elevation of 3,200 feet. The landscape is chaparral, oak woodlands, and grasslands, and the campsites are set in a grove of oaks. When full, the lake covers 1,500 surface acres, but water levels can fluctuate wildly

here. Catch rates for bass can be excellent, and some bass are big; the lake record for large-mouth bass weighed 19 pounds, 3 ounces, and the lake record for trout weighed 9 pounds, 6 ounces. Boat rentals are available nearby; motor boats are allowed only on Friday and Saturday. No swimming is allowed. The lake is just south of Cleveland National Forest and only seven or eight miles from the California/Mexico border. The Pacific Crest Trail passes through the park, and the surrounding national forest has hiking and horseback-riding trails. San Diego is about a 45-minute drive from the campground.

RV sites, facilities: There are 86 sites and a group area for tents or RVs of any length; many sites have full hookups (30 amps). Ten cabins are also available. Picnic tables and fire grills are provided. Restrooms have flush toilets and showers, and drinking water is available. A store, a boat ramp, and rowboat rentals are nearby. Leashed pets are permitted.

Reservations, fees: Reservations are accepted ($3 reservation fee) at 858/565-3600 or 877/565-3600. Sites are $12–16 per night, $25–50 per night for the group area, plus $1 per pet per night, $5 per day for boat launching. Open year-round.

Directions: From El Cajon, drive east on I-8 to Pine Valley, then continue east for four miles to the exit for Buckman Springs Road/County Road S1. Take that exit, turn south (right), and drive 5.5 miles to Oak Drive. Turn right (south) on Oak Drive and drive 1.5 miles to Lake Morena Drive. Turn left on Lake Morena Drive and drive to the park entrance on the right.

Contact: San Diego County Parks Department, Lake Morena County Park, 619/579-4101, fax 619/478-5327, www.sdparks.org.

43 LAKE MORENA RV PARK

Scenic rating: 6

near Campo

See map page 919

This camp is near the southern side of Lake Morena, a great lake for fishing and off-season vacations. It is one of three camps near the lake and the best for RVs. Lake Morena, at 3,200 feet, is a large reservoir in the San Diego County foothills and is known for big bass. It is also known for fluctuating water levels. Swimming is prohibited at this lake. (See the listing in this chapter for *Lake Morena County Park* for more information.)

RV sites, facilities: There are 41 sites with full or partial hookups (30 and 50 amps) for RVs up to 40 feet. No tents. Picnic tables are provided. Restrooms have flush toilets and showers. A dump station, a nine-hole pitch-and-putt golf course, propane gas, and a coin laundry are available. Some facilities are wheelchair accessible. Leashed pets are permitted.

Reservations, fees: Reservations are recommended. Sites are $28 per night. Some credit cards are accepted. Open year-round.

Directions: From El Cajon, drive east on I-8 to Buckman Springs Road. Take the Buckman Springs off-ramp, turn right (south) on Buckman Springs Road, and drive 5.5 miles to Oak Drive. Turn right on Oak Drive and drive 1.5 miles to Lake Morena Drive. Turn left on Lake Morena Drive and drive a short distance to the park on the right (2330 Lake Morena Drive).

Contact: Lake Morena RV Park, 619/478-5677, fax 619/478-5031.

44 COTTONWOOD

Scenic rating: 4

in the McCain Valley Recreation Area
See map page 919

This camp is on the western edge of the McCain Valley Recreation Area. Like most Bureau of Land Management camps, it is little known and little used. It is occasionally frequented by backcountry horsemen. The elevation is 4,000 feet.

RV sites, facilities: There are 29 sites for tents or RVs up to 35 feet (no hookups). Picnic tables and fire grills are provided. Drinking water and vault toilets are available. Two group horse corrals are also available. Leashed pets are permitted.

Reservations, fees: Reservations are not accepted. Sites are $6 per night. Open year-round.

Directions: From El Cajon, drive east on I-8 for 70 miles to the Boulevard/Campo exit. Take that exit right, then at the frontage road, turn left immediately and drive east (just south of the interstate) for two miles to McCain Valley Road. Turn left on McCain Valley Road and drive about 13 miles to the campground.

Contact: Bureau of Land Management, El Centro Field Office, 760/337-4400, fax 760/337-4490.

45 MOUNTAIN PALM SPRINGS PRIMITIVE CAMP AREA

Scenic rating: 4

in Anza-Borrego Desert State Park
See map page 919

A plus for this camping area is easy access from County Road S2, but no water is a giant minus. Regardless of pros and cons, only hikers will get the full benefit of the area. A trail leads south to Bow Willow Creek (and Bow Willow) and onward into Bow Willow Canyon. The Carrizo Badlands Overlook is on the southeast side of Sweeney Pass, about a 10-minute drive south on County Road S2. The elevation is 760 feet.

RV sites, facilities: This is a primitive, open camping area for tents or RVs of any length; no hookups. Vault toilets are available. No drinking water is available. Fires are permitted in metal containers. Garbage and ashes must be packed out. Leashed pets are permitted, but not on trails or in wilderness.

Reservations, fees: Reservations are not accepted. There is no fee for camping. Open year-round.

Directions: From El Cajon, drive east on I-8 for about 75 miles to the town of Ocotillo (the first town after crossing from San Diego County to Imperial County) and County Road S2/Imperial Highway. Turn north (left) on County Road S2/Imperial Highway and drive 27.5 miles to the campground entrance road on the left (about 0.5 mile past the Bow Willow

CALIFORNIA

campground turnoff). Turn left and continue 0.75 mile to the camp.

Contact: Anza-Borrego Desert State Park, 760/767-4205; Colorado Desert District, 760/767-5311, fax 760/767-3427, www.parks .ca.gov.

46 OUTDOOR WORLD RETREAT

🚶 🏕 ♿ 🚐 ⛺

Scenic rating: 4

in Boulevard

See map page 919

This retreat sits on 163 acres and has hiking trails. The elevation is 3,800 feet. The town of Boulevard is centrally situated for a wide variety of recreation possibilities. About 10 miles to the north is Mount Laguna, with hiking trails available. About 30 minutes to the south is the nearest point of entry to Mexico at Tecate. Fishing at Lake Morena or Lake Cuyamaca is also a possibility, as is soaking in nearby hot springs. A casino is four miles away. A train museum is available in Campo, about 16 miles away.

RV sites, facilities: There are 151 sites for tents or RVs up to 45 feet with full or partial hookups (20, 30, and 50 amps), a primitive tent camping area, and a group camping area for up to 1,000 people. Some sites are pull-through. Picnic tables and fire rings are provided at some sites. A clubhouse, restrooms with showers, horseshoes, volleyball, a coin laundry, a gift shop, a general store, Wi-Fi Internet access, a group campfire area, and organized activities and classes are available. Golf carts are allowed. Some facilities are wheelchair accessible. Leashed pets are permitted, with some breeds prohibited.

Reservations, fees: Reservations are accepted by website or telephone at 888/703-0009. Sites are $20–33 per night, $3 per person per night for more than two people, $3 per night for an additional vehicle, $3 per night per pet. Weekly, monthly, and group rates available. Some credit cards accepted. Open year-round.

Directions: From El Cajon, drive east on I-8 for approximately 50 miles (past Alpine) to the Crestwood/Live Oak Springs Road exit. Take that exit and turn east and drive 0.5 mile to Church Street. Turn right and drive 4.2 miles to Highway 94. Turn left (east) and drive 1.1 miles to the resort on the right.

Contact: Outdoor World Retreat, 619/766-4480, www.outdoorworldrvpark.com.

THE SOUTHERN DESERTS

There is no region so vast in California – yet with

fewer people – than the broad expanse of Anza-Borrego Desert State Park, Joshua Tree National Park, Mojave National Preserve, the Salton Sea, and endless Bureau of Land Management (BLM) land. And yet the area is best-loved not for the desert, but for the boating, water sports, and recreation of the Colorado River. Each of these respective areas has distinct qualities, separate and special, yet they are also joined at the edges.

What often attracts people to this region for the first time is a party at the Colorado River. On big weekends, it can even seem as if there is a party within close vicinity of every boat ramp on the river. The weather is hot, the boats are fast, and the body oil can flow as fast as the liquid refreshments. Campgrounds are available throughout this region for the best access to the water.

The rest of the area is far different.

Anza-Borrego (covered in the *San Diego and Vicinity* chapter) is so big that it seems to stretch to forever. That is because it does. The park covers 600,000 acres, the largest state park in California. The landscape features virtually every type of desert terrain, but most obvious are canyons, badlands, and barren ridges. In spring, the blooming cholla can be impressive. This is habitat for the endangered desert bighorn, and seeing one can be the highlight of a lifetime of wildlife-viewing.

Joshua Tree National Park, on the other hand, features a sweeping desert landscape edged by mountains and peppered with the peculiar Joshua tree. It is best known by most as the place where the high desert (Mojave Desert, 4,000 feet elevation) meets the low desert (Colorado Desert). This transition and diversity create the setting for a similar diversity in vegetation and habitat. The strange piles of rocks often appear to have been left there by an ancient prehistoric giant, as if chipped, chiseled, and then left in rows and piles.

The national park is far different from Mojave National Preserve. The highlights here are the Kelso Dunes, a series of volcanic cliffs, and a forest of Joshua trees. It is remote and explored by relatively few visitors. The Mojave is a point of national significance because it is where three major landscapes join: the Sonoran Desert, the Colorado Desert, and the Mojave Desert.

The Salton Sea and the endless BLM desert land provide one of the most distinct (and strange) lakes and terrain on earth. The Salton Sea, created in an accident from a broken dike, is one of the largest inland seas in the world. The desert land of the BLM is under BLM control only because no other agency wanted it.

Throughout this barren area, campgrounds are sprinkled in most of the best spots. Some are remote. Some consist of nothing but flat parking areas. Some are simple staging areas for OHV riders, and some serve as a base camp for a weekend party. Somewhere amid all this, a place like no other, you will likely be able to find a match for your desires.

Includes:

- Angeles National Forest
- Brite Valley Aquatic Recreation Area
- Calico Ghost Town Regional Park
- Colorado River
- Imperial Sand Dunes Recreation Area
- Joshua Tree National Park
- Lake Havasu
- Moabi Regional Park
- Mojave Narrows Regional Park
- Mojave National Preserve
- Mojave River
- Palm Springs
- Picacho State Recreation Area
- Providence Mountains State Recreation Area
- Pyramid Lake
- Red Rock Canyon State Park
- Saddleback Butte State Park
- Salton Sea State Recreation Area
- Senator Wash Recreation Area
- Taylor Lake
- Tecopa Hot Springs Park
- Tehachapi Mountain Park
- Wiest Lake

CALIFORNIA

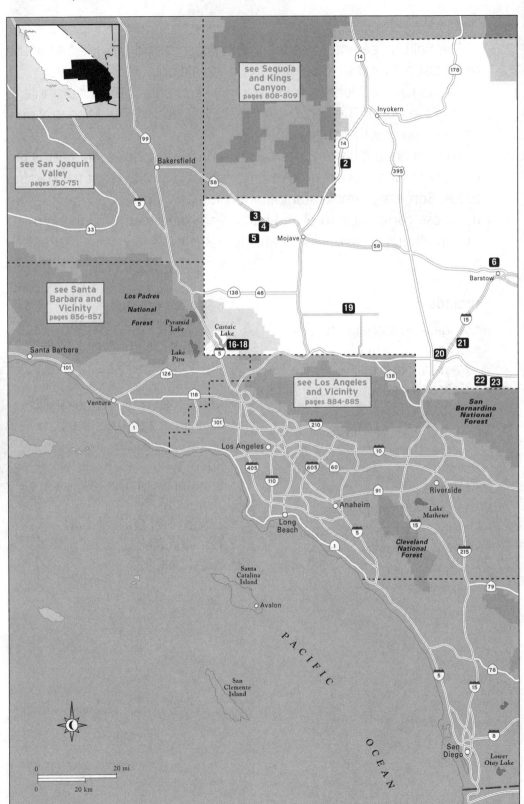

CALIFORNIA

see Sequoia
and Kings
Canyon
pages 808-809

see San Joaquin
Valley
pages 750-751

see Santa
Barbara and
Vicinity
pages 856-857

see Los Angeles
and Vicinity
pages 884-885

Bakersfield

Inyokern

Mojave

Barstow

Los Padres
National
Forest

Pyramid
Lake

Castaic
Lake

Lake
Piru

Santa Barbara

Ventura

Los Angeles

Anaheim

Long
Beach

Riverside

Lake
Mathews

San
Bernardino
National
Forest

Cleveland
National
Forest

Santa
Catalina
Island

Avalon

San
Clemente
Island

San
Diego

Lower
Otay Lake

PACIFIC

OCEAN

2
3
4
5
6
16-18
19
20
21
22
23

0   20 mi
0   20 km

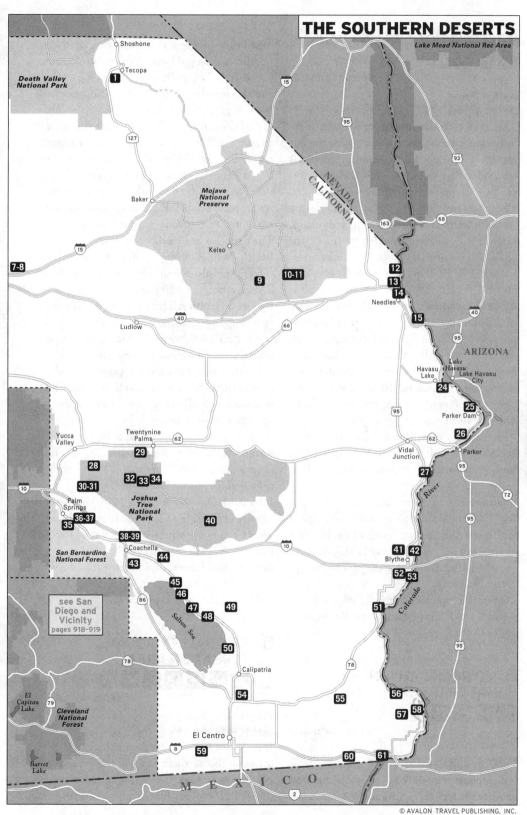

THE SOUTHERN DESERTS

Lake Mead National Rec Area

Death Valley National Park

Shoshone

Tecopa

1

7-8

Baker

Mojave National Preserve

Kelso

9   **10-11**

Ludlow

12

13

14

Needles

15

NEVADA / CALIFORNIA

ARIZONA

Havasu Lake

Lake Havasu

Lake Havasu City

24

25

Parker Dam

26

Vidal Junction

Parker

27

Yucca Valley

Twentynine Palms

29

28

32 **33** **34**

30-31

Palm Springs

36-37

35

Joshua Tree National Park

40

38-39

Coachella

44

San Bernardino National Forest

43

45

46

47 **48**

49

Salton Sea

50

Blythe

41 **42**

52 **53**

51

Colorado River

see San Diego and Vicinity pages 918-919

Calipatria

54

55

56

57 **58**

El Capitan Lake

Cleveland National Forest

El Centro

59

60 **61**

Barret Lake

M E X I C O

CALIFORNIA

1 TECOPA HOT SPRINGS PARK

Scenic rating: 3

north of Tecopa

See map page 947

This Inyo County campground is out there in no-man's-land, and if it weren't for the hot springs and the good rockhounding, all you'd see around here would be a few skeletons. Regardless, it's quite an attraction in the winter, when the warm climate is a plus and the nearby mineral baths are worth taking a dunk in. Rock hounds will enjoy looking for amethysts, opals, and petrified wood in the nearby areas. The elevation is 1,500 feet. Nobody gets here by accident.

RV sites, facilities: There are 250 sites for tents or RVs of any length with partial hookups (30 amps). Some sites are pull-through. Picnic tables and fire grills are provided. Restrooms have flush toilets and showers. A dump station is available. There is no drinking water. Groceries and propane gas are available within 10 miles. Leashed pets are permitted.

Reservations, fees: Reservations are accepted. Sites are $14–17 per vehicle per night. Weekly and monthly rates are available. Open year-round.

Directions: From Baker, drive north on Highway 127 for 58 miles to a county road signed for Tecopa Hot Springs (south of the junction of Highway 178 and Highway 127). Turn right (east) and drive five miles to the park and campground entrance.

Contact: Tecopa Hot Springs Park, 760/852-4481, Inyo County Parks and Recreation, 760/873-5577.

2 RED ROCK CANYON STATE PARK

Scenic rating: 8

near Mojave

See map page 946

This unique state park is one of the prettiest spots in the region year-round. What makes it worthwhile in any season is the chance to see wondrous geologic formations, most of them tinted red. The park has paleontology sites and the remains of 1890s-era mining operations. A great, easy hike is the two-mile walk to Red Cliffs Natural Preserve, where there are awesome 300-foot cliffs and columns, painted red by the iron in the soil. Part of this area is closed February–June to protect nesting raptors. For those who don't hike, a must is driving up Jawbone Canyon Road to see Jawbone and Last Chance Canyons. Hikers have it better. The park also has excellent wildflower blooms March–May. A primitive off-highway vehicle (OHV) trail also is available; check regulations. The elevation is 2,600 feet.

RV sites, facilities: There are 50 sites for tents or RVs up to 30 feet (no hookups). Picnic tables and fire grills are provided. Drinking water, pit toilets, a dump station, a picnic area, seasonal exhibits, a seasonal campfire program, and a seasonal nature trail are available. In spring and fall, rangers lead nature walks. Some facilities are wheelchair accessible. Leashed pets are permitted in the campground only.

Reservations, fees: Reservations are not accepted. Sites are $12 per night, $5 per additional vehicle. Open year-round.

Directions: Drive on Highway 14 to the town of Mojave (50 miles east of the Los Angeles Basin area). Continue northeast on Highway 14 for 25 miles to the park entrance on the left.

Contact: Red Rock Canyon State Park, Mojave Desert Information Center, 661/942-0662, fax 661/940-7327, www.parks.ca.gov.

3 BRITE VALLEY AQUATIC RECREATION AREA

Scenic rating: 7

at Brite Lake

See map page 946

Brite Valley Lake is a speck of a water hole (90 acres) on the northern flank of the Tehachapi Mountains in Kern County, at an elevation of 4,000 feet. No gas motors are permitted on the lake, so it's perfect for canoes, kayaks, or inflatables. No swimming is permitted. Use is moderate, primarily by picnickers and anglers. The lake is stocked with trout in the spring and catfish in the summer. Other species include bluegill. A golf course is nearby.

RV sites, facilities: There are 12 sites with partial hookups (20 amps) for RVs of any length and a tent camping area. Picnic tables and fire grills are provided. Drinking water, restrooms with flush toilets and showers, a dump station, a playground, reservable picnic pavilions, and a fish-cleaning station are available. Supplies are available about eight miles away in Tehachapi. Leashed pets are permitted.

Reservations, fees: Reservations are not accepted. Sites are $15–20 per night for each vehicle. Boat launching is $3 per day. Open late April–late October.

Directions: From Bakersfield, drive east on Highway 58 for 40 miles toward the town of Tehachapi. Take the Highway 202 exit and drive three miles west to Banducci Road. Turn left and drive for about one mile to the park on the right.

Contact: Tehachapi Valley Recreation and Parks District, 661/822-3228, fax 661/823-8529.

4 INDIAN HILL RANCH AND RV PARK

Scenic rating: 7

near Tehachapi
See map page 946

This is a unique park with two seasonal ponds stocked with largemouth bass and catfish. Crappie and bluegill are other fish species. The campground is open year-round and offers spacious, private sites with oak trees and a view of Brite Valley. A bonus is the hiking trails in the park. The elevation is 5,000 feet. Although this area is known for being windy, this campground is somewhat sheltered from the wind.

RV sites, facilities: There are 46 sites for RVs; many have full hookups, and nearly half are pull-through. Tents are allowed with RVs

only. Picnic tables and fire pits are provided. Restrooms have flush toilets and showers (seasonal). A dump station, a coin laundry, Wi-Fi, propane, and two stocked fishing ponds are available. Small leashed pets are permitted, with certain restrictions.

Reservations, fees: Reservations are accepted. Sites are $20–40 per night. Monthly and group rates available. Some credit cards accepted. Open year-round, with some sites closed November–mid-May.

Directions: Drive on Highway 58 to Tehachapi and Exit 148 for Tehachapi/Highway 202. Take that exit to Tucker Road. Turn right and drive south one mile to Highway 202/Valley Boulevard. Turn right (west) and drive four miles to Banducci Road. Turn left and drive 0.75 mile to Arosa Road. Turn left and drive 1.7 miles to the park at 18061 Arosa Road.

Contact: Indian Hill Ranch and RV Park, 661/822-6613, www.indianhillranch.com.

5 TEHACHAPI MOUNTAIN PARK

Scenic rating: 6

southwest of Tehachapi
See map page 946

This county park is overlooked by most out-of-towners. It is a pretty spot covering 5,000 acres on the slopes of the Tehachapi Mountains, with elevations in the park ranging 5,500–7,000 feet. The roads to the campgrounds are steep, but the sites are flat. Trails for hikers and equestrians are available, but no horses are allowed at the campground. An interpretive trail, Nuooah Nature Trail, is available. This park is popular not only in spring but also in winter, with the elevations sometimes high enough to get snow (chains often required for access). The park lies eight miles southwest of the town of Tehachapi on the southern side of Highway 58 between Mojave and Bakersfield. Woody's Peak, at almost 8,000 feet, overlooks the park from its dominion in the Tehachapi Mountains, the dividing line between the San Joaquin Valley and the Los Angeles Basin.

CALIFORNIA

RV sites, facilities: There are 61 sites for tents or RVs of any length (no hookups), a group campsite for up to 40 people, and group lodging with 10 cabins for a minimum of 40 people. Picnic tables and fire grills are provided. Drinking water (natural spring) and chemical toilets are available. Some facilities are wheelchair accessible. Leashed pets are permitted.

Reservations, fees: Reservations are accepted for the group site and group cabins only. Sites are $14 per night per vehicle, $275 per night for the group site, and $2 per pet per night. Reserve the group site and cabins at 661/868-7002. Open year-round, weather permitting.

Directions: In Tehachapi, take Tehachapi Boulevard to the Cury Street exit. Take that exit south and drive about three miles to Highline Road. Turn right on Highline Road and drive two miles to Water Canyon Road. Turn left on Water Canyon Road and drive three miles to the park.

Contact: Kern County Parks Department, info line 661/868-7000, www.co.kern.ca.us/parks/index.htm.

6 OWL CANYON

Scenic rating: 3

near Barstow

See map page 946

The primary attraction of Owl Canyon camp is that the surrounding desert is sprinkled with exposed fossils of ancient animals. Guess they couldn't find any water, heh, heh. Well, if people try hiking here without a full canteen, there may soon be some human skeletons out here, too. Actually, rangers tell us that the general public is unlikely to spot fossils here because it takes some basic scientific knowledge to identify them. The sparse BLM land out here is kind of like an ugly dog you learn to love: After a while, when you look closely, you learn it has a heart of gold. This region is best visited in the spring and fall, of course, when hiking allows a fresh, new look at what may appear to some as a wasteland. The beauty is in the detail of it—tiny critters

and tiny flowers seen against the unfenced vastness, with occasional fossils yet to be discovered. The elevation is 2,600 feet.

RV sites, facilities: There are 31 sites for tents or RVs of any length (no hookups). Picnic tables and fire grills are provided. Vault toilets are available. There is no drinking water. Leashed pets are permitted.

Reservations, fees: Reservations are not accepted. Sites are $6 per night. Open year-round.

Directions: Drive on I-15 to Barstow to the exit for 1st Street. Take that exit and drive north on 1st Street (crossing the Mojave River Bridge) for 0.75 mile to Irwin Road. Turn left and drive eight miles to Fossil Bed Road. Turn left and drive two miles to the campground on the right.

Contact: Bureau of Land Management, Barstow Field Office, 760/252-6000, fax 760/252-6099.

7 CALICO GHOST TOWN REGIONAL PARK

Scenic rating: 4

near Barstow

See map page 947

Let me tell you about this ghost town: There are probably more people here now than there have ever been. In the 1880s and 1890s it was a booming silver mine town, and there are still remnants of that. Alas, it now has lots of restaurants and shops. Recreation options include riding on a narrow-gauge railroad, touring what was once the largest silver mine in California, and watching an old-style melodrama with villains and heroes. This is a 480-acre park with self-guided tours, hiking trails, gold panning, summer entertainment, and museum, with festivals held through the year. Whatever you do, don't take any artifacts you may come across, such as an old nail, a jar, or anything; you will be doomed with years of bad luck. No foolin'. A park representative told us the story of a man from the East Coast who nabbed a beautiful rock on his visit. He then was plagued with years of bad luck, including broken bones, disappointment in his love life, and several family deaths. In desperation, he flew back to California and returned the rock to its rightful place.

RV sites, facilities: There are 252 sites for tents or RVs up to 45 feet; 104 have full or partial hookups (20, 30, and 50 amps), and some are pull-through. There are also three group camping areas, six cabins, and a bunkhouse. Fire pits are provided. Restrooms have flush toilets and showers. Drinking water and three dump stations are available. A pay phone, restaurants, and shops are on-site. Groceries, propane gas, and laundry facilities are available 10 miles away. Leashed pets are permitted.

Reservations, fees: Reservations are accepted ($2 reservation fee) at 800/TO-CALICO (800/862-2542). Sites are $18–22 per night, $1 per night per pet. Some credit cards accepted. Open year-round.

Directions: From Barstow, drive northeast on I-15 for seven miles to the exit for Ghost Town Road. Take that exit and drive north on Ghost Town Road for three miles to the park on the left.

Contact: Calico Ghost Town Regional Park, San Bernardino County, 760/254-2122, fax 760/254-2047, www.calicotown.com.

8 BARSTOW/CALICO KOA

🧍🏊🐕🚣♿🚐🏕️

Scenic rating: 3

near Barstow

See map page 947

Don't blame us if you end up way out here. Actually, for vacationers making the long-distance grind of a drive on I-15, this KOA can seem like the promised land. It has received awards for its cleanliness, and a nightly quiet time ensures that you have a chance to get rested. Vegetation screening between sites enhance privacy. But hey, as long as you're here, you might as well take a side trip to Calico Ghost Town, about three miles northeast at the foot of the Calico Mountains. A unique side trip is the Calico Early Man Site, about five miles to the north; tours are

available. Primitive stone tools are believed to have been discovered here in 1942. Rockhounding, hiking, and an outlet mall are other nearby options. The elevation is 1,900 feet.

RV sites, facilities: There are 78 sites for tents or RVs of any length with full or partial hookups (30 and 50 amps); many are pull-through. Picnic tables and fire grills are provided. Drinking water, restrooms with flush toilets and showers, a dump station, modem access, a playground, heated swimming pool, recreation room, a convenience store, propane gas, ice, and coin laundry are available. Some facilities are wheelchair accessible. Leashed pets are permitted.

Reservations, fees: Reservations are accepted at 800/KOA-0059 (800/562-0059). Sites are $20–33 per night, $2.50 per person per night for more than two people. Some credit cards accepted. Open year-round.

Directions: From Barstow, drive northeast on I-15 for seven miles to the exit for Ghost Town Road. Take that exit and drive left under the freeway to a frontage road at the Shell gas station. Turn left at the frontage road and drive 0.25 mile to the campground on the right.

Contact: Barstow/Calico KOA, 760/254-2311, fax 760/254-2247, www.koa.com.

9 PROVIDENCE MOUNTAINS STATE RECREATION AREA

🧍🐕🚐🏕️

Scenic rating: 8

near Mitchell Caverns

See map page 947

This remote desert park, at 4,300 feet, offers guided tours of Mitchell Caverns ($2–4 tour fee, discounts available). These tours are available daily early September through Memorial Day weekend and on weekends Memorial Day to early September. It's a good idea to make a reservation for the tour; phone 760/928-2586. The cavern tours are the reason most people visit and camp at this park. The caverns are classic limestone formations. There are additional recreational opportunities. From the campground Nina Mora Overlook Trail is a short (quarter-mile) walk to a lookout of the Marble Mountains and the valley below. Another short hike with a great view is the steep, one-mile hike (one-way) on Crystal Springs Trail, the best of the bunch. Another hike is Mary Beale, an interpretive trail accessible from the visitors center, a one-mile loop.

RV sites, facilities: There are six sites for tents or RVs up to 31 feet (no hookups). Picnic tables and fire grills are provided. Drinking water and flush toilets are available. A pay phone is available nearby. Leashed pets are permitted in the campground only.

Reservations, fees: Reservations are not accepted. Sites are $12 per night, $5 per night per additional vehicle. Open year-round.

Directions: Drive on I-40 to Essex Road (near Essex, 116 miles east of Barstow). Take that road and drive north on Essex Road for 16 miles to the park at road's end.

Contact: Providence Mountains State Recreation Area, 760/928-2586; Mojave Desert Information Center, 661/942-0662, fax 661/940-7327, www.parks.ca.gov.

10 MID HILLS

Scenic rating: 4

in the Mojave National Preserve

See map page 947

This is a primitive campground among the junipers and piñon trees in a mountainous area at 5,600 feet. It is one of two little-known camps in the vast desert that is now managed by the National Park Service. About two-thirds of the campsites were burned in the 2005 Hackberry Fire. Most of the piñon and juniper trees burned as well. An eight-mile one-way trail starts across from the entrance to Mid Hills and meanders down to the Hole-in-the-Wall Campground. It's a pleasant walk in spring and fall.

RV sites, facilities: There are 26 sites for tents or RVs up to 22 feet (no hookups). Picnic tables and fire grills are provided. Drinking water and vault toilets are available. Leashed pets are permitted.

Reservations, fees: Reservations are not accepted. Sites are $12 per night. Open year-round.

Directions: Drive on I-40 to Essex Road (near Essex, 116 miles east of Barstow). Take that exit and drive north on Essex Road for 10 miles to Black Canyon Road. Turn north, drive nine miles (at Hole-in-the-Wall Campground, the road becomes dirt), and continue seven miles to Wild Horse Canyon Road. Turn left and drive two miles (rough, dirt road) to the campground on the right.

Contact: Mojave National Preserve, Baker Information Center, 760/733-4040, fax 760/733-4027, www.nps.gov/moja.

11 HOLE-IN-THE-WALL/ BLACK CANYON GROUP AND HORSE CAMP

Scenic rating: 6

in the Mojave National Preserve

See map page 947

This is the largest and best-known of the camps in the vast Mojave National Preserve; the campgrounds are at 4,400 feet in elevation, with a group camp and equestrian camp across the road from a family camp. An interesting side trip is to the Mitchell Caverns in the nearby Providence Mountains State Recreation Area.

RV sites, facilities: There are 35 sites for tents or RVs of any length (no hookups), one group site for up to 50 people, and an equestrian camp. Picnic tables and fire grills are provided. Drinking water, vault toilets, and a dump station are available. Leashed pets are permitted.

Reservations, fees: Reservations are not accepted. Sites are $12 per night. Make reservations for the group camp and horse camp at 760/928-2572; $25 per night, including horse corral if needed. Open year-round.

Directions: Drive on I-40 to Essex Road (near Essex, 116 miles east of Barstow). Take that exit and drive north on Essex Road for 10 miles to Black Canyon Road. Turn north and drive nine miles to the campgrounds.

Contact: Mojave National Preserve, 760/733-4040, fax 760/733-4027, www.nps.gov/moja.

12 RAINBO BEACH RV AND MOBILE HOME RESORT

Scenic rating: 6

on the Colorado River
See map page 947

The big bonus here is the full marina, making this resort on the Colorado River the headquarters for boaters and water-skiers. And headquarters it is, with tons of happy folks who are extremely well lubed, both inside and out. This resort boasts 800 feet of river frontage. A 70-site mobile home park is adjacent to the RV park. (For boating details, see the listing in this chapter for *Needles Marina Park*.)

RV sites, facilities: There are 64 sites with full hookups (30 and 50 amps) for RVs, a grassy area for tents, and three park-model cabins. Some sites are pull-through. Picnic tables are provided. Restrooms have showers. A coin laundry, heated swimming pool, spa, recreation room, and restaurant are available. A boat dock is available nearby. Leashed pets are permitted.

Reservations, fees: Reservations are accepted. Sites are $25–28 per night, $16 per night for tents. Seasonal rates available. Some credit cards accepted. Open year-round.

Directions: Drive on I-40 to Needles and River Road. Turn north on River Road and drive 1.5 miles to the resort on the right.

Contact: Rainbo Beach RV and Mobile Home Resort, 760/326-3101, fax 760/326-5085.

13 NEEDLES MARINA PARK

Scenic rating: 6

on the Colorado River
See map page 947

Bring your suntan lotion and a beach towel. This section of the Colorado River is a big tourist spot where the body oil and beer can flow faster than the river. There are a ton of hot bodies and hot boats, and waterskiing dominates the adjacent calm-water section of the Colorado River. However, note that upstream of the Needles-area put-in is the prime area for waterskiing. Downstream is the chance for canoeing or kayaking. Meanwhile, there's an 18-hole golf course adjacent to the camp, but most folks head for the river. Compared to the surrounding desert, this park is almost a golden paradise. A mobile home park is adjacent to the RV park.

RV sites, facilities: There are 158 sites for tents or RVs with full hookups (30 and 50 amps), along with six cabins. Some sites are pull-through. Picnic tables are provided. Restrooms have flush toilets and showers. Drinking water, a heated pool, a spa, a recreation room, Wi-Fi, modem access, a playground, a picnic area, a boat ramp, boat slips, a store, gas, and laundry facilities are available. Leashed pets are permitted.

Reservations, fees: Reservations are accepted. Sites are $30–32 per night, $3.50 per night for air conditioning, $2.50 per pet per night. Some credit cards accepted. Open year-round.

Directions: Drive on I-40 to Needles and the exit for J Street. Take that exit and drive to Broadway. Turn left on Broadway and drive 0.75 mile to Needles Highway. Turn right (north) on Needles Highway and drive 0.5 mile to the park on the left.

Contact: Needles Marina Park, 760/326-2197, fax 760/326-4125, www.needlesmarinapark.com.

14 NEEDLES KOA

Scenic rating: 2

near the Colorado River
See map page 947

At least you've got the Needles KOA out here, complete with swimming pool, where you can get a new start. Side trips include venturing to the nearby Colorado River or heading north to Lake Mead. Of course, you could always go to Las Vegas. Nah.

RV sites, facilities: There are 93 pull-through sites for tents or RVs of any length with full hookups (30 and 50 amps) and 18 pull-through sites with partial hookups (30 and 50 amps). Five cabins are also available. Restrooms have flush toilets and showers. Drinking water, a recreation room, a swimming pool, a playground, a store, a snack bar, propane gas, and a coin laundry are available. Some facilities are wheelchair accessible. Leashed pets are permitted.

Reservations, fees: Reservations are accepted at 800/562-3407. Sites are $22–32 per night, $2 per person per night for more than two people. Some credit cards accepted. Open year-round.

Directions: Drive on I-40 to Needles and the exit for West Broadway. Take that exit to Needles Highway. Turn northwest on Needles Highway and drive 0.75 mile to National Old Trails Highway. Turn left and drive one mile to the park on the right (5400 National Old Trails Highway).

Contact: Needles KOA, 760/326-4207, fax 760/326-6329, www.koa.com.

15 MOABI REGIONAL PARK

Scenic rating: 7

on the Colorado River
See map page 947

Campsites are situated in the main area of the park along 2.5 miles of shoreline peninsula. This park features 24 group areas. The adjacent Colorado River provides the main attraction, the only thing liquid around these parts that isn't contained in a can or bottle. The natural response when you see it is to jump in the water, and everybody does so, with or without a boat. You'll see lots of wild and crazy types having the times of their lives on the water. The boating season is a long one here, courtesy of that desert climate. Fishing is good here for catfish, smallmouth bass, bluegill, striped bass, and sometimes crappie.

RV sites, facilities: There is a large grassy area for tents and more than 600 sites for RVs or tents—155 with full or partial hookups (20, 30, and 50 amps), and a few are pull-through. There are also 24 group camping areas. Picnic tables and fire grills are provided at most sites. Restrooms have flush toilets and showers. A coin laundry, a store, ice, a dump station, a covered picnic area, a marina, bait, and a boat ramp are

available. Volleyball, basketball, horseshoes, and a putting green are also available. An 18-hole golf course is nearby. Some facilities are wheelchair accessible. Leashed pets are permitted.

Reservations, fees: Reservations are accepted. Sites are $15–35 per night per vehicle, $1 per night per pet. Long-term rates available in the winter, with limit of five months. Some credit cards accepted. Open year-round.

Directions: From Needles, drive east on I-40 for 11 miles to Park Moabi Road. Turn left on Park Moabi Road and continue 0.5 mile to the park entrance at the end of the road.

Contact: Moabi Regional Park, 760/326-3831, fax 760/326-3272; San Bernardino County, 760/326-4777, www.co.san-bernardino.ca.us/parks/moabi.htm.

16 LOS ALAMOS

Scenic rating: 4

near Pyramid Lake in Angeles National Forest
See map page 946

Los Alamos is at an elevation of 2,600 feet near the southern border of the Hungry Valley State Vehicular Recreation Area and about 2.5 miles north of Pyramid Lake. Pyramid Lake is a big lake, covering 1,300 acres with 20 miles of shoreline, and is extremely popular for waterskiing and fast boating (35-mph speed limit), as well as for sailboarding (best at the northern launch point), fishing (best in the spring and early summer and in the fall for striped bass), and swimming. A lifeguard is on duty at the boat launch area during the summer season.

RV sites, facilities: There are 93 sites with no hookups and three group sites for tents or RVs up to 40 feet that can accommodate up to 25 people each. Picnic tables and fire pits are provided. Drinking water and flush toilets are available. A boat ramp is at the Emigrant Landing Picnic Area. Some facilities are wheelchair accessible. Leashed pets are permitted.

Reservations, fees: Reservations are not accepted for individual sites but are required for group sites at 661/248-6725. Sites are $14 per night, $65 per night for a group site. Open year-round.

Directions: Drive on I-5 to eight miles south of Gorman and the Smokey Bear Road exit. Take the Smokey Bear Road exit and drive west about three-quarters of a mile and follow the signs to the campground.

Contact: Angeles National Forest, Santa Clara/Mojave Rivers Ranger District, 661/296-9710, fax 661/296-5847; Recreation Resource Management, 661/248-6725.

17 OAK FLAT

Scenic rating: 3

near Pyramid Lake in Angeles National Forest

See map page 946

Oak Flat is just a short drive from Pyramid Lake, at 2,800 feet near the southwestern border of Angeles National Forest. Pyramid is surrounded by national forest, quite beautiful, and is a favorite destination for folks with powerboats, especially those towing water-skiers. The lake covers 1,300 acres and has 20 miles of shoreline. Water sports are popular in the summer, and fishing for striped bass can be good in the spring and fall. Other species are largemouth bass, catfish, crappie, and bluegill. (For more information on Pyramid Lake, see the listing for *Los Alamos* in this chapter.)

RV sites, facilities: There are 27 sites for tents or RVs up to 18 feet (no hookups). Picnic tables and fire pits are provided. Vault toilets are available. No drinking water is available. Garbage must be packed out. Leashed pets are permitted.

Reservations, fees: No reservations are accepted, and there is no camping fee. An Adventure Pass ($30 annual fee or $5 daily fee) per parked vehicle is required. Open year-round.

Directions: Drive on I-5 to six miles north of Castaic to Templin Highway. Take Templin Highway west and drive three miles to the campground.

Contact: Angeles National Forest, Santa Clara/Mojave Rivers Ranger District, 661/296-9710, fax 661/296-5847.

18 COTTONWOOD

Scenic rating: 5

near the Warm Springs Mountain Lookout in Angeles National Forest

See map page 946

Cottonwood Camp is at 2,680 feet in remote Angeles National Forest along a small stream. The camp is on the north flank of Warm Springs Mountain. A great side trip is to the Warm Springs Mountain Lookout (4,023 feet), about a five-mile drive. Drive south on Forest Road 7N09 for three miles, turn right (west) on Forest Road 6N32, and drive for 1.5 miles to Forest Road 7N13. Turn left (south) and drive a mile to the summit.

RV sites, facilities: There are 22 sites for tents or RVs up to 22 feet (no hookups). Picnic tables and fire pits are provided. Vault toilets are available. No drinking water. Garbage must be packed out. Supplies are available less than four miles away in the town of Lake Hughes. Leashed pets are permitted.

Reservations, fees: No reservations are accepted and there is no camping fee. An Adventure Pass ($30 annual fee or $5 daily pass per parked vehicle) is required. Open year-round.

Directions: Drive on I-5 to the Tehachapis near the small town of Castaic and Lake Hughes Road. Turn northeast on Lake Hughes Road and drive 27 miles to the campground on the right.

Contact: Angeles National Forest, Santa Clara/Mojave Rivers Ranger District, 661/296-9710, fax 661/296-5847.

19 SADDLEBACK BUTTE STATE PARK

Scenic rating: 8

near Lancaster

See map page 946

This 3,000-acre park was originally established to preserve ancient Joshua trees. In fact, it used to be called Joshua Tree State Park, but folks kept getting it confused with Joshua Tree National Park, so it was renamed. The terrain is

CALIFORNIA

sparsely vegetated and desertlike, with excellent hiking trails up the nearby buttes. The best hike is Saddleback Loop, a five-mile trip that features a 1,000-foot climb to Saddleback Summit at 3,651 feet. On rare clear days, there are fantastic views in all directions, including the Antelope Valley California Poppy Preserve, the surrounding mountains, and the Mojave Desert. On the typical hazy day, the poppy reserve might as well be on the moon; you can't even come close to seeing it. The elevation is 2,700 feet.

RV sites, facilities: There are 30 sites for tents or RVs up to 30 feet (no hookups). A group camp is available for up to 30 people. Picnic tables, shade ramadas, and fire grills are provided. Drinking water, flush toilets, and a dump station are available. A visitors center is nearby. Some facilities are wheelchair accessible. Leashed pets are permitted in the campground only.

Reservations, fees: Reservations are not accepted for individual sites, but the group camp may be reserved at 800/444-PARK (800/444-7275) or www.reserveamerica.com ($7.50 reservation fee). Sites are $12 per night, $5 per night for an additional vehicle, $66 per night for the group site. Open year-round.

Directions: Drive north on Highway 14 to Lancaster and the exit for Avenue J. Take that exit and drive east on Avenue J for 17 miles to the park entrance on the right.

Or drive south on Highway 14 to Lancaster to the exit for 20th Street west. Take that exit, turn left, and drive to Avenue J. Turn east on Avenue J and drive 17 miles to the park entrance on the right.

Contact: Saddleback Butte State Park, Mojave Desert Information Center, 661/942-0662, fax 661/940-7327, www.parks.ca.gov.

20 DESERT WILLOW RV PARK

Scenic rating: 2

in Hesperia

See map page 946

This is an RV park for I-15 cruisers looking to make a stop. Silverwood Lake, a 1,000-acre recreation lake with fishing, boating, and water sports, is 18 miles to the south. The elevation is 3,200 feet.

RV sites, facilities: There are 176 sites with full hookups (30 and 50 amps) for RVs; some are pull-through. No tents. Note that only 17 sites are available for overnight campers. Restrooms have showers. Cable TV hookups, ice, a coin laundry, propane gas, a swimming pool, an indoor spa, and a library are on the premises. Some facilities are wheelchair accessible. Leashed pets are permitted.

Reservations, fees: Reservations are accepted at 800/900-8114. Sites are $35 per night, $5 per person for more than two people, $1 per pet per night. Monthly rates available. Open year-round.

Directions: Drive on I-15 to Hesperia and Exit 143. Take that exit to Main Street. Turn west and drive to the park on the right (12624 Main Street West).

Contact: Desert Willow RV Park, 760/949-0377, fax 760/949-4334.

21 SHADY OASIS VICTORVILLE KOA

Scenic rating: 3

near Victorville

See map page 946

Most long-distance trips on I-15 are grueling endurance tests with drivers making the mistake of trying to get a decent night's sleep at a roadside rest stop. Why endure the torture, especially with a KOA way out here, in Victorville of all places? Where the heck is Victorville? If you are exhausted and lucky enough to find the place, you won't be making any jokes about it.

RV sites, facilities: There are 136 sites for tents or RVs of any length, many with full or partial hookups (30 amps) and some pull-through, and eight cabins. Picnic tables and fire grills are provided. Drinking water, restrooms with flush toilets and showers, a recreation room, a seasonal heated swimming pool, a playground, modem access, a convenience store, propane gas, and a coin laundry are available. Some facilities are wheelchair accessible. Leashed pets are permitted.

Reservations, fees: Make reservations at 800/KOA-3319 (800/562-3319); $24–40 per night, $2 per person for more than two people, $1 per night for an additional vehicle. Some credit cards accepted. Open year-round.

Directions: Drive on I-15 to Victorville and Stoddard Wells Road (north of Victorville). Turn south on Stoddard Wells Road and drive a short distance to the campground (16530 Stoddard Wells Road).

Contact: Shady Oasis Victorville KOA, 760/245-6867, fax 760/243-2108, www.koa.com.

22 HESPERIA LAKE CAMPGROUND

Scenic rating: 5

in Hesperia
See map page 946

This is a slightly more rustic alternative to Desert Willow RV Park in Hesperia. There is a small lake/pond for recreational fishing and there is a small fishing fee, but no fishing license is required. No boating or swimming is allowed, but youngsters usually get a kick out of feeding the ducks and geese that live at the pond.

RV sites, facilities: There are 58 sites for tents or RVs up to 40 feet with partial hookups (20, 30, and 50 amps) and two group areas for tents. Picnic tables and fire pits are provided. Drinking water, restrooms with flush toilets and showers, a playground, horseshoe pits, and a fishing pond are available. Some facilities are wheelchair accessible. Leashed pets are permitted in the camp, with certain restrictions, but not around the lake.

Reservations, fees: Reservations are accepted at 800/521-6332. Sites are $20 per night, $2 per night per pet. Some credit cards accepted. Open year-round.

Directions: Drive on I-15 to Hesperia and the exit for Main Street. Take that exit and drive east on Main Street for 9.5 miles (the road curves and becomes Arrowhead Lake Road) to the park on the left.

Contact: Hesperia Lake Campground, 760/244-5951 or 800/521-6332.

23 MOJAVE NARROWS REGIONAL PARK

Scenic rating: 7

on the Mojave River
See map page 946

Almost no one except the locals knows about this little county park. It is like an oasis in the Mojave Desert. There are actually two small lakes here: the larger Horseshoe Lake and Pelican Lake. No private boats are allowed; rental rowboats and pedal boats are available on weekends. Swimming and water/body contact are prohibited. It is at 2,000 feet and provides a few recreation options, including a pond stocked in season with trout and catfish, horseback-riding facilities, and equestrian trails. Hiking includes a wheelchair-accessible trail. The Mojave River level fluctuates here, almost disappearing in some years in summer and early fall. One of the big events of the year here is on Father's Day in June, the Huck Finn Jubilee. Note: The gate closes each evening.

RV sites, facilities: There are 110 sites for tents or RVs of any length, including seven pull-through and 42 with full hookups (15 and 30 amps). Fourteen group areas are also available. Picnic tables and barbecue grills are provided. Drinking water, restrooms with flush toilets and showers, a dump station, a snack bar, a playground, picnic shelters, bait, boat rentals, horse rentals, and horseback-riding facilities are available. A store, propane gas, and coin laundry are available three miles from the campground. Leashed pets are permitted.

Reservations, fees: Reservations accepted for RVs and groups. Sites are $22 per night, $1 per night per pet, $5 per day fishing fee. Weekly and group rates available. Some credit cards accepted. Open year-round.

Directions: Drive on I-15 to Victorville and the exit for Bear Valley Road. Take that exit and drive east on Bear Valley Road for six miles to Ridgecrest. Turn left on Ridgecrest, drive three miles, and make a left into the park.

Contact: Mojave Narrows Regional Park, 760/245-2226, www.co.san-bernardino.ca.us/parks/mojave.htm.

24 HAVASU LANDING RESORT & CASINO

Scenic rating: 6

on western shore of Lake Havasu

See map page 947

Situated on the western shore of Lake Havasu, this full-service resort is run by the Chemehuevi Indian Tribe. It even includes a casino with slot machines and a card room. The resort is in a desert landscape in the Chemehuevi Valley. A boat shuttle operates from the resort to the London Bridge and Havasu City, Arizona. A mobile home park is within the resort, and an airstrip is nearby. Some of the RV sites are rented for the entire winter. Permits are required for off-road vehicles and can be obtained at the resort. This is one of the most popular boating areas in the southwestern United States. The lake is 45 miles long, covers 19,300 acres, and is at the low elevation of 482 feet. Havasu was created when the Parker Dam was built across the Colorado River.

RV sites, facilities: There are 180 sites with full hookups (30 and 50 amps) for RVs up to 35 feet, three large tent camping areas, and mobile home and RV rentals. Picnic tables, restrooms with flush toilets and showers, a dump station, a coin laundry, picnic areas, a restaurant and lounge, a casino, 24-hour security, a 24-hour marina with gas dock, bait and tackle, a general store and deli, boat launches, boat slips, a fish-cleaning room, dry storage, a boat shuttle, and a boat launch and retrieval service are available. An airport is nearby. Leashed pets are permitted.

Reservations, fees: Reservations are accepted at 800/307-3610. Sites are $25–30 per night for RV sites, $15–20 per night for tent sites, $2 per person per night for more than two people, and $6 per night per additional vehicle. Holiday rates are higher. Weekly and monthly rates are available. A boat-launch fee is charged. Some credit cards are accepted. Two ATMs are on-site. Open year-round.

Directions: From Needles, drive south on Highway 95 for 19 miles to Havasu Lake Road. Turn left and drive 17.5 miles to the resort on the right.

From Blythe, drive north on Highway 95 for 79 miles to Havasu Lake Road. Turn right and drive 17.5 miles to the resort on the right.

Contact: Havasu Landing Resort & Casino, 760/858-4593 or 800/307-3610, www.havasulanding.com. For general information about Lake Havasu, contact the Lake Havasu Tourism Bureau, 928/453-3444 or 800/2-HAVASU (800/242-8278), www.golakehavasu.com; Lake Havasu Area Chamber of Commerce, 928/855-4115, www.havasuchamber.com.

25 BLACK MEADOW LANDING

Scenic rating: 6

south of Lake Havasu on the Colorado River

See map page 947

This area of the Colorado River attracts a lot of people, so reservations are highly recommended. Hot weather, warm water, and proximity to Las Vegas make this one of the top camping and boating hot spots in the West. Vacationers are here year-round, although fewer people use it in the late winter. Black Meadow Landing is a large resort with hundreds of RV sites, lodging, and a long list of amenities. Once you arrive, everything you need for a stay should be available within the resort.

RV sites, facilities: There are 350 sites with full hookups (30 amps) for RVs up to 40 feet, and tent camping is available. Park-model cabins, kitchen cabins, and a motel are also available. Restrooms have flush toilets and showers. Drinking water, picnic tables, picnic areas, horseshoes, a restaurant, a convenience store, a recreation room (winter only), bait and tackle, propane, a full-service marina, a boat launch, boat slips, boat and RV storage, a swimming lagoon, and a five-hole golf course are available. Leashed pets are permitted.

Reservations, fees: Reservations are accepted at 800/7-HAVASU (800/742-8278). Sites are $25–52 per night, $6 per person per night for more than two people, $25 per night for tent sites, and $6 per night for an additional vehicle. Monthly rates are available. Some credit cards are accepted. Open year-round.

Directions: From Southern California, take I-10 east to Blythe and turn north on U.S. 95. Continue to Vidal Junction at the intersection of U.S. 95 and Highway 62. Turn east on Highway 62 and drive to Earp and Parker Dam Road. Continue straight on Parker Dam Road and drive to a Y intersection and Black Meadow Landing Road (near Parker Dam). Bear left on Black Meadow Landing Road and drive approximately nine miles to the resort at the end of the road.

From Northern California, drive to Barstow and I-40. Turn east on I-40 and drive to Needles. Continue east on I-40 to Arizona Highway 95. Drive south on Arizona Highway 95 to Lake Havasu City. Continue south to the Parker Dam turnoff. Turn west and drive across the dam to a Y intersection and Black Meadow Landing Road. Bear right on Black Meadow Landing Road and drive approximately nine miles to the resort at the end of the road. Note: Towed vehicles are not allowed to cross the dam.

Contact: Black Meadow Landing, 760/663-4901, www.blackmeadowlanding.com. For general information about the Colorado River and Lake Havasu, contact the Lake Havasu Tourism Bureau, 928/453-3444 or 800/2-HAVASU (800/242-8278), www.golakehavasu.com; Lake Havasu Area Chamber of Commerce, 928/855-4115, www.havasuchamber.com.

26 RIVERLAND RESORT

Scenic rating: 6

on the Colorado River near Parker Dam

See map page 947

This resort is in the middle of a very popular boating area, particularly for waterskiing. Summer is the busiest time because of the sunshine and warm water. In the winter, even though temperatures can get pretty cold, around 40°F at night, the campground fills with retirees from the snow or rain country. Even though the resort is way out there on the Colorado River, there are plenty of services, including a convenience store, swimming beach, and full-service marina. Insider's tip: One of the best spots for catfish is a few miles down the road below Parker Dam.

RV sites, facilities: There are 60 sites with full hookups (50 amps) for RVs up to 40 feet. Picnic tables are provided. Tent camping and park-model cabins are available. Restrooms have flush toilets and showers. Drinking water, cable television, Wi-Fi, a convenience store, a coin laundry, a full-service marina, a boat launch, boat slips, boat and RV storage, a swimming beach, a fishing pier, bait, a recreation room (winter only), and horseshoe pits are available. An ATM is within five miles, and an 18-hole golf course is seven miles away. Leashed pets are permitted.

Reservations, fees: Reservations are accepted at 760/663-3733. Sites are $26 per night, $2 per person per night in summer, and $2 per pet per night. Monthly rates are available. Some credit cards are accepted. Open year-round.

Directions: From Southern California, take I-10 east to Blythe and turn north on U.S. 95. Continue to Vidal Junction at the intersection of U.S. 95 and Highway 62. Turn east on Highway 62 and drive to Earp and Parker Dam Road. Continue straight on Parker Dam Road and drive five miles to the resort on the right.

Contact: Riverland Resort, 760/663-3733.

27 LOST LAKE RESORT

Scenic rating: 6

on the Colorado River in Parker Valley

See map page 947

If you're looking for a remote spot on the Colorado River, this is it. This is kind of like an oasis in the middle of the desert. Direct access to the Colorado River is provided, and this is one of a few places around that sell fishing licenses for this stretch of the Colorado River. The Parker Valley section of the river is part of

CALIFORNIA

the Colorado River Indian Reservation, and the tribe requires that all anglers obtain a permit. One of the best spots for big catfish, including large flathead catfish and channel catfish, is below Parker Dam. If you catch a razorback sucker, a rare event, it must be released. It is an endangered species. Note that about half of the sites are filled with long-term or permanent renters.

RV sites, facilities: There are 150 sites with full hookups (30 amps). Tent camping is available. Picnic tables are provided at most sites. Restrooms have flush toilets. Showers, a coin laundry, a convenience store, a café, a recreation room (winter only), boat and RV storage, a boat launch, bait and tackle, fishing licenses, and a full-service marina are available. Leashed pets are permitted.

Reservations, fees: Reservations are accepted at 760/664-4413. Sites are $30 per night per vehicle. Monthly rates are available in winter. Some credit cards are accepted. Open year-round.

Directions: From Southern California, take I-10 east to Blythe and turn north on U.S. 95. Drive for 31 miles to the resort on the right.

Contact: Lost Lake Resort, 760/664-4413.

28 BLACK ROCK CANYON AND HORSE CAMP

Scenic rating: 4

in Joshua Tree National Park

See map page 947

This is the fanciest darn public campground this side of the desert. Why, it actually has drinking water. The camp is at the mouth of Black Rock Canyon, at 4,000 feet elevation, which provides good winter hiking possibilities amid unique (in other words, weird) rock formations, which are about a half hour drive from the campground. Show up in summer and you'll trade your gold for a sip of water. The camp is near the excellent Black Rock Canyon Visitor Center and a trailhead for a four-mile round-trip hike to a rock wash. If you scramble onward, the route continues all the way to the

top of Eureka Peak, 5,518 feet, an 11-mile round-trip. But hey, why not just drive there?

RV sites, facilities: There are 100 sites for tents or RVs up to 35 feet (no hookups) and 15 equestrian sites for up to six people and four horses per site. Picnic tables and fire grills are provided. Drinking water, flush toilets, and a dump station are available. The horse camp has hitching posts and a water faucet, and no tents are allowed. Some facilities are wheelchair accessible. Leashed pets are permitted, but not on trails.

Reservations, fees: Reservations are accepted at 800/365-CAMP (800/365-2267) or http://reservations.nps.gov. Sites are $10 per night, plus a $15 park entrance fee per vehicle. Open year-round, weather permitting.

Directions: From the junction of I-10 and Highway 62 near Palm Springs, drive northeast on Highway 62 for 22.5 miles to Yucca Valley and Joshua Lane. Turn right (south) on Joshua Lane and drive about five miles to the campground.

Contact: Joshua Tree National Park, 760/367-5500, fax 760/367-6392; Black Rock Nature Center, 760/367-3001, www.nps.gov/jotr.

29 INDIAN COVE CAMPGROUND

Scenic rating: 4

in Joshua Tree National Park

See map page 947

This is one of the campgrounds near the northern border of Joshua Tree National Park. The vast desert park, covering 1,238 square miles, is best known for its unique granite formations and scraggly looking trees. If you had to withstand the summer heat here, you'd look scraggly too. Drinking water is available at the Indian Cove Ranger Station.

RV sites, facilities: There are 101 sites for tents or RVs up to 35 feet (no hookups) and a group camp with 13 sites for tents only for up to 60 people. Drinking water is available at the Indian Cove Ranger Station. Vault toilets, picnic tables, and fire grills are provided. Gas, groceries, and laundry services are available in Twentynine Palms or Joshua Tree, 7–12 miles away. Leashed pets are permitted, but not on trails.

Reservations, fees: Reservations are accepted at 800/365-CAMP (800/365-2267) or http://reservations.nps.gov. Sites are $10 per night, $20–35 per night for group sites, plus a $15 per vehicle park entrance fee. Open year-round.

Directions: From the junction of I-10 and Highway 62 near Palm Springs, drive northeast on Highway 62 for 22 miles to Yucca Valley, continue to the small town of Joshua Tree, and then continue nine miles to Indian Cove Road. Turn right and drive three miles to the campground.

Contact: Joshua Tree National Park, 760/367-5500, fax 760/367-6392, www.nps.gov/jotr.

30 SKY VALLEY RESORT

Scenic rating: 2

near Palm Springs
See map page 947

This 140-acre park is much like a small town, complete with RV homes, an RV park, and park-model rentals and seasonal restaurants. One of the best adventures in California is just west of Palm Springs, taking the aerial tram up from Chino Canyon to Desert View, a ride/climb of 2,600 feet for remarkable views to the east across the desert below. An option from there is hiking the flank of Mount San Jacinto, including making the ascent to the summit (10,804 feet), a round-trip butt-kicker of nearly 12 miles. Golf courses are nearby.

RV sites, facilities: There are 618 sites with full hookups (30 amps) for RVs up to 42 feet. No tents allowed. Restrooms have showers. Cable TV, four swimming pools, nine natural hot mineral whirlpools, two laundry rooms, two large recreation rooms, fitness centers, a children's playroom, a seasonal grocery store, a chapel program, seasonal tennis and golf lessons, a business center with modem access, Wi-Fi, a social director, shuffleboard, tennis,

horseshoes, a crafts room, and walking paths are available. Propane gas is nearby. Some facilities are wheelchair accessible. Leashed pets are permitted.

Reservations, fees: Reservations are accepted at 888/893-7727 or by website. Sites are $38–39.50 per night, $5 per person per night for more than two people. Monthly rates available. Some credit cards accepted. Open year-round.

Directions: Drive on I-10 to the Palm Springs area and the Palm Drive exit (to Desert Hot Springs). Take that exit and drive north on Palm Drive for three miles to Dillon Road. Turn right on Dillon Road and drive 8.5 miles to the park on the right (74-711 Dillon Road).

Contact: Sky Valley Resort, 760/329-2909, fax 760/329-9473, www.skyvalleyresort.com.

31 SAM'S FAMILY SPA

Scenic rating: 3

near Palm Springs
See map page 947

Hot mineral pools attract swarms of winter vacationers to the Palm Springs area. The therapeutic pools are partially enclosed. This 50-acre park, 13 miles outside of Palm Springs, provides an alternative to the more crowded spots. And this is one of the few parks in the area that allows tent campers. A mobile home park is adjacent to the RV park. The elevation of Sam's Family Spa is 1,000 feet. (For information on the tramway ride to Desert View west of Palm Springs, or the hike to Mount San Jacinto, see the listing in this chapter for *Sky Valley Resort*.)

RV sites, facilities: There are 170 sites for RVs up to 42 feet with full hookups (30 and 50 amps). Four mobile home rentals and a motel are also available. Picnic tables are provided. There is a separate area with barbecues. Restrooms have showers. A playground, heated swimming pool, heated wading pool, four hot mineral pools, sauna, Wi-Fi, a coin laundry, and a convenience store are available. Some facilities are wheelchair accessible. Leashed pets are permitted in the campground only.

CALIFORNIA

Reservations, fees: Reservations are accepted online only; no telephone reservations. Sites are $38 per night. Weekly and monthly rates available. Some credit cards accepted. Open year-round.

Directions: Drive on I-10 to the Palm Springs Area and the Palm Drive exit (to Desert Hot Springs). Take that exit and drive north on Palm Drive for about two miles to Dillon Road. Turn right (east) on Dillon Road and drive 4.5 miles to the park on the right (70-875 Dillon Road).

Contact: Sam's Family Spa, 760/329-6457, fax 760/329-8267, www.samsfamilyspa.com.

32 HIDDEN VALLEY

Scenic rating: 7

in Joshua Tree National Park

See map page 947

This is one of California's top campgrounds for rock-climbers. Set at 4,200 feet in the high desert country, it is one of several camping options in the area. A trailhead is available two miles from camp at Barker Dam, an easy one-mile loop that features the Wonderland of Rocks. The hike takes you next to a small lake with magical reflections of rock formations off its surface. The RV sites here are snatched up quickly, and this campground fills almost daily with rock-climbers.

RV sites, facilities: There are 45 sites for tents or RVs up to 25 feet (no hookups). Picnic tables and fire grills are provided. Vault toilets are available. No drinking water is available. Leashed pets are permitted.

Reservations, fees: No reservations are accepted. Sites are $5 per night, plus a $15 park entrance fee per vehicle. Open year-round.

Directions: From the junction of I-10 and Highway 62 near Palm Springs, drive northeast on Highway 62 for 22 miles to Yucca Valley, then continue to the small town of Joshua Tree and Park Boulevard. Turn south on Park Boulevard and drive 14 miles to the campground on the left.

Contact: Joshua Tree National Park, 760/367-5500, fax 760/367-6392, www.nps.gov/jotr.

33 RYAN

Scenic rating: 4

in Joshua Tree National Park

See map page 947

This is one of the high desert camps in the immediate area (see also Jumbo Rocks in this chapter). Joshua Tree National Park is a forbidding paradise: huge, hot, and waterless (most of the time). The unique rock formations look as if some great artist made them with a chisel. The elevation is 4,300 feet. The best hike in the park starts here—a three-mile round-trip to Ryan Mountain is a 1,000-foot climb to the top at 5,470 feet. The view is simply drop-dead gorgeous, not only of San Jacinto, Tahquitz, and San Gorgonio peaks, but of several beautiful rock-studded valleys as well as the Wonderland of Rocks.

RV sites, facilities: There are 31 sites for tents or RVs up to 25 feet (no hookups). Picnic tables and fire grills are provided. Vault toilets are available. No drinking water is available. Hitching posts are available (bring water for the horses). Leashed pets are permitted.

Reservations, fees: Reservations are accepted only for equestrian sites at 760/367-5541. Sites are $5 per night, and there is a $15 park entrance fee per vehicle. Open year-round.

Directions: From the junction of I-10 and Highway 62 near Palm Springs, drive northeast on Highway 62 to Twentynine Palms and Utah Trail. Turn right (south) on Utah Trail and drive about 20 miles to the campground entrance on the left.

Contact: Joshua Tree National Park, 760/367-5500, fax 760/367-6392, www.nps.gov/jotr.

34 JUMBO ROCKS

Scenic rating: 4

in Joshua Tree National Park

See map page 947

Joshua Tree National Park covers more than 1,238 square miles. It is striking high-desert country with unique granite formations that seem to change color at different times of the

CALIFORNIA

day. This camp is one of the higher ones in the park at 4,400 feet, with adjacent boulders and rock formations that look as if they have been strewn about by an angry giant. It is a popular site for rock-climbing.

RV sites, facilities: There are 125 sites for tents or RVs up to 35 feet (no hookups). Picnic tables and fire grills are provided. Vault toilets are available. No drinking water is available. Leashed pets are permitted.

Reservations, fees: Reservations are not accepted. Sites are $5, and there is a $15 park entrance fee per vehicle. Open year-round.

Directions: From the junction of I-10 and Highway 62 near Palm Springs, drive northeast on Highway 62 to Twentynine Palms and Utah Trail. Turn right (south) on Utah Trail and drive about nine miles to the campground on the left side of the road.

Contact: Joshua Tree National Park, 760/367-5500, fax 760/367-6392, www.nps.gov/jotr.

35 HAPPY TRAVELER RV PARK

Scenic rating: 1

in Palm Springs
See map page 947

Are we having fun yet? They are at Happy Traveler, which is within walking distance of Palm Springs shopping areas and restaurants. The Palm Springs Air Museum has a collection of World War II aircraft. A casino is one mile away.

RV sites, facilities: There are 130 sites with full hookups (30 and 50 amps) for RVs up to 40 feet. No tents or tent trailers. Picnic tables are provided. Restrooms have showers. Cable TV, a swimming pool, a spa, a clubhouse, shuffleboard, propane, seasonal activities, and a coin laundry are available. Leashed pets are permitted.

Reservations, fees: Reservations are accepted. Sites are $35.50 per night. Monthly rates available. Credit cards are not accepted. Open year-round.

Directions: Drive on I-10 to Palm Springs and Highway 111/Palm Canyon Drive. Take Palm Canyon Drive and drive 12 miles south

to Mesquite Avenue. Turn right on Mesquite Avenue and drive to the park on the left (211 West Mesquite).

Contact: Happy Traveler RV Park, 760/325-8518, fax 760/778-6708, www.happytravelerrv.com.

36 OUTDOOR RESORT OF PALM SPRINGS

Scenic rating: 6

near Palm Springs
See map page 947

This is considered a five-star resort, beautifully landscaped, huge, and offering many activities: swimming pools galore, golf course, tons of tennis courts, spas, and on and on. The 137-acre park is four miles from Palm Springs. Note that this is a lot-ownership park with lots for sale. About a quarter of the sites are available for rent to vacationers. One of the best adventures in California is just west of Palm Springs, taking the aerial tram up from Chino Canyon to Desert View, a ride/climb of 2,600 feet for remarkable views to the east across the desert below.

RV sites, facilities: There are 1,213 sites with full hookups (50 amps) for RVs up to 45 feet. No tent camping. RV rentals are also available. Restrooms have showers. Eight swimming pools, spas, 14 lighted tennis courts, a 27-hole golf course, two clubhouses, a snack bar, café, a beauty salon, a coin laundry, Wi-Fi, modem access, a convenience store, shuffleboard, and planned activities are available. Some facilities are wheelchair accessible. Leashed pets are permitted.

Reservations, fees: Reservations are accepted at 800/843-3131 (California only). Sites are $60–70 per night, $1 per pet per night with a two-pet maximum. RV rentals are $85–115 per night. Some credit cards accepted. Open year-round.

Directions: Drive on I-10 to the Palm Springs area and continue to Cathedral City and the exit for Date Palm Drive. Take that exit and drive south on Date Palm Drive for two miles to Ramon Road. Turn left and drive to the resort on the right (69-411 Ramon Road).

CALIFORNIA

Contact: Outdoor Resort, 760/324-4005, www .outdoorresort.com.

37 PALM SPRINGS OASIS RV RESORT

Scenic rating: 2

in Cathedral City
See map page 947

This popular wintering spot is for RV cruisers looking to hole up in the Palm Springs area for awhile. Palm Springs is only six miles away. This is a seniors-only park, meaning that you need to be at the magic age of 55 or above to qualify for a stay.
RV sites, facilities: There are 140 sites with full hookups (30 and 50 amps) for RVs up to 45 feet. No tents. Restrooms have showers. Cable TV, Wi-Fi, modem access, two swimming pools, a spa, tennis courts, a coin laundry, and propane gas are available. An 18-hole golf course is adjacent to the park. Children and people under age 55 are not allowed. Some facilities are wheelchair accessible. Leashed pets are permitted, with a two-pet maximum.
Reservations, fees: Reservations are accepted. Sites are $41 per night, $2 per person per night for more than two people. Weekly and monthly rates available. Some credit cards accepted. Open year-round.
Directions: Drive on I-10 to the Palm Springs area and continue to Cathedral City and the exit for Date Palm Drive. Take that exit and drive south on Date Palm Drive for four miles to Gerald Ford Drive and the park on the left corner (36-100 Date Palm Drive).
Contact: Palm Springs Oasis RV Resort, 760/328-4813 or 800/680-0144, fax 760/328-8455.

38 INDIAN WELLS RV PARK

Scenic rating: 2

in Indio
See map page 947

Indio is a good-sized town midway between the Salton Sea to the south and Palm Springs

to the north, which is about 20 miles away. In the summer, it is one of the hottest places in America. In the winter, it is a favorite for "snow-birds," that is, RV and trailer owners from the snow country who migrate south to the desert for the winter. About one-half of the sites are filled with long-term renters.
RV sites, facilities: There are 381 sites with full hookups (50 amps) for RVs up to 45 feet; most are pull-through. No tents. Restrooms have showers. Cable TV, Wi-Fi, three swimming pools, two therapy pools, horseshoes, basketball, volleyball, shuffleboard courts, a putting green, planned activities, ice, a dog run, a picnic area, and a coin laundry are available. Some facilities are wheelchair accessible. Leashed pets are permitted, with a maximum of two.
Reservations, fees: Reservations are accepted at 800/789-0895. Sites are $41 per night, $2.50 per person per night for more than two people. Weekly and monthly rates available. Some credit cards are accepted. Open year-round.
Directions: Drive on I-10 to Indio and the exit for Jefferson Street. Take that exit, stay in the right lane, and drive to the light at Jefferson. Turn right at Jefferson and drive south for three miles to the park on the left (47-340 Jefferson Street).
Contact: Indian Wells RV Park, 760/347-0895, fax 760/775-1147.

39 OUTDOOR RESORTS INDIO

Scenic rating: 7

in Indio
See map page 947

For owners of tour buses, motor coaches, and lavish RVs, it doesn't get any better than this in Southern California. Only RVers in Class A motor homes are allowed here. This resort bills itself as the "ultimate RV resort" and has been featured on the Travel Channel and in the *Wall Street Journal*. About 25 percent of the sites are available for rent; the other sites are owned by motor home RVers. This park is close to golf, shopping, and restaurants. Jeep tours of the surrounding desert canyons and organized recreational events are available.

RV sites, facilities: There are 419 sites with full hookups (50 amps) for Class A motor homes with a minimum length of 28 feet. No trailers or pickup-truck campers. Restrooms have showers. Cable TV, Wi-Fi, modem access, swimming pools, tennis courts, a sauna, spas, massage service, a hair salon, a café, a fitness center, a clubhouse, a coin laundry, and an 18-hole golf course are available. Some facilities are wheelchair accessible. Leashed pets are permitted, with a two-pet maximum.

Reservations, fees: Reservations are accepted. The winter rates are $60–70 per night, summer rates are $40–50 per night, plus $5 per night for electricity. Some credit cards accepted. Open year-round.

Directions: Drive on I-10 to Indio and the exit for Indio Boulevard/Jefferson Street. Take that exit, stay in the right lane, and drive to the light at Jefferson. Turn right at Jefferson and drive south for three miles to Avenue 48. Turn left and drive 0.25 mile to the park on the left side of the road (80-394 Avenue 48).

Contact: Outdoor Resorts Indio, 760/775-7255 or 800/892-2992 (outside California), www.outdoor-resorts-indio.com/.

40 COTTONWOOD

Scenic rating: 4

in Joshua Tree National Park

See map page 947

If you enter Joshua Tree National Park at its southern access point, this is the first camp you will reach. The park visitors center, where maps are available, is a mandatory stop. This park is vast, high desert country, highlighted by unique rock formations, occasional scraggly trees, and vegetation that manages to survive the bleak, roasting summers. This camp is at 3,000 feet. A trailhead is available here for an easy one-mile nature trail, where small signs have been posted to identify different types of vegetation. You'll notice, however, that they

all look like cacti (the plants, not the signs, heh, heh).

RV sites, facilities: There are 62 sites for tents or RVs up to 35 feet (no hookups), and a group campground has three sites for 15–20 people each. Picnic tables and fire grills are provided. Drinking water and flush toilets are available. Some facilities are wheelchair accessible. Leashed pets are permitted.

Reservations, fees: Reservations are accepted only for group sites at 800/365-CAMP (800/365-2267). Sites are $10 per night, and group sites are $25 per night. The park entrance fee is $15 per vehicle. Open year-round.

Directions: From Indio, drive east on I-10 for 35 miles to the exit for Pinto Basin Road/Twenty-nine Palms (near Chiriaco Summit). Take that exit and drive north for seven miles (entering the park) to the campground on the right.

Contact: Joshua Tree National Park, 760/367-5500, fax 760/367-6392, www.nps.gov/jotr.

41 MIDLAND LONG TERM VISITOR AREA

Scenic rating: 4

west of Blythe

See map page 947

Like its neighbor to the south (Mule Mountain), this camp is attractive to snowbirds, rock hounds, and stargazers. Geodes and agates can be collected. The desert landscape is extremely stark. The campground is on the southwest slope of the Big Maria Mountains, a designated wilderness. The campsites are situated on flattened desert pavements consisting of alluvium. The campground elevation is 250 feet.

RV sites, facilities: There are numerous dispersed sites for tents or RVs of any length (no hookups). No drinking water or toilets are available. A dump station is nearby and is available from mid-September to mid-April. Leashed pets are permitted.

Reservations, fees: Reservations are not accepted. The fee is $30 for 14 nights, $140 per

CALIFORNIA

season. Fees are charged September 15–April 15. Summer is free, with a 14-day limit. Open year-round.

Directions: From Blythe, drive east on I-10 a short distance to Lovekin Boulevard. Turn left and drive about eight miles to the campground on the right.

Contact: Bureau of Land Management, Palm Springs Field Office, 760/251-4800, fax 760/251-4899.

42 MAYFLOWER COUNTY PARK

Scenic rating: 6

on the Colorado River
See map page 947

The Colorado River is the fountain of life around these parts and, for campers, the main attraction of this county park. It is a popular spot for waterskiing. There is river access here in the Blythe area. Fishing is good for channel and flathead catfish, striped bass, large- and smallmouth bass, bluegill, and crappie. This span of water is flanked by agricultural lands, although there are several developed recreation areas on the California side of the river south of Blythe near Palo Verde.

RV sites, facilities: There are 152 sites with partial hookups (30 and 50 amps) for RVs of any length and 25 tent sites. Picnic tables and fire grills are provided. Drinking water, restrooms with flush toilets and free showers, a dump station, and a boat ramp are available. Leashed pets are permitted.

Reservations, fees: Reservations are not accepted. Sites are $16–18 per night, plus a $2 boat-launch fee and $1 per night per pet. Monthly rates available. Some credit cards accepted. Open year-round.

Directions: Drive on I-10 to Blythe and Highway 95. Take Highway 95 north (it becomes Intake Boulevard) and drive 3.5 miles to 6th Avenue. Turn right at 6th Avenue and drive 2.5 miles to Colorado River Road. Bear left and drive 0.5 mile to the park entrance.

Contact: Mayflower County Park, 760/922-

4665; Riverside County, 760/922-9177, www.riversidecountyparks.org.

43 LAKE CAHUILLA COUNTY PARK

Scenic rating: 7

near Indio
See map page 947

Lake Cahuilla covers just 135 acres, but those are the most loved 135 acres for miles in all directions. After all, water out here is as scarce as polar bears. This 710-acre Riverside County park provides large palm trees and a 10-acre beach and waterplay area. In the winter it is stocked with trout, and in the summer, with catfish. Other species include largemouth and striped bass, crappie, and carp to 30 pounds. No swimming is allowed. Only car-top boats are permitted (no gas motors), and a speed limit of 10 mph is enforced. An equestrian camp is also available, complete with corrals. Equestrian and hiking trails are available on nearby public land. Morrow Trail is popular, and the trailhead is near the park's ranger station. A warning: The wind can really howl through here, and temperatures well over 100°F are typical in the summer.

RV sites, facilities: There are 55 sites with partial hookups (30 and 50 amps) and 10 sites with no hookups for RVs, a primitive camping area for tents or RVs (no hookups), and a large group area with horse corrals. Maximum RV length is 45 feet. Fire grills and picnic tables are provided. Restrooms have showers. A dump station, seasonal swimming pool, and a primitive (hand-launch) beach boat launch are available. No gas motors are allowed. Some facilities are wheelchair accessible. Leashed pets are permitted.

Reservations, fees: Reservations are accepted at 800/234-PARK (800/234-7275; $7.50 reservation fee). Sites are $13–18 per night, $1 per pet per night. Weekly rates are available during the winter. Maximum stay is two weeks. Some credit cards accepted. Open year-round, closed Tuesday–Thursday May–October.

Directions: Drive on I-10 to Indio and the exit for Monroe Street. Take that exit and drive south on Monroe Street to Avenue 58. Turn right (west) and drive two miles to the park at the end of the road.

Contact: Lake Cahuilla County Park, 760/564-4712, fax 760/564-2506, www.riversidecounty parks.org.

44 HEADQUARTERS

Scenic rating: 5

in the Salton Sea State Recreation Area
See map page 947

This is the northernmost camp on the shore of the giant Salton Sea, one of the campgrounds at the Salton Sea State Recreation Area. Salton Sea is a vast, shallow, and unique lake, the center of a 360-square mile basin and one of the world's inland seas. Salton Sea was created in 1905 when a dike broke and, in turn, the basin was flooded with saltwater. The lake is 35 miles long, but it has an average depth of just 15 feet. It is at the recreation area headquarters, just south of the town of Desert Beach at an elevation of 227 feet below sea level. Fishing for tilapia is popular, and it is also one of Southern California's most popular boating areas. Because of the low altitude, atmospheric pressure allows high performance for many ski boats. If winds are hazardous, a red beacon on the northeast shore of the lake will flash. If you see it, get to the nearest shore. The Salton Sea is about a three-hour drive from Los Angeles. Use is moderate year-round but lowest in the summer because of temperatures that can hover in the 110° range for days.

RV sites, facilities: There are 25 sites for tents or RVs (no hookups), 15 sites with full hookups (30 amps) for RVs up to 40 feet, and several hike-in/bike-in sites. Picnic tables, fire grills and shade ramadas are provided. Drinking water, restrooms with flush toilets and coin showers, a dump station, a fish-cleaning station, and a visitors center with Wi-Fi access are available. A store is within two miles. Some facilities are wheelchair accessible. Leashed pets are permitted in the campgrounds and on roadways only.

Reservations, fees: Reservations are accepted at 800/444-PARK (800/444-7275) or www .reserveamerica.com ($7.50 reservation fee). Sites are $12–23 per night, and $2 per person per night for hike-in/bike-in sites. Boat launching is $3 per day. Open year-round.

Directions: From the Los Angeles area, take I-10 east to Indio and the exit for the Highway 86 Expressway. Take that exit and drive south for 12 miles to 66th Avenue. Turn left and drive less than one mile to Mecca and Highway 111. Turn right (south) on Highway 111 and drive 12 miles to the entrance on the right.

Contact: Salton Sea State Recreation Area, 760/393-3052 or 760/393-3059, www.parks .ca.gov.

45 MECCA BEACH

Scenic rating: 4

in the Salton Sea State Recreation Area
See map page 947

This is one of the camps in the Salton Sea State Recreation Area on the northeastern shore of the lake. Waterfront sites, which are not available at nearby Headquarters campground, are the big attraction. (For details, see the listing in this chapter for *Headquarters.*)

RV sites, facilities: There are 110 sites for tents or RVs of any length, 10 with full hookups (30 amps), and several hike-in/bike-in sites. Picnic tables and fire grills are provided. Drinking water, restrooms with flush toilets and showers, an amphitheater, and a fish-cleaning station are available. A dump station is one mile north of Headquarters campground, and a store is within 3.5 miles. Leashed pets are permitted in the campgrounds and roadways only.

Reservations, fees: Reservations are accepted at 800/444-PARK (800/444-7275) or www.reserveamerica.com ($7.50 reservation fee). Sites are $12–23 per night, $3 per person per night for hike-in/bike-in sites. Boat launching is $3 per day. Open year-round.

CALIFORNIA

Directions: From the Los Angeles area, take I-10 east to Indio and the exit for the Highway 86 Expressway. Take that exit and drive south for 12 miles to 66th Avenue. Turn left and drive less than one mile to Mecca and Highway 111. Turn right (south) on Highway 111 and drive 12.5 miles to the entrance on the right.

Contact: Salton Sea State Recreation Area, 760/393-3052 or 760/393-3059, www.parks.ca.gov.

46 CORVINA BEACH

Scenic rating: 5

in the Salton Sea State Recreation Area
See map page 947

This is by far the biggest of the campgrounds on the Salton Sea. The campground is actually more of an open area on hard-packed dirt, best for parking an RV. (For details about the Salton Sea, see the listing for *Headquarters* in this chapter.)

RV sites, facilities: There are 250 primitive sites with no hookups in an open area for tents or RVs of any length and some hike-in/bike-in sites. Drinking water and chemical toilets are available. Fire are permitted in metal containers only. A store and gas station are available within five miles. Leashed pets are permitted in the campground and on roadways only.

Reservations, fees: Reservations are not accepted. Sites are $7 per night, $2 per person per night for hike-in/bike-in sites. Boat launching is $3 per day. Open year-round.

Directions: From the Los Angeles area, take I-10 east to Indio and the exit for the Highway 86 Expressway. Take that exit and drive south for 12 miles to 66th Avenue. Turn left and drive less than one mile to Mecca and Highway 111. Turn right (south) on Highway 111 and drive 14 miles to the entrance on the right.

Contact: Salton Sea State Recreation Area, 760/393-3052 or 760/393-3059, www.parks.ca.gov.

47 SALT CREEK PRIMITIVE AREA

Scenic rating: 4

in the Salton Sea State Recreation Area
See map page 947

The addition of water at this campground is a big plus, even though the campground consists of just an open area on hard-packed dirt. Waterfront campsites are a bonus. Birding hikes take place during winter months. Several trails leave from camp, or nearby the camp, and head one to two miles to the Bat Cave Buttes, which are in the Durmid Hills on Bureau of Land Management property. There are bats in the numerous caves, which can be explored, although not large numbers of bats because of OHV traffic nearby. From the buttes, which are up to 100 feet above sea level, hikers can see both the north and south ends of the Salton Sea simultaneously. This is the only easily accessible place to view both shores of the Salton Sea. Many people believe the buttes are the southernmost point of the San Andreas Fault; the fault does not exist above ground south of here. (For details on the Salton Sea State Recreation Area, see the listing for *Headquarters* in this chapter.)

RV sites, facilities: There are 200 primitive sites for tents or RVs of any length (no hookups) and several hike-in/bike-in sites. Drinking water and chemical toilets are available. Fires are permitted in metal containers only. Leashed pets are permitted in the campgrounds and on roadways only.

Reservations, fees: Reservations are not accepted. Sites are $7 per night, $2 per person per night for hike-in/bike-in sites. Open year-round.

Directions: From the Los Angeles area, take I-10 east to Indio and the exit for the Highway 86 Expressway. Take that exit and drive south for 12 miles to 66th Avenue. Turn left and drive less than one mile to Mecca and Highway 111. Turn right (south) on Highway 111 and drive 17.5 miles to the entrance on the right.

Contact: Salton Sea State Recreation Area, 760/393-3052 or 760/393-3059, www.parks.ca.gov.

CALIFORNIA

48 BOMBAY BEACH

Scenic rating: 5

in the Salton Sea State Recreation Area

See map page 947

All in all, this is a strange-looking place, with the Salton Sea, a vast body of water, surrounded by stark, barren countryside. This camp is in a bay along the northeastern shoreline, where a beach and nature trails are available. The campground is a flat, open area. Nearby to the south is the Wister Waterfowl Management Area. The Salton Sea is California's unique saltwater lake set below sea level, with fishing for tilapia a possibility.

RV sites, facilities: There are 200 sites for tents or RVs of any length (no hookups) and several hike-in/bike-in sites. Drinking water and chemical toilets are available. Fires are permitted in metal containers only. A store, a restaurant, a marina, and a boat launch are nearby in Bombay Beach. Leashed pets are permitted.

Reservations, fees: Reservations are not accepted. Sites are $7 per night, $2 per person per night for hike-in/bike-in sites. Open year-round.

Directions: From the Los Angeles area, take I-10 east to Indio and the exit for the Highway 86 Expressway. Take that exit and drive south for 12 miles to 66th Avenue. Turn left and drive less than one mile to Mecca and Highway 111. Turn right (south) on Highway 111 and drive 25 miles to the campground entrance on the right.

From Calipatria, drive north on Highway 111 to Niland, then continue north 18 miles to the entrance on the left.

Contact: Salton Sea State Recreation Area, 760/393-3052 or 760/393-3059, www.parks .ca.gov.

49 FOUNTAIN OF YOUTH SPA

Scenic rating: 4

near the Salton Sea

See map page 947

Natural artesian steam rooms are the highlight here, but close inspection reveals that nobody seems to be getting any younger. This is a vast private park on 90 acres, set near the Salton Sea. While this park has 1,000 sites for RVs, almost half of the sites have seasonal renters. This park is popular with snowbird campers, and about 2,000 people live here during the winter. (See the listing in this chapter for nearby *Red Hill Marina County Park* for side-trip options.)

RV sites, facilities: There are 835 sites for tents or RVs with full hookups (30 and 50 amps) and 165 sites for tents or RVs (no hookups). Restrooms have flush toilets and showers. Cable TV, natural artesian steam rooms, swimming pools, an artesian mineral water spa, three freshwater spas, recreation halls, dump stations, a fitness room, a library, picnic areas, a nine-hole golf course, horseshoes, organized activities, a craft and sewing room, Wi-Fi, modem access, a coin laundry, a barber shop, a beauty parlor, massage services, church services, propane gas, and groceries are available. Some facilities are wheelchair accessible. Leashed pets are permitted.

Reservations, fees: No reservations accepted. Winter rates are $15–29 per night, summer rates are $15–24 per night, $1 per person per night for more than two people. Weekly and monthly rates available. Some credit cards are accepted. Open year-round.

Directions: From the Los Angeles area, take I-10 east to Indio and the exit for the Highway 86 Expressway. Take that exit and drive south for 12 miles to Avenue 62. Turn right and drive less than one mile to Mecca and Highway 111. Turn left (south) on Highway 111 and drive 44 miles to Hot Mineral Spa Road. Turn left (north) on Hot Mineral Spa Road and drive approximately four miles to Coachella Canal Road. Turn right and drive approximately 1.5 miles to the park on the left.

From Calipatria, drive north on Highway 111 to Niland, and then continue north for 15 miles to Hot Mineral Spa Road. Turn right (north) on Hot Mineral Spa Road and drive approximately four miles to Coachella Canal Road. Turn right and drive about 1.5 miles to the park on the left.

Contact: Fountain of Youth Spa, 888/8000-SPA (888/800-0772) or 760/354-1340, fax 760/354-1558, www.foyspa.com.

50 RED HILL MARINA COUNTY PARK

Scenic rating: 3

near the Salton Sea

See map page 947

It's called Red Hill Marina, but you won't find a marina here; it washed away in the mid-1970s. This county park is near the south end of the Salton Sea, one of the weirdest places on the planet. Set 228 feet below sea level, it's a vast body of water covering 360 square miles, 35 miles long, but with an average depth of just 15 feet. It's an extremely odd place to swim, as you bob around effortlessly in the highly saline water. Note that swimming is not recommended in this park because of the muddy shore. Fishing is often good for corvina in spring and early summer. Hundred of species of birds stop by this area as they travel along the Pacific Flyway. Several wildlife refuges are in the immediate area, including two separate chunks of the Imperial Wildfowl Management Area, to the west and south, and the huge Wister Waterfowl Management Area, northwest of Niland. (For side-trip options, see the listing in this chapter for *Bombay Beach*.)

RV sites, facilities: There are 40 sites for RVs or tents; some sites have partial hookups. Picnic tables, cabanas, and barbecue pits are provided. Restrooms have flush toilets and showers. A concession stand, beer, bait, fishing and hunting licenses, and a boat launch are available. The water at this park is not certified for drinking. Leashed pets are permitted.

Reservations, fees: Reservations are not accepted. Sites are $7–12 per night, $2 per night for each additional vehicle, with a 14-day limit. Open year-round.

Directions: From Mecca, drive south on Highway 111 to Niland, and continue to Sinclair Road. Turn right and drive 3.5 miles to Garst Road. Turn right and drive 1.5 miles to the end of Garst Road at Red Hill Road. Turn left on Red Hill Road and drive to the park at the end of the road.

From El Centro, drive north on Highway 111 to Brawley and Highway 78/Main Street. Turn west (left) on Highway 78/Main Street and drive a short distance to Highway 111. Turn right (north) and drive to Calipatria. Continue north on Highway 111 just outside of Calipatria to Sinclair Road. Turn left on Sinclair Road and drive to Garst Road. Turn right and drive 1.5 miles to where it ends at Red Hill Road. Turn left at Red Hill Road and drive to the end of the road and the marina and the campground.

Contact: Red Hill Marina, tel./fax 760/348-2310; Imperial County, 760/482-4384.

51 PALO VERDE COUNTY PARK

Scenic rating: 5

near the Colorado River

See map page 947

This is the only game in town, with no other camp for many miles. It is near a bend in the Colorado River, not far from the Cibola National Wildlife Refuge. A boat ramp is available at the park, making it a launch point for adventure. This stretch of river is a good one for powerboating and waterskiing. The best facilities for visitors are available here and on the west side of the river between Palo Verde and Blythe, with nothing available on the east side of the river.

RV sites, facilities: There are 20 sites for tents or RVs of any length (no hookups). Picnic tables, fire rings, and shade ramadas are available. Restrooms have flush toilets. No drinking water. A boat ramp is available. A store, a coin laundry, and propane gas are available in Palo Verde. Leashed pets are permitted.

Reservations, fees: Reservations are not accepted. There is no fee for camping. Open year-round.

Directions: Drive on I-10 to Highway 78 (two

miles west of Blythe). Take Highway 78 south and drive about 20 miles (three miles past Palo Verde) to the park entrance road on the east side.

Contact: Palo Verde County Park, Imperial County, 760/482-4384.

52 RIVIERA RV RESORT

Scenic rating: 6

near the Colorado River
See map page 947

This RV park is set up for camper-boaters who want to hunker down awhile along the Colorado River and cool off. Access to the park is easy off I-10, and a marina is available, both big pluses for those showing up with trailered boats. Swimming lagoons are another bonus. A golf course is within 10 miles. Note that about half of the sites are rented year-round.

RV sites, facilities: There are 287 sites with full hookups (30 and 50 amps) for RVs of any length; some sites are pull-through. Tents are allowed, and seven park-model cabins are available. Picnic tables are provided. Restrooms have showers. A heated swimming pool, a spa, cable TV, Wi-Fi, modem access, a coin laundry, a telephone room, a convenience store, a card room, 24-hour security, RV and boat storage, an arcade, a recreation center, boat ramps, boat fuel, and propane gas are available. Some facilities are wheelchair accessible. Leashed pets are permitted, with certain restrictions.

Reservations, fees: Reservations are accepted at 800/RV-DESTINY (800/783-3784). Sites are $35–39 per night on weekends, $29 per night Sunday–Thursday, $2 per person for more than two people, $10 per night for an additional vehicle. Tent sites are $20 per night. Holiday rates are higher. Monthly rates available. Some credit cards accepted. Open year-round.

Directions: Drive on I-10 to Blythe and continue east for two miles to the exit for Riviera Drive. Take that exit east and drive two miles to the park on the right (14100 Riviera Drive).

Contact: Riviera RV Resort, 760/922-5350, fax 760/922-6540, www.reynoldsresorts.com.

53 DESTINY McINTYRE RV RESORT

Scenic rating: 3

on the Colorado River
See map page 947

This RV park sits on the outskirts of Blythe on the Colorado River, with this stretch of river providing good conditions for boating, water-skiing, and other water sports. A swimming lagoon is a big plus, along with riverfront beach access. Fishing is an option, with a variety of fish providing fair results, including striped bass, largemouth bass, and catfish roaming the area.

RV sites, facilities: There are 160 sites with full hookups (30 and 50 amps) for RVs of any length, including 11 pull-through sites, and 40 tent sites. Picnic tables and fire rings are provided. Drinking water, restrooms with flush toilets and showers, a dump station, propane gas, a store, bait, ice, and a boat ramp and boat fuel are available. Some facilities are wheelchair accessible. Leashed pets are permitted November–April only.

Reservations, fees: Make reservations at 800/RV-DESTINY (800/783-3784). Sites are $19–37 per night on weekends, $25 per night Sunday–Thursday November–March, $10–25 per night for a tent site, $4 per person per night for more than two people, $10 per night for an additional vehicle. Monthly rates available. Some credit cards accepted. Open year-round.

Directions: Drive on I-10 to Blythe to the exit for Intake Boulevard south. Take that exit and drive south on Intake Boulevard for 6.5 miles to the junction with 26th Avenue (it takes off to the right) and the park entrance on the left. Turn left and enter the park.

Contact: Destiny McIntyre RV Resort, 760/922-8205, fax 760/922-5695, www.destinyrv.com/mcintyrervresort.htm.

CALIFORNIA

54 WIEST LAKE COUNTY PARK

Scenic rating: 4

on Wiest Lake

See map page 947

This is a developed county park along the southern shore of Wiest Lake, which adjoins the Imperial Wildfowl Management Area to the north. Wiest Lake is just 50 acres, set 110 feet below sea level, and a prized area with such desolate country in the surrounding region. Waterskiing and sailboarding can be excellent, although few take advantage of the latter. Swimming is allowed when lifeguards are on duty. The lake is most popular for fishing, with trout planted in winter and catfish in summer. The lake also has bass and bluegill. The Salton Sea, about a 20-minute drive to the northwest, is a worthy side trip.

RV sites, facilities: There are 24 sites with full hookups (50 amps) for RVs up to 45 feet and 20 tent sites. Picnic tables and fire grills are provided. There is no drinking water. Restrooms have flush toilets and showers. A boat ramp and a dump station are available. A store, a coin laundry, and propane gas are available within five miles. Leashed pets are permitted.

Reservations, fees: Reservations are not accepted. Sites are $7–12 per night, $2 per night for each additional vehicle. Open year-round.

Directions: From El Centro, drive north on Highway 111 to Brawley and Highway 78/Main Street. Turn west (left) on Highway 78/Main Street and drive a short distance to Highway 111. Turn right (north) on Highway 111 and drive four miles to Rutherford Road (well signed). Turn right (east) and drive two miles to the park entrance on the right.

Contact: Wiest Lake County Park, tel./fax 760/344-3712; Imperial County, 760/482-4384.

55 IMPERIAL SAND DUNES RECREATION AREA

Scenic rating: 1

east of Brawley

See map page 947

Gecko, Roadrunner, and Midway campgrounds are three of the many camping options at Imperial Sand Dunes Recreation Area. There isn't a tree within a million miles of this camp. People who wind up here all have the same thing in common: They're ready to ride across the dunes in their dune buggies or off-highway vehicles. The dune season is on a weather-permitting basis. Note that several areas are off-limits to motorized vehicles and camping because of plant and habitat protection; hiking in these areas is allowed. There are opportunities for hiking on this incredible moonscape. Other recreation options include watching the sky and waiting for a cloud to show up. A gecko, by the way, is a harmless little lizard. I've had them crawl on the sides of my tent. Nice little fellows.

RV sites, facilities: There are numerous dispersed sites for tents or RVs of any length (no hookups). Vault toilets and a trash bin are available. No drinking water is available. A few sites have camping pads. Leashed pets are permitted.

Reservations, fees: Reservations are not accepted. Sites are $25 per week, $90 per season, with a 14-day stay limit every 28 days. Open year-round.

Directions: From Brawley, drive east on Highway 78 for 27 miles to Gecko Road. Turn south on Gecko Road and drive three miles to the campground entrance on the left. To reach Roadrunner Camp, continue for two miles to the campground at the end of the road.

Contact: Bureau of Land Management, El Centro Field Office, 760/337-4400, fax 760/337-4490. For more information on closed areas, contact the Imperial Sand Dunes ranger station at 760/344-3919 (closed in the summer).

CALIFORNIA

56 PICACHO STATE RECREATION AREA

Scenic rating: 6

near Taylor Lake on the Colorado River

See map page 947

To get here, you really have to want it. Picacho State Recreation Area is way out there, requiring a long drive north out of Winterhaven on a spindly little road. The camp is on the southern side of Taylor Lake on the Colorado River. The park is the best deal around for many miles, though, with boat ramps, waterskiing, good bass fishing, and, occasionally, crazy folks having the time of their lives. The sun and water make a good combination. This recreation area includes eight miles of the lower Colorado River. Park wildlife includes wild burros and bighorn sheep, with thousands of migratory waterfowl on the Pacific Flyway occasionally taking up residence. More than 100 years ago, Picacho was a gold-mining town with a population of 2,500 people. Visitors should always carry extra water and essential supplies.

RV sites, facilities: There are 58 sites for tents or RVs up to 35 feet (no hookups), two group sites for up to 100 people, and two boat-in campsites. Picnic tables and fire grills are provided. Drinking water, pit toilets, a dump station, solar showers, and two boat launches are available. Some facilities are wheelchair accessible. Leashed pets are permitted.

Reservations, fees: Reservations are accepted only for group sites at 760/996-2963. Sites are $10 per night. Group sites are $37.50 per night for up to 12 vehicles. Boat-in group sites are $22.50 per night for up to 15 people and $1.50 per person per night for additional people. Open year-round.

Directions: From El Centro, drive east on I-8 to Winterhaven and the exit for Winterhaven/4th Avenue. Take that exit to Winterhaven Drive. Turn left on Winterhaven Drive and drive 0.5 mile to County Road S24/Picacho Road. Turn right and drive 24 miles (crossing rail tracks, driving under a railroad bridge and over the American Canal, the road becoming dirt for the last 18 miles) to the campground. The road is not suitable for large RVs. The drive takes one to two hours from Winterhaven. In summer, thunderstorms can cause flash flooding, making short sections of the road impassable.

Contact: Picacho State Recreation Area, c/o Salton Sea State Recreation Area, 760/393-3059 or 760/996-2963 (reservations), www.parks .ca.gov.

57 SENATOR WASH RECREATION AREA

Scenic rating: 6

near Senator Wash Reservoir

See map page 947

Senator Wash Reservoir recreation area features two campgrounds, named (surprise) Senator Wash South Shore and Senator Wash North Shore. This recreation area is approximately 50 acres, with many trees of various types and several secluded camping areas. At Senator Wash North Shore (where there are fewer facilities than at South Shore), these campsites are both on the water as well as further inland. Gravel beaches provide access to the reservoir. Boat ramps are nearby. This spot provides boating, fishing, OHV riding, wildlife-viewing, and opportunities for solitude and sightseeing.

RV sites, facilities: There are numerous dispersed sites for tents or RVs of any length (no hookups). No drinking water is available. At South Shore, there are restrooms with flush toilets, outdoor showers, and drinking water. A buoyed swimming area and a boat ramp providing boat-in access to campsites at North Shore are available about 0.25 mile from South Shore. At North Shore, there are two vault toilets but no drinking water; a boat ramp is approximately 0.25 mile away. Some facilities are wheelchair accessible. No camping allowed at the boat ramp. Leashed pets are permitted.

Reservations, fees: Reservations are not accepted. Sites are $5 per night. There is a year-round maximum 14-day limit for every 28 days. Open year-round.

CALIFORNIA

Directions: Drive on I-8 to Yuma, Arizona, and the exit for 4th Avenue. Take that exit and drive to Imperial Highway/County Road S24. Turn north and drive 22 miles to Senator Wash Road. Turn left and drive about three miles south to Mesa Campground. Turn left and drive 200 yards to the South Shore Campground access road on the right. Turn right and drive to the reservoir and campground.

Contact: Bureau of Land Management, Yuma Field Office, 928/317-3200, fax 928/317-3250.

58 SQUAW LAKE

Scenic rating: 6

near the Colorado River
See map page 947

Take your pick. There are two camps near the Colorado River in this area (the other is Senator Wash). This one is near Squaw Lake, created by the nearby Imperial Dam on the Colorado River. These sites provide opportunities for swimming, fishing, boating, and hiking, featuring direct boat access to the Colorado River. Wildlife includes numerous waterfowl, as well as quail, coyotes, and reptiles. A speed limit of 5 mph is enforced on the lake; no wakes permitted. The no-wake zone ends at the Colorado River.

RV sites, facilities: There are 125 sites with no hookups for RVs of any length and dispersed sites for tents. Picnic tables and barbecue grills are provided. Four restrooms with flush toilets and outdoor showers are available. Drinking water is available at a central location. Two boat ramps are nearby. Some facilities are wheelchair accessible. Leashed pets are permitted.

Reservations, fees: Reservations are not accepted. Sites are $5 per night. There is a year-round maximum 14-day limit for every 28 days. Open year-round.

Directions: Drive on I-8 to Yuma, Arizona, and the exit for 4th Avenue. Take that exit and drive to Imperial Highway/County Road S24. Turn north and drive 22 miles to Senator Wash Road. Turn left and drive about four miles

(well signed) to the lake and campground on the right.

Contact: Bureau of Land Management, Yuma Field Office, 928/317-3200, fax 928/317-3250.

59 RIO BEND RV AND GOLF RESORT

Scenic rating: 5

near El Centro
See map page 947

This resort is at 50 feet below sea level near Mount Signal, about a 20-minute drive south of the Salton Sea. For some, this region is a godforsaken wasteland, but hey, that makes arriving at this park all the more like coming to a mirage in the desert. This resort is a combination RV park and year-round community with park models for sale. Management does what it can to offer visitors recreational options, including a nine-hole golf course. It's hot out here, sizzling most of the year, but dry and cool in the winter, the best time to visit.

RV sites, facilities: There are 500 sites for RVs of any length, 67 with full or partial hookups (30 and 50 amps); some sites are pull-through. No tents. Picnic tables are provided. Cable TV and restrooms with showers are available. A convenience store, a café, a heated swimming pool, a spa, shuffleboard, volleyball, horseshoes, two small stocked lakes for catch-and-release fishing, a nine-hole golf course, a library, a pool table, a club room, organized activities, and modem access are available on a seasonal basis. A small store is nearby. Some facilities are wheelchair accessible. Leashed pets are permitted.

Reservations, fees: Reservations are accepted. Sites are $27–38 per night, $3 per person for more than two people. Weekly, monthly, and annual rates available. Some credit cards accepted. Open year-round.

Directions: From El Centro, drive west on I-8 for seven miles to the Drew Road exit. Take that exit and drive south on Drew Road for 0.25 mile to the park on the right (1589 Drew Road).

Contact: Rio Bend RV and Golf Resort, 760/352-7061 or 800/545-6481, www.riobend rvgolfresort.com.

60 MIDWAY

Scenic rating: 6

in the Imperial Sand Dunes Recreation Area

See map page 947

This is off-highway-vehicle headquarters, a place where people bring their three-wheelers, four-wheelers, and motorcycles. That's because a large area has been set aside just for this type of recreation. Good news is that this area has become more family-oriented because of increased enforcement, eliminating much of the lawlessness and lunatic behavior of the past. As you drive in, you will enter the Buttercup Recreation Area, which is part of the Imperial Sand Dunes Recreation Area. You camp almost anywhere you like, and nobody beefs. Note that several areas are off-limits to motorized vehicles and camping because of plant and habitat protection; hiking in these areas is allowed. (See listing in this chapter for *Imperial Sand Dunes Recreation Area* for more options.)

RV sites, facilities: There are several primitive sites for tents or RVs of any length (no hookups). Vault toilets and a trash bin are available. No drinking water is available. Leashed pets are permitted.

Reservations, fees: Reservations are not accepted. Sites are $25 per week, $90 per season. Open year-round, weather permitting.

Directions: From El Centro, drive east on I-8 for about 40 miles to Gray's Wells Road (signed Sand Dunes). Take that exit and drive (it bears to the right) to a stop sign. Continue straight on Gray's Wells Road and drive three miles to another stop sign. To reach Buttercup Recreation Area, turn left and drive a short distance. To reach Midway, continue straight on Gray's Wells Road for 1.5 miles (the road turns from pavement to dirt and then dead-ends); camping is permitted anywhere in this region.

Contact: Bureau of Land Management, El Centro Field Office, 760/337-4400, fax 760/337-4490. For more information on closed areas, contact the Imperial Sand Dunes ranger station at 760/344-3919 or the BLM office in Yuma, Arizona, 928/317-3200.

61 SANS END RV PARK

Scenic rating: 5

in Winterhaven

See map page 947

Sans End is only seven miles from Mexico, and lots of people who stay here like to cross the border for shopping and fun. The high season at this RV park is January to March, and no wonder, because it is blazing hot here in the summer. The Colorado River provides recreational opportunities near Imperial Dam. Boat ramps are available in Yuma and Winterhaven. Some areas of this stretch of water are marshy wetlands that provide an opportunity for duck hunting in the fall and early winter. For anglers, there are some big catfish roaming these waters. The park is surrounded by palm trees, shielding your view of the junkyard across the road.

RV sites, facilities: There are 167 sites for RVs and a few sites for tents. Restrooms, showers, a recreation hall with a pool table, a coin-operated laundry, and shuffleboard are available. Leashed pets are permitted.

Reservations, fees: Reservations are not accepted. The fee is $21 per night. Open year-round.

Directions: Drive on I-8 to the exit for Winterhaven Drive (just west of Yuma, Arizona). Turn left (if arriving from the west) and drive a short distance to the park on the right.

Contact: Sans End RV Park, 2209 West Winterhaven Drive, Winterhaven, CA 92283, 760/572-0797.

CALIFORNIA

RESOURCES

Resources

NATIONAL FORESTS

The Forest Service provides many secluded camps and allows camping anywhere except where it is specifically prohibited. If you ever want to clear the cobwebs from your head and get away from it all, this is the way to go.

Many Forest Service campgrounds are quite remote and have no drinking water. You usually don't need to check in or make reservations, and sometimes, there is no fee. At many Forest Service campgrounds that provide drinking water, the camping fee is often only a few dollars, with payment made on the honor system. Because most of these camps are in mountain areas, they are subject to winter closure because of snow or mud.

Dogs are permitted in national forests with no extra charge and no hassle. Leashes are required for all dogs in some places. Always carry documentation of current vaccinations.

National Forest Adventure Pass - California

Angeles, Cleveland, Los Padres, and San Bernardino National Forests require an Adventure Pass for each parked vehicle. Daily passes cost $5; annual passes are available for $30. You can buy Adventure Passes at national forest offices in Southern California and dozens of retail outlets and online vendors. The new charges are use fees, not entrance fees. Holders of Golden Age and Golden Access (not Golden Eagle) cards can buy the Adventure Pass at a 50 percent discount at national forest offices only, or at retail outlets for the retail price. A Golden Eagle passport is honored in lieu of an Adventure Pass.

When you buy an annual Adventure Pass, you can also buy an annual second-vehicle Adventure Pass for $5. Major credit cards are accepted at most retail and online outlets and at some Forest Service offices. You can buy Adventure Passes by telephone at 909/382-2622, -2623, -2621, or by mail at San Bernardino National Forest, Pass Program Headquarters, 602 South Tippecanoe Avenue, San Bernardino, CA 92408-2607. Checks should be made payable to USDA Forest Service.

You will not need an Adventure Pass while traveling through these forests, nor when you've paid other types of fees such as camping or ski pass fees. However, if you are camping in these forests and you leave the campground in your vehicle and park outside the campground for recreation, such as at a trailhead, day-use area, near a fishing stream, etc., you will need an Adventure Pass for your vehicle. You also need an Adventure Pass if camping at a no-fee campground. More information about the Adventure Pass program, including a listing of retail and online vendors, can be obtained at www.fsadventurepass.org.

Northwest Forest Pass - Oregon and Washington

A Northwest Forest Pass is required for certain activities in some Washington national forests and at Columbia River Gorge National Scenic Area. The pass is required for parking at participating trailheads, nondeveloped camping areas, boat launches, picnic areas, and visitors centers.

Daily passes cost $5 per vehicle; annual passes are $30 per vehicle. Combined recreation passes for Washington and Oregon are also available. You can buy Northwest Forest Passes at national forest offices and dozens of retail outlets and online vendors. Holders of Golden Age and Golden Access (not Golden Eagle) cards can buy the Northwest Forest Pass at a 50 percent discount at national forest offices only, or at retail outlets for the retail price. Major credit cards are accepted at most retail and online outlets and at some Forest Service offices.

More information about the Northwest Forest Pass program, including a listing of retail and online vendors, can be obtained online at www.fs.fed.us/r6/passpermits/ or www.naturenw.org. You can also phone 800/270-7504.

National Forest Reservations
Some of the more popular camps and most of the group camps are on a reservation system. Reservations can be made up to 240 days in advance, up to 360 days in advance for groups. To reserve a site call 877/444-6777 or visit www.ReserveUSA.com. The reservation fee is usually $9 for a campsite in a national forest, and major credit cards are accepted. Holders of Golden Age or Golden Access passports receive a 50 percent discount for campground fees, except for group sites.

National Forest Maps
National forest maps are among the best you can get for the price. They detail all backcountry streams, lakes, hiking trails, and logging roads for access. They cost $7 or more, and they can be obtained in person at Forest Service offices or by contacting the U.S. Forest Service, Attn: Map Sales, P.O. Box 8268, Missoula, MT 59807, 406/329-3024, fax 406/329-3030, www.fs.fed .us/recreation/nationalforeststore. Major credit cards are accepted if ordering by telephone.

Maps are also available from an interpretive organization: Nature of the Northwest, 800 NE Oregon Street, Suite 177, Portland, OR 97232, 503/872-2750, www.naturenw.org.

Forest Service Information
Forest Service personnel are most helpful for obtaining camping or hiking trail information. Unless you are buying a map, Adventure Pass, or Northwest Forest Pass, it is advisable to phone in advance to get the best service. For specific information on a national forest, contact the following offices:

California
Pacific Southwest Region
1323 Club Drive
Vallejo, CA 94592
707/562-USFS (707/562-8737)
fax 707/562-9130
www.fs.fed.us/r5/

Angeles National Forest
701 North Santa Anita Avenue
Arcadia, CA 91006
626/574-1613
fax 626/574-5233
www.fs.fed.us/r5/angeles/

Cleveland National Forest
10845 Rancho Bernardo Road, No. 200
San Diego, CA 92127-2107
858/673-6180
fax 858/673-6192
www.fs.fed.us/r5/cleveland/

Eldorado National Forest
100 Forni Road
Placerville, CA 95667
530/622-5061
fax 530/621-5297
www.fs.fed.us/r5/eldorado/

Humboldt-Toiyabe National Forest
1200 Franklin Way
Sparks, NV 89431
775/331-6444
fax 775/355-5399
www.fs.fed.us/r4/htnf/

Inyo National Forest
351 Pacu Lane, Suite 200
Bishop, CA 93514
760/873-2400
fax 760/873-2458
www.fs.fed.us/r5/inyo/

Klamath National Forest
1312 Fairlane Road
Yreka, CA 96097-9549
530/842-6131
fax 530/841-4571
www.fs.fed.us/r5/klamath/

Lake Tahoe Basin Management Unit
35 College Drive
South Lake Tahoe, CA 96150
530/543-2600
fax 530/543-2693
www.fs.fed.us/r5/ltbmu/

Lassen National Forest
2550 Riverside Drive
Susanville, CA 96130
530/257-2151
fax 530/252-6448
www.r5.fs.fed.us/r5/lassen/

Los Padres National Forest
6755 Hollister Avenue, Suite 150
Goleta, CA 93117
805/968-6640
fax 805/961-5729
www.fs.fed.us/r5/lospadres/

Mendocino National Forest
825 North Humboldt Avenue
Willows, CA 95988
530/934-3316
fax 530/934-7384
www.fs.fed.us/r5/mendocino/

Modoc National Forest
800 West 12th Street
Alturas, CA 96101
530/233-5811
fax 530/233-8709
www.fs.fed.us/r5/modoc/

Plumas National Forest
P.O. Box 11500
159 Lawrence Street
Quincy, CA 95971

530/283-2050
fax 530/283-7746
www.fs.fed.us/r5/plumas/

San Bernardino National Forest
602 South Tippecanoe Avenue
San Bernardino, CA 92408-2607
909/382-2600
fax 909/383-5770
www.fs.fed.us/r5/sanbernardino/

Sequoia National Forest
Giant Sequoia National Monument
1839 South Newcomb Street
Porterville, CA 93257
559/784-1500
fax 559/781-4744
www.fs.fed.us/r5/sequoia/

Shasta-Trinity National Forest
3644 Avtech Parkway
Redding, CA 96002
530/226-2500
fax 530/226-2470
www.fs.fed.us/r5/shastatrinity/

Sierra National Forest
1600 Tollhouse Road
Clovis, CA 93611
559/297-0706
fax 559/294-4809
www.fs.fed.us/r5/sierra/

Six Rivers National Forest
1330 Bayshore Way
Eureka, CA 95501
707/442-1721
fax 707/442-9242
www.fs.fed.us/r5/sixrivers/

Stanislaus National Forest
19777 Greenley Road
Sonora, CA 95370
209/532-3671
fax 209/533-1890
www.fs.fed.us/r5/stanislaus/

Tahoe National Forest
631 Coyote Street
Nevada City, CA 95959
530/265-4531
fax 530/478-6109
www.fs.fed.us/r5/tahoe/

Oregon
USDA Forest Service
Pacific Northwest Region 6
333 SW 1st Avenue
P.O. Box 3623
Portland, OR 97208-3623
503/808-2468
www.fs.fed.us/r6/

Deschutes National Forest
1001 SW Emkay Drive
Bend, OR 97702
541/383-5300
fax 541/383-5531
www.fs.fed.us/r6/centraloregon/

Fremont-Winema National Forests
1301 South G Street
Lakeview, OR 97630
541/947-2151
fax 541/947-6399
www.fs.fed.us/r6/frewin/

Malheur National Forest
431 Patterson Bridge Road
P.O. Box 909
John Day, OR 97845
541/575-3000
fax 541/575-3001
www.fs.fed.us/r6/malheur/

Mount Hood National Forest
16400 Champion Way
Sandy, OR 97055
503/668-1700
fax 503/668-1794
www.fs.fed.us/r6/mthood/

Ochoco National Forest
3160 NE 3rd Street

Prineville, OR 97754
541/416-6500
fax 541/416-6695
www.fs.fed.us/r6/centraloregon/

Rogue River-Siskiyou National Forest
333 West 8th Street
P.O. Box 520
Medford, OR 97501-0209
541/858-2200
fax 541/858-2205
www.fs.fed.us/r6/rogue-siskiyou/

Siuslaw National Forest
4077 SW Research Way
P.O. Box 1148
Corvallis, OR 97339
541/750-7000
fax 541/750-7234
www.fs.fed.us/r6/siuslaw/

Umatilla National Forest
2517 SW Hailey Avenue
Pendleton, OR 97801
541/278-3716
fax 541/278-3730
www.fs.fed.us/r6/uma/

Umpqua National Forest
2900 NW Stewart Parkway
Roseburg, OR 97470
541/672-6601
fax 541/957-3495
www.fs.fed.us/r6/umpqua/

Wallowa-Whitman National Forest
1550 Dewey Avenue
P.O. Box 907
Baker City, OR 97814
541/523-6391
fax 541/523-1315
www.fs.fed.us/r6/w-w/

Willamette National Forest
211 East 7th Avenue
Eugene, OR 97401
541/225-6300

fax 541/225-6337
www.fs.fed.us/r6/willamette/

Washington

Colville National Forest
765 South Main Street
Colville, WA 99114
509/684-7000
fax 509/684-7280
www.fs.fed.us/r6/colville/

Gifford Pinchot National Forest
10600 NE 51st Circle
Vancouver, WA 98682
360/891-5000
fax 360/891-5045
www.fs.fed.us/r6/gpnf/

Mount Baker-Snoqualmie National Forest
21905 64th Avenue West

Mountlake Terrace, WA 98043-2278
425/775-9702 or 800/627-0062
www.fs.fed.us/r6/mbs/

Okanogan and Wenatchee National Forests
215 Melody Lane
Wenatchee, WA 98801-5933
509/664-9200
fax 509/664-9280
www.fs.fed.us/r6/wenatchee/

Olympic National Forest
1835 Black Lake Boulevard SW
Olympia, WA 98512-5623
360/959-2402
fax 360/956-2330
www.fs.fed.us/r6/olympic/

NATIONAL PARKS AND RESERVATIONS

The West Coast's national parks are natural wonders, ranging from the spectacular yet crowded Yosemite Valley in California to the breathtaking Crater Lake National Park in Oregon to the often fog-bound Olympic National Park in Washington. Reservations for campsites are available five months in advance for many of the national parks. In addition to campground fees, expect to pay a park entrance fee ranging $10–20 per vehicle (you can buy an annual National Parks Pass that waives entrance fees). This entrance fee is valid for seven days. For an additional fee, a Golden Eagle sticker can be added to the National Parks Pass, thereby eliminating entrance fees at sites managed by the U.S. Fish and Wildlife Service, the U.S. Forest Service, and the Bureau of Land Management. Various discounts are available for holders of Golden Age and Golden Access passports, including a 50 percent reduction of camping fees (group camps not included) and a waiver of park entrance fees.

For Yosemite National Park reservations, call 800/436-PARK (800/436-7275) or visit the http://reservations.nps.gov. Major credit cards accepted.

For all other national parks, call 800/365-CAMP (800/365-2267) or visit the http://reservations.nps.gov. Major credit cards are accepted.

For information about each of the national parks in California, Oregon, and Washington, contact the parks directly at the following telephone numbers or addresses:

California

National Park Service
Pacific West Region
One Jackson Center
111 Jackson Street, Suite 700
Oakland, CA 94607

510/817-1304
www.nps.gov

Cabrillo National Monument
1800 Cabrillo Memorial Drive
San Diego, CA 92106-3601

619/557-5450
fax 619/226-6331
www.nps.gov/cabr

Channel Islands National Park
1901 Spinnaker Drive
Ventura, CA 93001
805/658-5730
fax 805/658-5799
www.nps.gov/chis

Death Valley National Park
P.O. Box 579
Death Valley, CA 92328-0579
760/786-3200
fax 760/786-3283
www.nps.gov/deva

Devils Postpile National Monument
P.O. Box 3999
Mammoth Lakes, CA 93546
760/934-2289 (summer only)
fax 760/934-8896 (summer only)
www.nps.gov/depo
For year-round information, contact Sequoia
and Kings Canyon National Parks

Golden Gate National Recreation Area
Fort Mason, Building 201
San Francisco, CA 94123-0022
415/561-4700
www.nps.gov/goga

Joshua Tree National Park
74485 National Park Drive
Twentynine Palms, CA 92277-3597
760/367-5500
fax 760/367-6392
www.nps.gov/jotr

Lassen Volcanic National Park
P.O. Box 100
Mineral, CA 96063-0100
530/595-4444
fax 530/595-3262
www.nps.gov/lavo

Lava Beds National Monument
1 Indian Well Headquarters
Tulelake, CA 96134
530/667-2282
fax 530/667-2737
www.nps.gov/labe

Mojave National Preserve
2701 Barstow Road
Barstow, CA 92311
760/733-4040 (information)
fax 760/252-6174
www.nps.gov/moja

Pinnacles National Monument
5000 Highway 146
Paicines, CA 95043
831/389-4485
fax 831/389-4489
www.nps.gov/pinn

Point Reyes National Seashore
Point Reyes Station, CA 94956-9799
415/464-5100
fax 415/464-5149
www.nps.gov/pore

Redwood National and State Parks
1111 2nd Street
Crescent City, CA 95531
707/464-6101
fax 707/464-1812
www.nps.gov/redw

**Santa Monica Mountains National
Recreation Area**
401 West Hillcrest Drive
Thousand Oaks, CA 91360
805/370-2301
fax 805/370-1850
www.nps.gov/samo

Sequoia and Kings Canyon National Parks
47050 Generals Highway
Three Rivers, CA 93271-9651
559/565-3341
www.nps.gov/seki

Smith River National Recreation Area
P.O. Box 228
10600 Highway 199 North
Gasquet, CA 95543
707/457-3131
fax 707/457-3794
www.fs.fed.us/r5/sixrivers

Whiskeytown National Recreation Area
P.O. Box 188
14412 Kennedy Memorial Drive
Whiskeytown, CA 96095
530/246-1225 or 530/242-3400
fax 530/246-5154
www.nps.gov/whis

Yosemite National Park
P.O. Box 577
Yosemite National Park, CA 95389
209/372-0200 for 24-hour recorded message
www.nps.gov/yose

Oregon

Columbia River Gorge National Scenic Area
902 Wasco Avenue, Suite 200
Hood River, OR 97031
541/308-1700
fax 541/386-1916
www.fs.fed.us/r6/columbia/forest/

Crater Lake National Park
P.O. Box 7
Crater Lake, OR 97604
541/594-3000
fax 541/594-3010
www.nps.gov/crla

Crooked River National Grassland
813 SW Highway 97
Madras, OR 97741
541/475-9272
fax 541/416-6694
www.fs.fed.us/r6/centraloregon

Hells Canyon National Recreation Area
Wallowa Mountains Visitor Center
88401 Highway 82

Box A
Enterprise, OR 97828
541/426-5546
fax 541/426-5522
www.fs.fed.us/hellscanyon

Oregon Dunes National Recreation Area
Visitor Center
855 Highway Avenue
Reedsport, OR 97467
541/271-6000
fax 541/271-6019
www.fs.fed.us/r6/siuslaw/

Washington

Hells Canyon National Recreation Area
Snake River Office
2535 Riverside Drive
P.O. Box 699
Clarkston, WA 99403
509/758-0616
fax 509/758-1963
www.fs.fed.us/hellscanyon

Lake Roosevelt National Recreation Area
1008 Crest Drive
Coulee Dam, WA 99116
509/633-9441
fax 509/633-9332
www.nps.gov/laro

Mount Rainier National Park
55210 238th Avenue East
Ashford, WA 98304
360/569-2211
fax 360/569-2170
www.nps.gov/mora

**Mount St. Helens National
Volcanic Monument**
42218 NE Yale Bridge Road
Amboy, WA 98601
360/449-7800 or 360/274-0962 (Mount St. Helens Visitor Center)
fax 360/449-7800
www.fs.fed.us/r6/gpnf

North Cascades National Park
810 State Route 20
Sedro-Woolley, WA 98284-1239
360/856-5700
fax 360/856-1934
www.nps.gov/noca

Olympic National Park
600 East Park Avenue
Port Angeles, WA 98362-6798
360/565-3130 or 800/833-6388
fax 360/565-3015
www.nps.gov/olym

STATE PARKS

The state parks systems provide many popular camping spots in spectacular settings. These campgrounds include drive-in numbered sites, tent spaces, and picnic tables, with showers and bathrooms provided nearby. Reservations are often necessary during the summer. Although many parks are well known, there are still some little-known gems in the state parks systems where campers can enjoy seclusion, even in the summer.

California

Most of the state park campgrounds are on a reservation system, and campsites can be booked up to seven months in advance at these parks. There are also hike-in/bike-in sites at many of the parks, and they are available on a first-come, first-served basis. Reservations can be made by telephone or online by phoning 800/444-PARK (800/444-7275) or visiting www.reserveamerica.com. The reservation fee is usually $7.50 for a campsite. Major credit cards are accepted for reservations but are generally not accepted in person at the parks.

Camping discounts of 50 percent are available for holders of the Disabled Discount Pass, and free camping is allowed for holders of the Disabled Veteran/Prisoner of War Pass.

For general information about California state parks, contact:

California Department of Parks and Recreation
Public Information Office
P.O. Box 942896
1416 9th Street
Sacramento, CA 94296
916/653-6995 or 800/777-0369
fax 916/653-6995
www.parks.ca.gov

Oregon

Reservations can be made for many Oregon state parks through Reserve America at 800/452-5687. Online reservations for Oregon state parks can be made through www.reserveamerica.com. A nonrefundable reservation fee of $6 is charged for a campsite, and the reservation fee for group sites is higher. Major credit cards are accepted for reservations, and credit cards are accepted at some of the parks during the summer. Under this system, reservations can be made throughout the year, up to nine months in advance. Discounts may be available for certain user groups; check for current status.

For general information regarding Oregon state parks, contact:

Oregon State Parks
725 Summer Street NE, Suite C
Salem, OR 97301

800/551-6949
www.oregonstateparks.org.
www.oregon.gov/OPRD/PARKS/

Washington
Many of the state park campgrounds are on a reservation system, and campsites can be booked up to nine months in advance at these parks. Reservations can be made by telephone at 888/CAMPOUT (888/226-7688) or online at www.parks.wa.gov/reserve.asp. The reservation number is open 7 A.M.–8 P.M. (Pacific standard time) almost every day of the year. Major credit cards are accepted for reservations, and credit cards are accepted at some of the parks during the summer. A $7 reservation fee is charged for a campsite, and the reservation fee for group sites is higher. Discounts are available (group camps excluded) for Washington State pass holders of disabled, limited-income, and off-season senior citizen status. Disabled veterans pass holders are not charged any fees.

General information regarding Washington state parks can be obtained by contacting:

Washington State Parks and Recreation Commission
7150 Cleanwater Lane
P.O. Box 42650
Olympia, WA 98504-2650
360/902-8844
www.parks.wa.gov

BUREAU OF LAND MANAGEMENT
Most of the areas managed by the BLM are primitive and in remote areas. Parking and access are usually free. Often there is also no fee for camping. Holders of Golden Age or Golden Access passports receive a 50 percent discount, except for group camps, at BLM fee campgrounds.

California
Bureau of Land Management
California State Office
2800 Cottage Way, Suite W-1834
Sacramento, CA 95825-1886
916/978-4400
fax 916/978-4416
www.blm.gov/ca

California Desert District Office
22835 Calle San Juan de los Lagos
Moreno Valley, CA 92553
951/697-5200
fax 951/697-5299
www.blm.gov/ca/cdd

Alturas Field Office
708 West 12th Street
Alturas, CA 96101
530/233-4666
fax 530/233-5696
www.blm.gov/ca/alturas

Arcata Field Office
1695 Heindon Road
Arcata, CA 95521-4573
707/825-2300
fax 707/825-2301
www.blm.gov/ca/arcata

Bakersfield Field Office
3801 Pegasus Drive
Bakersfield, CA 93308
661/391-6000
fax 661/391-6040
www.blm.gov/ca/bakersfield

Barstow Field Office
2601 Barstow Road
Barstow, CA 92311
760/252-6000
fax 760/252-6099
www.blm.gov/ca/barstow

Bishop Field Office
351 Pacu Lane, Suite 100
Bishop, CA 93514
760/872-5000
fax 760/872-5050
www.blm.gov/ca/bishop

Eagle Lake Field Office
2950 Riverside Drive
Susanville, CA 96130
530/257-0456
fax 530/257-4831
www.blm.gov/ca/eaglelake

El Centro Field Office
1661 South 4th Street
El Centro, CA 92243
760/337-4400
fax 760/337-4490
www.blm.gov/ca/elcentro

Folsom Field Office
63 Natoma Street
Folsom, CA 95630
916/985-4474
fax 916/985-3259
www.blm.gov/ca/folsom

Hollister Field Office
20 Hamilton Court
Hollister, CA 95023
831/630-5000
fax 831/630-5055
www.blm.gov/ca/hollister

Palm Springs/South Coast Field Office
P.O. Box 581260
North Palm Springs, CA 92258-1260
760/251-4800

fax 760/251-4899
www.blm.gov/ca/palmsprings

Redding Field Office
355 Hemsted Drive
Redding, CA 96002
530/224-2100
fax 530/224-2172
www.blm.gov/ca/redding

Ridgecrest Field Office
300 South Richmond Road
Ridgecrest, CA 93555
760/384-5400
fax 760/384-5499
www.blm.gov/ca/ridgecrest

Ukiah Field Office
2550 North State Street
Ukiah, CA 95482
707/468-4000
fax 707/468-4027
www.blm.gov/ca/ukiah

Oregon

Oregon State Office
3333 West 1st Avenue
P.O. Box 2965
Portland, OR 97208
503/808-6002
www.blm.gov/or

Burns District
28910 Highway 20 West
Hines, OR 97738
541/573-4400
fax 541/573-4411
www.blm.gov/or/districts/burns

Coos Bay District
1300 Airport Lane
North Bend, OR 97459-2000
541/756-0100
fax 541/751-4303
www.blm.gov/or/districts/coosbay

Eugene District
P.O. Box 10226
2890 Chad Drive
Eugene, OR 97440-2226
541/683-6600
fax 541/683-6981
www.blm.gov/or/districts/eugene

Lakeview District
1301 South G Street
Lakeview, OR 97630
541/947-2177
fax 541/947-6399
www.blm.gov/or/districts/lakeview

Medford District
3040 Biddle Road
Medford, OR 97504
541/618-2200
fax 541/618-2400
www.blm.gov/or/districts/medford

Prineville District
3050 NE 3rd Street
Prineville, OR 97754
541/416-6700
fax 541/416-6798
www.blm.gov/or/districts/prineville

Roseburg District
777 NW Garden Valley Boulevard
Roseburg, OR 97470
541/440-4930
fax 541/440-4948
www.blm.gov/or/districts/roseburg

Salem District
1717 Fabry Road SE
Salem, OR 97306
503/375-5646
fax 503/375-5622
www.blm.gov/or/districts/salem

Vale District
100 Oregon Street
Vale, OR 97918-9630
531/473-3144
fax 541/473-6213
www.blm.gov/or/districts/vale

Washington

Spokane District
1103 North Fancher Road
Spokane, WA 97212
509/536-1200
fax 509/536-1275
www.blm.gov/or/districts/spokane

U.S. ARMY CORPS OF ENGINEERS CAMP RESERVATIONS

Some of the family camps and most of the group camps operated by the U.S. Army Corps of Engineers are on a reservation system. Reservations can be made up to 240 days in advance, and up to 360 days in advance for groups. To reserve a site, call 877/444-6777 or visit www.ReserveUSA.com. The reservation fee is usually $9 for a campsite, but group site reservation fees are higher. Major credit cards are accepted. Holders of Golden Age or Golden Access passports receive a 50 percent discount for campground fees, except for group sites.

California

South Pacific Division
333 Market Street
San Francisco, CA 94105
415/977-8272
fax 415/977-8316
www.spn.usace.army.mil

Sacramento District
1325 J Street
Sacramento, CA 95814
916/557-5100
www.spk.usace.army.mil

Los Angeles District
915 Wilshire Boulevard, Suite 980
Los Angeles, CA 90017-3401
213/452-3908
fax 213/452-4209
www.spl.usace.army.mil

Oregon
Portland District
333 SW 1st Avenue
P.O. Box 2946
Portland, OR 97208-2946

503/808-5150
fax 503/808-4515
www.nwp.usace.army.mil

Washington
Walla Walla District
201 North 3rd Avenue
Walla Walla, WA 99362-1876
509/527-7020
fax 509/527-7824
www.nww.usace.army.mil

DEPARTMENT OF NATURAL RESOURCES – WASHINGTON

The Department of Natural Resources manages more than five million acres of public land in Washington. All of it is managed under the concept of "multiple use," designed to provide the greatest number of recreational opportunities while still protecting natural resources.

The campgrounds in these areas are among the most primitive, remote, and least known of the camps listed in the book. The campsites are usually free, and you are asked to remove all litter and trash from the area, leaving only your footprints behind. Due to budget cutbacks, some of these campgrounds have been closed in recent years; expect more closures in the future.

The 2005 Major Public Lands Map is now available at all DNR regional offices or at www.dnr.wa.gov.

For more information, contact the Department of Natural Resources at the appropriate state or regional address:

State of Washington
1111 Washington Street SE
P.O. Box 47001
Olympia, WA 98504-7001
360/902-1000
fax 360/902-1775
www.dnr.wa.gov

Northeast Region
225 South Silke Road
P.O. Box 190
Colville, WA 99114-0190
509/684-7474
fax 509/684-7484

Northwest Region
919 North Township Street
Sedro Woolley, WA 98284-9384

360/856-3500
fax 360/856-2150

Olympic Region
411 Tillicum Lane
Forks, WA 98331-9271
360/374-6131
fax 360/374-5446

Pacific Cascade Region
601 Bond Road
P.O. Box 280
Castle Rock, WA 98611-0280
360/577-2025
fax 360/274-4196

Southeast Region
713 Bowers Road

Ellensburg, WA 98926-9301
509/925-8510
fax 509/925-8522

South Puget Sound Region
950 Farman Avenue North
Enumclaw, WA 98022-9282
360/825-1631
fax 360/825-1672

STATE FORESTS
California
Jackson Demonstration State Forest
802 North Main Street
Fort Bragg, CA 95437
707/964-5674
fax 707/964-0941

Mountain Home Demonstration State Forest
P.O. Box 517
Springville, CA 93265
559/539-2321 (summer) or 559/539-2855
(winter)

Oregon
Oregon Department of Forestry
2600 State Street
Salem, OR 97310
503/945-7200
fax 503/945-7212
www.odf.state.or.us

Tillamook State Forest
Forest Grove District
801 Gales Creek Road
Forest Grove, OR 97116
503/357-2191
fax 503/357-4548
http://oregon.gov/ODF/FIELD/FG/
aboutus.shtml

Tillamook State Forest
Tillamook District
5005 3rd Street
Tillamook, OR 97141-2999

503/842-2545
fax 503/842-3143
http://oregon.gov/ODF/FIELD/
TILLAMOOK/aboutTillamook.shtml

County/Regional Park Departments–California
Del Norte County Parks
840 9th Street, Suite 11
Crescent City, CA 95531
707/464-7230
fax 707/464-5824
www.co.del-norte.ca.us

East Bay Regional Park District
P.O. Box 5381
Oakland, CA 94605-0381
510/562-PARK (510/562-7275) or
510/544-2200
fax 510/635-3478
www.ebparks.org

Humboldt County Parks
1106 2nd Street
Eureka, CA 95501
707/445-7651
fax 707/445-7409
www.co.humboldt.ca.us/

Marin Municipal Water District
220 Nellen Avenue
Corte Madera, CA 94925
415/945-1455
fax 415/927-4953
www.marinwater.org

Midpeninsula Regional Open Space District
330 Distel Circle
Los Altos, CA 94022-1404
650/691-1200
fax 650/691-0485
www.openspace.org

Sacramento County Regional Parks
3711 Branch Center Road
Sacramento, CA 95827

916/875-6961
fax 916/875-6050
www.sacparks.net

San Diego County Parks and Recreation Department
2454 Heritage Park Row
San Diego, CA 92110
858/694-3049
fax 619/260-6492
www.co.san-diego.ca.us/parks

San Luis Obispo County Parks Department
1087 Santa Rosa Street
San Luis Obispo, CA 93408
805/781-5930
fax 805/781-1102
www.slocountyparks.org

San Mateo County Parks and Recreation Department
455 County Center, 4th floor
Redwood City, CA 94063-1646
650/363-4020
fax 650/599-1721
www.eparks.net

Santa Barbara County Parks and Recreation Department
610 Mission Canyon Road
Santa Barbara, CA 93105
805/568-2461
fax 805/568-2459
www.sbparks.com

Santa Clara County Parks Department
298 Garden Hill Drive
Los Gatos, CA 95032-7669
408/355-2200
fax 408/355-2290
www.parkhere.org

Sonoma County Regional Parks
2300 County Center Drive, Suite 120-A
Santa Rosa, CA 95404
707/565-2041

fax 707/579-8247
www.sonoma-county.org/parks

Information Services

Lake County Visitor Information Center
P.O. Box 1025
6110 East Highway 20
Lucerne, CA 95458
707/274-5652 or 800/525-3743
fax 707/274-5664
www.lakecounty.com

Mammoth Lakes Visitors Bureau
P.O. Box 48
437 Old Mammoth Road, Suite Y
Mammoth Lakes, CA 93546
888/GO-MAMMOTH (888/466-2666) or
760/934-2712
fax 760/934-7066
www.visitmammoth.com

Mount Shasta Visitors Bureau
300 Pine Street
Mount Shasta, CA 96067
530/926-4865 or 800/926-4865
fax 530/926-0976
www.mtshastachamber.com

The Nature Conservancy of California
201 Mission Street, 4th floor
San Francisco, CA 94105-1832
415/777-0487
fax 415/777-0244
www.nature.org/california

Plumas County Visitors Bureau
550 Crescent Street
P.O. Box 4120
Quincy, CA 95971
530/283-6345 or 800/326-2247
fax 530/283-5465
www.plumascounty.org

Shasta Cascade Wonderland Association
1699 Highway 273
Anderson, CA 96007

530/365-7500 or 800/474-2782
fax 530/365-1258
www.shastacascade.com

OTHER VALUABLE RESOURCES

California Department of Transportation
Highway Information
916/445-7623 or 800/427-ROAD
(800/427-7623)
www.dot.ca.gov

Nature of the Northwest Information Center
800 NE Oregon Street, Suite 177
Portland, OR 97232
503/872-2750
www.naturenw.org

Oregon Department of Transportation
Traveler Information
503/588-2941 or 800/977-ODOT
(800/977-6368)
www.oregon.gov/ODOT

Tacoma Power
P.O. Box 11007
Tacoma, WA 98411
253/502-8000 or 888/502-8690 (Fishing and Recreation Hotline)
tacomapower.com

Pacific Gas and Electric Company
Corporate Real Estate/Recreation
5555 Florin-Perkins Road, Room 100
Sacramento, CA 95826
916/386-5164
fax 916/923-7044
www.pge.com/recreation

Washington State Department of Transportation
Washington State Highway Information:
800/695-ROAD (800/695-7623)
Greater Seattle Area Information:
206/DOT-HIWY (206/368-4499)
www.wsdot.wa.gov

Washington State Ferries Information
206/464-6400 or 888/808-7977
www.wsdot.wa.gov

MAP RESOURCES

Map Link
30 South La Patera Lane, Unit 5
Goleta, CA 93117
805/692-6777 or 800/962-1394
fax 805/692-6787 or 800/627-7768
www.maplink.com

Nature of the Northwest Information Center
800 NE Oregon Street, Suite 177
Portland, OR 97232
503/872-2750
www.naturenw.org

Olmsted and Bros. Map Company
P.O. Box 5351
Berkeley, CA 94705
tel./fax 510/658-6534

Tom Harrison Maps
2 Falmouth Cove
San Rafael, CA 94901-4465
tel./fax 415/456-7940 or 800/265-9090
www.tomharrisonmaps.com

U.S. Forest Service
Attn: Map Sales
P.O. Box 8268
Missoula, MT 59807
406/329-3024
fax 406/329-3030
www.fs.fed.us/recreation/nationalforeststore

U.S. Geological Survey
Branch of Information Services
P.O. Box 25286, Federal Center
Denver, CO 80225
303/202-4700 or 888/ASK-USGS
(888/275-8747)
fax 303/202-4693
www.usgs.gov

Acknowledgments

CALIFORNIA

U.S. Forest Service

Matt Mathes, Pacific Region Headquarters

Jerry Reponen, Los Angeles River Ranger District, Angeles National Forest

Patrick Hersey, San Gabriel Ranger District, Angeles National Forest

Kirsten Johansen, Santa Clara–Mojave Ranger District, Angeles National Forest

Ann Carey, Descanso Ranger District, Cleveland National Forest

Jeff Wells, Palomar Ranger District, Cleveland National Forest

Jake Rodriguez, Trabuco Ranger District, Cleveland National Forest

Billy Brown, Amador Ranger District, Eldorado National Forest

Pete Robinson, Georgetown Ranger District, Eldorado National Forest

Nancy Platt, Christy Schroeder and Fay Buel, Pacific Ranger District, Eldorado National Forest

Joyce Pratt, Placerville Ranger District, Eldorado National Forest

Eric Pignata, Bridgeport Ranger District, Humboldt-Toiyabe National Forest

Mike May, Carson Ranger District, Humboldt-Toiyabe National Forest

Kitty VanStelle, Mammoth Lakes Ranger Station and Visitor Center, Inyo National Forest

Cathie Morgan and Adam Smith, Mono Basin Scenic Area and Visitor Center, Inyo National Forest

Kendrah Madrid, Mount Whitney Ranger District, Inyo National Forest

Carol Puryear, Britta Suppes and John Louth, White Mountain Ranger District, Inyo National Forest

Susan Reynolds, Goosenest Ranger District, Klamath National Forest

Veronica Selvage, Happy Camp and Oak Knoll Ranger Districts, Klamath National Forest

Charlie Krause, Scott River and Salmon River Ranger Districts, Klamath National Forest

Barbara Jackson, Almanor Ranger District, Lassen National Forest

Mario Guajardo, Eagle Lake Ranger District, Lassen National Forest

Mary Lou Schmierer, Hat Creek Ranger District, Lassen National Forest

Nicole Karres, Monterey Ranger District, Los Padres National Forest

Rick Howell, Mount Pinos Ranger District, Los Padres National Forest

Joe Sigorino, Ojai Ranger District, Los Padres National Forest

Jim Lopez, Santa Barbara Ranger District, Los Padres National Forest

Helen Tarbet, Santa Lucia Ranger District, Los Padres National Forest

Tony Kanownik, Covelo Ranger District, Mendocino National Forest

Gary Hayton, Grindstone Ranger District, Mendocino National Forest

Ray Linnet, Red Bluff Recreation Area, Mendocino National Forest

Debbie McIntosh, Upper Lake Ranger District, Mendocino National Forest

Jean Breakfield, Big Valley Ranger District, Modoc National Forest

Stephen Riley, Devil's Garden Ranger District, Modoc National Forest

Mike Kegg, Doublehead Ranger District, Modoc National Forest

Kathy Kempa, Warner Mountain Ranger District, Modoc National Forest

Pandora Valle and Bill Benson, Beckwourth Ranger District, Plumas National Forest

Mary August, Feather River Ranger District, Plumas National Forest

Judy Abrams, Mount Hough Ranger District, Plumas National Forest

Jonathan Cook-Fisher and Audrey Scranton, Mountaintop Ranger Station, San Bernardino National Forest

Roman Rodriguez, San Jacinto Ranger District, San Bernardino National Forest

Carol Hallacy, Hume Lake Ranger District, Sequoia National Forest

Sherry Montgomery, Kern River Ranger District, Kernville, Sequoia National Forest

Geri Adams, Kern River Ranger District, Lake Isabella, Sequoia National Forest

Carol Zeigler, Tule River–Hot Springs Ranger District, Sequoia National Forest

Cindy Beckstead, Big Bar Ranger District, Shasta-Trinity National Forest

Pat Smith, Hayfork Ranger District, Shasta-Trinity National Forest

Les Lloyd, McCloud Ranger District, Shasta-Trinity National Forest

Don Lee, Mount Shasta Ranger District, Shasta-Trinity National Forest

Cathy Southwick, Shasta Lake Ranger District, Shasta-Trinity National Forest

Marla Peckinpah, Mary Ellen Grigsby and Steve Gut, Weaverville Ranger District, Shasta-Trinity National Forest

Judy Hanevold, Yolla Bolly Ranger District, Shasta-Trinity National Forest

Patrice Yakovetic and Linda McPhail, Bass Lake Ranger District, Sierra National Forest

Debbie Arndt, High Sierra Ranger District, Sierra National Forest

Jim Lasell, Lower Trinity Ranger District, Six Rivers National Forest

Vonnie Harding and Dave Williams, Orleans Ranger District, Six Rivers National Forest

Karey Dean, Six Rivers National Forest, Smith River National Recreation Area

Diane Arthur, Calaveras Ranger District, Stanislaus National Forest

Jan Cargill, Groveland Ranger District, Stanislaus National Forest

Bill Seib, Mi-Wok Ranger District, Stanislaus National Forest

Walt Moneski, Summit Ranger District, Stanislaus National Forest

Jan Welsh, American River Ranger District, Foresthill Ranger Station, Tahoe National Forest

Susanne Johnson, Lake Tahoe Basin Management Unit, Tahoe National Forest

Ricardo Buitron, Sierraville Ranger District, Tahoe National Forest

Lydia Olson and Heather Newell, Yuba River Ranger District, North, Tahoe National Forest

Rene Smith, Yuba River Ranger District, South, Tahoe National Forest

U.S. Army Corps of Engineers

Linda Clapp, Lake Sonoma Recreation Area, San Francisco District

Phil Deffenbaugh, Lake Kaweah, Sacramento District

Tom Ehrke, Hensley Lake, Sacramento District

Hector Galvan, Island Park and Deer Creek Point Campgrounds, Sacramento District

Kathy Guynes, Englebright Lake, Sacramento District

Denice Hogan, Black Butte Lake, Sacramento District

Joanne Jackson, Cordoniz Recreation Area, Sacramento District

Valerie Mavis, Lake Mendocino, San Francisco District

Donna Nelson, Acorn and Oak Knoll Campgrounds, Sacramento District

Dwayne Urquhart, Tule Campground, Sacramento District

Dale Verner, Martis Creek Lake, Sacramento District

Bureau of Land Management

Claude Singleton, Alturas Field Office

Clarence Killingsworth, Arcata Field Office

Steve Larsen and Kenneth Hock, Bakersfield Field Office

Bob Raver, Barstow Field Office

Jeff Yanez, Bishop Field Office

Susan Richey and Terry Knight, Carson City
Field Office

Jim Hunt, Eagle Lake Field Office

Dallas Meeks, El Centro Field Office

Lou Cutajar, Folsom Field Office

Mona Daniels, Palm Springs Field Office

Mike Hoffman, Redding Field Office

Beth Lefebvre, Ukiah Field Office

Mirabella Lopez and Mark Lowans,
Yuma Field Office

National Parks

Yvonne Menard, Channel Islands
National Park

Terry Baldino and Alicia Alvarado, Death
Valley National Park

Shanda Ochs, Lassen Volcanic National Park

Mike Wagman, Sequoia and Kings Canyon
National Parks

Brent Gordon and Michele Woods, Yosemite
National Park

Kale Bowling-Schaff, Lava Beds National
Monument

Pete Lundberg, Devils Postpile National
Monument

Ina Webb, Pinnacles National Monument

Linda Slater, Mojave National Preserve

Erin Foley, Golden Gate National
Recreation Area

Susan Davis, Susan Doniger, Celia Riechel
and Debbie Wiest, Redwood National and
State Parks

John Dell'Osso, Point Reyes National Seashore

Tricia Ford, Whiskeytown National
Recreation Area

State Parks

Ruth Coleman, Roy Stearns and Balenda
Gray, Sacramento Headquarters

Ellen Absher, Mount San Jacinto State Park

John Arnold, Half Moon Bay State Beach

Ryan Banovitz, Bolsa Chica State Beach

Jill Bazemore, Emma Wood State Beach

Steven Bier, Salton Sea State Recreation Area

Avis Boutell and Star Sandoval, Bay Area Sector

Lynda Burman, Indian Grinding Rock State
Historic Park

Joshua Bynum, Crystal Cove State Park

Kathy Dolinar and Kent Miller, Ocotillo
Wells State Vehicular Recreation Area

Robert Carpenter, Henry Cowell Redwoods
State Park

Brandon Carroll, Big Basin Redwoods
State Park

Eric Carter, Prairie Creek Redwoods
State Park

Taya Chase, Jeanette Fenske and Liz
Hamman, Humboldt Redwoods State Park

Joni Coombe, Pfeiffer Big Sur State Park

Suzanne Downing, San Juan Bautista Section

Donna Galyean, Humboldt Lagoons
State Park

Dave Garcia, Limekiln State Park

Michael Grant, Butano State Park

Balenda Gray, Sacramento Headquarters

Greg Hall, Tolowa Dunes State Park

Ted Hannibal, Hollister Hills State Vehicular
Recreation Area

John Hardcastle, Benbow Lake State
Recreation Area

Kathy Hernandez, Folsom Lake State
Recreation Area

Jacque Hoffman, Fort Ross State Historic Park

Laura Itogawa, Cuyamaca Rancho State Park

Travis Johnson, Palomar Mountain State Park

Gary Kinney, Seacliff State Beach

Nathan Kogen and Mike Selbo, Sunset
State Beach

Lawani Kolley, Sierra District

John Kolsrud, Austin Creek State
Recreation Area

Mike Lair, China Camp State Park

Sheri Larue, Malakoff Diggins State
Historic Park

William Lutton, Turlock Lake State
Recreation Area

Valerie Marshall, Mendocino District

Dan Martin, Woodson Bridge State Recreation Area

Melissa McGee, Standish-Hickey State Recreation Area

Maria Mendez, Colusa–Sacramento River State Recreation Area

Bill Mentzer, Marin Sector

Lynn Mochizuki, Point Mugu State Park

Javier Morales, Patrick's Point State Park

Cecelia Moreno, Auburn State Recreation Area

Dan Murray and Alison Strachan, Channel Coast District

Sean Nichols and Mark Pupich, Grover Hot Springs State Park

Jerelyn Oliveira, Colonel Allensworth State Historic Park

Denise Peterson, Brannan Island State Recreation Area

Shirley Plumhuf, McArthur–Burney Falls State Park

Christa Quick, Angeles District

Mary Rafuse, Castle Crags State Park

Kellen Riley, San Simeon State Park

Carol Schmal, South Carlsbad State Beach

Rachel Shaw, San Elijo State Beach

Dan Smith, Samuel P. Taylor State Park

Jason Smith, Sonoma Coast State Beach

Shannon Stalder, Grizzly Creek Redwoods State Park

Mike Stanley, Portola Redwoods State Park

Erin Steinart, Bothe–Napa Valley State Park

Veneta Stewart, Donner Memorial State Park

Sarah Straws and Bob Young, Calaveras Big Trees State Park

Katie Sundvall, Richardson Grove State Park

Debborah Tanner, Four Rivers Sector

Theresa Tate, New Brighton State Beach

Charlie Thompson, Sinkyone Wilderness State Park

Bob Thornton, Andrew Molera State Park

Jennifer Tustison, Orange Coast District

Mckeena Vanrillaer, Salt Point State Park

John Verhoeven, Fremont Peak State Park

Tony Villareal, Pismo State Beach/Oceano Dunes State Vehicular Recreation Area

Karen Vreeland, Millerton Lake State Recreation Area

Shelley Waltman-Derr, Clear Lake State Park

Melissa Weaver, San Luis Reservoir State Recreation Area

Kathy Williams, Silverwood Lake State Recreation Area

Bob Williamson, Carnegie State Vehicular Recreation Area

Susan Wilson, Morro Bay State Park

Adam Wollter, Sugarloaf Ridge State Park

Tyson Young, Caswell Memorial State Park

State Forests

Wayne Connor, Boggs Mountain Demonstration State Forest

Lois Kauffman, LaTour Demonstration State Forest

Alan Frame, Mountain Home Demonstration State Forest

Other

Randy Akana, Siskiyou County Public Works

Doug Allen, Edward Ancheta, Mike Ekdao, John Heenan, Theresa Nance, Fred Griggs and Reggie Zapata, Santa Clara County Parks

Joe Anderson, Napa Valley Exposition

Marian Ardohain and Amy Tischman, Merced Irrigation District

Steve Benson, Huntington Beach City Parks

Tim Bolla, Richard Chandler and Marilea Linne, Solano County Parks

Christopher Burdette, The Presidio Trust

Cheryl Bynum and Martha Martinez, Imperial County Parks

Dolores Canali, Cindy Donald, Duane Forest, Randal Higgins, Ruben Rodriguez, Susan Storey, Riverside County Parks

Julie Cloherty, San Diego County Parks

Peggy Davidson, Nevada Irrigation District

Anna Diaz and Ann Springer, San Luis Obispo County Parks

Brent Doan, Lake Casitas Municipal Water District

Joy Feller, Nevada County Fairgrounds

Irene Flores, Karen Montanye, Juisa Powell, and Mary Sheehan, San Bernardino Regional Parks

Pam Gallo, Ventura County Parks

Clay Garland, Santa Barbara County Parks

Colleen Ghiglia, Lompoc Parks and Recreation

Patty Guida, New Melones Visitors Center, U.S. Bureau of Reclamation

Michelle Gilroy and Dennis Redfern, California Department of Fish & Game

Sherie Harral, Shasta Dam, U.S. Bureau of Reclamation

José Gutierrez, Sacramento Municipal Utility District

Heidi Gutnecht, City of San Diego

Chuck Hamilton and Ychelle Tillemans, Inyo County Parks

David Haverty and Donna LaGraffe, Sonoma County Regional Parks

Darlene Hennings, Placer County Facilities Services

Connie Jackson, Marty Johnson and Danae Schmidt, Stanislaus County Parks and Recreation

Sara Johnston and Karen White, United Water Conservation District

Tracy Kves, Northern California Power Agency

Cynthia McDonald, Joy Vandell, Ross Jackson and Mike Drury, Pacific Gas and Electric

Kathy McGadden, Greg Smith, and Jim Spreng, Monterey County Parks

Bill Minor, Humboldt County Public Works

Janet Morrison, Fresno County Parks

Dave Moore, San Mateo County Parks

Julie Ola, Alpine County Public Works Department.

John Parsons, Stancy Perich and John Wilbanks, Kern County Parks and Recreation

Don Pearson, Eldorado Irrigation District

Pam Phelps, City of Escondido

Christina Phillips, Hoopa Valley Tribal Council

Neil Pilegard, Tulare County Parks and Recreation

Patty Sereni, Napa County Fairgrounds

Ron Slimm, Orange County Parks

Alicia Smolke, San Joaquin County Parks

Pat Sotelo, Livermore Area Recreation and Park District

Laurie Swanson, Tahoe City Public Utilities District

Sue Vanderschans, Turlock Irrigation District

Roberta Warden, El Dorado Irrigation District

Amy Welch, Mono County Public Works

Jerry Wright, Yolo County Parks

OREGON

U.S. Forest Service

Beth McGuire, Deschutes National Forest, Bend–Fort Rock District

Lacie Knotts, Deschutes National Forest, Crescent District

Alice Ray, Fremont-Winema National Forest, Bly District

Vickie Zacharias, Fremont-Winema National Forest, Klamath District

Kathy Knowles, Fremont-Winema National Forest, Lakeview District

Hannah O'Leary, Fremont-Winema National Forests, Paisley District

Sheryl Raugust and Cheryl Wood, Malheur National Forest, Emigrant Creek District

Kitty Filbin and Sandy Loop, Mount Hood National Forest, Barlow Ranger District

Dianne Porter and Diana Wiley, Mount Hood National Forest, Clackamas River Ranger District

Kevin Slagle, Mount Hood National Forest, Hood River Ranger District

Susan Aldridge, Mount Hood National Forest, Zigzag Ranger District

Jackie Ringulet, Siskiyou National Forest, Chetco Ranger District

Judy Dangelo, Siskiyou National Forest, Galice District

Irene Kammerer, Siskiyou National Forest, Gold Beach Ranger District

Nita Allen, Siskiyou National Forest, Powers Ranger District

Donna Bodden, Siuslaw National Forest, Hebo District

Judy Ashard, Siuslaw National Forest, Waldport District

Cindi Doherty, Umatilla National Forest, Heppner Ranger District

Dana Croll and Dennis Scott, Umpqua National Forest, North Umpqua District

Dani Pavoni, Willamette National Forest, Detroit Ranger District

Wanda Hall and Esther Kelso, Willamette National Forest, McKenzie River District

Joyce Crebs, Willamette National Forest, Sweethome District

Michalene Kilbury, Winema National Forest, Chemult District

Nancy Carlsen, Wallowa Mountains Visitors Center

U.S. Army Corps of Engineers

Ken Cardwell and Julian Rose, Portland District

Larry Lassiter, ACE/Willamette National Forest, Recreation Information, Cottage Grove

Bureau of Land Management

Fred McDonald, Burns District

Janice Lloyd and Reg Pullen, Coos Bay District

Mark Wilkening, Eugene District

Lynn Hubble, Klamath Falls District

Peggy Ward, Medford District

Donna Anderson, Prineville Dist

Gregg Morgan, Roseburg District

Debra Drake, Claire Gregory, Traci Meredith and Josh Weathers, Salem District

Bob Alward, Vale District

National Parks and Grasslands

Nancy Kennedy, Crater Lake National Park

Roland Giller, Crooked River National Grassland

State Parks

Chris Havel, Oregon State Parks media office

Irene Shockey, Collier Memorial State Park

Darryl Fitzwater, Cove Palisades State Park

Michelle Saner, Detroit Lake State Park

Mike Stein, Fort Stevens State Park

Gerald Riste, Goose Lake State Park

Paul Pearson, Jessie M. Honeyman Memorial State Park

Leslie Hensley, Joseph H. Stewart State Park

Gail Jeffers, Lake Owyhee State Park

Stephanie Turk, La Pine State Park

Wally Judd, Milo McIver State Park

Marcia Esteben and Mark Smith, Nehalem Bay State Park

Delan Coonce, Prineville Reservoir State Park

Kristy Raines, Silver Falls State Park

Jerry Wilson, Viento State Park

Matt Rippee, Wallowa Lake State Park

State Forests, Heritage and Recreation Areas

Jim Ramirez, Champoeg State Heritage Area

Jim Anderson, Deschutes State Recreation Area

Jim Hutton, Emigrant Springs State Heritage Area

Margie Grosse, Tillamook State Forest, Forest Grove District

Debbie Queen, Tillamook State Forest, Tillamook Distric

Dennis Bradley, Unity Lake State Recreation Site

Other

Emily Snider, Clackamas County

Linda Salle, Columbia County

Joan Dage, Kathy Hammons and Bonnie Watts, Douglas County

Cory VanSickle, Hood River County

Jill Hammond, Jackson County

Kristi Tyler, Josephine County

Gary Gooch, Lane County

Melissa Franconi, Linn County

Sandi Putman, Morrow County

Alma Franzen, Tillamook County Parks

Val Jones, Portland General Electric

Bill Doran, Portland Metro Regional Parks

Ian Macek, Port of Cascade Locks

WASHINGTON

U.S. Forest Service

Harriet Schrader, Colville National Forest, Newport Ranger District

Seth Krohn, Colville National Forest, Republic Ranger District

Trish Goldsmith, Colville National Forest, Sullivan Ranger District

George McNicholl, Colville National Forest, Three Rivers Ranger District

Leo Zacher, Gifford Pinchot National Forest, Cowlitz Ranger District

Betty Transtrom, Gifford Pinchot National Forest, Mount Adams Ranger District

Bill Uyesugi, Gifford Pinchot National Forest, Mount St Helens National Volcanic Monument

Virginia Doty and Heidi Hooper, Mount Baker–Snoqualmie National Forest, Darrington Ranger District

Ann Dunphy, Mount Baker–Snoqualmie National Forest, Mount Baker Ranger District

Pam Young, Mount Baker–Snoqualmie National Forest, Skykomish Ranger District

Christina Perez, Okanogan and Wenatchee National Forests, Chelan Ranger District

Mike Ames and Nancy Jones, Okanogan and Wenatchee National Forests, Cle Elum Ranger District

Monte Bowe, Okanogan and Wenatchee National Forests, Entiat Ranger District

Stefani O'Connor and Greg Thayer, Okanogan and Wenatchee National Forests, Leavenworth Ranger Station

Kathy Corrigan, Okanogan and Wenatchee National Forests, Methow Valley Ranger District

Debbi Brewer, Kevin Hill and Doug Jenkins, Okanogan and Wenatchee National Forests, Naches Ranger District

Marne Planque, Okanogan and Wenatchee National Forests, Tonasket Ranger District

Terri Halstead and Steve Kiefe, Okanogan and Wenatchee National Forests, Wenatchee River Ranger District

DJ Coughlin, Okanogan and Wenatchee National Forests, White River Ranger District

Molly Ericson and Susan Graham, Olympic National Forest, Quilcene Ranger District

U.S. Army Corps of Engineers

Greg Webb, Portland District

Don Disbro, Craig Rockwell, Walla Walla District

National Parks

Lynne Brougher, Lake Roosevelt National Recreation Area

Linda Belcher, North Cascades National Park

Carla Bamer, Olympic National Park, Sol Duc campground

State Parks

Patrick Hutnik, Keah Jorgenson, Sandy Mealing, Virginia Painter, Joyce Riley and Hilary Schult, State Park Information

Greg John, Bay View State Park

Ted Morris, Birch Bay State Park

Adam Fahlenkamp, Brooks Memorial State Park

Roy Johnson, Camano Island State Park

Tracy Zuern, Cape Disappointment State Park

Fritz Osborne, Columbia Hills State Park

Ryan Layton, Conconully State Park

Mike Kessler, Daroga State Park

Johnny Johnson, Dash Point and Saltwater State Parks

Rick Blank, Deception Pass State Park

Brett Bayne, Fort Casey State Park

Lori Bond, Fort Flagler State Park

Stephen Wood, Grayland Beach State Park

Geoff Shufelt, Ike Kinswa State Park

Julie Rose, Illahee State Park

Jane O'Neil, Kanasket-Palmer State Park

Seth Mason-Todd, Kitsap Memorial State Park

Matthew Smith, Kopachuck State Park

Rod Jacques, Lake Chelan State Park

Colleen Hawley, Lake Easton State Park

Roger Poier, Lake Wenatchee State Park

Scott Chalfant, Larrabee State Park

Catherine Tanner, Lewis and Clark State Park

John Wennes, Lincoln Rock State Park

Desi Caillier, Maryhill State Park

Evan Johnson, Millersylvania State Park

Dan Kraft, Moran State Park

Jim Schmidt, Ocean City State Park

Ben Cornell and Peter Fry, Pacific Beach State Park

Toni Buechler, Potholes State Park

Darrela Standfill, Potlatch State Park

Debbie Greiner, Rasar State Park

Lori Cobb, Riverside State Park

Fred Remlinger, Rockport State Park

Sally Boyer, Schafer State Park

Gordon Bell and Tina Lynch, Seaquest State Park

Joe Vella, Sequim Bay State Park

Dennis Felton, Sun Lakes State Park

Stan Chance, Twenty-Five Mile Creek State Park

Craig Benner, Wenatchee Confluence State Park

Paul McEvers, Wenberg State Park

Mike Thomas, Yakima Sportsman State Park

State Department of Natural Resources

Arne Johnson, Sportsman's Camp, Northeast Region

Paul McFarland, Northwest Region

Brian Poehlein and Christine Redmond, Paciific Cascade Region North

Vanessa Seldao, Southeast Region

Other

Gary Robinson, City of Anacortes

Cathy Mether, City of Auburn

Caryn Foley, City of Chehalis

James Hayter, City of Chelan

Dianne Roberts, City of Coulee

Karen Sweeney, City of Entiat

Flora Matt, Chelan County

Elke Schuster, Pend Oreille County

Rusty Regan, Skagit County

Marcie Allen, Snohomish County

Janel Goebel and Terry Jeffries, Whitman County

Chris Wenger, Port of Port Townsend

Steve McClain, Port of Wahkiakum No. 2

Debbie Snell, Port of Whitman County

Julaine Nelson and Meghan Wright, Tacoma Power

Index

www.moon.com

For helpful advice on planning a trip, visit www.moon.com for the **TRAVEL PLANNER** and get access to useful travel strategies and valuable information about great places to visit. When you travel with Moon, expect an experience that is uncommon and truly unique.

*"A smart new look provides just one more reason to travel with Moon Outdoors.
Well written, thoroughly researched, and packed full of useful information and
advice, these guides really do get you into the outdoors."*

—GORP.COM

ALSO AVAILABLE AS FOGHORN OUTDOORS ACTIVITY GUIDES:

250 Great Hikes in
   California's National Parks
Baja Camping
California Fishing
California Golf
California Hiking
California Recreational
   Lakes & Rivers
California Waterfalls
California Wildlife
Camper's Companion
Easy Biking in Northern
   California
Easy Hiking in Northern
   California

Easy Hiking in Southern
   California
Georgia & Alabama Camping
Great Lakes Camping
Maine Hiking
Massachusetts Hiking
Montana, Wyoming & Idaho
   Camping
New England Biking
New England Cabins
   & Cottages
New England Camping
New England Hiking
New Hampshire Hiking
Oregon Hiking

Pacific Northwest Hiking
Southern California
   Cabins & Cottages
Tom Stienstra's Bay Area
   Recreation
Utah Camping
Utah Hiking
Vermont Hiking
Washington Boating
   & Water Sports
Washington Fishing
Washington Hiking

MOON WEST COAST RV CAMPING

Avalon Travel Publishing
1400 65th Street, Suite 250
Emeryville, CA 94608, USA
www.moon.com

Senior Research Editor: Stephani Stienstra
Research Editor: Kathie Morgan
Editor: Sabrina Young
Series Manager: Sabrina Young
Acquisitions Manager: Rebecca K. Browning
Copy Editor: Deana Shields
Graphics Coordinator: Tabitha Lahr
Production Coordinators: Tabitha Lahr, Sean Bellows
Interior Designer: Darren Alessi
Map Editor: Kevin Anglin
Cartographers: Kat Bennett, Chris Markiewicz, Kat Smith,
    Suzanne Service
Proofreader: Kay Elliott
Indexer: Greg Jewett

ISBN-10: 1-56691-845-6
ISBN-13: 978-1-56691-845-9
ISSN: 1546-9786

Printing History
1st Edition – 2004
2nd Edition – June 2007
5 4 3 2 1

KEEPING CURRENT

We are committed to making this book the most accurate and enjoyable RV camping guide to the West Coast. You can rest assured that every campground in this book has been carefully reviewed in an effort to keep this book as up-to-date as possible. However, by the time you read this book, some of the fees listed herein may have changed and campgrounds may have closed unexpectedly.

If you have a favorite gem you'd like to see included in the next edition, or see anything that needs updating, clarification, or correction, please drop us a line. Send your comments via email to feedback@moon.com, or use the address above.